WORLD TAX SERIES

THE LAW SCHOOL OF

INTERNATIONAL PROGRAM IN TAXATION

OLIVER OLDMAN,
Professor of Law and Director of the International Program in Taxation

CLIFFORD P. GRECK,
Administrative Director of the International Program in Taxation

ELISABETH A. OWENS,
Lecturer on Law and Research Associate in Law

BOLESLAW A. BOCZEK,
Research Associate in Law and Editor, World Tax Series

CHARLES K. COBB, JR.,
Research Associate in Law and Editor, World Tax Series

REX L. COLEMAN,
Research Associate in Law and Editor, World Tax Series

MARTIN NORR,
Research Associate in Law and Editor, World Tax Series

CONSULTING EDITORS,
for countries included in the World Tax Series

CORRESPONDENTS,
for all countries included in the World Tax Series

in consultation with
THE UNITED NATIONS SECRETARIAT

HARVARD UNIVERSITY

WORLD TAX SERIES

TAXATION IN
ITALY

HARVARD LAW SCHOOL

INTERNATIONAL PROGRAM IN TAXATION

COMMERCE CLEARING HOUSE, INC.
CHICAGO 1964

The law stated in this volume includes
the existing laws, decisions, and admin-
istrative instructions as of 1 January 1964,
except that laws and decrees of major
importance promulgated between 1 Janu-
ary 1964 and 1 March 1964 were given
consideration.

PRINTED IN THE UNITED STATES OF AMERICA
COMMERCE CLEARING HOUSE, INC.
CHICAGO, ILLINOIS

TAXATION IN ITALY

*This volume of the World Tax Series is
primarily the work of the following staff
member and correspondent:*

Charles K. Cobb, Jr.

and

Francesco Forte
(Correspondent)

With the aid of the following associate:

Boleslaw A. Boczek

Earlier volumes in the WORLD TAX SERIES

TAXATION IN BRAZIL

TAXATION IN THE UNITED KINGDOM

TAXATION IN MEXICO

TAXATION IN AUSTRALIA

TAXATION IN SWEDEN

TAXATION IN INDIA

TAXATION IN THE FEDERAL REPUBLIC OF GERMANY

TAXATION IN THE UNITED STATES

TAXATION IN COLOMBIA

Reports are being prepared on other countries, as well as supplements to the published volumes.

ACKNOWLEDGMENTS

This volume of the World Tax Series is the joint work of Charles K. Cobb, Jr., LL.B., Editor of the World Tax Series, and Francesco Forte, Professor of the Science of Finance and of Tax Law at the University of Turin. They were assisted in the preparation of the work by Boleslaw A. Boczek, LL.M., A.M., Dr. Jur., Ph.D.

Mr. Cobb, who was the staff member responsible for the volume, wrote Part II, revised the drafts of Part I and Part III, and had final responsibility for the substance of the entire volume. Professor Forte prepared the original drafts of most of Part I, based on his course book at the University of Turin, *Il sistema tributario italiano e la politica fiscale italiana*. He also assisted in the general planning of the work and reviewed the entire manuscript, making numerous suggestions which were incorporated in the text. Dr. Boczek prepared the original drafts of Part III and of the discussion of the succession taxes in Chapter 3. Dr. Lionello Jona Celesia of the University of Turin supplied many citations and clarifications to Part II. Dr. Mario Rey of the University of Turin assisted Professor Forte in the preparation of the statistical tables in Chapter 1.

Many other experts in the Italian tax system provided valuable assistance at various stages of the preparation of the volume. Useful preliminary notes on different aspects of the system were supplied by the following: Dr. Osvaldo Poli, District Director of Direct Taxes at San Remo; Professor Euclide Antonini of the University of Urbino; Dr. Anna Miraulo of the Associazione fra le Società Italiane per Azioni; Professor Luigi Pezzolo of the University of Padua; Dr. Filippo Gazzero, Inspector of Direct Taxes at Palermo; Dr. Eugenio Righi, Director of the Consumption Tax Office at Sesto San Giovanni (Milan); and Avv. Comm. Giuseppe Greco of Rossano Calabro. The arrangements for these notes were made either by Professor Forte or by Professor Roy P. Franchino, who was in charge of the early stages of the volume, prepared preliminary drafts of some chapters, and made a translation of the *Testo unico* of the direct taxes. Dr. Franco Romani, a student in the International Program in Taxation in 1959-1960, assisted Professor Franchino.

The following made helpful comments on the drafts or furnished information in response to queries: Dr. Bernardetto Bernardinetti, Director General of the Direct Taxes; Dr. Lelio Zappalà, Dr. Matteo Vizzini, Dr. Gino Manna, and Dr. Mario Giardinieri, all of the General Directorate of Direct Taxes at Rome; Dr. Osvaldo Poli, District Director of Direct Taxes at San Remo; Dr. Ezio Manfredi of the Direct Tax Office at Biella; Dr. Primiano Picarelli, Inspector of Indirect Taxes at Milan;

Dr. Eugenio Righi, Director of Consumption Taxes at Sesto San Giovanni; Professor Federico Maffezzoni of the University of Parma; Professor Victor Uckmar of the University of Pisa; Professor Euclide Antonini of the University of Urbino; Dr. Anna Miraulo of the Associazione fra le Società Italiane per Azioni; Dr. Marco Vitale of the Milan office of Arthur Andersen & Co.; and Mr. Theodore A. Coshnear, American consultant to Studio Legale Avvocato Giovanni M. Ughi at Milan. Although every effort has been made to describe the tax system as it is in fact administered, nothing in this volume is to be taken as an expression of official opinion.

The authors further acknowledge the advice received in the preparation of the volume, particularly Chapter 11, from the Fiscal and Financial Branch of the Bureau of Economic Affairs of the United Nations Secretariat.

Mr. Cobb wishes to thank particularly the various individuals who performed services essential to the completion and publication of the volume. Miss Gretchen A. Hovemeyer, Mrs. Jeanne Merenhole Littas, and Mrs. Anne T. Chiarenza copyedited the manuscript. Mrs. Mary C. Dransfield and Mrs. Wendell M. Fairbanks prepared the Index. The citations were checked and the tables of references prepared by Anthony Oldcorn, Teaching Fellow in Romance Languages at Harvard College. The manuscript was typed by Mrs. Anita Safran, Miss Ellen Gordet, Miss Margot Johnson, Mrs. Mara Bernstein, Mrs. Ellin Royds, Mrs. Marion Abe, and Mrs. Margaret E. Fitzgerald.

Finally, we wish to acknowledge the gifts of the Ford Foundation and of the contributors listed at the end of the book, which have made possible the preparation and publication of the World Tax Series.

CONTENTS

*A detailed Table of Contents for each chapter
appears at the beginning of the chapter.*

Preface   xv

Introduction   xvii

Glossary, Abbreviations, and Sources   xxi

Bibliography   xxxiii

PART I.   DESCRIPTION OF THE TAX SYSTEM

Chapter 1
Introduction to the Tax System

1/1. Historical Background of the Fiscal System   6
1/2. Constitutional Principles Affecting Tax Policy   13
1/3. Tax Legislation   25
1/4. Tax Administration   38
1/5. The Financial Policy of the Local Entities   57
1/6. Outline and Evolution of the Tax System in Relation
      to the Economic Structure   77

Chapter 2
Summary of Taxes on Income

2/1. Introduction   148
2/2. "Objective" Taxes on Income   149
2/3. The Complementary Progressive Tax and the Family Tax 181
2/4. The Corporation Tax   196

Chapter 3

Taxes on Capital

3/1. Introduction 208

3/2. Tax on Corporate Assets 208

3/3. Tax on Bonds 211

3/4. The Inheritance Tax 212

3/5. The Estate Tax 255

3/6. Taxation of Gifts 259

3/7. Betterment Contributions and Taxation of Increases in Value of Building Lots 261

Chapter 4

Taxes on Transactions

4/1. Introduction 275

4/2. The General Tax on Receipts 276

4/3. Registration Taxes 279

4/4. Stamp Taxes 284

4/5. Taxes on Production and Consumption 293

4/6. State Fiscal Monopolies 314

4/7. Fees for Governmental Concessions 317

4/8. Customs Duties 322

PART II. ANALYSIS OF THE INCOME TAX

Chapter 5

Classes of Taxpayers

5/1. Individuals 330

5/2. Corporations and Similar Entities 333

5/3. Other Taxpayers 338

5/4. Nonresidents 344

5/5. Tax-Exempt Persons 344

Chapter 6

Principles of Income Determination

6/1. Concept of Taxable Income   354
6/2. Books and Records   373
6/3. Accounting Periods   377
6/4. Accounting Methods   381
6/5. Valuation of Assets   383
6/6. Reserves   385
6/7. Branch Accounting   387
6/8. Attribution Rules   388
6/9. Other Methods of Determining the Tax Base   389

Chapter 7

Income from Business

7/1. Gross Income   395
7/2. Deductions   401
7/3. Depreciation and Amortization   415
7/4. Net Losses from Operations   423
7/5. Nondeductible Expenses   425

Chapter 8

Income from Personal Services

8/1. Remuneration for Services As an Employee   430
8/2. Income from Professional Services and Independent Work   438
8/3. Income from Miscellaneous Services   441
8/4. Income-Spreading Provisions   441

Chapter 9

Income from Capital and Capital Transactions

9/1. Interest   445
9/2. Dividends and Other Distributions   448
9/3. Pensions, Annuities, and Insurance   461
9/4. Rent   463
9/5. Royalties   476

9/6. Presumed Income 477
9/7. Taxation at Source 477
9/8. Capital Gains and Losses 477
9/9. Organization, Reorganization, and Dissolution of Business 483

Chapter 10

Income from Special Activities and from Miscellaneous Sources

10/1. Natural Resource Extraction 496
10/2. Agriculture and Forestry 500
10/3. Insurance 517
10/4. Banking and Credit 518
10/5. Investment Companies 522
10/6. Industrial Incentives 523
10/7. Miscellaneous Sources 536

Chapter 11

International Aspects of Income Taxation

11/1. Introduction 541
11/2. Taxation of Income Produced Abroad 549
11/3. Taxation of Income of Nonresidents and Foreign Enterprises 555
11/4. Tax Treaties 566

Chapter 12

Computation of Tax

12/1. Individuals 590
12/2. Corporations and Similar Entities 605
12/3. Other Taxpayers 611
12/4. Nonresident Taxpayers 612
12/5. Forms of Return 613

Chapter 13

Administration and Procedure

13/1. Returns 647
13/2. Assessment 654
13/3. Payment of Tax 663

13/4. Protests and Appeals   674
13/5. Refunds   686
13/6. Time Limits on Assessment and Collection   688
13/7. Interest, Penalties, and Prosecutions   689

PART III. ANALYSIS OF TAXES OTHER THAN INCOME TAX

Chapter 14

The General Tax on Receipts

14/1. History of the Tax   706
14/2. Persons Subject to the Tax   708
14/3. Taxable Receipts   715
14/4. Nontaxable Receipts   723
14/5. Determination of the Tax Base   731
14/6. The Tax Rates   733
14/7. Assessment and Collection   737
14/8. International Aspects   747
14/9. Penalties   753
14/10. Time Limits   756

Chapter 15

The Registration Tax

15/1. Introduction   761
15/2. Persons Subject to the Tax   763
15/3. Taxable Transactions   765
15/4. Exemptions and Reductions   775
15/5. Valuation   780
15/6. Tax Rates   782
15/7. Assessment and Collection   787
15/8. Penalties   791
15/9. Time Limits   794
15/10. Protests and Appeals   795
15/11. International Aspects   795
         References   797
         Index   835

PREFACE

The World Tax Series consists of volumes on the tax systems of countries throughout the world. Each volume covers a single country and contains a description of the tax system as a whole and a detailed analysis of the most important taxes, especially the income tax. As far as possible, the contents are arranged according to a uniform pattern, which is explained in the Introduction.

The United Nations, and the League of Nations before it, had long recognized the need for providing systematic information on national tax systems, and had initiated a series of publications dealing especially with the taxation of foreign income and foreign taxpayers. In August 1951, the Economic and Social Council of the United Nations passed the following resolution, which was recommended to it by the Fiscal Commission, where the United States delegate had originally proposed it:

The Economic and Social Council
Having in mind that the promotion of trade and investment between countries is of great importance in the economic development of Member countries;
Having in mind that the establishment of a modern tax structure constitutes an important factor in attracting foreign trade and investment and in promoting national development;
Having in mind that the availability of comprehensive and authentic information on the tax systems of Member countries serves these aims; and
Having in mind that the United Nations is best suited to obtain the basic information on national tax systems from Member governments;
Requests the Secretary-General to consider:
(a) The publication of a world tax service, providing a continuous service of information on national tax laws and administration;
(b) Keeping this service on a current basis by the publication of loose-leaf or booklet supplements;
(c) Inviting governments in each of the countries to be covered by the world tax service to cooperate in supplying the legislative documentation and other materials;
(d) The possible cooperation of universities in this undertaking.

The Harvard Law School offered to cooperate in response to this resolution. Officials of the United Nations Secretariat, working in close collaboration with members of the Law School faculty, prepared an outline and plan of organization for the contemplated series of volumes on national tax systems. Further discussion led, in 1952, to the establishment at the Law School of the International Program in Taxation, which has been carried forward as part of the Harvard Law School program in International Legal Studies. Training and research activities were started with the aid of a grant from the Ford Foundation. The World Tax Series project was undertaken as a part of the tax program in 1954, when the minimum financial support necessary to commence this work was obtained from the contributions of corporations and corporate foundations.

An advisory board, composed of persons familiar with international tax problems, assisted the staff by making recommendations on the scope and arrangement of the Series. The final arrangement of the material was worked out with the advice of consultants from the United Nations Secretariat and from tax publishing houses.

A uniform method of preparation is generally followed for all of the volumes of the World Tax Series. Preliminary drafts are prepared by the staff, with the assistance of consultants and correspondents. Ordinarily, the latter contributors are residents of the foreign country whose tax law is being described—members of the government, the academic community, or others who are knowledgeable in tax law.

The World Tax Series is designed to present a comprehensive survey of the various tax systems; it is not expected that the volumes will furnish final answers to all the questions that can arise under particular tax laws. The over-all description of the tax structure and the more detailed analysis of the principal taxes in each volume of the Series provide basic tools for comparative tax research. This research has hitherto been difficult because of the lack of any convenient source where information could be obtained on a comparative basis.

The Series also provides tax practitioners in the United States and elsewhere with technical information which will enable them to discuss tax questions with their advisors abroad. The Series may be useful to government officials engaged in tax reforms or in international tax negotiations. The information on the techniques used in other countries may be helpful to teachers of taxation as well as to those carrying on technical assistance in the fiscal field.

INTRODUCTION

The World Tax Series seeks to achieve two basic goals: (1) to describe each tax system in its own legal and administrative terms, and (2) to present each system so it can be compared, point by point, with others. Therefore, each volume in the Series presents in Part I a description of the tax system of a country and in Part II a detailed analysis, under uniform topic headings, of its income tax. If, in any country, taxes other than the income tax require detailed treatment, they are covered in Part III.

Part I

The four chapters of Part I describe the background and the entire tax structure in its own setting.

Chapter 1 gives the background information needed for an understanding of the tax structure as a whole. Chapter 2 summarizes taxes on net income. It serves as more than an introduction to their detailed analysis in Part II, in that it presents an over-all perspective of income taxes in terms of their own legislative and administrative design. Chapter 3 describes the various taxes on capital, and Chapter 4 describes taxes on transactions. Those taxes which are analyzed in detail in Part III are merely summarized here.

Readers should examine Part I to understand the framework of the whole tax system before they look up any specific point of law in Part II or III.

Part II

In Part II of each volume, Chapters 5 through 13 contain a detailed analysis of the national income tax, and these chapters generally have the same titles and the same major subdivisions in each volume. As the Table of Contents shows, the analysis follows the over-all sequence of answering these questions: Who pays the income tax? What is the tax imposed on? How is the tax computed? How is the tax administered?

Although this sequence is broad enough to embrace all of the problems presented by any income tax, it is designed primarily for analysis of detailed provisions, and does not follow the legislative and administrative pattern of the particular country's income tax, which is described in Chapter 2.

Part III

In Part III, the taxes other than the income tax that deserve detailed treatment are analyzed. These taxes differ in each volume, but they usually include those which are summarized in Chapters 3 and 4. Where a particular tax is an integral part of the income tax structure, it may be included in Part II.

Location of Certain Material

Individuals, corporations, and other taxpayers. In describing who pays the income tax, each volume makes the basic distinction between individuals and corporations. Where the distinction is between physical persons and juridical persons, the latter are referred to as "entities" in the Series. The first section of Chapter 5 of each volume describes the status of individuals as taxpayers, and the second describes the status of corporations. The various types of organization and association, some of which are taxpayers and some of which are not, are described separately, and, as far as possible, in terms of comparison and contrast with the tax status of individuals and of corporations.

The international aspects of income taxation. In order to emphasize international problems related to income taxation, the definitions of resident and nonresident are included among the criteria identifying the various classes of taxpayers described in Chapter 5, at the beginning of the analysis of the income tax. There are references throughout the income tax chapters to the sections of Chapter 11 ("International Aspects of Income Taxation") where equivalent problems are discussed in relation to nonresidents or to foreign income. The last section of Chapter 11, relating to tax treaties, covers only the major effects of those treaties on the basic internal law. The United Nations series on International Tax Agreements, of which nine volumes have been published so far (in English, French, and Spanish editions), provides full texts of the agreements and comprehensive data on their current status.

Schedular and global income tax system. The characterization of a system as "schedular" or "global" is retained in the descriptive material on income taxes in Part I, but it does not affect the arrangement of Part II.

Income tax return forms. An important part of each volume in the Series is the reproduction in Chapter 12 of the country's most recent available individual and corporate income tax return forms, with translations where necessary. The forms are not always facsimiles, but they show each item in the position corresponding to its place on the page of the original return.

The Numbering System

Each topic covered by the volumes in the Series is numbered. These numbers furnish a complete system of cross reference. By giving the same numbers to the same topics in each book, considerable uniformity has been provided throughout the Series. In Part I, only the chapter titles are identical, but in Part II both the chapter titles and the major headings within each chapter are virtually the same in every volume. The number and the content of the chapters in Part III vary; generally, a separate chapter is devoted to each of the principal taxes requiring analysis.

Each chapter is indicated by its number followed by a diagonal stroke. Thus, 5/ always refers to Chapter 5. The major headings within each chapter are numbered consecutively following the stroke. For example, in every volume, Chapter 7 is "Income from Business," and the second major heading is "Deductions." Thus, its number is 7/2. Subheadings are numbered consecutively following the period (for example, "Compensation for Services" under "Deductions" is usually 7/2.3), but rules of taxation vary so widely from country to country that these subheadings cannot be uniform. In general, where the same subject matter appears in different countries, the titles and numbers of the subheadings are the same in each volume, but the editorial staff of the Series considered it unwise to impose a perhaps artificial and misleading uniformity merely for its own sake.

Cross references and references in the Index are made to heading numbers rather than pages. Thus, 9/10.5 is a reference to Chapter 9, tenth major heading, fifth subheading. The Table of Contents in the front of the book lists each major heading, its title, and the number of the page on which it begins. An examination of the detailed Table of Contents at the beginning of each chapter will familiarize the reader with the workings of the system.

Citations

The form used in citing a volume of the World Tax Series is as follows: WTS: *Italy.*

In each volume, there are many citations to relevant sections of laws and regulations, but few direct quotations or translations. The substance and effects of tax provisions are explained instead of merely paraphrased. Wherever possible, examples further clarify the explanations, but there are no explicit comparisons with laws of any other country.

Glossary, Abbreviations, and Sources

Each volume of the Series has a list of the books containing the tax law of the country (Sources), the names of their publishers, an explanation of how they are cited, and a list of abbreviations used in the text and the footnotes. The terminology common to the volumes is covered in the Glossary, which appears together with the Sources directly after this Introduction. The Glossary may also include definitions which are relevant for each particular volume.

Bibliography

The Bibliography lists books, articles, and other works either used as source material for the text or recommended for further reference. A few secondary sources repeatedly cited in the volume are covered only in Sources. Generally, however, the specific references to general sources are also included in the Bibliography.

References

At the end of the text, the section of the volume called References contains a table of statutes, regulations, and other source material cited in the volume and the numbers of the sections of the volume in which they appear. In common law countries, a table of cases is also provided. The References section is designed to help readers find the application or interpretation of any particular section of a statute, regulation, or judicial decision.

The Index

All subjects and terms in the Index, both in English and in the language of the taxing country, are in one alphabetical list. Each foreign word or term in the list is cross-referenced to its English equivalent. In addition to consulting the Index, readers are advised to use the detailed Table of Contents at the beginning of each chapter.

GLOSSARY, ABBREVIATIONS, AND SOURCES

The Glossary, Abbreviations, and Sources below are designed as an aid to the reader. The Glossary defines many of the important terms used in this volume. The Abbreviations and the Sources sections, among other functions, explain the most commonly used citations.

GLOSSARY

In the preparation of the World Tax Series volumes, a standard vocabulary is being developed. The standardized terms which are used consistently throughout the Series apply principally to income taxation; with respect to the definition of technical tax terms, this Glossary applies to the income tax.

Allowance. Any part of net income on which the tax rate is zero. As opposed to deductions, "allowances" do not correspond to actual expenditures but are specific amounts or amounts based on percentages, established by the income tax law. They differ from exemptions in that they apply to amounts or percentages of income, while exemptions apply to types of income. The most common "allowances" are those granted to the taxpayer for himself and for his dependents (often called personal exemptions).

Credit. Amount that a taxpayer is permitted to subtract from his tax after he has computed the tax by applying the income tax rates to taxable income. "Credits" are usually granted by a government for taxes already paid, for example, for tax withheld on wages or salaries during the taxable period. Other frequent examples are the fixed amount a taxpayer is allowed to subtract from his total tax liability for dependents, and a credit for foreign taxes on income earned abroad. A "credit" against tax must not be confused with a deduction from income.

Deduction. Amount that the law declares a taxpayer may subtract from his gross taxable income in arriving at his net income. "Deductions" may include both expenses incurred in acquiring gross income, such as wages and rent, as well as other disbursements, such as medical expenditures and interest due on personal debts, which are not directly related to an income-earning activity.

Depreciation deduction. Annual prorated deduction allowed for the gradual exhaustion or obsolescence of property used in the production of income. Called "capital allowance" in some countries.

Estimated income. Amount estimated to have been received.

Exclusion. Amount received by a taxpayer which is not considered within the concept of income for tax purposes. Examples of "exclusions" might be gifts, life insurance proceeds, or capital receipts.

Exemption (as applied to classes of taxpayers). The elimination, by law, of a class of individuals and/or entities from the application of the income tax. Foreign diplomatic personnel and charitable institutions are examples of persons frequently exempt from tax.

Exemption (as applied to income). The elimination, by law, of an item of income from the scope of the income tax, even though that item is recognized as income. An example of an exempt item might be interest from certain government securities.

Gross income. The total of all items included in the concept of income that a taxpayer receives during a taxable period.

Gross profits. Gross income less cost of goods sold.

Gross receipts. Total amount, in cash and in goods, services, or other benefits, received by a taxpayer during the taxable period. In addition to items that are within the definition of gross income, "gross receipts" is used to include any items received which are not so considered.

Immovable property. Ordinarily, land and interests therein, buildings, and fixtures. Whether or not a particular interest is considered to be an interest in "immovable property" depends on the law of each country.

Imputed income. Amount derived by a taxpayer from the use or occupancy of his own property or from personal efforts on his own behalf. Examples are the rental value of an owner-occupied residence or the value of home-grown produce consumed by the taxpayer and members of his household. Also called "presumptive income."

Movable property. Property that is not "immovable property."

Net income. The amount remaining after subtracting exempt income and deductions from gross income. The term for income as reduced by taxes is "net income after tax."

Taxable income. Amount obtained after subtracting allowances from net income, to which the income tax rates are applied in computing tax liability.

Tax avoidance. Minimization of taxes by legal means.

Tax evasion. Minimization of taxes by illegal means.

ABBREVIATIONS

ACM . . . . *Applicazione dei contributi di miglioria per le opere eseguite dallo Stato o col suo concorso* (Application of the Betterment Contributions for Works Carried Out by the State or with Its Assistance)

App. . . . . *Corte d'Appello* (Court of Appeal)

Arch. fin . . . . *Archivio finanziario* (Periodical)
art. . . . . *articolo* (article)
Boll. trib. informazioni. . . . . . *Bollettino tributario d'informazioni* (Periodical)
Cass. . . . . *Corte Suprema di Cassazione*
(Supreme Court of Cassation)
CC . . . . *Codice civile* (Civil Code)
CEDAM . . . . .Casa Editrice Dott. Antonio Milani
C.M. . . . . *Circolare ministeriale* or *Circolare
del Ministero delle Finanze*
(Ministerial Circular)
Comm. Centr. . . . . *Commissione Centrale delle Imposte Dirette*
(Central Commission of Direct Taxes)
Comm. Prov. . . . . *Commissione Provinciale delle Imposte Dirette*
(Provincial Commission of Direct Taxes)
Cons. az. . . . . *Consulente delle aziende* (Periodical)
Const. . . . . .Constitution of the Italian Republic
Corte Cost. . . . .*Corte Costituzionale* (Constitutional Court)
CP . . . .*Codice penale* (Penal Code)
CPC . . . .*Codice di procedura civile*
(Code of Civil Procedure)
CPP . . . .*Codice di procedura penale*
(Code of Criminal Procedure)
Dir. e prat. trib. . . . .*Diritto e pratica tributaria* (Periodical)
D.L. . . . .*Decreto-legge* (Decree-Law); *Decreto
legislativo* (Legislative Decree)
D.L.C.P.S. . . . .*Decreto legislativo del Capo Provvisiorio dello Stato*
(Legislative Decree of the Provisional Head of State)
D.L.L. . . . .*Decreto legislativo luogotenenziale* (Lieutenancy
Legislative Decree); *Decreto legge luogotenenziale*
(Lieutenancy Decree-Law)
D.L.P. . . . .*Decreto-legge presidenziale* (Presidential Decree-Law);
Decreto legislativo presidenziale (Presidential Legislative Decree)
D.P. *or* D.P.R. . . . .*Decreto del Presidente della Repubblica*
(Decree of the President of the Republic)
ECA . . . .*Enti comunali di assistenza* (Communal Assistance Entities)
Foro it. . . . .*Il foro italiano* (Periodical)
Giorn. degli economisti . . . .*Giornale degli economisti e annali di
economia* (Periodical)
Giur. comp. Cass. . . . .*Giurisprudenza completa della Corte Suprema
di Cassazione* (Periodical)
Giur. cost. . . . .*Giurisprudenza costituzionale* (Periodical)
Giur. imp. or *Giur. imp. dir.* . . . . . .*Giurisprudenza delle imposte* (Periodical)
Giur. it. . . . .*Giurisprudenza italiana, Rivista universale di
giurisprudenza e dottrina* (Periodical)
Giust. trib. . . . .*La giustizia tributaria e le imposte dirette* (Periodical)
IAF . . . .*imposta sugli incrementi di valore delle aree fabbricabili*
(tax on the increase in value of building lots)
IB . . . .*Nuove norme sulla imposta di bollo*
(New Rules on the Stamp Tax)
ICAP . . . .*imposta sulle industrie, i commerci, le arti e le professioni*
(tax on industries, businesses, arts, and professions)

IGE ....*imposta generale sull'entrata* (general tax on receipts);
Istituzione di una imposta generale sull'entrata (Decree-Law
Instituting a General Tax on Receipts)

IGE Reg. ....*Regolamento per l'esecuzione del R.D.L. 9 gennaio 1940,
n. 2, istitutivo di una imposta generale sull'entrata*
(Regulations on the Execution of R.D.L.
9 January 1940, n. 2, Instituting a
General Tax on Receipts)

I.M. ....*Istruzione ministeriale* (Ministerial Instruction)

Imp. dir. erariali ....*Le imposte dirette erariali* (Periodical)

Jus ....*Jus—Rivista di scienze giuridiche* (Periodical)

L. ....*Legge* (Law)

L. Cost....................*Legge costituzionale* (Constitutional Law)

LCP ....*Legge comunale e provinciale* (Communal and Provincial Law)

LD ....*Legge doganale* (Customs Law)

LR ....*Testo unico di legge del registro*
(*Testo unico* of Registration Law)

L.R................................*Legge regionale* (Regional Law)

LS ....*Legge tributaria sulle successioni* (Succession Tax Law)

MSD ....*Modificazioni delle imposte sulle successioni e sulle donazioni*
(Modifications of the Taxes on Successions and Gifts)

n...................................*numero* (number); note

nn...................................*numeri* (numbers)

Nuova rass. comm. ....*Nuova rassegna commerciale* (Periodical)

Nuova riv. trib....................*Nuova rivista tributaria* (Periodical)

para...................................paragraph

Rass. dir. pubbl..................*Rassegna di diritto pubblico* (Periodical)

Rass. mens. imp. dir. ......*Rassegna mensile delle imposte dirette* (Periodical)

RDFSF ....*Rivista del diritto finanziario e scienza delle finanze*
(Periodical)

R.D.L. ....*Regio decreto-legge* (Royal Decree-Law); *Regio
decreto legislativo* (Royal Legislative Decree)

Riv. dir. comm. ....*Rivista del diritto commerciale e del diritto
generale delle obbligazioni* (Periodical)

Riv. dir. proc. ....*Rivista di diritto processuale* (Periodical)

Riv. dott. comm. ....*Rivista dei dottori commercialisti* (Periodical)

Riv. int. sc. econ. e comm. ....*Rivista internazionale di scienze economiche
e commerciali* (Periodical)

Riv. it. sc. econ. ....*Rivista italiana di scienze economiche* (Periodical)

Riv. leg. fisc. ....*Rivista di legislazione fiscale* (Periodical)

Riv. not. ....*Rivista del notariato* (Periodical)

Riv. pol. ec. ....*Rivista di politica economia* (Periodical)

Riv. soc. ....*Rivista delle società* (Periodical)

Riv. trib. ....*La rivista tributaria* (Periodical)

Riv. trim. dir. pubbl. ......*Rivista trimestrale di diritto pubblico* (Periodical)

R.M. ....*Risoluzione ministeriale* (Ministerial Resolution)

R.M. or r.m. ....*ricchezza mobile* (movable wealth); *imposta di
ricchezza mobile* (tax on income from movable wealth)

Sard. ....*Sardo* (Sardinian)

Sez. ....*Sezione* (Section)

Sez. un....................*Sezioni unite* (United Sections)

Sic. ....*Siciliano* (Sicilian)

GLOSSARY AND SOURCES

Studi urbinati .... *Studi urbinati di scienze giuridiche ed economiche*
(Periodical)
SVIMEZ .... *Associazione per lo Sviluppo dell'Industria nel Mezzogiorno*
TD .... *Tariffa doganale* (Customs Tariff)
Temi trib. .... *Temi tributaria* (Periodical)
Trent. .... Trentino-Alto Adige
Trib. .... *Tribunale* (Tribunal)
T. U. .... *Testo unico* (unified text of legislation)
TUCG .... *Testo unico delle leggi vigenti in materia di tasse sulle conces-
sione governative* (*Testo unico* of the Laws in Force on the
Fees for Governmental Concessions)
TUFL ...... *Testo unico per la finanza locale* (*Testo unico* of Local Finance)
UTET .... Unione Tipografico-Editrice Torinese
Verb. conf. .... *Verbale delle conferenze degli Ispettori Compartimentali
delle Imposte Dirette* (Minutes of Meetings of the
Compartmental Inspectors of Direct Taxes)
WTS .... World Tax Series

SOURCES

Listed below are the principal primary and secondary sources of tax
law relied upon in the preparation of this volume. The list of sources,
which does not purport to be exhaustive, includes all sources to which
reference is made in the text or footnotes and a number of additional
materials useful for further research.

Legislation

The Italian taxes are levied and modified by separate laws and decrees;
there is no single code of tax law. For some of the more important taxes,
the law has been codified in a "unified text" (*testo unico*); an example
is D.P.R. 29 January 1958, n. 645, the *Testo unico* of the laws on the direct
taxes. Modifications of the law governing a tax may be made either in the
form of a law or decree modifying the *testo unico* or other basic legislation, or in the form of an independent law or decree.

Current laws and decrees are published daily in the official gazette
(*Gazzetta ufficiale della Repubblica italiana*) and republished annually
in the official collection of laws and decrees (*Raccolta ufficiale delle leggi
e dei decreti*). Both of these publications are issued at Rome by the
government publications office, Istituto Poligrafico dello Stato. All laws
and decrees are also published unofficially in the periodicals *La legislazione italiana*, *Le leggi*, and *Lex*.

Current tax legislation is published not only in the collections and
periodicals described above, but also in monthly bulletins of the Ministry
of Finance and in certain tax periodicals. Tax legislation in force has
been compiled in unofficial "tax codes" (*codici fiscali*); these general compilations of tax law are listed below.

ARENA, C., and SCANDALE, E. *Le leggi fiscali, annotate con la dottrina, la giurisprudenza, e le normali ministeriali* (7th ed.) (3 volumes). Bologna: Dott. Cesare Zuffi, Editore, 1954-1960.

CORDARO, P. *Codice fiscale* (3d ed.). Torino: UTET, 1961.

GIANNINI, A. D., and SCOCA, S. *Codice delle leggi tributarie* (3d ed.). Milano: Giuffrè, 1962.

Unofficial "codes" are also published for most of the important taxes; in some cases, these contain annotations to decisions and administrative instructions. Some of the treatises and commentaries on particular taxes also quote the applicable legislation in some detail. The codes and commentaries on the legislation governing particular taxes are listed under the appropriate headings in the Bibliography.

Laws and decrees are generally cited by date, number, and article. In this volume, references to the *Testo unico* of the direct taxes, which is the principal source of the law on national income taxation, are designated by article in the following manner: art. 3. References to certain other frequently cited laws and decrees are designated by an abbreviation of the title, followed by an article reference. For example, "IGE art. 24" is a reference to the basic law of the general tax on receipts (*imposta generale sull'entrata* or IGE). The abbreviations of other frequently cited legislation are given in the list of abbreviations immediately preceding this section.

Decisions (Giurisprudenza)

Extracts from selected decisions of the Constitutional Court (Corte Cost.), the Supreme Court of Cassation (Cass.), Courts of Appeal (App.), Tribunals (Trib.), and various administrative organs are reported unofficially and annotated in general legal periodicals, of which the most important are *Il foro italiano* (*Foro it.*) and *Giurisprudenza italiana* (*Giur. it.*). Selected decisions of the courts and of the Central Commission for Direct Taxes (Comm. Centr.) regarding tax matters are reported or abstracted in various tax periodicals. In this volume, decisions are cited by an abbreviation of the name of the court or commission, date, and usually number.

Abstracts (*massime*) and periodical citations of decisions can be found in various digests (*massimari*), some of which are periodicals and some of which are compilations covering a number of years. For convenience, those of both types are listed below.

Massimario del Foro italiano. Roma: Soc. ed. Foro Italiano, 1931–. Published monthly.

Massimario della Giurisprudenza delle imposte dirette, di registro e di negoziazione (*Tributi erariali e locali*), *Anni 1940-1950.* Compiled by A. BERLIRI, with M. C. DEZZA and M. MALTAURO. Milano: Giuffrè, 1952.

Massimario della Giurisprudenza delle imposte (Tributi erariali e locali),
   Anni 1951-1957. Compiled by A. BERLIRI, M. C. DEZZA, and M.
   MALTAURO. Milano: Giuffrè, 1959.
Massimario della Giurisprudenza italiana. Torino: UTET, 1931–. Pub-
   lished monthly.
Massimario delle imposte dirette. Edited by F. MASSAFRA and S. BIASCO.
   Roma: Jandi Sapi Editori, 1958.
Massimario tributario. Edited by A. GIAQUINTO, F. MIRMINA, and G.
   Rosso. Roma: AEI, 1952–. Published bimonthly; jurisprudence
   of the civil and penal sections of the Court of Cassation and juris-
   prudence of the Central Tax Commission, with notes and com-
   mentaries.
Massimario tributario. Milano: Giuffrè, 1962–. Published monthly;
   supplementing *Giurisprudenza delle imposte* with abstracts of decisions of the Supreme Court of Cassation and the Central Tax Commission, printed on cards.
Le massime del registro, notariato e ipoteche. Roma: Tipografia "Le
   Massime" di G. Farri, 1863–. Published fortnightly.

Administrative Instructions and Ministerial Decrees

Ministerial decrees (D.M.) are published in the *Gazzetta ufficiale* and
are reported in periodicals and discussed in treatises in the same manner
as legislation. Ministerial instructions (I.M.), resolutions (R.M.), and
circulars (C.M.) are published for the use of the tax administration and
not primarily for the general public, but are available in the monthly
bulletins issued by the Ministry of Finance and in an annual collection,
Raccolta delle circolari, issued by the Ministry. Circulars or extracts
therefrom also appear in the tax periodicals and in the codes and treatises
listed in the Bibliography for the various taxes.

Periodicals

Listed below are the periodicals cited or used in the preparation of this
volume as sources of tax legislation, decisions, administrative instructions,
or commentary on tax law, tax policy, or public finance. Other reference
works and commentaries cited or used in the preparation of the volume
are listed in the Bibliography.

Annali di economia. Milano: Università Bocconi Editrice, 1924-1939.
   Published annually.
Annali di statistica. Edited by ISTITUTO DI SCIENZE ECONOMICHE E COM-
   MERCIALI. Genova: Tipografia C. Morando, 1933-1940. Published
   semiannually.

Archivio finanziario. *Annali degli studi tributari a cura dell'Istituto di Finanza Pubblica dell'Università di Ferrara.* Padova: CEDAM, 1950–. Published annually. Cited: *Arch. fin.*

Bollettino tributario d'informazioni. Milano: 1934–. Published fortnightly. Cited: *Boll. trib. informazioni.*

Bollettino ufficiale: legislazione e disposizioni ufficiali. Roma: Ministero delle Finanze, Direzione Generale delle Imposte Dirette. Published monthly.

Bulletin for International Fiscal Documentation. Amsterdam: International Bureau of Fiscal Documentation, 1948–. Published bimonthly.

Consulente delle aziende. Milano: 1925–. Published three times a month. Cited: *Cons. az.*

Diritto e pratica tributaria. Padova: CEDAM, 1926–. Published bimonthly. Cited: *Dir. e prat. trib.*

Il diritto fallimentare. Milano: Giuffrè, 1926–. Published monthly.

Economia e storia. Rivista italiana di storia economica e sociale. Milano: Giuffrè, 1962–. Published quarterly.

Economia internazionale. Edited by ISTITUTO DI ECONOMIA INTERNAZIONALE. Genova: Camera di Commercio, Industria e Agricoltura, 1948–. Published semiannually.

The Economist. London: The Economist Newspaper, Limited, 1843–. Published weekly.

European Taxation. Amsterdam: International Bureau of Fiscal Documentation, 1961–. Published fortnightly.

Il foro italiano. Roma: Soc. ed. Foro Italiano, 1876–. Published monthly. Cited: *Foro it.*

Il foro padano. Milano: 1946–. Published monthly.

Il foro siciliano. Palermo: Tipografia Valguarnera, 1879–. Published monthly.

Giornale degli economisti e annali di economia. Padova: CEDAM, 1886–. Until 1939: *Giornale degli economisti.* Cited: *Giorn. degli economisti.*

Giurisprudenza completa della Corte Suprema di Cassazione. Roma: Edizione dell'Istituto Italiano di Studi Legislativi, Ministero di Grazia e di Giustizia, 1945-1957. Published three times a year.

Giurisprudenza costituzionale. Milano: Giuffrè, 1956–. Published quarterly. Cited: *Giur. cost.*

Giurisprudenza delle imposte. Edited by ASSOCIAZIONE FRA LE SOCIETÀ ITALIANE PER AZIONI. Milano: Giuffrè, 1954–. Published quarterly; formerly: *Giurisprudenza delle imposte dirette* (1928-1947), *Giurisprudenza delle imposte dirette, di registro e di negoziazione* (1947-1954). Cited: *Giur. imp.* or *Giur. imp. dir.*

Giurisprudenza italiana, Rivista universale di giurisprudenza e dottrina.
Torino: UTET, 1849–. Published monthly. Cited: *Giur. it.*

Giurisprudenza siciliana. Milano: Giuffrè, 1947–. Published quarterly.

Giurisprudenza toscana. Milano: Giuffrè, 1950–. Published bimonthly.

La giustizia tributaria e le imposte dirette. Roma: 1924–. Published
monthly. Cited: *Giust. trib.*

Le imposte dirette. Published monthly, 1878-1918; last published at
Roma: Casa Editrice Italiana.

Le imposte dirette erariali. Frascati: Casa Editrice Tuscolana, 1958–.
Published monthly. Cited: *Imp. dir. erariali.*

Italian Report. New York: Italian Information Center. Published
monthly.

Jus–Rivista di scienze giuridiche. Milano: Università Cattolica del
Sacro Cuore, 1940-1943, 1950–. Published quarterly. Cited: *Jus.*

*Le leggi [e i decreti secondo l'ordine della inserzione nella Gazzetta
ufficiale].* Roma: Soc. ed. Foro Italiano, 1911–. Published fortnightly.

La legislazione fiscale italiana. Milano: Casa Editrice O.R.T., 1956–.
Published monthly.

La legislazione italiana. Milano: Giuffrè, 1943–. Published weekly.

Lex–Legislazione italiana. Torino: UTET, 1909–. Published semiannually.

Massimario tributario. Edited by A. GIAQUINTO, F. MIRMINA, and G.
Rosso. Roma: AEI, 1952–. Published bimonthly; jurisprudence of
the civil and penal sections of the Court of Cassation and jurisprudence of the Central Tax Commission, with notes and commentaries.

Massimario tributario. Milano: Giuffrè, 1962–. Published monthly;
supplementing *Giurisprudenza delle imposte* with abstracts of decisions of the Supreme Court of Cassation and the Central Tax Commission, printed on cards.

Nuova rivista tributaria. Roma: 1945–. Published monthly. Cited:
Nuova riv. trib.

Raccolta ufficiale delle sentenze e ordinanze della Corte costituzionale.
Roma: Istituto Poligrafico dello Stato, 1956–. Published annually.

Rassegna della Stampa–Problemi fiscali. Roma: Associazione fra le
Società per Azioni Italiane, 1956–. Published monthly.

Rassegna di diritto e tecnica doganale e delle imposte di fabbricazione.
Roma: 1952–. Published monthly.

Rassegna di diritto pubblico. Napoli: Morano, 1946–. Published quarterly. Cited: *Rass. dir. pubbl.*

Rassegna di finanza pubblica. Published at Roma.

Rassegna economica. Roma: Associazione fra le Società Italiane per Azioni, 1945–. Published monthly.

Rassegna mensile delle imposte dirette. Roma: 1951–. Published monthly. Cited: *Rass. mens. imp. dir.*

The Reporter. New York: 1949–. Published fortnightly.

Rivista dei dottori commercialisti. Published at Milano. Cited: *Riv. dott. comm.*

Rivista del diritto commerciale e del diritto generale delle obbligazioni. Appiano Gentile (Como): Casa Editrice Dr. Francesco Vallardi, 1903–. Published monthly. Cited: *Riv. dir. comm.*

Rivista del notariato. Milano: Giuffrè, 1947–. Published bimonthly. Cited: *Riv. not.*

Rivista delle società. Milano: Giuffrè, 1956–. Published bimonthly. Cited: *Riv. soc.*

Rivista di diritto finanziario e scienza delle finanze (and *Rivista italiana di diritto finanziario*). Milano: Giuffrè, 1937–. Published quarterly. Cited: *RDFSF.*

Rivista di diritto processuale. Padova: CEDAM, 1946–. Published quarterly. Cited: *Riv. dir. proc.*

Rivista di legislazione fiscale. Roma: 1906–. Published monthly. Cited: *Riv. leg. fisc.*

Rivista di politica economia. Roma: 1911–. Published monthly; before 1921: *Rivista delle società commerciali.* Cited: *Riv. pol. ec.*

Rivista internazionale di scienze economiche e commerciali. Edited by UNIVERSITÀ COMMERCIALE LUIGI BOCCONI, MILANO. Padova: CEDAM, 1954–. Published monthly. Cited: *Riv. int. sc. econ. e comm.*

Rivista italiana di scienze economiche. Bologna: Nicola Zanichelli Editore, 1928-1943. Before 1935: *Rivista italiana di statistica, economia e finanza.* Cited: *Riv. it. sc. econ.*

La rivista tributaria. Napoli: Casa Editrice Dott. Eugenio Jovene, 1931–. Published bimonthly. Cited: *Riv. trib.*

Rivista trimestrale di diritto pubblico. Milano: Giuffrè, 1951–. Published quarterly. Cited: *Riv. trim. dir. pubbl.*

Schedario tributario. Milano: Giuffrè, 1962–. Published monthly; reports circulars and instructions of the tax administration.

Sintesi economica. Roma: Unione Italiana delle Camere di Commercio, Industria e Agricoltura, 1948–. Published monthly.

Studi economici. Napoli: Facoltà de Economia e Commercio dell'Università di Napoli, 1945–. Published bimonthly.

Studi urbinati di scienze giuridiche ed economiche. Edited by UNI-
VERSITÀ DI URBINO. Milano: Giuffrè, 1927 to 1940, 1947-1948 to
present. Published annually. Cited: *Studi urbinati.*

Temi tributaria. Torino: Unione Industriale di Torino, 1959–. Published
bimonthly. Cited: *Temi trib.*

NAPOLETANO, V. *Dizionario bibliografico delle riviste giuridiche italiane
su leggi vigenti (1865-1954).* Milano: Giuffrè, 1956 (with annual
supplement).

BIBLIOGRAPHY

The material in most of the sections of this bibliography is divided into two parts: books and articles.

Constitutional and Public Law Background

ADAMS, J. C., and BARILE, P. *The Government of Republican Italy.* Boston: Houghton Mifflin, 1961.

BARTHOLINI, S. *Il principio di legalità dei tributi in materia di imposte.* Padova: CEDAM, 1957.

BATTAGLINI, M., and MININNI, M. *Codice della Corte Costituzionale* (2d ed.). Padova: CEDAM, 1960.

CORTE COSTITUZIONALE. *Sentenze Concernenti la Regione Siciliana, Atti Processuali* (2 volumes). Milano: Giuffrè, 1960.

ESPOSITO, C. *La Costituzione italiana—Saggi.* Padova: CEDAM, 1954.

FERRUCCIO, P. *Codice costituzionale.* Bologna: Nicola Zanichelli Editore, 1954.

GIARDINA, E. *Le basi teoriche del principio della capacità contributiva.* Milano: Giuffrè, 1961.

GIULIANI, G. *La Corte Costituzionale.* Milano: Giuffrè, 1962 (1963 supplement).

KOGAN, N. *The Government of Italy.* New York: Thomas Y. Crowell, 1962. Crowell Comparative Government Series.

LA BARBERA, G. *Lineamenti di diritto pubblico della regione siciliana.* Milano: Giuffrè, 1958.

MINISTERO PER LA COSTITUENTE. *Rapporto della Commissione Economica.* Roma: Istituto Poligrafico dello Stato, 1946.

MORTATI, C. *Istituzioni di diritto pubblico* (6th ed.). Padova: CEDAM, 1962.

PEASLEE, A. J. *Constitutions of Nations* (2d ed.) (3 volumes). The Hague: Nijhoff, 1956.

Raccolta di costituzioni italiane (2 volumes). Torino: Tipografia Economica, 1852. Contains Statute of Carlo Alberto (*Statuto degli Stati Sardi*).

RANELLETTI, O. *Istituzioni di diritto pubblico* (14th ed.) (2 volumes). Milano: Giuffrè, 1953, 1954.

SANDULLI, A. M. *Codice della legislazione amministrativa* (2 volumes). Roma: Casa Editrice Stamperia Nazionale, 1962.

UCKMAR, V. *Principi comuni di diritto costituzionale tributario.* Padova: CEDAM, 1959.

ZANOBINI, G. *Corso di diritto amministrativo* (6 volumes). Milano: Giuffrè, 1958-1959.

BERLIRI, A. "Appunti sul fondamento e il contenuto dell'art. 23 della Costituzione," *Jus*, 1958, 327.

FORTE, F. "Note sulla nozione di tributo nell'ordinamento finanziario italiano e sul significato dell'art. 23 della Costituzione," *RDFSF*, 1956, I, 248.

————. "Note sulle norme tributarie costituzionali italiane," *Jus*, 1957, 372.

LICCARDO, G. "Ancora sulla natura giuridica delle circolari amministrative e sulla loro influenza nel processo tributario," *Rass. dir. pubbl.*, 1955, 318.

MAFFEZZONI, F. "Valore positivo dei principi costituzionali in materia tributaria," *Jus*, 1956, 316.

MANZONI, I. "Sul problema della costituzionalità delle leggi tributarie retroattive," *RDFSF*, 1963, I, 519.

SANDULLI, A. M. "Natura, funzione ed effetti delle pronunce della Corte Costituzionale sulla legittimità delle leggi," *Riv. trim. dir. pubbl.*, 1959, 23.

UCKMAR, V. "Contrasto fra alcune norme del T. U. imposte dirette e la legislazione precedente," *Dir. e prat. trib.*, 1959, I, 18.

————. "La potestà regolamentare in materia tributaria," *Studi in onore di Achille Donato Giannini*. Milano: Giuffrè, 1961.

ZINGALI, G. "Il concetto di tributo nella più recente elaborazione giurisprudenziale," *Arch. fin.*, 1956, 220.

Economic Data

BIBLIOTECA DELLA RIVISTA "ECONOMIA E STORIA." *L'economia italiana dal 1861 al 1961. Studi nel 1° centenario dell'unità d'Italia.* Milano: Giuffrè, 1961.

BRUNI, L. *Aspetti strutturali delle industrie italiane; ampiezza degli impianti, concentrazione territoriale ed intensità di capitale* (Associazione per lo Sviluppo dell'Industria nel Mezzogiorno (SVIMEZ), Serie monografie, 5). Roma: Giuffrè, 1961.

CEE, COMMISSIONE. *Relazione sulla evoluzione della situazione sociale nella Comunità* (annexed to *Quarta relazione generale sulla attività delle Comunità*). Luxemburg: Servizi Pubblicazioni della Comunità Europea, 1961.

CENTRO DI AZIONE LATINA, CASSA DI RISPARMIO DELLE PROVINCIE LOMBARDE. *Italy's Economy 1961*. Milano: Giuffrè, 1961.

CLOUGH, S. B. *The Economic History of Modern Italy*. New York: Columbia University Press, 1964.

CORBINO, E. *Annali dell'economia italiana*. Roma (Città di Castello): Soc. an. Tip. "Leonardo da Vinci," 1931-1938.

FORTE, F. *Evoluzione e lineamenti del sistema tributario. Appendice.* Torino: Cooperativa Libraria Universitaria Torinese, Editrice, 1964.

ISTITUTO CENTRALE DI STATISTICA (ISTAT). *Annuario statistico italiano.* Roma: Istituto Poligrafico dello Stato. Published annually.

————. *Bollettino mensile di statistica*. Roma: Istituto Poligrafico dello Stato. Published monthly.

————. *Compendio statistico italiano*. Roma: Istituto Poligrafico dello Stato. Published annually; published in English under the title *Italian Statistical Abstract*.

————. *Il valore della lire nei primi 100 anni dell'unità d'Italia*. Roma: 1961.

————. *Indagine statistica dello sviluppo del reddito nazionale dell'Italia dal 1861 al 1956.* Roma: 1957.

————. *Indicatori mensili* (supplement to *Bollettino mensile di statistica*. Roma: Istituto Poligrafico dello Stato.

————. *Sommario di statistiche storiche italiane, 1861-1955.* Roma: 1958.

Istituto per la Ricostruzione Industriale (IRI). *Annual Report (Abridged Version).* Roma: Istituto per la Ricostruzione Industriale.

Lutz, V. *Italy: A Study in Economic Development.* London, New York, Toronto: Oxford University Press, 1962.

Milone, F. *L'Italia nell'economia delle sue regioni.* Torino: Edizioni Scientifiche Einaudi, 1955.

Ministero del Bilancio e Ministero del Tesoro. *Relazione generale sulla situazione economica del paese.* Roma: Istituto Poligrafico dello Stato. Published annually.

Ministero del Tesoro, Ragioneria Generale dello Stato. *Il bilancio del Regno d'Italia negli esercizi finanziari dal 1862 al 1912-13.* Roma: Tipografia dell'Unione Editrice, 1914.

————. *Il Bilancio dello Stato dal 1913-14 al 1929-30.* Roma: 1931.

————. *Il Bilancio dello Stato negli esercizi finanziari dal 1930-31 al 1941-42.* Roma: Istituto Poligrafico dello Stato, 1951.

————. *Il bilancio italiano nel primo cinquantennio della unificazione del regno.* Roma: G. Bertero, 1911.

————. *Note informative sul bilancio dello Stato per gli esercizi finanziari dal 1945-46 al 1955-56.* Roma: Istituto Poligrafico dello Stato, 1956.

Ministero dell'Agricoltura, Industria e Commercio. *Bilanci comunali per l'anno 1899.* Roma: 1901.

————. *Bilanci provinciali per l'anno 1899.* Roma: 1901.

Ministero delle Finanze. *Relazione generale sulla amministrazione delle finanze, esercizio 1911-12.* Roma: 1913.

————, Direzione Generale dei Servizi per la Finanza Locale. *Finanze delle amministrazioni comunali e provinciali.* Roma: Ministero delle Finanze, Direzione Generale dei Servizi per la Finanza Locale. Published annually.

————. *Imposte comunali sui consumi.* Roma: Istituto Poligrafico dello Stato. Published annually.

Ministero delle Finanze, Direzione Generale del Catasto e dei Servizi Tecnici Erariali. *Rivista del catasto e dei servizi tecnici erariali.* Roma: Ministero delle Finanze, Direzione Generale del Catasto e dei Servizi Tecnici Erariali. Published bimonthly.

Ministero delle Finanze, Direzione Generale delle Dogane e Imposte Indirette. *Statistica delle imposte di fabbricazione.* Roma: Ministero delle Finanze, Direzione Generale delle Dogane e Imposte Indirette. Published annually.

Ministero delle Finanze, Direzione Generale delle Imposte Dirette. *La gestione delle imposte dirette dal 1914 al 1925.* Roma: Provveditorato Generale dello Stato, 1926.

————. *La gestione delle imposte dirette dal 1926 al 1930.* Roma: Istituto Poligrafico dello Stato, 1932.

————. *La gestione delle imposte dirette dal 1931 al 1940.* Roma: Istituto Poligrafico dello Stato.

————. *L'attività tributaria dal 1949-50 al 1954-55.* Roma: Istituto Poligrafico dello Stato, 1955. Report of the Minister of Finance (Tremelloni) to the President of the Council of Ministers.

————. *Relazione generale della Direzione Generale delle imposte dirette, esercizio 1902-03.* Roma: 1904.

MINISTERO DELLE FINANZE, DIREZIONE GENERALE DELLE TASSE E DELLE IMPOSTE INDIRETTE SUGLI AFFARI. *Relazione sull'attività dell'Amministrazione delle tasse ed imposte dirette sugli affari.* Roma: Istituto Poligrafico dello Stato. Published annually.

MINISTERO DELLE FINANZE, ISPETTORATO GENERALE PER IL LOTTO E LE LOTTERIE. *Il gioco del lotto in Italia.* Roma: Ministero delle Finanze, Ispettorato Generale per il Lotto e le Lotterie. Published annually.

MINISTERO DELLE FINANZE, SERVIZIO DI STATISTICA, STUDI E STAMPA. *Annuario statistico finanziario.* Roma: Ministero delle Finanze, Servizio di Statistica, Studi e Stampa. Published annually.

————. *Dati sulla statistica dei redditi.* Roma: Ministero delle Finanze, Servizio di Statistica, Studi e Stampa. Published annually.

ORGANISATION FOR EUROPEAN ECONOMIC CO-OPERATION (OEEC). *Economic Conditions in Member and Associated Countries of the OEEC: Italy.* Paris: 1961.

PARRAVICINI, G. *La politica fiscale e le entrate del Regno d'Italia 1860-1890.* Torino: ILTE (Industria Libreria Tipografica Editrice), 1958.

PEDONE, A. *Il sistema tributario e la concentrazione industriale.* Milano: Giuffrè, 1963.

POZZANI, S. *L'economia italiana. Situazione e problemi.* Milano: Edizioni di Comunità, 1961.

RÉPACI, F. A. *La finanza italiana nel ventennio 1913-1932.* Torino: Giulio Einaudi, Editore, 1934.

————. *Le finanze dei comuni, delle provincie e degli enti corporativi.* Torino: Giulio Einaudi, Editore, 1936.

ROSSI, G. DE. *Profili e problemi dell'autonomia regionale siciliana.* Milano: Giuffrè, 1962.

SVIMEZ (ASSOCIAZIONE PER LO SVILUPPO DELL'INDUSTRIA NEL MEZZOGIORNO). *Informazioni SVIMEZ.* Roma: 1947—. Published weekly.

————. *Serie "Studie."* Roma: Giuffrè.

————. *Un secolo di statistiche italiane nord e sud 1861-1961.* Roma: 1961.

————, CENTRO PER GLI STUDI SULLO SVILUPPO ECONOMICO. *Serie "Monografie."* Roma: Giuffrè.

————. *Serie "Ricerche."* Roma: Giuffrè.

TAGLIACARNE, G. *Il reddito di lavoro subordinato nelle provincie e regioni d'Italia.* Roma: Edizioni La Fiaccola, 1956.

UNIONE ITALIANA DELLE CAMERE DI COMMERCIO, INDUSTRIA E AGRICOLTURA. *Compendio economico italiano 1963* (7th ed.). Milano: Giuffrè, 1963. Available in English edition.

VOLPI, F. *Le finanze dei comuni e delle province nel Regno d'Italia dal 1860 al 1890.* Torino: ILTE (Industria Libreria Tipografica Editrice), 1962.

AMOROSO, L. "La pressione tributaria nei grandi paesi d'Europa alla vigilia della guerra," *Riv. pol. ec.*, 1960, 561.

"Italy: New Wave or Interlude?" *The Economist*, 28 March 1964, 1233.

STERLING, C. " 'Apertura a Sinistra': Second Round," *The Reporter*, 21 November 1963, 28.

TREMELLONI, R. "Alcune riflessioni sulla spesa pubblica in Italia," *RDFSF*, 1962, I, 241.

Historical Background

ALBRECHT-CARRIÉ, R. *Italy from Napoleon to Mussolini.* New York: Columbia University Press, 1950.

BARBARODO, B. *Le finanze della Repubblica Fiorentina. Imposta diretta e debito pubblico fino all'istituzione del Monte.* Firenze: Leo S. Olschki, Editore, 1929.

CALISSE, C. *A History of Italian Law.* Boston: Little, Brown, 1928. Italian edition, Florence, 1902.

CIPOLLA, C. M. (ed.). *Storia dell'economia italiana. Saggi di storia economica.* Torino: Edizioni Scientifiche Einaudi, 1959.

DE'STEFANI, A. *La restaurazione finanziaria 1922-1925.* Bologna: Nicola Zanichelli Editore, 1926.

DI RENZO, F. "Imposta (Diritto intermedio)," 8 *Novissimo digesto italiano* 305. Torino: UTET, 1962.

IZZO, L. *La finanza pubblica nel primo decennio dell'unità italiana.* Milano: Giuffrè, 1962.

LUZZATO, G. *An Economic History of Italy from the Fall of the Roman Empire to the Beginning of the Sixteenth Century.* Translated by P. JONES. London: Routledge & Kegan Paul, Limited, 1961.

MINISTERO DEL TESORO, RAGIONERIA GENERALE DELLO STATO. *Istituzione e magistrature finanziarie e di controllo della Repubblica di Genova dalle origini al 1797.* Roma: Istituto Poligrafico dello Stato, 1952.

————. *Magistrature contabili e di controllo della Repubblica di Venezia dalle origini al 1797.* Roma: Istituto Poligrafico dello Stato, 1950.

————. *Organi contabili e di controllo del Regno di Napoli (1130-1860).* Roma: Istituto Poligrafico dello Stato, 1950.

MORSELLI, E. (ed.). *Storia della finanza pubblica* (13 volumes). Padova: CEDAM, 1960-1962.

PITIGLIANI, F. *The Italian Corporative State.* London: P. S. King & Son, Limited, 1933.

SMITH, D. M. *Italy, A Modern History.* Ann Arbor, Mich.: The University of Michigan Press, 1959.

SOLMI, A. *L'amministrazione finanziaria del Regno Italico nell'alto medio evo.* Pavia: Tipografica Cooperativa, 1932.

WELK, W. G. *Fascist Economic Policy.* Cambridge, Mass.: Harvard University Press, 1938.

General Works on Taxation and Public Finance

ANTONINI, E. *Studi di diritto tributario.* Milano: Giuffrè, 1959.

ARENA, C. *Finanza pubblica* (2 volumes). Torino: UTET, 1964.

———— and SCANDALE, E. *Le leggi fiscali, annotate con la dottrina, la giurisprudenza, e le normali ministeriali* (7th ed.) (3 volumes). Bologna: Dott. Cesare Zuffi, Editore, 1954-1960.

ASSOCIAZIONE FRA LE SOCIETÀ ITALIANE PER AZIONI. *La distinzione tra imposte dirette e indirette (Uno studio di storia delle dottrine finanziarie)* (volume XXIII of *Quaderni*). Roma: 1957.

BENNATI, A. *La gestione finanziaria dello Stato.* Milano: Giuffrè, 1961.

BENTIVENGA, C. *Elementi di contabilità di Stato* (3d ed.). Milano: Giuffrè, 1960.

BERLIRI, A. *Principi di diritto tributario* (2 volumes). Milano: Giuffrè, 1952, 1957.

Bosisio, O. *Imposte e tasse*. Milano: L. di G. Pirola, 1960.

Buchanan, J. M. " 'La Scienza delle Finanze': The Italian Tradition in Fiscal Theory," *Fiscal Theory and Political Economy, Selected Essays*. Chapel Hill, N. C.: The University of North Carolina Press, 1960.

Cordaro, P. *Codice fiscale* (3d ed.). Torino: UTET, 1961.

————. *Dizionario del contribuente* (2d ed.). Torino: UTET, 1959.

Cosciani, C. *La riforma tributaria*. Firenze: "La Nuova Italia," 1950.

De Nardo, V. *Il costo dei tributi in Italia*. Milano: Giuffrè, 1960.

De Viti De Marco, A. *Principii di economia finanziaria*. Torino: Giulio Einaudi, Editore, 1934. English edition, *First Principles of Public Finance*, translated by E. P. Marget and published in 1936 by Harcourt, Brace, New York.

Einaudi, L. *Il sistema tributario italiano* (3d ed.). Torino: Giulio Einaudi, Editore, 1935.

————. *Miti e paradossi della giustizia tributaria* (3d ed.). Torino: Giulio Einaudi, Editore, 1959.

————. *Principî di scienza della finanza*. Torino: Edizioni Scientifiche Einaudi, 1956.

———— and Répaci, F. A. *Il sistema tributario italiano* (5th ed., 1954; 6th ed., 1958). Torino: Edizioni Scientifiche Einaudi.

Fanno, M. *Elementi di scienza delle finanze* (24th ed.). Torino: S. Lattes & C., Editori, 1959.

Fasiani, M. *Principi di scienza delle finanze* (2 volumes). Torino: Giappichelli, 1951.

Forte, F. *Il sistema tributario italiano e la politica fiscale italiana* (volume 1, 1962). Torino: Cooperativa Libraria Universitaria Torinese, Editrice.

————. "Imposta (Scienza delle finanze)," 8 *Novissimo digesto italiano* 310. Torino: UTET, 1962.

Giannini, A. D. *I concetti fondamentali del diritto tributario*. Torino: UTET, 1956.

————. *Istituzioni di diritto tributario* (8th ed.). Milano: Giuffrè, 1960.

———— and Scoca, S. *Codice delle leggi tributarie* (3d ed.). Milano: Giuffrè, 1962.

Studi in onore di Achille Donato Giannini. Milano: Giuffrè, 1961.

Giardina, E. *Le basi teoriche del principio della capacità contributiva*. Milano: Giuffrè, 1961.

Gloria, A. *Il prontuario del contribuente italiano* (17th ed.). Padova: Gregoriana Editrice, 1961-1962.

Griziotti, B. "Diritto finanziario," 4 *Nuovo Digesto Italiano* 1056. Torino: UTET, 1938.

————. *Primi elementi di scienza delle finanze* (6th ed.). Edited by F. Forte. Milano: Giuffrè, 1957. A revised edition, edited by G. Parravicini, was published in 1962.

————. *Primi lineamenti delle dottrine finanziarie in Italia nell'ultimo cinquantennio*. Padova: CEDAM, 1930.

————. *Principii di politica, diritto e scienza delle finanze*. Padova: CEDAM, 1929.

————. *Saggi sul rinnovamento dello studio della scienza delle finanze e del diritto finanziario*. Milano: Giuffrè, 1953.

———— et al. *La politica finanziaria italiana. Studi sui problemi monetari e finanziari*. Milano: Soc. an. Istituto Editoriale Scientifico, 1926.

Studi in memoria di Benvenuto Griziotti. Edited by UNIVERSITÀ DI PAVIA, FACOLTÀ DI GIURISPRUDENZA, ISTITUTO DI FINANZA. Milano: Giuffrè, 1959.

HARVARD LAW SCHOOL INTERNATIONAL PROGRAM IN TAXATION. *World Tax Series: Taxation in Australia.* Prepared by W. W. BRUDNO and K. O. SHATWELL. Boston: Little, Brown, 1958. Cited: WTS: *Australia.*

————. *World Tax Series: Taxation in Brazil.* Prepared by H. J. GUMPEL and RUBENS GOMES DE SOUSA. Boston: Little, Brown, 1957. Cited: WTS: *Brazil.*

————. *World Tax Series: Taxation in Colombia.* Prepared by G. J. EDER, J. C. CHOMMIE, and H. J. BECERRA. Chicago: Commerce Clearing House, 1964. Cited: WTS: *Colombia.*

————. *World Tax Series: Taxation in the Federal Republic of Germany.* Prepared by H. J. GUMPEL and C. BOETTCHER. Chicago: Commerce Clearing House, 1963. Cited: WTS: *Germany.*

————. *World Tax Series: Taxation in India.* Prepared by W. W. BRUDNO, C. K. COBB, JR., and NANI A. PALKHIVALA. Boston: Little, Brown, 1960. Cited: WTS: *India.*

————. *World Tax Series: Taxation in Mexico.* Prepared by H. J. GUMPEL and H. B. MARGÁIN. Boston: Little, Brown, 1957 (1961 supplement). Cited: WTS: *Mexico.*

————. *World Tax Series: Taxation in Sweden.* Prepared by M. NORR, F. J. DUFFY, and H. STERNER. Boston: Little, Brown, 1959. Cited: WTS: *Sweden.*

————. *World Tax Series: Taxation in the United Kingdom.* Prepared by W. W. BRUDNO and F. BOWER. Boston: Little, Brown, 1957 (1961 supplement). Cited: WTS: *United Kingdom.*

————. *World Tax Series: Taxation in the United States.* Prepared by M. A. CHIRELSTEIN, L. DAY, E. A. OWENS, and S. S. SURREY. Chicago: Commerce Clearing House, 1963. Cited: WTS: *United States.*

LA VOLPE, G. *Sistema di contabilità nazionale. Struttura dei finanziamenti e dei pagamenti dell'Italia* (2 volumes). Milano: Feltrinelli Editore, 1960.

MAFFEZZONI, F. "Diritto finanziario," 5 *Novissimo digesto italiano* 845. Torino: UTET, 1960.

MESIANO, F., and PISCIOTTA, F. *Codice della contabilità pubblica.* Roma: Jandi Sapi Editori, 1959.

MILANO, CAMERA DI COMMERCIO, INDUSTRIA E AGRICOLTURA. *Atti del Convegno degli esperti fiscali dei paesi del M.E.C., 8-9 maggio 1959.* Milano: Giuffrè, 1960.

MINISTERO DEL TESORO, RAGIONERIA GENERALE DELLO STATO. *Legge e regolamento per l'amministrazione del patrimonio e per la contabilità generale dello Stato* (14th ed.). Roma: Istituto Poligrafico dello Stato, 1959.

————. *Nuovi concetti sulla impostazione strutturale del Bilancio dello Stato.* Roma: 1959.

MINISTERO DELLE FINANZE. *Sintesi dei lavori della Commissione per lo Studio della Riforma Tributaria.* Roma: Istituto Poligrafico dello Stato, 1963.

MORSELLI, E. *Le imposte in Italia* (7th ed.). Padova: CEDAM, 1962.

STAMMATI, G. *La finanza pubblica* (2d ed.). Bologna: Nicola Zanichelli Editore, 1960.

STEVE, S. *Il sistema tributario e le sue prospettive.* Milano: Rizzoli Editore, 1947.

————. *Lezioni di scienza delle finanze* (3d ed.). Padova: CEDAM, 1960.

SULLIVAN, C. K. *The Search for Tax Principles in the European Economic Community.* Cambridge, Mass.: Harvard Law School International Program in Taxation, 1963.

VANONI, E. *Opere giuridiche* (2 volumes). Edited by F. FORTE and C. LONGOBARDI. Milano: Giuffrè, 1961, 1962.

National Income Taxation

In General

ANGELI, D. (ed.). *Commento, Testo unico imposte dirette.* Milano: Edizioni Consulente delle Aziende, 1959.

ASSOCIAZIONE FRA LE SOCIETÀ ITALIANE PER AZIONI. *La perequazione tributaria (Disposizioni legislative e Atti parlamentari)* (2 volumes) (volume XXII of *Quaderni*). Roma: 1956.

BANCA COMMERCIALE ITALIANA. *Testo unico delle leggi sulle imposte dirette.* Milano: 1964.

BERLIRI, A. *Il testo unico delle imposte dirette (Esposizione istituzionale dei primi otto titoli).* Milano: Giuffrè, 1960.

BERLIRI, L. V. *L'imposta di ricchezza mobile.* Milano: Giuffrè, 1949.

COCIVERA, B. *Guida alle imposte dirette* (4th ed.). Torino: UTET, 1961.

————. *Raccolta delle circolari ed istruzioni ministeriali relative all'imposta di r.m. e complementare progressiva sul reddito.* Milano: Giuffrè, 1957 (with supplements).

DE ANGELIS, F., POTENZA, G., and TESTA, A. *Testo unico delle leggi sulle imposte dirette* (2d. ed.). Milano: Giuffrè, 1960.

FONTANA, S. *Note sulle imposte dirette secondo il nuovo T.U.* Torino: Giappichelli, 1960.

MANDÒ, M. *Imposta di ricchezza mobile* (2d ed.). Vicenza: Arti Grafiche delle Venezie, 1959.

MESIANO, V., PISCITELLI, I., and CECCARELLI, L. *Commento teorico-pratico alle norme integrative della legge sulla perequazione tributaria* (2d ed.). Roma: Jandi Sapi Editori, 1957.

QUARTA, O. *Commento alla legge sulla imposta di ricchezza mobile* (2d ed., 1902-1905; 3d ed., 1917-1920) (3 volumes). Milano: Società Editrice Libraria.

ZAPPALÀ, L., MARIONETTI, A., and LANZA, F. *L'imposta sui redditi di ricchezza mobile.* Napoli: Casa Editrice Dott. Eugenio Jovene, 1957.

ZAPPALÀ, L., and PIETRANTONIO, L. *Codice delle imposte dirette erariali (Edizione aggiornata con il Testo unico 29-1-1958 N. 645).* Frascati: Casa Editrice Tuscolana, 1959.

CASTELLINO, O. "Note sulla progressività dell'imposta complementare," *Giorn. degli economisti*, 1963, 168.

Classes of Taxpayers (Chapter 5)

ASSOCIAZIONE FRA LE SOCIETÀ ITALIANE PER AZIONI. *L'imposta sulla società (documenti e scritti vari)* (volume XXI of *Quaderni*). Roma: 1954.

BOIDI, A. *Commento alla legge sulla imposta complementare progressiva sul reddito* (2d ed.). Torino: UTET, 1956.

————. *L'imposta sulle società e sulle obbligazioni.* Torino: UTET, 1959.

BRUNETTI, A. *Trattato del diritto delle società* (2d ed.) (3 volumes). Milano: Giuffrè, 1948-1950.

COSCIANI, C. *The effects of differential tax treatment of corporate and non-corporate enterprises* (O.E.E.C. Project No. 314). Paris: The European Productivity Agency of the Organisation for European Economic Co-operation, 1959.

FRÈ, G. *Società per azioni, Commentario del Codice Civile.* Bologna: Nicola Zanichelli Editore, 1959.

"Istituzione di una imposta sulle società e modificazioni in materia di imposte indirette sugli affari," *Relazione al disegno di legge presentato al Senato dal Ministero delle Finanze,* 26 January 1954. *Atti Parlamentari, Legislatura II,* 1953-1954 (Stampato n. 359).

MERLINO, R. *L'imposta complementare progressiva sul reddito* (2d ed.). Roma: Centenari, 1960.

NAPOLITANO, L. *La imposta sulle società.* Milano: Giuffrè, 1955.

PEDEMONTE, E. *Costituzione e amministrazione delle società commerciali con speciale riguardo agli obblighi tributari* (14th ed.). Genova: Di Stefano Editore, 1959.

POLI, O. *Imposta sulle società e imposta sulle obbligazioni* (2d ed.). Cuneo: Ghibaudo, 1961.

TRABUCCHI, A. *Istituzioni di diritto civile* (12th ed.). Padova: CEDAM, 1960. The 14th edition of this work was published in 1964.

ALLORIO, E. "Imposta sulle società ed enti formati con dotazione statale," *Scritti giuridici in onore di Mario Cavalieri* 293. Padova: 1960.

FORTE, F. "Sulla politica fiscale nei confronti delle piccole società di capitali," *Temi trib.,* 1959, 30.

MAFFEZZONI, F. "L'imposta di ricchezza mobile sugli interessi dei contributi versati a un fondo di previdenza," *Giur. comp. Cass., Sez. Civ.,* 1947, vol. 26, 244.

POLI, O. "Cespiti e redditi nell'imposta di ricchezza mobile," *RDFSF,* 1955, II, 311.

Principles of Income Determination (Chapter 6)

BISCOTTO, A., and OZZOLA, G. *Il processo tributario di accertamento.* Roma: Società Grafica Romana, 1961.

BOCCHI, A. *Contabilità fiscale* (3d ed.). Milano: Edizioni Consulente delle Aziende, 1958.

CECCHERELLI, A. *Il linguaggio dei bilanci* (6th ed.). Firenze: Felice le Monnier, 1956.

FERRERO, G. *Le analisi di bilancio.* Milano: Giuffrè, 1961.

GIANNETTA, E., SCANDALE, G., and SESSA, M. *Teoria e tecnica nell'accertamento del reddito mobiliare* (2d ed.). Roma: Soc. A.B.E.T.E., 1958.

GRILLO, R. *Il bilancio delle società per azioni nella determinazione del reddito economico e del reddito fiscale* (3d ed.) (2 volumes). Milano: Giuffrè, 1955, 1959.

————. *Le riserve di bilancio nella economia di azienda e nel diritto tributario.* Milano: Giuffrè, 1950.

MAZZA, G. *Scritture e bilanci in una impresa di media dimensione* (2 volumes). Milano: Giuffrè, 1963.

MINISTERO DELLE FINANZE, DIREZIONE GENERALE DELLE IMPOSTE DIRETTE. *Rivalutazione per conguaglio monetario (Legge 11 febbraio 1952, n. 74).* Roma: Istituto Poligrafico dello Stato, 1955.

MINNITI, F. *Le norme sulla perequazione tributaria e la svalutazione della moneta* (2d ed.). Napoli: Edizioni Scientifiche Italiane, 1951.

MONTUORI, L. *La determinazione dei redditi soggetti all'imposta di R.M.* Torino: Giappichelli, 1963.

———. *Note sulle tassazioni in base al bilancio.* Torino: Giappichelli, 1960.

NAPOLITANO, L. *Il reddito nella scienza delle finanze e nel diritto tributario.* Milano: Giuffrè, 1953.

PELLINGRA, G. *Dell'accertamento induttivo in materia tributaria* (2d ed.). Roma: Bardi Editore, 1960.

———. *La determinazione analitica e induttiva del reddito fiscale nell'imposizione tributaria.* Milano: Giuffrè, 1962.

TRAINA-PORTANOVA, S. *Spese e passività deducibili nell'imposta di ricchezza mobile* (3d ed.). Milano: Giuffrè, 1956.

ARDIGÒ, F. "Sul requisito dell'intento speculativo per l'imposizione del plusvalore nelle vendite d'immobili," *RDFSF,* 1938, II, 301.

BOIDI, A. "Ancora sui tributi deducibili ai fini dell'imposta complementare," *Dir. e prat. trib.,* 1959, II, 417.

———. "Le imposte e tasse deducibili in sede d'imposta complementare sul reddito," *Dir. e prat. trib.,* 1958, II, 447.

CICOGNANI, A. "Ancora della detraibilità dell'imposta patrimoniale ai fini dell'imposta complementare," *Boll. trib. informazioni,* 1957, 1089.

COLOMBO, G. E. "Riserve facoltative e riserve occulte nel bilancio delle società per azioni," *Riv. dir. comm.,* 1960, I, 176.

DUS, A. "I ricavi nel nuovo T.U. delle imposte dirette," *RDFSF,* 1959, I. 113.

FORTE, F. "Alcune osservazioni sulla personalizzazione delle imposte reali sul reddito," *Studi urbinati,* 1957-1958, vol. 26, 3.

GIUSSANI, B. "Del concetto di reddito mobiliare e del trattamento tributario degli assegni alimentari," *RDFSF,* 1940, II, 3.

GRIZIOTTI, B. "I concetti giuridici dogmatici di reddito di r.m. e di capacità contributiva. L'imposizione degli assegni alimentari," *RDFSF,* 1940, II, 11.

———. "L'autonomia del diritto finanziario nella determinazione della capacità contributiva e del reddito imponibile. La intassabilità in r.m. delle plusvalenze monetarie nominali," *RDFSF,* 1938, II, 107.

———. "Le imposte sugli incrementi di valore nei capitali e sulle rendite dei redditi (interessi, salari e profitti)," *Giorn. degli economisti,* 1910, vol. 40, 625; vol. 41, 648.

JONA CELESIA, L. "Detraibilità dell'imposta di successione in sede di applicazione dell'imposta complementare," *Jus,* 1963, 249.

VANONI, E. "Intorno alla deducibilità ai fini dell'imposta sui redditi di R.M. della imposta straordinaria sul capitale delle società per azioni," *RDFSF,* 1943, II, 57.

———. "Stabilità ed unicità dell'accertamento dei redditi 'una tantum' nell'imposta complementare," *RDFSF,* 1942, II, 53-60, 109-113. Reprinted in 1 VANONI, *Opere giuridiche* 455. Milano: Giuffrè, 1961.

WUELLER, P. H. "Concepts of Taxable Income III: The Italian Contribution," 54 *Political Science Quarterly* 555 (1939). New York: Columbia University, Academy of Political Science.

Income from Business (Chapter 7)

AMADUZZI, A. *L'azienda nel suo sistema e nell'ordine delle sue rilevazioni.* Torino: UTET, 1953.

ASCARELLI, T. *Corso di diritto commerciale. Introduzione alla teoria dell'impresa* (3d ed.). Milano: Giuffrè, 1962.

————. *Studi in tema di società.* Milano: Giuffrè, 1952.

ASSOCIAZIONE FRA LE SOCIETÀ ITALIANE PER AZIONI. *Problemi fiscali degli ammortamenti* (volume XXV of *Quaderni*). Roma: 1960.

BOCCHI, A. *Contabilità fiscale* (3d ed.). Milano: Edizioni Consulente delle Aziende, 1958.

BRUNI, A. *L'organizzazione aziendale nel quadro delle istituzioni economiche europee.* Milano: Giuffrè, 1962.

CECCHERELLI, A. *Il linguaggio dei bilanci* (6th ed.). Firenze: Felice le Monnier, 1956.

DE GREGORIO, A. *Corso di diritto commerciale. Imprenditori e società* (6th ed.). Roma: Soc. ed. Dante Alighieri, 1960.

FERRARA, F. *Gli imprenditori e le società* (2d ed.). Milano: Giuffrè, 1946. The fourth edition of this work was published in 1962.

FERRI, G. *Manuale di diritto commerciale* (reprint of 2d ed.). Torino: UTET, 1961.

GIANNETTA, E., SCANDALE, G., and SESSA, M. *Teoria e tecnica nell'accertamento del reddito mobiliare* (2d ed.). Roma: Soc. A.B.E.T.E., 1958.

GRAZIANI, A. *Manuale di diritto commerciale* (4th ed.). Napoli: Morano, 1955.

GRILLO, R. *Il bilancio delle società per azioni nella determinazione del reddito economico e del reddito fiscale* (3d ed.) (2 volumes). Milano: Giuffrè, 1955, 1959.

————. *Le riserve di bilancio nella economia di azienda e nel diritto tributario.* Milano: Giuffrè, 1950.

MAZZA, G. *Scritture e bilanci in una impresa di media dimensione* (2 volumes). Milano: Giuffrè, 1963.

MONTUORI, L. *Note sulle tassazioni in base al bilancio.* Torino: Giappichelli, 1960.

ONIDA, P. *Il bilancio d'esercizio nelle imprese* (3d ed.). Milano: Giuffrè, 1945.

————. *Le discipline economiche aziendali.* Milano: Giuffrè, 1951.

TRAINA-PORTANOVA, S. *Spese e passività deducibili nell'imposta di ricchezza mobile* (3d ed.). Milano: Giuffrè, 1956.

ZAPPA, G. *Il reddito d'impresa* (4th reprint of 2d ed.). Milano: Giuffrè, 1950.

BERLIRI, A. "Questioni in tema di applicazione dell'imposta di r.m.," *Foro it.,* 1951, I, 1575. Untitled annotation to Trib. Bologna 27 June 1950.

BERLIRI, L. V. "In tema di 'avulsione' dei redditi ai fini dell'imposta di ricchezza mobile," *Foro it.,* 1948, I, 223. Untitled annotation to Cass., Sez. I, 22 February 1947, n. 253.

COLOMBO, G. E. "Riserve facoltative e riserve occulte nel bilancio delle società per azioni," *Riv. dir. comm.,* 1960, I, 176.

CROXATTO, G. "Tassabilità in R.M. dei proventi di natura commerciale e degli avanzi di gestione degli enti pubblici," *Dir. e prat. trib.,* 1960, II, 401.

DUS, A. "Le 'spese e passività' deducibili ai fini del calcolo del reddito mobiliare nel nuovo testo unico delle imposte dirette," *RDFSF,* 1958, I, 333-345.

Forte, F. "Detraibilità di spese per sinistri nell'imposta di r.m.," *RDFSF*, 1950, II, 101.

Giannini, A. D. "L'avulsione dei redditi in tema d'imposta di ricchezza mobile," *Giur. comp. Cass., Sez. Civ.*, 1946, vol. 22, 526.

Giussani, B. "Avanzi di gestione ed imposta di ricchezza mobile," *Giur. it.*, 1954, I, 2, 421.

Greco, G. "Interessi passivi delle banche—Categoria di tassazione," *Rass. mens. imp. dir.*, 1958, 170.

————. "Presunzione di interessi, avulsione dei redditi, renunzia agli interessi e cessazione dei redditi con riferimento all'imposta di R.M.," *RDFSF*, 1956, II, 308.

Grillo, R. "Imposta di ricchezza mobile, cat. A: interessi passivi e mancata rivalsa della relativa imposta, indetraibilità di essa," *Giust. trib.*, 1961, 393.

Jona Celesia, L. "Deducibilità degli interessi dal reddito lordo delle aziende di credito," *RDFSF*, 1962, II, 173.

Onida, P. "Il reddito d'esercizio e la politica degli ammortamenti dei dividendi nei bilanci delle società per azioni," *Riv. dott. comm.*, 1951, III, 65.

Poli, O. "La tassazione delle partecipazioni agli utili come compenso di prestazioni di opera," *RDFSF*, 1959, II, 335.

Rotondi, A. "Imposta di r.m. sui redditi *'una tantum,'*" *Dir. e prat. trib.*, 1951, II, 283.

Income from Personal Services (Chapter 8)

Ferri, G. *Manuale di diritto commerciale* (reprint of 2d ed.). Torino: UTET, 1961.

Greco, P. *Lezioni di diritto commerciale.* Roma: Edizioni Ricerche, 1958.

Panusa, G., and Merlino, R. *La legislazione tributaria sui redditi di lavoro subordinato* (2d ed.). Roma: Tipografia Squarci, 1955.

Rubino, D. *L'appalto* (3d ed.) Torino: UTET, 1958.

Montuori, L. "Le plusvalenze, le perdite e l'avviamento nella determinazione del reddito derivante dall'esercizio delle arti e professioni," *RDFSF*, 1963, II, 194.

Income from Capital and Capital Transactions (Chapter 9)

Armocida, P. *Il nuovo catasto urbano e l'imposta sul reddito dei fabbricati.* Milano: Giuffrè, 1962.

Evidente, P. *L'imposta sui fabbricati con particolare riguardo al nuovo catasto edilizio urbano* (rev. 2d ed.). Napoli: Morano, 1957.

Frè, G. *Società per azioni Commentario del Codice Civile.* Bologna: Nicola Zanichelli Editore, 1959.

Giannetta, E., Scandale, G., and Sessa, M. *Teoria e tecnica nell'accertamento del reddito mobiliare* (2d ed.). Roma: Soc. A.B.E.T.E., 1958.

Pedone, A. "Le régime fiscal comparé au processus de la concentration des entreprises (Italie)," *Cahiers de droit fiscal international (Studies on International Fiscal Law)*, 1963, vol. XLVIIIa, 153. Paris: Association Internationale de Droit Financier et Fiscal and International Fiscal Association.

Piazza, G. *Ritenuta d'acconto o imposta sugli utili delle società—Nominatività dei titoli azionari.* Milano: Edizione Consulente delle Aziende, 1963.

POLI, O. *Imposta complementare sui redditi derivanti da partecipazioni in società e imposta cedolare.* Milano: Giuffrè, 1963.

PORZIO, M. *L'estinzione della società per azioni.* Napoli: Casa Editrice Dott. Eugenio Jovene, 1959.

RUMBOLDT, T. *Le imposte fondiarie.* Torino: UTET, 1961.

SANTORO, F. *Esenzioni ed agevolazioni fiscali in materia di imposte dirette ordinarie erariali e di tributi degli enti territoriali.* Roma: Casa Editrice Carlo Colombo, 1954 (1957 supplement).

SCATÀ, U. *Esenzioni e riduzioni di imposte a favore della nuova proprietà edilizia* (4th ed.). Roma: Studio Tributario Scatà, 1961.

VIZZINI, M. *Fabbricati e terreni nell'imposizione diretta erariale.* Milano: Giuffrè, 1959. The second edition of this book was published in 1964.

ARDIGÒ, F. "Sul requisito dell'intento speculativo per l'imposizione del plus-valore nelle vendite d'immobili," *RDFSF,* 1938, II, 301.

BOSELLO, F. "La tassazione dell'avviamento nella cessione di quote sociali," *RDFSF,* 1963, II, 187.

CRISTOFARO, A. "Concetto di plusvalori patrimoniali con particolare riferimento al nostro ordinamento tributario," *Temi trib.,* 1961, 760.

CROXATTO, G. "Assoggettabilità degli incrementi patrimoniali all'imposta di ricchezza mobile," *Dir. e prat. trib.,* 1959, II, 177.

————. "Su taluni casi controversi di tassabilità del avviamento," *Riv. int. sc. econ. e comm.,* 1962, 1067.

DI PAOLO, G. "La tassazione delle plusvalenze e sopravvenienze," *Cons. az.,* 1962, 152.

————. "Società immobiliari ed imposta di R.M.," *Temi trib.,* 1960, 14.

FALSITTA, G. "Tassabilità del avviamento nel caso di scioglimento di società e assegnazione dell'azienda all'unico socio o ad uno dei soci," *RDFSF,* 1963, II, 301.

FASIANI, M. "L'imposizione degli incrementi patrimoniali," MINISTERO PER LA COSTITUENTE, *Rapporto della Commissione Economica,* 1946, vol. 5, II, 429.

FERRO, F. "La tassazione degli incrementi patrimoniali nella imposta di ricchezza mobile," *Nuova riv. trib.,* 1960, 348.

FORTE, F. "L'imponibilità degli utili derivanti a società dall'acquisto di azioni proprie nella imposta di R.M.," *RDFSF,* 1950, II, 301.

————. "Sulla politica fiscale nei confronti delle piccole società di capitali," *Temi trib.,* 1959, 30.

GIUSSANI, B. "Del concetto di reddito mobiliare e del trattamento tributario degli assegni alimentari," *RDFSF,* 1940, II, 3.

GRIZIOTTI, B. "Ancora sull'imponibilità degli assegni alimentari fra coniugi," *RDFSF,* 1940, II ,99.

————. "I concetti giuridici dogmatici di reddito di r.m. e di capacità contributiva. L'imposizione degli assegni alimentari," *RDFSF,* 1940, II, 11.

————. "Le imposte sugli incrementi di valore nei capitali e sulle rendite dei redditi (interessi, salari e profitti)," *Giorn. degli economisti,* 1910, vol. 40, 625; vol. 41, 648.

JONA CELESIA, L. "Sulla tassabilità in complementare dei redditi di r.m. delle società di capitali," *RDFSF,* 1962, II, 3.

LICCARDO, G. "Importanza dell'intento speculativo nella determinazione del reddito," *Riv. trib.,* 1952, 408.

LONGOBARDI, C. "Il concetto di reddito mobiliare e l'imponibilità degli assegni alimentari fra coniugi," *Giur. comp. Cass., Sez. Civ.*, 1947, vol. 25, 146.

MAFFEZZONI, F. "Motivi e limiti di efficacia della abolizione del 'solve et repete,'" *Riv. dir. proc.*, 1961, 641.

MAZZILLI, T. "In tema di tassazione delle plusvalenze aziendali," *Nuova rass. comm.*, 1959, 249.

MONTUORI, L. "Le plusvalenze, le perdite e l'avviamento nella determinazione del reddito derivante dall'esercizio delle arti e professioni," *RDFSF*, 1963, II, 194.

————. "Osservazioni sulla nominatività fiscale dei dividendi e sulla ritenuta cedolare d'acconto," *RDFSF*, 1963, I, 544.

NAPOLITANO, L. "Cessione del pacchetto azionario ed avviamento dell'azienda sociale," *Dir. e prat. trib.*, 1956, II, 3.

PICCATTI, P. "La circolazione dell'azienda ed il realizzo dell'avviamento," *Temi trib.*, 1963, 671.

POLI, O. "Il reddito di avviamento nelle trasformazioni di società," *Imp. dir. erariali*, 1962, 336-350.

————. "Redditi derivanti da partecipazioni in società di persone o di capitali e imposta complementare," *Imp. dir. erariali*, 1963, 161.

ROMANI, A. "Alcune riflessioni in tema di presupposti dell'imposta di ricchezza mobile," *RDFSF*, 1960, I, 370.

SCOTTO, A. "Sulla tassabilità di un premio di avviamento nella trasformazione di società di capitale in società di persone," *Riv. soc.*, 1957, 263.

Income from Special Activities and from Miscellaneous Sources (Chapter 10)

CENTRO DEMOCRATICO DI CULTURA E DI DOCUMENTAZIONE. *Repertorio della legislazione sul Mezzogiorno d'Italia (1860-1956)*. Roma: Edizioni di Cultura e di Documentazione, 1958.

CONFEDERAZIONE GENERALE DELL'INDUSTRIA ITALIANA (CONFINDUSTRIA). *Legislation for the Development of Southern Italy*. Roma: Laboratorio Arti Grafiche, 1958.

CORRADO, T. *Il trattamento fiscale dell'esercizio cinematografico*. Milano: Giuffrè, 1963.

EINAUDI, L. *La terra e l'imposta* (3d ed.). Torino: Giulio Einaudi, Editore, 1960.

GALIPÒ, G. *Le agevolazioni fiscali per l'industrializzazione del Mezzogiorno*. Roma: Editore Nuova Rivista Tributaria, 1961.

NITTO, A. *Le agevolazioni per lo sviluppo industriale del Mezzogiorno. Con particolare riguardo a quelle doganali*. Roma: Edizioni Scambi e Dogane, 1962.

REALE, G. *Agevolazioni fiscali per l'industrializzazione del Mezzogiorno d'Italia e delle isole. Benefici vari per l'industria*. Roma: Appollonio, 1962.

RUMBOLDT, T. *Le imposte fondiarie*. Torino: UTET, 1961.

SANTORO, F. *Esenzioni ed agevolazioni fiscali in materia di imposte dirette ordinarie erariali e di tributi degli enti territoriali*. Roma: Casa Editrice Carlo Colombo, 1954 (1957 supplement).

SVIMEZ (ASSOCIAZIONE PER LO SVILUPPO DELL'INDUSTRIA NEL MEZZO-GIORNO). *Agevolazioni per l'industrializzazione e lo sviluppo economico del Mezzogiorno* (4th ed.). Roma: 1954.

————. *Informazioni SVIMEZ*. Roma: 1947—. Published weekly.

————. *La legislazione per il Mezzogiorno, 1861-1957* (2 volumes). Roma: Giuffrè, 1957.

————. *Rassegna di giurisprudenza sulle leggi per l'industrializzazione del Mezzogiorno.* Edited by M. Annesi. Roma: Giuffrè, 1960.

————. *Summary of measures to promote industrialization in Southern Italy.* Rome: 1961.

Vizzini, M. *Fabbricati e terreni nell'imposizione diretta erariale.* Milano: Giuffrè, 1959. The second edition of this book was published in 1964.

Einaudi, L. "Discutendo con Fasiani e Griziotti di connotati dello Stato e di catasto ed imposta fondiaria," *RDFSF*, 1943, I, 178.

Jona Celesia, L. "Deducibilità degli interessi dal reddito lordo delle aziende di credito," *RDFSF*, 1962, II, 173.

————. "In tema de deducibilità dell'imposta di r.m. cat. A pagata dalle banche," *RDFSF*, 1963, II, 291.

International Aspects of Income Taxation (Chapter I I)

Collection Jupiter. *Recueils pratiques du droit des affaires dans les pays du Marché Commun* (volume 5: *Régimes fiscaux*). Paris: Éditions Jupiter, 1958-1962.

Common Market Reporter. Chicago: Commerce Clearing House, 1962.

Federal Tax Treaties and Related Matters. Englewood Cliffs, N. J.: Prentice-Hall, 1958.

Friedmann, W. G., and Pugh, R. C. (eds.). *Legal Aspects of Foreign Investment.* Boston: Little, Brown, 1959.

Income Taxes Outside the Commonwealth, Compiled by Direction of the Board of Inland Revenue. London: Her Majesty's Stationery Office, March 1961.

League of Nations. *Double Taxation and Fiscal Evasion (Collection of International Agreements and Internal Legal Provisions for the Prevention of Double Taxation and Fiscal Evasion).* Geneva: 1928.

————. *London and Mexico Model Tax Conventions, Commentary and Text.* Geneva: 1946.

————. *Taxation of Foreign and National Enterprises.* Geneva: 1933.

Miraulo, A. "Imposizione doppia," 8 *Novissimo digesto italiano* 283. Torino: UTET, 1962.

Nortcliffe, E. B. *Common Market Fiscal Systems.* London: Sweet & Maxwell, Limited, 1960.

Organisation for Economic Co-operation and Development, Fiscal Committee. *Draft Double Taxation Convention on Income and Capital.* Paris: Organisation for Economic Co-operation and Development, 1963.

Organisation for European Economic Co-operation. *The Elimination of Double Taxation—Report of the Fiscal Committee of the Organisation for European Economic Co-operation.* Paris: 1958.

————. *The Elimination of Double Taxation—Second Report of the Fiscal Committee of the Organisation for European Economic Co-operation.* Paris: 1959.

————. *The Elimination of Double Taxation—Third Report of the Fiscal Committee of the Organisation for European Economic Co-operation.* Paris: 1960.

————. *The Elimination of Double Taxation—Fourth Report of the Fiscal Committee of the Organisation for European Economic Co-operation.* Paris: 1961.

PASETTI, G., and TRABUCCHI, A. *Codice delle comunità europee.* Milano: Giuffrè, 1962.

PIAZZA, G. *Tassazione degli stranieri.* Milano: Edizioni Consulente delle Aziende, 1961.

Tax Treaties. Chicago: Commerce Clearing House, 1959.

UCKMAR, V. *La tassazione degli stranieri in Italia.* Padova: CEDAM, 1955 (1959 supplement).

UNITED NATIONS, DEPARTMENT OF ECONOMIC AND SOCIAL AFFAIRS. *International Tax Agreements* (9 volumes, with supplements). New York: 1948—. The *World Guide to International Tax Agreements* (volume VIII and supplement 1) includes comprehensive information on all international tax agreements which existed on 1 June 1960. This information is kept up to date.

UNITED STATES CONGRESS, STAFF OF THE JOINT COMMITTEE ON INTERNAL REVENUE TAXATION. *Legislative History of United States Tax Conventions* (4 volumes). Washington, D. C.: United States Government Printing Office, 1962.

VAN WINENDAELE, J., and WOUTERS, H. *Le droit des sociétés anonymes dans les pays de la Communauté Économique Européenne.* Bruxelles: Établissements Émile Bruylant, 1961.

BERLIRI, A. "Sulla tassazione delle redevances," *Giur. imp.*, 1959, 735.

CROXATTO, G. "Le convenzioni fra Italia e Svezia al fine di evitare le doppie imposizioni," *Dir. e prat. trib.*, 1959, I, 26.

————. "Sulla tassabilità delle 'redevances' corrisposte a società straniere per la utilizzazione in Italia di beni immateriali," *Giur. it.*, 1963, I, 2, 733.

DE LIBERO, A. "Legal Aspects of Doing Business in Italy," *Common Market Reporter*, ¶ 9034. Chicago: Commerce Clearing House, 1962.

MASSIMINO, F. "Lo stabilimento permanente nel diritto fiscale nazionale ed internazionale," *RDFSF*, 1957, 201.

UCKMAR, V. "Contrasto fra alcune norme del T.U. imposte dirette e la legislazione precedente," *Dir. e prat. trib.*, 1959, I, 18.

General Tax on Receipts

BIGIAVI, W. *La professionalità dell'imprenditore.* Padova: CEDAM, 1947.

CECCARELLI, L., MESIANO, V., and PISCITELLI, I. *Codice dell'imposta generale sull'entrata.* Roma: Jandi Sapi Editori, 1955.

DE BONO, C. *Dizionario dell'imposta generale sull'entrata.* Milano: Giuffrè, 1954.

DE NARDO, V. *Rimborsi all'esportazione.* Milano: Giuffrè, 1962.

DUE, J. F. *Sales Taxation.* London: Routledge & Kegan Paul, Limited, 1957.

GIORGIS, V. *Imposta generale sull'entrata* (20th ed.). Roma: Nuova Rivista Tributaria, 1961.

JANDOLO, M. *Rassegna di giurisprudenza sulla imposta generale sull'entrata.* Milano: Giuffrè.

MANDÒ, M. *Imposta generale sull'entrata* (14th ed.). Vicenza: Arti Grafiche delle Venezie, 1960.

MONTAGNI, A. *IGE.* "*Merci in lavorazione*" (3d ed.). Milano: Giuffrè, 1956.

ORGANISATION FOR EUROPEAN ECONOMIC CO-OPERATION. *The Influence of Sales Taxes on Productivity.* Paris: 1958.

ROMANI, A. *L'entrata imponibile nel sistema dell'I.G.E.* Milano: Giuffrè, 1958.

FORTE, F. "Sulla esenzione dalla imposta generale sull'entrata per i giornali periodici aventi carattere prevalentemente politico," *Dir. e prat. trib.*, 1956, I, 113.

PUGLIESE, M. "I soggetti passivi dell'obbligazione tributaria nel diritto italiano," *Riv. it. sc. econ.*, 1935, 337.

Registration, Succession, and Stamp Taxes

BERLIRI, A. *La legge del bollo* (2d ed.). Milano: Giuffrè, 1957.

————. *Le imposte di bollo e di registro.* Milano: Giuffrè, 1961. The second edition of this work was published in 1964.

————. *Le legge di registro* (4th ed.). Milano: Giuffrè, 1960.

D'AMATI, N. *L'imposta di bollo.* Torino: UTET, 1962.

DE BONO, C. *Le successione legittime e testamentarie nelle leggi tributarie.* Milano: Giuffrè, 1963.

————. *L'imposta sulle successioni e l'imposta sull'asse globale ereditario netto.* Milano: Giuffrè, 1955.

FISICARO, C., and GIAMMATTEI, G. *Imposte sulle assicurazioni private.* Milano: Giuffrè, 1964.

GIORGIS, V. *Imposte di bollo e di pubblicità. Tassa di bollo sui documenti di trasporto* (5th ed.). Roma: Nuova Rivista Tributaria Editrice, 1961.

GRECO, G. *Imposte di bollo e di registro nei procedimenti in materia civile, penale e amministrativa* (2d ed.). S. Maria C. V.: Ernesto Schiano, 1955.

———— (ed.). *Imposte ipotecarie.* Piacenza: Casa Editrice La Tribuna, 1961.

GRISOLIA GESANO, E. (ed.). *Rassegna di giurisprudenza sulla imposta di successione.* Milano: Giuffrè, 1958.

GUGLIELMI, G., and AZZARITI, G. *Le imposte di registro.* Torino: UTET, 1959.

JAMMARINO, E. *Commento alla legge sulle imposte di registro* (3 volumes). Torino: UTET, 1959. The second edition of this work was published in 1962.

PEPE, M. (ed.). *Rassegna di giurisprudenza sulla imposta di registro.* Milano: Giuffrè, 1959.

PERRICONE, L. *Aziende e società nell'imposta di registro.* Milano: Giuffrè, 1950.

————. *Trattato del diritto tributario del registro, Parte generale.* Milano: Giuffrè, 1962.

PUGLIESE, M. "Come ripristinare l'imposta di successione," B. GRIZIOTTI *et al., La politica finanziaria italiana. Studi sui problemi monetari e finanziari* 189-229. Milano: Soc. an. Istituto Editoriale Scientifico, 1926.

RASTELLO, L. *Il tributo di registro.* Roma: Soc. A.B.E.T.E., 1955.

ROTONDI, A. *Lineamenti di diritto tributario: Le imposte di registro, di successione ed ipotecarie.* Milano: Giuffrè, 1962.

SANTI, G. (ed.). *Rassegna di giurisprudenza sulla legge del bollo.* Milano: Giuffrè, 1959.

SERRANO, F. *Le imposte sulle successioni* (4th ed.). Torino: UTET, 1961.

STAMMATI, G., ARMANI, A., and CECCARELLI, L. *Codice della imposta di registro.* Roma: Jandi Sapi Editori, 1959.

————. *Codice delle imposte di successione, ipotecarie, e del gratuito patrocinio.* Roma: Jandi Sapi Editori, 1959.

UCKMAR, A. *La legge del registro* (5th ed.) (3 volumes). Padova: CEDAM, 1958.

BRACCINI, R. "Requisiti per la registrazione a tassa fissa della cessione di quote di società a responsabilità limitata," *Dir. e prat. trib.*, 1962, II, 116.

CELORIA, C. "Cessione di azienda e legge di registro," *Il foro padano*, 1956, I, 209.

GRIZIOTTI, B. "Il principio della realtà economica negli articoli 8 e 68 della legge di registro," *RDFSF*, 1939, II, 202.

————. "Il regime della legge di registro per gli atti nulli, annullabili e revocabili nel controllo dell'interpretazione funzionale," *RDFSF*, 1941, II, 260.

————. "Il regime delle pertinenze nel Codice Civile vigente e gli immobili per destinazione secondo l'art. 47 della legge del registro e la legge di successione," *RDFSF*, 1953, II, 112.

GUALANDI, L. "Le imposte di registro ed ipotecarie relative agli atti di assegnazione di immobile a socio de cooperativa edilizia priva di contributo statale," *Riv. leg. fisc.*, 1954, 481.

PICCATTI, P. "Ancora sul regime fiscale della circolazione di quote delle società a responsabilità limitata," *Temi trib.*, 1961, 226.

————. "Regime fiscale della circolazione di quote della società responsabilità limitata," *Temi trib.*, 1960, 147.

PUGLIESE, M. "I soggetti passivi dell'obbligazione tributaria nel diritto italiano," *Riv. it. sc. econ.*, 1935, 337.

RASTELLO, L. "Le pertinenze: Aspetti civilistici ed aspetti tributari," *RDFSF*, 1954, I, 354.

SCIELLO, G. "Le pertinenze e le imposte sui trasferimenti," *Riv. not.*, 1952, 478.

SERRANO, F. "L'imposta di successione nel pensiero di Luigi Einaudi," *Dir. e prat. trib.*, 1962, 5.

VANONI, E. "Sulla presunta responsabilità del mandatario per la tassa di registro," *Foro. it.*, 1933, I, 1798.

VIRGILIO, A. "Successione di commerciante dichiarato fallito dopo la morte," *RDFSF*, 1955, II, 337.

Other National Taxes

ALESSI, R. *Monopoli fiscali, imposte di fabbricazione, dazi doganali.* Torino: UTET, 1956.

AMMINISTRAZIONE AUTONOMA DEI MONOPOLI DI STATO. *Raccolta delle principali disposizioni riguardanti l'Amministrazione Autonoma dei Monopoli di Stato* (2 volumes). Roma: 1954.

CATELLO, A. *Istruzioni di contabilità per l'amministrazione delle dogane e delle imposte di fabbricazione.* Roma: Edizioni "Scambi e Dogane," 1960.

DE LITALA, L. *Diritto delle assicurazioni sociali* (4th ed.). Torino: UTET, 1959.

DE NARDO, V. *Rimborsi all'esportazione.* Milano: Giuffrè, 1962.

GALIPÒ, G. *Imposte di fabbricazione. Oli minerali.* Catania: Edizioni Paoline, 1958.

GRISOLIA, F. *Codice delle esenzioni e riduzioni nelle tasse e imposte sugli affari* (3d ed.). Milano: Giuffrè, 1963.

SANTENIELLO, G. (ed.). *Rassegna di giurisprudenza sulle leggi doganali e leggi sul monopolio.* Milano: Giuffrè, 1957.

STAMMATI, G., and CECCARELLI, A. *Le tasse sulle concessioni governative.* Roma: Jandi Sapi Editori, 1961.

Local Finance

BENVENUTI, F., and SEPI, O. *Codice comunale e provinciale.* Roma: Jandi Sapi Editori, 1959.

BONARETTI, L. *La procedura coattiva per la riscossione delle imposte di consumo.* Milano: Giuffrè, 1963.

BOSISIO, O. *L'imposta di famiglia ed altre imposte comunali* (6th ed.). Milano: L. di G. Pirola, 1962.

CECCARELLI, L., MESIANO, V., and PISCITELLI, I. *Codice delle imposte di consumo.* Roma: Jandi Sapi Editori, 1958.

COCIVERA, B. *Guida ai tributi locali* (2d ed.). Torino: UTET, 1958.

CORRADO, T. *L'imposta sugli incrementi di valore delle aree fabbricabili e il contributo di miglioria specifica.* Milano: Giuffrè, 1963.

DI GIULIO, G. *Le imposte di consumo.* Brescia: Casa Editrice F. Appollonio & C., 1959.

GAGLIARDI, M. (ed.). *Rassegna di giurisprudenza sulle imposte di consumo.* Milano: Giuffrè, 1961.

INGROSSO, G. *Le finanze locali.* Napoli: Casa Editrice Dott. Eugenio Jovene, 1962.

NOBILE, G. A. *L'imposta di famiglia* (3d ed.). Napoli: Casa Editrice Dott. Eugenio Jovene, 1954.

PERINI, M. M. G., and LEATI, G. B. *Trattato sulle imposte di consumo.* Padova: CEDAM, 1957.

PIACENTINI, A. *Il diritto tributario degli enti locali.* Udine: Libreria Editrice "Aquileia," 1958.

PROVINI, G. *L'imposta di famiglia* (3d ed.). Padova: CEDAM, 1956.

RÉPACI, F. A. *Le finanze dei comuni, delle provincie e degli enti corporativi.* Torino: Giulio Einaudi, Editore, 1936.

ROSSI, G. DE. *Profili e problemi dell'autonomia regionale siciliana.* Milano: Giuffrè, 1962.

SAVINO, G. *I tributi locali.* Milano: L. di G. Pirola, 1963.

SVIMEZ (ASSOCIAZIONE PER LO SVILUPPO DELL'INDUSTRIA NEL MEZZO-GIORNO). *La finanza locale nella politica di sviluppo.* Written by T. SCIPIONE. Roma: Giuffrè, 1962.

TAMBORINO, F. *Come si applica l'imposta sulle aree fabbricabili* (2d ed.). Milano: Consulente Immobiliare, 1963.

VITO, F., *et al.* (eds.). *L'imposta sulle aree fabbricabili.* Milano: Società Editrice "Vita e Pensiero," 1962.

VOLPI, F. *Le finanze comunali di un grande centro urbano (Milano).* Milano: Feltrinelli Editore, 1959.

———. *Le finanze dei comuni e delle province nel Regno d'Italia dal 1860 al 1890.* Torino: ILTE (Industria Libreria Tipografica Editrice), 1962.

ZINGALI, G. *Del riparto dei tributi tra lo stato e la regione siciliana e della necessità di aggiornare i criterii.* Milano: Giuffrè, 1960.

ALLORIO, E. "Profili giuridico-formali del problema della valutazione del reddito agli effetti dell'imposta di famiglia con riferimento all'accertamento del reddito compiuto ai fini delle imposte erariali," *Giur. it.*, 1960, I, 1, 28.

CELLITTI, V. "L'autonomia dell'imposta di famiglia nel diritto e nella pratica," *Giust. trib.*, 1953, 393.

——. "Sul principio dell'autonomo accertamento per l'imposta di famiglia," *Giust. trib.*, 1961, 1.

DE MITA, E. "Autonomia finanziaria e potestà tributaria delle regioni a statuto normale," *RDFSF*, 1963, I, 497.

FORTE, F. "In tema di autonomia dell'imposta di famiglia e di norme interpretative," *Giur. it.*, 1963, I, 1, 409.

——. "Sulla determinazione dell'imponibile nell'imposta di famiglia," *Giur. it.*, 1960, I, 1, 5.

GIANNINI, M. S. "I proventi degli enti pubblici minori e la riserva della legge," *RDFSF*, 1957, I, 1.

GUZZARDI, F. "Valutazione dei redditi per l'imposta di famiglia," *Giust. trib.*, 1961, 281.

INGROSSO, G. "Imposta di famiglia," *Rass. fin. pubbl.*, 1958, 504.

JACONDINI, A. "L'imposta di famiglia," *Difesa fiscale*, 1962, 81.

——. "Sull'obbligo della motivazione degli accertamenti ai fini dell'imposta di famiglia," *Rass. mens. imp. dir.*, 1961, 747.

PROVINI, G. "La valutazione dei redditi nell'imposta di famiglia," *Dir. e prat. trib.*, 1958, II, 344.

RASTELLO, L. "Aspetti tributari del turismo," *Temi trib.*, 1963, 5.

STEVE, S. "La riforma dei tributi locali," *RDFSF*, 1963, I, 479.

Administration and Procedure

ALLORIO, E. *Diritto processuale tributario* (3d ed.). Torino: UTET, 1955. The fourth edition of this book was published in 1962.

——. *La vita e la scienza del diritto in Italia e in Europa.* Milano: Giuffrè, 1957.

BERLIRI, A. *Il processo tributario.* Reggio Emilia: 1940.

BISCOTTO, A., and OZZOLA, G. *Il processo tributario di accertamento.* Roma: Società Grafica Romana, 1961.

BONARETTI, L. *La procedura coattiva per la riscossione delle imposte di consumo.* Milano: Giuffrè, 1963.

CELLITTI, V. *Il concordato tributario nel diritto e nella pratica con riferimento alla riforma Vanoni.* Ancona: Industria Tipografica E. Venturini, 1953.

COCIVERA, B. *Il concordato tributario.* Milano: Società Editrice Libreria, 1948.

D'ANGELILLO, A. *Le frodi fiscali* (2d ed.) (3 volumes; volume 1: *Le alterazione dei bilanci e l'imposta di ricchezza mobile*). Milano: Giuffrè, 1963.

DE'STEFANI, A. *L'ordinamento finanziario italiano.* Edited by F. G. LUPARELLO. Roma: Jandi Sapi Editori, 1957.

FERRITO, G. *L'ordinamento dell'amministrazione finanziaria dello Stato.* Palermo: Editore Lo Monaco, 1959.

FLORIO, N. *L'esecuzione forzata esattoriale.* Campobasso: Casa Molisana del Libro, Editrice, 1962.

GAZZERO, F. *Il domicilio e le notificazioni fiscali.* Milano: Sigurtà M., 1961.

————. *La dichiarazione tributaria nell'accertamento e nel contenzioso* (2d ed.). Milano: Sigurtà M., 1960.

GIORGETTI, A. *L'evasione tributaria.* Roma (Città di Castello): Istituto Italiano Edizioni Giuridiche, 1958.

GRECO, G. *Le imposte nei procedimenti in materia civile, penale e amministrativa (Imposte di bollo, di registro, sulle successioni, ipotecarie, sull' entrata e di ricchezza mobile).* Milano: Giuffrè, 1963.

GUZZARDI, F., and SIMONCINI, G. (eds.). *Legislazione sulla riscossione delle imposte dirette.* Roma: Industria Grafica Moderna, 1959.

LAPORTA, E. *La riscossione delle imposte dirette.* Roma: Casa Editrice Stamperia Nazionale, 1960.

MALINVERNI, A. *Principi di diritto penale tributario.* Padova: CEDAM, 1962.

MERLINO, R. *Dizionario dell infrazioni e delle relative conseguenze nel campo delle imposte dirette.* Milano: Giuffrè, 1961.

MINISTERO DELLE FINANZE, DIREZIONE GENERALE DEGLI AFFARI GENERALI E DEL PERSONALE. *Disposizioni in materia di contenzioso penale tributario.* Roma: Istituto Poligrafico dello Stato, 1961.

PARLATO, A. *Il responsabile d'imposta.* Milano: Giuffrè, 1963.

PELLINGRA, G. *Dell'accertamento induttivo in materia tributaria* (2d ed.). Roma: Bardi Editore, 1960.

————. *La determinazione analitica e induttiva del reddito fiscale nell'imposizione tributaria.* Milano: Giuffrè, 1962.

PICOZZI, L. *Codice esattoriale.* Milano: Giuffrè, 1962.

PISATURO, M. *Il fallimento fiscale nella dottrina e nella giurisprudenza* (2d ed.). Roma (Città di Castello): Editoriale Giuridica, 1960.

RASTELLO, L. *La pena pecuniaria nel diritto tributario.* Roma: 1959.

SCANDALE, E. *La riscossione delle imposte dirette* (8th ed.). Napoli: Casa Editrice Dott. Eugenio Jovene, 1960.

SPINELLI, G. *Norme generali per la repressione delle violazioni delle leggi finanziarie.* Milano: Giuffrè, 1957.

VINCIGUERRA, S. *I delitti doganali. Parte generale.* Milano: Giuffrè, 1963.

AZZARITI, G., *et al.* "Studio per una riforma del contenzioso tributario," *RDFSF*, 1951, I, 99.

BARILE, P. "Sulla permanenza attuale delle giurisdizioni speciali," *Riv. dir. proc.*, 1954, II, 81.

FORTE, F. "Osservazioni sui progetti di riforma dell'organizzazione per la risoluzione delle controversie tra fisco e contribuente," *Temi trib.*, 1962, 459.

GAZZERO, F. "I costi d'imposizione e di riscossione delle imposte dirette e ripercussioni di essi nel MEC," *Boll. trib. informazioni*, 1959, 835.

GUARINO, G. "Contenzioso tributario e giurisdizioni speciali," *Foro it.*, 1954, III, 110.

JONA CELESIA, L. "Per l'abolizione degli aggi di riscossione delle imposte dirette," *Riv. int. sc. econ. e comm.*, 1964, n. 2, n. 3, n. 4.

MAFFEZZONI, F. "Ragioni ed obiettivi di una riforma del contenzioso tributario," *Riv. dir. proc.*, 1962, 400.

MICHELI, G. A. "Considerazioni sulla incostituzionalità del 'solve et repete,'" *Giur. cost.*, 1961, 1183.

————. "Parere sullo schema di disegno di legge concernente la riforma del contenzioso tributario," *Giur. imp.*, 1962, 759.

PICOZZI, L. *Codice esattoriale.* Milano: Giuffrè, 1962.

Poli, O. "La maggiorazione del reddito per omessa dichiarazione," *Imp. dir. erariali*, 1962, 1217.

————. "Maggiorazione del reddito. Dichiarazioni tardive e ricorsi contro il ruolo," *Imp. dir. erariali*, 1962, 449.

————. "Natura giuridica dell'atto di liquidazione dell'imposta sulle società," *Imp. dir. erariali*, 1962, 673.

Sandulli, A. M. "Sulla sopravvivenza delle giurisdizioni speciali al termine fissato per la loro 'revisione,'" *Giur. cost.*, 1956, 965.

Tesauro, A. "Le giurisdizioni speciali e le commissioni tributarie," *Rass. dir. pubbl.*, 1954, I, 401.

PART I

DESCRIPTION OF THE TAX SYSTEM

The first four chapters of this volume describe the tax system and its background. The income tax is described generally in Part I, and in detail in Part II. Other taxes are treated in Part I, and those of special importance in Part III as well.

CHAPTER 1

INTRODUCTION TO THE TAX SYSTEM

1/1. Historical Background of the Fiscal System
   1/1.1   Origins of the Italian Financial System
   1/1.2   Political Influences After the *Risorgimento*
   1/1.3   The Fascist Period
   1/1.4   The Second World War and Subsequent Reconstruction
   1/1.5   Development since 1955

1/2. Constitutional Principles Affecting Tax Policy
   1/2.1   In General
   1/2.2   Legality of Taxation
   1/2.3   Contribution in Accordance with Ability To Pay
   1/2.4   Progressivity of the Tax System
   1/2.5   General Principles Promoting Justice and Equality
   1/2.6   Provisions Authorizing Government Intervention in the Economy
   1/2.7   Provisions Protecting Certain Liberties
   1/2.8   Decisions of the Constitutional Court on Principles Affecting Taxation

1/3. Tax Legislation
   1/3.1   The Legislature
       a.   Composition and election
       b.   Laws
       c.   Decree-laws
       d.   Presidential decrees
       e.   International treaties
   1/3.2   The Executive
       a.   The President of the Republic
       b.   The Council of Ministers

    c. Regulations
    d. Ministerial decrees
    e. Ministerial circulars
1/3.3 The National Economic and Labor Council
1/3.4 Budget Policy
    a. In general
    b. Approval of budgets
    c. New taxes and new expenditures

1/4. Tax Administration

1/4.1 Ministry of Finance
1/4.2 Direct Taxes
1/4.3 Fees and Indirect Taxes on Transactions
1/4.4 Customs Duties and Indirect Taxes on Manufacturing and Consumption
1/4.5 Fiscal Monopolies
1/4.6 Cadaster and Revenue Technical Services
1/4.7 General Matters and Personnel: Intendancies of Finance
1/4.8 Finance Guard
1/4.9 Central Tax School
1/4.10 Taxpayer Remedies
    a. Constitutional provisions regarding jurisdiction
    b. The status of the tax commissions
    c. District Tax Commission
    d. Provincial Tax Commission
    e. Central Tax Commission
    f. Appeals to the ordinary courts
    g. Appeals to special courts
    h. Census commissions
    i. Appeals regarding customs duties ' and taxes on manufacturing and consumption
    j. Appeals regarding local taxes
1/4.11 Representation of Taxpayers
1/4.12 Inspection, Search, and Seizure
1/4.13 Proposals for the Reform of Tax Litigation

1/5. The Financial Policy of the Local Entities

1/5.1 Units of Local Government
1/5.2 The Structures of Local Government
1/5.3 Legislative and Administrative Functions of Local Governments

1/5.4 Expenditures of Local Governments

1/5.5 Receipts of Local Governments
    a. In general
    b. Patrimonial receipts
    c. Autonomous local taxes
    d. Local surtaxes on state taxes
    e. Participations in yields of state taxes
    f. Subsidies
    g. Movements of capital
    h. Loans

1/5.6 Limitations on the Tax Powers of Local Entities

1/5.7 The Chamber of Commerce, Industry, and Agriculture

1/6. Outline and Evolution of the Tax System in Relation to the Economic Structure

1/6.1 National Income and Total Fiscal Burden
    a. In general
    b. Deficit
    c. Social insurances

1/6.2 Burden of Total National Taxes

1/6.3 Burden of Total Local Taxes

1/6.4 Burden of Compulsory Social Insurances

1/6.5 The Public Debt

1/6.6 Classification of Taxes

1/6.7 Yields of National Direct Taxes
    a. In general
    b. Classification of direct taxes
    c. Objective taxes on income
    d. Personal taxes on income
    e. Succession taxes
    f. Taxes on wealth

1/6.8 Yields of National Indirect Taxes
    a. In general
    b. Taxes on exchanges
    c. Registration and mortgage taxes
    d. Miscellaneous transaction taxes
    e. Manufacturing taxes
    f. Motor vehicle taxes
    g. Customs duties
    h. Fiscal monopolies
    i. Lotteries

1/6.9 Yields of Local Taxes
    a. In general
    b. Direct taxes and surtaxes
    c. Indirect taxes

1/6.10 Economic Considerations Affecting the Structural
       Evolution of the Tax System
    a. International balance of payments
    b. Composition of the national product
    c. Size and organization of units of production
    d. Growth of employment income
    e. Size and pattern of public expenditure
    f. Behavior of prices
    g. Internal dynamics of various sectors
    h. Consumption expenditures
    i. Regional differences in economic activities

1/1. Historical Background of the Fiscal System

1/1.1 Origins of the Italian Financial System

The unitary Italian state was founded in 1861 with the proclamation of the Kingdom of Italy. In that year, as a result of the victories of Garibaldi, the political structure and the juridical and financial system of the Piedmontese state [1] were extended to southern Italy, formerly ruled by the dynasty of the Bourbons of Naples, and to a substantial part of central Italy—excluding Rome and a large part of Latium which remained under the Pontifical government until 1870. In 1860, the Piedmontese order had been extended to Lombardy.[2] Since the structure of the new national state was essentially that of the old Piedmontese-Sardinian Kingdom of Savoy, it can be said that, for a limited part of the national territory, the Italian financial structure has a tradition which dates back more than 100 years.

Prior to unification, two types of public finance system had existed in the Italian territory. The first type can be called "modern" or "Piedmontese-Lombard-Tuscan." Generally speaking, it had undergone the effects of the Middle Ages of the communes, the Renaissance, the effects of the "progressive" mercantilism characteristic of northern Italy, and, finally, the influence, rapid but deep, of the Enlightenment, the French Revolution, and the Napoleonic period. It had, that is, received the

---

[1] The old Piedmontese state included, roughly, Liguria, Piedmont, and Sardinia, besides other regions of Savoy which now belong to France.

[2] Veneto remained under Austria until 1866; the regions of Trento and Trieste belonged to Austria until 1918, at the end of the First World War.

effects of the modern conception of the state as an institution which should be organized to perform certain functions as efficiently as possible, and whose actions should insofar as possible be predictable to the citizens.

The second type of public finance system can be called "Bourbon," from the principal state in which it was found, that of the Bourbons of the south. The Bourbon system applied substantially also in the Pontifical state and thus, in pre-unification Italy, came to cover almost all of the center-south: half of Italy both in terms of population and in terms of area, a little less than half perhaps in terms of national income. More empirical, more approximative, this system was constructed on much less rational lines than the Piedmontese-Lombard-Tuscan system. With regard to the rights of the citizens, the powers of the sovereign and his court, and the development and administration of direct taxation, the "Bourbon" type of state remained unaffected by the Enlightenment and the French Revolution. This does not mean that the "Bourbon" state intervened less in the economic life of its citizens. In the period before the French Revolution, there were in the south great and even oppressive instances of intervention and of regulation, of a mercantilist origin. Moreover, the feudal regime itself was full of restrictions and controls. But these regulations were of a very different type from those which arose as a result of the Enlightenment and of the subsequent experiences and doctrines which shook Western Europe in the period of the French Revolution and the Napoleonic period.

The process of unification was based on the expansion of the Piedmontese system to all of Italy, a large part of which had diverse traditions and experiences. The process of unification which officially began in 1860 did not develop everywhere with the same success; long after 1861, the new system remained merely a superficial superimposition. Even in the regions of its origin, the Piedmontese system had not reached complete maturity in 1860, and, above all, it had not been transfused into the consciousness of the mass of citizens, or even into that of all of the ruling and political-administrative classes. However, it must be remembered that the Piedmontese state, until the Statute of Carlo Alberto and the liberally inspired government of Cavour, was still not democratic, but conservative and authoritarian, with extensive feudal survivals. Authoritarianism and paternalism could not fail to subsist in the Lombardo-Veneto territory, which, before its annexation to Piedmont in 1860, had been subjected first to the rule of Spain and then to that of the Austro-Hungarian kingdom. In conclusion, if, in the Italy of 1860, there were important elements of response to the new times, there were also, even in the more evolved northern part, considerable components of the old illiberal mold, which had deep roots. The attitude of the citizens toward the state and toward the tax administration often reflected that lack of confidence which an individual may have toward a public authority that is not a genuine expression of his political beliefs and seems to be opposed to his interests.

1/1.2 Political Influences After the *Risorgimento*

The liberal conception which was affirmed in Italy in the *Risorgimento* was considerably different from the type of liberalism and free economy of other European countries. In Italy, the liberal movement was strongly influenced by elements of interventionism and of public activism. The dominant theme of the *Risorgimento* was the moral and civil restoration of the nation. With this ultimate goal, one faction of the ruling class, the "historical right," fought for a form of "active" liberalism under which the state would play an active role in political and economic life. But the doctrine of the "historical right" was not familiar to, or accepted by, the majority of the persons included in the dominant group. The men of the ruling class, of which the Piedmontese government, now the national government, availed itself, and the men who influenced this government, were very often in conflict with themselves; they wavered between the old and the new, between the pre-Enlightenment conceptions and the new conceptions.

Apart from the ruling class, which had the direct or indirect responsibility of government and of administration, there existed a large mass of people with different ways of life, customs, and interests: agricultural laborers and poor farmers; the small-business class; well-to-do agricultural landowners with small or medium-sized properties and minor state bureaucrats; army officers of the lower ranks; and, finally, workers employed by the new industrial enterprises. Obeying the law, for the masses, often meant a mechanical acceptance of what had been devised by others.

The two leading movements in modern Italian political life, the Socialist and the Catholic, were in a precarious or indifferent position with relation to the state during the entire nineteenth century. The Socialists, who began to organize politically and spread among the masses around 1885 and who became rather quickly a movement of growing importance, initially criticized the state as an expression of the exploitation of the masses by the capitalist bourgeoisie. It was only at the turn of the century that there appeared among the Italian Socialists, especially among those of more moderate tendencies, another "reformist" movement, which saw in the state and particularly in the local entities, if controlled democratically by an informed populace, the means for gradually modifying the relations with capitalism and with the bourgeoisie, and for modifying the bourgeoisie itself. But on this theme, the Italian Socialists long remained substantially uncertain and divided.

The Catholics, from the political point of view, maintained for the entire nineteenth century an attitude of protest and of distrust toward the state because of the "Roman question," which arose because of the occupation of Rome by the Kingdom of Italy and the suppression of other temporal powers of the Catholic Church, such as the vast landed wealth of the ecclesiastical organizations and of the Catholic religious organs. Only in the first years of the twentieth century did the Catholic movement make its entry in the political arena, departing from its hostile attitude toward the state and taking up, although hesitantly, a more positive role.

These remarks are very important for an understanding of the vicissitudes of the Italian tax system, as well as of many other aspects of the Italian economic and juridical system. Often, to an outside observer, the Italian fiscal system may appear as an ingenious scheme which has little to do with the realities of administrative interpretation, practice, or public opinion.

This split between law and fact could not be avoided in the first years of Italian national life, precisely because there was a profound difference between the thought and action of the government officials on the one hand and the population on the other. First of all, for the officials and civil service employees sent by the north to administer the south, there was the obstacle of different customs, mentality, and often language. An aggravating circumstance was that the southern power groups were not at all disposed to help the new Piedmontese administrators in their relations with the citizens of the south (*Mezzogiorno*). The old local ruling class tried to eliminate and weaken the influence of these new administrators, or else to channel their efforts into the groove of its own old methods, forms of conduct, and regime.

Unification, in effect, for the south was accompanied by a worsening of its economic situation, especially because of an increased fiscal burden and greater competition from the industrial economy of the north. The "southern question"—the problem of economic depression and underdevelopment of the south—was already serious in the last decades of the nineteenth century, but was faced squarely neither then nor during the first decades of this century when economic conditions in the rest of Italy had greatly improved.

Furthermore, the idea of the equality between a citizen and the public administration in the field of law, including fiscal law, had difficulty in making progress. In case of doubt in a tax question, for example, neither the government nor the taxpayer should be favored; the dispute should be resolved according to justice and equity. For a long time, this rule was not followed in Italy either in doctrine or in practice. Instead, there was oscillation between protecting the private property of the taxpayer and protecting the accounts of the treasury. Naturally, the resolution of a dispute depended not only on the personal opinion of the judge, but also on the nature of the private interests involved.

1/1.3 The Fascist Period

The monetary inflation and the political and social instability that followed the First World War, and then the fascist period, had a great impact on the fiscal system. The changes made by the fascist regime were very substantial in all fields. But in the fiscal field, they are important probably not so much because of the specific measures adopted with regard to tax policy as because of the omission of measures of tax modernization and because of the authoritarian regime in which fiscal policy operated.

It cannot be said that there existed a precise doctrine of fascism in the field of economy and public finance. From an initial period of favoring the abolition of restrictions on private business and of a fiscal policy encouraging private capital (the so-called "productivism" of the Minister of Finance De Stefani, a "fascist liberal"), the fascist government passed —through the experiences of the depression of 1930—to a corporative period of interventionism in economic life and of the strengthening of the tax system, as it sought at first self-sufficiency and protectionism and then the bases of a war finance. In the last period of fascist rule, there took place a vast tax reform, authored by Paolo Thaon di Revel, which involved a broad intervention by the state in economic and financial policy. But it is doubtful how far the doctrines of Thaon di Revel were in accord with fascism and with corporativism. On the whole, it can be said that eclecticism was the salient characteristic of the experiences and innovations of fascism in the economic field and that the only constant was the authoritarian regime in which these experiences were framed.

The divergence between what was written in the laws and what functioned in practice became increasingly greater—although always within certain limits which enabled the two systems to function in a regular and harmonious way.

The phenomenon of tax evasion was characteristic of this divergence between law and practice. Tax evasion was largely permitted and, it might be said, even legislatively preordained—for example, through the absence of provisions for identifying the holders of shares in assessing the taxes on income and wealth. But not all laws were evaded. The practice allowed a margin of tolerance; evasion for certain matters or up to a certain quantitative limit was considered reasonable and permissible. Disregarding or disobeying some of the laws was permitted within certain limits, or to certain persons, or under certain circumstances.

In the fascist state, practice developed in the most diverse ways. It could originate at the center, in relations between the ministries and large industrial enterprises, or at the periphery, in relations between the thousands of communal tax offices and influential local men or the general populace. But it would be inappropriate to say that this diversity arose in the fascist period. In Italy, it had much earlier roots, and the new regime furnished only additional reasons for its much greater vigor.

1/1.4 The Second World War and Subsequent Reconstruction

The period of the Second World War and the subsequent period of inflation were characterized by the collapse of a number of fiscal structures. The entire system of direct taxation entered a crisis. Many other Italian taxes broke down almost completely. The sole tax which remained efficient was the general tax on receipts (*imposta generale sull'entrata* or IGE), instituted by Thaon di Revel at the beginning of the war, in preparation for imminent necessities and with an eye to the contingencies of violent change, on the basis of the experiences of the German tax system. The organization of many tax offices was disrupted by loss of personnel and destruction of buildings. In 1945, with the end of the war and its controls, inflation gave the last blows to the tottering fiscal edifice.

There began a period of reconstruction. Having inherited the troublesome wartime tax legislation, the inefficiencies which had been accumulating during the war, a partially destroyed administrative apparatus, and the administrative and legislative confusion resulting from the splitting of sovereignty over the national territory, the postwar governments had a very hard task. But they succeeded in managing it respectably, in part with Anglo-American financial help, and in 1947-1948 there began a determined recovery in public finance. Profound innovations were introduced meanwhile into the general principles of government, with the adoption of the new Italian Constitution of 1947 (1/2).

The new political structure of Italy under the Constitution of 1947 involved the resumption of a movement interrupted in 1922, when the country had passed from parliamentary institutions to a dictatorial regime. But together with this resumption, it was necessary also to initiate a completely new system in order to adjust the structure of the fiscal system and of the general economic and financial policy to the new socioeconomic orientations of the West, especially in America and in northern Europe. Moreover, the new structure had to take account of the evolution of the Italian economy. The economic and social ideologies that had nourished the development of the Italian tax system up to a certain point by now no longer seemed acceptable to the great majority of the parties and of the public. New arrangements became necessary for the distribution of the fiscal burden and for tax assessment. Italy, from an agricultural-industrial country, was increasingly on its way to becoming a prevalently industrial country. The family and artisan enterprise was being replaced more and more by the corporation and the large enterprise. Incomes had risen, and their sources were more diverse.

One of the most important needs, perhaps not noticed by everyone, was pointed out by Ezio Vanoni, the most influential policymaker in public finance in the recent period: to return to a situation of coincidence between what was written in the law and what was practiced. Together with this need, there was another, which Vanoni saw as strictly connected with it. This involved the adoption of an administrative concept, which had been considered little even in the periods of the best administration, under which the base of the hierarchy would fully comprehend the decisions at the summit and the administration as a whole would understand the problems of the general public. Italian fiscal devices have always been rather incomprehensible to the population, and the Italian governments and their fiscal administrations have made little effort to make the tax system known and understandable to the man in the street. The central government, moreover, has always shown little awareness of the differing situations of the various localities.

The picture of Italian finances in the period following that of immediate reconstruction was not reassuring from the point of view of monetary stability. The problem of increasing revenues to check the dangers of inflation and to lighten the disequilibrium in the balance of international payments was acute and constant. In addition, there was the problem of distributing the fiscal burden on production so as to facilitate the process of full employment and the strengthening of industry, which was coming out of a long protectionist phase and which, from 1951 on, in consequence of a courageous course of economic policy pressed forward by the Minister of Commerce (La Malfa), faced the open competition of the great international markets.

In 1949, as a result of the work of Vanoni, a tax reform intended to resolve this mass of problems was started. The death of Vanoni in 1955 resulted in a weakening of the ideological and political current which had favored this reform and which had sought to promote a coherent design of revision in the various aspects of the fiscal structure. This loss was the more serious in that, for a number of reasons of political tactics, Vanoni had not been able to give a complete and explicit public statement of his design for tax reform and of the various stages through which it had to pass.

1/1.5   Development since 1955

Since 1955, there has been a structural evolution of a neocapitalist type, through which the economic situation has been greatly modified. The Italian fiscal system today, in the aggregate, provides a high revenue. It is capable of expanding its yields at a higher rate than the growth of the national income, to provide the large requirements for the public expenses of the new epoch and to maintain stable prices. The per capita national income of Italy has climbed at an average rate of over 5% a year, in a regime of almost complete monetary stability, of continuous improvements in the balance of payments and of currency reserves, and of continuous reduction of unemployment. On the legislative plane, the work of reform which has been carried out between 1951 and 1958 and which has emerged in the *Testo unico* of the laws on direct taxes (2/1), issued in 1958 and in force since 1960, is very important. But because of the rapid growth of the economy, many tax problems have been rendered even more delicate, in particular the taxation of capital gains and computation of capital losses, the taxation of enterprises on the balance sheet basis, and assessment of wealth in the form of shares and bonds. And especially in the administrative realm, there are many unsolved problems: in the concrete methods of tax assessment, in the organization of the tax offices, and in the proceedings of tax jurisdiction and control.

1/2.   Constitutional Principles Affecting Tax Policy

1/2.1   In General

The Italian Constitution of 1947 [3] lays down express principles that taxes cannot be levied except by law (1/2.2), that all are required to contribute to the public expenses in accordance with their ability to pay (1/2.3), and that the tax system as a whole should be progressive (1/2.4). A number of other provisions of the Constitution are relevant to tax policy. These may be classified as general principles promoting justice and equality, which furnish means of specifying the requirements regarding ability to pay and progressivity (1/2.5); provisions authorizing government intervention in the economy, which bear on the use of tax policy for extrafiscal purposes (1/2.6); provisions for the protection of certain liberties, which may impose extrafiscal limitations on tax policy (1/2.7); and provisions limiting methods of investigation, which bear on the assessment of taxes (1/4.12).

The Constitution of 1947 also provides for the establishment of the Constitutional Court, whose function in the interpretation of constitutional provisions regarding taxation is discussed at 1/2.8.

The provisions of the Constitution dealing with the tax powers of the regional, provincial, and communal governments are discussed at 1/5.5.

1/2.2   Legality of Taxation

Article 23 of the Italian Constitution provides that "no levy, personal or patrimonial, may be imposed except on the basis of the law." This

---

[3] The Constitution of 1947 is hereinafter cited: "Const."

rule has clear historical continuity with the principle stated in article 30 of the Statute of Carlo Alberto of 4 March 1848, according to which "no tax may be imposed or collected except as consented by the chambers and sanctioned by the King." In the centuries preceding the Albertine Statute, Piedmont had had a long tradition of affirming the principle that taxes could not be applied except as approved by the representatives of the tax-payers; the experience involved is very similar to that which the English had undergone. The principle of the legality of tax, for this and other reasons, had found a natural place among the general rules of the new Italian Kingdom, although its application was not as broad as at first might appear. It survived unaltered until the fascist epoch. During that time, it underwent a profound change of meaning. Representative democracy having been suppressed, the legal basis of taxation no longer had the same significance. The chambers were no longer the expression of the representatives of the taxpayers; they were an expression of the existing dictatorial regime. Moreover, the laws themselves were increasingly replaced by decree-laws of the government (cited in the codes as "R. D. L.": *regio decreto-legge*) converted mechanically—and not always rapidly—into laws by the legislature (1/3.1c).

After the Second World War, there was a return to the system of elective chambers. Suffrage was extended to all adult men and to women. A change was made in the manner of choosing representatives to the chambers; while, in the pre-fascist period, the King had appointed "notables" from among specified categories of citizens to the Senate, and the Chamber of Deputies had been elected by a single-member constituency, the Deputies are now elected by citizens at least 21 years of age through a system of proportional representation, and the Senate members are elected by citizens at least 25 years of age through a system approaching proportional representation, but retaining characteristics of a single-member constituency.[4]

Article 23 of the Constitution has given rise to various questions.[5] Most of these arise from the fact that a large part of the fiscal laws existing in Italy were enacted either in the fascist period, in which the canon of legality of taxation had lost its original significance, or in the postwar period, in which, despite the existence of the Statute of Carlo Alberto, a close scrutiny of fiscal arrangements was not possible. A complete abrogation of these laws, which were more or less openly contrary to a

---

[4] For a description in English of the Italian electoral system, see Adams and Basile, *The Government of Republican Italy* 163 *et seq.*

[5] On these questions, see Bartholini, *Il principio di legalità dei tributi in materia di imposte;* Forte, "Note sulla nozione di tributo nell'ordinamento finanziario italiano e sul significato dell'art. 23 della Costituzione," *RDFSF*, 1956, I, 248; Giannini, "I proventi degli enti pubblici minori e la riserva della legge," *RDFSF*, 1957, I, 1; Berliri, "Appunti sul fondamento e il contenuto dell'art. 23 della Costituzione," *Jus*, 1958, 327.

rigorous application of the principle of the legality of taxation, would undoubtedly have produced legislative and administrative chaos.

Moreover, there is no doubt that there are two ways of interpreting article 23. Under a strict interpretation, the law would describe all the taxes minutely—not an easy matter, especially in a system like the Italian, in which legislation customarily leaves problems to be worked out through administrative practice. An elastic interpretation would not demand that such detail be included in the fiscal law, but merely that the law contain the essential elements of the taxes, from which, through logical developments and administrative supplementations, their concrete applications could be deduced. The elastic interpretation, apart from its practical advantages for fiscal administration, seems to respond better to the statement in article 23 that no levy may be imposed "except on the basis" of the law. It has been appropriately observed that for an institution to have a basis in the law is not the same thing as for it to be completely regulated in the law.

The Italian Constitutional Court (*Corte Costituzionale*) generally has chosen an elastic interpretation. Following an elastic interpretation, for example, the system of revaluing taxable income from agricultural land (12/1.1) is not unconstitutional. A system of revaluation was necessary because many of the cadasters employed in Italy for the evaluation of income from lands were made more than 100 years ago and were brought up to date hastily in 1923, and even more hastily in 1938. As used in the cadasters, the values of lira do not correspond to present values. Also, the agricultural economy has changed radically with regard to cultivation methods, costs, receipts, wages, and relations of ownership. Since it was deemed too costly to revise the entire content of the 1938 cadaster —the one still in use—a multiplier, a coefficient of revaluation, is now used to give a current value to the income. To avoid glaring inequalities, this coefficient is customarily low; it is determined yearly by the Ministry of Finance, on the basis of economic conditions, and published in a decree. The grounds for considering this process constitutional can be found in the legislation which declares the income from land taxable and establishes the cadasters, and in the law which authorizes the tax administration to establish the coefficients of revision on the basis of economic changes. Moreover, these coefficients are formally concerned with technical problems in the assessment of the taxes and do not explicitly affect the rate or the definition of the taxable income. Thus, the principle of the legality of the tax, intended in an elastic sense, is saved. This elastic interpretation permits the overcoming of great problems in the valuation of taxable income; moreover, it permits the government to lessen the burden of agricultural taxation according to the circumstances.

In the field of penal law also, the Italian Constitution establishes the principle of legality, stating in article 25 that "no one may be punished except in force of a law effective before the act committed" and adding that "no one may be subject to security measures except in the cases provided by law." Thus, the entire subject of the penal tax law and a large part of the subject of the penal tax procedural law is reserved to legislation.

1/2.3 Contribution in Accordance with Ability To Pay

Article 53 of the Constitution provides that "all are required to contribute to the public expenditures in proportion to their ability to pay [*capacità contributiva*]," thus setting forth, first, the principle of the "universality" of taxation, and, secondly, the principle of "juridical equality" in the tax field.[6]

Article 53 can be compared to article 25 of the Albertine Statute, according to which the citizens "contribute without distinction in proportion to their own property to the burdens of the state." In place of ability to pay, the Albertine Statute refers to property. Furthermore, while the Constitution poses the criterion of progressivity of taxes, the rule of the Albertine Statute seems to be satisfied with proportionality; however, the expression "in proportion" used in the Statute does not specifically define a criterion of allocation which is proportional rather than progressive or regressive. It lends itself to being understood purely in the sense of "in ratio" or "in relation" to property.

A third principle which seems to be contained in the first paragraph of article 53 of the Constitution is that of the connection between the duty to pay taxes and the financing of public expenditures. "All," it says, "are required to contribute to the public expenditures . . . ." In article 25 of the Albertine Statute, the statement was much less explicit and did not refer to the "public expenditures" but generically to the "burdens of the state."

The language of article 53 seems able to sustain the thesis that the principle of taxing both Italians and aliens, to the extent that they receive the benefit of the public expenditures, is a general principle of the Italian system. Article 53 says only "all," and not "all those who benefit from the public expenditures," are required to contribute. But to give a reasonable meaning to "all" in the provision, it seems logical to suppose that "those who benefit from the public expenditures" is understood. Otherwise, anyone anywhere in the world could be taxable in Italy on the basis of any of his property or activities, wherever located, without other limit than the practical possibility of taxing him and without other foundation than that of extracting from him money to finance Italian public expenditures. This "cynical" rule of taxation could be followed in

---

[6] On these questions, see Forte, "Note sulle norme tributarie costituzionali italiane," *Jus,* 1957, 372, and literature there cited; Giardina, *Le basi teoriche del principio di capacità contributiva* 425 *et seq.*

fact by a government or by a state; but it is difficult to suppose that a state would wish to make this rule part of its constitution.[7]

There is thus a rule which can serve to determine, in doubtful cases, the general criterion for the taxability of persons or property not belonging entirely to Italy: a connection must be made between the taxable matter and the advantages, even if general, to be derived from Italian public expenditures. One might think that this rule could be the constitutional basis for the principle of the territoriality of taxation (2/2.5). The principle of territoriality—of taxing income and transactions in the place where they are generated, and wealth and property in the place where they are situated—might appear to some as a corollary of the canon of taxation with relation to the public expenditure, since public expenditures benefit those properties which are situated in Italy and those events productive of income and of economic transactions which are carried out in Italy. It seems impossible, however, to state that article 53 entirely excludes principles other than that of territoriality as rules of the international limitation of taxation—that article 53 would exclude the criterion of citizenship, for example. The citizen who does not reside in his own state or resides there only for limited periods, and the citizen who, although residing there permanently, obtains certain income abroad and reinvests it abroad, can enjoy definite advantages from national public expenditures.

If the criterion of territoriality is not the only one permitted by the Constitution or for purposes of the international limitation of taxation, it nonetheless undoubtedly appears to be a general principle of the Italian tax system. Thus, the principle of territoriality is established as a general rule for the direct taxes by article 6 of the *Testo unico* of the laws on direct taxes (2/1), which states that "the taxes are applicable if their bases arise in the territory of the state" (11/1.1). The *Testo unico* of the laws on direct taxes is recent, but with regard to the principle of territoriality, it did no more than render explicit a long and confirmed legislative tradition in Italian direct taxation.

The principle of territoriality is also at the base of the general tax on receipts (14/), the chief Italian indirect tax. This tax extends to receipts obtained in payment for the transfer of goods or the furnishing of services "carried out in the state" (14/8.1). The principle of territoriality is at the base of the manufacturing taxes, which extend only to production carried on in Italy and to imports for consumption in Italy, and are refunded or not applied to merchandise destined for export (4/5.2). The registration tax extends to "transactions executed in Italy" (15/), and the succession tax extends to property located in Italy at the moment at which the suc-

---

[7] Maffezzoni, "Valore positivo dei principi costituzionali in materia tributaria," *Jus*, 1956, 316; see also Giardina, *Le basi teoriche del principio di capacità contributiva* 412-414, and literature there cited.

cession takes place, independently of the place of death of the decedent and of his citizenship (3/4.14a).

The principle of territoriality, finally, is used also for the local income and consumption taxes, in the delimitation of the tax powers of the various communes among themselves. The personal tax on income (family tax) of the communes is applied to those who reside in the commune (2/3). The communal taxes on consumption are applied to goods introduced into the commune which are consumed there (4/5.8).

1/2.4 Progressivity of the Tax System

An analysis of the second paragraph of article 53 of the Constitution, according to which the tax system "is based on criteria of progressivity," [8] shows that not all taxes must be progressive; only the tax system in the aggregate must follow this principle. Proportional or regressive taxes are thus allowed, provided that they are accompanied by others so progressive as to make the net result a progressive "system." Nonetheless, certain regressive taxes, structured in such a way as to render impossible the development of a satisfactory progressivity in conformity with the principles of ability to pay, might not be allowable.

Article 53, second paragraph, refers to the "tax" system and not to the "financial" system; what should be progressive according to article 53, therefore, is the system of levies and not the aggregate effect, which is the resultant of the system of levies and of public expenditures. Progressivity of the financial system as a whole is ensured by the operation of other principles of the Constitution regarding the effects of expenditures.

For purposes of this rule, are obligatory social security contributions included among the taxes? From an economic point of view, they seem to be taxes. But according to the opinion of an authoritative group of Italian jurists, they are not taxes in a juridical sense since they are regulated and organized in a manner considerably different from the taxes of the state and of the local entities.[9] The question is serious and gives rise to uncertainties (1/6.1c).

Finally, does the expression "tax system" refer only to the system of the state, or to the state system plus the systems of all local entities together; or, finally, does it refer to each individual tax system taken separately? The interpretation of the rule most in conformity with the letter and with the spirit of the constitutional language seems to be that by "tax system" is meant all of the tax systems affecting the taxpayer: the central fiscal system, the regional, communal, and provincial systems, and possibly the "parafiscal" system of social security.

---

[8] See Giardina, *Le basi teoriche del principio di capacità contributiva* 451 *et seq.*; Forte, "Note sulle norme tributarie costituzionali italiane," *Jus,* 1957, 372.

[9] See Zingali, "Il concetto di tributo nella più recente elaborazione giurisprudenziale," *Arch. fin.,* 1956, 220.

1/2.5 General Principles Promoting Justice and Equality

The principles contained in article 53 of the Constitution regarding ability to pay and progressivity find some elements of specification in other constitutional provisions. First, the principle of the equality of citizens before the law is established in article 3 of the Constitution, which adds, "it is the task of the Republic to remove the obstacles of an economic and social order which, limiting the fact of liberty and the equality of the citizens, impede the full development of the human person and the effective participation of the workers in the political, economic, and social organization of the country." [10]

Article 4 of the Constitution fixes the importance of work and of its income:

> The Republic recognizes for all citizens the right to work and promotes the conditions which render this right effective.
> Every citizen has the duty to carry out, according to his own possibilities and his own choice, an activity or a function which contributes to the material or spiritual progress of society.

Together, these provisions seem to point out a constitutional foundation for discrimination in favor of income from work and against income from capital. Discrimination in favor of earned income is established in the state and local taxes, in the form of lower rates applied to income from work as against other income. "Unearned" income deriving from particular situations or from fortunate opportunities cannot, on the other hand, be said to have a treatment less favorable than other income; indeed, it often has a more favorable treatment (for example, capital gains of individuals are not taxed in the absence of specific "speculative intent"). It should be added that discrimination in favor of income from work in the Italian direct tax system is considerable only on the legislative plane, that is, for the nominal rates, and not on the practical plane of the rates actually applied. In assessment, income from work as an employee does not escape taxation, while income of other kinds frequently does. Moreover, fewer deductions for expenses of production are allowed from income from work as an employee than from other kinds of income.

Another rule which is interesting in the specification of the concept of ability to pay is that of article 31: "the Republic facilitates, with economic measures and other provisions, the formation of the family, and the fulfillment of the duties related thereto . . . ." This rule amply justifies the system of allowances for family burdens and the reliefs provided for large families, adopted in the taxation of income by the state and by the communes. It should be noted, however, that the weight of the taxes on consumption in Italy carries, for large families, a fiscal burden greater than for other families, in the measure in which the

---

[10] See Esposito, *La Costituzione Italiana* 29.

former are obliged to spend a larger part of their income on taxable consumption goods.

1/2.6 Provisions Authorizing Government Intervention in the Economy

Ability to pay and progressivity must be considered also from an extra-fiscal point of view. Exemptions for industrialization and for economic development are very good examples of tax measures provided for the purpose of directing the economy. Today in Italy, these are widespread; they are given especially for the benefit of the south (*Mezzogiorno*), but also in lesser measure for the depressed areas of the center-north. The policy of tax exemptions for the south goes back to the beginning of the century, but it was episodic and limited for a long time. Today, new enterprises and enterprises which make new investments in the south are given favored treatment for the direct taxes (10/6), for customs duties (on machinery) (4/8.1), and for certain transaction taxes (taxes on credit and similar operations) (4/2.4).

Article 53 (1/2.3) establishes the duty of "all" to contribute to the public expenditures, placing at the base of the fiscal system the criterion of the "universality" of taxes. It also lays down the rule of ability to pay. Can exemptions for vast areas of the national territory be allowed, in view of the constitutional principle of the universality of taxation? The admissibility of an extrafiscal policy directed toward economic regulation may be drawn from articles 41, 42, 43, and 44 of the Constitution, which are the fundamental articles concerning public intervention in the economy and the relations between policy and economy in the Italian system.

Article 41 establishes that "private economic initiative is free" but specifies that it "cannot be carried out in conflict with social utility or in such a manner as to bring injury to security, to liberty, to human dignity." Finally, the article declares expressly that "the law determines the appropriate programs and controls so that public and private economic activity can be directed and coordinated to social ends." Extrafiscal finance for social purposes therefore seems to be allowed by the Italian Constitution, given that article 41 permits controls and programs suitable for directing the private and public economy to those ends.

The controls of extrafiscal finance are precisely the ones most easily accepted by those wishing to avoid too strong an interference by the state in the market economy but disposed to accept a certain amount of public intervention. In reconciling directivist needs and the need for respect for the initiative of individuals (a reconciliation reflected by the language of articles 41 and 42), therefore, the acceptance of fiscal instruments of intervention appears as a natural result.

But it is necessary to clarify for what ends the regulation is allowed. In saying "social end" in distinction to "individual end," the Constitution does not mean necessarily to allude to problems of distributive justice, but to something which concerns the collectivity or the majority of persons as distinguished from that which interests particular individuals. These expressions thus authorize the belief that considerations of the economic development of the collectivity are among the objects for which article 41 of the Constitution allows planning and control of the market economy.

The same is true with regard to the "social function" of property, mentioned in article 42, which recognizes private property and affirms the duty of the state "to render it accessible to all." This, evidently, can be fulfilled not only by a policy of redistribution, but also by a policy of economic development. In addition, article 44, on the subject of agriculture, along with redistributive ends, explicitly sets forth productive ends: "for the purpose of achieving the rational exploitation of the soil and of establishing equitable social relations, the law imposes duties and restrictions on private landed property, sets limits to its extension according to the agrarian regions and zones, promotes and imposes the improvement of the lands, the transformation of the landed estate [*latifondo*], and the reformation of the productive units; assists the small and medium-sized farms [*proprietà contadina*]."

Article 47 of the Constitution declares that "the Republic encourages and protects saving in all its forms," and adds that it "favors the access of popular saving to the ownership of the dwelling, to the direct ownership of the cultivator, and to the direct and indirect share investment in the great productive groups of the country." Here one finds a basis for the policy of fiscal reliefs and incentives for building, which has taken various forms: (1) exemptions from or reductions in the registration taxes for purchase of immovable property on which dwellings to be used by the owners already exist or will be built (15/4.1); (2) facilitation of loans to building cooperatives and of the purchase of low-cost dwellings by those who inhabit them; and, more generally, (3) 25-year exemptions from the tax on income from buildings for buildings used as dwellings (9/4.2b).

Article 44, last paragraph, states that "the law provides measures for the benefit of mountainous zones." In fact, for agriculture in the mountainous zones of Italy, a total abolition of income taxes has been provided for some years. This policy could perhaps have been considered unconstitutional because contrary to the principle of universality of tax in article 53 of the Constitution, if favored treatment were not expressly allowed for mountainous zones.

Recognizing the social function of "cooperation of a mutual character and without ends of private speculation," article 45 of the Constitution adds that "the law promotes it and favors its growth with the most suitable means and ensures, with the appropriate checks, its character and its purposes." Cooperatives, indeed, even apart from the laws relative to building cooperatives previously mentioned, receive a favored fiscal treatment in the Italian system, conditioned on the requirement that these enterprises not only have the juridical vestment of the cooperative, but also its substance (in practice, this check is not always easy to make). The most important instance of favored fiscal treatment for cooperatives is found in the field of the tax on corporations and other collective entities, under which cooperatives are in part exempt and in part subjected to reduced rates (5/5.10).

Finally, article 45, second paragraph, provides for the protection of the artisan class and has found application in various fiscal rules by which, in matters of direct taxes, it is desired to ensure to artisan enterprises the more favorable treatment allowed to income from independent work instead of the less favorable treatment given to enterprise income (7/1.2b).

With regard to progressivity, an important limitation on extrafiscal finance results from article 42, which establishes that "private property is recognized and guaranteed by the law, which determines the modes of its acquisition and enjoyment and its limits for the purpose of assuring the social function and rendering it accessible to all" and that "private property can be, in the cases provided by the law, and subject to indemnity, expropriated for reasons of general interest." From this rule, it can be inferred that the criterion of progressivity cannot reach "confiscatory progressivity," that is, rate levels such as to eliminate private property.

1/2.7 Provisions Protecting Certain Liberties

Extrafiscal finance can be directed to other goals besides those of economic productivity and social justice. Article 16 of the Constitution states: "every citizen may circulate and sojourn freely in any part of the national territory, subject to the limitations which the law establishes generally for reasons of health and of security." From this rule can be inferred a prohibition against discriminatory fiscal measures which would place an obstacle to the circulation of citizens within the country. Local authorities—without this constitutional prohibition—could be tempted to adopt measures of direct or indirect taxation, designed to prevent migrations from undesired areas, or to prevent the settling in their locality of merchants, industries, and professionals who would compete with local interests.

A direct prohibition against obstructing the free circulation of goods and capital in Italian territory exists in a narrower though more definite way by virtue of article 120, which establishes that the regions "may not adopt measures obstructing in any way the free circulation of persons and of things among the regions." For regional finance, therefore, the prohibition of taxes prejudicing the free movement of goods and of capital is fixed with greater rigor than for local finance.

The regions are new in the Italian administrative structure: so new that, more than 15 years after the adoption of the Constitution, the regions of ordinary statute for which it provides have not yet been established (1/5.1). Fear that the regions could fragment Italy into many units, which would attain political as well as administrative autonomy and which would impede the functioning of the unitary state, is alive in many Italians, perhaps in part because of the historical memory of the Italian political and economic situation before the national unification. It is understandable that the Constitution contains limits for the regions, while it does not for the communes, with which the Italian system has been familiar for a long time and which are smaller and by themselves not in a position, without special constitutional legislation, to present the same dangers of fragmentation and particularism. Moreover, communal finances are regulated by laws of the state, and, thus, the state can, even without constitutional imposition, attempt to remove obstacles to the free circulation of goods. With the entry into force of the treaty establishing the European Economic Community (Common Market), the free circulation of goods was established, as a general rule, for the Common Market area. It also may be noted that article 5 of the Constitution says: "the Republic is one and indivisible and promotes local autonomies."

Article 18 of the Constitution states that "the citizens have the right to associate, without authorization, for ends which are not forbidden to individuals by the penal law." This article, as regards specifically liberty of association in trade unions, is accompanied by article 39, providing that "the organization of trade unions is free" and that "on the trade unions can be imposed no other duty than their registration at the local or central offices, according to the rules of law." Thus, discriminatory taxation against associations which are not prohibited by the penal law, and in any event against trade union associations, whose lawfulness the Constitution explicitly states in general outline, would not be allowed. Moreover, it is forbidden to require citizens to enter into associations which impose obligations to pay taxes and levies.[11]

Liberties outside the economic sphere are provided in certain articles of the Constitution. Article 21 begins: "all have the right to manifest freely their own thought by word, writing, and any other means of broadcast"; it adds, "the press cannot be subject to authorizations and censorships." Although the liberty of thought and of the press is here safeguarded absolutely, it seems evident that the Constitution does not intend to annul penal prohibitions established, in the common laws, for

---

[11] See Corte Cost., ord. 16 March 1962, n. 110 (*Foro it.*, 1962, II, 252), declaring that the question of the constitutionality of a law requiring a hunting license to be validated by a hunting association, which imposed a fee, was not manifestly unfounded.

certain crimes committed through manifestations of thought, such as offenses to the head of state, insults, or obscene writings and speeches. It may be noted that today in Italy, exemptions from the general tax on receipts are allowed for periodicals of a political character (14/4.6i). It seems likely that, given article 21, the limitation of these exemptions to publishers supporting certain political causes would not be deemed constitutional.

Finally, article 20 states that "the ecclesiastical character and the purpose of religion or of worship of an association or institution cannot be the occasion of special legislative limitations nor of special fiscal burdens on its formation, juridical capacity, or any other form of activity." This rule has been considered to apply not primarily to the Roman Catholic religion, but to other forms of worship. With regard to the Roman Catholic religion, article 7 provides that "the state and the Catholic Church are, each in its own order, independent and sovereign" and adds that "their relations are regulated by the Lateran Treaties." The Lateran Treaties are concerned not only with the avoidance of fiscal discrimination against the Catholic Church, but with the availability, to entities of worship and religion of that Church, of the fiscal reliefs granted to entities of education and welfare (5/5). The entities of Catholic religion and worship thus enjoy a favored treatment, guaranteed to them by the Constitution. Similar non-Catholic entities today do not enjoy specific fiscal reliefs; however, discriminatory taxation against them, consisting of "special fiscal burdens" not borne by other taxpayers, is forbidden.

1/2.8   Decisions of the Constitutional Court on Principles Affecting Taxation

The second paragraph of article 53, establishing that the tax system is based on the criterion of progressivity (1/2.4), gives specification to the rule of the first paragraph, which places equalization according to ability to pay at the basis of the tax (1/2.3).

During the debates on the drafts of the constitutional rules, article 53 was regarded with some scepticism by many of the most authoritative jurists and politicians of the period, who held the opinion that such an article was unenforceable and not to be considered binding. This tendency has now been completely reversed. The Constitution, and in particular its rules on the law of the economy, such as that of article 53, are important in practice, as directives to the ordinary legislator and as principles for the interpretation and application of the existing system.

This new tendency has its roots in the evolution of the Italian society and economy. The parliamentary regime, universal suffrage, and the large political parties and associations have made the general public aware of the structural problems of the country and have nourished broad political discussions on the concrete application of the various constitutional principles. The current active debate on limitations on the relations between public and private initiative has often brought to light the crucial importance of the interpretation of the constitutional rules.

Another reason for the new tendency has been the institution of the Constitutional Court and of procedures of constitutional interpretation of which the country had no previous experience (1/4.10g). The Constitutional Court obviously has a greater sensitivity to, and a greater tendency to affirm the importance of, the Constitution and its operative scope than had the Court of Cassation, which concerned itself principally with ordinary laws.[12]

1/3. Tax Legislation

1/3.1 The Legislature

a. COMPOSITION AND ELECTION. The Italian national legislature is a bicameral Parliament composed of the Chamber of Deputies and the Senate of the Republic (Const. art. 55). The Deputies are elected for five years (Const. art. 60) by direct universal suffrage of the voters in the proportion of one Deputy for every 80,000 inhabitants or major fraction thereof (Const. art. 56).[13] The Senate is elected for six years (Const. art. 60) by regions, each region having one Senator for every 200,000 inhabitants or major fraction thereof (Const. art. 57).[14] Senators are chosen by direct suffrage of voters who have passed the twenty-fifth year of age (Const. art. 58).[15]

b. LAWS. All taxes, in their essential outlines, must have a definition in the law, according to article 23 of the Constitution (1/2.2). For the enactment of the laws, there is first an ordinary procedure, which in turn can be of two types, normal or abbreviated. The ordinary procedure is regulated by articles 70-74 of the Constitution. Article 70 establishes that "the legislative function is exercised collectively by the two chambers." Article 71 specifies that "the initiation of the laws belongs to the government, to each member of the chamber and to the organs and entities on which it may be conferred by constitutional law."[16]

Article 72 provides that every draft bill presented to a chamber must be examined by a committee (*commissione*) and then by the chamber

---

[12] On these questions, see Sandulli, "Natura, funzione ed effetti delle pronunce della Corte Costituzionale sulla legittimità delle leggi," *Riv. trim. dir. pubbl.*, 1959, 23.

[13] D.P.R. 30 March 1957, n. 361.

[14] Valle d'Aosta has one Senator; each other region must have not fewer than six.

[15] L. 6 February 1948, n. 29.

[16] In practice, the sole entity thus empowered is the National Economic and Labor Council spoken of in article 99 of the Constitution. However, this body does not have legislative initiative for fiscal matters (1/3.3).

Popular initiative may be exercised by the submission of a draft bill by at least

DESCRIPTION OF TAX SYSTEM   26

itself, which votes on each article of the bill and then on the whole bill. In addition, article 72 states that the rules of the chamber may establish abbreviated procedures for draft bills whose urgency is declared, and may further establish in what cases and forms the examination and the approval of draft bills may be referred to limited committees of Deputies or Senators. (These committees, including permanent committees, are composed in such a way as to reflect the proportions of the parliamentary parties.) Until the moment of its final approval, however, the draft bill must be sent back to the chamber if the government or one tenth of the members of the chamber or one fifth of the members of the committee requests that it be discussed and voted in the chamber itself, or that it be subjected to the final approval of the chamber without discussion. Under article 72 of the Constitution, the procedure for approval of the laws by committees cannot be used for the budget law, for the law approving the receipts and expenditures, or for draft bills on constitutional or electoral matters, authorization to ratify international agreements, and legislative delegation (1/3.1d).

When one chamber has approved the text of a draft law, it is the duty of the other to discuss it and approve it either by the normal procedure or by an abbreviated procedure. If the second chamber, in the course of the debate, approves amendments to the draft law already approved by the first chamber, the amended draft must return to the first chamber to be discussed there anew. This process continues until both chambers approve the same legislative text.

Approval by both chambers does not suffice to give effect to laws. Article 73 of the Constitution states that "the laws are promulgated by the President of the Republic within a month of their approval." If the chambers, each by an absolute majority of its own members, declare the urgency of a law, however, the law is promulgated within the time limit established by the law itself. The duty of the President of the Republic is not purely formal, for, under article 74, "the President of the Republic, before promulgating a law, may, in a message giving reasons to the chambers, request a new deliberation." Only if the chambers insist on approving the law must it then be promulgated. Under article 73, last paragraph, "the laws are published immediately after promulgation and become effective the fifteenth day following their publication, unless the laws themselves establish a different time limit." Publication is made in the Official Collection of Laws and Decrees (*Raccolta ufficiale delle leggi e dei decreti*) and in the Official Gazette (*Gazzetta ufficiale*).

50,000 electors. Const. art. 72. A popular referendum may be called to decide on the total or partial abrogation of a law or of an act having the force of law, on the request of 500,000 electors, but this procedure is not available for tax or budget laws. Const. art. 75.

Besides the ordinary procedure for enacting a law, there are two special procedures which have considerable importance both in general and in tax matters: use of a decree-law that is later converted into law (1/3.1c), and use of a proxy law (*legge delega*), delegating to the government the power to issue a legislative provision by decree of the President of the Republic (1/3.1d).

c. DECREE-LAWS. Use of a decree-law is provided for in article 77 of the Constitution, which states: "when, in extraordinary cases of necessity and of urgency, the government adopts, on its own responsibility, provisional measures with force of law, it must the same day present them for conversion to the chambers, which, even if dissolved, are specially convoked and meet within five days." If, within 60 days of the publication of a decree-law, the chambers do not approve its conversion into law, the decree-law loses its efficacy from the beginning. However, under article 77, "the chambers may regulate by law the juridical relations arising on the basis of decrees not converted."

Considerable use of the decree-laws is made in the tax field. One reason is that the announcement of some taxes causes great disturbances in the market. In other cases, use of the decree-law arises out of urgent fiscal needs. For manufacturing and analogous taxes, the decree-law is now used systematically. A "foreclosing decree" (*decreto catenaccio*) is issued by surprise, thereby having the double advantage of hastening the flow of the required revenue and avoiding market disturbances.

In the fascist period, the legislative function was debased by considerable abuse of the decree-law procedure. The entire tax field (and in large part, the rest of the legislative field) was generally modified by decree-laws. There was no time limit, as there is today, for the conversion of the decree-law into law. Moreover, Parliament had little authority as compared to the government, and, in the last analysis, it was the government that legislated instead of the Parliament. Parliament merely approved, within an indefinite period and without discussion, the decree-laws presented by the government for conversion.

One decree-law enacted during the fascist period provided that "the Ministry of Finance has the power, in the manner and with the forms established by the laws and regulations, to impose national, provincial, and communal taxes, and to manage the funds of the state," and added that "no tax, in any form, may be established in favor of any entity, without the previous consent of the Ministry of Finance." [17] The principle of the legality of taxation thus was transformed by this decree-law, mechanically converted into law by Parliament one year later, into the principle that taxation was reserved to the government. One who glances

---

[17] Article 1 of R.D.L. 7 August 1936, n. 1639, converted in L. 7 June 1937, n. 1016, on the reform of the tax structure.

over the Italian tax codes even today will still find important legislative provisions headed "R.D.L." ("royal decree-law").

The presentation of the recent reform of the taxation of profits from shares (9/2.7) in the form of a draft bill instead of a decree-law is probably a reaction to such abuse of the decree-law procedure—even though the effect of this reform on the stock market might have been thought to justify the use of a decree-law.

d.   PRESIDENTIAL DECREES. Article 76 of the Constitution provides: "the exercise of the legislative function cannot be delegated to the government except with definition of directive principles and standards and only for a limited time and for defined objects." Decrees issued on the basis of such a delegation are called "presidential decrees" since their approval by the President of the Republic, under the Italian constitutional system, has the value of "issue" and not of simple "promulgation" as in the case of the laws (1/3.1b). Any act of the President of the Republic having the force of law must be countersigned by the minister proposing it and by the President of the Council of Ministers (Const. art. 89).

In the tax field, there has been frequent recourse to the presidential decree. The most conspicuous example in recent years is the *Testo unico* of the laws on the direct taxes, which took effect on 1 January 1960 (2/1). This *Testo unico* is based on article 63 of the Law of 5 January 1956, n. 1, on tax equalization, known as the "Tremelloni law," from the name of the Minister of Finance who presented it to Parliament. Article 63 of that law provided:

> The government of the Republic, having heard a parliamentary commission composed of five senators and five deputies, is authorized to issue, within 18 months of the entry into force of this law, unified texts concerning the different direct taxes, the general provisions, and also the rules on collection, eliminating the provisions in conflict with the provisions contained in the Law of 11 January 1951, n. 25, and in this law, and adding, besides the changes useful for a better coordination, those necessary for attainment of the following criteria:
>
> (1) adaptation of the provisions to the requirement of simplification in the application of the taxes and to that of a rational organization of the services;
>
> (2) perfection of the rules concerning the activity of the tax administration for purposes of the assessment of income.

The time limit established by article 63 of the Tremelloni law was not sufficient for the preparation of the *Testo unico*, and the time limit was extended to 31 January 1958.[18] When completed, the *Testo unico* gave rise to many judicial controversies, especially with respect to whether it had exceeded the legislative delegation.[19] At present, the principal

---

[18] L. 30 July 1957, n. 654.

[19] See Uckmar, "Contrasto fra alcune norme del T.U. imposte dirette e la legislazione precedente," *Dir. e prat. trib.*, 1959, I, 18.

question resolved by the Constitutional Court in validating the *Testo unico* concerns the tax period.[20]

e. INTERNATIONAL TREATIES. Italy has entered into several international treaties; these include not only treaties for the avoidance of double taxation, but treaties of broader scope such as that establishing the European Economic Community (Common Market). International treaties are concluded by the government, but they must be approved by Parliament in a law (Const. art. 80) and ratified by the President of the Republic. Only when they do not involve modifications of law, financial burdens, or changes in the national territory may the treaties concluded by the government be ratified directly by the President of the Republic without approval by Parliament.

1/3.2 The Executive

a. THE PRESIDENT OF THE REPUBLIC. The Italian government is not a presidential government. The office and the functions of the head of the state, the President of the Republic, are quite distinct from the office and the functions of the head of the government, the President of the Council of Ministers (1/3.2b). The President of the Republic is elected by Parliament, in joint session of its members (Const. art. 83),[21] for a term of seven years (Const. art. 85). He has the following functions (Const. art. 87): represent the nation; send messages to the chambers of Parliament; authorize the presentation to the chambers of draft bills initiated by the government; promulgate laws, issue decrees having the force of law (1/3.1), and issue regulations (1/3.2c); call elections of new chambers and fix the time of their first meeting; call a popular referendum in the cases provided by the Constitution; nominate, in cases specified by law, the officials of the state; fulfill various military duties; preside over the High Council of the Magistracy (1/4.10a); grant pardons and commute penalties; confer honors; accredit and receive diplomatic representatives; ratify international agreements, on authorization, when necessary, of the chambers; nominate the President of the Council of Ministers and, on the proposal of the latter, the ministers (Const. art. 92); dissolve one or both of the chambers before the expiration of their elected terms (Const. art. 88).

In the fiscal field, the President of the Republic has modest functions. His influence may be exercised particularly in the choice of the heads of the great public holding companies (1/3.4a), in refusal to promulgate certain laws, and in sending messages to Parliament. The fact that the President of the Republic nominates the President of the Council of

---

[20] See Corte Cost. 9 June 1961, n. 30.

[21] One delegate from Valle d'Aosta and three from each other region, elected by the Regional Councils, participate in the election.

Ministers and, on the latter's proposal, the ministers normally does not mean that the President of the Republic can assume responsibility for the choice of the various ministers or impose his choices on the head of the government.

b. THE COUNCIL OF MINISTERS. The head of the government is the President of the Council of Ministers. Under article 95 of the Constitution, he "directs the general policy of the government and is responsible for it." In addition, he maintains the unity of political and administrative action by promoting and coordinating the activities of the ministers. According to article 95, second paragraph, "the ministers are responsible collectively for the acts of the Council of Ministers and individually for the acts of their ministries." Each minister performs the normal tasks of administration within the ambit of his own ministry. But when he prepares a draft bill which he wishes to submit for the approval of the Parliament, he must first present the bill for approval to the Council of Ministers. The Council, having given its approval, will in turn present the draft bill to the chambers. The screening by the Council of Ministers limits considerably a minister's margin of legislative maneuver.

Article 95 of the Constitution, in the last paragraph, entrusts to the ordinary law the organization of the presidency of the Council, and the number, the functions, and the organization of the ministries. In Italy, at one time, all financial policy was in the hands of the Minister of Finance. At present, the Minister of Finance retains responsibility for the public receipts; responsibility for the public expenditures and for the public debt and the supervision of the monetary, credit, and banking system have been transferred to the Minister of the Treasury. In the postwar period, the office of Minister of the Budget was created to coordinate all economic and financial policy and to summarize in a general report (*Relazione generale sulla situazione economica del paese*) the policies followed in the previous year. This report is presented to the Parliament each year by the Minister of the Budget jointly with the Minister of the Treasury, but is essentially the work of the former. There is at present a plan to extend the duties of the Ministry of the Budget, transforming it into a "Ministry of the Budget and of Planning [*Programmazione*]." In 1962, in fact, the Minister of the Budget presented, with his general report, an additional document (*Nota aggiuntiva*) setting forth the guidelines of a policy of national planning. Subsequently, he established a national planning commission, whose first report, drawn in very general terms, was presented in July 1963. But the hierarchy among the three ministers is not at all clear, although they are formally on an equal footing. The function of the Minister of the Budget in all fields of public finance is purely "additional" to, and not "substitutive" of, that of the other ministers. It is an office difficult to place in the structure of the Italian government, and which perhaps will find its definition when the creation of the proposed Ministry of the Budget and of Planning has been carried out.

Finally, it should be mentioned that, in order to separate fiscal activity from activity of an economic-productive character, many capital properties which were formerly administered by the Ministry of Finance, such as thermal establishments and various mining establishments, are now controlled by the Ministry of State Participations, which also controls most other public enterprises. The Ministry of Finance has retained almost exclusively the administration of those activities in the capital business field which are inseparably connected with fiscal aspects: that is, the fiscal monopolies of salt and tobacco (4/6); the lottery (1/6.8i, 4/6.7); and certain public properties (for example, the seashores) called "public domain" (*demaniali*) because they are inalienable and devoted permanently to public use (4/7.1).

The Ministry of Finance, whose structure is described at 1/4, is the ultimate source of tax policy. Tax policy is the subject of lively and constant discussion not only within the government, but also among academic experts and representatives of business groups such as the Association of Italian Corporations (*Associazione fra le Società Italiane per Azioni* or *Assonime*) and its affiliate, the General Federation of Italian Industry (*Confederazione Generale dell'Industria Italiana* or *Confindustria*). To assist in the discussion and planning of major reforms, the government may organize a special study committee. The most recent study committee, composed of 15 experts from the government, the universities, and business, was appointed by the Fanfani government in 1962 to study a reform of the entire Italian tax system with a view to its simplification, to the achievement of a more equitable distribution of the tax burden, and to more effective enforcement.[22] This committee recommended a number of reforms, particularly the replacement of the "objective" taxes on income by a system of personal taxation of the income of individuals and of corporations (see 2/3, 2/4), the replacement of the general tax on receipts (4/2, 14/) by a value-added tax, and the abolition or simplification of certain other indirect taxes. The work of the committee has been published only in summary form; [23] the implementation of its recommendations has been delayed by the problems of inflation and international balance of payments facing the Italian economy at the end of 1963.[24]

---

[22] See *Corriere della Sera*, 11 August 1962, 6; *Corriere della Sera*, 29 September 1962, 6.

[23] Ministero delle Finanze, *Sintesi dei lavori della Commissione per lo Studio della Riforma Tributaria.*

[24] For discussion of these problems, see "Italy: New Wave or Interlude?" *The Economist*, 28 March 1964, 1233; Sterling, "'Apertura a Sinistra': Second Round," *The Reporter*, 21 November 1963, 28.

c. REGULATIONS. Article 87 of the Constitution gives the President of the Republic the authority to issue regulations. Like any act of the President of the Republic, a regulation must be countersigned by the minister proposing it; to have the force of law, such an act must also be countersigned by the President of the Council of Ministers (Const. art. 89).

The Italian administrative system permits various kinds of regulations: executory, independent, and delegated. All of them are important in the tax field. Although article 23 of the Constitution establishes that no levy can be imposed except on the basis of the law (by "law" is meant a law in the formal sense), this rule does not require that all tax matters be contained in the laws integrally and in detail—only a legislative basis is required (1/2.2). A certain margin of maneuver, not easy to define, is left for regulatory action on the part of the finance administration. In fact, the offices of the finance administration today have very great regulatory powers, so great as to arouse, in some important cases, suspicions of violation of article 23.

Executory regulations (*regolamenti esecutivi*) "are connected always with a previous law and have the purpose of establishing the particular rules necessary to its execution." [25] Independent or autonomous regulations (*regolamenti indipendenti*), on the other hand, flow from a simple "discretionary power granted by a law to the executive power regarding a given subject matter which in this way comes to be governed solely by the rules of the regulation." [26] Delegated regulations (*regolamenti delegati*), finally, find their source in an express rule of law which authorizes the government to carry out regulatory activities in a field which otherwise would not be open to it. A delegated regulation must be distinguished from a presidential decree issued on the basis of a legislative delegation (1/3.1d). The delegation which lies at the base of the presidential decree is exhausted in a definite time, by the issue of a single measure. In contrast, the legislative authorization to issue regulations on certain matters gives the government permanent competence in those matters. "Delegated regulations," although not contrary in principle to the new Constitution, have aroused suspicions of unconstitutionality, both in general and particularly in tax matters. [27]

d. MINISTERIAL DECREES. The greatest suspicions of unconstitutionality are directed at an anomalous class of regulations: those issued in the form of "ministerial decrees" (*decreti ministeriali*). They are published directly by the ministerial authority, without the formalities prescribed by

---

25 1 Zanobini, *Corso di diritto amministrativo* 72.
26 1 Zanobini, *Corso di diritto amministrativo* 73.
27 See 1 Zanobini, *Corso di diritto amministrativo* 73.

the Constitution for acts of the President.[28] One group of jurists considers that ministerial decrees are not improper if they are founded on authorizations contained in a law, and are issued by the government to supplement, apply, or modify that law. The law instituting the general tax on receipts in 1940,[29] for example, authorizes the Ministry of Finance to issue administrative regulations in the form of ministerial decrees. For various manufacturing taxes, even in quite recent times, the ministerial decree has been the means of specifying the criteria for granting exemption to certain uses, kinds, or quantities of products normally taxed.

e. MINISTERIAL CIRCULARS. The role of the ministerial circular (*circolare ministeriale*) in the Italian tax system is considerable. An example of fundamental importance is the ministerial circular containing the tables of rates of amortization and depreciation allowed for the various kinds of assets in the determination of business income (7/3.1). Another example is the ministerial circular which provides for the classification of the incomes of artisans and of small enterprises as professional rather than business income (7/1.2b).

Ministerial circulars are not regulations in the proper sense since the administration does not issue them for the use of the public. Rather, they are instructions issued by the administration to its own officials who are obliged to obey them because of the hierarchical relation which exists between the officials and the administration to which they belong. Some jurists state, however, that when a circular involves the exercise of a normative power expressly delegated by the law to the administration, it is no longer limited to internal measures of the administration, binding only for its officials, but has the power to bind persons outside the administration, thus meeting the criteria for external regulations. The circulars then would become a subspecies of, or a species related to, the delegated or autonomous regulations, discussed at 1/3.2c.[30]

1/3.3 The National Economic and Labor Council

Among the auxiliary organs provided for in the Constitution, the National Economic and Labor Council (*Consiglio Nazionale dell'Economia e del Lavoro* or CNEL) has an important role. The Council is composed of experts and of representatives of the productive sectors of the economy, and acts as a consulting organ of the chambers and of the government for the matters allocated to it by law. It has legislative

---

[28] See 1 Zanobini, *Corso di diritto amministrativo* 75.

[29] R.D.L. 9 January 1940, n. 2, converted in L. 19 June 1940, n. 762. See Chapter 14.

[30] For discussion, see Ranelletti, *Istituzioni di diritto pubblico* 574-577; Liccardo, "Natura giuridica delle circolari ministeriali," *RDFSF*, 1952, II, 136; Liccardo, "Ancora sulla natura giuridica delle circolari amministrative e sulla loro influenza nel processo tributario," *Rass. dir. pubbl.*, 1955, 318.

initiative and may assist and advise in the drafting of economic and social legislation according to the principles, and within the time limits, established by law (Const. art. 99).

Taxation has been removed from among those matters on which CNEL has legislative initiative.[31] However, for tax matters, CNEL may carry out "studies and investigations," [32] give opinions to the chambers and to the government at their request, and furnish "observations and proposals" to the chambers and to the government, even on its own initiative, concerning legislative plans.[33]

In the tax field, until recently, the contribution required of, and furnished by, CNEL has been very modest. But the tendency seems to be changing. In the summer of 1962, for example, the government asked CNEL for an opinion on the government's plan for the reform of tax litigation procedure (1/4.13).

1/3.4 Budget Policy

a. IN GENERAL. The Constitution, in article 81, states four fundamental rules regarding the budget of the state. The first is as follows: "the chambers approve each year the budget and the revenue and expenditure account presented by the government." In this statement is contained the principle of an annual budget estimate and an annual budget of revenues and expenditures, and also the principle of the legality of these two supreme documents for the management of public finance.

Article 81 then states that "the provisional functioning of the budget cannot be granted except by law and for periods not exceeding in the aggregate four months." This provision authorizes the use of a provisional budget period (*esercizio provvisorio*), subject to the principle of legality and also to a temporal limitation.

The third and fourth provisions of article 81 concern the relations between the estimated budget on the one hand and the taxes and the public expenses on the other. The third paragraph of article 81 provides that the law approving the budget cannot establish new taxes or new expenditures. The last paragraph of article 81 provides that "any other law [other than the law approving the budget] providing for new or greater expenditures must specify the means for meeting them." This provision establishes the relative inviolability of the balance between revenues and expenditures fixed in the budget law—the surplus or the deficit fixed by that law cannot be changed by new uncovered expenditures. On the other hand, the balance may be varied in the inverse direction since, under the Constitution, new receipts can be established

---

[31] L. 5 January 1957, n. 33, art. 10.

[32] L. 5 January 1957, n. 33, art. 12.

[33] L. 5 January 1957, n. 33, art. 8.

without identifying the expenditures which, in the course of the budget period, they would be used to meet.

The budgets involved in article 81 are "accrual" budgets (*bilanci di competenza*) and not "cash" budgets (*bilanci di cassa*). Although the Constitution does not specify this, there can be no doubt of it, given the system of ordinary budget laws and the Italian tradition in the matter, antedating the Constitution. Usually, however, the duty to spend is assumed, and any unspent balance passes to the cash budget as a "negative residuum."

The regions, the provinces, the communes, and the universities have budgets separate from that of the state. No rule of "universality of the budget" requires the consolidation of the budgets of these other entities with that of the state; such a rule would be contrary to the principle of the financial autonomy of the regions and the local entities established by articles 5, 119, and 128 of the Constitution (1/5.5c) and to the need of autonomy for the centers of culture and learning. The receipts and expenditures for social security, moreover, not only do not flow into the state budget, but do not even flow into a single, unified social security budget.

The receipts and expenditures of public enterprises, that is, the enterprises which the state controls through the possession of their patrimony or of the majority thereof, are not completely consolidated with the budget of the state. The manner in which the budgets of these enterprises are handled depends on the nature of the enterprise. A public enterprise organized in a manner similar to a private enterprise has a centralized financial management, independent of that of the state. The Ministry of State Participations supervises the budget of the enterprise, or rather, the budgets of the large entities (similar to "holding companies") into which such enterprises are incorporated.[34] The so-called "autonomous" public enterprises (*aziende autonome*) are controlled more directly by the state administration. The state railways, the post office, the state telegraph, the state long-distance telephone service, and the state monopolies are the major autonomous enterprises. The budgets of these enterprises are separate from that of the state but are attached to it, and their net surpluses or deficits are reflected in it. Only the positive balances which these enterprises are obliged to give to the state are included in the budget of the state as patrimonial receipts; a part of the profits is retained by the enterprise for self-financing.

---

[34] Examples of these entities are the National Petroleum Entity (*Ente Nazionale Idrocarburi* or ENI), the Institution for Industrial Reconstruction (*Istituto per la Ricostruzione Industriale* or IRI), and the National Electricity Entity (*Ente Nazionale Elettrico* or ENEL). Further information on these enterprises may be found in the *Report of the Ministry of State Participations*.

Finally, there is a group of seemingly anomalous independent public
entities which is composed of enterprises that are not true and proper
producers of goods and services, but entities of control and distribution
or credit entities independent of the state. The budgets of these enterprises are neither attached to that of the state nor subjected to the control
of the Ministry of State Participations. Examples of these entities are
the Bank of Italy, the Fund for the South, the Deposit and Loan Fund,
the Building Increment Fund, the Fund for Small Farming Property, the
Fund for Winter Relief, and the Fund for the Training of Workers. It is
difficult to establish the number and the boundaries of these special man-
agements. The Fund for the South (*Cassa per il Mezzogiorno*), for
example, which is primarily responsible for the economic development
of southern Italy and the islands, is supported by an annual contribution
from the state. The Fund, however, has its own budget of expenses and
receipts, and this budget is not attached to that of the state. Entities such
as the Fund for the South, although independent of the ordinary bureaucracy of the state, are subject to controls and examinations by branches of
the government and by the Court of Accounts (*Corte dei Conti*). The
Fund for the South, for example, is under the control of a Committee of
Ministers for the South and is entrusted in particular to the Minister for
the Fund for the South. This Minister is responsible for general guidance
of the activities of the Fund.

b. APPROVAL OF BUDGETS. Article 81 requires not only that Parliament
approve the estimated budget (*bilancio preventivo*) each year, but also
that it approve the financial reports (*rendiconto*), that is, the budget of
receipts and expenditures (*bilancio consuntivo*). The estimated budget
to be approved each year is the estimated budget for the budget period
immediately following. Approval of the budgets of receipts and expenditures is several years behind.

If neither the estimated budget nor the provisional budget has been
voted, both the basis for the public expenditures and the basis for the
levy of taxes are lacking. For the expenditures, this consequence is evident. The individual administrative offices cannot "appropriate" the
funds for their spending activities in a particular budget period if the
budget which allocates the amount of their funds for the financial year
under consideration has not been approved.

For taxes, it is generally considered that two kinds of authorizations
are necessary: the individual tax laws, which require the citizens to pay
the various taxes, and (2) the budget laws, which, in combination with
the tax laws, permit the administration to carry out the activity of fiscal
levy for the budget period under consideration.

If the chambers do not succeed, before the end of the financial year,
in approving the budget for the budget period immediately following,

recourse is made to the provisional budget period. Recourse to the provisional budget period is now a constant practice since it is practically never possible to terminate the discussion of the estimated budget on or before 30 June, which marks the end of each financial year.[35]

c. NEW TAXES AND EXPENDITURES. Under the rule of the third paragraph of article 81, new taxes and new expenditures cannot be established in the same law that approves the budget. In addition, neither the budget nor the budget law makes any reference to the taxes and expenditures established in the legislation in force. These taxes and expenditures, therefore, are not necessarily subject to annual revision, as under the systems of some other European countries. Before the approval of the budget law, and simultaneously with the debate on the budgets, however, laws for new receipts or new expenditures for the coming financial year may be presented to and approved by the chambers.

If laws involving new or increased expenditures are deliberated after the budget has been approved, the means of covering these expenditures must be specified (Const. art. 81, para. 4). This rule was intended to accomplish three objectives. In the first place, it would limit budget deficits and the expansion of currency and of the public debt connected with them. Expenditures met by increasing the public debt or the issue of new currency would not be "covered" within the meaning of article 81. Secondly, it would place an obstacle to the expansion of public expenditure, by encouraging the habit of keeping in mind that each individual expense, in one way or another, had to be covered. A third purpose, perhaps more doctrinal, was to lead the Parliament to improve the technique, and thus the content, of its own processes of financial decision-making; in theory, comparisons "at the margin" between increments of expenditure and increments of possible burdens necessary for making an expenditure can lead more readily to rational choices than comparisons of aggregate quantities.

One means of circumventing the fourth paragraph of article 81 has been the establishment of a "global fund for draft bills not yet approved." By recourse to this expedient, it is possible to bring to approval, after the budget has been approved, laws which involve new expenditures, specifying their coverage not by a specific additional receipt, but by this global fund. However, the possibilities of the global fund are not unlimited: an enlargement of the fund sufficient to meet all contingencies could result in an inflated deficit which the government would have to justify in Parliament.

---

[35] The financial year of the government has been changed to the calendar year by article 1 of L. 1 March 1964, n. 62, and is therefore now uniform with the tax period in force for the national and local taxes. During July of each year, the budget of receipts and expenditures for the preceding year and the estimated budget for the following year are to be presented to Parliament.

Another method of tempering the rigor of article 81, fourth paragraph, is the presentation, during the financial year, of "notes of variation" increasing the estimates of receipts already approved. The government may find that the actual receipts are greater than those estimated in the approved budget, and that a correction is necessary to take account of the difference between what has occurred and what was anticipated. Thus, while the global fund described above provides a means of overstating expenditures in the budget, the note of variation makes it possible to understate receipts in the budget.

Because the last paragraph of article 81 requires specification of the means of covering expenditures other than those in the already approved budget, the Minister of Finance often has found it necessary to make recourse to indirect taxes—such as those on manufacturing—which are easily applied and rapidly collected, or else to increases in the rates of certain indirect taxes on very simple transactions—such as the stamp taxes and the fees for governmental concessions.

In recent times, there has been a rather energetic divergence from this tendency. The Minister of Finance has taken advantage of the opportunity presented by the specification requirement to introduce re- forms of direct taxation, already studied beforehand and designed in such a way as to bring structural improvements to this sector of the Italian fiscal system. The new coupon tax (9/2.7) and the requirements for the registration of shares and for reporting dividends distributed (9/2.8) were brought about in this manner. Less satisfactory, however, have been measures increasing the rates of certain direct taxes without accompanying reforms to strengthen the structure of the taxes and render them more equitable.

1/4. Tax Administration

1/4.1 Ministry of Finance

The Ministry of Finance is subdivided into General Directorates (*Dire- zioni Generali*). Each General Directorate has jurisdiction over a certain sector of activity and has at its head a Director General, who is usually a career official of the public administration but is not necessarily chosen from the bureaucracy which he heads. There are eight General Direc- torates, complemented by four other special divisions which do not have the form of a General Directorate but which are very similar to it. Five of the General Directorates have charge of five different branches of taxation: direct taxes; fees and indirect taxes on transactions; customs duties and indirect taxes on manufacturing and consumption; local finance; and extraordinary finance (this last is in process of termination, in view of the progressive expiration of the extraordinary finance measures of the war and postwar periods). The remaining three are the General Directorate of General Personnel Matters; the General Directorate of the Public Domain (that is, of the capital receipts, for that business, now small in amount, which has not been transferred from the Ministry of Finance to the Ministry of State Participations); and the General Directorate of the Cadaster and of the Revenue Technical Services (concerned with the assessment of taxes requiring particular knowledge of the quality of commercial articles or of engineering) (10/2.2).

The four divisions which are not General Directorates, but which approach them closely, are the General Inspectorate for Lotto and the Lotteries, the Independent Administration of the State Fiscal Monopolies, the Corps of the Finance Guard (*Guardia di Finanza*), and the Central Tax School.

1/4.2 Direct Taxes

The General Directorate of the Direct Taxes (*Direzione Generale delle Imposte Dirette*) is divided by territory into numerous branch offices, and by subject matter into various central divisions. The peripheral offices are called District Offices of Direct Taxes; at the head of each of them is a District Procurator (*Procuratore*). They carry out the activity of assessing those taxes over which the General Directorate has jurisdiction and dispatch, in general, the work which directly relates to the taxpayers; they also represent the tax administration before the organs charged with resolving controversies between the administration and the taxpayers. The 662 District Offices of Direct Taxes are located in the principal communes of the country. There is one in at least every provincial capital. Since the provinces in Italy number slightly less than 100, there are on the average six District Offices of Direct Taxes per province. In the large cities—Milan, Rome, Genoa, Naples, and Turin—instead of a single Direct Tax Office, there are three: one dealing with taxpayers taxed on the balance sheet basis (6/1.2b); one dealing with payers of the taxes on land and buildings (9/4.1, 9/4.2), the cadaster (10/2.2), and the card index (9/2.8); and one dealing with the remaining activities and the other taxpayers.

The District Offices of Direct Taxes are grouped into 14 Compartmental Inspectorates, each of which is directed by a Compartmental Inspector and has its office in a large city. The Inspectors in these offices supervise the work of the District Offices. The Inspectorate issues directives on the criteria of estimate to be used in the assessment of the various enterprises and economic activities (7/1.1). The Compartmental Inspectors meet often in conferences for the purpose of coordinating their work and of comparing and bringing up to date the criteria of estimate.

The General Directorate of the Direct Taxes is made up of nine divisions, plus a special service that coordinates accounting practices. Most of the divisions have jurisdiction, separately, for the principal direct taxes. Other divisions are concerned with personnel, legislative studies, printing, and statistics.

1/4.3   Fees and Indirect Taxes on Transactions

The General Directorate of the Fees and Indirect Taxes on Transactions (*Direzione Generale delle Tasse e delle Imposte Indirette sugli Affari*) administers the general tax on receipts (14/), the registration tax (15/), stamp taxes (4/4), and analogous taxes, such as the succession taxes (3/4, 3/5). These taxes are usually classified for administrative purposes as indirect taxes on transactions and constitute the most productive part of the Italian fiscal system (1/6.8).

The General Directorate of the Fees and Indirect Taxes on Transactions is divided by subject matter into 15 divisions and a number of special offices, and along territorial lines into branch offices.

Of the branch offices, there are 941 Registry Offices (*Uffici di Registro*), each of which is directed by a Registry Procurator (*Procuratore di Registro*), who performs the same services with regard to the indirect taxes as the District Procurator for the direct taxes (1/4.2). Besides the Registry Offices, there are 97 offices of the keepers of the registers of immovable property and mortgages (*conservatori dei registri immobiliari ed ipotecari*), located chiefly in the provincial capitals. The Registry Offices are of two kinds: offices with combined branches and single-branch offices. The offices with combined branches are found in the less important localities, and their jurisdiction extends to all of the taxes administered by the General Directorate of the Fees and Indirect Taxes on Transactions. The single-branch offices are found in the more important localities and either are concerned with a single tax or perform a single function for a group of taxes. Thus, there is an office for the general tax on receipts, a succession office, a stamp office. But there are also offices performing functions regarding "public acts," "private acts," and "judicial acts." There are also 32 "mixed offices of registry and mortgages," which perform the duties of Registry Offices and the duties of the keepers of the registers of immovable property and mortgages.

The organization of the Registry Offices has recently been supplemented by machine accounting centers, or First Offices of the General Tax on Receipts, which have been established in Milan, Genoa, Florence, Rome, and Palermo, and which have jurisdiction over the divisions of the territory where those cities are located. In the machine accounting centers, accounting for the part of the general tax on receipts that is paid through postal current accounts (14/7.1) is carried out with the use of punched cards, classified and read automatically by machine.

The Registry Offices are directed by 14 Compartmental Inspectorates, each headed by a Compartmental Registry Inspector and situated in a large city. At Rome, there are also a Compartmental Inspectorate for the Control of the Motor Vehicle Operation Fees (4/5.5), supervising the collection of these taxes by the Automobile Club of Italy, and a Compartmental Inspectorate for the Control of the Taxes on Public Shows (4/5.4), supervising the collection of those taxes by the Italian Society of Authors and Publishers (*Società Italiana degli Autori ed Editori* or SIAE).

1/4.4 Customs Duties and Indirect Taxes on Manufacturing and Consumption

The General Directorate of the Customs Duties and Indirect Taxes (those on manufacturing and on consumption) (*Direzione Generale delle Dogane e delle Imposte Indirette*) administers the border duties, license fees, and other customs duties levied at the Italian border on imports. It also supervises other customs matters, such as those concerning exempt merchandise and merchandise in transit between countries. In addition, it handles the manufacturing taxes (4/5.2), and the corresponding border surtaxes, which are levied on imports of products subject to the manufacturing taxes (4/5.2d).

The General Directorate of the Customs Duties and Indirect Taxes is subdivided by subject matter into six central offices and eight divisions. Along territorial lines, it is divided into 174 Customs Offices (*Uffici Doganali*) and 34 Technical Offices of the Manufacturing Taxes (*Uffici Tecnici delle Imposte di Fabbricazione*), which have jurisdiction, respectively, over the border taxes and the internal taxes under the General Directorate. Some Customs Offices are located at the border, but others are found in the interior, in important trade centers. The Customs Offices are grouped into 33 customs jurisdictions, which, in turn, are supervised by the nine Customs Compartments of Inspection (*Compartimenti Doganali d'Ispezione*), each headed by a Compartmental Inspector. The Inspectorates have functions analogous to the Inspectorates set up for the direct taxes (1/4.2) and for the fees and indirect taxes on transactions (1/4.3). The Customs Inspectorates are located at Genoa, Turin, Milan, Venice, Trieste, Rome, Naples, Bari, and Palermo.

1/4.5 Fiscal Monopolies

The state fiscal monopolies (tobacco, salt, quinine, playing cards, and cigarette papers) are not administered by a General Directorate, but by a semiautonomous administration of the monopolies. The reason for this is to give the fiscal monopoly a greater independence than is given to other tax activities. The administration of the monopolies has not only the function of collecting a tax—the monopoly tax, included in the price of the goods sold subject to the regime of legal monopoly in the monopoly stores (4/6.1)—but also functions of an economic character in the field of production and selling.

Besides the Ministry of Finance, a Council of Administration, assisted by a Director General, presides over the administration of the monopolies. Under the Director General are six services: general administration and personnel; accounting control and administration; cultivation of tobacco by private farmers; tobacco processing; salt works; and sales offices. Operations of sale in bulk and the bulk warehouses are managed by the monopoly, while retail sale is made exclusively by private businesses, the so-called "monopoly stores" (*privative*) of salt and tobacco.

The administration of the monopolies is subdivided along territorial lines into 11 Compartmental Directorates, which supervise the cultivation of tobacco; 22 Compartmental Offices, which are concerned with sales; 19 works and 4 manufacturing sections for the manufacture of tobacco products; 7 salt works, 3 laboratories for the refinement of salt and 2 for the production of quinine, plus an experimental factory equipped with a laboratory; and 25 storehouses for monopoly goods, with 597 warehouse and sale offices under them as organs of secondary distribution. The retail monopoly stores attached to this administration number about 50,000. The farmers who furnish the tobacco to the monopoly, under concession, number about 1,200. The Italian Tobacco Enterprise (*Azienda Tabacchi Italiani* or ATI) is a corporation concerned with the production and international activities relating to tobacco products, salt, and quinine.

1/4.6 Cadaster and Revenue Technical Services

The General Directorate of the Cadaster and of the Revenue Technical Services (*Direzione Generale del Catasto e dei Servizi Tecnici Erariali*) is subdivided into six technical services, an office of general technical matters, a study office, a machine accounting office, and two divisions, one for personnel matters and one for accounting services. Of the six services, one has charge of the new urban building cadaster, which will have to be kept up to date (since the new building cadaster is based on rents of the year 1939, it is already anachronistic at its birth) (9/4.2d). Three other services are concerned with surveys, the consideration of protests, and the keeping of the land cadasters (10/2.2). Another service is in charge of estimate operations for buildings, for the tax on buildings, and for other purposes such as estimates for the determination of expropriation indemnities and of market value for the registration and succession taxes. The sixth service administers, maintains, and provides technical and administrative assistance concerning the immovable properties of the state and the furnishings and equipment of the central offices of the various financial administrations.

Territorially, the General Directorate of the Cadaster and of the Revenue Technical Services is divided into Technical Cadastral Offices (*Uffici*

Tecnici del Catasto), which have the duty of developing the new agricultural cadasters, and into Revenue Technical Offices (*Uffici Tecnici Erariali*), situated in each provincial capital, which have the following duties: technical assistance regarding the immovable property of the state; the keeping of the old land cadaster; the establishment of the new urban building cadaster; claims for indemnity arising out of war, and assessment of damages relative thereto; estimates for purposes of the assessment values of immovable property for the registration and succession taxes and for state betterment contributions; estimates for the payment of indemnities for expropriation by the public administration of the state or minor entities; and, in general, technical assessments carried out in the interests of the financial administration.

1/4.7 General Matters and Personnel: Intendancies of Finance

The General Directorate of General Matters and of Personnel (*Direzione Generale degli Affari Generali e del Personale*) regulates employment, promotion, and other matters regarding the personnel of the Ministry of Finance. It also has the functions of equipping the finance administration buildings, making contracts on behalf of the financial administration, and administering pensions. It has duties of administrative study and coordination, and also of supervision over the Intendancies of Finance, the offices which must carry out, at the peripheral level, the coordinative functions of this General Directorate. The activity of coordination at the center, indeed, has remained until now at an almost completely theoretical stage because of the difficulty of bringing the Directorates concerned with the various taxes, each of which claims jurisdiction in relation to its field, under the controls of this General Directorate.

In each provincial capital, there is an Intendancy of Finance, directed by an Intendant (*Intendente di Finanza*). In theory the Intendant of Finance supervises all of the financial offices concerned with the various taxes and under the various General Directorates, which have their seats in the province, and also supervises all public receipts, reporting to the Ministry of Finance on the course of the tax activity which is carried on in the province. In practice, the work of observing and of informing the Ministry is largely symbolic since the Intendancy does not have study offices and cognitive instruments at its disposal even remotely comparable to those required for a good economic research bureau; nor does it keep archives on the structure of the income, employment, transactions, and fiscal and other conditions of the province. Moreover, since the peripheral offices of the various taxes are subject to supervision by Inspectors dependent in turn on their respective General Directorates, and since the Intendant of Finance is not authorized by any detailed administrative

DESCRIPTION OF TAX SYSTEM   44

provision to make his own checks on these offices and coordinate them among themselves, his possibilities in the matter are very limited.

1/4.8   Finance Guard

The Corps of the Finance Guard (*Guardia di Finanza*) is a military organization which originally was created and developed to control evasion of customs duties and the fiscal monopolies, especially at the border. It was used later to check evasion of the manufacturing taxes; only in 1923 were the duties of the Finance Guard extended also to the other taxes. But the historical origins of the Finance Guard as a military frontier guard strongly influence its structure and activities even now. Under the law, the Commanding General of the Finance Guard must be chosen from among the career generals of the army corps. His second in command is a division general in the Corps of the Finance Guard and is chosen from among its officers; the chief of staff is a colonel of the Finance Guard. His staff also contains a brigadier general of the army, who is concerned particularly with the military training of personnel of the Corps. The Corps of the Finance Guard has slightly less than 1,000 officers, about 8,500 noncommissioned officers, and about 25,000 troops. It is subdivided into 5 zone commands and 16 territorial legions. In addition, there is an Institute of Instruction, which supervises the academy and the schools for the officers, noncommissioned officers, and troops.

In 1923, the duties of the Finance Guard were extended beyond their traditional limits for the purpose of combating "fiscal frauds, the evasion of taxes, and in particular organized smuggling, through studies and observations and positive action directed to focus toward a single objective the various organs of control and of civil and military police." [36] To meet the new duties, there was formed, at the center, a technical office for the tax police, which was placed under a general of the Finance Guard. Moreover, contingents of soldiers in civilian dress were organized for the special services of investigation. These peripheral groups were named "nuclei of Investigative Tax Police" (PTI).

In 1926, the functions of the Investigative Tax Police were enlarged to include "powers and rights of investigation, of access, of inspection, of control, of requiring information, which belong by law to the different financial offices charged with the application of the direct and indirect taxes." [37] In 1937, the new functions of the Finance Guard were further developed by the establishment of a nucleus of PTI in each provincial capital and the provision for stronger ties between it and the local branches of the financial administration. But these ties, notwithstanding the new measures, are still weak.

---

[36] R.D.L. 14 June 1923, n. 1281, art. 1.
[37] R.D.L. 3 January 1926, n. 63.

1/4.9   Central Tax School

Mention should be made, finally, of the Central Tax School (*Scuola Centrale Tributaria*), instituted in 1949. It was dedicated at first to training the officials of the General Directorate of Fees and Indirect Taxes on Transactions, which had been the Directorate most interested in the School; but its duties were soon extended to the training of the accounting auditors of the direct taxes and of other categories of personnel for all of the General Directorates. The School is directed by a university professor, and its courses are given partly by university professors and partly by officials of the fiscal administration. The establishment of this School has been considered one of the most important steps toward the modernization of the Italian fiscal machinery.

1/4.10   Taxpayer Remedies

a. CONSTITUTIONAL PROVISIONS REGARDING JURISDICTION. Article 113 of the Constitution provides that "against the acts of the public administration is always allowed the jurisdictional protection of rights and legitimate interests before the organs of ordinary and administrative jurisdiction," and that "such jurisdictional protection cannot be excluded or limited to particular means of attack or for defined categories of acts." Under article 102 of the Constitution, "the jurisdictional function is exercised by ordinary magistrates instituted and regulated by the rules of the judicial system," and "extraordinary judges or special judges cannot be instituted." In the ordinary courts, however, it is possible to institute specialized sections for defined matters, with or without the participation of qualified citizens outside the magistracy. The rule of article 102, at first view, establishes that special judges in the tax field are incompatible with the Italian constitutional system. Today, a large part of tax litigation, however, is in fact carried on by special judges, quite apart from the ordinary magistracy: that is, by the tax commissions. Whether these commissions are proper is an important question, still widely debated and in practice not resolved.

The explanation of the assignment of jurisdiction to the ordinary magistracy is found chiefly in the guarantees which tradition and the Constitution itself have set up for the ordinary magistracy. Article 104 of the Constitution states, "the magistracy constitutes an order autonomous and independent of any other power." Article 105 establishes that "to the High Council of the Magistracy, under the rules of the judiciary system, belong appointment, assignment, transfers, promotions and disciplinary measures with regard to the magistrates." The High Council of the Magistracy, in turn, has been constructed in such a way as to insure its greatest possible independence of the government. Under article 104 of the Constitution, paragraphs 2-7, the Council is presided over by the

President of the Republic himself. It includes, by law, the First President and the Procurator General of the Court of Cassation (which is the highest ordinary court for all nonconstitutional questions); two thirds of the other members are elected by all of the ordinary magistrates from among those belonging to the various categories, and one third by the Parliament in joint session from among ordinary university professors in juridical matters and lawyers who have had 15 years of service. The Council elects a vice-president from among the members designated by the Parliament. The elected members of the Council remain in office four years and are not immediately re-electable. They may not, while in office, be inscribed in the professional registers, or be members of Parliament or of a Regional Council. The nomination of the magistrates takes place by competition (Const. art. 106), and the magistrates are not removable and cannot be relieved or suspended from service or assigned to other offices or functions without their consent, except as a result of a decision of the High Council of the Magistracy (Const. art. 107).

The prohibition in article 102 of the institution of extraordinary judges and special judges is not incompatible with the existence of organs of administrative jurisdiction. Thus, under article 103, the Court of Accounts (*Corte dei Conti*) is given jurisdiction over public expenditures and public accounts, but not over taxes. Article 103 also assigns to the Council of State (*Consiglio di Stato*) and the other organs of administrative justice "jurisdiction for the protection, as against the public administration, of legitimate interests, and, in particular matters specified by the law, also of subjective rights." [38]

When subjective rights are not involved, but mere legitimate interests, jurisdictional protection is traditionally given not by the ordinary courts but by the organs of administrative justice. At the vertex of these (except for certain matters) is the Council of State; and in the first instance and for lesser questions, the Provincial Administrative Board has jurisdiction. The Provincial Administrative Board and the Council of State, even after the new Constitution, retained full powers in litigation relative to legitimate interests and functions in litigation for certain subjective rights—such as relations of public employment—which, being intertwined almost indistinguishably with legitimate interests, had traditionally been entrusted to these organs of administrative justice.

---

[38] A "subjective right" is a right which one person has against another by virtue of a legal duty of the latter toward him, arising out of some relationship between them, such as the right of a taxpayer to recover, from the public administration, a tax not due. A "legitimate interest" is the interest which one person has in the enforcement of a duty imposed on another (such as an official or organ of the public administration) regardless of any relationship between them, and merely as a person affected by the enforcement of a duty to the public at large. See Trabucchi, *Istituzioni di diritto civile* 44; 1 Zanobini, *Corso di diritto amministrativo* 187 *et seq.*

Since administrative jurisdiction in tax matters is generally exercised by special tax commissions, however, the Council of State and the other organs of general administrative jurisdiction have no functions in the tax field (1/4.10g).

Article 103 mentions not only the Court of Accounts, the Council of State, and the military tribunals, but also "the other organs of administrative justice." It has been maintained that this phrase is equivalent to a general permission for the existence of special administrative jurisdictions. Naturally, even the supporters of this thesis have taken account of the fact that it could not be maintained unconditionally in the face of the language of article VI of the Transitory and Final Provisions of the Constitution, which requires, within five years of the entry into force of the Constitution, the "revision" of all of the special jurisdictions with the exception of only three: the Council of State, the Court of Accounts, and the military tribunals. But to surmount the stumbling block of article VI, it has been maintained that what is required is "revising," and not "abolishing," the special jurisdictions. Revision, it is said, is a different thing from abrogation; it can also mean merely transformation. From a purely literal point of view, any transformation whatever would suffice. But since this could not have been intended and since the Constitution provides no directives for the way in which the "revision" is to be carried out, it is reasonable to assume that the requirement looks to the abolition of the special nature of the jurisdiction.

It is also argued that although article VI requires the revision of the special jurisdictions within five years, it does not provide that these jurisdictions should automatically be considered lapsed if the revision is not carried out. It is certain that new special jurisdictions cannot be created, and it is certain that the old must be revised; but until such a revision is made, the old system continues in effect.[39]

b. THE STATUS OF THE TAX COMMISSIONS. As noted at 1/4.10a, a large part of tax litigation is carried out by administrative tax commissions, which have exclusive competence over most questions regarding the valuation of tax bases, and which in most cases must be appealed to before an appeal can be taken to the ordinary courts. Thus, if the tax commissions do not have the nature of organs of jurisdiction but perform functions of purely administrative character, the existing procedures violate the requirement of jurisdictional protection against acts of the public administration (Const. art. 113). If, on the other hand, they are

---

[39] The Constitutional Court has upheld the survival of the special jurisdictions in Corte Cost. 11 March 1957, n. 41 (*Giur. it.*, 1957, I, 1, 509); Corte Cost. 15 June 1960, n. 41 (*Giur. cost.*, 1960, 660). See also Barile, "Sulla permanenza attuale delle giurisdizioni speciali," *Riv. dir. proc.*, 1954, II, 81; Guarino, "Contenzioso tributario e giurisdizioni speciali," *Foro it.*, 1954, III, 110; Sandulli, "Sulla sopravvivenza delle giurisdizioni speciali al termine fissato per la loro 'rivisione,'" *Giur. cost.*, 1956, 965.

organs of jurisdiction, they violate the prohibition against the institution of extraordinary or special judges (Const. art. 102) (1/4.10a).[40] The second interpretation appears to be the less unfavorable to the continued existence of the commissions, pending the reform required by article VI of the Constitution's Transitory and Final Provisions (1/4.10a). Some recent proposals for the reform of tax litigation are discussed at 1/4.13.

c. DISTRICT TAX COMMISSION. With regard to the direct taxes (except the tax on income from landowning (1/4.10h)) and the indirect taxes on transfers, the taxpayer, having had notice of assessment or of correction of an assessment, and not wishing to accept the assessment, can attempt to persuade the administration to conclude an agreement (*concordato*) (13/2.4), or else he can make an appeal to the District Tax Commission (13/4.2). This Commission has a territorial jurisdiction coincident with that of the District Tax Office and is situated in the same commune as that Office.[41] The District Tax Commission is composed of a president, a vice-president, eight working members, and four substitute members. These are not career judges belonging to a specialized corps but are chosen from among ordinary taxpayers. The members of the Commission are not nominated by an organ impartial both to the interests of the tax administration and to those of the taxpayer, but by the Intendant of Finance. They are chosen from among the payers of the direct taxes residing in the district of the Direct Tax Office, on the basis of a designation made by the Mayors of the communes in the district of a number triple that of the members. The number of persons to be designated from each commune is established by the Intendant of Finance with the Prefect (the official who represents the Ministry of the Interior, the state executive power, at the provincial level), taking account of the relative importance of the different productive activities operating in the district of each Direct Tax Office. The District Commissions have a term of four years.[42]

d. PROVINCIAL TAX COMMISSION. When the appeal to the District Commission has been completed, the taxpayer or the tax administration or both may appeal against its decision to the Provincial Tax Commission (13/4.3). The Provincial Commission has its seat in the capital of the

---

[40] The jurisdictional nature of the tax commissions has been upheld by the Constitutional Court in Corte Cost. 26 January 1957, n. 12 (*Giur. cost.*, 1957, 288); Corte Cost. 11 March 1957, n. 41, n. 42 (*Giur. cost.*, 1957, 511, 516; Corte Cost. 13 July 1963, n. 132 (*Temi trib.*, 1963, 555). For the contrary view, see Giannini, *Istituzioni di diritto tributario* 188; Tesauro, "Le giurisdizioni speciali e le commissioni tributarie," *Rass. dir. pubbl.*, 1954, I, 400, 405.

[41] R.D.L. 7 August 1936, n. 1639 (converted in L. 7 June 1937), n. 1016, art. 31.

[42] The appointment and qualifications of members and the functioning of the District Commissions are governed by R.D. 8 July 1937, n. 1516; and R.D.L. 13 March 1944, n. 88.

province and is similar in structure and source to the District Commission. It is composed of a president, a vice-president, eight working members, and four substitute members; one half of this total is chosen from among the residents of the province who are payers of the direct taxes, and the other half from among magistrates of the ordinary judicial system or active or retired officials of the state. The members of the Commission are named directly by the Minister of Finance, instead of by the Intendant of Finance; but in practice, the Ministry usually follows the designations made to it by the branch tax offices. Those members of the Commission chosen from among the payers of the direct taxes are selected from a group of citizens, triple the necessary number, nominated by the Prefect of the province. The Prefect must nominate six working members and three substitute members in relation to the relative importance of the productive activities operating in the province, and another three working members and three substitute members from among the persons expert in matters of leases and of valuation.[43]

Both the District Commissions and the Provincial Commissions are subdivided into two separate sections, one competent for controversies which involve the direct taxes affecting movable property and persons, and the other competent for controversies which involve the taxes on transfers of goods or property (that is, the general tax on receipts, the registration and similar taxes, and the succession taxes) and also the tax on income from buildings. To this second section belong the persons expert in matters of leases and valuation. The Ministry of Finance has the power to provide for the formation of additional sections; thus, for the general tax on receipts paid by annual fee (*abbonamento*) (14/7.3), there often exist special sections in the Provincial Commissions.

e. CENTRAL TAX COMMISSION. If the taxpayer or the administration is not satisfied with the decision of the Provincial Commission in cases involving legal questions, either may appeal to the Central Tax Commission. The Central Tax Commission, unlike the District Commissions and the majority of the Provincial Commissions, is an organ of litigation composed of specialists. It consists of a president and of 25 members, five of them with functions of vice-president. The vice-presidents are chosen from among active or retired magistrates of the judicial or administrative systems, of not less than the third grade (one of the highest grades in the hierarchy of the public administration). The other members are chosen from among the following categories of active or retired magistrates or officials: Councilors of State; Councilors of the Court of Accounts; magistrates of not less than the fourth grade; state advocates of not less

---

[43] The appointment and qualifications of members and the functioning of the Provincial Commissions are governed by R.D. 8 July 1937, n. 1516; R.D.L. 13 March 1944, n. 88; and D.L. 8 April 1948, n. 514.

than the fourth grade; officials of the central financial administration of not less than the grade of director at the head of a division.

The Central Tax Commission is subdivided into five sections, whose composition and specific competence in matters of direct and indirect taxes are determined annually by a measure of the President of the Republic. For certain particularly difficult controversies, the Central Commission is convoked in "united sections" (*sezioni unite*).[44]

f. APPEALS TO THE ORDINARY COURTS. On completion of the procedure in any of the tax commissions, the parties to controversies involving the direct taxes and the taxes on transfers can turn to the ordinary courts under the rules discussed at 13/4.9. For the taxes on transfers of property, at least some of the decisions and some commentators consider that it is possible to appeal to the courts even without awaiting completion of an appeal before the commissions, or even without filing any appeal whatever to these commissions. The question, however, is controverted, and there are those who maintain that this possibility exists only for some of the taxes on transfers.

The Italian court system is a unified system.[45] The lowest court is that of the Conciliator (*Conciliatore*), who has a limited civil jurisdiction, and who is not a career judge but is chosen from among the educated men of the community. The next highest court is that of the Magistrate (*Pretore*), who has original jurisdiction over minor civil and criminal matters in his district and appellate jurisdiction over the decisions of the Conciliator. There are about 1,000 districts. The lowest court having competence in tax matters is the Tribunal (*Tribunale*) (13/4.9a), which consists of three judges; it has original jurisdiction over civil and criminal matters not within the competence of the lower courts and appellate jurisdiction over decisions of the Magistrates. There are 150 Tribunals in Italy. A decision of a Tribunal may be appealed to a Court of Appeals (*Corte d'Appello*), of which there are 23, each consisting of five judges. The highest court is the Supreme Court of Cassation (*Corte Suprema di Cassazione*), composed of more than 150 judges, of whom only seven hear a particular case. The Court is divided into several civil and criminal sections, the highest ranking judges of which meet together in "united sections" to hear the most important cases.

g. APPEALS TO SPECIAL COURTS. The Constitutional Court (*Corte Costituzionale*) decides all controversies relating to the constitutional legitimacy of national and regional laws and acts having the force of law

---

[44] The appointment and qualifications of members and the functioning of the Central Commission are governed by R.D. 8 July 1937, n. 1516; and D.L.L. 12 October 1944, n. 334.

[45] The court structure is based on R.D. 30 January 1941, n. 12.

(Const. art. 134). The Court is composed of 15 judges. One third of the judges are nominated by the President of the Republic, one third by a joint session of the chambers, and one third by the supreme ordinary and administrative magistracies. The judges are selected from among the active or retired magistrates of the high ordinary and administrative jurisdictions, ordinary university professors of law, and lawyers who have practiced at least 20 years (Const. art. 135).[46] They remain in office for 12 years (Const. art. 135).[47]

Before the Constitution of 1947, there did not exist either a supreme tribunal in constitutional matters or a special procedure for the resolution of controversies on the constitutionality of the ordinary laws. Under the authority of the Statute of 1848, which remained in effect, at least formally, until 1947, the supreme tribunal for every type of controversy was the Court of Cassation, which, on the most important questions, met in "united sections." The judgment of the Court of Cassation on the incompatibility of an ordinary law with the Statute had the same effect as a judgment on the incompatibility of an administrative measure with ordinary law. The lower judge passed on all questions including those of constitutional conformity in the first or in the second instance, and the Court of Cassation then decided in the last instance on all juridical questions. Now, however, when a lower tribunal recognizes a question of constitutionality regarding an ordinary law, it must suspend judgment and send the case to the Constitutional Court.[48] If the Constitutional Court judges that the law is incompatible with the Constitution, the law ceases to have effect as soon as the judgment of the Court has been issued (Const. art. 136).[49]

Although the Council of State (*Consiglio di Stato*), the highest administrative organ of the state, serves as a court for appeals against administrative acts, its jurisdiction is limited to cases falling within the competence neither of the ordinary courts nor of an administrative adjudicating body (13/4.11).

h. CENSUS COMMISSIONS. For the tax on income from landowning, the litigation procedure is different from that provided for the other direct taxes. In matters of controversy relative to the determination of the estimates and other questions of fact regarding the land cadaster and its revisions, the taxpayer may appeal in the first instance to the Communal Census Commission, in the second instance to the Provincial Census Commission, and in the third instance to the Central Census Commission (10/2.2g). The Communal Census Commissions in the capitals

---

[46] L. Cost. 11 March 1953, n. 87, arts. 1-4.
[47] L. Cost. 11 March 1953, n. 87, art. 4.
[48] L. Cost. 11 March 1953, n. 87, art. 23.
[49] L. Cost. 9 February 1948, n. 1.

of provinces with a population exceeding 50,000 inhabitants are composed of a president, eight working members, and four substitute
members; in smaller communes, they are composed of five working
members and three substitutes. All are named by the Intendancy of
Finance of the province from among persons designated by the Mayor
of each commune in a number triple that of the members. The Provincial Census Commissions, located in the provincial capitals, are composed
of nine working members and four substitute members, named by the
Minister of Finance. The Central Census Commission, finally, is formed
of 19 working members and six substitutes, named by the Minister of
Finance and presided over either directly by the latter or by the vice-
president, named by him.[50] These Commissions, besides duties in the
field of litigation, also have functions regarding the making of estimates.
Questions of "fact" or "simple estimation" are within the exclusive
jurisdiction of the Commissions (10/2.2g); other questions may be
appealed to the ordinary courts, but it is not settled whether appeal to the
courts is conditioned on prior appeal to the Commissions.[51]

i. APPEALS REGARDING CUSTOMS DUTIES AND TAXES ON MANUFACTURING
AND CONSUMPTION. In the field of the customs duties and the taxes on
manufacturing and consumption, the Chambers of Commerce are competent for litigation in the first instance, and the Ministry of Finance in
the second.[52] In customs matters, these bodies are competent for the
classification of merchandise under the schedule of duties, and controversies on this subject are removed from the competence of the ordinary
courts. The various laws concerning the different taxes on manufacturing,
similarly, usually provide the same litigation procedures for controversies
arising out of the determination of the kinds of products or of raw
materials taxed, for purposes of the application of the appropriate schedule
or of the characterization of exempt goods.

j. APPEALS REGARDING LOCAL TAXES. The special organs of litigation for
local finance are, in the first instance, the Communal Commission for
Local Taxes,[53] and in the second instance, the Provincial Administrative
Board, sitting in an administrative capacity, in which is instituted a special
section for local taxes (TUFL arts. 282, 283).[54] For the provincial taxes,
the Provincial Administrative Board, sitting in an administrative capacity,

---

[50] The appointment and qualifications of members and the functioning of the
Census Commissions are governed by L. 8 March 1943, n. 153; D.L.L. 23 November
1944, n. 403; D.L.C.P.S. 14 October 1947, n. 1472; and D.L. 8 April 1948, n. 514.
[51] See Giannini, *Istituzioni di diritto tributario* 215-219.
[52] R.D. 9 April 1911, n. 330, arts. 2, 3.
[53] R.D.L. 14 September 1931, n. 1175, arts. 278-281. This decree is the *Testo
unico* of local finance; it is hereinafter cited: "TUFL."
[54] See D.L.L. 12 October 1944, n. 334, art. 3.

is competent in the first degree. The special section of the Provincial Administrative Board is competent in the second degree. An appeal to the Central Commission for the Direct Taxes against the decisions of the Provincial Administrative Board is allowed, but only for questions of legitimacy (TUFL art. 284 *bis*).[55]

For local finance, the *Testo unico* of local finance has explicitly established that no application can be made to the judiciary authority until the proceedings before the above-mentioned organs of litigation have been completed; no application to the judiciary authority can ever be made for questions on the estimation of income or questions of fact relative to the assessment of the tax base (TUFL, art. 285).[56]

The Communal Commission for Local Taxes is composed of members numbering from 30 to 90, depending on the size of the commune, except in unusual cases in which the number can be increased. The members must have the qualifications specified for election to the Communal Council (1/5.2), and two thirds of them are chosen by the Communal Council and one third by the Prefect, from among the taxpayers of the commune (TUFL art. 278).[57]

1/4.11 Representation of Taxpayers

A delicate question is that of the representation of taxpayers in controversies about tax matters. A first point in this regard involves the right which former tax officials have at present to transform themselves, so to speak, into "taxpayers' lawyers" in judgments before the tax commissions, and more generally, to represent taxpayers in fiscal questions in contacts with tax officials.[58] The former official often keeps particular bonds of friendship with the tax officials, not infrequently reinforced by sentimental ties of regional origin; the result is considerable disturbance both in the administration of this delicate subject and in its litigation phase.[59]

A related point is that of the qualifications for being a fiscal consultant. In general, to represent taxpayers in fiscal questions today, there are far fewer formalities required than for the exercise of the legal profession or for the exercise of the profession of business consultant (*commercialista*).

---

[55] See R.D. 5 September 1938, n. 1530.

[56] As amended by R.D.L. 26 December 1936, n. 2394, art. 3.

[57] As amended by L. 2 July 1952, n. 703, art. 47.

[58] Under article 13 of D.P.R. 29 January 1958, n. 645 (*Testo unico* of the laws on the direct taxes), the Ministry of Finance may authorize former functionaries of supervisory and technical rank who have retired after at least 20 years of service to assist and represent taxpayers in matters regarding the direct taxes. Generally speaking, former members of the tax administration are prohibited for two years after the termination of their employment from assisting or representing taxpayers in the geographical "compartments" in which they exercised their functions during their last five years of service.

[59] See Allorio, *Diritto processuale tributario* 475.

In Italy, while the possession of a degree and inscription in the professional lists are required for lawyers (*avvocati*) and for doctors of business, and specific examinations are provided for admission to these professions, no such requisites exist with regard to the profession of tax consultant. On the contrary, not even a degree is required.[60] As a result, former officials from even the lowest grades of the administration, or "experts" of other origin, often dedicate themselves to this activity; and, frequently, the fiscal consultant is an expert not so much in tax matters as in the personnel of the various offices.

1/4.12   Inspection, Search, and Seizure

The Constitution contains a number of rules which regulate the rights of the citizen in proceedings of the administration with regard to tax assessment. Article 14 establishes that "the domicile is inviolable"; that "inspections or searches or seizures cannot be made except in the cases and ways established by the law according to the guarantees prescribed for the protection of personal liberty"; and, finally, that "assessments and inspections for reasons of public health and safety and for economic and fiscal ends are regulated by special laws." This provision would seem to permit the enactment of laws allowing the fiscal authorities and the tax police to make inspections and searches in official places or even in dwellings, and also to make seizures, for example, of accounting books, invoices, and other documents; however, it does not allow such operations to be carried out on the basis of mere administrative or police provisions, but only on the basis of provisions of law specifying when and how inspections, searches, and seizures are to be made. Moreover, it can be inferred from article 14 that, for fiscal matters, there can be "special" rules, possibly more severe than those relating to other matters such as health, public security, or business.

Another provision of the Italian Constitution important in this connection is article 15, which says that "the liberty and the secrecy of correspondence and of every other form of communication are inviolable," and that "their limitation can occur only through an act of the judicial

---

[60] Under article 12 of D.P.R. 29 January 1958, n. 645 (*Testo unico* of the laws on the direct taxes), authority to represent anyone before tax offices in direct tax matters must be conferred in writing and can be exercised only by the persons described below.

1. Spouse or relatives within the fourth degree.
2. Persons inscribed in the registries of advocates, procurators, doctors of business, and accountants, and also persons inscribed in the registries of engineers, architects, and other technical professions.
3. Persons previously belonging to the tax administration (see note 58 *supra*).

Taxpayers may be represented before the Census Commissions by procurators or agents (R.D. 12 October 1933, n. 1539, art. 140), and in local tax matters, before the Communal Commissions, by a fiduciary (TUFL art. 280). See also Allorio, *Diritto processuale tributario* 473-474.

authority, supported by reasons, with the guarantees established by the law." The possibility of intercepting, for purposes of fiscal assessment, correspondence or communication by telegraph, telephone, or radio is thus removed from the decision of the administrative authority and can be carried out only on decision of the courts.

Between the provisions of article 14 and article 15, there is thus an important difference: the first gives the administrative fiscal authority the possibility of inspection, search, and seizure on the basis of a law; the second permits interception on the part of the administrative fiscal authority only on the basis of a judicial authorization, which, in its turn, can be given only on the basis of a law. Clearly, this greatly reduces the field of action of the tax administration—even in the presence of a law which provides the necessary power.

1/4.13   Proposals for the Reform of Tax Litigation

For several reasons, the reform of tax litigation, under the principles discussed at 1/4.10b, has been greatly delayed. Both taxpayers and the tax administration fear that a reform devised in a certain way would in practice develop differently and thus unreasonably weaken their position. Thus, although the present state of affairs is unsatisfactory for everyone, reform is not easy. There is also a financial problem. To institute a litigation procedure satisfying the demands for unity, independence, and specialization, a large sum would have to be spent for the tax judges, whereas only a modest figure is spent on the present commissions, which employ only part-time personnel.

Numerous plans have been prepared by private students, by political groups, and in the Ministry for the reform of tax litigation.[61] One solution—which has had few supporters—would be the complete abolition of the present system of tax commissions and the transfer of all controversies involving subjective rights in tax matters to the ordinary magistracy. This solution, which is conceptually the most straightforward, nonetheless involves the greatest practical difficulties, since it would be necessary to ask of the ordinary judge a competence in fiscal matters and in valuation which he does not usually have.

Another similar but more realistic solution would be to entrust all tax litigation to "specialized sections" of the ordinary magistracy which would be specially formed to deal with tax matters. This solution, favored by many, is explicitly permitted by the language of article 102 of the Constitution, which foresees the possibility that specialized sections of the ordinary magistracy could be instituted (1/4.10a). This solution, with

---

[61] Forte, "Osservazioni sui progetti di riforma dell'organizzazione per la risoluzione delle controversie tra fisco e contribuente," *Temi trib.*, 1962, 459; Micheli, "Parere sullo schema di disegno di legge concernente la riforma del contenzioso tributario," *Giur. imp.*, 1962, 759; Maffezzoni, "Ragioni ed obiettivi di una riforma del contenzioso tributario," *Riv. dir. proc.*, 1962, 570.

some qualification, has been supported in a 1951 plan made privately, but with the support of the Minister of Finance Vanoni, by seven authoritative experts.[62] The main difficulty with this solution is of a financial character. The members of the present tax commissions receive almost symbolic compensation, and they require a small number of secretarial and auxiliary personnel. To replace the commissions with career judges, paid at the same rates as the ordinary magistracy, and to endow them with secretarial personnel and with the necessary equipment, would involve a considerable expense.

For the purpose of tempering this disadvantage, some modifications have been suggested. One involves appointing to specialized sections, in addition to the robed judges, tax experts chosen by the ordinary magistracy in such a manner as to avoid partiality between the tax administration or the taxpayer (whereas the members of the tax commissions today are normally named by the tax administration).

Another suggested modification would be to supplement the specialized sections in some manner with nonmember experts, who, although not carrying on a true and proper jurisdictional activity, would carry out work preliminary or preparatory to the work of the judge. In this way, the present tax commissions would be utilized, but appropriately improved by eliminating from their functions those jurisdictional duties to which they are not adapted. In turn, two formulations of this modification have been presented. First of all, it has been suggested that the tax commissions remain as organs of litigation for the tax administration. These commissions would decide on taxpayer appeals not as jurisdictional organs, but as administrative organs, in a "hierarchic" way. Furthermore, the taxpayer would have the right to omit the phase of litigation in the commissions and appeal directly to the ordinary judge. Finally, before an ordinary judge, the taxpayer would not be bound by the way in which he had set up his claims and his arguments for the administrative proceedings, since two completely distinct proceedings would be involved. For the purpose of inducing taxpayers to make preliminary application to the administrative tax commissions in the largest possible number of cases, it has been suggested that taxpayers who wished to apply directly to the ordinary judge would not have a right, even if successful, to reimbursement of the procedural expenses sustained. There is doubt, however, as to the constitutionality of this device, given the rule of article 113 of the Constitution, which forbids any limitation on the right of the citizen to jurisdictional protection as against acts of the public administration (1/4.10a).

The second formulation of the change under examination involves subjecting all fiscal controversies to the opinion of commissions of experts,

---

[62] See Azzariti *et al.*, "Studio per una riforma del contenzioso tributario," *RDFSF*, 1951, I, 99.

before taking them to the ordinary judge. In substance, under this method, the present tax commissions would serve as preparatory organs, which would begin by making a careful examination of the question, above all in its most specialized aspects, to permit the ordinary judge then to decide more rapidly upon it. To this effect was the plan of Trabucchi, Minister of Finance in the Fanfani government of 1961-1962.

A last solution for the problem of tax litigation is the institution of a special tax magistracy, completely separate from the ordinary magistracy, to which would be transferred every controversy on tax matters, except for appeals to the Supreme Court of Cassation on questions of violation of law, and appeals to the Constitutional Court on questions of constitutional legitimacy. It may be observed that this solution could be adopted only if the Constitution were first revised to permit the existence of special fiscal jurisdictions. Many consider an appropriate constitutional revision opportune. The danger in establishing a special jurisdiction to settle matters in one field, it is argued, arises when the real reason for its establishment lies not in the difficulties and technical particulars of the subject matter, but in the desire of the political power to apply standards different from those applied by the regular courts. A special independent fiscal judge—a specialist who could judge with competence and independence on tax matters whose technicalities require special skills—would not present this danger.

1/5. The Financial Policy of the Local Entities

1/5.1 Units of Local Government

Italy is not a federation or confederation, but a unitary state. The "state" is the highest political unit, under which three other levels of government are recognized. The communes, the lowest level, have existed since medieval times, and the provinces since national unification. The third level—the regions—was first established in the Constitution of 1947 and has not yet been fully instituted. All three of these levels of government are endowed with powers in the field of public finance. The terms "local entities" and "local finance" are frequently used to refer to all three levels.

Article 114 of the Constitution establishes that "the Republic is divided into regions, provinces and communes," and article 115 states, "the regions are formed in independent entities with their own powers and functions according to the principles fixed by the Constitution." Article 116 then specifies that "to Sicily, Sardinia, Trentino-Alto Adige, to Friuli-Venezia Giulia, and to Valle d'Aosta are given particular forms and conditions of autonomy according to special statutes, adopted by constitutional laws." Thus, there are two types of regions: those of "special statute," which are regulated by special constitutional laws and enjoy a particular condition, and those of "ordinary statute," which are all of the others. The regional structure in Italy, however, has remained in its first stages until now; almost all of the regions of special statute have been instituted (except that of Friuli-Venezia Giulia, now in process of formation), but those of ordinary statute are still to be instituted.

The unitary state from the beginning was constituted as a centralized state: first, because of the need of knitting together the various parts of the country, and secondly, because of the ideological currents prevailing in the *Risorgimento* and in the formation of the Statute of Carlo Alberto. The republicans, especially the followers of Mazzini, were of federalist inspiration and, in general, supporters of broad local autonomy. But the monarchists were centralists, whether they were right-wing liberals, like the men of the historical right who ruled Italy until 1876 (1/1.2), or traditional conservatives inspired by the traditions of the Piedmontese state or of the other Italian states existing before unification. Under the historical right, as soon as the new national state had been formed, the communes and the provinces were recognized. The elective character of the communal and provincial councils was established, but the mayor of the commune and the head of the province were named by the crown. Rejected, however, was the proposal of Minghetti [63] to recognize the regions, even if only as associations of provinces.

The historical left, numbering among its ranks many men of republican background, had from the beginning opposed the course of centralization. But having attained power, it did not make many changes, especially in this matter, chiefly for reasons of a financial character. However, suffrage was extended, and the office of Mayor, for all capitals of provinces and for all communes of more than 10,000 inhabitants, became elective. At the head of the province was placed a President elected by the Provincial Council. Giolitti [64] made some reforms to satisfy the new needs of the cities, in connection with industrial development and urbanization, but was substantially a centralist.

The period immediately following the First World War was a period of opposition to any type of authoritarianism and paternalism, and of development of decentralization in every field. The new Catholic party of Sturzo had local autonomy and decentralization as fundamental points of its program.

The Socialists viewed local autonomy with great favor, to the extent that it coincided with the municipalization of the public services, the development of the cooperative movement, and the carrying out of urban and fiscal reforms. The local administrations were often considered by the new popular parties as a proving ground for the reforms they

---

[63] Prime Minister, 1863-1864 and 1873-1876.
[64] Prime Minister, 1892-1893, 1903-1905, 1906-1909, 1911-1914, and 1920-1921.

would carry out at the national level when they achieved decisive political strength.

Fascism, which came to power in 1922, sought to create the "strong state," and clearly wanted for this purpose a considerable measure of centralization, which it expressed by enlarging the controls of the central government over the local territorial entities. In addition, the public organs of general jurisdiction were rather quickly reinforced at the provincial and communal levels by the organs of the national fascist party, with broad political functions, organized into provincial federations and communal branches. Later, the corporative structures, organized both by sector and by provincial subdivisions, were added. All these developments decreased further the significance of the local territorial entities, and in particular of the provinces.

The Constitution of 1947 reacted against the centralized control over local government. Thus, article 5 of the Constitution states, "the Republic, one and indivisible, recognizes and promotes the local autonomies; brings about in the services under the state the broadest administrative decentralization; and conforms the principles and the methods of the legislation to the needs of autonomy and decentralization." Besides articles 114 and 115 establishing the regions, articles 128 and 129 regarding the provinces and communes must also be read in the light of article 5. Article 128 establishes that "the provinces and the communes are autonomous entities within the range of the principles fixed by the general laws of the Republic, which determine their functions," and article 129 provides, in the first paragraph, that "the provinces and the communes are also organs of state and regional decentralization." Thus, it is necessary to distinguish between the provinces and communes as local entities and the provinces and communes as local agencies of the jurisdiction of the state and the regions. Every province is a local entity, and, as an expression of local autonomy, has its own Provincial Council, and a President of its provincial administration. In addition, however, there is the administrative provincial jurisdiction of the state, carrying out national policy at the provincial level. In every province, the Minister of Internal Affairs has under him a Prefect (*Prefetto*), who represents the central executive power in the province, supervises the conduct of the public administration therein, and guards public order and security.[65]

1/5.2 The Structures of Local Government

The governments of the communes and the provinces are at present founded on standards of a representative democracy. Each commune is governed by a Communal Council (*Consiglio Communale*), elected for

---

[65] See R.D. 3 March 1934, n. 383, art. 19, as amended by L. 8 March 1949, n. 277. The decree of 1934 is the *Testo unico* of communal and provincial law and is hereinafter cited: "LCP."

four years, which approves the estimated budget for the current year and the budget of receipts and expenditures for the preceding year. The Communal Council elects the Municipal Board (*Giunta Municipale*), which is the "government" of the commune and which lasts for four years. The members of the Board, called "assessors" (*assessori*), each have jurisdiction in a defined sector, such as welfare, buildings, education, or transportation, and correspond on the communal level to the ministries of the central government. There is, generally, an assessor for taxes or for finances. The Mayor (*Sindaco*), who is elected by the Communal Council, also remains in office for four years.

Similarly, each province has a Provincial Council (*Consiglio Provinciale*), elected for four years, which is responsible for the formation of the provincial budget and approves the budget of receipts and expenditures for the preceding year. The Provincial Council elects, for a term of four years, the President of the provincial administration and the Provincial Administrative Board (*Giunta Provinciale Amministrativa*), who are, respectively, the head of the "government" of the province and the members thereof, each operating within the jurisdiction of a specified assessor's office. The province also normally has an office of assessor for finances.

For the ordinary regions, the Constitution provides an analogous structure: the Regional Council (*Consiglio Regionale*), which is the regional parliamentary assembly, the Regional Board (*Giunta Regionale*), which is the "government" of the region, and the President of the Regional Board (Const. art. 121). The mechanism of election of the Regional Council has been entrusted by the Constitution to the ordinary laws (Const. art. 122); it can be either of first grade (direct election by the citizens of the region) or of second grade (election by the Provincial Councilors of the provinces in the region in question, or election by the Communal Councilors of the communes in the region). The President and members of the Regional Board, on the other hand, are to be elected by the Regional Council from among its own members (Const. art. 122); the ordinary law will have to establish the term of the regional legislature and decide whether the Board and its President will be elected for the entire term of the legislature.

The ordinary regions also will be subdivided territorially at the communal and provincial levels. But only as an exception will they have their own communal and provincial offices, distinct from those of the local communal and provincial entities themselves. Indeed, article 118 of the Constitution, third paragraph, establishes that "the region normally exercises its administrative functions by delegating them to the provinces, to the communes, or to other local entities, or making use of their offices."

1/5.3   Legislative and Administrative Functions of Local Governments

At present, the communes and provinces are subjected to strong controls not only of legitimacy or legality (*legittimità*), but also of merit or policy (*merito*), by the organs of the state administration, principally by the Prefect, the Provincial Administrative Board in its administrative capacity (which is presided over by the Prefect himself), and the Ministry of Internal Affairs.[66] In the Ministry of Internal Affairs, there is a Central Commission for Local Finance, one of whose functions is to advise on questions relating to local finance submitted to it by the Minister of Internal Affairs or the Minister of Finance (LCP art. 328). When the regions are established, the controls of legitimacy should pass, as a rule, to the appropriate organ of the region. Naturally, there will probably also be a control by the state administrative authority on the acts of the region itself. But the legitimacy of the acts of the provinces and communes will have to be transferred from the direct control of the state administration to that of the regional administration.

Article 117 of the Constitution grants the regions of ordinary statute the power to issue legislative rules "within the limits of the fundamental principles established by the laws of the state, provided that those rules be not in conflict with the national interest and with the interest of other regions." Their jurisdiction would extend to the following areas: ordering of the offices and of the administrative entities under the region; communal districts; urban and rural local police; fairs and markets and the artisan class; public welfare and health and hospital assistance; artisan and professional instruction and scholastic assistance in general; museums and libraries of local entities; urban affairs; tourism and the hotel industry; the road system, aqueducts, and public works of regional interest; lake ports; tramways, motor vehicle transportation lines of regional interest, and lake navigation; mineral and thermal waters, quarries and peat bogs, fishing in interior waters; agriculture and forests. New constitutional laws, moreover, could extend further the legislative jurisdiction of the regions.

As can be seen, the legislative subject matter assigned to the regional government is very broad. It involves delicate sectors of economic policy in fields such as professional education, urban road systems, and agriculture, which are particularly important in Italy today.

The region also is given administrative competence in all fields in which it can legislate, except for matters of exclusively local interest in those fields—in which case the administration may be allocated by the laws of the state to the communes, the provinces, or the Chambers of Commerce. The state may also delegate to a region the exercise of other administrative functions (Const. art. 118). Since, normally, the region will have to act by delegating its administrative functions to the

---

[66] See L. 9 June 1947, n. 530; LCP art. 102.

communes and provinces, or by making use of their offices, these local entities could—in the end—carry out for the regions functions which the state has delegated to the latter, thus carrying decentralization a step further.

Even after the institution of the regions, the provinces and communes will have their own independent functions since, under article 128 of the Constitution, the provinces and communes are "autonomous entities." The communes and the provinces will certainly regulate at least those questions that are "of exclusively local interest" over which the regions normally have administrative jurisdiction. But they presumably will also continue to have the functions assigned to them by the present communal and provincial law (1/5.4).

1/5.4   Expenditures of Local Governments

The basic communal and provincial law of 1934 classifies the expenditures of the communes and of the provinces as obligatory and optional, but lists only the ordinary obligatory expenditures. "Obligatory expenditures" are those which the communes are required under various laws to undertake, some representing matters of local concern and others matters of national concern for which the government prefers to delegate responsibility. They are listed under the following headings: patrimonial charges; general expenses; local police, health, and hygiene; public security and justice; public works; education; agriculture; assistance and welfare; and worship (LCP art. 91).

The actual picture of the present powers of the communes is considerably less restricted than this 1934 classification might lead one to think. The urgency of certain problems and the recognition of new needs in local life brought about, even in the period before the democratic restoration, some enlargement of horizons and some changes of direction. Since the democratic restoration, there have been various legislative reforms, and, especially, new interpretations and changes in practice, which have led to broader conceptions of the functions of local entities in the field of urban affairs and social welfare.

The functions and expenditures of the communes may be divided into the economic classifications described below.

1. *General administration of the local entity.* Collection of taxes and fees; administration of loans and patrimonies; payment of taxes to other public entities; compensation and reimbursement of expenses to the Mayor and to the communal administrators; central bureaucracy of the entity; expenses of representation and the like.
2. *Formation and keeping of the population registers, archives of national interest, and the like.* Services of civil status (births, marriages, deaths, and the related proofs); registers of the resident population (*anagrafe*); that part of national censuses carried out on the communal territory;

expenses for the notarial archives; expenses for the formation of the new cadaster.

3. *Military, defense, and public order.* Maintenance and custody of military cemeteries and tombs; contribution to expenses of conscription; lodging for *carabinieri* and troops in transit; rifle ranges; requisition of animals and vehicles.

4. *Justice.* Premises and furniture for the judiciary offices of the Conciliators.

5. *Agriculture.* Nurture of trees; control of locusts; construction and maintenance of storage facilities for fertilizer.

6. *Local police.* Supervision of traffic and of the road system; supervision of the exercise of business and of accommodations open to the public (police of the food supply); various functions of the protection of order; contributions to the fire department.

7. *Urban affairs.* Formation and carrying out of regulatory plans and of urban regulations; carrying out of programs of acquisition (possibly with expropriation) and infrastructural endowment of areas for low-cost and popular housing.

8. *Primary urbanization.* Construction, maintenance, cleaning, and illumination of the communal streets and squares; construction and maintenance of ditches and aqueducts; contributions for the construction of roads connecting isolated communes.

9. *Education.* Building, furnishing, maintenance, heating, and lighting of the elementary schools and of the offices of the school inspectors and educational directors, and compensation of building employees; the same charges plus secretarial expenses for the professional technical schools, classical high schools, and training colleges; the same charges (excluding secretarial expenses) for the communal industrial and technical schools.

10. *Health.* Office and service of hygiene (including personnel); contributions to the provincial laboratory of hygiene and prevention of disease (the large communes, instead of giving this contribution, may institute and operate laboratories of their own); vaccinations, prevention of infectious diseases, and contributions to clinics for the prevention and cure of venereal diseases; contribution to provincial antituberculosis associations; communal pharmacy, if any; salaried doctor and midwife; free supply of medicines to the indigent; hospital charges for the care of the sick indigent not receiving assistance from social insurance or welfare entities; transportation of mentally ill to mental hospitals.

11. *Social assistance.* Premises for the committee of the institution for maternity and infancy; support of those unable to work; contributions for the assistance of abandoned infants; transportation of remains of poor persons to the cemetery and provision of funeral coffins.

12. *Various equipment for community premises.* Slaughterhouse (construction, operation, and veterinaries); fairs and markets; parks, gardens, villas, and sports fields; cemeteries.

13. *Tourism.* Contributions to the provincial entity for tourism and (where they exist) resort businesses.

14. *Various public works.*

15. *Various public services.*

Considered optional are all current nonobligatory functions and expenditures having as their object services and offices of public utility which are carried on, even in charge of different entities, within the administrative district of the commune (LCP arts. 92, 312). The making of optional expenditures is limited in various ways, besides the general limitation imposed by the need to undertake obligatory expenses first. Optional current expenditures may not exceed 20% of total ordinary receipts if the commune applies the immovable property surtaxes at a rate less than the second limit for those taxes (1/5.6), and may not exceed 10% of total ordinary receipts if the rate of the surtaxes is higher than the second limit (LCP art. 314). Moreover, the Provincial Administrative Board has an "audit of merit" on the optional expenditures of the individual commune; that is, the Board may refuse or grant authorization for the commune to make the expenditures, on the basis of its own appraisal of their public utility, or their cost, even if the expenditures do not exceed the specified percentages of 10% or 20%. Furthermore, and this is the primary purpose of the "audit of merit" of the Provincial Administrative Board, optional expenditures can be made by the individual commune only if it has been shown that the means exist to meet them without detriment to the obligatory expenses (LCP art. 316). Finally, the optional current expenditures cannot be financed through loans (1/5.5h). The result of the present arrangement is that many communes, after meeting obligatory expenditures for functions that might better be assigned to the state, have insufficient receipts to make optional expenditures for functions —such as urban planning—which are more properly within their sphere.

The administrative classification of obligatory and optional expenditures of the provinces is identical, under the existing legislation of local finance, to that of the expenditures of the communes (LCP arts. 312, 314). The obligatory expenditures of the provinces can be classified under the same economic scheme as the one used for the expenditures of the communes (LCP art. 144).

1. *General administration of the local entity.* The content of this class is analogous to that of the expenses of the communes.
2. *Archives and records.* Expenditures for the formation of the cadaster and for the premises and functioning of the Provincial Census Commissions; supplying of the premises and other expenses for the state archives.
3. *Defense and public order.* Expenditures for the premises of the conscription offices; expenditures for the premises for the police headquarters and the commissariats of public security; contributions for firing-range camps.
4. *Agriculture.* Contributions to the Provincial Inspectorate of Agriculture; contributions for the control of locusts and Argentine ants; indemnities for the destruction of animals having infectious diseases; various duties regarding hunting and fishing.
5. *Local police.* Supervision of hunting and fishing.
6. *Urban affairs.* Making and carrying out plans regarding provincial streets and other public works under provincial jurisdiction.

7. *Urbanization and infrastructure.* Construction and maintenance of provincial streets and contributions for certain water works; various contributions for the maintenance of banks and shores against rivers and tides.

8. *Education.* Expenses for secretarial and building personnel, construction, maintenance, furnishing, heating, lighting, for the technical business institutes, surveyors, and scientific high schools; similar expenses (except those for personnel) for the agrarian institutes and the institutes of higher learning.

9. *Health.* Provincial laboratory of hygiene and prevention of disease; preventive service for infectious diseases; sanitary inspections for epidemics; disinfection service; supply of smallpox vaccine and quinine, cure of pellagra and rabies; construction of the headquarters and offices of the provincial antitubercular association; contributions for the expenses of the health bureau and its personnel; provincial mental hospitals and assistance to the mentally infirm.

10. *Social assistance.* Assistance for illegitimate infants, abandoned or threatened with abandonment; assistance to the blind and to deaf-mutes; furnishing of premises and personnel to the maternity and infancy bureau; expenses of the functioning of the provincial committee of assistance and welfare.

11. *Various equipment of community premises.* Construction, furnishing, and office personnel for the barracks of the fire department.

12. *Tourism.* Contributions to the provincial entity for tourism.

1/5.5   Receipts of Local Governments

a. IN GENERAL. Just as some local expenditures are made according to precise rules laid down by legislation and by the state administration, rather than autonomously by the local entity, not all receipts of the local entity are collected by it autonomously.

A classification of actual or current receipts (that is, in which the public debt is not counted) of the local entity is formulated below; each type of receipt is endowed with a progressively lower grade of autonomy, down to its total absence.

1. Completely autonomous patrimonial receipts and local taxes.

2. Partly autonomous patrimonial receipts and local taxes. The state fixes a maximum limit to the rates and places restrictions on exemptions, deductions, and reliefs.

3. Autonomous surtaxes on taxes levied by other entities. The local entity chooses the rate it will apply; the assessment belongs to the other entity.

4. Partly autonomous surtaxes on taxes levied by other entities.

5. Partly autonomous additionals and shares of taxes assessed by other entities.

6. Nonautonomous surtaxes, additionals, and participations in the yield of taxes collected by other entities on a tax base located in the territory of the local entity; participations in the yield of taxes of other entities. These can be measured by economic criteria such as the need of the

local entity, or they can be distributed according to the amount of some of the entity's expenses.

7. Subsidies, which can be distributed in the ways mentioned in item 6.

8. Assistance given from time to time.

Of these types of receipts, only completely autonomous taxes and sur-taxes are absent from Italian local finance; this is a consequence of the constitutional principle, which has been explained at 1/2.2, that taxation must have a basis in the law.

b. PATRIMONIAL RECEIPTS. Prominent among the autonomously levied patrimonial receipts are those which the communes, the provinces, and the regions of special statute have (and which, presumably, the regions of ordinary statute will have) from the patrimonial forests. Included also in this class are various other patrimonial assets, such as areas zoned for building, which may be transferred or developed for purposes of profit.

The local entities have numerous other patrimonial or semipatrimonial receipts derived from enterprises and services. The communes receive the earnings from the municipalized services (tramways, electric buses, gas and electric companies, communal pharmacies, milk centers, public baths, general and slaughterhouse markets, and communal swimming pools); the receipts of cemeteries; fees for public-bill posting (4/5.12); fees for the collection of rubbish; fees for the occupation of public spaces and areas (4/5.11); and fees for weighing and measuring (4/5.13). (These last four classes, juridically, are considered by some students to be taxes, rather than prices.)[67] For the provinces, the major sources of revenue are the fees for the occupation of public spaces and areas and the receipts from highways. The regions will have receipts from regional businesses, such as transportation businesses, operation of high-ways, and the like.

In most cases, however, the patrimonial and semipatrimonial receipts deriving to the local entities from the exercise of "enterprises or services" do not figure as entirely autonomous receipts since there is a state control over the fee schedules or the conditions of operation or both. In some cases, in fact, the schedules which the communes and the provinces apply are established rather rigidly by the law; this is true, for example, of the fees for the occupation of public spaces and areas and the fees on public-bill posting. It should also be added that, when a coercive element can be found in the nature of the receipt, the levy of receipt comes within the scope of article 23 of the Constitution, which requires that it have a basis in the law.[68]

---

[67] On this question, see Forte, "Note sulla nozione di tributo nell'ordinamento finanziario italiano e sul significato dell'art. 23 della Costituzione," *RDFSF*, 1956, I, 248.

[68] See Forte, "Note sulla nozione di tributo nell'ordinamento finanziario italiano e sul significato dell'art. 23 della Costituzione," *RDFSF*, 1956, I. 248.

c. AUTONOMOUS LOCAL TAXES. As a result of article 23 of the Constitution (1/2.2), there cannot be completely autonomous communal and provincial taxes in the Italian system. Every tax must have a basis in the law, and thus the tax autonomy of the communes and of the provinces cannot be absolute and can be exercised only as long as this precept is not violated. Given the principle of the autonomy of the local entities and of the regions, however, the rule of legality here, under the ordinary · legislation in force, can have a particularly broad flexibility.

Besides a general autonomy (Const. art. 115), the Constitution gives the regions a certain measure of financial autonomy [69] and, more specifically, of tax autonomy.[70] But a region cannot institute import, export, or transit duties between regions, adopt measures in any way obstructing the free circulation of persons and things between regions, or limit the right of citizens to exercise their profession, employment, or work in any part of the national territory (Const. art. 120). For the communes and the provinces, the Constitution formulates explicitly only a generic recognition of autonomy,[71] from which tax autonomy can be inferred only by interpretation.

The major taxes through which the fiscal autonomy of the local entities is exercised at present are the communal family tax (a personal progressive tax on income) (2/3) and the communal consumption taxes (4/5.8) (TUFL art. 10). For these taxes, especially for the family tax, the national laws on local finance leave to the commune a particularly broad margin of maneuver. For the family tax, the law does not specify the rates which must actually be applied to the various classes of income, but only the maximum rates within which the progressive scale of actual rates, to be selected by the individual local entity, must range (2/3.4b). Moreover, the law does not define very specifically the taxable object of the family tax, describing it only as the "well-being" or means (*agiatezza*), inferred from income and other indices (2/3.3b). The amount of the exemptions for minimum income, of the fixed deduction for the head of the family and for the members of the family dependent on him, and the reductions for income produced entirely or predominantly through labor, are not made precise by the law, which limits itself only to foreseeing generically the possibility of such exemptions and reliefs (2/3.4a). In the face of this situation, the fiscal administration of the state has

---

[69] "The regions have financial autonomy in the forms and within the limits established by the laws of the Republic, which coordinate them with the finance of the state, of the provinces, and of the communes." Const. art. 119, first paragraph.

[70] "To the regions are given their own taxes and shares of national taxes, in relation to the needs of the regions for the expenses necessary to the fulfillment of their normal functions." Const. art. 119, second paragraph.

[71] "The provinces and the communes are autonomous entities within the ambit of the principles fixed by general laws of the Republic, which determine their functions." Const. art. 128.

responded by issuing circulars limiting the power of action of the communes; the organs of control and supervision under the Ministry of Internal Affairs provide for further limiting the autonomy of the local entities with regard to the application of these taxes (2/3.6).

The provinces and the communes both impose autonomously the betterment contributions, which reach benefits derived from improvements made by public works and from the aggregate of activities furnished by the local entities to immovable property (TUFL art. 10) (3/7.1). These taxes have been used rather little in the past by the local entities because of the complexity of their assessment procedures and because of the low rates permitted by the law. The tax autonomy granted to the local entity in this field did not work very well. But a recent reform of these taxes has increased the revenue yield and made their assessment easier (3/7.3). The levies are now compulsory for a large number of communes, and, in the future, it may be less easy for the individual local entity to refuse to apply them by alleging that the yield will not justify undergoing the administrative difficulties.

The other autonomous taxes which the communes are authorized to impose (TUFL art. 10) are the taxes on the leasehold value of dwellings (2/3.7), on public and private carriages (TUFL arts. 137-147), on servants (2/2.9), on pianos (if the commune does not impose the family tax) and billiard tables (TUFL arts. 155-160), on businesses (*imposta di patente*) (2/2.9), and on visitors (*imposta di soggiorno*) (4/5.9); fees for public weighing and measuring and the renting of public counters (4/5.13); and fees for the collection of rubbish (TUFL arts. 268-272). The tax on cattle (*imposta sul bestiame*) (TUFL arts. 122-126) and the power to require the contribution of work on public roads and in combating locusts (TUFL art. 10(7))[72] were abolished as of 1 January 1961.[73] The communes are also required to impose license taxes (4/5.10), the tax on signs (4/5.12), and the tax on dogs (TUFL arts. 130-136).

d. LOCAL SURTAXES ON STATE TAXES. The communes apply surtaxes to almost all of the objective taxes of the state, in particular, to the taxes on income from movable wealth from enterprises and independent work (categories B and C/1) and on income from the ownership of buildings and of agricultural land (TUFL art. 10) (2/2.9). The provinces apply surtaxes on the same sources (2/2.9). For the regions, the use of surtaxes on income from movable wealth from enterprises and independent work has been suggested in governmental studies.

---

[72] See also L. 30 August 1868, n. 4613, arts. 5-7; L. 4 July 1895, n. 390.

[73] L. 16 September 1960, n. 1014, art. 15. From 1961 through 1970, 1.6% of the yield of the general tax on receipts is set aside in a special fund, to be distributed among the communes to compensate them for the yield lost by the abolition of the tax on cattle. L. 21 October 1960, n. 1371, art. 2.

Formally, the local surtax on income from movable wealth from enterprises and from independent work—the "communal tax on industry, commerce, arts, and professions" (usually abbreviated "ICAP")—is an independent tax of the communes, on which the provinces apply a surtax.
But, in reality, ICAP is a surtax since it does not have an independent
taxable base; the communal rate of ICAP (and also the provincial rate)
is applied to the income assessed by the state administration against the
payers of the state tax on income from movable wealth of categories
B and C/1. The local entity must accept the assessments of the state;
its only autonomy consists in establishing, in a uniform manner for all
of the taxpayers, a rate which is within the maximum established by the
law. The communal surtaxes on income from lands and on income from
buildings do not differ at all, in mechanism, from the ICAP; for these
also, the local entity must accept the state assessment and may only vary
the rate uniformly within the maximum established by the law.

To the normal rates of a certain number of national taxes and provincial
and communal surtaxes is added a uniform rate, now 10% for most taxes,[74]
of which three fifths is distributed among the provinces [75] and the balance
among the communes. The aggregate rate of this "additional" is not
computed on taxable income, but on the proceeds (or on the rate multiplied by the taxable income) of those taxes. This additional, which was
instituted for the benefit of the communes in 1937 and for the benefit of
the provinces in 1946, takes its name, "additional for ECA," from the fact
that its proceeds go to finance the communal assistance entities (*enti
comunali di assistenza*) and similar entities of the provinces. The taxes
on which it is levied are very numerous: the objective taxes of the state
on income from landowning, income from buildings, agrarian income, and
income from movable wealth; the personal tax of the state on individuals
("complementary"); the state succession, registration, and mortgage
taxes; the communal and provincial surtaxes on the national taxes on land
and buildings; the ICAP and its provincial surtax; the family tax and a
number of lesser communal taxes and fees, which have the common
characteristic of being collected through "rolls"—thus, the tax on signs,
the tax on dogs, the tax on *espresso* coffee machines, the special health
contribution, the fee for the occupation of public spaces and areas, the
fee for the collection and removal of rubbish, and the license tax.[76]

The proceeds of the communes from the additional for ECA flow into
a special fund of the Minister of Internal Affairs,[77] who distributes four
fifths of the fund, according to standards which he sets, to the Prefects
of the provinces; each Prefect then divides the amount received among

---

[74] R.D.L. 30 November 1937, n. 2145; L. 10 December 1961, n. 1346. See 2/2.9.
[75] D.M. 20 July 1946.
[76] See R.D.L. 30 November 1937, n. 2145, art. 1.
[77] D.L. 7 November 1954, n. 1025, arts. 2, 3.

the communal assistance entities of the communes in his province. The remaining fifth of the fund stays at the disposition of the Minister of Internal Affairs "to meet subsequent needs inherent in the supplementation of the budgets of the said entities." [78] The proceeds from the additional for ECA belonging to the provinces, on the other hand, are subdivided among them every six months on the basis of the population as determined in the last official census.[79]

A further additional of 5%, for the purpose of obtaining funds for aid to areas where serious natural calamities have occurred—such as Polesine, Salernitano, and Calabria, which have had floods and earthquakes—is added to all national, communal, and provincial taxes and surtaxes collected through rolls (exclusive of ECA and collection fees) for the years 1955-1956 through 1966-1967.[80]

e. PARTICIPATIONS IN YIELDS OF STATE TAXES. In addition to receiving proceeds from the taxes levied and collected autonomously by them, local entities receive a share of the proceeds from certain state taxes. Although this method of local finance is of more recent origin than the autonomous taxes and the surtaxes, it has assumed great importance in the finances of both the communes and the provinces and is the predominant method by which the regions of special statute are financed. The principal instance of participation in yield is the allocation to the communes and the provinces of a share of the general tax on receipts (14/1).[81] Since 1952, 7.5% of the total yield of the general tax on receipts has been divided among all of the communes. The division is made in proportion to the population resident in each commune as determined in the last national decennial census. A further 1% of the yield of the general tax on receipts is divided, in the same manner, among the communes of the small islands. Although this percentage is small, it constitutes a significant participation considering that the over-all population of these communes is a small fraction of the national population (and will become still smaller with the increasing exodus from the land). The provinces participate, also on the basis of population, in the division of another 2.5% of the annual yield of the general tax on receipts.

The local entities also participate in the total proceeds from other state taxes. First of all, the communes are entitled to 75% of the yield of the national tax on public shows (4/5.4) collected in their territories. The participation in this tax was instituted in 1923 and substantially enlarged in 1948 and in 1959.[82] Moreover, the communes enjoy specified

---

[78] D.P.R. 19 August 1954, n. 968, art. 17, on the decentralization of the services of the Ministry of Internal Affairs.

[79] See D.M. 20 July 1946.

[80] L. 26 November 1955, n. 1177, art. 18.

[81] See L. 2 July 1952, n. 703; L. 16 September 1960, n. 1014, art. 16.

[82] D.L. 26 March 1948, n. 261, art. 2; L. 20 December 1959, n. 1102, art. 4.

percentages of the yields of the general tax on receipts levied in their
territories on wine and livestock. This participation, first instituted in
1948,[83] and the participation in the yield of the national tax on shows are
distinguished from the other shares which the communes are given since
they do not have an equalizing function but constitute a means through
which each commune retains levies made on economic activities carried
on its territory.

The provinces, finally, receive one third of the total yield of the tax
on the operation of motor vehicles (4/4.5), which is divided among them
every four months in proportion to the area and to the length of the provincial streets.[84] The second index for the division is based on a criterion
of benefit since it places the division in relation to the presumable use of
the provincial streets and to the expenditure for streets in each province.
The first index, on the other hand, has an equalizing function since it
favors the provinces which have a low density of streets in relation to their
area and which would receive less if the division were made on the basis
of the length of streets alone. It is supposed that these provinces have particular problems in the aggregate distribution of public services because
of a low density of population or a modest economic development, or both.

By far the predominant part of the receipts of the regions of special
statute comes from participations in the proceeds of the state taxes. The
ministerial studies and the work of the Tupini Commission have foreseen
that these participations will also play a prominent role in the finances
of the regions of ordinary statute.

The regions of special statute enjoy the participations listed below.

1. *Sicily.* All proceeds from the state taxes levied on the island, excluding those from the taxes on manufacturing, the customs duties, and the
   fiscal monopolies.[85]
2. *Sardinia.* Nine tenths of the yield of the taxes on income from landowning, agrarian income, income from buildings, and income from
   movable wealth, the stamp tax, the fees for governmental concessions,
   the mortgage tax, taxes in substitution of registration and stamp taxes,
   manufacturing taxes, taxes on gas and electric energy, and the monopoly
   tax on tobacco, received on the island; six tenths of the taxes on manufacturing received on the island; and a share of the yield of the general
   tax on receipts levied on the island "to be determined by estimate for
   each financial year by agreement between the state and the region, in
   relation to the expenses necessary to fulfill the normal functions of the
   region." [86]

---

[83] Suspended by L. 2 July 1952, n. 703, art. 2; now governed by L. 18 December
1959, n. 1079, art. 5.

[84] D.P. 5 February 1953, n. 39, art. 10.

[85] See R.D.L. 15 May 1946, n. 455 (Stat. Reg. Sic.), arts. 36-39; D.L. 12 April
1948, n. 507.

[86] L. Cost. 26 February 1948, n. 3 (Stat. Sard.), art. 8; see also D.P.R. 9 May 1949,
n. 250, arts. 32-38.

3. *Trentino-Alto Adige.* The proceeds of the mortgage tax collected there and the proceeds of the state tax on gas and electric energy levied on electric energy and gas "consumed" there (it would have been quite different had the provision been that the tax was to be levied on the electricity "produced" in the region, given that Trentino-Alto Adige produces an important part of the electricity consumed in the rest of northern Italy); as well as a percentage of the yield of lotto, and of the monopolies and fees and taxes on transactions collected in the territory of the region, "determined each year by agreement between the government and the President of the Regional Board." [87]

4. *Valle d'Aosta.* Besides the receipts of the province of Aosta, including participations, nine tenths of the yield of the taxes on income from buildings, income from landowning, agrarian income, succession, registration, and stamp taxes, substitution of registration and stamp taxes, mortgage tax, and governmental concessions collected in the region, as well as eight tenths of the yield of the tax on income from movable wealth and nine tenths of the yield of the complementary tax collected in the region.[88]

f. SUBSIDIES. The subsidies, like the participations in the proceeds from state taxes, were introduced recently into Italian local finance, and in fact are now more frequently used than participations. The subsidies have two purposes: (1) to contribute to meeting certain expenses of the local entities which concern important national matters (expenses for school buildings, streets, and the like), and (2) to make up, for a limited period, losses in the provincial and communal revenues caused by the abolition—because of the agricultural crisis and the requirements of agricultural reform—of the surtaxes on agrarian income, the tax on livestock, and the communal tax on the consumption of wine.

One of the more important subsidies of recent years was made by a law of 1954 which appropriated L. 1,500 million annually until 1963-1964 for the building of schools.[89] This provision proved to be insufficient in the face of the vast need for new schools, and it was supplanted by a 1960 law establishing a plan under which the annual appropriation over a period of several years would gradually increase. The 1960 law provides L. 8,000 million for the communes and L. 2,000 million for the provinces for the financial year 1959-1960; the appropriations are doubled for 1960-1961, tripled for 1961-1962, and quadrupled for 1962-1963. For subsequent financial years, the appropriations cannot be less than those of

---

[87] See L. Cost. 26 February 1948, n. 5 (Stat. Trentino-Alto Adige), arts. 60-70; D.P.R. 30 June 1951, n. 574, arts. 57-63. Under articles 67 and 68 of the Statute, the provinces of the region receive nine tenths of the yield of the state taxes on income from landowning, agrarian income, income from buildings, and income from movable wealth.

[88] See L. Cost. 26 February 1948, n. 4 (Stat. Valle d'Aosta), art. 12; L. 29 November 1955, n. 1179, art. 2.

[89] See L. 9 August 1954, n. 645, arts. 1, 2.

1962-1963 and will be determined on the basis of the increase in the expenditures to which the state contributes.[90]

The method of distributing school subsidies has also been profoundly modified. Previously, the ministerial authorities established discretionally, case by case and without any predetermined general criterion, what local entities to assist and to what extent. Now, however, the granting of subsidies is based on objective indices resulting from a systematic evaluation. The state school subsidies to the communes are distributed half in proportion to the number of pupils enrolled in the state elementary and middle schools in the territory of each commune, and half in proportion to the number of inhabitants in each commune between six and fourteen years of age. State school subsidies to the provinces are distributed three fourths in proportion to the number of pupils enrolled in the state middle schools in the territory of each province, and one fourth in relation to the population resident in each province.[91]

Subsidies have been used increasingly in the financing of the provincial road systems. The first broad intervention by the state was made in a law of 1958, which authorized the Ministry of Public Works to give contributions of up to 80% of the expense necessary for the systematization of those roads, within the limits of an appropriation of L. 180,000 million.[92] The percentage of the contribution is determined at the discretion of the state, taking account of "the budgetary conditions of the individual provincial administrations." No general objective criterion was preestablished. In 1959-1960, a new contribution of L. 20,000 million was appropriated, to be divided in the same manner.

The law on the systematization of the communal and provincial budgets of 1960 also represented a considerable improvement in the method of dividing the road subsidies. It provided that the state would pay to the provinces, for each kilometer of communal street or of improvement, classified as provincial, following the entry into force of the above law of 1958, an annual contribution of L. 300,000 to meet their ordinary maintenance expenses.[93]

In the case of highways, the provinces receive the same treatment as the other public and private entities which request a concession from the National Autonomous Road Enterprise (*Azienda Nazionale Autonoma Strade* or ANAS) for the construction and operation of highways. Under the law of 1961 on the plan for new streets and highways, state contributions cannot exceed 4% a year, for 30 years, of the aggregate cost of the works; but the rate may be raised to 4.5% in the case of highway

---

[90] L. 16 September 1960, n. 1014, art. 7.
[91] L. 16 September 1960, n. 1014, art. 8.
[92] L. 12 February 1958, n. 126, art. 18.
[93] L. 16 September 1960, n. 1014, art. 10.

arteries directly connected with the European road and highway network. The contribution is granted by the president of ANAS (who is the Minister of Public Works) on the basis of his evaluations, within a range of figures provided for each year, in increasing and then declining amounts, until 1999.[94]

Until now, the most important subsidy in the field of regional finances has been the "fund of solidarity," which the state pays annually to Sicily on the basis of a provision of the Sicilian Statute.[95] The purpose of this fund is the development of regional public works. Its functions overlap, however, with those of the Fund for the South, and also with the functions of the state regarding public works of national interest. The overlap in functions has resulted in controversies on the annual amount of the fund to be given to Sicily. But above all, such controversies are nourished by the lack of precise standards in the laws regulating the fund and by the absence of regional economic planning in which the urgency and the significance of the various public works could be evaluated.

g. MOVEMENTS OF CAPITAL. The review of the expenses and of the receipts completed up to now concerns only "current" expenses and receipts. It does not include receipts from the "movement of capital" —receipts which do not increase the wealth of the local entity, but only express a change in the composition of its patrimony. Loans are the principal type of such receipts. The receipts which an entity obtains by selling land of its own on the market are also usually receipts from the movement of capital since they are balanced by the removal of the asset sold from the accounts.

Corresponding to the distinction between current receipts and receipts from the movement of capital is the distinction between current expenditures and expenditures from the movement of capital. The current expenditures constitute a net actual diminution in the wealth of the entity considered. It is important to note that, under the Italian legislation on the accounting system of the state and of local finance, for a certain expenditure to be considered an expenditure from the movement of capital, it is not sufficient that it be accompanied by the acquisition of a corresponding patrimonial value; the asset must also be fruitful of receipts in a measure adequate to its value (LCP art. 290). In other words, when the commune spends L. 1,000 million to build a school, this is a current expenditure since the school which is acquired is not fruitful of receipts, but is used to provide a service gratuitously to the public.

The general rule is clear and its reason evident, but doubts can arise in concrete applications. A doubtful case of great importance at present is that of the purchase of building lots by the local entity. For purposes

---

[94] L. 24 July 1961, n. 729.
[95] R.D.L. 15 May 1946, n. 455 (Stat. Reg. Sic.), art. 38.

of financing such purchases through loans, and for purposes of expanding them beyond the narrow limits provided for optional expenses, it could be maintained that these investments are not current expenses, but expenditures from the movement of capital. The state organs of control, once averse to this thesis, now seem inclined to it.

h. LOANS. The local entities are not free to contract loans at their pleasure. In the first place, no loan can be made if the budgeted interest on all loans and other debts exceeds one fourth of the ordinary actual receipts appearing in the budget of receipts and expenditures of the preceding year (LCP art. 300). In the second place, loans cannot be used to finance optional expenditures (LCP art. 299). Thirdly, the amortization of loans and the payment of the interest on them must be guaranteed, and their means determined (LCP art. 299). For this purpose, not all receipts of the local entities can be delegated, but only certain ones, principally those from the surtaxes on income from landowning and income from buildings, and three fourths of the receipts from the consumption taxes (net of the so-called "supercontributions") (4/5.8d). All other taxes collectible through rolls are delegable for the payment of certain loans only in exceptional cases. Participations in the yields of state taxes are never delegable. Moreover, receipts delegable can be determined only on the basis of receipts obtained in the past, not on estimates of future yield. For the consumption taxes, for example, the average yield in the last three-year period controls.

1/5.6 Limitations on the Tax Powers of Local Entities

Formerly, the law established the limits of the rates of the communal and provincial surtaxes on income from landowning and income from buildings; in order to impose the surtaxes within each of the limits, the provinces and communes were required to have instituted certain other taxes.[96] The present law, however, provides a single set of maximum rates for these provincial and communal surtaxes (12/1.1, 12/1.3). A province or commune may be authorized to exceed these rates in order to balance its budget, provided it (1) has applied all the taxes contemplated by existing laws at their maximum rates, (2) has imposed ICAP or the provincial additional thereto at certain specified rates, and (3) in the case of a commune, has applied certain additionals to the family tax (2/3) or to the tax on leasehold values (2/3.7).[97] The imposition of super-contributions (*eccedenze*) on the communal or provincial surtaxes on income from landowning may be authorized by the Provincial Administrative Board (LCP art. 306).[98] If the budget of a commune remains un-

---

[96] See TUFL arts. 254, 255.
[97] L. 16 September 1960, n. 1014, art. 20.
[98] As modified by L. 16 September 1960, n. 1014, art. 3.

balanced, the levy of further supercontributions on the surtax on income from landowning and other taxes may be authorized by the Central Commission for Local Finance (LCP art. 332).[99] Similarly, the Central Commission for Local Finance may authorize provinces to impose further supercontributions on the surtax on income from landowning and on other taxes (LCP art. 336).[100]

Communes which already apply supercontributions to the surtax on income from landowning can introduce supercontributions on merchandise of the first group (so-called "schedule" goods) on which the communal consumption taxes are imposed (4/5.8b) (LCP art. 332).[101]

Local taxes are also subject to restrictions connected with the size of the population of the commune. The communes are divided into nine classes, as shown in Table 1 below.

Table I: *Classes of Communes*

Class	Population	
	Lower Limit	Upper Limit
A	500,000	. . . . . .
B	200,000	500,000
C	100,000	200,000
D	60,000	100,000
E	30,000	60,000
F	15,000	30,000
G	10,000	15,000
H	5,000	10,000
I	. . . . . .	5,000

Source: TUFL art. 11.

The rates of the following taxes vary depending on the class of the commune: the tax on leasehold values (2/3.7); the family tax (2/3); the tax on signs (4/5.12); the sewer contribution; and the fee for the occupation of space above and below ground by liquid-fuel pumps (4/5.11).[102]

The restrictions on the application of certain local taxes give rise to various questions. In the first place, the requirement of applying the maximum rates of the consumption taxes on "schedule" goods before the rates on "extra-schedule" goods (4/5.8b) appears unsatisfactory. Many of the "extra-schedule" goods—for example, jewels, furs, furnishings, electrical appliances, toys, or flowers—represent greater taxable capacity

---

[99] As modified by L. 16 September 1960, n. 1014, art. 23.
[100] As modified by L. 16 September 1960, n. 1014, art. 23.
[101] As modified by D.P.R. 19 August 1954, n. 968, art. 5.
[102] See Cocivera, *Guida ai tributi locali* 11.

than some of the schedule goods, such as gas used for lighting, bottled gas for heating and cooking, electricity for lighting, and cheese. Another question arises regarding the practice of varying the rates of the family tax according to the population of the commune. The theory which seems to have prevailed is that the taxpayers in the larger communes have a greater fiscal capacity, or that the communes have greater needs. But even if the communes with a more intense economic activity can bear a greater fiscal burden, it is not clear that the most populous are also those with the most intense economic activity.

The entire subject of local finance in Italy is at present the object of lively discussion. The budgets of almost all of the communes and of many of the provinces are in considerable difficulties, and problems in the field of urban affairs, construction of housing and schools, social welfare, and hospitals are very serious. The communes of the less developed zones are in financial difficulties because of the poverty of the taxable subject matter within their jurisdiction. The communes of the zones which have been industrialized or which are in the process of intense industrialization are in financial difficulties because of the influx of inhabitants and new enterprises, and because—in the larger centers—fiscal congestion and the rise in the cost of living in building zones have increased expenses enormously and forced the local public debt to high levels. It is generally agreed that reforms in local finance will be necessary.

1/5.7 The Chamber of Commerce, Industry, and Agriculture

Various functions regarding the economic life of the province are performed by the Chamber of Commerce, Industry, and Agriculture (*Camera di Commercio, Industria e Agricoltura*). This is a public body which is supposed to be elective;[103] but, in the absence of an electoral law, its members are appointed by the Ministers of Industry and of Agriculture. It is empowered to impose a surtax on income from business and industrial activities (2/2.9, 12/1.4d).

1/6. Outline and Evolution of the Tax System in Relation to the Economic Structure [104]

1/6.1 National Income and Total Fiscal Burden

a. IN GENERAL. In 1961, the Italian national income in current lire was L. 20,840,000 million, gross of expenditures for depreciation and plant. The net national income was L. 18,905,000 million (about $30,045 mil-

---

[103] D.L. 21 September 1944, n. 315.

[104] Most of the tables in 1/6 are selected from those prepared by Dr. Mario Rey for inclusion in an appendix to Forte, *Evoluzione e lineamenti del sistema tributario.* In

lion), implying an income per inhabitant of L. 373,447 (about $600) since the population of Italy now exceeds 50 million.[105] Table 2 shows the growth of the national income since 1861 in market prices.

In 1863, the national income per capita was L. 76,463 in 1960 lire.[106] In 1901, it had risen to around L. 110,478. It reached L. 130,000 shortly before the First World War, to fall to around L. 116,000 in 1922, at the time of the "march on Rome" of the fascists. In 1926, at the end of the "financial restoration" authored by De Stefani, it was L. 146,887. After the depression, in 1931, the per capita income was L. 161,941. It then increased slightly, reaching L. 173,616 per capita in 1939. But it fell rather quickly and considerably as a result of the second world conflict, so that, in the immediate postwar period, the level reached before the war had been halved. Only in 1950 did it again exceed the level of 1938.

Subsequently, there has been a much greater development, not only in the absolute figures, but also in the percentages of increase, of the national income. In 1960, a per capita income figure of L. 342,335 was reached, and in 1961, L. 373,662 (in terms of 1960 lire). That is, in little more than a decade, there has been an increase in the national income such as to double the income per inhabitant. Since the population in these

---

most cases, the tables giving receipts of national taxes are based on sources which give figures for the financial year of the Italian government, which runs from 1 July to 30 June; for purposes of the tables included in 1/6, the figures given for financial years in the original sources have been converted to calendar-year figures by the computation of moving averages.

Where practicable, sources are indicated at the foot of each table. Certain data used in the preparation of several tables are based on information found in the sources listed below.

1. Data on tax receipts and budgets of the national government, published by the Ragioneria Generale dello Stato: *Il Bilancio del Regno d'Italia dal 1862 al 1912-13*; *Il Bilancio dello Stato dal 1913-14 al 1929-30*; *Il Bilancio dello Stato dal 1930-31 al 1941-42*; *Note informative al Bilancio dello Stato dal 1945-46 al 1955-56*.

2. Data relative to local finance: Ministero dell'Agricoltura, Industria e Commercio, *Bilanci comunali per l'anno 1899 and Bilanci provinciali per l'anno 1899*; Répaci, *Le finanze dei comuni, delle provincie e degli enti locali corporativi*; Volpi, *Le finanze dei comuni e delle provincie del Regno d'Italia dal 1860 al 1890*.

In addition, various data regarding population, national income, national and local tax receipts, social security contributions, and economic conditions have been taken from the *Relazione generale sulla situazione economica del paese*, published annually by the Ministry of the Budget and the Ministry of the Treasury.

[105] The lira is at present worth approximately $0.00161 in United States currency, or 620 to the dollar.

[106] The value of the 1960 lira is obtained on the basis of coefficients of variation of the purchasing power of money, inferred from the behavior of wholesale prices computed by the Central Statistical Institute (*Istituto Centrale di Statistica*). All figures given in 1/6 are in terms of 1960 lire unless otherwise indicated.

Year	Population (Thousands)	Coefficients for Change in Value of Lira*	Net National Income (Millions of Lire) Current Lire	Net National Income (Millions of Lire) 1960 Lire	Net National Income Index of Variation (1952 = 100)	Per Capita Net National Income Current Lire	Per Capita Net National Income 1960 Lire	Per Capita Net National Income Index of Variation (1952 = 100)
1863	22,340	287.9622	5,932	1,708,192		265.5	76,463	
1871	27,059	275.0307	8,590	2,362,514		317.5	87,310	
1881	28,953	287.6323	9,303	2,675,843		321.3	92,420	
1891	30,989	294.3763	11,106	3,269,343		358.4	105,500	
1901	33,158	298.5767	12,269	3,663,238		370.0	110,478	
1911	35,918	263.4869	17,973	4,735,650		500.4	131,846	
1921	38,469	46.4060	88,893	4,125,169		2,310.8	107,234	
1923	39,166	45.6634	106,955	4,883,929		2,730.8	124,698	
1926	40,307	40.1508	147,458	5,920,557		3,658.4	146,887	
1931	41,832	66.3416	101,482	6,732,478		3,658.4	160,941	
1938	43,851	51.8701	139,820	7,252,472	79.1	3,185.5	165,389	86.2
1939	44,334	49.7234	154,798	7,697,083	84.0	3,491.6	173,616	90.5
1947	46,091	1.0054	5,495,000	5,524,673	60.3	119,220.0	119,864	62.5
1948	46,542	0.9530	6,454,000	6,150,662	67.1	138,670.0	132,153	68.9
1949	46,899	1.0035	6,963,000	6,987,371	76.3	148,468.0	148,988	77.7
1950	47,262	1.0592	7,711,000	8,167,491	89.1	163,154.0	172,813	90.1
1951	47,538	0.9294	8,836,000	8,212,178	89.6	185,872.0	172,750	90.1
1952	47,774	0.9843	9,303,000	9,156,943	100.0	194,729.0	191,672	100.0
1953	48,091	0.9880	10,193,000	10,070,684	109.9	211,952.0	209,409	109.2
1954	48,434	0.9970	10,848,000	10,815,456	118.1	223,975.0	223,303	116.5
1955	48,730	0.9880	11,871,000	11,728,548	128.0	243,608.0	240,684	125.5
1956	48,974	0.9715	12,779,000	12,414,798	135.5	260,934.0	253,498	132.2
1957	49,214	0.9620	13,728,000	13,206,336	144.2	278,945.0	268,345	140.4
1958	49,530	0.9793	14,718,000	14,413,337	157.3	297,153.0	291,002	151.8
1959	49,901	1.0092	15,777,000	15,922,148	174.6	316,166.0	319,075	166.4
1960	50,232	1.0000	17,197,000	17,197,000	187.7	342,351.0	342,351	178.5
1961	50,623	0.9979	18,905,000	18,865,300	202.6	373,447.0	373,662	191.2

*Based on wholesale prices (1960 =1).

Sources: ISTAT, *Sommario di statistiche storiche italiane* 216; ISTAT, *Il valore della lira nei primi 100 anni dell'unità d'Italia*; ISTAT, *Indagine statistica sullo sviluppo del reddito nazionale dell'Italia dal 1861 al 1956*; SVIMEZ, *Un secolo di statistiche italiane nord e sud*, Chapter XI; *Relazione generale sulla situazione economica del paese.*

years has been continuously increasing, it is clear that, in absolute figures, the increase in income appears even greater.

Table 3 shows the total of state and local tax receipts and the fiscal burden, expressed as a relation between tax receipts and national income. The state and local tax receipts composed about 9.5% of the national income in 1863; in 1871, about 12.5%; at the turn of the century, almost 16%; shortly before the First World War, about 15%; and in 1921, about 17%. In 1926, the terminal year of De Stefani's "financial restoration," it was about 16%, rising to 21.9% in 1931, a year of economic crisis. In 1939, it was 20%. In the immediate postwar years, it underwent a difficult phase of recovery: in 1949, the level of receipts was still 17.5% of national income, decidedly modest as compared with past normal levels. The level of 20%, previously attained in 1939, was reached in 1953. There has been no great departure from this percentage in subsequent years, but there has been a slow, regular increase to about 23.8% in 1961.

Another view of the fiscal burden may be obtained by considering the average amount of taxes paid by each inhabitant, that is, the total amount of income which, in terms of constant money, he must sacrifice to the fisc. Table 3 also shows the per capita receipts of national and local taxes, in 1960 lire.

The fiscal expansion seems, at least until now, to have operated positively in the economic system, given that the years of the greatest expansion in the national income have also been those of the greatest expansion in public finance. Above all in the last period, which has been the most dynamic of the Italian economy, there has been the greatest increase in per capita taxes.

The forward drive of the Italian economy in the 15-year period 1946-1961 is comparable to the phases of explosive growth of other western and eastern economic systems, which have marked their passage from backwardness to development; in the preceding 90 years, there were never such striking phases of economic development in Italy. It took 80 years of national life to double the national income per inhabitant. Five years, from 1946 to 1951, were enough in which to reconstitute the income halved by the war, and another 10 years to double the income of 1951.

b.   DEFICIT. Current public expenditures are covered by current receipts or by the public debt; and since by far the larger part of the current receipts consists of taxes, by adding the fiscal burden to the deficit, the annual increase in the public debt, one comes very close to the aggregate level of the current public expenditure.

Figures on the surplus or deficit are given in Table 4. The deficit is today a negligible percentage of the national income. In 1962, the deficit was about 1.3% of national income, and the percentage has not varied

Table 3: *Tax Receipts of the National and Local Governments*

Year	Tax Receipts (Millions of Lire) Current Lire	Tax Receipts (Millions of Lire) 1960 Lire	Index of Variation (1952 = 100)	Percent of National Income	Per Capita Tax Receipts (1960 Lire)	Index of Variation (1952 = 100)
1863	565	162,601		9.510%	7,182	
1871	1,072	294,832		12.480	10,902	
1881	1,445	415,730		15.530	14,358	
1891	1,724	507,357		15.520	16,370	
1901	1,930	576,236		15.720	17,379	
1911	2,691	709,032		14.970	19,739	
1921	15,314	710,661		17.230	18,473	
1923	18,016	831,804		17.040	21,244	
1926	23,348	937,440		15.830	23,254	
1931	22,252	1,476,100		21.920	35,283	87.0
1938	27,827	1,443,389	79.7	19.899	32,911	92.0
1939	31,036	1,543,215	85.2	20.046	34,803	69.1
1949	1,222,518	1,226,797	67.8	17.557	26,163	83.2
1950	1,404,171	1,487,298	82.2	18.210	31,469	84.3
1951	1,682,532	1,517,275	83.8	18.476	31,910	100.0
1952	1,839,132	1,810,257	100.0	19.769	37,838	111.9
1953	2,060,594	2,035,866	112.5	20.216	42,326	126.7
1954	2,328,973	2,321,986	128.3	21.469	47,938	139.1
1955	2,594,981	2,563,841	141.6	21.860	52,621	151.3
1956	2,886,458	2,804,194	154.9	22.588	57,250	163.0
1957	3,155,633	3,035,719	167.7	22.987	61,687	176.9
1958	3,385,490	3,315,411	183.1	23.002	66,936	196.9
1959	3,685,141	3,719,044	205.4	23.358	74,513	212.9
1960	4,047,538	4,047,538	223.6	23.536	80,555	234.8
1961	4,506,684	4,497,220	248.4	23.839	88,835	

Sources: See note 104 *supra.*

Table 4: *Surplus or Deficit of the Budget of the State*

Fiscal Year	Global Surplus (+) or Deficit (−)°	Current Surplus (+) or Deficit (−)° — Current Lire	Current Surplus (+) or Deficit (−)° — 1960 Lire	Current Surplus or Deficit as Percentage of National Income	Current Per Capita Surplus (+) or Deficit (−) (1960 Lire)
1863	+ 102	− 382	− 110,016	6.439%	− 4,923
1871	+ 43	− 47	− 12,925	0.547	− 478
1881	+ 51	+ 53	+ 15,264	0.570	+ 527
1890-1891	+ 46	− 77	− 22,099	0.693	− 731
1900-1901	+ 41	+ 69	+ 20,493	0.562	+ 621
1910-1911	+ 79	+ 11	+ 3,135	0.061	+ 80
1920-1921	− 14,634	− 17,409	− 731,178	19.583	− 21,000
1922-1923	− 395	− 3,029	− 138,414	2.832	− 3,531
1925-1926	+ 2,536	+ 468	+ 19,188	0.317	+ 466
1930-1931	+ 466	− 504	− 29,232	0.497	− 799
1937-1938	− 9,534	− 11,174	− 614,570	7.992	− 13,218
1938-1939	− 12,035	− 12,277	− 638,404	7.931	− 13,769
1948-1949	− 553,416	− 496,512	− 473,176	7.131	− 10,624
1949-1950	− 177,025	− 297,044	− 314,629	3.852	− 6,657
1950-1951	− 220,897	− 173,530	− 181,206	1.964	− 3,393
1951-1952	+ 360,793	+ 391,636	+ 363,830	4.210	+ 8,069
1952-1953	− 320,099	− 505,712	− 497,620	4.961	− 10,389
1953-1954	− 171,234	− 324,931	− 321,031	2.995	− 6,688
1954-1955	− 136,034	− 308,292	− 307,367	2.597	− 6,251
1955-1956	− 137,846	− 293,602	− 290,078	2.298	− 5,825
1956-1957	− 86,092	− 147,946	− 143,655	1.078	− 2,893
1957-1958	− 263,442	− 224,634	− 216,098	1.526	− 4,441
1958-1959	− 222,651	− 124,134	− 121,527	0.787	− 2,511
1959-1960	− 6,984	− 320,802	− 320,802	1.865	− 6,385
1960-1961	− 573,075	− 294,848	− 294,848	1.560	− 5,814
1961-1962	− 735,224	− 285,167	− 276,313	1.335	− 5,458

°Millions of lire.

Sources: See note 104 *supra.*

significantly in the last decade. Added together, the tax receipts of the state and the local entities and the deficit make up a total of about 25% of the national income.

In the past, there have been wide oscillations in the amount of the deficit. Some budgets were closed with heavy deficits, especially in the first period after the unification—in 1863, for example, the deficit was 6.4% of national income. Since then, however, the deficits have gradually diminished. At present, percentages are comparable to past normal percentages.

c. SOCIAL INSURANCES. The compulsory contributions to social insurance may be added to the fiscal burden of the state and local entities and to the deficit (1/2.4, 1/6.4). These contributions were instituted in the last century, but their accounting has been inadequate until recently. It is possible, however, with some reliability, to fit this element into the picture of the financial economics of the last decade. In 1960 lire, the tax burden per inhabitant inclusive of social insurances has risen from L. 51,734 in 1952 to L. 132,138 in 1961. As a percentage of income, it has passed in those years from 27% to 35.4%. Table 5 shows total receipts from national and local taxes and social insurance contributions, as a percentage of national income and per inhabitant.

Table 5: *Receipts of National and Local Taxes and Social Insurances*

Year	Receipts (Millions of Lire) Current Lire	1960 Lire	Index of Variation (1952 = 100)	Percent of National Income	Per Capita Receipts (1960 Lire)	Index of Variation (1952 = 100)
1949	1,639,649	1,645,378	66.5	23.547%	35,087	67.8
1950	1,848,574	1,958,010	79.1	23.970	41,423	80.1
1951	2,156,490	2,004,242	81.0	24.406	42,154	81.5
1952	2,513,939	2,474,470	100.0	27.019	51,734	100.0
1953	2,874,860	2,840,361	114.8	28.206	59,058	114.2
1954	3,575,142	3,265,316	132.0	30.189	67,410	130.3
1955	3,680,817	3,636,747	147.0	31.010	74,644	144.3
1956	4,137,014	4,019,109	162.4	32.278	82,067	158.6
1957	4,442,578	4,373,760	176.8	32.357	86,831	167.8
1958	4,847,737	4,747,389	191.9	32.942	95,862	185.3
1959	5,301,453	5,350,226	216.2	33.598	107,186	207.2
1960	6,170,257	6,170,257	249.4	35.876	122,801	237.4
1961	6,703,210	6,689,133	270.3	35.459	132,138	255.4

Sources: See note 104 *supra*.

1/6.2   Burden of Total National Taxes

Table 6 shows the amount and growth of the burden of the national taxes. The tax receipts of the state per inhabitant have increased, from 1863 to the present, about 14 times, and from 1871, 9.1 times. In the last decade, they have increased almost two and one half times. In the past, they doubled twice: once in the decade after unification, and again in the period between 1920 and 1930. As a percentage of national income, they have gone from about 10% at the end of the first decade of the Kingdom of Italy to the present 21%.

Table 6: *Tax Receipts of the National Government*

Year	Receipts (Millions of Lire)		Index of Variation (1952 = 100)	Percent of National Income	Per Capita Receipts (1960 Lire)	Index of Variation (1952 = 100)
	Current Lire	1960 Lire				
1863	433	124,590		7.29%	5,575	
1871	843	231,850		9.82	8,574	
1881	1,104	317,647		11.87	10,971	
1891	1,309	385,224		11.78	12,427	
1901	1,474	440,085		12.01	13,273	
1911	1,968	518,531		10.95	14,435	
1921	13,013	603,881		14.64	15,697	
1923	15,022	695,088		14.24	17,754	
1926	19,194	770,664		13.01	19,116	
1931	17,650	1,170,796		17.39	27,986	
1938	22,501	1,167,129	75.4	16.09	26,611	82.1
1939	25,423	1,264,118	81.7	16.42	28,508	88.0
1947	526,016	528,853	34.1	9.57	11,471	35.3
1948	842,078	802,500	51.8	13.05	17,246	53.2
1949	1,041,504	1,045,149	67.5	14.96	22,289	68.7
1950	1,197,539	1,268,433	81.9	15.53	26,838	82.8
1951	1,395,513	1,296,990	83.7	15.79	27,277	84.1
1952	1,572,845	1,548,151	100.0	16.91	32,412	100.0
1953	1,756,627	1,735,547	112.1	17.23	36,081	111.3
1954	1,975,542	1,969,615	127.2	18.21	40,663	125.4
1955	2,215,981	2,189,389	141.4	18.67	44,936	138.6
1956	2,483,359	2,412,583	155.8	19.43	49,255	151.9
1957	2,712,542	2,609,465	168.5	19.76	53,025	163.5
1958	2,914,214	2,853,890	184.3	19.80	57,618	177.7
1959	3,182,984	3,212,267	207.4	20.17	64,357	198.5
1960	3,521,376	3,521,376	227.4	20.47	70,079	216.2
1961	3,972,016	3,963,675	256.0	21.01	78,296	241.6

Sources: See note 104 *supra*.

1/6.3 Burden of Total Local Taxes

The amount of the tax receipts of the local entities since 1863 is presented in Table 7. As a percentage of national income, the level of these receipts has remained roughly stationary as compared with the national tax receipts. As in 1871, tax receipts are now between 2.6% and 3% of the national income.

There have been certain variations, however. In 1863, the local tax receipts were around 2.2% of income. In 1871, they had risen to 2.6%.

Table 7: *Tax Receipts of the Local Governments*

Year	Receipts (Millions of Lire)		Index of Variation (1952=100)	Percent of National Income	Per Capita Receipts (1960 Lire)	Index of Variation (1952=100)
	Current Lire	1960 Lire				
1863	132	38,011		2.225%	1,607	
1871	229	62,982		2.666	2,328	
1881	341	98,083		3.665	3,387	
1891	415	122,166		3.737	3,943	
1901	456	136,151		3.717	4,106	
1911	723	190,501		4.023	5,304	
1921	2,301	106,780		2.589	2,776	
1923	2,994	136,716		2.799	3,490	
1926	4,154	166,786		2.817	4,138	
1931	4,602	305,304		4.535	7,297	
1938	5,326	276,260	105.4	3.809	6,300	114.8
1939	5,613	279,097	106.5	3.626	6,295	114.7
1949	181,014	181,648	69.3	2.600	3,874	70.6
1950	206,632	218,865	83.5	2.680	4,631	84.4
1951	237,019	220,285	84.0	2.682	4,633	84.5
1952	266,287	262,106	100.0	2.862	5,486	100.0
1953	303,967	300,319	114.6	2.982	6,245	113.8
1954	353,431	352,371	134.4	3.258	7,275	132.6
1955	379,000	374,452	142.9	3.193	7,685	140.1
1956	403,099	391,611	149.4	3.154	7,995	145.7
1957	443,091	426,254	162.6	3.228	8,662	157.9
1958	471,276	461,521	176.1	3.202	9,318	169.8
1959	502,157	506,777	193.4	3.183	10,156	185.1
1960	526,162	526,162	200.7	3.060	10,476	191.0
1961	534,668	533,545	203.6	2.828	10,539	192.1

Sources: See note 104 *supra.*

After a decade, they had risen again to 3.665%. After a rise to about 4% in 1911, there followed a phase of decline, and, on the eve of the "march on Rome," the percentage had returned to the level of 1871. In 1931, it registered the highest point of the century—4.535%; but in 1939, it returned to the level of 1881. In 1952, the percentage was 2.86%, the same as at the time of addition of Rome to Italy. But there then followed a phase of slow increase until 1958, and thence a phase of equally gradual decline. Thus, in 1961, the level was about that of 1952.

At the beginning of the Kingdom of Italy, the tax receipts of the local entities represented a little less than one third of the aggregate total of the state receipts (Tables 6 and 7). In 1871, they were already only a little less than one fifth. In 1891, they were a little over one third. In 1921, they had returned to one fifth. In 1939, they were considerably less than one fifth. Today, the tax receipts of the local entities amount to about one seventh of the tax receipts of the state.

In lire of constant purchasing power per inhabitant, the receipts of the local entities have naturally undergone a considerable growth, given the imposing increase of the national income. They have risen from about L. 1,600 in the first period of unification to L. 10,539 in 1961.

It should be added, to avoid misunderstanding regarding the growth of the finance of the local entities, that the available finances of those entities are not exhausted by their tax receipts and that to their taxes and their surtaxes on state taxes must be added the tax receipts of the state which the state passes to the local entities (1/5.5e). These have increased in the last period, both as a percentage of income and per capita, and this increase lessens the significance of the constancy of the amount of the local tax receipts with respect to national income. The fiscal autonomy of these entities has diminished, however, both because the receipts which do not belong to the entities increased proportionally and because the total of these receipts and those belonging to the entities has not sufficed to meet the development of expenditures, causing an increase in the indebtedness of the local entities.

In conclusion, two characteristics in the evolution of the local fiscal structures can be pointed out: on the one hand, the diminished comparative weight of local finance, and, on the other, the diminished comparative weight of local tax autonomy in the face of the great expansion of the tax receipts of the state.

1/6.4 Burden of Compulsory Social Insurances

An important new fact of the last period is the development of the compulsory social insurances (1/2.4, 1/6.1c); the expansion of the social insurances since their inception is presented in Table 8. In 1962, they amounted to 12.29% of national income. In 1952, with income much lower

Table 8: *Social Insurance Contributions*

Year	Contributions (Millions of Lire)		Index of Variation (1952=100)	Percent of National Income	Per Capita Contributions (1960 Lire)	Index of Variation (1952=100)
	Current Lire	1960 Lire				
1945	25,810	64,997	9.8	2.16%	1,416	10.2
1946	89,418	160,827	24.2	3.23	3,486	25.1
1947	224,246	225,457	33.9	4.08	4,890	35.2
1948	332,385	316,763	47.7	5.15	6,806	49.0
1949	417,121	418,581	63.0	5.99	8,924	64.2
1950	444,403	470,712	70.9	5.76	9,954	71.6
1951	523,958	486,967	73.9	5.93	10,244	73.7
1952	674,807	664,213	100.0	7.25	13,896	100.0
1953	814,266	804,495	121.1	7.99	16,732	120.4
1954	946,169	943,330	142.0	8.72	19,472	140.1
1955	1,085,836	1,072,806	161.5	9.15	22,023	158.5
1956	1,250,556	1,214,915	182.9	9.79	24,817	178.6
1957	1,286,945	1,238,041	186.4	9.37	25,144	180.9
1958	1,462,247	1,431,978	215.6	9.94	28,926	208.2
1959	1,616,312	1,631,182	245.6	10.24	32,673	235.1
1960	2,122,719	2,122,719	319.6	12.34	42,246	304.0
1961	2,196,526	2,191,913	330.0	11.62	43,303	311.6
1962	2,625,098	2,542,670	382.8	12.29		

Source: *Relazione generale sulla situazione economica del paese.*

than at present, they already composed 7% of national income; with the expansion of income, there has also been a percentage expansion of social security, and in lire per inhabitant the expansion is still greater. By now, the social insurances are in second position in the field of tax levies, clearly displacing the taxes of the local entities. In 1952, they were, in 1960 lire, L. 13,896 per inhabitant, and, in 1961, L. 43,303 per inhabitant, having tripled in a decade. No other group of fiscal levies has had a similar increase in this or in any other period. Table 9 shows social insurance receipts by source for 1955 and 1959.

The factors which have determined the imposing growth of the social insurances are essentially three. The first is the continuous increase in the number of persons employed in industrial activities which, because of their size, are assessed by social security and required to submit to the levy of the insurances. These levies theoretically ought to concern also even the small entrepreneurs of the industries covered; but often in practice, for the weakest and smallest enterprises and for enterprises situated in certain underdeveloped zones, there have been many gaps in the assessments, especially with regard to certain types of insurance. With the development of industrialization, this group of more modest activities is itself being industrialized, and its employees, like the workers in larger industries, become increasingly subject to the social insurances.

The second factor is of institutional character and concerns changes in the financial system. A continuous enlargement of the number of beneficiaries has taken place; today, the benefits are extended even to independent workers in agriculture, and, in growing numbers, those employed in the tertiary sector. The impetus to the inclusion of direct cultivators and artisans has been given by the fact that, to the financing derived from compulsory contributions to the social insurances, there have from the beginning been added state donations and supplements derived from the general tax system.

Naturally, the increase in wages per employee has itself brought about a growth in the volume of the receipts of the social insurances through the compulsory contributions.

1/6.5 The Public Debt

A fourth great element of public receipts is the public debt, whose history is shown in Table 10. At the beginning of the Kingdom of Italy, the public debt constituted an enormous burden on national income: in 1880, the total outstanding debt was about 105% of the national income. The state had to pay interest on it, at about 5% of the debt and therefore of the national income. Thus, half of the tax receipts of the state in that epoch went to the payment of interest on the debt—a situation not very reassuring, either for the state, which had so many needs to meet by

Table 9: *Social Insurance Receipts* by Source, 1955 and 1959*

(Millions of Current Lire)

Source	1955 Amount	Percent	1959 Amount	Percent
Insured persons	141,815	10.30%	282,784	13.3%
Employers	1,060,585	77.05	1,562,686	73.5
State and public entities	106,813	7.70	167,199	7.5
Investment income and other receipts	67,266	4.80	121,631	5.7
Total	1,376,479		2,134,300	

*Insurance for sickness, maternity, old age, invalidism, and the like; professional accidents and illnesses; unemployment; family allowances.
Source: EEC, *Relazione sulla evoluzione della situazione sociale nella Comunità nel 1960.*

Table 10: *Public Debt*

Year	Public Debt (Millions of Lire)		Index of Variation (1952=100)	Percent of National Income	Per Capita Public Debt (1960 Lire)	Index of Variation (1952=100)
	Current Lire	1960 Lire				
1863	3,945.12	1,136,045		66.505%	49,840	
1871	8,372.30	2,302,639		97.461	85,058	
1881	9,825.60	2,826,160		105.505	97,264	
1890-1891	12,289.00	3,617,590		110.656	116,570	
1900-1901	12,993.00	3,879,407		105.905	116,756	
1910-1911	12,605.00	3,321,252		70.132	92,286	
1920-1921	84,215.00	3,908,081		94.737	101,574	
1922-1923	94,113.00	4,297,520		87.060	108,409	
1925-1926	89,209.00	3,581,813		60.497	88,749	
1930-1931	91,422.00	6,065,082		90.106	144,925	
1937-1938	135,418.00	7,024,145	230.6	96.850	159,963	251.8
1938-1939	143,672.00	7,143,860	234.6	92.812	161,058	253.5
1948-1949	2,138,430.00	2,145,915	70.5	30.768	45,755	72.0
1949-1950	2,548,640.00	2,699,519	88.6	33.125	57,106	89.9
1950-1951	2,801,520.00	2,603,733	85.5	31.741	54,722	86.1
1951-1952	3,094,260.00	3,045,680	100.0	33.354	63,528	100.0
1952-1953	3,433,280.00	3,392,081	111.4	33.842	70,191	110.5
1953-1954	3,858,340.00	3,846,765	126.3	35.731	78,876	124.2
1954-1955	4,200,990.00	4,150,578	136.3	35.598	84,387	132.8
1955-1956	4,538,302.00	4,408,960	144.8	35.904	88,923	140.0
1956-1957	4,789,120.00	4,607,133	151.3	35.388	92,236	145.2
1957-1958	5,094,750.00	4,989,289	163.8	35.313	99,217	156.2
1958-1959	5,347,630.00	5,396,828	177.2	35.057	106,429	167.5
1959-1960	5,813,930.00	5,813,930	190.9	33.936	113,662	179.9
1960-1961	5,900,500.00	5,888,109	193.3	31.211	116,313	183.1

Sources: Corbino, *Annali dell'economia italiana* (vols. 1-5); Répaci, *La finanza italiana nel ventennio 1913-1932; Relazione generale sulla situazione economica del paese.*

expenditure, or for the holders of the public debt, in Italy and abroad, who could fear for the solvency of the state. Since certain expenditures are rigid, a drop in the yield of the taxes or the failure to create new debt could make it difficult for the state to pay interest and reimburse the loans falling due. Today, the situation is different; in 1961, the public debt was just over 30% of the national income for the year. Only a bare 2% of the national income must be set aside for the payment of interest on the public debt, but the state, by itself, levies 20% of the national income. This means that only one tenth of the state tax receipts today go to the payment of interest on the public debt. It can be added that it is of course easier to sustain this debt with the present high income per inhabitant, which permits a more abundant flow of savings invested in public or private securities.

The great improvement in the debt situation in Italy occurred essentially since the Second World War. In the preceding 80 years, the heavy burden of the public debt was always one of the characteristics of Italian finance. In the most recent decrease, the influence of the level of the deficit, remaining constant or slightly progressing in absolute volume in current lire during a period of a much more dynamic increase in the national income, has been fundamental. The improved debt situation which existed at the beginning of this decade in contrast to the prewar situation is explained in an entirely different way. In 1950, Italy found itself with a public debt reduced to less than one half of the prewar public debt, not as a result of an expansion of real income or of repayment of the public debt, but chiefly through the annulment of the old public debt in real terms by the enormous monetary devaluation. By 1950, the lira had about one fiftieth of its worth in 1939. This means that a public debt of 100 in 1939 was reduced to 2 in 1950.

1/6.6 Classification of Taxes

In the Italian system, taxes levied on income or on wealth are usually called "direct taxes." Thus, all other taxes are "indirect taxes." Included among the direct taxes are the national objective taxes on income (landowning, buildings, movable wealth, agrarian income, and the related surtaxes and additionals) (2/2); the communal family tax and the national complementary progressive tax on income, which are personal taxes on income (2/3); the national tax on the capital assets and profits of corporations (2/4, 3/2); the recently instituted communal taxes on the increase in value of building land (3/7.3); an ordinary tax on wealth, not now in effect, but whose reintroduction is advocated in several circles; and the various extraordinary taxes on wealth of the past; which, despite extended installments, are now almost completely exhausted (3/1).

Pressing the classification to its limits, it could be said that the social insurances should be distinguished into two groups. The contribution

falling on the employer can be classified as an indirect tax in that it does
not apply to income or wealth as such, but to total wages paid by
the employer. The gross payroll obviously is not the same thing as the
income of the enterprise; it is not an income, but an expense of production. The contribution paid by the worker (the total of workers'
contributions is very small in comparison with the total of compulsory
contributions), however, should be considered a direct tax since it is
measured on the income of the worker, that is, on his wages. But it is
clear that, in Italy, the problems of the compulsory social insurances are
separate from the problems of the rest of the tax system—first, because they
are connected, partly on an actuarial basis, with particular benefits of
certain public expenditures, the expenditures of the social insurances
themselves; secondly, because they are administered by particular agencies, the institutions for the social insurances, and do not flow directly
into the budget of the state; and finally, because their structure is conditioned by a number of elements partly of a historical character and partly
connected with the type of entity and the purpose. For these reasons,
the contributions to the social insurances can be classified separately,
rather than among the direct taxes or the indirect taxes.

Both the estate tax (3/5), which is considered as affecting the deceased
person and thus figures as a tax on the total wealth of the deceased, and
the inheritance tax (3/4), which is considered as bearing on the heirs
and legatees and which, from the economic point of view, bears on net
income or capital gains, should be included among the direct taxes in a
classification of an economic and political character. In the analyses of
this chapter, these taxes will therefore be considered with the direct
taxes, even though in the Italian fiscal system, from the juridical and
administrative point of view, the two succession taxes are classified among
the taxes on transfers, together with the registration fees and taxes
(15/1.1), from which they derive (3/4.1).

1/6.7   Yields of National Direct Taxes

a. IN GENERAL. The burden of the national direct taxes on the national
income has varied, as may be seen in Table 11. In 1871, the direct taxes
totaled 4% of national income. Considering that the aggregate fiscal
burden at that time was 9.8%, this means that the direct taxes constituted
about 40% of the national tax burden. In 1961, they were 5.15% of the
income, and thus nearly the same share of the national income as 90
years ago. Since the fiscal burden of the national taxes today is a little
more than double that of 1870, it is clear that the direct taxes have lost
much ground as a percentage of total national tax receipts. In other
words, the direct taxes have simply followed the growth of the national
income, while the growth of the national tax system in the aggregate has

Table 11: *Receipts of National Direct Taxes*

Year	Receipts (Millions of Lire)		Index of Variation (1952 =100)	Percent of National Income	Percent of Total National Tax Receipts	Per Capita Receipts (1960 Lire)	Index of Variation (1952=100)
	Current Lire	1960 Lire					
1863	147	42,233		2.47%	33.90%	1,889	
1871	343	94,335		4.00	40.69	3,492	
1881	408	117,455		4.39	36.98	4,057	
1891	465	136,770		4.18	35.50	4,410	
1901	530	158,229		4.32	35.95	4,773	
1911	563	148,332		3.13	28.61	4,129	
1921	4,863	225,672		5.47	37.37	5,866	
1923	5,407	246,902		5.06	35.52	6,310	
1926	6,167	247,610		4.18	32.13	6,140	
1931	5,086	337,413		5.01	28.82	8,063	
1938	6,648	344,832	99.5	4.75	29.55	7,856	108.3
1939	7,360	365,964	105.6	4.75	28.96	8,247	113.6
1947	126,966	127,652	36.8	2.31	24.14	2,769	38.2
1948	198,265	188,947	54.5	3.07	23.54	4,060	55.9
1949	225,445	226,234	65.3	3.24	21.65	4,821	66.4
1950	244,988	259,491	74.9	3.18	20.46	5,491	75.7
1951	302,414	281,064	81.1	3.42	21.67	5,911	81.5
1952	352,202	246,672	100.0	3.79	22.39	7,257	100.0
1953	384,589	379,974	109.6	3.77	21.89	7,898	108.8
1954	427,922	426,638	123.1	3.94	21.66	8,808	121.4
1955	480,812	475,042	137.0	4.05	21.70	9,748	134.3
1956	567,229	551,063	159.0	4.44	22.84	11,256	155.1
1957	620,381	596,806	172.2	4.52	22.87	12,129	167.1
1958	692,002	677,678	195.5	4.70	23.75	13,677	188.5
1959	759,656	766,644	221.1	4.81	23.87	15,347	211.5
1960	833,149	833,149	240.3	4.84	23.66	16,570	228.3
1961	973,404	971,360	280.2	5.15	24.51	19,192	264.5

Sources: See note 104 *supra.*

been much higher than that of national income.

Between 1870 and 1961, the national direct tax burden varied considerably. Before the beginning of this century, the share of the direct taxes remained around 4% of income. However, in the first decade of the 1900's, which was among the most prosperous of the national economic life, the growth of the direct taxes was not equal to that of income: in 1911, they had fallen to about 3% of the national income. During the turbulent years of the period immediately preceding the accession of the fascists to power, the share of the direct taxes was restored to its former level: in 1921, they reached 5.47% of national income, the maximum point registered in the 100 years of Italian unity. In 1926, after the first fascist period of finance, the direct taxes were 4.18% of national income. In 1931, they were again 5.01%. In 1939, they had fallen back to 4.75% of national income. Their structural deterioration began to be evident; they suffered severely because of the war, more than did the other elements of the tax system.

In the postwar period, the national direct taxes were less important than in the preceding 80 years. In fact, in 1950, the percentage was 3.18%, and, in 1951, it was 3.42%, less than in 1901 and slightly more than in 1863. Then began the phase of "tax equalization" (*perequazione tributaria*), during which efforts were made to improve the structure and quality of the direct tax system (2/1). By 1961, the percentage which the direct taxes constitute of the national income slowly and irregularly had arrived at 5.15%.

In 1960 lire per inhabitant, absolute values are, of course, considerably greater today than 90 or 100 years ago, when the national income was much smaller: the unchanged percentage means a great expansion, in lire per inhabitant, of over-all purchasing power. The direct taxes per inhabitant in 1960 lire are five times greater today than in 1871. In 1951, the year of the beginning of tax equalization, the value of direct taxes per inhabitant was L. 5,911, only slightly higher than in 1901 (L. 4,773), even though, in the meantime, the national income had increased considerably.

b. CLASSIFICATION OF DIRECT TAXES. The direct taxes are divided into two types: the objective taxes (*imposte reali*), that is, those which apply to income or wealth as such (2/2.1, 2/2.2), and the personal taxes, that is, those which consider income or wealth in relation to the persons who receive it (2/3, 6/1.1a). Until 1923, there existed in the state fiscal system only three objective taxes on income (with the exception of certain extraordinary or transitory taxes): the tax on income from the ownership of agricultural land, the tax on income from the ownership of buildings not devoted to agriculture, and the tax on income from movable wealth (movable capital, enterprises, professional and artisan activities, and work as an employee); there was one personal tax (that on transfers as a result of death).

In 1923, another objective tax was instituted, that on agricultural income, intended to reach income from agricultural enterprises conducted by the landowners themselves (2/2.3). A personal tax on income, the "complementary progressive" tax (2/3), was introduced in 1926. In 1945, a new succession tax was instituted, on the global value of the inheritance as measured on the aggregate of the property of the deceased; it is described in this volume as the "estate tax" (3/5). In the year 1954, a new personal tax on corporations and other collective capital entities was instituted in part on the profits of those entities and in part on their capital assets (the share and bonded capital) (2/4, 3/2). Since national unification, there have been several extraordinary or transitory direct taxes, especially in the periods around the wars. Most of these have been introduced as "extraordinary," with the stated purpose of being employed for a limited period of time; others, although introduced as "ordinary," were not in existence for long, so that in effect they were "transitory." Since a complete list of these taxes would be too long, mention is made here of only a few (1/6.7f, 3/1).

During the First World War, an "extraordinary" complementary tax was imposed on income exceeding L. 10,000 (about L. 4 million in present lire). In the Italian data on tax receipts, the diminishing installments of this tax were grouped with the receipts of the complementary progressive tax on income after the institution of the latter. In 1926, a tax of a permanent character on bachelors was introduced (included in the complementary tax in the statistics in Table 15 at 1/6.7d) for the purpose of encouraging marriages and increasing the population. This tax died with the fall of fascism. Also to be mentioned are the tax on the proceeds from bearer securities issued by companies, which was instituted in 1935 and abrogated in 1946, and the extraordinary progressive tax on income distributed by business companies in excess of 6% of capital plus reserves, introduced in 1936 and abrogated in 1948. The yields of these two taxes were modest.

Of particular importance are the extraordinary or transitory taxes on wealth (1/6.7f), whose imposition, as a result of extended installments, lasted from the first postwar period until 1960. In 1920, in the framework of postwar finance, provision was made for an extraordinary progressive tax on wealth with installments intended to last until 1938. Its yield was considerable. In 1936-1938, to meet the financial burdens of the Ethiopian war, an extraordinary tax on immovable property, an extraordinary tax on the capital of corporations, and an extraordinary tax on industrial and commercial businesses were instituted; their yields were rather small. In 1939, the installments of the 1920 extraordinary tax on wealth having expired, an ordinary proportional tax on wealth was introduced. This was abrogated in 1948, and in its place were introduced two extraordinary proportional taxes on wealth of individuals and of collective entities, to last until 1951 and 1957 respectively, and an extraordinary progressive tax on wealth of individuals with installments to end in 1960. All three of these taxes applied to the values of wealth in 1947. Their yield was considerable. During the two wars and the two postwar periods, there were various minor taxes on war and contingency profits and excess profits, on increases in the values of wealth resulting from the war, and on the compensation of managers and directors of companies. Of insignificant yield was the tax on "regime profits," instituted in the last postwar period to reach profits realized by taking advantage of the fascist regime. Finally, it should be mentioned that an additional to various national and local taxes to meet damages from floods and earthquakes has been instituted (2/2.9); this additional gives rather considerable receipts.

c. OBJECTIVE TAXES ON INCOME. Beneath the stability of the aggregate yields of the direct taxes as a percentage of national income is concealed in reality a profound structural rearrangement. Some direct taxes have lost importance and others have developed *ex novo* or have acquired an importance which they did not have in the beginning. To be noted first of all is the enormous decline in yield of the immovable property taxes, those on income from agricultural ownership and on income from buildings. The yield of the tax on income from agricultural ownership (including, after 1923, the tax on agrarian income) is shown in Table 12. The landowning tax on agricultural income in 1863 was 1.972% of national income and, in 1871, 1.496%. In 1863, its yield was more than three quarters of the total direct tax yield and, in 1871, still more than one third. In 1901, it had been reduced to 0.84% of the national income and, in 1911, to 0.46%. The decline has been continuous. In 1931, the share was about 0.15% and, in 1939, about 0.10% of the national income. By 1961, the tax on income from landowning no longer had much importance among the state taxes; it represented only 0.042% of the national income. The surtaxes imposed by the local entities on income from landowning had more significance, as is shown in Table 32 (1/6.9b); their yield today is about nine times that of the state tax. But even with the addition of the local levies, the taxation of ownership of agricultural land gives a yield which constitutes a very small percentage of national income, about 0.40%. In 1951, the yield of the local taxes was about five times that of the state tax; in all, the yield of the state and local taxes on income from landowning was 0.566% of national income, a great decline as against 1871. It must be noted, however, that, in 1939, the percentage had already fallen below 0.9%.

The importance of the tax on income from buildings has declined similarly, as shown in Table 13. This is somewhat surprising, especially considering that this tax covers also the imputed income of the premises inhabited by the owner himself. The decrease has been caused by the profusion of exemptions for new buildings and by the rent controls on old buildings in effect since the war. The yield of this tax was 0.594% of national income in 1871; at that time, the yield amounted to one third of that of the state tax on agricultural ownership. At the beginning of

Table 12: *Receipts of Tax on Income from Landowning*

Year	Receipts (Millions of Lire) Current Lire	1960 Lire	Index of Variation (1952 = 100)	Percent of National Income	Percent of National Direct Taxes	Per Capita Receipts (1960 Lire)	Index of Variation (1952 = 100)
1863	117°	36,692		1.972%	79.59%	1,508	
1871	128	35,339		1.496	37.45	1,306	
1881	126	36,371		1.359	30.97	1,256	
1891	106	31,336		0.959	22.91	1,012	
1901	103	30,786		0.840	19.45	928	
1911	83	21,819		0.461	14.71	608	
1921	117	5,429		0.131	2.41	140	
1923	118	5,388		0.110	2.18	137	
1926	148	5,942		0.100	2.40	147	
1931	150	9,951		0.148	2.95	238	
1938	150	7,781	92.9	0.107	2.26	177	101.7
1939	150	7,459	89.1	0.097	2.04	168	96.6
1947	5,944	5,976	71.4	0.108	4.68	129	74.1
1948	7,939	7,566	90.3	0.123	4.00	163	93.7
1949	8,160	8,189	97.8	0.117	3.62	174	100.0
1950	8,473	8,975	107.2	0.110	3.46	190	109.2
1951	8,456	7,859	93.8	0.096	2.80	166	95.4
1952	8,509	8,375	100.0	0.091	2.42	174	100.0
1953	8,165	8,067	96.3	0.080	2.12	168	96.6
1954	7,842	7,818	93.3	0.072	1.83	160	92.0
1955	8,024	7,928	94.7	0.068	1.67	164	94.3
1956	8,073	7,843	93.6	0.063	1.42	160	92.0
1957	8,159	7,849	93.7	0.059	1.32	158	90.8
1958	8,180	8,011	95.7	0.056	1.18	163	93.7
1959	8,094	8,168	97.5	0.051	1.07	163	93.7
1960	8,107	8,107	96.8	0.047	0.97	161	92.5
1961	7,948	7,931	94.7	0.042	0.82	156	89.7

°Immovable property tax including also tax on income from buildings.
Sources: See note 104 *supra*.

the century, it had risen to 0.73% and almost equalled in importance the tax on agricultural ownership, which had meanwhile declined. There followed a period of percentage decline in the yield from the tax on buildings, coinciding with urban expansion. At the outbreak of the Second World War, this tax gave only 0.222% of the national income and, in 1951, less than 0.01% of national income. As the rent controls narrowed and the area subject to them was reduced, the percentage increased, but very slowly, and the tax was still only 0.058% of the national income in 1961.

DESCRIPTION OF TAX SYSTEM   98

Table 13: *Receipts of Tax on Income from Buildings*

Year	Receipts (Millions of Lire) Current Lire	Receipts (Millions of Lire) 1960 Lire	Index of Variation (1952=100)	Percent of National Income	Percent of National Direct Taxes	Per Capita Receipts (1960 Lire)	Index of Variation (1952=100)
1871	51	14,024		0.594%	14.86%	519	
1881	63	18,253		0.682	15.54	630	
1891	80	23,609		0.721	17.26	761	
1901	90	26,839		0.732	16.95	809	
1911	102	27,002		0.569	18.20	751	
1921	173	8,028		0.195	3.56	209	
1923	185	8,448		0.173	3.42	216	
1926	301	12,085		0.204	4.88	300	
1931	329	21,826		0.324	6.47	522	
1938	341	17,688	1,338.0	0.244	5.13	403	1,492.6
1939	344	17,105	1,293.9	0.222	4.67	385	1,425.9
1947	334	336	25.4	0.006	0.26	7	25.9
1948	352	335	25.3	0.005	0.18	7	25.9
1949	409	410	31.0	0.006	0.18	9	33.3
1950	551	584	44.2	0.007	0.22	12	44.4
1951	806	749	56.7	0.009	0.27	16	59.3
1952	1,343	1,322	100.0	0.014	0.38	27	100.0
1953	2,369	2,341	177.1	0.023	0.62	49	181.5
1954	3,441	3,431	259.5	0.032	0.80	71	263.0
1955	4,297	4,245	321.1	0.036	0.89	87	322.2
1956	5,281	5,130	388.0	0.041	0.93	105	388.9
1957	6,372	6,130	463.7	0.047	1.03	125	463.0
1958	7,446	7,292	551.6	0.051	1.07	148	548.1
1959	8,652	8,732	660.5	0.055	1.14	175	648.1
1960	9,766	9,766	738.7	0.057	1.17	194	718.5
1961	10,933	10,910	825.3	0.058	1.12	216	800.0

Sources: See note 104 *supra*.

The picture changes appreciably even if the surtaxes of the local entities, shown in Table 32 (1/6.9b), are taken into account. In 1939, the surtaxes of the local entities slightly exceeded the national tax, so that taxes on the ownership of buildings yielded about 0.7% of the national income, nearly as much as the tax on agricultural ownership. In 1951, the buildings taxes yielded barely 0.29% of national income, and 0.257% of national income in 1960, about half that of the tax on agricultural ownership. It should be added, however, that, since 1923, the tax on income from movable wealth on enterprise income, rather than the tax on buildings, has been applied to industrial factories owned by the entrepreneur himself (9/4.2); this explains in part the subsequent decline of the tax on buildings.

The third type of objective tax consists of the so-called "movable wealth taxes," those on income derived from any source other than the ownership of agricultural land or of buildings. Table 14 shows that over the past 100 years, as could have been expected, there has been an increase in these taxes as a percentage of national income. The national movable wealth tax was about 1.63% of national income in 1871 and 1.95% in 1951; today, it is 2.817%. But it is important to notice that the increase in the movable wealth tax has not matched the percentage decline in the agricultural ownership and buildings taxes. Indeed, in 1871, the combined yields of these three objective taxes together—land-owning, buildings, and movable wealth—constituted more than 3.7% of national income. The combined yield was about 3.9% of income in 1901, but fell to 2.72% in 1911, and to 1.82% in 1921. It then increased to 3.99% in 1931; but, in 1939, it had fallen back to 3.11%. In 1951, it just exceeded 2%; and, as a result of the great decline in the yield of the two immovable property taxes, the yield of these three objective taxes was just under 2.92% of national income at the end of 1961.

Modifications in the economic structure have brought about a lightening of the burden on certain sectors in contraction or in difficulties but have not brought about a corresponding aggravation of the burden on other sectors in process of expansion and undergoing a net gain. In conclusion, the system of objective direct taxation has shown slight capacity of adaptation to the growth of the economic system.

d. PERSONAL TAXES ON INCOME. The progressive personal (complementary) tax on income has been in effect since 1925. Table 15 shows the gradual increase in the yield of this tax, which, in the fascist period, amounted to a modest 0.40% to 0.50% of the national income. The structural weaknesses of this tax are thrown into relief by the fact that the percentage of national income which it represented in 1939 was lower than in 1936. Today, the complementary tax yields about the same percentage of income as during the period 1931-1939. There was a considerable decline in the interim: in 1949, it was only 0.318%; in 1954, it was still 0.305%.

The personal tax on income and capital assets of corporations and other collective entities, although of much more recent origin than the complementary tax, has succeeded in a brief space of time in placing itself second in importance, after the tax on income from movable wealth, among the direct taxes (Table 16). In 1954, the year of its institution, it gave a yield of 0.372% of national income, more than the complementary tax. The yield of the corporation tax and the percentage by which it exceeds that of the complementary tax have increased steadily.

e. SUCCESSION TAXES. The taxes on successions and gifts (Table 17) are a very modest source of revenue: 0.265% of national income in 1961.

Table 14: *Receipts of Tax on Income from Movable Wealth*

Year	Receipts (Millions of Lire)		Index of Variation (1952=100)	Percent of National Income	Percent of National Direct Taxes	Per Capita Receipts (1960 Lire)	Index of Variation (1952=100)
	Current Lire	1960 Lire					
1863	14	4,000		0.234%	9.47%	179	
1871	140	38,642		1.636	40.95	1,428	
1881	184	52,798		1.973	44.95	1,823	
1891	234	68,890		2.107	50.37	2,223	
1901	293	87,510		2.389	55.28	2,639	
1911	304	80,226		1.694	54.08	2,233	
1921	1,325	61,488		1.490	27.25	1,598	
1923	2,458	112,241		2.298	45.46	2,866	
1926	3,861	155,022		2.618	62.61	3,846	
1931	3,566	236,574		3.514	70.11	5,655	
1938	3,983	206,599	114.9	2.846	59.91	4,707	125.0
1939	4,330	215,302	119.7	2.794	58.83	4,852	128.9
1947	54,909	55,206	30.7	0.999	43.25	1,198	31.8
1948	89,141	84,951	47.2	1.380	44.96	1,825	48.5
1949	113,932	114,331	63.6	1.637	50.54	2,437	64.7
1950	139,111	147,346	81.9	1.806	56.78	3,118	82.8
1951	172,588	160,403	89.2	1.952	57.07	3,373	89.6
1952	182,711	179,842	100.0	1.962	51.88	3,765	100.0
1953	187,684	185,432	103.1	1.842	48.80	3,855	102.4
1954	217,083	216,432	120.3	2.004	50.73	4,469	118.7
1955	251,590	248,571	138.2	2.120	52.33	5,102	135.5
1956	295,598	287,173	159.7	2.315	52.11	5,864	155.7
1957	335,708	322,951	179.6	2.444	54.11	6,562	174.3
1958	375,021	367,258	204.2	2.545	54.19	7,414	196.9
1959	416,918	420,754	234.0	2.643	54.88	8,430	223.9
1960	464,698	464,698	258.4	2.703	55.78	9,250	245.7
1961	532,660	531,541	295.6	2.817	54.72	10,500	278.9

Sources: See note 104 *supra*.

Table 15: *Receipts of National Personal Taxes on Income of Individuals**

Year	Receipts (Millions of Lire)		Index of Variation (1921 =100)	Index of Variation (1952 =100)	Percent of National Income	Percent of National Direct Taxes	Per Capita Receipts of Complementary Tax**	Index of Variation (1952 =100)
	Current Lire	1960 Lire						
1921	106	4,919	100.0		0.119%	2.18%	128	
1923	173	7,900	160.6		0.162	3.20	202	
1926	284	11,403	231.8		0.193	4.61	283	
1931	435	28,859	586.7		0.429	8.55	690	
1938	649	33,664	684.4	109.3	0.465	6.21	769	119.2
1939	703	34,956	710.6	113.5	0.454	6.21	788	122.1
1947	7,874	7,917	160.9	25.7	0.143	6.20	172	26.7
1948	14,220	13,552	275.5	44.0	0.220	7.17	291	45.1
1949	22,165	22,243	452.2	72.2	0.318	9.83	474	73.5
1950	25,125	26,612	541.0	86.4	0.326	10.26	563	87.3
1951	30,171	28,041	570.0	91.1	0.341	9.98	590	91.4
1952	31,281	30,790	625.9	100.0	0.336	8.88	645	100.0
1953	27,764	27,431	557.6	89.1	0.272	7.22	570	88.4
1954	33,049	32,950	669.8	107.0	0.305	7.72	680	105.4
1955	39,338	38,866	790.1	126.2	0.331	8.18	797	123.6
1956	45,015	43,732	889.0	142.0	0.352	7.94	893	138.5
1957	52,076	50,097	1,018.4	162.7	0.379	8.39	1,019	158.0
1958	61,629	60,353	1,226.9	196.0	0.418	8.90	1,219	189.0
1959	69,051	69,686	1,416.6	226.3	0.438	9.09	1,396	216.4
1960	74,116	74,116	1,506.7	240.7	0.431	8.90	1,475	228.7
1961	84,711	84,533	1,718.5	274.5	0.480	8.70	1,669	258.8

*Including complementary progressive tax on income, former complementary tax on income, former complementary tax on income above L. 10,000, and former tax on bachelors.

**1960 lire.

Sources: See note 104 *supra.*

Table 16: *Receipts of Corporation Tax and Tax on Bonds*

Year	Receipts (Millions of Lire)		Index of Variation (1954=100)	Percent of National Income	Percent of National Direct Taxes	Per Capita Receipts (1960 Lire)	Index of Variation (1954=100)
	Current Lire	1960 Lire					
1954	40,285	40,164	100.0	0.372%	9.41%	829	100.0
1955	48,443	47,862	119.2	0.408	10.08	982	118.5
1956	63,885	62,064	154.5	0.500	11.26	1,267	152.8
1957	80,426	77,370	192.6	0.586	12.96	1,572	189.6
1958	95,423	93,448	232.7	0.648	13.79	1,887	227.6
1959	111,749	112,777	280.8	0.709	14.71	2,260	272.6
1960	128,141	128,141	319.0	0.745	15.38	2,550	307.6
1961	144,362	144,059	358.7	0.763	14.83	2,846	343.3

Sources: See note 104 *supra.*

Table 17: *Receipts of Taxes on Gratuitous Transfers**

Year	Receipts (Millions of Lire)		Index of Variation (1952=100)	Percent of National Income	Percent of National Direct Taxes	Per Capita Receipts (1960 Lire)	Index of Variation (1952=100)
	Current Lire	1960 Lire					
1863	16	4,472		0.262%	10.59%	200	
1871	23	6,359		0.269	6.74	235	
1881	35	10,033		0.375	8.54	347	
1891	44	12,935		0.396	9.46	418	
1901	44	13,161		0.359	8.31	397	
1911	56	14,658		0.310	9.88	409	
1921	226	10,488		0.254	4.65	272	
1923	292	13,334		0.273	5.40	340	
1926	96	3,854		0.065	1.56	95	
1931	137	9,089		0.135	2.69	217	
1938	218	11,308	72.2	0.156	3.28	258	78.7
1939	232	11,536	73.7	0.150	...	260	79.3
1947	4,336	4,359	27.8	0.079	3.42	95	29.0
1948	6,726	6,410	41.0	0.104	3.39	138	42.1
1949	13,705	13,753	87.9	0.197	6.07	293	89.3
1950	15,581	16,503	105.4	0.202	6.36	349	106.4
1951	13,956	12,971	82.9	0.158	4.61	272	82.9
1952	15,903	15,653	100.0	0.171	4.56	328	100.0
1953	19,712	19,475	124.4	0.193	5.13	405	123.5
1954	24,031	23,959	153.1	0.222	5.62	494	150.6
1955	27,083	26,758	170.9	0.228	5.63	549	167.4
1956	31,538	30,639	195.7	0.247	5.56	625	190.6
1957	34,539	33,227	212.3	0.251	5.57	675	205.8
1958	37,750	36,969	236.2	0.256	5.46	746	227.4
1959	41,602	41,985	268.2	0.264	5.48	841	256.4
1960	43,923	43,923	280.6	0.256	5.27	874	266.5
1961	50,264	50,158	320.4	0.265	5.16	990	301.8

*Taxes on inheritance, gifts, and estates, and the *imposta de manomorta* (a tax imposed from 1923 to 1954, in place of the succession and registration taxes, on the income and property of certain charitable and ecclesiastical entities).
Sources: See note 104 *supra*.

The quantitative changes in the yield of this tax reflect changes brought about by successive political regimes. The yield constituted about 0.26% of income in 1863, rose to 0.27% in 1871, and was brought to 0.37% in 1881. In 1891, it constituted about 0.39% and remained at about 0.36% at the beginning of the century, while the development of the new forms of industrial wealth and the reduced importance of agricultural wealth, for which this form of taxation was particularly structured, undermined the tax base. In 1923, the tax yield was about 0.27% of national income. The fascist period marked a distinct decline in the yield; the tax had showed itself in crisis by the second decade of the twentieth century. But the fascist regime preferred to decrease the importance of the tax rather than resolve the crisis. In 1926, the percentage was 0.065%. In 1931, it was 0.135% and, in 1939, 0.15%, of national income. In its last years, the fascist regime adopted a more favorable attitude towards wealth taxation; but by then, because of the war, it was too late for a systematic reform of the taxation of successions.

In 1945, the tax was supplemented by a new tax on the total value of the estate (the "estate" tax). In 1949, the combined yield of the succession taxes was equal to 0.197% of the national income, a very modest figure, but still higher than the percentage in 1931. There ensued a slow rise, but the yield has remained about 0.26% for several years. Although the tax rates are very high and growing in real terms as a result of the intervening devaluation of the lira, especially between 1946 and 1951, the machinery of assessment in use at present has not permitted any substantial increases in the yield of this tax with relation to the national income.

f. WEALTH TAXES. The Italian fiscal system does not contain at present an ordinary general tax on wealth. But as a result of the extraordinary taxes on wealth with extended installments, and the ordinary tax on wealth in effect from 1939 to 1947, some form of general taxation of wealth has always been in operation during the last 40 years. Statistics on these taxes are given in Table 18.

In 1939, the ordinary tax on wealth furnished a yield of about 0.9% of national income—about twice that of the complementary tax. In 1950, the extraordinary tax yielded as much as the complementary tax: as a percentage of income, slightly less than one half of the figure for 1939. There followed a period of expansion in the yield of taxes on wealth, as a result of the assessment efforts of the tax offices (legally, the taxes were due on wealth possessed at a certain date; the base year for the postwar taxes was 1947). In 1953, the year of their maximum yield, the taxes on wealth reached almost 1% of national income, nearly three and one half times the complementary tax—partly because of a temporary decline of the latter as a percentage of income. After that, however, as

Table 18: *Receipts of Transitory and Extraordinary Direct Taxes on Wealth*

Year	Receipts (Millions of Lire)		Index of Variation (1921 = 100)	Index of Variation (1952 = 100)	Percent of National Income	Percent of National Direct Taxes	Per Capita Receipts (1960 Lire)	Index of Variation (1921 = 100)	Index of Variation (1952 = 100)
	Current Lire	1960 Lire							
1921	2,916	135,320	100.0		3.280%	59.96%	3,517	100.0	
1923	2,181	99,591	73.6		2.039	40.34	2,543	72.3	
1926	1,477	59,304	43.8		1.002	28.95	1,472	41.9	
1931	469	31,114	23.1		0.462	9.22	744	21.2	
1938	1,166	60,481	44.7	70.0	0.834	17.54	1,369	39.2	76.2
1939	1,403	69,762	51.6	80.7	0.906	19.06	1,572	44.7	86.9
1947	47,992	48,251	35.7	55.8	0.873	37.80	1,047	29.8	57.9
1948	70,271	66,968	49.5	77.5	1.089	35.44	1,439	40.9	79.5
1949	54,311	54,501	40.3	63.1	0.780	24.09	1,161	33.0	64.2
1950	41,008	43,436	32.1	50.3	0.532	16.74	919	26.1	50.8
1951	55,235	51,335	37.9	59.4	0.625	18.26	1,079	30.7	59.6
1952	87,795	86,417	63.9	100.0	0.945	24.93	1,809	51.4	100.0
1953	101,857	100,635	74.4	116.5	0.999	26.48	2,091	59.5	115.6
1954	74,946	74,721	55.2	86.5	0.691	17.51	1,542	43.8	85.2
1955	53,352	52,712	39.0	61.0	0.449	11.10	1,082	30.8	59.8
1956	52,863	51,356	38.0	59.4	0.414	9.32	1,049	29.8	58.0
1957	45,771	44,032	32.5	51.0	0.333	7.38	894	25.4	49.4
1958	37,050	36,283	26.8	42.0	0.252	5.35	730	20.8	40.4
1959	28,411	28,672	21.2	33.2	0.180	3.87	575	16.3	31.8
1960	23,088	23,088	17.1	26.7	0.134	2.77	459	13.1	25.4
1961	19,323	19,282	14.2	22.3	0.102	1.99	381	10.8	21.1

Sources: See note 104 *supra*.

was inevitable, they declined sharply, even in absolute figures. In 1961, their yield was already reduced to below one quarter that of the complementary tax—about 0.1% of national income. In a short time, with the exhaustion of the installments still due, their extinction will be complete.

1/6.8 Yields of National Indirect Taxes

a. IN GENERAL. There are several groups of national indirect taxes. Around the time of the First World War, a general tax on exchanges of goods was instituted; its modern successor is the general tax on receipts, or IGE (4/2, 14/). There is a group of taxes on transfers and transactions, almost all of which existed, in different forms, in the pre-unification states: the registration tax (4/3.2, 15/), stamp tax (4/4.2), fees for governmental concessions (4/7), and substitute taxes for stamp and registration (4/3.1). Also classified as indirect taxes are those on particular goods and economic activities, such as transportation (4/4.4), automobiles (4/5.5), advertising (4/5.3), shows (4/5.4), and playing cards (4/5.2a). In addition, there are border duties (4/5.8), two consumption taxes levied at the border on coffee and cocoa (4/5.2a), and manufacturing taxes on various goods (4/5.2). Finally, there are the taxes levied through fiscal monopolies (salt, tobacco, matches, and cigarette packages and papers (4/6)), the receipts from lotto and lotteries (4/6.7), and the single tax on games of skill and football pools (4/5.7).

The observations which may be made about the national indirect taxes are somewhat different from those made for the direct taxes. As a percentage of income, the direct taxes are today not far from their level in 1871 (1/6.7a); the total indirect taxes of the state as a percentage of the national income climbed, in the same period, to 15.86%, about two and one half times their 1871 level. Table 19 shows the behavior of the national indirect taxes as a whole. The various groups of indirect taxes are discussed in the subsections below.

b. TAXES ON EXCHANGES. Noteworthy, first of all, is the continuous development of the general tax on exchanges (4/2, 14/), which now provides more than 28% of the yield of all national indirect taxes as against 16% in 1939 (Table 20). As a percentage of income, the tax on exchanges was 0.153% in 1921, 0.992% in 1931, and 1.871% in 1939. In 1951, the percentage had already doubled to 3.653% and in 1961 exceeded 4.5%, amounting to an increase of almost two and one half times over the already high figure of 1939. In 1939, the exchange tax provided a little less than one tenth of the total yield of the indirect taxes; in 1961, it provided between one fifth and one fourth.

Table 19: *Receipts of National Indirect Taxes*

Year	Receipts (Millions of Lire)		Index of Variation (1952 =100)	Percent of National Income	Percent of National Tax Receipts	Per Capita Receipts (1960 Lire)	Index of Variation (1952 =100)
	Current Lire	1960 Lire					
1863	286	82,357		4.82%	66.10%	3,686	
1871	500	137,515		5.82	59.31	5,082	
1881	696	200,192		7.48	63.02	6,914	
1891	844	248,454		7.60	64.50	8,017	
1901	944	281,856		7.69	64.05	8,500	
1911	1,405	370,199		7.82	71.39	10,306	
1921	8,150	378,209		9.17	62.63	9,831	
1923	9,815	448,186		9.18	64.48	11,444	
1926	13,027	523,044		8.83	67.87	12,976	
1931	12,562	833,383		12.38	71.18	19,923	
1938	15,853	822,297	68.4	11.34	70.45	18,755	74.6
1939	18,063	898,154	74.6	11.67	71.04	20,261	80.5
1947	399,050	401,201	33.4	7.26	75.86	8,702	34.6
1948	643,813	613,553	51.1	9.98	76.46	13,186	52.4
1949	816,059	818,915	68.2	11.72	78.35	17,468	69.4
1950	952,551	1,008,942	84.0	12.35	79.54	21,347	84.7
1951	1,093,099	1,015,926	84.6	12.37	78.33	21,366	84.9
1952	1,220,643	1,201,479	100.0	13.12	77.61	25,155	100.0
1953	1,372,038	1,355,573	112.8	13.46	78.11	28,183	112.0
1954	1,547,620	1,542,977	128.4	14.27	78.34	31,855	126.6
1955	1,735,169	1,714,347	142.7	14.62	78.30	35,188	139.9
1956	1,916,130	1,861,520	154.9	14.99	77.16	37,999	151.1
1957	2,092,161	2,012,659	167.5	15.24	77.13	40,896	162.6
1958	2,222,212	2,176,212	181.1	15.10	76.25	43,941	174.7
1959	2,423,328	2,445,623	203.6	15.36	76.13	49,010	194.8
1960	2,688,227	2,688,227	223.7	15.63	76.34	53,509	212.7
1961	2,998,612	2,992,315	249.1	15.86	75.49	59,104	235.0

Sources: See note 104 *supra*.

Table 20: *Receipts of Taxes on Exchanges**

Year	Receipts (Millions of Lire)		Index of Variation (1921 = 100)	Index of Variation (1952 = 100)	Percent of National Income	Percent of National Indirect Taxes	Per Capita Receipts (1960 Lire)	Index of Variation (1921 = 100)	Index of Variation (1952 = 100)
	Current Lire	1960 Lire							
1921	136	6,311	100.0		0.153%	1.67%	164	100.0	
1923	447	20,412	323.4		0.418	4.55	521	317.7	
1926	830	33,325	528.0		0.563	6.37	827	504.3	
1931	1,007	66,806	1,058.5		0.992	8.02	1,597	973.8	
1938	2,358	122,310	1,938.0	35.0	1.686	14.87	2,789	1,700.6	38.1
1939	2,896	143,999	2,281.7	41.2	1.871	16.03	3,248	1,980.5	44.4
1947	150,256	151,067	2,393.7	43.3	2.733	37.65	3,276	1,997.6	44.8
1948	223,319	212,823	3,372.2	60.9	3.462	34.69	4,574	2,789.0	62.6
1949	254,230	255,120	4,042.4	73.1	3.651	31.15	5,441	3,317.7	74.4
1950	281,785	298,467	4,729.2	85.5	3.653	29.58	6,314	3,850.0	86.4
1951	324,264	301,371	4,775.2	86.3	3.669	29.66	6,337	3,864.0	86.7
1952	354,805	349,235	5,533.6	100.0	3.816	29.07	7,312	4,458.6	100.0
1953	393,031	388,315	6,152.9	111.2	3.854	28.65	8,073	4,922.6	110.4
1954	440,711	439,389	6,962.1	125.8	4.061	28.48	9,072	5,531.7	124.0
1955	492,936	487,021	7,716.8	139.5	4.152	28.41	9,994	6,093.9	136.7
1956	548,824	533,183	8,448.3	152.7	4.293	28.64	10,884	6,636.6	148.8
1957	597,605	574,896	9,109.2	164.6	4.353	28.56	11,680	7,122.0	159.7
1958	636,445	623,271	9,875.7	178.5	4.326	28.64	12,585	7,673.8	172.1
1959	703,002	709,470	11,241.6	203.1	4.454	29.01	14,214	8,667.1	194.4
1960	787,990	787,990	12,485.7	225.6	4.580	29.31	15,681	9,561.6	214.5
1961	867,994	866,171	13,724.5	248.0	4.593	28.95	17,112	10,434.2	234.0

*Tax on exchanges and general tax on receipts (IGE).
Sources: See note 104 *supra*.

c. REGISTRATION AND MORTGAGE TAXES. As a percentage of national income, the yield of the registration (15/) and mortgage (4/3.3) taxes is among the most stable (Table 21). The percentage has increased in the last 100 years from about 0.5% to about 0.8%.

Table 21: *Receipts of Registration and Mortgage Taxes*

Year	Receipts (Millions of Lire) Current Lire	1960 Lire	Index of Variation (1952 = 100)	Percent of National Income	Percent of National Indirect Taxes	Per Capita Receipts (1960 Lire)	Index of Variation (1952 = 100)
1863	29	8,351		0.489%	10.14%	374	
1871	43	11,826		0.501	8.60	437	
1881	64	18,408		0.688	9.19	636	
1891	67	19,723		0.603	7.93	636	
1901	65	19,407		0.530	6.88	586	
1911	105	27,666		0.584	7.47	770	
1921	618	28,679		0.695	7.58	745	
1923	823	37,581		0.769	8.39	959	
1926	1,252	50,269		0.849	9.61	1,247	
1931	915	60,703		0.902	7.28	1,452	
1938	1,127	58,458	80.1	0.806	7.11	1,332	87.1
1939	1,394	69,314	95.0	0.901	7.72	1,563	102.2
1947	20,670	20,782	28.5	0.376	5.18	451	29.5
1948	29,856	28,453	39.0	0.464	4.64	612	40.0
1949	42,814	42,964	58.9	0.615	5.25	917	60.0
1950	55,219	58,488	80.2	0.716	5.80	1,238	81.0
1951	65,941	61,286	84.0	0.746	6.03	1,288	84.2
1952	74,126	72,962	100.0	0.798	6.07	1,529	100.0
1953	82,359	81,371	111.6	0.807	6.00	1,691	110.6
1954	84,906	84,651	116.0	0.783	5.49	1,748	114.3
1955	83,427	82,426	113.0	0.702	4.81	1,690	110.5
1956	87,799	85,297	116.9	0.687	4.58	1,742	113.9
1957	94,605	91,010	124.8	0.689	4.52	1,847	120.8
1958	101,410	99,311	136.2	0.689	4.56	2,004	131.1
1959	113,357	114,400	156.8	0.719	4.68	2,294	150.0
1960	127,369	127,369	174.6	0.741	4.74	2,537	165.9
1961	151,808	151,489	207.7	0.804	5.06	2,994	195.8

Sources: See note 104 *supra.*

d. MISCELLANEOUS TRANSACTION TAXES. As a percentage of national income, the various taxes on transactions, after a 50-year period of relative stability, have undergone a considerable increase (Table 22). In 1930, they were about 1.5% of income and about 1.4% in 1939. In the last decade, their rise has been gradual but continuous, and their percentage, which was 1.031% in 1951, reached 2.105% in 1961.

e. MANUFACTURING TAXES. The various manufacturing taxes (4/5.2), in the last decade, remained at around 1.5% of national income (Table 23). They had had greater weight in the period between 1920 and 1940, and were about 1.5% of national income in 1939.

Table 22: *Receipts of Miscellaneous Transaction Taxes**

Year	Receipts (Millions of Lire)		Index of Variation (1952=100)	Percent of National Income	Percent of National Indirect Taxes	Per Capita Receipts (1960 Lire)	Index of Variation (1952=100)
	Current Lire	1960 Lire					
1863	26	7,487		0.438%	9.09%	335	
1871	53	14,577		0.617	10.60	539	
1881	75	21,572		0.806	10.78	745	
1891	115	33,853		1.035	13.63	1,092	
1901	126	37,621		1.027	13.35	1,135	
1911	179	47,164		0.996	12.74	1,313	
1921	1,133	52,578		1.275	13.90	1,367	
1923	986	45,024		0.922	10.05	1,150	
1926	1,542	61,913		1.046	11.84	1,536	
1931	1,548	102,697		1.525	12.32	2,454	
1938	2,124	110,172	102.2	1.519	13.40	2,512	111.3
1939	2,207	109,740	101.9	1.426	12.22	2,476	109.8
1947	34,135	34,319	31.8	0.621	8.55	744	33.0
1948	53,426	50,915	47.2	0.828	8.30	1,094	48.5
1949	67,484	67,720	62.8	0.969	8.27	1,444	64.0
1950	79,676	84,393	78.3	1.033	8.36	1,785	79.1
1951	91,145	84,710	78.6	1.031	8.34	1,781	78.9
1952	109,487	107,768	100.0	1.177	8.97	2,256	100.0
1953	134,465	132,851	123.3	1.319	9.80	2,762	122.4
1954	165,752	165,255	153.3	1.528	10.71	3,412	151.2
1955	193,269	190,950	177.2	1.628	11.14	3,918	173.7
1956	209,861	203,880	189.2	1.642	10.95	4,162	184.5
1957	222,501	214,046	198.6	1.621	10.63	4,522	192.8
1958	238,256	233,324	216.5	1.619	10.72	4,711	208.8
1959	262,132	264,544	245.5	1.661	10.82	5,300	234.9
1960	318,079	318,079	295.2	1.850	11.83	6,333	280.7
1961	398,016	397,180	368.6	2.105	13.27	7,845	347.7

*Stamp, substitute for registration and stamp, advertising, radio and television, public shows, playing cards, governmental concessions, and the like.
Sources: See note 104 *supra*.

Table 23: *Receipts of National Manufacturing and Consumption Taxes**

Year	Receipts (Millions of Lire)		Index of Variation (1952=100)	Percent of National Income	Percent of National Indirect Taxes	Per Capita Receipts (1960 Lire)	Index of Variation (1952=100)
	Current Lire	1960 Lire					
1863	23	6,623		0.388%	8.04%	297	
1871	109	29,978		1.269	21.80	1,108	
1881	139	39,981		1.494	19.97	1,381	
1891	104	30,615		0.936	12.32	987	
1901	148	44,189		1.206	15.68	1,332	
1911	245	64,554		1.363	17.44	1,797	
1921	1,193	55,362		1.342	14.64	1,439	
1923	1,971	90,003		1.843	20.08	2,298	
1926	2,148	86,244		1.457	16.49	2,140	
1931	1,866	123,793		1.839	14.86	2,960	
1938	2,156	111,832	81.3	1.542	13.60	2,550	88.5
1939	2,314	115,060	83.6	1.495	12.81	2,595	90.1
1947	43,329	43,563	31.7	0.788	10.86	945	32.8
1948	74,430	70,932	51.5	1.154	11.56	1,524	52.9
1949	102,236	102,594	74.5	1.469	12.53	2,189	76.0
1950	122,358	129,602	94.2	1.587	12.85	2,743	95.2
1951	134,206	124,731	90.6	1.519	12.28	2,624	91.1
1952	139,812	137,617	100.0	1.502	11.45	2,880	100.0
1953	146,738	144,977	105.3	1.439	10.69	3,013	104.6
1954	156,020	155,552	113.0	1.438	10.08	3,211	111.5
1955	178,626	176,482	128.2	1.505	10.29	3,623	125.8
1956	202,286	196,521	142.8	1.583	10.56	4,013	139.3
1957	210,926	202,911	147.4	1.537	10.08	4,123	143.2
1958	217,245	212,748	154.6	1.476	9.78	4,295	149.1
1959	229,604	231,716	168.4	1.455	9.47	4,642	161.2
1960	241,797	241,797	175.7	1.405	8.99	4,811	167.0
1961	249,335	248,811	180.8	1.319	8.36	4,915	170.7

*Not including petroleum and gasoline taxes or border surtaxes.
Sources: See note 104 *supra*.

Table 24: *Receipts of Motor Vehicle Fees and Manufacturing Taxes on Petroleum and Gasoline*

Year	Receipts (Millions of Lire)		Index of Variation (1952=100)	Percent of National Income	Percent of National Indirect Taxes	Per Capita Receipts (1960 Lire)	Index of Variation (1952=100)
	Current Lire	1960 Lire					
1911	5	1,317		0.028%	0.36%	37	
1921	132	6,126		0.148	1.62	159	
1923	175	7,991		0.164	1.78	205	
1926	194	7,789		0.132	1.49	194	
1931	440	29,190		0.434	3.50	698	
1938	2,047	106,178	73.2	1.464	12.91	2,421	79.7
1939	2,799	139,176	95.9	1.808	15.50	3,139	103.3
1947	28,434	28,588	19.7	0.517	7.13	620	20.4
1948	55,119	52,528	36.2	0.854	8.56	1,129	37.2
1949	72,947	73,202	50.4	1.048	8.94	1,561	51.4
1950	98,534	104,367	71.9	1.278	10.34	2,209	72.7
1951	124,720	115,915	79.9	1.411	11.41	2,438	80.2
1952	147,425	145,110	100.0	1.585	12.08	3,038	100.0
1953	178,522	176,380	121.5	1.751	13.01	3,667	120.7
1954	221,200	220,536	152.0	2.039	14.29	4,553	149.9
1955	265,771	262,581	181.0	2.239	15.32	5,389	177.4
1956	300,793	292,220	201.4	2.354	15.70	5,967	196.4
1957	357,951	344,349	237.3	2.607	17.11	6,996	230.3
1958	395,849	387,655	267.1	2.690	17.81	7,828	257.7
1959	435,209	439,213	302.7	2.758	17.96	8,800	289.7
1960	470,227	470,227	324.0	2.734	17.49	9,360	308.1
1961	529,649	528,537	364.2	2.802	17.66	10,442	343.7

Sources: See note 104 *supra.*

f. MOTOR VEHICLE TAXES. The automobile fees (4/5.5), and especially the manufacturing taxes on petroleum and gasoline (4/5.2), have shown a considerable growth (Table 24). As a percentage of national income, the aggregate yield of these taxes increased steadily from 0.028% in 1911 to about 2.8% in 1961. During the decade from 1951 to 1961, the percentage almost doubled.

g. CUSTOMS DUTIES. Since World War II, the yield of the customs duties (4/8.1) has declined sharply as a percentage of the total indirect tax yield (Table 25). They now provide about 1.3% of national income, slightly less than in 1939, whereas they were about 2% between 1926 and 1931 and also between 1891 and 1914 (having reached 2.54% in 1890). Between 1861 and 1871, they had been at about 1%, and the percentage increased by one half in the course of another decade.

To understand the recent decline of customs duties, it helps to keep in mind the succession of (1) protectionist but not prohibitive policies which, even in the absence of favorable circumstances, resulted in conspicuous customs yields (between 1880-1890 and in 1930); (2) low tariff policies in a regime of economic expansion, also providing a conspicuous (although not always equally high) customs yield; (3) policies of extreme protectionism, which had a sharply negative effect on the customs yield (the autarky of the period immediately preceding the Second World War); (4) policies of considerable protectionism, in a regime of redevelopment of international exchanges interrupted and disturbed by war (the years following the First and Second World Wars); and (5) a "common market" period, with a drastic reduction in duties, which prevented any percentage increase in yield notwithstanding the strong economic expansion and the conspicuous expansion of international exchanges connected with it.

h. FISCAL MONOPOLIES. The yield of the fiscal monopolies (4/6) remains conspicuously important as a percentage of national income (due chiefly to the yield of tobacco), although a percentage decline occurred in the period immediately before the last war (Table 26). In 1961, the yield was 2.526% of national income.

i. LOTTERIES. As a percentage of national income, the yield from lotto and the lotteries (4/6.7) today is minor in comparison to its role in the first 50 years of national life (Table 27). However, the addition of the yield from the tax on games of skill and football pools (4/5.7), of recent institution, maintains the total yield at around 0.30%.

1/6.9 Yields of Local Taxes

a. IN GENERAL. The following examination of the structural evolution which has taken place in local finance is limited in some cases to the

Table 25: *Receipts of Customs Duties*＊

Year	Receipts (Millions of Lire) Current Lire	Receipts (Millions of Lire) 1960 Lire	Index of Variation (1952=100)	Percent of National Income	Percent of National Indirect Taxes	Per Capita Receipts (1960 Lire)	Index of Variation (1952=100)
1863	59	16,990		0.995%	20.63%	761	
1871	81	22,277		0.943	16.20	823	
1881	157	45,158		1.688	22.56	1,560	
1891	230	67,707		2.071	27.25	2,185	
1901	257	76,734		2.095	27.22	2,315	
1911	362	95,382		2.014	25.76	2,655	
1921	1,324	61,442		1.489	16.24	1,597	
1923	1,908	87,126		1.784	19.44	2,225	
1926	3,069	123,223		2.081	23.56	3,057	
1931	3,210	212,957		3.163	25.55	5,091	
1938	2,047	106,178	117.4	1.464	12.91	2,421	128.0
1939	2,173	108,049	119.5	1.404	12.03	2,438	128.9
1947	24,818	24,952	27.6	0.452	6.22	542	28.6
1948	49,175	46,864	51.8	0.762	7.64	1,007	53.2
1949	62,530	62,749	69.4	0.898	7.66	1,338	70.7
1950	58,538	72,595	80.3	0.889	7.20	1,536	81.2
1951	78,043	72,533	80.2	0.883	7.14	1,525	80.6
1952	91,863	90,421	100.0	0.987	7.53	1,892	100.0
1953	111,403	110,066	121.7	1.093	8.12	2,289	121.0
1954	128,901	128,514	142.1	1.188	8.33	2,653	140.2
1955	144,630	142,894	158.0	1.218	8.34	2,932	155.0
1956	169,636	164,801	182.3	1.327	8.85	3,364	177.8
1957	185,609	178,556	197.5	1.352	8.87	3,628	191.8
1958	183,565	179,765	198.8	1.247	8.26	3,629	191.8
1959	199,913	201,752	223.1	1.267	8.25	4,043	213.7
1960	228,750	228,750	253.0	1.330	8.51	4,553	240.6
1961	250,698	250,698	277.2	1.326	8.36	4,941	261.2

＊Including border surtaxes except that on petroleum.
Sources: See note 104 *supra*.

Table 26: *Receipts of Fiscal Monopolies*

Year	Receipts (Millions of Lire)		Index of Variation (1952=100)	Percent of National Income	Percent of National Indirect Taxes	Per Capita Receipts (1960 Lire)	Index of Variation (1952=100)
	Current Lire	1960 Lire					
1863	111	31,964		1.871%	38.81%	1,431	
1871	147	40,430		1.711	29.40	1,494	
1881	188	54,075		2.021	27.01	1,868	
1891	253	74,477		2.278	29.98	2,403	
1901	281	83,900		2.290	29.77	2,530	
1911	401	105,658		2.231	28.54	2,941	
1921	3,316	153,882		3.730	40.69	4,000	
1923	3,118	142,378		2.915	31.77	3,635	
1926	3,514	141,090		2.383	26.97	3,500	
1931	3,055	202,674		3.010	24.32	4,844	
1938	3,479	180,456	69.0	2.487	21.95	4,114	75.2
1939	3,747	186,314	71.3	2.421	20.74	4,203	76.8
1947	90,389	90,877	34.8	1.644	22.65	1,971	36.0
1948	147,286	140,364	53.7	2.283	22.88	3,017	55.1
1949	196,054	196,740	75.3	2.815	24.02	4,196	76.7
1950	222,237	235,339	90.0	2.881	23.33	4,980	91.0
1951	242,845	225,700	86.4	2.749	22.22	4,748	86.8
1952	265,547	261,378	100.0	2.854	21.75	5,471	100.0
1953	286,106	282,673	108.1	2.806	20.85	5,876	107.4
1954	306,545	305,625	116.9	2.827	19.81	6,310	115.3
1955	328,927	324,980	124.3	2.771	18.96	6,670	121.9
1956	349,402	339,444	129.9	2.735	18.23	6,931	126.7
1957	368,442	354,441	135.6	2.685	17.61	7,204	131.7
1958	390,321	382,241	146.2	2.654	17.56	7,721	141.1
1959	418,345	422,194	161.5	2.652	17.26	8,457	154.6
1960	447,373	447,373	171.1	2.601	16.64	8,902	162.7
1961	477,458	476,455	182.3	2.526	15.92	9,412	172.0

Sources: See note 104 *supra*.

Table 27: *Receipts of Lotto and Lotteries*

Year	Receipts (Millions of Lire)		Index of Variation (1952=100)	Percent of National Income	Percent of National Indirect Taxes	Per Capita Receipts (1960 Lire)	Index of Variation (1952=100)
	Current Lire	1960 Lire					
1863	38	10,943		0.641%	13.29%	490	
1871	67	18,427		0.780	13.40	681	
1881	73	20,997		0.785	10.49	725	
1891	75	22,078		0.675	8.89	712	
1901	67	20,005		0.546	7.10	603	
1911	108	28,457		0.601	7.69	792	
1921	298	13,829		0.335	3.66	359	
1923	387	17,672		0.362	3.94	451	
1926	478	19,192		0.324	3.67	476	
1931	520	34,498		0.512	4.14	824	
1938	515	26,713	90.0	0.368	3.25	609	98.0
1939	533	26,503	89.3	0.344	2.95	598	96.3
1947	5,983	6,015	20.3	0.109	1.50	131	21.0
1948	9,707	9,251	31.2	0.151	1.51	199	32.0
1949	15,623	15,678	52.8	0.224	1.91	334	53.8
1950	21,441	22,710	76.5	0.278	2.25	480	77.3
1951	26,855	24,959	84.1	0.304	2.46	526	84.7
1952	30,163	29,689	100.0	0.324	2.47	621	100.0
1953	31,176	30,802	103.8	0.306	2.27	640	103.1
1954	35,092	34,987	117.8	0.324	2.27	723	116.4
1955	39,238	38,767	130.6	0.330	2.26	794	127.9
1956	40,584	39,427	132.8	0.318	2.12	805	129.6
1957	44,530	42,838	144.3	0.324	2.13	870	140.1
1958	48,431	47,428	159.8	0.329	2.18	956	153.9
1959	50,039	50,499	170.1	0.317	2.06	1,012	163.0
1960	53,537	53,537	180.3	0.312	1.99	1,067	171.8
1961	58,102	57,980	195.3	0.307	1.93	1,142	183.9

Sources: See note 104 *supra*.

Table 28: *Current Receipts of the Communes*
(Millions of Current Lire)

Receipts	1951 Amount	Percent of Local Taxes	Percent of Total Receipts	1961 Amount	Percent of Local Taxes	Percent of Total Receipts
Land surtax	18,027	9.5%	6.1%	37,954	8.4%	4.7%
Buildings surtax	1,604	0.8	0.5	17,540	3.9	2.2
ICAP	21,295	11.2	7.2	60,459	13.3	7.5
Family and leasehold value taxes	32,965	17.3	11.1	87,039	19.0	10.6
Cattle tax and agrarian income additional	14,486	7.6	4.9	1,575	0.4	0.2
Consumption taxes	93,040	48.9	31.3	216,778	47.7	26.9
Other taxes°	8,799	4.7	2.9	33,195	7.3	4.1
Total local tax receipts	190,216	100.0%	64.0%	454,540	100.0%	56.2%
Taxes on public shows	12,200		4.1	22,215		2.7
General tax on receipts (IGE)	14,723		4.9	60,310		7.4
Total participations in national taxes	26,923%		9.0%	82,525		10.1%
Total tax receipts	217,139		73.0%	537,065		66.3%
Patrimonial income and profits from municipal services	20,777		7.0	53,856		6.7
Other nontax receipts	59,295		20.0	218,316		27.0
Total nontax receipts	80,072%		27.0%	272,172		33.7%
Total communal receipts	297,211		100.0%	809,237		100.0%

°Various taxes, fees, and contributions (for example, taxes on dogs, carts, servants, billiard tables, licenses, and *espresso* coffee machines, and sewer contributions).

Sources: For 1951: Ministero delle Finanze, *L'attività tributaria dal 1949-50 al 1954-55*; for 1961: *Relazione generale sulla situazione economica del paese.*

most recent period, given the difficulty of collecting homogeneous data for the entire 100-year period since 1861. The increased importance, as a percentage of the total receipts of the local entities, of participations in the yields of national taxes as against yields from taxes levied and collected independently has already been noted at 1/5.5e. Even nontax receipts, as a result of the increased importance of state subsidies, have increased as a percentage of total receipts. The receipts of the communes are analyzed in Table 28, of the provinces, in Table 29, and of the regions, in Table 30. The total tax receipts of the local entities are presented in Table 7 (1/6.3).

b. DIRECT TAXES AND SURTAXES. The total yields of local direct taxes and surtaxes are given in Table 31. It is necessary to point out the long-term growth in importance of the personal taxation of income by the communes (2/3), which constituted 0.21% of national income in 1899, 0.29% in 1939, and 0.50% in recent years (Table 32). But from this percentage increase must be subtracted—in the long run—the percentage decline undergone by the communal and provincial surtaxes on income from lands (2/2.9), which fell from 0.77% in 1899 to 0.41% in 1960 and to 0.37% in 1961, and of the communal and provincial surtaxes on buildings (2/2.9), which fell from 1.19% in 1899 to 0.21% in 1960 (Table 32).

In 1862, the local surtaxes on landowning and on buildings together were close to 0.90% of national income, whereas, at present, they are 0.58% (Table 32). The decline has been gradual and continuous after an initial phase of development: in 1883, they reached almost 2% of income, and they remained at this level until the end of the century. But in 1914, they declined to 1.82%; in 1921, to 1.63%; in 1927, to 1.25%. They rose—after a short period of moderate percentage expansion—to 1.28% in 1939. The present percentage is less than one half of that of 1939.

The surtaxes on movable wealth of the local entities gave 0.37% of income in 1927 and reached 0.46% immediately before the Second World War (Table 32). This percentage has been regained in the last decade, and in some recent years has been slightly exceeded.

c. INDIRECT TAXES. The yields of the indirect taxes of the local entities are presented in Table 33. The communal consumption taxes (4/5.8) have always had great importance. Statistics for the consumption taxes are presented in Table 34. Their yield in 1961 was 1.38% of national income. As can be seen from Table 35, the average weight of the consumption tax yield is very unequal in various parts of the national territory. On the basis of the data for 1959, against a national average of about L. 4,000 per inhabitant, the average amount of consumption taxes paid per inhabitant in northern and central Italy is about L. 5,108, and the

Table 29: *Current Receipts of the Provinces*
(Millions of Current Lire)

Receipts	1951 Amount	Percent of Local Taxes	Percent of Total Receipts	1961 Amount	Percent of Local Taxes	Percent of Total Receipts
Land surtax	23,556	50.8%	28.9%	31,628	37.7%	12.5%
Buildings surtax	1,366	2.9	1.7	21,461	25.6	8.4
Agrarian income additional	3,726	8.0	4.6	1,018	1.2	0.4
ICAP additional	17,491	37.7	21.5	29,500	35.1	11.6
Other Taxes°	263	0.6	0.3	343	0.4	0.1
Total local tax receipts	46,402	100.0%	57.0%	83,950	100.0%	33.0%
Automobile fees	3,465		4.2	20,667		8.1
General tax on receipts (IGE)				17,738		7.0
Additionals to national and local taxes	11,797		14.5	31,683		12.5
Total participations in national taxes	15,262		18.7%	70,088		27.6%
National contributions and reimbursements	12,510		15.3	55,240		21.7
Other nontax receipts	7,351		9.0	45,011		17.7
Total nontax receipts	19,861		24.3%	100,251		39.4%
Total provincial receipts	81,525		100.0%	254,289		100.0%

°Fee for circulation of automobiles and animal-drawn vehicles, betterment contribution, and fee for occupation of public spaces and areas.

Sources: For 1951: Ministero delle Finanze, *L'attività tributaria dal 1949-50 al 1954-55*; for 1961: *Relazione generale sulla situazione economica del paese*.

Table 30: *Current Receipts of the Regions*
(Millions of Current Lire)

Receipts	1951		1961	
	Amount	Percent	Amount	Percent
Patrimonial income	972	2.5%	3,611	3%
Regional taxes	401	1.1	1,174	1
Participations in national taxes	34,606	90.0	105,151	87
Miscellaneous	2,426	6.4	10,933	9
Total	38,405	100.0%	120,869	100%

Sources: For 1951: Ministero delle Finanze, *L'attività tributaria dal 1949-50 al 1954-55*; for 1961: *Relazione generale sulla situazione economica del paese*.

average for southern Italy and the islands about L. 2,071. Table 36 gives the yield per inhabitant in the provincial capitals. The average yield per inhabitant in cities of over 350,000 inhabitants exceeds L. 5,000, even in the south. But the cities of the north and center have a particularly high burden per inhabitant: L. 12,438 in Milan, L. 11,116 in Genoa, L. 7,948 in Turin; about L. 10,000 each in Venice, Bologna, Florence; and barely L. 7,715 in Rome. The average in Naples is L. 5,112, and in Catania, L. 5,612. Among the large communes, the only exception is Palermo, where the average is L. 4,195.

1/6.10   Economic Considerations Affecting the Structural Evolution of the Tax System

a. INTERNATIONAL BALANCE OF PAYMENTS. For an understanding of the structural evolution of the fiscal system, the problems which it has met, and the problems which it faces in the future, it is important to keep in mind certain changes that have taken place in the Italian economy. The first change to be noted is that which has taken place in the balance of payments, that is, in the balance of transactions abroad.[107] Table 37 shows the general balance of current payments. Traditionally in deficit, this balance has recently become positive. The increase of exports has exceeded the increase of imports, and there has been a large

---

[107] Including both the balance of imports and exports and the other headings—tourism, freights, remittances of immigrants, gifts, investments abroad and from abroad, payments of interest and royalties on patents and copyrights abroad and from abroad—which involve Italy's receipts and disbursements of currency in relation to other countries.

Table 31: *Receipts of Local Direct Taxes*

Year	Receipts (Millions of Lire)		Index of Variation (1952=100)	Percent of National Income	Percent of Local Tax Receipts	Per Capita Receipts (1960 Lire)	Index of Variation (1952=100)
	Current Lire	1960 Lire					
1863	90	25,917		1.517%	68.18%	1,160	
1871	157	43,180		1.828	68.56	1,596	
1881	239	68,744		2.569	70.09	2,374	
1891	269	79,187		2.422	64.82	2,555	
1901	293	87,483		2.388	64.25	2,638	
1911	533	140,439		2.966	73.72	3,911	
1921	1,529	70,955		1.720	66.45	1,844	
1923	1,937	88,450		1.811	64.70	2,258	
1926	2,511	100,819		1.703	60.45	2,501	
1931	2,963	196,569		2.920	64.39	4,699	
1938	3,376	175,113	114.2	2.415	63.39	3,994	124.5
1939	3,569	177,473	115.7	2.306	63.58	4,004	124.8
1949	115,542	115,946	75.6	1.659	63.83	2,472	77.0
1950	131,324	139,098	90.7	1.703	63.55	2,943	91.7
1951	143,784	133,633	87.2	1.627	60.66	2,811	87.6
1952	155,769	153,323	100.0	1.674	58.50	3,209	100.0
1953	172,483	170,413	111.1	1.692	56.74	3,543	110.4
1954	208,364	207,739	135.5	1.921	58.95	4,290	133.7
1955	221,313	218,657	142.6	1.864	58.39	4,486	139.8
1956	234,887	228,193	148.8	1.838	58.27	4,659	145.2
1957	264,314	254,270	165.8	1.925	59.65	5,166	161.0
1958	282,695	276,843	180.6	1.921	59.99	5,590	174.2
1959	300,135	303,135	197.7	1.904	59.81	6,075	189.3
1960	324,274	324,274	211.5	1.886	61.63	6,457	201.2
1961	317,838	317,171	206.9	1.681	59.45	6,264	195.2

Sources: See note 104 *supra.*

Table 32: *Receipts of Communal and Provincial Direct Taxes*
(Millions of Lire)

Year	Surtax on Income from Landowning Current Lire	1960 Lire	Percent of National Income	Surtax on Income from Buildings Current Lire	1960 Lire	Percent of National Income	Total Surtaxes on Immovable Property Current Lire	1960 Lire	Percent of National Income	Taxes on Movable Wealth Current Lire	1960 Lire	Percent of National Income	Family and Leasehold Value Taxes Current Lire	1960 Lire	Percent of National Income
1862							68.0	18,720	0.88%	5.0					
1871							127.4			2.3			6.6		
1883							193.0	57,765	1.99	3.4			9.2		
1889							201.7			3.8			17.7		
1899	87	27,040	0.77%	134	41,647	1.19%	221.0	68,687	1.97				24.0	7,459	0.21%
1914	161	42,198	0.86	188	49,275	1.01	349.0	91,473	1.82				41.0	10,746	0.22
1921							1,399.0	64,914	1.63						
1927							1,568.0	74,950	1.25	459.0	21,940	0.37%			
1930							1,621.0	93,856	1.44	549.0	31,787	0.49			
1938	1,173	60,879	0.85	730	37,887	0.53	1,903.0	98,766	1.38	613.0	31,815	0.44	409.0	21,227	0.30
1939	1,212	60,358	0.79	748	37,250	0.49	1,960.0	97,608	1.28	704.0	35,059	0.46	440.0	21,912	0.29
1951	41,286	38,371	0.47	2,460	2,286	0.28	43,746.0	40,657	0.50	38,310.0	35,605	0.43	35,650.0	33,133	0.40
1952	45,225	44,515	0.49	3,627	3,570	0.04	48,852.0	48,085	0.53	37,483.0	36,895	0.40	31,194.0	30,704	0.34
1953	46,234	15,679	0.46	8,579	8,476	0.08	54,813.0	54,155	0.54	37,729.0	37,276	0.37	42,431.0	41,922	0.42
1954	54,371	54,208	0.50	13,709	13,668	0.13	68,080.0	67,876	0.63	44,769.0	44,635	0.42	53,570.0	53,409	0.50
1955	60,792	60,062	0.51	16,261	16,066	0.14	77,053.0	76,128	0.65	52,609.0	51,978	0.45	50,672.0	53,409	0.43
1956	65,301	63,440	0.52	20,700	20,110	0.16	86,001.0	83,550	0.68	53,647.0	52,118	0.43	54,927.0	53,362	0.44
1957	67,522	64,956	0.49	26,034	25,045	0.19	93,556.0	90,001	0.68	67,525.0	64,959	0.49	60,211.0	57,923	0.44
1958	68,839	67,414	0.47	27,931	27,353	0.19	96,770.0	94,767	0.66	74,156.0	72,621	0.51	67,014.0	65,627	0.46
1959	68,869	69,503	0.44	28,445	28,707	0.18	97,314.0	98,210	0.62	75,242.0	75,934	0.48	79,024.0	79,751	0.50
1960	69,181	69,181	0.41	33,968	33,968	0.20	103,149.0	103,149	0.60	82,496.0	82,496	0.48	83,810.0	83,810	0.49
1961	69,582	69,582	0.37	39,001	39,001	0.21	108,583.0	108,583	0.58	87,552.0	87,552	0.46	87,039.0	87,039	0.46

Sources: See note 104 *supra*; Ministero delle Finanze, *Relazione della Direzione Generale delle Imposte Dirette, Esercizio 1902-03* and *Relazione generale sulla amministrazione delle finanze, Esercizio 1911-12.*

Table 33: *Receipts of Local Indirect Taxes*

Year	Receipts (Millions of Lire)		Index of Variation (1952=100)	Percent of National Income	Percent of Local Tax Receipts	Per Capita Receipts (1960 Lire)	Index of Variation (1952=100)
	Current Lire	1960 Lire					
1863	42	12,094		0.708%	31.82%	447	
1871	72	19,802		0.838	31.44	732	
1881	102	29,339		1.096	29.91	1,013	
1891	146	42,979		1.315	35.18	1,388	
1901	163	48,668		1.329	35.75	1,468	
1911	190	50,062		1.057	26.28	1,393	
1921	772	35,825		0.869	33.55	932	
1923	1,057	48,266		0.988	35.30	1,232	
1926	1,643	65,967		1.114	39.55	1,637	
1931	1,639	108,735		1.615	35.61	2,598	
1938	1,950	101,147	93.0	1.394	36.61	2,306	101.3
1939	2,044	101,634	93.4	1.320	36.42	2,291	100.6
1949	65,472	65,702	60.4	0.941	36.17	1,402	61.6
1950	75,308	79,767	73.3	0.977	36.45	1,688	74.1
1951	93,235	86,652	79.7	1.055	39.34	1,822	80.0
1952	110,518	108,783	100.0	1.188	41.50	2,277	100.0
1953	131,484	129,906	119.4	1.290	43.26	2,702	118.7
1954	145,067	144,632	133.0	1.337	41.05	2,985	131.1
1955	157,687	155,795	143.2	1.329	41.61	3,199	140.5
1956	168,212	163,418	150.2	1.316	41.73	3,336	146.5
1957	178,777	171,984	158.1	1.303	40.35	3,496	153.5
1958	188,581	184,678	169.8	1.281	40.01	3,728	163.7
1959	201,785	203,642	187.2	1.279	40.19	4,081	179.2
1960	201,888	201,888	185.6	1.174	38.37	4,019	176.5
1961	216,830	216,374	198.9	1.147	40.55	4,275	187.7

Sources: See note 104 *supra*.

Table 34: *Receipts of Communal Consumption Taxes*

Year	Receipts (Millions of Lire)		Index of Variation (1952=100)	Per Capita Receipts (1960 Lire)	Index of Variation (1952=100)
	Current Lire	1960 Lire			
1863	41.7	12,444.576	0.580%	557.03	
1871	71.7	20,434.055	0.800	755.16	
1881	98.3	29,305.510	1.030	792.00	
1889	141.0	42,930.791	1.420	1,404.34	
1899	158.8	51,158.642	1.410	1,563.48	
1912	200.6	50,763.194	1.080	1,405.79	
1921	772.3	37,129.558	0.871	965.18	
1926	1,642.0	68,300.796	1.140	1,694.51	
1931	1,639.0	112,854.331	1.640	2,697.79	
1936	1,861.0	124,774.467	1.730	3,904.08	
1938	1,921.0	103,229.353	1.390	2,354.09	
1939	2,034.0	104,778.052	1.330	2,363.38	
1951	93,040.0	89,578.912	1.050	1,883.49	
1952	110,306.0	112,467.997	1.190	2,346.65	100.00
1953	131,183.0	134,265.800	1.290	2,778.38	118.39
1954	144,736.0	146,935.987	1.340	2,992.45	127.52
1955	153,315.0	154,863.481	1.300	3,213.93	136.95
1956	165,810.0	170,320.032	1.310	3,437.26	146.47
1957	180,404.0	187,133.069	1.330	3,751.13	159.85
1958	187,204.0	190,779.596	1.290	3,795.02	161.72
1959	201,535.0	217,687.780	1.270	4,292.96	182.93
1960	201,624.0	201,200.589	1.170	3,933.38	167.61
1961	261,778.0	261,778.000	1.380	5,781.44	246.36

Sources: ISTAT, *Annuario statistico, 1961,* and *Sommario di statistiche storiche italiane,*
1861-1955.

Table 35: *Receipts of Communal Consumption Taxes by Region, 1959*

Region	Population°	Total Receipts (Thousands of Lire)	Per Capita Receipts (Lire)
Northern Italy	22,346,151	115,806,316	5,108
Central Italy	9,299,903	42,102,523	4,521
Southern Italy	12,791,510	24,694,692	1,931
Islands	6,270,252	13,019,178	2,071
Total	50,707,816	195,622,709	3,806

°Population as of 31 December 1959.
Source: Ministero delle Finanze, *Imposte comunali di consumo nel 1959.*

Table 36: *Receipts of Communal Consumption Taxes*
in Provincial Capitals, 1959
(Thousands of Current Lire)

Commune	Receipts	Population on 31 December 1959	Per Capita Receipts
Agrigento	120,766	46,258	2,611
Alessandria	600,922	80,234	2,734
Ancona	634,085	98,172	6,459
Aosta	178,259	30,354	5,862
Arezzo	282,251	73,176	3,857
Ascoli Piceno	171,337	49,625	3,453
Asti	279,051	58,294	4,787
Avellino	147,648	41,861	3,527
Bari	1,448,247	313,351	4,622
Belluno	194,615	30,896	6,299
Benevento	174,937	55,161	3,171
Bergamo	972,980	113,489	8,573
Bologna	4,203,969	426,621	9,854
Bolzano	627,048	84,794	7,395
Brescia	1,498,892	164,575	9,108
Brindisi	287,199	68,555	4,190
Cagliari	1,005,208	171,946	585
Caltanisetta	192,960	63,219	3,052
Campobasso	111,957	32,559	3,439
Caserta	159,762	49,033	3,258
Catania	2,037,370	363,048	5,612
Catanzaro	226,080	72,012	3,139
Chieti	166,923	44,988	3,710
Como	564,840	76,914	7,344
Cosenza	296,026	74,249	3,987
Cremona	683,627	72,119	9,479
Cuneo	268,783	44,926	5,983
Enna	71,659	29,730	2,410
Ferrara	1,174,004	148,861	7,887
Firenze	4,397,276	428,955	10,251
Foggia	512,803	116,450	4,404
Forli	368,132	88,929	4,140
Frosinone	73,242	31,757	2,306
Genova	8,431,145	758,491	11,116
Gorizia	472,049	42,456	11,119
Grosseto	224,767	49,371	4,553
Imperia	204,075	33,815	6,035
L'Aquila	211,407	58,420	3,619
La Spezia	957,365	121,058	7,908
Latina	132,359	48,033	2,757
Lecce	241,943	72,507	3,337
Livorno	1,258,000	159,517	7,886
Lucca	628,670	87,804	7,160
Macerata	192,162	36,633	5,246
Mantova	525,612	60,331	8,712
Massa e Carrara	235,543	56,011	4,205
Matera	84,719	37,466	2,261
Messina	992,000	248,523	3,992
Milano	18,302,475	1,471,471	12,438

(Thousands of Current Lire)

Commune	Receipts	Population on 31 December 1959	Per Capita Receipts
Modena	889,317	130,910	6,793
Napoli	5,881,069	1,150,393	5,112
Novara	641,961	83,231	7,713
Nuoro	68,680	22,019	3,119
Padova	266,674	194,706	6,506
Palermo	2,479,312	591,041	4,195
Parma	955,626	134,878	7,085
Pavia	541,215	73,326	7,381
Perugia	622,083	109,531	5,680
Pesaro e Urbino	285,841	63,099	4,530
Pescara	424,372	83,035	5,111
Piacenza	641,078	84,475	7,589
Pisa	682,753	87,575	7,796
Pistoia	440,408	82,424	5,343
Potenza	122,609	39,954	3,069
Ragusa	118,802	56,177	2,115
Ravenna	507,715	109,799	4,624
Reggio Calabria	506,744	152,343	3,326
Reggio Emilia	695,760	113,568	6,126
Rieti	182,919	35,450	5,160
Roma	15,301,369	1,983,286	7,715
Rovigo	236,045	46,251	5,104
Salerno	518,608	110,953	4,674
Sassari	305,781	86,425	3,538
Savona	553,705	71,458	7,749
Siena	423,744	59,492	7,123
Siracusa	212,481	82,944	2,572
Sondrio	96,235	17,527	5,491
Taranto	636,154	192,821	3,299
Teramo	105,637	42,761	2,170
Terni	521,347	94,825	5,498
Torino	7,519,122	946,029	7,948
Trapani	139,438	77,795	1,792
Trento	572,437	71,226	8,037
Treviso	479,982	73,898	6,495
Udine	650,266	83,300	7,806
Varese	384,589	62,138	6,189
Venezia	3,460,392	345,537	10,015
Vercelli	299,012	49,235	6,073
Verona	2,000,227	210,124	9,519
Vicenza	683,162	93,587	7,300
Viterbo	200,724	48,114	4,172
Trieste	2,467,047	282,776	8,724
Total	112,949,591	15,526,424	7,274

Source: Ministero delle Finanze, *Le imposte comunali di consumo nel 1959.*

Table 37: *General Balance of Current Payments*
(Thousand Millions of Current Lire)

	1958			1959			1960			1961		
	Credits	Debits	Balance	Credits	Debits	Balance	Credits	Debits	Balance	Credits	Debits	Balance
Goods and services												
Goods f.o.b.°	1,576.8	1,815.1	− 238.0	1,775.4	1,859.6	− 84.2	2,231.6	2,627.7	− 396.1	2,567.7	2,900.0	− 332.3
Shipping and insurance	271.2	287.3	− 16.1	281.6	309.1	− 27.5	334.2	400.9	− 66.7	382.1	462.5	− 80.4
Travel abroad	307.3	50.2	+ 275.1	331.2	51.1	+ 280.1	401.6	59.0	+ 342.6	471.9	67.3	+ 404.6
Income from capital	33.3	54.7	− 21.4	57.5	61.4	− 3.9	52.3	70.9	− 18.6	55.5	87.7	− 32.2
Income from services	85.4	9.3	+ 76.1	93.8	11.6	+ 82.2	107.3	13.1	+ 94.2	153.0	15.1	+ 137.9
Governmental services and miscellaneous	193.0	121.8	+ 71.2	203.8	141.1	+ 62.7	229.8	178.9	+ 51.1	256.1	218.1	+ 43.6
Total	2,467.0	2,338.4	+ 128.6	2,743.3	2,433.9	+ 309.4	3,356.8	3,350.5	+ 6.3	3,886.3	3,750.7	+ 135.6
Unilateral transfers												
Emigrant remittances	117.8	--	+ 117.8	100.1	--	+ 100.1	133.7	--	+ 133.7	144.2	--	+ 144.2
Miscellaneous°°	54.6	13.5	+ 41.1	31.8	16.2	+ 15.6	25.8	11.4	+ 14.4	34.3	7.5	+ 26.8
Total	172.4	13.5	+ 158.9	131.9	16.2	+ 115.6	159.5	11.4	+ 148.1	178.5	7.5	+ 171.0
Extraordinary governmental receipts	61.6	--	+ 61.6	44.8	--	+ 44.8	54.4	--	+ 54.4	36.5	--	+ 36.5
Total	2,701.0	2,351.9	+ 349.1	2,920.0	2,450.1	+ 469.9	3,570.7	3,361.9	+ 208.8	4,101.3	3,758.2	+ 343.1

°Data on foreign commerce furnished by the *Istituto Centrale di Statistica* less notes and insurance, plus welfare donations, less ships' stores and other items.

°°Private gifts, reparations, contribution to Somalia, miscellaneous contributions.

Source: *Relazione generale sulla situazione economica del paese.*

DESCRIPTION OF TAX SYSTEM   128

expansion of foreign tourism in Italy, large enough not only to remove the deficit in the balance of imports as against exports, but to result in a surplus.

Since a diminution in the yield from foreign tourism does not seem to be in the offing, but rather an increase in it, and a further increase in the imbalance between imports and exports also is improbable, it can be argued that—apart from a conspicuous spontaneous structural excess of Italian investments abroad as against foreign investments in Italy—the Italian balance of payments can be regarded with tranquillity. In the last 90 years, except for the first decade of this century, it was not possible to say this.

Continuation of a favorable balance of payments would facilitate the adoption of stronger measures of reform of the tax system and provide new possibilities of expansion in the field of public expenditures. Expansion in public expenditures has been undertaken recently, and those problems of reform of the indirect taxes which could compromise the yield necessary for the increased public expenditures have been postponed.

But the fear of internal inflationary pressures due to a price-wage spiral is more acute today than five years ago because, full employment having almost been reached, the power of the unions in the field of wage demands has grown considerably, and the willingness to use this power has been strengthened. At the same time, the market power of oligopolistic enterprises has grown, and thus the possibility that these enterprises will incorporate the wage increases in their prices (instead of absorbing them out of profits) has been increased.

b. COMPOSITION OF THE NATIONAL PRODUCT. Modifications have taken place in the extent to which the agricultural, industrial, and tertiary sectors contribute to the Italian national product; Table 38 compares the value added and the net product in 1951 and 1961.

In the five-year period 1861-1865, agricultural production was slightly less than three times industrial production. The tertiary activities (trade,

Table 38: *Value Added and Net Product of the Private Sector (Thousand Millions of Current Lire)*

Sector	Value Added		Net Product	
	1951	1961	1951	1961
Agriculture, forests, and fisheries	2,391	3,297	2,222	3,031
Industry	3,626	8,467	3,144	7,200
Tertiary activities	1,901	5,587	1,741	5,093

Source: *Relazione generale sulla situazione economica del paese* (1951 and 1961).

credit, services of the public administration, and various other services) gave to the national product a contribution slightly higher than that of industry. Agriculture alone thus gave a higher contribution than did industry and the tertiary sector—about 60% of the national income.

In the five-year period 1885-1890, the contribution to the national product of industry and the tertiary sector together equaled that of agriculture; agriculture had registered (in current lire) an increase of 25% against an increase of over 33% for industry and slightly less than 100% for the tertiary sector.

In 1906-1910, industry and the tertiary sector together noticeably exceeded agriculture. Industry alone, however, always contributed only a little more than one half as much as agriculture. Not until 1931-1935 did industry equal agriculture, and not until 1936-1940 did it exceed agriculture by as much as 10%.

The comparative decline of agriculture as against industry has become particularly accentuated in the last 10 years. In 1951, the agriculture, forests, and fishing sector had a product of L. 2,222,000 million, as against industry's L. 3,144,000 million. In 1961, the sector of agriculture, forests, and fishing gave L. 3,031,000 million, and industry L. 7,200,000 million. From barely one third less than industry, agriculture fell in a decade to less than one half. In the meantime, there has been a certain increase in the absolute volume of agriculture, so that the volume is comparable to that of agriculture's best years—but industry has had a far greater growth. If, in addition, the tertiary activities are considered along with industry, the weight of agriculture in the decade appears even further diminished. The contribution of the tertiary sector has had an increase greater than that of industry: from L. 1,741,000 million in 1951 to L. 5,093,000 million in 1961. In 1961, agriculture, gross of depreciation (which is rather higher in industry than in agriculture), was slightly less than one third of industry and less than one fifth of the total national product.

These modifications are very significant for the fiscal system. First of all, certain traditional taxes (on income from landowning, registration, and succession) can no longer serve their original function. Furthermore, the methods of tax assessment are outdated. Indeed, in an agricultural economy, the budgets of the economic units, like crops, are characterized by recurring fluctuations; but in an industrial economy like the present one, there are great differences in the rates of growth of the various subsectors contributing to the dynamics of the whole. Traditional agriculture is an activity of recurring natural cycles. But the same agriculture industrialized presents new characteristics. The growth of industries in the narrow sense is tied to changes in technology and in the accumulation of capital. In an industrial economy, practically nothing is recurrent. For the tax system, this implies that a method of assessment like the Italian, which is based on stable averages over several years, no longer follows

DESCRIPTION OF TAX SYSTEM

the actual behavior of income. Today, the new and different fluctuations require an assessment on analytic bases adapted to reach the amount and the direction of the variations.

c. SIZE AND ORGANIZATION OF UNITS OF PRODUCTION. The size of the business unit subjected to assessment has grown with the passage of the Italian economy from an agricultural one based traditionally on the small holding to an economy of industries and industrialized services. An important change has occurred also in the nature and the economic-organizational characteristics of the units of production which are tax-payers. The agricultural economy involves individuals for the most part; they do not use much accounting, and they need secure, stable, and simplified relations with the tax administration, rather than flexible relations based on the complex concrete situations of the large modern business. But the productive unit and taxpayer in the present structure is, rather, an enterprise endowed with an elaborate accounting setup, often a company, whose relations with the tax administration are depersonalized (or could be so) and which desires (or would be disposed) to deal with the tax administration not on the basis of uniform elementary rules, but on the basis of procedures appropriately devised to take account of business forces and of the variety of economic-accounting situations.

d. GROWTH OF EMPLOYMENT INCOME. Income from work as an employee has undergone a significant quantitative modification with important fiscal consequences (Tables 39 and 40). Income from work as an employee has grown considerably, both in the aggregate and per employee, in connection with the development of industry and the expansion of the tertiary sector. There has been an increase in the number of persons engaged in commerce and working as salaried employees rather than as entrepreneurs or members of the family group of the entrepreneur. Similarly, there has been a rise in the compensation of agricultural workers, under the pressure of the increased manpower requirements for industry, which has diminished the supply of manpower for agriculture.

In 1954, income from work as an employee constituted 38.1% of the national income and, by 1961, had risen to 42.84%. During the same time, the national income had increased greatly, both total and per capita, so that the total volume and the volume per capita of income from work as an employee has risen even more than indicated by these two percentages.

The increase in income from work as an employee and its diversification renders indirect taxation always less acceptable and raises new problems regarding the qualitative discrimination of taxable incomes as an indirect means of carrying out quantitative discrimination (2/2.7a). More glaring, on the other hand, becomes the inequality of a personal progressive tax.

Table 39: *Income from Employment and Its Relation
to National Income, 1954 and 1961
(Thousand Millions of Current Lire)*

Sector and Branch	Amount 1954	Amount 1961	Percent 1954[°°]	Percent 1961
Private sector	2,579.6	6,960.9	72.8%	77.5%
Agriculture, forests, fisheries	235.6[°]	493.6	6.6	5.5
Industrial activities	1,721.0	4,174.1	48.7	46.5
Tertiary activities	307.0	2,293.2	8.6	25.5
Family allowances of all of the private sector	316.0	--	8.9	--
Public sector	961.0	2,026.0	27.2	22.5
Total	3,540.6	8,986.9	100.0%	100.0%
Share of national income	38.1%	42.8%		

[°]Transportation included.

[°°]The percentage figures of this column can be compared with those of the succeeding
column only with some caution because family allowances for the private sector are treated
separately, whereas in the other column these allowances are merged in the figures for the
appropriate branches of the private sector.

Sources: Tagliacarne: *Il reddito di lavoro dipendente nelle province e regioni d'Italia*;
Relazione generale sulla situazione economica del paese (1961).

Table 40: *Labor Force and Value Added Per Employee
in the Major Sectors, 1951 and 1961*

Sector	Labor Force (Millions)		Value Added Per Employee (Lire)	
	1951	1961	1951	1961
Agriculture	8,261	5,907	289,432	558,151
Industry	6,290	8,012	576,471	1,056,790
Other activities	5,026	6,348	378,233	880,120
Total	19,577	20,267		

Sources: For 1951: SVIMEZ, *Un secolo di statistiche italiane nord e sud*; for 1951 and
1961: *Relazione generale sulla situazione economica del paese*.

in which fixed incomes from employment are assessed exactly, while incomes from capital, enterprise, or occasional activities escape in large measure—as is the case in Italy today.

e. SIZE AND PATTERN OF PUBLIC EXPENDITURE. The increase in the public expenditure as a share of national income is easily reconstructed by taking account of the tax receipts and the contributions to social security, and of the relative constancy of the deficit as against national income in the last decade. For public investment expenditures, the estimate of the annual total is complicated by accounting irregularities connected with the inadequacy of the present structure in quickly reflecting commitments of public expenditure. Large programs of expenditure are often not completed by the end of the financial year for which they have been placed in the budget. Thus, while the accrual budget shows a deficit—even if slight—between receipts and expenditures, the cash budget shows a surplus resulting from the deferred disbursement of expenditure combined with prompt cash receipts. This complicates the deflationary action of the fiscal system. If the Minister of Finance computes the annual investment expenditures on the basis of the accrual deficit, the fiscal system may operate in the short run in a manner somewhat less deflationary than would be wished; on the other hand, if he makes the computation on the behavior of the cash budget, he risks putting off to future periods, difficult to make precise, an inflationary wave of uncertain size.

Apart from this, it must be noted that the expansion of public investments which has taken place, in the total of the public expenditures, also opens new views on the problem of distribution of taxation between the two great aggregates, consumption and saving, and on the problem of the choice between tax receipts and receipts obtained by an increase in the public debt. On these points, the increase which has taken place in the last decade in the share of aggregate public and private investments also deserves mention. In 1951-1955, these investments were nearly one fourth of private consumption. In 1960, they were one third of private consumption and, in 1961, more than one third. This, however, represents a short-term tendency, which is connected with an increase in wages smaller than the increase in productivity and which could undergo considerable changes in the years to come. The national economic balance sheet for 1951 and 1961 is given in Table 41; recent figures on the behavior of consumption, investment, and savings are given in Tables 42, 43, and 44.

The total public expenditure of the national and local governments has risen from about 17% of the net national income in the nineteenth century to about 20% in the 1920's, 25% in 1939, and 33% in 1962.[108] As

---

[108] The statements in this paragraph are based on an article by Tremelloni, "Alcune riflessioni sulla spesa pubblica in Italia," *RDFSF*, 1962, I, 241.

Table 41: *National Economic Balance Sheet, 1951 and 1961*
(Thousand Millions of Current Lire)

Resources and Uses	1951	1961
Resources		
Gross national income at market prices	9,606	20,975
Imports of goods and services	1,323	3,751
Total resources	10,929	24,726
Uses		
Private consumption	6,840	13,194
Public consumption	737	2,288
Total consumption	7,577	15,482
Gross fixed investments	1,835	5,058
Inventory variations	194	300
Total gross investments	2,029	5,538
Exports of goods and services	1,018	3,886
Total uses	10,929	24,726

Source: *Relazione generale sulla situazione economica del paese* (1951 and 1961).

may be seen in Table 45, in the period 1953-1962, the total current and capital expenditures of the national government, net of debt repayments, have risen from L. 2,672,000 million to L. 5,015,000 million, in 1961 lire, an increase of 88%. The average annual rate of increase has been 8.2%, higher than the rate of increase of the national income. All the major heads of expenditure have increased during this period; but increases exceeding the over-all rate of 88% have occurred in public education (162%), economic action and intervention (111%), and financial and unclassifiable charges (100%). Increases below the average rate were made in expenditures for social security (74%), military expenditures (36%), and institutional and general expenses of administration (55%). In 1961-1962, 49.6% of the national expenditure went for economic intervention, welfare and health assistance, and public education. Of the entire expenditure of the state, regions, provinces, and communes for that year, 57% was divided among education (17%), welfare and health assistance (15%), and economic intervention (25%).

Table 42: *Consumption, Investment, and Production of Industry,
Agriculture, and the Tertiary Sector
(Millions of Current Lire)*

Year (Average)	Private Consumption at Current Prices	Gross Investment at Current Prices	Agriculture, Forests, and Fisheries°	Industrial Activities°	Tertiary Activities°
1861-1865	6,950	789	4,249	1,461	1,650
1866-1870	7,683	935	4,826	1,659	1,938
1871-1875	9,158	1,027	5,806	1,904	2,362
1876-1880	9,276	996	5,613	1,930	2,559
1881-1885	8,765	1,249	5,066	2,008	2,666
1886-1890	9,184	1,317	5,031	2,098	2,972
1891-1895	9,416	1,012	5,217	1,948	3,122
1896-1900	9,834	1,159	5,407	2,103	3,250
1901-1905	10,782	1,888	5,961	2,603	3,662
1906-1910	13,310	3,038	6,825	3,817	4,565
1911-1915	16,421	3,055	8,373	4,927	5,807
1916-1920	50,328	4,937	26,003	16,529	13,181
1921-1925	92,627	20,835	44,389	33,979	30,897
1926-1930	110,027	25,783	45,780	40,103	40,669
1931-1935	80,740	17,157	27,938	28,540	36,470
1936-1940	111,295	29,569	40,374	46,729	49,431
1941-1945	501,267	24,941	281,170	117,593	116,006
1946-1950	4,804,000	1,333,000	1,994,000	2,197,000	1,379,000
1951-1955	8,236,000	2,377,000	2,569,000	4,308,000	2,535,000
1956	9,953,000	3,130,000	2,711,000	5,395,000	3,324,000
1957	10,449,000	3,456,000	2,754,000	6,182,000	3,326,000
1958	10,506,000	3,576,000	2,982,000	6,258,000	3,911,000
1959	11,356,000	3,935,000	3,004,000	6,791,000	4,596,000
1960	12,199,000	4,732,000	2,993,000	7,593,000	5,110,000
1961	13,194,000	5,358,000	3,297,000	8,467,000	5,587,000

°Gross of corrections and depreciation.
Sources: ISTAT, *Indagine statistica sullo sviluppo del reddito nazionale dell'Italia dal
1861 al 1956*; *Relazione generale sulla situazione economica del paese* (1957,
1959, 1960, and 1961).

f. BEHAVIOR OF PRICES. In the last decade, prices were almost stable, as a result of a number of factors of an international character, such as the reduction of the barriers to international trade, the establishment of international competition, and the expansion of markets, which have permitted the enjoyment of decreasing costs of production on a large scale; the reduction in international prices of raw materials; and the soft wage policy of the trade unions, more concerned with increasing employment and with the accumulation of capital of enterprises than with wages. Almost all of these factors are now dying out, and the problem of maintaining stable internal prices is becoming delicate. There is no problem with the

Table 43: *Savings, 1954-1959*
(Thousand Millions of Current Lire)

Year	Bank Deposits and Current Accounts (Including Postal Savings Banks)	Fiduciary Deposits for Business Categories on 31 December	Aggregate Deposits for Business Categories on 31 December
1954	3,655.4	2,391.3	4,527.0
1955	4,141.7	2,783.4	5,218.8
1956	4,697.3	3,244.4	5,891.0
1957	5,309.5	3,751.2	6,586.9
1958	6,181.8	4,492.1	7,664.7
1959	7,083.1	5,217.5	8,961.1

Source: SVIMEZ, *Un secolo di statistiche italiane nord e sud 1861-1961.*

Table 44: *Gross Investments by Major Categories, 1951 and 1961*
(Thousand Millions of Current Lire)

Investment	1951 Value	1951 Percent	1961 Value	1961 Percent
Agriculture	265	14.5%	539	10.7%
Industry	700	38.1	1,590	31.4
Transportation and communications	270	14.7	892	17.6
Dwellings	} 485	} 26.4	1,192	23.6
Public works			485	9.6
Miscellaneous	115	6.3	360	7.1
Total fixed investments	1,835	100.0%	5,058	100.0%
Inventory variations	194		300	
Total gross investments	2,029		5,358	

Source: *Relazione generale sulla situazione economica del paese* (1951 and 1961).

balance of payments, however, because the other currencies have also slipped as much as—and sometimes more than—the Italian currency.

The policy of the Bank of Italy at present tends to favor the employment of Italian capital abroad when the accumulation of reserves of foreign currencies appears excessive. In 1962, along with the positive policy in this direction adopted by the Bank of Italy, a certain migration abroad of private capital has taken place, which has been caused by political changes (the seating of a government of the "center-left," considered unfavorable to the growth of private capital because of its fiscal measures),

Table 45: *Current Expenditures of the State*
(Millions of Current Lire)

Year	General Administration		National Defense and War Charges		Justice and Public Order		International Relations		Public Instruction	
	Amount	Percent	Amount	Percent	Amount	Percent	Amount	Percent	Amount	Percent
1913-1914	402	17.3%	833	28.1%	225	9.7%	29	1.3%	155	6.7%
1922-1923	1,763	10.6	6,023	14.6	1,327	8.0	317	1.9	981	5.9
1930-1931	3,014	14.4	5,013	24.0	1,568	7.5	730	3.5	1,505	7.2
1939-1940	5,014	11.7	34,346	29.8	1,998	5.4	2,294	6.2	2,741	7.4
1950-1951	179,923	10.9	617,026	22.5	145,528	8.8	27,068	1.7	178,584	10.8
1951-1952	212,380	11.0	598,554	20.6	158,279	8.2	25,237	1.3	210,332	10.9
1952-1953	235,187	10.4	530,832	21.3	164,881	7.3	29,068	1.3	229,349	10.1
1953-1954	236,474	10.3	471,675	19.6	170,186	7.4	29,486	1.3	252,534	10.9
1954-1955	268,779	10.3	477,088	17.6	182,947	7.0	34,531	1.3	289,816	11.1
1955-1956	285,462	10.2	464,825	16.4	187,608	6.7	30,020	1.1	325,016	11.6
1956-1957	312,191	10.7	523,290	16.9	200,727	6.8	29,904	1.0	380,656	13.0
1957-1958	414,700	12.5	553,253	16.4	217,067	6.6	37,990	1.2	421,031	12.7
1958-1959	421,697	12.5	555,704	16.3	222,416	6.6	33,051	1.0	462,746	13.7
1959-1960	492,698	12.3	607,260	15.0	237,613	5.9	34,857	0.9	517,630	12.9
1960-1961	599,111	13.8	648,431	14.8	250,898	5.8	40,850	0.9	610,675	14.0

(Millions of Current Lire)

Year	Social Welfare and Assistance		Economic Action and Intervention		Unclassifiable Financial Charges*		Charges of Independent Businesses of the State**	Total
	Amount	Percent	Amount	Percent	Amount	Percent	Amount	Amount
1913-1914	20	0.9%	302	13.0%	534	23.0%	238	2,738
1922-1923	76	0.5	1,955	11.7	7,801	46.8	1,969	22,212
1930-1931	211	1.0	3,065	14.7	5,785	27.7	--	20,891
1939-1940	532	1.4	5,858	15.8	7,606	20.6	--	60,389
1950-1951	76,855	4.7	364,612	22.1	303,998	18.5	--	1,893,594
1951-1952	109,202	5.7	469,088	24.3	345,754	18.0	--	2,128,826
1952-1953	164,417	7.3	565,944	25.0	389,870	17.3	--	2,309,591
1953-1954	162,207	7.0	539,320	23.4	463,917	20.1	--	2,326,199
1954-1955	187,680	7.2	587,831	22.6	594,149	22.9	--	2,622,821
1955-1956	211,084	6.6	682,053	24.4	617,052	22.0	--	2,803,150
1956-1957	195,480	6.7	673,348	23.0	640,768	21.9	--	2,956,364
1957-1958	226,788	6.8	794,447	24.0	657,951	19.8	--	3,323,227
1958-1959	255,241	7.6	725,799	21.6	695,858	20.7	--	3,372,512
1959-1960	272,084	6.8	1,100,580	27.4	758,752	18.8	--	4,021,474
1960-1961	320,441	7.4	1,094,843	25.2	790,623	18.1	--	4,355,872

*Includes debt interest, interventions for the benefit of the local entities, war pensions, and war damage indemnities.

**Formerly charged against the budget of the state.

Source: Tremelloni, "Alcune riflessioni sulla spesa pubblica in Italia," *RDFSF*, 1962, I, 241, 257-262.

the nationalization of electric energy, and the preparation of a policy of economic planning. This migration, of a temporary character, together with the interventions of the Bank of Italy, has lightened the problem of excessive currency reserves, which could have manifested itself in the balance of payments.

In 1962, the index of wholesale prices had begun to rise (in conformity with a trend in western Europe), and the indexes of the cost of living and of consumer prices showed even more marked increases, suggesting also that the phase of spontaneously almost stable prices is at an end. A problem new for Italy but already common in many western economies is appearing: sustaining total demand and maintaining a high rate of growth of the economic system, while at the same time controlling inflationary tensions and keeping prices and the cost of living at a stable or almost stable level.

g. INTERNAL DYNAMICS OF VARIOUS SECTORS. Also worthy of consideration are the internal dynamics of the industrial sector, of the agricultural sector, and of private expenditures for consumption. The discussion here is limited to changes of the last decade. To be noticed in the composition of the structure of industry, shown in Table 46, is the comparative decline of the sector of textiles, clothing, apparel, furnishings, skins, and leather, which passed in the last decade from 21.1% to 9.5% of the total, and a less sharp decline of the sector of food, beverages, and tobacco. These declines contrast with the exceptional expansion of the mechanical sector, which in 1961 occupied the position of primacy held by textiles in 1951, and the expansion of the building industry, which replaced in importance the sector of food, beverages, and tobacco. The chemical and similar industries, the extractive industries, and metallurgy have realized a progress equal to the vast progress registered by the industrial system as a whole.

As a result of these and other transformations, the Italian productive machinery is now, much more than 10 years ago, founded on industries which are closely connected with the most advanced phase of technological progress, with investments, and with the production of instrumental goods. This change implies new problems regarding the fiscal treatment of investments, depreciation, and expenses of research and study.

The agricultural sector, in the decade just closed, also showed important internal changes. As can be seen in Table 47, there has been considerable expansion in the sector of wood cultivation—from 24.6% to 28.5% of total agricultural production. Among the forms of wood cultivation, the growing of fruit trees, and most recently the growing of trees for the paper industry, moved ahead. Among the forms of herbaceous cultivation, those of vegetables and flowers developed increasingly. Thus, a transformation is in progress in Italy; certain traditional kinds of agricul-

Table 46: *Value Added and Net Product
of Industrial Activities, 1951 and 1961
(Thousand Millions of Current Lire)*

Industry	Value Added		Percent of Total Industrial Production	
	1951	1961	1951	1961
Extraction of natural resources	101	208	2.7%	2.5%
Manufacturing				
Food, beverages, tobacco	581	898	15.5	10.6
Textiles, clothing, apparel and furnishings, skins and leather	793	807	21.1	9.5
Metallurgy	262	550	7.0	6.5
Mechanical	696	1,923	18.6	22.7
Building materials and the like		276		3.3
Chemicals and the like (petro-chemicals, cardboard, paper, and rubber)	534	1,205	14.2	14.2
Miscellaneous (wood, graphics, photography, phonographs, cinematography)	248	668	6.6	7.9
Total	3,114	6,327	83.0%	74.7%
Electricity, gas, water	227	527	6.1	6.2
Building	306	1,405	8.2	16.6
Value added	3,748	8,467	100.0%	100.0%
Net product	3,213	7,200		

Sources: For 1951: ISTAT, *Indagine statistica sullo sviluppo del reddito nazionale dell'Italia dal 1861 al 1956*; for 1961: *Relazione generale sulla situazione economica del paese.*

tural production (wheat, wine, olive oil, citrus fruits, and silk) are diminishing in importance, while other, formerly secondary, kinds of production (fruits other than citrus, flowers, vegetables, and poplars) are increasing. This presents problems regarding the assessment of the agricultural taxes, based on the cadaster and on the maintenance, for the entire agricultural-forestry area, of the cadastral method, which is being slowly revised.

h. CONSUMPTION EXPENDITURES. Among the consumption expenditures of the Italian population, as shown in Table 48, a considerable percentage

DESCRIPTION OF TAX SYSTEM   140

decline was registered under the general heading "food and beverages," which in 1951 still occupied 58.6% of the total expenditure, but which in 1952 had fallen to about 54% and by 1961 to 48.1%. Of increased importance, on the other hand, are expenditures for the rental of dwellings. Formerly, almost all dwellings were subjected to rent control from the

Table 47: *Value Added and Net Product of the Principal Agricultural Activities, 1951 and 1961 (Thousand Millions of Current Lire)*

Class of Production	Amount		Percent of Total Agricultural Production	
	1951	1961	1951	1961
Products of herbaceous cultivation	913	1,322.0	35.6%	35.6%
Products of wood cultivation	629	1,057.1	24.6	28.5
Forage cultivation	27	25.2	1.0	0.7
Products of animal husbandry	992	1,307.7	38.7	35.2
Gross saleable production	2,561	3,712.0	100.0%	100.0%
Less: Purchase of goods and services	508	561.6	19.7	15.1
Value added	2,053	3,150.4	80.3%	84.9%
Less: Depreciation	173	262.5	6.8	7.1
Net product	1,880	2,887.9	73.4%	77.8%

Sources: For 1951: ISTAT, *Indagine statistica sullo sviluppo del reddito nazionale dell'Ita dal 1861 al 1956*; for 1961: *Relazione generale sulla situazione economica del paes*

Table 48: *Common Expenditures by General Categories, 1951 and 1961 (Thousand Millions of Current Lire)*

Category	1951		1961	
	Amount	Percent of Total	Amount	Percent of Total
Food and beverages	4,371	58.6%	6,647	48.1%
Tobacco	286	3.8	574	4.2
Clothing and other personal effects	1,200	16.1	1,329	9.7
Rent	104	1.4	1,016	7.4
Shows, books, newspapers, and other recreational and cultural expenditures	95	1.3	697	5.0
Miscellaneous	1,400	18.8	3,537	25.6
Gross total	7,456	100.0%	13,800	100.0%
Less duplications			606	
Net total	7,456		13,194	

Source: *Relazione generale sulla situazione economica del paese* (1951 and 1961).

time of the war and thus remained at artificially low levels because not revalued in proportion to the postwar monetary depreciation. Both the expenditures for shows and entertainments and the "miscellaneous" expenditures (such as for transport, durable domestic goods, electricity, heating, and sanitation) have acquired a much greater role than before. Within the broad headings of Table 48, expansion has been registered in expenditures for meat, durable goods for domestic use, and personal transportation.

It must be pointed out that the headings for which a constant percentage or slight decrease has been registered, given the great absolute increase of total expenditure, may be rather dynamic in absolute volume. Some of these headings of expenditure have expanded along with the expansion of consumption, which in these years has been considerable.

The growth of consumption in these years necessitates changes in the collection of factual data and in the objectives of indirect taxation. The exemptions of certain categories of expenditure for food, important in the budgets of citizens of low income, today can be put into effect more easily than several years ago, when they would have undermined the base of indirect taxation.

The policy of rate discrimination for general indirect taxation has acquired new importance. Formerly, it appeared of slight significance because the popular classes tended to consume mostly the basic necessities. Now, consumption by the popular classes tends to be differentiated; that of the classes of higher consumption has been extended.

The important development of new types of mass consumption characteristic of an "abundant" society, such as expenditure for automobiles, creates also in Italy new problems for indirect taxation, within the framework of a policy balancing private and public consumption: this is a theme which draws attention in the current formulation of a policy of planning.

i. REGIONAL DIFFERENCES IN ECONOMIC ACTIVITIES. A structural characteristic of the Italian economy which has particular importance for tax policy is the differences in economic activities among the various parts of Italy. The regional distribution of receipts from various national taxes, in percentages of the total receipts, is shown in Tables 49, 50, and 51.

The difference in income per inhabitant in northwestern Italy (pivoted on the "Turin-Genoa-Milan industrial triangle"), the rest of northern and central Italy, and southern Italy may be mentioned first of all in this connection. In the last 10 years, Italian tax policy has been broadly influenced by the problem of the retardation of the south. There have been many laws enacted to encourage the industrial development of the south, including reliefs from both the direct taxes and the indirect taxes. In addition, many laws granting tax reliefs have been enacted

Table 49: *Percentage Distribution of Principal National Tax Receipts in the Regions of Ordinary Statute, 1958*

Region	Permanent Direct Taxes	Fees and Indirect Taxes on Transactions	Other Receipts			Total Other Receipts	Aggregate Total
			Manu-facturing Taxes	Tobacco	Lotto and Football Pools		
Piemonte	14.447%	13.629%	8.550%	9.195%	9.919%	8.929%	11.857%
Lombardia	34.276	30.574	19.733	18.475	17.700	19.045	26.554
Veneto	6.673	7.090	13.356	8.570	6.064	10.775	8.508
Friuli-Venezia Giulia	2.142	2.901	2.925	3.127	3.289	3.037	2.817
Liguria	7.866	8.667	10.785	5.317	8.709	8.339	8.395
Emilia-Romagna	5.851	7.243	13.660	9.473	6.966	11.367	8.669
Toscana	6.213	6.696	7.229	8.680	7.088	7.823	7.062
Umbria	0.699	0.779	0.363	1.532	0.801	0.886	0.807
Marche	1.029	1.570	2.395	2.541	1.302	2.342	1.786
Lazio	14.436	10.544	6.894	11.698	12.488	9.328	10.749
Abruzzi e Molise	0.616	1.029	1.186	2.361	1.343	1.688	1.223
Campania	3.650	5.311	7.708	10.186	17.007	9.488	6.709
Puglia	1.472	2.709	4.583	5.552	5.368	5.050	3.433
Basilicata	0.014	0.272	0.012	0.724	0.320	0.392	0.298
Calabria	0.616	0.986	0.621	2.561	1.636	1.511	1.133
Total	100.000%	100.000%	100.000%	100.000%	100.000%	100.000%	100.000%

Source: Forte, *Evoluzione e lineamenti del sistema tributario*, Appendix, Table 52.

Table 50: *Percentage Distribution of National Permanent Direct Taxes in the Regions of Ordinary Statute, 1958*

Region	Landowning	Agrarian Income	Buildings	Movable Wealth	Complementary Progressive Tax on Income	Corporation Tax and Tax on Bonds
Piemonte	11.688%	13.800%	11.767%	14.502%	12.300%	19.719%
Lombardia	15.000	11.412	25.250	35.105	27.947	46.453
Veneto	11.829	10.404	6.863	6.690	7.091	3.221
Friuli-Venezia Giulia	2.710	3.556	2.916	2.126	2.744	0.427
Liguria	0.662	0.902	6.705	7.968	8.619	7.558
Emilia-Romagna	14.059	15.605	7.963	5.626	6.714	3.205
Toscana	6.606	10.036	8.178	6.227	7.171	2.946
Umbria	2.343	3.874	1.043	0.613	0.862	0.499
Marche	3.571	5.148	1.915	0.951	1.294	0.242
Lazio	5.928	6.263	13.726	14.463	16.353	12.895
Abruzzi e Molise	2.780	3.237	1.730	0.519	0.935	0.090
Campania	6.352	4.670	5.765	3.418	4.888	2.395
Puglia	11.518	7.430	4.289	1.153	2.007	0.295
Basilicata	1.101	0.955	0.515	0.114	0.197	0.005
Calabria	3.853	2.707	1.373	0.525	0.878	0.050
Total	100.000%	100.000%	100.000%	100.000%	100.000%	100.000%

Source: Forte, *Evoluzione e lineamenti del sistema tributario*, Appendix, Table 53.

Table 51: *Percentage Distribution of Certain Indirect Taxes in the Regions of Ordinary Statute, 1958*

Region	Inheritance and Gift Taxes	Estate Tax	Registration Tax	General Tax on Receipts[*]	Import Equalization Tax	Stamp Tax
Piemonte	11.814%	11.754%	12.224%	12.442%	18.860%	8.825%
Lombardia	25.890	28.343	22.628	34.435	44.783	25.996
Veneto	8.052	7.319	7.328	7.141	3.434	6.814
Friuli-Venezia Giulia	2.556	1.897	1.802	3.168	4.494	2.396
Liguria	6.586	6.453	6.283	10.528	13.799	5.360
Emilia-Romagna	8.355	12.096	7.671	6.701	2.476	9.057
Toscana	8.977	5.871	6.949	6.445	2.663	8.058
Umbria	1.151	0.843	0.927	0.580	- -	1.468
Marche	2.631	1.436	1.641	1.289	0.170	2.806
Lazio	10.461	15.394	18.986	8.437	4.800	12.807
Abruzzi e Molise	1.168	1.094	1.291	0.716	0.100	2.103
Campania	5.059	3.374	6.666	5.136	3.729	7.016
Puglia	5.040	2.941	3.890	2.131	0.629	4.519
Basilicata	0.444	0.205	0.399	0.167	- -	0.746
Calabria	1.816	0.980	1.315	0.684	0.063	2.029
Total	100.000%	100.000%	100.000%	100.000%	100.000%	100.000%

[*]About 90% retained by the state.

Source: Forte, *Evoluzione e lineamenti del sistema tributario*, Appendix Table 54.

with the idea of developing a modern tertiary sector (provisions such as reliefs for tourists and hotel plant, and the abolition of the obligatory nominativity of share certificates in Sicily and Sardinia, to attract to those regions the offices of large enterprises and favor the local development of private financing).

Another reflection of the differences in the distribution of economic activities is the territorial concentration of the seats and central offices of corporations—by far the majority are located in the provinces of Milan, Genoa, and Turin. This has great importance with regard to the distribution of the work of the various tax offices. The tax offices of Milan, Turin, and Genoa collect the greater share of the corporation tax, the registration and stamp taxes on acts of companies or in connection with their activities, the movable wealth tax on income of enterprises, the general tax on receipts, and the other taxes which affect the business world. Even when the production or the capital to which these taxes apply is not localized in Milan, Turin, and Genoa, in many cases the taxes are collected there because the legal offices and the central administrations of the firms are in those cities.

The Italian fiscal apparatus has not always adjusted itself, up to now, to this territorial concentration of business offices, which would involve a corresponding concentration of personnel of the tax administration. But this is one of the larger tasks which will have to be faced in the future, in the fiscal administrative reform, together with the mechanization of the recording and accounting services.

CHAPTER 2

SUMMARY OF TAXES ON INCOME

2/1. **Introduction**

2/2. **"Objective" Taxes on Income**

    2/2.1   The Concept of Income

    2/2.2   The "Productive Sources" of Income

        a. In general

        b. Pure capital

        c. Mixed capital and work

        d. Pure work

        e. Rate discriminations

    2/2.3   Agrarian Income

    2/2.4   Imputed Income

        a. In general

        b. Immovable property

        c. Pure work

        d. Movable property

    2/2.5   Territoriality

    2/2.6   Capital Gains

        a. Gains forming part of the national product

        b. The objective taxation of gains

    2/2.7   "Personalization" of the Objective Taxes

        a. Effects of qualitative discrimination

        b. Income from landowning

        c. Income from buildings

        d. Income from movable capital

        e. Income from shareholding

        f. Enterprise income

        g. Standard allowance and rate reduction

        h. Compensation of gains and losses

2/2.8   Effects of the Complexity of the System

2/2.9   Local Taxes and Surtaxes; Additionals and Fees

2/3.   The Complementary Progressive Tax and the Family Tax

2/3.1   Historical Background

2/3.2   Persons Subject

2/3.3   Tax Bases
         a.   Complementary tax
         b.   Family tax

2/3.4   Computation and Rates of Tax
         a.   Allowances
         b.   Rates

2/3.5   International Aspects

2/3.6   Jurisdiction of Communes To Impose the Family Tax

2/3.7   Communal Tax on Leasehold Values

2/3.8   Administration and Procedure

2/3.9   Collection and Payment

2/4.   The Corporation Tax

2/4.1   Historical Background

2/4.2   Tax Base

2/4.3   Rates of Tax; Relation Between Income and Assets

2/4.4   Persons Subject

2/4.5   Intercorporate Distributions

2/4.6   Public Enterprises

2/1.   Introduction

The taxation of income in Italy began with a tax on the presumed income from land, which was split shortly after national unification into a tax on income from agricultural land and a tax on income from buildings. A few years later, a tax intended to cover all income from sources other than land or buildings was introduced—the so-called "tax on income from movable wealth." These three taxes, together with the tax on agrarian income, which was added later to give special treatment to a particular class of income from movable wealth, form a system of "objective" taxation on income: a system designed to tax all income having a "productive source" in Italy at rates varying according to the nature of the source and independently of the amount of income received from that source, or from other sources, by the person who owns it. The development of this system and the problems connected with its functioning are discussed in 2/2.

Independently of this system, there existed even before unification a rudimentary form of taxation of income of persons, regardless of source. After unification, this method of taxation was left to the communes, and it developed during this century into what is now the local "family tax," a progressive tax on the "well-being" or "aggregate means" of the family unit. In the meantime, the national government instituted in 1925 a "complementary progressive" tax on the aggregate income of each taxpayer and his family, including the incomes subject to the various objective taxes. These two "personal" taxes, their relationship to each other, and their relationships to the objective taxes are discussed in 2/3.

In 1955, the government, completing the structure of its direct tax system, introduced another "personal" tax, the corporation tax. This tax, which consists of a tax on "taxable assets" and a tax on income exceeding a certain percentage of taxable assets, together with a tax on bonds, is described in 2/4; more detailed discussion of the taxable-assets component of the tax and of the tax on bonds is also given in 3/2.

In 1951 and again in 1956, the entire structure of the direct taxes underwent an extensive revision, particularly the assessment procedures.[1] Since then, the laws governing all the direct taxes have been consolidated into a single law, the *"Testo unico delle leggi sulle imposte dirette"* (consolidated text of the laws on the direct taxes), which became effective 1 January 1960.[2] This new law, with explanatory references to earlier provisions where necessary, is the basis of the detailed discussion of the various taxes on income and their application to specified categories of persons, activities, and situations, which constitutes Part II of this volume.

2/2. "Objective" Taxes on Income

2/2.1 The Concept of Income

In Italy, there exists a system of "objective" taxes (*imposte reali*) which, in principle, attempts to tax without gaps or duplications the entire "national product"— that is, all the new wealth which is produced in the country during the year—according to the nature of the components of that product. As will be seen, however, the system departs from this general principle in certain cases in which imputed income is not taxed (2/2.4) and in certain cases involving the territoriality principle (2/2.5).

The most rigorous theoretical formulation of the basic concept of the system has been given by De Viti De Marco during the first decades of this century. A tax, De Viti De Marco maintains, is the compensation for

---

[1] These reforms were instituted by the so-called "Vanoni law" (L. 11 January 1951, n. 25) and the so-called "Tremelloni law" (L. 5 January 1956, n. 1).

[2] D.P.R. 29 January 1958, n. 645.

the cost which the state bears for the furnishing of its public services.[3] According to De Viti, the hypothesis can be made that the public services benefit each particle of the national product in uniform measure, or, in other words, that "the consumption of public services is proportional to the income of each citizen." [4]   In this hypothesis, he recognizes that there is a certain margin of approximation because there are concrete cases in which the consumption of public services is not equal for each particle of income.   But a part, however small, of the tax structure is necessarily arbitrary; and this hypothesis, in his opinion, is less arbitrary than any other which could be taken in a general way.   Under this principle, deductions made for expenses in arriving at the net income of one taxpayer must be included in the taxable income of the persons to whom the payments were made.[5]   Thus, the purification of an enterprise's income of its expenses of production, that is, the passage from its gross income to its net income, is not a way of eliminating from taxation a part of the national product.   Rather, it is a way of taxing precisely, in the hands of the owner of each factor, the share of the national product which belongs to him.

It is necessary to distinguish, says De Viti, the "external" relations between one business and another and the "internal" relations among entrepreneur, workers, and capitalists, who—in a single business—are owners of the private factors of production (the fourth factor is that represented by gratuitous public services, the cost of which is met by the state through taxes).   In the "external" relations between one enterprise and another, the purification of the individual enterprise's income of the cost involved in purchases which it makes from different enterprises is in reality a method of allocating to each enterprise the income of the agents of production which belong to it.   This income belonging to the agents of production of the individual enterprise today is called "value added," but the concept is exactly that defined by De Viti.

The global income of each enterprise thus having been established, one passes to the "internal" purification, that is, to the allocation of the income among the various agents of production.   The deduction from the enterprise's earnings of expenses for wages for the use of work as an employee, of interest for the use of movable capital, and of rent for the use of immovable capital is a way of allocating income among the productive agents operating inside the enterprise.   Thus, in reality, the passage from gross to net income which the fisc makes when it taxes each individual taxpayer is only a way of specifying exactly the income imputable to the productive factors of which that taxpayer is the owner.   If a taxpayer

---

[3] De Viti De Marco, *Principii di economia finanziaria* 84.   This book has been published in English translation under the title *First Principles of Public Finance.*

[4] De Viti De Marco, *Principii di economia finanziaria* 89.

[5] De Viti De Marco, *Principii di economia finanziaria* 196.

failed to make the full purification necessary for arriving at his income, there would be a "duplication" of tax. On the other hand, there would be a tax gap (*salto*) if expenses were deducted in excess of the compensation belonging to each other taxpayer for the factors owned by him, or if the other taxpayers were not taxed on the compensation belonging to them as owners of factors external or internal to the enterprise of which the first taxpayer was agent.[6]

The last, but most fundamental, point of De Viti's formulation is the rule that income placed in savings must also be taxed if gaps are to be avoided: or, to take the matter from another point of view, the taxation of income placed in savings does not involve duplication. Income saved in one tax period is used to increase production in other tax periods, with the employment of more raw materials, more labor, and more public services.[7]

2/2.2 The "Productive Sources" of Income

a. IN GENERAL. The Italian "objective" taxes and the sources of income to which they apply are listed below.

1. The tax on income from landowning ("land tax"—*imposta fondiaria* or *imposta sui terreni*), which is applied to the income arising from agricultural land by virtue of ownership thereof (10/2.2).
2. The tax on income from the ownership of buildings ("tax on buildings"— *imposta sui fabbricati*), which is applied to the income from buildings as property, when these are not employed for agricultural purposes or in activities of industrial, commercial, or artisan character carried on by their owners (9/4.2).
3. The tax on agrarian income (*imposta sul reddito agrario*), which has as its object the agrarian income obtained from the exercise of agricultural enterprise on lands held by virtue of ownership, usufruct, or other property right (10/2.3).
4. The tax on income from movable wealth (*imposta sui redditi di ricchezza mobile*—or, more briefly, "R.M."), which is applied to the income deriving from a movable source and any other income which has not been subjected to the two taxes on the fruits of immovable property mentioned above.

Although there are formally four taxes, there are only three from the economic point of view, since the tax on agrarian income affects income that conceptually falls within the definition of income from movable wealth (2/2.3).

In distinguishing between the taxes on landowning income and building income on the one hand and the taxes on movable wealth income and agrarian income on the other, the civil law distinction between movable property and immovable property is an aid. However, the

---

[6] De Viti De Marco, *Principii di economia finanziaria* 190-196.
[7] De Viti De Marco, *Principii di economia finanziaria* 205-206.

civil law concept of movable property and the fiscal concept of productive source of income from movable wealth do not coincide perfectly
since there are productive sources of income from movable wealth which
it would be difficult for the civil lawyer to classify as "property." The
basic concept of the tax on income from movable wealth is to tax the
income arising from some "productive source" other than immovable
property (2/2.2) (except for income covered by the tax on "agrarian
income"; this is discussed further at 2/2.3); it is understandable how
the economic concept of "productive source" would not necessarily coincide with that of a property or an identifiable group of properties of
movable nature. For example, "pure work" is a productive source, but
it is not a property, either movable or immovable, in the civil juridical
sense. Furthermore, an enterprise is, from the objective point of view, a
collection of movable and immovable properties and of rights of various
kinds, organized for certain ends productive of a profit; thus, one cannot
say that the "source" of the income of the enterprise is a movable property or a pure collection of movable properties. What one can say is
that the source is not an immovable property or a mere collection of
immovable properties: the object of the tax on income from movable
wealth is specified better negatively than positively.

Reinforcing this last point is a further consideration—that the tax on
income from movable wealth also has the function of a "residual" tax.
That is, this tax reaches, in addition to income from movable wealth in
the strict sense (but excepting income falling under the tax on agrarian
income), all income from immovable property which is excluded by
definition from the bases of the immovable property taxes (or from the
basis of the tax on agrarian income), provided that such income is not
explicitly or implicitly exempted from the bases of those taxes (6/1.1e).

b. PURE CAPITAL. The tax on income from movable wealth is divided
into categories which are distinguished in relation to the kind (*qualità*)
of income.

Included in category A is income from movable capital. Category A
rounds out the triptych of the taxes on income from pure ownership: the
tax on income from landowning and on income from agricultural property; the tax on income from buildings and on income from nonagricultural buildings and the land appurtenant to them; and the tax on income
from movable wealth, category A, on income from movable property.

Income from shareholding is not considered income from "pure capital."
Instead, the share company itself is taxed on its profits under category B
(2/2.2c) of the tax on income from movable wealth, whether the income
is distributed in the form of dividends or in another form, and even if the
income is not distributed at all but is retained for self-financing. For
the tax on income from movable wealth, income from pure capital is

generally that which, from an abstract point of view, does not involve for the taxpayer any participation except a credit right in the enterprise which produces the income, and which therefore does not involve in reality a variable income, but a fixed monetary income.[8] Thus, interest deriving from bonds, bank deposits, and savings accounts, interest deriving from loans, and interest payable under certain insurance contracts are included in category A for the tax in question (9/1). It must be specified that income from securities of the public debt, present and future, is exempt from this tax (9/1.2), a fact which, of course, greatly reduces the tax base of category A.

Bond certificates are not registered, but the tax on income from movable wealth of category A is levied "at the source" on the issuing companies and entities. These companies have the right, seldom exercised, to withhold the tax from the interest which they pay on the certificates (9/1.1). For bond interest, therefore, the tax is rather difficult to evade. Evasion of tax is easier with regard to interest on loans, because of the rule that the borrower cannot deduct the interest charges on loans as an expense of production for purposes of the movable wealth tax of category B unless the lender can be ascertained by the tax administration (7/2.5). Because banking secrecy makes it difficult to assess the exact amount of bank deposits, there is also a possibility of evasion for the tax on interest paid by banks to depositors, which is levied at the source against the banks (the banks, if they wish, then recover the amount of the tax from the depositors).

c. MIXED CAPITAL AND WORK. Category B of income from movable wealth covers, in general, "enterprise" income, that is, income deriving not from a pure employment of capital, but from an employment of capital and other productive factors, among which the predominant component is the entrepreneurial activity. The so-called "agrarian income" is in reality, as will be seen at 2/2.3, a subspecies of income from movable wealth of category B; for this reason, it was stated above that, in substance, the Italian objective taxes are three: taxes on land, on buildings, and on movable wealth.

The tax on income from movable wealth of category B is applied to income of the entrepreneur (7/1.2a) arising from the directive work of the enterprise, as well as to income from the work of persons who also make a substantial contribution of their own capital to the business (in the objective sense, an aggregate of physical property and of advances for circulating capital, permanently employed in the business). It can be said that category B is an intermediate category, definable practically rather than logically, between category A, fixed income from capital (2/2.2b),

---

[8] Lottery winnings, however, are an exception (10/7.1).

and category C, fixed and variable income from work (2/2.2d). Income which, to a certain extent, is traceable to movable capital, and is reducible neither to category A nor to category C, will fall automatically into category B, "mixed" income (from capital and work). Thus, income from directive and executive work or work of an entrepreneurial nature, which is not included in income of "pure work," as defined in 2/2.2d, falls automatically into category B. Included in category B, finally, is agricultural income, which can be traced to an agricultural enterprise (and not to the mere ownership of the land) which is not subject to the tax on agrarian income (2/2.3).

d. PURE WORK. Category C/1 of income from movable wealth includes, in principle, income from independent work (8/2); category C/2 includes income from work as an employee (*lavoro subordinato*) (8/1). With the use of the same letter, the identity of the point of departure—income from work—is emphasized. By income from independent work is meant income deriving from artisan activities, professions, or similar activities; or from small enterprises, which are defined in the ministerial circulars on the basis of the number of employees and of the capital invested (7/1.2b).

But it must be pointed out that the so-called "independent worker" is also an "entrepreneur" as regards himself and his own professional or artisan activity (or his own family business). Moreover, with respect to independent professionals and artisans, the confines of category C/1 are not at all definable in terms of "pure work." Even if only a small amount of physical equipment is used, the gain of the professional or artisan no longer derives only from his "pure" work. It is clear that practically no professional would be included in the category of independent workers if it were required that his income be derived solely from his work. Thus, inclusion in this category must be determined also quantitatively, and not merely qualitatively: a small amount of capital and a small amount of work provided by others distinguish the work of the professional and of the artisan from that of persons who receive "mixed" income taxed in category B.

To classify an enterprise which makes clothing, for example, recourse is had—on the basis of ministerial circulars—to the criterion of the number of employees, excluding members of the family of the entrepreneur; and to the criterion of whether the enterprise has separate juridical personality. If a professional office (for example, of advertising consultants) is organized as a company having its own juridical personality (a corporation, limited liability company, cooperative with shares, or limited partnership with shares), it is always taxed in category B, rather than in category C/1, because the law admits to category C/1 only the income of individuals (*persone fisiche*) (8/2.1). The same is true as regards retail stores: thus, the income of the supermarket is taxed at the rate applicable to category B, and the income of the grocery shop is taxed at the rate applicable to category C/1—as a small enterprise or artisan enterprise.

Category C/2, in most cases, at first appears easier to delineate because it is the category of income from work as an employee. But not even the contents of category C/2 show themselves to be homogeneous or completely clear. Included in this category, besides income of pure work as an employee, is a series of assimilable incomes, among which is, first of all, income deriving from pensions. The original basis for a pension is, of course, work as an employee. But the pension is income "deferred," and the deferral involves for it, inevitably, the presence of an element of capital: like any "deferred" payment, it contains the interest compounded on the original sum (9/3.1). Certain other types of capital income, such as life annuities, insurance contracts, and subsidies (9/3), are also taxed in category C/2; the characteristic of these types of income is that they are "fixed" but are considered worthy of taxation to a lesser degree than the fixed incomes of category A.

Category A and category C/2 are, as a rule, the two categories of "fixed" income. The first is taxed at high rates and the second at low rates, and, for the most part, the distinction between the two is made on the basis of their sources: movable capital and work as an employee.

e. RATE DISCRIMINATIONS. Regarding the discrimination of rates (12/1.4c), it can be said that rates were originally higher in category A than in category B, in deference to the principle that where the proportion of capital is higher, the rate should be higher (2/2.7a). But for some time, income of category B has been subjected to the national tax at slightly progressive rates, some higher and some lower than those which apply to income of category A. Since there is a local surtax on income of category B and none on income of category A (2/2.9), the number of cases in which category B income is in practice taxed less than category A income tends to be reduced.

On the other hand, the policy has persisted of taxing income of category C/1 to a lesser degree than income of categories A and B because the factor of work predominates more in category C/1 than in category B. This remains true even if the income of category C/1 bears a local surtax, as distinct from income of category A. The national rates for category C/1 and category C/2 are the same, but income of category C/1 is subject in addition to a local surtax (2/2.9).

2/2.3 Agrarian Income

Income from the conduct of an agricultural "enterprise," as distinct from that arising from the ownership of the land itself, would in principle be income from movable wealth, taxed in category B or in category C/1 according to the size of the enterprise. However, it is considered that, when the owner cultivates his own land—and thus is an agricultural entre-preneur—the burden of two taxes, the land tax on the income from owner-ship and the movable wealth tax on the income from the enterprise, would be excessive. If, theoretically, such a person enjoys the sum of the two incomes, he often receives in reality less than only one of the two: many such agricultural owner-entrepreneurs are marginal operators who must put together capital, work, and enterprise to achieve low incomes, and under these conditions, barely survive. These and other considerations led, for a time, to the total exemption of the enterprise income of owner-entrepreneurs from movable wealth taxation. When the decision was reached to abrogate this exemption in 1923, it did not seem proper to apply the rather severe treatment prescribed for movable wealth of cate-gory B. It was found fair and opportune to work out a special treatment through the institution of the tax on agrarian income, which, as compared to the tax on movable wealth of category B, involves considerable miti-gations both in the rate (12/1.2) and in the definition of the tax base (10/2.3).

In the case of the individual agricultural owner-entrepreneur, the tax on agrarian income applies to the income attributable to the enterprise. There exists, however, a situation in which the agricultural entrepreneur is more properly co-entrepreneur: the best known forms of this are *mezzadria, colonia parziaria,* and *soccida* (10/2.3). One of the entre-preneurs is the owner, but the other is not. In such a case, the problem of how to split the enterprise income for purposes of treatment for the tax on income from movable wealth and the tax on agrarian income has been met by subjecting all the income of the enterprise in question to the tax on agrarian income, even for the part which does not concern the owner-ship (10/2.3a).

The income of an agricultural enterprise in which at least one of the entrepreneurs is owner does not include income from the activity of work, directive or otherwise, carried on by the entrepreneur and by the mem-bers of his family, since compensation for all work is among the expenses taken into account in the determination of income from landowning, and since the income of directive work which is part of the basis of the tax on agrarian income does not include the compensation for directive work, but only the "surplus" attributable to it (10/2.3b). On the other hand, income from directive work of the entrepreneur is included in the income of a nonagricultural enterprise taxed in category B or in category C/1. Income from directive work of the entrepreneur and the members of his family which is excluded from the tax on agrarian income is excluded also from income from movable wealth of category C/2—since the latter reaches only "remuneration" for work "as an employee," which directly assumes the character of a payment—as well as from category C/1.

2/2.4   Imputed Income

a. IN GENERAL. "Imputed" (*figurativo*) income means all those economic advantages flowing to a person which fall into either of the classes described below.

1. Economic advantages which do not receive a monetary measure on the market (or a measure reducible to a monetary valuation) because they are not the object of a bilateral transaction.[9]

2. Economic advantages which, even if on the surface seem to receive on the market an authentic monetary valuation (or a valuation reducible to money), in reality do not receive it since they are the object of an intrinsically fictitious transaction—of a contract in which the two parties are in substance identical in the same person or in persons bound by narrow family ties who do not have opposed or distinct interests but convergent or common interests.   Such a fictitious transaction is not made always or necessarily for purposes of fraud; it can have a completely honest origin and serve a function of "internal accounting"; what is important is that the price of remuneration fixed in this way can also diverge somewhat from the correct remuneration or imputed income, which expresses the intrinsic value of that economic quantity and which is established by looking at the market value that similar quantities would have in comparable circumstances.

"Imputed" income of the first type, for example, is the advantage which an individual derives from the habitation of a villa owned by him; or that which the family of an agricultural owner-entrepreneur draws by consuming products from its land. To imputed remunerations of the second type belong, for example, amounts which a company pays to another company, closely connected with it, for the use of raw materials which the latter produces; or amounts which a father established in a profession gives to his son to compensate him for work carried out in the father's professional office, which the son will one day inherit. "Imputed" income, thus, is totally or partially lacking in certain exterior requisites of money value and contractuality which usually characterize income. This often involves particular problems of assessment and valuation; it also results sometimes in the complete exclusion of income from the tax base.

b. IMMOVABLE PROPERTY. In the sector of income from immovable property, in the Italian objective taxes, imputed incomes are subject to tax. This applies not only under the tax on buildings, for imputed rents which the owner of a dwelling and his family lose if they do not rent the premises to others, but also under the land tax: when the commodities which the

---

[9] It must be understood that the term "transaction" (*transazione*) is used here in the sense accepted by economists, in the field of economic accounting, and not in the sense accepted by the civil law. In the latter, a "transaction" is a particular contract in which a compromise on contested rights is made between the parties (15/3.3j).   In economic accounting, a bilateral "transaction" is any exchange, any transfer of properties or values in exchange for others.   There are three types of transactions: money for money, property for money, and property for property.   Gifts (of money or property) are unilateral transactions.

owner of the land and his family produce are consumed by them directly, the value of the commodities is included in the landowning income assessed cadastrally for this tax. As regards buildings, the presumed rental value is subject to the tax on buildings not only when the dwelling is inhabited by the owner, but also when the premises are devoted to artistic or professional activities carried on by the owner which are taxed in category C/1. On the other hand, if premises are used for manufacturing or for the carrying on of other productive activities, specifically serving a business activity taxed in category B or category C/1 and not susceptible of other use without radical transformation, the income from the premises is included in the movable wealth income of the business if the owner of the business also owns the premises (9/4.2a).

c. PURE WORK. The policy of the Italian tax legislator is less rigorous for imputed income from pure work and from pure movable capital than for imputed income from the ownership of land and buildings. This policy does not establish the general rule of including in income from pure movable capital or from pure work income which does not have the character of monetary or monetizable "remuneration," but rather, that such income is excluded unless, although not having any monetary character as such, it is included in income which has monetary character or lends itself easily to monetary valuation.

With regard to income from pure work, the exclusion of imputed income resulting from executive agricultural labor of the entrepreneur who is a direct cultivator, of the members of his family, and of his co-entrepreneurs and the members of their families, has been pointed out (2/2.3). To obtain this result, it has been sufficient for the legislator to establish the exclusion of the income from the base of the tax on agrarian income, given that, for category C/2, taxation is confined to "remuneration" actually received for work carried on (8/1.1), and, for category C/1 (as for category B), taxation is confined to "proceeds" (*ricavi*) of an activity of independent work (8/2.1). Of itself, the value of executive work of the persons in question which is carried on without giving rise to a "remuneration" or to "proceeds" (in money or in kind) is not taxable in category C/1, in category C/2, or in category B. An "imputed wage" for work not connected with the production of other income never has tax importance: the housewife who carries on domestic work in her household does not produce taxable income even if a case of "imputed remuneration" for work as an employee could be made out.

Similarly, income from independent work which does not receive a true remuneration, but only an imputed one, is not taxable in category C/1. A doctor who treats members of his own family and a dentist who drills the teeth of his own children are not taxed for these services. Nor is a professional taxed who furnishes services to his friends free of charge.

On the other hand, a professional (or any other person taxed in category C/1) must include in his taxable proceeds the value of the work which the members of his family carry out for him gratuitously because the work of these persons gives rise to proceeds, not necessarily for their own benefit, but for the benefit of the person for whom they work. Just as the value of activities for which "remuneration" is not actually received but which provides advantages to the taxpayer or to members of his family or his friends is not included in the concept of income of categories C/1, C/2, or B, no deduction is provided, as an expense, for the monetary value of work which members of a family carry on without compensation, from the income of the professional (8/2.1). As a result, even if a part of the income, strictly speaking, has the nature of imputed compensation for work as an employee, it is subjected to the higher rate of tax applicable to income from independent work.

This general rule, that income which does not assume directly a monetary expression is not imputed independently but also is not deducted as an expense from the gross total of other income which includes it, applies as well to income from movable wealth of category B. Thus, income from work of members of an entrepreneur's family which does not take the form of true wages or of true professional compensation but remains "imputed income" because the work is furnished without contractual payment is not taxed independently as income of category C/1 or category C/2, but neither is it deducted, as an expense, from the enterprise income of category B in which such wages and compensation are included. The consequence is that, in family enterprises taxed in category B or category C/1, a part of the income from work is taxed under the higher rates of enterprise income.

The legislator has also wished to guard against the temptation of the taxpayer to attribute to himself and members of his immediate family fictitious relations of work or fictitious contractual compensation for true relations of work. As a result, the imputed compensation for the work of the taxpayer, his wife, and unemancipated minor children is never deductible as an expense from income of category B or category C/1 of the enterprise or the professional activity, and it is never taxed in category C/1 or category C/2 as the income of the worker, even when the work is performed under regular professional contracts of work as an employee for compensation which formally appears as true remuneration (7/2.1, 8/2.2).

The rule that income imputed to the work of members of the family is not independently taxed is applied only when the work is of a personal character, that is, when the worker is an individual and family ties can be shown between the entrepreneur and the other persons. The situation changes when the enterprise is a juridical person. The *Testo unico* originally also denied independent taxation of compensation received by directors of corporations and similar entities for their services as such, as income from work in category C/2 or category C/1, and included such compensation in the enterprise income of such entities. A recent law has modified this rule, however, establishing that, in general, compensation paid to directors is deductible from the enterprise income (7/2.3c) and is included in the income of the director in category C/1 (8/2.1). However, amounts which directors receive as compensation remain taxable as enterprise income in category B when they are given in the form of participations in profits. This solution reduces also the possibility that those who control the enterprise might succeed in passing off, as income from work, compensation received in the form of a dividend for their own capital invested or left in the enterprise.

For members of the families of directors of capital companies, the legislation in force makes no disposition, so that all wages and professional compensation paid to the wife or to the son (even if a minor) of a director are deductible from the income of a corporation, a solution, it is noted, that is diametrically opposed to that in force for personal enterprises.

d. MOVABLE PROPERTY. The use which the owner makes of a piece of movable property, when he does not make it the object of a bilateral transaction or employ it in the production of other goods, does not give rise to taxable income: the use which an owner makes personally of his automobile, or which a friend makes of it gratuitously, does not involve taxable income. The use of an automobile granted gratuitously by the owner to his firm enters automatically into the income (of category B or category C/1) of the enterprise; whereas rental of an automobile, granted by the owner for hire to his own firm, is income of category C/1 (artisans and small enterprises) for the owner, and it is deducted as an expense of producing income of category B or category C/1 of the firm which rents it.

The last group of questions which must be considered regarding imputed income concerns income obtainable from the gratuitous or semigratuitous transfer of movable things, or their transfer at a price artificially higher than the market price. In considering gratuitous transfers of products by an enterprise taxed in category B, it must be noted that such operations are conceptually similar to the gratuitous furnishing of services by a professional whose income is taxed in category C/1 to the members of his family or his friends. But fiscally, in the Italian objective taxes, the treatment in the two cases is different. At first sight, it might appear that gifts of products made by an enterprise taxed in category B to private consumers should also be excluded from objective taxation since they do not form part of the "proceeds" of the enterprise (and, of course, they are not taxable as income of the private recipients of the gifts since the Italian objective taxes only strike income in the hands of the owner of the source which has "produced" it). But closer reflection shows that this is not possible because of the notion of enterprise accepted in Italian commercial law and understood in Italian tax law, and because of the accepted notion of "proceeds" in Italian business accounting, based on the double entry system.

In Italian commercial law, the enterprise has a profit purpose, and, in Italian tax law, profit is always presumed in the activities of the enterprise. Moreover, in the double-entry system of accounting, any part of the product of the enterprise which is given to others, even if gratuitously, is registered among the products before being given, and then among the transfers of products. The transfer of the "product," given the presumption of profit, must give rise to "proceeds" in the system of accounts of the enterprise. These proceeds often will be balanced by an expense or corresponding negative entry, so as to take account of the fact that, for this product, the enterprise in reality receives nothing. Thus, from the fiscal point of view, if the enterprise is taxed on the basis of its accounting records, deductibility of the gift can be considered only if there is an entry of expense which balances the value of the product gratuitously transferred. But the only deductible expenses are those "inherent in the production of income" (7/2.1); gifts to private persons, except in certain cases when they have the character of advertising and thus figure as "inherent" in the production of income, do not constitute part of the expenses which serve to produce income. That gifts of products are not deductible in determining net income is supported also by the consideration that gratuities of enterprises have been "exempted" only up to 5% of the declared income, by an express provision of law issued in 1956, provided that the specific purpose of the gratuity is instruction, education, social assistance, religious worship, or welfare (7/2.4).

In the case of transfers of products at artificial prices, there are no provisions for imputed proceeds relative to operations between financially connected enterprises that both operate completely on national territory. On the other hand, there are explicit provisions for imputed proceeds from operations involving connected enterprises, where the connection involves enterprises operated in part abroad:

> In the income of persons who carry on their activity in the territory of the state on behalf of foreign companies, firms, and associations, through the sale or disposal of raw materials or merchandise, or through the manufacturing of goods, are included amounts paid to a foreign company, firm, or association in the form of a price higher than the current price for raw materials, products, or merchandise, or in the form of brokerage fees, participations in receipts, commissions, premiums, and the like ... (11/2.4).[10]

---

[10] D.P.R. 29 January 1958, n. 645 (*Testo unico* of the laws on the direct taxes), art. 113.

The case is particularly important with regard to petroleum enterprises. By virtue of internal agreements, refining enterprises connected with large international companies which control the extraction of raw petroleum are often accustomed to file balance sheets showing small profits or even losses, in which the purchase of raw petroleum from the associated companies appears at an artificially high price. The rule described above has the effect of removing from these operations the result of an undervaluation of income produced in Italy.

As was said above, analogous rules do not exist in the relations between enterprises that both operate on national territory. The reason for this is probably in the basic concept of the Italian system of objective taxes: that of reaching entirely, and as a rule only once (that is, without duplications), all of the national product. It is clear that, when the undervaluation of the profits of a certain Italian company is translated into an inflation of the receipts of a foreign company, there is an allocation to a foreign company of a share of the Italian national product, which should be subject to the objective taxes in Italy. On the other hand, when the undervaluation of the profits of a certain company operating in Italy is translated into an inflation of the proceeds of another company also operating fully in Italy, there is simply a displacement of part of the proceeds of one Italian enterprise to another enterprise. It is indeed true that, through this expedient, the burden of the objective taxes in Italy can be reduced because the taxable profit of one enterprise can be reduced by carrying a part of it to reduce the negative account of another enterprise. But this internal displacement is fully consistent with the concept of taxing once, without duplications, the national product (2/2.1).

2/2.5   Territoriality

As a rule, the Italian fiscal legislator is inspired for the objective taxes by the concept of reaching only, and entirely, the "national" product (2/2.1). Territoriality does not concern the residence or the domicile of the operator to whom the product comes, but the place where the productive factor is employed: even if the owner is abroad, the fruit of the productive factor is taxed in Italy whenever the factor itself is employed on national soil. This distinction is rather important for interest on capital. Such interest is taxed in Italy, if the capital in question is employed in Italy, even if the person who receives it resides abroad (or if he is a citizen of a foreign country residing in Italy).

The criterion of territoriality, in the above sense, is not formulated explicitly for each of the objective taxes in the definitions of their respective tax bases, but by a general rule in the *Testo unico* of the direct taxes, under which the taxes are applicable only if their bases (*presupposti*) arise in the territory of the state (11/1.1). For the tax on income from movable wealth, however, it was found necessary to give a detailed definition of the manner in which the principle of territoriality is expressed (11/1.3); the application of the criterion in question for income from movable wealth is not always as obvious as for income from an immovable asset, whose connection with national territory is immediately evident.

For income from movable wealth of category A, the law does not say expressly that it is taxed in Italy when the movable capital involved is employed in Italy. But it says so indirectly by the general pronouncement that "income owed by persons domiciled or resident in the state" is taxed in Italy (11/1.2).

In the case of Italian enterprises indebted to foreigners for amounts employed abroad, the basic criterion of territoriality of the productive factor is modified in favor of the Italian tax system (11/1.1). That is, in this case, the Italian objective taxes are applied to an amount which, strictly speaking, does not form part of the Italian national product, but of the foreign product.

A problem also arises in the treatment of income from pure capital where only a part of the capital is employed abroad, and a part is employed in Italy: while the credit is utilized in operations outside national territory, a mortgage guarantee on it is given on property situated in Italy. Here it can indeed be said that "national" capital, even if under the form of a guarantee for other capital situated abroad, participates in the formation of the income of pure capital in question. This income is taxed in Italy in its entirety under the tax on income from movable wealth of category A (11/1.2).

But the hardest problems concern income from movable wealth of category B (11/1.3). The general principal fixed by Italian law is that income deriving from business activities exercised in the state ("business," here, usually covers industrial, commercial, and artisan activities) is taxed in Italy. But certain business activities are carried on partly in Italy and partly abroad: for example, in the case of a foreign firm which essentially manufactures a product abroad but completes the productive cycle (for example, with assembly) and carries out the sale in Italy. A rigorous application of the principle of territoriality of productive factors in this case would involve taxing in Italy only the part of the income of the enterprise involving the activity exercised on national territory—the employment in Italy of productive factors. However, such an application of this principle would give rise to considerable complications in tax assessment. Thus, the Italian law, in accepting the principle, has made two modifications dictated by practical reasons: one against, and the other in favor of, the Italian tax system.

The first of the two modifications is the rule that, in the case of foreign enterprises, only the income imputable to activities carried on in Italy by such enterprises through the central office, branches, or other permanent establishments (*organizzazioni stabili*) is included in the tax base of the tax on income from movable wealth of category B (11/3.5). By virtue of this rule, not every productive factor operating in Italy, but only those involved in "permanent establishments," are taxed in Italy for the income produced by them. Some of the national product, as a result, is excluded from movable wealth taxation.

The second modification, which results in the inclusion in the tax base of certain components of the foreign product, is the rule that the income of an enterprise formed in Italy deriving from activities exercised abroad is considered produced in Italy unless the activities are carried on through a permanent establishment abroad having a separate administration and accounting (11/2.3). That is, such income is conclusively presumed to be produced in Italy even if in reality it is not. To forestall elusive maneuvers, such as placing the official office of the company abroad (perhaps in a border city), the above rule is applied also to any company formed abroad but having in Italy the central office of its administration or the principal object of its enterprise—that is, to any company which, considering the true location of its directive center, can be called Italian, independently of the place of its formation and the location of its official legal office.

For income from independent work, category C/1 of income from movable wealth, the principle of territoriality of the productive factor is followed in full. The law establishes that only that income from independent work which derives from an activity exercised in Italy is taxable under the Italian movable wealth tax. The surgeon who has an office in Italy and normally works there, but who, on one occasion, goes to New York to perform an operation, or the Italian lawyer who goes to Paris to deal with a legal question for a client who has a lawsuit there, is not subject to tax in Italy on the income from the specific activity carried on abroad. And, inversely, the American expert who is called by a firm operating in Italy to give advice, or the German architect who builds villas on the Italian coast for his fellow countrymen, is, at least in principle, taxed in Italy in category C/1 on the income from such work even if he has no professional office in Italy and goes there only on single, isolated cases, and even if the contract to work in Italy was made abroad with persons who customarily do not reside in Italy (11/1.4).

The application of the principle of territoriality in the case of income from work as an employee is only in part analogous to that provided for income from independent work. Income from work as an employee carried on in Italy is taxed in Italy, even if the person in question is employed by a foreign firm. But also subject to tax in Italy, in category C/2 of income from movable wealth, is income from work as an employee which is carried on abroad by employees of a person domiciled or resident in Italy who does not have a distinct organization with separate administration and accounting to which the compensation can be charged (11/1.5). Remuneration paid by a firm domiciled in Italy to employees abroad is subject to tax in category C/2 for those persons. The only way in which the firm could avoid the creation of this liability would be to have the duty to pay the remuneration in question arise, from the beginning, at its branch or at its parent office domiciled abroad. Finally, Italian tax is applied to remuneration paid to persons who work abroad on behalf of the Italian public administration (11/1.5).

To complete the picture, two important points must be added. The first is that, by virtue of international treaties with various countries, the application of the territoriality principle to different classes of income can be modified with respect to income of citizens of the countries with which those treaties are concluded (11/2.1). The second point concerns a "closing rule" (*norma di chiusura*) established for the tax on income from movable wealth by the *Testo unico* of the direct taxes: the rule is that the base of this tax includes income produced abroad by persons domiciled or resident in Italy which, by reason of an international agreement, is not taxed in the other country (11/2.2). It is possible to say that, in view of this rule, the Italian movable wealth tax exercises a "residual" function from the international point of view, as well as from the internal economic point of view, in that it taxes any income which does not fall under the other objective taxes and which is not otherwise taxable in Italy. It taxes any income of persons domiciled or resident in Italy, which, as a result of international agreements, is not taxed abroad. Taken together, these two rules would appear to permit the movable wealth tax to apply to income of persons domiciled or resident in Italy not taxed abroad because of international agreements, even if such income happened to be of a nature (rather than of a territorial origin) different from that of the income normally subject to the tax on income from movable wealth (11/2.1). However, this is a hypothesis rather than a reality.

2/2.6   Capital Gains

a.   GAINS FORMING PART OF THE NATIONAL PRODUCT.   Increases in the market value of assets—lands, buildings, securities, agricultural investments, and merchandise—sometimes form a part of the national product and sometimes do not. It is necessary, therefore, to compare the treatment of such gains under the objective taxes with their economic origins.

Excluding changes in the general level of prices, increases in the capital value of assets can arise in the four ways listed below.

1.   The failure of an enterprise to distribute profits, permitting self-financing and thus an increase in the productive capacity of the enterprise, which is reflected in the value of the shares represented by its share capital.

2. The increase in the productive capacity of an enterprise, or of other assets, with the capital employed remaining constant, connected with the improvement of the prospects of transactions or with improvements in organization.
3. The diminution of the general market interest rate, which causes an asset giving a fixed income to have a higher value. For example, a share with a yield of 5, when the average interest rate demanded on the market is 5%, will have a capital value of 100; but when the market interest rate falls to 4% and the share continues to yield 5, other conditions being equal, it will have a capital value not of 100 but of 125, since 5 represents 4% of 125.
4. The increase in the price of immovable property or other specific assets included in the capital of the enterprise, deriving not from the expectation that they will give a larger contribution to the national product, but from the expectation that the compensation for them and for their products will rise on the market as compared with other prices.

The capital gains specified under item 1 certainly form part of the national product. The distributed and undistributed profits of an enterprise are already subjected entirely to the movable wealth tax (at least in theory) in the hands of the enterprise itself. If the shareholder of a corporate enterprise is taxed on the capital gain corresponding to the undistributed profits of the corporation, there is, from the economic point of view, a duplication in objective taxation.

Article 7 of the *Testo unico* of the direct taxes establishes the general rule that the same tax cannot be applied more than once to the same tax basis, even against different taxpayers. But this rule is not sufficient to render illegal, and thus to remove from Italian objective taxation, the duplication just described because, from a juridical point of view, the capital gain on securities which the shareholder obtains constitutes a different taxable basis from that of the undistributed profit which has already borne the movable wealth tax in the hands of the company to which the shares relate (9/2.1).

The Italian fiscal legislator appraises economic phenomena only through the juridical outlines in which they appear; thus, the prohibition mentioned above does not serve to eliminate this or other duplications of tax which can be traced in the Italian system of objective taxes, starting from the theoretical model of net product inspired by De Viti and examining economic reality as it exists under its multiple juridical forms. Starting from concepts of income other than the "objective" one of income as national "product," this taxation appears justifiable and the duplication vanishes.

The second class of capital gains listed above involves those which can be traced to an increase in the capacity of future yield—expressing the greater contribution of the assets to the national income. The inclusion of these gains in the base of the movable wealth tax involves including in the present tax base not an element of the present national product, but the discount of increases in the future product which will go to form part of the national product of future years.   Prima facie—within the present annual cycle—it seems obvious here to state that a duplication is involved. But after closer examination, this no longer appears to be true.   In effect, if, every year, the entire value of the national product for that year must be reached, one would have to be able to evaluate it at its full value.   Now if, in subsequent years, one recognizes that the goods produced in a certain base year have a higher value than foreseen, the product of that base year, strictly speaking, would have to be "revalued" as a result.   If the fisc has measured its tax on the valuation of the product which was set forth in the base year, the fact that, in the subsequent year in which the new higher valuation emerges, it requires a further share of tax does not constitute a fiscal duplication from the point of view of the integral taxation of the new product; it constitutes, on the other hand, a way of recovering, even if with a displacement of some years, an omitted levy to fill a gap which otherwise would be created in favor of certain parts of the product.   Houses, or land investments, or those assets which compose a given enterprise before constituting capital put to use, have formed part of the national product of the years in which they were created.   Therefore, the taxation of this class of capital gains fits perfectly in the theory of taxing the national product without gaps and without duplications.

The third class of capital gains involves those deriving from variations in the market rate of interest, with respect to securities, buildings, and other investments.   Even for these gains, it cannot certainly be said that there is a corresponding increase in the national product.   Naturally, in the measure in which the diminution of the market rate depends on past, present, and future variations in national income, the latter are at the base of the phenomenon.   But these increases in national product are already reached, in the framework of movable wealth taxation, through the taxation of the factors which are responsible for them.   To take account of them again through the taxation of capital gains arising by way of the reduction of the interest rate would mean a duplication.   However, it can correctly be maintained that these increases of capital are actually a revaluation of investment property, which must be carried to correct the values assigned to this property in the years in which they were produced.   A decrease in the market interest rate indicates a disposition to renounce present goods in view of future goods, on conditions that are more burdensome than before the decrease: there is a disposition to be content with lower present consumption, for the sake of the future.   But this implies that durable goods devoted to investments, that is, goods which give rise to future benefits at the expense of omitted present consumption, must increase in value if they continue to allow the production of a certain flow of future goods.   Indeed, they permit giving the same quantity of future goods in exchange for present goods, while—by hypothesis—one is now content with a lesser quantity. Therefore, such capital gains can approach, for purposes of the application of the theory of the taxation of income produced, those of the second class, and the considerations expounded for that class also apply to them.

The last class of capital gains involves those deriving from an increase in the value of goods which is due not to a revision of the appraisal of their contribution to the national product or to a revision of the discount rate between present and future goods (that is, of the current market interest rate), but to a revision of the estimate of the share which they are in the position to secure for themselves in the national product in whose creation they participate. Houses can increase in value because it is estimated that rents will rise in comparison with other prices; shares of a given enterprise can rise in value because it is estimated that the enterprise will be in a position to increase more than can be foreseen its own market power and thus the proceeds per unit of product, or because it is estimated that the enterprise will be in a position to distribute to the productive factors which participate in it, together with the entrepreneurial factor (intended in the broad sense to embrace the entire share capital and the person managing it), a larger share of the product obtained than had been foreseen. In these cases, the inclusion in the tax base of capital gains raises questions related to those which we have seen in examining item 2. What is involved is a correction of evaluation of properties which at one time appeared in the national product at a lower price. Thus, the points already developed also are applicable here.

b. THE OBJECTIVE TAXATION OF GAINS. Italian fiscal legislation does not generally distinguish among the four classes described above. All gains falling under them—whether from investments in land, buildings, securities, agriculture, or merchandise—are subjected to identical treatment under the tax on income from movable wealth. The treatment of the four classes has followed an identical historical evolution. This treatment results in the taxation of certain gains which do not form part of the national product under the principles discussed at 2/2.7a, and in the exclusion from taxation of some gains which do.

The inclusion of capital gains in category B of income from movable wealth has been long established, under the decisions, and was limited to gains deriving from professional speculative activities (9/8.2). Increments of capital obtained by private persons, not by virtue of a professional speculative activity, but through occasional transactions, originally were excluded because it seemed that a true "productive source" was lacking for such gains. Subsequently, gains on operations of sale, not arising out of a specific professional activity directed toward this objective, but carried out by business enterprises, were included in the tax base on the assumption that all activities of a business enterprise are activities professionally organized to obtain a profit, and that a speculative intent, and thus a productive source of capital gain, could always be conclusively presumed therein.   Finally, it was established that gains on occasional sales made by private persons should be included in the tax base, provided it could be shown that they had been motivated by a speculative intent.   In such sales, it was decided, there is also a productive source of capital gain, even though more fleeting.

The picture resulting from the decisions has been completed with the recent provision of law that, for enterprises taxed on the balance sheet basis (corporations and similar entities) (6/1.2b), a capital gain is includible in income from movable wealth, not only when there is a sale or other transaction comparable in its economic effects to a sale, but also whenever the enterprise recognizes the existence of the gain by inscribing it in the balance sheet, thus increasing in its own accounting record the value of the asset responsible for the gain (9/8.1).   The conclusive presumption of the productive "source" is thus strengthened because, even before sale, a speculative intent is assumed to be implicit and inherent in the enterprise.

The reason for the taxation of capital gains on lands and on other assets obtained by speculative activity or with speculative "intent" lies in the recognition, which Italian jurisprudence has been able to make rather easily, that those who pursue these gains receive the compensation for a "productive source" which they own, that is, for an activity of independent work or of an enterprise.   And since the basic principle of the objective tax is to tax any income deriving from a source of work and capital, separately or taken together, it seemed logical to include the gains in question in the base of the movable wealth tax.   But, from the point of view of the theory of the income produced, this is not logical: there is a conceptual difference between the existence of a source in work and in capital, on the one hand, and its application to the creation of one or more particles of national product, on the other.   A comparison between the case of the agent or broker and that of the professional operator who buys and sells lands for profit on his own account can clarify this point.   The first offers a service to individuals in their private transactions, in the same manner as lawyers or business consultants offer theirs.   The second, on the other hand, does not work so much to produce the service to others, contributing to the national product with his own service, as to assure himself a part of the national capital or of the national product which corresponds to the employment of other factors.

In other words, not all of the employment of work and of capital emerges in the national product.   This does not mean that the speculator in lands or other assets does not also offer some service to the national product while he is carrying on his speculative operations. In fact, he acts in part as a broker or agent: he performs functions analogous to those of the merchant. But he gains by profiting from his knowledge or skill in production in order to transfer to himself a share of the wealth and of the national product created by the acts of others. The fisc makes no distinction and, in principle, includes the entire gain of the speculator under the movable wealth tax, while excluding other capital gains. With regard to the theory of income produced, this is an error since the value of the asset either is or is not part of the national product, independently of who appropriates it and the manner in which he does so. Speculative intent characterizes the activity of certain persons, through whose action specific goods come to receive a new valuation on the market. But the valuation is one account, and the production of goods is another account. The source of production of goods is capital and work, but not, generally, the capital and the work which are connected with the speculative activity. The production of certain goods in a base year and the subsequent market adjustment of their values can very well occur without the intervention of a speculative activity or any similar activity on the part of the persons owning those goods.

Thus, the search for a speculative activity operates as a reference to certain personal elements and removes from its true terms the problem of objective taxation inspired by a scheme of De Viti's type (2/2.1). Reasoning from the subjective point of view of the "merits" of the taxpayers, compensation for activities not resulting in new national product appears even more suitable for taxation than compensation which represents new wealth. But the objective tax should not take personal elements into account. In practice, it is difficult to put personal elements aside in a concrete fiscal system, given that the system in the final analysis affects taxpayers, that is, persons. Thus it is that the concept of fiscal income as equal to the sum of the net national product is almost unknowingly deflected to compromises which, however understandable, represent a serious flaw in the system.

The deflection goes further when taxation is extended to include all operations of enterprises, by conclusively presuming their speculative nature. Capital gains are involved in such operations; but even more clearly than those of professional operators, such gains are distinct from the furnishing of a service contributing to the national product. They express only the circumstance that the distribution of national wealth has been modified and is being modified in favor of those who have property rights on certain parts of the national soil, which benefit from production of other sectors. From the personal point of view, this appears to be an element of taxable capacity, but, objectively, neither work nor capital presently employed by the owner is the direct and explicit source of it. There is no longer at the base of the tax the capital factor or the work factor, but the absolute presumption of them: a fiction of a scheme which expresses a mistaken causal relationship.

Capital gains resulting from a pure increase in the general price level are taxed in principle since, under the Civil Code, all money obligations are extinguished by payment at their nominal value (CC art. 1277). However, gains resulting from large devaluations of money in inflationary periods have been exempted from tax by special legislation, as after World War II (9/8.1).

2/2.7 "Personalization" of the Objective Taxes

a. EFFECTS OF QUALITATIVE DISCRIMINATION. In Italy—especially since World War II, and more particularly from the time of the 1951 reform, known as the Vanoni reform—there has been a greater tendency toward personalization of the objective taxes; that is, there has been a tendency to adapt the system of the "seven rates" always more to the personal conditions of the taxpayers.

Before World War II, by virtue of ministerial provisions, the wages of workers in industries generally were excluded from income from movable wealth of work as an employee, and, thus, the problem of not cutting into the minimum incomes of wage earners was largely, but roughly, resolved without need for measures of personalization.

The tendency toward personalization of the objective taxes could not be developed without great difficulties, first of all in assessment. From a certain theoretical point of view, the tax on income of objective character, discriminated qualitatively, can be considered as a type standing by itself to be opposed to another type, discriminated quantitatively, as has been done until now. But from another point of view, in a tax system with broad evasion possibilities and with broad difficulties of assessment, especially for certain types of income, the objective tax, discriminated qualitatively, may be imagined as an indirect, rough instrument for attempting to realize—through the higher taxation of income from capital and from enterprises in contrast to income from work, especially of workers and employees who usually have lower total incomes— that type of progressivity which such a system does not attain directly through quantitative discrimination.

The evolution toward personalization in Italy has always been conditioned by this substitutive function of objective taxation. The theoretical need of moving toward personalization was accompanied by the practical need of maneuvering the qualitative discrimination of taxable incomes (which forms the operative substitute of a personal tax) precisely to attempt to satisfy the new demands of progressivity.

From another point of view, the rate discrimination by kind of income has an independent function of its own even where its substitutive function is lacking. First of all, income from capital is obtained with less trouble than income from work; and besides, capital can increase in value without the increases (better known as "capital gains") being easily taxable as current income. Often, the important argument can be added that income flowing in whole or in part from capital is less fortuitous, more stable, than income from work and thus involves a lesser need for saving.[11]

Today, the thesis prevails among Italian students of taxation that it would be opportune to abandon the qualitative discrimination of income in taxing income, but that it would likewise be opportune to safeguard the principle of it, substituting for the objective taxes on income a discrimination made through a tax on wealth, under which "established" (*fondati*) incomes are automatically taxed more than others, in relation to the participation of capital in their production. This second system could substitute a "continuous" discrimination based on wealth for the "discontinuous" and complex discrimination based on the nature of income as a way of presuming the existence of a certain quantity of wealth in its creation.

b. INCOME FROM LANDOWNING. As against industrial activities which were still weak and often subject to crises until about 10 years ago, land seemed the best, most solid, and most certain investment in the prevalently agricultural economy, and it therefore also appeared as a particularly suitable base for national and local taxation. Today, the picture is profoundly changed. Agriculture in Italy is undergoing deep transformations and, in large part, is in crisis. It is still possible sometimes to derive good income from ownership of agricultural lands; but to do so, it is necessary to add to the immovable capital much movable capital, much work, and many diverse skills.

Moreover, a considerable part of land ownership is in the hands of small agricultural owner-entrepreneurs (2/2.3) whose incomes are rather low both in absolute terms and above all in comparison to what can be obtained in other occupations, even as an employee or as a manual laborer.

Finally, the Italian land cadasters (10/2.2c), based in the best of hypotheses on incomes of 1938, are by now largely inaccurate, so that the assessments which are obtained from them by multiplying the base values by certain general coefficients of adjustment present a very faint reference

---

[11] In addition, one who derives income from capital, all other conditions being equal, finds himself in a better economic situation than one who has income from work, because the former can realize on the market the capital value of his prospective income, while the latter cannot (except where slavery is allowed). On this point, see Steve, *Il sistema tributario e le sue prospettive* 124 *et seq.*

to the real average conditions of the landowning income of the various taxpayers.

To distinguish these incomes—as proceeds of pure capital, more established and more secure, less troublesome to obtain—from established and semiestablished incomes of other types (such as those from enterprises) no longer appears satisfying as a general principle. Given the imprecision of the cadastral data, moreover, the objective taxation of lands appears to be a very imperfect means for distinguishing taxpayers with different amounts of income. Often, the machinery seems to operate in reverse, increasing the tax on those taxpayers worse off than average, not on those better off.

The harshness of the rates of this objective tax has led to the need for broad exemptions. Since the idea of personalization of the taxation of landowning income has gained little headway, the idea has spread of indiscriminately reducing this fiscal burden by introducing a low rate of national taxation; this remedy, however, is largely offset by the possibility of high rates of local surtaxes (12/1.1). A recent provision also exempts income from landowning (and agrarian income) from taxation if such income falls below a certain figure (12/1.1).

It may be said that the unpersonalized objective tax, in this field, tends to destroy itself. The personal conditions of the various owners have become very different; and a uniform objective tax whose rate is established by looking only to the quality of the income is thus no longer satisfactory today because, in order to be able to treat marginal operators equally, it is necessary to allow many of those above the margin to escape their proper burden, and, in order to treat the latter in proportion to their capacity, it is necessary to burden the former unbearably.

c. INCOME FROM BUILDINGS. Certain economic and institutional factors have affected the application of the tax on income from buildings: first, the control of rents, which was adopted in the war economy and is still in force, although in process of gradual elimination; and second, the 25-year exemptions for new buildings, which are still in effect (9/4.2b). Thus, the base of the tax on buildings is today singularly narrow because, on the one hand, new houses are largely exempt from it and because, on the other hand, buildings under rent control do not have an income equal to what they could have in a free market. Owners of old houses, if they have the means, often have already provided, or are providing now, for pulling down the old houses in order to build new ones exempt from tax and from rent control. Those with lesser means who have old houses are bearing the full weight of the tax, besides that of the rent control (which has often caused a reduction in the quality of the houses).

It is true that the rise in values of urban lands and the resulting opportunities for investment have permitted many to recoup these damages or to obtain large additional gains. But it has been a very unequal process of growth, so that the qualitative taxation of objective income appears decidedly unsuitable as a substitute for a tax system aimed at taking account of personal differences of income and wealth and of the movement of capital gains and losses.

It is evident that between the class of owners who rent buildings and that of owners who use their own apartments, there is a profound socio-economic difference, and, in this respect also, the thesis that qualitative discrimination can serve as an indirect instrument of quantitative discrimination appears always weaker. On the contrary, the absence of personalization has led to the erosion of the base of the tax by giving greater force to the demands for maintenance of the exemption for houses of new construction.

d. INCOME FROM MOVABLE CAPITAL. Income from pure movable capital in category A theoretically should be established fixed income, to be contrasted with mixed income from capital and work of category B, which is variable income to which the entrepreneurial activity contributes as well as capital (although, in practice, an investor in bonds may not have a less risky income than one who invests in shares of larger enterprises, since the former is subject to risks of monetary devaluation). Today, however, with the cumulative effect of the rates levied by the local entities and with the recent changes in the national rates, income of category B, in the last analysis, is often taxed more heavily than income of category A, so that the discrimination operates in reverse of what was originally intended. The legislator seems today to behave as if he were admitting that enterprise income was "more established," and thus less insecure, than income from pure capital. In the particular case of the relationship between shares and bonds, this seems sufficiently plausible; but it opens a breach in all of the old conceptions of the qualitative discrimination of incomes characterized by the presence of different quantities of capital in the production of income, on which the Italian objective movable wealth system was originally based.

An important part of income from pure movable capital, income from securities of the public debt, is exempt by law from the objective taxes (9/1.2). Another part, although it bears a rate of objective tax higher than income from pure work, involves the advantage of a much broader possibility of evasion for purposes of the succession taxes and of the personal progressive taxes of the state (the complementary tax) and of the commune (the family tax), since bonds need not be registered. For taxpayers of the higher income brackets, these are not negligible advantages, given the high rates of those taxes. In these conditions, it certainly cannot be said that the objective taxation of income from pure movable capital in Italy carries out a broad function as an indirect instrument of progressivity, of quantitative discrimination of taxable incomes.

e. INCOME FROM SHAREHOLDING. With respect to the theoretical basis of the qualitative discrimination of incomes as such, the treatment of movable wealth incomes flowing to single individuals as shareholding income gives rise to considerable perplexities. The profits out of which distributions are made to shareholders are subject to the tax on income from movable wealth in category B, but the distributions themselves are not subject to any objective tax (9/2.1a).

On the one hand, from the point of view of the typical shareholder, the profits which he draws from his share of investments differ hardly at all from an income from pure capital. If it is imagined that the company in economic substance pays the tax of movable wealth of category B on this income "on behalf of" the shareholder (in the same way that it formally pays on behalf of the bondholders the movable wealth tax on interest received by them), then one is obliged to treat movable wealth income from shareholding as income from pure capital. On the other hand, from the point of view of the enterprise, the profits taxed in category B do not appear as income of pure capital. Thus, if it is imagined that the movable wealth tax bearing on this income remains charged against the enterprise, for purposes of qualitative discrimination, one is driven to consider the income as mixed because it is obtained with an effort of work (entrepreneurial) as well as simple capital.

f. ENTERPRISE INCOME. There is a series of minor inconsistencies in the qualitative discrimination of enterprise income as it is carried out today.

If a professional or a small entrepreneur taxed in category C/1 devotes a part of his own savings to the purchase of the premises in which his activity has its office, he becomes subject, on the income inherent in his activity, to an objective rate of pure capital and to another of pure work. But if the same taxpayer employs the same amount of money, not to purchase the premises where he carries on his activity, but to purchase instrumental goods (as in the case of a doctor who equips himself with radiological apparatus), he will pay only the tax on income from work—and not that on income from capital or mixed income—on the higher income which he obtains in this manner and which derives from the employment of capital.

In the present economy, the capital endowment of small entrepreneurs and of professionals tends in many cases to become considerable. In many activities, the fact that the enterprise has few employees no longer suffices to assure that the activity of its owner is an activity consisting almost entirely of pure work.

g. STANDARD ALLOWANCE AND RATE REDUCTION. Against this background, the measures of personalization which have been introduced into the objective taxes have a very limited effect. The standard allowance of L. 240,000 (12/1.4b) and the reduction of the rate by one half on the next L. 720,000 (12/1.4c) have been granted only for certain categories of the tax on income from movable wealth for individuals but have not been extended to all the objective categories of income. These measures do not extend to income from landowning, agrarian income, income from buildings, or income from movable capital, or to income of personal or family companies. Also excluded is all movable wealth income of nonfamily corporations and similar entities: this is in appearance perfectly justified since the "personalization" concerns individuals; but, in reality, it can be criticized with respect to the shareholding income going to typical individual shareholders.[12]

Suppose that an agricultural business is conducted by the owner. Both he—the head of the family—and his wife work there. If the treatment of movable wealth income were in effect, there would be an allowance of L. 480,000 for the tax on agrarian income and the tax on landowning. But, in actuality, if the landowning income exceeds a minimum amount, the landowning income and the agrarian income are taxed entirely (12/1.1, 12/1.2). For income from agricultural enterprise and agricultural ownership, besides, there is no reduction to one half of the rate for the next L. 720,000 of income after the standard allowance has been taken. Thus, the small agriculturalist finds himself with a differential burden of tax, higher than that which falls, for example, on the small merchant.

To introduce this type of personalization for agriculture, however, the great difficulty presented by the use of the cadastral method of assessment in the taxation of these types of income would have to be overcome. In order to achieve personalization, it presumably would be necessary to pass from an objective and automatic method of assessment, such as the cadastral method, to one permitting consideration of the economic conditions of the taxpayer. This group of assessments would have to be based on the returns of income, involving, obviously, great labor for the Direct Tax Offices, which already face a difficult situation.

Problems analogous to those seen for the taxation of agricultural income are posed for the personalization of the tax on income from buildings. Here the practical obstacle of greater work for the Tax Offices is again presented; even with the activation of the new urban building cadaster, the tax will be based on market rents when these are substantially higher

---

12 Along with these incomplete developments, another aspect seems particularly open to discussion: the failure to extend these measures of personalization to those local surtaxes, and independent taxes similar to surtaxes (2/2.9), which are imposed on the same categories of income.

than the cadastral values (9/4.2c), and the taxpayer will therefore still have to report the income on his return.

An example will show some of the inequalities which this creates. Suppose that a taxpayer has a "mixed" annual income from capital and work of L. 1 million (taxed in category C/1), derived from a small enterprise in which his contribution of capital can be valued at from L. 10 million to L. 12 million (and can thus be considered responsible for half of his annual income). Another taxpayer has an annual income of L. 1 million obtained half through work and half through the rent from ownership of buildings valued at L. 10 million to L. 12 million. The first will enjoy the allowance of L. 240,000 and the reduction of the rate by one half on the next L. 720,000. The second will enjoy these benefits only for the L. 500,000 derived from pure work. Moreover, a widow receiving an income of L. 500,000 a year from building ownership will enjoy no allowance, even though perhaps needing it more than the first two taxpayers and having the same value of ownership.

One might think that, except for the classes of small agricultural owners, these points would be marginal because—except in the case of "widows and orphans"—rather few persons now having small savings invested in buildings or in the form of fixed income from movable capital would find themselves without an income from work of at least L. 720,000 to L. 960,000 a year. But the points made above are not at all marginal when the circumstances listed below are taken into account.

1. The measures of personalization are granted at present, entirely, to the extent that they can be taken advantage of, to each member of the family receiving movable wealth income of categories C/2, C/1, or B. Cases in which the owner of a small enterprise is not the head of the family, but the wife or other dependent, are very frequent.

2. These measures are applied starting with the income subject to the lowest rate (category C/2). If it were established that the measures should start with the category of income taxed with the highest rate or that a proportional reduction should be made on all three categories, the denial of personalization for income from pure ownership would become rather more meaningful.

3. The amount of income to which the basic allowance applies could be increased (L. 240,000 is by now less than the vital minimum for any family, if a minimum of civil dignity is also to be included in it); and allowances could be given for dependent children (as is already done, if only in limited measure, for the complementary tax).

The system of the basic allowance and of the reduction of rate on income on the next L. 720,000 of income for individuals taxed in categories B and C/1 is extended to personal companies subject to movable wealth taxation in category B. But for personal companies, also, the allowance is available only once, even if the company is formed by several individuals, each entitled to a share of the income produced by it. Now

DESCRIPTION OF TAX SYSTEM   178

if it is the concept of the "person" which is important, it is reasonable to give a basic allowance and an initial rate reduction for each member of the enterprise.

The problem evidently is that, from the point of view of yield, the state—with these broadened reliefs—could sustain considerable losses in a system of taxation which already, as a result of evasions, is not considered satisfactory.

For incomes whose taxation is carried out through direct withholding by the state or withholding at the source by the employer, the basic allowance of L. 240,000 and the reduction of the rate by one half for the next L. 720,000 are applied, according to the expression of the law, in "annualized" measure. That is, if a person is paid on a monthly basis, the amount of the allowance for the income of each month is calculated by dividing L. 240,000 by 12, thus reducing the monthly compensation by L. 20,000 (12/1.4b). The rate reduction is made in the same way; for each payment period of a month, the halved rate is applied on L. 60,000 (12/1.4c). For persons who work only several months of the year and who clearly cannot obtain income of category C/2 except in those months, this system results in a discrimination which can be very severe. Such is the case for seasonal workers—for example, agricultural laborers or building workers—who work only six months of the year. The same problem arises for youths who enter their first occupation, not at the beginning of the year, but during the year. On the other hand, it is clear that the liquidation of the tax would indeed be much more complex if, in the computation of the tax due on each pay envelope, it were necessary to take account of differences in the total annual income of each recipient of income from employment.

h. COMPENSATION OF GAINS AND LOSSES. In the strictly objective system of taxing the various separate incomes according to their sources, in force until a few years ago, it could happen that, in a certain business period, a taxpayer who had a loss for a certain source of income and an equal or lesser gain for another had to pay the full tax on the second even if the algebraic sum of the two incomes taken together was zero or negative. Marking a step forward, article 95 of the *Testo unico* of the direct taxes establishes that, as regards each person, the objective taxes are measured on the basis of the aggregate net result of all the activities and operations productive of income classifiable in the same category (7/1.1, 7/4.1).

Still denied, however, is compensation between incomes of different categories of movable wealth belonging to the same person, and compensation between different objective taxes. Suppose an artisan or small entrepreneur or professional is the owner of the premises in which he exercises his activity. He is taxed separately, on the one hand, under the tax on buildings for the figurative income from ownership; and on the other hand, under the tax on income from movable wealth of category C/1 for his professional activity, net of the presumed expense for the premises. In case his professional activity gives a negative balance, this taxpayer is not in a position to set off the loss on the professional income against the imputed income from the buildings because the income from the buildings does not belong to the same category of income as the enterprise income. This is profoundly illogical since, in reality, the building where he works cooperates indistinguishably in the production of his movable wealth income. Medium-sized and large entrepreneurs taxed in category B, on the other hand, have the right to set off losses of the exercise of the enterprise against income from ownership of the buildings in which the enterprise is carried on, by virtue of the rule that the owner of a building who carries out in it his own economic activity subject to tax in category B is taxed on both of the types of income entirely in category B (9/4.2a).

Article 95 establishes compensation for incomes of the same category obtained by the same "person." However, as a result of the definition which the *Testo unico* of the direct taxes gives of "person" (*soggetto*), the situation can arise rather frequently where the same individual has two economic activities which, from the subjective point of view, are fiscally separate and belong to different taxpayers. Consider, for example, the case of two activities, of which one, being a partnership enterprise carried on by an individual together with other persons, belongs to the one subject—namely, the partnership—from the point of view of the objective tax; and of which the other, carried on by the same individual, belongs from the point of view of the movable wealth objective tax to a different taxpayer—namely, the individual.

In cases of this kind, the compensation provided for by article 95 is not allowed because there are formally two distinct persons. This rule might appear particularly subject to discussion from the point of view of the rigor of the tax system: on the one hand, for the personal taxes in the Italian system, the partnership resolves itself into the single individuals which make it up, and its income is taxed to each member in accordance with his share. On the other hand, for the national and communal personal taxes on income, the incomes of different persons forming part of the same family are cumulated.

2/2.8   Effects of the Complexity of the System

Perhaps the principal defect of an aggregate system of taxation of income in which so many qualitative and quantitative discriminations and diversifications exist together—as in the present Italian system, in contrast with a system of the Anglo-Saxon type—is that the taxpayer cannot easily adopt, in the payment of the tax, the procedure which is known in the United States as "self-assessment." The Italian taxpayer is not in a position to compute by himself, at the bottom of the form of the return of income, the taxes owed by him. He reports the income, but not the amount of taxes which this requires him to pay. And only rarely does a person know exactly the rate applicable to each of his own incomes. The citizen, thus, is hardly "tax conscious." Besides, since the computation of the taxes is now the responsibility of the tax administration, it is not possible to adopt, at present, the rule that the tax be paid upon the filing of the return. The bill specifying the amount of taxes due will reach the taxpayer later, and the majority of persons are in a position only to know the general total of it and the amount of the bimonthly installments, and not to identify the various taxes, surtaxes, and additionals which compose this total.

The Italian system of taxing income is very complex, and it requires considerable technical knowledge even for taxpayers who are individuals, and who do not have the particular questions and particular duties of corporations. The logic of the Italian system—although very interesting for the economist and for the fiscal expert—is less easily comprehensible to the common man. The reasons for the complexity of the Italian system are that an attempt has been made up to now to make the qualitative discrimination of incomes in taxing the income from wealth instead of the wealth itself, and that the system is now in a phase of transition toward a single personal tax absorbing all of the objective taxes. This transition is the aim which Italy seems to be setting up for the next five years in its own tax policy—and also in relation to its obligations in connection with the Common Market tax harmonization. The present tax policy thus will complete the reform begun by Vanoni in 1951 with the introduction of the obligatory single annual return of income for all taxpayers.

2/2.9 Local Taxes and Surtaxes; Additionals and Fees

In considering the burden of the objective taxation of income, mention should be made of local taxes and surtaxes imposed on the bases of the national objective taxes, and of certain additionals and fees which are computed on the taxes themselves.

Income from landowning (12/1.1) and income from buildings (12/1.3) are subject to communal and provincial surtaxes at rates which may exceed those of the national taxes. Income from movable wealth of categories B and C/1 is subject to a communal tax on industries, commerce, arts, and professions (ICAP) and a provincial "additional" thereto (12/1.4d), even if the income is exempt under a special law from the tax on income from movable wealth.[13] In all the cases described above,

---

[13] Any industry, business, art, or profession producing income which cannot be subjected to the tax on income from movable wealth, or in any way has not yet been assessed for purposes of that tax, is subject to the communal license tax (*imposta di patente*), which consists of a fixed fee, graduated in seven categories taking account of the nature of the activity, the place in which it is carried on, the personnel em-

there are also surtaxes, at varying rates, for the benefit of the local Chambers of Commerce (12/1.4d). In addition, those who conduct industries, businesses, arts, or professions in a commune recognized as a place of resort, health, or tourism are subject to a special contribution, known as the *contributo di cura*, at the rate of 1% of the income subject to ICAP.[14] If ICAP is not imposed, the contribution is computed on the income subject to the tax on income from movable wealth of categories B and C/1, including income exempt from that tax. The contribution is inscribed in the roll and collected in the same manner as the other local taxes.

On the objective taxes and the related taxes and surtaxes are also computed the "additionals" described below.

1. An additional for the benefit of the communal welfare entities (ECA), applicable to the national, provincial, and communal taxes on land-owning and on buildings, the tax on income from movable wealth, the tax on agrarian income, the complementary tax; the registration, mortgage, and succession taxes; all communal and provincial taxes collectible through rolls; [15] and the corporation tax.[16] For the tax on landowning income and the related surtaxes, the tax on agrarian income, and the tax on income from movable wealth of category C/2 when imposed at 4% (12/1.4d), the additional is 5% of the tax; in all other cases, it is 10% of the tax.
2. An additional to meet expenses of earthquake relief in Calabria, imposed on all national, communal, and provincial ordinary taxes, surtaxes, and contributions, collectible through rolls from 1955-1956 through 1966-1967.[17] The additional is 5% of the taxes, net of collection fees and the additional for ECA.

All the taxes collected through rolls are subject to collection fees (13/3.7).

2/3. The Complementary Progressive Tax and the Family Tax

2/3.1 Historical Background

There are two progressive personal taxes on income of individuals: the complementary tax (*imposta complementare progressiva*), which is imposed by the state, and the family tax (*imposta di famiglia*), which is imposed by the commune. From a historical point of view, the oldest of the two is the family tax, which existed in various parts of Italy before the national unification. However, it was set up in a rudimentary way, in part as a tax on expenditures, and was levied on the more well-to-do persons, rather than being an income tax of a general character. In some states, it was a state tax, in others a local tax. It must be remembered,

---

ployed, and the number of premises or the rental paid for them (TUFL arts. 165-167). The maximum tax is L. 2,400.

[14] L. 4 March 1958, n. 174, art. 8.
[15] R.D.L. 30 November 1937, n. 2145, art. 1.
[16] L. 10 December 1961, n. 1346, art. 1.
[17] L. 26 November 1955, n. 1177, art. 18.

however, that some states had an area equal to, or little larger than, that of the present local provincial entities, and a smaller population. With the national unification, the family taxes were replaced, for the benefit of the central government, by the new, stronger, objective taxes on income, which were extended from Piedmont to all the national territory. The family tax was left to the local finances, but, in part by reason of the uncertainties of the legislation, it did not receive much attention.

Only toward the end of the last century did it begin to be regarded as an important instrument for the benefit of the local entities, in the framework of the new ideals of personal progressive taxation which, under the stimulus of the most advanced political currents and of the extension of the right to vote, were emerging together with a growth in the fiscal requirements of the cities. From the beginning of this century, a certain number of large communes applied it: Milan, for example, instituted it in 1908 and began to apply it in 1909. From 1923 to 1926, the application of the family tax—in all of Italy—was suspended under fascist tax policy, and from 1926 to 1945, its application was allowed only in communes with less than 30,000 inhabitants. The tax on leasehold values, described at 2/3.7, was instituted for the larger communes. In 1945, on the fall of fascism, the family tax was extended anew to all communes, on authorization of the Provincial Administrative Board, except to those—in practice, very few—which applied the tax on leasehold values generally.[18]

The introduction of the complementary progressive tax on income (6/1.1f) is rather more recent—1925—and its development is even more disappointing than that of the family tax.[19] The yield of the family tax was formerly rather close to that of the complementary tax but has exceeded it considerably in recent years (1/6.7d). It is important to notice that the lowest rate of the family tax is at a level near that of the lowest complementary tax rate, but that the highest family tax rate—which cannot exceed 12%—is lower than the highest complementary tax rate; also, for purposes of the family tax, there are reductions for income from work notably broader than under the complementary tax. The maximum rate of the complementary tax was 50% until 1962; now it has been increased to 65%, for incomes exceeding L. 500 million (12/1.5c).

The difference in yield is evidently due to the different intensity of assessment on the part of the state 'and on the part of the local entities.

---

[18] The family tax is regulated by articles 111-121 of the *Testo unico* of local finance. The imposition of this tax may be authorized by the Provincial Administrative Board for communes which do not apply generally the tax on leasehold values; and its application precludes the application of the tax on servants (TUFL arts. 149-152) and the tax on pianos (TUFL arts. 155-160). These taxes, which are imposed at fixed annual rates, are not of great importance.

[19] The complementary progressive tax is now regulated by articles 130-144 of the *Testo unico* of the direct taxes.

The state is bound by an analytic and formalized assessment, which, above all for income from capital, enterprise income, and professional income, often gives slender results for a number of reasons. Inductive assessment based on the style of living and other facts can be employed only in a supplementary way; and the national fisc, particularly in the larger centers, encounters great difficulty in gathering indicia of the way of living and other facts suitable for challenging the results of the analytical assessments, under the procedures provided by law (13/2.2, 13/2.3). The commune, for the family tax, makes full recourse to the style of living and to rougher inductive criteria, which permit, at least for certain classes of income, an assessment more severe if not more fair.

It is just the difference in yield, in the strictness in the assessments, which stands in the way of the unification of these two taxes. The communes, if the unification were made in the hands of the state, fear the loss of a considerable part of their receipts from personal taxation and the necessity of adapting themselves in this field to the practice, until now less efficient, of the state. The complementary tax, as noted above, is more recent than the family tax and has had, on the whole, a more difficult development. Although the tax was one of the first accomplishments of fascist fiscal policy, the latter should not be credited with a courageous (even if not fruitful) innovation. In fact, the last years of the nineteenth century and the first twenty years of this century saw a continuous succession of plans for the introduction of a personal progressive tax on income. When the fascists reached power, the new personal tax on income was already about to be launched, with the actuation of the Meda plan; Meda, Minister of Finance and one of the leaders of the Popular Party (called today the Christian Democracy), with the assistance of Luigi Einaudi and of other experts, had prepared a harmonious and robust plan for a personal tax on income, against which the complementary tax launched by De Stefani in 1925 appears as a compromise directed in large part to deprive the new tax of its spirit and its foundations.

2/3.2   Persons Subject

Both the complementary tax and the family tax aim at the family group rather than at individual persons. With respect to both taxes, Italian citizens and foreigners are treated alike. The payer is an individual (*persona fisica*) and is liable for tax on his own total income and the total incomes of the persons included in his family nucleus.

For the complementary tax, the taxpayer is formally the head of the family, but his income includes all income of other persons over which, under the civil law, he has free disposition or administration without the duty to render an accounting. The income of the wife is cumulated with that of her husband (5/1.2). A wife legally and actually separated from her husband is subject to the tax for that income of which she can freely dispose (5/1.2).

The family tax, on the other hand, is imposed on the family as a unit, considered as a union of persons related by blood (*parentela*) or marriage (*affinità*),[20] who live together in the same house and constitute an economic unit, even if they do not have a single and undivided patrimony (TUFL art. 112).[21] Also considered as separate families are the persons specified below (TUFL art. 113).[22]

1. Single persons, even if living with others to whom they are not related by blood or marriage.
2. Persons under guardianship who have their own income, even if living with their guardians.
3. Persons who live with their families without any participation in the economic unit thereof, even if bound to them by ties of blood or marriage.
4. Groups of persons who live together for purposes of instruction, education, or worship (TUFL art. 114).

For the family tax, the "family" is defined on the basis of independent economic concepts, while, for the complementary tax, reference is made exclusively to the concepts of the civil law. What is important for the family tax is that the persons living together form an economic unit, and it is not necessary, as for the complementary tax, that the head of the family have the free disposition or administration, without the duty of rendering an accounting, over the property of the members (other than the wife). It is clear that the patrimonies of persons living together can be separate, from the point of view of the civil law; this situation gives rise to unitary taxation under the family tax, but not under the complementary tax. The concept of the family for the family tax is also broader than for the complementary tax in that individuals living together are grouped in a single nucleus. For example, a community of monks is taxed under the family tax on the sum of the individual incomes.

For these two taxes, it seems at first view that the taxpayer, if he wishes to reduce the burden of the tax, should have an interest in appearing not as a dependent, but as a separate person. In practice, just the opposite occurs. A desire to reduce the burden of the tax leads young people to make themselves seem still to belong to the original family, especially with regard to the family tax. The reason for this lies in the approximative way with which, often for the family tax and less often for the complementary tax, the taxable income is assessed on the

---

[20] *Parentela* binds persons descended from a common ancestor (see CC arts. 74-77); *affinità* binds persons related by marriage (see CC art. 77).
[21] As substituted by L. 2 July 1952, n. 703, art. 28.
[22] As modified by L. 2 July 1952, n. 703, art. 29.

basis of indicia of the style of living. Now it is sufficiently evident that a person who lives on his own, especially if he is of a certain social condition, cannot fail to have a minimum of income which causes a certain taxable income to be attributed to him. If this person appears as a dependent of others, these presumptions and indicia of capacity for income do not arise. Thus, the tendency exists for such a person to try to create the impression that he is a member of the family, while perhaps having a very successful professional office.

2/3.3 Tax Bases

a. COMPLEMENTARY TAX. The object of the complementary tax is the aggregate income of the family exceeding the taxable minimum, established at L. 720,000 annually (12/1.5c). Included in the aggregate income are the amounts, added algebraically, resulting from the various incomes assessed or assessable for the various objective taxes (6/1.1f), unless the style of living and other circumstances and factual information lead to a consideration of these assessments as unreliable (13/2.3). Thus, in principle, there does not exist an independent assessment for this tax; those already made for the various objective taxes are applied. But just as the assessments made for the various objective taxes are sometimes made with particular criteria, the law foresees certain adjustments, in the employment of these criteria, for purposes of the complementary tax. The biggest adjustments involve the income for the landowning tax and the tax on agrarian income, which are expressed in cadastral lire of 1938 (12/1.1, 12/1.2).[23] Then, certain incomes are exempt from the objective taxes (such as those from houses and new construction), but not from the personal tax, and therefore require an *ad hoc* evaluation for that tax. In addition, aggregate income for the complementary tax includes certain incomes subjected to the objective taxes in the hands of other taxpayers, and it is therefore necessary to make other adjustments to identify the proper share. Finally, deduction is allowed for other income taxes paid or withheld during the year, including the family tax (6/1.5e), and for certain other expenditures not deductible for the objective taxes (6/1.5a).

For incomes produced by companies which do not have juridical personality, the system of pro rata attribution to the members is used (5/3.2). For incomes produced by companies or entities with their own juridical personalities, the system used is that of attribution of the part

---

[23] The fact that the coefficients of adjustment can lead to an income lower than the true one does not, in general, justify recourse to the inductive assessment which has been spoken of. In practice, however, it is difficult to establish whether the difference in the style of living of the taxpayer as against the income determined for the objective taxes results from the insufficiency of the coefficients applied to his landowning income or from the fact that the assessment of other incomes for purposes of the direct taxes is defective.

which each taxpayer has "actually" received, "on any basis and in any form" (9/2.1). Attention must be paid to the phrase last quoted. This expression is intended, first of all, to render taxable the profits which corporations and similar entities distribute to their members as something other than profits: the name and the juridical form of such distributions do not matter. To be taxable—in principle—it is sufficient that the amounts or the property in question be traceable to net profits of the company which are such from the point of view of the objective taxes. In the second place, the expression involves including in the taxable profits not only profits paid out in money, but also those distributed to the members in kind (9/2.2); not only those given under the form of allocations of amounts or of division of property, but also those paid out through the allocation of realizable economic benefits of various kinds (the gratuitous use of a lodging, the remission of a debt contracted against the company, the obtaining of services from the company with discounts such as to give rise to the presumption of the paying out of a true profit). It must be said that, in practice, in the investigation of these benefits in kind or favorable treatments by the company toward the member which are translated into true profit, rather often the Italian tax administration does not make much headway—except against certain corporations with a family base where these phenomena are very noticeable, and easily identifiable—because the administration is already absorbed with a series of preliminary problems of analytical assessment of the objective incomes.

The expression "on any basis and in any form" has also been interpreted extensively by the tax authority in such a way as to permit the taxation under the complementary tax, pro rata, against the individual members, of undistributed profits of corporations of a family character, both on the assumption that, in such companies, the member and the entity tend to be identical and on the assumption that those profits, by some hidden route, find their way to the member. This position of the Italian tax authorities, however, is scarcely convincing in principle because there exists today a tax on corporations which is aimed at reaching both corporations of a family character and those of a larger base, and because the provision described above always requires some "receipt": to presume this absolutely, solely because a company has a family base, seems a little too bold. Better founded, on the other hand, is the thesis of the fisc of considering as surreptitiously distributed the profits of corporations with a family base which have not appeared in the balance sheet; for these profits, the company does not officially appear as the owner, and thus the thesis that they have been appropriated by the members without having passed through the company appears rather reasonable—even if, in a rigorous formulation, proof by the company or the members to the contrary should be allowed.

b. FAMILY TAX. As against the relative precision of the rule for the assessment of the complementary tax, the imprecision and empiricism of the rule for the family tax is striking. The tax is imposed on the well-being or means (*agiatezza*) of the family, which are inferred from the family's income or earnings (*proventi*) of any kind, and from any other apparent index of well-being (TUFL art. 117). First, the object of the tax is rendered uncertain by the indeterminacy of the word "well-being," which is not a juridical term currently used outside of the tax system, and which, in accepted Italian usage, has a meaning significantly different from that of "style of living" or "volume of expenditures." Then, it is not clear whether the "income" serves as a pre-eminent condition and measure for the assessment of a certain element, "well-being," or serves as merely one of different indicia of means which, altogether, give rise to an aggregate estimate of well-being; or, finally, whether the income is not itself the proper object of the tax, and the indicia of means of other kinds are only elements for determining the income when it does not appear by analytical assessment of the resources of the taxpayer.[24]

A reading of the subsequent paragraphs in the law, which define the tax base, not only does not reduce, but even increases, the perplexities. One would expect an analytical list such as that for the complementary tax. But the law states only that, in the determination of the taxable income, account must be taken of the factors listed below (TUFL art. 117).

1. Income or earnings, whatever their origin, the manner and the place in which they are produced, net of expenses of production, of taxes, surtaxes and fees (including the objective taxes and the complementary tax), and of annuities, rents, and other patrimonial charges.
2. The nature of the income or earnings—whether they are patrimonial, industrial, or professional.
3. Any other index of individual wealth, inferred from the leasehold value of the dwelling, from the luxury of the house, from the social position.
4. The make-up (*costituzione*) of the family: the number, age, sex, and condition of its members.

Finally, to complicate the situation still a little more, there is the provision: "in the determination of the incomes or earnings of workers' families the coefficient of unemployment for the year is taken into account" (TUFL art. 117).

These rules seem to be the fruit of a compromise of very different points of view, in the sense that they involve not only rules for the determination of the total of the taxable income, but also rules for

---

[24] On the difficulties presented by these criteria, and on the question of whether the family tax is to be regarded as a tax on income or as partly a tax on expenditure, see Forte, "Sulla determinazione dell'imponibile nell'imposta di famiglia," *Giur. it.*, 1960, I, 1, 5; Allorio, "Profili giuridico-formali del problema della valutazione del reddito agli effetti dell'imposta di famiglia con riferimento all'accertamento del reddito compiuto ai fini delle imposte erariali," *Giur. it.*, 1960, I, 1, 28.

the determination of the rates of tax. The two criteria are superimposed in such a way that it is not clearly established when one is to operate and when the other is to operate. This problem is discussed further at 2/3.4.

Sometimes reference to "well-being" is more or less explicitly used to define in the concrete the notion of income; undistributed profits of corporations with a family base, controlled by the taxpayer, have been considered in some decisions as income of the taxpayer, insofar as they are included in his well-being.[25] Since 1945, however, a long battle has developed between the communes and the taxpayers regarding the problem of whether the notion of income for the family tax can be defined independently of that for the complementary tax, and, also, whether the assessment made by the state for the objective taxes and for the complementary tax should also govern for the family tax. Pre-1945 legislation contained a provision according to which the assessments made for the objective taxes were also valid for purposes of the assessment of income for the family tax (TUFL art. 119). But a law of 1945 repealed this provision, without making other specifications.[26] The communes considered this to mean that they were free to make independent assessments, and the same opinion has been adopted in a rather large part of the doctrine. The problem was, and is, particularly great, not only because of extensive evasion of the national taxes on income, but also because, as has been said, the revalued cadastral figures of 1938 used in determining landowning and agrarian income for the national taxes are adopted as well for purposes of the complementary tax, following a modest mean coefficient (12/1.5a). In individual cases, the landowning income at times can be much higher than the cadastral income, and at times it can be notably lower. The communes in which agricultural economy is important have attempted to make their own assessments of landowning incomes, seeking to correct the cadastral estimates where they are defective; the reaction of the best-endowed taxpayers and of the organizations which represent the interests of landowners,[27] however, has been to deny that, even after 1945, the assessment of the family tax is independent of that of the complementary tax.

The Court of Cassation has accepted this thesis, affirming that "in a tax system technically and harmoniously well-ordered the concept of income can be only one," and stating that the repeal made in 1945 should be understood—given this general principle of the single assessment—to be solely concerned with the prohibition of including incomes

---

[25] See, for example, Comm. Centr. 8 February 1951, n. 20288; Provini, *L'imposta di famiglia* 77-80.

[26] D.L.L. 8 March 1945, n. 62.

[27] These associations have not concerned themselves at all with the interests of those small landowners who, possessing marginal or declining lands, can have cadastral assessments higher than the actual income.

which have "entirely" escaped state taxation within the scope of the family tax.[28] The communes, however, supported by decisions of the administrative commissions, have continued to adopt the solution of independence, and a law put forward in 1960 on the initiative of members of Parliament who are particularly close to the interests of the local entities expressly declared this independence.[29] The Court of Cassation, however, has not been satisfied with this law and has denied retroactive application, considering it valid only after 1960. Recently, a new draft law was filed to establish the principle of independence explicitly for the period before 1961; but the legislature adjourned without having approved the draft.[30] Thus, the situation remains unsettled. There are those who propose to unify the two personal taxes in a single national tax, calling the communes to collaborate in the assessment of the state tax; while others would like simply to abolish any local autonomy for the tax on income, assigning to the communes a share of the state tax.

2/3.4 Computation and Rates of Tax

a. ALLOWANCES. For the complementary tax, there is a basic personal allowance of L. 240,000, and a further allowance of L. 50,000 for each dependent (12/1.5b). For the family tax, the Provincial Administrative Board determines, with respect to each class of commune, on the basis of proposals which the communal councils have the power to present, the amount of income corresponding to the fundamental living requirements of the family, to be exempted from tax in relation to the number of members of the family (TUFL art. 118). The limits within which the allowance may range have been established by a ministerial circular; they are shown in Table 52.

For families entitled to the allowance for large families described at 5/1.3, there is a further allowance of L. 500,000.[31] The allowance is reduced by one half when the number of dependent children is reduced to not less than five. The allowance is granted in addition to the personal

---

[28] Cass., Sez. un., 14 August 1959, n. 2542 (*Giur. it.*, 1960, I, 1, 3), with comment of Forte, "Sulla determinazione dell'imponibile nell'imposta di famiglia" (p. 5), and of Allorio, "Profili giuridico-formali del problema della valutazione dell reddito agli effetti dell'imposta di famiglia con riferimento all'accertamento del reddito compiuto ai fini delle imposte erariali" (p. 28). On this problem, see also Cocivera, *Guida ai tributi locali* 576; Provini, *L'imposta di famiglia* 48; Celliti, "Sul principio del autonomo accertamento per l'imposta di famiglia," *Giust. trib.*, 1961, 1.

[29] L. 16 September 1960, n. 1014, art. 18.

[30] See Forte, "In tema di autonomia dell'imposta di famiglia e di norme interpretative," *Giur. it.*, 1963, I, 1, 409.

[31] L. 14 June 1928, n. 1312, as modified by D.L.P. 27 June 1946, n. 87, art. 6, and D.L.P. 1 September 1947, n. 892.

allowance just described, but it is not taken into account in determining the rate of tax.[32]

Table 52: *Range of Allowance for Income Subject to the Family Tax, by Class of Commune*

Class of Commune	Allowance (Lire)	
	Lower Limit	Upper Limit
A	L. 240,000	L. 360,000
B	225,000	335,000
C	210,000	315,000
D	195,000	290,000
E	180,000	270,000
F	165,000	245,000
G	150,000	225,000
H	135,000	200,000
I	120,000	180,000

Source: C. M. 2 April 1953, n. 2/4025/5 (Annex).

b. RATES. The complementary tax is applied at progressive rates ranging from 2% on a taxable income of L. 240,000 or less to 65% on a taxable income of L. 500 million or more; no tax is imposed if income before personal allowances does not exceed L. 720,000 (12/1.5c).[33] The maximum rate of the family tax, 12%, is applicable under the complementary tax to a taxable income of approximately L. 10 million. The complementary tax is subject to the additional for ECA of 10% of the tax, the additional for Calabrian relief of 5%, and the collection fees (12/1.5c).

The rate structure of the family tax is very different. The family tax makes by itself both a discrimination by type of income and a discrimination by the aggregate total of income, which the state makes by the combined systems of objective taxes and personal tax. Moreover, in practice, for taxpayers with incomes of L. 12 million or more, the family tax is a proportional tax at the rate of 12%. The law provides that the Provincial Administrative Board is to determine, for each class of commune, the classification of taxable incomes [34] and the rates, to be graduated in direct ratio to income and inverse ratio to the population of the communes in the province in such a way that the maximum rate of 12% is applied to incomes of not less than L. 12 million (TUFL art. 118).[35] However, the rate schedule presently in force has been estab-

---

[32] C.M. 7 February 1949, n. 501; C.M. 17 March 1949, n. 500280.

[33] A draft law to raise the limit to L. 960,000 was placed before Parliament in 1963.

[34] This includes, according to current administrative instructions, the discrimination of incomes according to their source as patrimonial, industrial, or professional.

[35] As modified by L. 2 July 1952, n. 703, art. 30.

lished for all classes of commune by the Ministry of Finance. Under this schedule, progressive rates beginning at 2% for income of L. 200,000 and rising to 12% for income of L. 12 million or above are applied to the taxable income, net of the personal allowance; these rates are shown in Table 53.

Table 53: *Rates of the Family Tax*

Taxable Income Net of Allowance (Lire)	Rate [*]
L. 200,000	2.00%
300,000	2.17
400,000	2.31
500,000	2.43
600,000	2.55
700,000	2.67
800,000	2.78
900,000	2.89
1,000,000	3.00
1,500,000	3.52
2,000,000	4.00
2,500,000	4.47
3,000,000	4.92
3,500,000	5.36
4,000,000	5.79
4,500,000	6.19
5,000,000	6.63
6,000,000	7.45
7,000,000	8.24
8,000,000	9.62
9,000,000	9.78
10,000,000	10.53
11,000,000	11.27
12,000,000	12.00

[*] The rates are graduated on the basis of the formula:
$$y = 2 + 0.003282 \, (x - 200)^{\,0.8556}$$
where y is the percentage rate, and x the income expressed in thousands of lire.

For income falling between steps on the table, the rate is determined in practice by attributing the increment of the rate proportionately to the increment of income between the two steps. C.M. 2 April 1953, n. 2/4025/5 (Annex).

Source: C.M. 2 April 1953, n. 2/4025/5 (Annex).

The family tax may be increased by additionals not exceeding 20% of the tax.[36] An additional of 10% of the tax for ECA and an additional of 5% for Calabrian relief are applied (2/2.9).

The commune has the power to apply coefficients of reduction up to a maximum of 50% for income from work as an employee and income

---

[36] L. 16 September 1960, n. 1014, art. 20.

of artisans and direct cultivators, with respect to that part of the income which is attributable to manual labor, and it has the possibility of graduating the benefit inversely with respect to the total of the income and of fixing limits beyond which the benefit is excluded.[37] This system—of applying the full rate to a reduced income, rather than a partial rate to the full income—is understandably convenient for computation purposes because it permits a number of practical manipulations of the taxable income (in reality, manipulations of the rate on the various components of the income) to be made with considerable simplicity; it not only does not give rise to any inconvenience whatever, but constitutes an advantage. Perplexities can exist in principle, however,[38] and also from the general civic and political point of view of the education of the taxpayer and his perception of fiscal duty.

2/3.5 International Aspects

For the complementary tax, the rules relative to international aspects are given with precision: aggregate income includes income produced in Italy belonging to persons wherever resident and income of residents which is produced abroad and enjoyed in Italy or is not taxable in the other country by reason of an international agreement (11/1.1). It is to be observed that the expression "enjoyed" (*goduti*) does not mean only "consumed" but can also indicate "employed" or "utilized," as in the case of investments. Income of residents which is produced and enjoyed abroad is taxed only if it would escape all taxation, in Italy and elsewhere, as a result of an international agreement. The principle of citizenship has no effect outside of treaties.

As the result of an agreement between a foreign country and Italy, an Italian citizen producing income abroad may not be subjected to taxation in the foreign country. If this Italian citizen resides in Italy, and only in this case, he will be taxed in Italy on that income, even for the part enjoyed abroad (11/2.2). Since the complementary tax in principle applies to the algebraic sum of incomes subject to the objective taxes, the concept of income "produced in Italy" for purposes of the various objective taxes is also employed for purposes of the complementary tax. And since, for the objective taxes, some share of income produced abroad is considered in certain cases to have been produced in Italy, even if in fact it was not (2/2.5), the complementary tax itself comes to cover also certain income produced and enjoyed abroad belonging either to Italian residents or to foreign residents—in the absence of international agreements.

---

[37] L. 16 September 1960, n. 1014, art. 18.

[38] It is obvious that also for incomes other than those from work, with this system, the scale of progressivity is attenuated because these incomes are added to incomes from work which are valued only in part.

The family tax in principle reaches income which the taxpayer has produced abroad, provided it can be considered to contribute to his "well-being." This is questionable with respect to income which a taxpayer resident in Italy produces abroad and does not enjoy in Italy, that is, which does not affect his aggregate economic condition in Italy; but all this is very fluid, and controversies—especially involving cinema actors—are not lacking. In practice, given the commune's limited means of assessment, a taxpayer who produces his own income and reinvests it abroad succeeds in removing it, in any case, from the reach of the family tax, unless he is a well-known person whose activities abroad and high compensation, as with certain cinema actors, are widely publicized. Aliens are subject to the family tax unless exempted by provision of an international agreement (TUFL art. 114) (11/4.2).

2/3.6 Jurisdiction of Communes To Impose the Family Tax

In the relations among communes with regard to the family tax, the principle of territoriality operates with reference to the "person" of the head of the family. The family tax is owed entirely to the commune in which the head of the family has his habitual dwelling for purposes of the Civil Code (TUFL art. 115) (11/2.2). Here, however, difficulties arise. The Civil Code concept of residence is based on facts: a person cannot claim for civil law purposes to have a residence in one place, if he does not actually reside in that place. But in the modern world, a concrete check of his actual residence is rather difficult to make. Moreover, the very concept of residence in a single commune, given the various means of rapid transportation available today, is almost devoid of content. Today, a person can "stay habitually" in several places. These are problems which make the functioning of the family tax faulty. Indeed, a kind of "fiscal contraband" carried on by the local entities has resulted, involving a tendency to lower the rates to attract taxpayers, who pay less to a commune after agreeing to transfer their fiscally valid "residence" there, through various artifices and expedients directed to establish the fact of habitual dwelling. There are communes around Turin, Milan, Bologna, Rome, and other large cities which have a very high yield per inhabitant from the family tax. This is not due to a high average rate or particular severity of assessment; rather, it is due to the fact that there are many taxpayers "imported" from the metropolis who have in fact dwellings both in the metropolis and in the small commune (where often they have a villa or an industrial enterprise).

The problem of the division of the tax among the various communes also presents other sensitive aspects. The finances of certain communes—the so-called "dormitory" communes—can appear artificially rich. Those of the so-called "factory" or "tertiary" communes can appear artificially poor, however. This discrepancy arises because of the different purposes which these communes serve and which permit them to have a larger or smaller number of persons shown as "in fact" resident there. If the tax were attributed pro rata to each commune connected in any way with the taxpayer under the territoriality principle, these problems would be resolved easily enough. But others would arise, probably, on the method of dividing the aggregate receipts obtained from each individual taxpayer.

2/3.7 Communal Tax on Leasehold Values

Something similar to "pro rata" division is done, not under the family tax, but under the tax on leasehold values, which gives a considerable yield to touristic communes. The tax on leasehold values is due from anyone, Italian citizen or foreigner, who keeps at his own disposition, in the territory of a commune, a dwelling house furnished with his own property or that of others (TUFL art. 101), on condition that he is not subjected to the family tax in the commune (TUFL art. 111). Even if the commune generally applies the family tax, it can have recourse to the tax on leasehold values for those persons who fulfill the requirements for it and who are not subject to the family tax in that commune. The tax on the leasehold value is owed for the entire year only if the habitation "is kept at the disposition" of the taxpayer for more than six months of the year; if it is "held at his disposition for a lesser period," the tax is due for six months. There is no need for the taxpayer to stay a single day in this dwelling in order to owe the tax in question: it is sufficient that the dwelling be "at his disposition."

The tax base is the real or presumed rent (and from this the tax takes its name) (TUFL art. 104).[39] The rate is progressive, from 5% to 9%, depending on the class to which the commune belongs (less, for communes of lesser population) and on the size of the rent (there are five categories of rent for rate purposes) (TUFL art. 102).[40]

The original purpose of the tax was to reach the taxpayer's aggregate style of living through the index of expenditure on the dwelling, and thus to realize income expended. But now, as has been said above, its function is much narrower: to give to communes a source of revenue from persons who live there from time to time, in a house of their own, receiving the benefits of the expenditures of the local entity.

---

[39] As substituted by D.L.L. 8 March 1945, n. 62, art. 15.

[40] As modified by R.D.L. 9 September 1937, n. 1769, art. 1. The tax may be increased by additionals of up to 20% of the tax (L. 16 September 1960, n. 1014, art. 20); the additionals of 10% for ECA and 5% for Calabrian relief are also applied (2/2.9).

2/3.8 Administration and Procedure

. For the complementary tax, the procedures of assessment are based on the annual return of income (13/1.1) and are governed by the rules relating to the administration of the direct taxes (13/2.1).

For the family tax, the system is rather different since there is no compulsory annual return.[41] When he begins his residence in a commune, the taxpayer is required only to file a return, with which he begins his relations with that commune, and which serves for all the subsequent years. But many taxpayers fail to file this report since there are only negligible penalties. The consequence is that, while the assessments for the complementary tax have an annual base and vary, when the system functions, with the variations in the income of the taxpayer, the assessments of the family tax, in practice and perhaps even in principle, are stable plurennially and are usually remade after a certain number of years on the initiative of the Tax Office itself. The larger and more energetic communes succeed in collecting ample yields. The others are contented with much less. Since, as a last resort, the communes always have the assessment of the complementary tax made by the state to refer to, the more active communes can assess all the income that the state assesses for the complementary tax, plus all that which they are able to assess effectively on their own accounts.

Thus, the often higher yield of the family tax as against that of the complementary tax—notwithstanding the lower rates—does not necessarily mean that the communal offices are more efficient. It means rather that these offices, given the flexibility of the tax, are able to utilize the methods both of the state assessments and of their own. The consequences of this are harmful, in turn, for the base of the complementary tax, whose taxpayers are rather little inclined, even for this tax, to enumerate analytically their own classes of income.

A taxpayer who has filed a return or received a notice of assessment for the family tax may appeal to the Communal Commission for Local Taxes (TUFL art. 277)[42] and thence to the special section for local taxes of the Provincial Administrative Board (TUFL art. 282). Further appeal, on grounds of legality (*legittimità*) only, is allowed to the Central Tax Commission (TUFL art. 284 *bis*) (1/4.10e). On any question not involving estimation of income or determinations of fact relative to taxable income, appeal may be made to the ordinary courts from decisions of the Provincial Administrative Board or the Central Commission.

---

[41] Assessments for the family tax and other local taxes are governed by TUFL art. 274 *et seq*.

[42] It appears that a person may appeal against inadequate assessments against others, even though not himself inscribed in the same roll; but very little use has been made of this provision.

An appeal to the special section for local taxes of the Provincial Administrative Board is provided for a taxpayer who is notified of the application of the same tax in more than one commune of the same province, or to the Minister of Finance if the same tax is applied in different provinces (TUFL art. 289).[43]

2/3.9 Collection and Payment

Except in the cases in which it is provisionally withheld (13/3.5), the complementary tax is inscribed in the rolls and collected in the manner provided for the direct taxes of the state (13/3.1). The family tax is inscribed in the local tax rolls under the procedures provided for the local taxes (TUFL arts. 286-290). The tax is ordinarily collected by the communal tax collectors in six bimonthly installments, on the due dates provided for the collection of the national direct taxes (TUFL art. 297) (13/6.2).

2/4. The Corporation Tax

2/4.1 Historical Background

Since 1955, there has existed another form of national personal taxation, in addition to that on income of individuals: personal taxation of juridical persons. An independent tax is applied to the income and assets of corporations and of other collective entities taxed on the balance sheet basis (such as credit institutions, insurance institutions, and public entities of various kinds; there are exemptions for the communes, provinces, and universities, to which, on the other hand, the movable wealth tax and the general tax on receipts are applied) and of all foreign companies and associations (even if personal) operating in Italy through a permanent establishment, even if not taxable on the balance sheet basis (6/1.1g). This taxation fulfills the function of covering that which can be defined as the "aggregate taxable capacity" presented by these entities but lacking in individuals and in personal companies and associations.

As is well known, in a fiscal system with a high personal progressive tax on income, it is not possible to do without some form of taxation on corporations and similar organizations of capital if one is to avoid the collection of great problems connected with companies of convenience (*società di comodo*) and the use of the corporate structure to escape the personal tax legally through nondistribution of profits.

It can perhaps at first glance appear strange that the corporation tax was not introduced in Italy until 1954 and that, even then, it encountered

---

[43] As substituted by L. 2 July 1952, n. 703, art. 52.

very great opposition. But this fact does not appear strange at all if the difficult development of the personal taxation of income in Italy, of which this phenomenon is in part effect and in part cause, is considered. Before 1954, at any rate, there existed a modest taxation of corporate assets, through the so-called "negotiation tax" (*imposta di negoziazione*). This tax arose originally as an indirect tax on the true or presumed transfer of shares and bonds. The base of the tax consisted of the aggregate share and bond capital of any corporation (and of shares of limited liability companies), and the rate was levied annually, independently of the actual circulation of securities, in proportion only to their potentiality of circulation. This potentiality was generally presumed, however, and valuation took place, in substance, on the market value of negotiation of securities. This tax, of which the bases and premises were very limited, was abrogated in 1954, giving way to the new corporation tax.

The corporation tax introduced in Italy is not similar to the majority of corporation taxes existing in other Western countries—the United States, Canada, West Germany, and Great Britain. The corporation tax in the other foreign systems generally reaches the aggregate income of those enterprises, with more or less generous deductions for the expenses of production and for other expenditures which seem deserving of encouragement. The Italian corporation tax has two components. The first strikes the assets of the enterprise (paid-in capital plus reserves, at their official nominal balance sheet value) (3/2.3). The second, on aggregate income, reaches not the entire aggregate income, but the "excess" over normal profit; it is applicable to the profit which exceeds 6% of the value of the taxable assets.

2/4.2 Tax Base

The base of the corporation tax, as regards aggregate income, is not determined independently; following the principle that governs also for the complementary tax on the income of individuals (2/3.3a), the assessments made for the objective taxes are adopted when available. In the case of the exemption of certain income from the objective taxes, the rules valid for the objective taxes are adopted for purposes of the assessment of that income for the corporation tax. A question arises here, as for the complementary tax, with regard to the imputation to the taxpayer —in this case, the corporation or collective entity—not only of income of which the taxpayer itself is the productive source, but also of income which arises from other productive sources belonging to it. On the basis of the law in force, profit for the corporation tax includes "amounts received by way of distribution or division of the profits of companies and associations of any type" (9/2.1c). The difference is evident between this formulation and the rather broad one in effect for the complementary tax, for which are included in the taxable income "the profits on whatever basis and in whatever form received by the taxpayer" (9/2.1b). Unlike the provision for the complementary tax, however, the law governing the corporation tax includes in the tax base, besides the various incomes to which are applied the taxes on lands, on buildings, on agrarian income, and on movable wealth income expressly mentioned, "any other income not included" under the other headings. This throws doubts on the actual restrictive effect of the above-mentioned provision regarding distributions.

As in the case of the complementary tax, the tax base for the income component of the corporation tax is the "algebraic" sum of the various elements of income included in it (6/1.1g); this means, naturally, that, if for a certain source of income, the corporation has losses, these are compensated with the gains from other sources of income. It should be noted, however, that this rule generally reduces itself in practice to the allowability of compensation of any losses in the enterprise income of the corporation with gains deriving from other incomes. In fact, there can never be negative incomes from buildings, lands, or securities in portfolio, owned by the corporation; [44] for income of category A and for gains deriving from participations in other enterprises, the income can be zero—when no profit is distributed and no interest is paid out—but generally never becomes negative.[45]

Moreover, as in the complementary tax, in determining the tax base for the income component of the corporation tax, deduction is allowed for the taxes related to the individual classes of income inscribed in the rolls whose collection begins during the tax period (6/1.5e). The possibility of deducting the objective taxes on the various incomes, which vary between 20% and 30% of the total taxable income, reduces substantially the likelihood that the profit will exceed 6% of the value of the assets and thus be taxable. Because the burden of the objective taxes (if the assessments are accurate) is around 25% to 30% of the taxable income, a global profit, to be reached by the corporation "profit" tax, must exceed 8% to 9% before taxes.

---

[44] With respect to exempt incomes, however, the income is positive but does not give rise to tax. It should be remembered that the corporation tax includes in its base also all incomes exempt from the objective taxes which are not expressly exempted from the corporation tax: thus, interest on the public debt and incomes from houses, new construction, or new enterprises built in the south, which are more or less fully excluded from the objective taxes, fall under the corporation tax.

[45] There are certain cases in which the income may be negative: (a) that of a company which manages, under lease, an agricultural business taxed in category B of movable wealth, which closes with a loss in a certain year; (b) that of a corporation which participates in a personal company and which thus, where the latter closes with a loss, bears pro rata the burden of the loss.

There remains, finally, the deduction, in determining the base of the tax on corporate profits, of "the expenses, charges, and losses inherent in the production of the various classes of income, insofar as by their nature they are not deductible in the determination of those incomes" (6/1.5b). By virtue of this rule, a company which possesses immovable property can deduct interest charges on loans with which it has financed the purchase or the construction of its own building, the expense of administration of the property, and perhaps also insurance regarding the property (if it is possible to show that these are not included in the lump-sum deduction for expenses under the tax on buildings, and that besides, they are "inherent" in the production of the income). The company can also deduct for the corporation tax those capital losses for which deduction has been denied for purposes of the immovable property taxes. Deduction is not allowed, inexplicably, for losses carried forward under the provision applicable to the movable wealth tax (7/4.2).

As explained at 3/2.3, the taxable assets consist of the subscribed and paid-in capital, plus reserves shown in the balance sheet, plus profits carried forward from prior business periods, less losses carried forward from prior business periods. By taxing only the aggregate income exceeding 6% of the taxable assets, the intention is to introduce an instrument which would leave immune from taxation the incomes of those enterprises presumed to be endowed with less economic strength. Thus, the existing dual structure of the Italian economic system is taken into consideration as containing on the one hand enterprises of a technological level comparable to those of the other large countries, and on the other hand enterprises which have a lower technological level with a lower wage structure but which do not yet have the capacity for growth and the productivity of the large modern enterprise. The problem of productivity is rather great in an economy which, like that of Italy eight years ago, is just on the way to leaving a long phase of protectionism and of economic errors, and, in the case of the Italian economy, the emphasis was on favoring the drive to its growth by means of the accumulation of capital.

Considering the weakness of the Italian tax assessments, which was especially great in 1955 when the severe rules for assessment on the balance sheet basis (launched in 1956) were still lacking, the excluded 6% meant (and perhaps still means) in practice a percentage generally much higher.

2/4.3 Rates of Tax; Relation Between Income and Assets

The rates of the corporation tax are 0.75% of the value of the taxable assets, and 15% of the profits above 6% of the value of the taxable assets (12/2.2c). This rate structure was designed as a means of obstructing automatically the evasion of the tax.

The taxable assets are defined as the subscribed and paid-in capital plus reserves shown in the balance sheet (3/2.3). Thus, in substance, the taxpayer is free to give the value which he wishes to the taxable assets. But if he undervalues his own assets for tax purposes to pay a lower rate on a smaller figure for taxable assets, the assets which the fisc considers for purposes of the relation between profit and assets to determine the allowance of the 6% excluded from the tax on profits is also diminished. Thus, if the taxpayer undervalues the assets, he also undervalues the base on which the exclusion of profit is calculated. If, for example, a company has a profit of 5 and has actual assets of 100 but leads the fisc to believe it has assets of 50, the company makes ᴀ saving of 50% in its tax on assets, but its profit of 5 is placed in relation with assets of 50, giving place to a greater profit of 10%. A true valuation of assets would have shown a profit of only 5%. As a result, the company, which has saved 0.75% on half the value of its assets, is required to pay 15% on 40% of its profit, which is 2. The savings made on the taxation of assets in this example is 0.372, but the higher taxation on profits is 0.3. The maneuver of undervaluation thus is resolved in a net saving of tax of 0.072, that is, of only one fifth of the total tax which the corporation hoped to save.

The aim of the "pincer" structure of the tax was to ensure that maneuvers of the taxpayer directed to undervaluing either the assets or the profits would result in increasing the tax on the other. But the "pincers" lose much of their effect if the taxpayer can succeed in making profits escape taxation from the beginning. To the extent that the movable wealth tax does not function and income from buildings escapes imposition, companies have ample possibility for undervaluing corporate assets. Moreover, all corporations which have a sufficiently low ratio of profit to assets can undervalue the latter to reduce the burden on assets, without fear of encountering the rate on profits. The corporation tax is applied indiscriminately to corporations which have productive enterprises and corporations which manage immovable property (and which often in addition are family companies of convenience). Among immovable property companies, there are those which hold building lots and prosper, not by collecting rents but by speculating in land transactions. These companies for many years do not have profits in the balance sheet, or at least have only profits offset by charges sustained for financing obtained from banks for purchase of the lands (which then are sold). Given the possibility of specifying at will the taxable assets for the corporation tax, and given the absence of profits, these corporations can reduce practically to zero the burden on their assets. In the year in which it sells the lands or builds upon them, an enterprise can eventually revalue its capital if it wishes to reduce the rate on the profit.

But this is a problem which it has to face only in the year of "realization." In all the preceding years, it can lower its own land capital to minimum levels.

Thus, the "pincers" in reality show themselves much less efficient than the ingenious builders of this scheme may have supposed. The device would be rather more efficient if "physical" valuation of the assets were required: that is, the inclusion in assets not only of balance sheet reserves but also of "hidden" reserves, which are simply correction headings serving to render the nominal balance sheet value of the assets, increased by "reserves" of every kind, equal to the market value of the physical assets of the enterprise (6/6.1). The consideration of the assets at the market value instead of the nominal value could be an efficient means of paralyzing and discouraging certain immovable property companies of convenience which manage buildings and building lots and of reducing speculation in building lots. For this last purpose, rather than making any discrimination with the corporation tax, the Italian legislature has introduced in 1963 a complex tax on increases in the values of building lots, allocated to the communes (3/7.3). Thus, all of the reliefs which the corporation tax gives to benefit the accumulation and the productivity of small corporations devoted to production also end, in large measure, by nourishing fiscal evasions, speculative movements, and so forth. In the end, this results in preventing assistance from being given to small industrial corporations in the desirable measure.[46]

2/4.4 Persons Subject

The scope of the corporation tax does not reach certain associative forms which contemplate limited liability of the members, nor does it reach certain other instruments devised specifically for the purpose of eluding it. It does not affect a vast number of companies of convenience (*società di comodo*).

For example, outside the corporation tax are simple limited partnerships (*società in accomandita semplice*)—personal companies in which only some of the members, the *accomandanti,* have joint and unlimited liability for the debts and other obligations of the company, while others, the *accomandatari,* are liable only within the limits of the capital contributed (5/3.3). It can easily be understood how the limited partnership can fulfill all the functions of a corporation: to permit the "true" members, who clothe themselves as *accomandatari,* to find themselves in the same juridical position as if they were in a corporation or a limited liability company, it is sufficient to take as *accomandante* a person who holds no property or a willing professional. Moreover, the limited

[46] See Forte, "Sulla politica fiscale nei confronti delle piccole società di capitali," *Temi trib.*, 1959, 30.

partnership has the advantage, on the fiscal plane, of not being subjected to the corporation tax, since it is considered a personal company; and, for this same reason, it is not subject to the duties of keeping accounting records for the analytical assessment or to the rules on the fiscal liability of directors, which concern corporations and similar entities both for the tax on movable wealth and for the corporation tax (6/1.2b).

The point has been reached at which corporations now form limited partnerships, so that, although they are corporations, they are able to pour off a substantial part of their activity and their assets into personal companies subject to fewer fiscal controls—and thus to elude most of the rules provided for them for purposes of the immovable wealth taxes and the corporation tax.

Another common device is the use of foreign corporations having their legal offices in "tax havens." The most flourishing species is that of Liechtenstein corporations, which offer particular advantages because of the civil and fiscal laws of that country. The nature of Liechtenstein companies is between that of a foundation, in which the assets and the purpose of the entity predominate—the members being unimportant —and that of a corporation, in which the members have a power of disposition and enjoy the fruits of the enterprise. According to convenience, the normal corporation becomes the foundation when the members "disappear," or else the members "re-emerge" and the enterprise again becomes a normal corporation. A corporation-foundation of this kind can be useful to Italian taxpayers for eluding both the personal taxes on income and the succession taxes. At times, the mechanism is perfected so that the corporation, although a Liechtenstein corporation, appears Swiss, after opening an office in one of several places in Switzerland, thus permitting direct participation in this large international financial market. At other times, the taxpayer resorts to a completely Swiss company, protected by Swiss banking secrecy, and controls it in the strictest anonymity through a local banking institution.

For purposes of the Italian corporation tax, foreign companies and associations are taxed if they operate in Italy through a permanent establishment whether or not they have the nature of corporations and thus are enterprises required to be taxed on the balance sheet basis (11/3.4). But this provision, which would seem sufficient to discourage foreign companies of convenience, such as those of Liechtenstein and Switzerland, often is ineffective in the face of the characteristics of the corporation tax and the difficulty of checking those enterprises when they are not required to be taxed on the balance sheet basis. The taxable assets for purposes of the corporation tax, when foreign companies and associations not required to be taxed on the balance sheet basis are involved, consists of the aggregate amount of assets devoted to operations or in any manner employed in Italy on 31 December of the tax year (11/3.4). But how is the value of the assets determined? The secrecy which generally protects these companies makes this determination rather difficult. Furthermore, following the official interpretation in force,[47] here also the assets are not the value of the property physically identified and existing on national territory, but the amounts constituting its financial countervalue—that is, the aggregate investment of funds in the state, net of loans made in Italy whose interest is subjected to the Italian objective taxes. This treatment results in a net advantage for foreign companies not required to be taxed on the balance sheet basis in Italy, which function as companies of convenience. At the same time, the regime is very burdensome to all the other foreign companies, which are obliged to pay the tax even if they have a juridical form which, for the corresponding Italian companies, would not involve subjection to the tax.

Another common device is to create an Italian partnership with a Swiss or Liechtenstein entity as one of the partners. The partnership need not fulfill the accounting requirements for corporations and is not subject to the corporation tax; and the income paid to the Swiss or Liechtenstein partner (which often represents an Italian individual) is not subject to the Italian personal taxes.

2/4.5 Intercorporate Distributions

The corporation tax is applied to every company on profits and assets already taxed in other companies in which the first controls participation. The only modification in the application of this principle is the reduction of the rate by 25% for "financial companies" (investment or holding companies); these, however, are defined in a very restrictive way (10/5), probably to discourage monopolistic concentrations carried out by grouping of companies into holding companies and to favor independent enterprises over those, large or small, which form themselves into financially integrated groups of complex structure. Obviously, given the modest rates of the corporation tax, it is very doubtful whether this effect takes place. Credit firms and institutions enjoy a rate reduction of 25% even if they do not have the requisites of holding companies (10/4.2).

2/4.6 Public Enterprises

Public enterprises are in principle subject to the corporation tax just as are private companies, a measure taken to prevent their receiving preferential fiscal treatment. The same rule applies also to the objective taxes, to the general tax on receipts, and to the registration tax, the stamp tax, and other taxes. However, for corporations and entities with state

---

[47] C.M. 1 June 1955, n. 351690.

participation, the rate reduction to which investment companies are entitled is 40%, instead of 25% (5/2). Probably it was deemed desirable to take account of the fact that, for reasons of centralized public control, these enterprises are organized into multilevelled structures, a complexity which they would perhaps not have if they were private; and of the fact that these financial structures, integrated in grades in order to increase their sizes, are desired by the state itself, so that it would not be very logical to penalize them for tax purposes. Businesses of the state, whose budgets are attached to that of the state (mail and telegraph, national railways, tobacco monopoly), are exempt, as are businesses of the local entities insofar as they "in fact carry on as monopolies services of public utility" (municipal tramway and bus lines, subways, municipal milk businesses, and the like) (5/5.11). Besides, the new National Electric Entity (*Ente Nazionale Elettrico* or ENEL), which carries on all the production and distribution of electrical energy, and is organized like the English public corporations (for electricity, coal, and so on), is exonerated both from the corporation tax and from the national and local objective taxes on income; it is subjected instead to a single special tax measured on the kilowatt-hours produced.

Special exemptions and reductions are provided for cooperative societies (5/5.10), even though it is not always easy to distinguish, among these, the societies which have truly the purposes of cooperatives, and the societies which in practice have ends identical to those of ordinary corporations.

CHAPTER 3

TAXES ON CAPITAL

3/1. Introduction

3/2. Tax on Corporate Assets

   3/2.1   In General
   3/2.2   Persons Subject
   3/2.3   Taxable Assets
   3/2.4   Computation and Rates of Tax

3/3. Tax on Bonds

   3/3.1   Basis and Persons Subject
   3/3.2   Taxable Value
   3/3.3   Computation and Rates of Tax
   3/3.4   Administration and Procedure

3/4. The Inheritance Tax

   3/4.1   In General
       a.   General description
       b.   History of the succession taxes
   3/4.2   Persons Subject
   3/4.3   The Tax Base
       a.   In general
       b.   Usufruct
       c.   Use and habitation
       d.   Fideicommissary (trust) substitution
       e.   Annuities
       f.   Emphyteusis
       g.   Partnership shares
       h.   Credits
       i.   Life insurance proceeds
       j.   Supervening assets

3/4.4 Exemptions

    a. In general
    b. Art collections
    c. Securities of public debt
    d. Special tax on transfers of motor vehicles

3/4.5 Valuation

    a. In general
    b. "Salable" (market) value
    c. Immovable property
    d. Annuities in kind
    e. Business enterprises and partnership interests
    f. Movable property
    g. Securities

3/4.6 Deductions

    a. Debts
    b. Expenses of the last illness and funeral expenses
    c. Time limits for proving the existence of debts
    d. The estate tax

3/4.7 Computation and Rates

    a. In general
    b. Progressive rates
    c. Proportional rates
    d. Reduction in case of successive deaths
    e. Credit for taxes on previous gifts
    f. Additionals

3/4.8 Returns

    a. In general
    b. Persons filing
    c. Time limits for filing
    d. Form and content

3/4.9 Assessment

3/4.10 Payment

    a. In general
    b. Persons subject
    c. Time limits
    d. Payment in installments
    e. Preference of the state
    f. Legal subrogation
    g. Refunds
    h. Compulsory collection

3/4.11 Protests and Appeals

3/4.12 Time Limits for Assessment and Collection
      a.   The limitation periods
      b.   Interruption of the limitation periods

3/4.13 Penalties
      a.   Penalties against taxpayers
      b.   Penalties against other persons
      c.   Increased and reduced penalties

3/4.14 International Aspects
      a.   In general
      b.   Credits, securities, and annuities
      c.   Foreign debts
      d.   Tax treaties

3/5.   **The Estate Tax**

3/5.1 History and Sources

3/5.2 Relation to the Inheritance Tax

3/5.3 The Tax Base

3/5.4 Persons Subject

3/5.5 Computation and Rates of Tax

3/5.6 Returns

3/6.   **Taxation of Gifts**

3/7.   **Betterment Contributions and Taxation of Increases in Value of Building Lots**

3/7.1 In General

3/7.2 The Specific Betterment Contributions of the Local Entities
      a.   In general
      b.   The tax basis
      c.   Valuation
      d.   Rates
      e.   Assessment, appeals, and payment

3/7.3 The New Local Tax on the Increases in Value of Building Lots
      a.   In general
      b.   Tax basis and valuation
      c.   Rates and credits
      d.   Assessment, appeals, and payment

3/7.4 The National Betterment Contributions

3/1. Introduction

During the past 40 years, both individuals and collective entities have been subject to a series of taxes on wealth (*patrimonio*) (1/6.7b, 1/6.7f). There is now no general tax on the wealth of individuals, but the net assets of corporations and similar entities are subject to the corporation tax (3/2), which, since 1954, has replaced the former "negotiation tax" (2/4.1). A tax is also imposed on the outstanding bonds of corporations and similar entities (3/3).

Until 1942, gratuitous transfers of property and property rights, both at death and inter vivos, were subject to one levy: an inheritance or gift tax respectively, imposed on the property received by each heir, legatee, or donee. In 1942, Italy introduced an estate tax levied upon the aggregate value of the estate (or donation); thus, at the present time, gratuitous transfers are, as a rule, subject to two taxes.

There is no tax on immovable property as capital. The presumed income from the ownership of agricultural land is subject to the tax on income from landowning (10/2.2), and the presumed income from the ownership of buildings is subject to the tax on income from buildings (9/4.2). Increases in the value of lands resulting from the execution of public works and the carrying on of public services are subject to the special national and local taxes described at 3/7.

3/2. Tax on Corporate Assets

3/2.1 In General

The corporation tax, levied by the state since 1954, is based on the possession of assets (*patrimonio*) or of income by corporations and similar entities required to be taxed on the balance sheet basis, or by foreign companies and associations operating in Italy through a permanent establishment, even if not required to be taxed on the balance sheet basis (3/2.2). Although the tax consists of two components, one imposed on assets and the other on income, it is regarded as a unitary personal tax, serving for corporations and similar entities the same function as the complementary tax for individuals (2/3.1). Since the corporation tax includes a tax on income (2/4) and is a part of the system of direct taxes, regulated by the *Testo unico* of the direct taxes, many of the provisions governing its application are discussed in Part II of this volume. The discussion in this chapter will be concerned principally with the component of the tax which applies to capital assets, with cross references to more detailed discussions in Part II of provisions which are relevant to both the capital asset and the income components of the tax.

3/2.2 Persons Subject

The corporation tax is payable by any entity formed in Italy which is required to be taxed on the balance sheet basis (6/1.1g, 6/1.2b). The principal entities subject to the tax are corporations (5/2.2), limited liability companies (5/2.3), limited partnerships with shares (5/2.4), cooperative societies (5/2.5), mutual insurance companies (5/2.6), and many public entities (5/2.7). A foreign company or association is subject to the tax if it operates in Italy through a permanent establishment, even if not required to be taxed on the balance sheet basis (11/3.4).

Exemption from the tax is granted to certain cooperative societies (5/5.10); local authorities, Chambers of Commerce, and certain public enterprises (5/5.11); associations for reclamation, improvement, irrigation, and waterworks, and certain agrarian associations; certain welfare, provident, and assistance entities (5/5.6); and nonprofit educational, scientific, and cultural institutions (5/5.7). For certain cooperative societies, the tax on capital assets is imposed only on assets exceeding L. 5 million in value,[1] and the tax on income is applied at a reduced rate (5/5.10). The entire tax is reduced by 25% for credit firms and institutions (10/4.2) and for certain holding companies (10/5), and by 40% for companies with prevailing government participation (10/5).

3/2.3 Taxable Assets

The taxable assets (*patrimonio imponibile*) consist of the sum of the amounts listed below (art. 147).[2]

1. The subscribed and paid-in capital (*capitale*) of a company; or, in the case of any other association, the net assets (*patrimonio netto*) shown in the balance sheet.[3]
2. Ordinary and extraordinary reserves of any kind (6/6) shown in the balance sheet, including the surcharge (*sovraprezzo*) on the issuance of new shares (9/9.3), reserve funds for the amortization of immovable property to revert to the grantor of a concession (7/3.10), and positive

---

[1] D.P.R. 29 January 1958, n. 645, art. 152. This is the *Testo unico* of the laws on the direct taxes, and, as in Part II of this volume, an article of this decree will hereinafter be cited: "art."

[2] See also C.M. 1 June 1955, n. 351690.

[3] Subscribed and paid-in capital consists of the fully paid shares and capital subscribed in any manner, through contributions made in cash, in kind, or in credits (see CC art. 2440), including shares issued against allotment of profits to employees involving a corresponding increase in capital (see CC art. 2349), but not including shares (*azioni di godimento*) issued to former holders of redeemed shares (see CC art. 2353). Capital subscribed and not paid (which appears in the assets of the company as a credit against the members) and capital paid in but not subscribed (payments into capital account which appear as debts of the company to its members) are not included under this definition. Increases and decreases of capital which have been decided upon are effective only when they appear in the balance sheet (C.M. 1 June 1955, n. 351690).

monetary revaluation funds, but not reserves and funds used to cover specific burdens and charges on behalf of third persons.

3. Profits of previous business periods carried forward.

From this sum are deducted losses of previous business periods carried forward (art. 147). If the assets include immovable property subject to gratuitous retransfer to the grantor of the concession, usually a governmental authority (7/3.10), that proportion of the total value of the property which the time elapsed since the granting of the concession bears to the total term of the concession is also deducted from the taxable assets, and the assets include the related amortization fund reserves (art. 147), which regenerate, for the benefit of the shareholders, the capital invested in the property reverting to the grantor.

In the case of a foreign company or association not required to be taxed on the balance sheet basis (11/3.4), including a foreign corporation or similar entity neither having its head office nor carrying on the principal activities of its enterprise in Italy (11/3.3), the taxable assets consist of the aggregate amount of capital devoted to operations in Italy, or in any manner employed in Italy, on 31 December of the tax period (art. 147) (11/1.1). The taxable assets employed in Italy are assessed case by case, on the basis of information furnished by the taxpayer or available to the Tax Office. They are not limited to paid-in capital, but may include other financing provided by the members or by third persons; the value of loans contracted and employed in Italy is deducted if the interest paid thereon has been subjected to the tax on income from movable wealth.[4] If a foreign company or association has no permanent establishment in Italy, it incurs no liability for the corporation tax by holding shares in an Italian company; but if it has a permanent establishment in Italy, the value of shares is included in its taxable assets even if the activity of the Italian company is in no way connected with that of the permanent establishment in Italy (11/3.6b). In order to obtain credit for the coupon tax withheld from dividends under the rules discussed at 9/2.7a, the foreign company must declare the shares for purposes of the corporation tax liability of the permanent establishment (9/2.7c).

The taxable assets of an entity required to be taxed on the balance sheet basis are determined on the basis of information appearing in the balance sheet (art. 150).

3/2.4 Computation and Rates of Tax

To the taxable assets, determined as described at 3/2.3, the tax is applied at the rate of 0.75% (art. 146), except in the case of credit firms and institutions (10/4.2) and holding companies (10/5), for which there

---

[4] C.M. 1 June 1955, n. 351690.

are reduced rates. If income determined for purposes of the corporation tax results in a net loss, the entire tax is reduced as explained at 12/2.2. The additional for communal assistance entities (ECA) is applicable to the corporation tax under present law; the additional for Calabrian relief is not payable on the tax paid directly into the Treasury on the basis of the return, but is payable on tax inscribed in the rolls as a result of a corrected assessment (12/2.2c). An example of the computation of the tax is given at 12/2.5.

3/3. Tax on Bonds

3/3.1 Basis and Persons Subject

The tax on bonds (*imposta sulle obbligazioni*) is based on the existence of bonds and similar securities, issued in Italy by entities required to be taxed on the balance sheet basis (6/1.2b), or by foreign companies and associations operating in Italy through a permanent establishment (11/3.4), even if not required to be taxed on the balance sheet basis (art. 156). The tax is reduced to one fourth for regions, provinces, and communes (5/5.11), for credit firms and institutions (10/4.2), and for certain holding companies (10/5) for which a reduction of the corporation tax is provided (art. 159).

The tax is payable by the entity issuing the securities; on securities issued on or after 26 August 1954, the issuing entity has a right of recovery (*facoltà di rivalsa*) against the holders of the securities (art. 156). The tax does not apply to securities issued before 26 August 1954 which were exempt from the former "negotiation tax" (2/4.1) or included in a system of payment of taxes through an annual fee (*abbonamento*) (art. 159).

3/3.2 Taxable Value

The tax is measured on the aggregate value of the securities outstanding, obtained from the balance sheet of the entity; the value of securities issued during the second half of the business period is reduced to one half (art. 158). In the case of a foreign company or association not required to be taxed on the balance sheet basis (11/3.4), the securities taken into account are those appearing in the balance sheet on 31 December of the tax period.

The value of securities listed on the stock exchange is the last price paid before the close of the business period; the value of unlisted securities or of securities listed but not priced is the nominal value (art. 158).

3/3.3 Computation and Rates of Tax

The tax is imposed at the rate of 0.5% on the taxable value of the securities (art. 157). For certain classes of entities, the tax is reduced to one fourth (3/3.1). An example of the computation of the tax is given at 12/2.5.

3/3.4 Administration and Procedure

The taxable value of securities is reported in Schedule F (*Quadro F*) of the annual return form for entities required to be taxed on the balance sheet basis (12/5.3). In general, the provisions governing returns, assessment, collection, appeals, penalties, and time limits for the tax on bonds are those applicable to the corporation tax. They are described in detail in Chapter 13.

3/4. The Inheritance Tax

3/4.1 In General

a. GENERAL DESCRIPTION. The inheritance tax is a progressive levy imposed upon heirs and legatees with respect to the transfer of ownership, usufruct, use, or enjoyment of property, or of any other right, either by intestacy or by testamentary disposition, by reason of the death or of the declared or presumptive absence of the person to whom the right belongs.[5] The tax is also applied to gifts inter vivos of the rights specified above (3/6).

For purposes of the law, the transfers described above are taxable insofar as the transferee or transferees are enriched thereby; this enrichment constitutes the tax basis and is made up of the total value of the decedent's property diminished by the value of the items deductible under the law (*netto delle passività*). The tax is payable not only with respect to property passing to the decedent's heirs, but also to property passing to his legatees (LS art. 2). In Italy, an inheritance may pass either by law or by testament (CC art. 457). In the absence of a testament, the inheritance passes by law, in accordance with the provisions of the Civil Code, to legitimate descendants, legitimate ascendants, collaterals, natural relatives, the spouse, and the state (CC art. 565). All persons who inherit by law are heirs. Persons who inherit under a testament are heirs if they take property under a "universal" disposition (*a titolo universale*), comprising the entire property of the testator or a share of the entire property; they are legatees if they take property under a "particular" disposition (*a titolo particolare*) (CC art. 588). Testa-

---

[5] R.D.L. 30 December 1923, n. 3270, art. 1. This decree is the basic inheritance tax law, an article of which will hereinafter be cited: "LS art."

mentary dispositions cannot prejudice the rights which are reserved by law to the persons (*legittimari*) who have a legal right to inherit (CC art. 457)—namely, legitimate, legitimated, and adopted children, legitimate ascendants, natural children, and spouses (CC arts. 536-564).

In providing for the taxation of successions by reason of the declared or presumed absence of the owners of property (LS art. 1), the inheritance tax law follows the old Civil Code of 1865.[6] Under the Civil Code of 1942, the tax obligation arises only after the judicial declaration of absence (CC art. 49) or presumptive death (CC arts. 58-68).

With regard to the territorial application of the inheritance tax, the Italian law follows the principle of *lex rei sitae*: in order to be subject to the tax, the property must be located in Italy at the moment of the decedent's death. The place of death, the nationality, the domicile, and the residence of the decedent are irrelevant for purposes of the tax (LS art. 20). The territorial application of the inheritance tax is discussed more fully at 3/4.14.

b. HISTORY OF THE SUCCESSION TAXES. The succession taxes in Italy have a long history. Before the unification of the country, various succession taxes were levied in the Italian states, and several of the taxes were governed by the French registration law of 22 Frimaire (VII) (12 December 1799).[7] In general, the richer northern states taxed successions more heavily than the south, where fixed fees were prevalent. After the unification of Italy, an inheritance tax was introduced by the Law of 21 April 1862, n. 585, which also included provisions concerning the registration tax. The rates were proportional and extremely moderate: 0.5% for direct descendants and slightly higher for other grades of relationship. The law was subsequently modified in details but not in its essentials. In 1897, a *testo unico* integrated the laws regulating inheritance and registration taxes.[8] The first important modification was the introduction of the principle of progressivity in 1902.[9] Further modifications brought increased, in certain cases even confiscatory, tax rates.[10] Such a heavy burden of taxation caused evasion and pressure for the reduction of rates. The government, instead of combating evasion and introducing reasonable rates, found a radical solution by repealing the tax on transfers

---

[6] Civil Code (1865) arts. 20-22.
[7] Serrano, *Le imposte sulle successioni* 9-10.
[8] R.D. 20 May 1897, n. 217.
[9] L. 23 January 1902, n. 25.
[10] L. 23 April 1911, n. 509; R.D. 27 September 1914, n. 1042; D.L.L. 21 April 1918, n. 629; R.D.L. 24 November 1919, n. 2163 (introducing a complementary tax); L. 24 September 1920, n. 1300. See also Serrano, *Le imposte sulle successioni* 11-12. For the rate tables, see De Bono, *L'imposta sulle successioni e l'imposta sull'asse globale ereditario netto* 387-395.

between ascendants and descendants, between spouses, between brothers and sisters, between uncles and nephews, and between decendants of brothers and sisters of the decedent, if they succeeded by the right of representation of their parents.[11] This reform, a part of the financial *"ristorazione"* of De Stefani, the Minister of Finance in the first Mussolini governments, was intended to favor accumulation of wealth within the close family group (*nucleo familiare*). Another purpose was to remove discrimination between southern Italy, where estates, consisting mainly of immovable property, were generally taxed, and northern Italy, where estates, consisting of movable wealth, could more easily escape taxation.[12] The new provisions were converted into a special law on successions, included in a text separated for the first time from the text of the registration law.[13] The 1923 decree, with subsequent modifications, is still in force. Also in force are the regulations [14] which contain detailed provisions for the application of the inheritance tax law. In 1930, the inheritance tax was reintroduced for many family relationships,[15] but tax exemption was retained for transfers of estates (1) between parents and children if there was more than one child, (2) between parents and descendants of their children if there was more than one descendant, and (3) between spouses with more than one child. This law, in force until 31 March 1945, was one of the pillars of the tax policy favoring population growth established by Mussolini. In 1935, additional criteria of taxation were introduced, under which the rates of tax varied according to the age, civil status, and family conditions of the heirs and other beneficiaries.[16] Further tax reliefs for families having more than four children were provided in 1940,[17] and, in 1942, special rates for transfers to legally unrecognized and unrecognizable natural children and reduced rates for transfers to adopted children were enacted.[18]

The year 1942 is a turning point in the history of succession taxes in Italy because, in that year, a separate tax on the aggregate net value of

---

[11] R.D. 20 August 1923, n. 1802.

[12] See Einaudi and Répaci, *Il sistema tributario italiano* 273 (5th ed., 1954); the evasion was facilitated by absence of legal provisions on obligatory nominativity of securities. See Fanno, *Elementi di scienza delle finanze* 200. It has been contended that, instead of abolishing the tax because of the discriminations due to unequal evasion, it would have been better to attempt to eliminate the sources of the evasion. See Pugliese, "Come ripristinare l'imposta di successione," in Griziotti *et al., La politica finanziaria italiana. Studi sui problemi monetari e finanziari* 189-229.

[13] R.D.L. 30 December 1923, n. 3270.

[14] R.D. 23 March 1902, n. 114.

[15] R.D.L. 30 April 1930, n. 431.

[16] R.D.L. 26 September 1935, n. 1749, Annex B, converted in L. 28 May 1936, n. 1027. This law was in force until 31 March 1945.

[17] L. 29 June 1940, n. 877.

[18] L. 19 January 1942, n. 23.

the estate, the *imposta sul valore netto globale delle successioni,* was instituted.[19]

In 1945, the provisions of 1930, 1935, 1940, and 1942 were repealed, and the treatment of successions between ascendants and descendants, and between spouses, was made uniform; the provisions concerning the estate tax were also recodified.[20] The reform of 1945 made the succession taxes more productive; but, despite the progressive devaluation of currency, their yield soon decreased because of ineffectiveness of assessment.[21] To relieve this difficulty in part, a law was passed in 1949 introducing new tax rates within new brackets. In particular, the exemption limits for successions in the direct line and between spouses were raised to L. 750,000, and the exemption limit for the estate tax was fixed at L. 500,000. The same law also modified certain provisions of the 1923 decree.[22] Some of the more recent legislative provisions concern (1) the extension to foreign entities of the tax reliefs favoring successions and gifts having welfare, religious, or cultural purposes;[23] (2) the valuation of farm property;[24] and (3) the equivalent treatment of adopted children and legitimate natural children.[25]

There are no special gift taxes in Italy, but the inheritance tax and the estate tax are, in general, applicable to gifts; as applied to gifts, these taxes are also sometimes referred to as gift tax and tax on the aggregate value of gifts, respectively. Also, the registration tax law of 1923 has some application to the taxation of gifts (15/3.3g).

The rates of the inheritance tax are very high, especially on smaller bequests (3/4.7b), and, as a result, there is an unfair burden on those who cannot escape the tax. Diminution of the rates and measures to reduce tax evasion are targets of the present Italian tax policy in this field. However, the large flow of capital abroad (often coming back as officially "foreign" capital lent to Italian institutions and enterprises) casts doubt on the possibilities of success of these policies. Some tax experts favor the abolition of the tax and recommend reliance on a permanent tax on net wealth.

3/4.2 Persons Subject

In general, the inheritance tax is payable by natural persons or entities receiving property, that is, heirs or legatees in the case of transfers by

---

[19] R.D.L. 4 May 1942, n. 434, converted in L. 18 October 1942, n. 1220, in force until 31 March 1945. This tax, called the "estate tax" in this volume, is discussed at 3/5.

[20] D.L.L. 8 March 1945, n. 90. This decree, on modifications of the taxes on successions and gifts, is the basic estate tax law; an article of this decree will hereinafter be cited: "MSD art."

[21] See Fanno, *Elementi di scienza delle finanze* 201-202.

[22] L. 12 May 1949, n. 206.

[23] L. 10 February 1953, n. 59.

[24] L. 20 October 1954, n. 1044.

[25] L. 20 November 1955, n. 1123.

reason of death and donees in the case of gratuitous acts inter vivos. With respect to successions, the tax is applied on the basis of testamentary dispositions even if the testament has been contested in court, except when the testament is voided in whole or in part by a final judicial decision rendered in protest proceedings between the party concerned and the tax administration. However, the tax is not applied on the basis of testamentary provisions which violate the rights reserved to the close family group, the *legittimari* (LS art. 6) (3/4.1a).[26] In cases of intestate succession, the tax is applied on the basis of Book 2 of the Civil Code. The various categories of beneficiaries are discussed at 3/4.7b. Persons liable for payment are specified at 3/4.10.

Bequests of any sort for the benefit of provinces, communes, and other Italian legal entities or institutions legally recognized, founded or to be founded, are exempt if the specific purpose of the gift is welfare, instruction, or education.[27] This exemption has been extended, on the condition of reciprocity, to bequests to legally recognized foreign institutions, whether they have their seat in Italy or abroad.[28]

By virtue of the concordat of 1929 with the Holy See, the exemption of transfers for purposes of welfare, instruction, and education has been extended to transfers for purposes of worship and religion which are made for the benefit of church entities.[29] If the purpose of worship and religion is not explicitly declared in the testament, it is considered implicit unless the testator specifically designated a purpose not exempt from the tax.[30] The exemption also applies to transfers for the benefit of foreign church entities.[31] It apparently also includes legally recognized religious entities other than the Catholic Church.[32]

Exemption is granted to transfers to the surviving spouses and other heirs and legatees who are direct descendants or ascendants of soldiers killed in war and of persons whose deaths resulted from war (MSD art. 16).[33] Total exemptions are granted only to direct line descendants and ascendants and to surviving spouses. If there are no surviving spouses and no direct descendants or ascendants, brothers and sisters and their first-degree descendants receive up to L. 300,000 free of tax, and the tax on the excess is reduced to one half.[34]

---

[26] As amended by R.D.L. 26 September 1935, n. 1749.

[27] R.D.L. 9 April 1925, n. 380.

[28] L. 10 February 1953, n. 59. See also C.M. 14 April 1953, n. 177124 (*Riv. leg. fisc.*, 1953, 715).

[29] L. 27 May 1929, n. 810, art. 29.

[30] I.M. 10 April 1930, n. 92127.

[31] L. 10 February 1953, n. 59.

[32] R.D. 28 February 1930, n. 289, art. 12, implementing L. 24 June 1929, n. 1154, on religious entities allowed by the state.

[33] There must exist a direct causal nexus between the death and the state of war. Comm. Centr., Sez. un., 8 November 1946, n. 84911 (*Dir. e prat. trib.*, 1950, II, 54).

[34] R.D.L. 19 August 1943, n. 734, art. 2.

3/4.3 The Tax Base

a. IN GENERAL. The inheritance tax is payable with respect to the net value of the decedent's property passing to each heir or legatee. In addition, for purposes of determining the applicable rate brackets, the value of inter vivos gifts made by the decedent to the heirs and legatees must be added to the value of inheritance shares and legacies received by the respective beneficiaries. The decedent's motive in making the gift inter vivos and the time at which it was made are immaterial. The law allows as a credit against the inheritance tax the taxes which would be due on those gifts and donations if passing at death under the laws currently in force (LS art. 3) (3/4.7e). The law prescribes certain rules and establishes presumptions with regard to the determination of the various elements of the taxable property to be included in the tax base.

Immovable property (CC art. 812) is considered as belonging to the decedent if the decedent is inscribed as the owner in the register of immovable property. If the decedent is not inscribed as the owner in the register, the law presumes that he was the owner if he is inscribed in the rolls of the tax on income from landowning or the tax on income from buildings and has paid on his own account at least one installment of the tax, or, if there is evidence of an agreement (*convenzione*) which makes him the presumptive owner of the property (LS art. 22). The decedent's ownership of the property might be inferred, for example, from a receipt for the payment of the price of the property, a contract of lease, a consent to record mortgage, or a mortgage redemption.

These presumptions are rebuttable. The effectiveness of the contrary proof varies from case to case.[35] However, the mere declaration of ownership included in the testament is not sufficient to prove, for purposes of the inheritance tax, that the immovable property belongs to the estate left by the decedent.[36]

Under general principles, movable property in the possession of the decedent at the time of his death, including securities found in a safe deposit box registered under his name, is presumed to be his property and thus is included in his estate. The heir may rebut the presumption, proving that it belongs to someone else, but the exclusion of any item of the decedent's property is governed by the strict rules concerning the deduction of the liabilities prescribed by articles 45 through 50.[37]

---

[35] Cass. 15 February-31 March 1921 (*Riv. leg. fisc.*, 1921, 214); Comm. Centr., Sez. VI, 18 February 1952, n. 33116 (*Rass. tasse*, 1952, 413). See also De Bono, *L'imposta sulle successioni e l'imposta sull'asse globale ereditario netto* 108; Serrano, *Le imposte sulle successioni* 115.

[36] Comm. Centr., Sez. VI, 4 April 1952, n. 35020 (*Rass. tasse*, 1953, 253). See also De Bono, *L'imposta sulle successioni e l'imposta sull'asse globale ereditario netto* 108.

[37] See De Bono, *L'imposta sulle successioni e l'imposta sull'asse globale ereditario netto* 109.

The law sets up certain specific presumptions with regard to the existence of jewelry, money, and household furniture. Property transmitted by reason of death is presumed to include, first, jewelry and money in the amount of 2% of the gross value of the rest of the property of the decedent; and second, household furniture (*mobilia*) in the amount of 5% of the total gross value of the estate, including money and jewelry already assessed in the presumptive way (LS art. 31). The concept of the *mobilia*, unknown in the Civil Code of 1942, is taken from the old Civil Code of 1865 where *mobilia* is defined, in article 423, as "movables intended for use and decoration of apartments." It appears that it should be interpreted in this sense for tax purposes. The concept does not include collections of paintings, sculptures, and the like, which are exempt from the tax (3/4.4b). From the presumed value of the *mobilia* are specifically excluded horses, carriages and other equipages, grain, wine, hay, other foodstuffs, and anything that was the object of trade or other business of the decedent. All of these goods must be declared according to their market value. The presumed values are computed on the taxable property located in Italy, without regard to the nationality or domicile of the decedent.[38] The presumptions operate to the detriment of those who leave immovables, which lend themselves to easy assessment, and favor precisely those who leave securities, participations in companies, jewelry, money, and other objects difficult of assessment.

The presumptions of article 31 do not apply if higher values are shown by acts or declarations of the parties, or if lower values (or the complete absence of jewelry, money, or funiture) are shown by inventories made in connection with guardianship, on a claim of benefit of inventory, in bankruptcy, or on the affixing of seals under a court order made immediately after the opening of the succession.

If the property includes industrial or commercial enterprises, their net value is taken into account.

b. USUFRUCT. Full right to property consists of two rights: the bare legal title (*nuda proprietà*) and the right to enjoy and use (*usufrutto*). These two rights are usually vested in one person, but it often happens that one person has the right to enjoy and use the property, that is, the right of usufruct (CC arts. 978-1020) (9/4.1), whereas what remains, that is, the bare legal title, is left to another. The law subjects usufruct to tax (LS art. 1) and lays down elaborate provisions for the determination of the tax base in cases of transfer of usufruct (LS art. 23) or of the transfer of bare title only (LS art. 24).

---

[38] Comm. Centr., Sez. VII, 25 July 1940, n. 30237 (*Riv. leg. fisc.*, 1941, 888); Cass., Sez. I, 6 April 1929 (*Riv. leg. fisc.*, 1929, 576).

The value of usufruct is based on the value of the full ownership, taking into account the actual or presumed duration of the usufruct and the age of the usufructuary. If the usufruct is constituted for an indefinite period of time or for not less than 10 years, the tax is applied on one half of the value of the whole property if the usufructuary or the person for whose life the duration of the usufruct is established has not yet reached the age of 50 years, and on one quarter if he has reached that age. If the usufruct is limited for a period of time less than 10 years, its value is presumed to be equal to as many twentieths of the total value as there are years of its duration. However, if the usufructuary has reached 50 years of age, the value of the usufruct cannot exceed five twentieths of the value, even though it was constituted for more than five years. These presumptions greatly aggravate the burden of the inheritance tax. If the usufruct is enjoyed by a widow of 52 years, in good health, who may easily live at least 20 more years, it is unreasonable to reduce the value of the bare ownership by only one quarter when it can give no income until the usufructuary dies. And if the usufruct goes to a child of only 5 years, the value of the bare ownership is reduced by only one half, although on the market a property which may yield no income for 60 years will not command a price equal to one half of the price of a comparable property not burdened with a usufruct. It would be more equitable to determine the value of the usufruct by reference to actuarial tables of survival. Under the present rules, the total of inheritance, estate, and mortgage taxes on the bare ownership of a property burdened with a usufruct, together with the tax which may be due on income from buildings, may approach the actual market value of the bare ownership and thus induce the legatee to refuse the bequest.

Usufruct may be transferred jointly to more than one person (*usufrutto congiunto*). In such cases, the tax is applied to each share as if no joint usufruct existed, subject, however, to a reassessment of a higher tax due in case of accretion (*accrescimento*) of a lapsed share (CC art. 678). The age of each usufructuary and the grade of relationship between each usufructuary and the decedent are taken into account in the determination of the tax base.[39]

The law provides that, in the case of a later usufruct constituted for a term of years, the tax is applied with respect to the first beneficiary who is subject to it, except for a possible modification when the subsequent transfer occurs. If, however, the usufruct is for the benefit of several persons successively, only the age of the first beneficiary or beneficiaries for whom the institution of usufruct is valid (CC art. 698) is taken into account (LS art. 23).[40]

---

[39] Comm. Centr. 12 June 1939, n. 16494.

[40] Under article 698 of the Civil Code, a testamentary provision under which usufruct or an annuity is left to several persons successively, that is, upon the death of

On the transfer of the bare ownership by reason of death, the person receiving the bare ownership pays the tax computed on the difference between the full value of the property and that of the usufruct (LS art. 24). The duration of the usufruct cannot exceed the life of the usufructuary, and a usufruct constituted for the benefit of a juridical person cannot exceed 30 years (CC art. 979) (9/4.1). Usufruct can also cease by prescription (by failure for 20 years to enjoy and use the usufruct), by total destruction of the property, or, which is of interest here, by merger of usufruct and ownership in the same person (CC art. 1014). The merger, as a rule, takes place on the death of the usufructuary or the person for whose life the usufruct was established, or on the expiration of the term for which it was established. It may also be effected by sale. On the termination of usufruct, the beneficiary (person who then receives the full ownership, whether the bare owner or the usufructuary) [41] must pay the tax on the value of the usufruct deducted when the bare ownership of the property was taxed (LS art. 24), since the usufruct then passes for a second time. One should note that the right of the tax authority to collect the tax on the full ownership arises on the death of the testator, and only for reasons of economic convenience and equity is the full payment postponed until the merger; the taxpayer has the option of making immediate payment on the death of the testator. Thus, in cases of gratuitous transfers of bare ownership, both usufruct and bare ownership are, on the death of the decedent, taxed separately on their respective taxable bases, but the taxation, as taxation of full ownership, is completed by subjection to tax of the value of usufruct at the time of the merger of usufruct and bare ownership.

Postponing payment of the tax until merger causes considerable inconvenience to the taxpayer because the tax administration tends to discourage such a choice by adopting a rigid attitude in reaching an agreement on the value of the estate (3/4.9). The administration also inscribes a preference against the property concerned for payment of the taxes due on merger. Thus, in practice, many prefer to pay the taxes on the full ownership at the time of acquiring bare ownership. As a result, at the time of the succession, the property is burdened with the tax on the transfer of bare ownership plus the taxes on the two successive transfers of usufruct. Measures of this kind bear most heavily on the ownership of small holdings of buildings or of agricultural land, penalizing those forms of distribution of property which try to avoid excessive

---

the first usufructuary, is valid only to the benefit of those who, on the testator's death, are first called to benefit thereby. The rationale of this prohibition is that a sequence of usufructs would considerably reduce the value of the property and would be an obstacle to the improvement thereof. See Cass. 19 October 1957, n. 3985 (*Riv. not.*, 1958, 808). See also Serrano, *Le imposte sulle successioni* 203-206.

[41] Cass. 29 March 1932.

subdivision of property by giving the ownership to one person and the usufruct to others.

Joint and several liability in the case of merger of usufruct and bare ownership is discussed at 3/4.10b.

c. USE AND HABITATION. The rules governing the transfer of the right of ownership (LS art. 22) and the right of usufruct (LS art. 23) are also applicable to the transfer of the rights of use or habitation. This is similar to the pattern of the civil law under which the provisions relating to usufruct are applied, as far as they are compatible, to use and habitation (9/4.1). Use is the right to receive that amount of the profits of the property which satisfies the needs of the user and his family. The needs are valued according to the social status of the user (CC art. 1021). Habitation is the right of a person to live in the house of another. The right of habitation is limited to the needs of the person and his family (CC art. 1022).

d. FIDEICOMMISSARY (TRUST) SUBSTITUTION. A distinction must be made between usufruct and the institution of fideicommissary (trust) substitution (*sostituzione fedecommissaria*), introduced by the Civil Code of 1942 (CC arts. 692-699). An ordinary substitution (*sostituzione ordinaria*) is one by which the testator substitutes another (*sostituito*) in the place of his instituted heir in the event that the latter cannot or will not accept the inheritance (CC arts. 688-691). In trust substitution, the testator transfers the ownership and the use and enjoyment of the property to his son, or to his brother or sister, as instituted heir, but imposes upon him or her the duty not to dissipate the property, but to hand it over intact, upon his death, to all children born or to be born of the instituted heir, or to a public entity (CC art. 692). In trust substitution, the bare ownership does not pass directly to the *sostituito* (the subsequent heir); he acquires it, along with usufruct, only upon the death of the original beneficiary (*istituito*).

With respect to the original heir, the inheritance tax is applied to the value of the full ownership of the property that is the object of trust substitution, and is due in the amount of one half of that value if the original heir has not reached the age of 50 years, and one quarter if he has reached that age.[42] Upon his death (even if it occurred within the two-year period for which a 50% reduction is allowed (3/4.7d),[43] the subsequent heir must pay the tax on the total value of the property at the time of transfer. If transfer to a subsequent heir does not take place (for example, if the original heir dies without issue), then the heirs of

---

[42] L. 12 May 1949, n. 206, art. 6.
[43] L. 12 May 1949, n. 206, art. 3.

the original heir must pay the tax computed on the total value of the inheritance at the time of the testator's death, a credit being allowed for what was paid by the original heir. If the original heir inherits other property, free of the fideicommissary bond, from the same testator, he is taxed on the total value of the property inherited; subsequently, the proportion of the total tax applied which is attributable to the value of the trust property is determined, and that proportion is reduced to one half or one quarter, according to the age of the original heir. These rules apply also in the case of a legacy (CC art. 697).

e. ANNUITIES. The Italian civil law distinguishes between a perpetual annuity (*rendita perpetua*) (CC art. 1861) and a life annuity (*rendita vitalizia*) (CC art. 1872), the latter being established for the life of the creditor or another person. The perpetual annuity may be a land annuity (*rendita fondiaria*), in consideration for a transfer of immovable property, or a simple annuity, in consideration for capital secured by mortgage on immovable property (CC arts. 1863, 1864).

The taxable amount of an annuity or pension is determined in accordance with the rules listed below (LS art. 26).

1. If the annuity or pension is established during the decedent's life by an act specifying the capital amount, the tax is applied to the capital amount.
2. If the annuity or pension is established by testament of the decedent, or is established during the decedent's life by an act not specifying the capital amount, the tax is applied to 20 times the annual amount if the term is indefinite or is 20 years or more; if the term is less than 20 years, the tax is applied to the annual amount multiplied by that number of years.
3. If an annuity or pension established by testament of the decedent is limited to the life of the beneficiary or another person, or is limited to a term of 10 or more years but can cease earlier by reason of the death of the beneficiary or another person, the tax is applied to 5 or 10 times the annuity or pension, according to whether or not the person by whose life the annuity is limited has reached the age of 50; if the annuity or pension is to be paid for a period of less than 10 years, the amount subject to tax is the amount of the annual payment multiplied by the number of years for which the annuity is established, if the beneficiary has not reached 50 years of age at the time of the decedent's death. If he has reached that age, the annual payment may not be multiplied by more than five.

If there is more than one beneficiary, each of whom enjoys a share of the annuity, or pension, the annuity is divided into as many parts as there are beneficiaries, and each is taxed separately. However, if the testator has established the right of accretion, the tax is always reassessed on the death of a beneficiary, and the procedure is the same as in the case of joint usufruct (LS art. 26) (3/4.3b).

If an annuity is established in kind, the value is capitalized in accordance with the same rules (LS art. 27). The rules for valuation of the property constituting the annuity are discussed at 3/4.5.

Life annuities for legally unrecognized and unrecognizable natural children are valued by reference to the maximum annual pension to which a natural child would be entitled if the affiliation were judicially declared or acknowledged (CC art. 580) and are calculated at the rate of 5% of the value of the amount of the share from which the pension would be paid.[44]

f. EMPHYTEUSIS. Among the property rights (*diritti reali*) which may be transferred at death are those connected with the civil-law institution of emphyteusis (*enfiteusi*), by which land is transferred to the transferee (*enfiteuta*) either in perpetuity or for a definite term of not less than 20 years, for an annual rent (*canone*), upon the condition that the *enfiteuta* improve the property, and with the right to dispose, either inter vivos or at death, of the right transferred (CC arts. 957-977) (9/4.1). Emphyteusis is not subject to revocation by the grantor, except in cases explicitly provided by the law, for example, nonpayment of the rent or the deterioration of the substance of the land. Two rights result from emphyteusis: *dominio diretto*, the right of the grantor to bare ownership without use, and *dominio utile*, the right of the grantee to use without ownership.

In transfers of emphyteusis on death, the value of the transferee's right is considered to correspond to the value of the full ownership, decreased by 20 times the amount of the annual rent.[45] The taxable basis of the grantor's interest (*dominio diretto*) is the capital formed by multiplying the amount of the annual rent by 20. If a special law permits the enfranchisement (*affrancazione*) of the emphyteusis, by means of less than 20 annual payments, then the taxable value of the grantor's interest is represented by the amount specified by the law (LS art. 30). The capital value of the ground rents burdening the transferred land is deducted from the value of the land itself.[46]

g. PARTNERSHIP SHARES. Partnership shares in general or shares of limited partnerships are considered movable or immovable according to the nature of the elements constituting the property of the partnership. If the property includes both movables and immovables, the partnership

---

[44] L. 19 January 1942, n. 23, art. 1.

[45] In cases of emphyteusis established prior to 1865, the 1923 law also provided for the deduction of the so-called *laudemio*, the sum of money which, under the rules prevailing before the Civil Code of 1865, used to be paid to the grantor by the grantee if the latter disposed of the emphyteutical land.

[46] Comm. Centr., Sez. VII, 14 April 1948, n. 97052 (*Riv. leg. fisc.*, 1949, 762).

shares up to the amount of the value of the immovables are considered to be immovables (LS art. 29).[47]

h. CREDITS. In the case of the transfer of credits (*crediti*), the tax is applied to their amount. Whether or not a credit bears interest is irrelevant for the determination of the taxable amount, unless the interest, being already mature and due before the death of the decedent, is included in the principal obligation (LS art. 28). For purposes of the inheritance tax, all rights, obligations, and actions whose exclusive object is a sum of money are considered credits (LS art. 29). Thus, a credit is transferred if the beneficiary of the estate acquires the right to a sum of money on the basis of any obligation or bond (loan, rent, sale, for example) which arose between the decedent and a third party.[48] On the other hand, rights and obligations which have as their object movable property, as well as shares of business companies, are treated in the same manner as movable property (LS art. 29). Thus, if the heir or another beneficiary acquires the right to a sum of money which is already part of the property of the decedent at the moment of his death, such a sum of money should be considered movable property.[49] The question of contested or uncollectible credits is discussed in 3/4.10g.

i. LIFE INSURANCE PROCEEDS. The 1923 law does not discuss life insurance proceeds; proceeds of a life insurance policy taken out by the decedent for the benefit of third parties, including heirs, are not subject to the tax because the sum insured was never part of the property of the decedent. Under the civil law, the beneficiaries have their own independent right to the insurance proceeds payable to them directly (CC art. 1920).[50] However, if the insurance policy has matured for the benefit of the decedent himself prior to his death, the proceeds of the insurance are part of the assets of the inheritance and are subject to tax.[51]

j. SUPERVENING ASSETS. In discussing the time limits within which the return must be filed, the 1923 law mentions the duty to declare any assets supervening in the estate (LS art. 54). The law refers to the unforeseen assets which were not a part of the estate at the moment of the death of the decedent. The tax authority must be notified of the value of these assets. Such supervening assets might arise, for example, if the heir obtained the annulment of a transfer made by the decedent before his death.

---

[47] Comm. Centr., Sez. VI, 17 December 1951, n. 30839 (*Riv. leg. fisc.*, 1952, 1043); Comm. Centr., Sez. VI, 16 June 1952, n. 37532 (*Riv. leg. fisc.*, 1952, 1320).
[48] Serrano, *Le imposte sulle successioni* 81-83.
[49] Serrano, *Le imposte sulle successioni* 81-83.
[50] See Stammati, Armani, and Ceccarelli, *Codice delle imposte di successione* 77.
[51] Serrano, *Le imposte sulle successioni* 86-87.

3/4.4 Exemptions

a. IN GENERAL. For various economic, political, and social reasons, transfers of certain assets of the estate are not subject to the inheritance tax, regardless of the beneficiary. Also, certain beneficiaries are exempt from the tax to which they would, under general provisions, be subject (3/4.2b). The exemptions are specified by the law and cannot be extended to other cases by analogy.

b. ART COLLECTIONS. Transfers of collections of paintings, statues, porcelain objects, books, prints, medals, and similar objects are exempt unless they are objects of a trade or business. However, the exemption terminates if the collection is sold within a decade of the death of the decedent. In such a case, the price received would be the taxable amount for the purposes of the tax (LS art. 21). The prevailing opinion is that a single object of art can be entitled to the exemption.[52]

c. SECURITIES OF PUBLIC DEBT. Under special provisions, transfers of certain securities of public debt, either in the form of loans or in the form of consolidated annuities (*rendite consolidate*) or Treasury bonds, have been exempted from the inheritance tax both in order to encourage their purchase and because, in any case, such securities are payable "to bearer" and, thus, can be transferred by simple delivery. Among the exempt securities are those listed below.

1. The redeemable loan at 3.5%.[53]
2. The national loan at 5%.[54]
3. The redeemable loan at 5%.[55]
4. The reconstruction loan at 5%.[56]
5. The reconstruction loan at 3.5%.[57]
6. The land reform loan at 5%.[58]
7. The redeemable loan at 5% "Trieste." [59]
8. The redeemable debt at 5% for the indemnification of Italian property lost abroad as a result of the peace treaty.[60]
9. Long-term Treasury bonds whenever issued.[61]

---

[52] De Bono, *L'imposta sulle successioni e l'imposta sull'asse globale ereditario netto* 83; Serrano, *Le imposte sulle successioni* 109.
[53] R.D.L. 3 February 1934, n. 60.
[54] R.D.L. 20 September 1935, n. 1684.
[55] R.D.L. 5 October 1936, n. 1743.
[56] D.L.L. 22 February 1946, n. 43.
[57] D.L.C.P.S. 26 October 1946, n. 262.
[58] L. 12 May 1950, n. 230, art. 8; L. 22 October 1954, n. 974, art. 8.
[59] L. 22 October 1954, n. 974, art. 3.
[60] L. 29 October 1954, n. 1050, art. 5.
[61] The first exemption of this type was established by article 2 of R.D.L. 26 May 1943, n. 398.

However, the exempt securities do not include the "Annuity of 1906 at 3.5%" or the ordinary annual bonds.[62]

d. SPECIAL TAX ON TRANSFERS OF MOTOR VEHICLES. Transfers of motor vehicles at death are subject only to a special tax on transfer of motor vehicles, instead of inheritance and estate taxes.[63] This is not an exemption, but only a different method of taxation.

Reductions of tax in the case of successive deaths are discussed at 3/4.7d.

3/4.5 Valuation

a. IN GENERAL. The rules and procedures for the assessment of the value of property transferred at death are, in general, the same as those for purposes of other taxes on gratuitous transfers and taxes on transfers for a consideration, in particular, the registration taxes.[64] Differences exist, however, in the valuation of securities (3/4.5g) and rural land property (3/4.5c).

b. "SALABLE" (MARKET) VALUE. As a general rule, the decedent's assets are valued at the "salable," or market, value (*valore venale*) in common commerce at the date of death, even if no value was declared in the return (LS art. 34).[65] The phrase "salable value in common commerce," as explained by ministerial instruction, means something "that would result from free contract of sale, hence independent of the particular conditions of buyer and seller and of the possible abrupt perturbances of the real property market, or of normal temporary oscillations of the economic factors." In other words, it must be a "normal value of the market and not an exceptional one."[66]

c. IMMOVABLE PROPERTY. The rules governing the valuation of immovable property for the succession taxes are, in general, the same as those for the registration tax (15/5.2). Immovable property is taxable at the market value (*valore venale*) in common commerce at the date of the death of the decedent. In order to determine this market value,

---

[62] Serrano, *Le imposte sulle successioni* 110.

[63] D.L.L. 18 June 1945, n. 399, art. 9, and Table, Annex A, containing the tax rates. See also I.M. 10 August 1945, n. 90960, making it clear that, for purposes of succession taxes, motor vehicles are deemed not to form part of the estate.

[64] The valuation rules for indirect taxes, in general, are governed, first of all, by R.D.L. 7 August 1936, n. 1639, and R.D. 8 July 1937, n. 1516, which modified the applicable provisions of the 1923 *Testo unico* on the inheritance tax and the corresponding *Testo unico* on the registration tax (15/1.1). The modifying provisions of the new decrees will be cited here as applied to the succession taxes.

[65] As modified by R.D.L. 7 August 1936, n. 1639, art. 15.

[66] I.M. 10 October 1934, n. 361.

one must, in principle, consider: (1) transfers, partitions, and judicial appraisals made within the previous three years with respect to the property concerned or to other property in the same locality and in analogous conditions; (2) net income from the property, taking into account the average capitalization rate adopted in the locality for similar immovable investments at the time of the transfer; [67] and (3) the current market value (*valore corrente di mercato*) of the property at the time of the transfer.[68]

Special rules govern the valuation of rural land, except forests and building lots, which are subject to the general rules. Rural land is not subject to the assessment of value if the value declared is not lower than that calculated on the basis of tables compiled by the Central Census Commission for purposes of the former extraordinary progressive tax on wealth. The tables are brought up to date according to coefficients determined each year by the Commission and approved by the Minister of Finance. When a new cadaster is instituted, the Commission determines new coefficients on the basis of the income appearing in the new cadaster.[69]

d. ANNUITIES IN KIND. Annuities paid in kind or commodities are capitalized according to the rules described at 3/4.3e. The parties concerned must declare the value of the payments. If the tax administration considers the declared value untrue, the average annual price of the goods or commodities, taken from local market reports, is used as the basis of capitalization. If no place of payment is specified, the market report of the place of transfer, or the report of the market nearest thereto, is taken as the basis for the appraisal. The administration computes the average by determining the average annual price of the commodities for each of the 10 years preceding the transfer, excluding the highest and lowest averages, and taking one eighth of the aggregate total of the remaining annual prices (LS art. 27).

e. BUSINESS ENTERPRISES AND PARTNERSHIP INTERESTS. The market value is also taken into account in the valuation of business enterprises and partnership interests. Additional rules exist for determining the quantity and value of merchandise existing at the date of death of the decedent and the kind and value of any other goods, including good will and patents; the tax authorities have the power to examine business records and to take into account the data therefrom, the assessments made for purposes of the direct taxes, and any other appropriate elements. Refusal to

[67] R.D.L. 7 August 1936, n. 1639, art. 16.
[68] R.D.L. 5 March 1942, n. 186, art. 1, converted with modifications in L. 21 June 1942, n. 840.
[69] L. 20 October 1954, n. 1044, art. 1.

submit the records is subject to the penalties provided by articles 42 and 254 of the *Testo unico* on the direct taxes (13/7.3).[70]

f. MOVABLE PROPERTY. Movable property is taxable at the value declared or resulting from inventory estimates or from a contract concerning the property, effected during the six months before or after the death of the decedent. The value of commodities and commercial articles is determined from market reports, from listings and books of Chambers of Commerce, or from records and books of commercial intermediaries, taking as basis the market report or contract nearest in time to the date of death of the decedent (LS art. 34).

Presumptions with respect to jewels, money, and household furniture are discussed at 3/4.3a.

g. SECURITIES. Securities listed on the stock exchange are valued at the latest compensation price (*prezzo di compenso*) established by the administrative committee of the stockbrokers of the exchange nearest to the place of the decedent's death.

The value of unlisted securities is their value on the date of death, as established by an expert's certificate by the administrative committee of the nearest exchange. The expert's certificate must be enclosed with the return if a return is required (MSD art. 11).

3/4.6 Deductions

a. DEBTS. Debts of a personal nature, resulting from obligations incurred by the decedent prior to his death, are deductible from total assets in determining the value of the estate. Encumbrances on property are taken into account in determining the value of the property which they encumber and therefore are not deductible from total assets. "Objective" taxes levied on property (6/1.1a) are deductible only to the extent of unpaid installments due prior to the death of the decedent. Objective taxes not yet due for periods prior to the death of the decedent become, when due, a charge against the property itself; they are neither legally due at the time of death nor personal to the decedent.

In order to be deductible, a debt must be certain, liquidated, and legally existent at the time of the decedent's death (LS art. 45). Debts owed to the public administration which are certain at the time of death are deductible even if liquidated after the decedent's death. Thus, taxes due from the decedent with respect to a period prior to his death are deductible even if not formally assessed until afterwards (LS arts. 45, 50).[71]

---

[70] R.D.L. 7 August 1936, n. 1639, art. 19.

[71] For purposes of the succession taxes, social insurance agencies are considered units of public administration. L. 12 May 1949, n. 206, art. 4.

In order to be recognized as a deduction, the debt must also satisfy the strict conditions laid down by the law concerning supporting evidence. Debts whose existence can be proved only by acknowledgment in the decedent's testament are considered legacies and are not deductible.[72] Besides being certain, liquidated, and legally existent at the date of death, the debt must result from a public act (*atto pubblico*) (CC art. 2699) (see 15/3.1) or a judgment bearing a date prior to the death of the deceased; from a private act (*scrittura privata*) (CC art. 2702) (see 15/3.1) bearing a certain date (that is, subjected to registration) prior to the decedent's death; or from a bill of exchange or an obligatory business account made prior to the decedent's death (LS art. 45).

In order to prove the existence of a debt by a public act, the taxpayer must produce a copy thereof (exempt from the stamp tax) declared by a notary, Magistrate, or the Mayor of the town, to be identical with the original (LS art. 48). A judgment must be final and prior to the date of death; the finality clause (*passaggio in giudicato*) (CPC art. 324) may bear a date after death (LS art. 45), but not later than two years after the filing of the return (LS art. 50). A private act that serves as the proof of the debt must have acquired a certain date (that is, must have been registered) prior to the death of the decedent in one of the ways specified by article 2704 of the Civil Code, but not by the supervening death or physical incapacity to write on the part of the person who signed it. The authentication of the signature must be registered prior to the death of the decedent even if prepared in the form prescribed by article 2703 of the Civil Code (that is, certified by a notary or other authorized public official) (LS art. 45). The law requires also that the copy of the private act produced as evidence of the debt (exempt from stamp tax) be provided with a signature (*visto*) of a notary, Magistrate, or Mayor certifying the signature.[73]

Debts resulting from business activities exercised in Italy or from bills of exchange may be deducted under the general provisions described above, but the law also provides a different method of proving their existence if the general rules cannot be satisfied. The existence of business debts (*debiti commerciali*) may be proved by producing the debtor's business records if properly kept. Debts resulting from bills of exchange

[72] App. Bologna 12 January 1934 (*Riv. leg. fisc.*, 1934, 408); Comm. Centr. 30 January 1940, n. 21811 (*Riv. leg. fisc.*, 1940, 556); Comm. Centr., Sez. un., 9 July 1945, n. 77517 (*Riv. leg. fisc.*, 1947, 472); Comm. Centr., Sez. VII, 7 November 1947, n. 92817 (*Riv. leg. fisc.*, 1949, 344); Comm. Centr., Sez. VI, 3 December 1956, n. 87103 (*Riv. leg. fisc.*, 1958, 1103). *Contra*, Cass., Sez. I, 22 January 1935 (*Riv. leg. fisc.*, 1937, 350). It has been held, however, that evidence by witness is admissible to prove the existence of debt, but only to forestall regarding the debt as a disguised legacy and thus to avoid the payment of the tax on the said legacy; Cass. 23 March 1937 (*Riv. leg. fisc.*, 1937, 350).
[73] D.P.R. 2 August 1957, n. 278, art. 8; L. 18 March 1958, n. 228; R.M. 23 July 1958, n. 122011.

may be proved by annotation in the properly kept business records of the debtor or the creditor (LS art. 45). Liabilities of enterprises (*passività delle aziende*) may be proved under any of the rules described above. Liabilities which are proved are admitted in their total even if they exceed the assets of the enterprise (LS art. 45).[74] An enterprise (*azienda*) is an institution of civil law meaning "a complex of things (*beni*) organized by the entrepreneur for the exercise of the enterprise" (CC art. 2555) (7/1.2a). Thus, it is also a complex of various legal relationships, both assets and liabilities. For purposes of the succession taxes, the assets and liabilities of a business enterprise must be declared separately on the respective pages of the return. Since proved debts are admitted in their entirety, any excess of debts over assets is deducted from the aggregate gross value of the estate.

The debts of employers to their employees, resulting from wages, salaries, and other remuneration of any kind, are deductible from the estate up to the amount due at the time of death, even if the labor relationship has been terminated, and even if the payments were not liquidated until after death. For this purpose, among the business records required by article 45 are also included the register of employees (*libro matricola*) and the payroll book (*libro paga*), signed and kept according to the law.[75]

In all cases, the law requires that if the debt is to be allowed as a deduction, there must be produced not only the documentary evidence specified above but also a declaration by the heir or legatee and by the creditors or successors in title (*aventi causa*) attesting that the debt existed in total or in part at the time of the decedent's death. If the creditor or successor in title refuses to furnish the debtor with the evidence of the debt, to permit the making of an authenticated copy, or to issue the declaration of the existence of the debt, he is liable for damages (LS art. 48).

Since a decree adjudging the decedent bankrupt deprives him of the power to dispose of the property, it has been held that the creditors of the bankrupt estate must be satisfied first, and only afterward can the inheritance tax be collected on any excess of the estate remaining.[76]

b. EXPENSES OF THE LAST ILLNESS AND FUNERAL EXPENSES. Expenses of the last illness during the six months preceding the decedent's death are deductible if they are of a strictly medical (*sanitario*) character and are

---

[74] As modified by R.D.L. 26 September 1935, n. 1749, Annex B, art. 11.

[75] L. 12 May 1949, n. 206, art. 4.

[76] Cass. 16 November 1931 (*Foro it.*, 1932, 169); Cass. 11 December 1931 (*Giur. it.*, 1932, 174); Cass., Sez. I, 13 March 1961; App. Torino 18 January 1935 (*Riv. leg. fisc.*, 1936, 43). See Serrano, *Le imposte sulle successioni* 146-153. See also Virgilio, "Successione di commerciante dichiarato fallito dopo la morte," *RDFSF*, 1955, II, 337.

supported by the proper receipts of physicians, surgeons, chemists, hospitals, and sanatoria (LS art. 46). The law also permits the deduction of funeral expenses, evidenced by proper receipts, up to a maximum of L. 40,000 (LS art. 46).[77] Receipts relative to expenses of the last illness and funeral expenses must be certified for the authenticity of the signatures of the respective professionals and artisans who are not public officials or functionaires, if the receipts are submitted to Registry Offices located outside of the commune in which they were issued.[78]

c. TIME LIMITS FOR PROVING THE EXISTENCE OF DEBTS. The deduction of debts from the assets of the estate may be allowed even after the collection of the taxes, provided that the existence of the debts is proved according to the law within two years following the filing of the return. In such a case, the excess of the tax paid is refunded (LS art. 50). This rule also applies to the deduction of expenses of the last illness and funeral expenses.[79]

Article 50 of the inheritance tax law provides that

in case of debts to public administrative offices, not liquidated at the moment of the opening of the succession [that is, the death of the decedent] the justification (giustificazione) is allowed even after the expiration of two years following the filing of the return if it is proved by a certificate of the creditor administration that one month prior to that expiration the liquidation has not yet taken place. In this case the justification must be submitted within two months from the date of the liquidation.

Some decisions have held that evidence of the debt (that is, the certificate) may be submitted after the expiration of the two-year term prescribed, if within two months of the liquidation.[80] However, the official resolution of the Minister of Finance interpreted the provision as meaning that the proof of the existence of the debt must be submitted within the general time limit of two years, and that only the justification (by which the Ministry meant the justification of the exact amount) may be produced within two months of the liquidation.[81]

d. THE ESTATE TAX. The tax on the aggregate value of the estate is deducted from the value of the estate before the distribution of the shares of the estate (MSD art. 13).

---

[77] As modified by L. 12 May 1949, n. 206, art. 7.

[78] R.M. 23 July 1958, n. 122011.

[79] R.D. 22 May 1910, n. 316, art. 8.

[80] Cass. 28 April 1932 (Riv. leg. fisc., 1932, 444); Comm. Centr., Sez. VI, 13 November 1950, n. 17364 (Riv. leg. fisc., 1952, 362); Comm. Centr., Sez. VI, 9 January 1954, n. 55700 (Riv. not., 1954, 422).

[81] R.M. 18 January 1954, n. 170758. Comm. Centr., Sez. VI, 13 April 1953, n. 46704. See also Serrano, Le imposte sulle successioni 159-162.

3/4.7 Computation and Rates

a. IN GENERAL. Unlike the estate tax, which is applied to the estate as a whole, the inheritance tax is levied and computed separately on the distributive share of each of the heirs or legatees. Except in the cases described at 3/4.7c, for which proportional rates are provided, the tax is applied at progressive rates (LS art. 2).

When a beneficiary renounces his share and it passes to another person, the tax is nonetheless payable at the rate applicable to the first beneficiary if that is higher than the rate applicable to the second (LS art. 15).

b. PROGRESSIVE RATES. The present system of rates for the inheritance (and gift) tax has been in force since 31 May 1949.[82] In a table annexed to the 1923 decree (subsequently modified), beneficiaries are divided into five categories according to their degree of relationship with the decedent (see Table 54). Within each category, the tax is graduated in brackets into which the value of the estate or of each share of the estate or legacy is divided (LS art. 2). The rates are progressive within each category.

The five categories of beneficiaries are listed below.[83]

1. Direct line ascendants and descendants, including legally recognized natural children.
2. Spouses.
3. Brothers and sisters.
4. Uncles, aunts, nephews, nieces.
5. Great-uncles, great-aunts, great-nephews, great-nieces, cousins, other relatives beyond the fourth degree, persons related by marriage, strangers.

Beneficiaries in categories 1 and 2 are entitled to an allowance of L. 750,000, by which the taxable amount is reduced. The rate schedule is applied to the amount exceeding the allowance. The total amount of the succession taxes, the mortgage tax (4/3.3), the surcharges, and cadastral fees can in no case exceed the net value of the property on which those taxes, surcharges, fees, and penalties are imposed (LS art. 102).

Specific provisions govern the relationships of adoption and so-called "affiliation."[84] An adopted child succeeding to the property of his

---

[82] L. 12 May 1949, n. 206, Annex A, Tables 1 and 3. Rate tables for the years 1862-1949 may be found in De Bono, *L'imposta sulle successioni e l'imposta sull'asse globale ereditario netto* 385-395.

[83] On relationship under the civil law, see articles 74-78 of the Civil Code.

[84] "Affiliation" was introduced into the Italian civil law by articles 404-413 of the Civil Code of 1942. Affiliation is related to both guardianship and adoption; but, unlike the adopted person, the affiliated person does not enter into a family relationship with the affiliating person and does not acquire new status.

Table 54: *Rates of the Inheritance Tax*

Taxable Value of Inheritance (Lire)		I Ascendants and Descendants *	II Spouses *	III Brothers and Sisters	IV Uncles, Aunts, Nephews, Nieces	V Other Relatives, Persons Related by Marriage, and Strangers
Lower Limit	Upper Limit					
0	1,000,000	1%	2%	3%	5%	15%
1,000,000	2,500,000	2	3	5	8	20
2,500,000	5,000,000	3	4	8	12	25
5,000,000	10,000,000	6	8	16	19	40
10,000,000	15,000,000	9	12	22	25	46
15,000,000	25,000,000	12	16	28	32	52
25,000,000	50,000,000	16	20	34	41	60
50,000,000	75,000,000	20	25	41	51	70
75,000,000	100,000,000	25	30	48	60	74
100,000,000	250,000,000	29	34	54	64	77
250,000,000	500,000,000	32	37	57	67	79
500,000,000	—	35	40	60	70	80

* For categories I and II, there is a tax-free allowance up to L. 750,000 (L. 12 May 1949, n. 206, art. 2).
Source: L. 12 May 1949, n. 206.

adoptive parent is treated in the same way as a natural child. If the adoptive parent succeeds by testament to his adopted child's property, the tax is payable in half of the amount that would be due if the relationship of adoption did not exist. This latter provision is also applicable to succession by the affiliating person to the property of the affiliated.[85] A legally unrecognized or unrecognizable natural child succeeding to his natural parent's property is subject to tax at the rate of one and one fourth times the rate of the first category (direct line ascendants and descendants). An heir who acquires the estate by right of representation is subject to the tax at the rate which corresponds to the grade of relationship between the heir and the decedent (LS art. 10; MSD art. 1).

The rate schedule provided by the law establishes the proportional rate to be applied within each bracket, depending on the amount of the inheritance, for each class of beneficiary (Table 54). The total share of each beneficiary is divided among the appropriate brackets, and the rate applicable to each bracket is multiplied by the amount of the share falling within that bracket; the total tax of the beneficiary is the sum of the resulting amounts.

Example 1
A sister leaves an estate of L. 14 million to her brother. Using the rate schedule provided by the law and reproduced in Table 54, the brother's tax would be computed as shown below.

| Bracket | | | | |
Lower limit	Upper limit	Amount	Rate	Tax
0	1,000,000	1,000,000	3%	30,000
1,000,000	2,500,000	1,500,000	5	75,000
2,500,000	5,000,000	2,500,000	8	200,000
5,000,000	10,000,000	5,000,000	16	800,000
10,000,000	15,000,000	4,000,000	22	880,000
		14,000,000	(14.2)	1,985,000

In practice, this cumbersome process of computation can be dispensed with, because the Ministry of Finance has prepared a ready-made computation table for arriving at the amount of tax due. Using this table, the entire taxable amount is multiplied by the rate for the highest bracket into which a share of the taxable amount would fall, and this result is then reduced by the fixed figure (in the column entitled "Reduction") which corresponds to that rate and bracket (see Table 55). This "reduction" represents the difference between the amount determined by applying the marginal rate to the lower limit of the top bracket and the tax due on the lower limit of that bracket as determined from the rate schedule provided in the law (Table 54).

---

[85] L. 20 November 1955, n. 1123.

Table 55: *Computation Table for the Inheritance Tax*

Taxable Value of Inheritance (Lire)		I Ascendants and Descendants *		II Spouses *		III Brothers and Sisters		IV Uncles, Aunts, Nephews, Nieces		V Other Relatives, Persons Related by Marriage, and Strangers	
Lower Limit	Upper Limit	Rate %	Reduction (Lire)	Rate %	Reduction (Lire)	Rate %	Reduction (Lire)	Rate %	Reduction (Lire)	Rate %	Reduction (Lire)
0	1,000,000	1	—	2	—	3	—	5	—	15	—
1,000,000	2,500,000	2	10,000	3	10,000	5	20,000	8	30,000	20	50,000
2,500,000	5,000,000	3	35,000	4	35,000	8	95,000	12	130,000	25	175,000
5,000,000	10,000,000	6	185,000	8	235,000	16	495,000	19	480,000	40	925,000
10,000,000	15,000,000	9	485,000	12	635,000	22	1,095,000	25	1,080,000	46	1,525,000
15,000,000	25,000,000	12	935,000	16	1,235,000	28	1,995,000	32	2,130,000	52	2,425,000
25,000,000	50,000,000	16	1,935,000	20	2,235,000	34	3,495,000	41	4,380,000	60	4,425,000
50,000,000	75,000,000	20	3,935,000	25	4,735,000	41	6,995,000	51	9,380,000	70	9,425,000
75,000,000	100,000,000	25	7,685,000	30	8,485,000	48	12,245,000	60	16,130,000	74	12,425,000
100,000,000	250,000,000	29	11,685,000	34	12,485,000	54	18,245,000	64	20,130,000	77	15,425,000
250,000,000	500,000,000	32	19,195,000	37	19,985,000	57	25,745,000	67	27,630,000	79	20,425,000
500,000,000	—	35	34,185,000	40	34,985,000	60	40,745,000	70	42,630,000	80	25,425,000

* For categories I and II, there is a tax-free allowance up to L. 750,000 (L. 12 May 1949, n. 206, art. 2).
Source: I.M. 16 June 1949, n. 121579.

Example 2

As in *Example 1*, a sister leaves an estate of L. 14 million to her brother In the computation table provided by the Ministry (Table 55), the rate corresponding to this amount is 22%. The tax is computed as shown below

L. 14,000,000 × .22	3,080,000
Less: reduction	1,095,000
Tax L. 1,985,000	

c. PROPORTIONAL RATES. In certain specified cases, the inheritance tax is applied at proportional rates without regard to the taxable amount (LS art. 2). Subject to a proportional tax at 5% are transfers for the benefit of the persons and entities listed below (LS art. 11).

1. Juridical persons and legally recognized Italian institutions, founded or to be founded, whose main purpose is charity or the education, instruction, or training for a profession, art, or craft, of persons of any condition or nationality. These institutions also include libraries, art galleries, and museums founded for purposes of instruction.[86]
2. Provinces, communes, and other legal entities if the main purpose of the donation is health or public utility.[87]
3. Foundations intended to reward talent (*virtù*) and merit (*merito*), or having other purposes of public utility.
4. Societies of mutual assistance, registered in accordance with the Law of 15 April 1886, n. 3818.

The specification of "purposes of public utility" in item 2 gives rise to many uncertainties, discriminations, and contradictions, since it leaves to the tax administration the power to decide whether or not a bequest is publicly "useful." In practice, the administration's severely restrictive interpretation of the phrase has rendered the provision largely ineffective. The absence of explicit exemptions and reductions for bequests to entities carrying on scientific research and for bequests to entities for the development of the arts and of archaeology is a hindrance to development in these areas. It is also unfortunate that exemption is granted only for bequests to entities and not for bequests to individuals for similar purposes.

Subject to tax at the rate of 3% are legacies, not exceeding L. 2,000 annually, to servants of the decedent for their support (LS art. 12), or to relatives of the decedent within the fourth degree for their support.[88]

d. REDUCTION IN CASE OF SUCCESSIVE DEATHS. When, as a result of the death of the first beneficiary, property included in one succession is

---

[86] Certain gifts to such institutions are exempt from tax entirely (3/4.2b).

[87] Gifts to such entities for instruction or welfare are exempt from tax entirely (3/4.2b).

[88] Report of the Minister of Finance on R.D. 30 December 1923, n. 3270; see Stammati, Armani, and Ceccarelli, *Codice delle imposte di successione* 45.

subject to a second succession opened within two years of the opening of the first, the tax rate on the second succession is reduced by one half (LS art. 19).[89] The reduced tax is computed on the valuation of the property made for the second succession, regardless of the value attributed to it for the first succession.

The reduction does not apply to property in the second succession which was not included in the first, or to property which in the first succession was totally exempt from the tax.

e. CREDIT FOR TAXES ON PREVIOUS GIFTS. The tax base of each heir or legatee includes the value of all inter vivos gifts made by the decedent, without regard to when the gifts were made or to the donor's motives (3/4.3a). The rate of tax is determined by reference to, and is applied to, this cumulative total. The tax which would be due on the total of the previous gifts, under the current rate schedule, is then subtracted as a credit from the inheritance tax payable on the cumulative total (LS art. 3). Since, presumably, the previous gifts have been subjected cumulatively to the tax on gifts (3/6), the net result is the taxing of the cumulative total of the inheritance plus previous gifts at the current rate applicable to it, refunding taxes payable at the current rates on the value of the previous gifts.

f. ADDITIONALS. On the amount of the inheritance tax are computed the additional for communal assistance entities (ECA) at 10% of the tax and the additional for Calabrian relief at 5% of the tax (2/2.9).

3/4.8 Returns

a. IN GENERAL. As in the case of other indirect taxes, the succession taxes are administered by the Registry Office (*Ufficio del Registro*), headed by the Registrar (*Procuratore del Registro*), within whose jurisdiction the decedent was domiciled or had been residing for at least 10 years at the date of his death (LS art. 61). If the decedent had neither domicile nor 10-year residence in Italy, the return is submitted to the Registry Office within whose jurisdiction the greater part of the estate property is located (LS art. 61). The Registry Offices are local organs of the General Directorate of the Fees and Indirect Taxes on Transactions, Division VII of which deals with the two succession taxes, the mortgage taxes, and the valuation of property (1/4.3). It is to the Registry Office that all transfers by death must be reported by filing a written return (*denunzia*). The practical consequence is that the succession taxes fall principally on immovables possessed by individuals, since this is the field in which the registration taxes operate most

---

[89] As substituted by L. 12 May 1949, n. 206, art. 3.

effectively. Even if the succession is totally exempt from the tax, the return must be filed for purposes of the cadastral registration of immova ble property, the mortgage tax, and the estate tax (LS art. 51; MSD art 11). The return for purposes of the inheritance tax is valid also for the estate tax (LS art. 53; MSD art. 11). A transfer taking place on the ful fillment of a suspensive condition (a condition on whose fulfillment, in the future, a transfer is to take place), the execution of a conditiona transfer depending on death before the condition was fulfilled, or the merger of usufruct with bare ownership must be declared to the Registry Office at which the conditional transfer or the transfer of bare ownership has been declared. The declaration of the renunciation of an inheritance or legacy, the declaration of the execution of donation subject by testament to the possibility of survival, or the declaration of supervening assets, the termination of contestability, and dubious col lectibility of estate credits must be filed with the Office at which the succession has been registered (LS art. 63).

b. PERSONS FILING. In principle, the heirs are jointly and severally liable for filing the return (LS art. 55). The duty falls upon an heir who has been called to succession even if the testament is contested or if he repudiates the succession.[90] The heirs must declare the entire estate, including the property bequeathed to legatees (LS art. 55), but the legatees must also file returns for their bequests. If heirs or legatees do not have legal capacity, the duty to file the return falls upon their legal representative as provided by the Civil Code. The duty falls also upon administrators of estates and testamentary executors (LS art. 55).

c. TIME LIMITS FOR FILING. The law prescribes ordinary and extraordi- nary time limits for filing the return. The ordinary time limits are four months if the decedent died in Italy, six months if he died abroad in Europe, and eighteen months if he died abroad, but not in Europe. For the heirs, these time limits run from the date of the death; for guardians, curators, and testamentary executors and administrators, from the date of the legal notification of their appointment; in the case of succession to the estate of an absent person, from the date of taking possession of the absent person's property; and, if the property is under distraint, from the date on which the heirs take possession (LS art. 55). The time limit for filing the return declaring the succession of soldiers or other persons attached to the armed forces who died in war is one year from the day of the transcription of the act of death in the register of civil

---

[90] The declaration of succession in the return does not mean the acceptance of inheritance. Cass. 2 January 1942 (*Riv. leg. fisc.*, 1942, 180); Comm. Centr., Sez. VI, 21 January 1943, n. 65284 (*Riv. leg. fisc.*, 1943, 620).

status if the death occurred in Europe, and three years if it occurred outside of Europe (LS art. 55).

For successions accepted with the "benefit of inventory" (*col beneficio d'inventario*),[91] the time limit runs from the expiration of the time limit prescribed for the preparation of the inventory or, if the inventory was completed before the expiration of that time limit, from the date of the closing thereof. But, in any case, the return must be filed within one year of the date of the death if it occurred in Italy; within fourteen months if the death occurred abroad in Europe; or within twenty-four months if the death occurred abroad, but not in Europe. These provisions are not applicable if the declaration of the acceptance of the inheritance with the benefit of inventory was not made in accordance with article 484 of the Civil Code, before the expiration of the ordinary time limits (LS art. 56).[92]

The ordinary time limits and those established for the inheritances of soldiers who died in war are also applicable to the returns declaring the merger of usufruct with bare ownership, the fulfillment of a condition of survival, the acquisition of supervening assets (*sopravvenienze*) in the estate, and the termination of the contestability and dubious collectibility of the estate credits (LS art. 57). The fulfillment of a suspensive condition attached to transfers at death, or the execution of the transfer for the fulfillment of the condition must be declared in the return by the persons concerned within 20 days following the date of the fulfillment of the condition or execution of the transfer. The renunciation of an inheritance or legacy must be declared within the same time limits by the person who benefits thereby (LS art. 58). The day of the death of the deceased is not included in the time limits set for filing the return.

d. FORM AND CONTENT. The return is prepared on a special form distributed free of charge by the administration and must be signed by the declaring person.[93] If the person filing the return is not one of the persons required to do so under article 55, he must attach to the return a power of attorney issued to him by at least one of those persons. In any case, the return must specify the domicile and residence of the heir

---

[91] If an heir accepts an inheritance "with benefit of inventory," his property is kept distinct from that of the decedent, with the result that the heir retains toward the inheritance all the rights and duties which he had toward the decedent except those extinguished by death; that the heir is not liable for the payment of estate debts and legacies beyond the value of his inheritance; and that the legatees and the creditors of the estate have preference against the estate over the creditors of the heir (CC art. 490).

[92] See also Comm. Centr., Sez. VII, 14 July 1947, n. 91672 (*Riv. leg. fisc.*, 1949, 148). The provisions of article 56 are also applicable to legatees. See Comm. Centr., Sez. VI, 9 November 1949, n. 6875 (*Riv. leg. fisc.*, 1951, 162).

[93] By virtue of the stamp tax law (D.P.R. 25 June 1953, n. 492, Table, Annex B, art. 9), the returns are exempt from the stamp tax (4/4.2d).

(LS art. 51). The return is, as a rule, filed in one copy; but two copies must be filed of a return declaring the merger of usufruct with bare ownership, the fulfillment of a suspensive condition by death or by execution before the condition was fulfilled, the renunciation of an inheritance or legacy, the acquisition of supervening assets in the estate, or the termination of the contestability or dubious collectibility of the estate credits (LS art. 54).

The return must contain a detailed specification of immovable and other property of the estate, with the declaration of the value, and with sufficient information regarding the nature, location, or importance of the various components of the estate (LS art. 51). Industrial and commercial enterprises, as property of an estate, must be declared in the part of the return pertaining to assets; the components, including the value of good will, must be listed separately (LS art. 51).[94] The description of annuities and credits must specify their legal bases with the dates and places of registration, the name of the debtors, and the amounts already due both for capital and for interest or annuities at the date of the death. Debts must be documented in the manner prescribed by the law; debts which are not properly evidenced are not taken into account by the Registry Office (LS art. 51).

In the case of testamentary succession, an authenticated copy of each testament must be attached to the return. After registration, the copy is returned to the person filing the return if that person submits a copy of the testament provided with his signature (LS art. 51).

The return must be registered by the Registry Office to certify the date of filing. If the tax is paid according to the assessment of the Registrar, the Registrar may not delay the registration of the return or other declarations by more than three days. If requested, he must also issue a receipt, free of charge (LS art. 60).

A return which does not contain the information necessary for the assessment of the tax, or which is not signed by the authorized person, is considered irregular or incomplete. The Registrar must specify the irregularity by an annotation written on the return, and must return it to the taxpayer, instructing him to rectify the return within the time limits prescribed by the law (LS art. 55), but not within less than eight days. An irregular return is deemed not to have been submitted until it has been rectified. If the taxpayer does not recognize the irregularity and insists on filing the return as it stands, the Registrar issues a receipts with an express reservation of the surcharges to be applied (LS art. 52).

---

[94] For a detailed description of the return form, see Cordaro, *Dizionario del contribuente* 1094. For the detailed provisions concerning the return, see R.D. 23 December 1897, n. 549; R.D. 23 March 1902, n. 114.

3/4.9 Assessment

The return filed by the taxpayer is examined by the tax administration. If the value of the transfer or the elements necessary for the determination thereof appear in the return, the tax (and the mortgage tax and cadastral fees) is assessed on the basis of the value declared by the taxpayer or that determined by the tax administration on the basis of the elements supplied by the taxpayer (LS art. 34).

In cases of transfers at death of immovable property, ships, industrial and commercial enterprises, and partnership shares, the values appearing in the declarations of the parties and those determined by the Registry Office are subject to revision. If the Office claims the declared or the determined value is lower than the market value at the date of the transfer, it notifies the taxpayer of the market value ascribed to the property by the administration (LS art. 36).[95] Differences in value not exceeding 12% are not contested by the administration.[96] The time limit for notification of contested value is one year from the date of payment of the tax or from the date of the grant of an extension (LS art. 37).[97] A second notification may be sent if the first has not reached the taxpayer (LS art. 37).[98] Within 30 days of a first or second notification the taxpayer may appeal to the District Tax Commission (LS art. 37) (1/4.10c).[99] If the taxpayer has not appealed within this time limit, he forfeits the right to challenge the value of which he has been notified; the administration may, however, reduce this value by a decision supported by reasons if the assessment was found to be defective or erroneous (LS art. 37).

If the return does not disclose the value or elements necessary for an assessment, the Registrar requests one or more of the taxpayers to complete the return by making an estimating declaration signed by them. If the party fails to make the declaration or file the return within the assigned time limit, the Registrar determines the value ex officio.

With respect to transfers of industrial and commercial enterprises and of partnership shares, the administration, in order to assess the quantity and value of the merchandise existing at the date of the transfer, and the kind and value of other property of any nature, including good will and patents, has the right to inspect the accounting records, and may take account of their results. The administration may also make use of assessments made for purposes of the tax on income from movable wealth and other direct taxes, and of any other appropriate element. Refusal to produce the accounting records results in their inadmissibility in

---

[95] As amended by R.D.L. 7 August 1936, n. 1639, art. 20.
[96] I.M. 21 April 1938, n. 8478.
[97] As amended by D.L.C.P.S. 21 January 1947, n. 25, art. 1.
[98] As amended by L. 12 June 1930, n. 742, art. 8.
[99] As amended by R.D.L. 7 August 1936, n. 1639, art. 21.

administrative or judicial proceedings (13/2.3) and the imposition of the penalties provided for nonfulfillment of requests for information in the assessment of the direct taxes (13/7.3).[100]

After the value has been assessed by the Registry Office, the taxpayer may refuse to accept the assessment if he alleges the value of the property to be less than that assessed by the Office by more than one tenth in the case of immovable property, or by more than one eighth in the case of ships, industrial and commercial enterprises, and partnership shares. In such cases, the taxpayer has the right to appeal to the District Tax Commission within 30 days of the service of the notice of assessment (LS art. 34).[101] If he fails to appeal, he forfeits the right to challenge the assessed value (LS art. 38).[102] Appeals to District Commissions may also be filed with respect to the valuation of rural land made by the Registry Office.[103]

At any stage of the assessment proceedings, except after the final decision of the District Commission, the value of the estate may be established by agreement (*concordato*) between the administration and the taxpayer (LS art. 44).[104] This results in the right to a reduction by one quarter of the tax base assessed by the administration.[105] With the signing of such an agreement, the taxpayer relinquishes his right to appeal the assessment of the administration; thus, he loses not only the possibility of a reduction of the amount assessed on appeal, but also the possibility of deferral of payment of the tax pending conclusion of the appeal.

3/4.10 Payment

a. IN GENERAL. The inheritance tax is paid directly to the Registry Office, which issues a receipt for the payment. The receipt, issued as a separate sheet detached from the counterfoil register, must specify the name of the Office, the nature of the tax or the cause of the complementary or supplementary tax (LS art. 5) (15/7.2), the date of collection, the number of the sheet, the registration number, and the amount of the tax, spelled out in words (LS art. 67).[106] If the taxpayer pays the tax by a postal money order, the receipt thereof cannot serve as evidence of payment.[107]

---

[100] R.D.L. 7 August 1936, n. 1639, art. 19.

[101] As modified by R.D.L. 7 August 1936, n. 1639, art. 17.

[102] As amended by L. 12 June 1930, n. 742, art. 38; R.D.L. 7 August 1936, n. 1639, art. 21.

[103] L. 20 October 1954, n. 1044, arts. 1-2.

[104] As modified by R.D.L. 7 August 1936, n. 1639, art. 14.

[105] C.M. 25 April 1950, n. 131556.

[106] An incomplete receipt cannot serve as evidence of payment. Cass. Roma 29 December 1877; Cass. Roma 15 May 1894.

[107] *Relazione Avvocatura dello Stato 1920* 445.

b. PERSONS SUBJECT. In the case of transfers at death, each heir is liable for payment of the total amount of tax due, but has a right of recovery against the other coheirs and legatees; the legatees are liable for the taxes due on property bequeathed to each of them (LS art. 66). In the case of a transfer at death which is subject to a suspensive condition, all persons who benefit by the fulfillment of the condition are jointly and severally liable for payment of the taxes (LS art. 66). In the case of the merger of usufruct with bare ownership, those effecting the merger, their heirs, and any other successors in title (*aventi causa*) are jointly and severally liable for payment of the taxes (LS art. 66).

In the case of renunciation of an inheritance or legacy, the person who benefits thereby is liable for the succession tax that would be due from the disclaiming heir or legatee, unless he is himself liable for a higher amount of tax by reason of this relationship with the deceased (LS art. 15).

The law imposes the duty to declare transfers at death not only on the heirs and legatees of the decedent, but also on their guardians or curators, administrators of the estate, and testamentary executors (LS art. 55) (3/4.8b). These persons, known in theory as *responsabili d'imposta*, although personally liable for the fulfillment of formalities described by the law in the matter of tax assessment,[108] are not bound to pay the tax out of their own means, but only from their own shares of the estate.[109] Persons who have paid the tax for the person subject to it are deemed to have entered into all the rights and preferences of the tax administration and, in order to secure reimbursement, have the right to obtain from the Magistrate (*Pretore*) an order of payment to be executed within 24 hours (LS art. 69).[110]

Persons who commit offenses subject to pecuniary penalties (3/4.13c, items 1-4) are also liable for payment of the inheritance tax on the property involved in the transgressions.

In accordance with the rules of civil law, the heir who accepts an inheritance with the benefit of inventory is liable for the tax only to the extent of the assets bequeathed to him by the decedent (LS art. 70).

c. TIME LIMITS. Payment of the inheritance tax is, as a rule, due within two months of the expiration of the time limit set for the filing of the return (LS art. 64). Heirs who accept the succession with the benefit of inventory, guardians, curators, administrators, sequestrators, and testamentary executors must pay the tax within two months of the

---

[108] Article 72 makes these persons personally liable for the payment of the surcharge for failure to file the return or late filing thereof.

[109] See Serrano, *Le imposte sulle successioni* 248, 254-355.

[110] Compare similar provisions in article 98 of R.D. 30 December 1923, n. 3269. See also article 1203 of the Civil Code, on subrogation.

expiration of the time limit set for filing the return if they had been granted possession of the estate property, and, in any case, not later than six months from the expiration of the time limit set for filing the return.[111]

Special provisions govern the time limits for the payment of tax by juridical persons (5/2.1). Under Italian civil law, juridical persons can accept donations or successions and legacies only with governmental authorization, without which the acceptance has no effect (CC art. 17). The acceptance must be made with benefit of inventory unless the juridical person is a company (CC art. 473). A juridical person must file the return within the time limit prescribed by law, and pay the tax within three months of the authorization or the declaration of the benefit of inventory. If the juridical person does not make the declaration of benefit of inventory, it must file the return under the general rule of article 55, whether or not it has been authorized to accept the inheritance (LS art. 71).[112] If the juridical person has not applied for the authorization within one year of the decedent's death, the tax becomes collectible and must be paid within 20 days of the request of the Registrar; notice that the tax is due is made through a court official or messenger. A juridical person to which authorization to accept an inheritance or legacy has been denied has the right to a refund of the tax paid, provided that application is made within six months of the day on which it received the knowledge of the refusal. After the refund, however, the tax administration has the right to collect the tax from those who benefited by the refusal of the authorization, provided that it requests payment within six months from the date of the refund (LS art. 71).

d. PAYMENT IN INSTALLMENTS. Mitigating the general rule of the law that no public authority or official may suspend the collection of the inheritance tax without becoming personally responsible therefore (LS art. 8), the law provides that, at the request of the taxpayer, payment of the tax and possibly of the surcharges by installments may be allowed. Payment is spread over a maximum of six years, and interest at 5% is due on the unpaid balance. If immovable property or shares of commercial or industrial companies are concerned, the privilege must be granted if the taxpayer requests it; if movable property is involved, it is within the Registrar's discretion to grant permission. As security for the deferred tax amount, the law allows the administration to place a mortgage on the immovable property of the estate and any other security which the administration deems appropriate. In any case, the administration's

---

[111] R.D.L. 26 September 1935, n. 1749, Annex B, art. 13.
[112] I.M. 10 September 1866, art. 23.

credit is entitled to a preference (3/4.10e) against all property of the estate during the entire installment period. The deferral of payment must always be based on a written act; if such an act was drafted before the expiration of the time limit fixed for the payment of the tax, the taxpayer incurs no surcharges. In the case of late payment of an installment by more than 20 days, the entire amount of tax becomes collectible in one payment with the related interest and surcharges for the tax due. The power to grant the deferral lies with the Registry Office (LS art. 65).[113]

e. PREFERENCE OF THE STATE. Under Italian civil law, certain debts are selected for first payment, that is, preferred above others, and paid first out of the estate's assets (CC arts. 2745-2783). Such a preference (*privilegio*) is established first of all for the credits of the state arising from taxation. For the collection of succession taxes, the state has a preference against the movable or immovable property to which the taxes relate. The preference also guarantees the payment of taxes due on the higher value assessed in the valuation procedure (LS art. 68).[114] The preference lasts over the period of installment payments until the full satisfaction of the tax and the related interest (LS art. 65). The prevailing opinion is that the preference also extends to the collection of surcharges and collection expenses.[115]

f. LEGAL SUBROGATION. On the basis of the civil law rules on subrogation (CC arts. 1201-1205), the inheritance tax law repeats the provisions found in article 98 of the registration law (15/2.3)—that all those who have paid the inheritance tax for the persons subject enter into all rights, actions, and preferences of the administration and, in order to recover the sum paid, may obtain from the Magistrate (*Pretore*) of their place of residence an order of payment to be executed within 24 hours. In the execution of this order, it is no defense that the taxes paid were not due, or that they were overpaid. The tax debtor may not appeal against the tax administration unless he can prove that he has reimbursed those who paid the tax for him (LS art. 69). According to the prevailing judicial decisions and doctrine, jointly and severally liable heirs who are subrogated to the rights of the administration under the general rule

---

[113] L. 12 May 1949, n. 206, art. 5; R.D.L. 7 August 1936, n. 1639, art. 14. For the other provisions concerning the payment by installments, see R.D. 23 March 1902, n. 114, arts. 14-18.

[114] As amended by R.D.L. 7 August 1936, n. 1639. On the range of the privilege, see CC arts. 2758, 2772.

[115] Comm. Centr., Sez. VII, 18 February 1943, n. 66798 (*Riv. leg. fisc.*, 1943, 554); Comm. Centr., Sez. VII, 26 May 1947, n. 90214 (*Riv. leg. fisc.*, 1948, 848). *Contra*, see Uckmar, 3 *La legge del registro* 126-129.

of civil law are not entitled to the preference or to the Magistrate's order.[116]

g. REFUNDS. The general rule is that except for cases expressly provided by the law, taxes regularly (*regolarmente*) collected in accordance with the law cannot be refunded as a result of the nonfulfillment of a condition to which a transfer was subject, or due to any other ulterior event (LS art. 7). A tax is "regularly" collected if the tax official collecting it did not commit any error of fact or law to the detriment of the taxpayer. By "ulterior events" are meant events following the death of the decedent which might modify the legal status of the heirs with regard to the inheritance.[117] Refund of tax would be due if the collection had been based on a testament subsequently annulled or if a new testament were discovered. Refund is allowed in cases of inheritances of property of which the taxpayer was deprived by eviction or other deprivation (*spoglio*).[118] The conditions for refund are that deprivation must result from a cause existing prior to the death of the decedent and that it must be in pursuance of a final and enforceable judicial decision pronounced in proceedings between the tax administration and the party concerned (LS art. 9).[119]

The law itself orders a refund of the tax in cases where no taxable basis exists. Thus, the heir or the legatee has the right to a refund of the tax paid on a credit whose judicial contestability or dubious collectibility has not previously been sufficiently proved if he proves either of these conditions within two years of the date prescribed for the filing of the return (LS art. 32). The right to a refund also obtains if the debt is proved within two years of the date for the filing of the return (LS art. 50), and also if the tax was paid for the inheritance of a person declared absent who subsequently returns (LS art. 55).

Subject to the interruptions of limitation periods discussed at 3/4.12b, the action of the taxpayer for the refund of the tax is barred after the lapse of three years from the date of payment (LS art. 86).

---

[116] Compare article 65 with article 1203, n. 3, of the Civil Code. See Cass. 12 November 1928 (*Riv. leg. fisc.*, 1929, 8677); Trib. Bari 12 March 1930 (*Foro it.*, 1930, 207). See also Berliri, *Le leggi di registro* 410 *et seq. Contra*, Cass., Sez. I, 4 January-23 February 1938 (*Riv. leg. fisc.*, 1938, 359). See also De Bono, *L'imposta sulle successioni e l'imposta sull'asse globale ereditario netto* 344-346; Serrano, *Le imposte sulle successioni* 301-302.

[117] See Serrano, *Le imposte sulle successioni* 270.

[118] *Spoglio* is a general term for the deprivation of a thing, suffered by the heir, besides the specific case of eviction. See R.M. 6 August 1903, n. 52723.

[119] See Comm. Centr., Sez. V, 25 May 1959, n. 17176. See also Serrano, *Le imposte sulle successioni* 271-273; De Bono, *L'imposta sulle successioni e l'imposta sull'asse globale ereditario netto* 99-102.

h. COMPULSORY COLLECTION. The first stage in the procedure of compulsory collection of the succession taxes, surcharges and pecuniary penalties on these taxes, and any other tax within the jurisdiction of the Registry Offices, is an injunction issued by the Registry Office. The injunction is an order to pay the sum due within 30 days. If the taxpayer fails to comply with the order, the Office proceeds to execution.

The injunction for the collection of pecuniary penalties is issued at the request of the Intendant of Finance (LS art. 92).[120] The injunction, endorsed and rendered executory by the competent Magistrate, is delivered to the taxpayer (LS art. 92).[121] The taxpayer may challenge the injunction either administratively or in court. In the latter case, his appeal must be served, to avoid the sanction of nullity, on the state administration through the state legal office (*Avvocatura dello Stato*) (LS art. 93).[122] In general, the time limit for filing the appeal to the courts is six months from the service of the administrative decision (LS art. 94). The jurisdiction lies with the civil court of the seat of the state legal office in whose district the Registry Office in question is located (LS art. 95).[123] If the taxpayer resorts to judicial proceedings without exhausting administrative remedies (or before the expiration of 90 days for filing the administrative appeal), the administration cannot be required to pay the litigation expenses even if it loses the suit (LS art. 96).

3/4.11 Protests and Appeals

On the administrative side, disputes concerning the application of succession taxes, as well as registration and mortgage taxes, and those regarding the assessment of value in transfers inter vivos and at death are within the jurisdiction of the administrative commissions for direct taxes, whatever the nature of the controversy and the presumed value of the property involved.[124]

Controversies over the determination of value are decided in the first instance by the District Commission and in the second instance by the Provincial Commission. The decision of the Provincial Commission is final (*definitivo*), but the taxpayer may appeal to the courts if he alleges gross and evident error in appraisal or defective or insufficient calculation in the determination of value.[125] All other disputes are decided in the first instance by the Provincial Commission and in the second instance

---

[120] As amended by R.D. 13 January 1936, n. 2313, art. 1.
[121] As amended by R.D.L. 7 August 1936, n. 1639, art. 40.
[122] As amended by R.D. 30 October 1933, n. 1611, art. 11; see also art. 9.
[123] R.D. 30 October 1933, n. 1611, art. 7.
[124] R.D.L. 7 August 1936, n. 1639, art. 28. Transfers at death of automobiles are within the jurisdiction of the Intendant of Finance and the Minister of Finance, D.L.L. 18 June 1945, n. 399, art. 11.
[125] R.D.L. 7 August 1936, n. 1639, art. 29. For procedure governing these cases, see R.D.L. 7 August 1936, n. 1639, and R.D. 8 July 1937, n. 1516 (13/4.9).

by the Central Commission, but appeal may be made to the courts within six months of the service of the decision of the Commission.[126]

The time limit for appeals against the assessment notice and against decisions of the commissions of first and second instance is 30 days. Appeals are filed either with the Secretariat of the Commission or with the Registry Office.[127] Decisions of the Provincial Commission may also be challenged within the time limit prescribed for judicial appeals by the so-called "revocation appeal" (*ricorso di revocazione*), which is allowed under the circumstances prescribed by civil procedure, such as subsequent discovery of new facts, fraud, error in fact, or conflict with previous final decision.[128] In other cases, rules relative to the procedure before administrative commissions of direct taxes (13/4) are applicable to administrative litigation regarding taxes on transfer of property.[129]

3/4.12 Time Limits for Assessment and Collection

a. THE LIMITATION PERIODS. The tax administration is barred from demanding payment after the expiration of the limitation periods listed below (LS art. 86).[130]

1. Three years from the filing of the first or subsequent return.
2. Three years from the filing of the return, in cases of taxes on property omitted from the return, or of the supplementary tax.
3. Twenty years from the day of the death of the decedent in cases where no return has been filed.

The time limit for demanding payment of taxes on transfers subject to a suspensive condition, for merger of usufruct with bare ownership, for renunciation of an inheritance or legacy, for the fulfillment of a condition of survival, for supervening assets in the estate, and for the final settlement of the estate credits is three years from the date of the filing of the return. If no return was filed, the time limit is 20 years from the date on which the return was due (LS art. 87). The periods of limitation for surcharges are the same as for the taxes themselves; for pecuniary penalties, the limitation period is five years from the day on which the contravention was committed (LS art. 88).[131]

b. INTERRUPTION OF THE LIMITATION PERIODS. The running of the limitation period is interrupted by the service of an injunction or other act

---

[126] R.D.L. 7 August 1936, n. 1639, art. 29, para. 4. See also article 94 of the inheritance tax law.

[127] R.D.L. 7 August 1936, n. 1639, arts. 28, 29, 41; R.D. 8 July 1937, n. 1516, arts. 37, 45.

[128] R.D. 8 July 1937, n. 1516, art. 44; CPC art. 395. See also 13/4.9c.

[129] L. 7 August 1936, n. 1639, art. 31.

[130] On periods of limitation, see CC arts. 2934-2963.

[131] As amended by L. 7 January 1929, n. 4, art. 17.

of compulsory proceedings, or by any judicial demand, whether an action for payment or refund of the tax or direct action to cause a valuation of the transferred property by the tax commissions. A limitation period interrupted by a judicial demand remains suspended for the duration of the judicial proceeding instituted by the demand, and a limitation period interrupted by injunction remains suspended during the proceeding opposing the injunction. The limitation period is not interrupted if the judicial demand is barred through lapse of time; but, when the limitation period is interrupted by an injunction of the administration, the interruption continues in effect even if the injunction becomes ineffective through the extinction of the proceedings (LS art. 89).

A limitation period validly interrupted is completed with the running of a whole new term equal to that fixed by the law (LS art. 89).

A taxpayer's administrative claim for refund of the tax, or opposing the administration's claim for payment, interrupts the limitation period in favor of both parties. The request must be filed on stamped paper with the Registry Office in which the tax was paid, or which claims the payment. Even if not requested to do so, the Registry Office must issue a receipt, which is the only proof that the appeal was filed on time. Appeals for refund must be accompanied by the original receipt of the tax paid (LS art. 90).

3/4.13 Penalties

a. PENALTIES AGAINST TAXPAYERS. The penalties listed below are applicable for the violation by the taxpayer of the provisions on succession taxes.

1. A "pecuniary penalty" [132] of six times the amount of the tax, for signing a false declaration concerning the existence of alleged debts. The violators are jointly and severally liable for payment without prejudice to more severe penalties prescribed by the penal code (LS art. 49).

2. A surcharge equal to six tenths of the tax due, but not less than L. 12, is imposed on the heirs and legatees for failure to file the return within the prescribed time limits (LS art. 72).[133]

3. For filing an incomplete return, a surcharge equal to one and one fifth times the amount of the tax due on the property omitted (LS art. 72). The same surcharge is imposed for insufficient declaration of value under article 43.[134] The surcharge is not due if the omissions or under-

---

[132] It should be considered a surcharge, according to L. 7 January 1929, n. 4. See 13/7.1. See also Serrano, *Le imposte sulle successioni* 336-338.

[133] As modified by D.L.C.P.S. 5 October 1947, n. 1208, art. 1, para. 2, increasing the amounts six or three times, because of the devaluation of currency. See 3 Uckmar, *La legge del registro* 174-180; De Bono, *L'imposta sulle successioni e l'imposta sull'asse globale ereditario netto* 333-334. However, Serrano (*Le imposte sulle successioni* 339-340) believes that the minimum of L. 12 is not subject to this increase.

[134] As modified by L. 12 June 1930, n. 742, art. 12. Article 43 of the inheritance tax law provides that, if the value assessed by the commission, diminished by one

evaluations have been supplemented in subsequent returns registered before the time limit for the payment of the tax.

4. A surcharge of 24% of the tax is imposed for late payment of the tax or surcharge; and also in cases of omission, insufficient valuation or higher value assessed by agreement (*concordato*), if payment is not made within 20 days of the day on which the notice of payment was served (LS art. 75) (4/3.3).[135]

If the inheritance is exempt from the inheritance tax, the surcharges described in items 1, 2, and 4 are applied to the mortgage tax. Guardians, curators, testamentary executors, and other administrators are personally (*in proprio*) liable for the payment of the surcharge due for an omitted or late return (LS art. 72). A surcharge for a late return and a surcharge for an incomplete return can be applied simultaneously. However, if a return is filed on time with items omitted, there is a surcharge for the omitted items but not for the late return.[136] The penalties described in items 1, 2, and 3 are also applicable to returns filed on the merger of usufruct with bare ownership, fulfillment of a suspensive condition, renunciation of the inheritance or legacy, supervening assets in the estate, and the termination of judicial contestability and dubious collectibility of the inheritance credits (LS art. 74).

A pecuniary penalty of from L. 1,000 to L. 12,000 is imposed jointly and severally upon the beneficiaries who have failed to declare previous gifts from the decedent in their succession tax returns. If a declaration is false, the party guilty of the false statement is subject to a fine of from L. 2,000 to L. 24,000 (MSD art. 14).[137]

b. PENALTIES AGAINST OTHER PERSONS. The provisions of Title IV of the inheritance tax law define certain duties of public officials and other persons, designed to insure the observance of the law. Failure to comply with these duties results in the imposition of the pecuniary penalties listed below.

1. A penalty of L. 72 is imposed on officials and judicial officers who, contrary to the provisions of article 77, issue acts or make decisions at the request of the beneficiaries, before receiving proof of the payment of the tax or of authorization to postpone payment of tax. Such officials are also liable for the payment of the tax and surcharges, with the right of recovery from the taxpayer (LS arts. 79, 80).

2. Bailees (*detentori*) of the estate money or securities are subject to a pecuniary penalty in the amount of the tax due on the property if they

---

fourth, exceeds the value declared by the taxpayer, a pecuniary penalty is imposed under article 72, besides the tax due on the difference.

[135] The penalty for late payment of the registration tax has been reduced to 10%. See R.D. 13 January 1936, n. 2313, art. 1 (15/8.2).

[136] See Serrano, *Le imposte sulle successioni* 340.

[137] The amounts of the penalties and fines are given here as increased by D.L.C.P.S. 5 October 1947, n. 1208.

transfer it to the beneficiaries without having received proof of the payment of the tax (LS art. 81).

3. Those who open safe deposit boxes after the owner's death, without a notary's or Registrar's inventory, are subject to a penalty of L. 3,000 (LS art. 82).

4. Credit institutions, banking companies, and other entities which continue operations with respect to the securities belonging to the estate, without receiving proof of payment or authorization to postpone payment of tax, are subject to a penalty equal to the tax due on the securities issued by them (LS art. 83).

5. Persons charged with keeping the register of civil status who fail to make quarterly reports to the Registry Office of deaths which occurred in the preceding three months incur the penalty of L. 80 for each of the omitted or late transmissions, and L. 36 for each death omitted from the reports (LS art. 84).

c. INCREASED AND REDUCED PENALTIES. The 1923 inheritance tax law provides, in one case, for an exceptional increase in the surcharge, that is, in connection with the oath administered to the heir by the Magistrate with regard to the declaration in the return of annuities, bonds, securities, and any other property. If the heir refuses to sign the oath and does not appear on the date prescribed, and if subsequently an omission is found in the return, the surcharge on the omitted item is raised to twice the amount of the tax. The same surcharge applies if an omission is found after the signing of the oath. On the other hand, the surcharge is reduced to one tenth of its amount if, before signing the oath, the heir discloses knowledge of property omitted from the return and not assessed ex officio by the tax administration (LS art. 73).

The surcharges for late filing of the return or late payment are reduced by one half, but not to less than to L. 12, if the taxpayer pays the sum due before the delivery of the injunction. These surcharges are reduced to one tenth of their amount, but not to less than L. 12, if the return is filed and payment is made within 60 days of the respective due dates (LS art. 76).[138]

3/4.14 International Aspects

a. IN GENERAL. The principle of *lex rei sitae* governs the application of the succession taxes: the transfer is subject to tax if the property involved is located in Italy at the moment of the "opening of the succession," that is, at the death of the decedent. Transfers of property located abroad are not subject to tax. The place of death, the nationality, and the place of residence of the decedent are immaterial in determination of tax liability (LS art. 20). However, the principle of extra-

---

[138] The amounts of the surcharges are given here as increased by D.L.C.P.S. 5 October 1947, n. 1208, art. 2.

territoriality (that is, nontaxability) is applied, in cases of reciprocal treatment, to property of foreign diplomatic and consular representatives located in Italy.

In order to be subject to the tax, the location of movable property in Italy must be of a permanent character. For instance, movable property in the possession of a foreign tourist who happens to be in Italy at the moment of his death is ordinarily not subject to tax. Similarly, property located outside of Italy in an accidental way is ordinarily subject to tax. Money deposited in foreign banks and located abroad at the moment of death is not subject to taxation even if it is subsequently withdrawn by consular authorities and transferred to Italy.[139]

Under the present system, however, transfers of certain movable property, such as share certificates, have been able to escape the succession taxes by taking advantage of the numerous loopholes in the requirements for the registration of share certificates and by the formation of foreign corporations. It is possible to form or use a corporation, limited liability company, or any other form of company even for the ownership of houses, building lots, and agricultural estates. Companies formed in Liechtenstein, having a structure between that of a foundation and that of a corporation, can prevent identification of the names of the owners of participations. The shares or the certificates representing the participations can be deposited with a Swiss bank or investment company which issues a "share certificate" transmissible by delivery like a baggage check; or, even more simply, the certificates which represent the participations of a limited partnership, with the name in blank, can be left with an Italian bank, permitting the heirs to come into possession only in the case of death.

The presumptions of article 31 with respect to the existence of money, jewelry, and household furniture (3/4.3a) in proportion to the property located in Italy are also applicable to successions of nonresident aliens. Ships of Italian registry are included in the tax basis even if they are located outside of the Italian territorial waters; for the cargo, the location of its final destination is decisive.[140]

b. CREDITS, SECURITIES, AND ANNUITIES. Special rules are laid down by the law regarding the international aspects of the taxability of credits (*crediti*), securities, and annuities. Credits are presumed to be located in Italy if they are collectible (*esigibili*) in Italy; are secured by property located in Italy; are in consideration of contracts relating to immovable property situated in Italy; or depend on contracts made between Italian citizens in Italy (LS art. 20).

---

[139] R.M. 18 June 1906, n. 53059.
[140] Serrano, *Le imposte sulle successioni* 64-65.

For purposes of succession taxes, pensions and annuities (*titoli di rendita*) issued by foreign governments, as well as shares and bonds of foreign companies or other entities having their seat abroad, are considered located in Italy if the contracts or securities are located in Italy (LS art. 20). The law, however, provides relief from double taxation of these securities. If the recipient proves, within three years from the payment of the tax, that, by virtue of a foreign law, a tax measured on their value for the same inheritance has been paid or at least assessed on the securities, the tax due in Italy on the value of the succession is remitted or refunded. If the assessed value of the securities was lower than it would be according to the Italian rules, Italy taxes the difference.

c. FOREIGN DEBTS. Mortgage debts encumbering immovable property located abroad are not deductible from the inheritance estate. If the estate includes immovable property located abroad and immovable property located in Italy, the debts which are not secured by mortgage are deductible only in proportion to the value of that part of the estate which is located in Italy (LS art. 47). Evidence of debts incurred abroad must be given according to the general rules discussed at 3/4.6a and 3/4.6c. A debt resulting from a public act must be authenticated by an Italian consul before the death of the decedent; his signature must, in turn, be certified by the Italian Foreign Ministry.[141] A debt based on a foreign judgment is not deductible unless it is made enforceable in Italy by a judgment of the Court of Appeals under the rules of civil procedure (CPC arts. 796-797).

d. TAX TREATIES. Italy is a party to tax treaties for the avoidance of double taxation in succession tax matters with the United States [142] and Sweden.[143] These treaties deal only with estate and inheritance taxes and do not apply to gift taxation.

The treaty with the United States contains detailed rules on the situs of various types of property and on property rights: immovable property is deemed to be situated at the place where the land is located; tangible personal (movable) property and bank and currency notes, at the place where such property or currency is located at the time of death or, if in transit, at the place of destination; debts (*crediti*), at the place where

---

[141] See Serrano, *Le imposte sulle successioni* 158; De Bono, *L'imposta sulle successioni e l'imposta sull'asse globale ereditario netto* 147.

[142] Agreement for the Avoidance of Double Taxation and the Prevention of Fiscal Evasion with Respect to Death Duties, signed in Washington, 30 March 1955; 6 *United Nations International Tax Agreements* 247 (1956). In Italy, the treaty has been implemented by L. 19 July 1956, n. 943.

[143] Convention for the Avoidance of Death Taxation in the Matter of Inheritance Taxes, signed at Stockholm, 20 December 1956, 7 *United Nations International Tax Agreements* 324 (1958).

the debtor resides or, if the debtor is a corporation, at the place in or under the laws of which the corporation was created or organized; ships or aircraft, at the place of registration; good will as a trade, business, or professional asset, at the place where the trade, business, or profession is carried on; patents, trademarks, and designs, at the place where they are registered or used; copyrights, franchises, rights to artistic or scientific works, and rights or licenses to use copyrighted materials, artistic or scientific works, patents, trademarks, or designs, at the place where the rights arising therefrom are exercisable. All other property is deemed to be situated in the country in which the decedent was domiciled at the time of his death.[144] The convention with Sweden does not contain express situs rules. However, both treaties follow the rule of *lex rei sitae;* the United States convention stipulates that the state which imposes tax in the case of a decedent who was a national of or was domiciled in the other state shall "take no account of property situated outside that state in determining the rate and the amount of tax."[145]

Under the treaty with Sweden, immovable property, including accessory rights to royalties granted for the use of immovable property or for the operation of a mine, as well as debts secured by immovable property, are liable to tax only in the state in which the property is situated.[146] Assets invested in a commercial or industrial undertaking, or connected with the exercise of a liberal profession, or attributable to a permanent establishment, in one contracting state, are liable to tax only in that state.[147] Other assets are liable to tax in the state in which the decedent was domiciled at the time of his death.[148] The treaty with Sweden also provides rules concerning the deduction of debts.[149]

The problem of domicile is solved by the two treaties in different ways. Under the treaty with the United States (which refers to nationals of or persons domiciled in one of the contracting states), the question of whether or not the decedent was, at the time of his death, a national of or domiciled in one of the contracting states (also, whether a debtor resided therein) is determined in accordance with the law in force in that state.[150] Under the convention with Sweden, the decedent is deemed

---

[144] Treaty with the United States, art. III(1).

[145] Treaty with the United States, art. IV.

[146] Treaty with Sweden, art. 3.

[147] Treaty with Sweden, art. 4. The term "permanent establishment," as understood by the convention, means "a place where special installations are permanently utilized or where special arrangements have been made for carrying on an activity, such as the seat of management offices, branch establishments, workshops, warehouses, mines or mineral deposits which are being worked." Treaty with Sweden, art. 4.

[148] Treaty with Sweden, art. 5. Compare the Treaty with the United States, art. III(1).

[149] Treaty with Sweden, art. 6.

[150] Treaty with the United States, art. III.

to have been domiciled in the state of his "actual residence and dwelling."
In case of doubt or of double domicile, the question is settled by special
agreement between the highest fiscal authorities of the contracting countries. The decision involves the determination of the location of "the
strongest personal and economic ties" of the decedent at the time of
his death. Only if this point cannot be conclusively determined is the
nationality of the decedent taken into account. If the decedent had no
actual residence or dwelling in either Italy or Sweden, he is deemed to
have been domiciled in the state in which he had been living. If he had
been living in both Italy and Sweden, the question of domicile is settled
by a special agreement between the highest fiscal authorities of the two
states.[151]

The treaty with the United States provides a tax credit procedure
under which one country shall allow against its tax a credit for the
amount of the tax imposed by the other country on property situated
in the other state and included in the respective tax bases by both states;
the amount of the credit, however, cannot exceed the portion of the tax
imposed by the former state which is attributable to such property.[152]
Under the United States treaty, each country, when imposing tax in the
case of a decedent who was not a national of or domiciled in a given
state, agrees to grant any exemption which would be allowable if the
decedent had been domiciled in that state, in the proportion which
the value of the property subject to tax bears to the value of the property which would have been subjected to its tax if the decedent had
been domiciled in that state.[153] The two treaties provide for administrative assistance in cases of double taxation contrary to the treaty provisions.[154]

3/5. The Estate Tax

3/5.1 History and Sources

The first bill introducing an estate tax was submitted to the Italian
Parliament in 1914. Under that bill, estates valued at less than L. 10,000
were exempt; the rates for estates with a value of L. 10,000 or more were
progressive and ranged from 1% to 6%. The bill, however, met with strong
opposition and was withdrawn.[155] It was not until 1942 that the inheritance tax was complemented by an estate tax levied on the net
value of the entire estate (*imposta sul valore netto globale delle successioni*).[156] Since that time, there have existed two independent taxes on

---

[151] Treaty with Sweden, art. 5.
[152] Treaty with the United States, art. V.
[153] Treaty with the United States, art. IV.
[154] Treaty with the United States, art. VIII; Treaty with Sweden, art. 9.
[155] See Serrano, *Le imposte sulle successioni* 22.
[156] R.D.L. 4 May 1942, n. 434, modified and converted in L. 18 October 1942,
n. 1220.

gratuitous transfers at death (and on gifts), one levied on the entire estate and the other (the inheritance tax), on the share of each heir and legatee, levied after the estate tax has been paid. The 1942 law was repealed in 1945 by a legislative decree [157] which modified the structure of the succession taxes in general; this 1945 decree has remained the legal basis of the estate tax until today. The law of 12 May 1949, n. 206, contains the latest rates for the inheritance and estate taxes.

3/5.2 Relation to the Inheritance Tax

The estate tax is applied independently of the inheritance tax; the amount of the estate tax, however, is one of the deductions allowed in computing the taxable basis for the inheritance tax (MSD art. 13). The 1945 decree specified in particular, but not by way of limitation, that the provisions of the 1923 inheritance tax law regarding the filing of the return, determination of the taxable value, valuation, deductions, payment, preferences, limitation periods, procedures concerning controversies, and penalties are, unless otherwise provided by the decree of 1945, applicable to the estate tax (MSD art. 11). However, transfers exempt from the inheritance tax must nonetheless be reported and valued for purposes of the estate tax (MSD art. 11).

3/5.3 The Tax Base

The estate tax is due at the "opening of the succession," that is, at the decedent's death, before the distribution of the estate among the heirs and the other beneficiaries, in the case of estates whose aggregate net value is at least L. 500,000 (MSD art. 6).[158] That part of the estate transferred to direct descendants or direct ascendants or the surviving spouse is exempt if it does not exceed L. 3 million, and is taxed at one half the regular rate if it exceeds L. 3 million (3/5.5).

In order to thwart attempts to minimize the burden of the progressive rates by making gifts before death, the computation of the estate tax, following the rule applied to the inheritance tax, requires inclusion (*coacervo*) in the decedent's estate of all gifts and donations made by the decedent to his heirs or legatees on or after 12 May 1942, that is, the date on which the estate tax was first introduced in Italy. The taxes which would be due on these gifts and donations (3/6.2) are credited against the amount of the estate tax (MSD art. 10).[159]

---

[157] D.L.L. 8 March 1945, n. 90, modifications of the taxes on successions and gifts; an article of this decree will hereinafter be cited "MSD art."

[158] As modified by L. 12 May 1949, n. 206, art. 8. The original law of 1942 had fixed the taxable minimum at L. 50,000; it was raised in 1945 to L. 250,000, and finally to L. 500,000 in 1949.

[159] See I.M. 6 April 1945, n. 120156.

If there is more than one heir or legatee, the tax computed on the entire estate is distributed among the heirs and legatees in proportion to the value of their respective shares. Some of the beneficiaries may be entitled to reductions or exemptions (MSD art. 8).

3/5.4 Persons Subject

Theoretically, the decedent is the person subject to the estate tax,[160] and his debt is left to his heirs who become liable for payment. The law states that all of the heirs are jointly and severally liable for the payment of the entire tax. A legatee is liable only for his proportional share of the tax. An heir who has paid the entire tax has the right of recovery against each co-heir and legatee, limited to the tax share ascribed to that co-heir or legatee under the rules laid down by the law (MSD art. 12). However, in case of fidecommissary (trust) substitution (3/4.3d), the estate tax is charged exclusively to the instituted heir.[161] Usufructuaries are liable immediately, as well as the holders of bare ownership, each in proportion to the value received.[162]

3/5.5 Computation and Rates of Tax

The net value of the estate is determined by deducting from its gross value, including previous gifts, and bequests and gifts exempt from the inheritance tax, the expenses allowed as deductions for inheritance tax purposes (3/4.6). No tax is imposed on an estate whose net value is less than L. 500,000 (MSD art. 6).[163] If the net value of the estate exceeds L. 500,000, the entire net value, including the first L. 500,000, is subject to tax. In order to prevent the net value of an estate which slightly exceeds this limit from being reduced by the tax to an amount lower than it would have been if it had not exceeded the limit, the law provides that the amount of the tax can in no case exceed the difference between the net value of the estate and L. 500,000 (MSD art. 6).[164] An estate or part of an estate transmitted to the surviving spouse or to direct descendants or direct ascendants, including legally recognized natural children, but not adopted children,[165] is not subject to tax if its net value is L. 3 million or less, and is subject to tax at one half the

---

[160] Einaudi, criticizing the 1914 bill, called the tax *l'imposta sul morto*, the tax on the dead. See Serrano, *Le imposte sulle successioni* 22. See also Serrano, "L'imposta di successione nel pensiero di Luigi Einaudi," *Dir. e prat. trib.*, 1962, 5-12.

[161] L. 12 May 1949, n. 206, art. 6.

[162] See Comm. Centr., Sez. VI, 7 May 1951, n. 23509. See also R.M. 31 March 1952, n. 190631; R.M. 30 April 1954, n. 178646.

[163] As modified by L. 12 May 1949, n. 206, art. 8.

[164] L. 12 May 1949, n. 206, art. 8.

[165] Comm. Centr. 19 July 1949, n. 100077 (*Riv. leg. fisc.*, 1949, 879).

regular rate if its net value exceeds L. 3 million (MSD art. 7).[166] The rate applicable to the balance of the estate is that appropriate to the total value of the estate, including the part transferred to the spouse or to direct descendants or direct ascendants. In no case may the total tax due exceed the difference between the net value of the total estate and L. 3 million.

Table 56: *Rates of the Estate Tax*

Aggregate Net Value Exceeding L. 500,000 (Lire)		
Lower Limit	Upper Limit	Rate of Tax
0	1,000,000	1%
1,000,000	2,500,000	2
2,500,000	5,000,000	3
5,000,000	10,000,000	6
10,000,000	15,000,000	9
15,000,000	25,000,000	12
25,000,000	50,000,000	16
50,000,000	75,000,000	20
75,000,000	100,000,000	25
100,000,000	250,000,000	29
250,000,000	500,000,000	32
500,000,000	—	35

Source: L. 12 May 1949, n. 206, art. 8.

The rates of the estate tax are progressive. Except for the operation of the taxable limits and marginal relief provisions described above, there is no differentiation between beneficiaries; the rates in force since 31 May 1949 (Table 56) are the same as the inheritance tax rates for the first category of beneficiaries and are applied in the same manner (3/4.7b). Table 57, the computation table, gives the marginal rate of tax for each bracket with the "reduction" to correct for the difference between the marginal rate for that bracket and the marginal rates for the lower brackets.

The tax attributable to previous gifts included in the total estate is credited against the estate tax in the same manner as in the case of the inheritance tax (3/4.7e). As in the case of the inheritance tax (3/4.7d), a reduction of the estate tax is made for a second succession following within two years of the first.[167]

On the amount of the estate tax are computed the additional for communal assistance entities (ECA) at 10% of the tax, and the additional for Calabrian relief at 5% of the tax (2/2.9).

---

[166] As modified by L. 12 May 1949, n. 206, art. 9.
[167] See Comm. Prov. Cremona 10 June 1955 (Cordaro, *Dizionario del contribuente* 479).

Table 57: *Computation Table for the Estate Tax*

Aggregate Net Value Exceeding L. 500,000 (Lire)			
Lower Limit	Upper Limit	Rate of Tax	Reduction (Lire)
0	1,000,000	1%	0
1,000,000	2,500,000	2	10,000
2,500,000	5,000,000	3	35,000
5,000,000	10,000,000	6	185,000
10,000,000	15,000,000	9	485,000
15,000,000	25,000,000	12	935,000
25,000,000	50,000,000	16	1,935,000
50,000,000	75,000,000	20	3,935,000
75,000,000	100,000,000	25	7,685,000
100,000,000	250,000,000	29	11,685,000
250,000,000	500,000,000	32	19,185,000
500,000,000	—	35	34,185,000

Source: I.M. 16 June 1949, n. 121579, rates and reductions for category I for the inheritance tax.

3/5.6 Returns

The return filed for purposes of the inheritance tax is valid also for the estate tax. The filing of a return is compulsory even if the transfer is exempt from the inheritance tax (MSD art. 11).

3/6. Taxation of Gifts

Gifts, donations (*donazioni* or *atti di liberalità*) (CC arts. 769-809), and, in general, gratuitous transfers inter vivos are subject to the inheritance tax (3/4) and to the estate tax (3/5) in the same manner as transfers at death. With respect to gifts, these two taxes have been called the "tax on gifts" and the "tax on the aggregate value of gifts" respectively. The tax on gifts is a registration tax;[168] under the 1923 registration tax law, gratuitous transfers were subject to progressive rates fixed according to the grade of relationship between the donor and the donee.[169] These rates were, with one exception, the same as the rates of the inheritance tax.[170]

The 1945 decree reforming taxation at death also contains rules concerning the taxation of gifts. The decree explicitly states that the new

---

[168] See 2 Uckmar, *La legge del registro* 160-166; Berliri, *Le leggi di registro* 263, calls it a registration tax on gifts.

[169] R.D. 30 December 1923, n. 3269, arts. 4, 44 (15/6.2).

[170] R.D. 30 December 1923, n. 3269, Schedule, Annex A, art. 139, subjected gifts between spouses, brothers and sisters, and uncles and nephews to the rates applicable to transfers for consideration whereas those transfers were exempt from the inheritance tax.

succession tax rates (subsequently modified in 1949) are also applicable to gifts and donations (MSD art. 3). Under this decree, gifts also became subject to the tax on the aggregate value of the estate (MSD art. 9).

The rule of cumulating prior gifts (*coacervo*) made by the donor to the same donee is applicable both to the regular gift tax and to the tax on the aggregate value of the gifts (MSD arts. 4, 10) (3/4.3a). Against the tax payable on each successive gift, a credit is given for the tax which would be payable at current rates on the value of all previous gifts (see 3/4.7e).

There is a presumption that transfers of immovable property for consideration between relatives within the third degree are gifts and thus are subject to tax at progressive rates; these rates may be higher than those applicable to transfers for consideration under the registration tax. This presumption is rebuttable, however, by the buyer's proving, on the basis of registered documents bearing certain date, that at the moment of the transfer he possessed an amount sufficient to pay for the property.

A gift is not considered to exist until it has been accepted, and the rate applicable is that which is in force at the moment of acceptance.[171] The rates of the two gift taxes are, in principle, the same as the respective rates of the two death taxes, with the differences listed below.

1. The L. 750,000 personal allowance under the inheritance tax for transfers to direct line ascendants and descendants, and to spouses, is not applicable for purposes of gift taxation.[172]

2. The rates for the establishment of civil or military dowry or family wealth are reduced to one half. Donations on account of marriage enjoy the reduction only if there is no direct line relationship between the donor and the donee (MSD art. 3).[173]

3. Gifts not accepted and inter vivos donations subject to the condition of survival are subject to a fixed fee of L. 200.[174]

4. Gratuitous inter vivos transfers of artistic collections to scholarly institutions are exempt from all registration taxes under certain conditions (15/4.3).

The rules governing returns, assessment, payment, and other procedural matters are the same as for transfers at death (3/4). The contracting parties must produce a notarized declaration stating the degree of relationship existing between them; failure to do so results in the imposition of a pecuniary penalty of from L. 1,000 to L. 12,000, for which both the parties and the notary are jointly and severally liable.

---

[171] Comm. Centr., Sez. VII, 13 October 1947, n. 92132.

[172] Comm. Centr., Sez. VI, 27 June 1955, n. 73598; Comm. Centr. 6 February 1956, n. 78608 (*Riv. leg. fisc.*, 1956, 745).

[173] R.D. 30 December 1923, n. 3269, art. 61. See Cass., Sez. I, 16 March 1957, n. 921.

[174] R.D. 30 December 1923, n. 3269, Schedule, Annex A, Part I, arts. 78, 105 (15/3.3f).

A false declaration results in a fine of from L. 2,000 to L. 24,000 (MSD art. 5).[175]

The international aspects of the taxation of gifts, except for the application of treaties, are the same as those described for succession taxes at 3/4.14.

3/7. Betterment Contributions and Taxation of Increases in Value of Building Lots

3/7.1 In General

Until 1963, the communes had the power, under the *Testo unico* of local finance, to impose a "specific" betterment contribution (*contributo di miglioria*) which taxed the increase in value of developed rural and urban property other than building lots (*aree fabbricabili*), or that part of an increase in value which was attributable to public works carried out by the commune (TUFL arts. 236-246). The provinces could also impose the "specific" betterment contribution, but only on extra-urban property, other than building lots, the value of which had increased as a result of provincial works. In addition, the communes could impose a "generic" betterment contribution on undeveloped land that was suitable for building lots and had increased in value as a result of urban expansion and of public works carried out by the communes. Since 1938, the state also could impose a "specific" betterment contribution on increases in value resulting from works of the state or from works carried out by the provinces, communes, and other public entities with the assistance (*concorso*) of the state (3/7.4).[176]

These taxes were rather unsuccessful in raising revenue, partly because of the low rates and partly because the imposition of the contributions was not obligatory and the procedures were cumbersome. With the recent increases in value resulting from public works or, in general, from industrial, residential, and tertiary development, and with the growth of cities, the demand for new ways of taxing undeveloped land has become more insistent. The need has been most evident in the large industrial cities, such as Turin and Milan, and in those cities which are in the course of industrial development, such as Bologna. The formation and actuation of intercommunal regulatory plans, embracing the chief commune of a metropolis and communes of the surrounding area, require large expenditures and necessitate the cooperation of the local entities.

In 1963, the specific and generic betterment contributions of the provinces and communes were abolished and replaced by two more effective

---

[175] See R.M. 29 November 1952, n. 163772; R.M. 29 August 1953, n. 166955.

[176] R.D.L. 28 November 1938, n. 2000, on the application of betterment contributions for works carried out by the state or with its assistance; an article of this decree-law will hereinafter be cited: "ACM art."

taxes (3/7.2, 3/7.3), and the specific betterment contribution of the state, still governed by the 1938 law, was strengthened.[177] The power to impose the generic betterment contribution, now called the "tax on the increase in value of building lots" (*imposta sull'incremento di valore delle aree fabbricabili*), has been extended to the provinces, regions, and associations of territorial public entities, in addition to the communes (3/7.3). Similarly, specific betterment contributions may now be levied not only by the communes and provinces, but by the regions and by associations of territorial public entities (3/7.2).

The basic improvements in the betterment-contribution system under the 1963 law include streamlined assessment and appeal procedures, increased rates, an enlarged tax base, and obligatory imposition of the tax in some communes.

3/7.2 The Specific Betterment Contributions of the Local Entities

a. IN GENERAL. The local entities and associations of local entities have the power to impose specific betterment contributions on the increases in value of immovable property resulting from the carrying out of public works and certain other municipal activities (3/7.2b).

An entity is permitted to tax only the increase in value of property within its territorial jurisdiction. Thus, even if the work which one commune carries out gives rise to a direct or indirect increase in value of immovables situated in another commune, these increases in value are not taxable. However, an association of local entities, such as an association for the actuation of an intercommunal regulatory plan, can apply the specific betterment contribution throughout the entire jurisdiction of the communes which belong to it. The revenue resulting from this tax is not combined with that of other communal taxes to become part of the operating budget of the commune. Rather, one half of the yield must be devoted to expenditures for the purchase and expropriation of lots, or of buildings and zones having a historical and esthetic (*ambientale*) character, and to expenditures for the systemization of the road networks and the public services (IAF art. 46).

The specific betterment contribution must be instituted within one year of the approval of execution of the works or the introduction of the services (IAF art. 36).

b. THE TAX BASIS. The specific betterment contributions of the local entities are applicable to the increases in value described below (IAF arts. 31, 32).

---

[177] L. 5 March 1963, n. 246, on the tax on the increases in value of building lots; an article of this law will hereinafter be cited: "IAF art."

1. Increases in the value of immovable property, rural or urban, including building lots (*aree fabbricabili*), resulting directly or indirectly from the execution of individual public works or from the introduction of public services.

2. Increases in the value of immovable property resulting from the modifications of detailed regulatory plans, which make possible a more fruitful exploitation of land or buildings, or from the lapse of limitations imposed by plans for popular housing.

The new law specifies that the contribution can be levied on any increase which is a direct or indirect consequence of the improvements. It is not necessary that the immovable property benefited be sold. The causal tie between public works or public services and increases in value does not have to be immediate, but the increases must be specifically traceable to the works or services. Thus, it appears that increases in the value of immovables not immediately adjacent to the land on which the work has been carried out or the service furnished can be taxed. However, when an increase in value results from concurrent causes besides the execution of public works or the introduction of public services, the contribution is applied only on that part of the increase which is attributable to the works or services (IAF art. 37).

While the old legislation allowed only the taxation of the benefits of "public works," the specific betterment contributions can now be levied on increases in value resulting from the "introduction of public services." Thus, the new law takes into account the advantages resulting from the introduction of public transportation lines (tramways, local trains, buses, electric buses) by local authorities. The municipal enterprise which carries on the service has a right to a share of the revenue "proportional to the expenditures sustained by it" in the introduction of the public service (IAF art. 33). Since the law refers only to the "introduction" of services, these expenditures include plant expenditures, but not expenses of management.

Although benefits resulting from the original approval of regulatory plans are not taxable, the specific betterment contribution can be imposed on increases in value resulting from modifications of these plans. The power to impose this contribution lies only with the communes and not with associations of territorial public entities, among which the associations for the carrying out of the intercommunal plans have particular importance. However, persons listed as owners of immovable property at a "date preceding that of the deliberation which approved the regulatory plan and the plan of the zone to be devoted to popular housing" are exempt from the contribution on increases in values resulting from modifications in the regulatory plan or in a plan for popular housing (IAF art. 32).

The imposition of the specific betterment contribution on increases in value resulting from modifications in detailed regulatory plans has tempered, to some extent, the disparities between burdens and benefits which urban planning involves for individual owners. However, the Ministry of Public Works recently advanced a radical solution, in the form of a draft urban law which contemplates the expropriation, at pre-established prices, of all lands situated in the area of detailed regulatory plans and their sale at public auction to private persons, except for a part to be reserved for the construction of the works of the local entities. This plan, if approved, would eliminate the necessity of betterment contributions, because the base auction price would be increased by interest and administrative costs, and by costs sustained by the local entity for works of urbanization (such as streets, schools, water pipe lines, and sewers).

c. VALUATION. The increase in value is the difference between the current market price after the execution of the public work, the approval of the modification of a regulatory plan, or the lapse of a limitation imposed by a housing plan, and the market price on 1 January of the year preceding that of the decision to undertake the public works, the decision to modify the plan, or the lapse of the restriction (IAF art. 37).

In application, it is necessary to determine what part of an increase in value is the result of the execution of a public work and what part results from conditions not specifically traceable to the public work. The law explicitly refers to "individual" (*singole*) works and public services; the causal tie must be between the various individual works or individual services and the increase in value, and not globally between a complex of works or services and the increase in value.

d. RATES. The administration of the local entity has the power to impose the contribution at a rate not exceeding 33% (IAF art. 33).[178]

e. ASSESSMENT, APPEALS, AND PAYMENT. The tax is imposed as a result of a decision of the local entity, which specifies the owners of the properties benefited by the improvements and the increases in value to be taxed (IAF art. 36). The decision must be published, and the pertinent portions must be served on the persons concerned. The decision is subject to approval by the Provincial Administrative Board or, in the case of imposition by an association of entities belonging to different provinces, by the Minister of Finance (IAF arts. 36, 44). Appeals are allowed

---

[178] Under the old system, the rates of the betterment contributions could not exceed 15% of the increase in value attributable to the improvement; and the total amount of the specific contribution, moreover, could not exceed 30% of the cost sustained by the public entity for the execution of the work (TUFL art. 238).

only under the procedures of local finance (TUFL arts. 277-294; IAF art. 36) (1/4.10j).

If the taxpayer appeals the decision instituting the levy for the properties which he owns, the tax is immediately inscribed against him in the roll for collection. However, the amount inscribed in the roll is not that specified by the administration, but that specified by the taxpayer in his appeal (IAF art. 36). When the taxpayer appeals on questions of estimation of value, he is required to specify his own estimate; otherwise, that of the administration controls.

Payment is made in 10 equal annual installments, including interest at 5%, on amounts made final following the assessment proceeding (IAF art. 38). A taxpayer who pays immediately is entitled to a reduction of 15%, which may diminish the incentive to dilatory appeals. If the property is transferred, on the other hand, all installments still unpaid will be collected immediately.

3/7.3 The New Local Tax on the Increases in Value of Building Lots

a. IN GENERAL. The communes have the power to impose a tax on the increases in value of building lots transferred or used for building (3/7.3b). The imposition of the tax is obligatory for communes having a population exceeding 30,000, for capitals of provinces, for tourist and health resorts, and for the communes in the environs (*communi limitrofi*) of communes having 300,000 or more inhabitants (IAF art. 1).

In the case of persons who are corporations or similar entities (*società di capitali*), and all other persons owning building lots, the value of which is not less than L. 100 million, the tax is imposed when 10 years have elapsed from the date the tax was instituted, even if there has been no transfer of or building on the property concerned (IAF art. 3). Moreover, under the same provision, the tax is applied at the end of every succeeding ten-year period. This procedure is an improvement over the old law for the generic betterment contribution, under which taxation was to occur at the time of passage of ownership, or, if there had been no passage of ownership for five years, or one accompanied by taxation more than three years before, at the time of building (TUFL art. 241).

To accelerate the application of the tax on lots and to increase its present yield, the new law has established a certain retroactivity for the first application of the tax. It provides that the communes in which imposition is obligatory have the power to make the first period for which the increase is computed, that which began 10 years before the date of the institution of the tax (IAF art. 25). A retroactivity of 10 years can also be established by communes with fewer than 30,000 inhabitants, provided that they are located near communes with more than 30,000 inhabitants, are included in zones of urban expansion or in intercommunal plans of urban expansion, and are authorized to do so by the Provincial Administrative Board (IAF art. 25). For other communes, the maximum retroactivity is three years (IAF art. 5). However, because of the retroactivity of the tax and because of the liability of the present owners for tax on increases in value occurring before they acquired the properties, it is presumable that there will be many appeals to the Constitutional Court asserting violation of the nonretroactivity of tax laws under article 53 of the Constitution, and encroachment of rights of property and private initiative, under articles 41 and 43.

Special provision is made with respect to lots built up before 1958 which were purchased not more than three years before the construction by a person who now undertakes to resell them, or to demolish the existing buildings, for the purpose of new building. The increase in value of such lots may be taxed only on the condition that the volume of the new building or the number of rooms exceeds by a certain percentage that of the pre-existing building, and that, in the computation of the increase in value, account be taken of the variation in the number of rooms and in volume (IAF arts. 8-11). These cases are frequent in the Italian cities, both as a result of the renewal of the old central quarters, and as a result of the elimination of modest rural and semirural houses, or industrial factories, in zones of new metropolitan expansion which absorb old peripheral and country villages.

The building lots specified below are exempt from application of the tax (IAF arts. 14, 15).

1. Lots belonging to the state or to local entities.
2. Lots belonging to the independent institutions for popular housing, or to public entities for low-cost and popular building.
3. Lots belonging to welfare and assistance entities, religious, educational, or health entities.
4. Lots permanently restricted to use as parks and gardens by urban planning regulations, or on which building is permanently forbidden by a restriction of the law.
5. Lots restricted exclusively to popular housing by regulatory plans.
6. Lots restricted by their owners or by regulations to use as parks and gardens of private dwellings.
7. Lots restricted by their owners to the service or enlargement of pre-existing industrial and artisan factories, business firms, or health, welfare, assistance, educational, or religious institutions carried on by the owners.
8. Lots included in industrial zones, restricted by law to industrial building under special license, provided that there is the possibility of expropriation at the price current at the time of the zoning or at a price measured by the capitalization of the landowning income alone.
9. Lots restricted by regulatory plans to the construction of schools, squares, streets, churches, and, in general, to uses incompatible with the building of houses or industrial structures.

The yield of the tax on building lots, like the specific betterment contribution, does not become part of the operating budget of the local entity; one half of it must be devoted to the acquisition of lots, or of buildings or zones having historical or esthetic character, and to expenditures for the systemization of the road networks and of the public services (IAF art. 46). However, the proceeds of this tax, as distinguished from those of the specific betterment contribution, can be used for loans even beyond the normal limit of one fourth of the yield (1/5.5h), but not beyond one half of the average annual collections made in the preceding five years (IAF art. 47).

The tax on building lots is allowed as a deduction for purposes of the movable wealth tax (and the related local surtaxes) as applied to taxable capital gains, and for purposes of the tax on corporate profits insofar as applicable (IAF art. 24).

b. TAX BASIS AND VALUATION. The basis of the tax is the increase in value, computed as the difference between the market value of the building lot at the date of application of the tax and the market value at the moment of transfer or of utilization for building (IAF art. 2). It is no longer restricted to the increase in value "attributable to the expansion of the inhabited area and to the aggregate of public works carried out by the commune," as under prior legislation (see TUFL art. 236).

The initial or final value of a lot determined by assessment for the registration (15/5.2) and the succession (3/4.5) taxes is valid also for purposes of determining the taxable increase for the tax on building lots, unless the owner or the commune can show that it is in error by at least one third of the actual value (IAF art. 4). In a period of considerable rise in the prices of land, the final value (the positive component) is, on the average, much higher than the initial value (the negative component), and thus a percentage error of one third in the final value bears much more heavily on the net taxable amount than an error of the same percentage in the initial value. Thus, the taxpayer gains more from an undervaluation by the Registry Office of the final value than he loses from an undervaluation of the initial value.

The Registry Offices, in cases of assessment concluded by agreement, always give a reduction of one fourth with respect to the estimate they originally made. The effect of the undervaluations described above can be great; however, it appears that the Registry Offices often make slight overvaluations to compensate for this reduction.

c. RATES AND CREDITS. The rates of the new levy are established by a complex progressive scale (see Table 58) (IAF art. 21). On the average,

DESCRIPTION OF TAX SYSTEM

this progressive scale should permit a levy of not less than 15% of the increase in value.

Table 58: *Rates of Tax on Increase in the Value of Building Lots*

Taxable Increase in Value, Divided by Number of Years for Which Gain Is Computed, As a Percentage of the Initial Value		Rate of Tax on Excess Over Lower Limit
Lower Limit	Upper Limit	
—	30%	15%
30%	50	20
50	100	25
100	300	30
300	500	40
500	—	50

Source: L. 5 March 1963, n. 246, art. 21.

The application of the rate schedule is illustrated by the two examples below.

Example 3

A piece of agricultural land becomes urban land by being included in the area of expansion of a large commune, and can be converted to residential building. The value changes from L. 500 per square meter to L. 10,500 per square meter in 10 years. The total gain is L. 10,000 per square meter and the average annual gain, L. 1,000 per square meter, is equal to 200% of the initial value. The tax per square meter is computed as shown below.

Percentage of average annual gain over initial value	Average annual gain (Lire)	Gain over 10 years (Lire)	Rate	Tax (Lire)
30%	150	1,500	15%	225
20	100	1,000	20	200
50	250	2,500	25	625
100	500	5,000	30	1,500
Total 200%	1,000	10,000	(25.5)	2,550

Example 4

A piece of land already converted to residential use, located in the central zone of a city, changes over 10 years from a value of L. 10,000 per square meter to a value of L. 40,000 per square meter. The total gain is L. 30,000 per square meter, and the average annual gain, L. 3,000 per square meter, is equal to 30% of the total gain; the tax, at the rate of 15%, is L. 4,500 per square meter.

From these two examples, it can be seen that since the progressivity of the rates is based on the percentage of gain, not on the absolute size, an operator who has had a large increase in value in absolute terms can be taxed at a more modest rate than an operator with a smaller gain. It can also be supposed that, in general, the rate is higher for those who possess lands not yet urbanized than for those who have building lots already prepared for use.

The net yield of this new tax on building lots is lowered considerably by the credit given against it for the communal tax on industry, commerce, arts, and professions (ICAP) (2/2.9), which is applied to gains subjected to the tax on income from movable wealth (IAF art. 24): that is, gains on the sale of lands of persons who carry out that operation with speculative intent, or of companies for which speculative intent is conclusively presumed (9/8.1). However, as a result of the improved assessment procedures for the new local tax on building lots, it is hoped that assessments for both ICAP and the tax on income from movable wealth will be more effective, and that, even if the yield of the new tax is reduced by the credit for ICAP, the yield of both taxes taken together will increase.

d. ASSESSMENT, APPEALS, AND PAYMENT. The decision to impose the tax must be approved by the Provincial Administrative Board (IAF art. 44). Whenever property or property rights in land subject to the tax are transferred, a return must be filed with the commune by the notary or public official registering the transfer, within 20 days of registration; assessment of the tax is made on the basis of this return. For property transferred by a private act, the transferor must file a return within five days of registration (IAF art. 6). The taxpayer is required to ascertain the tax and pay it in a single payment to the Communal Treasury Office (IAF art. 6). In the case of building, the return must accompany the request for a license to build; within 90 days of the service of a notice of approval of the license by the commune, the taxpayer must pay one twenty-fourth of the tax, ascertained by him, on the basis of his return (IAF art. 7). The balance of the tax must be paid to the Communal Treasury Office in 23 equal bimonthly installments, beginning at the end of the first bimonthly period after the first payment. A taxpayer who pays the tax in a single payment has the right to a reduction of 15% of the total tax due.

If taxpayers are liable for the tax independently of the transfer of, or building on, property because 10 years have elapsed from the date from which the taxable increase is calculated (except in the period of the first application of the tax), they must file a return within 30 days of the end of that 10 years, accompanied by payment of one twelfth of the tax (IAF art. 12). The balance of the tax must be paid in 11 equal bimonthly installments, with a reduction of 10% for payment of the entire tax at one time. Finally, taxpayers liable for the tax in the first period of application, either because of transfer or the passing of 10 years, must file a return within the 60-day period from the date of the notice of the Mayor of the institution of the tax, and one twelfth of the amount of the tax must accompany the return (IAF arts. 27, 43). Appeals are allowed only under the procedures of local finance (IAF art. 18) (1/4.10j).

In order to prevent the underreporting of values and also to aid the communes in acquiring building lots to further the building and urban and economic development of their territories, a commune has the power to purchase a lot at the value declared by the taxpayer, increased by legal interest accruing from the date of the return (IAF art. 13). Notice of the decision to purchase must be served within 12 months of the filing of the return. If the owners do not agree to the purchase, the commune, within the next six months, can expropriate the lot at the declared value (IAF art. 13).

3/7.4   The National Betterment Contributions

The state has the power to impose a betterment contribution (*contributo di miglioria*) on the increase in the value of immovable property resulting from a public work carried out by the state, directly or by concession (ACM art. 1; IAF art. 35). The contribution is also imposed on increases in value resulting from the execution of a complex of public works or from important transformations of existing public works (ACM art. 1). Exemption is granted to certain property of the Holy See, the state, provinces, communes, and certain other public entities (ACM art. 2). These betterment contributions, enacted in 1938, remain in effect under the 1963 law, but with notable increases in rates and some changes in procedure.

The increase in value is determined at the completion of the work. Any advantage resulting from the public work that is capable of economic valuation is taken into account (ACM art. 5)—for example, the degree of improvement in access to light and view, in transportation and communications, and in health or cultural conditions. From the increase in value are deducted the expenses sustained and the presumed compensation for work furnished by the owner to improve the property, as well as the value of goods transferred by the owner, without payment, for the execution of the work (ACM art. 6). The rate to be applied to the resulting basis is 25% (ACM art. 7; IAF art. 35).[179]

The owners of immovable property affected by the work must be notified of the imposition of the contribution at some time between the start of the work and three years following its completion (ACM art. 8). The imposition of the contribution is administered by the Intendant of

---

[179] The former limitation of the total tax yield to 30% of the expenditure made has been abolished.

Finance; the increases in value are determined by the Revenue Technical Office. Appeals regarding the imposition of the contribution may be made to the Registry Office and thence to the District and Provincial Tax art. 12). Appeals regarding the amount of the increase in value may be made to the Registry Office and thence to the District and Provincial Tax Commissions; appeal may be made to the courts in cases of evident error of valuation or absence or insufficiency of computation in the determination of value (ACM art. 14).

The Intendant of Finance provides for inscription of the contribution in the roll for collection beginning in the year following imposition; the total contribution is divided into five equal annual installments. One or more installments may be paid in advance, with interest for the advance payment discounted (ACM art. 15).

The amounts collected are accounted for under a special heading in the budget (ACM art. 16). When works are executed by communes, provinces, or other entities with the support of the state, the proceeds of the betterment contribution are divided among the entities participating in the expense, in proportion to the share borne by each (ACM art. 19).

CHAPTER 4

TAXES ON TRANSACTIONS

4/1. Introduction

4/2. The General Tax on Receipts
4/2.1 Historical Background
4/2.2 Persons Subject
4/2.3 Tax Base
4/2.4 Exclusions
4/2.5 Exemptions

4/3. Registration Taxes
4/3.1 In General
4/3.2 The Registration Tax
    a. In general
    b. Taxable transactions
    c. Rates
    d. Valuation
4/3.3 Mortgage Tax
4/3.4 Tax on Insurance
4/3.5 Tax on Secured Loans
4/3.6 Motor Vehicle Registration Fees

4/4. Stamp Taxes
4/4.1 In General
4/4.2 The Stamp Tax
    a. In general
    b. Documents subject to tax when executed
    c. Documents subject to tax when used
    d. Exemptions and reductions
    e. Rates

273

      f.   Payment
      g. Appeals
      h. Violations and penalties

4/4.3 Stamp Tax on Stock Exchange Contracts
      a. In general
      b. Rates
      c. Administration and collection

4/4.4 Stamp Tax on Transportation Documents

4/5. **Taxes on Production and Consumption**
4/5.1 In General
4/5.2 Manufacturing Taxes
      a. In general
      b. Products taxed and rates
      c. Administration
      d. International aspects

4/5.3 Advertising Tax
      a. In general
      b. Notices to the public
      c. Advertising in newspapers, magazines, and other printed matter
      d. Cinema, radio, television, and mobile advertising
      e. Exemptions
      f. Rates of tax
      g. Administration and procedure

4/5.4 Tax on Public Shows
4/5.5 Motor Vehicle Fees
4/5.6 Radio and Television Reception Fees
4/5.7 Tax on Games of Skill and Football Pools
4/5.8 Local Consumption Taxes
      a. In general
      b. Taxable goods
      c. Exclusions and exemptions
      d. Rates and valuation
      e. Assessment and payment
      f. Administration and collection
      g. Appeals
      h. Penalties

4/5.9 Local Visitors Tax
4/5.10 Local License Taxes
4/5.11 Local Fee for the Occupation of Public Spaces and Areas

4/5.12 Local Tax on Signs

4/5.13 Local Fee for Public Weights and Measures and the Renting of Public Counters

4/5.14 Local Fee for the Circulation of Animal-Drawn Vehicles

4/6. State Fiscal Monopolies

4/6.1 In General

4/6.2 Salt

4/6.3 Tobacco

4/6.4 Cigarette Packages and Papers

4/6.5 Matches

4/6.6 Cigarette Lighters and Flints

4/6.7 Lotto and Lotteries

4/7. Fees for Governmental Concessions

4/7.1 In General

4/7.2 Rates

4/7.3 Assessment and Collection

4/7.4 Appeals

4/8. Customs Duties

4/8.1 In General

4/8.2 Rates

4/8.3 Temporary Importation

4/8.4 Administration and Procedure

4/8.5 Penalties

4/1. Introduction

Taxes on transactions furnish a large part of the tax receipts for both national and local finance (1/6.8). The national government levies a general tax on receipts (4/2), manufacturing taxes (4/5.2), and miscellaneous taxes on certain forms of public consumption, among which are the fiscal monopolies (4/6) and the fees on governmental concessions (4/7). Consumption taxes are levied by the communes on certain goods consumed within their borders (4/5.8); the communes also impose a variety of local fees for governmental services and for the use of public resources (4/5.9-4/5.14). Registration taxes (4/3) and stamp taxes (4/4) on documents having legal effects are levied by the national government; these taxes, as well as those on public consumption, represent in part payment for the governmental services performed.

Imported goods which would have been subject to the manufacturing taxes if produced domestically are subject to a border duty (4/5.2d) and, in addition to any customs duty which may be applicable, to an equalization tax corresponding to the general tax on receipts which would have been payable on transfers of those goods if they had been produced or sold domestically (14/8.5). Exported goods are exempt both from the manufacturing taxes (4/5.2d) and from the general tax on receipts (14/8.3).

4/2. The General Tax on Receipts

4/2.1 Historical Background

The general tax on receipts (*imposta generale sull'entrata* or IGE), the most important indirect tax levied by the national government in terms of scope and yield (1/6.8b), is described in detail in Chapter 14; the discussion here is limited to general comments on some of the more important aspects of the tax.

The IGE, instituted in 1940, replaced the tax on exchanges (*imposta sugli scambi*) (14/1), which had a similar but narrower tax base: receipts from transfers of goods inherent in the carrying on of "business activities." "Business activities" meant economic and productive activities in the sense of those carried on by a "business entrepreneur" in a "business transaction" (*atto di commercio*), as defined in the now-abolished Commercial Code of 1865. The IGE, born out of a need for enlarging this tax base to provide additional revenue for Italy's anticipated entry into the Second World War, is applied, in general, to all receipts from professional activities, receipts of business enterprises, and receipts of nonmerchants from "occasional business transactions" (14/3.1).

In addition, the IGE rates are higher than those of the old tax on exchanges, and their structure is less complex. The tax on exchanges had exempted exchanges involving amounts up to L. 1 (now equivalent to about L. 70), and had provided gradually increasing rates of from 0.3% on exchanges involving amounts between L. 1 and L. 10 (prewar lire) to 3% on exchanges involving amounts exceeding L. 1,000. Instead of these progressive rates, which often led a businessman to divide one transaction involving large amounts into several smaller transactions in order to reduce the tax, IGE was imposed at a standard general rate of 2% in 1940. From October 1944 to December 1946 and from November 1947 to 31 December 1948, the general rate was raised to 4%; today it is 3.3%.

4/2.2 Persons Subject

IGE is payable, in general, by "individuals, juridical persons, and entities of all kinds, both national and foreign" (14/2.1). Thus, the existence of juridical personality in the technical sense (5/2.1) is not necessary for the existence of a taxable subject.

In order to diminish inequality of tax burden between products which are both produced and sold to the public by a single enterprise and products which are produced by one enterprise and then sold to another for resale to the public, transfers of goods by a producer to its own retail outlets are taxed in the same manner as transfers by a producer to an independent retailer (14/2.2). On the other hand, sales of goods through agents and other commercial intermediaries are treated in the same manner as direct sales (14/2.3).

4/2.3 Tax Base

Because of the breadth and simplicity of its tax base, the general tax on receipts withstood the political and economic disasters resulting from the Second World War and became a pillar of the financial reconstruction. The yield of the tax increases with the expansion of the volume of economic activities, because IGE is applied to all receipts from the transfer of goods and the furnishing of services.

In application, IGE obeys the territoriality principle; it is imposed only on receipts from the furnishing of services and the transfer of goods carried out in Italy (2/2.5; 14/8.1). The receipts must represent, in some way, a payment for the transfer of goods or the furnishing of services (14/4.5); this requirement is known as "mutuality" (*corrispettività*). Thus, receipts which are entirely gratuitous are not taxable. Operations involving the transfer of goods or services for payment that are explicitly excluded from the scope of IGE are discussed at 4/2.4 and 14/4.

While the taxable object of most indirect taxes is defined with reference to legal concepts, the taxable object of IGE is defined with reference to economic concepts. The IGE law refers to the transfer of goods and the furnishing of services, rather than to types of contracts. Transactions are defined in terms of the furnishing of one economic utility in exchange for another.

4/2.4 Exclusions

Taxable receipts do not include amounts received as capital, such as amounts constituting payment for the transfer of immovable property, businesses, public and private securities, or resulting from the creation or extinction of debts (14/4.2). This exclusion is justified in part by the fact that these capital receipts are usually subject to the registration tax or to some other type of transfer tax.

Amounts received by the state, the provinces, the communes, and other public entities in the form of taxes or compulsory contributions, participations in tax receipts, and certain fees are not taxable (14/4.4). Not all taxes forming part of the price of the goods or services are excluded, but only taxes received by the imposing entity by virtue of the power of imposition. Amounts received from the sale of monopoly goods and the sale of stamped paper are also excluded (14/4.4). In many other cases, however, IGE is applied to receipts which incorporate a tax, such as sales of petroleum, sugar, and other goods, the price of which includes a manufacturing tax. The distinction is one between receipts of taxes by governmental bodies and taxes passed on to the seller as part of the price of the goods or services.

The IGE law also excludes contributions and related accessory payments made for social security and for other forms of welfare established by law, collective contract, or business regulations (14/4.3).

Exclusion is also provided for amounts received by the state from the direct management of public services, such as the mails and the railways, and from the exercise of the game of lotto and of the lotteries (14/4.4). But this exclusion does not apply to the receipts of the independent public enterprises, even those derived from the furnishing of public services. Thus, IGE is applied to the receipts of STET, a telephone company under the Institution for Industrial Reconstruction (*Istituto per la Ricostruzione Industriale* or IRI) whose services can be included within the concept of "public service," because IRI is independent of the state, being endowed with its own juridical personality, and STET is organized as a corporation, the majority of whose shares are owned by IRI. It was deemed desirable to treat such independent public enterprises in the same way as private enterprises, even from the point of view of IGE, to permit a better survey of costs and to avoid altering the structure of competition between private and public enterprises.

There are two particularly important exclusions of receipts from the furnishing of services: interest and other returns received for the furnishing of credit services, except when received by credit institutions as enterprise income (14/3.8, 14/4.2); and, in general, all compensation classifiable as income from employment (8/1.1) for purposes of the tax on income from movable wealth (14/4.3).

Amounts received for the exportation of raw materials, goods, or products, amounts received for freight, and other payments for international services are excluded (14/8.3). This exclusion results from the operation of the principle of territoriality, on the basis of which only the furnishing of services and transfers of goods carried on in Italy are taxable. In the same manner, amounts received for the processing or repair in Italy of temporarily imported materials, goods, and products of foreign origin are excluded (14/8.4b).

Receipts from the operation of railway, tramway, and internal navigation facilities by private enterprises under concessions are excluded from IGE, because these enterprises are subject to the special stamp tax on transportation documents (4/4.4, 14/4.10).

As of 1 January 1963, receipts from the leasing of urban immovable property were excluded from IGE (14/3.6). In addition to IGE at 3.3%, these receipts had previously been subject to the registration tax at 0.5% (plus additionals of about 0.1%) and to the graduated stamp tax. As a result of exclusion from IGE and the stamp tax, the rate of the registration tax on these receipts has been increased to 4% on the rental of property not yet listed in the cadaster, and to 6% of the cadastral yield of property listed in the cadaster (15/6.3d).

4/2.5 Exemptions

In principle, IGE applies to each transfer from the beginning of production to consumption; the tax on each transfer is based on the total price, which includes the IGE paid at earlier stages. However, certain transfers at the final stage have been exempted: receipts from the sale of goods to the public in premises licensed for retail sale, sales by itinerant vendors, purveyances (*somministrazioni*) in public accommodations, and sales to private consumers by artisan workshops, shops, market stands, recreation clubs, and the like (14/4.8). Other transfers are exempted at intermediate stages. Exemption is granted, for example, to commercial auxiliaries of a parent firm, stores for selling goods produced by the owner's workshops, government stockpiling agencies, and cooperative supply associations (14/2.2-14/2.4). Transfers by a parent firm to its own retail outlets, however, are treated in the same manner as transfers to independent retailers (14/2.2b).

Also exempt are receipts from retail services (*prestazioni al dettaglio*) performed by persons classified as "artisans" under the tax on income from movable wealth (14/4.8b).

Certain other exemptions from IGE seem merely to be exceptions to the general definition of the taxable object. These include the exemption of receipts from the sale of bread and milk for direct consumption (14/4.6e), certain types of wheat and flour and spaghetti (*pasta alimentare*) (14/4.6g), and newspapers, magazines, and periodicals of a predominantly political character (14/4.6i).

4/3. Registration Taxes

4/3.1 In General

Documents having legal effects are, in general, subject to registration and to the registration tax, either under the general registration tax law described in Chapter 15 or under one of several special laws applicable to specific classes of documents. While a registration tax may be regarded in part as a fee for the protection afforded by the state to the legal effects of a document, a stamp tax (4/4) which may be levied on the same document serves in part as a fee for the authentication of the document as such. The registration taxes and the stamp taxes are all levied by the national government.

Certain taxes levied in the past in substitution of the registration and stamp taxes on specific classes of documents have been abrogated. These are the negotiation tax (2/4.1) [1] and the tax on the capital of foreign companies.[2]

4/3.2 The Registration Tax

a. IN GENERAL. This chapter gives a general description of the structure and functioning of the registration tax (*imposta di registro*); the tax is described in detail in Chapter 15.

Originally, the registration tax was merely a fee (*tassa*) payable on the act of inscription of a document in a public register. The fee was considered to be payment for a service rendered by the state: protection of ownership and other property rights in immovables. Registration of a document serves two functions: (1) establishing the legal existence of an act or transaction, and (2) establishing the date at which the act or transaction occurred.

The present law governing the registration tax [3] was enacted in 1923, the year in which De'Stefani, the Minister of Finance of the first fascist government after the march on Rome, began a broad reorganization of the Italian system of public finance.

b. TAXABLE TRANSACTIONS. Attached to the registration tax law are five annexes which specify the various types of taxable transactions and the rates applicable to each. The Schedule, Annex A, specifies the transactions and transfers subject to progressive, proportional, graduated, or fixed tax. Annex B specifies transactions which are required to be registered, but which are subject to a reduced tax or a fixed fee. Annex C specifies the transactions to be registered without payment of tax. Annex D lists the transactions to be registered only if produced in judicial or administrative proceedings or referred to in documents subject to registration. Annex E contains a specification of the transactions exempt from registration.

The registration tax is applied according to the nature and the effects of a transaction, rather than according to the title or the apparent form of the document evidencing the transaction (15/3.1). A transaction which is not specified by name in the schedule is taxed at the rate established by the schedule for the transaction with which it has the greatest similarity in nature and effect.

---

[1] First levied by R.D. 30 December 1923, n. 3280, arts. 1-9; replaced by R.D.L. 15 December 1938, n. 1975, supplemented by D.L.C.P.S. 5 September 1947, n. 1173; abrogated by L. 6 August 1954, n. 603, art. 26.

[2] Levied by R.D. 30 December 1923, n. 3280, arts. 10-19; abrogated by L. 6 August 1954, n. 603, art. 26.

[3] R.D. 30 December 1923, n. 3269.

c. RATES. The rates of the registration tax are progressive, proportional, graduated, or fixed, depending on the nature of the act or document. The progressive rates are applied to inter vivos gratuitous transfers of property.[4]

The proportional rates are applied to transfers, for consideration, of ownership, usufruct, use, enjoyment, or any other property right in movable or immovable property. Acts which contain obligations or releases from obligations for payment of money or the performance of services are also subject to proportional rates (15/6.3).

The graduated rates decrease as the taxable amount increases; they apply, in general, to acts which do not contain obligations or releases, but attribute values or rights without transferring them (15/6.4). A typical example is a declaration of already existing rights which have become the object of some controversy.

The fixed rates are applied to all other acts not previously specified that can serve as legal titles of documents (15/6.5). They are also applied, under special rules, in many cases in which the proportional or graduated tax would normally be due (15/4.5b).

d. VALUATION. Except in cases where a fixed rate applies, the amount of tax due depends on the tax base. The taxable value is the value appearing in the act, contract, or report, or the value declared by the taxpayer at the request of the Registry Office. The Registry Office checks whether the value declared corresponds to the market value at the date of the transfer. Property exchanged for securities is valued at the listed price of the securities on the date of the transfer. If the value stated by the taxpayer is lower than the market value, the tax administration proceeds to correct and liquidate the difference in tax (the "complementary" or "supplementary" tax) (15/7.2). If the market value is lower than that appearing in the act, contract, report, or declaration of the taxpayer, the tax administration considers valid the estimate made by the taxpayer. In the case of agreement (*concordato*) between the taxpayer and the tax administration, the law authorizes the tax administration to reduce the taxable value agreed upon by one quarter.

4/3.3 Mortgage Tax

A mortgage tax (*imposta ipotecaria*) is imposed for inscriptions, renewals, transcriptions, cancellations, and other entries made in public registers of immovable property.[5] The tax is proportional in the case of original inscriptions and their renewal; transcriptions of documents and judgments involving transfers of ownership of immovables or of rights

---

[4] Gratuitous transfers at death are subject to the inheritance tax, which was originally a branch of the registration tax (3/4.1).

[5] L. 25 June 1943, n. 540.

capable of mortgage; and inscriptions for subentry or subrogation, for transfer of credits not conditioned on death, for cancellation or reduction of a mortgage or pledge, and for restriction of a mortgage. Under the Schedule (Table A) attached to the law, the maximum proportional rate is 2.5%. The tax is graduated when applied to entries for transfers of credits at death and to entries and inscriptions for deferral or grant of priority or of mortgage rank. The tax is a fixed fee for other mortgage formalities [6] and for certain cases specified in the law that would normally be subject to gradual or proportional tax.[7] In certain cases, the proportional rate is reduced to a fraction of the normal rate. There is also a table of exemptions (Table C).

The proportional tax on transcriptions of documents or judgments transferring ownership of immovable property or of rights capable of mortgage, and on transcriptions of certificates of reported succession involving immovable property, as well as the fixed tax and surcharges connected with those documents, must be paid to the Registry Office within the time limit established for the payment of the registration and succession taxes. In all other cases, the tax is paid to the keeper of the register of immovable property at the time of the inscription. Table D lists the fees (*emolumenti*) to be paid to the keeper of the register at the time of inscription; these range from L. 10 to L. 200.

4/3.4 Tax on Insurance

An insurance fee (*tassa sulle assicurazioni*) is imposed on insurance policies issued in Italy by companies and enterprises, domestic or foreign, or by single individuals, except policies insuring exclusively property situated abroad.[8] Certain insurance policies issued abroad that are subject to the tax are listed below (LTA art. 1).

1. Policies which are to be used in Italy.
2. Policies insuring immovable or movable property situated in Italy, ships of Italian registry, or goods transported by ships of Italian registry.
3. Life insurance policies of persons domiciled in Italy.
4. Maritime policies insuring goods transported by ships of foreign registry for Italian persons or firms which have paid the insurance.

The taxable value of marine and air insurance is the amount of the accumulated premium if it is declared, or the insured amount if the premium is not declared; the tax is payable once for the duration of the policy (LTA art. 5). Marine or air insurance issued by enterprises in Italy must be registered within five days at the Registry Office; insurance issued

---

[6] In these cases, the fixed fee is L. 1,000 (about $1.61). L. 21 July 1961, n. 707, art. 1.

[7] In these cases, the fixed fee is L. 2,000 (about $3.22). L. 21 July 1961, n. 707, art. 1.

[8] R.D. 30 December 1923, n. 3281, art. 1. This decree is the tax law on insurance; it will hereinafter be cited: "LTA."

abroad must be registered within two months if issued in Europe, and within six months if issued outside Europe (LTA art. 6). The tax is payable at the time of registration (LTA art. 8). For other types of insurance, the tax is based on the premiums paid (LTA art. 16), and it includes the stamp tax due on policies and receipts (LTA art. 18).

The taxable value of life annuity contracts is the capital amount which forms the basis of the annuity payments; these contracts must be registered (LTA art. 28), and the tax is payable at the time of registration (LTA art. 29).

The rates of tax on various types of insurance are listed below (LTA Annex A, Schedule).

1. Marine and air: 2% of the accumulated premium or insured amount.
2. Other transportation: 20% of the total premium.
3. Baggage (without policy): 10% of the total premium.
4. Accident and life: 2% of each premium payment.
5. Civil liability: 9% of each premium payment.
6. Animals, and weather damage to farms: 2% of each premium payment.
7. Breakage of glass: 9% of each premium payment.
8. Fire damage: 18% of each premium payment.
9. Receipts of nonmaritime contracts exempt from registration taxes: 1% of the receipted amount.
10. Solvency: 2% of each premium payment.
11. Fidelity of employees: 5% of each premium payment.
12. Life annuity contracts: 1% of the capital amount.

The tax is reduced to one fourth of the normal rate for life insurance contracts that secure payments for popular or low-cost housing (LTA Annex B). Exemption is provided for life annuity contracts made by mutual aid societies or by provident institutions for railroad personnel; for employment accident insurance; for insurance furnished by the national fund for social security; and for the insurance of cattle in Sardinia (LTA Annex C). Special rates are provided for insurance against the risks involved in the production of motion pictures.[9]

Insurance companies are required to file reports on their operations with the Registry Office (LTA art. 33). Surcharges are imposed for omitted or late payment. The collection of the taxes and surcharges is governed by the provisions of the registration tax (LTA art. 39) (15/7).

4/3.5 Tax on Secured Loans

In place of the stamp and registration taxes on loans or subsidies made by savings banks, companies, and institutions on the deposit or pledge of goods, securities, or commercial paper (*valori*), there is a special fee (*tassa sulle anticipazioni o sovvenzioni contro deposito o pegno*) based on the amount and duration of each operation.[10] The tax is assessed

---

[9] R.D.L. 3 March 1938, n. 261, art. 1.
[10] R.D. 30 December 1923, n. 3280, art. 20. This decree is the law on fees replacing stamp and registration fees; it will hereinafter be cited: "LTSBR."

every six months on the basis of a report of transactions filed with the local Registry Office (LTSBR art. 21). The rates are L. 0.005 per day for each L. 5,000 loaned if guaranteed by the state or by securities of the state; L. 0.01 per day for advances guaranteed by other securities; [11] and 0.01% per day for loans guaranteed by other property (LTSBR Annex A, art. 5).

Advances made by private pawnshops are subject to a special tax in place of stamp and registration taxes on the basis of a report of transactions filed every six months (LTSBR arts. 23, 24). The tax rate is 2.35% of the amount advanced, and the tax is payable every six months (LTSBR Annex A, art. 6).

4/3.6 Motor Vehicle Registration Fees

Acquisitions and transfers of motor vehicles must be registered with the Automobile Club of Italy,[12] to which small fixed fees (*emolumenti*) are payable in accordance with a schedule issued by the Minister of Finance.[13] Before registration with the Automobile Club of Italy, the documents evidencing the acquisition or transfer must be registered in accordance with the law governing the registration tax. The rates of the registration tax vary according to the type and horsepower of the vehicle; [14] they range from L. 500 for motorcycles to L. 40,000 for the largest industrial trucks.[15]

4/4. Stamp Taxes

4/4.1 In General

All stamp taxes are levied by the national government. Payment of the tax is evidenced by a stamp or some other mark; in some cases, the stamp or mark serves to authenticate a document, and, in other cases, for example, the tax on advertising, the use of the stamp is merely a matter of administrative convenience.

Certain taxes which are considered stamp taxes in Italy have been classified for purposes of this volume as taxes on production or consumption: the tax on advertising (4/5.3), the fees for governmental concessions (4/7), the tax on public shows (4/5.4c), the tax on playing cards (4/5.2a), and the motor vehicle fee (4/5.5).

---

[11] R.D.L. 19 August 1943, n. 738, art. 13.

[12] D.L.L. 18 June 1945, n. 399.

[13] D.M. 15 June 1953.

[14] D.L.L. 18 June 1945, n. 399, art. 2; R.D. 30 December 1923, n. 3269, Schedule, Annex A, art. 3 *bis*.

[15] A decree of 23 February 1964 has introduced a new tax on the sale to consumers of new automobiles and motor boats for personal use. The rate for automobiles, applied to the sale price, is 5% plus an additional percentage computed by taking into account the length and width of the car and the cylinder capacity. See D.L. 23 February 1964, n. 26.

4/4.2 The Stamp Tax

a. IN GENERAL. The stamp tax (*imposta di bollo*) is of ancient origin, but has been remodeled and reorganized many times. The most recent general revision was enacted in a presidential decree,[16] a *Testo unico* on the stamp tax, issued by the government on the basis of a legislative delegation (1/3.1d).[17]

The stamp tax is applied to all papers on which are drawn civil, administrative, judicial, and extrajudicial acts, and also on certain writings, registrations, printed matter, and drawings specified in the rate schedule (IB art. 1). "Paper" (*carta*) means any material, suitable for the compilation or reproduction of writings and designs, that can function as a document or embody a transaction.

The yield of the stamp tax is slightly less than that of the complementary progressive tax on income (1/6.7d, 1/6.8e).

b. DOCUMENTS SUBJECT TO TAX WHEN EXECUTED. The stamp tax is due on certain civil documents, administrative documents, and documents presented before jurisdictional organs, when they are executed (IB art. 2; IB Schedule, Annex A, art. 1). Among the civil documents are documents issued or certified by public officials; registers kept by notaries or other public officials; bills of exchange (*cambiali*), business documents, and commercial paper of various types; bonds, including securities of the public debt; receipts, notes, accounts, invoices, and the like; releases and discharges of various kinds; accounting registers and books; savings bank and current account books; and copies and extracts of books of professional agents.

An "ordinary" receipt—any written declaration issued for the total or partial discharge of a pecuniary obligation or for payment in money or money's worth (IB art. 7)—is generally not subject to registration, but is subject to the stamp tax at a proportional rate. However, a receipt which is "not ordinary"—one involving liberation from an obligation resulting from an earlier written agreement subject to a proportional tax on registration within a fixed time limit (15/6.3) or resulting from a court order (IB art. 7)—is subject to the stamp tax at a fixed rate (4/4.2e).

If a document evidences a transaction that is subject to the general tax on receipts (IGE), the IGE payable on the transaction includes the stamp tax which would otherwise be due on the receipt for payment, provided that the receipt is placed, simultaneously or later, on the document under which IGE was collected.[18] If the receipt is issued separately, it is subject to the stamp tax, but the stamp tax is applied at a reduced

---

[16] D.P.R. 25 June 1953, n. 492. This decree is called the "new rules on the stamp tax"; it is hereinafter cited: "IB."

[17] L. 27 December 1952, n. 3596, art. 1.

[18] R.D.L. 9 January 1940, n. 2, art. 24.

rate if the document specifies the essential elements of the document on which IGE has already been paid. If IGE is not paid separately for each transaction, but in a single annual payment for all receipts actually obtained during a defined period (14/7.3g), it includes the stamp tax which would be payable on the receipts issued for the individual payments. The stamp tax is due separately on bills issued to clients by professionals and artists, independently of the IGE due on the payments, and also on notes, bills, invoices, and similar documents issued in relation to the acts described below.

1. Transactions for which IGE is paid in annual fixed fees or by subscription contracts subject to reconciliation (14/7.4).
2. Transfers of merchandise for which IGE is due in one payment, at specific rates, according to the value, weight, or volume of the merchandise. Exception is made for sale documents issued by the firm required to pay IGE when it is paid directly on these documents.
3. Transfers of cattle, sheep, and pigs, made before the slaughtering of the animals, and transfers of grapes and wines, made before payment of the local consumption tax.

Bills, invoices, and other documents issued in connection with the use of telephone service or the supply of gas, water, and electricity are exempt from the stamp tax. Foreign invoices relative to imported merchandise for which IGE has been paid at the time of importation are exempt from the stamp tax, provided that they specify the essential elements of the customs bill and evidence the payment of IGE.

The stamp tax is payable on bills, invoices, and similar documents issued in relation to transactions which do not result in receipts taxable under IGE if the documents specify the price or value of the commodity.[19]

On leases of urban immovable property, the registration tax now replaces both IGE and the stamp tax (15/6.3).

c. DOCUMENTS SUBJECT TO TAX WHEN USED. In some cases, the stamp tax is due only when documents are used, that is, when presented or produced in judicial or administrative proceedings, filed at a Registry Office for registration, or inserted in public acts (*atti pubblici*) (IB art. 2; IB Schedule, Annex A, Part II). These documents may be classified under the headings listed below.

1. Certain documents regarding the public interest, the state, and public entities (for example, registries and other documents of governmental administration).
2. Documents in certain contractual matters (chiefly relating to employment).
3. Correspondence and telegrams embodying business transactions.
4. Documents related to the movement of goods (documents required by law to accompany shipment, if not taxed when executed).
5. Exchanges of farm property.

---

[19] R.D.L. 9 January 1940, n. 2, art. 25; R.D. 26 January 1940, n. 10, art. 111.

6. Professional drawings, computations, and accounting work.
7. Foreign securities.
8. Other documents and writings of foreign origin which would be subject to tax when executed if drawn in Italy.
9. Acts and writings not expressly contemplated in the Schedule.
10. Acts for which the stamp tax replaces the registration tax under the registration law.

Foreign documents and writings which would be subject to tax if drawn in Italy are not subject to tax when drawn, but only when used in Italy; they are considered used when filed at a public office or in any way made effective in Italy between private persons (IB art. 2). Bills of exchange and other business documents issued abroad are considered used when presented, delivered, sent, receipted, accepted, endorsed, guaranteed, or otherwise negotiated in Italy. By virtue of a special rule, however, the tax on a receipt issued abroad must be paid by the addressee within three days of the date on which he receives it (IB Schedule, Annex A, art. 64). Securities issued abroad are considered used when transferred or negotiated in Italy or reported in public or private acts or writings other than statements of assets (IB art. 2).

Acts subject to tax when used are taxed at the rates in force at the time of use; acts drawn on free (unstamped) paper must be subjected to extraordinary stamping if they are to be used for a purpose different from that for which they were created (IB art. 6).

d. EXEMPTIONS AND REDUCTIONS. Exemptions from the stamp tax are provided for specified documents listed in Table B annexed to the decree. The exemptions are very numerous and are established in response to a social need to favor taxpayers who are less well-to-do or are in need of assistance. In these cases, free (unstamped) paper is used. The exempt documents concern: the public interest, the state, and public entities (for example, the exercise of legislative powers); civil status; the public debt and saving in general (for example, treasury bonds and postal bonds); welfare and the indigent; employment and pensions; public health; schools; social security; passports and immigration; companies (chiefly cooperative societies); guardianship and affiliation of children; certain judicial matters; and miscellaneous other documents (including holographic wills, lottery tickets and lotto drawing slips, contracts between administrative offices of the state). Other exemptions are contained in a number of special laws.

For bills of exchange and other business documents issued in Italy and payable abroad, the rates are reduced by one half (IB Schedule, Annex A, art. 5).

e. RATES. Most of the documents specified in the Schedule, Annex A, are subject to tax at fixed rates, ranging from a few lire to a few hundred lire. The fixed rates are applied to each sheet contained in the document; thus the tax is roughly proportional to the length of the document. The law requires that stamped paper have precisely defined dimensions and contain a prescribed number of lines, with margins of a certain size (IB art. 5). Examples of the documents to which fixed rates are applied are listed below.

1. Notarized documents and documents received by administrative officials: L. 200 (IB Schedule, Annex A, art. 1).
2. Private writings containing contracts of lease or sublease: L. 100. Private writings containing other contracts or declarations involving the creation, transfer, recognition, or extinction of rights: L. 200 (IB Schedule, Annex A, art. 2).
3. Copies of extracts issued by any public official or authority: L. 200 (IB Schedule, Annex A, art. 3).
4. Certificates of liquidation of stock exchange contracts: L. 200 (IB Schedule, Annex A, art. 12).
5. Receipts other than "ordinary" receipts (4/4.2b): L. 100 (IB Schedule, Annex A, art. 20).
6. Import licenses: L. 50 (IB Schedule, Annex A, art. 29).
7. Accounting books and registers: L. 10 per page (IB Schedule, Annex A, art. 33).
8. Savings-bank books: L. 15 per sheet (IB Schedule, Annex A, art. 34).
9. Copies and extracts of records of vital statistics: L. 100 per sheet (IB Schedule, Annex A, art. 36).
10. Administrative petitions and appeals: L. 100 to L. 400 per sheet, depending on the official or agency to which the appeal is made (IB Schedule, Annex A, art. 38).
11. Use in court of government registers, documents, and other papers, or of business correspondence and telegrams: L. 40 to L. 80 per sheet, depending on the court (IB Schedule, Annex A, arts. 48, 57).

For certain other documents, the rates are graduated according to the amount involved in the transaction or to the dimensions of the paper. Documents for which the rate depends on the value are: protests of bills of exchange (IB Schedule, Annex A, art. 11); securities of the public debt of the state (IB Schedule, Annex A, art. 16); negotiable securities of local governments or of corporations or other entities (IB Schedule, Annex A, art. 17); subscriptions to newspapers, magazines, and other printed matter (IB Schedule, Annex A, art. 26); and acts before the Magistrate (IB Schedule, Annex A, art. 43). The rates for these documents are less than L. 200, except in the case of negotiable securities of local governments or of corporations or other entities; for these, the maximum rate is L. 1,200, applicable to securities whose nominal value exceeds L. 750,000 (IB Schedule, Annex A, art. 17). The rate applicable to professional drawings, computations, and accounting work, when used as described at 4/4.2c, is L. 50, L. 100, or L. 200, depending on the dimensions of the paper (IB Schedule, Annex A, art. 62).

Finally, proportional rates, usually expressed in lire per thousand or fraction of a thousand, are applied to the amounts involved in certain documents. Thus, bills of exchange and other business documents issued and payable in Italy are taxed at rates ranging from L. 1 to L. 12 per thousand, depending on the face amount and the term; the rates are halved for documents issued in Italy but payable abroad (IB Schedule, Annex A, art. 5). For "ordinary" receipts (4/4.2b), accounts, and invoices, the rate is L. 2 per thousand, with a maximum of L. 2,000 for amounts exceeding L. 1,000,000 if the transaction is not subject to IGE; if the document shows that IGE has already been paid on an earlier document, or if IGE has been paid by an annual fee (14/7.3) or *una tantum* (14/6.4), the maximum rate of the stamp tax is L. 50 (IB Schedule, Annex A, art. 19). The rate for endorsement of import licenses is L. 1 per thousand (IB Schedule, Annex A, art. 29). For foreign securities taxable when used in Italy (4/4.2c), the rate is 1.2% in the case of interest-bearing securities and bonds of foreign governments, and 2.4% in the case of securities of foreign local governments or foreign corporations not subject to the tax on bonds (3/3) (IB Schedule, Annex A, art. 63).

f. PAYMENT. The "ordinary" method of paying the stamp tax is by the purchase of stamped paper, which is watermarked and carries an impress of the amount of tax (IB arts. 4, 5); the paper is distributed by the state through the fiscal monopoly stores (IB art. 46) (4/6.1) in various standard values. This method is required for many business documents subject to tax when executed, such as receipts, and for acts presented before the jurisdictional organs.

However, other methods of payment have developed in the course of the long history of the tax. One method is the purchase of stamps to be affixed to unstamped paper; these stamps are impressed or endorsed by the Registry Office or other duly authorized offices. Another method is the punching of unstamped paper by the Registry Office. Clearly, not all documents lend themselves to being drawn on special watermarked and stamped paper—for example, registers of enterprises. The schedule attached to the decree specifies the methods of payment applicable to each document; for some documents, a choice among the various methods is provided. For each method, the decree describes in some detail the procedure for its application (IB arts. 10-21).

Still another method (*in modo virtuale*) consists of payment of the tax to the Registry Office or to other duly authorized offices without the material affixing of a stamp or endorsement (IB art. 4). This method simplifies collection but is less efficient than the others from the point of view of assessment. To obtain authorization to pay the tax without stamping, the taxpayer must file with the Registry Office a statement of the presumed number of taxable documents of each type to be issued during the year and a facsimile of the imprint to be applied to each document. The tax is paid provisionally every three months, and is paid finally on the basis of the documents actually issued as of 31 March of each year. At the request of the taxpayer, the Intendant of Finance may permit payment of the tax on defined categories of acts or writings by this method on the basis of a special agreement with the taxpayer (IB art. 23).[20]

Provision is also made for suspension of payment of the stamp tax during judicial proceedings involving state administrative offices, entities treated for tax purposes in the same manner as state offices, or persons granted the right of free legal assistance (*gratuito patrocinio*) (IB arts 25, 26). Under this procedure, called reservation on account (*prenotazione a debito*), a document presented or produced in judicial proceedings is stamped, but payment of tax is suspended until the proceedings benefit the person who had the document stamped.[21]

g. APPEALS. Administrative appeals on the application of the stamp tax and surcharges (4/4.2h) are decided by the Intendant of Finance; if the amount of tax and surcharge contested exceeds L. 50,000, the Intendant's decision may be appealed to the Ministry of Finance within 30 days of notification of his decision (IB art. 30). An appeal to the courts against a decision of the Intendant or the Ministry cannot be made more than six months after the notification of the decision. Appeal to the courts in revocation for errors of fact or of computation is allowed under the conditions established by article 395 of the Code of Civil Procedure (IB art. 30).

h. VIOLATIONS AND PENALTIES. The determination of violations of the stamp tax decree is entrusted to the officials of the General Directorate of the Fees and Indirect Taxes on Transactions, who, along with the tax police (1/4.8), have the power to inspect stamped books, registers, and writings (IB art. 42). The penalties imposed are summarized below.

1. Magistrates and other public officials who fail to observe the duties imposed on them are subject to a pecuniary penalty of from L. 500 to L. 1,000 (IB art. 35).
2. Any person who draws acts or writings on which tax is due when executed or makes use of acts or writings on which tax is due when used, paying no tax or insufficient tax, is subject to a pecuniary penalty of from L. 1,000 to L. 10,000 for each act. For bills of exchange and other business acts, and for releases, the pecuniary penalty is from 50 to 100 times the amount of the tax not paid, with a minimum of L. 300 (IB art. 36).
3. When the tax is payable directly at the Registry Office (*in modo virtuale*), a surcharge (*sopratassa*) of 60% of the tax is imposed for omitted or late

---

[20] As substituted by D.P.R. 4 February 1955, n. 72.
[21] See the discussion of provisions governing registration on account at 15/7.2c.

filing of the return, of 120% of the tax evaded for filing a false return, and of 12% of the tax for failure to make payment within 20 days following the due date (IB art. 37).

4. For failure to observe other duties or prohibitions specified in the decree and the schedule, a pecuniary penalty of from L. 500 to L. 5,000 is imposed for each infraction (IB art. 38).

The tax not paid and any supplement are always due in addition to any penalty or surcharge (IB art. 39). Falsification, counterfeiting, or alteration of the values stamped on the paper, and the unauthorized keeping for sale, use, and sale of stamped paper, are also subject to penalties under the Penal Code (IB art. 40).

Any person who signs, receives, accepts, or negotiates documents that violate the requirements of the stamp tax decree, or transcribes or states them in other acts or writings, is responsible for the violation of the decree; responsible also is any person who, without first providing the required stamp, makes use of a document or writing on which tax is due only in the case of use (IB art. 33).

Judges and other public officials are forbidden to give effect to documents not stamped in the proper form (IB arts. 27, 28). Judicial and other public officials who give effect to unstamped documents in violation of the decree are jointly responsible for the violation with the parties to the document. Except in the case of bills of exchange and other business documents, a party to whom an act or writing not in proper form is remitted, and who has not participated in the formation of it, is free from any responsibility for the violation if he presents the document at the Registry Office for regularization within 15 days of receiving it.

4/4.3 Stamp Tax on Stock Exchange Contracts

a. IN GENERAL. Stock exchange contracts (*contratti di borsa*) are subject to a special stamp tax based on the value of their subject matter.[22] The contracts listed below are considered stock exchange contracts for purposes of this tax (LTCB art. 1).

1. Contracts whose objects are securities of the public debt of the state, provinces, communes, or other public entities; shares and bonds of corporations, including certificates of farm credit institutions; and, in general, any security of an analogous nature, either national or foreign, whether or not listed on a stock exchange. Any such contract made in conformity with commercial usages is included, whether made in or outside a stock exchange, in cash or on time, on premium, or in *riporto* (9/2.8).
2. Sales of monetary values, whether in ingots or in foreign exchange, whether or not made on a stock exchange.
3. Term sales (*a termine*) of commodities and goods, contracted according to the usages of the commodities exchange, whether made in or outside of the exchange, if made through registered exchange agents (*mediatori*).

---

[22] R.D. 30 December 1923, n. 3278, art. 1. This decree is the law on fees on stock exchange contracts; it is hereinafter cited: "LTCB."

Operations of discount of bills of exchange (*sconto di cambiali*) are not included (LTCB art. 1). Contracts executed abroad have legal effect in Italy only if subjected to this tax, even when an agreement has been made to resolve them by a payment limited to the difference of stock exchange prices (LTCB art. 8). The tax does not apply to term and *riporto* contracts (9/2.8) involving securities or monetary values whose agreed term exceeds 135 days, or to term contracts involving goods and commodities whose agreed term exceeds 180 days; these contracts are subject instead to the tax on secured loans (LTCB art. 15) (4/3.5).[23]

Letters, telegrams, and other writings issued by the parties in relation to contracts subject to the tax, for which stamped sheets have been used, are exempt from regular stamp and registration taxes, even if judicial or administrative use is made of them (LTCB art. 7).

b. RATES. The rates of tax on contracts involving securities or monetary values, in lire per L. 100,000 or fraction thereof, are graduated according to the duration of the contract (up to 135 days); according to whether the contract calls for payment in cash, on term, or in *riporto* (9/2.8); and according to whether the contract is concluded directly between the parties, through bankers or private persons, through exchange agents or banks registered under specified provisions, or through ordinary exchange agents. The maximum tax is L. 300 per L. 100,000 of value in the case of term contracts concluded directly between the parties for more than 90 days but not more than 135 days. In the case of cash contracts involving exclusively securities of the state or guaranteed by the state, except when concluded by ordinary exchange agents, the tax is reduced to one half.[24]

The rates of tax on contracts involving commodities and goods are graduated according to the value of the goods; according to the duration of contract (up to 180 days); and according to whether the contract is concluded directly between exchange agents, directly between parties allowed to bid from the floor, or transmitted through exchange agents or persons allowed to bid from the floor. The maximum tax is L. 2,700 in the case of contracts exceeding L. 6 million in value, made for not less than 120 days or more than 180 days and transmitted through authorized persons.[25]

c. ADMINISTRATION AND COLLECTION. Special forms are required for the execution of contracts subject to the tax (LTCB art. 3). The tax is paid either by the purchase of stamped paper or by stamping at the Registry

---

[23] As modified by L. 10 November 1954, n. 1079, art. 1.

[24] The rates are found in L. 10 November 1954, n. 1079, Table A, as substituted by D. L. 30 June 1960, n. 589.

[25] L. 10 November 1954, n. 1079, Table B.

Office (LTCB art. 4). Direct payment of tax (*in modo virtuale*) by credit firms on cash stock exchange transactions may be authorized by the Minister of Finance.[26] If one of the parties to a contract is abroad, the tax due for a contract executed in Italy is paid by the person allowed to deal in the official market, or by the party residing in Italy (LTCB art. 8). Various provisions are made for the keeping of records for and the administration of various kinds of transactions (LTCB arts. 9-15).[27]

Penalties are provided for failure to observe the rules established by the decree and for improper use by the tax administration of information obtained in the course of enforcement (LTCB arts. 16-21).

4/4.4 Stamp Tax on Transportation Documents

A stamp tax is levied on documents for the transportation of persons, baggage, and goods: railroad tickets and invoices; bus tickets; documents for transport by land; passenger tickets, baggage checks, and invoices for transport by sea; passenger tickets, baggage checks, and bills of lading for transport by air.[28] Although fixed rates of up to L. 100 are provided for most documents, some rates are graduated on the basis of the weight of the goods shipped or the speed of travel. However, proportional rates of up to 3% of the transportation price are provided for railroad passenger tickets and baggage checks and certain railroad invoices, and tickets and other documents for bus and interurban motor vehicle transport.

In some cases, the tax is paid at the time of issue of the ticket or document, and payment is evidenced by stamping or punching. In other cases, the tax is paid directly (*in modo virtuale*) on the filing of an annual return at the Registry Office. The decree law contains special provisions regarding administration and penalties.

4/5. Taxes on Production and Consumption
4/5.1 In General

The national government imposes manufacturing taxes and consumption taxes on certain activities. The consumption taxes are often partly fees for the performance of public services. The fiscal monopolies and the fees for governmental concessions may be regarded as taxes on production or consumption, but they are treated separately in this volume (4/6, 4/7). The communes also levy consumption taxes on certain goods, as well as taxes which are partly fees for the use of public facilities or resources.

---

[26] D.L. 30 June 1960, n. 589 (converted in L. 14 August 1960, n. 826), art. 2 *bis*.
[27] See also R.D.L. 20 December 1932, n. 1607.
[28] D.L. 7 May 1948, n. 1173, art. 1, and Annex A, Schedule.

4/5.2 Manufacturing Taxes

a. IN GENERAL. The state levies taxes on the manufacture of various goods produced in Italy; there are corresponding border surtaxes imposed on the same goods if imported from abroad. In most cases, the Italian manufacturer must also pay an annual license fee.

The principles which regulate the manufacturing taxes are uniform. When certain goods are subject to a manufacturing tax, those who wish to manufacture those goods at the stage at which the tax is imposed—the so-called "final" stage—must obtain a manufacturing license. In this way, the tax administration learns of each factory in which those goods are manufactured, its location, its capacity, and the names of those who manage it.

Control is exercised over production in two ways. The taxpayer must make a report of intention to manufacture, giving the days and hours he works, the quantities of raw materials processed, the kinds of materials employed, and the product he will obtain. He must also keep a register of processing, which shows the purpose for which the material employed in the factory is used. The other method of control involves the recording of movements of raw materials in a special register of shipments received and sent out, and the storing of raw materials in warehouses isolated from the rest of the factory.

The tax is levied on the processed product as such; but because the tax is sometimes higher than the price of the processed product net of tax, payment of tax may be delayed until the moment of sale. In the time intervening between production and sale, the product must be kept in special warehouses, called "fiduciary warehouses," subject to controls similar to those for checking customs warehouses, pending payment of duty or pending export. This system is reinforced by the keeping of a register of goods received and sent out, and by a check by the Finance Guard (1/4.8). Often an advance on the tax due at the moment of sale is required. When the product is subsequently sold, goods which have borne the manufacturing tax must often be accompanied by a consignment note (*bolletta di accompagnamento*), which enables the Finance Guard to ascertain whether the goods shipped have regularly borne the tax or are contraband.

In addition to the taxes described at 4/5.2b, the taxes listed below can be classified as manufacturing taxes.

1. The tax on matches, received through a private monopoly (4/6.5).
2. The tax on automatic lighters (4/6.6).
3. The tax on playing cards, formally a stamp tax but actually a manufacturing tax on this product.[29]

---

[29] R.D. 30 December 1923, n. 3277.

A tax on mercury and its compounds [30] was suspended in 1959 [31] and abolished in 1961.[32] Two taxes that are called "consumption" taxes are levied exclusively at the border on products of tropical origin: coffee and cocoa.[33]

b. PRODUCTS TAXED AND RATES. The law imposing each manufacturing tax lists the specific or ad valorem rates applied to production or importation and the annual license fee, if applicable. The rates and fees applicable to each classification of commodities are summarized below.

1. *Beer.*[34] The manufacturing tax and corresponding border surtax is L. 400 per hectoliter. The annual license fee is L. 2,500 for factories producing not more than 300 hectoliters annually and L. 7,500 for factories producing more than 300 hectoliters annually.
2. *Coffee substitutes.*[35] The manufacturing tax is L. 4,000 per quintal (100 kilograms). The license fee is L. 2,500.
3. *Threads and textile fabrics.*[36] The manufacture of threads of various natural and artificial textile fibers is taxed at rates graduated according to the length or to the specific weight of the fiber, in lire per kilogram. The importation of fabrics made from threads subject to the manufacturing tax is subject to a corresponding border surtax. The license fee is graduated according to the number of spindles or spinnerettes employed, up to a maximum fee of L. 30,000.
4. *Gas and electric energy.*[37] The consumption of electric energy is taxed at fixed or graduated rates per kilowatt-hour, depending on the use and the monthly consumption; the consumption of gas for lighting or heating is taxed at a fixed rate per cubic meter. Exemption is made for electricity or gas used for the lighting of public areas by governmental and other public bodies; on condition of reciprocity, for electricity and gas consumed by diplomatic offices; for electric energy used in the state railroads and electric traction cables; for electricity and gas used for scientific and teaching purposes, but not illumination, in public institutions; for electricity used in the generation or transformation of other electricity; for electricity used in communications; for electricity produced in ships or other vehicles for use thereon; and for gas used in manufacturing processes in industrial factories, including bakeries. The annual license fee is graduated according to the productive capacity of the works.
5. *Sugar, glucose, maltose, and sugar products.*[38] Taxes and border surtaxes are imposed in lire per quintal on various kinds and grades of products, up to a maximum of L. 6,200 for first-grade sugar. Reductions are

---

[30] D.L. 24 November 1954, n. 1068, converted in L. 10 December 1954, n. 1166.

[31] L. 9 May 1959, n. 266.

[32] L. 16 December 1961, n. 1425.

[33] D.L.P. 14 October 1946, n. 206, art. 1; D.L. 11 March 1950, n. 50, arts. 12, 13.

[34] D.M. 8 July 1924 (*Testo unico* for the tax on beer).

[35] D.M. 8 July 1924 (*Testo unico* for the tax on coffee substitutes), art. 1; substituted by D.L.L. 26 April 1945, n. 223, Annex E; modified by D.L. 11 March 1950, n. 50, art. 5.

[36] D.L.P. 3 January 1947, n. 1; D.M. 10 March 1949, Table A.

[37] D.M. 8 July 1924 (*Testo unico* for the tax on the consumption of gas and electric energy).

[38] D.M. 8 July 1924 (*Testo unico* for the tax on sugar); L. 14 August 1960, n. 822.

provided for sugar used for certain purposes, and special provisions are made for molasses. The annual license fee varies according to the kind and grade of the product; the highest is L. 15,000 for sugar factories and refineries.

6. *Seed oils.*[39] The manufacturing tax is L. 6,000 per quintal of raw oil produced. The rate of the corresponding border surtax depends on the type of product imported. The maximum annual license fee is L. 25,000.

7. *Petroleum and petroleum products.*[40] The taxes and border surtaxes on various products are given in lire per quintal. The tax on crude oil is L. 6,000; as of 1963, the tax on gasoline was L. 11,200. Special rates are provided for products used for certain purposes.

8. *Electric light bulbs.*[41] The manufacturing tax and border surtax are imposed at specific rates according to wattage. The maximum rate is L. 300 for vapor or fluorescent lamps exceeding 100 watts. The maximum annual license fee is L. 7,500.

9. *Spirits.*[42] Spirits and alcohols used in their manufacture are subject to a manufacturing tax and corresponding border surtax of L. 40,000 per anhydrous hectoliter. Spirits employed in the manufacture of vinegar are taxed at lower rates. Alcohols employed exclusively for industrial purposes or exported are exempt. Special provisions are made for various types of alcoholic beverages and alcohol products. Maximum sales prices of spirits may be established annually by the Minister of Finance.[43]

10. *Liquid animal oils and fats for foodstuffs.*[44] Animal oils and fats with a solidification point not higher than 30° centigrade, except butter and pork lard, are subject to a manufacturing tax and corresponding border surtax of L. 25,000 per quintal produced. Products intended for further use in various manufacturing processes are excluded. The annual license fee is L. 15,000.

11. *Liquid vegetable oils.*[45] Liquid vegetable oils with a solidification point not higher than 12° centigrade are subject to a manufacturing tax and corresponding border surtax of L. 16,000 per quintal. The annual license fee is L. 15,000.

12. *Methane gas.*[46] The rate of tax on distribution and the corresponding border surtax is L. 1 per cubic meter at normal temperature and pressure. The gas subject to this tax is not subject to the manufacturing tax on gas and electric energy (item 4 above). Exemptions are given for biological

---

[39] D.P. 22 December 1954, n. 1217.

[40] D.L. 28 February 1939, n. 334. The rates are established by D.L. 3 December 1953, n. 878 (converted in L. 31 January 1954, n. 2), art. 1; L. 11 June 1959, n. 405; and L. 13 July 1960, n. 661. Exemptions and reductions are provided for products devoted to certain public and other uses. By L. 31 December 1962, n. 1852, the tax was revised to take account of products developed by new chemical techniques to replace or supplement already existing petroleum products. In L. 21 February 1963, n. 263, a reduced rate was provided for oil for domestic heating. A decree of 23 February 1964 increased the tax on gasoline; see D.L. 23 February 1964, n. 25. There is also a tax on gases liquefied by compression. D.L. 24 November 1954, n. 1071; L. 11 June 1959, n. 405.

[41] R.D.L. 16 June 1938, n. 954, art. 1; D.L.L. 26 April 1945, n. 223, Annex B, substituted by D.L.C.P.S. 21 October 1946, n. 236.

[42] D.M. 8 July 1924, art. 14, as modified by D.L. 8 September 1951, n. 750.

[43] R.D.L. 27 April 1936, n. 635, art. 10.

[44] D.L. 20 November 1953, n. 843.

[45] D.L. 26 November 1954, n. 1080.

[46] D.L. 6 October 1955, n. 873, converted in L. 3 December 1955, n. 1110.

methane used by the producer for his own purposes; for methane produced by the chemical industry for the synthesis of other chemical products; for methane used to drive machines for the extraction or compression
of gas; and for methane coming from certain sources. The license fee is
graduated according to the amount of gas to be produced annually, up to
a maximum of L. 10,000. Methane gas in cylinders is subject to an
additional fee of L. 3 per cubic meter, due from anyone who bottles gas
extracted in Italy or imports gas in cylinders.[47]

13. *Fatty acids of animal or vegetable origin.*[48] The rate of the manufacturing tax and corresponding border surtax is L. 25,000 per quintal.
Products employed for industrial uses other than the preparation of edible
oils are excluded. The annual license fee is L. 15,000.

14. *Margarine.*[49] The manufacturing tax and the corresponding border
surtax are imposed at the rate of L. 12,000 per quintal. Margarine
destined exclusively for industrial or artisan factories for the preparation
of food or candy is exempt.

15. *Radio and television receiving equipment.*[50] The invoice price, including
customs duties and any other fees, is subject to a "radio broadcast fee"
of 5%, payable by the manufacturer or importer with a right of recovery
from anyone who purchases the equipment for resale (4/5.6).

16. *Phonograph records and other devices for the reproduction of sound.*[51]
The invoice price, including customs duties and any other fees, is subject
to a tax of 10%, payable by the manufacturer or importer with a right of
recovery from anyone who purchases the equipment for resale.

c. ADMINISTRATION. The manufacturing taxes are administered by the
Technical Offices of the Manufacturing Taxes (1/4.4). Each of the laws
under which these taxes are levied contains its own provisions for the
filing of a report of intention to manufacture; inspection and supervision
of factories by agents of the Technical Offices; control of movements of
raw materials and products, and supervision of warehouses; the keeping
of records and registers; assessment and payment of tax into the Treasury,
normally in advance, on the basis of a return showing the expected production for a specified period; payment by annual fee (*abbonamento*)
by agreement with the administration under specified conditions; refund
of tax on products exported; and relief from tax on goods accidentally
destroyed while in the factory warehouse. Controversies regarding the
application of these taxes are resolved under the rules provided for
customs controversies (4/8.4).

Each law defines the acts which constitute violations of its provisions
and prescribes penalties for them; these penalties often involve imprisonment and, in general, are more severe than those imposed for violations
of other taxes. The crime (*reato*) of contraband has been defined as a

---

[47] L. 27 May 1959, n. 360, as modified by L. 13 July 1960, n. 661.
[48] D.L. 31 October 1956, n. 1194.
[49] L. 11 June 1959, n. 450; L. 16 June 1960, n. 623, art. 1.
[50] L. 15 December 1960, n. 1560.
[51] L. 1 July 1961, n. 569.

type of tax evasion consisting either of a fraud [52] or of an action that is conclusively presumed to have the capacity of defrauding the tax administration. For example, processing by means and at times other than those provided in the report of intention to manufacture is deemed to be contraband, even if it can be shown that the processing took place accidentally or that the taxpayer made a declaration and later changed his mind without changing the declaration.

d. INTERNATIONAL ASPECTS. Corresponding to each manufacturing tax, there is a border surtax of the same amount on imported goods of the same type, payable at the time of importation. From a formal point of view, these are not manufacturing taxes, but import taxes; however, their purpose is not to obstruct the circulation of goods between various countries—the usual purpose of customs duties—but to equalize national and foreign goods on the domestic market.

The fiscal burden on exported goods is eliminated in two ways. One is by refunding at export the tax paid on goods processed and exported, a system called "draw-back." The other is the so-called "temporary import" system, applied to materials which are imported from abroad for the manufacture of goods normally subject to a manufacturing tax in Italy, but which it is known are to be exported abroad; instead of requiring payment of tax and then refunding it at the time of export, these goods are exempted from the border surtax. If the goods are subsequently "nationalized"—for example, if the importer changes his mind and sells the processed goods internally—the importer will nationalize the product not on entry into customs, where he had obtained a license for temporary import, but later, when the goods leave manufacturing and the warehouse and enter the market.

4/5.3   Advertising Tax

a. IN GENERAL. Advertising, by any method, for any purpose, and in any form, is subject to a special stamp tax (*imposta di pubblicità*).[53] The tax is paid by the "ordinary" method by the application of stamps, by the "extraordinary" method through the application of a stamp punch by the Registry Office, or directly (*in modo virtuale*) on the basis of a return filed with the Registry Office (IP art. 3). The marks must be cancelled, with the date written or impressed partly on the mark and partly on the paper. The sale of marks is governed by the rules

---

[52] L. 25 September 1940, n. 1424.

[53] D.P.R. 24 June 1954, n. 342. This decree is called the "new rules on the advertising tax"; it is hereinafter cited: "IP." Formerly, the taxation of advertising was regulated by the stamp tax decree of 1923, R.D. 30 December 1923, n. 3268. Advertising along public roads is governed by a special ministerial decree, D.M. 20 August 1947.

applicable to the distribution and sale of stamped paper (IP art. 4) (4/4.2f). The tax is not included in the annual-fee method of payment (*abbonamento*) of fees and indirect taxes on transactions which some institutions and entities enjoy under legal provisions in force.

b. NOTICES TO THE PUBLIC. Payment of the tax on public notices made on paper or cardboard or on transfers is evidenced by a mark or a punched stamp (IP art. 6). For notices made by painting or any other means on material other than paper, and for luminous or illuminated signs, the tax is due quarterly on the basis of a return to be filed at the Registry Office prior to the appearance of the advertisement, on special forms furnished by the tax administration (IP arts. 7, 8). For notices distributed by hand, by mail, or dropped from an airplane, the tax is paid in advance upon the filing of a return at the Registry Office (IP art. 9). Advertising stamped or printed on bills, tickets, receipts for public services, contest cards, playing cards, matchbooks, packages of cigars, cigarettes, and other monopoly goods, forms used by the postal and telecommunications administration, and advertising stamped on correspondence sent out by that administration are subject to tax on the basis of a return to be filed quarterly at the Registry Office (IP art. 10). The tax is due at the time of filing and is paid by the advertising contractor, with a right of recovery against the advertiser. The tax is determined on the basis of the invoice price paid for the advertising.

c. ADVERTISING IN NEWSPAPERS, MAGAZINES, AND OTHER PRINTED MATTER. The tax on advertising in newspapers, magazines, and other printed matter is payable by the publisher or the advertising firm which arranges for the insertion, with a right of recovery against the advertiser; the tax due is determined on the basis of the amount collected for the advertising service, as shown in duplicate order books (IP art. 11). Daily and weekly periodicals must publish their rate schedules in each issue; periodicals published less often must keep the Registry Office informed of their rate schedules (IP art. 13). Tax must be paid quarterly at the Registry Office in the commune of publication, on the filing of a return, but the taxpayer may apply to the Ministry of Finance for authorization to pay the tax provisionally, subject to adjustment, if the annual taxable amount exceeds L. 500 million (IP art. 14).

d. CINEMA, RADIO, TELEVISION, AND MOBILE ADVERTISING. The tax on cinema, radio, and television advertising is payable by whoever provides the advertising, either directly or through third persons, with a right of recovery against the advertiser (IP arts. 15, 16). The tax is assessed and collected in the same manner as in the case of periodical advertising.

DESCRIPTION OF TAX SYSTEM

The tax on mobile advertising is paid directly (*in modo virtuale*) or the basis of a return filed with the Registry Office before the advertising appears (IP art. 17). The tax is paid at the time of the filing of the return.

e. EXEMPTIONS. Exemption from the advertising tax is provided for certain civil advertising, including various types of notices displayed at business or professional offices or on the business property, certain advertising by street vendors, certain tourist propaganda, and certain notices whose publication is required by civil and commercial laws; for notices and communications regarding the public interest, the state, or public entities; for notices and communications regarding social security and employment; and for inscriptions on monuments and gravestones (IP Annex B).

f. RATES OF TAX. The rates for the tax on advertising are given in the Schedule, Annex A, that is attached to the decree. Publicly exhibited notices on paper or cardboard are taxed at rates of up to L. 20 per square meter or fraction thereof; these rates are graduated according to the dimensions of the notice, the length of time for which it is exhibited, and, if it involves public shows, whether or not it has illustrations. Distributed notices are taxed at rates graduated according to the number of copies; the maximum tax is L. 2,000 for 5,000 or more copies. On notices and signs made of materials other than paper or cardboard, a tax of up to L. 100 per square meter or fraction thereof is due, in quarterly installments; on luminous or illuminated signs, up to L. 500 per square meter or fraction thereof, at rates graduated according to the number of messages and to the size of type; and for the display of products in windows, L. 1,000 for each square meter or fraction thereof. Daily rates are applied for the use of loudspeakers (L. 100), mobile advertising by persons, whether on foot, on bicycles, or on motorcycles (L. 100), advertising by automobile (L. 3,000), and aerial advertising (L. 2,000). Percentage rates are provided for the types of advertising listed below.

1. Tables and signs distributed to insured persons by insurance companies and displayed publicly on buildings and other insured property: 1% of the value insured, payable annually.
2. Insertions in newspapers, periodicals, and other printed matter: 4% of the advertising price.
3. Advertising printed on receipts for public services, packages of monopoly goods, and the like: 2% of the advertising price.
4. Cinema advertising: 12% of the advertising price.
5. Radio and television advertising: 4% of the advertising price.

g. ADMINISTRATION AND PROCEDURE. Enforced collection of the advertising tax is governed by the provisions applicable to the registration taxes (IP art. 18) (15/7). Pecuniary penalties and surcharges are provided for violations; and falsification, counterfeiting, and alteration of marks evidencing payment are punishable under the Penal Code.

Administrative appeals may be made to the Intendant of Finance, whose decision may be appealed within 30 days to the Minister of Finance if the amount of tax and surcharge contested exceeds L. 50,000. An appeal in revocation is allowed for errors of fact or of computation, as well as in the cases specified in the Code of Civil Procedure. Appeals to the courts against decisions in administrative appeals must be made within six months of notification of the decision. Action by the state for the collection of taxes, pecuniary penalties, and surcharges is barred after five years. The taxpayer may appeal within one year of payment for the refund of taxes unduly paid, unless payment of the tax was evidenced by a stamp or punch.

4/5.4   Tax on Public Shows

The gross receipts from shows (*spettacoli*), games, and other forms of entertainment are subject to a tax levied by the state at proportional rates depending on the nature of the entertainment.[54] The rates are, for example, 3% for fairs and exhibitions, 15% for plays and concerts, and 36% for games at which bets are taken (other than horse races and horse shows). The tax on games at which bets are not taken, and on horse races and horse shows, is graduated according to the price charged for admission.[55] The rates on motion pictures are progressive according to admission prices and range from a minimum of 5% to a maximum of 45% for ordinary shows, and to a maximum of 37.5% for shows including live acts.[56] The tax is due even for benefit performances and performances given for purposes other than the profit of the promoter.

This tax is administered by the General Directorate of the Fees and Indirect Taxes on Transactions (1/4.3). The collection of the tax is delegated to the Italian Society of Authors and Publishers (*Società Italiana degli Autori ed Editori* or SIAE), which retains a collection fee from the amounts collected. Of the yield of the tax, 75% is returned to the communes from which it was collected.[57] There are a number of special provisions dealing with the application of the tax to various types of entertainment.[58]

4/5.5   Motor Vehicle Fees

The operation of motor vehicles and attached trailers on streets and in other public areas and of motor boats in public waters is subject to an

---

[54] R.D. 30 December 1923, n. 3276, art. 1; L. 26 November 1955, n. 1109, art. 1, and Table A.

[55] L. 26 November 1955, n. 1109, Table B.

[56] L. 26 November 1955, n. 1109, Table C.

[57] D.L. 26 March 1948, n. 261, art. 2; L. 20 December 1959, n. 1102, art. 4.

[58] See Cordaro, *Codice fiscale* 355 *et seq.*

annual tax.[59] Motor vehicles of foreign diplomatic and consular representatives are exempt on the conditions of reciprocal treatment; exemption is also made for vehicles used for certain public purposes (TUTA art. 17). Exemptions and reductions are provided also for vehicles for certain other uses. Vehicles imported temporarily by persons regularly residing abroad are exempt for three months on the condition of reciprocal treatment (TUTA art. 18). They are subject to special provisions for the following nine months (TUTA art. 8). One third of the proceeds of the tax is divided among the provinces as explained at 1/5.5e.

The rate of tax varies with the type, horsepower, and size of each vehicle. For passenger automobiles, the rates are graduated from L. 5,000 for 5 horsepower (CV) to L. 237,100 for 45 horsepower, plus L. 8,500 for each horsepower over 45.[60] Payment is made at the local office of the Automobile Club of Italy and is evidenced by the fixing of a countersign-disc to the vehicle.

Appeals may be made to the Intendant of Finance, and then to the Minister of Finance; their decisions may be appealed to the courts within six months of notification (TUTA art. 39).

4/5.6 Radio and Television Reception Fees

Owners of radio and television receiving equipment are required to pay a subscription fee (*canone di abbonamento*) for reception.[61] The fee must be paid each year, without notice being sent to the taxpayer. The fee includes the fee for payment by current postal account, the postage fee for delivery of the inscription booklet for radio reception, and the general tax on receipts (which is paid into the Treasury by the tax administration); hence these taxes need not be paid separately.[62] When reception is broadcast in public places or outside the family home, or the equipment is employed in any manner for profit, the user must enter into a special subscription contract with the Italian Radio Broadcast Company (*Società Radio Audizioni Italia* or SRAI), concessionary of closed-circuit receptions.[63]

Payment of the fee for private use is made only by current postal account, in advance, either annually or semiannually, by means of a special "inscription booklet" issued by the Registry Office. Tourists and travelers may obtain a license for temporary importation of receivers upon payment of a fixed fee of L. 200 and deposit of customs duties, the latter to be

---

[59] D.P. 5 February 1953, n. 39, arts. 1, 2. This decree is the *Testo unico* of the laws on the automobile fees; it is hereinafter cited: "TUTA."

[60] L. 21 May 1955, n. 463, Schedule C, as substituted by L. 27 May 1959, n. 356, art. 1.

[61] R.D.L. 21 February 1938, n. 246, as modified by subsequent legislation.

[62] D.L.L. 1 December 1945, n. 834, art. 3.

[63] R.D.L. 21 December 1944, n. 458.

refunded if the taxpayer leaves Italy within three months. Military hospitals and other military establishments are exempt.

Sellers of radio equipment are required to keep special registers of purchases and sales of equipment and of equipment received for repairs.[64]

The annual rates for home use are L. 3,300 for radio receivers and L. 12,000 for television sets. Lower rates are provided for hospitals, clinics, clubs, and other organizations; the rates for commercial use, as in hotels and on ships, are somewhat higher.

There is also a "radio broadcast fee" (*tassa di radiodiffusione*) of 5% of the invoiced price of radio and television receiving equipment, plus customs duties and other fees, if any, payable by the manufacturer or importer with a right of recovery against anyone who purchases the equipment for resale.[65]

4/5.7   Tax on Games of Skill and Football Pools

There is a special tax on the gross receipts from games of skill and football pools.[66] This tax replaces all transactions taxes (except the stamp taxes on bills of exchange, court fees, and advertising), and all other direct or indirect taxes otherwise due from the promoters, including the tax on income from movable wealth and the complementary tax payable on the winnings (6/1.1). The rates vary from a minimum of 33%, if the receipts do not exceed L. 300 million, to 45%, if the receipts exceed L. 1,500 million.[67]

4/5.8   Local Consumption Taxes

a. IN GENERAL. The consumption taxes (*imposte di consumo*) have a very ancient origin; once called "internal tolls" (*dazi interni*), they were levied both by the state and by the communes after the national unification, but are now levied exclusively by the communes. Until 1930, the taxes were imposed on the passage of goods through the toll barrier in closed communes and on the introduction of goods into retail shops or warehouses in open communes; these earlier duties, however, were an obstacle to commerce between the towns, were unequal in burden, and were difficult to administer.[68]

Today, the consumption taxes, imposed on a wide variety of goods in common use, are the principal form of indirect taxation of the communes; their yield is more than double that of the family tax. The taxes are payable by the producer, the wholesaler, or the retailer in accordance

---

[64] L. 12 November 1949, n. 996.
[65] L. 15 December 1960, n. 1560.
[66] D.L. 14 April 1948, n. 496, art. 1; L. 22 December 1951, n. 1379.
[67] L. 27 May 1959, n. 358, art. 1.
[68] See Einaudi, *Il sistema tributario italiano* (3d ed., 1935) 231-233.

with the rules established for the particular category of goods taxed (4/5.8e). The taxes are imposed on goods brought into the commune, or produced in the commune, for use or consumption therein; in the latter case, they are paid when the goods are sold. The rates are fixed by the communes, within limits established by law. Some commodities are taxed at specific rates, but most are taxed at ad valorem rates applied on the basis of a schedule of values that reflects the average prices of the preceding 12 months (4/5.8d).

b. TAXABLE GOODS. The law lists certain goods ("schedule" goods) which the communes are required to tax, but it also provides a second list of goods ("extra-schedule" goods) for which imposition is optional. However, if the commune decides to increase the rates of the tax on the "schedule" goods beyond the ordinary level, it must extend the tax to all goods in the second list. The goods in both lists are very numerous. The "schedule" goods that give the most significant yield are listed below.[69]

1. Electric energy for illumination, and gas.
2. Meats.
3. Building materials.
4. Alcoholic beverages other than wine;[70] nonalcoholic beverages.
5. Poultry, rabbits, game, and fish.
6. Candy.
7. Cheese and dairy products; butter and its substitutes.
8. Certain household furniture (including radios, phonographs, and television sets), phonograph records, furs, fine soaps, and perfumes.

The "extra-schedule" goods that provide the greatest yield are listed below (TUFL art. 20).

1. Electric household equipment such as refrigerators, stoves, and furnaces.
2. Precious objects.
3. Toys.
4. Timepieces.
5. Materials for furnishings.
6. Textiles and clothing goods.
7. Glass and crystal products.
8. Shoes.
9. Sporting goods.
10. Various foodstuffs.
11. Flowers.
12. Paper wrappings, boxes, and cellophane.

c. EXCLUSIONS AND EXEMPTIONS. Categories of goods not included in either list of taxable goods are automatically excluded from taxation.

---

[69] R.D. 14 September 1931, n. 1175, art. 20. This decree is the *Testo unico* of local finance; it is hereinafter cited: "TUFL."

[70] The tax on wine was abolished as of 1 January 1962 by article 8 of L. 18 December 1959, n. 1079. Sparkling wine, however, is subject to a national tax of L. 500 per bottle if purchased in a luxury establishment, as well as to the general tax on receipts at 8% of its sale price. L. 18 December 1959, n. 1079, arts. 12, 13.

n addition, the law specifically exempts certain goods which do fall within the categories in the lists of taxable goods (TUFL art. 20).

1. Bread, spaghetti (*pasta alimentare*), and flours, rice, most vegetables, milk, eggs, and fresh fruit.
2. Paper destined for newspapers, scholarly reviews, or educational, scientific, political, religious, or cultural publications.
3. Glass or ceramic objects having no commercial or artistic value.
4. Bicycle tires and tubes.
5. Cloth of cotton or of raw or bleached hemp.
6. Work shoes.
7. Electric light bulbs under 100 watts.
8. Sewing machines for home use.

Exemption is also provided for goods destined for heads of state, diplomatic personnel, various state and public services, and some charitable organizations (TUFL art. 29). Also exempt are materials employed in the construction of temporary buildings or the construction and repair of industrial factories, farm buildings, and works for agrarian improvement; building materials used by tenants for minor repairs to urban buildings (TUFL art. 30);[71] and, if requested by the owner, materials employed in the reconstruction or substantial remodeling of buildings destroyed or damaged by war.[72] Small quantities of beverages and materials for their manufacture (TUFL art. 3), and small quantities of perfume and certain foodstuffs,[73] may be brought into a commune by hand free of tax. Until 1967, the communal administrations may grant total or partial exemptions to enterprises which provide for the installation, transformation, enlargement, or reactivation of technically organized industrial factories in southern and insular Italy, the operation of which they assume.[74] The law also exempts used movable property belonging to families already resident in a commune or moving into it (TUFL art. 29).

Meats prepared in qualified establishments and destined for export or for further processing by businesses in the commune in which the establishment is located or in other communes are exempt (TUFL art. 30). Goods exported abroad are not subject to the consumption taxes, and any tax paid on them can be refunded (TUFL art. 51).

d. RATES AND VALUATION. The rates of tax are established by the Mayor, subject to approval by the Provincial Administrative Board and to formal ratification by the Ministry of Finance (TUFL art. 21). The rates so determined must lie within the limits specified in the schedule issued under the decree (TUFL arts. 22, 95). The rates applicable to a class

---

[71] See CC art. 1609.
[72] D.L.L. 8 March 1945, n. 62, art. 9.
[73] See R.D. 30 April 1936, n. 1138, art. 102; D.L.L. 8 March 1945, n. 62, art. 5.
[74] L. 29 July 1957, n. 634, art. 33.

of goods or commodities may be graduated according to their kind and value. The maximum rates at present apply to all communes, regardless of class.[75]

The values of the taxable goods, to which the rates are applied, are determined annually for homogeneous groups of communes by a provincial committee named by the Prefect and composed of seven members, including the Intendant of Finance and representatives designated by certain public offices. This committee fixes the values of the goods for the various communes or groups of communes in the province on the basis of the average prices of the preceding 12 months (TUFL art. 22).

A single value is not necessarily established for an entire province, as the groups of communes within a single province may differ with respect to "local conditions of production and of business" (TUFL art. 22). Between the capital of the province and the other communes, there usually are considerable differences in the average prices: populated centers have notably different characteristics and sizes. The average values must take account of the differences in value of diverse products included in the same general category of taxable goods. Moreover, the value of a single product of a national manufacturer, sold everywhere at the same price, may vary greatly from commune to commune, because its value must be averaged with those of competing local products whose value may vary in accordance not only with quality but with local market conditions.

When average values have been established, the rates are set; some will be lower than the maximum set by the law and others equal to it. On the basis of the average values and the rates, the commune establishes in a concrete figure the amount of the tax per unit of measure—applicable for the year beginning on the following 1 January. Therefore, from a scheme which is predominantly one of an ad valorem tax, a scheme of tax per unit of measure results. The amounts of tax are listed in a guidebook (*prontuario*) used by the agents charged with assessment of the tax.

The fixed maximum rate for alcoholic beverages having the strongest proof is L. 150 per liter. Fixed maximum rates are also provided for low-heat gas and for electricity. Other maximum rates range from 1.5% on certain foods to 15% on perfumes and furs.

Luxury goods are generally taxed at higher rates than raw materials or goods for normal consumption. Thus, the maximum rate is 3% on biscuits and similar products of ordinary quality, but 10% on biscuits and candy intended for luxury consumption. Electric energy is taxed at L. 10 per kilowatt-hour and gas at the rate of L. 1.5 per cubic meter.

---

[75] L. 2 July 1952, n. 703, art. 24; L. 18 December 1959, n. 1079, art. 1. See also LPC art. 306, substituted by D.P.R. 19 August 1954, n. 968, art. 3.

For building materials, the rate is 8% of the value. For meats of all kinds, the rate is 4%. For nonalcoholic beverages, the rate ranges from 10% to 25% of the value. For fine furniture, the rate is 10%, and for ordinary furniture, 5%. For refrigerators, it is 4%; for phonographs and radios, 10%; for textiles and clothing goods, 4%. These rates can be increased by 50% of their amount when the commune cannot meet its expenditures after having applied the rates on the "extra-schedule" goods.

e. ASSESSMENT AND PAYMENT. The theoretical basis of taxability is the entry of goods into a commune for the purpose of consumption or use therein. The tax on alcoholic beverages is payable at the time of sale by the wholesaler or producer, or on consumption by the wholesaler and his family; if the sale is to consumers, the tax is payable by the whole-saler, and if the sale is to a retailer, the tax is payable by the retailer (TUFL art. 32). Beverages brought in from other communes or from abroad are taxed in the commune in which they are consumed (TUFL art. 35).

The tax on meat is payable when the animals are slaughtered; meat coming from other communes or from abroad is taxed in the same manner as beverages (TUFL art. 37). Gas for lighting and electricity are taxed at the time of consumption, by assessment against the producer, who has a right of recovery from the consumer (TUFL art. 38). Building construction materials are taxed on the basis of metric calculation; the tax is assessed on the basis of completed work (TUFL art. 39).

In the case of certain beverages and of cheese and dairy products, and of other goods for which such treatment is authorized by the Minister of Finance, local regulations may provide for payment of the tax by the wholesaler every 15 days on the basis of a register (TUFL art. 42). The tax on mailed packages, plus a collection fee of 5% of the tax, is paid by the addressee (TUFL art. 46). Durable goods whose arrival in the commune of final consumption is easy to check (such as furniture, radios, and refrigerators) are taxed in the commune of final consumption rather than in the commune of purchase.

Goods that enter a commune for purposes other than final consumption or use must be accompanied by a consignment note (*bolletta di accompagnamento*) specifying the origin and destination of the goods, their quantity, kind, and typical commercial denomination if there is one (TUFL arts. 35, 40). If the consignment note does not show receipt of the communal consumption tax, the goods must be taxed. A consignment note is not necessary, however, if the goods are (1) accompanied by a note verifying payment of the tax in another commune; (2) carried by hand by travelers in quantities not exceeding prescribed limits; (3) certain beverages and foodstuffs, sent other than by parcel post, in quantities not exceeding certain limits; (4) fresh fish, not limited in weight; or (5) sent by parcel post (TUFL art. 40).

In addition, all wholesale merchants of goods subject to tax are required to keep a register of "loading and unloading" and to obtain a special license (the issuance of which is a means of checking the fulfillment of the duty to keep the register) (TUFL arts. 33, 40). In the case of a transfer of goods to a retail merchant in the same commune, the latter is immediately liable for the tax (TUFL arts. 32, 33). In the case of a transfer to a retail merchant in another commune, it is necessary to issue a consignment note (except as noted above). In the case of a transfer to another wholesale merchant in another commune, the note must accompany the goods, and the transfer must be inscribed in the register of the wholesaler who receives the goods (TUFL art. 35). Transfers to another wholesaler in the same commune are governed by particular regulations, case by case (TUFL art. 34). Finally, in the case of sale to a consumer, the wholesaler is immediately liable for the tax if the transfer takes place in the same commune, or to issue a consignment note (except as noted above) if the goods are sent to another commune (TUFL arts. 32, 35).

A traveler is required to declare goods which he carries with him and which are taxable in the communes through which he is traveling (TUFL art. 40). In providing with a consignment note goods which are sent, the commune of origin is required to inform the commune of destination thereof (TUFL art. 35). When a vehicle enters a commune carrying objects which are taxable, it must stop at the tollhouse (*casello daziario*) and make a report of the goods transferred. The absence of a consignment note where one is prescribed is an infraction of the consumption tax regulations, punishable by pecuniary penalties. If the person produces the note and shows that the goods are in transit, payment of tax does not take place. If an enterprise transports several goods of different types into various communes, each type transported must be supplied with a separate consignment note; and, in each commune, it is necessary to specify which goods are to remain there and which are in transit.

Payment by annual fee (*abbonamento*) has been introduced for some goods. The Communal Council may authorize collection under an *abbonamento* agreement made with individual taxpayers and may provide for collection by general obligatory annual fee in the case of the taxes on candy, cocoa, and chocolate, and other goods if circumstances render collection of tax by the ordinary method difficult (TUFL art. 44). The settlement of controversies regarding the annual fee is within the jurisdiction of the Communal Commission for Local Taxes; an appeal may be made to the special section for local taxes of the Provincial Administrative Board, and further appeal may be made to the Minister of

Finance on questions of legitimacy (1/4.10j). Payment by annual fee occurs by *forfait* on the basis of a presumed movement of goods.

Provision is made for refunds of overpayments of tax (TUFL art. 50); of tax paid on goods exported abroad (TUFL art. 51); of tax paid by schedule on meat taken into another commune after slaughter if a new tax is paid by schedule in the other commune (TUFL art. 52); and of tax paid by schedule on other goods taken to a retail business in another commune if a new tax is paid by schedule in the other commune (TUFL art. 53).

f. ADMINISTRATION AND COLLECTION. Two methods are used to assess and collect the consumption taxes: direct management by the communal administration (TUFL arts. 71-75) and concession in *appalto* to private firms (arts. 76-89). In the case of direct management (*gestione diretta* or *gestione in economia*), the tax is assessed and collected by public officials employed by the governmental body endowed with the power of imposition. In the case of collection under *appalto*, on the other hand, the local government determines the taxable values and the rates, but entrusts the functions of assessment and collection to private "excisemen" (*gabellieri*). The *appalto* system is used primarily by those communes which lack the financial means and the administrative personnel necessary to form an efficient organization for direct management.[76] In some instances, however, use of the *appalto* system is not a choice to be made by the commune; the Prefect, in concurrence with the Provincial Administrative Board, may compel a commune to collect taxes by *appalto* if he considers direct management unsuitable to the needs of the commune (TUFL art. 93).

The system of collection in *appalto* is divided into two fundamental types: fixed-rent *appalto* (*a canone fisso*) and fee *appalto* (*ad aggio*). The fixed-rent system is generally adopted by the communes with the weakest finances, in particular the small agricultural communes, because it guarantees in advance a certain yield: the commune receives from the firm a fixed amount at *forfait*, and the firm then collects from the taxpayer as much as possible.[77] The main disadvantage of this system is that while efficient management increases the yield of the tax, the increase flows not into the public treasury, but into the hands of the *appaltatore*.

Under fee *appalto*, the commune pays the firm collecting the tax a percentage of the tax collected, as compensation. The commission-basis of this compensation stimulates the firm to levy the highest possible

---

[76] Even populous communes resort to *appalto*, especially in southern Italy, where only four or five communes, among them capitals of provinces, use direct management. Naples, which has one million inhabitants, uses the *appalto* system. There are also conspicuous cases of *appalto* management in the north; Florence is one example.

[77] Besides the fee and fixed-rent systems, there is also a combination system of a fee and a guaranteed minimum return to the commune (TUFL art. 86).

amount on the taxpayer. If the rates of tax are increased, the collection fee on the increased proceeds is 4%. If new taxes are instituted, the fee on the increased proceeds is limited to between one fifth and one third of that established in the *appalto* contract already in effect, but may not be less than 4% in any case (TUFL art. 80). In actuality, this fee is often as high or higher than 15% of the proceeds.

The contract of *appalto* is generally awarded through a competition in which each firm offers its services, reducing its percentage fee or increasing the fixed rent that it offers. For fee *appalto*, the "award of the management" takes place through private bidding among persons or firms "who have an adequate organization in the matter, and who give full assurance of honest administration through solvency, correctness, and technical competence" (TUFL art. 86). "Private bidding" consists of inviting particular firms to compete; it does not permit everyone interested to enter the competition. Furthermore, when the bidding becomes fruitless, or when certain reasons make it advisable to dispense with the bidding, the Prefect can authorize the award of management on fee through private agreements (TUFL art. 86). Thus, the possibility of competition can be excluded entirely.

The *appaltatore* awarded management assumes, for the five years of its contract, all of the rights and duties of the commune toward the taxpayer, and the powers of its agents are equal for tax purposes to those of the communal officers. During the year following the termination of the *appalto*, it retains fiscal preferences for the collection of consumption taxes in arrears (TUFL art. 78). On the demand of the Mayor, the Prefect, after consulting the Provincial Administrative Board, can authorize the commune to confirm for another five years the appointment of the *appaltatore* in office, provided that the conditions of the new contract are not in any respect more burdensome for the commune than the contract in force (TUFL art. 88).

The *Testo unico* of local finance offers other solutions to the problem of collection faced by communes with weak administration. One is the association (*consorzio*) of several communes for the collection of taxes through direct management; the communes do not have to lie within the boundaries of the same province (TUFL art. 71). However, the smaller communes often fear that the association would result in the loss of their autonomy in favor of the larger communes. Another possibility open to the smallest communes is, with the authorization of the Prefect, the collection through agreements made with businesses and private persons for the compulsory payment of an annual fee (*abbonamento*) (TUFL art. 44).

g. APPEALS. Administrative appeals regarding the assessment and collection of the consumption taxes are made to the Mayor in the first instance, then to the Prefect, and finally to the Minister of Finance. The decision of the Minister of Finance may be appealed to the courts within three months of notification (TUFL art. 91).

h. PENALTIES. Places where taxable goods are manufactured, deposited, or sold are subject to supervision by officers of the tax administration (TUFL art. 54); agents of the local tax offices have the power to take possession of the goods involved and the containers or vehicles in which they are transported (TUFL art. 62).

Severe penalties are provided for evasion of the consumption taxes. Acts committed with the intent to avoid payment of the tax result in a mulct (*multa*) (13/7.1) of from two to twenty times the tax due, in addition to payment of the tax itself. A third violation can lead to the closing of the taxpayer's business for a period of from 15 days to six months (TUFL art. 55); a fourth violation can result in imprisonment for up to three months (TUFL art. 56). Evasions of this type of tax are not contraventions, but delicts, which are infractions of particular gravity in the penal law (13/7.1). There is, however, the possibility of converting a mulct into a fine (TUFL art. 59), which is the penalty for offenses of lesser gravity.

Fifty percent of the receipts from pecuniary penalties goes to the commune, even if management is by *appalto*; 15% to the profit of the group of agents of the consumption taxes; 5% to the state; and 30% to a special fund for rewards conferred on persons who have contributed to the discovery and assessment of the crime (TUFL art. 70).

4/5.9 Local Visitors Tax

The local visitors tax (*imposta di soggiorno*) is imposed in health and tourist resorts, the complete list of which is established by a decree of the Minister of Internal Affairs, in concert with the Minister of Finance and the Minister of Public Instruction.[78] The tax is payable by any person taking temporary lodging in a hotel, boardinghouse (*pensione*), inn, cure establishment, or sanatorium, and, except as provided in the interministerial decree, by any person living temporarily for more than five days in a villa, apartment, furnished room, or other lodgings. Exemptions are granted to persons decorated for military valor, war invalids, diplomatic personnel, state employees on official business, priests in a commune for their ministry, members of religious orders living in ecclesiastical brotherhoods, persons visiting in houses owned by them,

---

[78] R.D.L. 24 November 1938, n. 1926, art. 1; D. Intermin. 25 June 1940; D.M. 10 August 1952. The visitors tax is systematized in the 1938 decree-law, hereinafter cited: "IS."

For further discussion of this tax, see Rastello, "Aspetti tributari del turismo," *Temi trib.*, 1963, 5.

children under three years of age, students, patients in public hospitals
and welfare institutions, persons on business for enterprises, and others
(IS art. 7).

The tax is imposed at fixed rates per person per day, graduated from
L. 10 (inns) to L. 200 (luxury-class hotels).[79] Fixed rates per person
are provided for an entire stay of more than seven days but less than
120 days in villas, apartments, furnished rooms, and other lodgings.[80]
The tax is reduced to one half for servants, children under 12 years of
age, and members of families having not less than five dependent children
whose parents visit in the commune for health or bathing cures (IS art.
4). Reductions are also provided for large groups of persons organized
by authorized tourist and travel bureaus, or by scholastic institutions for
purposes of instruction (IS art. 4).

The proceeds of the tax are divided between the national agency for
the protection and assistance of maternity and infancy and various provincial and local agencies concerned with the encouragement of tourism
(IS art. 7).

A special "health contribution" (*contributo di cura*), based on income
subject to the local tax on industry, commerce, arts, and professions
(ICAP), is imposed on persons who conduct business or professional
activities in health or tourist resorts (2/2.9).

4/5.10 Local License Taxes

The communes impose license taxes (*imposte di licenza*), which are
based on the presumed free-market rental value of the premises listed
below (TUFL art. 183).[81]

1. *Hotels, inns, boardinghouses, restaurants, snack bars, and other places
   in which alcoholic or nonalcoholic beverages are sold.* The premises on
   whose value the tax is determined are limited to the area in which food
   and drink normally are consumed. The rates range from 10% to 20% for
   establishments in which alcoholic beverages are sold at retail, and from
   5% to 7.5% for establishments in which beverages no stronger than wine
   are sold at retail (TUFL arts. 184, 185).[82]
2. *Bathing establishments, automobile or carriage repair shops, and stables.*
   The rate is 4% of the rental value (TUFL art. 187).[83]
3. *Public dance halls, billiard rooms, and halls for other legally permitted
   games.* The rates range from 10% to 20% of the rental value (TUFL
   art. 189).[84]

The owners of cafés, bars, and other establishments in which *espresso*
coffee is sold and consumed must pay to the commune an annual tax for

---

[79] L. 4 March 1958, n. 174.
[80] L. 4 March 1958, n. 174.
[81] As substituted by L. 2 July 1952, n. 703, art. 33.
[82] As modified by L. 2 July 1952, n. 703, art. 34.
[83] As substituted by L. 2 July 1952, n. 703, art. 36.
[84] As substituted by L. 2 July 1952, n. 703, art. 38.

each *espresso* coffee machine, in addition to the ICAP or *imposta di patente* (2/2.9), if imposed (TUFL art. 190).[85] The rates are determined according to the class of the commune and the size of the machine.

4/5.11 Local Fee for the Occupation of Public Spaces and Areas

A fee is payable to the commune for the occupation of public spaces and areas along streets and avenues and in squares and public markets; private areas serving public travel; and spaces above and below ground (TUFL art. 192). The fee is graduated according to the area occupied. The space or area is classified by the communal or provincial administration (TUFL art. 194). The rate schedule determined by the province or commune is subject to approval by the Provincial Administrative Board. Special rates may be provided for temporary occupation. The taxpayer may free himself permanently from the burden of the tax on balconies, verandas, and other permanent structures by making a single payment of 20 times the annual tax (TUFL art. 195). The law provides special rate schedules for electric lines,[86] for subsurface pipes and conduits, and for fuel pumps and tobacco vending machines (TUFL arts. 197, 198).[87]

Exemption is made for poles, wires, and tunnels belonging to the state administration or used by the state for telegraph, telephone, or the transmission of electric energy; mailboxes; timetables for public transportation; traffic signs, clocks for the convenience of the public, flagpoles, and miscellaneous other structures (TUFL art. 200).

4/5.12 Local Tax on Signs

All signs, inscriptions, notices, and the like exhibited within developed areas (other than ports and the public domain) are subject to an annual local tax (TUFL art. 201). The rates are fixed within a maximum and a minimum established by law for each class of commune (TUFL art. 202) [88] and are graduated by the Mayor according to the importance of the streets on which the signs are exhibited or from which they are visible (TUFL art. 204). Communes recognized as places of cure, sojourn, or tourism may be authorized by the Provincial Administrative Board to impose the rate schedule provided for communes one class higher (TUFL art. 203).

4/5.13 Local Fee for Public Weights and Measures and the Renting of Public Counters

The communes are authorized to carry on public weighing and measuring and the renting of counters for a fee; this authorization does not

---

[85] As modified by D.L.P. 29 March 1947, n. 177, art. 16, and L. 2 July 1952, n. 703, art. 31.

[86] D.M. 26 February 1933; L. 2 July 1952, n. 703, art. 39.

[87] L. 2 July 1952, n. 703, art. 39.

[88] L. 2 July 1952, n. 703, art. 31.

preclude private persons from using their own weights, measures, and counters in the sale of their own merchandise, or from the limited, free furnishing of these services to private persons (TUFL art. 209). The rates are determined by the Mayor, subject to the approval of the Provincial Administrative Board, after hearing the opinion of the Chamber of Commerce (TUFL art. 212).

4/5.14   Local Fee for the Circulation of Animal-Drawn Vehicles

The circulation of animal-drawn vehicles on public streets or on streets traveled by the public is subject to an obligatory annual fee levied for the benefit of the provinces, communes, and associations of communes (TUFL art. 214). The fee is based on the type of vehicle and the gross weight; the maximum that may be charged is L. 4,000.

The tax is collected by the provincial administration and is divided between the province and the communes in proportion to the expenditures sustained by them for the maintenance of their respective streets (TUFL art. 215). The tax is collected by the communal collectors through the sale of metal countersigns which are affixed to the vehicle as proof of payment of tax (TUFL arts. 216, 217). Exemption is provided for vehicles of certain government, church, and diplomatic officials, of certain public entities, and of the armed forces and other public services; for agricultural carts and farm machines that use public roads only to go by the shortest route from one farm to another of the same enterprise; and for vehicles kept on deposit for purposes of sale (TUFL art. 220).

4/6.   State Fiscal Monopolies

4/6.1   In General

The fiscal monopolies are a form of consumption tax, collected by the state on the production or sale of certain goods through a monopoly enterprise. The monopolies are managed by a semiautonomous agency of the national government (1/4.5) under the Ministry of Finance. The sale prices of monopoly goods are proposed by the Minister of Finance and established by a decree of the President of the Republic, after hearing the Council of Ministers.[89] The decree specifies the share of each price to be received by the supplier, the monopoly administration, and the seller; the balance constitutes the tax paid to the state.

4/6.2   Salt

The extraction, processing, collecting, introduction, and sale of salt are subject to a state monopoly.[90] With certain exceptions, salt may

---

[89] L. 19 December 1958, n. 1085, art. 1.

[90] L. 17 July 1942, n. 907, art. 1. This is the law on the monopoly of salt and tobacco; it is hereinafter cited: "LMST."

be produced or introduced in Italy only by the state monopoly administration. Salt can be sold only at the prices established for each grade by presidential decree (LMST art. 19).[91] Special prices may be established for salt destined for certain industrial purposes and for salt used in the preparation of products which are to be exported.

On the importation of salt, a customs duty is also payable.[92]

4/6.3 Tobacco

The manufacture, preparation, introduction, and sale of tobacco and tobacco products are subject to a state monopoly; the production, manufacture, preparation, importation, and sale of tobacco substitutes are forbidden (LMST art. 45). Private persons may be permitted to cultivate tobacco in certain cases as provided by law (LMST art. 45).

The monopoly administration has the power to cultivate tobacco directly and to grant concessions for the cultivation of tobacco for supplying state factories or for export (LMST art. 49). Except in specified cases, tobacco may be manufactured or imported only by the monopoly administration. Tobacco and tobacco products can be sold only at prices established by presidential decree (LMST art. 54).[93]

A customs duty is also payable on imported tobacco.[94]

4/6.4 Cigarette Packages and Papers

The importation and sale of cigarette packages and papers are reserved to the state, and sale is entrusted to the state monopoly administration.[95] A special license from the monopoly administration is required for the manufacture of cigarette packages and papers either for supplying the monopoly or for export.[96] The prices for the sale of these goods to the public are established by the Minister of Finance.[97]

4/6.5 Matches

A license is required for the manufacture of matches;[98] and matches can be sold only at the established price.[99] Matches are exempt from

---

[91] D.P. 14 December 1948, n. 1421; D.M. 22 April 1958; L. 19 December 1958, n. 1085, art. 1.

[92] L. 19 December 1958, n. 1085, art. 2. See also L. 11 April 1959, n. 137. Regarding salt imported from other member countries of the EEC, see D.P.R. 9 March 1961, n. 390.

[93] See L. 19 December 1958, n. 1085, art. 2; D.P.R. 18 April 1959, n. 167.

[94] L. 19 December 1958, n. 1085, art. 2.

[95] R.D.L. 13 January 1936, n. 70, art. 1; converted in L. 4 June 1936, n. 1342. Regarding products imported from other member countries of the EEC, see D.P.R. 9 March 1961, n. 390.

[96] R.D.L. 13 January 1936, n. 70, art. 3.

[97] R.D.L. 13 January 1936, n. 70, art. 11.

[98] L. 8 August 1895, n. 486, Annex E, art. 3.

[99] R.D.L. 5 April 1925, n. 396, art. 1.

the consumption taxes,[100] but those made of wax or wood are subject to a manufacturing tax and corresponding border surtax.[101] The prices for the sale of matches to the public and the rates of tax are established every two years in a decree of the Minister of Finance.[102]

4/6.6 Cigarette Lighters and Flints

A fixed fee is due on every lighter flint made or imported for consumption in Italy, independently of the import duty.[103] A similar fee on lighters and on replacement parts was abolished in 1956 and replaced by an annual fee of L. 300 for the possession of lighters.[104] Annual collection is made through the sale of a countersign mark which the user places on the lighter or on any document of personal identification.[105]

4/6.7 Lotto and Lotteries

Public lotto games are held under the supervision of the Intendants of Finance.[106] Five winning numbers out of a total of 90 numbers are chosen each week at public drawings in specified cities (LLP arts. 3, 4). Tickets are sold in denominations of L. 150, L. 200, L. 300, and L. 500 (LLP art. 8).

Lotteries are prohibited except by authorization of special laws for national lotteries, enacted on the proposal of the Minister of Finance (LLP art. 39).[107] The conduct of authorized lotteries is entrusted to the Inspector General of Lotto and Lotteries. The Intendant of Finance may, however, authorize lotteries to be conducted by public entities for certain welfare or cultural purposes (LLP art. 40).[108] On operations of lotteries authorized by the Intendants of Finance, a lottery fee of 10% of the gross receipts is payable if the gross receipts exceed L. 100,000 (LLP art. 41). Lottery tickets and lotto drawing slips are exempt from the stamp tax (4/4.2d). Prizes won in national lotteries are exempt from the tax on income from movable wealth (LLP art. 39), but are subject to the complementary tax (10/7.1).

The Ministry of Finance can authorize the communes, provinces, and other public entities to add prizes, to be awarded by the drawing of

[100] R.D.L. 5 April 1925, n. 396, art. 3.
[101] R.D. 11 March 1923, n. 560, arts. 1, 7.
[102] R.D. 11 March 1923, n. 560, art. 5.
[103] R.D.L. 26 February 1930, n. 105, art. 1. The fixed fees and prices of flints are established by D.P. 10 March 1950, n. 52.
[104] L. 11 January 1956, n. 2, arts. 1, 2.
[105] L. 11 January 1956, n. 2, art. 3.
[106] R.D.L. 19 October 1938, n. 1933, art. 1, converted in L. 5 June 1939, n. 973. This decree-law is the reform of the laws on public lotto; it is hereinafter cited: "LLP."
[107] Substituted by D.L.P. 27 June 1946, n. 122, art. 1.
[108] Substituted by L. 15 July 1950, n. 585, art. 2.

lots, to loans contracted for works of public utility, provided that the amounts so destined do not exceed one fifth of the annual interest and provided that the loans are represented by bonds meeting certain requirements (LLP art. 42).

Contests and prize operations of any kind intended to favor or promote specific products, or having only partly commercial ends, including the sale of goods to the public with offers of prizes or gifts in any form, must be authorized in advance (LLP art. 43). An offer contained in an advertisement of prizes to be awarded to participants on designation by lot, or in regard to skill or other defined requisites, is considered a prize contest. An offer of prizes to all those buying a certain quantity of merchandise from one firm and an offer of gifts to those purchasing certain merchandise are considered prize operations (LLP art. 44). Prize contests and operations are subject to lottery fees and fixed license fees (LLP arts. 45-49). Exemption is provided for contests and operations in which the prizes consist of national lottery tickets, or of lottery bets, under conditions determined by the administration. Also exempt are contests and operations conducted by savings banks to encourage and diffuse the habit of saving. In both cases, authorization must be obtained in advance from the Minister of Finance (LLP art. 50).

The fees must be paid before issuance of the authorization by the Minister of Finance or the Intendant of Finance.

4/7. Fees for Governmental Concessions

4/7.l In General

The fees for governmental concessions (*tasse sulle concessioni governative*) were recently codified in a *Testo unico*.[109] These taxes existed before the unification of Italy and were incorporated into the fiscal system of the unified state.

The fees on governmental concessions are divided into two parts. The first and more important part consists of fees which are applied to a wide variety of concessions, authorizations, acts, declarations, and administrative measures (TUCG art. 1).[110] The second part consists of office fees (*diritti di segreteria*), collected by the Registry Offices for the execution of acts in public form in the ministries, state administrative

---

[109] Approved by D.P.R. 1 March 1961, n. 121. This decree is the *Testo unico* of the laws in force regarding fees for governmental concessions; it is hereinafter cited: "TUCG."

[110] In granting a "concession," the state removes a prohibition and permits the exercise by another of an activity which it considers its own; in making an "authorization," the state allocates the right to carry on an activity which it does not consider its own. On this subject, see Mortati, *Istituzioni di diritto pubblico* 310-311. The concession, therefore, in principle represents something more than the authorization, and, at the same time, governmental intervention is more penetrating in an activity subject to concession than in an activity subject to authorization.

units, and public offices, for copies of such acts, and for research in the archives (TUCG art. 1). These fees retain the character of compensation for the cost of drafting the documents involved; the maximum fee is L. 50 (TUCG Table Annex B).

The fees on governmental concessions are levied on the basis of the transactions stipulated in the documents and thus, from a technical point of view, are to be distinguished from the stamp tax (4/4.2), which is levied on the basis of the documents themselves. The remainder of this discussion concerns the part of the tax relating to concessions and authorizations.

The acts for which the fees on governmental concessions are due, in addition to any stamp tax which may be applicable, are classified under the headings listed below (TUCG Table Annex A, Schedule).

1. Citizenship and civil status.
2. Juridical persons.
3. Heraldry, titles, coats of arms, decorations, and honors.
4. Hygiene, health, and zootechny.
5. Passports and legalizations.
6. Bearing of arms, hunting, fishing.
7. Public security and order.
8. Commerce and industry (various inspections, registrations, and authorizations).
9. Industrial property (patents, trademarks, and the like).
10. Intellectual property (copyrights).
11. Public works and mining.
12. Public waters.
13. Beach and seacoast.
14. Land, river, and maritime transport services.
15. Deposit and loan banks, public debt, and social security institutions.
16. Professions and arts.
17. Telegraphic, telephonic, and radiophonic communications; radioelectric equipment and materials; broadcasting.
18. Accounting machines (for sale of tickets to public shows and the like).

Some of the fees retain their original character of payment for the administrative services connected with the granting of the concessions and authorizations. For example, the fees for authorizations to produce mineral water, carbonated soft drinks, and various food products such as preserved meats and bread are primarily justified by the services of health and sanitary inspection carried out by the public administration in connection with the production of those goods. Similarly, authorizations are required for many activities involving some form of inspection or supervision for reasons of public safety or public security: in this category are declarations of inhabitability of new houses and authorizations or licenses for elevators, cinemas, entertainments, fairs and markets, printing, driving motor vehicles, bearing arms, and hunting and fishing, to list a few.

In other cases, however, the fees have become high enough to constitute a form of transaction tax on the activities authorized. Thus, the fees for opening and operating pharmacies are determined in accordance with a rough estimate of the probable gain to be realized from the exercise of an activity which is permitted to a limited number of persons. The fees for insurance activities, credit activities, and a variety of other occupations serve a similar function. The fees for authorizations to open and operate hotels and restaurants, cinemas, and establishments for the sale of alcoholic beverages also serve in part as taxes on what may be regarded as voluptuary expenditures.

During the corporative period of the fascist regime, most economic activities were subjected to licensing, and the concession fees were often designed to tax monopoly yields permitted by the government in order to give a certain arrangement to the industrial structure. Although this course of economic policy is no longer followed, some of the restrictions remain in the form of business licenses. The taxation of gains resulting from activities of a monopoly character also figures in the fees for concessions to operate bus lines, for patents and copyrights, for concessions to carry out public works, and for furnishing supplies or services to the state under contracts of *appalto*.

Finally, some fees constitute payment for the right to use public resources—for example, fees for mineral exploration and mining concessions (which are in addition to the royalties (*canoni*) provided by the mining laws for the exploitation of mines); fees for finding and using public waters; and fees for occupying lakeshores, seashores, and beaches.

The total yield of the fees is only slightly less than that of the complementary progressive tax on income (1/6.7d).

4/7.2 Rates

The fees are levied at specific rates, which are quite high in some cases. The acts for which the fees are due are very numerous; a few examples are listed below by way of illustration.

1. *Pharmacies.* The fees for authorizations to open pharmacies are graduated according to the number of inhabitants in the commune. The rates range from L. 20,000 for pharmacies in communes of not more than 5,000 inhabitants to L. 800,000 for pharmacies in communes of more than 500,000 inhabitants. The annual operating fee is one fifth of the opening fee (TUCG Table Annex A, Schedule, art. 15).
2. *Establishments producing brand medicines.* The fees for authorization to produce brand medicines are graduated in accordance with the number of nonadministrative employees, from L. 40,000 for a factory employing less than five workers to L. 1 million for a factory employing more than 500 workers (TUCG Table Annex A, Schedule, art. 16).
3. *Establishments producing carbonated beverages.* The maximum fee for the authorization of the Ministry of Health to open establishments for

the production of mineral water, applicable to those producing artificial mineral water, is L. 150,000; the maximum annual operating fee is L. 37,500 (TUCG Table Annex A, Schedule, art. 22). The maximum fee for the authorization to open carbonated soft drink plants, applicable to those employing more than 100 workers, is L. 80,000, and the annual operating fee is one half of that figure (TUCG Table Annex A, Schedule, art. 24).

4. *Declarations of inhabitability of new houses.* The fee for the Mayor's declaration of inhabitability of new houses is L. 5,000 per room for luxury houses, L. 200 for popular and low-cost housing and rural houses, and L. 1,000 for other houses (TUCG Table Annex A, Schedule, art. 29).

5. *Hotels and restaurants.* Fees for the authorization issued by the Mayor for the opening of hotels, restaurants, inns, day hotels, rooms for rent, bars, cafés, and taverns, as well as for the sale of nonalcoholic beverages in such establishments, vary according to the population of the communes in which they are operated; hotels and restaurants are, in addition, differentiated by classes which reflect the rates they are permitted to charge their customers. The fees for the authorization to open and the annual inspection of the authorization range from L. 1,000 for small accommodations in communes of not more than 10,000 inhabitants to L. 90,000 for luxury hotels and restaurants regardless of location (TUCG Table Annex A, Schedule, art. 30).

6. *Cinema theaters.* The fee for the license issued by the police to open and operate cinema theaters varies with the class of the theater and the population of the commune. The maximum opening fee is L. 600,000, with a maximum annual license-inspection fee of L. 90,000 (TUCG Table Annex A, Schedule, art. 75).

7. *Establishments selling alcoholic beverages.* Establishments selling alcoholic beverages are differentiated according to category, the strength of the beverages they are permitted to sell, and the population of the commune in which they are located. The annual fees payable by establishments selling wine range, for example, from L. 3,000 to L. 9,000 in communes having not more than 10,000 inhabitants, and from L. 15,000 to L. 180,000 in communes having more than 500,000 inhabitants (TUCG Table Annex A, Schedule, art. 83). The fees are considerably higher for establishments selling "superalcoholic" beverages—beverages having an alcoholic content exceeding 21% by volume (TUCG Table Annex A, Schedule, art. 84).

8. *Inspection of accounting books.* The fee for the inspection of accounting books (CC art. 2215) is graduated according to the number of pages, with a maximum of L. 1,400 for each book (TUCG Table Annex A, Schedule, art. 108).

9. *Registration of enterprises.* The annual fee for inscription in the register of enterprises is L. 6,000 (TUCG Table Annex A, Schedule, art. 110).

10. *Registration of companies.* Fees must be paid for the inscription in the register of enterprises of the bylaws of companies and acts increasing their capital. The maximum fee is L. 16,000, for inscription of the bylaws of a corporation with a capital exceeding L. 2 million, plus L. 3,000 for each additional million or fraction thereof (TUCG Table Annex A, Schedule, art. 111).

11. *Patents.* The documents necessary for a patent application are taxed at modest fixed rates; a graduated tax is also due for the printing and

publication of the description of the invention, ranging from L. 4,500 (not more than 10 pages) to L. 120,000 (more than 100 pages). The fee for keeping a patent in force increases from L. 1,000 in the first year to L. 35,000 in the fifteenth year (TUCG Table Annex A, Schedule, art. 136).

12. *Public works.* The fee is L. 5,000 for a concession for public works whose aggregate cost does not exceed L. 500,000; L. 10,000 for public works whose aggregate cost exceeds L. 500,000 but not L. 10 million; and L. 10,000, plus L. 1,500 for each additional million or fraction thereof, for works whose aggregate cost exceeds L. 10 million (TUCG Table Annex A, Schedule, art. 146). Additional fees are provided for certain classes of works.

13. *Extraction of petroleum and natural gas.* The fee for a permit for petroleum extraction is L. 40,000 (TUCG Table Annex A, Schedule, art. 163); the fee for a concession to extract oil or gas is L. 80,000 (TUCG Table Annex A, Schedule, art. 166).

4/7.3   Assessment and Collection

Assessment and collection of the fees for the various authorizations are governed by special rules for the various classes of acts (4/7.1). Payment is made either at the Registry Office (the ordinary manner) or by purchasing from the tax administration a special mark which must be presented to the appropriate office for cancellation, in the manner provided for the stamp tax (4/4.2f), when the document in question is issued (TUCG art. 3). Except as provided in the rules laid down for the various classes of acts, the fees are not due from entities which are authorized under particular laws to pay the fees and indirect taxes on transactions by the annual-fee method (*abbonamento*) (TUCG art. 4). The fees for acts involving entities treated for tax purposes in the same manner as state administrative units, the administration of the fund for worship, or persons entitled to free legal assistance (*gratuito patrocinio*) are reserved on account (*prenotate a debito*) (TUCG art. 5) in the same manner as under the registration taxes (15/7.2c). Fees for judicial acts required in executory proceedings for the collection of the direct taxes are reduced by one half and must be reserved on account and recovered from the taxpayer losing the case.

Omitted or late payment of the tax affects the efficacy of the act. The concessions, authorizations, acts, declarations, and administrative measures have no effect if payment of the fee has not been made; when the measure has temporary duration and the payment of the fee is late, however, the efficacy of the measure is limited to the time remaining from the date of payment to the expiration of the time limit of the measure (TUCG art. 2). Thus the taxpayer is induced to pay the tax to avoid loss of the permission which he wants.

4/7.4 Appeals

Administrative appeals on questions regarding the application of the fees are made to the Intendant of Finance, whose decision on a matter involving fees and surcharges exceeding L. 50,000 may be appealed to the Minister of Finance (TUCG art. 14). Final administrative decisions may be appealed to the courts within six months (TUCG art. 15).

4/8.   Customs Duties

4/8.1 In General

Although the present customs law (*legge doganale*) was enacted in 1940,[111] the rates have recently undergone considerable revision. The duties on imports from other members of the European Economic Community (EEC) have been reduced, and those on imports from countries outside the EEC have been adjusted to approach the Common Market external tariff. In general, there has been a substantial diminution of the customs protection of the Italian economy (1/6.8c).

Customs duties (*diritti doganali*) are due and collectible when goods subject to them pass the customs barrier (*linea doganale*) (LD art. 4). "Customs duties" include all "border duties" (*diritti di confine*) that the Customs Offices are required to collect, not only import and export tolls (*dazi*), but manufacturing surtaxes (4/5.2), monopoly duties (4/6.1), and any other tax or surtax levied for the benefit of the state (LD art. 7).

Since 1945, Italy has imposed no export duties.[112] Exported goods are exempted from internal indirect taxes, such as IGE (14/8.3), the manufacturing taxes (4/5.2), and the communal consumption taxes (4/5.8). However, special taxes on exports may become necessary in trade between Italy and other member countries of the EEC. For example, exports of Italian refrigerators to France rose from 22,000 units in 1961 to 136,000 units in 1962. At the request of France, the EEC Commission authorized France to impose a tax on Italian refrigerators to compensate for the difference between the French and Italian prices unless Italy itself should impose a compensatory tax of its own. This Italy did early in 1963.[113]

4/8.2 Rates

The present rate schedule (*tariffa doganale*) of import duties went into effect on 1 February 1959.[114] The schedule established temporary rates for some commodities, lower than those presently in force, to expire not later than 31 December 1961; the higher permanent rates were applied to imports not covered by reductions or exemptions under the

---

[111] L. 25 September 1940, n. 1424; this law is hereinafter cited: "LD."
[112] See D.L.L. 8 August 1945, n. 498.
[113] D.P.R. 12 February 1963, n. 169.
[114] D.P.R. 26 December 1958, n. 1105, art. 1; this decree is hereinafter cited: "TD."

treaties involving the EEC and other European organizations, by the General Agreement on Tariffs and Trade (GATT), or other customs treaties.

In the rate schedule, the commodities subject to import duty are classified under 99 headings, which in turn are arranged in 21 sections, following the nomenclature established by the treaty signed by Italy at Brussels on 11 January 1951.[115] At present, the rates are all computed ad valorem.

The duties on goods imported from countries which discriminate against Italian exports can be increased by up to 50% of the schedule rates, and, if exempt, such goods can be subjected to a duty of up to 25% of their value; specified foreign goods which are subjected to restrictions if exported abroad from Italy can be subjected to analogous restrictions when imported into Italy.[116] Italy can also increase its import duties to compensate for subsidies granted on the export of the goods from the other country; and on specified goods, to compensate for favored treatment which the exporting country gives to similar goods coming from other countries, as against goods coming from Italy.[117] All such discriminations are established by decree-laws under article 77 of the Constitution (1/3.1c).[118] The government also has the power to introduce compensatory anti-dumping fees against goods whose importation in large quantities "occasions or threatens to occasion notable damage to domestic production or notably impedes the development of domestic production." [119]

The members of the European Economic Community have agreed to reduce their internal tariffs for imports from the Common Market area in steps of 10% on prescribed dates.[120] Under the treaty, the member nations have also agreed to adjust their external tariffs, those applying to imports from nonmember countries, to conform with a common external tariff.

In accordance with the treaty instituting the European Atomic Energy Community (Euratom),[121] Italy has exempted from import duty certain commodities imported from other member countries which are provided with the appropriate certificate issued by the customs administration of the exporting country; goods imported from member countries without certificate and goods imported from other countries are subject

---

[115] Ratified and executed by L. 31 October 1952, n. 1976.

[116] TD, Preliminary Provisions, art. 8.

[117] TD, Preliminary Provisions, arts. 9, 10.

[118] TD, Preliminary Provisions, art. 11.

[119] L. 11 January 1963, n. 39.

[120] Treaty instituting the European Economic Community, signed at Rome, 25 March 1957 (ratified and executed by L. 14 October 1957, n. 1203), art. 14. See also D.P.R. 29 December 1958, n. 1103.

[121] Concluded at Rome, 25 March 1957, ratified and executed by L. 14 October 1957, n. 1203.

to common tariffs.[122] Similar provisions are made for coal and steel commodities imported from members of the European Coal and Steel Community (TD art. 2), pursuant to the treaty establishing that community.[123] Italy is also a party to the General Agreement on Tariffs and Trade (GATT) [124] and to numerous other treaties modifying its customs arrangement with various countries.

4/8.3 Temporary Importation

Temporary importation without duty can be authorized for foreign goods to be processed in a specified manner in Italy, and subsequently exported abroad, or as a special relief for international trade (LD art. 57).[125] Refunds of duty and other border charges paid on raw materials employed in the manufacture of products that are subsequently exported can be allowed on products specified in a presidential decree.[126]

4/8.4 Administration and Procedure

The owner of imported or exported goods must file a declaration within 15 days of the arrival of the goods at maritime customs or border railroad stations, and immediately on the arrival of the goods in other cases (LD arts. 16-19). Ministerial decrees establish the lists of goods for whose importation [127] or exportation [128] authorization is required. On payment of import duties, for which both the owner and the consignee of the goods are liable (LD art. 5), the taxpayer receives an import license (*bolletta di importazione*), without which the goods cannot be imported (LD art. 54).

The resolution of controversies between taxpayer and the customs administration regarding the classification, value, or origin of goods is governed by a special *Testo unico*.[129] The taxpayer can appeal to the Chamber of Commerce (1/5.7) in whose jurisdiction the Customs Office is located; the Chamber can name a board of experts, whose opinion it may accept at its discretion.[130] Further appeal is allowed to the Minister of Finance, who, except in specified cases, must seek the opinion of a

---

[122] D.P.R. 29 December 1958, n. 1104, arts. 1, 2.

[123] Treaty instituting the European Coal and Steel Community, signed at Paris 18 April 1951, ratified and executed by L. 25 June 1952, n. 766.

[124] This agreement, concluded at Geneva, 30 October 1947, and the tariff agreement annexed to Protocol of Annecy of 10 October 1949 were ratified and executed by L. 5 April 1950, n. 295.

[125] Temporary import and re-export are governed by special laws; L. 18 December 1913, n. 1453; L. 11 April 1938, n. 709.

[126] TD, Preliminary Provisions, art. 16.

[127] D.M. 31 October 1962, Table A.

[128] D.M. 28 September 1962.

[129] R.D. 9 April 1911, n. 330; see also TD, Preliminary Provisions, art. 3.

[130] The taxpayer must pay a fee for the services of such experts. See TD, Preliminary Provisions, art. 28; D.M. 1 October 1953.

Consulting College of Customs Experts, the president and members of which are chosen by the Minister of Finance, the Minister of Foreign Commerce, and certain other government officials. The decision of the Minister of Finance is issued in a decree supported by reasons and may or may not be in conformity with the vote of the College of Experts. The determination of the Minister of Finance regarding the classification of goods is final; on questions of law not involving the classification of goods, appeals may be made to the ordinary courts. Clearance of the goods through customs is suspended until a controversy is resolved, unless the duty demanded by the customs administration has been deposited in its entirety, the required report has been made, and samples have been taken for the resolution of the controversy.

4/8.5   Penalties

The penalties provided for contraband by the customs law include mulcts (*multe*) of from two to ten times the amount of the duties due, and, in some cases, imprisonment (LD arts. 97-116). Smaller fines are provided for lesser offenses which constitute contraventions rather than delicts (LD arts. 117-130). Amounts collected as penalties are divided among the Treasury, the persons who assist in the discovery of the violations, and the provident funds to which the persons discovering the violations belong (LD art. 144).

PART II

ANALYSIS OF THE INCOME TAX

The presentation of the income tax of Italy in Part II follows the uniform system adopted by the World Tax Series. This method of presentation does not necessarily follow the system of Italian law. The reader is advised to refer to Chapter 2 for a brief survey of the Italian income tax system as a whole.

CHAPTER 5

CLASSES OF TAXPAYERS

5/1. Individuals

   5/1.1   In General
   5/1.2   Married Persons
   5/1.3   Minors and Other Incompetent Persons
   5/1.4   Other Dependents

5/2. Corporations and Similar Entities

   5/2.1   In General
   5/2.2   Corporations
   5/2.3   Limited Liability Companies
   5/2.4   Limited Partnerships with Shares
   5/2.5   Cooperative Societies
   5/2.6   Mutual Insurance Companies
   5/2.7   Governmental Bodies and Public Enterprises
   5/2.8   Other Entities Taxed As Corporations

5/3. Other Taxpayers

   5/3.1   In General
   5/3.2   General Partnerships
   5/3.3   Simple Limited Partnerships
   5/3.4   Noncommercial Partnerships
   5/3.5   Associations in Participation
   5/3.6   *De Facto* Companies
   5/3.7   Separate Businesses and Activities
   5/3.8   Associations and Foundations
   5/3.9   Estates of Deceased Persons

5/4. Nonresidents

5/5. Tax-Exempt Persons

   5/5.1   Diplomatic Representatives and Employees of Foreign
           Governments
   5/5.2   Clergy

5/5.3   Teachers, Authors, and Inventors
5/5.4   Government Officials and Employees
5/5.5   Religious and Charitable Institutions
5/5.6   Provident Institutions
5/5.7   Educational Institutions
5/5.8   Mutual Aid Societies
5/5.9   Professional Associations
5/5.10 Cooperative Societies
5/5.11 Governmental Bodies and Public Enterprises

5/1. Individuals

5/1.1 In General

The Italian income tax system consists of two types of taxes. The "objective" taxes are based on the possession of immovable property capable of producing income and on the production of income from movable wealth (2/2). The "personal" taxes are based on the taxpayer's possession of income which is subject to the "objective" taxes and of certain other receipts (2/3, 2/4, 6/1.1a).

For all taxpayers, the objective taxes are based on the possession of immovable property in Italy and on the production in Italy of income from movable wealth (11/1.1). Thus, an individual owning immovable property in Italy or exercising an activity in Italy is subject to the appropriate tax on income therefrom, regardless of his citizenship, domicile, or residence. If an individual is domiciled or resident in Italy (11/2.2) or carries on an enterprise formed in Italy (11/2.3a), income from his activities carried on abroad may be considered, under certain conditions, to have been produced in Italy, and thus subjected to the tax on income from movable wealth. If an individual carries on a business enterprise, his income therefrom is assessed under the rules applicable to business enterprises (art. 8) (7/1.2).[1]

The personal tax applicable to individuals is the complementary progressive tax (6/1.1f). An individual's income for purposes of this tax, regardless of his citizenship or residence, includes all income produced in Italy (11/1.1). If an individual is resident in Italy under the tests described at 11/2.2, his income for purposes of the complementary tax also includes income produced abroad which is consumed by him in Italy or which is nontaxable in another country by virtue of an international agreement.

For purposes of the tax on income from movable wealth, an individual is entitled to a personal allowance (art. 89) (12/1.4b), and to a

---

[1] Throughout Part II of this volume, "article" ("art."), when used alone, refers to an article of D. P. R. 29 January 1958, n. 645, the *Testo unico* of the laws on the direct taxes, which became effective 1 January 1960.

eduction of the rates of tax on the next L. 720,000 income, applied in
rder to categories C/2, C/1, and B (art. 90) (12/1.4c). Income from
vork as an employee, as well as from pensions and length-of-service and
ocial security payments, is exempt from tax if it does not exceed certain
imits (12/1.4a). A standard allowance and allowances for dependents
re also deducted from net aggregate income for purposes of the
omplementary tax (art. 138) (12/1.5b).

Each individual who has income subject to tax must file an annual
eturn, except as explained at 13/1.1a.

/1.2   Married Persons

For the objective taxes, the incomes of a husband and his wife are
computed and taxed separately; there is no aggregation of income for rate
urposes. However, the husband reports, in separate statements attached
o his own return (12/5.2), the income of his wife and income of any
other person over which he has free disposition or administration without
he duty to render an accounting.

For purposes of determining the basis and rate of the complementary
ax, the income of the wife is aggregated with that of her husband (art.
131), and the husband receives an allowance for her as a dependent
(art. 138) (12/1.5b). There is no splitting of income between husband
and wife for rate purposes. Both incomes are reported on the return
of the husband, or of the spouse having the power of free disposition or
administration without the duty to render an accounting. If a wife is
legally and actually separated from her husband, however, she is subject
separately to the complementary tax on income over which she has the
power to dispose freely (art. 131). The husband may deduct from his
income, in place of the personal allowance for each child entrusted to
the custody of a separated wife, as much of the annual support allowance
paid to the wife as is required by a court decree or a certified document;
this annual payment is included in the income of the wife (art. 138)
(9/3.1), who must file a separate return. The wife may deduct the
basic personal allowance and an allowance for each child entrusted
to her custody and for any other person dependent on her.

The incomes of husband and wife are also aggregated for purposes
of the family tax imposed by the communes (2/3.2).

5/1.3   Minors and Other Incompetent Persons

The age of majority in Italy is 21 (CC art. 2);[2] but a minor is automatically emancipated by marriage (CC art. 390) and may be emancipated under the supervision of a curator (*curatore*), with the consent

---

[2] Under various provisions of the Civil Code, however, legal capacity for certain
purposes is acquired at different ages.

of his parent or guardian, after attaining the age of 18 (CC arts. 391, 392).

For purposes of the objective taxes, the income of a minor is treated as his own income, and is taxed separately from that of his parent or guardian. The person having direction or control of an unemancipated minor's affairs is responsible for filing a return of the minor's income; if he has free disposition or administration of the income without the duty to render an accounting, he includes it in separate statements attached to his own return (12/5.2). After emancipation, a minor is responsible for filing his own return, and is capable of fulfilling most acts connected with taxation, although the assistance of his *curatore* is required for acts beyond simple administration of his affairs, such as the commencement of judicial proceedings (CC art. 394).[3]

Any income of the minor over which the parent or guardian has the power of free disposition or administration without obligation to render an accounting must be included in the income of the parent or guardian for purposes of the complementary tax (art. 131); the minor is not subject to tax separately on that income. The taxpayer is entitled to dependent allowances (12/1.5b) for unemancipated minor children, including recognized natural children, adopted children, and affiliated children (art. 138). Dependent allowances are also granted for unrecognized natural children, stepchildren, and foundlings, if they are living with the taxpayer, and for children who have reached the age of majority or are emancipated, if they are permanently unable to work, or are wholly engaged in study or in a continuous apprenticeship and are of an age not exceeding 25 years (art. 138). Income of an unemancipated minor child is also aggregated with that of his parent for purposes of the family tax levied by the communes (2/3.2).

A taxpayer who is responsible for seven or more dependent children of Italian nationality, including legitimate children and recognized natural children, is entitled to the special reliefs described below (art. 161).[4]

1. The allowance deductible from net aggregate income for purposes of the complementary tax is increased to L. 5 million, in addition to the regular allowances for dependent family members (12/1.5b).
2. An aggregate reduction of L. 5 million is allowed, in proportion to the amounts of income assessed, in the income assessed for the tax on income from landowning, the tax on agrarian income, the tax on income from buildings, and the tax on income from movable wealth, after deduction of the standard allowance (12/1.4b).

War widows with six children are entitled to these reliefs as long as they remain unmarried. Persons with fewer than seven children, but not

---

[3] See Giannini, *Istituzioni di diritto tributario* 85.
[4] As modified by L. 27 June 1961, n. 551, art. 10.

ewer than five, are entitled to the relief in half measure (art. 163).[5] If a person meeting the required conditions is associated with the owner of a farm in the conduct of an agricultural enterprise, the relief with respect to the tax on agrarian income is applied within the limits of his share (art. 161). On the death of the parents, the reliefs remain available to a child who has assumed the status of head of the family and who is responsible for not fewer than four dependent brothers or sisters. A married daughter is not considered dependent; a son of more than 28 years of age is not considered dependent unless he is incapable of work and is without means of providing directly for his own support (art. 162). The reliefs described above run from 1 January of the year following that in which the required conditions are fulfilled to 31 December of the year in which the conditions cease to exist (art. 164).[6]

The tax return of an incompetent person is filed by his guardian (*tutore*). Unless the guardian's relationship to the incompetent gives him free disposition or administration of the latter's income without the duty to render an accounting, the return is completely separate from that of the guardian's own income, and the incompetent person is subject to the complementary tax as a separate taxpayer.

5/1.4 Other Dependents

The aggregate income of an individual for purposes of the complementary tax includes income of any other person over which he has the power of free disposition or administration without obligation to render an accounting (art. 131). The taxpayer is entitled to dependent allowances (12/1.5b) for parents and parents-in-law over 60 years of age, for a widowed mother or mother-in-law, if living with the taxpayer, and for persons related to the taxpayer by consanguinity or marriage who have a right to support and actually exercise it (art. 138). The allowance for family dependents does not apply to persons who are in a position to maintain themselves with their own income in which the taxpayer does not have rights of usufruct (9/4.1) without the obligation to render an accounting (art. 138).

5/2.   Corporations and Similar Entities

5/2.1   In General

In Italian law, the term "company" (*società*) refers to any organization in which two or more persons contract to confer property or services for the exercise in common of an economic activity for the purpose of

---

[5] As modified by L. 27 June 1961, n. 551, art. 10.

[6] Procedure for claiming the reliefs is set forth in article 165 and is further explained in C.M. 3 August 1961, n. 500816.

ANALYSIS OF INCOME TAX

sharing its profits (CC art. 2247). A corporation (5/2.2) acquires "juridical personality" by inscription in the register of enterprises (CC art. 2331). Other forms of company which have juridical personality are subject to tax in the same manner as corporations. These companies are discussed in 5/2; the taxation of companies lacking juridical personality is discussed in 5/3.

5/2.2 Corporations

The Italian equivalent of the corporation is the *società per azioni,* the liability for whose obligations is limited to its assets (*patrimonio*) and whose participations are represented by shares (CC art. 2325). The management of the corporation is entrusted to a sole director (*amministratore unico*) or to a board of directors (*consiglio di amministrazione*) (CC arts. 2380, 2381), chosen by the ordinary shareholders' meeting (*assemblea ordinaria*) (CC arts. 2364, 2383), and is supervised by a board of overseers or auditors (*collegio sindacale*) (CC art. 2397).

For corporations, as for all other taxpayers, the objective taxes (6/1.1a) are based on the possession of immovable property in Italy and on the production in Italy of income from movable wealth (11/1.1). Thus, a corporation owning immovable property in Italy or carrying on an activity in Italy is subject to the appropriate tax on income therefrom, regardless of its nationality, domicile, or residence. Under certain conditions, income produced abroad by a corporation domiciled or resident in Italy (11/2.2) and income derived from activities carried on abroad by a corporation formed in Italy or having its head office or the principal object of its enterprise in Italy (11/2.3a) may be considered produced in Italy and thus subject to the tax on income from movable wealth.

A corporation is required to be taxed on the balance sheet basis (*in base al bilancio*) for purposes of the tax on income from movable wealth if it is formed in Italy, or if it has its head office or carries on the principal activities of its enterprise in Italy (6/1.2b). A foreign corporation which neither has its head office nor carries on the principal activities of its enterprise in Italy may elect to be taxed on the balance sheet basis if it has one or more secondary offices with a permanent representative in Italy (11/3.3). Entities taxed on the balance sheet basis are subject to special rules of assessment of the tax on income from movable wealth (6/1.2b, 13/2). The income of a corporation carrying on business activities is also assessed under the rules specifically applicable to business enterprises (art. 8) (7/1.2).

The personal tax applicable to corporations is the corporation tax, which is composed of a tax on taxable assets or "patrimony" (3/2) and a tax on profits exceeding 6% of the taxable assets (2/4, 6/1.1g). A corporation formed in Italy is subject to this tax on its entire assets and on its entire income (11/2.1). A corporation formed abroad is subject to the corporation tax if it operates in Italy through a permanent establishment, but its taxable income for the corporation tax is limited to income attributable to its investment in Italy. If it has its head office or carries on the principal activities of its enterprise in Italy, its entire assets are subject to tax; if it neither has its head office nor carries on the principal activities of its enterprise in Italy, its taxable assets are limited to assets employed in Italy (11/3.3).

If a corporation or a similar entity is exempt from the corporation tax, amounts withheld from distributions of profits payable to it, under the rules discussed at 9/2.7a, are not credited or refunded; hence such withholdings constitute a separate tax on those entities (9/2.7c).

As explained at 9/2.1, a distribution of corporate profits to shareholders is not subject, as such, to the tax on income from movable wealth, since it has already been taxed as the profits of the corporation; but it is included in the shareholder's income for purposes of the complementary tax if the shareholder is an individual, or for purposes of the corporation tax if the shareholder is a corporation.

Any corporation having income or assets subject to tax is required to file a single annual return for all of its income and assets (13/1.1a), signed by the proper officers (13/1.1b). A branch is not a separate taxpayer (art. 8) (6/7), and its income is reported on the return of the principal office.[7] In practice, an Italian branch of a foreign company files the return of its income subject to tax under the rules discussed at 11/3.5. A subsidiary (*società sussidiaria* or *società-figlia*), being a separate taxpayer, must file a separate return of its own income.

5/2.3 Limited Liability Companies

A limited liability company (*società a responsibilità limitata*) is a juridical person (CC arts. 2331, 2475); liability for its debts is limited to the assets of the company, but the members' participating equity is not represented by shares (CC art. 2472). It is not permitted to issue bonds (CC art. 2486). Unless the charter provides otherwise, the directors must be shareholders (CC art. 2487), and there must be a board of overseers or auditors if the capital is not less than L. 1 million (CC art. 2488).

A limited liability company is required to be taxed on the balance sheet basis (art. 8) and is treated for tax purposes in the same manner as a corporation (5/2.2). Distributions to members are taxed in the same manner as corporate distributions (9/2.1).

---

[7] The generic term for a branch or agency is *filiale*, which, in some contexts, also appears to cover subsidiaries. A *succursale* is a branch responsible for operations in a defined geographic area.

5/2.4   Limited Partnerships with Shares

A limited partnership with shares (*società in accomandita per azioni*) is a juridical person (CC art. 2464) composed of one or more general partners (*soci accomandatari*) whose liability for the company obligations is unlimited and of one or more limited partners (*soci accomandanti*) whose liability is limited to their participations in the subscribed capital (CC art. 2462). The participating equity of the members is represented by shares. The company is directed by the general partners (CC art. 2465), and there is a board of overseers or auditors (CC arts. 2464, 2468).

A limited partnership with shares is required to be taxed on the balance sheet basis (art. 8) and, is treated for tax purposes in the same manner as a corporation (5/2.2). Distributions to shareholders are taxed in the same manner as corporate distributions (9/2.1).

5/2.5   Cooperative Societies

An enterprise which has as its purpose the mutual benefit of the members may take the form of a cooperative society (*società cooperativa*) (CC art. 2511), which is a juridical person (CC arts. 2331, 2519). A cooperative society of unlimited liability is liable for its obligations to the extent of its assets; in the case of forced administrative liquidation or bankruptcy, the members have unlimited secondary liability for the obligations of the society in proportion to their shares of the capital (CC arts. 2513, 2541). A cooperative society of limited liability is liable for its obligations to the extent of its assets; the participating equity of the members can be represented by shares, and the charter may provide that, in the case of forced administrative liquidation or bankruptcy of the society, the members shall be jointly and secondarily liable in proportion to their shares of the capital (CC art. 2514). In general, a cooperative society is managed under the rules governing the management of corporations (CC art. 2516)(5/2.2).

A cooperative society, whether of limited or unlimited liability, is required to be taxed on the balance sheet basis (art. 8) and is treated for tax purposes in the same manner as a corporation (5/2.2), with the exceptions listed below.

1. For purposes of the tax on income from movable wealth, a cooperative society is entitled to the same standard allowance and rate reduction as an individual or a partnership (arts. 89, 90) (12/3.2).
2. A cooperative society is exempt from the tax on income from movable wealth on income realized through the processing, transformation, or sale of agricultural products contributed to it by its members (art. 84) (10/2.4).

3. A consumer cooperative society or production and labor cooperative society is allowed special deductions for certain distributions to its members (art. 111) (7/2.14).
4. Certain cooperative societies are exempt from the corporation tax or are subject to it at a reduced rate (5/5.10).

Distributions by cooperative societies to their members are taxed in the same manner as corporate distributions (9/2.1). However, the provisions governing the withholding of the coupon tax from distributions of profits do not apply to cooperative societies with unlimited liability (9/2.7a).

5/2.6   Mutual Insurance Companies

In the case of a mutual insurance company, the obligations of the company are guaranteed by its assets, and the members must be insured by the company (CC art. 2546). Such a company is subject to the laws regulating insurance and, in general, to the rules governing cooperative societies of limited liability (CC art. 2547).

A mutual insurance company is required to be taxed on the balance sheet basis (art. 8) and is subject to the corporation tax in the same manner as a corporation (5/2.2). Special rules governing the taxation of income from an insurance business are discussed at 10/3.

5/2.7   Governmental Bodies and Public Enterprises

The state and its subdivisions are, in principle, no less subject to taxation than private entities.[8] Provinces, communes, and public entities recognized as juridical persons are juridical persons of the public law (CC art. 11) and are subject to the direct taxes on income derived from income-producing property held by them unless exempted by special provisions.[9] But income derived by the state or other public entities from taxes cannot, of course, be the object of further taxation.

Regions, provinces, communes, and other public entities are required to be taxed on the balance sheet basis as juridical persons (art. 8) but are entitled to the exemptions described at 5/5.11. Moreover, most public enterprises are organized as corporations and, except as noted at 5/5.11, are treated for tax purposes in the same manner as any other corporation. Joint enterprises can be formed between private business entities and state enterprises in any of the regular forms of business organization (5/3.1) and are taxed according to the form adopted.

5/2.8   Other Entities Taxed As Corporations

In addition to the entities described at 5/2.2-5/2.7, a juridical person formed in Italy and required by law or by its own charter and bylaws to

---

[8] Giannini, *I concetti fondamentali del diritto tributario* 207, 232-233.

[9] C. M. 2 May 1955, n. 301660, withdraws immunity from the tax on income from movable wealth from certain public enterprises on the ground that there is no legislative provision granting such an immunity to the state itself.

5/3.

prepare a balance sheet (*bilancio*) or annual financial report (*rendiconto*) is required to be taxed on the balance sheet basis (art. 8) and is therefore subject to the corporation tax (art. 145) (6/1.1g) unless expressly exempted. Entities of public interest which are subject to public control, such as banks, insurance companies, hospitals, and foundations, are required to prepare a balance sheet. Public entities, including public enterprises which are public entities, such as certain banks, are required to prepare financial reports.

An enterprise not required to be taxed on the balance sheet basis may elect to be so taxed by complying with certain conditions (6/1.2b). This election affects the method of assessment of the tax on income from movable wealth (13/2) but does not subject the enterprise to the corporation tax.

5/3.   Other Taxpayers

5/3.1   In General

The category of persons subject (*soggetti passivi*) to the obligations of the income and other direct taxes includes not only individuals (5/1) and corporations and other entities required to be taxed on the balance sheet basis (5/2), but all other juridical persons, companies, associations, and organizations of persons or property not belonging to persons required to be taxed on the balance sheet basis,[10] even if lacking juridical personality, for which a "tax basis arises in a unitary and independent manner" (art. 8). There are juridical persons which are not required to be taxed on the balance sheet basis because they are not required to prepare balance sheets or annual financial reports (5/3.8). All companies other than those described at 5/2 lack juridical personality. There are also organizations which are neither companies nor juridical persons. As explained in the sections following, all such taxpayers are subject to the objective taxes, but in general they are not subject to any personal tax; instead, the income of the company, association, or organization is allocated among the members for purposes of their own personal tax liability. However, amounts withheld under the rules discussed at 9/2.7a from profits payable to organizations of persons or property which are neither companies nor juridical persons are not credited against the personal tax liability of the members; hence such withholdings constitute a separate tax on these organizations (9/2.7c).

The income of a company carrying on a business activity is assessed under the special rules applicable to business enterprises (art. 8) (7/1.2). Under article 2249 of the Civil Code, a company having a business activity as its object must be organized as a corporation (5/2.2), limited

---

[10] This qualification excludes a branch, whose income is included in that of the principal office (5/2.2), from taxation as a separate entity.

liability company (5/2.3), limited partnership with shares (5/2.4), general partnership (5/3.2), or simple limited partnership (5/3.3).

5/3.2 General Partnerships

A general partnership (*società in nome collettivo*) is a company in which all the members are liable without limitation for the obligations of the company (CC art. 2291).[11] It is not a juridical person. Provision may be made for "conjunctive direction" by several directing members, all of whom must agree to the carrying out of company operations; or the agreement of a majority of the members, determined according to the share of each in the profits, may be required for the direction of the company or for specified acts (CC arts. 2257-2259). In the absence of any such provision or requirement, each member disjunctively (that is, individually) has the power of direction; disagreements are resolved by a majority of the members, determined according to the share of each in the profits (CC arts. 2257, 2293).

For partnerships, as for all other taxpayers, the objective taxes (6/1.1a) are based on the possession of immovable property in Italy and on the production in Italy of income from movable wealth (11/1.1). Thus, a partnership owning immovable property in Italy or carrying on an activity in Italy is subject to the appropriate tax on income therefrom, regardless of nationality, domicile, or residence. Under certain conditions, however, income produced abroad by a partnership domiciled or resident in Italy (11/2.2) and income derived from activities carried on abroad by a partnership formed in Italy or having its head office or the principal object of its enterprise in Italy (11/2.3a) may be considered produced in Italy, and thus subjected to the tax on income from movable wealth.

A partnership is not required to be taxed on the balance sheet basis for purposes of the tax on income from movable wealth, but a business enterprise carried on by a general partnership formed in Italy may elect to be so taxed (6/1.2b). A business enterprise carried on by a partnership formed abroad may make such an election if it has one or more secondary offices with a permanent representative in Italy (art. 104) (11/3.4).

For purposes of the tax on income from movable wealth, a partnership is entitled to a single personal allowance (art. 89) (12/3.1), and to a reduction of the rates of tax on the next L. 720,000 of income, applied, in order, to categories C/2, C/1, and B (art. 90) (12/3.1).

A general partnership formed in Italy is not subject to the corporation tax (6/1.1g) unless it was created by a foreign company which has supplied the majority of its capital and which uses it as a means of carrying on its own operations in Italy (11/2.3b). However, a foreign partnership

---

[11] An agreement limiting the liability of any member or members has no effect against third parties.

is subject to the corporation tax on its assets employed in Italy, and on its income referable either to assets employed in Italy or to a permanent establishment in Italy if it operates in Italy through a permanent establishment (11/3.4).

Under the principle that a tax cannot be applied more than once to the same basis, even if different taxpayers are involved (6/1.1a), a member of a general partnership is not subject to the tax on income from movable wealth on partnership profits distributed to him (art. 83), since the tax has already been assessed against the partnership. Since the liability of a member for one of the personal taxes has a different basis, however, the inclusion of the partnership profits in the member's income for the appropriate personal tax does not violate the prohibition against double taxation (6/1.1a). If the shareholder is an individual, his income for purposes of the complementary tax includes that proportion of the net income of the partnership, whether distributed or not, in which he has the right to participate in the profits (art. 135) (9/2.1b). If a corporation or other entity required to be taxed on the balance sheet basis (5/2) is a member of a partnership, its income for purposes of the corporation tax includes all amounts received by way of distribution or division of the profits of the partnership (art. 148) (9/2.1c).[12] The objective taxes paid on the income of the partnership are deductible in determining the shareholders' income for the personal taxes (6/1.5e).

Any partnership possessing income or capital subject to tax is required to file a single annual return (13/1.1a), signed by its legal or designated representative (13/1.1b).

5/3.3 Simple Limited Partnerships

A simple limited partnership (*società in accomandita semplice*) is a company composed of general partners (*soci accomanditari*) having unlimited liability for the obligations of the company and of limited

---

[12] For example, Cass., Sez. I, 11 January 1962, n. 21 (*Giur. imp.*, 1962, 377), which holds that, since a personal company having a corporation and several individuals as members is not possible, no assessment of the tax on income from movable wealth can be made against a claimed *de facto* company consisting of a corporation and several private entrepreneurs. There are several other decisions holding that a corporation or similar entity may not be a member of a general partnership or a simple limited partnership. See Cass. 14 June 1958, n. 8024 (*Dir. fall.*, 1958, II, 444); Cass. 23 September 1958, n. 3035 (*Dir. fall.*, 1958, II, 585); Cass. 3 April 1959, n. 993 (*Dir. fall.*, 1959, II, 393). The chief argument for this position seems to be that the assets of the shareholders of a corporation or similar entity would not be available to satisfy the debts of the partnership of which it was a member. However, there is considerable support in the doctrine for the view that this is not an obstacle to a partnership having a corporation as a member, since the corporation and not its shareholders would participate in the partnership, and the assets of the corporation itself would be fully available to satisfy the debts of the partnership. See Graziani, *Diritto delle società* 81-82; Ascarelli, *Studi in tema di società* 55; 1 Brunetti, *Trattato del diritto delle società* 205.

partners (*soci accomandanti*) whose liability is limited to their contributions to the capital of the company; the participating equities of the members cannot be represented by shares (CC art. 2313). The direction of the company is in the hands of the general partners (CC art. 2318) under the same rules which govern the direction of a general partnership (CC art. 2315) (5/3.2). A simple limited partnership is not a juridical person.

A simple limited partnership and its members are subject to tax in the same manner as a general partnership and its members (5/3.2).

5/3.4 Noncommercial Partnerships

A noncommercial partnership (*società semplice*) is a form of company, requiring no particular form of contract (CC art. 2251), which may be used for the exercise of any economic activity other than a business activity (CC art. 2249). Since it cannot conduct a business activity, it cannot elect to be taxed on the balance sheet basis (6/1.2b). In all other respects, a noncommercial partnership and its members are taxed in the same way as a general partnership and its members (5/3.2).

5/3.5 Associations in Participation

The association in participation (*associazione in partecipazione*) is an ancient form of joint venture in which the associate (*associato*) contributes capital to the active member (*associante*) and receives a share of the profits of an enterprise or of one or more transactions conducted by the latter (CC art. 2549). The management of the enterprise or transactions is in the hands of the active member (CC art. 2552), and third parties have rights and obligations only against him (CC art. 2551).

Under the general principles discussed at 5/3.1, an association in participation and its members are subject to tax in the same manner as a general partnership and its members (5/3.2); but the association is not entitled to a personal allowance (art. 89) or to a rate reduction (art. 90) for purposes of the tax on income from movable wealth.[13]

5/3.6 De Facto Companies

An entit_ lacking legal capacity under private law, such as a company irregularl˙ or illegally formed, may nonetheless have legal capacity for

---

[13] The association in participation was expressly considered a single taxpayer under article 29 of R. D. L. 24 August 1877, n. 4021, as modified by article 4 of L. 8 June 1936, n. 1231, and was expressly required to file a return under article 2 of D.P.R. 5 July 1951, n. 573. Although the failure of article 8 of the present *Testo unico* to name expressly such associations has led some commentators to doubt that they may be treated as single taxpayers (see Berliri, *Il testo unico delle imposte dirette* 18), the terms of the article seem sufficient to include them. See 5/3.1.

tax purposes (*capacità giuridica tributaria*).[14] Although not mentioned specifically in the present law, such a company appears to be clearly within the definition of persons subject to the tax obligation (5/3.1).[15]

5/3.7 Separate Businesses and Activities

Tax liability for income from business activities falling in category B of the tax on income from movable wealth must be measured by reference to the net aggregate result of all of the taxpayer's activities and operations producing income classifiable in that category (art. 95) (7/1.1). Thus, although the literal definition of a person subject to the tax would include a business (*azienda*), defined as a complex of property organized by an entrepreneur for the conduct of the enterprise (CC art. 2555), the tax law treats income from one or more business activities as the income of the person carrying on the activities and not as the income of the business itself. Income from professional activities, similarly, must be measured by reference to the net aggregate result of all of the taxpayer's activities and operations producing income classifiable in category C/1 (art. 95) (8/2.1); the income derived by a taxpayer from diverse professional activities is therefore taxed as his own income and not as the income of the separate activities. As a result, a taxpayer may set off losses sustained in one business during the year against his income from other businesses in the same year (7/4.1).

Prior to the tax reform law of 1956, income from occasional business activities carried on by certain taxpayers (7/1.1), income from certain occasional professional activities, and income from certain contracts for the performance of particular services distinct from the taxpayer's normal and ordinary activity (8/4) were assessed *una tantum* (or *una volta tanto*), apart from the income from the taxpayer's normal activities. These provisions served to exclude occasional income of irregular activities from tax bases which, under the system of assessment then in use, would have continued in effect for subsequent years; they were abrogated in 1956.[16]

The separate taxation of separate activities was consistent with the "objectivity" of the tax on income from movable wealth, which was originally a proportional tax imposed on income from a productive source, regardless of the economic situation of the taxpayer (2/2, 6/1.1e). How-

[14] For discussions of the relationship between legal capacity for tax purposes and legal capacity in general, see Berliri, *Il testo unico delle imposte dirette* 15; Giannini, *Istituzioni di diritto tributario* 82; Mandò, *Imposta di ricchezza mobile* 21.

[15] A *de facto* company (*società di fatto*) was expressly considered to be a single taxpayer under article 29 of R. D. L. 24 August 1877, n. 4021, as modified by article 4 of L. 8 June 1936, n. 1231, and was required to file a return under article 2 of D.P.R. 5 July 1951, n. 573.

[16] L. 5 January 1956, n. 1, art. 24.

ever, as a result of the personal allowance (art. 89) (12/1.4b) and of
the introduction of progressive rates on certain categories of income
(art. 90) (12/1.4c), the tax now takes account of personal elements
extraneous to the activity producing the income (2/2.7g, 6/1.1a).[17]

5/3.8 Associations and Foundations

Associations (*associazioni*) and foundations (*fondazioni*) are private
institutions. The foundation is primarily an organization of property,
whereas the association is primarily an organization of persons; [18] both
are used chiefly for the carrying on of nonprofit activities. A foundation
or an association can acquire juridical personality by recognition rendered by a government decree (CC art. 12). The structure and
administration of an association not recognized as a juridical person is
governed by agreement of the members (CC art. 36). A foundation or
an association is subject to the income and other direct taxes, but it is
not required to be taxed on the balance sheet basis, and therefore is
not subject to the corporation tax, unless it has juridical personality and
is required by law or by its bylaws to prepare a balance sheet or annual
financial report (5/2.8).

5/3.9 Estates of Deceased Persons

The heirs of a taxpayer are jointly and severally liable for his tax
obligations (art. 16), whether or not already inscribed in the roll for
collection.[19] For the benefit of the heirs, all time limits pending on the
date of death, including those for the filing of the return and for con-
testing the assessment, are extended by six months (art. 16). The heirs
of a person who has filed a return or a protest, or against whom a proceeding for assessment or rectification has been initiated, must inform the
Tax Office of their identity within six months of the taxpayer's death; if
this is not done, documents and acts involving the taxpayer have effect
with respect to the heirs even if notice thereof is sent to only one of them,
or is sent collectively and impersonally to the last fiscal domicile of the
decedent (art. 16). If the basis of a tax terminates with the death of the
decedent, as in the case of the complementary tax, a report of
termination may be filed (art. 144) (13/1.5); if such a report is not filed
and no notice of assessment has been served, the heirs may appeal against
inscription in the roll for partial or total nonexistence of the tax liability
(art. 188) (13/4.6).

Since an inheritance is acquired by acceptance, which becomes effective as of the death of the decedent (CC arts. 456, 459), an heir becomes

---

[17] See Poli, "Cespiti e redditi nell'imposta di ricchezza mobile," *RDFSF*, 1955,
II, 311.

[18] See Trabucchi, *Istituzioni di diritto civile* 103.

[19] See De Angelis, Potenza, and Testa, *Testo unico delle leggi sulle imposte
dirette* 80.

subject, from the time of acceptance, to taxes on income which arises on his share of the property at any time after the decedent's death. An heir who does not accept is not liable for any taxes on income from the property of the estate, whether arising before or after the death of the decedent. An heir may accept an inheritance "with the benefit of inventory" (*col beneficio d'inventario*), in which case his liability for payment of the debts of the inheritance, including taxes, is limited to the value of the property coming to him (CC art. 490).

A legacy, if not renounced, is acquired without the need of acceptance (CC art. 649). The ownership of specified property and the right to the income therefrom pass to the legatee at the moment of the testator's death (CC arts. 649, 669). The legatee immediately becomes subject to the taxes on income thereafter arising from the property, but he is not liable for taxes on income which arose before the death of the testator.

Prior to acceptance of an inheritance, the administration of the property thereof, including the filing of returns and the payment of taxes on past and current income, is in the hands of the named heir (*chiamato all'eredità*) (CC art. 460) or, under certain conditions, of an administrator (CC arts. 641-644).

An unclaimed inheritance is administered by a *curatore* (CC arts. 528-532). If one or more testamentary executors are appointed, however, the administration of the entire estate is in their hands (CC arts. 700, 703).

5/4. Nonresidents

The taxation of income of a nonresident, including a foreign company having neither its head office nor the principal object of its enterprise in Italy, is discussed at 11/3.

5/5. Tax-Exempt Persons

5/5.I Diplomatic Representatives and Employees of Foreign Governments

Ambassadors and other diplomatic agents of foreign states are exempt from the tax on income from movable wealth on the income derived from the exercise of their duties in Italy (art. 84), and are exempt from the complementary tax on their entire income (art. 132). Consuls, consular agents, and officials and employees of diplomatic and consular offices of foreign states are similarly exempt from the tax on income from movable wealth with respect to the income derived from the exercise of their duties in Italy, provided that they are neither Italian citizens nor Italians not belonging to the Republic (for example, residents of the Vatican or of the Republic of San Marino) and provided that reciprocity is granted (art. 84). Persons who qualify for this exemption are exempt from the complementary tax on their entire income, provided that they do not exercise a business or professional activity in Italy (art. 132).

Employees of the Food and Agriculture Organization of the United Nations (FAO) are exempt from Italian direct taxes on their wages and salaries, regardless of citizenship.[20] Employees of a number of other international organizations are exempt from all Italian direct taxes on their wages and salaries, provided that they are not citizens of Italy. The most important of these organizations are the International Monetary Fund (IMF),[21] the International Commission of the World Health Organization (WHO),[22] the Organization for European Economic Co-operation (OEEC) (now OECD),[23] the North Atlantic Treaty Organization (NATO),[24] the Council of Europe,[25] the European Coal and Steel Community (CECA),[26] and agencies of the United Nations.[27] The organizations themselves are exempt from the direct taxes on their own income.

5/5.2 Clergy

Remuneration of any kind paid by the Holy See, the central entities of the Catholic Church, or entities managed directly by the Holy See, whether or not in Rome, to their permanent and temporary dignitaries, officers, and employees, is exempt from the tax on income from movable wealth (art. 84) and from the complementary tax (art. 134), whether or not the recipients are members of the clergy.

There is no general exemption for the income of the clergy. Contributions made to the Church in payment for special offices or ministries in favor of the contributor are included in the income of category C/2 of the celebrating priest; they are generally subject to the tax on income from movable wealth,[28] and therefore also to the complementary tax.

5/5.3 Teachers, Authors, and Inventors

No general exemption is granted to teachers or authors. There is no provision for the spreading of income of an author or inventor from the

---

[20] L. 9 January 1951, n. 11. See Boidi, *Commento alla legge sulla imposta complementare progressiva sul reddito* 108.

[21] L. 23 March 1947, n. 132.

[22] D. L. 13 April 1948, n. 917.

[23] L. 4 August 1948, n. 1107.

[24] L. 10 November 1954, n. 1226; L. 30 November 1955, n. 1335, n. 1338.

[25] General Agreement on Privileges and Immunities, 2 September 1949; L. 27 October 1951, n. 1578.

[26] L. 25 June 1952, n. 766.

[27] Resolution of the United Nations General Assembly for the Unification of Privileges and Immunities, 21 November 1947; L. 24 July 1951, n. 1740.

[28] C. M. 22 January 1941, n. 690.

sale of a copyright or patent, and such income is generally taxed in the year in which it becomes payable (8/4).

5/5.4 Government Officials and Employees

The government payments listed below are exempt from the tax on income from movable wealth and from the complementary tax.

1. The annual grant of the President of the Republic (arts. 84, 134).
2. The allowance and per diem of members of Parliament.[29]
3. Family supplements paid to state employees, war pensions, extra payments annexed to medals for military valor, pensions for the decorations of the Military Order of Italy, and grants annexed to certain pensions (art. 134).[30]
4. Special supplementary allowances paid to employees of the state, of local entities, and of institutions of public law.[31]

The pay and perquisites of personnel of the Italian armed forces of grades inferior to noncommissioned officer are exempt from the tax on income from movable wealth (art. 84), but not from the complementary tax.

5/5.5 Religious and Charitable Institutions

No general exemption from the objective taxes on income is provided for religious or charitable institutions. However, buildings devoted to the exercise of worship allowed by the state are excluded as bases of the tax on income from buildings, since they are not considered capable of producing income (art. 77) (9/4.2a). Certain buildings belonging to the Holy See are exempt from the tax on income from buildings (art. 78) (9/4.2b).

Contributions and bequests received by the Church in compensation for the celebration of masses and religious offices are, in principle, income subject to the tax on income from movable wealth, even if subsequently taxed as part of the income of the celebrating priest under the rules discussed at 5/5.2. Contributions and bequests requiring no services on the part of the clergy are considered capital receipts and thus are not subject to tax. It appears, however, that income of the Church and income of the clergy are seldom assessed in practice.

Certain public entities of welfare and assistance are exempted from the direct taxes on their income by special laws conferring such exemption [32] or making them "equivalent for tax purposes to units of the state

---

[29] L. 9 August 1948, n. 1102, art. 3.
[30] L. 8 April 1952, n. 212, art. 29.
[31] L. 27 May 1959, n. 324, arts. 1, 16.
[32] See Mandò, *Imposta di ricchezza mobile* 81.

administration."[33] Charitable institutions to which exemption has not been granted are subject to the objective taxes.

Church welfare institutions, provident and social assistance entities and institutions, and entities whose objectives are equated by law to social welfare and instruction (entities of worship and religion of the Catholic Church)[34] are exempt from the corporation tax (art. 151).

5/5.6 Provident Institutions

Certain public entities furnishing provident or social security insurance as monopolies are granted special exemptions from the tax on income from movable wealth. The principal institution of this kind is the *Istituto Nazionale della Previdenza Sociale* (INPS), which manages obligatory and optional insurance and other provident funds for designated categories of workers. The annual income of the funds of the institution and the income of special funds managed by the institution are exempt from the tax on income from movable wealth.[35] Shares of participation, amounts devolved as increments of the individual accounts of the participants, and pensions, allowances, subsidies, and indemnities to be paid as insurance benefits under the law are also exempt (8/1.3b). Similar provisions apply to the *Istituto Nazionale per l'Assistenza di Malattia* (INAM),[36] which furnishes insurance against illness, and the *Istituto Nazionale per l'Assicurazione contro gli Infortuni sul Lavoro* (INAIL),[37] which furnishes insurance against occupational illness and accidents occurring at work. A number of other provident and social insurance entities are exempt from the direct taxes as a result of having been made "equivalent for tax purposes to units of the state administration," although there is, in fact, no general exemption for the state or its offices (5/5.5).[38] In the absence of a special exemption, however, the interest received by a provident or social security fund is subject to the tax on income from movable wealth in category A.[39]

Provident entities and institutions, whether public or private,[40] are exempt from the corporation tax if they are legally formed and recognized (art. 151).

---

[33] See Mandò, *Imposta di ricchezza mobile* 86-89; Zappalà, Marionetti, and Lanza, *L'imposta sui redditi di ricchezza mobile* 194-196.

[34] See Lateran Treaty of 11 February 1929, art. 29, approved by L. 27 May 1929, n. 810.

[35] R. D. L. 4 October 1935, n. 1827, art. 122, converted in L. 6 April 1936, n. 1155.

[36] L. 11 January 1943, n. 138, art. 35.

[37] R. D. 17 August 1935, n. 1765, art. 71.

[38] On this question, see Mandò, *Imposta di ricchezza mobile* 86-89; Zappalà, Marionetti, and Lanza, *L'imposta sui redditi di ricchezza mobile* 194-196; Giannetta, Scandale, and Sessa, *Teoria e tecnica nell'accertamento del reddito mobiliare* 345-346.

[39] Cass., Sez. I, 3 September 1947, n. 1559. See Maffezzoni, "L'imposta di ricchezza mobile sugli interessi dei contributi versati a un fondo di previdenza," *Giur. comp. Cass., Sez. Civ.*, 1947, vol. 26, 244.

[40] See C. M. 29 July 1957, n. 351420.

Amounts withheld under the rules discussed at 9/2.7a from profits distributed to entities required to be taxed on the balance sheet basis which are exempt from the corporation tax are not credited or refunded; hence such withholdings constitute a separate tax on those entities (9/2.7c).

5/5.7 Educational Institutions

School playgrounds, agricultural school lands, public zoos, and other school lands are excluded from the scope of the tax on income from landowning as lands devoted exclusively to gratuitous public services (10/2.2a). However, school buildings owned by the state or other public entities with territorial jurisdiction are generally not part of the public domain and therefore are not excluded from the tax on income from buildings under the rules applicable to public buildings, which are discussed at 9/4.2a. Universities and institutes of higher education are exempt from the direct taxes on contributions and allowances made by the state, by other entities, or by private persons.[41] Limited exemptions from the direct taxes are also provided for the *Accademia d'Italia*,[42] the *Accademia Nazionale dei Lincei*,[43] and *Istruzione Media Commerciale*.[44]

Nonprofit educational institutions, scientific bodies, academies, historical, literary, and scientific research and experiment foundations, associations having purely cultural purposes, and institutes for study and experimentation of general interest whose purposes and activities are nonprofit are exempt from the corporation tax (art. 151).

Amounts withheld under the rules discussed at 9/2.7a from profits distributed to entities which are required to be taxed on the balance sheet basis and which are exempt from the corporation tax are not credited or refunded; hence such withholdings constitute a separate tax on those entities (9/2.7c).

5/5.8 Mutual Aid Societies

Mutual aid societies are exempt from the corporation tax (art. 151). Mutual aid housing societies are exempt from the tax on income from movable wealth on profits paid to member-tenants to decrease the rental or purchase price of housing (10/6.6).

5/5.9 Professional Associations

There are no special exemptions from the direct taxes for professional associations, and such associations are therefore subject to tax unless

---

[41] R.D. 31 August 1933, n. 1592.
[42] R.D.L. 17 January 1935, n. 67.
[43] D.L.L. 28 September 1944, n. 359.
[44] R.D.L. 15 May 1924, n. 749.

exempt from the corporation tax as nonprofit institutions under article 151 (5/5.7).[45]

5/5.10 Cooperative Societies

Income realized by cooperative societies and other associations through the processing, transformation, or sale of agricultural products contributed by their members is subject to tax as the income of the members and is therefore excluded from the income from movable wealth of the societies or associations themselves (10/2.4). Cooperative and mutual aid societies are exempt from the tax on income from movable wealth on profits paid to member-tenants to decrease rental or purchase prices (10/6.6).

Cooperative societies of unlimited liability (5/2.5) are exempt from the corporation tax, provided that they furnish goods, services, and opportunities of work only to their own members and do not carry on operations with nonmembers beyond the limits expressly stated by their special laws (art. 151).[46]

Labor and consumer cooperative societies of limited liability (5/2.5) and associations of such societies, and cooperative societies furnishing services among direct cultivators, are exempt from the corporation tax provided that the paid-in capital does not exceed L. 4 million, the taxable assets do not exceed L. 8 million, and the bylaws expressly provide for the conditions listed below (art. 151).[47]

1. Prohibition of distribution of dividends greater than the legal rate of interest applicable to the capital actually paid in.
2. Prohibition of distribution of the reserves among the members during the life of the enterprise.
3. Devolution, in case of the dissolution of the society, of all of the assets of the enterprise—less only the capital paid in and any matured dividends —to purposes of public utility which are for mutual benefit.

The exemption does not apply if the administration finds that at any time during the past five years either of the conditions listed in items 1 and 2 has not in fact been observed.[48] The tax is imposed at reduced rates on cooperatives or associations of cooperatives which satisfy all of the conditions except the limitation on capital, and on cooperatives

---

[45] Contributions and membership fees paid to certain organizations, notably trade unions, are excluded from the general tax on receipts (IGE) (14/4.5).

[46] See also C. M. 1 June 1955, n. 351690.

[47] See D. L. 14 December 1947, n. 1577, art. 26, ratified with modifications by L. 2 April 1951, n. 302.

[48] It is the position of the tax administration that a cooperative society which has lost its right to exemption for failure to observe either of these two prohibitions is permanently barred from enjoyment of the exemption, even after five years have elapsed from the date of the violation. C. M. 1 June 1955, n. 351690. For a criticism of this view, see Poli, *Imposta sulle società e imposta sulle obbligazioni* 8.

established by law or in fulfillment of legislative provisions for social utility or public interest (art. 152) (12/3.2). The reliefs are available, under the same conditions, to cooperative societies and other associations realizing income through the processing, transformation, or sale of agricultural products contributed by their members, insofar as the activities giving rise to the income are a part of the normal exercise of agriculture according to the techniques which govern it (arts. 84, 151) (10/2.4).

Building cooperatives are not subject to the corporation tax when contracts of sale of the lodgings have been stipulated with the individual allottees within three years of the approval of the construction.[49]

5/5.11 Governmental Bodies and Public Enterprises

As explained at 5/2.7, governmental bodies and public enterprises are, in principle, taxpayers, and therefore are subject to the objective taxes if they own property capable of producing income, or engage in activities productive of income, subject to those taxes. However, buildings devoted to gratuitous public services are excluded from the basis of the tax on income from landowning (art. 49) (10/2.2a); structures in the public domain which do not produce income and are owned by the state or other public entities with territorial jurisdiction are excluded from the basis of the tax on income from buildings (art. 77) (9/4.2a). Moreover, public entities with territorial jurisdiction are exempt from the tax on income from buildings with respect to buildings, and their appurtenances, constructed for supplying drinkable water (art. 78) (9/4.2b).

Although governmental bodies and public enterprises, when subject to tax, are required to be taxed on the balance sheet basis for purposes of the tax on income from movable wealth (5/2.7), regions, provinces, communes, associations of communes, and Chambers of Commerce are specifically exempted from the corporation tax (art. 151). Exemption from the corporation tax is also granted to the independent enterprises of the state whose accounts are attached to the financial report of the administration of the state (art. 151).[50] Exemption is also granted to enterprises of the regions, provinces, communes, and associations of communes, insofar as they in fact provide, as monopolies, services of public utility, and to associations for reclamation, improvement, irrigation, and water works (art. 151).

Amounts withheld under the rules discussed at 9/2.7a from profits distributed to entities required to be taxed on the balance sheet basis which are exempt from the corporation tax are not credited or refunded; hence such withholdings constitute a separate tax on those entities (9/2.7c).

---

[49] L. 19 July 1961, n. 659, art. 4.

[50] See R. D. 23 May 1924, n. 827, arts. 145, 146; C. M. 1 June 1955, n. 351690. The principal enterprises in this category are the state railways, the state highway system, the postal and telecommunications systems, the telephone system, and the tobacco and salt monopolies.

A number of the entities and enterprises for whose income special exemptions or other concessions have been made are public entities or enterprises. A general classification of the provisions is given below.

1. Certain public enterprises are formed under the Mininstry of State Participations for the purpose of holding participations in, or financing, other companies and are therefore subject to the corporation tax at a reduced rate (10/5).
2. Certain public entities, chiefly entities supplying industrial or agricultural credit (10/4.2), and certain government holding companies (10/5), pay an annual fee (*quota di abbonamento*) in place of the tax on income from movable wealth, but are still subject to the corporation tax.
3. Certain public entities whose objectives are to aid specified sections of the economy are exempt from the tax on income from movable wealth entirely, but are subject to the corporation tax. Examples are the *Ente Nazionale per le Piccole Industrie* (ENPI),[51] the *Istituto Nazionale di Credito per le Piccole Industrie e l'Artigiane*,[52] and the *Consorzio per Sovvenzioni su Valori Industriali.*[53]
4. A number of welfare and assistance institutions which have been granted special exemptions from the tax on income from movable wealth, and are exempt from the corporation tax, are, in fact, public or quasi-public entities (5/5.6).

---

[51] R. D. L. 26 December 1926, n. 2334.
[52] R. D. L. 14 March 1927, n. 372, art. 1.
[53] R. D. L. 13 November 1928, n. 2579.

CHAPTER 6

PRINCIPLES OF INCOME DETERMINATION

6/1. Concept of Taxable Income

6/1.1 Definition and Determination of Taxable Income
    a. In general
    b. Tax on income from landowning
    c. Tax on agrarian income
    d. Tax on income from buildings
    e. Tax on income from movable wealth
    f. Complementary tax
    g. Corporation tax

6/1.2 Methods of Determining Actual Income
    a. Net income method
    b. Net worth comparison method

6/1.3 Exclusions

6/1.4 Tax-Exempt Income

6/1.5 Deductions
    a. In general
    b. Expenses of production or maintenance of income
    c. Depreciation
    d. Interest
    e. Taxes
    f. Contributions for social security, insurance, and charity

6/2. Books and Records

6/2.1 Laws Relating to Books and Records
6/2.2 Books and Records Required
6/2.3 Registration and Inspection of Books and Records
6/2.4 Form of Entries
6/2.5 Weight Given to Book Entries

6/3. Accounting Periods
  6/3.1 Tax Year and Base Year
  6/3.2 Calendar Year and Fiscal Year
  6/3.3 Change of Accounting Period
  6/3.4 Commencement of Operations
  6/3.5 Termination of Operations
  6/3.6 Mergers and Reorganizations

6/4. Accounting Methods
  6/4.1 In General
  6/4.2 Installment Sales
  6/4.3 Long-Term Contracts

6/5. Valuation of Assets
  6/5.1 Inventories
  6/5.2 Accounts Receivable
  6/5.3 Securities
  6/5.4 Fixed Assets
  6/5.5 Intangibles
  6/5.6 Revaluations and Devaluations

6/6. Reserves
  6/6.1 In General
  6/6.2 Reserves Required by Law
  6/6.3 "Hidden Reserves"

6/7. Branch Accounting

6/8. Attribution Rules
  6/8.1 Income of Family Members
  6/8.2 Payments to Foreign Companies

6/9. Other Methods of Determining the Tax Base
  6/9.1 Estimated Income
  6/9.2 Presumed Income
  6/9.3 Income Determined by Agreement

6/1. Concept of Taxable Income

6/1.1 Definition and Determination of Taxable Income

a. IN GENERAL. The Italian income tax system is composed of two groups of taxes. The first group, known as the "real" or "objective" taxes (*imposte reali*), consists of four separate taxes, imposed for the most part at proportional rates (12/1) on income from different productive sources. The second group, known as the "personal" taxes (*imposte personali*), is imposed on the total income of individuals, on the one hand, and of corporations, on the other.

Two of the objective taxes, the tax on income from landowning and the tax on income from buildings, are imposed on an owner's presumed income from immovable property in Italy. A third tax, the tax on agrarian income, is levied on the presumed income of an agricultural enterprise carried on by the owner of land in Italy. Each of these taxes exhausts the owner's liability for the objective taxes on income from its productive source; actual income from those sources is not taxable as such. The fourth tax, the tax on income from movable wealth, is imposed on all actual income from sources not subject to the other three taxes; it is a schedular tax, taxing different categories of income at separate rates. In determining the tax on income from movable wealth, individuals, partnerships, and cooperative societies are entitled to a personal allowance (12/3.1) and to a reduced rate of tax on income below a certain figure (12/3.2). There is also a limited progression of the rates of tax applicable to business income (12/1.4c). Apart from these provisions, however, the tax on income from movable wealth and the other objective taxes take no account either of the taxpayer's personal circumstances or of his total resources (2/2).[1]

The personal taxes are imposed on all income subject to the objective taxes and on certain other receipts which are exempt from the objective taxes or which have borne the objective taxes in the hands of another taxpayer. These taxes are the complementary progressive tax on individuals and the corporation tax. The latter consists of a tax on assets (3/2) and a tax on income above a specified percentage of the taxable assets (2/4).

Strictly speaking, it is not the income, but the "production" or productive source of the income, which is the basis (*presupposto*) of an objective tax, whereas the basis of a personal tax is the "possession" of the income itself. The law forbids the imposition of the same tax on the same basis more than once, even where different taxpayers are involved (art. 7). This principle forbids the taxation, as income from movable wealth, of distributions of corporate profits which have been subject to the tax on income from movable wealth when earned, since the basis of that tax is the exercise of a business activity by the corporation. It, however, does not forbid the inclusion of such distributions in a shareholder's income for purposes of the complementary tax or the corporation tax, even though the profits have borne the tax on income from movable wealth and the corporation tax in the hands of the

---

[1] See Forte, "Alcune osservazioni sulla personalizzazione delle imposte reali sul reddito," *Studi urbinati*, 1957-1958, vol. 26, 3.

corporation; the possession of the profits by the corporation and their subsequent possession by the shareholder constitute separate bases of taxation (9/2.1).

b. TAX ON INCOME FROM LANDOWNING. The tax on income from landowning (*imposta sul reddito dominicale dei terreni*) is levied on the landowner's presumed income from the ownership of agricultural land in Italy (10/2.2). Net income is determined by means of a cadastral register of property and schedules of estimated values of the produce of the land, with its appurtenant buildings and equipment, and of the landowner's estimated expenses. The cadastral net income, which is given in 1939 lire, is multiplied by a revaluation coefficient of 12 (12/1.1).

c. TAX ON AGRARIAN INCOME. The tax on agrarian income (*imposta sul reddito agrario*) is levied on the presumed income from the exercise of an agricultural enterprise by the landowner, alone or with others, on land situated in Italy (10/2.3). This tax is a tax on income produced by an activity, which, if not taxed separately, would be treated as income from movable wealth (2/2.3); the tax on income from landowning, on the other hand, is a tax on the income resulting from the ownership of immovable property. Net income for the tax on agrarian income is determined by means of a cadastral register of property and schedules of estimated values of the income attributable to the circulating capital and directive labor of the enterprise, and of the estimated expenses of the enterprise. The cadastral net income, which is given in 1939 lire, is multiplied by a revaluation coefficient of 12 (12/1.2).

d. TAX ON INCOME FROM BUILDINGS. The tax on income from buildings (*imposta sul reddito dei fabbricati*) is levied on the landowner's presumed income from buildings situated in Italy which are used neither in agriculture nor in a business carried on by the landowner himself (9/4.2). Gross income is the rent determined by means of a new urban building cadaster which went into effect on 1 January 1962 (9/2.4d).

e. TAX ON INCOME FROM MOVABLE WEALTH. The basis of the tax on income from movable wealth (*imposta sul reddito di ricchezza mobile*) is the production of an actual net income derived from the employment of capital, of labor, or of both capital and labor, or of income derived from any other source which is not subject to any of the other objective taxes (art. 81).[2] The tax may be regarded as applicable to any income

---

[2] On the classical concept of income whose source is a productive activity, see 1 Quarta, *Commento alla legge sull'imposta di ricchezza mobile* (3d ed., 1917) 129, 137; Pugliese, *I concetti di reddito in economia e finanza*; Giannini, *Istituzioni di diritto tributario* 327; Giannini, "Il concetto di reddito mobiliare nel diritto tributario italiano," *Riv. pol. ec.*, 1935, 397, 592; Einaudi, *Il sistema tributario italiano* (3d

which is excluded from the scope of the other three objective taxes, but not to income which is exempt from any of them (6/1.4). Thus, although income as such is not defined in the law, the basis of the tax on income from movable wealth is broad enough to encompass any receipt or benefit which would ordinarily be regarded as income and whose productive source is not the basis of one of the other objective taxes.[3]

Although, in general, a capital receipt or a return of capital is not taxable, annuity installments are treated as income even though part of the aggregate potential amount of the installments represents the capital price paid for the annuity (9/3.1). The law also specifically taxes as business income certain receipts which otherwise might not be considered income. The most important of these receipts are certain capital gains (9/8), the profits of a mutual insurance company (5/2.6), and amounts derived from cancellation of indebtedness or from the recovery of previously deducted expenses (7/1.3e).

Income may be in kind (8/1.4) as well as in money, and may be occasional (art. 81), as in the case of capital gains (9/8), lottery winnings (10/7.1), and earnings from occasional business or professional activities.[4] If immovable property is rented, rental income attributable to furniture and other movables contained therein is included in the

---

ed., 1935) 61 *et seq.*; Berliri, *L'imposta di ricchezza mobile* 2 *et seq.*; Berliri, *Il testo unico delle imposte dirette*; Montuori, *Note sulle tassazioni in base al bilancio* 86 *et seq.*; Napolitano, *Il reddito nella scienza delle finanze e nel diritto tributario*. More recently, Italian fiscal theorists have tended to regard income as net receipts—the algebraic sum of income produced and of increases and decreases in wealth; see Dus, "I ricavi nel nuovo T. U. delle imposte dirette," *RDFSF*, 1959, I, 113-127; Griziotti, *Principî di politica diritto e scienza delle finanze*; Griziotti, "Le imposte sugli incrementi di valore nei capitali e sulle rendite nei redditi (interessi, salari e profitti)," *Giorn. degli economisti*, 1910, vol. 40, 625, vol. 41, 648; Griziotti, "I concetti giuridici dogmatici di reddito di r.m. e capacità contributiva. L'imposizione degli assegni alimentari," *RDFSF*, 1940, II, 11 *et seq.*; Ardigò, "Sul requisito dell'intento speculativo per l'imposizione del plusvalore nelle vendite d'immobili," *RDFSF*, 1938, II, 301.

[3] For general discussions of the concept of income for purposes of the tax on income from movable wealth considered as a residual tax, compare Griziotti, "I concetti giuridici dogmatici di reddito di r.m. e di capacità contributiva. L'imposizioni degli assegni alimentari," *RDFSF*, 1940, II, 11, and Giussani, "Del concetto di reddito mobiliare e del trattamento tributario degli assegni alimentari," *RDFSF*, 1940, II, 3.

[4] Income from occasional activities other than the taxpayer's normal activity and income from separate businesses carried on by a single taxpayer, other than a corporation or similar entity, were formerly subject to separate taxation in order to avoid distortion of subsequent assessments under the methods of assessment then in force (6/9.2, 8/4). However, each taxpayer is now subject to tax on the net aggregate result of all his business or professional activities which produce income taxable in the same category (5/3.7).

rental income for purposes of the tax on income from buildings; however, imputed income of movable property is not otherwise taxed (2/2.4d).

The tax on income from movable wealth is a schedular tax, imposed at separate rates (12/1.4c) on the four categories of income listed below (art. 85).

1. *Category A.* Income from capital, including perpetual annuities (art. 86) (9/3.1) and income from capital given in loan or otherwise employed so as to derive income in a definite amount (9/1.1); prizes from loan lotteries; and winnings from lotteries, prize contests, and bets (10/7.1).

2. *Category B.* Income to whose production capital and labor contribute jointly, including income from a business other than a small business (7/1.2); income from speculative operations, even if occasional (9/8.2); and interest received by credit firms and institutions or by other persons in the conduct of a business enterprise, exclusive of interest derived from securities held (7/1.3b). For business enterprises, business income includes capital gains, under the rules explained at 9/8.1, and certain windfalls (7/1.3e).

3. *Category C/1.* Income from independent work of an individual, such as that produced in the exercise of an art, profession (8/2, 8/3), or small private enterprise based predominantly on the personal labor of the taxpayer and the members of his family (7/1.2b).

4. *Category C/2.* Income from work as an employee (8/1.1) and certain income which, at the time of production, is, strictly speaking, the result neither of capital nor of labor, such as pensions (8/1.3), annuities (9/3.1), subsidies, and the like.[5]

Net business or professional income is determined by deducting allowable expenses and depreciation from gross income (7/2, 8/2.2). The taxable income of an individual, of a partnership or similar company (5/3.1), or of a cooperative society (5/2.5) is determined by deducting the allocable share of a standard allowance (12/1.4b) from net income from employment, net professional income, and net business income.

Income subject to the tax on income from movable wealth is income which is produced in Italy or is considered to have been produced in Italy under the rules explained at 11/1.

f. COMPLEMENTARY TAX. The complementary progressive tax (*imposta complementare progressiva sul reddito*) is based on the "possession" by an individual, regardless of citizenship, of net aggregate income, including income of members of his family attributed to him (6/8.1), which exceeds a taxable minimum (arts. 130, 131) (12/1.5c).

The aggregate income includes the revalued net income determined for the taxes on income from landowning and agrarian income (12/1.1,

---

[5] Pensions and annuities are considered to have been produced by the contract under which they are paid. The payments, however, represent capital formed with income produced by work as an employee and interest produced by the capital so formed. In general, these two components are not taxed as such when produced.

12/1.2); for purposes of the complementary tax, the revalued net income for these taxes is further multiplied by coefficients of revaluation established annually by the Minister of Finance in relation to the market prices of agricultural products and their means of production (art. 135) (12/1.5a). It also includes the net income determined for the taxes on income from buildings and income from movable wealth, or for substitutive taxes (art. 135). Aggregate income for the complementary tax is not limited to income subject to the objective taxes (art. 133), but includes, specifically, the receipts listed below, which are not subject to the objective taxes on income (art. 135).

1. Income derived from participation in a noncommercial partnership, general partnership, or simple limited partnership, in that proportion of the net income of the company which corresponds to the share in which the taxpayer has the right to participate in the profits of the company (5/3.1).

2. Income derived from participation in a corporation, limited partnership with shares, limited liability company, or cooperative society, in an amount equal to the profits received by the taxpayer, on whatever basis and in whatever form (9/2.1b).

3. Interest from state securities or from bonds whose income is exempt from the tax on income from movable wealth (9/1.1).

4. Income derived from serving as a director of a company (8/1.2).

5. Any other income, even if occasional.

In the absence of an express contrary provision, aggregate income for purposes of the complementary tax includes all income which would have been subject to one of the objective taxes but for a special exemption.

Net aggregate income for the complementary tax is determined by deducting interest payments not deductible for the tax on income from movable wealth and taxes related to income, other than the complementary tax itself, which have been paid or withheld during the year (art. 136) (6/1.5e). Taxable income, to which the progressive rates are applied, is determined by deducting from the net aggregate income a standard allowance and allowances for the persons dependent on the taxpayer (art. 138) (12/1.5b). It should be noted, however, that the net aggregate income may be estimated by the tax administration if there is evidence that the taxpayer's income exceeds the amount determined in the foregoing manner (6/9.1).

Income of an individual for purposes of the complementary tax includes income produced in Italy, regardless of the taxpayer's residence or citizenship (11/1.1); income of a resident individual also includes income produced abroad which is "enjoyed" by him in Italy or which, by virtue of an international agreement, is not taxable in another country (11/2.2).

g. CORPORATION TAX. The corporation tax (*imposta sulle società*) is based on the "possession" of assets or income by a taxable entity. It is composed of two parts, the first of which is a proportional tax on assets, which are defined as subscribed and paid-in capital, plus reserves, plus profits of previous business periods carried forward (3/2.3). The second component is a proportional tax on the amount by which aggregate income exceeds 6% of the taxable assets (art. 146). The tax is imposed on any entity required to be taxed on the balance sheet basis (6/1.2b) which is formed in Italy or has its head office or the principal object of its enterprise in Italy, and also on any foreign company or association operating in Italy through a permanent establishment, even if not required to be taxed on the balance sheet basis (art. 145). In determining the aggregate income of a foreign company or association, only income and expenses related to capital devoted to operations in Italy or employed in Italy, or related to a permanent establishment of the entity in Italy, are taken into account (11/2.1, 11/3.3). Enterprises which elect to be taxed on the balance sheet basis even though not required to be so taxed are not subject to the corporation tax (6/1.2b). Certain entities are exempt from the tax (5/5), and the tax is imposed at reduced rates on the assets and income of credit firms and institutions (10/4) and of investment companies (10/5).

Aggregate income for purposes of the corporation tax includes the revalued net income determined for the taxes on income from landowning and agrarian income. The revalued net income for these taxes is multiplied by coefficients of revaluation which are established annually by the Minister of Finance in relation to the market prices of agricultural products and their means of production (art. 148) (12/2.2b). The aggregate income also includes the net income determined for the tax on income from buildings and the net income from movable wealth of category B, disregarding any loss carried forward for purposes of that tax (7/4.2), but increased by certain payments to directors which were deducted in determining income from movable wealth (art. 148) (7/2.3c). Aggregate income includes, in addition, the receipts listed below, which are not subject to the objective taxes (art. 148).

1. Amounts received by way of distribution or division of the profits of a company or association of any type (9/2.1c).[6]
2. Interest income not included in income from movable wealth of category B (9/1.1).
3. Income exempt from the objective taxes, or substitutive taxes, including income subject in any way to temporary or permanent moderation or to reduction of tax, determined with the criteria applicable to those taxes.

---

[6] Special provisions applicable to holding companies are discussed at 10/5.

4. Any income not otherwise included, such as income produced abroad by a corporation which was formed in Italy or which has its head office or carries on the principal activity of its enterprise in Italy (11/2.1).

From aggregate income are deducted expenses, charges, and losses connected with the production of the various classes of income which, by their nature, were not deductible in the determination of net income of those classes. Ordinary taxes on income and business losses resulting from the application of the provisions relating to the tax on income from movable wealth are also deductible (art. 148) (7/4).

6/1.2 Methods of Determining Actual Income

a. NET INCOME METHOD. For purposes of the taxes on income from landowning, agrarian income, and income from buildings, net income is determined by means of cadastral registers of property and schedules of estimated values for gross income and expenses. In principle, the net income from movable wealth of an individual or of a company not taxed on the balance sheet basis (6/1.2b) is the difference between actual gross income, including realized capital gains when taxable (9/8.1), and actual deductible costs, charges, and losses, determined analytically, that is, by taking account of each item of gross income and of deductible costs (13/2.2). However, the provisions authorizing estimated assessments (6/9.1, 13/2.3) and assessments by agreement (6/9.3, 13/2.4) are broad, and such assessments are very common.

b. NET WORTH COMPARISON METHOD. In determining the net income of entities which are taxed on the balance sheet basis, including both those which are required and those which elect to be so taxed, unrealized capital gains and losses appearing in the balance sheet are taken into account (7/1.3d). Except in those cases in which income is estimated (6/9.1) or determined by agreement (6/9.3), net income of these entities is determined, in the first instance, by a comparison of opening and closing net worth as reflected in the opening and closing balance sheets (13/2.2). Certain assets, however, must be valued in accordance with special rules (6/5); adjustments must also be made, as in the case of any business enterprise, for certain expenses which are not deductible (7/5).

It should also be noted that, in determining the net income of any business enterprise, whether or not taxed on the balance sheet basis, the costs of raw materials, merchandise, and securities are determined by a comparison of successive balance sheet values (6/5).

The entities listed below are required to be taxed on the balance sheet basis if they have been formed in Italy (art. 8).

1. Corporations (5/2.2).
2. Limited liability companies (5/2.3).

3. Limited partnerships with shares (5/2.4).
4. Cooperative societies (5/2.5).
5. Mutual insurance companies (5/2.6).
6. Other juridical persons which are required by law or by their bylaws to prepare a balance sheet (*bilancio*) or an annual financial report (*rendiconto*) (5/2.8).

An entity formed abroad is required to be taxed on the balance sheet basis if its form is one of the first five specified above and it has its head office or carries on the principal activities of its enterprise in Italy (art. 8). All entities which are required to be taxed on the balance sheet basis are subject to the corporation tax (6/1.1g).

The law provides that income of entities required to be taxed on the balance sheet basis is to be determined on the basis of the information which can be inferred from the balance sheet and from the profit and loss statement, or from the annual financial report. It also gives the tax administration the power to check the items in the balance sheet against accounting books, records, and documents and the power to examine and compare book entries with information gathered ex officio (art. 119) (13/2.2). The income of such an entity is assessed under the normal rules applicable to business enterprises only if the entity has failed to comply with certain requirements regarding returns and records (13/2.3). Entities required to be taxed on the balance sheet basis are subject to a number of special provisions, which are summarized below.[7]

1. The tax period, for purposes of the tax on income from movable wealth of categories A and B and for the corporation tax, is the business period (art. 3) (6/3.1).
2. Even if not a business enterprise, an entity required to be taxed on the balance sheet basis is subject to the rules of the *Testo unico* which apply to business enterprises if it carries on business activities (art. 8) (7/1.2a).
3. The return must be filed within one month of the approval of the balance sheet or annual financial report by the shareholders (art. 21) (13/1.1c).
4. The return must be accompanied by a copy of the balance sheet and of the profit and loss statement, or of the annual financial report, and a list of the names of the directors and auditors or overseers for the period covered by the balance sheet (art. 28) (13/1.3).
5. Special accounting records are required, and special rules are prescribed for the keeping of accounting records (arts. 43-45) (6/2).
6. Income from movable wealth includes windfalls related to the property of the entity even if not related to the enterprise (7/1.3e), as well as certain unrealized capital gains on which other companies and enterprises are not taxed (arts. 105, 106) (9/8.1).

---

[7] For discussion of the assessment of income on the balance sheet basis, see Montuori, *Note sulle tassazioni in base al bilancio;* Grillo, *Il bilancio delle società per azioni;* Ceccherelli, *Il linguaggio dei bilanci.*

7. Expenditures for which special records are prescribed are not deductible for purposes of the tax on income from movable wealth unless such records have been kept (arts. 105, 109) (6/2).

8. The deduction of interest charges is limited to the proportion between income subject to the tax on income from movable wealth and gross receipts (arts. 105, 110) (7/2.5).

9. A limited carry-forward of losses is permitted (arts. 105, 112) (7/4.2).

10. Certain payments to foreign enterprises may be attributed to an Italian company required to be taxed on the balance sheet basis (arts. 105, 113) (11/2.4).

11. Special provisions are made for returns and assessments in the case of merger, reorganization, or liquidation (arts. 22, 124, 125) (9/9, 13/1.3c).

12. A special allowance is granted against income from movable wealth for profits invested in the south (10/6.3).

13. Entities required to be taxed on the balance sheet basis are subject to the tax on income from movable wealth on interest and premiums payable by them which have the character of income from capital; these entities have a right of recovery against the recipient through withholding (13/3.4).

14. Entities required to be taxed on the balance sheet basis must attach to their annual returns lists of shares purchased or sold in the course of the business period, except shares purchased or sold by credit firms acting as intermediaries, and of shares given and taken in *riporto* in the course of the business period (9/2.8, 13/1.3).

Other special provisions applicable to particular classes of entities subject to tax on the balance sheet basis are discussed at 5/2.

Business enterprises (7/1.2a) which are not included in the category of persons required to be taxed on the balance sheet basis may elect to be so taxed by following the procedure described at 13/1.3 (art. 104). The exercise of this option does not render the enterprise liable for the corporation tax. A company formed abroad may make this election if it has one or more secondary offices in Italy with a permanent representative (*rappresentanza stabile*) and if it complies with certain requirements with respect to the preparation and publication of its balance sheet (art. 104) (13/1.3). An enterprise which has made this election must attach to its return a copy of its balance sheet and of its profit and loss statement (art. 104) and is subject to all provisions governing the determination of income of entities required to be taxed on the balance sheet basis (art. 105). Such an enterprise must also observe the special rules provided for the keeping of accounting records by entities required to be taxed on the balance sheet basis (art. 45) (6/2.2). The election, however, neither permits the enterprise to change its tax period from the calendar year nor affects the date on which it must file a return. Such an enterprise is not eligible for the special allowance granted to entities required to be taxed on the balance sheet basis for profits invested in the south (10/6.3) and is not subject to the requirement of furnishing lists of shares purchased and sold, or of shares given or taken in *riporto*.

Whenever the phrase "taxed on the balance sheet basis" is used in this volume, it refers collectively to entities required to be taxed on the balance sheet basis and enterprises electing to be so taxed.

6/1.3 Exclusions

Each of the objective taxes is structured in such a way that it excludes from its scope income which is taxable under any of the others. Thus, relief from the tax on agrarian income is granted to owners of estates under lease (10/2.3a), because the actual rental income from the lease is subject to the tax on income from movable wealth; income from certain rural structures which are appurtenant to the land is subject to the tax on income from landowning and is therefore excluded from the tax on income from buildings (10/2.2a); and income from structures used by their owner in his business is excluded from the tax on income from buildings because it is considered to have been included in the income from movable wealth derived from the business carried on in them (9/4.2a). Certain other structures which are not considered to produce income are excluded from the basis of the tax on income from buildings (9/4.2a).

The receipts listed below are expressly excluded from the basis of the tax on income from movable wealth (art. 83).[8]

1. Amounts received as a result of the distribution or division of the profits of a company or association of any type (9/2.1a).
2. A surcharge on the issuance of shares by a company (9/9.3).
3. Equalization payments made by subscribers to new shares of a company which are issued during the business period (9/9.3).

For purposes of the tax on income from movable wealth, capital gains are considered income only when produced by a speculative or business activity, under the rules described at 9/8.1. Gifts (*donazioni*) are not considered income for the tax on income from movable wealth unless they are the counterpart of services or some other condition to be performed by the donee.[9] The basis of the tax on income from movable wealth is the "production" of income (6/1.1e), and a gift which has no counterpart in goods or services furnished to the donor is not considered to have a productive source. Bequests (*legati*) are not considered income

---

[8] Amounts set aside as actuarial reserves by fixed premium or mutual life insurance companies, although "excluded" under article 83, are treated as deductions for purposes of this volume (10/3). Contributions received from the state or other public entities, also "excluded" under article 83, are treated as exempt for purposes of this volume (6/1.4).

[9] The value of a gift of property made by an entity to its president as remuneration for his services is taxable as income from movable wealth, even if the gift is an act of liberality. Comm. Centr. 16 December 1930, n. 15606.

for the tax on income from movable wealth, even in the case of a bequest
to an executor (8/3.1). Income from property given or bequeathed is
subject to the tax on income from movable wealth, even if its value
has been capitalized for purposes of the gift tax or the succession tax.
Whether allowances for support received from a member of one's family
or from a legally separated spouse may be considered income is discussed at 9/3.1. A return of capital, such as that portion of a lump-sum
payment of life insurance benefits which represents a repayment of the
premiums (9/3.2), is not considered income. Casualty insurance proceeds are not considered income if the premiums were not deducted
as a business expense (9/3.3). The repayment of a debt is merely the
replacement of one asset by another and therefore does not constitute
income. Except as noted at 8/1.4, benefits not convertible into money
or money's worth are excluded from income.

The principle that the same tax cannot be applied more than once to
the same basis (6/1.1a) precludes the taxation, as income from movable
wealth, of distributions of corporate profits which have already been
taxed as profits earned, but does not preclude their inclusion in the
shareholder's income for the complementary tax or the corporation tax
(9/2.1b, 9/2.1c). With this exception, receipts which are not considered
income for purposes of the tax on income from movable wealth are not
considered income for the personal taxes.

6/1.4 Tax-Exempt Income

As explained at 5/5, certain classes of taxpayers are exempt either from
the tax on income from movable wealth or from the corporation tax with
respect to certain classes of income. The discussion in this section is
limited to classes or categories of income which are exempt from one
or more of the taxes without regard to the status of the taxpayer. It
should be noted that, although any income which is excluded expressly
or by definition from the taxes on income from landowning, agrarian
income, and income from buildings is included in income for the tax
on income from movable wealth (art. 81), exemption of all or part of
the presumed income from any of those taxes does not subject actual
income from the same source to liability to the tax on income from
movable wealth.

With respect to the tax on income from landowning, permanent exemptions are granted for certain classes of mountainous lands, and full
or partial temporary exemptions are granted for various types of new
cultivation (10/2.2f). In the absence of a special provision, such as that
for agrarian income described at 10/2.3c, exemption from the tax on
income from landowning does not confer exemption from the tax on
agrarian income or the tax on income from movable wealth for any

income derived from the exercise of an agricultural enterprise on the land. Various exemptions from the tax on income from buildings are provided for new construction (9/4.2b).

The receipts listed below are exempt from the tax on income from movable wealth.

1. Social security and welfare contributions paid by the taxpayer's employer in accordance with provisions of law or of a collective bargaining contract (art. 87) (8/1.3).[10]
2. Subsidies received from the state or from other public entities for purely charitable purposes (art. 84).
3. Amounts of any kind received from the state or other public entities which do not constitute a participation (*concorso*) in production expenses or other deductible charges (art. 83).
4. Interest from certain government securities and loans (9/1.2).

In addition to the standard allowance granted against certain categories of income from movable wealth (12/1.4b), income from work as an employee, as well as from pensions and length-of-service and social security payments, is exempt from the tax on income from movable wealth if it does not exceed certain limits (12/1.4a).

A large number of exemptions and special reliefs, chiefly related to the tax on income from movable wealth, were provided by separate laws and have been continued in effect by article 274 of the *Testo unico*. The most important of these exemptions and reliefs are related to credit activities (10/4) and industrial production (10/6). It should be noted that an exemption or relief from "any direct tax" applies only to the taxes levied on the "production" of the income (6/1.1a), that is, to the objective taxes, the communal tax on industry, commerce, arts, and professions (ICAP), the provincial additional thereto, and the Chamber of Commerce tax (2/2.9), but not to the complementary tax, the family tax (2/3), or the corporation tax (2/4).

Individuals are exempt from the complementary tax on war pensions, payments annexed to certain war pensions, and certain wage supplements for family expenses paid to public employees and employees of entities assimilated to state administrative offices (art. 134) (5/5.4). Income exempt from the tax on income from movable wealth or from any of the other objective taxes is, in general, subject to the complementary tax unless the contrary is expressly provided (art. 133). Similarly, income exempt from the objective taxes is generally included in income for the corporation tax (art. 145) (6/1.1g).

---

[10] The "exemption" of gratuities paid to employees by enterprises and of gratuities paid to anyone on behalf of certain entities (art. 84) is actually a reduction of gross income allowed for a disbursement and therefore is treated as a deduction for purposes of this volume (6/1.5f, 8/1.3b). Similarly, the allowance of an employee's social security and welfare contributions (art. 87) is an allowance for a disbursement of the employee and is therefore also treated as a deduction (6/1.5f, 8/1.3a).

6/1.5   Deductions

a. IN GENERAL. The provisions governing each tax on income prescribe
the deductions which may be taken from gross income in determining
net income for that tax, and deductions may be made only in accordance
with those provisions.

b. EXPENSES OF PRODUCTION OR MAINTENANCE OF INCOME. For purposes
of the taxes on income from landowning and agrarian income, the average ordinary expenses of earning the presumed income have been taken
into account in the schedules of estimated values by which average ordinary income is determined (10/2.2, 10/2.3); no other deductions are
permitted. In determining gross income for the tax on income from
buildings, the owner-lessor of a building is permitted to deduct expenses
which he assumes under the contract of lease which would otherwise be
chargeable to the tenant (9/4.2c). The only deduction from gross income
for the tax on income from buildings is a standard allowance for maintenance, repairs, and all other expenses and losses (9/4.2c).

In general, expenses "inherent in" (*inerente a*) the production of business or professional income are deductible in determining net income of
categories B or C/1 of income from movable wealth (7/2.1, 8/2.2).
Amounts set aside as reserves are deductible only in accordance with
the rules explained at 6/6. Special rules are prescribed for the deduction
of certain expenditures by entities required or electing to be taxed on
the balance sheet basis (arts. 108-112); expenses for which such entities
are required to keep special accounting records (6/2.2) are deductible
only if such records are properly kept (art. 109). Business enterprises
are permitted to deduct from business income realized capital losses
(7/2.7) and certain unrealized losses on assets (6/5). An individual is
not permitted to deduct capital losses not connected with the exercise
of a business enterprise unless they result from speculative operations
(9/8.2).

With the exceptions noted at 7/2.1, in determining the net income
for a tax period, only those expenses and losses may be deducted which
are actually incurred in earning income of that period; losses of one
tax period may not be set off against the income of another except in
accordance with the express provisions described at 7/4. If an expense
is underestimated in the year in which it is incurred, the excess cannot
be deducted from income of a later year to which it does not relate,
unless it can be balanced against a taxable hidden reserve (6/6.3) or can
be classified as a general expense attributable to more than one year.
If a business enterprise overestimates an expense, the assessment may be
modified under the rules discussed at 13/2.3. Any recovery of an expense
previously allowed as a deduction must be added to income as a

ANALYSIS OF INCOME TAX   368

windfall in the year in which the account is settled (7/1.3e). Expenses
attributable to more than one business period (7/2.1) and expenses
connected with certain types of contracts, the income from which may
be spread over the contract term (8/4), may also be spread over the
business periods to which the income is attributable. No deduction from
gross income is permitted in the case of income from capital given in
loan or otherwise employed so as to derive income in a definite amount
(9/1.1), or in the case of a perpetual annuity (9/1.3), if that income is
taxable under category A of the tax on income from movable wealth
(art. 86).

Aggregate income for the complementary tax includes net income from
movable wealth and, thus, is already net of expenses deductible in
determining that income (6/1.1f). Expenses which have been taken
into account in the formation of the schedules of estimates for the tax
on income from landowning (10/2.2) or for the tax on agrarian income
(10/2.3), or under the fixed deduction for determining income from
buildings (9/4.2c), have already been considered in determining the
aggregate income for the complementary tax and therefore cannot be
deducted again in determining net aggregate income.[11]

In determining net aggregate income for the complementary tax, the
taxpayer may deduct expenses, charges, and losses inherent in the production of income subject to the tax which, because of their nature, not
their amount, were not deductible in the determination of the aggregate
income (art. 136). Expenses incurred in earning income subject to the
complementary tax, but excluded or exempted from the objective taxes
(6/1.1f), including income produced abroad but "enjoyed" in Italy by
a resident (11/2.2), may be deducted. Expenses of producing income
subject to the objective taxes which have not been taken into account
in determining aggregate income for the complementary tax, such as
expenses of performing services as an employee, within certain limits
(8/1.9), and expenditures for reconstruction of an asset, the income
from which is subject to the tax on income from landowning (10/2.2)
or to the tax on income from buildings (9/4.2c), may also be deducted.
Other examples of expenses which are neither normally taken into account nor separately deductible in determining net income subject to
the objective taxes are interest paid by the owner of a building on a
loan for construction; extraordinary expenses for the rebuilding of a
retaining wall washed away by flooding; betterment contributions (3/7)
paid in reimbursement of expenses sustained for the construction of
works of reclamation; expenses and charges sustained for the purchase
and administration of shares and other securities when these do not form

---

[11] C. M. 12 March 1925; Boidi, *Commento alla legge sulla imposta complementare
progressiva sul reddito* 207-208.

part of the normal activity of the purchaser; and mortgage charges and other annual charges and fees which bear on income from immovable property. Expenditures which were not deductible in determining aggregate income because they were not inherent in the production of income from movable wealth, as in the case of appropriation of the profits of an enterprise by the taxpayer or his family (7/2.3c), cannot be deducted in determining net aggregate income for the complementary tax.[12]

The standard allowance deductible from the net income of categories B, C/1, and C/2 of income from movable wealth (12/1.4b), the basic personal allowance and the allowances for dependents which are deductible from net aggregate income for the complementary tax (12/1.5b), and the reliefs for large families provided under the complementary tax (5/1.3) also take account, to a limited extent, of the living expenses of individuals and their families (2/2.7g).

Income for purposes of the corporation tax, like aggregate income for the complementary tax, is determined net of expenses already taken into account in determining net income for the various objective taxes (6/1.1g). As in the case of the complementary tax, the taxpayer, in determining income subject to the corporation tax, may deduct those expenses, charges, and losses inherent in the production of the various classes of income subject to the tax which, because of their nature, not their amount, were not deductible in the determination of those classes of income (art. 148). Thus, deduction is allowed for expenses inherent in the production of income subject to the corporation tax but excluded or exempt from all of the objective taxes (6/1.1g); deduction is also permitted for expenses inherent in the production of income subject to the objective taxes which were not within the categories specified as deductible in determining income for those taxes.[13] For purposes of the corporation tax, foreign companies and associations operating in Italy are permitted to deduct only those expenses which relate to the employment of capital in Italy or, in some way, to a permanent establishment in Italy (art. 148) (11/2.1).

---

[12] C. M. 12 March 1925.

[13] In this last respect, the *Testo unico* modified the law as it existed under article 5 of L. 6 August 1954, n. 603. Income assessed for movable wealth of category B and income from landowning, agrarian income, and income from buildings were treated as net of all expenses inherent in the production of those classes of income, whether or not actually taken into account in the method of determining net income. See C. M. 1 June 1955, n. 351690; see also Boidi, *L'imposta sulle società e sulle obbligazioni* 171-178; Poli, *Imposta sulle società e imposta sulle obbligazioni* 136-144. The new provision permits the deduction of any expenses not taken into account in determining the various classes of income, without regard to the class of income with which the expense was connected. C. M. 18 December 1959, n. 84.

c. DEPRECIATION. A business enterprise or a person receiving income from the exercise of an art or profession is permitted to deduct depreciation both of the original cost of physical assets relating to the conduct of the activity, and of expenditures for the improvement of such assets (7/3, 8/2.2). The costs of certain intangibles, including good will, and of successful scientific research may be amortized as explained at 7/3.9. Expenses which relate to the formation of a company and to the increasing of its capital are deductible over a five-year period (7/2.13). Thus, in general, capital expenditures for entering into or expanding a business enterprise are depreciable. Entities required to be taxed on the balance sheet basis and enterprises which have elected to be so taxed are not allowed to deduct depreciation for which they have not kept the prescribed records (6/2.2, 7/3.1).

Depreciation of buildings and equipment subject to the tax on income from landowning (10/2.2) is not allowed separately, but is taken into account in the formation of the schedules of estimated values. In the case of buildings subject to the tax on income from buildings, depreciation is not allowed separately, but is covered by the standard deduction (9/4.2c).

d. INTEREST. Interest is deductible from business or professional income under the conditions explained at 7/2.5 and 8/2.2. Interest which is not deductible for purposes of the tax on income from movable wealth is deductible for the complementary tax provided that the recipient and his domicile are specified (art. 136). Interest not taken into account in the determination of net income for the tax on income from landowning or for the tax on income from buildings also may be deducted as an expense related to the production of income subject to the complementary tax or to the corporation tax (6/1.5b).

e. TAXES. Taxes which are considered expenses of producing business or professional income are deductible in determining net income from movable wealth (7/2.8). Income taxes are never considered expenses of producing income.

Net aggregate income for purposes of the complementary tax is determined by deducting, in addition, taxes related to (*afferenti*) income, either on particular classes or in the aggregate, but exclusive of the complementary tax itself, which are inscribed in the rolls for collection (13/3.6a), and whose collection is begun in the year or has been made during the year through withholding (art. 136). Taxes which are deductible under this provision include the objective taxes on income, together with surtaxes and additionals; the local tax on industry, commerce, arts, and professions (2/2.9); and the communal family tax, which is imposed on aggregate income (2/3). The present law makes it clear that the deduction applies only to taxes related to income, thus excluding taxes on capital.[14] It should be noted that deductibility is governed by the time of payment of the taxes and is not limited to taxes related to income of the current tax period.[15]

Similarly, net income for purposes of the corporation tax is determined by deducting ordinary taxes related to (*afferenti*) the various classes of income which have been inscribed in the rolls for collection and whose collection is begun during the tax period (art. 148). Ordinary taxes inscribed in the rolls after the closing of a liquidation or after the reorganization of a company are deductible from the aggregate income of the last business period for which the corporation tax is applied (art. 148). Deductible under these provisions are the objective taxes, with surtaxes and additionals; the communal tax on industry, commerce, arts, and professions, and the provincial additional thereto; the Chamber of Commerce tax; and all other periodic and recurring taxes which are measured on income included in aggregate income for the corporation tax (2/2.9).[16] Taxes paid through an annual fee (*in abbonamento*) in substitution of the tax on income from movable wealth and of certain indirect taxes are also deductible insofar as they do not represent expenses of production deductible in determining net income for the tax on income from movable wealth.[17] The corporation tax itself is not deductible from aggregate income.[18] Whether the tax on bonds is deductible for purposes of the corporation tax, if not already deducted in determining net income from movable wealth (7/2.8), depends on the use to which the capital

---

[14] See De Angelis, Potenza, and Testa, *Testo unico delle leggi sulle imposte dirette* 708. The question of the deductibility of taxes on capital under the prior law is discussed in Boidi, *Commento alla legge sulla imposta complementare progressiva sul reddito* 223, 225 *et seq.* A recent case holding succession taxes deductible is Comm. Centr., Sez. III, 25 May 1960, n. 29038 (*Temi trib.*, 1960, 566). The tax administration has always considered succession taxes and other taxes on capital nondeductible; see C. M. 1 December 1953, n. 501370; C. M. 27 July 1958, n. 500701. For discussion, see Boidi, "Le imposte e tasse deducibili in sede d'imposta complementare sul reddito," *Dir. e prat. trib.*, 1958, II, 1447; Boidi, "Ancora sui tributi deducibili ai fini dell'imposta complementare," *Dir. e prat. trib.*, 1959, II, 417; Cicognani, "Ancora della detraibilità dell'imposta patrimoniale ai fini dell'imposta complementare," *Boll. trib. informazioni*, 1957, 1089; Vanoni, "Intorno alla deducibilità ai fini dell'imposta sui redditi di R. M. della imposta straordinaria sul capitale delle società per azioni," *RDFSF*, 1943, II, 57.

[15] Cass., Sez. I, 16 December 1960, n. 3261. For a discussion of this question, see Boidi, *Commento alla legge sulla imposta complementare progressiva sul reddito* 222.

[16] Boidi, *L'imposta sulle società e sulle obbligazioni* 186.

[17] Boidi, *L'imposta sulle società e sulle obbligazioni* 187.

[18] C.M. 1 June 1955, n. 351690; Poli, *Imposta sulle società e imposta sulle obbligazioni* 150. See, however, Boidi, *L'imposta sulle società e sulle obbligazioni* 189-190. Whether the asset component of the corporation tax may be deducted from income from movable wealth as an expense of producing income is discussed at 7/2.8.

borrowed is to be put.[19] As in the case of the complementary tax, the deductibility of taxes related to income is governed by the time of payment rather than by the tax period in which the taxed income is produced.[20]

When income which has already borne an income tax in another country is subject to the complementary tax because "enjoyed" in Italy (11/2.2), the tax paid abroad clearly is not included in the amount enjoyed in Italy. Although opinions differ as to whether income produced abroad is subject to the corporation tax (11/1.1), such income, if included, would be net of taxes paid abroad,[21] unless, by virtue of a treaty provision (11/4.3b), Italy gave a credit for taxes paid abroad by Italians.

f. CONTRIBUTIONS FOR SOCIAL SECURITY, INSURANCE, AND CHARITY. Social security and welfare contributions paid by an employee in accordance with provisions of law or of a collective bargaining contract are deductible from the employee's income from movable wealth of category C/2, even if computed on the basis of his remuneration (art. 87) (8/1.3a). An individual is permitted to deduct, for purposes of the complementary tax, any additional amounts withheld or paid for social security purposes and any premiums for life insurance purchased by him for his benefit or for members of his family living with him for whose maintenance he is legally responsible (art. 136) (8/1.3a).

The deduction from an employer's business income of social security contributions and insurance premiums paid on behalf of employees is discussed at 7/2.4; the taxation of benefits ultimately received by employees is discussed at 8/1.3b.

A taxpayer is permitted to deduct up to 5% of declared income from movable wealth for gratuities paid on behalf of legally recognized entities, institutes, or associations when the specific purpose of the gratuities is instruction, education, social assistance, worship, or charity (art. 84).[22] Within the same limitation, an enterprise is permitted to deduct amounts paid as gratuities, for the purposes specified, to employees (7/2.4). Since the law regards such amounts as "exempt" from the tax on income from movable wealth, not as deductible in determining net income, they must be included in the payor's income for the complementary tax or the corporation tax.

---

[19] See Poli, *Imposta sulle società e imposta sulle obbligazioni* 154.

[20] See De Angelis, Potenza, and Testa, *Testo unico delle leggi sulle imposte dirette* 777; see also, for critical comment, Boidi, *L'imposta sulle società e sulle obbligazioni* 178-186; Poli, *Imposta sulle società e imposta sulle obbligazioni* 145-149.

[21] See C. M. 1 June 1955, n. 351690.

[22] The percentage is computed on the net income before deduction of the gratuities themselves. See L. 5 January 1956, n. 1, art. 28; De Angelis, Potenza, and Testa, *Testo unico delle leggi sulle imposte dirette* 358. The provision does not exempt the gratuities from tax in the hands of the recipient.

6/2. Books and Records

6/2.1 Laws Relating to Books and Records

The basic requirements for the keeping of books and records by business enterprises are established by the Civil Code. The tax law prescribes special rules for the keeping of books and records by entities taxed on the balance sheet basis (6/2.2, 6/2.3, 6/2.4). The Tax Office has the power to inspect all books and records which the taxpayer is required to keep or to preserve (art. 42).

The manner in which books and records are used in assessment is described at 6/2.5.

6/2.2 Books and Records Required

Any business enterprise except a small business (7/1.2) is required to keep a journal (*libro giornale*), a statement of assets and liabilities (*libro degli inventari*), and any other accounts which are required by the nature and size of the enterprise. Also required to be preserved are the originals of letters, telegrams, and invoices received and copies of letters, telegrams, and invoices sent out (CC art. 2214). The statement of assets and liabilities must be closed annually with the balance sheet (*bilancio*) and the profit and loss statement (*conto dei profitti e delle perdite*) and must contain a specification and valuation of all assets and liabilities of the entrepeneur outside the enterprise (CC art. 2217). Thus, an individual entrepreneur must list all his personal assets and liabilities, as well as those of his business, since there is no distinction between them. In the case of a company, whether formed as a corporation or similar entity (5/2) or as a partnership (5/3), the assets and liabilities of the entrepreneur are those belonging to the company itself; only after the assets of a partnership have been exhausted are the members liable for payment of its debts with their own assets (CC art. 2304).

A corporation is required to keep a register of shareholders (*libro dei soci*), a register of bonds (*libro delle obbligazioni*), and minute-books of the sessions and decisions (*libri delle adunanze e delle deliberazioni*) of the shareholders' assembly (*assemblea*), of the board of directors (*consiglio di amministrazione*), of the board of overseers (*collegio sindacale*), of the executive committee (*comitato esecutivo*), if any, and of the bondholders' meeting (*assemblea degli obbligazionisti*) if bonds have been issued (CC art. 2421). These requirements apply also, insofar as appropriate, to limited partnerships with shares (CC art. 2464), limited liability companies (CC art. 2490), cooperative societies (CC art. 2516), and mutual insurance companies (CC art. 2547).

In addition, an entity required to be taxed on the balance sheet basis (art. 43), or an enterprise which has elected to be so taxed (art. 45) (6/1.2b), is required by the tax law to keep the records listed below.

1. An outline of the accounts (*quadro dei conti*), accompanied by notes explaining the content of each account and the system of accounting adopted.
2. A note explaining the criteria followed in the valuation of the various assets entering into the capital accounts (6/5).
3. A schedule of depreciable assets and their depreciation funds, showing separately, by year of acquisition, the elements of each group, the original cost, revaluations, and devaluations (6/5.6), the depreciation taken in each business period, and reductions through the elimination of assets (7/3.6).
4. A special journal showing all amounts paid to individuals: (a) by way of compensation, reimbursement of expenses, and the like, for the performance of professional, artistic, brokerage, or any other kind of independent services; (b) by way of copyright or of fees or earnings for the transfer or licensing for use of patents, designs, processes, formulas, trademarks, and the like; and (c) by way of interest, commissions, premiums, brokerage, and the like, for the acceptance of funds in deposit, loan, security, or current account, whatever the form, the name, and the method of the transaction, except when received by credit firms and institutions (10/4.4).
5. An entity which carries on industrial activities for the production of goods or services must keep special warehouse records (*registrazioni di magazzino*) which indicate, separately, by quantity and quality, the movements of raw materials, of partially processed materials for sale, of finished products, and of goods to be used in the manufacturing process; such records should make it possible to follow changes between annual inventories (6/2.4).
6. An entity which carries on activity as a dealer or broker in transactions involving goods is required to maintain warehouse records which specify the movements of merchandise, separately, by quantity and quality, and make it possible to follow changes between annual inventories.

6/2.3   Registration and Inspection of Books and Records

The accounting books required by the Civil Code, before being placed in use, must be numbered consecutively on each page and stamped on each leaf by the office of the registry of enterprises or, under the provisions of special laws, by a notary (CC arts. 2215, 2421), and must be inspected annually by the office of the registry of enterprises or by a notary (CC arts. 2216, 2421). Other books of an enterprise may also be stamped and inspected in the same manner at the option of the entrepreneur (CC art. 2218). Loose-leaf or card systems may be used for inventory provided that the sheets used for tabulation are numbered, inspected, and stamped.[23] The statement of assets and liabilities must be filed for inspection, within three months of the closing of the books, with the office of the registry of enterprises or with a notary (CC art. 2217).

All accounts must be kept in accordance with the rules of ordered bookkeeping, without blank spaces, interlineations, or transfers to the

---

[23] See C. M. 1 March 1956, n. 350660; C. M. 30 June 1958, n. 351060.

margin (CC art. 2219). Erasures are not permitted, and cancelled items must remain legible (CC art. 2219).

The schedule of depreciable assets, the special journal of payments to individuals, and the special records of inventory which entities taxed on the balance sheet basis are required to keep (6/2.2) must be numbered and stamped in the same manner as other accounts (art. 44). All of these records, except the schedule of depreciable assets, must be inspected annually (art. 44; CC art. 2216).[24]

The required books, records, and other documents must be preserved for 10 years (art. 44; CC art. 2220). As part of the assessment procedure, the Tax Office may inspect the writings, accounting books, records, and documents which the taxpayer is required by law to keep or to preserve (art. 42) (13/2.2). Books which the taxpayer refuses to produce for inspection cannot be taken into consideration for purposes of assessment (6/2.5).

The return of an entity required to be taxed on the balance sheet basis or of a business enterprise other than a small business (7/1.2) must contain a certification of the receipt of payment of the fee for governmental concessions (4/7) which is due at the time of the first inspection of the books and accounting records (art. 24). The fee for governmental concessions is collected by the Registry Office in whose jurisdiction the enterprise, entity, or company has its fiscal domicile (13/1.1d).

6/2.4   Form of Entries

The Civil Code requires that the balance sheet and the profit and loss statement reflect clearly and precisely the economic situation of the company and the profits incurred or losses suffered (CC art. 2423). The balance sheet must be accompanied by a report of the directors on the conduct of the operations of the company. The Civil Code also prescribes certain accounts which must appear in the balance sheet (CC art. 2424).

The tax law requires that the accounting records of entities required to be taxed on the balance sheet basis be kept in such a manner as to show clearly and distinctly the positive and negative items in the determination of income, in conformity with the type of return in effect at the start of the business period (art. 44). Devaluations, revaluations (6/5.6), and depreciation (7/3.1) must be recorded in the general journal and in individual accounts with separate and distinct entries for categories of assets which are alike in nature and in period of depreciation. The inventory book must indicate, in addition to the items prescribed by the

---

[24] In practice, the books are taken to the Chancellor of the Tribunal (13/1.1c), who stamps them, without actual inspection, if the fee for governmental concessions has been paid.

ANALYSIS OF INCOME TAX   376

Civil Code or by special laws, the quantity of assets, classified in categories by nature and value, and the value attributed to each category of assets (art. 44) (6/5). If the inventory does not reveal the components of each category and their location, the detailed lists used in compiling the inventory must be kept available to the tax officers. These requirements apply also to enterprises electing to be taxed on the balance sheet basis (art. 45) (6/1.2b).

In other respects, no special method of keeping books is prescribed. Subject to the powers of the tax administration to check the books against information gathered ex officio (6/2.5) and, in certain cases, to assess income by estimate (6/9.1), the accounts will be accepted provided that they show clearly and separately the positive and negative elements involved in the determination of income and provided that the journal and the register of amounts paid (6/2.2) reflects the day-to-day operations of the enterprise.

6/2.5 Weight Given to Book Entries

The Tax Office may inspect the writings, accounting books, records, and documents which the law requires a taxpayer to keep or preserve (art. 42). In the case of business enterprises not taxed on the balance sheet basis, the tax law provides that income is to be determined on the basis of the economic situation of the firm, as derived from the information furnished by the taxpayer and gathered ex officio (art. 118) (13/2.3). Under this method of determining income, the taxpayer's books and records are one source of information on which the authorities may rely. On the other hand, accounting books, records, writings, and documents which the taxpayer refuses to produce cannot be taken into consideration for purposes of assessment, administrative proceedings, or litigation (art. 42). The taxpayer's declaration that he does not possess accounting books, records, writings, and documents, and their concealment from a requested inspection, constitute refusals to produce (art. 42). A business enterprise other than a small business (7/1.2) has the burden of proof against the assessment of the Tax Office when it appears from a report of inspection (6/2.3) that it has not kept the required accounting records, has failed to keep them in accordance with the provisions of the Civil Code, or has refused to produce them (art. 118).

The income of entities taxed on the balance sheet basis is determined from the information which can be inferred from the balance sheet and the profit and loss statement or from the annual financial report (arts. 118, 119). However, the tax administration can use the accounting books, records, and documents to check the entries in the balance sheet and can check the entries in the records themselves against information gathered ex officio (art. 119). The conditions under which the Tax Office may modify or correct entries in the balance sheet or estimate the tax-payer's income without regard to the balance sheet are discussed at 6/9.1 and 13/2.3.

6/3.   Accounting Periods

6/3.1   Tax Year and Base Year

The financial year (*esercizio finanziario*) of the Italian government begins on 1 July and ends on the following 30 June. However, the income taxes are assessed for a tax period (*periodo d'imposta*) (6/3.2) which may coincide with the financial year in the case of an entity required to be taxed on the balance sheet basis, but otherwise does not. For each tax period, the direct taxes are measured with reference to the bases (*presupposti*) existing in that period (art. 4); hence, under the Italian tax system, the "tax year" and the "base year" are identical.[25]

There is a separate tax obligation for each tax period (art. 3), and, in general, net income for each period is determined by deducting from the gross income produced during the period the expenses incurred during the period for the production of that income (6/1.5b). However, by using the accounting rules described at 6/4.1, recognition of gross income or expenses may be postponed until after the year of production, especially in the case of business income. Income actually produced in prior years is also taken into account under the provisions governing inscription in the balance sheet of a corporation or similar entity of gains not previously taxed (7/1.3d), recoupment of previously deducted expenses or losses (7/1.3e), and the capitalization, distribution, or appearance in the balance sheet of "hidden reserves" (6/6.3). Expenses related to the production of income of other years is taken into account under the provisions governing the deduction of bad debts (7/2.10), the carrying-forward of net operating losses by entities or companies taxed on the balance sheet basis (7/4.2), and the deduction of taxes related to income in determining net income for the complementary tax and the corporation tax (6/1.5e). The provisions governing valuation (6/5) and reserves (6/6) may also result in the compensation of losses against gains over income years.

Under the principle which forbids retroactivity of a law a change in the tax law applies, in general, only to the assessment of income produced after the effective date of the law; however, it appears that a change in

---

[25] Before the effective date of the *Testo unico*, tax was assessed for the financial year by reference to the income of a base year, under the presumption that the amount had not changed. For corporations, limited partnerships with shares, limited liability companies, and entities required by law to compile balance sheets, the base year was the business period ending during the financial year; for other taxpayers, the base year was the calendar year ending before the start of the financial year. See L. 11 January 1951, n. 25, art. 18. The income of the financial year was conclusively presumed to be equal to the income of the base year.

the law may, by express provision, apply to the assessment of all income of the tax period during which the change was enacted. A change cannot apply to the assessment of income of a tax period which expired before the enactment of the change.[26]

6/3.2 Calendar Year and Fiscal Year

For taxpayers not required to be taxed on the balance sheet basis, the tax period (6/3.1) for all types and sources of income is the calendar year (art. 3).[27] For taxpayers required to be taxed on the balance sheet basis (6/1.2b), the business period or fiscal year (*esercizio sociale*) is the tax period for purposes of the tax on income from movable wealth of categories A and B, and for the corporation tax (art. 3); however, on 31 March of each year, these taxpayers must file returns of wages and salaries paid by them in the preceding calendar year.

Since the shareholders' assembly must meet at least once a year and is charged with approving the balance sheet (CC art. 2364), the business period of a corporation or similar entity normally cannot exceed 12 months, although the period in which a company changes its accounting period may be longer or shorter as a result.

The Tax Office is authorized to assess income "inductively" or by estimate (13/2.3), and certain sanctions are applicable in the case of a false return (13/7.4); otherwise, no sanctions are provided for the incorrect choice of tax period.

6/3.3 Change of Accounting Period

When a company not required to be taxed on the balance sheet basis (6/1.2b) decides, during the course of and without closing the business period, to reorganize as an entity required to be taxed on the balance sheet basis, or vice versa, the fractions of the calendar year or business period before and after the change are separate tax periods for purposes of the tax on income from movable wealth of categories A and B and for the corporation tax (art. 3). There are no restrictions on the change of accounting periods by an entity taxed on the balance sheet basis if the entity is not transformed thereby into one not taxed on the balance sheet basis. When a change is made, the tax period of the entity ends at the time of change. Special provisions to avoid the necessity for adjustments of this kind were in effect for the years 1959 to 1961, when many com-

---

[26] See Giannini, *I concetti fondamentali del diritto tributario* 49-50. However, article 2 of L. 10 December 1961, n. 1346, enacts an increase of the additional for communal assistance entities, applicable to taxes collectible from 1 January 1961, even if referable to income of previous tax periods (2/2.9).

[27] It appears, however, that some local Tax Offices allow enterprises that elect to be taxed on the balance sheet basis to use the business period instead of the calendar year.

panies were adopting the calendar year as their business period in order to have the same tax period for all their income.

6/3.4 Commencement of Operations

The taxes on income are owed from the period in which their bases arise to the period in which their bases end (art. 5). When a business is commenced, the first tax period of an enterprise not required to be taxed on the balance sheet basis runs from the commencement of business to the end of the current tax period (6/3.2). The first tax period of an entity required to be taxed on the balance sheet basis runs to the date fixed for the closing of the business period, which may be more or less than 12 months away.

By virtue of a special provision, the assessment of the taxes on income from landowning and agrarian income is made against the owner inscribed in the cadastral register on 31 August of the year preceding the tax period (10/2.2b, 10/2.3a). But, although a person who purchases agricultural lands after 31 August of any year is not subject to tax on the income of that tax year, or of the following tax year, he is jointly and severally liable with the previous owner for the payment of taxes on income arising after the date of the transfer (13/3.1). An increase in the assessable income of the land resulting from the commencement of new operations by a landowner does not take effect until the tax year following that in which the change occurs (10/2.2e, 10/2.3b).[28] Income from a new building is subject to the tax on buildings from the day on which the building becomes actually suitable for the use to which it is to be devoted, or on which a special exemption terminates; under the provisions currently in force, however, income from all new buildings is exempt for varying periods (9/4.2b).

For purposes of the corporation tax, the income of the period during which the company commenced operations is annualized, and the tax is computed on that amount of annualized income which exceeds 6% of the taxable assets; the tax payable for the first period is that proportion of the annual tax which the first period bears to the entire year.[29]

6/3.5 Termination of Operations

Except in the case of income from landowning and agrarian income, the final period for assessment of the taxes on income is that in which the basis of taxation ends (art. 5). The income assessed is that attributable to the final tax period down to the date of termination.[30]

---

[28] It should be noted that the change does not actually take effect until it is inscribed in the cadastral register, at the instance either of the taxpayer or of the Tax Office.

[29] C.M. 1 June 1955, n. 351690.

[30] Under the system in effect before the *Testo unico* (6/3.1), the income for the year of termination of an enterprise not required to be taxed on the balance sheet

In the case of liquidation of an entity required to be taxed on the balance sheet basis, the corporation tax is computed on the amount of annualized income exceeding 6% of taxable assets; the tax payable is that proportion of the annual tax which the final tax period bears to the entire year. If the liquidation extends over more than one year, the taxable assets are determined from the closing balance sheet of each year.[31]

In the case of termination of the tax basis during the tax period, the taxpayer may file a report to that effect in the same manner prescribed for filing of a return (art. 30) (13/1.5). The filing of the report does not relieve the taxpayer of the requirement of filing a return for the period during which the termination took place (art. 30), but merely precludes provisional inscription in the roll (13/3.6a), for later tax periods, of the amount of tax assessed for the year of termination.

A taxpayer who is registered as the owner of agricultural land on 31 August of any year is liable for the taxes on income from landowning and agrarian income from that land for the succeeding tax period, even if he has sold the land and terminated the agricultural enterprise (10/2.2b, 10/2.3a). If the termination of agricultural operations results in a decrease in the amount of income assessable for the tax on agrarian income or for the tax on income from landowning, the decrease takes effect from the base year following the filing of a request therefor, unless the request is filed before 31 January of the base year (10/2.2e, 10/2.3b).

6/3.6 Mergers and Reorganizations

In the case of a merger of entities taxed on the balance sheet basis, the company or entity surviving or resulting from the merger is responsible for compiling a closing balance sheet; this balance sheet will serve as the basis for the final determination of the tax due for the last business period of any entity which has ceased to exist (9/9.7). When a change in the form of a company requires a change of accounting periods for tax purposes, the fractions of the year or business period before and after the change are separate tax periods (6/3.3), and a balance sheet must be compiled for the period before the reorganization if the entity was taxed on the balance sheet basis during that period (9/9.4).

When a company not required to be taxed on the balance sheet basis is transformed into a company required to be taxed on the balance sheet basis, liability for the corporation tax is determined as if operations had been commenced during the year (6/3.4); when a company required to be taxed on the balance sheet basis is transformed into a company not

---

basis, or of an enterprise required to be taxed on the balance sheet basis whose business period did not coincide with the financial year, did not serve as the tax base of any year; the basis of the assessment for the final period was the income of the year preceding that of termination.

[31] C.M. 1 June 1955, n. 351690.

required to be taxed on the balance sheet basis, liability for the corporation tax is determined as if dissolution or liquidation of the company had been completed in the course of the year (6/3.5).[32]

6/4. Accounting Methods

6/4.1 In General

The Italian direct tax laws make no provision for a choice between cash and accrual accounting methods. The accounting method to be used must be inferred for each tax and each category of income by examining the applicable provision governing the determination of the income.

The types of income listed below are expressly subject to tax in the amount received by the taxpayer.

1. Income from work as an employee, for the tax on income from movable wealth (art. 87) (8/1.1).
2. Income derived from serving as a director of a company, interest from state securities or from bonds, and any other income, even if occasional, for the complementary tax (art. 135) (8/2.1).
3. Income derived from participation in a corporation, limited partnership with shares, limited liability company, or cooperative society, on whatever basis and in whatever form it is received by the taxpayer, for the complementary tax (art. 135) (9/2.1b).
4. Amounts received by way of distribution or division of the profits of a company or association of any type, for the corporation tax (art. 148) (9/2.1c).

Although not explicitly stated in the law, it appears that a taxpayer may be considered, in any of these cases, to have received income when it is placed at his disposal, as when wages or salary are paid, interest is deposited in a bank, or a distribution of profits is declared. It should also be noted that in the case of income from work as an employee, the tax is normally paid by the employer and recovered from the employee through withholding (13/3.4).

In all other cases, it must be assumed that income becomes subject to tax when "produced" (6/1.1a), under the rules governing the determination of income of each type, whether or not it has been received.[33] Thus, for purposes of the tax on income from movable wealth, income from business and professional activities is the "gross proceeds" (*ricavi lordi*), which include receipts and credits (7/1.1) less the expenses connected with the production of the income, including payments and debts (7/2.1) and the value of goods produced but not sold (6/5.1). Business receipts and expenses are taken into account only when they become fixed and certain; receipts not taxed in the year of production and expenses related to the production of income of other years are taken into account under

---

[32] C.M. 1 June 1955, n. 351690.
[33] See Zappalà, Marionetti, and Lanza, *L'imposta sui redditi di ricchezza mobile* 30.

ANALYSIS OF INCOME TAX   382

the rules summarized at 6/3.1. Income derived from the exercise of an art or profession consists of the amount of compensation for activities carried on during the year, after deduction of the expenses connected with the exercise of those activities (art. 115); as in the case of business income, credits and debts which have become settled during the year are taken into account.[34]

The spreading of amounts received which are attributable to more than one year is permitted in the case of long-term contracts (6/4.3), piecework by employees (8/1.1), and liquidation of a company (9/9.9). The spreading of business and professional expenses covering more than one year, including certain capital expenses, is also permitted (7/2.1).

Income from capital given in loan or otherwise employed so as to derive an income in a definite amount and income from perpetual annuities, are included in income from movable wealth in the amount shown in the contract or security from which the income arises unless a greater amount is proved to have been received (art. 86) (9/1.1). In most cases, however, the tax on income from movable wealth on such income is paid by the person who pays the income and is subject to recovery from the recipient through withholding (13/3.4).

For the taxes on income from landowning and agrarian income, no problem of accounting methods arises because the production of income is presumed (10/2.2, 10/2.3). The production of income is also presumed in the case of income from buildings, even if the income is measured by the rent appearing in the contract of lease (9/4.2c).

6/4.2   Installment Sales

Since the gross proceeds of a business include both receipts and credits (6/4.1), the total price of goods sold for a price payable in installments is included in the income of the year of sale. Interest payable by reason of deferred payment of the purchase price is included in income of the year in which it becomes due; it is taxed in category B unless the credit, by "*avulsione*," becomes a separate capital asset, in which case it is taxed in category A (7/1.3b). There is no allowance for risks of collection; a loss on a credit is deductible only in the year in which the credit becomes worthless (7/2.10).

6/4.3   Long-Term Contracts

Income derived from contracts for the execution of a specific work or service (*appalti*), contracts of supply (*forniture*), administrations (*amministrazioni*), and services required by court order, guardianship, and the like, which cover more than one year or business period, is deter-

---

[34] See *Guida pratica per la compilazione della dichiarazione unica dei redditi nell'anno 1962*; see, however, Cass. 3 August 1960, n. 2283. For discussion of the interpretation of article 115, see Berliri, *Il testo unico delle imposte dirette* 234.

mined on the basis of the share of receipts and expenses proportionately attributable to the activity carried on in each tax period (6/3.1); this determination of income takes account of the risk connected with accomplishing the work (art. 116) (8/4). The time of the receipt of payment is immaterial.

6/5.   Valuation of Assets

6/5.1   Inventories

Raw materials and merchandise must be valued at the cost or price of acquisition, or market value at the close of the business period, whichever is lower (art. 102). Once a valuation has been made for a business period in accordance with this provision, it can be maintained by the taxpayer for succeeding business periods (art. 102). When there is a decrease in quantity, inventory identification must be made by the last-in-first-out (LIFO) method (art. 102).[35]

There is no requirement that inventories be valued at market on the discontinuance of a business or upon distribution of inventory among the partners, associates, or shareholders, unless the taxpayer has regularly valued its inventories at market value.

Under prior law, taxpayers were permitted to compute profit or loss from realization on "permanent stock," the raw materials and merchandise indispensable for the normal functioning of the business, by deducting the cost of replacement from the receipts realized on sale.[36] Taxpayers who, before 1 January 1960, exercised the option to use this method of computation may continue to do so (art. 289).

6/5.2   Accounts Receivable

Accounts receivable, or credits (*crediti*), are normally valued at their nominal value. If they are valued at their presumable value of realization, as required by the Civil Code for corporations and similar entities (CC art. 2425), the difference between nominal value and presumable value of realization must be recorded as a devaluation in the general journal and in the individual accounts (art. 44) (6/5.6). Since amounts transferred to reserves for bad debts are not deductible (6/6.1), the devaluation constitutes a "hidden reserve" which is taxed when it is capitalized or distributed, or otherwise appears in the balance sheet (6/6.3).

6/5.3   Securities

For the determination of gains taxable as income from business (7/1.3d, 9/8.1), shares, bonds, and interest-bearing securities must be valued at

---

[35] The development and the operation of the rules governing the valuation of inventory are discussed in Montuori, *Note sulle tassazioni in base al bilancio* 185-204.
[36] L. 11 January 1951, n. 25, arts. 9, 10, 11.

not less than their cost of acquisition or their market value at the close of the business period, whichever is lower (art. 103). Once a valuation has been made for a business period in accordance with this provision, however, it can be maintained by the taxpayer for succeeding business periods.[37]

The cost of securities issued by the same entity and having the same characteristics is determined by dividing the total purchase price by the number of securities held, including those acquired gratuitously (art. 103). The taxpayer nonetheless has the option of valuing securities individually at cost, provided he has given written notice to the District Office of Direct Taxes before the start of the business period; if not revoked, such notice also continues in effect for succeeding business periods. If this option is elected, securities already held at the start of the business period are considered to have been acquired at the start of the business period and are valued at their average cost in the normal manner; securities disposed of are then considered to be those acquired most recently (LIFO).

The value of similar securities at the close of the business period is the average of the purchase prices paid during the last three months of the business period or the market price at the date of the close of the business period, whichever is lower (art. 103). In the case of shares not quoted on the stock exchange, the proportionate share of any decrease in the capital value between the last regularly approved balance sheet of the issuing company before the date on which the shares were acquired and the most recent balance sheet, or of any decrease appearing from decisions adopted by the issuing company in accordance with article 2446 of the Civil Code, must be taken into account. In the case of bonds and other interest-bearing securities not quoted on the stock exchange, the proportionate share of any decrease in value evidenced by certain and precise elements must be taken into account.

Participations other than shares must be valued in an amount not exceeding that obtained from the last balance sheet of the enterprise to which they refer (CC art. 2425).

6/5.4 Fixed Assets

For purposes of depreciation, fixed assets are valued at original cost in accordance with the rules explained at 7/3.3.

6/5.5 Intangibles

As explained at 7/3.9, intangibles cannot be valued at more than purchase price or cost, and the value must be reduced each year in

---

[37] For examples of the method of valuing securities, see C. M. 15 April 1957, n. 350860.

proportion to the period of exploitation, the life of the assets, or the loss or diminution of their utilization.

6/5.6   Revaluations and Devaluations

Monetary revaluations and devaluations must be shown in the schedule of depreciable assets and their depreciation funds which entities taxed on the balance sheet basis are required to keep (art. 43) (6/2.2).[38] Active monetary revaluation funds are included in the taxable assets of an entity for purposes of the corporation tax (art. 147).

Capital gains resulting from revaluation for monetary equalization, made in conformity with the Law of 11 February 1952, n. 74, are not subject to the tax on income from movable wealth (9/8.1).

Reserves formed by devaluations of inventory, securities, or other assets are subject to the tax on income from movable wealth when inscribed in the balance sheet (6/6.3).

6/6.   Reserves
6/6.1   In General

The Civil Code requires the maintenance of a "legal reserve" (*riserva legale*) (6/6.2) to protect the integrity of capital. A company may also establish reserves for losses on credits, for renewal of machinery, or for other needs which may arise in the course of business. Such reserves may be required by the bylaws (*riserve statuarie*) or may be established at the discretion of the directors or shareholders (*riserve facoltative*).

With the exceptions noted at 7/2.1, only those liabilities or expenses connected with the production of income for the business period which become fixed during the business period are permitted to be deducted. In general, therefore, provisions to legal, bylaw, or discretionary reserves are not deductible for tax purposes. However, special provisions of the *Testo unico* permit the deduction, for purposes of the tax on income from movable wealth, of amounts transferred to funds providing allowances for length of service and retirement (6/6.2, 7/2.3e), and to life insurance actuarial reserves (10/3).

Reserves formed with a surcharge received on the issue of new shares are not subject to the tax on income from movable wealth (9/9.3).

It should also be noted that, for purposes of the corporation tax, taxable assets include ordinary and extraordinary reserves of any kind shown in the balance sheet and active monetary revaluation funds, with the exclusion of reserves and funds to be used to cover specific burdens and charges or on behalf of third persons (art. 147) (3/2.3); they also

---

[38] For discussion of the tax treatment of monetary revaluations, see Zappalà, Marionetti, and Lanza, *L'imposta sui redditi di ricchezza mobile* 17-28.

include amortization fund reserves for property subject to gratuitous retransfer to the grantor under a contract of concession (art. 147) (7/3.10).

6/6.2 Reserves Required by Law

One twentieth of the net annual profits of a corporation or similar entity (5/2) must be set aside as a reserve fund until the fund equals one fifth of the capital of the company (CC art. 2428).[39] If diminished for any reason, the reserve fund must be restored to the amount required by law. The fact that the annual provision to this reserve fund is required by law does not render it deductible for tax purposes (6/6.1).

When a corporation or similar entity has not provided for the formation of a social security fund or other form of social security insurance, it is required to make periodic payments to provide allowances for length of service (anzianità) and retirement (quiescenza) (CC art. 2429). These payments are deductible for purposes of the tax on income from movable wealth under the rules explained at 7/2.4.

A credit firm or institution must set aside annually not less than one tenth of its net profit for an ordinary reserve until the fund equals 40% of capital.[40] That part of the annual provision to a legal or bylaw reserve which exceeds one twentieth of the net profit is subject to the tax on income from movable wealth at one half the normal rate (10/4.2).

6/6.3 "Hidden Reserves"

For all enterprises organized as business companies under the Civil Code (5/3.1), income which has escaped taxation in previous business periods is included in taxable income for the business period in which it is capitalized or distributed, or otherwise appears in the balance sheet (art. 107) (7/1.3f).[41] This provision permits the taxation of previously untaxed income, provided that it appears in the balance sheet, even after the expiration of the time limit for modifying the assessment for the year in which the income was actually earned (13/6.1).[42] Before the expira-

---

[39] A cooperative society must set aside one fifth of its annual profits, regardless of the total amount of the fund (CC art. 2536).

[40] R.D.L. 7 September 1926, n. 1511.

[41] Despite the express language of the law, the intent of which is confirmed by administrative instructions (C. M. 18 December 1959, n. 84), it appears that, in practice, this provision is not applied to a company not required to be taxed on the balance sheet basis unless it has elected to be so taxed. See Montuori, Note sulle tassazioni in base al bilancio 147. The original purpose of the provision was to remove an inequality between entities required to be taxed on the balance sheet basis, whose income could otherwise be assessed only on the basis of the current year's balance sheet, and other enterprises, whose income is subject to inductive assessment (13/2.3). See L. 8 June 1936, n. 1231, art. 19; L. 5 January 1956, n. 1, art. 22; Montuori, Note sulle tassazioni in base al bilancio 144.

[42] See Ceccherelli, Il linguaggio dei bilanci 492.

tion of the time limit, however, the tax authorities can modify the assessment for the year in which the income was actually earned to take account of income discovered (13/2.5), whether or not that income has appeared in the balance sheet.[43] Amounts taxed under this provision are included in income only for purposes of the final adjustment of the assessment and do not form part of the basis of the provisional assessment for future business periods (13/3.6a).[44]

Income of previous business periods may have escaped taxation by the concealment of receipts in a special account, sometimes transitory; by excessive assessments of costs and debts, or the inclusion of fictitious costs and expenses; by the total or partial devaluation of assets, or the omission of assets from the balance sheet; or by the valuation of inventory below cost.[45] The reductions in income created by the use of such devices are frequently called "hidden reserves" (*riserve occulte*). Such reserves may come to light, and therefore be subject to taxation, when they are transformed into open reserves, or when they emerge in the balance sheet either through the realization of assets in which they are embodied or through their use to cover expenses and losses in business periods after that in which they were established.[46]

6/7. Branch Accounting

A branch and its head office constitute a single taxable entity, and the profits of the branch are taxed as the profits of the principal organization (5/2.2). There are no special requirements concerning accounting for branch income.

Income derived by an enterprise operating both in Italy and abroad from a branch or permanent establishment in Italy is subject to tax in Italy (11/3.5). Conversely, an enterprise formed in Italy, or having its head office or the principal object of its enterprise in Italy, is not subject to tax on income derived from activities exercised abroad by a foreign branch or other permanent establishment abroad which has separate administration and accounting (11/2.3).

When a branch or affiliate in Italy does not have separate administration and accounting, the income allocated to the branch for purposes of the communal tax on industry, commerce, arts, and professions, and related surtaxes (2/2.9) is determined empirically, in proportion to receipts, to labor employed, or to expenses directly imputable to the branch.

---

[43] See C. M. 15 April 1957, n. 350860; Montuori, *Note sulle tassazioni in base al bilancio* 148.

[44] See L. 5 January 1956, n. 1, art. 22; Montuori, *Note sulle tassazioni in base al bilancio* 148.

[45] See C.M. 15 April 1957, n. 350860; Montuori, *Note sulle tassazioni in base al bilancio* 149.

[46] See C.M. 15 April 1957, n. 350860; Montuori, *Note sulle tassazioni in base al bilancio* 152.

However, a share of the income is always allocated to the head office. The income of a branch and the income of the head office are reported on a single return (5/2.2).

6/8. Attribution Rules

6/8.1 Income of Family Members

In principle, the structure of objective taxation affords no opportunity for a family to reduce its total tax liability by spreading the income of some of its members among the others; income from each productive source or activity is taxed as a unit, at proportional rates, without regard to the identity or personal circumstances of the taxpayer. As a result of the limited "personalization" (2/2.7g) which has been introduced for the tax on income from movable wealth, however, the total tax liability of a family on the income which its members collectively derive from a family business, whether the business is nominally owned by one of the members of the family or by a family partnership, may be higher than would be the case if the business employed outside labor and the members of the family were employed elsewhere. This possibility is not a consequence of any direct attribution of business income, taxed at progressive rates (12/1.4c), to the head of the family, because, in any event, the income of a business enterprise has a single basis and is therefore taxed as a unit. The higher total tax liability results from the operation of the rules described below.

1. In determining net income from movable wealth, an enterprise is not permitted to deduct compensation paid to the taxpayer's wife or unemancipated minor children, or to partners, for their work in the business (7/2.3c). The income attributable to their work is therefore taxed not as income from work as an employee, but at the higher progressive rates applicable to business income (2/2.4c), unless the enterprise qualifies as a small business taxable in category C/1 (7/1.2b).
2. In determining net taxable income from the business, whether carried on by an individual or by a partnership, use may be made only once of the standard allowance (12/1.4b) and of the rate reduction (12/1.4c) provided for income below certain limits.

The aggregate income of an individual for purposes of the complementary tax includes not only his own income, but the income of his wife (5/1.2) and also that of other persons over which he has the power of free disposition without the obligation to render an accounting (5/1.3). Thus, for purposes of the complementary tax, devices to divide income among members of a family, such as family partnerships, do not reduce the total tax liability of the family unless some members of the family are independent. But since the income of a person living independently is likely, under the existing procedures, to be assessed at a higher figure than the income of a dependent, both for the complementary tax and for the family tax (2/3.2), the motive for members of a family to appear independent is not as strong as it would be if the complementary tax and the family tax were always assessed by the analysis of separate items of receipts and expenditures.

A family corporation or other closely held corporation is subject to the corporation tax, and, in principle, a shareholder is not liable for the complementary tax on the profits of a corporation unless a distribution has actually been declared. There remains the possibility, however, that undistributed profits of a family corporation or a closely held corporation could be included in the incomes of its shareholders for purposes of the complementary tax (9/2.1b).

6/8.2   Payments to Foreign Companies

If an entity taxed on the balance sheet basis carries on activity in Italy on behalf of a foreign company or association, through the sale or disposal of raw materials or merchandise, or through the manufacturing of goods, its income includes amounts paid to the foreign company, firm, or association in the form of a price higher than the current price for raw materials, products, or merchandise, or in the form of brokerage fees, royalties, commissions, premiums, and the like, if the payments are not subject to withholding (art. 113) (11/2.4).

Other relations between Italian companies and foreign companies which may result in the former being subject to tax on income produced by the latter are discussed at 11/2.3b.

6/9.   Other Methods of Determining the Tax Base

6/9.1   Estimated Income

The income of a business enterprise not taxed on the balance sheet basis is determined on the basis of the economic situation of the firm (art. 118) (13/2.3). The income of any other taxpayer not taxed on the balance sheet basis is assessed by a determination of the various receipts and deductions, unless the taxpayer has failed to file a return or has failed to furnish all information necessary to check the return (art. 117) (13/2.3).

The income of an entity or enterprise taxed on the balance sheet basis may be determined on the basis of the economic situation of the business deduced from information furnished by the taxpayer or collected by the Tax Office, if the taxpayer has failed to file a return in the proper manner, or has not kept the required accounting records in the prescribed manner, or has refused to produce them, or if the appearance of serious or repeated irregularities in the entries justifies the conclusion that the balance sheet is unreliable (13/2.3). In all other cases, the determination of income must be based on information obtained from the balance sheet and profit and loss statement (13/2.2); however, individual items in the balance sheet may be modified or corrected, by estimate if necessary, on the basis of any information available to the Tax Office (13/2.3). If the taxpayer fails to file a return, the assessment is based on income of the preceding tax period, increased by 10% for all income from movable wealth except category C/2, and any increment may be assessed by estimate (ex officio) (13/2.3).

For purposes of the complementary tax, the net aggregate income may be determined by estimate, with reference to the taxpayer's way of living or other circumstances, if these are such as to justify the presumption of a net income greater than that resulting from an analytical assessment (13/2.3). Income so determined is not eligible for any deductions other than the standard allowances for the complementary tax (12/1.5c).

Detailed reasons must accompany a notice of assessment of income which the taxpayer has reported, if the return contains a detailed specification of the receipts and deductions (13/2.1).

6/9.2 Presumed Income

The taxable income of a landowner from the ownership of agricultural land is based on the presumed income, derived from a schedule of estimated values; it is subject to the tax on income from landowning (10/2.2).

The taxable income of a landowner from the exercise of an agricultural enterprise on his own land is based on the presumed income from the circulating capital and directive labor of the enterprise, derived from a schedule of estimated values; it is subject to the tax on agrarian income (10/2.3). A taxpayer carrying on agriculture under a lease may elect to have the income therefrom, which is subject to the tax on income from movable wealth, based on the revalued presumed income for the tax on agrarian income (10/2.3).

The taxable income obtained by an owner from buildings not used in agriculture or in the owner's business is based on the presumed income derived from a new urban building cadaster which went into effect 1 January 1962; it is subject to the tax on income from buildings (9/4.2).

Once any of the objective taxes, including the tax on income from movable wealth, has been assessed against a taxpayer, the basis of the imposition of the tax is generally presumed to continue in existence until its termination is reported, either in the return or in a report of termination (13/1.5). Before World War II, the taxable income assessed for the tax on income from movable wealth was conclusively presumed to continue unchanged for three years; occasional income and income from separate businesses carried on by the same taxpayer were assessed separately, *una tantum* (8/4). In the doctrine, the complementary tax was regarded, even during this period, as applicable to actual income, including occasional income; [47] there were, however, decisions excluding occasional income from the basis of the tax.[48] The legislation now in force requires that occasional income be assessed in the same manner as other income, both for the tax on income from movable wealth (art. 95) (6/1.1e) and for the complementary tax (6/1.1f).

6/9.3 Income Determined by Agreement

The amount of taxable income may be determined by agreement between the taxpayer and the tax administration under the rules described at 13/2.4.

---

[47] See Vanoni, "Stabilità ed unicità dell'accertamento dei redditi 'una tantum' nell'imposta complementare," *RDFSF*, 1942, II, 53-60, 109-113, reprinted in 1 Vanoni, *Opere giuridiche* 455.

[48] See, for example, Comm. Centr., Sez. un., 12 November 1941, n. 53296; Vanoni, "Stabilità ed unicità dell'accertamento dei redditi 'una tantum' nell'imposta complementare," *RDFSF*, 1942, II, 53.

CHAPTER 7

INCOME FROM BUSINESS

7/1. Gross Income

7/1.1 In General

7/1.2 Activities Productive of Business Income
    a. In general
    b. Small businesses

7/1.3 Receipts and Gains Included in Business Income
    a. In general
    b. Interest
    c. Royalties
    d. Capital gains
    e. Windfalls
    f. "Hidden reserves"

7/2. Deductions

7/2.1 General Principles

7/2.2 Rent

7/2.3 Remuneration for Services Rendered
    a. Salaries and wages
    b. Bonuses and commissions
    c. Payments to owners, partners, and directors
    d. Profit sharing
    e. Payments for termination of employment
    f. Expense allowances and reimbursements

7/2.4 Pensions, Pension Plans, Social Security, and Welfare Payments

7/2.5 Interest

7/2.6 Repairs and Maintenance

7/2.7 Worthless Assets and Casualty Losses
7/2.8 Taxes
7/2.9 Insurance Premiums
7/2.10 Bad Debts
7/2.11 Charitable Contributions
7/2.12 Royalties
7/2.13 Organization Expenses
7/2.14 Distributions by Cooperative Societies
7/2.15 Expenditures for Research
7/2.16 Trade Association Dues

7/3. **Depreciation and Amortization**
7/3.1 In General
7/3.2 Assets Which Are Depreciable
7/3.3 Determination of Cost of Assets
7/3.4 Depreciation Methods
7/3.5 Depreciation Rates
        a. In general
        b. Accelerated depreciation
7/3.6 Disposition or Loss of Assets
7/3.7 Set-Off and Carry-Over of Unused Depreciation
7/3.8 Amortization of Leasehold Improvements
7/3.9 Amortization of Intangibles
7/3.10 Assets Reverting to Grantor of Concession
7/3.11 Obsolete Machinery

7/4. **Net Losses from Operations**
7/4.1 Set-Off in Current Year
7/4.2 Loss Carry-Over
7/4.3 Loss Carry-Over by Branches
7/4.4 Loss Carry-Back
7/4.5 Losses on Foreign Exchange

7/5. **Nondeductible Expenses**
7/5.1 In General
7/5.2 Payments to Owners, Partners, and Directors
7/5.3 Payments to Nonresidents
7/5.4 Payments for Which the Required Records Have Not Been Kept

7/1. Gross Income

7/1.1 In General

Income from the exercise of business enterprises or from business activities (7/1.2a) is taxed in category B of the tax on income from movable wealth (6/1.1e) as "income to whose production capital and labor contribute jointly" (art. 85).[1] Net income is determined by deducting from the gross proceeds (*ricavi lordi*) comprising business income (7/1.3) the amount of expenses and charges inherent in the production of that income (arts. 88, 91) (7/2). Income and expenses are determined in accordance with the accounting rules described at 6/4, and the cost of goods sold is valued in accordance with the inventory rules described at 6/5.1. Assessment of the income of a business enterprise required to be taxed on the balance sheet basis (such as a corporation) or electing to be so taxed (6/1.2b) is based on the balance sheet (13/2.2) unless the conditions for estimated assessment are fulfilled (13/2.3). Assessment of the income of an enterprise carried on by an individual or by a partnership or other personal company (5/3.1) is based on the economic situation of the firm, derived from information furnished by the taxpayer or gathered ex officio (13/2.2), unless the enterprise has elected to be taxed on the balance sheet basis. The tax period for income of category B is the business period for entities required to be taxed on the balance sheet basis and the calendar year for other enterprises (6/3.2).

The tax on income from movable wealth is applied on the basis of the net aggregate result of all the taxpayer's activities and operations producing income classifiable in category B (art. 95).[2] As a result, the losses (7/4.1) of one business, including a negative balance representing

---

[1] On the concept of enterprise income, see Zappa, *Il reddito d'impresa;* Zappa, *La determinazione del reddito nelle imprese commerciali. I valori di conto in relazione alla formazione del bilancio;* Amaduzzi, *L'azienda nel suo sistema e nell'ordine delle sue rilevazioni;* Onida, *Il bilancio d'esercizio dell'impresa;* Onida, *Le discipline economiche aziendali;* Onida, "Il reddito d'esercizio e la politica degli ammortamenti dei dividendi nei bilanci delle società per azioni," *Riv. dott. comm.,* 1951, III, 65.

[2] Prior to the tax reform law of 1956, income from industrial or commercial activities which were such as to be considered separate from the ordinary regular activity of a taxpayer other than a corporation or similar entity was assessed separately, *una tantum.* Otherwise, under the method of assessment then in effect, the assessment of the net aggregate result of the taxpayer's activities would not adequately have reflected annual fluctuations in income (6/9.2, 8/4). See L. 8 June 1936, n. 1231, art. 8. Income of category B derived by communes, provinces, and public entities from independent enterprises managed by them were assessed separately on the basis of their respective balance sheets; see L. 8 June 1936, n. 1231, art. 13. This provision was extended by R. D. L. 12 April 1943, n. 205, to all entities required to be taxed on the balance sheet basis. See Rotondi, "Imposta di r. m. sui redditi una tantum," *Dir. e prat. trib.,* 1951, II, 283; Berliri, "Questioni in tema di applicazione 'dell'imposta' di r. m.," *Foro it.,* 1951, I, 1575. The *una tantum* provisions were abrogated in 1956 by article 24 of L. 5 January 1956, n. 1. See C. M. 15 April 1957, n. 350860.

unused depreciation (7/3.7), may be set off against the profits of another carried on by the same taxpayer.

In the case of an enterprise formed in Italy or a company formed abroad having its head office or the principal object of its enterprise in Italy, the tax on income from movable wealth applies to income derived from business activity carried on in Italy (11/1.3) and to income derived from activities carried on abroad, except when the latter are carried on through a permanent establishment having separate administration and accounting (11/2.3a). In other cases, the tax on income from movable wealth is limited to income derived from an activity exercised in Italy through a branch or other permanent establishment (11/3.5a). Income produced abroad by a taxpayer domiciled or resident in Italy is considered as produced in Italy when it is not taxable in another country by virtue of an international agreement (11/2.2).

Business income subject to the tax on income from movable wealth is included in aggregate income for purposes of the complementary tax as explained at 6/1.1f, and for purposes of the corporation tax as explained at 6/1.1g.

7/1.2 Activities Productive of Business Income

a. IN GENERAL. Under the Civil Code, an entrepreneur (*imprenditore*)[3] is defined as one who exercises professionally an economic activity organized for the purpose of producing or exchanging goods or services (CC art. 2082).[4]

Business enterprises are subject to special rules regarding the method of assessment (13/2) and to special provisions regarding capital gains (7/1.3d), windfalls (7/1.3e), "hidden reserves" (7/1.3f), and deductions (7/2.1); business enterprises required to be taxed on the balance sheet basis or electing to be so taxed are subject to the special rules listed at 6/1.2b. Business enterprises are enterprises which carry on any of the activities listed below (art. 8; CC art. 2195).

1. An industrial activity directed to the production of goods or services.
2. Activity as a dealer in the distribution of goods.
3. Transport by land, water, or air.
4. Banking or insurance activity.
5. Any activity auxiliary to those specifically listed.

Unless otherwise provided, provisions of the *Testo unico* which refer to business enterprises apply also to entities required to be taxed on the

---

[3] On the concept of "entrepreneur," see Ferrara, *Gli imprenditori e le società* 1-70; Ferri, *Manuale di diritto commerciale* 27-86; Graziani, *Manuale di diritto commerciale* 13-32; De Gregorio, *Corso di diritto commerciale. Imprenditori e società* 5-54.

[4] An Italian company having the exercise of a business activity as its object must be organized in one of the forms specified for that purpose by the Civil Code (5/3.1). The rules governing foreign companies are discussed at 11/3.

alance sheet basis, and to credit firms and institutions, which carry on
usiness activities (art. 8).[5] Special rules regarding the taxation of busi-
ess income from the extraction of natural resources, agriculture, insur-
nce, and banking and investment, as well as special incentives for certain
idustrial and productive activities, are discussed in Chapter 10.

Income from speculative operations, even if occasional, is taxed as
usiness income (9/8.1, 9/8.2). Rental income derived by the owner
f land or buildings or of a property right in land or buildings generally
s not subject to the tax on income from movable wealth, but it is subject
ither to the tax on income from landowning (10/2.2) or to the tax on
icome from buildings (9/4.2), even if the taxpayer leases property as
regular business activity. Income from the subletting of land or build-
igs by a tenant is taxable as business income whether or not the taxpayer
s engaged in leasing property as a business (9/4.3).

. SMALL BUSINESSES. Income of an individual from an enterprise based
redominantly on his own personal labor or that of the members of his
amily is not taxed in category B but in category C/1 (art. 85), at the
ame rate as income from the independent work of an individual (8/2),
ut determined under the rules applicable to business income. The
icome from such an enterprise is considered to be based primarily on
abor and only to a negligible extent on capital (2/2.2d). The present
rovision of the *Testo unico* formalizes an already-existing administrative
ractice under which the income of artisans, small business and industrial
ctivities, and small agricultural leaseholds was taxed in category C/1
nder certain conditions.[6]

Thus, the income of artisans (*artigiani*) may be classified in category
C/1 rather than in category B if all the conditions listed below are
ulfilled.[7]

---

[5] Regarding the taxation of the management surplus (*avanzi di gestione*) resulting
rom the contributions of members to public entities carrying on both institutional
nd business activities, see Croxatto, "Tassibilità in R.M. dei proventi di natura
ommerciale e degli avanzi di gestione degli enti pubblici," *Dir. e prat. trib.*, 1960,
I, 401, commenting on Comm. Centr., Sez. III, 28 October 1959, n. 20600, and
Comm. Centr., Sez. II, 15 December 1958, n. 11014. See also Giussani, "Avanzi di
estione ed imposta di ricchezza mobile," *Giur. it.*, 1954, I, 2, 421.

[6] Compare article 2083 of the Civil Code, which classifies as small enterpreneurs
piccoli imprenditori) direct cultivators of land, artisans, small businessmen, and
hose who exercise a professional activity organized predominantly with their own
abor and that of the members of their families. Such entrepreneurs are relieved
rom the requirement of inscription in the register of enterprises (CC art. 2202)
nd from the requirement of keeping a journal and an inventory book (CC art.
2214) (6/2.2). Their income is taxed in category C/1, however, only if they meet
he further conditions prescribed for that purpose.

[7] C. M. 5 April 1946, n. 2160. These provisions have been temporarily continued
n effect by C. M. 18 December 1959, n. 304250.

1. The income derives predominantly from the work and personal participa
tion of the taxpayer and the members of his family, not from capita
employed.
2. The employment of capital is limited to the purchase of tools, machines
raw materials, and merchandise or products required for processing th
orders of customers, and does not extend significantly to the productio
of business products for the account of the enterprise.
3. The business does not have more than four regular employees in additio
to the taxpayer, including members of the taxpayer's family, whether o
not the taxpayer is required by law to support them, and not more tha
two apprentices or irregular or occasional workers.[8]

In exceptional cases, the income of an artisan who also carries on busines
or industrial activities may be apportioned between categories C/1 and B

Similarly, the income of certain small businesses, such as those o
vendors, peddlars, retailers of fruit and vegetables, small shopkeepers
and other small businesses whose income derives predominantly from
the personal activity of the owner rather than from capital, may be
classified in category C/1 provided the taxpayer furnishes his own service:
to the business [9] and provided the remuneration attributable to the work
done by the taxpayer and members of his family is not less than two
thirds of the aggregate net income of the enterprise as finally assessed.[1]
The remuneration attributable to the services performed by the taxpayer
and members of his family is determined on the basis of the yearly
compensation provided under labor contracts for workers with simila
duties or in fact paid by enterprises in the same sector of the economy
For purposes of computing the proportion (but not for purposes of com
puting the tax due on the net income of the enterprise), the income
finally assessed is increased by the remuneration allotted to children of
age and to emancipated minor children (5/1.3) which has been de
ducted in the determination of the income because it is subject to tax in
category C/2.[11]

The conditions under which income from small agrarian leaseholds
may be classified in category C/1 are discussed at 10/2.4.

---

[8] C. M. 5 April 1946, n. 2160, as modified by C. M. 4 June 1955, n. 302220.

[9] C. M. 18 December 1959, n. 304250. This instruction eliminates a former requirement that the taxpayer be assisted by not more than two persons, including members
of his family (C. M. 12 June 1946, n. 4080), and not more than one apprentice
(C. M. 4 June 1955, n. 302220).

[10] C. M. 18 December 1959, n. 304250. Under the former practice, in order to
avoid variations not connected with the relation between the capital and labor employed, the tax authorities calculated the income attributable to the capital of the
business at the presumed value of 8% of the fixed and circulating capital, computed
at current prices, by approximation if necessary, and added this income to the
remuneration attributable to work done by the taxpayer. The actual income of the
enterprise was taxed in category C/1 instead of in category B only if the income
from the capital, as so computed, did not exceed one fourth of the total. C. M.
12 June 1946, n. 4080.

[11] C. M. 18 December 1959, n. 304250.

7/1.3   Receipts and Gains Included in Business Income

a. IN GENERAL. In addition to income produced by normal business transactions (7/1.1), income from movable wealth of category B includes the gains and receipts described in the succeeding subsections.

Income from movable wealth does not include distributions of the profits of companies and associations (9/2.1a), surcharges received by companies on the issue of new shares (9/9.3), equalization payments made by subscribers to new shares (9/9.3), or subsidies paid by the state or other public entities which do not constitute contributions to expenses of production or other deductible charges (art. 83) (6/1.3).

b. INTEREST. Interest received by credit firms and institutions (10/4) or by other persons in the exercise of business enterprises, exclusive of interest on securities held, is included in category B of income from movable wealth as business income (art. 85). Thus, as in the case of interest received by a bank in its credit operations (10/4.1) and interest received from a customer when payment is delayed or made in installments (6/4.2), interest received in the course of business is taxed as business income. However, when a credit becomes overdue, becomes the object of a judgment, or becomes collectible by a method outside the normal collection of business credits, so that it becomes a capital asset outside the ordinary flow of business transactions, the interest becomes taxable in category A as income from pure capital.[12]

c. ROYALTIES. Income derived by a business enterprise from the licensing of intellectual property is taxed in category B as business income (9/5).

d. CAPITAL GAINS. Even if occasional, income from speculative operations is taxable as business income in category B of income from movable wealth (9/8.2). In the case of capital gains (*plusvalenze*) derived by business enterprises from the sale of assets, speculative intent is conclusively presumed; and all assets belonging to a business enterprise organized as a company are considered as related to the enterprise (9/8.3). The capital gains of a business enterprise are subject to tax not only if realized through the sale of assets, but also if distributed to the members of a company or inscribed in the balance sheet of a corporation or similar entity. The rules summarized here are treated in greater detail in 9/8.

[12] Cass., Sez. I, 29 July 1940, n. 2575; Cass., Sez. un., 25 February 1944, n. 115; Cass., Sez. I, 22 February 1947, n. 253. Such a change of category is sometimes called "avulsion" (*avulsione*). See Giannini, *Istituzioni di diritto tributario* 352, n. 102; see also Berliri, "In tema di 'avulsione' dei redditi ai fini dell'imposta di ricchezza mobile," *Foro it.*, 1948, I, 223; Greco, "Presunzione di interessi, avulsione dei redditi, renunzia agli interessi e cessazione dei redditi con riferimento all'imposta di R. M.," *RDFSF*, 1956, II, 308.

ANALYSIS OF INCOME TAX   40(

Gain or loss on the sale of depreciable assets is determined on th∢ basis of the depreciated cost (7/3.6). The valuation of securities i discussed at 6/5.3.

In all cases, the net gain subject to the tax on income from movabl∢ wealth is included in income for the complementary tax (art. 133) an∢ in income for the corporation tax (art. 148). Special rules relating t∢ the transfer of assets on the liquidation or reorganization of a busines∢ are discussed at 9/9.

e. WINDFALLS. The business income of any enterprise includes windfall∢ (*sopravvenienze attive*) obtained in the exercise of the enterprise including those resulting from the recoupment of amounts allowed a∢ deductions in previous business periods and amounts derived from th∢ subsequent nonexistence of a debt (arts. 100, 106). Business income of an entity required to be taxed on the balance sheet basis include∢ windfalls obtained in any manner during the business period, wherea∢ windfalls includible in the income of any other enterprise, including on∢ electing to be taxed on the balance sheet basis, are limited to thos∢ obtained in the exercise of the enterprise (art. 106).

Windfalls are exceptional receipts whose connection with a productive cause must be sought in previous business periods. They include the receipts listed below.[13]

1. Receipts connected with a productive cause in an earlier business period such as a penalty or deposit recoverable for previous nonfulfillment of ∢ contract, or a contribution paid by the state to a railroad to cover losse∢ of previous years.
2. Recovery on any basis of amounts allowed as deductions from income from movable wealth of previous business periods, including the diversior to other purposes, for which deduction is not allowed, of annual depreciation costs or provisions to retirement funds or other reserves.[14]
3. The supervening nonexistence, total or partial, of an originally valid debt.

Amounts advanced to a corporation by a shareholder to pay debts of the corporation or to reconstitute its reserves, refunds of direct taxes, and contributions for the operation of associations do not constitute new wealth resulting from productive causes (6/1.1e); thus, they are not considered income.[15] However, dividends not collected by shareholders are included in the profit of the year in which the right to collection lapses.[16]

f. "HIDDEN RESERVES." In the case of an enterprise formed as a company regulated by article 2200 of the Civil Code as a business com-

---

[13] Montuori, *Note sulle tassazioni in base al bilancio* 110-114.
[14] Comm. Centr., Sez. II, 11 June 1955, n. 72945.
[15] See Montuori, *Note sulle tassazioni in base al bilancio* 114-115.
[16] Comm. Centr., Sez. II, 14 June 1948, n. 98897.

pany,[17] even if not required to be taxed on the balance sheet basis, amounts subtracted from the tax base in previous business periods must be included in business income of the period in which they are capitalized or distributed or otherwise appear in the balance sheet, unless the assessment for the original period can still be reopened (6/6.3).

7/2. Deductions

7/2.1 General Principles

Net income of category B for the tax on income from movable wealth is determined by deducting from gross income subject to the tax the amount of expenses and charges inherent in (*inerente a*) the production of that income (art. 91). Although the present law contains no detailed enumeration of the expenses which are deductible, there is no doubt that it covers such ordinary business expenses as the consumption of raw materials and means (6/5.1), wages, salaries, and commissions (7/2.3), and rent (7/2.2), all of which were specified in the original law governing the tax on income from movable wealth.[18] A business enterprise is also permitted to deduct its general expenses or overhead, but the deduction is limited to that part which is imputable to activities productive of income subject to the tax (art. 96).[19] As a result of this provision, expenses which cannot be identified with the production of particular income subject to tax in category B, such as legal expenses, general office expenses, the rental of the building in which a company has its office, and general administrative salaries, are not deductible insofar as they are attributable to the production of income excluded or exempted from income from movable wealth of category B. It appears that the allocation of general expenses between income of category B and other income is not necessarily made in proportion to the amounts of income but may be based on costs or on some other method of determining the relative importance of the services afforded to the production of income of category B and to the production of other income.[20]

---

[17] The forms of company covered by this provision are the corporation (5/2.2), limited liability company (5/2.3), limited partnership with shares (5/2.4), cooperative society (5/2.5), general partnership (5/3.2), and simple limited partnership (5/3.3).

[18] R. D. L. 24 August 1877, n. 4021, art. 32. See also R. D. 11 July 1907, n. 560, art. 55; C. M. 1 July 1902, n. 11959. On the concept of *inerenza* of expenses as developed in the doctrine and the decisions, see 2 Quarta, *Commento alla legge sull'imposta di ricchezza mobile* (2d ed., 1902) 184; Traina-Portanova, *Spese e passività deducibili nell'imposta di ricchezza mobile* 21-36; Montuori, *Note sulle tassazioni in base al bilancio* 171-183; Dus, "Le 'spese e passività' deducibili ai fini del calcolo del reddito mobiliare nel nuovo testo unico delle imposte dirette," *RDFSF*, 1958, I, 333-345.

[19] This provision is derived from article 23 of L. 5 January 1956, n. 1.

[20] See C. M. 15 April 1957, n. 350860.

The deduction of interest charges is subject to the special rules discussed at 7/2.5. Business enterprises are permitted, under special provisions, to deduct expenses attributable to more than one business period, including: lump-sum dismissal and retirement payments (art. 97) (7/2.3e), expenses of forming companies or increasing their capital (7/2.13), depreciation on certain physical assets and intangibles (7/3), losses realized on the sale or destruction of assets (7/2.7, 7/3.6), losses on credits becoming uncollectible during the business period (7/2.10), and unrealized losses resulting from decreases in the book value of inventory (6/5.1) and securities (6/5.3). Entities or enterprises taxed on the balance sheet basis are allowed a limited carry-forward of net operating losses (7/4.2) but are subject to special limitations regarding capital losses deriving from devaluations (7/2.7), the registration of depreciation (7/3.1), payments for independent services (7/2.3), payments of royalties (7/2.12), interest charges (7/2.5), and certain payments made to foreign companies, firms, and associations (11/2.4).

Although the assessment of the income of a business enterprise not taxed on the balance sheet basis is based on the firm's economic situation as derived from any information available, the Tax Office normally has the burden of proving an assessment that disregards deductions supported by the accounting records required under the rules described at 6/2.2. If deductions are not supported by the required accounting records, however, the taxpayer has the burden of proof against the assessment of the Tax Office (13/2.3). Deduction of expenses cannot be based on an estimate or on a percentage of gross income, even if the expenses are not easily identifiable or demonstrable.[21] The existence and the amount of the expense must be proved.[22] Subject to the special rules noted above regarding formation expenses and expenses covering more than one year, the deduction of an expense is permitted only in the year in which its existence and amount become definite under standard accounting rules (6/4.1). An expense which is the means of earning income is deductible as inherent in the production of income regardless of whether it was opportune to incur such an expense in order to achieve a certain profit.[23]

In determining net aggregate income for the complementary tax, deduction is allowed for certain expenses which, by their nature (not because of their amount), were not deductible in determining net income from movable wealth (6/1.5b); for interest not deductible in determining income from movable wealth (7/2.5); and for taxes related to income (art. 136) (6/1.5e, 7/2.8).

---

21 Comm. Centr., Sez. I, 24 March 1956, n. 80477.
22 Comm. Centr., Sez. II, 23 June 1948, n. 99181.
23 Comm. Centr. 12 October 1960, n. 32148.

In determining the aggregate income for the corporation tax (6/1.1g), any loss carried forward for the tax on income from movable wealth (7/4.2) and any excessive remuneration to directors which has been deducted in determining net income of category B (7/2.3c) must be added back. As in the determination of other types of income, however, expenses connected with the production of business income which, by their nature, were not deductible in the determination of income from movable wealth (6/1.5b), as well as ordinary taxes related to the various classes of income and inscribed in the rolls during the year (6/1.5e), are deductible from aggregate income (art. 148). For the corporation tax, also, the deductible expenses of a foreign company or association are limited to expenses relating to capital employed in Italy or to a permanent establishment in Italy (art. 148) (11/3.3).

7/2.2 Rent

Rent paid for immovable property used in the business is deductible as an expense of producing income of category B, or as a general expense, under the principles discussed at 7/2.1.

If the business is carried on in premises owned by the entrepreneur, the business income subject to the tax on income from movable wealth in category B is considered to include any income attributable to the buildings, which therefore is specifically excluded from the tax on income from buildings provided the building is devoted specifically to the exercise of a business activity and is not susceptible of other use without radical transformation (9/4.2a).

7/2.3 Remuneration for Services Rendered

a. SALARIES AND WAGES. Salaries and wages taxed in category C/2 as income of the employee (8/1.1) are deductible as expenses of the production of income of category B, or as general expenses, under the principles discussed at 7/2.1.

Restrictions on the deductibility of compensation paid to the taxpayer or to members of his family are discussed at 7/2.3c.

b. BONUSES AND COMMISSIONS. Bonuses and commissions paid to employees are deductible as expenses of the production of income of category B, or as general expenses, under the principles discussed at 7/2.1, insofar as they are taxed in category C/2 (8/1.1) of the income of the employee.

Production and labor cooperative societies are permitted to deduct amounts paid to their members as a supplement to wages previously paid to them, up to the amount of current wages paid for similar work elsewhere (art. 111).

Compensation, reimbursement of expenses, and similar payments for professional, artistic, brokerage, or other independent services are also

ANALYSIS OF INCOME TAX   404

deductible under the principles discussed at 7/2.1; but, in the case of
entities and enterprises taxed on the balance sheet basis, the deduction
is conditioned on the keeping of the prescribed journal of payments made
to individuals (6/2.2) (art. 109).

Compensation paid to aliens or to Italians domiciled abroad for professional or artistic services performed in Italy is subject to provisional
withholding of tax under the rules described at 13/3.5. No deduction
is allowed for brokerage fees and commissions, not subject to provisional
withholding, paid by a corporation or other entity required to be taxed
on the balance sheet basis to a foreign enterprise for which it carries
on activity in Italy through the sale, disposal, or manufacture of goods
(11/2.4).

c. PAYMENTS TO OWNERS, PARTNERS, AND DIRECTORS. Amounts regarded
as remuneration for activities of the taxpayer, his wife, or his unemancipated minor children for the production of income are not deductible
in determining net income of category B (art. 94). Compensation paid
to children who have attained majority or who have been emancipated
as a result of marriage or of a judgment of a tutelary judge is deductible
provided that the children have no other occupation, either of work or
of study, that their services are regularly performed according to a normal
daily schedule, and that the compensation does not exceed the amount
which would be paid to strangers performing the same duties.[24]

Under the principle stated above, compensation paid by *de facto*
companies and general partnerships to their members for personal services furnished by them in the business is not a deductible expense in
determining net income of category B.[25] However, salaries paid by a
simple limited partnership to partners who serve in the management of
the enterprise (5/3.3) are deductible in determining net income of
category B, but the amount to be deducted is subject to reduction if
clearly excessive.[26] Similarly, compensation paid to shareholders of a
corporation or similar entity (5/2) who are also employees thereof is
deductible.[27] By virtue of a recent modification of the *Testo unico*,
compensation paid to directors, auditors, or overseers, excluding participations in the net profits of the business period, may be deducted in
determining net income from movable wealth of an entity required to
be taxed on the balance sheet basis (art. 108).[28] The deduction is subject
to the conditions that the required withholding of tax have been made

---

[24] C. M. 20 March 1952, n. 301340.

[25] See *Verb. conf.* November 1957, De Angelis, Potenza, and Testa, *Testo unico
delle leggi sulle imposte dirette* 500.

[26] Comm. Centr., Sez. II, 16 November 1956, n. 86364.

[27] C. M. 7 December 1954, n. 303932.

[28] This provision was introduced by article 1 of L. 21 April 1962, n. 226. Formerly,
compensation paid to directors for their services as such was not deductible.

(13/3.5); that the compensation be set by the by-laws, the shareholders' meeting, or other competent governing body; and that the compensation be registered in the prescribed journal of payments made to individuals (6/2.2).[29] Payments which are deductible include not only regular compensation for services as a director, but daily allowances, fees for attendance at meetings, and reimbursements (either fixed-sum or specific) of expenses in relation to the performance of the duties as a director.[30] If, in addition to the performance of his duties as such, a director performs managerial or other functions as a regular employee, his remuneration for those services is deductible in the same manner as any other remuneration, provided a regular employment relation is established and the payments are included in the recipient's income of category C/2.[31]

Salaries, compensation, and other payments to directors or partners which have been allowed as deductions in determining income from movable wealth of category B must be added to income for purposes of the corporation tax if they exceed normal remuneration and do not represent simply reimbursement of expenses (art. 148).

d. PROFIT SHARING. Remuneration to employees may be made in the form of participation in profits (CC art. 2099). Remuneration in this form is taxable in category C/2 of the employee's income (8/1.1) and is allowable as a deduction from gross income of category B under the principles discussed at 7/2.1.[32] Shares of profits paid to members of the board of directors of a corporation are not deductible unless given for regular services as an employee, as distinguished from the performance of the duties of a director (7/2.3c). Shares of profits not deducted from gross income of category B are deductible from the payor's aggregate income for the complementary tax,[33] provided they are not paid to the taxpayer himself or to members of his family.

The taxation of employees and directors receiving shares of profits is discussed at 8/1.6.

---

[29] C. M. 15 June 1962, n. 60.

[30] C. M. 15 June 1962, n. 60.

[31] C. M. 18 December 1959, n. 84; C. M. 15 April 1960, n. 350900. See also Montuori, *Note sulle tassazioni in base al bilancio* 263-264. This principle, established before the recent amendment of article 108 of the *Testo unico*, does not seem to be affected by the amendment.

[32] Comm. Centr., Sez. un., 21 February 1940, n. 22715; Comm. Centr., Sez. I, 28 May 1958, n. 5633 (*RDFSF*, 1959, II, 4). However, it is doubtful whether shares of profits may be deducted when they are not supplemental to a fixed remuneration but constitute the entire remuneration for the services rendered. In the latter case, the person performing the services might not be considered an employee but a participant in the risks of the enterprise; if so, his share of the profits would be neither taxable as compensation in category C/2 nor deductible from the income of the enterprise. See Poli, "La tassazione delle partecipazioni agli utili come compenso di prestazioni di opera," *RDFSF*, 1959, II, 335.

[33] Comm. Centr. 1 October 1932, n. 40667. See Boidi, *Commento alla legge sulla imposta complementare progressiva sul reddito* 209-210.

e. PAYMENTS FOR TERMINATION OF EMPLOYMENT. Indemnities required by law or by contract upon termination of employment are regarded as attributable to more than one business period and hence deductible in each period in the amount of the share attributable to that period (art. 97). The share attributable to each business period is determined by the position of each individual employee in accordance with the legal and contractual provisions which regulate the employment relation; the share is set aside each year in a special fund for termination and retirement payments (*indennità di licenziamento e quiescenza*).

Such indemnities are based on the total compensation payable, at the time of termination of employment, for a base period, multiplied by the number of years of service. In each year, the employer is permitted to deduct the amount set aside as payable to each employee, in case of dismissal, on account of that year's service, plus any adjustment which may be required to spread increases in the rate of compensation over the past years of service.[34] If the indemnity due on termination of employment exceeds the amounts set aside annually, the excess is a negative windfall deductible from income of the year in which the indemnity is paid; if the amounts set aside annually exceed the indemnity actually due, the difference is a windfall includible in income of the business period in which the employment terminates (7/1.3e).[35]

f. EXPENSE ALLOWANCES AND REIMBURSEMENTS. In determining the employer's net income of category B, the deduction of expense allowances or of reimbursements made to employees is governed by the principles discussed at 7/2.1. Such payments are deductible in full if they are inherent in the production of income subject to tax in category B, or, if they constitute general expenses, they are deductible in the proportion attributable to activities productive of income subject to tax in category B.

7/2.4   Pensions, Pension Plans, Social Security, and Welfare Payments

Any pension payable by law or contract upon termination of employment is deductible over the period of employment under the provision described at 7/2.3e.[36]

Under admininstrative instructions, social security and welfare contributions (*contributi previdenziali ed assistenziali*) made by employers or employees, in compliance with provisions of law or contract, are

---

[34] See Montuori, *Note sulle tassazioni in base al bilancio* 266-267. The payment of these indemnities is governed by articles 2120 and 2121 of the Civil Code. Within the limits established by law, the base period for calculation of the indemnity is determined by contract.

[35] See Montuori, *Note sulle tassazioni in base al bilancio* 267-268. It appears that before 1 January 1960, practically all amounts set aside for indemnity funds for workers were taxed and therefore deductible when actually paid out.

[36] See Montuori, *Note sulle tassazioni in base al bilancio* 269-270.

deductible from the employer's income of category B (art. 87) provided that they are either deposited in a special independent fund (*cassa autonoma*) established for this purpose or are used to pay the premiums of insurance on the employee's life.[37] However, the Central Commission has held that amounts set aside in social security funds established by the competent organs of a company are deductible even if not deposited in an independent fund.[38] Social security and welfare funds established by an employer for the benefit of employees cannot be diverted from the purpose for which they have been set aside and cannot be reached by creditors either of the employer or of the employee (CC art. 2117).

An enterprise is permitted to deduct up to 5% of its declared income for amounts paid as gratuities to employees for instruction, education, social assistance, religious worship, or charity (art. 84) (6/1.5f).

The taxation of employees on social security and welfare contributions and benefits is discussed at 8/1.3.

Amounts expended by an enterprise for the acquisition of land and on plans for the construction of housing for its own employees are not deductible as expenses connected with the production of income; however, a business may deduct the contributions which it is required[39] to make for the construction of housing for its employees.[40]

7/2.5 Interest

The deduction of interest charges by business enterprises not taxed on the balance sheet basis is limited, under the principles explained at 7/2.1, to interest which is inherent in the production of income subject to the tax on income from movable wealth in category B or which is imputable, as a share of general expenses, to activities productive of such income.[41] Interest payments deductible under these provisions include interest on borrowings for circulating capital, for the construction of new plant, or for the purchase of securities.[42] It appears not to have

---

[37] C. M. 19 January 1934, n. 600.

[38] Comm. Centr. 30 June 1939, n. 16967.

[39] See L. 28 February 1949, n. 43, providing for contributions to INA-Casa (an autonomous division of the *Istituto Nazionale delle Assicurazioni*) by government, employers, and employees.

[40] C. M. 26 September 1952, n. 351700.

[41] See C. M. 15 April 1957, n. 350860, interpreting L. 5 January 1956, n. 1, art. 23. Under the law prior to 1956, a special provision permitted the deduction of annual charges (*annualità passive*), even on loans secured by mortgage, burdening income from movable wealth, provided the debt was justified and the identity and the domicile of the creditor in Italy were ascertained. See R. D. L. 24 August 1877, n. 4021, art. 31. See also Traina-Portanova, *Spese e passività deducibili nell'imposta di ricchezza mobile* 71 *et seq.*, 370 *et seq.*; Giannetta, Scandale, and Sessa, *Teoria e tecnica nell'accertamento del reddito mobiliare* 499, 521, 525-527.

[42] See Montuori, *Note sulle tassazioni in base al bilancio* 297. For a discussion of the deductibility of interest on money borrowed for investment in industrial plants, see Traina-Portanova, *Spese e passività deducibili nell'imposta di ricchezza mobile* 370-404.

been settled whether interest on money borrowed for the construction of new plant which is not yet completed when the interest is paid is deductible from current income or must be amortized as part of the cost of the plant itself.[43]

However, there are several conditions and limitations on the deductibility of interest. Unless the taxpayer is a credit firm or institution (10/4.1), interest charges are deductible from business income only if owed to a person domiciled, resident, or having a permanent establishment in Italy, or if the payor of the interest is required to pay the category A tax with a right of recovery from the recipient through withholding (art. 92) (13/3.4). The deduction of interest charges by entities or enterprises taxed on the balance sheet basis, moreover, is limited to the ratio between the amount of gross receipts composing income subject to tax in category B and the aggregate amount of gross receipts (art. 110); and it is immaterial whether or not a higher proportion of the borrowing on which the interest is payable is actually employed in the activity subject to tax in category B.[44] This provision does not preclude the operation of other limitations on the deduction of interest when the purpose for which the capital borrowed by the company was employed can be established. If it were shown that borrowed funds had been used for purposes not productive of income subject to tax in category B, such as for the purchase of buildings not used in the exercise of the business, for the purchase of agricultural land, or for the construction of plants whose income is exempted from the tax on income from movable wealth, the interest payable on such borrowings would not be inherent in the production of income subject to tax in category B and therefore would be nondeductible in its entirety.[45]

If interest is owed to a credit firm or institution and an official request for certification of the debt by the creditor has been made (13/2.2), the interest charges are not deductible if the certification has not been filed (art. 93). The filing of the certificate does not prevent an estimated assessment in a proper case, however (13/2.3).

[43] See Montuori, *Note sulle tassazioni in base al bilancio* 297. For a discussion of this problem, see Traina-Portanova, *Spese e passività deducibili nell'imposta di ricchezza mobile* 418-431.

[44] See Berliri, *Il testo unico delle imposte dirette* 292-293. For purposes of this provision, the aggregate amount of gross receipts does not include income from shares in which the taxpayer is required by law to invest in order to be classified as an investment company under the corporation tax (C. M. 15 April 1957, n. 350860), nor does it include income from treasury bonds in which a credit firm is required to invest in order to issue checks (C. M. 7 December 1957, n. 352040) or holds as security against checks issued (C. M. 23 December 1957, n. 352114).

[45] See Giannetta, Scandale, and Sessa, *Teoria e tecnica nell'accertamento del reddito mobiliare* 525-527; Montuori, *Note sulle tassazioni in base al bilancio* 295, 296-297.

In order to deduct payments to individuals by way of interest, commissions, premiums, brokerage, and similar payments for the acceptance of funds on deposit, loan, security, or current account, entities taxed on the balance sheet basis, other than credit firms and institutions, must keep the journal of payments to individuals prescribed by article 43 (6/2.2) (art. 109).

For purposes of the complementary tax, interest not deductible under the tax on income from movable wealth is deductible if the recipient and his domicile are specified (art. 136). For purposes of the corporation tax, interest which, by its nature (not because of its amount), was not deductible in determining net income from movable wealth may be deducted if it is an expense inherent in the production of income subject to the corporation tax (7/2.1), on condition of the filing of a certificate, if requested, for interest charges owed to a credit firm or institution (art. 148). Interest deductible for purposes of the corporation tax by a foreign company or association is limited to interest relating to capital employed in Italy or to a permanent establishment in Italy (art. 148) (11/3.3).

7/2.6 Repairs and Maintenance

Expenditures for the repair and maintenance of assets are deductible as expenses of the production of income, or as general expenses, under the principles discussed at 7/2.1, provided they do not increase the value of the assets. Expenditures for the repair and maintenance of leased premises are deductible by the tenant as expenses of the production of income if they are made necessary by the tenant's use of the premises; in other cases, they are deductible only if the tenant is required by an express contract to make them. Expenditures for the improvement of assets related to the business, including expenditures for extraordinary maintenance, and including expenditures on buildings which are not subject to the tax on income from buildings (9/4.2), are deductible at annual rates determined by reference to the remaining life of the assets, as affected by the improvements made (art. 98) (7/3.5).

7/2.7 Worthless Assets and Casualty Losses

Losses arising from the total or partial destruction of assets related to the enterprise (*relativi all'impresa*) are deductible (art. 99) in the year in which the destruction occurs. The provision applies to losses resulting from extraordinary natural causes, such as fire or flood, and is not limited to losses resulting from the activity productive of income.[46] Losses arising from the sale of depreciable property related to the enterprise at a price lower than the undepreciated cost (7/3.6), and losses arising

---

[46] See Cass., Sez. I, 1 December 1936; Forte, "Detraibilità di spese per sinistri nell'imposta di r. m.," *RDFSF*, 1950, II, 101.

from the sale of property related to the enterprise having no undepreciated cost at less than the last value recognized for the determination of income, are deductible (art. 99) in the year of sale. In effect, property related to the enterprise includes any property connected with the enterprise but is not limited to property necessary to the production of income. Losses on credits are deductible in the year in which the credits become worthless, as explained at 7/2.10. Other losses inherent in the activity productive of income, such as losses through theft of stock in trade of the business,[47] are deductible (art. 99) in the year in which they occur.

Book (that is, unrealized) losses (*minusvalenze*) on raw materials, merchandise, shares, bonds, and other interest-bearing securities are deductible in accordance with the valuation rules described at 6/5 (art. 101).

An entity required to be taxed on the balance sheet basis or an enterprise electing to be so taxed is not permitted to deduct capital losses arising from devaluations not registered in the general journal in the prescribed manner (art. 109) (6/2.2).

In determining income for the corporation tax, losses inherent in the production of the various classes of income are deductible to the extent that, by their nature (not because of their amount), they are not deductible in the determination of income for the objective taxes (art. 148). Under this provision, losses on assets productive of income excluded or exempt from the tax on income from movable wealth but productive of income subject to the corporation tax may be deducted.

Recovery (as by insurance) of a loss previously deducted must be included in income as a windfall in the year of receipt (art. 100) (7/1.3e).

7/2.8 Taxes

Taxes imposed on the exercise of business activities, other than taxes on income, may be deducted as expenses of the production of income, or as general expenses, under the principles discussed at 7/2.1, in determining net income for the tax on income from movable wealth of the year in which they are paid. Among the taxes which may be deducted are those listed below.

1. Local consumption taxes (*imposte di consumo*) (4/5.8).
2. Registration taxes on contracts for the performance of specified work and contracts of supply (15/3.3i).
3. Manufacturing taxes (*imposte di fabbricazione*) (4/5.2).[48]
4. The general tax on receipts (*imposta generale sull'entrata*) (14/), even if paid as an annual fee.[49]
5. Customs duties (4/8).[50]

---

[47] Comm. Centr., Sez. III, 11 March 1959, n. 14440.
[48] Comm. Centr. 6 March 1873, n. 13772.
[49] C. M. 13 May 1952, n. 301430.
[50] Comm. Centr. 24 September 1870, n. 12949.

6. Local license taxes (4/5.10).
7. The fee for occupation of public spaces and areas (*tassa di occupazione di spazi ed aree pubbliche*) (4/5.11).
8. The fee for the exercise of governmental concessions (4/7).[51]
9. Stamp taxes (4/4).
10. The tax on the circulation of vehicles (4/5.5).

The registration and stamp taxes payable on the formation of a company or the contribution of capital thereto are deductible in equal parts over the five years following the year in which the formation or contribution occurs (7/2.13).[52]

A question has arisen as to whether the tax on bonds (3/3) may be considered part of the cost of the financing obtained through the issuance of bonds and thus deducted as an expense inherent in the production of income. On bonds issued after the effective date of the Law of 6 August 1954, n. 603, under which the tax was first levied, however, the issuer has a right of recovery of the tax against the holder (3/3.1). If the issuer exercises this right, he recovers the expense of the tax, and any resulting increase of the cost of financing is reflected in increased interest charges, which the issuer of the bond may deduct.[53] It has recently been held that, when a credit institution fails to exercise its right to recover the tax on income from movable wealth of category A on interest paid to its depositors, its payment of the tax on behalf of the depositors is a part of the cost of financing and thus is deductible, as an expense of producing income, from the institution's income of category B.[54] On the same principle, the tax on bonds would probably also be deductible, in determining income of category B, by an issuer who failed to exercise his right of recovery of the tax against the holder.[55] It has also been contended that the asset component of the corporation tax is deductible in determining business income,[56] but this contention is not accepted by the tax administration.[57]

---

[51] Comm. Centr., Sez. III, 4 March 1941, n. 38141.
[52] C. M. 25 May 1957, n. 351190.
[53] Since income from capital given in loan generally is included in income without any deduction (art. 86) (9/1.1), the holder of the bond is not permitted to deduct the tax recovered from him in determining his net income of category A.
[54] Comm. Centr., Sez. I, 12 October 1960, n. 32148 (*RDFSF*, 1962, II, 173). See, however, Comm. Centr. 15 December 1930, n. 15569. See also Greco, "Interessi passivi delle banche—Categoria di tassazione," *Rass. mens. imp. dir.*, 1958, 170; Grillo, "Imposta di ricchezza mobile, cat. A: interessi passivi e mancata rivalsa della relativa imposta, indetraibilità di essa," *Giust. trib.*, 1961, 393; Jona Celesia, "Deducibilità degli interessi dal reddito lordo delle aziende di credito," *RDFSF*, 1962, II, 173. It appears that the rule stated in the text is not accepted by the tax administration.
[55] See Poli, *Imposta sulle società e imposta sulle obbligazioni* 152-154. Before the 1960 decision cited in note 54 *supra*, deduction of the tax on bonds was not allowed when the right of recovery was not exercised; see C. M. 15 June 1956, n. 351038.
[56] Comm. Prov. Milano 5 June 1959.
[57] It has also been rejected by the Central Commission. Comm. Centr., Sez. II, 6 December 1961, n. 51283.

Taxes related to income which have been inscribed in the rolls for collection (13/3.6a) and for which payment begins in the year or has been made during the year through withholding are deductible from income subject to the complementary tax (art. 136) (6/1.5e). If the enterprise is a partnership or other "personal" company, the taxes and other allowable deductions are deducted from the net income allocable among the members. Ordinary taxes related to income which have been inscribed in the rolls and whose collection is begun during the tax period are deductible for purposes of the corporation tax (art. 148) (6/1.5e). For both the complementary tax and the corporation tax, the deductible taxes include the objective taxes on income and the applicable surtaxes, additionals, and collection fees (2/2.9, 6/1.5e).

Taxes paid abroad, other than income taxes, are deductible in determining income from movable wealth if they constitute expenses inherent in the production of income subject to the tax on income from movable wealth in Italy under the rules discussed at 11/1.3 and 11/2.2. Income taxes, whether paid in Italy or abroad, are not regarded as expenses of producing income from movable wealth and therefore are not deductible in determining net income from movable wealth. However, income produced abroad which was subject to the complementary tax or the corporation tax would ordinarily be net of any income taxes paid abroad, except where Italy gave a credit against the corporation tax under a treaty provision for taxes paid abroad by Italians.

7/2.9 Insurance Premiums

Premiums paid for insurance against the insolvency of debtors are an expense of the production of income and are deductible since they take the place of the loss which would result from a bad debt if there were no insurance.[58] Premiums for the insurance of property related to the enterprise against losses connected with the production of income or resulting from extraordinary causes, such as fire, flood, or theft, are deductible under the same conditions as the losses themselves (7/2.7).[59]

Insurance proceeds are included in gross income in the year in which they become collectible (7/1.3d).

7/2.10 Bad Debts

Losses on uncollectible credits are deductible in determining income from movable wealth (art. 99), but only in the business period in which the credit becomes worthless.[60] If the debtor is undergoing bankruptcy, the credit is allowed as a deduction only in the business period in which

---

58 C. M. 8 June 1932, n. 5169.
59 See C. M. 1 July 1902, n. 11959.
60 Comm. Centr. 1 March 1932, n. 34551.

the bankruptcy proceeding is terminated because only then do the existence and amount of the loss become certain.[61] If the debtor, although insolvent, is not subject to bankruptcy proceedings, the creditor must show that judicial proceedings for recovery have been begun but have been abandoned because the debt cannot be collected. If the debt is small, however, the Tax Office may allow its deduction on the basis of documentary proof.[62] Premiums paid for insurance against the insolvency of debtors are deductible (7/2.9); and, if the insurance proceeds do not cover a loss, the difference between the loss and the insurance proceeds may also be deducted.[63] No deduction is allowed, however, for provisions to a reserve for bad debts.

Recovery of a debt previously deducted as uncollectible must be included in income of the business period of recovery as a windfall (art. 100).

7/2.11 Charitable Contributions

An enterprise is permitted to deduct amounts paid as gratuities to employees, or on behalf of legally recognized entities, institutes, or associations, when the specific purpose of the gratuities is instruction, education, social assistance, religious worship, or charity (art. 84). The deduction is limited to 5% of the declared net income from movable wealth (6/1.5f). Since the law regards these amounts as "exempt" from the tax on income from movable wealth, they are included in the income of the enterprise for the complementary tax or the corporation tax.

7/2.12 Royalties

Fees paid for the use of a copyright or for the licensing for use of patents, designs, processes, formulas, trademarks, and other intellectual property in the production of income subject to tax in category B are deductible under the principles discussed at 7/2.1; but, in the case of entities and enterprises taxed on the balance sheet basis, the deduction of such payments is conditioned on the keeping of the prescribed journal of payments made to individuals (6/2.2) (art. 109). If patents or other intellectual property are used outside Italy, the fees paid for their use are deductible only if the assets are used for the production of income subject to tax in Italy in category B of income from movable wealth (7/2.1).

Royalties and other payments made to aliens or Italians domiciled abroad for the use or transfer of patents and other intellectual property are subject to provisional withholding of tax under the rules described

---

[61] C. M. 23 April 1957, n. 300635.

[62] Ministerial Note 25 February 1957, n. 352173.

[63] C. M. 8 June 1932, n. 5169.

at 13/3.5. If a corporation or other entity required to be taxed on the balance sheet 'basis pays any commissions or fees not subject to withholding under those rules to a foreign enterprise for which it acts in Italy through the sale, disposal, or manufacture of goods, deduction of such fees for purposes of the tax on income from movable wealth is not allowed (11/2.4).

Even when this provision is not applicable, the tax authorities customarily give careful scrutiny to royalty payments made by Italian companies to foreign enterprises, in order to insure that high royalties are not being used to remove profits from taxation.

Fees paid to the state or other public entity for the grant of a concession are deductible in determining income from movable wealth whether set as a fixed amount or measured by production or gross receipts.[64]

The amortization of the cost of intangible assets is discussed at 7/3.9.

7/2.13 Organization Expenses

Expenses relating to the formation of a company and to increases in its capital are deductible in the five business periods following that in which they are incurred, at a rate not exceeding one fifth for each period (art. 97). Prior to the tax reform law of 1956, registration taxes on contributions of capital to companies and other formation expenses were not deductible because they were not directly and specifically charges on the income produced in the year in which they were incurred.[65] However, such expenses have more recently been considered to represent costs of obtaining the financing required for the business and therefore entitled to the same treatment as interest on money borrowed for fixed capital by an individual enterprise.[66] Professional fees, expenses of the issue and sale of shares, and registration and stamp taxes (7/2.8) are deductible under this provision. The value of good will, however, is amortized as an intangible under the rules discussed at 7/3.9.

7/2.14 Distributions by Cooperative Societies

In determining net income from movable wealth, consumer cooperative societies are permitted to deduct amounts, other than dividends, which they distribute to their members in the form of refunds of part of the price of goods purchased (art. 111). Production and labor cooperative societies may deduct amounts paid to their members to supplement wages, up to the going wage (7/2.3b).

---

[64] See Giannetta, Scandale, and Sessa, *Teoria e tecnica nell'accertamento del reddito mobiliare* 431.

[65] See Traina-Portanova, *Spese e passività deducibili nell'imposta di recchezza mobile* 33, 39–41, 50.

[66] The deduction was specifically allowed by C.M. 25 May 1957, n. 351190, in application of the provision for carry-forward of losses contained in article 25 of L. 5 January 1956, n. 1.

7/2.15   Expenditures for Research

Expenses sustained during the year for studies, research, or experiments are deductible from business income in accordance with the principles discussed at 7/2.1.[67] It appears that expenditures for buildings, machinery, plant, or other assets used in research and having a useful life of more than one year must be depreciated under the normal depreciation rules described at 7/3.[68]

7/2.16   Trade Association Dues

Dues paid to a trade association are deductible as general expenses of the production of business income, provided the functions of the association are not confined to protecting the interests of its members as a class but include the furnishing of administrative and technical services which the members would otherwise have to provide individually at their own expense. Such services include collecting information indispensable to the carrying on of the industry or business, distributing statistical data, and giving administrative consultation and assistance.[69]

7/3.   Depreciation and Amortization

7/3.1   In General

Beginning in the business period in which the assets are put to use, a business enterprise is permitted to depreciate the costs of immovable property, plant, machinery, and movable property (7/3.2) in annual amounts (7/3.5) determined in relation to the life (*durata*) of the assets (art. 98). Expenditures for improving assets, including those of extraordinary maintenance, are deductible in annual amounts determined in relation to the remaining life of the improved assets, taking into account any prolongation resulting from the expenditures made (art. 98). The costs of certain intangibles may be amortized (7/3.9), and expenses relating to the formation of companies and increasing their capital are deductible over a five-year period (7/2.13).

The cost of new plant and expenditures for the enlargement, transformation, and reconstruction of existing plant may be depreciated at accelerated rates, beginning in the business period in which the expense was sustained; accelerated depreciation may also be permitted for assets subjected to unusually intensive operation (7/3.5b).

---

[67] C. M. 13 April 1960, n. 350890. It is now immaterial whether the research has been successful or unsuccessful. Under earlier instructions, expenses of successful research, as well as copyright payments and payments for the acquisition of or the right to use patents, designs, processes, formulas, trademarks, and similar intangibles, had to be amortized under the rules described at 7/3.9. See C. M. 1 March 1957, n. 350620.

[68] C. M. 13 April 1960, n. 350890.

[69] C. M. 29 March 1924, n. 4314.

During the tax years 1957, 1958, and 1959, entities taxed on the balance sheet basis were also permitted to deduct a specified percentage of the amount by which expenditures for new plant installed during each year exceeded the depreciation allowed for that year (10/6.1). This provision has not been renewed. There is, however, a special deduction for profits invested in southern Italy, which is limited to 50% of the profits and to 50% of the cost of the plants in which the investment is made (10/6.3).

The annual amounts (*quote*) of depreciation and consumption must be entered in an appropriate amortization and depreciation fund on the liability side of the balance sheet (CC art. 2425), leaving unaltered the values of the assets entered in the asset accounts. Entities required to be taxed on the balance sheet basis, and enterprises which elect to be so taxed, are required to keep schedules of depreciable assets and depreciation funds, and to record depreciation in the general journal and in individual accounts with separate and distinct entries for categories of assets which are alike in their nature and in their period of depreciation (6/2.2). Such entities are not permitted to deduct depreciation for which these requirements have not been observed (art. 109).

Depreciation is permitted only in accordance with the categories established by the table annexed to the administrative instructions on depreciation and cannot exceed the prescribed rates.[70] If less depreciation is taken than is permitted by the table, an entity or enterprise taxed on the balance sheet basis apparently may carry forward the unused balance in accordance with the provisions relating to losses (7/3.7).

Special rules relating to depreciation in the extraction of natural resources, agriculture, and banking are discussed in Chapter 10.

7/3.2   Assets Which Are Depreciable

The table attached to the administrative instructions on depreciation lists 43 groups of industries, some of which are further divided into subgroups (*specie*), specifying the rates of depreciation for various classes of physical assets in each category.[71] The amortization of intangibles, which is governed by the administrative instructions and by the Civil Code, is discussed at 7/3.9.

The most common categories of physical assets for which rates are provided are listed below.

1. Buildings devoted to the industry, including sheds, barracks, fixed water works, drains and pipes, tanks and reservoirs, streets and open places (*piazzali*), silos, and walled structures in general.

---

[70] C. M. 1 March 1957, n. 350620. Formerly, book depreciation taken in excess of the amount permitted in the table had to be subtracted from the depreciation fund in the business period during which the assessment became final and entered on the liability side of the balance sheet in an unrestricted taxable reserve fund; this procedure is now optional. C. M. 14 April 1959, n. 350710.

[71] C. M. 1 March 1957, n. 350620, Annex.

2. "Generic" plant, including all plant (*impianti*) not peculiar to a particular industry, and plant used for providing a service common to various industries—for example, plant for the production, storage, and distribution of energy; maintenance shops; railway junctions; transformers; parking spaces and gasoline pumps; installations for internal transport, loading, unloading, lifting, and weighing.
3. "Specific" plant, comprising machinery and plant typical of each industry, even if identical equipment could be found in other types of industry. For some specific plant, such as furnaces and their appurtenances, a special category with a different period of depreciation has been provided.
4. Miscellaneous equipment, small items, and laboratory equipment.
5. Office equipment (*mobili d'ufficio*).
6. Vehicles (*automezzi*).

The District Tax Offices are responsible for checking the allocation of particular assets among the various categories, with the assistance, if necessary, of the Revenue Technical Offices.

When the owner of a building leases it, the owner's income from the lease is subject to the tax on income from buildings (9/4.2). Even if the renting of buildings is one of the taxpayer's regular activities, the income therefrom is not taxed as business income. Depreciation is not allowed separately because it is taken into account under the standard deduction for the tax on income from buildings (9/4.2). On the other hand, income from the renting of machinery and equipment belonging to the taxpayer would normally be taxed either as business income or as income from independent work (7/1.2); in either case, depreciation of the machinery or equipment would be allowed.

The amortization of leasehold improvements by a tenant is discussed at 7/3.8; the deduction of contributions to an amortization fund to preserve intact the value of assets which are to revert to the grantor on the expiration of a concession is discussed at 7/3.10.

7/3.3   Determination of Cost of Assets

The total value to be depreciated is determined by adding to the original cost of the assets in each category accessory costs (of installation, assembly, or transportation), additions (*incrementi*) subsequent to the acquisition of the assets, increases resulting from monetary revaluation under the monetary revaluation law of 1952, and taxable capital gains inscribed in the balance sheet (7/1.3d, 9/8.1).[72] This value is diminished in consequence of the elimination of assets from production (7/3.6) or of completed depreciation. Depreciation which has not been completed at the end of the normal period may be extended (7/3.7).

---

[72] C. M. 1 March 1957, n. 350620. Regarding capital gains inscribed in the balance sheet, see also C. M. 15 April 1957, n. 350860.

7/3.4 Depreciation Methods

Depreciation must be calculated by the straight-line method; the prescribed rate of depreciation is applied annually to the actual cost of the asset to the taxpayer (7/3.3).

7/3.5 Depreciation Rates

a. IN GENERAL. The rates (*coefficienti*) of depreciation are established for categories of similar assets (7/3.1) employed in various groups and subgroups of industries.[73] An enterprise engaged in more than one industry applies the rates established for each of the industries to the assets employed in that industry. An asset which is employed for more than one kind of manufacture is depreciated at the rate established for the kind of manufacture in which it is predominantly used.

In general, the annual rate for the depreciation of buildings is 3%, although rates of up to 5% or 6% are provided for certain industries. For "generic" plant, the rates range from 6% to 12%. The rates for "specific" plant and machinery are usually in the neighborhood of 10%, but they are considerably higher in some industries. The rates for miscellaneous equipment and laboratory equipment range from 10% to 40%. In most industries, office equipment is depreciable at 10%, and vehicles at 20%. Pending further revision of the rates of depreciation to take account of current economic conditions, a ministerial circular of 31 October 1963 (n. 320590) provides for an increase of 20% in the rates given in the table.

The rates of depreciation are based on the average physical life of the assets in each category, making allowance for the prevalence of each type of asset in the category as a whole.

In the normal case, the rates given in the table represent the maximum, and no increase can be given to compensate for failing to take depreciation or for taking less depreciation than authorized in prior years. The treatment of unused depreciation is described at 7/3.7.

b. ACCELERATED DEPRECIATION. For new plant (*impianti*) and for the enlargement, tranformation, and reconstruction of existing plant, the period of depreciation may, at the taxpayer's request, be reduced by not more than two fifths (art. 98).[74] Under this provision, the accelerated depreciation (*ammortamento anticipato*) begins in the business period in which the expense was sustained, and not, like normal depreciation, in the period in which the assets are put to use. For the initial period

---

[73] C. M. 1 March 1957, n. 350620, Annex.

[74] Such accelerated depreciation is available also for ships. C. M. 14 May 1955, n. 351440. Under C. M. 2 April 1954, n. 350650, ships had been excluded from this provision.

and for each of the three succeeding periods, an additional amount not exceeding 15% of the total expenditure is added to the normal depreciation. The taxpayer must exercise the option for accelerated depreciation on the filing of the annual return for the period in which the expenditure was incurred, specifying the amounts of increased depreciation for which he requests a deduction (art. 98).

At the discretion of the Tax Office, an increase in the rate of depreciation may be permitted for plant which has been subjected to more intensive operation (*lavorazione*) than is normal for the industry as a whole (not merely for the particular enterprise).[75] For example, if operations were prolonged beyond the work hours normal for the industry, an increase in the rates of depreciation proportional to the lengthened use of the plant might be permitted. The working of machinery in shifts would not justify an increase, however, in an industry in which extra shifts were a part of normal operations and therefore presumptively taken into account in the establishment of ordinary rates.

7/3.6 Disposition or Loss of Assets

When depreciable property related to an enterprise is sold, any excess received over the undepreciated cost of the property is included in income for the year of sale (art. 100). If the undepreciated cost exceeds the sale price, the excess may be deducted as a loss (art. 99). If property related to an enterprise is totally or partially destroyed, the loss may be taken as a deduction (art. 99) (7/2.7); in the case of depreciable assets, the loss would normally be measured by the undepreciated cost. If the last value used for the determination of income differs from the undepreciated cost, however, that value is used instead of the undepreciated cost in computing the gain or loss (arts. 99, 100). In practice, when a depreciable asset is removed from production for any reason, its value or undepreciated cost is taken as a loss in the year in which the removal takes place, and any amount realized on subsequent sale of the asset is included in income of the year of sale.[76]

On the sale of a depreciable asset by an enterprise not formed as a company, only the gain accruing after 1 January 1957, as determined by reference to its value on the books of the enterprise on that date, is taken into account (7/1.3d); but if a loss is realized on the sale, it is taken into account in its entirety.[77]

No special allowance is made for obsolescence, and obsolescent machinery is treated in the same manner as any other asset sold or withdrawn from production.[78]

---

[75] C. M. 1 March 1957, n. 350620.
[76] C. M. 1 March 1957, n. 350620.
[77] C. M. 5 March 1958, n. 10.
[78] C. M. 1 March 1957, n. 350620.

7/3.7   Set-Off and Carry-Over of Unused Depreciation

The tax on income from movable wealth is applied to the net aggregate result of all the taxpayer's activities and operations producing income in category B (7/1.1). Thus, if a corporation or other entity required to be taxed on the balance sheet basis carries on different businesses involving similar or different economic activities, the depreciation for the assets used in each business is computed separately but included in the total figure for depreciation in the profit and loss account and the balance sheet of the corporation. If an individual or a collective entity not required to be taxed on the balance sheet basis carries on different businesses involving similar economic activities, the depreciation for all the assets used is reported on the schedule of "industrial, business, and artisan activities, and agricultural rentals" [79] and is subtracted from the gross income of all the businesses taken together. If an individual or a collective entity not required to be taxed on the balance sheet basis carries on different businesses involving different economic activities, it must file a separate schedule for each activity, and the taxpayer's net income of category B is determined by adding algebraically the gains and losses from the various activities. But since the assessment of enterprises not required to be taxed on the balance sheet basis is commonly made by the application of coefficients for the activities carried on to the volume of transactions (13/2.3), the recognition of a loss, for tax purposes, from an activity carried on by such an enterprise is apparently very rare.

Depreciation not absorbed by income of category B cannot be set off against income of other categories.

Since depreciation is considered a present cost of production in the year for which it is provided [80] and since depreciation at rates higher than those provided in the table is not permitted (7/3.1), unused depreciation of one year cannot be carried forward and set off against business profits of later years except under the provisions governing the carry-over of losses (7/4.2). If an asset has not been completely depreciated at the end of the normal period (the number of years resulting from dividing 100 by the annual rate), however, depreciation may continue to be taken at a rate not exceeding that provided in the table, on condition that the asset continues to be used in production.[81]

7/3.8   Amortization of Leasehold Improvements

Expenses for improvements to the building in which a business is carried on are depreciable if the improvements are related to the enter-

[79] In the individual return, Schedule F (12/5.2); in the return of collective entities not required to be taxed on the balance sheet basis, Schedule II (12/5.4).

[80] See Traina-Portanova, *Spese e passività deducibili nell'imposta di ricchezza mobile* 35.

[81] C. M. 1 March 1957, n. 350620.

prise, even if the building is leased from another. A lessee may also deduct expenditures for repairs and maintenance which are made necessary by his use of the premises for the business or which he is required by express contract to make (7/2.6).

7/3.9 Amortization of Intangibles

The law provides for deduction of amortization of the costs of the intangibles listed below, beginning with the business period in which the intangibles are put to use (art. 98; CC arts. 2425, 2427).

1. Industrial patent rights.
2. Rights to use works of the mind (*opere dell'ingegno*).
3. Rights of concession.
4. Trademarks.
5. Any difference between the amount owed on the maturity of a bond issue and the amount received at the time of issue.[82]
6. The value of good will (*avviamento*). [83]

The annual amounts (*quote*) of amortization are determined in relation to the period of exploitation (*sfruttamento*). If there is no period of exploitation, the amounts are determined in proportion to the life (*durata*) of the assets or to the loss or diminution of their utilization.[84] The amounts must be determined separately for each item of intangible property and may be carried over to diminish the value of the item entered in the asset side of the capital account.[85] Entities required to be taxed on the balance sheet basis and enterprises which elect to be so taxed are not permitted to amortize intangibles for which they have not kept the prescribed journal of payments to individuals (6/2.2) (art. 109).

Expenses for studies, research, or experiments are deductible from income as explained at 7/2.15.

7/3.10 Assets Reverting to Grantor of Concession

Many public utilities—electricity and gas supply, railroads and other public transportation—are operated under concessions from governmental

---

[82] It appears that this difference would be amortized only if the debt were contracted for the purchase of depreciable assets, of which the difference must be considered as a higher cost. If the debt were contracted for working capital, the difference would be deductible as interest paid, under the rules discussed at 7/2.5. See Giannetta, Scandale, and Sessa, *Teoria e tecnica nell'accertamento del reddito mobiliare* 493.

[83] The value of good will may be entered in the balance sheet when an amount has been paid for it on the acquisition of the business (9/9.4), and it must be amortized in subsequent years in accordance with the prudent estimation of the directors (*amministratori*) and the members of the board of overseers (*sindaci*). CC art. 2427.

[84] C. M. 1 March 1957, n. 350620; CC art. 2425. Article 98 of the *Testo unico* provides for determination of the annual amortization in relation to the life (*durata*) of the assets (7/3.1). The life of an asset can exceed its period of exploitation.

[85] C. M. 1 March 1957, n. 350620.

authorities (1/3.4a). Under the terms of these concessions, the technical equipment used in the operation devolves upon the grantor of the concession on expiration of the concession, and the grantee must maintain its value intact by means of an amortization fund, the annual contributions to which are deductible in the determination of taxable income.[86] The amortization is entered in the liability side of the balance sheet, but the value ascribed to the assets on the asset side is not changed.

In these cases, the basis for the amortization of the assets is the purchase price or the cost of manufacture, increased by accessory costs and diminished by any contributions made by the granting entity to the cost of the assets.[87] The amortization is spread over the period of the concession, starting with the year in which the concession is first exploited. If the plant is increased during the period of the concession, or if there is a monetary capital gain or a taxable economic capital gain, the annual amortization for the balance of the term is increased by an amount equal to the increase in value divided by the number of years remaining. A decrease in value during the term of the concession gives rise to a corresponding decrease in the annual amortization during the balance of the term. If an asset whose physical life is shorter than the duration of the concession is replaced, the value of the replacement is substituted for that of the original asset, and the annual amortization for the balance of the term is adjusted to take account of the difference between the cost of the replacement and the cost of the original asset.

On the expiration of the concession, when the plant actually devolves upon the grantor, any excess in the amortization fund over the initial book value of the installations actually devolved is included in income for the business period in which the devolution takes place. If the concession is extended and the depreciation fund shows a deficit, the depreciation may be continued until the end of the extension. In that case, the annual deduction may be determined in an amount not exceeding the maximum permitted during the term of the concession itself, or it may be fixed by dividing the undepreciated value by the number of years for which the concession is extended.

Since the physical life of plant which devolves gratuitously is generally shorter than the duration of the concession, the grantee usually incurs not only the expense of the original cost of the plant, but also the cost of one or more replacements, whereas, for purposes of the amortization fund, he is permitted to deduct only the cost of the assets which actually devolve to the grantor at the end of the concession. Formerly, the grantee was permitted to deduct the costs of extraordinary maintenance and restoration as business expenses in the year in which they were incurred.

---

[86] C. M. 1 March 1957, n. 350620.
[87] Comm. Centr., Sez. III, 26 March 1942, n. 53346; C. M. 1 March 1957, n. 350620.

To avoid having the cost of replacement fall entirely in the year in which it is incurred, however, the grantee is now permitted to deduct an annual allowance for depreciation (*deperimento*) and consumption (*consumo*) calculated at the rates provided in the table, and may no longer deduct either expenses for extraordinary maintenance increasing the value of the assets or expenses of restoration, although the deduction of ordinary maintenance expenses not increasing the value of the assets (*non incrementativa*) is still permitted. Depreciation funds established for this purpose must be included in the grantee's income in the business period in which the assets devolve upon the grantor.

When an entity subject to the corporation tax holds immovable property which is subject to gratuitous retransfer on the expiration of a concession, its taxable assets include the amortization fund reserves; and in determining the taxable assets, that proportion of the total balance sheet value which the time elapsed since the granting of the concession bears to the term of the concession is deductible (art. 147) (3/2.3).

7/3.11   Obsolete Machinery

No deduction is allowed, other than the normal depreciation deduction (7/3), for the obsolescence of machinery. If obsolete machinery is scrapped, sold, or retired from use, however, any excess of its undepreciated cost over the amount realized on the sale of the machinery may be deducted as a loss (7/3.6).

7/4.   Net Losses from Operations

7/4.1   Set-Off in Current Year

Since the tax on income from movable wealth is applied on the basis of the net aggregate result of all of the taxpayer's activities and operations producing income classifiable in category B (7/1.1) a net operating loss of one business can be set off against the profits of any other business carried on by the taxpayer which are subject to tax in the same year. However, a business loss cannot be set off against income of other categories. Since a company and each of its members are separate taxpayers, a member cannot set off losses of the company against profits of a personal business. However, it appears that a member of a company not required to be taxed on the balance sheet basis may deduct his share of the company's loss in determining his net aggregate income for the complementary tax.

Losses of the business period are deductible for purposes of the corporation tax if, and to the extent that, they result from the application of the provisions relating to the tax on income from movable wealth (art. 148). If the determination of aggregate income for purposes of the corporation tax results in a net loss, the tax is reduced at the rate of 10 times the proportion between the net loss and the taxable assets (art. 149) (12/2.2c). The reduction cannot exceed 90% of the tax, however.

7/4.2   Loss Carry-Over

It is a general principle of Italian income taxation that the taxes due for each tax period are determined separately with reference to the tax bases existing in that period (arts. 3, 4) (6/3.1). However, entities required to be taxed on the balance sheet basis may carry business losses forward up to and including the fifth business period after that in which the loss was sustained (art. 112). Enterprises which elect to be taxed on the balance sheet basis (6/1.2b) may carry forward losses in accordance with this provision if they have been taxed on the balance sheet basis for the three years prior to that in which the loss was sustained and will continue to be so taxed in the years for which the set-off is authorized. Other taxpayers are not permitted to carry forward business losses. Unused depreciation may be carried forward under these rules (7/3.7). Losses of one business can be carried forward against income of another, under the rules discussed above, only if both businesses are taxed on the balance sheet basis.

Losses of prior business periods are deductible in determining taxable capital for the asset component of the corporation tax (art. 147) (3/2.1), but not in determining income for the income component of that tax (art. 148).

7/4.3   Loss Carry-Over by Branches

Since a branch is not a separate entity or unit of assessment distinct from the head office of a corporation, the profit or loss of an Italian branch of a corporation formed in Italy or having its head office or the principal object of its enterprise in Italy is consolidated with that of the head office; and any net loss is treated in accordance with the principles discussed at 7/4.1 and 7/4.2. However, since income derived abroad by such a corporation through a branch having separate administration and accounting is not subject to the tax on income from movable wealth (11/2.3a), the computation of any net operating loss incurred by the foreign branch is made without reference to profits earned in Italy (6/7), and foreign losses of the branch cannot be set off against Italian income of the corporation.

Similarly, any net operating loss of an Italian branch of a foreign corporation having neither its head office nor the principal object of its enterprise in Italy is computed without reference to the income of the head office because only the income derived by the corporation through the branch is subject to tax in Italy (6/7, 11/3.5).

In the case of an Italian corporation, losses of a foreign branch are set off against income of the head office for the same year, for purposes of the corporation tax (11/2.1).

7/4.4 Loss Carry-Back

There is no provision for the carry-back of any loss to a year prior to that in which it has been sustained.

7/4.5 Losses on Foreign Exchange

There are no special rules regarding the tax treatment of losses on foreign exchange. Such losses are therefore taken into account when realized,[88] in accordance with the rules governing worthless assets (7/2.7) and losses on credits (7/2.10).

7/5. Nondeductible Expenses
7/5.1 In General

In determining net income from movable wealth of category B under the principles discussed at 7/2.1, no deduction is allowed for expenses not inherent in the production of income subject to tax in category B; for expenses inherent in the production of income not subject to tax in category B; or for general or overhead expenses attributable to activities not productive of income subject to tax in category B.[89] For interest charges owed by entities or enterprises taxed on the balance sheet basis, the limitation on the deduction of general or overhead expenses is given further specification: the proportion deductible is the ratio between gross receipts composing income subject to tax in category B and aggregate gross receipts (7/2.5).

Since the application of these principles to various important classes of expenditure has been discussed in 7/2, it is sufficient to point out here a few examples of expenditures whose deduction would not be allowed under them. The most obvious class includes capital expenditures for assets not related to the production of income subject to the tax on income from movable wealth, and expenditures in excess of the annual amounts allowed under the provisions governing the depreciation of assets related to the enterprise (7/3.1) or the provision for the deduction of expenses of forming companies and increasing their capital (7/2.13). Income taxes and other taxes levied on, or measured by, profits do not constitute expenses of the production of income and thus are not deductible for purposes of the tax on income from movable wealth; but taxes

---

[88] See Comm. Centr., Sez. un., 6 April 1932, n. 35619.

[89] For discussion of the allocation of expenses and losses between taxable income and nontaxable income, see Giannetta, Scandale, and Sessa, *Teoria e tecnica nell'accertamento del reddito mobiliare* 522-529.

related to income are specifically allowed as deductions in determining
income for the complementary tax and the corporation tax (7/2.8).
Authority exists for the deduction of contractual penalties,[90] but penalties
for violations of law are deductible, if at all, only if the violations are
caused by unforeseeable facts.[91] In general, it seems unlikely that fines
and penalties can be considered expenses inherent in the production of
income.[92]

Expenses for which deduction is not allowed under these principles
in determining net income from movable wealth may nonetheless be deducted in determining net aggregate income for purposes of the complementary tax or the corporation tax if they are inherent in the production
of income subject to whichever of those taxes is applicable (6/1.5b).

Since, as a general rule, expenses are deductible only when they are
actually incurred (7/2.1), amounts set aside as reserves for future
expenses (6/6.1) are not deductible, except under the special provisions
relating to retirement funds (7/2.4) and life insurance actuarial reserves
(10/3).

In the following sections are summarized the rules which specifically
disallow the deduction of expenses in determining net income from
movable wealth of category B.

7/5.2   Payments to Owners, Partners, and Directors

In determining income from movable wealth, no deduction is allowed
for the remuneration of the taxpayer, his wife, or unemancipated minor
children, or for remuneration of members of *de facto* companies, general
partnerships, and simple limited partnerships for work done by them in
the business (7/2.3c). Under present rules, shares of profits paid to
directors as part of their compensation for services as directors are not
deductible (7/2.3c). In determining income for the corporation tax,
excessive payments to partners or directors which have been deducted
in determining income from movable wealth must be added back
(7/2.3c).

7/5.3   Payments to Nonresidents

Interest payable by a taxpayer other than a credit firm or institution
is deductible from gross income from movable wealth of category B only
if it is owed to a person domiciled, resident, or having a permanent establishment in Italy, unless the payor is required to pay the category A tax
on the interest with a right of recovery against the recipient through

[90] C. M. 1 July 1902, n. 11959, citing Comm. Centr. 1 July 1877, n. 46687.
[91] C. M. 1 July 1902, n. 11959.
[92] See Giannetta, Scandale, and Sessa, *Teoria e tecnica nell'accertamento del reddito mobiliare* 492.

withholding (7/2.5, 13/3.4). A corporation or other entity required to be taxed on the balance sheet basis is not permitted to deduct certain payments to a foreign enterprise for which it carries on activities in Italy through the sale, disposal, or manufacture of goods, unless the payments are subject to provisional withholding (11/2.4). Otherwise, the deductibility of an expense is not conditioned on the recipient's being domiciled or resident in Italy, provided always that the expense is inherent in the production of income subject to tax in Italy (11/1.3), or is a general expense allocable to such income (7/2.1).

The apportionment of income from business activities exercised abroad by Italian enterprises and the apportionment of income from business activities exercised in Italy by foreign enterprises are discussed at 11/2.3c and 11/3.5b, respectively.

7/5.4   Payments for Which the Required Records Have Not Been Kept

Interest charges owed to credit firms and institutions, for which an official request for certification has been made, are not deductible unless the certification has been filed (7/2.5). No deduction is allowed for capital losses deriving from devaluations not registered in the prescribed manner (6/2.2, 7/2.7), for depreciation not registered in the prescribed manner (6/2.2, 7/3.1), or for expenses not registered in the prescribed manner in the journal of payments to individuals (6/2.2) (art. 109). The taxpayer has the burden of proving all other deductions which are not supported by the required accounting records (13/2.3) and, in practice, apparently also has the burden of proving the accuracy of accounting records.

CHAPTER 8

INCOME FROM
PERSONAL SERVICES

8/1. **Remuneration for Services As an Employee**

    8/1.1   In General

    8/1.2   Employment and Independent Work Distinguished

    8/1.3   Pension, Social Security, and Welfare Benefits
           a.   Contributions by employer
           b.   Payment of benefits

    8/1.4   Benefits in Kind

    8/1.5   Expense Reimbursements

    8/1.6   Profit Sharing

    8/1.7   Bonuses and Gratuities

    8/1.8   Termination Pay

    8/1.9   Deductions

    8/1.10 Withholding of Tax on Wages and Salaries

8/2. **Income from Professional Services and Independent Work**

    8/2.1   Gross Income

    8/2.2   Deductions

    8/2.3   Withholding of Tax

8/3. **Income from Miscellaneous Services**

    8/3.1   Gross Income

    8/3.2   Deductions

8/4. **Income-Spreading Provisions**

ANALYSIS OF INCOME TAX   430

8/1.   Remuneration for Services As an Employee

8/1.1   In General

"Income from work as an employee" (*reddito di lavoro subordinato*) whether received in the form of salaries, wages, allowances, grants, or any other remuneration, is subject to the tax on income from movable wealth in category C/2 (art. 85). Category C/2 also includes certain other income which, at the time of production, is, strictly speaking, the result neither of capital nor of labor. Examples of such income are pensions, life annuities, and subsidies (6/1.1e, 8/1.3).[1] In addition to the standard allowance applicable against income of category C/2 (12/1.4b), income from work as an employee, pensions, and length-of-service and welfare payments are exempt from the tax on income from movable wealth if they do not exceed certain limits (12/1.4a).

The income from work as an employee which is subject to tax is the income actually received in each payment period as a result of work done (art. 87). Remuneration payable under regular Italian accounting doctrine and practice is considered as received (6/4.1). In the case of piecework, if payment is made at the end of a work cycle which includes more than one pay period, the income for each period is determined by taking into account the proportionate share of the total wage for the job (art. 87). The tax period for income from work as an employee is the calendar year (art. 3) (6/3.1).

Income from work as an employee performed in Italy and income from work done abroad on behalf of the public administration or for a person domiciled or resident in Italy who does not have separate administration and accounting abroad to which the compensation can be charged are considered as produced in Italy (art. 82) and are therefore subject to the tax on income from movable wealth regardless of the residence status of the taxpayer (11/1.5). Compensation earned abroad by a person domiciled or resident in Italy is considered as produced in Italy if it is exempted from tax in the other country by virtue of an international agreement (11/2.2).

Aggregate income for the complementary tax includes all compensation considered as produced in Italy for the tax on income from movable wealth under the rules described above (6/1.1f) and compensation earned abroad by a person domiciled or resident in Italy which is either enjoyed in Italy or exempted from taxation in the other country by virtue of an international agreement (11/2.2).

---

[1] Category C/2 was formerly defined as "income of a fixed character from work." See R.D.L. 16 October 1924, n. 1613, art. 1; D.L.L. 19 October 1944, n. 384, art. 4. Prior to the enactment of the 1944 decree law, salaries, wages, pensions, and allowances paid by the state or other public entities were subject to tax in a separate category, category D.

Exemptions granted to certain classes of persons from the tax on income rom movable wealth or from the complementary tax on certain types f compensation are discussed at 5/5.

8/1.2 Employment and Independent Work Distinguished

Although income from work as an employee and income from inde->endent work are at present subject to the tax on income from movable vealth at the same rate (12/1.4c), the distinction between them is mportant because of differences in the applicable surtaxes and addiionals (2/2.9, 12/1.4d).

An employee (*prestatore di lavoro subordinato*) is one who binds iimself, for compensation, to work in an enterprise, furnishing intellectual r manual labor for, and under the direction of, the entrepreneur (CC art. 2094). Persons who are hired irregularly or seasonally,[2] or who may be imultaneously under contract to perform services for more than one >erson,[3] are considered as furnishing independent professional services, nd their income is taxable in category C/1 of income from movable .vealth under the rules discussed at 8/2.

Until recently, compensation paid to a director (*amministratore*) for iis services as such was not deductible as an expense of earning business ncome (7/2.3c) and was not included in the director's income for pur->oses of the tax on income from movable wealth. By a recent modifica-tion of the *Testo unico,* compensation paid in any form by a business enterprise to directors, excluding participations in net profits of the busi-ness period, is now deductible from the income of the corporation and is subject to provisional withholding of the tax on income from movable wealth (13/3.5).[4] The compensation is included in the recipient's pro-fessional income.[5]

Remuneration received by a director for services outside the scope of his duties as a director, and not exceeding current remuneration for the functions performed, is subject to tax in category C/2 (paid by the employer and recovered through withholding (13/3.4)) and is deduct-ible from the income of the corporation (7/2.3c), provided the existence of a regular relation of employment is established. If a director performs independent professional services for the corporation, for example, as a lawyer, his compensation for such services is taxed as ordinary

---

[2] Comm. Centr., Sez. II, 24 October 1953, n. 52485 (members of a band hired individually, and not as employees of the band leader, by a festival committee); Comm. Centr., Sez. III, 16 April 1947, n. 89084 (musicians hired to perform only for the opera or concert season).

[3] Ministerial Note 28 May 1941, n. 3087, De Angelis, Potenza, and Testa, *Testo unico delle leggi sulle imposte dirette* 388 (personnel hired on a temporary basis for the production of a film).

[4] L. 21 April 1962, n. 226, art. 1.

[5] C.M. 15 June 1962, n. 60.

professional income, without withholding, in category C/1.[6] For purposes of the complementary tax, income derived from serving as a director is included in income in the amount received by the taxpayer (art. 135).

Remuneration paid to partners is regarded not as compensation for work, but as a distribution of profits. Since this distribution is not deductible in determining the net income of the partnership from business (7/2.3c), the profits so distributed are taxed when earned by the partnership and are not again subject to the tax on income from movable wealth when distributed to the partner (5/3.2). However, the total share of each partner in the profits of the partnership is included in his income for purposes of the complementary tax, regardless of the amount actually distributed to him (5/3.2).

8/1.3   Pension, Social Security, and Welfare Benefits

a. CONTRIBUTIONS BY EMPLOYER. Social security and welfare contributions paid by an employer in compliance with provisions of law or of a collective bargaining contract are not included in an employee's income even if computed on the basis of his remuneration (art. 87). Similarly, the employee's compulsory contributions are not included in his income in the year in which they are made (art. 87).[7]

For purposes of the complementary tax, an employee may deduct amounts withheld or paid for social security purposes and premiums for life insurance contracted for by him for his own benefit or for members of his family living with him for whose maintenance he is legally responsible (art. 136), even if the contributions are not required by law or by contract.[8]

The contributions of the employer and the employee are deductible from the employer's business income under the conditions described at 7/2.4.

---

[6] C.M. 18 December 1959, n. 84; C.M. 15 June 1962, n. 60.

[7] Under administrative instructions in effect prior to the enactment of the *Testo unico*, if a life insurance policy was purchased for an employee, the entire premium was included in his income of category C/2 at the time of payment because the proceeds are excluded from income as a return of capital. C.M. 19 January 1934, n. 600. In order to make possible the uniform treatment of contributions to an independent social security fund (7/2.4) and the purchase of a life insurance policy, an independent social security fund could request that the employer's and employee's contributions be taxed in category C/2 at the time of payment into the fund, in which case distributions by the fund to the employee were not subject to tax. C.M. 14 July 1934, n. 7120. Insofar as they are applicable to contributions paid in compliance with law or contract, however, these provisions are now in conflict with article 87 of the *Testo unico*. According to the Ministry of Finance, the tax treatment of social security and welfare contributions and benefits is now under reconsideration.

[8] See C.M. 12 March 1925; De Angelis, Potenza, and Testa, *Testo unico delle leggi sulle imposte dirette* 708.

b. PAYMENT OF BENEFITS. Pensions, annuities, and subsidies paid by an
employer to a present or former employee are included in the employee's
income in category C/2 (arts. 85, 87)[9] except in the case of certain
military pensions and allowances to public employees, whose wages are
also exempt (5/5.4). In addition to the standard allowances applicable
against income of category C/2 (12/1.4b), pensions and length-of-service
and welfare payments are exempt from the tax on income from movable
wealth if they do not exceed certain limits (12/1.4a). Moreover, special
laws exempt from the tax on income from movable wealth pensions,
allowances (indennità), subsidies, and family grants (assegni familiari)
paid by the National Institute of Social Security (Istituto Nazionale
della Previdenza Sociale, or INPS); [10] pensions, allowances, and subsidies
paid by the National Institute of Health Insurance (Istituto Nazionale
per l'Assistenza di Malattia, or INAM); [11] and payments made by the
National Institute for Work Accident Insurance (Istituto Nazionale per
l'Assicurazione contro gli Infortuni sul Lavoro, or INAIL).[12] The institutions are exempt from the tax on income from movable wealth on their
own income (5/5.6).

In all other cases, pensions, annuities, subsidies, and social security
and welfare payments made to employees of private enterprises are
included in category C/2 of income from movable wealth at the time
of payment. Tax is imposed on the payor of the benefit, with the obligation to recover the tax from the recipient through withholding (13/3.4).
If the payments are made under a contract of insurance, only the interest
is subject to the tax, recoverable through withholding (9/3.2); but life
annuities are subject to tax in full (9/3.1). Amounts paid as gratuities
to an employee are included in the employee's income of category C/2
but are deductible in determining the taxable business income of the
employer under the limitations discussed at 7/2.11.

Benefit payments exempt from the tax on income from movable wealth
are nonetheless subject to the complementary tax (6/1.1f), with the
exception of family allowances paid out of funds managed by the
Istituto Nazionale della Previdenza Sociale [13] and pensions paid by that
institute as a result of direct compulsory insurance.[14] When a payment
on account of dismissal, length of service, social security, or termination
of employment are made in a lump sum, the amount of the payment

---

[9] This point has been clarified by the amendment to article 87 made by article
2 of L. 4 December 1962, n. 1682.
[10] R.D.L. 4 October 1935, n. 1827 (converted in L. 6 April 1936, n. 1155), art.
124; and R.D.L. 21 August 1936, n. 1632, art. 10.
[11] L. 11 January 1943, n. 138, art. 35.
[12] R.D. 17 August 1935, n. 1765, art 71.
[13] R.D.L. 17 June 1937, n. 1048, art. 23; R.D.L. 4 October 1935, n. 1827 (converted in L. 6 April 1936, n. 1155), art. 124.
[14] C.M. 15 February 1958, n. 500051.

which is subject to the tax on income from movable wealth is subject to the complementary tax separately from the other income of the taxpayer, at the rate applicable to the amount determined by dividing the total payment received by the number of years of service rendered (art. 140).

8/1.4 Benefits in Kind

The value of benefits in kind generally is subject to the tax on income from movable wealth (art. 81). Thus, the value of lodgings furnished by an employer to an employee is included in the employee's income of category C/2 in the amount of the presumed rent, as determined in accordance with the criteria used for the tax on income from buildings (9/4.2c), unless the lodgings are furnished in the interest of the employee's duties and he is required to occupy them as a condition of employment.[15] However, although a cash allowance for meals is included in income as explained at 8/1.5, no effort is made to collect tax on the value of meals furnished in kind.[16]

8/1.5 Expense Reimbursements

Per diem or other fixed travel payments (*trasferte*) not subject to a requirement of rendering an accounting and food payments (*panatiche*) made to maritime personnel are included in income to the extent of 40% of their amount (art. 87).

The reimbursement of expenses which are incurred by an employee while traveling and for which he renders an accounting to his employer is included in the employee's income only to the extent to which it represents the employee's normal living expenses, taking into account his grade and responsibility and the class of establishment which he usually frequents.[17] The Central Commission has held that when an employee is traveling for business reasons, his normal sustenance should be considered to be that part of the reimbursement of the living expenses which he would have incurred had he remained at the office, and that it is not proper for the tax administration to presume that one third of the entire reimbursement is income subject to withholding.[18] However, it appears that the practice in some districts is to exempt entirely from the employee's income of category C/2 reimbursements for travel ex-

---

[15] Comm. Centr., Sez. II, 2 March 1942, n. 52059.
[16] C.M. 27 March 1945, n. 770.
[17] C.M. 17 October 1936, n. 10560.
[18] Comm. Centr., Sez. III, 15 June 1945, n. 76996. It appears that, at present, the tax administration attempts to determine, under the rules laid down in the administrative instruction cited in footnote 17 *supra*, the proportion of a travel allowance which is subject to the requirement of rendering an accounting within a maximum limit of 40%.

penses based on the rendering of an accounting and to include entirely in that income other occasional reimbursements, such as expenses for meals not connected with traveling.

Risk allowances paid to bank employees in consideration of losses to which they are exposed through possible errors of calculation in collections and payments are taxable in full in category C/2.[19]

8/1.6 Profit Sharing

The sharing of profits of a corporation with employees in remuneration for services performed is subject to the tax on income from movable wealth in category C/2.[20] Shares of profits which are paid to directors solely in consideration of their services as such, however, are distributions of profits (9/2.5) rather than remuneration and therefore are subject to the tax on income from movable wealth only against the company and not against the recipient. For the same reasons, although profit sharing paid to regular employees is deductible from the income of the corporation as an expense of earning income, profit sharing paid to directors is normally a nondeductible appropriation of profits already earned (7/2.3d).

8/1.7 Bonuses and Gratuities

All bonuses and gratuities paid by an employer to an employee are subject to the tax on income from movable wealth in category C/2 as part of the employee's remuneration for work performed (art. 87). Although the employer is required to pay the tax on "service percentages" (*percentuali di servizio*) paid to the employee, with obligation of recovery of the tax from the employee as in the case of other income of category C/2 (13/3.4), he is not required to pay or collect the tax on tips paid to the employee directly by customers.[21] Although, in principle, such tips are subject to the tax on income from movable wealth and to the complementary tax, in practice, for administrative reasons, they are not assessed.

Special rules are provided for the payment and recovery of the tax on income from movable wealth and for provisional withholding of the complementary tax on bonuses in the form of an extra month's pay (*tredicesima mensilità*) and on Christmas and Easter bonuses (*gratifiche natalizie e pasquali*) (8/1.10, 12/1.6).

---

[19] Comm. Centr., Sez. I, 10 July 1946, n. 83514. It appears that the losses themselves would be deductible from income for the complementary tax but not from income from movable wealth (8/1.9).

[20] Comm. Centr., Sez. un., 21 February 1940, n. 22715.

[21] Comm. Centr. 8 May 1929, n. 95507.

8/I.8 Termination Pay

Termination payments based on length of service (*indennità di anzianità*), like pensions and social security payments, are treated as income from services as an employee and thus are included in income of category C/2 in the year of receipt (art. 87).[22] Termination payments based on length of service, as well as social security payments, are exempt from the tax on income from movable wealth if they are payable by law or under a collective labor contract and if their total amount does not exceed L. 1 million (12/1.4a). For termination payments based on length of service and social security payments made in a lump sum at the time of termination of employment, there is also a standard allowance for the tax on income from movable wealth of L. 40,000 for each year of service rendered (12/1.4b); a reduced rate is then applied to L. 60,000 for each year of service rendered (12/1.4c).

For payments on account of dismissal (*licenziamento*), length of service (*anzianità*), social security (*previdenza*), and for any other amount received in a lump sum in relation to termination of employment, the complementary tax is computed separately from the tax on the other income of the taxpayer (art. 140). For purposes of the complementary tax, the income from such payments, before allowances (12/1.5b), is computed in the same way as for the tax on income from movable wealth; but the rate applicable to such income is the rate corresponding to the amount determined by dividing the total payment received by the number of years of service rendered (art. 140).

8/I.9 Deductions

As explained at 8/1.5, reimbursements for certain expenses are excluded from an employee's income of category C/2 for the tax on income from movable wealth. Social security and welfare contributions paid by an employee in accordance with provisions of law or of a collective bargaining agreement are excluded when made from the employee's income of category C/2 (art. 87) (8/1.3a). The effect of each of these exclusions is the same as if the excluded amount were included in taxable income and allowed as a deduction. Apart from these provisions and the standard allowance (12/1.4b), no other deductions are allowed in determining income of category C/2. The tax on income from movable wealth of category C/2 is paid by the employer and recovered from the employee through withholding (13/3.4).

For purposes of the complementary tax, other expenses inherent in the production of income from work as an employee are deductible (art. 136) (6/1.5b). Until recently, the taxpayer could deduct itemized ex-

---

[22] As modified by L. 4 December 1962, n. 1682, art. 2.

penses for transportation (*trasporto*),[23] for the purchase of technical books and materials,[24] for the purchase of work tools, and for professional instruction.[25] Instead of itemizing these deductions, the taxpayer could, under administrative practice, take a standard deduction of 15% of the gross amount of the total remuneration of the members of his family who worked, but not exceeding L. 300,000 annually for each working member.[26] By a recent modification of the *Testo unico*, however, the taxpayer is allowed a standard deduction of 20% from income from work as an employee and from pensions, up to a maximum of L. 360,000 (art. 136).[27]

For purposes of the complementary tax, the taxpayer may also deduct interest not deductible for purposes of the tax on income from movable wealth (6/1.5d), taxes related to income which were paid during the year (6/1.5e), and certain social security contributions and life insurance premiums not deductible for purposes of the tax on income from movable wealth (8/1.3a).

Other measures providing limited relief for the living expenses of employees and their families are: the personal allowance deductible from income from movable wealth of category C/2 (12/1.4b), the reduced rate applicable to income of category C/2 above a certain limit, the basic personal allowances and allowances for dependents which are deductible from net aggregate income for the complementary tax (12/1.5b), and the reliefs for large families provided under the complementary tax (12/1.5b). If the taxpayer's wife has income from work as an employee, she is entitled to a personal allowance, in place of a dependent's allowance, for purposes of the complementary tax (12/1.5b).

8/1.10 Withholding of Tax on Wages and Salaries

The tax on income from movable wealth is withheld directly by the state on its payments of salaries, remuneration, pensions, and occasional compensation (13/3.3). All other private and public employers are required to pay the tax on income from movable wealth on payments of income from employment made by them and are required to recover the tax by withholding from each payment (13/3.4). Business enterprises must make a provisional withholding of the tax on income from movable wealth from any compensation paid to directors, auditors, and overseers, except shares of business profits (13/3.5). The complementary tax is withheld provisionally at special rates from all payments of income from employment (13/3.5).

---

[23] Comm. Centr. 22 March 1930, n. 3685.
[24] Comm. Prov. Napoli 8 May 1956.
[25] C.M. 25 February 1957, n. 500116, confirmed by C.M. 4 January 1960, n. 501519.
[26] C.M. 25 February 1957, n. 500116.
[27] As modified by L. 4 December 1962, n. 1682, art. 5.

The provisional withholdings are credited against the tax finally assessed; the payments and withholdings of the tax on income from movable wealth of category C/2 from payments of income from employment are final.

The computation of withholding on payments for length of service and for dismissal (8/1.8) and on bonuses (8/1.7) is described at 12/1.6.

8/2. Income from Professional Services and Independent Work

8/2.1 Gross Income

Income derived from the exercise of an art or profession is subject to the tax on income from movable wealth in category C/1 as "income from independent work of individuals" (art. 85).

Fees (*provvigioni*) paid to an independent broker are subject to tax in category C/1; however, commissions (*commissioni*) paid to an agent acting on behalf of a single firm as an employee are taxed in category C/2 as income from work as an employee (8/1.2). Compensation paid for professional services to a person who is not an employee is taxed as income from independent services, in category C/1, even if it is paid under an agreement requiring a fixed compensation by the month or by the year.[28] It appears that income of category C/1—income from the "independent work of individuals"—may also be earned by a professional firm, provided the firm's professional or artistic activities are carried on predominantly by individuals, without involving any important element of capital,[29] and are not carried out through the work of employees for salaries or other compensation taxed in category C/2. Category C/1 also includes income derived from carrying on an enterprise based predominantly on the personal labor of the taxpayer and the members of his family (art. 85), as in the case of artisans, small businesses, and small agricultural leaseholds (7/1.2b). The classification of income from personal services not rendered in the course of employment or in the exercise of a profession is discussed at 8/3. The net income of category C/1 is included in aggregate income for purposes of the complementary tax (art. 135).

The tax period for income of category C/1 is the calendar year (art. 3) (6/3.1). Gross professional income includes compensation for the activities carried on during the tax period (art. 115), even if not yet received (6/4.1). Interest accruing on uncollected professional fees apparently also would be taxed in category C/1, as the result of a professional activity, rather than in category A, as the result of an investment of

---

[28] Comm. Centr., Sez. un., 7 July 1947, n. 91418; Comm. Centr., Sez. I, 22 March 1946, n. 81623.

[29] Compare R.D.L. 24 August 1877, n. 4021, art. 54.

capital.[30] There is, however, no express provision to this effect. Capital gains resulting from nonspeculative dealings by an individual in property used in the exercise of an art or profession, or from the transfer of good will by a professional individual, are not considered income (9/8.1). Gains resulting from speculative dealings in property used in the exercise of a profession or art are taxed in category B as business income under the rules discussed at 9/8.2. Income derived from certain types of services rendered over more than one business period may be spread over the years in which the services are performed (8/4). With respect to each taxpayer, the tax is measured on the basis of the net aggregate result of all activities producing income classifiable in category C/1 (art. 95) (8/4).

The tax on income from movable wealth is applied to income from independent work derived from an activity exercised in Italy (art. 82), under the rules discussed at 11/1.4.

When a taxpayer carries on his professional or artistic activity in a building owned by him, the income attributable to the building remains subject to the tax on income from buildings and is not considered to be included in the income derived from the professional activity. The income attributable to a building whose owner carries on a business activity in it, on the other hand, is considered to be a part of the income from the business activity and is therefore excluded from the tax on income from buildings (9/4.2a). The difference is that income of category B includes income attributable to the capital invested in the enterprise, but income of category C/1 is in principle limited to income from the furnishing of independent services (2/2.2, 6/1.1e).

8/2.2 Deductions

The net income from the exercise of an art or profession consists of the difference between the compensation due for activities carried on during the year and the expenses inherent in (*inerente a*) the exercise of the activities (arts. 91, 115), even if not yet paid (6/4.1). The meaning of "inherent in" for expenses of professional activities is similar to its meaning for business enterprises (7/2.1). In addition, certain provisions limiting expenditures deductible from business income for

---

[30] See Berliri, *Il testo unico delle imposte dirette* 235-236. Interest received in the exercise of a business enterprise is by express provision taxed in category B (7/1.3b). As in the case of a business debt, when a professional debt becomes the subject of a judgment, it becomes a capital asset; and the interest, by *avulsione*, is thereafter taxable in category A as income from capital. Cass., Sez. I, 11 February 1946, n. 115; Comm. Centr., Sez. III, 20 July 1945, n. 77842; Comm. Centr., Sez. II, 13 May 1959, n. 16625.

purposes of the tax on income from movable wealth also apply to income from independent work in category C/1. These are listed below.

1. Interest charges are deductible only if owed to persons domiciled, resident, or having a permanent establishment in Italy, unless the payor of the interest is required to pay the category A tax with a right of recovery from the recipient through withholding (art. 92) (7/2.5).
2. Interest charges owed to credit firms and institutions are not deductible if the creditor has failed to comply with an official request for a certification of the debt (art. 92) (7/2.5).
3. Payments regarded as remuneration for activities carried on by the taxpayer, his wife, or unemancipated minor children for the production of income cannot be deducted (art. 94) (7/2.3c).

A taxpayer engaged in the exercise of an art or profession may spread payments due by law or by contract to employees for termination of employment, in the manner described at 7/2.3e (arts. 97, 115); he also may take depreciation for the cost of assets and expenditures for the improvement of assets as described at 7/3 (arts. 98, 115), excluding accelerated depreciation for new plant (7/3.1). The other deductions provided for determining the net income of business enterprises (7/2.1) are not allowed in determining net income from the exercise of arts or professions.

Since income attributable to a building in which the taxpayer exercises an art or profession is not included in income from movable wealth but is subject to the tax on income from buildings, expenses for repairs and maintenance, the cost of improvements, and depreciation of the building are taken into account only through the standard deduction provided for the tax on income from buildings (9/4.2c); they therefore may not be deducted separately from gross income of category C/1. However, if a taxpayer exercising an art or profession rents the premises in which he works, he is entitled to deductions, under the rules applicable to business enterprises, for expenses of repairs and maintenance (7/2.6) and for depreciation of improvements to the building (7/3.8).

8/2.3 Withholding of Tax

Provisional withholding of the tax on income from movable wealth and the complementary tax is required, in accordance with the provisions discussed at 13/3.5, from fees paid to persons domiciled in Italy by business enterprises for artistic services performed in Italy; from compensation paid to aliens, or to Italians domiciled abroad, for the exercise of arts or professions in Italy; and from payments made to aliens, or to Italians domiciled abroad, for copyrights or for the transfer or licensing of patents, designs, processes, formulas, trademarks, and other intellectual property.

8/3.   Income from Miscellaneous Services

/3.1   Gross Income

Income from independent personal services or activities outside the
limits of the taxpayer's regular occupation are subject to the tax on
ncome from movable wealth in category C/1 as income from independent
work (art. 85). Examples of such income are fees paid to the liquidators
of a business,[31] sales commissions earned by one not regularly engaged
in the profession of agent or broker, payments received by a nonprofes-
sional writer or inventor for the use of a patent or a copyright (9/5),
and prizes or awards won through the performance of services (10/7.1).
Speculative gains from dealings in property are taxed in category B
9/8.1).

A director's compensation for his services normally is taxed in category
C/1; but a director may also receive compensation taxed in category
C/2 for services as an employee and compensation taxable in category C/1
or the rendition of independent professional services to the corporation
(8/1.1). Compensation received under a will by an executor is not
included in income for purposes of the tax on income from movable
wealth or for purposes of the complementary tax (6/1.3), because it is
axed as a bequest under the succession tax (3/4).[32]

Income from occasional or isolated activities is consolidated with the
taxpayer's other income of category C/1 in the year in which it is payable; but income from certain services which are to be performed over
more than one year may be spread as explained at 8/4.

Payments to authors or inventors who are aliens or Italians domiciled
abroad are subject to provisional withholding of the tax on income from
movable wealth and the complementary tax (13/3.5).

3/3.2   Deductions

Net income from occasional or isolated services classified in category
C/1 is the difference between gross proceeds and the amount of expenses
and charges inherent in the production of the income (art. 91), subject
to the limitations listed at 8/2.2 for interest charges and payments regarded as remuneration for activities carried on by the taxpayer or
members of his family.

8/4.   Income-Spreading Provisions

A taxpayer who derives income from contracts for the execution of
specific work (*appalti*),[33] contracts of supply (*forniture*), administrations

---

[31] Comm. Centr. 10 January 1941, n. 35143.
[32] Comm. Centr. 3 October 1931, n. 27299.
[33] *Appalto* is a contract by which one party assumes the accomplishment of work
or service for a payment in money, furnishing the necessary means and carrying out

(*amministrazioni*) (for example, of property or of a succession, or of company in receivership), services under court order, services as a guar dian, or similar services which are to be performed over more than on year, is entitled to apply to each of the years a proportional share c the income and expenses of the work as a whole. In computing the shar attributable to each year, the risk connected with completing the wor. is taken into account (art. 116).[34]

Income derived from isolated or occasional activities other than thos to which the spreading provision described above applies, includin income derived by an author or inventor from the sale of a copyrigh or patent covering work produced by him, is included in income o category C/1 in the year in which it becomes payable.

Payments on account of dismissal, length of service, social security and other amounts received in a lump sum in relation to termination o employment are subject to the complementary tax in the year of receipt but the tax on such payments is applied separately from the other incom of the taxpayer at the rate applicable to the amount determined by dividing the total payment received by the number of years of servic rendered (8/1.3b).

Prior to the tax reform law of 1956, the Tax Offices were empowerec to make a separate assessment, *una tantum,* of income which member of the professions derived from administrations, services under cour order, services as a guardian, liquidation of businesses, arbitration o exchange, and similar services, whenever the amount or other circum stances relative to the method in which the profession was normally carried on made it possible to consider such income apart from the regula income assessed for the ordinary carrying on of professional activity.[3] Income from contracts of *appalto* and *forniture* could be assessed in th same manner if their amount, duration, method of execution, or othe circumstances made it possible for them to be considered distinct from the normal and ordinary activity of the taxpayer.[36] These provisions whose purpose was to prevent distortion of assessments established fo periods of more than one year (6/9.2), have been ineffective since 1 July 1957.[37]

---

the contract at his own risk (CC art. 1655). A contract which has the continuing or periodic furnishing of things or services as its object is known as *somministrazione* (CC arts. 1559-1677). See Ferri, *Manuale di diritto commerciale* 637-653; Greco, *Lezioni di diritto commerciale* 267-328; Rubino, *L'appalto.*

[34] See C.M. 15 April 1957, n. 350860.
[35] L. 8 June 1936, n. 1231, art. 7.
[36] L. 8 June 1936, n. 1231, art. 8.
[37] L. 5 January 1956, n. 1, art. 24.

CHAPTER 9

INCOME FROM CAPITAL
AND CAPITAL TRANSACTIONS

9/1. **Interest**
9/1.1 In General
9/1.2 Interest Payments by Government or Public Entities
9/1.3 Loan Premiums and Prizes
9/1.4 Capitalized Interest
9/1.5 Sales of Obligations with Accrued Interest
9/1.6 Sales of Interest
9/1.7 Exempt Interest

9/2. **Dividends and Other Distributions**
9/2.1 In General
    a. Basis of taxation of participations
    b. Complementary tax
    c. Corporation tax
9/2.2 Dividends in Kind
9/2.3 Stock Dividends and Other Bonus Securities
9/2.4 Distributions on Liquidation or in Reduction of Capital
9/2.5 Payments to Directors and Shareholders
9/2.6 Transfers of Accrued Dividends
9/2.7 Taxation of Dividends at Source
    a. In general
    b. Profits exempt from withholding
    c. Credit against complementary tax or corporation tax for amounts withheld
    d. Bearer shares
    e. Foreign securities
9/2.8 Registration of Shares

9/3. Pensions, Annuities, and Insurance
    9/3.1   Pensions and Annuities
    9/3.2   Life Insurance Proceeds
    9/3.3   Accident and Health Insurance Proceeds

9/4. Rent
    9/4.1   In General
    9/4.2   Tax on Income from Buildings
        a. In general
        b. Exemptions
        c. Determination of net income from buildings
        d. Urban building cadaster
        e. Appeals
    9/4.3   Rent Subject to Tax As Income from Movable Wealth
    9/4.4   Rental Income from Movables

9/5. Royalties

9/6. Presumed Income

9/7. Taxation at Source

9/8. Capital Gains and Losses
    9/8.1   In General
    9/8.2   Speculative Operations
    9/8.3   Property Related to an Enterprise
    9/8.4   Speculation and Transactions in Securities
    9/8.5   Sales of Patents and Copyrights
    9/8.6   Transactions in Other Assets
    9/8.7   Determination of Gain
    9/8.8   Capital Losses

9/9. Organization, Reorganization, and Dissolution of Business
    9/9.1   In General
    9/9.2   Sale of Assets or Business
    9/9.3   Purchase of Assets or Business
    9/9.4   Change of Form of Enterprise
    9/9.5   Exchange of Shares for Shares
    9/9.6   Creation of Subsidiaries
    9/9.7   Mergers of Corporations or Similar Entities
    9/9.8   Division of Corporate Assets Among Several Corporations

9/9.9   Cessation and Liquidation of Business
      a.   Sole proprietorship
      b.   Partnership or similar company
      c.   Corporation or similar entity

9/1.   Interest

9/1.1   In General

Interest on securities held, other than securities of public debt (9/1.2), is subject to the tax on income from movable wealth in category A, as income from capital (arts. 85, 86). Other interest—on a loan or mortgage (*ipoteca*), for example—is also included in income from movable wealth in category A, except interest received by credit institutions (10/4) or by other persons in the exercise of business enterprises, which is taxed as business income in category B (art. 85) (7/1.3b),[1] and certain interest which is exempt (9/1.7). Income from capital given in loan, or otherwise employed so as to derive income in a definite amount, is included in taxable income in the amount shown in the contract from which it arises, without any deduction (art. 86). If no stipulated interest appears in the contract, or if the interest received exceeds that appearing in the contract, the interest actually received may be assessed (art. 86).[2] Interest classified in category A as income from capital is subject to the tax on income from movable wealth if it is payable by persons domiciled or resident in Italy or if the capital is guaranteed by a mortgage on property located in Italy (11/1.6a). Interest classified in category B as income from business is subject to the tax on income from movable wealth if produced in Italy under the rules relating to business income (11/1.3). Entities required to be taxed on the balance sheet basis and credit firms and institutions are required to pay the tax on income from movable wealth due on all interest and premiums payable which have the character of income from capital (rather than of business income); they have a right of recovery against the recipient through withholding (13/3.4).

Termination of income of category A which is not subject to withholding must be proved in one of the ways listed below (art. 129).

1. Producing a notarized extract or copy of the document prepared by a notary, the notarized private writing, or the judicial decree which extinguishes the credit, or specifying the date of the registration of the document, writing, or decree.

---

[1] On the same principle, interest received in the exercise of a professional activity would probably be taxed in category C/1. See 8/2.1.

[2] When the Central Commission recognizes the existence of and estimates the value of income from capital for which no interest is stipulated, it must give the taxpayer a hearing (13/4.4).

2. Producing a notarized copy of a statement canceling the credit, or of a renunciation of interest payments, which has been served on the debtor.
3. Producing a notarized extract or copy of a judicial decree of execution against the property of a debtor (CPC art. 598), or of a decree closing bankruptcy.[3]

The tax period for income in category A is the business period if the taxpayer is an entity taxed on the balance sheet basis (art. 3) (6/1.2b). For all other taxpayers, it is the calendar year (6/3.2).

Income for purposes of the complementary tax includes all interest subject to the tax on income from movable wealth (6/1.1f). Interest from bonds and interest from public securities are subject to the complementary tax in the amount received (art. 135), unless exempted by special laws (9/1.2). Income for purposes of the corporation tax also includes all interest, either as income of category B or as interest not included in category B (art. 148) (6/1.1g).

Special rules governing credit firms and institutions are discussed at 10/4; special rules governing investment companies are discussed at 10/5.

9/I.2   Interest Payments by Government or Public Entities

Interest derived from loans made by credit firms and institutions to public entities is exempt from the tax on income from movable wealth (art. 84). Interest from bonds issued after 20 September 1926 by provinces, communes, and other public entities (*enti morali*) are also exempt from the tax on income from movable wealth.[4] Interest on treasury bonds,[5] interest on postal bonds,[6] and interest on certain securities of public debt are exempted from the tax on movable wealth by the laws under which the securities are issued. Such interest, however, is included in aggregate income for the complementary tax (art. 135) or for the corporation tax (art. 148), unless specially exempted therefrom by the laws under which the securities are issued.

When government interest payments are subject to the tax on income from movable wealth, the tax is withheld directly (13/3.3).

9/I.3   Loan Premiums and Prizes

When a loan is repayable at a premium, the premium is subject to the tax on income from movable wealth in category A, in the same manner as interest (9/1.1). Prizes payable on redemption to the holders of bonds selected by lot are usually exempted from the tax on income from movable wealth by the special laws under which the bonds are issued; they are, however, otherwise subject to tax. In the absence of a

---

[3] L. 16 March 1942, n. 267, art. 118 (4).
[4] R. D. L. 20 September 1926, n. 1643, art. 10.
[5] L. 8 August 1895, n. 486.
[6] D. M. 5 May 1930, art. 3.

special provision, premiums and prizes are included in aggregate income for the complementary tax or for the corporation tax.

If a loan is issued at a discount, the difference between the price of redemption and the discounted amount of the loan is apparently considered a capital receipt rather than income and is therefore not subject to tax; [7] the reduction in the amount received by the borrower, however, may be treated as a depreciable cost under the rules explained at 7/3.9.

9/1.4   Capitalized Interest

Interest is taxed when produced and available for withdrawal, whether or not withdrawn (6/4.1). Accrued interest which is not paid but capitalized, that is, added to the amount of the loan, so that it too bears interest, is therefore taxable; interest on the capitalized interest is included in taxable interest of subsequent years.

9/1.5   Sales of Obligations with Accrued Interest

Since the person paying interest on a bond pays the tax on income from movable wealth on the interest and is entitled to recover it from the recipient through withholding (13/3.4), a bondholder who sells an obligation "with interest" before the due date never bears the tax on income from movable wealth of category A. However, that part of the price which is attributable to the expectation of receiving interest might be included in his income of category B as a speculative gain (9/8.1).

9/1.6   Sales of Interest

As in the case of the sale of an obligation with accrued interest (9/1.5), a bondholder who sells interest before the due date, while retaining the bond on which it is paid, never bears the tax on income from movable wealth of category A. Since the transaction is clearly undertaken for gain, however, it is possible that the price received for the interest would be included in his income of category B (9/8.1). In any case, the buyer and the seller of the interest must each, in principle at least, include what he has received in his income for the complementary tax; for purposes of the complementary tax, however, the buyer would be able to offset the interest against the price paid for it, under the rules described at 6/1.5b.

Similarly, a bondholder who sells a security before its interest date and subsequently repurchases the same or a similar security does not pay the tax on income from movable wealth of category A on the difference between the price of sale and the price of repurchase. However, if the original security was held for speculation, the difference

---

[7] But see Cass. 21 October 1910.

between the original purchase price and the price of the sale may be
subject to tax in category B (9/8.1).

9/1.7   Exempt Interest

In addition to the exemptions for government interest payments (9/1.2)
and the exemptions granted to income of certain credit enterprises
(10/4.2), exemptions from the tax on income from movable wealth are
granted for the interest payments listed below.

1. Interest on bonds issued by corporations and limited partnerships with
   shares which furnish farm, agrarian, or mining credit.[8]
2. Interest received on fiduciary deposits with certain institutions for agrarian
   credit.[9]
3. Interest on loans for the construction, enlargement, or reconstruction of
   nonluxury dwellings begun on or before 31 December 1959 and completed on or before 31 December 1961 (9/4.2b3), and interest on loans
   for the first sale of such buildings if it takes place within four years
   of the day on which they are declared inhabitable or are actually
   inhabited.[10]
4. Until 31 December 1969,[11] exemption from the tax on income from
   movable wealth is granted for interest on loans for the construction of
   low-cost and popular housing,[12] on contributions to the amortization of
   loans for the repair and reconstruction of houses damaged by war,[13] and
   on advances made to cooperative societies by their members for the purchase of land for the start of construction of cooperative housing.[14]

Interest exempt from the tax on income from movable wealth under
the above provisions is nonetheless includible in aggregate income for
the complementary tax or for the corporation tax in the absence of a
special exemption (9/1.1).

Interest on bonds which are issued by corporations or by limited
partnerships with shares between 16 December 1959 and 30 June 1962,
and which are actually circulating, is subject to the tax on income from
movable wealth at one half the normal rate.[15]

9/2.   Dividends and Other Distributions

9/2.1   In General

a. BASIS OF TAXATION OF PARTICIPATIONS. For tax purposes, a company
or association of any type is a taxpayer distinct from its members and

[8] R. D. L. 20 September 1926, n. 1643, art. 10; R. D. L. 18 September 1934, n.
1465; C. M. 21 September 1934, n. 9460.
[9] R. D. L. 3 February 1936, n. 287, replacing R. D. L. 29 July 1927, n. 1509,
art. 21. See Mandò, *Imposta di ricchezza mobile* 91.
[10] L. 2 July 1949, n. 408, arts. 18, 19; L. 10 December 1957, n. 1218; L. 2
February 1960, n. 35, art. 1.
[11] L. 2 February 1960, n. 35, art. 2.
[12] R. D. 28 April 1938, n. 1165, art. 71.
[13] D. L. C. P. S. 10 April 1947, n. 261, art. 90.
[14] L. 2 July 1949, n. 408, art. 15.
[15] L. 25 November 1959, n. 1001; Ministerial Note 8 March 1960, n. 352412.

is liable for the tax on income from movable wealth on the income produced by its business activity (5/2.2, 5/3.2). Since this income cannot again be subjected to the tax on income from movable wealth (6/1.1a), amounts received by way of distribution or division of the profits of a company or association of any type are excluded from the members' or shareholders' income from movable wealth (art. 83).[16] Thus, there is no double taxation based on the "production" of income by a company.

A partnership or similar company, other than one formed abroad but operating in Italy through a permanent establishment (11/3.5a), is not liable for any personal tax. As explained at 5/3.2, however, each individual member of a partnership must include in his aggregate income for the complementary tax his entire share of the profits of the company, whether or not actually distributed to him. If an entity subject to the corporation tax should hold a participation in a partnership (5/3.2), aggregate income of such an entity for purposes of the corporation tax would include any amount which it received by way of distribution of the profits of the partnership.

The profits of a corporation or similar entity are included in its aggregate income for purposes of its own liability for the corporation tax (6/1.1g). Distributions of corporate profits received by an individual are included in his aggregate income for purposes of the complementary tax, under the rules discussed at 9/2.1b, and distributions of corporate profits received by a corporation are included in its aggregate income for the corporation tax, under the rules discussed at 9/2.1c; the principle which forbids double imposition of tax on the same basis does not prevent the application of the personal taxes to both the corporation and its shareholders (6/1.1a). In the absence of a special exemption, distributions of corporate income are subject to the personal taxes whether or not the income is exempt from the tax on income from movable wealth.[17]

Dividends may be paid only out of profits which are actually received and appear in the regularly approved balance sheet (CC art. 2433). Dividends may be paid not only out of profits of the current year, but out of profits earned and transferred to reserves in previous years. Transfers of profits or reserves to capital are subject to limited taxation under the new coupon tax, as explained at 9/2.3. It appears that if profits or reserves have been added to capital, their subsequent distribution is subject to tax only upon liquidation (9/2.4, 9/9.9c).

---

[16] Dividends received by an Italian enterprise as a result of participation in a foreign company engaged in a similar business in Italy may in an exceptional case be subjected to the tax on income from movable wealth, as explained at 11/2.3b, but the justification for taxing such dividends is the fact that the income of the foreign company is not itself subject to the tax on income from movable wealth.

[17] Comm. Centr., Sez. un., 21 February 1940, n. 22715.

ANALYSIS OF INCOME TAX   450

The so-called "coupon tax" (*imposta cedolare*) enacted in 1962 provides for withholding from distributions of profits by corporations and similar entities (9/2.7a). In most cases, the amounts withheld are credited against the liability of the recipient for the complementary tax or for the corporation tax. In certain cases, however, no credit is given, with the result that the withholding amounts to the imposition of a separate tax (9/2.7c). In the case of bearer shares, the withholding is also a separate tax, in addition to whichever personal tax is applicable (9/2.7d).

In determining net income from dividends, deductions are allowed only for certain extraordinary expenses, under the rules discussed at 6/1.5b.

A special allowance for profits invested in the form of participations in specified enterprises is described at 10/6.3b.

b. COMPLEMENTARY TAX. The income of an individual for purposes of the complementary tax includes all income derived from participation in a corporation, limited partnership with shares, limited liability company, or cooperative society (5/2), in an amount equal to the profits, on whatever basis and in whatever form received (*percepiti*) by the taxpayer (art. 135).

Under the original law imposing the complementary tax, income for that tax included income which individuals received from companies or entities of any type "as employees, . . . members, shareholders, bondholders, and on any other basis." [18] Although the law itself made no distinction between receipts from different types of companies, the tax administration, in its administrative instructions, took the position that the net aggregate income of a member of a partnership, simple limited partnership, or other "personal company" (5/3) should include his share of the income subject to the tax on income from movable wealth, or to other objective taxes on income, while in the hands of the company itself, whether or not actually distributed to him. [19] The profits of such companies were considered to be available to the members and therefore, in some sense, "received" by them. The Central Commission subsequently held that the income of a personal company assessed for the tax on income from movable wealth must be presumed to have been actually divided among the members, in the absence of proof to the contrary. [20] Under the present law, the proportion of the net income of such a company in which each member has the right to participate in the profits, whether

---

[18] R. D. 30 December 1923, n. 3062, art. 3.

[19] C. M. 12 March 1925.

[20] Comm. Centr. 8 March 1937, n. 98532. For a discussion of the application of this principle under the old law, see Boidi, *Commento alla legge sulla imposta complementare progressiva sul reddito* 47-52.

or not distributed, is included in the member's aggregate income for the complementary tax (5/3.2).

The tax administration also sought, under the old law, to subject shareholders and members of corporations and similar entities (5/2) to the complementary tax not only on dividends actually distributed to them, but also on their proportionate shares of undistributed profits retained as surplus or transferred to reserves in the company accounts.[21] This practice was based on the belief of the administration that income which would otherwise have been subjected to the complementary tax was escaping liability through the use, by individuals, of corporations having a limited share base, of closely held or individual corporations (*società familiari*), of real estate holding corporations (*società immobiliari*), and of various types of investment and holding companies.[22] However, the position of the administration was not accepted by the Central Commission [23] or by the courts.[24] Under the new coupon tax law, a part of reserves and other funds transferred to capital through the allotment of gratuitous shares or through gratuitous increases in the value of shares held is now subject to tax (9/2.3).

Although article 135 of the *Testo unico* expressly provides different treatment for the application of the complementary tax to the profits of personal companies and to the profits of corporations and similar entities, the provision taxing income derived from participation in a corporation or similar entity, "on whatever basis and in whatever form received by the taxpayer," seems not to clearly preclude the possibility of subjecting the undistributed profits of closely held corporations to the complementary tax, by analogy with the provision applicable to the profits of personal companies.[25] The enactment of the corporation tax in 1954, however, has perhaps rendered less urgent the problem of avoidance of the complementary tax by the use of closely held corporations (2/4.1), despite the radical differences in the structures and rates of the two taxes.

It appears nonetheless that in order to insure that shareholders will not be subjected to the complementary tax on the undistributed profits of a corporation, the omission of a distribution of dividends, as a result of

---

[21] See Boidi, *Commento alla legge sulla imposta complementare progressiva sul reddito* 52; Berliri, *Il testo unico delle imposte dirette* 359.

[22] See Boidi, *Commento alla legge sulla imposta complementare progressiva sul reddito* 70-73.

[23] Comm. Centr., Sez. un., 13 January 1937, n. 69279, n. 96282. See Boidi, *Commento alla legge sulla imposta complementare progressiva sul reddito* 53-55, 67-70.

[24] Cass., Sez. I, 10 March 1941, n. 698.

[25] The application of the complementary tax to the undistributed profits of closely held corporations is criticized on grounds of fiscal policy by Forte, "Sulla politica fiscale nei confronti delle piccole società di capitali," *Temi trib.*, 1959, 30; and on legal grounds by Boidi, *Commento alla legge sulla imposta complementare progressiva sul reddito* 54-74; and Merlino, *L'imposta complementare progressiva sul reddito* 115.

insufficient surplus or of transfer of the profits to reserves, must not only represent a result clearly supported by the balance sheet or by a decision of the shareholders' meeting, formally set forth in its resolution approving the balance sheet, but must be recognized by the tax administration in its assessment of the income of the corporation on the basis of the balance sheet.[26] It also appears that if the balance sheet is found unreliable and the income of the corporation is estimated under the rules discussed at 13/2.3, the tax administration may infer that the shareholders have received a portion of the difference between the profits assessed and the balance-sheet profits after adjustment for expenses and other charges not deductible in determining income from movable wealth (6/1.5b).[27] But it has also been stated that when the Tax Office wishes to attribute to the taxpayer a share of corporate profits greater than the dividend declared, it must show that the excess has actually been received by the taxpayer.[28] The taxation of transfers of profits or reserves to capital is discussed at 9/2.3.

Dividends and other distributions are subject to the complementary tax if declared out of profits subject to the tax on income from movable wealth; other distributions are not subject to the complementary tax unless received by a resident and either enjoyed by him in Italy or exempted from tax abroad by virtue of an international agreement (11/2.2).

c. CORPORATION TAX. The aggregate income of a corporation or similar entity for purposes of the corporation tax includes amounts received by way of distribution or division of the profits of a company or association of any type (art. 148) (6/1.1g), whether or not the profits have been subject to the corporation tax in the hands of the distributing company. However, special reductions of the corporation tax are made for credit firms and institutions (10/4.2) and investment companies (10/5).

If the recipient of a distribution is a corporation formed in Italy, its aggregate income for the corporation tax includes distributions received from any corporation, Italian or foreign; if the recipient is a corporation formed abroad which is subject to the corporation tax, its income for the corporation tax generally includes dividends declared by Italian corporations (11/3.6b).

---

[26] See Boidi, *Commento alla legge sulla imposta complementare progressiva sul reddito* 55-56.

[27] Cass. 10 March 1941; Comm. Centr. 23 July 1937, n. 10398; Comm. Centr., Sez. un., 1 June 1938, n. 6599; Comm. Centr. 6 June 1958, n. 6015. See also Boidi, *Commento alla legge sulla imposta complementare progressiva sul reddito* 55-56. This problem does not ordinarily arise for corporations with a larger share base, since the shareholder receives only the declared dividend, and the higher income assessed is kept at the disposal of the corporation as reserves.

[28] See De Angelis, Potenza, and Testa, *Testo unico delle leggi sulle imposte dirette* 692.

9/2.2   Dividends in Kind

A dividend in kind, such as the distribution of shares of another corporation, is subject to tax in the same manner as a dividend in cash and is valued at the market price on the date of distribution.

In order to receive a distribution of profits in kind, even in connection with liquidation of the company, the shareholder must pay to the company the amount corresponding to the withholding required under the provisions described at 9/2.7a, determined in relation to the value of the property allocated to him according to the last balance sheet of the company, subject to assessment of the actual value for purposes of the application of the various taxes.[29]

9/2.3   Stock Dividends and Other Bonus Securities

A corporation which increases its capital by transferring to it disposable reserves and special funds inscribed in the balance sheet may either issue new shares having the same characteristics as those already outstanding, assigning them to the shareholders in proportion to their previous holdings, or increase the nominal value of each of the outstanding shares (CC art. 2442).

If the taxpayer is an entity or enterprise taxed on the balance sheet basis, and if the increase in the nominal value of its holdings results in a gain under the valuation rules described at 6/5.3, the gain is included in business income under the rules described at 7/1.3d.

In other cases, an increase in the nominal value of the shares or the issue of new shares does not of itself give rise to tax liability. If the taxpayer is a business enterprise, any gain incurred on the shares, as determined by the valuation rules, is subject to the tax on income from movable wealth and to the appropriate personal tax when the shares are sold or distributed (7/1.3d). If the taxpayer is not a business enterprise and is not engaged in speculative operations, the gain is not taxed (9/8.4). With respect to the personal taxes, however, the new coupon tax law has introduced important modifications of these rules. For purposes of the withholding required under the provisions described at 9/2.7a, that part of the aggregate total of reserves and other funds transferred to capital after 1 January 1963, through allotment of gratuitous shares or through gratuitous increase in the nominal value of the shares held, which exceeds 25% of the aggregate total of the dividends allotted to the members after the same date, is considered distributed profit.[30]

According to the ministerial instructions, this provision is not merely a means of increasing the withholding, and thus of increasing the credit against the complementary tax or the corporation tax otherwise due, but

---

[29] L. 29 December 1962, n. 1745, art. 1.

[30] L. 29 December 1962, n. 1745, art. 1.

extends the complementary tax and the corporation tax, *pro tanto*, to undistributed profits of the corporation which are transferred to capital.[31] Funds formed with monetary revaluation balances exempt from tax or with surcharges paid by the members on the issue of shares are not considered funds transferred to capital.

9/2.4   Distributions on Liquidation or in Reduction of Capital

When a corporation or similar entity is liquidated, the gain realized by each shareholder is subject to tax under the rules explained at 9/9.9c. In order to receive distributions of profits in kind upon liquidation, the shareholder must pay to the company the amount corresponding to the withholding required under the provisions described at 9/2.7a (9/2.2). It appears, however, that shareholders are not taxed on other distributions in reduction of capital, even if the capital includes amounts transferred thereto out of previously earned profits of the corporation.

9/2.5   Payments to Directors and Shareholders

As a result of a 1962 law, compensation paid to directors for their services as such, excluding participations in net profits of the business period, are subject to provisional withholding of the tax on income from movable wealth, are included in the recipient's professional income (8/1.2), and are deductible from the corporation's income from movable wealth of category B (7/2.3c). Shares of profits paid to directors are treated as ordinary distributions of corporate profits and therefore, for purposes of the tax on income from movable wealth, are neither deductible from the income of the corporation (7/2.3d) nor included in the income of the recipient (8/1.6). Such payments are, however, included in the recipient's aggregate income for purposes of the complementary tax, in the full amount received (6/1.1f, 8/1.6). It is also possible that loans, advances, or other payments to shareholders out of profits could be regarded as having been received in some form by those shareholders and thus included in the base of the complementary tax, under the principles discussed at 9/2.1b.

9/2.6   Transfers of Accrued Dividends

For purposes of the complementary tax and the corporation tax, dividends are assessed against the registered owner of the shares (9/2.8). Hence the transfer of accrued dividends does not affect the shareholder's liability for tax thereon.

Although there are no decisions on the point, it appears that if the transfer of the right to receive dividends in an unknown amount involves

---

[31] C. M. 2 April 1963, n. 110.

speculation by either of the parties to the transaction, and if the trans-action is carried out through a written act, the gain resulting to either party might be subject to the tax on income from movable wealth in category B, under the rules governing speculative operations (9/8.2).

9/2.7 Taxation of Dividends at Source

a. IN GENERAL. As explained at 9/2.1a, corporate profits are subject to the tax on income from movable wealth only once, on "production," and cannot be subjected to that tax again in the hands of the shareholder. The tax liability discharged by the corporation paying the tax on income from movable wealth on the income produced is its own; the tax is not considered to have been paid on behalf of the shareholders and is not includible in their income.[32] The recipient of a dividend or other dis-tribution of corporate profits is subject to the complementary tax or to the corporation tax on the amount distributed, even though the corporation may also have been liable for the corporation tax on the profits (9/2.1c).

Until 1963, there was no withholding of the personal taxes from dis-tributions of corporate profits. At the end of 1962, however, a new law enacted a so-called "coupon tax" (*imposta cedolare*). Beginning on 1 January 1963, under this law, a withholding of 15% must be made from profits distributed, even provisionally, in any form and under any desig-nation, by corporations, limited partnerships with shares, limited liability companies, and cooperatives with limited liability.[33] The amounts with-held are paid to the Provincial Treasury Office every six months, in ac-cordance with the rules described at 13/3.5, and are credited against the complementary tax or the corporation tax due from the recipient of the distribution of profits, except in the case of profits payable to organi-zations of persons or property lacking juridical personality (other than companies), entities required to be taxed on the balance sheet basis which are exempt from the corporation tax, and aliens or Italians domi-ciled abroad not subject to the complementary tax or the corporation tax (9/2.7c). Profits payable on bearer shares are subject to withholding at the rate of 8%, as a separate tax, which is not credited against the com-plementary tax or the corporation tax (9/2.7d). There is a special provision for withholding at 15% by Italian banks from profits collected on

---

[32] Compare WTS: *United Kingdom*, 9/2.3; WTS: *India*, 9/2.4a.

[33] L. 29 December 1962, n. 1745, art. 1. As part of the counter-inflationary measures introduced early in 1964, the rate of withholding applicable to dividends which are subjected to the corporation tax or to the complementary tax has been reduced to 5%, effective 24 February 1964; the rate of withholding applicable to dividends which are not subject to the complementary tax or to the corporation tax, on the other hand, has been increased to 30%. A shareholder who does not wish to be identified as the owner of the shares for purposes of the complementary tax or the corporation tax may elect to have the withholding made at the 30% rate, paying no further tax on the dividends. The 1964 provisions are effective for three years from the effective date of the decree. See D.L. 23 February 1964, n. 27.

foreign securities and for the crediting of such withholding against the complementary tax or the corporation tax (9/2.7e). Distributions in kind can be received only after payment by the recipient of an amount of tax corresponding to the withholding (9/2.2). When gratuitous shares are distributed, or when capital is gratuitously increased, a part of the amount imputed to capital is considered distributed profit and thus is subjected to the complementary tax or the corporation tax (9/2.3). The law enacting this withholding also provides new measures for enabling the tax administration to keep a record of the owners of securities (9/2.8) and for reporting distributions of profits (13/1.4).

The new provisions apply to all profits the distribution of which is decided after 1 January 1963, and to the full amount of profits distributed before 1 January 1963 of which any part remains uncollected.[34] For purposes of the application of the complementary tax and the corporation tax, uncollected accounts are considered to have been acquired as of the date of the distribution decision.[35]

b. PROFITS EXEMPT FROM WITHHOLDING. If an individual produces a certificate of the competent Tax Office attesting that neither he nor any member of his family (apart from associated members) is inscribed in the complementary tax rolls for taxes then in course of collection (13/3.6), the withholding need not be made from profits payable on securities belonging to him.[36] This exemption from the withholding does not affect the application of the requirements regarding the production and deposit of securities, attestation and stamping of certificates, and other administrative duties of the distributing company, outlined at 9/2.8. In the request for the certificate and in the certificate itself (which are exempt from stamp tax) must be specified the shares on which the applicant intends to collect dividends without the application of withholding. Every six months, the Compartmental Inspectorate of Direct Taxes (1/4.2) must send each company a list of the persons for whom certificates have been issued, specifying the number of shares involved.

The duties of withholding and of making the communications and payments connected therewith are not applicable to the distributions listed below.[37]

1. Profits distributed by cooperative societies inscribed in the corporation register of the Prefect, if the total of the withholding does not exceed L. 200. If the total of the withholding exceeds L. 200, the duties are not applicable if the paid-in capital of the society does not exceed L. 40 million, the bylaws expressly provide for the three conditions listed at 5/5.10 for exemption from the corporation tax, and the first two of those conditions have been observed throughout the last five years.

---

[34] L. 29 December 1962, n. 1745, art. 22.
[35] L. 29 December 1962, n. 1745, art. 22.
[36] L. 29 December 1962, n. 1745, art. 1.
[37] L. 29 December 1962, n. 1745, art. 1.

2. Profits distributed, during the first five years from the beginning of their
   activity, by popular cooperative banks and cooperative societies satisfying
   the conditions listed in item 1, whatever the amount of their paid-in
   capital.
3. Amounts, exclusive of dividends, which consumer cooperative societies
   distribute among their members in the form of a refund of part of the
   price of goods purchased (art. 111).
4. Amounts paid by production and labor cooperative societies to their
   members as a supplement to wages previously paid, up to the amount
   of current wages (art. 111).

c. CREDIT AGAINST COMPLEMENTARY TAX OR CORPORATION TAX FOR
AMOUNTS WITHHELD. If the shareholder is an individual, the total of the
amounts withheld is credited against the complementary tax due from
him, for the year in which his right to the profits is acquired, on the net
aggregate income in which the profits are included.[38]

If the shareholder is a simple company, general partnership, simple
limited partnership, or cooperative society with unlimited liability, the
total of the amounts withheld is credited against the complementary tax
due from each member of the company in that proportion of the company's net income in which the member has the right of participation in
profits (5/3.2).[39]

If the shareholder is a corporation or similar entity required to be taxed
on the balance sheet basis (6/1.2b), the total of amounts withheld is
credited against the corporation tax due for the business period during
which the right to the profits was acquired. If the shares were owned
for less than a year at the time the right to the profits was acquired, the
credit is limited to one twelfth of the total amount withheld for each
month of uninterrupted ownership.[40]

The amounts to be credited under these provisions are deducted, under
the provisions described at 13/3.5, from the complementary tax to be
inscribed in the roll, and any excess of withholdings over the tax to be
inscribed in the roll is refunded under the provisions described at 13/5.[41]
If shares are given in *riporto* (9/2.8), the credit and refund apply to the
tax due from the *riportato*; if shares are the object of a purchase on time,
the credit and refund apply to the tax due from the buyer.[42]

In the absence of a contrary provision of an international agreement
(see 11/4.7a), no credit or refund is given for tax withheld on the distributions described below.[43]

1. Distributions of profits derived by a foreign company or association,
   operating in Italy through a permanent establishment, from shares not

[38] L. 29 December 1962, n. 1745, art. 3.
[39] L. 29 December 1962, n. 1745, art. 3.
[40] L. 29 December 1962, n. 1745, art. 3.
[41] L. 29 December 1962, n. 1745, art. 3.
[42] L. 29 December 1962, n. 1745, art. 8.
[43] L. 29 December 1962, n. 1745, art. 3.

included in the taxable assets for purposes of the corporation tax (11/3.3, 11/3.6b).[44]

2. Profits payable to organizations of persons or property lacking juridical personality (other than companies) (5/3.1).

3. Profits payable to corporations or other entities required to be taxed on the balance sheet basis but exempt from the corporation tax (5/5.11).

4. Profits payable to aliens or Italians domiciled abroad who are not subject to the complementary tax or to the corporation tax (11/3.1).[45]

In these cases, therefore, the withholding from distributions of profits is not a provisional payment of the complementary tax or the corporation tax, but a new and separate tax.[46] The withholding is also an independent tax in the case of gratuitous distributions of new shares or gratuitous increases in capital beyond certain limits (9/2.3), and, in the case of bearer shares, is in addition to any personal tax already applicable (9/2.7d).

d. BEARER SHARES. On profits allocated to bearer shares issued under the laws of regions with special statute (9/2.8), the withholding is made at the rate of 8%, as a separate tax, and not as a provisional withholding of the complementary tax or the corporation tax.[47] Hence no credit or refund is given if the amount withheld exceeds the normal personal tax liability. Since the coupon tax law makes no provision for excluding profits allocated to bearer shares from the complementary tax or from the corporation tax otherwise due, it is necessary to assume that the profits must be included as well in the aggregate income of whichever of the personal taxes is applicable—the coupon tax withheld being deductible in determining net aggregate income.[48] Distributions of dividends

---

[44] A foreign company or association having a permanent establishment in Italy and holding shares in an Italian enterprise is allowed credit against the corporation tax for the tax withheld from the dividends, provided that the shares and the dividends have been declared for purposes of the corporation tax due from the permanent establishment. C. M. 12 June 1963, n. 360120.

[45] The income from which tax is withheld must be considered as produced in Italy, under the rules discussed at 11/1.6b, and would therefore normally be subject to the complementary tax or the corporation tax, regardless of the citizenship or domicile of the recipient (11/3.2). The administrative instructions issued under the coupon tax law point out that the provision operates to subject to the complementary tax profits paid to aliens or Italians domiciled abroad whose net aggregate income produced in Italy does not exceed L. 720,000 (12/1.5b); and to subject to the corporation tax profits paid to foreign companies or associations not operating in Italy through a permanent establishment (11/3.3). C. M. 2 April 1963, n. 110. For further discussion of this provision, see Poli, *Imposta complementare sui redditi derivanti da partecipazioni in società e imposta cedolare* 242-246, 260.

[46] See Poli, "Redditi derivanti da partecipazioni in società di persone o di capitali e imposta complementare," *Imp. dir. erariali*, 1963, 161, 175.

[47] L. 29 December 1962, n. 1745, art. 10. The rate has been increased to 30% for three years from 24 February 1964. D.L. 23 February 1964, n. 27, art. 1.

[48] C. M. 2 April 1963, n. 110. For discussion of this point, see Poli, *Imposta complementare sui redditi derivanti da partecipazioni in società e imposta cedolare* 265.

⟩ holders of such shares are exempt from the communication require-
ents described at 9/2.8.

FOREIGN SECURITIES. Italians are now permitted to hold and to deal
1 foreign securities, but the securities must be deposited with the Bank
f Italy or other Italian bank, which collects the profits distributed and
ays them over to the owners. The bank is required to withhold tax,
t the rate of 15%, from profits distributed and to pay the withholdings
ver to the Provincial Treasury Office every six months, reporting the
ithholdings annually to the Minister of Finance; the withholdings are
redited against the complementary tax or the corporation tax of the
ecipients of the distributions, in accordance with the rules discussed at
/2.7c, and excess withholdings are refunded, under the rules described
t 13/5.[49]

/2.8 Registration of Shares

With the appropriate authorization, a company having its office in the
egion of Sicily,[50] in the region of Sardinia,[51] or in the region of Trentino-
lto Adige [52] may issue shares to bearer in furtherance of specified activi-
ies to be carried on in the region itself. The purpose of these
uthorizations is to encourage investment in the specified activities in
hose regions (10/6.1). Profits payable on bearer shares are subject to a
ax withheld at the rate of 8% as explained at 9/2.7d.

In all other cases, the shares of a company having its office in Italy
ust be registered (*nominative*).[53] Each share subject to registration
ust be listed, on the certificate and in the register of shareholders
6/2.2), in the name of a determinate physical or juridical person; dealers
re forbidden to have themselves fictitiously listed for shares belonging
⟩ their clients, and fiduciary companies which have listed in their own
ames shares belonging to third persons are required to declare the
lentities of the actual owners.[54] For tax purposes, a share belongs to
he person whose name is inscribed on it.[55]

Issuing companies, exchange agents, authorized credit firms, and no-
aries must communicate information regarding the issue of new shares
nd transfer of shares to the Central Section of the Tax Register (13/1.4),
vhich enters this information in the general card index of share certifi-
ates for use in the assessment of the direct taxes.[56] Exchange agents,

---

[49] L. 29 December 1962, n. 1745, art. 11.
[50] L.R.Sic. 8 July 1948, n. 32.
[51] L.R.Sard. 12 April 1957, n. 10.
[52] L.R.Trent. 8 August 1959, n. 10.
[53] R.D.L. 25 October 1941, n. 1148, art. 1.
[54] R.D. 29 March 1942, n. 239, art. 1.
[55] R.D.L. 25 October 1941, n. 1148, art. 2.
[56] R.D. 29 March 1942, n. 239, arts. 35-37, 40, 42.

credit firms, financial and fiduciary companies, and stock exchange
commission agents must keep, on stamped sheets sold by the tax adminis
tration, daily records of transactions on time and *riporto* transaction
regarding securities.[57]   These measures are designed to assist in the
assessment not only of dividends but of gains resulting from transfer
of shares (9/8.4).

The 1962 law enacting provisional withholding from distributions o
profits provides further measures for insuring that the tax administration
has accurate and timely information regarding the ownership of shares
The most important of these measures are summarized below.

1. A shareholder cannot obtain payment of profits without producing the
   securities held before the issuing company or its agent designated for the
   payment of dividends, and cannot participate in the shareholders' meet
   ing unless he has deposited the securities with the company or its desig
   nated agent at least five days in advance.[58]   An endorsee in possession
   of the securities on the basis of an unbroken series of endorsements ha
   the right to payment of the profits and to participation in shareholders
   meeting.

2. A security presented or deposited must be stamped after the last en
   dorsement, in a form approved by decree of the Minister of Finance
   to show that the required information concerning the ownership of the
   security has been supplied.[59]   Within 90 days, the issuing company must
   bring the register of shareholders up to date on the basis of the informa
   tion supplied.

3. Once a year, on or before 15 February, companies must communicate
   to the general card index of share certificates the required information
   regarding the ownership of securities on which they have paid profits
   during the preceding calendar year.[60]   Companies which have not paid
   profits must furnish the required information with regard to share
   certificates which have been deposited for purposes of participation in
   the ordinary shareholders' meeting.

4. When profits are paid on shares held in *riporto*, the *riportatore* must give
   the paying company or its designated agent a written declaration of the
   number of shares held and the required information about the *riportato*.[61]
   The company's communication to the card index must contain the re
   quired information regarding both the *riportatore* and the *riportato*
   Credit firms and exchange agents must make similar communications to

---

[57] L. 5 January 1956, n. 1, art. 17.   See also C. M. 30 November 1961, n. 500719
These records are subject to inspection and verification in the exercise of the powers
of the Tax Office listed at 13/2.2; L. 29 December 1962, n. 1745, art. 18.

[58] L. 29 December 1962, n. 1745, art. 4.

[59] L. 29 December 1962, n. 1745, art. 5; for the information required, see R. D
29 March 1942, n. 239, art. 4.

[60] L. 29 December 1962, n. 1745, art. 7.

[61] L. 29 December 1962, n. 1745, art. 8.

In a contract of *riporto*, the *riportato* transfers securities to the *riportatore* for a
determined price, and the *riportatore* undertakes to transfer an equal number of
securities of the same kind to the *riportato* at an agreed price at the expiration of the
time limit established (CC art. 1548).   While the shares are in the hands of the
riportatore, he has the voting rights, but the right to receive dividends and other
accessory rights and duties belong to the *riportato* (CC art. 1550).

the card index. These reports must be made within 30 days of the date on which the profits are paid. These provisions apply also to sales on time and to sales for cash with execution deferred.[62] Corporations and similar entities required to be taxed on the balance sheet basis must file, attached to the annual return, lists of shares given and shares taken in *riporto* during the business period.

5. Fiduciary companies must communicate annually to the card index and to the Tax Office, on or before 15 February, information regarding shares which they hold on behalf of third persons.[63]

9/3. Pensions, Annuities, and Insurance

/3.1   Pensions and Annuities

Except as provided by special laws (8/1.3b), pensions, life annuities (*vitalizi*), and subsidies are subject to the tax on income from movable wealth at the time of payment, as income of category C/2 (art. 85) 6/1.1e). State pensions and annuities are subject to direct withholding f the tax (13/3.3); entities required to be taxed on the balance sheet asis, credit firms and institutions, insurance enterprises, and other entities nd companies are required to pay the tax, with a right of recovery gainst the recipient through withholding (13/3.4). Payments of life nnuities are subject to tax and to withholding in their entirety, over the tandard allowance applicable to income of category C/2 (12/1.4b), because the uncertainty of the duration of the payments is considered to make it impossible to allocate them between income and return of capital. f an insurance company, under a "contract of capitalization," makes a ump-sum payment representing a return of capital paid as premiums, plus interest, only the interest is subject to tax.[64] If a taxpayer purchases n annuity for a term of years, either by an outright transfer of capital or by the periodic payment of premiums, that part of each annual payment which represents interest is included in income of category A. Compulsory social security and welfare contributions paid by an employer or by n employee are excluded from the employee's current income from movable wealth (8/1.3a). Both employers' and employees' compulsory contributions are deductible from the business income of the employer, under the conditions described at 7/2.4.

---

[62] In a sale of securities on time, the voting rights belong to the seller until the moment of delivery, but dividends collectible after the conclusion of the contract and before the expiration of the time limit are credited to the buyer (CC art. 1531).

These provisions replace those of the fourth and fifth paragraphs of article 17 of L. 5 January 1956, n. 1, which required communications to the card index regarding riporti and time transactions to be made at the time of the transaction. It was found impossible to keep the card index current by this method, primarily because of the use of the so-called "riporto staccato," closed weekly rather than monthly, which the administration accepted as exempt from the requirement of communication.

[63] L. 29 December 1962, n. 1745, art. 9.

[64] See Giannetta, Scandale, and Sessa, *Teoria e tecnica nell'accertamento del reddito mobiliare* 81-82.

Income from capital employed so as to derive an income in a definite amount and perpetual annuities (*rendite perpetue*) [65] are subject to the tax on income from movable wealth in category A as income from capital (art. 86) and are treated in the same manner as payments of interest (9/1.1).

With the exceptions noted at 8/1.3b, all pensions and life annuities are subject to the complementary tax (6/1.1f). No withholding of the complementary tax is provided for this class of income (13/3.5). The rate of the complementary tax on lump-sum payments for social security or termination of employment is determined by dividing the amount received by the number of years of service (8/1.3b). For purposes of the complementary tax, an individual may deduct amounts withheld or paid for social security purposes which have not already been deducted in determining net income from movable wealth (8/1.3a).

An allowance which a taxpayer receives from a member of his or her own family is not subject to the tax on income from movable wealth.[66] It also appears that a support allowance received by a wife from her husband under a legal separation is not included in her income for purposes of the tax on income from movable wealth.[67] A husband may deduct from his own income for the complementary tax, in place of the dependent allowances for his wife and the children entrusted to her (12/1.5b), the entire amount of an annual allowance paid to her under a court decree or certified document; this amount is then included in the wife's income for the complementary tax (art. 138).

9/3.2 Life Insurance Proceeds

Life insurance proceeds, like pensions, life annuities, and subsidies, are subject to the tax on income from movable wealth in category C/2 as income which is not the present result of either capital or labor (art.

---

[65] Under a contract of *rendita perpetua*, one party confers on the other the right to exact in perpetuity the periodic payment of an amount in money or in a certain quantity of other fungible goods, in consideration for the transfer of immovable property or for a payment of capital. A *rendita perpetua* can be established also as a burden (*onere*) on immovable property or capital transferred gratuitously (CC art. 1861).

[66] Comm. Centr. 8 July 1930, n. 9421.

[67] Cass., Sez. I, 22 February 1947, n. 254; Comm. Centr., Sez. un., 7 February 1948, n. 95317. Decisions to the contrary are: Comm. Centr. 6 June 1928, n. 86122; Comm. Centr., Sez. un., 22 March 1939, n. 14411 (*RDFSF*, 1940, II, 3); Comm. Centr., Sez. I, 15 October 1945, n. 78315. For discussion, see Longobardi, "Il concetto di reddito mobiliare e l'imponibilità degli assegni alimentari fra coniugi," *Giur. comp. Cass., Sez. Civ.*, 1947, vol. 25, 146; Giussani, "Del concetto di reddito mobiliare e del trattamento tributario degli assegni alimentari," *RDFSF*, 1940, II, 3; Griziotti, "I concetti giuridici dogmatici di reddito di r.m. e di capacità contributiva. L'imposizione degli assegni alimentari," *RDFSF*, 1940, II, 11; Griziotti, "Ancora sull'imponibilità degli assegni alimentari fra coniugi," *RDFSF*, 1940, II, 99.

5) (6/1.1e). The insurance company is required to pay the tax on the ntire amount payable under a life annuity, over the standard allowance pplicable to category C/2, and to pay the tax on the interest included 1 the payments of proceeds under contracts of capitalization or insurance, vith a right of recovery against the recipient through withholding 13/3.4). Thus, whereas the entire amount of a life annuity is subject o tax under the rules discussed at 9/3.1, a lump-sum payment or an nnuity for a term of years is taxed only insofar as it represents interest, ince the portion representing a return of capital is not regarded as ncome. The amount subject to the tax on income from movable wealth s also included in aggregate income for the complementary tax (6/1.1f).

Apart from the provisions governing the treatment of compulsory ocial security contributions (8/1.3a), life insurance premiums are not leductible in determining net income from movable wealth. For pur-poses of the complementary tax, an individual may deduct premiums paid or life insurance for his benefit or for the benefit of members of his family iving with him for whose maintenance he is legally responsible (art. 136) 8/1.3a).

/3.3   Accident and Health Insurance Proceeds

Accident insurance proceeds are not considered income, but reim-bursements of expenses, and therefore are subject neither to the tax on ncome from movable wealth nor to the personal taxes.

There are many organizations furnishing health insurance to em-ployees in different industries and occupations. Health insurance pro-ceeds are included in category C/2 of income from movable wealth as subsidies or similar payments of income which is the present result neither of labor nor of capital (art. 85) (6/1.1e); this rule does not apply to benefits paid by the *Istituto Nazionale per l'Assistenza di Malattia* (8/1.3b). When health insurance proceeds are taxable, the insurance company is required to pay the tax, with a right of recovery from the recipient through withholding (13/3.4). Payments of premiums required by law or by a collective bargaining contract are deductible, under the rules explained at 8/1.3a.

Except in the cases noted at 8/1.3b, health insurance proceeds are included in income for the complementary tax; deduction is allowed for amounts withheld or paid for health insurance under voluntary arrange-ments (8/1.3a).

9/4.   Rent

9/4.1   In General

Prior to the unification of Italy, the various systems of land taxation then in effect applied to all types of immovable property.[68] In 1865,

---

[68] Rumboldt, *Le imposte fondiarie* 3.

ANALYSIS OF INCOME TAX   464

however, income from buildings was subjected instead to a separate tax, which is described at 9/4.2.[69] In the course of the unification of the basic system of land taxation, the tax was further modified by the removal of mines, quarries, peat bogs, salt deposits, fishing lakes and ponds, and tuna fisheries from properties listed in the rural cadaster,[70] and by the subjection of the income derived from the exploitation of these resources to the tax on income from movable wealth.[71] As a result, the original land tax now applies only to lands suitable for agricultural production (10/2.2) and to roads and parks.

Land fit for agricultural production is presumed to give rise to income, measured by the average ordinary income obtainable from the land, net of expenses and losses, determined cadastrally. That part of the average ordinary income which can be considered to be the share of the land-owner, as such, or of the owner of a property right in the land is subject to the tax on income from landowning (10/2.2). The part which is attributable to the circulating capital and directive labor of an agricultural enterprise carried on by the landowner, alone or in association with others, is subject to the tax on agrarian income (10/2.3). Rent which the landowner or owner of a property right in the land actually receives, therefore, is not taxable as such. Income from landowning is computed in 1938 lire and multiplied by a revaluation coefficient of 12 (12/1.1). It is included in income for the complementary tax and income for the corporation tax, but must be further revalued, for this purpose, on the basis of current prices (12/1.5a).

The income presumed to arise from rural buildings is part of the basis of the tax on income from landowning for the agricultural lands on which the buildings are located (10/2.2). Income from buildings used by their owner in his business is taxed as a part of the owner's income from business under the tax on income from movable wealth in category B if the building is specifically devoted to that activity and cannot be devoted to other uses without radical transformation (9/4.2a). In all other cases, income from buildings is subject to the tax on income from buildings (9/4.2a), even if the renting of the property is a regular business activity of the taxpayer. For buildings listed in the new urban building cadaster, income is normally to be determined by revaluation of the 1938 rents obtained from the cadaster (9/4.2d). In other cases, the gross income is the rent specified in the contract of lease, if any, or the current rental income for similar buildings, whichever is higher; net income is determined by making a specified fixed deduction from gross income (9/4.2c).

---

[69] L. 26 January 1865, n. 2136; see Rumboldt, *Le imposte fondiarie* 113.

[70] L. 1 March 1886, n. 3682; R. D. 8 October 1931, n. 1572, art. 18.

[71] R. D. 6 December 1923, n. 2722 (mineral deposits and tuna fisheries); L. 11 July 1929, n. 1260 (fishing lakes and ponds). The taxation of income derived from the extraction of mineral resources is discussed at 10/1.

A person cannot be subject to the tax on income from landowning or the tax on income from buildings unless he is in possession of immovable property by virtue of ownership or other property right.[72] Ownership (CC art. 832) includes the power to create, in favor of others, certain "property rights," the holders of which then have the power to deal with the property, against strangers, in certain respects as if it were their own. Such rights are called property rights to distinguish them from contractual rights, which affect only the rights of the parties against each other. The most important of the property rights are described below.

1. Emphyteusis (*enfiteusi*) confers on its holder (the *enfiteuta*) the same rights that the owner of the soil would have to its fruits, and with respect to utilization of the products of the subsoil in accordance with special laws (CC art. 959). The holder has the duty to improve the estate and to pay the grantor a periodic rent (CC art. 960); he must also pay the taxes and other charges against the estate (CC art. 964).

2. Usufruct (*usufrutto*) confers on its holder (the *usufruttuario*) the right to enjoy movable or immovable property within the limits of its economic destination (CC art. 981). Usufruct cannot exceed the life of its holder or, if the holder is a juridical person (5/2.1), 30 years (CC art. 979). The holder has the right to possession (CC art. 982) and to receive all the fruits (CC art. 984), to enjoy quarries and peatbogs already in use, and to open new ones with the consent of the owner (CC art. 987). If he obtains authorization to carry on mining explorations or operations, he must indemnify the owner; but if the authorization is obtained by the owner or by a third person, the holder of the usufruct is indemnified for his reduced enjoyment of the estate. The holder of the usufruct must return the property in the condition in which he received it (CC arts. 989-1007). He is entitled to indemnity for improvements remaining on the property when it is returned to the owner (CC art. 985); he may make additions not altering the economic destination of the property, and may remove them if this can be done without harm to the property, or receive an indemnity for them (CC art. 986). He is liable for taxes, rents, and other annual charges against income (CC art. 1008).

3. Use (*uso*) confers on its holder the right to use movable or immovable property and the right to collect any income it produces to the extent required for the needs of himself and his family, according to his social condition (CC art. 1021). The holder's liability for taxes, repairs, and expenses is proportional to the share of the income that he uses (CC art. 1025). The provisions governing usufruct apply, insofar as compatible, to use (CC art. 1026).

4. Habitation (*abitazione*) confers on its holder the right to occupy a house within the limits of the needs of himself and his family (CC art. 1022). The holder's liability for taxes, repairs, and expenses is proportional to the part of the house that he occupies (CC art. 1025).

---

[72] Under article 1140 of the Civil Code, the possession (*possesso*) of property is that power over it which is manifested in the exercise of ownership (*proprietà*) or other property right (*diritto reale*).

The provisions governing usufruct apply, insofar as compatible, to habitation (CC art. 1026).
5. Superficies (*superficie*) confers on its holder the ownership of a building which is built and maintained by the owner of the soil (CC art. 952).

Actual rental income derived from the subletting of land or buildings by a person other than the owner or the holder of a property right therein is taxed as business income under the tax on income from movable wealth (7/1.2a, 9/4.3), as are actual rental income from the renting of movable property without land or buildings (9/4.4) and actual rental income from the furnishing of services or fuel. In rental contracts, the rent itself and the price paid for services and utilities are always distinguished.

Liability for the objective taxes on income derived from immovable property located in Italy is not affected by the taxpayer's residence (11/1.1). Rent received from property located abroad may be subject to the tax on income from movable wealth under the limited conditions discussed at 11/2.1.

Whether subject to the tax on income from buildings or to the tax on income from movable wealth, the income from a building is included in aggregate income for the complementary tax (6/1.1f) and for the corporation tax (6/1.1g), even if exempt from the applicable objective tax. In determining net aggregate income for the personal taxes, deductions are allowed only for the objective taxes paid (6/1.5e) and for extraordinary expenses (6/1.5b).

9/4.2   Tax on Income from Buildings

a. IN GENERAL. The tax on income from buildings (*imposta sul reddito dei fabbricati*) is based on the possession, by virtue of ownership, usufruct, or other property right (9/4.1), of fixed structures or portions of structures, of any kind and use, which are on or under the ground or secured firmly to the earth and which are capable of producing independent income (art. 69). The land occupied by a building and any land devoted indefinitely to serving or embellishing it are considered integral parts of the building (art. 69).

The tax on income from buildings is levied only on a person who is in possession of a building by virtue of ownership, usufruct, or other property right (art. 69). A person in possession of a building by virtue of a property right is liable for the tax whether or not he occupies the building himself. Income derived by a tenant from subletting a building is subject to the tax on income from movable wealth (6/1.1e, 9/4.3).

If a property right in a building is held by more than one person, each of them is liable jointly and severally for payment of the tax. But if there is more than one property right in a building, the owner of each right is liable for payment of the share of tax on that part of the net income which corresponds to his right, without joint and several liability for the shares owed by the other owners (art. 70). A person holding the "bare ownership" of property in which the usufruct or other right of enjoyment has been granted to another does not have possession and is therefore not liable for the tax.

Income from new structures, including those resulting from the enlargement or radical modification of pre-existing buildings, becomes subject to the tax from the day on which the structures actually become suitable for the use to which they are to be devoted, or on which an exemption provided by special law terminates (art. 79). All new buildings are exempt for varying periods, however, depending on their intended use (art. 274) (9/4.2b). The tax period for the tax on income from buildings is the calendar year (art. 3). When the ownership of a building changes hands during the year, the new owner is liable for the tax due for the portion of the year after the date of the transfer under the rules discussed at 13/3.1.

Income from certain rural structures is excluded from income from buildings because income from these structures is considered to have been taken into account for purposes of the tax on income from landowning (10/2.2). Similarly, income from structures and their appurtenances [73] devoted specifically to the direct exercise by the owner of a business activity (7/1.2a),[74] and not susceptible of other use without radical transformation, are not subject to the tax (art. 72), because the income from such structures is considered to form part of the income from the business itself.[75] However, this exclusion does not apply to income from a building only part of which is devoted to a business use—for example, a *pensione*, hotel, or theater on one floor of a building otherwise devoted to ordinary uses—unless the business use can be considered predominant

---

[73] Including, under certain conditions, lodgings provided for personnel of a factory if their presence is required by the needs of the enterprise, or if the factory is remote from centers of habitation. See Vizzini, *Fabbricati e terreni nell'imposizione diretta erariale* 32-34.

[74] Under prior law, the exclusion was applicable to industrial factories, to buildings devoted to theaters, motion-picture houses, and hotels, and also to buildings constructed for the special requirements of a specific industrial or business activity (L. 8 June 1936, n. 1231, art. 28). The present law imposes no restriction on the type of business to which the provision may apply and also makes no reference to the exclusion from the earlier provision, as interpreted by C.M. 28 June 1937, n. 6200, of structures originally built for ordinary uses and later devoted to the exercise of industrial or business activity. See De Angelis, Potenza, and Testa, *Testo unico delle leggi sulle imposte dirette* 286; Vizzini, *Fabbricati e terreni nell'imposizione diretta erariale* 24.

[75] Article 10 of L. 11 July 1942, n. 843, under which the exclusion from the tax on income from buildings was denied if the taxpayer was exempt, personally or as an entity, from the tax on income from movable wealth, has been abrogated by article 288C of the *Testo unico*. See De Angelis, Potenza, and Testa, *Testo unico delle leggi sulle imposte dirette* 287; Vizzini, *Fabbricati e terreni nell'imposizione diretta erariale* 30. See also 9/4.2b2.

and economically independent rather than accessory to the use of the rest of the building.[76] Similarly, the exclusion would not apply to income attributable to space devoted by an artisan to the exercise of his activity in his own dwelling,[77] nor would it apply to income from a building in which the owner exercised a small business, predominantly based on labor, whose income was taxed in category C/1 (7/1.2b).

The structures listed below are excluded from the scope of the tax (art. 77) because they are considered not capable of producing income.

1. Structures devoted to the exercise of religious worship allowed (*ammessi*) by the state.[78]
2. Structures in cemeteries and in dependent areas of cemeteries.
3. Structures in the public domain (*demanio pubblico*) (CC arts. 822, 824), not producing income and owned by the state or other public entities with territorial jurisdiction.[79]

b. EXEMPTIONS. In addition to the exclusions discussed at 9/4.2a, permanent exemption from the tax on income from buildings is granted to certain buildings belonging to the Holy See[80] and to buildings and their appurtenances belonging to public entities with territorial jurisdiction and constructed for the purpose of supplying drinkable water (art. 78). Buildings belonging to foreign governments and used as offices of their diplomatic representatives to the Italian Republic or to the Vatican or used as the dwellings of personnel assigned to their embassies are exempt from the tax on income from buildings by established practice.[81]

Even if the income of a building is exempt from the tax on income from buildings, it must nonetheless be assessed for purposes of the complementary tax and, except in the case of certain building cooperatives (5/5.10), for purposes of the corporation tax.

Temporary exemptions from the tax on income from buildings are granted, under specified conditions, for buildings of certain categories.[82] In general, these exemptions become effective when the buildings become actually inhabitable or suitable for the use to which they are destined.[83] The following paragraphs summarize these temporary exemptions.

1. *All buildings.* All new buildings, enlargements, and alterations not entitled to greater exemptions are exempt for two years from the date on which they become suitable for use.[84] This exemption and the

---

[76] C.M. 28 June 1937, n. 6200.
[77] See Vizzini, *Fabbricati e terreni nell'imposizione diretta erariale* 28.
[78] See Rumboldt, *Le imposte fondiarie* 152.
[79] See Rumboldt, *Le imposte fondiarie* 153.
[80] See Lateran Treaty of 11 February 1929, arts. 13-16, executed by L. 27 May 1929, n. 810.
[81] See Rumboldt, *Le imposte fondiarie* 165.
[82] Provisions enacted prior to the *Testo unico* have been continued in effect by article 274.
[83] L. 11 July 1942, n. 843, art. 7.
[84] L. 26 January 1865, n. 2136, art. 18; L. 11 July 1942, n. 843, art. 5.

one described at 9/4.2b2 are intended to take account of the possibility
that a building may not produce income during the first few years of its
existence.

2. *Buildings devoted to business activities.* Since 1889, new factories
requiring fixed machinery, other than floating structures, have been exempt from the tax on income from buildings for three years from the date
on which they become suitable for use.[85] It appears, however, that under
the *Testo unico* this exemption extends to all buildings devoted to business activities (arts. 72, 274).[86] When the income from the buildings is
excluded from the tax on income from buildings because the owner
carries on the business activity directly (9/4.2a), the exemption applies
to the tax on income from movable wealth.[87] When the income of an
industrial factory in the south is exempt from the tax on income from
movable wealth, and the factory is not operated by the owner of the
building, exemption of the owner from the tax on buildings may be
granted at the discretion of the tax administration (10/6.2a). There
is a special exemption for the reconstruction or repair of factories
damaged by war (9/4.2b10).

3. *Nonluxury dwellings.* New constructions, enlargements, or reconstructions of nonluxury dwellings begun on or before 31 December 1959
and completed on or before 31 December 1961 are exempt for 25 years.[88]
Under a recent provision, new constructions or enlargements of nonluxury
dwellings are exempt for 25 years if completed on or before 31 December
1961; the exemption is reduced for buildings completed within successive
years down to a five-year exemption for buildings completed after 31
December 1969.[89] The exemptions apply to offices and shops located in
the buildings, provided that not more than one fourth of the total area
of the floors above ground is devoted to stores; [90] if this limit is exceeded,
the exemption is restricted to that part of the building which is devoted
to habitation.[91]

---

[85] L. 11 July 1889, n. 6214, art. 8.

[86] See Vizzini, *Fabbricati e terreni nell'imposizione diretta erariale* 58-59.

[87] Ministerial Note 10 April 1961, n. 201259. For discussion, see De Angelis,
Potenza, and Testa, *Testo unico delle leggi sulle imposte dirette* 287; Vizzini, *Fabbricati e terreni nell'imposizione diretta erariale* 59-60. Although the tax commissions
and the doctrine have held that the income to be exempted should be determined
by the criteria governing the tax on income from movable wealth, it appears that the
Ministry requires the determination of such income to be based on the leasehold
value of the buildings. This problem is discussed in Giannetta, Scandale, and Sessa,
Teoria e tecnica nell'accertamento del reddito mobiliare 668-676.

[88] L. 2 July 1949, n. 408, art. 13; L. 27 December 1956, n. 1416; L. 2 February
1960, n. 35, art. 1. Interest on loans for this purpose is exempt under the provision
described at 9/1.7, item 3.

[89] L. 2 February 1960, n. 35, art. 1. Enlargements are included by virtue of article
5 of L. 11 July 1942, n. 843.

[90] L. 11 July 1942, n. 843, art. 7; L. 2 February 1960, n. 35, art. 1.

[91] L. 11 July 1942, n. 843, art. 7.

4. *Normal housing.* New constructions, enlargements, and certain reconstructions of normal housing (*abitazione civile*) between 1919 and 1937 are exempt for 25 years.[92] The exemption also applies to reconstructions on areas left vacant by the complete demolition of houses declared uninhabitable and to reconstructions made in the execution of standard urban plans (*piani regolatori*). Constructions begun after 1 December 1936 and completed on or before 31 December 1950 are entitled to two years of complete exemption; thereafter one twenty-fifth of the income becomes taxable each year until the income is fully taxed.[93] Reconstructions completed on or before 31 December 1957 of normal housing, on the same site or elsewhere, to replace those destroyed by war, are exempt for 25 years.[94]

5. *Popular and low-cost housing.* Popular and low-cost houses (*case popolari ed economiche*) built by communes or by autonomous institutes for popular and low-cost housing are exempt for 25 years.[95] Houses built with state contributions by other companies or entities are exempt for 25 years if completed on or before 31 December 1957.[96] Private constructions or enlargements of low-cost housing built between 5 July 1919 and 31 December 1937 are exempt for 25 years.[97] Private constructions or enlargements of popular housing made without state contribution are exempt for 25 years.[98] There is also a 15-year exemption for popular and low-cost housing built in places damaged by earthquakes.[99]

6. *Housing for particular categories of occupants.* Special 25-year exemptions are made, under specified conditions, for housing built for their own use by farmers, agricultural and other workers, and artisans;[100] for popular housing built by private employers for their employees;[101] for housing built or purchased by certain state agencies for their employees;[102] and for housing built for laborers in accordance with the 1949 plan for increasing employment of workers.[103]

7. *Schools, hospitals, and welfare institutions.* Exemption for 25 years is provided for constructions or enlargements of school buildings,

---

[92] R.D. 28 April 1938, n. 1165 (*Testo unico* of provisions on popular and low-cost housing), art. 168.

[93] R.D.L. 21 June 1938, n. 1094, arts. 2, 3.

[94] D.L.C.P.S. 10 April 1947, n. 261, as modified by D.L. 17 April 1948, n. 740, and by L. 25 June 1949, n. 409, art. 33.

[95] R.D. 28 April 1938, n. 1165, art. 160.

[96] R.D. 28 April 1938, n. 1165, art. 161, as amended by L. 2 July 1949, n. 408, art. 1, and by L. 27 December 1956, n. 1416.

[97] R.D. 28 April 1938, n. 1165, art. 161.

[98] R.D. 28 April 1938, n. 1165, art. 159.

[99] R.D. 28 April 1938, n. 1165, arts. 252, 274.

[100] R.D. 28 April 1938, n. 1165, art. 159; L. 11 July 1942, n. 843, art. 8; L. 2 July 1949, n. 408, art. 24.

[101] R.D. 28 April 1938, n. 1165, art. 159.

[102] R.D. 28 April 1938, n. 1165, arts. 323, 340, 392.

[103] L. 28 February 1949, n. 43.

barracks, hospitals, welfare houses, shelters, boarding schools, orphanages, and the like, built by entities between 5 July 1919 and 31 December 1937.[104] Constructions, enlargements, or reconstructions of such buildings begun after 1 December 1936 and completed on or before 31 December 1950 are entitled to the exemptions provided for normal housing built during the same period (9/4.2b4). At present, constructions, enlargements, and completions of such buildings are entitled to the same exemptions as nonluxury housing (9/4.2b3).[105]

8. *Hotels.* Exemption for 25 years is provided for popular hotels built by entities between 5 July 1919 and 31 December 1937 [106] and for constructions or enlargements of hotels, alpine refuges, and thermal establishments made between 7 October 1937 and 31 December 1953.[107]

9. *Repair of earthquake damage.* Besides the 15-year exemption for popular and low-cost housing built in places damaged by earthquakes (9/4.2b5), provision is made for 15-year exemption, in accordance with special laws, of repaired buildings in places damaged by earthquakes.[108]

10. *Repair of war damage.* In 1943, buildings rebuilt after war damage were granted the regular two-year exemption for new buildings, even if the old foundations and main walls were used; the increased income due to repairs to houses damaged by war was exempt for 10 years.[109] More recently, exemption for 25 years was granted to buildings reconstructed, on the same site or elsewhere, to replace those destroyed by war.[110] With respect to the reconstruction or the repair of property devoted to the exercise of an industrial or business activity qualifying as factories or buildings assimilated thereto,[111] the exemption is limited to 10 years;[112] in such cases, however, the exemption also applies to the tax on income from movable wealth if the income is excluded from the tax on income from buildings because the business activity is carried on directly by the owner of the building.[113]

11. *Renewal projects.* In addition to the exemptions for reconstructions described at 9/4.2b4 and 9/4.2b7, 25-year exemptions are made by special legislative provisions for construction carried under standard

---

[104] R.D. 28 April 1938, n. 1165, art. 168.
[105] L. 19 July 1961, n. 659, arts. 1, 2.
[106] R.D. 28 April 1938, n. 1165, art. 168.
[107] R.D.L. 16 December 1937, n. 1669, art. 17, as amended by L. 24 November 1941, n. 1506, art. 7; by R.D.L. 29 May 1946, n. 452, art. 12; by L. 28 June 1952, n. 677, art. 3 (modified by L. 17 December 1953, n. 935, art. 1).
[108] R.D.L. 21 June 1938, n. 1094, art. 7.
[109] R.D.L. 12 April 1943, n. 243, art. 6.
[110] L. 27 December 1953, n. 968, art. 69. See also the special provision relating to normal housing (9/4.2b4).
[111] See L. 8 June 1936, n. 1231, art. 8.
[112] L. 27 December 1953, n. 968, art. 70.
[113] See Vizzini, *Fabbricati e terreni nell'imposizione diretta erariale* 67.

urban plans (*piani regolatori*) and urban renewal plans (*piani di risana-mento*) [114] and for construction in specified regions.[115]

C. DETERMINATION OF NET INCOME FROM BUILDINGS. The net income from buildings listed in the new urban building cadaster is normally to be determined by revaluing the 1938 rents obtained from the cadaster (9/4.2d). The method of determining net income described here is that used before the new cadaster went into effect. It now applies to buildings which are not yet listed in the cadaster or whose cadastral income differs by more than a specified percentage from the actual gross income reduced by 25% (9/4.2d).

If a building is rented, and the contract of lease specifies a rent which is not less than current rents for buildings under analogous conditions, the gross income from the building consists of the rent appearing in the contract of lease (art. 74). If the contract of lease does not specify a rent less than that of current buildings under analogous conditions, or if the building is not rented, the gross income is determined by comparison with current rents for buildings under analogous conditions (art. 74). The conditions considered for this purpose include the location, use, and grade of the building, and whether or not the building is subject to rent control. A building or part of a building which is normally rented is not considered to produce income under these rules during any period in which it remains unoccupied.[116]

The gross income from buildings is increased by the amount of expenses which are assumed by the lessee under the contract, although chargeable by law or custom to the lessor (art. 74). The principal expenses normally chargeable to the lessor are those of improvements, ordinary and extraordinary maintenance, fire insurance premiums, and taxes on the building. Conversely, gross income is reduced by the amount of expenses which are assumed by the lessor under the contract, although chargeable by law or custom to the lessee (art. 74). Repairs of deterioration produced by use, heating, and light, and the furnishing of water and other utilities and services, are the principal expenses normally borne by the lessee (CC arts. 1575, 1576).[117]

The net income subject to the tax on income from buildings is determined by deducting from the gross income a standard allowance for maintenance, repairs, and all other expenses and losses; this allowance is equal to one fourth of the amount of gross income (art. 75). This deduction is increased to one third of gross income for buildings and

[114] See Rumboldt, *Le imposte fondiarie* 180.
[115] See Rumboldt, *Le imposte fondiarie* 181.
[116] See De Angelis, Potenza, and Testa, *Testo unico delle leggi sulle imposte dirette* 297; Vizzini, *Fabbricati e terreni nell'imposizione diretta erariale* 106.
[117] See C.M. 10 January 1952, n. 200100.

their appurtenances which are devoted to the exercise of a business activity by someone other than the owner and which are therefore not entitled to the exclusion for buildings devoted to the exercise of a business by the owner (art. 75) (9/4.2a). For buildings in the city of Venice or on the neighboring islands of Giudecca, Murano, and Burano, where the expenses of maintenance are particularly heavy, the deduction is two fifths of the gross income (art. 75).

For a building built and used for its intended purpose before 29 May 1946,[118] there is allowed, from gross income reduced by one quarter, a further deduction equal to four and one half times the taxable income assessed or assessable for the year 1938.[119] If the building was built after 31 December 1938, its taxable income is valued by comparison with the rents of buildings under analogous conditions already existing in 1938 in the same commune. This additional deduction was provided when the requirement of the annual return of actual income from buildings was introduced, in order to relieve the owners of buildings subject to rent control from the consequences of the disproportion between the permitted increases in rent and the growth of expenses as a result of rising prices.[120] The deduction is apparently applicable to all dwelling units built and used before 29 May 1946, the effective date of the law cited, whether or not they are actually subject to rent control.[121]

The increases of rent permitted by a recent extension of rent control are not taken into account for purposes of the tax and surtaxes on income from buildings.[122] Since this provision is considered the establishment of a method of assessing income rather than the grant of an exemption, the increases are similarly disregarded for purposes of the complementary tax.[123]

d. URBAN BUILDING CADASTER. When a separate tax on income from buildings was first levied in 1865, income was determined by reference to actual rent received.[124] In 1871, however, a cadaster of urban buildings was established which was used as the basis for the assessment of income from buildings until the introduction of the annual return in 1951.[125]

---

[118] The effective date of D.L.L. 24 April 1946, n. 350.
[119] L. 4 November 1951, n. 1219, art. 1(b).
[120] See C.M. 10 January 1952, n. 200100; Vizzini, *Fabbricati e terreni nell'imposizione diretta erariale* 110-114; Rumboldt, *Le imposte fondiarie* 142-147.
[121] C.M. 25 March 1959, n. 200400.
[122] L. 21 December 1960, n. 1521, art. 6.
[123] Ministerial Note 24 May 1961, n. 500240.
[124] See Rumboldt, *Le imposte fondiarie* 114.
[125] R.D. 5 June 1871, n. 267, approving the regulation for the formation of the building cadaster; R.D. 24 August 1877, n. 4024, regulations for the application of the tax on buildings; L. 11 July 1889, n. 6214, providing for a general revision of cadastral incomes; R.D. 30 December 1923, n. 3069, providing for a general revaluation of income from buildings. See also Rumboldt, *Le imposte fondiarie* 114-115.

The original assessments were made for rented buildings on the basis of the rents appearing in the leases then in effect; for unrented buildings, assessments were made on the basis of the rent which they were capable of yielding. Cadastral income was subject to "partial revision" by the Direct Tax Office when the actual or presumed income regularly exceeded one third of the gross cadastral income.

The formation of a new cadaster of urban buildings was provided for in 1939.[126] The formation of a cadaster required the determination of the location, area, ownership, and yield of each unit of urban immovable property in Italy. For each class and grade of property in a commune, the gross ordinary average yield, after deduction of all expenses and losses, except taxes and certain other charges on the property, is given by a schedule determined with reference to the average current prices of a base period fixed by law.[127] The deduction for expenses and losses is to be fixed as a percentage of income for each kind of property in each category.[128] It has been provided that, from the effective date of the new urban cadaster, and until rent control ceases or a general revision of the cadastral income of urban units is provided, the taxable income of urban units is to be determined by applying, to the cadastral yield defined with reference to the economic elements of the period 1937-1939, supplementary coefficients to be established by the Minister of Finance for the various categories of units.[129] The taxable income is to be determined by reference to the provisions previously in effect (9/4.2c), however, whenever the actual gross income of a unit, reduced by one fourth, exceeds by more than one fifth the cadastral income after application of the coefficients; taxable income may be so determined at the request of the taxpayer if, as a result of exemptions of increases in rent or reductions of increases allowed by the rent control laws, the actual gross income of the unit reduced by one fourth is lower by more than one fifth than the cadastral income after application of the coefficients.[130]

The cadastral operations are carried out by the Administration of the Cadaster and of the Revenue Technical Offices (1/4.6) with the assistance of the census commissions (10/2.2g).[131] Subject to the regulations for the formation of the new urban building cadaster, the Communal,

[126] R.D.L. 13 April 1939, n. 652, converted in L. 11 August 1939, n. 1249; as modified by D.L. 8 April 1948, n. 514, art. 2. Regulations for the formation of the cadaster are contained in D.P.R. 1 December 1949, n. 1142.

[127] D.P.R. 1 December 1949, n. 1142, art. 1. The three-year period 1937-1939 is taken as the basis. R.D.L. 13 April 1939, n. 652, art. 9, converted in L. 11 August 1939, n. 1249; as modified by D.L. 8 April 1949, n. 514, art. 2.

[128] R.D.L. 13 April 1939, n. 652, art. 9, converted in L. 11 August 1939, n. 1249; as modified by D.L. 8 April 1949, n. 514, art. 2.

[129] L. 23 February 1960, n. 131, art. 1.

[130] L. 23 February 1960, n. 131, art. 2.

[131] D.P.R. 1 December 1949, n. 1142, art. 2.

Provincial, and Central Census Commissions have functions similar to those that they exercise in the formation and keeping of the cadaster of agricultural lands (10/2.2g).[132]

The new urban building cadaster took effect on 1 January 1962 in the entire territory of Italy except the province of Trieste.[133] Because of the rapid growth of building construction in Italy in recent years, the formation and preservation of an accurate building cadaster is extremely difficult. The need for a cadaster arises from the necessity of combating avoidance of the tax through the under-reporting of actual rents under the old system.

e. APPEALS. Administrative appeals regarding the imposition of the tax on income from buildings are made to the administrative tax commissions under the rules applicable to the tax on income from movable wealth (13/4.1).[134] Under the new urban building cadaster, however, administrative appeals regarding the formation and keeping of the cadaster and the schedules of income are within the sole competence of the census commissions (10/2.2g).[135] The administrative tax commissions remain competent for controversies concerning the tax liability, errors, reductions of tax, and exemptions and reliefs established exclusively in relation to the person of the taxpayer (13/4.1).

In the first year of the application of the tax on income from buildings on the basis of the new urban building cadaster, taxpayers are permitted to appeal against the roll to the Intendant of Finance, within six months of the service of the collector's payment bill, for material errors, duplications, or nontaxability of the income inscribed in the roll; the Intendant of Finance has the power to accord suspension of the collection of tax in such cases.[136] Appeals may be made to the courts under the rules discussed at 13/4.9.

9/4.3   Rent Subject to Tax As Income from Movable Wealth

Rent from land or buildings, received by a sublessor or by a person other than the owner or holder of a property right therein (9/4.1), is subject to the tax on income from movable wealth (art. 81) (6/1.1e). The income is included in category B as income from business, determined under the rules discussed in Chapter 7, whether or not the

---

[132] L. 8 March 1943, n. 153, arts. 20-23.

[133] D.M. 4 December 1961. Coefficients of revision to be applied to the cadastral yield defined with reference to the period 1937-1939 have been established by D.M. 24 April 1963. These coefficients, by which the income is multiplied, range from 20 for rural dwellings to 75 for stores and shops.

[134] L. 8 March 1943, n. 153, art. 360.

[135] L. 8 March 1943, n. 153, as modified by D.L. 8 April 1948, n. 514, art. 5. The procedures are explained in Rumboldt, *Le imposte fondiarie* 237-251.

[136] L. 23 February 1960, n. 131, art. 4.

taxpayer is engaged in subletting land or buildings as a business activity, since capital and labor contribute jointly to the production of the income.

9/4.4 Rental Income from Movables

Income from the renting of movable property is subject to the tax on income from movable wealth in category B, determined under the rules discussed in Chapter 7, since capital and labor contribute jointly to its production. If a building is rented with furniture or other movables by the owner or holder of a property right (9/4.1), that portion of the rent received which is attributable to the building is subject to the tax on income from buildings, and the remainder is included in income from movable wealth of category B.

9/5. Royalties

When the owner of intangible property leases it to another or licenses another to use it, the payments received are subject to the tax on income from movable wealth, whether received periodically or in a lump sum (7/1.3).

If the recipient is a business enterprise, income derived from the licensing of intellectual property is classified in category B as income to whose production capital and labor contribute jointly (6/1.1e). Income derived by the owner or concessionary of mineral rights, as a result of leasing them to another, is taxed as explained at 10/1.1. Income derived by an author or an inventor from the licensing or leasing of copyrights, patents, processes, designs, formulas, trademarks, and other intellectual property is classified in category C/1 as income from independent work of an individual, whether the recipient is a professional or an amateur (8/3.1). Since the classification of income is determined by its productive source, copyright royalties classifiable in category C/1 continue to be classified in category C/1 as income from services, and not in category A as income from capital, when received by the heirs of the author.[137] Lump-sum or periodic payments received for the transfer of intellectual property are subject to the tax on income from movable wealth under the same rules (7/1.3; 9/8.5).

Expenditures incurred in order to earn royalties are deductible as business (7/2.12) or professional (8/2.2) expenses. Amortization of the cost of purchasing or acquiring patents and other intangibles is permitted under the rules described at 7/3.9.

The tax on income from movable wealth is applied to income payable for the transfer or licensing of assets created by work done in Italy or by an Italian enterprise; it is also applied to royalties and fees payable

---

[137] Comm. Centr., Sez. III, 28 November 1955, n. 76536; C.M. 7 March 1956, n. 300770.

by persons domiciled or resident in Italy (11/1.6c). Fees or earnings paid to aliens, or to Italians domiciled abroad, for the transfer or licensing of intellectual property are subject to provisional withholding of the tax on income from movable wealth and of the complementary tax, computed on the gross amount, as explained at 13/3.5.

9/6. Presumed Income

The taxation of presumed income from the ownership of immovable property is explained at 9/4.1, 9/4.2, and 10/2.2.

9/7. Taxation at Source

The provisions relating to the withholding of the tax on income from movable wealth from payments of income from capital are listed below.

1. The tax is withheld directly from certain government interest and annuity payments (13/3.3).
2. The tax payable on payments of specified interest and annuities made by specified private entities is paid by the person paying the income and recovered from the recipient through withholding (13/3.4).
3. The tax on the gross amount of fees or earnings paid to aliens, or to Italians domiciled abroad, for the transfer or licensing of intellectual property is subject to provisional withholding (13/3.5).

The complementary tax is withheld provisionally from the gross amount of fees or earnings paid to aliens, or to Italians domiciled abroad, for the transfer or licensing of intellectual property (13/3.5). Beginning in 1963, a special provisional withholding called the coupon tax, to be credited in most cases against the complementary tax or the corporation tax, must be made from all distributions of profits by corporations and similar entities (9/2.7a).

9/8. Capital Gains and Losses

9/8.I   In General

The taxation of capital gains (gains incurred on capital assets) is governed by the rules of the *Testo unico* stated below.[138]

---

[138] For a discussion of the general problem of the taxation of capital gains in Italy, see Associazione fra le Società Italiane per Azioni, *Annuario legale delle società per azioni*, 1942-1946, vol. XI, 112; 1947-1952, vol. XII, 153; 1952-1953, vol. XIII, 126; Cristofaro, "Concetto di plusvalori patrimoniali con particolare riferimento al nostro ordinamento tributario," *Temi trib.*, 1961, 760; Croxatto, "Assoggettabilità degli incrementi patrimoniali all'imposta di ricchezza mobile," *Dir. e prat. trib.*, 1959, II, 177; Di Paolo, "La tassazione delle plusvalenze e sopravvenienze," *Cons. az.*, 1962, 152; Di Paolo, "Società immobiliari ed imposta di R.M.," *Temi trib.*, 1960, 14; Fasiani, "L'imposizione degli incrementi patrimoniali," in Ministero per la Costituente, *Rapporto della Commissione Economica*, vol. 5, II, 429; 2 Fasiani, *Principi di scienza delle finanze* 125; Ferro, "La tassazione degli incrementi patrimoniali nella imposta di

1. Income from speculative operations, even if occasional (9/8.2), is subject to the tax on income from movable wealth (art. 81) and classified in category B as business income (art. 85).
2. Capital gains (*plusvalenze*) realized by a business enterprise (7/1.2a) on the sale of property related to the enterprise (9/8.3),[139] including good will (9/9.2, 9/9.9), at a price higher than its undepreciated cost (7/3.6) or higher than the last value recognized for the determination of income, are included in income from business (art. 100).[140]
3. In the case of a company regulated by article 2200 of the Civil Code as a business company,[141] all property owned by the enterprise is considered related to it for purposes of the provision described in item 2 above; in addition, gains are taxable as business income even if they are distributed to partners, members, or shareholders prior to the transfer of the property (art. 100).
4. Capital gains of an enterprise are included in taxable income of the business period in which they are realized, distributed, or inscribed in the balance sheet (art. 106). In the case of an entity required to be taxed on the balance sheet basis, this provision applies to capital gains incurred on any property of the enterprise; in the case of an enterprise not required to be taxed on the balance sheet basis, it applies only to capital gains incurred on property related to the enterprise, either in fact or by virtue of the presumption described in item 3 above.

The gains taxed under these provisions are included in income from movable wealth of category B and taxed at the normal rates applicable to business income (12/1.4c).

A gain realized by an individual on the sale of property not related to an enterprise carried on by him, and held for investment rather that for speculation, is not subject to tax. It should also be pointed out that the provision taxing gains realized by a business enterprise on the sale of property related to the enterprise does not apply to professions; thus, a gain realized on the sale of a capital asset related to the exercise of an art or profession, or on the transfer of good will in a professional practice, is not subject to tax unless shown to be speculative. Capital gains resulting from revaluation for monetary equalization made in con-

---

ricchezza mobile," *Nuova riv. trib.*, 1960, 348; Griziotti, "Le imposte sugli incrementi di valore nei capitali e sulle rendite nei redditi (interessi, salari e profitti)," *Giorn. degli economisti*, 1910, vol. 40, 625, vol. 41, 648; Mazzilli, "In tema di tassazione delle plusvalenze aziendali," *Nuova rass. comm.*, 1959, 249; Romani, "Alcune riflessioni in tema di presupposti dell'imposta di ricchezza mobile," *RDFSF*, 1960, I, 370.

[139] See C.M. 5 March 1958, n. 10.

[140] Prior to the enactment of article 20 of L. 5 January 1956, n. 1, gains realized by a business enterprise not formed as a company were taxed only if they had resulted from speculative operations. In determining the business income from nonspeculative transactions of an enterprise not formed as a company, therefore, only the gain accruing after 1 January 1957, the effective date of that provision, is taken into account. C.M. 5 March 1958, n. 10.

[141] The forms of company covered by this provision are the corporation (5/2.2), limited liability company (5/2.3), limited partnership with shares (5/2.4), cooperative society (5/2.5), general partnership (5/3.2), and simple limited partnership (5/3.3).

formity with the Law of 11 February 1952, n. 74, are not subject to the tax on income from movable wealth.[142]

Capital gains are subject to the tax on income from movable wealth only if produced in Italy or if considered produced in Italy under the rules applicable to income from business (11/1.3, 11/1.6d, 11/2.3).

Those capital gains which are subject to the tax on income from movable wealth under the rules stated above are included in aggregate income for the complementary tax (6/1.1f) or in aggregate income for the corporation tax (6/1.1g). Under the principles stated at 11/2.1, some capital gains resulting from speculative operations or from business dealings may be subject to the personal taxes whether or not considered produced in Italy for purposes of the tax on income from movable wealth.

The tax treatment of gains or losses on transfers of property in the course of the organization, reorganization, or dissolution of a business is discussed at 9/9.

9/8.2 Speculative Operations

When gains incurred on capital assets are considered income, the basis of taxation required by the concept of income (2/2.6, 6/1.1a) is considered to be an activity motivated by the intent to realize a profit.[143] Under the rules stated at 9/8.1, speculative intent is conclusively presumed in the case of gains realized on property related to an enterprise not carried on by a business company and in the case of gains incurred on any property belonging to an enterprise carried on by a business company, whether or not the property is related to the enterprise (9/8.3).[144] As a result, the actual existence of speculative intent need be shown only for gains realized by taxpayers who are not entrepreneurs and for gains realized by individual entrepreneurs on property not related to the enterprise.[145]

In the cases in which actual speculative intent must be shown, its presence or absence is a question of fact.[146] Certain types of property,

---

[142] L. 5 January 1956, n. 1, art. 20.

[143] See 1 Vanoni, *Opere giuridiche* 258-259; Liccardo, "Importanza dell'intento speculativo nella determinazione del reddito," *Riv. trib.*, 1952, 408. For criticism of the view that unanticipated gains from investment in property should be subject to less rigorous tax treatment than gains resulting from speculative activity, however, see 1 Vanoni, *Opere giuridiche* 262; Ardigò, "Sul requisito dell'intento speculativo per l'imposizione del plusvalore nelle vendite di immobili," *RDFSF*, 1938, II, 301.

[144] For the development of these presumptions in the decisions of the Central Commission, see 1 Vanoni, *Opere giuridiche* 255-257. The presumptions were embodied in the law, in substantially their present form, by article 20 of L. 5 January 1956, n. 1.

[145] See 1 Vanoni, *Opere giuridiche* 257-258, editors' footnote.

[146] For a brief summary of the development of the law regarding speculative intent, down to the reform law of 1956, see Zappalà, Marionetti, and Lanza, *Imposta sui redditi di ricchezza mobile* 8-11.

such as securities (9/8.4), tend to be more frequently the subject matter of speculation than others, for example, real estate. Although, under the rules stated at 9/8.1, income from an isolated transaction is taxable if the operation is speculative, frequency of transactions could presumably suggest a speculative intent which would not be inferable from any single transaction. Speculative intent has been inferred from the resale of immovable property recently purchased; [147] conversely, gain realized on the resale, after many years, of immovable property originally acquired as an investment has been held not to be speculative.[148] The intention to resell an asset at a profit must exist at the time of its acquisition if speculative intent is to be inferred.

9/8.3 Property Related to an Enterprise

On the ground that a business company exists for the purpose of making a profit, all acts of a company which could lead to gains or losses in the balance sheet are conclusively presumed to have a speculative foundation, whether or not they form a part of the company's regular activity.[149] This presumption is embodied in article 100 of the *Testo unico,* by virtue of which all property belonging to a business enterprise organized as a business company (CC art. 2200) is considered related to the enterprise. As a result of this provision, a gain sustained by such an enterprise on any property belonging to it is included in its gross business income under the rules discussed at 9/8.1. A gain realized on property by a business enterprise not organized as a company, however, is included in its business income only if the property transferred is related to the enterprise (art. 100) (9/8.1). Property related to the enterprise includes not only property which itself forms the object of the activity of the enterprise, but capital assets instrumental to the exercise of that activity, such as buildings, plant, machinery, and other depreciable assets.[150] It also includes any other assets owned by the enterprise which, as a result of their relation to the activity of the enterprise, ought to be considered part of the capital of the business.[151] Shares in similar enterprises may may be found, "with the support of other elements," to be related to

[147] Cass. 15 April 1916; Cass., Sez. un., 14 January 1927 (*Riv. leg. fisc.,* 1927, 250); Comm. Centr., Sez. I, 20 October 1948, n. 100768.

[148] Comm. Centr. Centr. 10 March 1921, n. 6228.

[149] Comm. Centr. 4 April 1928, n. 83883. See critical discussion in 1 Vanoni, *Opere giuridiche* 257-261; see also 2/2.6.

[150] C.M. 15 April 1957, n. 350860; C.M. 5 March 1958, n. 10. These instructions were issued under article 20 of L. 5 January 1956, n. 1, the legislative precedent of article 100 of the *Testo unico,* which provided that the gains in question should be taxed only when resulting from activities in some manner related (*afferenti*) to the conduct of the enterprise.

[151] C.M. 15 April 1957, n. 350860.

the enterprise.[152] The computation of gain or loss realized on the sale of depreciable assets related to the enterprise is discussed at 7/3.6.

9/8.4 Speculation and Transactions in Securities

Under the rules discussed at 9/8.1, gains realized by an individual from transactions in securities, except as a part of a business enterprise, are subject to tax only if they result from speculative operations (9/8.2). Gains realized from transactions in securities by a business enterprise other than a company are subject to tax only if the securities transferred are related to the enterprise, as in the case of securities held by a professional dealer in securities or shares of a business similar to that carried by the transferor (9/8.3). Since all property belonging to a business enterprise formed as a business company under article 2200 of the Civil Code is considered related to the enterprise, the business income of such an enterprise includes all gains sustained on securities held by it, under the rules discussed at 9/8.1. Thus, for example, any increase inscribed in the balance sheet of an Italian corporation in the value of shares of a foreign subsidiary is included in the Italian corporation's gross income from business, even if the gain has not been realized.

Securities held by business enterprises are valued in accordance with the rules discussed at 6/5.3; deduction is allowed for losses on shares, bonds, and other interest-bearing securities, determined in accordance with those rules (art. 101).

The collection by the Ministry of Finance of information regarding transactions in securities is discussed at 9/2.8 and at 13/1.4. The taxation of income from·securities transactions of banks is governed by the rules discussed at 10/4, and of income from transactions of investment companies, at 10/5.

The transfer of all of the outstanding shares of a corporation is treated as a transfer of the business with the consequent realization of the price of good will, under the rules discussed at 9/9.2.[153] The transfer of only a part of the outstanding shares is not treated as a transfer of the business,[154] even if more than a majority of the shares are transferred.[155]

If a corporation buys its own shares at a price lower than their nominal value and then reduces its capital by an amount corresponding to the nominal value of the shares purchased, the difference between the

---

[152] C.M. 15 April 1957, n. 350860.

[153] See Comm. Centr., Sez. un., 21 February 1955, n. 68742, with critical note by Napolitano, "Cessione del pacchetto azionario ed avviamento dell'azienda sociale," *Dir. e prat. trib.*, 1956, II, 3.

[154] Comm. Centr., Sez. un., 24 November 1945, n. 79346. See Berliri, *L'imposta di ricchezza mobile* 199.

[155] Comm. Centr., Sez. un., 21 February 1955, n. 68742.

nominal value of the shares purchased and the price paid for them is included in the business income of the corporation.[156]

9/8.5 Sales of Patents and Copyrights

Capital gains resulting from the transfer of patents, copyrights, and other intellectual property in exchange for lump-sum or installment payments are subject to the tax on income from movable wealth in category B if the recipient is a business enterprise. If the seller is an individual author or inventor not engaged in a business enterprise, the net gain is taxed in category C/1. Payments received by persons other than the original author or inventor who do not deal professionally in patents or copyrights are treated as capital receipts, subject to tax in category B if the transaction is speculative.[157]

Payments to aliens or to Italians domiciled abroad for the transfer of copyrights, patents, and other intellectual property are subject to provisional withholding of the tax on income from movable wealth and of the complementary tax, as explained at 13/3.5.

9/8.6 Transactions in Other Assets

The tax treatment of gains or losses on credits resulting from fluctuation in foreign exchange is governed by the general rules described at 9/8.1. Gains inscribed in the balance sheet are represented by the difference between the values at the opening and closing of the balance sheet, without reference to the original value of the credit.[158]

It should be noted that capital gains incurred on immovable property suitable for building may not only be subject to the income taxes under the rules discussed at 9/8.1, but are also subject to the tax on increases in the values of building lots which was introduced in 1963 (3/7).

The treatment of amounts received on termination of employment or on retirement is discussed at 8/1.8; of loan discounts and premiums, at 9/1.3; of annuities, at 9/3.1; of proceeds of life insurance policies and contracts of capitalization, at 9/3.2; and of proceeds of accident insurance policies, at 9/3.3.

9/8.7 Determination of Gain

In determining the amount of capital gain subject to the tax on income from movable wealth, the taxpayer may deduct the cost of the assets

---

[156] Comm. Centr., Sez. II, 19 January 1948, n. 94657. See also Giannetta, Scandale, and Sessa, *Teoria e tecnica nell'accertamento del reddito mobiliare* 639. For criticism of this method of computing the gains, see Forte, "L'imponibilità degli utili derivanti a società dall'acquisto di azioni proprie nella imposta di R.M.," *RDFSF*, 1950, II, 301.

[157] See Zappalà, Marionetti, and Lanza, *L'imposta sui redditi di ricchezza mobile* 33.

[158] C.M. 15 April 1957, n. 350860.

involved, reduced by depreciation if the asset is depreciable (7/3.2). If the taxpayer is a business enterprise, and the last value recognized for the determination of income is less than the cost, the gain is the difference between the sale price and the last value recognized for the determination of income (9/8.1). Expenses inherent in the purchase, holding, and sale of the asset are deductible in accordance with the rules provided for the category in which the gain is taxed (7/2.1, 8/2.2).

9/8.8   Capital Losses

Provision is made for the deduction by business enterprises of losses resulting from the total or partial destruction of property related to the enterprise (7/2.7); of losses from the sale of property related to the enterprise at a price less than the undepreciated cost, or less than the last value recognized for the determination of income, if this value differs from the undepreciated cost (7/3.6); of losses on credits (7/2.10); and of other losses inherent in the activity productive of income (art. 99). All property belonging to a business company is considered related to the enterprise for purposes of article 99 regarding losses, in the same manner as for article 100 regarding capital gains (9/8.3). Business enterprises may deduct realized or unrealized losses on shares, bonds, and other interest-bearing securities, in accordance with the valuation rules discussed at 6/5.3, provided that the securities are related to the enterprise (9/8.4).[159] Entities and enterprises taxed on the balance sheet basis may not deduct capital losses resulting from devaluations which have not been registered in accordance with the rules for keeping of accounting records (6/2.3, 7/2.7).

Capital losses deductible under the rules described above may be deducted from other income of category B in determining net income of that category (7/4.1). Entities taxed on the balance sheet basis may carry forward capital losses deductible in category B, under the rules described at 7/4.2.

9/9.   Organization, Reorganization, and Dissolution of Business

9/9.1   In General

With respect to the organization of business, the *Testo unico* contains special provisions exempting companies from tax on surcharges and equalization payments and permitting the deduction of expenses relative to the formation of companies and the increasing of their capital (9/9.3).

In the case of the transfer of a business, the *Testo unico* makes special provision for inclusion of the value of good will as a part of the gain

---

[159] It appears that if this requirement is met, the transaction giving rise to the loss need not be a part of the normal activity of the enterprise. Comm. Centr., Sez. II, 11 November 1950, n. 17275.

realized, under the rules normally applicable to capital gains sustained by enterprises (9/8.1); it also makes provision for determining the rate of the complementary tax on income connected with the realization of good will (9/9.2). With respect to the transferor, a termination of the tax basis takes place (6/3.5), and the purchaser of the business becomes liable for the payment of certain taxes already due (9/9.3). In the case of a change in the form of a business enterprise, special provisions exist regarding tax periods, the compilation of balance sheets, and the filing of returns (9/9.4, 9/9.6).

Income received as a result of the liquidation of a business is treated in the same manner as income from a transfer of the business, except that there is no value attributable to good will, and is subject to the complementary tax at a special rate. There are also special provisions (1) for determining the income, for purposes of the tax on income from movable wealth and the corporation tax, of a corporation or similar entity whose liquidation lasts for more than one year but not more than five years; (2) for the filing of returns during the liquidation of a corporation; and (3) for the personal liability of liquidators for unpaid taxes of the corporation. These provisions are discussed at 9/9.9c.

Apart from these provisions, the taxation of transfers and distributions on the organization, reorganization, or dissolution of a business is governed by the ordinary rules for the determination of business income (7/1), including those for capital gains (9/8.1). The application of the ordinary rules and of the special rules mentioned above to these transactions is discussed below.[160]

9/9.2 Sale of Assets or Business

Gain or loss realized on assets transferred to a business is treated, for income tax purposes, in the same manner as gain or loss on any other transfer of assets, under the rules explained at 9/8.1. Thus, if the transferor is an individual who is neither dealing nor speculating in the assets transferred, gain or loss is recognized for tax purposes only if the assets were related to a business previously carried on by the transferor; however, any gain realized on assets related to a business of the transferor is included in income from movable wealth of category B as business income (9/8.3). If the transferor is a business company, gains realized on any assets belonging to it are subject to tax, even if distributed to the members before realization (9/8.1). If the transferor is a corporation or similar entity, gains inscribed in the balance sheet are included in

---

[160] For a detailed treatment of the problems discussed in 9/9, see Giannetta, Scandale, and Sessa, *Teoria e tecnica nell'accertamento del reddito mobiliare* 679-708, and Piccatti, "La circolazione dell'azienda ed il realizzo dell'avviamento," *Temi trib.*, 1963, 671.

business income even if neither realized nor distributed. Transfer of an entire business would also involve taking account of "hidden reserves" of business properties and, therefore, their taxation as business income (7/1.3f). Inventory is valued in the normal manner (6/5.1), and gain or loss on depreciable assets is determined as explained at 7/3.6.

By express provision, the gain to be included in business income on the transfer of business assets includes the gain attributable to good will (*avviamento*) (art. 100).[161] The value of good will represents a capitalization of the future profits of the business, produced by the activity and the capital employed in the business, but subject to tax only when realized on transfer, either as part of the business or separately.[162] The value attributable to good will is subject to the tax on income from movable wealth even if the income from the exercise of the normal activity of the business transferred is entitled to a temporary exemption, since such exemptions do not apply to occasional speculations outside the activity for which they are provided.[163] It appears that, when the business itself is not transferred, gain on the sale of machinery or other instrumental assets is considered to have been made in the exercise of the activity of the enterprise and is thus entitled to such exemptions. Payment received for an agreement not to compete is considered part of the value of good will.[164] The transfer of shares in a business is not considered a transfer of the business unless the shares transferred represent the entire share capital of the enterprise (9/8.4).[165] If the income of the business transferred is classified in category C/1, under the rules discussed at 7/1.2b, the value attributable to good will is also classified in category C/1.[166]

If the price paid for a business includes the value of good will, the total gain on the transfer of a business, including good will, is the difference between the total price received and the transferor's last book value of the total net assets. When payment for assets or for a business is made in shares, the gain or loss is ordinarily measured by the difference between

---

[161] Under the system of assessment in effect prior to the *Testo unico*, the assessment of the income of the final period of a business was based on the income of the previous tax period, and the gain attributable to good will had to be assessed "*una tantum*"; see L. 8 June 1936, n. 1231, art. 8, abrogated by L. 5 January 1956, n. 1, art. 24.

[162] See 1 Vanoni, *Opere giuridiche* 270 *et seq.*; Zappalà, Marionetti, and Lanza, *L'imposta sui redditi di ricchezza mobile* 15-16.

[163] Comm. Centr. 25 February 1935, n. 72870. See Zappalà, Marionetti, and Lanza, *L'imposta sui redditi di ricchezza mobile* 42.

[164] Comm. Centr. 16 March 1937, n. 98848; Comm. Centr., Sez. II, 24 February 1951, n. 20995.

[165] Cass., Sez. un., 5 November 1936; Comm. Centr., Sez. un., 24 November 1945, n. 79346; Comm. Centr., Sez. un., 21 February 1955, n. 68742. See Zappalà, Marionetti, and Lanza, *L'imposta sui redditi di ricchezza mobile* 50.

[166] *Verb. conf.* October 1947, De Angelis, Potenza, and Testa, *Testo unico delle leggi sulle imposte dirette* 395.

the last book value of the net assets and the nominal value of the shares at the time of issue.[167]   It appears, however, that the value of good will may be estimated if it is not actually reflected in the nominal value of the shares.[168]   If there is no book value of the total net assets of a business, it appears that the Tax Office estimates the income attributable to good will by capitalizing the income from movable wealth at from two to five times its average amount in the last five tax periods, taking account of the age of the enterprise and of any previous transfers.   If the purchase price of the business is paid in the form of a life annuity or perpetual annuity, the value of good will is taken into account in the taxation of the periodic payments under the rules described at 9/3.1 and is apparently not taxed separately at the time of the transfer.[169]

A capital loss resulting from a transfer of assets or of a business may be deducted from the taxpayer's other income of category B of the current year (9/8.8); if the taxpayer is an entity or enterprise taxed on the balance sheet basis, such a capital loss may be carried forward, subject to the rules discussed at 7/4.2.

For purposes of the complementary tax, income received as a result of the liquidation of a business and income connected with the realization of good will on the transfer of a business are included in the taxpayer's income; the amount to be included in income for purposes of determining the rate of the complementary tax is determined by dividing the income by the number of years elapsed since the commencement of the business or since the preceding transfer of the business and adding the result to the taxpayer's other income (art. 140).   The number of years by which the income is divided for this purpose may not exceed fifty, and it is presumed to be five if not otherwise determinable.   The entire amount of the income is subject to the complementary tax at the rate so determined (art. 140).

When an entire business is transferred, a termination of the transferor's tax basis takes place (6/3.5), and the transferor may file a report of termination to prevent inscription in the rolls for future years (13/1.5).   Special problems regarding transformations, with the resulting dissolution of the company which previously owned the business, are discussed at 9/9.4.

9/9.3   Purchase of Assets or Business

On the purchase of assets or of an entire business, the purchase price is the cost for purposes of depreciation (7/3.3) and the determination of any future gain or loss (9/8.1).   Transferred inventories are taken into

---

[167] Comm. Centr. 30 April 1936, n. 87472; Comm. Centr., Sez. II, 19 May 1953, n. 48280.

[168] See C.M. 9 May 1960, n. 351110.

[169] See Piccatti, "La circolazione dell'azienda ed il realizzo dell'avviamento," *Temi trib.*, 1963, 671.

account and valued in the normal manner (6/5.1). Unabsorbed losses of the business cannot be carried forward by the transferee even if the transferor would have been entitled to carry them forward under the rules discussed at 7/4.2.

If a corporation issues fully paid shares in payment for assets or a business, the purchase price is ordinarily the nominal value of the shares, plus any surcharge (*sovraprezzo*) paid for the new shares, to equalize their current book value with that of the shares already outstanding.[170] Such a surcharge is part of the contribution of capital and is included in what must be restored to the shareholders on liquidation.[171] Both the surcharge and any adjustment paid by the recipient of the new shares to compensate for the fact that they have not been shareholders for the full period for which the dividend is paid are excluded from the income of the issuing company (art. 83) (6/1.3). The contribution of assets and good will is a contribution of capital and is not income of the company to which they are contributed.[172]

Expenses relating to the formation of companies and to increasing their capital are deductible in the five business periods following that in which they were sustained, at a rate not exceeding one fifth of the expense in each period (art. 97) (7/2.13).

The purchaser of a business is liable for payment of the taxes due from any previous owners on the income of the enterprise and on income of category C/2 for the tax period of the transfer and the preceding tax period, as well as for payment of any surcharges due for violations charged against any previous owner before the transfer (13/3.1).

9/9.4 Change of Form of Enterprise

If an individual transfers a business to a corporation, receiving shares in exchange, good will is realized even if the transferor becomes the sole shareholder of the corporation.[173] Similarly, good will is realized when an individual contributes a business to a limited liability company.[174] If an individual transfers a business to a partnership, retaining a participation

---

[170] See Einaudi, *Il sistema tributario italiano* (3d ed., 1935) 66-67. Frè, *Società per azioni. Commentario del Codice Civile* 554.

[171] If a corporation offers old shareholders an option to purchase newly issued shares at a price representing their nominal value increased by an amount covering expenses of issue plus an adjustment for the dividend of the year in course, and some of the shareholders do not exercise the option, any excess over the option price of the price thereafter received for the shares on the open market is not regarded as a surcharge in this sense but as income from movable wealth.

[172] Comm. Centr., Sez. un., 9 November 1946, n. 85001.

[173] Cass., Sez. un., 27 January 1943, n. 184. See Berliri, *L'imposta di ricchezza mobile* 198; Zappalà, Marionetti, and Lanza, *L'imposta sui redditi di ricchezza mobile* 49; Piccatti, "La circolazione dell'azienda ed il realizzo dell'avviamento," *Temi trib.*, 1963, 671.

[174] Comm. Centr., Sez. I, 20 July 1959, n. 19617.

in the partnership, good will is realized on that part of the business which does not represent the share retained. Gains realized are subject to tax under the rules discussed at 9/9.2, in the same manner as in the case of any other transfer of a business by an individual.

Under earlier decisions, it was held that when the form of a business was changed from a partnership to a corporation owned by the former partners, there was no realization of good will because there was no transfer or discontinuance, but only a change in the juridical form of the company.[175] A similar rule was applied to the transformation into a corporation of a *de facto* company having the same object and capital and the same members as its successor corporation,[176] and to the merger and dissolution of two or more partnerships into a newly formed corporation.[177] It appears, however, that the gain resulting from such a merger could be taxed as income of the individual members of the partnerships dissolved in the merger, even if the members received payment in the form of shares of the new corporation instead of in cash.[178]

Under the provisions of the *Testo unico* governing the taxation of gains distributed by companies and the taxation of hidden reserves of companies (9/8.1), it seems likely that, on the transformation of a partnership into a corporation or similar entity, gains on assets and good will would be taxed in the same manner as in the case of an outright transfer (9/9.2), even if the shareholders of the new corporation were identical with the previous owners of the business, and even if the shares of the new corporation were issued directly to the former partners.[179] Under present practice, however, the transformation of a corporation or similar entity into a partnership or sole proprietorship owned by the former shareholders is not considered a transfer of the business for purposes of the provisions regarding the taxation of the value of good will.[180]

---

[175] Cass. 7 May 1934. See Zappalà, Marionetti, and Lanza, *L'imposta sui redditi di ricchezza mobile* 48; but see Comm. Centr., Sez. II, 19 May 1953, n. 48280.

[176] Comm. Centr., Sez. un., 25 March 1931, n. 20441. See, however, Comm. Centr., Sez. III, 25 October 1940, n. 31481 (simple civil company); Berliri, *L'imposta di ricchezza mobile* 194.

[177] Comm. Centr., Sez. un., 25 May 1939, n. 15993; Comm. Centr., Sez. II, 17 January 1950, n. 8923.

[178] Comm. Centr., Sez. un., 25 May 1939, n. 15993; Comm. Centr. 17 October 1939, n. 18115. See Berliri, *L'imposta di ricchezza mobile* 186-194; Zappalà, Marionetti, and Lanza, *L'imposta sui redditi di ricchezza mobile* 49.

[179] A recent decision involving a *de facto* company is Comm. Centr., Sez. III, 19 February 1960, n. 25110. See, however, Comm. Centr., Sez. I, 19 January 1960, n. 23620. For the most recent administrative instructions, see C.M. 7 September 1956, n. 351253 (partnership); and C.M. 9 May 1960, n. 351110 (*de facto* company). For discussion, see Piccatti, "La circolazione dell'azienda ed il realizzo dell'avviamento," *Temi trib.*, 1963, 671, and literature cited therein; Piccatti, "In tema di tassabilità dell'avviamento nel caso di trasformazione di società," *Temi trib.*, 1960, 599.

[180] Comm. Centr., Sez. I, 19 January 1960, n. 23620; Comm. Centr., Sez. I, 23 November 1960, n. 34217. In C.M. 7 September 1956, n. 351253, the tax administration had taken the position that such transformations should be treated as

If such a transformation were to be taxed as a transfer, the aggregate
income of each shareholder for the complementary tax would include
his share of the undistributed profits of the corporation at the time of
the transformation (9/2.1b) and any gain realized by him through the
exchange of his shares for his participation in the reconstituted enterprise
(9/8.4); the rate of tax would be determined in accordance with the
special provision described at 9/9.2. It appears that, in any case, such
a transaction would be considered a liquidation for purposes of the
special rules for adjustment of the income of the corporation described
at 9/9.9c.

In the case of a reorganization of an entity required to be taxed on
the balance sheet basis into a company not required to be taxed on the
balance sheet basis, a balance sheet relative to the tax period prior to the
reorganization must be compiled (art. 124). In either type of transformation—that is, whether an entity required to be taxed on the balance
sheet basis changes into one not required to be so taxed, or an entity
not required to be so taxed changes into one required to be so taxed—
the fraction of the calendar year or business period before the change
and the fraction of the calendar year or business period after the change
are separate tax periods for purposes of the tax on income from movable
wealth of categories A and B and for the corporation tax, whether or
not there has been a closing of the business period (art. 3).[181] The return
for the tax period before the reorganization must be filed within three
months of the reorganization decision (art. 22). The taxable amounts
of the tax periods before the reorganization are provisionally inscribed
in the roll against the reorganized company in accordance with the ordinary rules (13/3.6a), and the taxable amounts of the fractions of the
year or business period before and after the reorganization are both
taken into account (art. 176).

9/9.5 Exchange of Shares for Shares

When persons owning shares in different companies exchange their
respective holdings, each party realizes a gain or loss on his original

transfers; but the Compartmental Inspectors, at a meeting of 16-19 May 1961, have re-
examined this position in the light of the cited decisions of the Central Commission
and have adopted a policy of not assessing the price of good will in the cases in
question, except under the regular provisions regarding the taxation of capital gains
of business enterprises, including good will (9/8.1), and the taxation of hidden
reserves (7/1.3f). See Poli, *Imposta sulle società e imposta sulle obbligazioni* 190-191.
Poli (p. 188) criticizes the legal bases of the current position of the tax administration; see also Poli, "Il reddito di avviamento nelle trasformazioni di società," *Imp.
dir. erariali*, 1962, 336-350; Scotto, "Sulla tassabilità di un premio di avviamento
nella trasformazione di società di capitale in società di persone," *Riv. soc.*, 1957, 263.

[181] From the fact that a transformation is possible without closing the balance
sheet, it should not be inferred that the companies existing before and after the
transformation are not distinct entities for tax purposes. See Poli, *Imposta sulle
società e imposta sulle obbligazioni* 188.

investment and makes a new investment. If a party to such a transaction is engaging in speculation, or is a business enterprise organized as a company of any type, any gain realized is taxable as business income (9/8.4).

Gains realized on the exchange of shares for other shares by banks and investment companies are taxable as business income, as explained at 10/5.

9/9.6   Creation of Subsidiaries

When a corporation transfers a branch or a part of its business to a subsidiary corporation, in exchange for shares of the subsidiary, the parent is subject to the rules regarding transfer (9/9.2), and the subsidiary is subject to the rules regarding purchase (9/9.3).

9/9.7   Mergers of Corporations or Similar Entities

When a corporation transfers its assets or business to another corporation in exchange for shares of the other corporation, the first corporation is subject to the provisions applicable to a transfer of assets by a corporation in exchange for shares (9/9.2); the corporation receiving the assets is taxed under the provisions applicable to an exchange of shares for assets (9/9.3). Under the rules stated at 9/8.1, gains resulting from the transfer are included in the income of the transferor, even if the shares issued in exchange are distributed directly to the shareholders of the transferor. The distribution of the shares of the transferee to the shareholders of the transferor would be taxed as a dividend in kind if the transferor had available profits or hidden reserves (9/2.2). If a reduction in capital resulted from the distribution, the consequences described at 9/2.4 would apply. Any gain realized by the shareholders on the exchange would be treated under the rules discussed at 9/9.5.

When one corporation is merged with another as a result of the acquisition by the second of all the outstanding shares of the first (*fusione per incorporazione*), there is no realization of good will by the corporation which has been absorbed.[182] If any gains resulting from the transaction (including the value of good will) appear in the balance sheet which the second corporation must compile for the final business period of the corporation which has been absorbed, under the rules stated below, these gains will form part of the income of that period, but will normally be assessed against the new company and the shareholders of the absorbed corporation. Any gain realized by the shareholders of the company which has been absorbed may be taxed under

---

[182] Comm. Centr. 15 November 1933, n. 55447; Comm. Centr. 21 June 1937, n. 101792; Cass., Sez. un., 4 March 1937. See also C.M. 28 June 1937, n. 6200, discussing L. 8 June 1936, n. 1231, art. 16.

ie rules discussed at 9/9.5,[183] whether the shares are paid for in money
r in shares of the purchasing company.[184] Unabsorbed losses of the
rst corporation can be carried forward by the second, under the rules
iscussed at 7/4.2. It appears likely that similar rules would apply when
hareholders of two or more corporations form a new corporation, receiv-
ig shares of the new corporation in exchange for the old shares (*fusione
erfetta*).

The entity surviving or resulting from a merger is responsible for com-
iling the closing balance sheet for the assessment of the tax due for the
nal business period of the company or companies extinguished by the
ierger (art. 124); within three months after the merger or incorporation,
he resulting entity must file the return for the final business period of
he extinguished company or companies (art. 22) (13/1.1c). For the
ntities surviving or resulting from a merger, the taxable amount for
urposes of provisional inscription in the roll for the period of the merger
ncludes the taxable amounts of all the entities participating in the
ierger (art. 176) (13/3.6a). For purposes of the corporation tax, ordi-
iary taxes inscribed in the rolls after the reorganization are deductible
rom the aggregate income of the last business period for which the
orporation tax is applied (art. 148).

/9.8   Division of Corporate Assets Among Several Corporations

If a corporation operating several businesses desires to have one of
hem carried on by a separate corporation owned directly by the share-
iolders of the original corporation, the transaction may be accomplished
)y transferring the business to a new corporation in exchange for its
;hares and distributing those shares to the shareholders of the old cor-
)oration. The formation of the new corporation and the transfer of the
iusiness in exchange for its shares would result in the tax consequences
:o the transferor described at 9/9.2. The provisions which would be
ipplicable to the new corporation are discussed at 9/9.4.

The distribution of the shares of the new corporation to the share-
iolders of the old would be taxed as a dividend in kind if the old
corporation had available profits or hidden reserves (9/2.2). If a reduction of capital resulted from the distribution, the consequences described
it 9/2.4 would apply.

9/9.9   Cessation and Liquidation of Business

a. SOLE PROPRIETORSHIP. On the death of an individual owner of a
business, his heirs are jointly and severally liable for the payment of

---

[183] Comm. Centr. 17 October 1939, n. 18115.
[184] See Zappalà, Marionetti, and Lanza, *L'imposta sui redditi di ricchezza mobile*
18.

taxes due on income earned prior to his death (13/3.1). The filing of a report of termination of the tax basis (6/3.5) prevents inscription in the roll for future years (13/1.5). Income produced by the business while it is in the hands of the heirs is included in their respective incomes from movable wealth of category B and their aggregate incomes for the complementary tax, in proportion to their rights to participate in the profits If the heirs sell or liquidate the business, gain realized on good will is included in their income, under the rules discussed at 9/9.2, even though it is the result of the previous activity of the deceased heir.[185]

b. PARTNERSHIP OR SIMILAR COMPANY. The sale by a partner of his interest in the firm, or the retirement or death of a partner, does not cause a discontinuance of the business if the firm continues in existence The partnership is subject to the tax on income from movable wealth on the entire income for the year (5/3.1), and also on any hidden reserves distributed to the partner or his heirs (7/1.3f). The withdrawing partner is subject to the complementary tax on his share of the profits to the date of withdrawal, whether or not distributed, and the profits for the balance of the year are divided among the remaining partners for purposes of their complementary tax liability.

Gain realized by the withdrawing partner on the transfer of his share, including any share of good will, is included in his income for the tax on income from movable wealth; [186] for determining the rate of the complementary tax, the value of good will is taken into account in the manner explained at 9/9.2.

If the partnership is dissolved, either on the death, retirement, or withdrawal of a partner, or following sale (9/9.2) or transformation (9/9.4) of the business, the partnership's business income includes all previously untaxed profits which are capitalized or distributed (7/1.3f) and any gain realized on the sale or distribution of partnership assets (9/8.1). If the business is being permanently discontinued, there is no value attributable to good will. The rate of complementary tax imputable to each partner's share of the income received as a result of the liquidation or connected with the realization of good will on the transfer of the business is determined in the manner described at 9/9.2.

c. CORPORATION OR SIMILAR ENTITY. If a corporation is dissolved during or after sale (9/9.2), transformation (9/9.4), or liquidation of the busi-

---

[185] Comm. Centr., Sez. un., 31 January 1942, n. 50514; Comm. Centr., Sez. II, 28 April 1956, n. 81431.

[186] See Comm. Centr. 1 December 1961, n. 50892; see also Piccatti, "La circolazione dell'azienda ed il realizzo dell'avviamento," *Temi trib.*, 1963, 671. Good will is not taxed on the purchase of the share of one partner by the remaining partners. Comm. Centr. 8 May 1961, n. 43503 (*Dir. e prat. trib.*, 1961, II, 393); C.M. 23 October 1961, n. 302187 (*Dir. e prat. trib.*, 1962, I, 132).

ness, its business income includes any previously untaxed income which is capitalized, distributed, or inscribed in the balance sheet (7/1.3f) and also any gain on corporate assets which is realized, distributed, or inscribed in the balance sheet (9/8.1). The gain or loss of the corporation is measured by its closing balance sheet, whether the assets themselves or the proceeds of their sale are distributed to the shareholders. If the assets are distributed directly to the shareholders, the gain or loss sustained by the corporation is determined by reference to the market value of the assets.[187]

If the liquidation of the corporation extends beyond the year in which it was begun, the income subject to the tax on income from movable wealth in each of the periods is adjusted on the basis of the final balance sheet of the liquidation, unless the liquidation continues for more than five business periods (including the first) or unless the liquidator fails to file the required return relating to the outcome of the liquidation within three months of the deposit of the final balance sheet, in addition to the regular return for each business period (arts. 22, 125) (13/1.1c). This adjustment of income is made by subtracting, from the net income of the period of liquidation, losses carried forward from periods prior to the liquidation and income on which tax has been inscribed in the roll during the period of liquidation.[188] For purposes of the corporation tax, the difference in income from movable wealth resulting from this adjustment is applied in equal parts to each of the business periods which have elapsed during the period of liquidation (art. 150).[189] Ordinary taxes inscribed in the rolls after the closing of the liquidation are deductible from the aggregate income of the last business period for which the corporation tax is applied (art. 148).

The liquidators of an entity required to be taxed on the balance sheet basis must file a return for each tax period of the liquidation; within three months of the deposit of the final balance sheet, they must also file a special return relating to the outcome of the liquidation (art. 22) (13/1.1c). The liquidators are personally liable for the payment of taxes owed by the entity for the period of liquidation and for the preceding tax period (13/3.1).

The treatment, for purposes of the tax on income from movable wealth, of any gain realized by a shareholder as a result of the liquidation is governed by the general rules relating to the taxation of capital gains on securities (9/8.4). Thus, if the shareholder is a professional investor

---

[187] See Giannetta, Scandale, and Sessa, *Teoria e tecnica nell'accertamento del reddito mobiliare* 700-701.

[188] See Giannetta, Scandale, and Sessa, *Teoria e tecnica nell'accertamento del reddito mobiliare* 699-700.

[189] It is probable, however, that the apportionment would take the lengths of the opening and closing periods of the liquidation into account. See Poli, *Imposta sulle società e imposta sulle obbligazioni* 235.

or a business enterprise, or is engaged in speculation, the difference
between the amount received on distribution and the last value taken
into account for tax purposes under the applicable rule, depending on
whether the taxpayer is an individual, a business company, or an entity
or enterprise taxed on the balance sheet basis, is included in category I
of income from movable wealth (9/8.1). The amount so determined is
also included in the income of the shareholder for purposes of the com
plementary tax or the corporation tax. It appears that the rate of the
complementary tax is based on the inclusion of the entire amount in the
aggregate income as distribution of profits (9/2.1b) without the rate
adjustment described at 9/9.2 for income received as a result of the
liquidation of a business.[190]

If the shareholder is an individual not engaged in dealing or speculation in securities, the difference between the amount distributed to the
shareholder on liquidation and the amount of his original investment is
considered to be income derived from participation in a corporation,
under the rules discussed at 9/2.1b and thus is not subject to the tax
on income from movable wealth; but it is included in his aggregate
income for purposes of the complementary tax in the year of distribution.

Shareholders cannot deduct unabsorbed losses sustained by the corporation before the liquidation.

---

[190] See Poli, *Imposta complementare sui redditi derivanti da partecipazione in
società e imposta cedolare* 51.

CHAPTER 10

................:
              :
              :
              :
              :
              :

INCOME FROM SPECIAL
ACTIVITIES AND FROM
MISCELLANEOUS SOURCES

10/1. Natural Resource Extraction

10/1.1 In General

10/1.2 Cost of Acquiring Mineral Rights or Concessions

10/1.3 Expenses of Exploration, Extraction, and Development

10/1.4 Depletion

10/1.5 Depreciation of Physical Assets

10/2. Agriculture and Forestry

10/2.1 In General

10/2.2 Tax on Income from Landowning

    a. Basis

    b. Persons subject

    c. Cadastral register and schedule of estimated values

    d. Determination of taxable income

    e. Changes in production or costs

    f. Exemptions

    g. Administration and procedure

10/2.3 Tax on Agrarian Income

    a. Basis and persons subject

    b. Determination of taxable income

    c. Exemptions

    d. Protests and appeals

10/2.4 Income from Movable Wealth

10/3. Insurance

10/4. Banking and Credit
    10/4.1 In General
    10/4.2 Exemptions and Reliefs
    10/4.3 Deductions
    10/4.4 Records and Returns

10/5. Investment Companies

10/6. Industrial Incentives
    10/6.1 In General
    10/6.2 Exemption for Industrial Factories Built in the South
        a. In general
        b. Technically organized industrial factories
        c. Factories which are expanded, converted, reactivated, or transferred
        d. Income derived from utilization of agricultural products
    10/6.3 Allowance for Agricultural or Industrial Investment in the South
        a. Direct investment
        b. Participation
    10/6.4 Exemptions for Other Industrial Zones
    10/6.5 Exemption for New Artisan Enterprises and New Small Industries
        a. In general
        b. Territories in which exemption may be granted
        c. Limitations on size of enterprise
        d. Industrial activities
        e. Reconstruction or expansion by existing enterprises
    10/6.6 Incentives for Particular Industries

10/7. Miscellaneous Sources
    10/7.1 Lotteries, Prizes, and Awards
    10/7.2 Speculative Operations
    10/7.3 Scholarships and Fellowships

10/1. Natural Resource Extraction

10/1.1 In General

Mines are part of the indisposable patrimony of the state; quarries and peat bogs are part of the indisposable patrimony of the state when the right to exploit them (*disponibilità*) is separated from the ownership of the land (CC art. 826). Mineral exploration may be carried on only with government permission, and a mine can be worked, even by the owner of the soil, only under a temporary concession granted by decree of the Minister of Industry and Commerce to a person having the suitable technical and economic resources. Quarries and peat bogs are left at the disposal of the owner of the soil; but the government may grant concessions to other persons having the suitable technical and economic resources when the owners of quarries or peat bogs do not work them or do not develop them sufficiently, and the owner is compensated for the value of the plant, usable equipment, and extracted minerals.[1]

Mines, quarries, peat bogs, and salt deposits, together with surface areas permanently occupied for the related extracting industries, are excluded from the land cadasters (10/2.2c).[2] The income derived from the exercise of the extracting activities, whether above or below ground, is subject to the tax on income from movable wealth in category B as business and industrial income, and not to the tax on income from landowning,[3] even if the land on which the quarry or mine is situated is subject to the tax on income from landowning.[4] If the owner of a mine or quarry leases it to another who carries on the extracting activity, both the rent received by the owner and the income derived by the lessee from the exercise of the extracting activity are subject to the tax on income from movable wealth.[5] An indemnity which the grantee of a mining concession pays to the usufructuary (9/4.1) of an estate as compensation for a limited enjoyment of the surface soil, and as damages for the injury resulting to him from the works of exploration and the exercise of the mine, does not constitute income.[6]

Concessionaries and operators of sulfur mines are subject to a special tax on the production or sale of raw sulfur, in substitution for all other taxes, direct or indirect, national or local.[7] The tax is a fixed fee applied when sulfur produced in Sicily is exported from the island either in the

---

[1] R. D. 29 July 1927, n. 1443, as modified by D. P. R. 28 June 1955, n. 620.
[2] L. 1 March 1886, n. 3682; R. D. 8 October 1931, n. 1572 (*Testo unico* of the laws on the new cadaster), art. 18.
[3] R. D. 6 December 1923, n. 2722, art. 1.
[4] Comm. Centr., Sez. I, 6 May 1946, n. 82273.
In principle, income from the exploitation of the surface was always subject to the tax on income from landowning, whereas income from the exploitation of the subsurface was always subject to the tax on income from movable wealth. Thus, the effect of the 1923 law was merely to substitute the tax on income from movable wealth for the tax on income from landowning as regards income from the exploitation of the surface, when that income did not arise from land devoted to agriculture but from land devoted to the exercise of activity connected with the exploitation of the subsurface. Even after that law, however, no further tax was imposed on income from the land, either from exploitation of the surface or from exploitation of the subsurface, if the tax on income from landowning had been paid.
[5] Comm. Centr. 9 February 1928, n. 82469.
[6] Comm. Centr. 7 July 1936, n. 90523.
[7] R. D. L. 22 September 1932, n. 1346.

raw state or as a manufactured product, or when sulfur is produced on the mainland. The single fee applies also to the processing required to separate the sulfur from slag.[8] A holder of a concession who grants the right to work the mine to another remains subject to the special treatment.[9] The Italian Sulfur Agency (*Ente Zolfi Italiani*), formed for the sale of Italian sulfur, is subject to the payment of an annual fee (*quota di abbonamento*) in substitution for all taxes except the provincial and communal surtaxes, insofar as they are taken into account in the rural cadaster.[10]

The National Petroleum Agency (*Ente Nazionale Idrocarburi*, or ENI) also pays an annual fee in substitution for all taxes, including the tax on income from movable wealth.[11]

10/1.2 Cost of Acquiring Mineral Rights or Concessions

Fees paid periodically for the grant of a concession to extract minerals are deductible from gross income whether set as a fixed amount or measured by production or gross receipts.[12] If a single payment is made for a concession to be exploited over a period of years, it may be amortized over the period of exploitation (7/3.9).

10/1.3 Expenses of Exploration, Extraction, and Development

Amounts which a mining company pays out for underground research are not regarded as capital expenditures but as expenses of production, and they are therefore deductible from income subject to the tax on income from movable wealth.[13] It appears that such amounts are deductible in the year in which they are actually sustained, under the general rules presently applicable to the deduction of expenses for research (7/2.15).[14] Expenditures for the purchase or construction of fixed assets, however, must be depreciated under the provisions discussed at 10/1.5. Expenditures for the shoring up and lining of shafts are considered as deductible expenses of production rather than as capital ex-

---

[8] Comm. Centr., Sez. III, 21 July 1941, n. 44759 (*Riv. leg. fisc.*, 1942, n. 16498).

[9] Comm. Centr., Sez. un., 6 February 1956, n. 78639 (*Riv. leg. fisc.*, 1956, n. 23575).

[10] R. D. L. 5 July 1934, n. 1128, arts. 1, 4; R. D. 28 September 1934, n. 1591; D.P.R. 1 August 1957, n. 649. See Vizzini, *Fabbricati e terreni nell'imposizione diretta erariale* 263-265.

[11] L. 10 February 1953, n. 136, art. 26.

[12] See Giannetta, Scandale, and Sessa, *Teoria e tecnica nell'accertamento del reddito mobiliare* 432.

[13] Comm. Centr., Sez. un., 26 July 1933, n. 53445; Comm. Centr., Sez. II, 9 June 1948, n. 98766. See Traina-Portanova, *Spese e passività deducibili nell'imposta di ricchezza mobile* 47-49.

[14] See also Comm. Centr., Sez. II, 14 June 1948, n. 98897; and Giannetta, Scandale, and Sessa, *Teoria e tecnica nell'accertamento del reddito mobiliare* 402.

penditures, whether required to facilitate the immediate extraction of minerals or incurred in furthering the orderly development of the working of the mine.[15]

The expenses of carrying on the mining operation, including the costs of the working or exploitation of the mine (for example, extraction, transportation, removal of water, ventilation, safety, and refilling) are deductible as expenses of the production of income under the rules discussed at 7/2.[16] Interest charges incurred in the production of income by the mining enterprise are deductible under the rules discussed at 7/2.5.

Expenses for restoring the surface to its former condition after excavation are considered as expenses of the production of income from the excavation itself and are therefore deductible in determining income from movable wealth.[17]

10/1.4 Depletion

No allowance is granted for depletion of mineral resources. However, the fee paid for the concession to extract mineral resources may be considered as allocable in part to the cost of the deposits themselves, and the allowance of a deduction for this fee (10/1.2) may therefore be considered as in the nature of a depletion allowance. Moreover, the tax administration recognizes in principle that the value of quarries should be depreciable since the land on which they are located will not be susceptible of further agricultural or industrial use.[18]

10/1.5 Depreciation of Physical Assets

The table of rates of amortization and depreciation (7/3.5) lists seven classes of industries for extraction of minerals.[19]

1. Iron ore and of ores of nonferrous metals.
2. Sulfur.
3. Fossil fuels.
4. Liquid and gaseous fuels.
5. Marble and similar stones, building stone, limestone, marl, and other stones.
6. Sand pits, gravel pits, and rubble pits.
7. Rock salt, natural salt springs, and the production of salt from sea water and by evaporation.

In each class, separate rates are provided for buildings and other structures; tunnels and shafts (excluding shorings and linings, deductible as

---

[15] See Traina-Portanova, *Spese e passività deducibili nell'imposta di ricchezza mobile* 49.

[16] See Giannetta, Scandale, and Sessa, *Teoria e tecnica nell'accertamento del reddito mobiliare* 402.

[17] Comm. Centr., Sez. un., 16 December 1931, n. 31938, n. 31939.

[18] *Verb. conf.* May 1958, De Angelis, Potenza, and Testa, *Testo unico delle leggi sulle imposte dirette* 536.

[19] C. M. 1 March 1957, n. 350620 (Annex), Group IV.

expenses of production as explained at 10/1.3); generic plant above ground; specific plant above ground; specific plant below ground; furnaces and their appurtenances; miscellaneous small equipment, including laboratory equipment and devices for exploration, office furniture and machines, and vehicles. The allowance for depreciation is governed by the rules described at 7/3.

10/2.   Agriculture and Forestry

10/2.1   In General

All Italian land fit for agricultural production is presumed to give rise to income, measured by the average ordinary income obtainable from the land, net of expenses and losses, determined cadastrally.[20] That part of the average ordinary income which can be considered as the share of the landowner as such, or of the owner of a property right in the land, is subject to the tax on income from landowning (10/2.2). The landowner or owner of a property right in the land (9/4.1) is subject to the tax whether or not the land is in fact used for agriculture, and actual income which he may derive from the land either by farming it himself or by leasing it to others is disregarded. That part of the average ordinary income which is attributable to the circulating capital and directive labor of an agricultural enterprise carried on by the landowner or by the owner of a property right in the land is subject to the tax on agrarian income (10/2.3). If the owner of the land or of a property right therein leases the land to a tenant, the income derived by the tenant from the exercise of an agricultural enterprise on the land is subject to the tax on income from movable wealth under the rules explained at 10/2.4.

No person other than the owner of land or of a property right therein can be subject to the tax on income from landowning or the tax on agrarian income. Actual rental income derived from the subletting of agricultural land by a person other than the owner of the land or of a property right therein is taxed as business income under the tax on income from movable wealth (7/1.2a, 9/4.3).

The fact that a taxpayer resides outside Italy does not affect his liability for the tax on income from landowning on Italian land which he owns or in which he has a property right, or his liability for the tax on agrarian income or for the tax on income from movable wealth on income derived from carrying on an agricultural enterprise on Italian land (11/1). The taxes on income from landowning and agrarian income do not apply to

---

20 For discussion of the merits of the cadastral method of assessment of agricultural income, see Einaudi, "Discutendo con Fasiani e Griziotti di connotati dello Stato e di catasto ed imposta fondiaria," *RDFSF*, 1943, I, 178 (with reply by Griziotti); Einaudi, *La terra e l'imposta* (vol. 2 of *Scritti di economia e di finanza*), reviewed by Griziotti in *RDFSF*, 1943, I, 48.

land situated outside Italy, but income derived from the exercise of an
agricultural enterprise abroad or from the renting of agricultural land
situated abroad might conceivably be subjected to the tax on income from
movable wealth through the application of the rules discussed at 11/2.1.

The cadastral income from landowning and the cadastral agrarian
income are expressed in 1938 lire and are multiplied by the revaluation
coefficient of 12 (12/1.1, 12/1.2). The resulting figures, further revalued
in accordance with the coefficients of variation fixed annually by the
Minister of Finance in relation to the market prices of agricultural products and their means of production (12/1.5a), are included in aggregate
income for purposes of the complementary tax (art. 135) (6/1.1f) or the
corporation tax (art. 148) (6/1.1g). When income from an agricultural
enterprise is subject to the tax on income from movable wealth, it is included in aggregate income for the complementary tax or the corporation
tax in the same manner as any other income from movable wealth of
category B (7/1.1).

10/2.2 Tax on Income from Landowning

a. BASIS. The presumed income from lands fit for agricultural production, not constituting appurtenances to urban buildings and not devoted
exclusively to gratuitous public services or to the exercise of specific
business activities, is subject to the tax on income from landowning
(*imposta sul reddito dominicale dei terreni*) if the income, assessed as
explained at 10/2.2d and multiplied by 12 (12/1.1), exceeds L. 600 (art.
49).[21]

Rural structures and portions of rural structures, with their appurtenances, are excluded from the basis of the tax on income from buildings
(9/4.2) if they belong to the owner of the land they serve and are devoted
to any of the uses listed below (art. 71).

1. The habitation of persons employed in the manual cultivation of the
   land, in the custody of the estates, animals, and rural buildings, or in the
   supervision of agricultural workers, and of dependent members of their
   families living with them.
2. Shelter for animals used for the cultivation of the lands or sustained by
   the lands.
3. The keeping of machines, implements, and other supplies needed for
   cultivation.
4. The storing, processing, or transforming of agrarian products, to the
   extent that these activities are included in the normal exercise of agriculture according to the techniques which govern it.

Such buildings are included in the rural cadaster, but the income attributable to them is exempt from the tax on income from landowning [22] be-

---

[21] As modified by L. 28 July 1961, n. 838, arts. 1, 2.
[22] R. D. 8 October 1931, n. 1572, art. 16. The purpose of this relief is to favor
the development of agriculture.

cause the buildings serve the farm and thus are not capable of producing an income independent of that resulting from the cultivation of the farm.[23] Apparently, the exemption does not derive from the fact that the income of the building is already included in the income from landowning because the exemption applies even if the building is not situated on the land which it serves.[24] Income from areas or buildings on agricultural land which are used for production outside the normal scope of agriculture is subject to the tax on income from movable wealth (9/4.1, 10/1.1, 10/2.3a). Income from buildings used neither for agriculture nor for industrial purposes is subject to the tax on income from buildings (9/4.2a).

b. PERSONS SUBJECT. As is explained at 9/4.1, property rights (*diritti reali*) must be distinguished from other kinds of rights affecting property, such as those arising under a lease or other contract. It is the possession of land by virtue of a property right—the most important for purposes of agricultural land are ownership, usufruct, and emphyteusis (9/4.1)—which forms the basis of the tax on income from landowning (art. 49).

If a property right is held jointly by two or more persons, all are jointly and severally liable for payment of the tax (art. 50). When there are several rights which confer possession of the same land, each possessor is liable for that share of the tax which is attributable to the part of the taxable income corresponding to his right, and he is not liable for any of the tax due from the other possessors (art. 50).

The possessors of rights in property are determined exclusively on the basis of the cadastral register as of 31 August of the preceding year (art. 51). However, the service of a notice of imposition on a person inscribed in the cadastral register is not effective against the actual holder of a property right if the latter is not responsible for the incorrectness of the cadastral entry (art. 51). Requests for annotation (*voltura*) of transferred property are made on stamped paper furnished by the cadastral administration and filed with the Registry Office, together with the documents to be registered.[25] Changes appearing in cadastral annotations do not give rise to supplemental inscriptions or to relief from tax unless one of the parties involved in the annotation is exempt from tax. Relief from tax is given to the person inscribed prior to the change (art. 51).

c. CADASTRAL REGISTER AND SCHEDULE OF ESTIMATED VALUES. The taxable income is that part of the average ordinary income obtainable from the land which can be considered as the share of the proprietor or landowner as such, net of expenses and losses (art. 52). It is determined by the

---

[23] See Rumboldt, *Le imposte fondiarie* 155 *et seq.*
[24] Comm. Centr. 16 April 1901, n. 80390.
[25] R. D. 8 October 1931, n. 1572, art. 55.

application of the schedule of estimated values established according to
the rules of the cadastral law (art. 52).

For this purpose, the agricultural land of Italy has been divided into
cadastral units (*particelle*), each of which comprises a continuous piece
of land or a building, situated in the same commune, belonging to the
same owner, of the same kind or class, and having the same use.[26] The
various holdings and cadastral units of each commune are shown on a
map. The lands of each commune are distinguished according to the
kind of cultivation or crop (*qualificazione*) and the grade of productivity
(*classificazione*). Each unit is then given a designation (*classamento*)
according to its kind of cultivation and its grade of productivity. Each
unit is considered by itself, without regard to its connection to other
units, to industrial operations carried on, or to personal relations of the
owner.[27]

For each commune, a schedule of estimated values (*tariffa d'estimo*)
is drawn up, which expresses in legal money the taxable income of a
hectare of land of each kind and grade.[28] The average ordinary quantities
of products and of means of production are determined for the methods
of cultivation which are judged ordinary for that commune at the time
of the assessment, and for a period of years sufficient to take account of
the ordinary vicissitudes of production, excluding maxima and minima
attributable to extraordinary causes.[29] For each grade of each of the
principal types of products of the commune are determined the gross
salable product produced by a standard parcel or cadastral unit (*parti-
cella tipo*), and the quantities of the means of production required to
produce that quantity of the product in a standard agricultural enterprise
are then determined.[30] In computing the net income of the standard
cadastral unit, the quantities of products and of means of production are
valued by reference to the average of current prices in the period between
1 January 1937 and the end of the revision of the schedule of estimates
which was provided by the 1939 law regarding the establishment of the
new cadaster.[31]

The income of each farm consists of the sum of the incomes of its
cadastral units, as determined by comparison with the standard units of
the commune. Lands devoted to recreation, or to cultivation requiring

[26] R. D. 8 October 1931, n. 1572, art. 2.
[27] R. D. 8 October 1931, n. 1572, art. 15.
[28] R. D. 8 October 1931, n. 1572, arts. 12, 13. A hectare is 10,000 square meters
or 2.471 acres.
[29] D. L. 4 April 1939, n. 589, art. 2.
[30] See Berliri, *Il testo unico delle imposte dirette* 120; Vizzini, *Fabbricati e terreni
nell'imposizione diretta erariale* 212-213; Einaudi and Répaci, *Il sistema tributario
italiano* (6th ed., 1958) 111-113.
[31] D. L. 4 April 1939, n. 589, art. 2. The revision is regarded as having been
completed on 31 December 1939. See Vizzini, *Fabbricati e terreni nell'imposizione
diretta erariale* 230.

special equipment for shelter or heating, or otherwise withdrawn from ordinary cultivation for some other use and not accessory to rural buildings are valued by comparison to the best contiguous lands.[32]

d. DETERMINATION OF TAXABLE INCOME. In determining the income from landowning of the standard cadastral units, the starting point is the gross salable product—that is, the total product less that part which is employed or consumed as a means of production, such as fertilizer, seeds, or fodder for animals. From the value of the gross salable product are deducted the "expenses of production" listed below.[33]

1. Expenses for materials and services purchased outside the enterprise.
2. Average annual expenses for maintenance and insurance of capital equipment, and depreciation thereon.
3. Compensation for manual labor.[34]
4. Compensation for work of direction, overseeing, and administration, relative to the management of the enterprise.
5. Interest on the fixed capital of the enterprise for the year, and interest on the circulating capital for six months, at 6%.[35]

The resulting amount is called the gross income of the land capital (*capitale fondiario*). To arrive at income from landowning, the following deductions relative to the land capital are made.[36]

1. The annual average expenses of maintaining land capital and the depreciation of those parts of it which must be periodically renewed, such as plant and buildings which are neither excluded nor exempt.[37]
2. General expenses falling on the owner, as distinguished from the agricultural enterprise, such as those relating to the sale of products belonging to the owner himself, to the collection of rents, or to the preservation of the land capital.

---

[32] R. D. 8 October 1931, n. 1572, art. 18.

[33] This discussion of the determination of income from landowning is based on Vizzini, *Fabbricati e terreni nell'imposizione diretta erariale* 213 *et seq.*, which quotes an administrative instruction of 25 July 1939.

[34] Compensation for manual labor is calculated on the basis of collective labor contracts, even when manual labor furnished by the owner himself is involved (D. L. 4 April 1939, n. 589, art. 2). As a result, the manual labor of the owner of land on his own farm, or of a *colono* or *mezzadro* (10/2.3a), is not subject to any of the direct taxes, whereas the labor of an employee on the farm is subject to the tax on income from movable wealth, as in the case of any other employee (2/2.2d). See Berliri, *Il testo unico delle imposte dirette* 115. It also may be noted that remuneration paid by a business enterprise to the owner-taxpayer or members of his family is not deductible in determining income from movable wealth (7/2.3c).

[35] The circulating capital consists of the sum of the "expenses of production" included in items 1-4. The sum of item 5 and the income attributable to the directive labor of the agricultural enterprise constitutes agrarian income (10/2.3b).

[36] See Vizzini, *Fabbricati e terreni nell'imposizione diretta erariale* 224, and form reproduced at 214.

[37] Depreciation on animals, machines, and equipment is already taken into account in determining the gross income of the land capital. See item 2 above.

In general, the schedules of estimated values do not take account of expenses for permanent works of preservation, drainage, and reclamation, of expenses of irrigation, or of decreases in income resulting from the burdens imposed by military servitude.[38]

Expenses incurred in the production of income subject to the tax on income from landowning which have not been taken into account in the determination of net income subject to tax may be deducted in determining net aggregate income for the complementary tax or in determining income subject to the corporation tax (6/1.5b). For example, extraordinary expenses for the total or partial reconstruction of an asset are not presumed to have been taken into account in the determination of income from landowning, and they are therefore deductible for purposes of the complementary tax.[39]

Because of the changes in the money values of land since the last schedules of estimated values were drawn up, the income determined by these schedules is multipled by a coefficient of revaluation as explained at 12/1.1.

e. CHANGES IN PRODUCTION OR COSTS. With the exception of certain improvements for which temporary exemptions are granted (10/2.2f), the taxable income may be increased if there has been an improvement in the kind of cultivation (*qualità di coltura*) or the grade of the land, or if the burden of expenses previously borne by persons subject to the tax for the maintenance of dams, drainage, and reclamation has been transferred to the state or to other public entities (art. 54). Increases take effect from the year following that in which they occur (art. 57), except when special exemptions apply (10/2.2f). Taxable income may be decreased for the reasons listed below (art. 55).

1. Substitution for the kind of cultivation recorded in the cadastral register of another for which the taxable income is lower.
2. Diminution of the productive capacity of the land because of natural exhaustion or other events in the nature of *vis major*, whether or not there is an accompanying change in the cultivation, or because of plant diseases or insects affecting cultivation.
3. Transfer to persons subject to tax of the burden of expenses for the maintenance of dams, drainage, or reclamation which were previously borne by the state or by other public entities.

Decreases take effect from the year in which a request is filed, if the request is filed before 31 January; otherwise, they take effect from the year following the filing of the request (art. 57). Increases or decreases under these provisions must be reported to the Revenue Technical Office or to the Tax Office on or before 31 January of the year following that in

---

[38] Vizzini, *Fabbricati e terreni nell'imposizione diretta erariale* 231.
[39] Comm. Centr. 20 July 1939, n. 17681. See also Boidi, *Commento alla legge sulla imposta complementare progressiva sul reddito* 210-211.

which they occur (art. 57); failure to report an increase within the prescribed time results in the application of a penalty surcharge (art. 247) (13/7.1).

The Administration of the Cadaster and of the Revenue Technical Services has the power to determine whether or not the kind of cultivation attributed to individual lands corresponds to that actually in use and to correct the cadastral entries to secure such correspondence.[40] However, improvements (*miglioramenti*) have effect in the cadaster only after five years from the time when the owner shows that he has introduced them, without prejudice to longer exemptions accorded by special laws (10/2.2f).

The taxable income may also be modified as a result of a revision of the qualification, classification, and designation of the lands of the entire cadastral commune because of permanent changes in the condition of cultivation of the lands (art. 56).[41] Such changes take effect from the year following that in which they are entered in the cadastral register (art. 57). A new revision cannot be made unless at least 10 years have elapsed since the preceding revision (art. 56).

Agricultural land on which urban buildings have been built is removed from the rural cadaster.[42]

f. EXEMPTIONS. Permanent exemption from tax is granted for lands situated at an altitude of not less than 700 meters above sea level, lands included in the list of mountainous lands compiled by the Central Census Commission (10/2.2g),[43] and lands included in mountain reclamation zones (art. 58).

Temporary exemption from the tax is granted, under the rules listed below, for lands subjected to various improvements (art. 59).

1. Full exemption from the tax is provided for income from lands on the appropriate government list, together with their appurtenant waters in the public domain, which are reforested under the direction and control of the forestry authority. The exemption lasts for 15 years in the case of coppice (*boschi cedui*), which is cut back periodically, and for 40 years in the case of tall trees (*boschi di alto fusto*). Privately owned coppice which has been transformed into forest and maintained as such in accordance with a specific plan of reforestation and conservation approved by the Ministry of Agriculture and Forests is exempt for 25 years.

---

[40] R. D. 8 October 1931, n. 1572, art. 45.

[41] Periodic and extraordinary audits are governed by the regulations for the keeping of the cadaster. These regulations, approved by R. D. 8 December 1938, n. 2153, and by D. M. 1 March 1959, are summarized in Vizzini, *Fabbricati e terreni nell'imposizione diretta erariale* 293-298.

[42] R. D. 8 December 1938, n. 2153, art. 131.

[43] Certain communes are included in this list, either automatically or on application, under the provisions of L. 25 July 1952, n. 991, and L. 30 July 1957, n. 657. See also C. M. 25 March 1959, n. 200400; C. M. 18 December 1959, n. 84.

2. A 10-year exemption from tax is granted for lands planted with olive trees which have been regrafted in accordance with law; the exemption applies only to the extent of the difference between the income from the lands planted with olive trees and the income attributable to the same lands without olive trees.[44]

3. The increment of income resulting from new fruit cultivation is exempt for periods ranging from 5 years to 25 years, depending on the kind of fruit and the average length of time required for the new cultivation to become productive. The exemptions do not apply to new plantings which constitute ordinary renewals necessary for maintaining cultivation under normal conditions, unless they are replacements for vines destroyed or damaged by phylloxera or citrus trees destroyed or damaged by root decay or dry rot.

4. The increment of income from land reclaimed under the laws governing redevelopment (*bonifica integrale*) is exempt from the tax for 20 years.[45]

5. The increment of income attributable to land improvements not otherwise specified is exempt for 5 years.[46]

The exemptions discussed in items 1 and 2 above take effect from the year following that in which the transformations are completed and must be requested, by application to the Tax Office, on or before 31 January of that year (art. 60). Late requests take effect, for the remainder of the exemption period, from the year following that in which they are filed. The exemptions discussed in item 3 take effect from the year following that in which the change in the kind or grade of cultivation takes place (art. 60). If the change is not reported to the Revenue Technical Office or to the Tax Office on or before 31 January of the year following that in which it takes place, the benefit of the exemption is limited to the period remaining after 1 January of the year following that in which the request for exemption is filed with the Tax Office.

In connection with the five-year plan for agricultural development, exemption from the taxes, surtaxes, and additionals on income from landowning and agrarian income is granted for five years from 1 January 1962 or from 1 January of any subsequent year in which the land is allotted to, or purchased by, the taxpayer, for the lands specified below.[47]

1. Lands purchased in accordance with the decree concerning welfare for the benefit of small farm property.[48]

---

[44] By the normal operations of estimate, the Technical Offices determine the kind and grade of cultivation which could be attributed to the land if it were not devoted to the cultivation of olives.

This exemption and the exemptions described in items 4 and 5 of the list have been extended by five years for transformations and improvements made or begun in the five-year period from 1960-1961 to 1964-1965. L. 2 June 1961, n. 454, art. 37. See also C. M. 20 July 1961, n. 204210.

[45] See footnote 44 *supra*.

[46] See footnote 44 *supra*.

[47] L. 2 June 1961, n. 454, art. 28; C. M. 20 July 1961, n. 204210.

[48] D. L. 24 February 1948, n. 114, and subsequent modifications.

2. Lands allotted as the property of ex-servicemen by the *Opera Nazionale Combattenti.*[49]
3. Lands allotted by the entities of farm colonization and transformation.[50]
4. Lands allotted to agricultural workers in accordance with the Sicilian regional law concerning agrarian reform.[51]

For lands classified as mountainous,[52] the exemption runs for eight years. Request for the exemption must be made within 90 days of the date from which the exemption begins; if the request is filed late, the exemption runs from 1 January of the following year. The exemption ceases if the lands are sold before the expiration of the period for which the exemption is granted.[53]

In case of a loss of at least two thirds of the ordinary produce of an estate as a result of accidents not contemplated in the formation of the schedule of estimated values,[54] the tax administration may grant relief from the tax for the year in which the loss occurs. Such relief must be requested from the Tax Office within 30 days after the occurrence of the accident (art. 61).

In case of natural events of exceptional character which have caused the loss of at least one half of the ordinary produce of estates, the Minister of Finance is authorized to grant relief from the taxes, surtaxes, and additionals of the year in the zones affected, defined in concert with the Ministers of the Interior, of the Treasury, and of Agriculture and Forests (art. 61).[55] The inspections requisite for the implementation of this provision are provided for by the offices of the tax administration with the collaboration, where necessary, of the Provincial Inspectorates of Agriculture and the Divisional Inspectorates of Forests (art. 61).[56] Pending such inspections, the tax on income from landowning, the tax on agrarian income, and the communal and provincial surtaxes and additionals on lands may be suspended in the defined zones; payment for the

---

[49] R. D. L. 16 September 1926, n. 1606, converted in L. 16 June 1927, n. 1100.

[50] L. 31 December 1947, n. 1629; L. 12 May 1950, n. 230; L. 21 October 1950, n. 841, and subsequent modifications and supplements; L. 31 March 1955, n. 240.

[51] L. R. Sic. 27 December 1950, n. 104.

[52] L. 25 July 1952, n. 991, and subsequent modifications and supplements; R. D. 13 February 1933, n. 215, art. 44; D. P. 7 February 1951, n. 69, art. 1.

[53] Reliefs are also granted against the stamp taxes and registration and mortgage taxes on transactions connected with the formation of small farm properties.

[54] Losses due to storms, floods, landslides, or volcanic activity generally are not contemplated in the formation of the schedules of estimated values. Common or recurrent plant diseases are usually taken into account in the formation of the schedules, but relief may be granted for destruction of crops by an unusual disease. See Vizzini, *Fabbricati e terreni nell'imposizione diretta erariale* 299-304.

[55] As modified by L. 21 July 1960, n. 739, art. 9. For the application of this provision, see C. M. 9 September 1960, n. 204650.

[56] As amended by L. 21 July 1960, n. 739, art. 9.

suspended contributions is made in 24 equal bimonthly installments running from the end of the period of suspension.[57]

Certain rural buildings are exempt from the tax on income from land-owning (10/2.2a).

In the absence of special provision to the contrary, income from the exercise of an agricultural enterprise is subject to the tax on agrarian income or to the tax on income from movable wealth, even if the income attributable to the land as such is exempt from the tax on income from landowning.

g. ADMINISTRATION AND PROCEDURE. The cadastral operations are under the direction and supervision of a general technical and administrative office, in the Ministry of Finance, which conducts the survey operations, either directly or through contracts of *appalto* (8/4), and carries out the assessment operations with the assistance of the Census Commission which is established in each commune.[58] The function of the latter is to cooperate with the Administration of the Cadaster and of the Revenue Technical Services in the formation and keeping of the new cadaster of rural lands and the new urban building cadaster (9/4.2d).[59] With regard to the cadaster of agricultural lands, the Communal Census Commission examines and approves the plan of the kinds and grades of the lands in the commune (10/2.2c), and it decides in the first instance on complaints of owners regarding the listing, description, and designation of their properties and on the apportionment of shares of the estimates among co-owners; it also has the power to file with the Provincial Census Commission complaints and observations on the plan of the schedule of estimates relative to the commune.

The Provincial Census Commission examines and approves the proposed schedules of estimates for the communes within its jurisdiction, decides in the first instance on controversies arising between the Administration of the Cadaster and of the Revenue Technical Services, on the one hand, and the Communal Census Commission, on the other, in regard to the plans of the kinds and grades of lands; it also decides on appeals brought by the landowner or by the administration against decisions of first instance by the Communal Census Commission.

The Central Census Commission is the final authority for decisions as to the proper execution of the assessment operations.[60] The Commission decides on appeals forwarded by the administration on: decisions of the

---

[57] L. 21 July 1960, n. 739, art. 11. The Minister of Labor and Social Security can suspend the unified agricultural contributions for a period of one year, beginning with the date of the measure defining the affected zones.

[58] R.D. 8 October 1931, n. 1572, arts. 19, 20.

[59] L. 8 March 1943, n. 153, art. 20.

[60] R.D. 8 October 1931, n. 1572, art. 23.

Provincial Census Commission on the merits of the plans of the kinds and grades of lands and the schedules of estimates; complaints of the Provincial Census Commission as to errors in the criteria followed by the administration in the designation (*classamento*) of the lands; complaints of the administration as to errors in the criteria followed by the Provincial Census Commission in its decisions on appeals of individual taxpayers in regard to the designation of lands; and complaints of the administration, Provincial or Communal Census Commissions, and landowners, on questions of principle (*massima*) or for violation of law (*legge*).[61] At the request of the Minister of Finance or of the General Directorate of the Cadaster and of the Revenue Technical Services, the Central Census Commission also gives its opinion on any question concerning the formation and keeping of the cadaster.

Administrative resolution of any other controversy between the administration and a landowner in regard to the land cadaster, and of controversies regarding the taxes on income from landowning and agrarian income other than those which are within the competence of the administrative tax commissions (13/4.1), is committed in the first instance to the Communal Census Commission and on appeal to the Provincial Census Commission, with appeal to the Central Census Commission reserved only for questions of principle or violations of law.[62]

Protests regarding the cadastral survey and the taxes on income from landowning and agrarian income may be made after the publication of the cadastral information resulting from the designation of the lands.[63] The information is published by the Communal Census Commission, which is required to give appropriate notice of the places and times at which the information can be examined, to invite the owners to examine it and file any complaints or observations, and to give notice of any intervening changes.[64] The documents must be available for examination for 60 consecutive days, within which period those concerned must file complaints or observations—if any—either directly or through a procurator or agent. At the end of this period, all of the documents relating to the publication must be sent to the competent Cadastral Office, which examines the observations and complaints, verifies them, and makes corrections when required. The documents, including the observations and complaints, are then sent back to the Communal Census Commission, which decides on the merits, in the first instance, within the peremptory

---

[61] L. 8 March 1943, n. 153, art. 22.

[62] L. 8 March 1943, n. 153, art. 23.

[63] The publication and the protest procedures are governed by article 127 *et seq.* of R.D. 12 October 1933, n. 1539, and are described in Vizzini, *Fabbricati e terreni nell'imposizione diretta erariale* 352-360.

[64] R.D. 12 October 1933, n. 1539, art. 131, as modified by D.L. 8 April 1948, n. 514, art. 5.

time limit of 30 days from the receipt of the documents.[65] In every case, the Commission must make its decision known to those concerned by depositing it at the town hall together with the original complaints and the opinion of the cadastral expert on each; the Commission must also have notice of the deposit published within three days from the date on which the papers are returned to the Cadastral Office. Those concerned may examine the decisions, complaints, and opinions within 30 days, during which time they may appeal to the Provincial Census Commission against the decision of the Communal Commission. The Provincial Commission must decide the appeals within 30 days after they are sent to it and must return them with the decisions to the Cadastral Office.

Final decisions of the Provincial Census Commission must be communicated to those concerned during the operations of activation of the new cadaster, and those concerned may appeal to the Central Census Commission for violation of law or questions of principle within the peremptory time limit, not to be less than 30 days, fixed by the General Directorate of the Cadaster.[66]

When the cadastral operations of a district are completed, the Cadastral Office sees that the plans of the schedules are communicated to the Provincial Census Commission and that each commune receives notification of the schedules relating to it and to the adjoining communes.[67] These plans must be available for inspection in the town hall for 30 days. The landowner may appeal to the Central Census Commission only on questions of principle or for violation of law. The Cadastral Office may appeal to the Provincial Census Commission, within 30 days from the return of the complaints and decisions to the town hall, from a decision of the Communal Census Commission regarding the cadastral information resulting from the designation of the lands.[68] The cadastral administration, or the Provincial Commission or a minority thereof, may appeal to the Central Census Commission regarding the criteria followed in the various communes in the application of the kinds and classes of lands.[69] The Communal Census Commission may file complaints regarding the qualification, classification, and schedules of the commune with the Central Census Commission within 60 days from receipt of notification of the plans.[70]

When changes are made in the cadastral listing of lands or in their income, either by assessment following proper notice or ex officio, the landowners concerned must be promptly notified on a form which the

---

[65] R.D. 12 October 1933, n. 1539, art. 157.
[66] R.D. 12 October 1933, n. 1539, arts. 162, 172.
[67] R.D. 12 October 1933, n. 1539, art. 164.
[68] R.D. 12 October 1933, n. 1539, art. 158.
[69] R.D. 12 October 1933, n. 1539, art. 161.
[70] R.D. 12 October 1933, n. 1539, art. 166.

Revenue Technical Office fills out and sends to the Mayor of the commune in which the land is situated.[71] Notification is carried out by the servers or messengers of the commune under the rules governing the application of the tax on income from movable wealth (13/2.1). The owner may complain against the act of the Revenue Technical Office within 30 days of receipt of notification of the change, of the decision of the Communal Census Commission in the first instance, or of the Provincial Census Commission on appeal. Appeal to the Central Census Commission against decisions of the Provincial Census Commission on appeal is allowed only on questions of principle or for violation of law. Complaints are filed with the census commissions by the Revenue Technical Office, to which they may be given either directly, through the Mayor, or through the District Office of Direct Taxes. The Revenue Technical Office examines the complaints and makes the necessary corrections when evident material errors are involved. In all other cases, it forwards the complaints to the census commission with its own opinion, which may be set forth at the foot of the complaint.

Controversies other than those involving simple estimation of income or questions of fact may be appealed to the courts under the rules explained at 13/4.9.[72]

10/2.3 Tax on Agrarian Income

a. BASIS AND PERSONS SUBJECT. The presumed income from the exercise of an agricultural enterprise on an estate is subject to the tax on agrarian income if the person exercising the enterprise possesses the estate by virtue of ownership, usufruct, or other property right (9/4.1, 10/2.2b), if the income from landowning, assessed as explained at 10/2.2d and multiplied by 12 (12/1.1), exceeds L. 600 (art. 62).[73] The tax is owed by the possessor of the estate, with a right of recovery against his associates in the conduct of the enterprise in proportion to the income received by them (art. 63).[74] The liability of joint owners of a single right and the liability

---

[71] Protests in connection with the keeping of old and new cadasters are governed by paragraphs 231-234 of D.M. 1 March 1949 regarding the keeping of the new cadasters. The provisions are set forth in Vizzini, *Fabbricati e terreni nell'imposizione diretta erariale* 358-360.

[72] L. 20 March 1865, n. 2248, Annex E.

[73] As modified by L. 28 July 1961, n. 838, arts. 1, 2.

[74] The person who carries on an agricultural enterprise may associate himself with others for the cultivation of a farm and for the exercise of the connected activities by means of a contract of *mezzadria* with an individual *mezzadro* or a farm family, which is required to furnish its entire labor to the farm, for the purpose of dividing the profits equally or in an agreed proportion (CC art. 2141 *et seq.*); or by means of a contract of *colonia parziaria* with one or more *coloni*, who are required to furnish their labor as needed for the purpose of dividing the profits as established by agreement or by custom (CC art. 2164 *et seq.*). In both cases, the enterprise is under the direction of the grantor of the contract. Another form of association, *soccida*, has as its object the raising and exploitation of the livestock

of owners of different rights in the same land (art. 68), and the effects of cadastral registration (art. 64), are governed by the rules applicable to the tax on income from landowning (10/2.2b).

Relief from the tax for estates under lease must be requested from the Tax Office within three months from the start of the lease. If the request is filed after the expiration of the time limit, the relief applies from the date of filing (art. 67). When an estate is leased, the owner remains subject to the tax on income from landowning (10/2.2b), and the income derived by the tenant from the conduct of the agricultural enterprise is subject to the tax on income from movable wealth (10/2.4).

The tax on agrarian income applies only to that part of the presumed income from the land, within the limits of the capacity of the estate, which is attributable to the exercise of activities directed to the cultivation of the estate; to forestry; to the breeding of animals; or to the processing, transformation, or sale of agricultural products when these activities form part of the normal exercise of agriculture according to the techniques which govern it (art. 65).[75] Income derived by a landowner or possessor from processing which falls within the normal exercise of agriculture according to the techniques which govern it also is subject to the tax on agrarian income, and not to the tax on income from movable wealth, even if the processing involved has not been taken into account in the formation of the schedules of estimated values.[76]

The normal exercise of agriculture includes the raising and sale of poultry, the breeding of cattle—for the farm itself or for others—with bulls which are in the service of the farm and maintained with the products of the farm,[77] the raising and marketing of queen bees in an apiary,[78] and the raising and sale of other animals, provided the activity is carried on within the limits of the capacity of the estate. Thus, in all cases, the animals must be raised and maintained with the products of the estate;

---

of the grantor or of both parties for the purpose of sharing the increase of the stock and the profits deriving therefrom (CC art. 2170 *et seq.*). For further description of these forms of association, which must be distinguished from contracts of lease (10/2.4), see Trabucchi, *Istituzioni di diritto civile* 302-304.

[75] A person who exercises these activities is an "agricultural entrepreneur" for purposes of article 2135 of the Civil Code. With regard to the processing, transformation, and sale of agricultural products, however, the Civil Code definition does not refer to the techniques governing the normal exercise of agriculture.

[76] Comm. Centr., Sez. un., 26 May 1953, n. 48558; Comm. Centr., Sez. un., 10 November 1951, n. 29243; Comm. Centr., Sez. I, 3 May 1958, n. 4605; Cass., Sez. un., 19 January 1957, n. 127, n. 128, departing from the earlier position that income not taken into account in the formation of the schedules of estimated values of agrarian income must be considered industrial income (Cass., Sez. un., 30 October 1951, n. 2651; Cass., Sez. I, 14 April 1953, n. 962). See C.M. 21 June 1957, n. 302020.

[77] C.M. 28 June 1937, n. 6200. See also Comm. Centr., Sez. un., 10 November 1951, n. 29243; Comm. Centr., Sez. II, 25 March 1946, n. 81693.

[78] Comm. Centr., Sez. III, 11 May 1942, n. 55406.

ANALYSIS OF INCOME TAX   514

any income attributable to investment in outside resources is income from movable wealth.

Whether particular kinds of processing of products fall within the normal exercise of agriculture is a question of fact. Examples of processing which are regarded as part of the normal productive cycle of agriculture when carried on by the grower are: making wine from grapes; drying, selecting, pressing, and packing tobacco; making butter and cheese from milk; making oil from olives;[79] soaking hemp to place it in condition for sale;[80] and husking rice.[81] On the other hand, cooking tomatoes to make a concentrate,[82] making jam from grapes,[83] and making railroad ties from forest wood[84] are regarded as outside the normal productive cycle of agriculture even when carried out by the cultivator of the land. In general, the mere fact that machinery is used in processing does not remove the processing from the normal agricultural productive cycle.[85] The selling of farm products at retail is usually regarded as outside the normal agricultural activity if it involves an independent commercial venture with labor and means foreign to the cultivation itself.[86]

When processing, transformation, or sale falling within the normal exercise of agriculture is carried out by a cooperative society or other association, rather than by an individual landowner, the income is nonetheless considered to have been subjected to the tax on agrarian income and is therefore exempted from the tax on income from movable wealth under a special provision, discussed at 10/2.4. Except for this provision, income derived by a taxpayer from processing the products of a farm not owned by him is treated as industrial income, subject to the tax on income from movable wealth.

Income from the sale of produce of nonagricultural land is not subject to the tax on agrarian income. Thus, the imputed income of a garden attached to a house is included in the income of the house for purposes of the tax on buildings (2/2.4). If the house is rented, any actual income derived by the lessee from the sale of produce, net of the rent paid to the lessor, is subject to the tax on income from movable wealth. Similarly, income derived from the sale of grass cut from land bordering a highway is subject to the tax on income from movable wealth.

---

[79] C.M. 28 June 1937, n. 6200.
[80] Comm. Centr., Sez. II, 3 November 1953, n. 52908.
[81] Comm. Centr. 25 March 1958, n. 3377.
[82] C.M. 28 June 1937, n. 6200.
[83] Comm. Centr., Sez. II, 29 May 1941, n. 42054.
[84] Comm. Centr., Sez. II, 7 October 1941, n. 45437.
[85] C.M. 28 June 1937, n. 6200. See, however, Comm. Centr., Sez. II, 9 October 1951, n. 27911.
[86] Comm. Centr., Sez. I, 22 March 1950, n. 11531; Comm. Centr. 6 December 1930, n. 15070; Comm. Centr., Sez. I, 16 July 1958, n. 7744.

b. DETERMINATION OF TAXABLE INCOME. The agrarian income is that part of the income of the estate which is attributable to the capital and to the directive work employed, within the limits of the potential of the land, in the exercise of agricultural activities (art. 65). Determination of the agrarian income is based on the application, to the individual cadastral units composing the estate (10/2.2c), of the schedules of estimated values established in accordance with the rules of the cadastral law (art. 65).[87] As in the case of the tax on income from landowning (10/2.2d), the cadastral income is in 1938 lire and is multiplied by the revaluation coefficient of 12 (12/1.2).

Increases and decreases in taxable income resulting from changes in the kind of cultivation or the grade of the land, changes in taxable income through cadastral revisions, and relief on account of adverse weather conditions may be made under the rules governing similar changes for the tax on income from landowning (art. 68) (10/2.2e).

The capital employed in the exercise of the agricultural activities consists of the sum of the amounts listed below, which have been deducted from gross income of farm capital in arriving at income from landowning (10/2.2d).[88]

1. Interest, at 6% for six months, on the circulating capital of the activities, determined for the purpose of arriving at gross income of land capital as explained at 10/2.2d.
2. Interest, at 6%, on living capital stock (*capitale scorte vive*), or animals.
3. Interest, at 6%, on the value of nonliving capital stock (*capitale scorte morte*), consisting of equipment and machines.

The income attributable to the directive work employed in the agricultural activities is not the remuneration which is or would be actually paid to a manager—which is an element of cost for the enterprise—but the surplus or higher income accruing to the owner and his associates as a result of the directive labor.[89]

c. EXEMPTIONS. Certain of the exemptions and reliefs granted for the tax on income from landowning also apply to the tax on agrarian income (art. 68). These are: the permanent exemptions for lands situated at an altitude not less than 700 meters above sea level, mountainous lands included in the list compiled by the Central Census Commission, and

---

[87] The income subject to this tax was first taxed separately by R.D. 4 January 1923, n. 16, having formerly been included in the basis of the tax on income from landowning. From 1923 until 1939, agrarian income was included in income from movable wealth of category B but taxed at a reduced rate. The determination of agrarian income by the cadastral method was introduced by article 4 of D.L. 4 April 1939, n. 589. See Griziotti, *Primi elementi di scienza delle finanze* 139.

[88] See Vizzini, *Fabbricati e terreni nell'imposizione diretta erariale* 231, and tables at 214 and 233.

[89] C.M. 23 May 1944, n. 3660.

lands included in mountain reclamation zones; the reliefs provided for loss of crops (art. 68); and the exemption for lands included in the five-year plan for agricultural development (10/2.2f).[90]

d. PROTESTS AND APPEALS. Administrative resolution of controversies relating to the tax on agrarian income is divided between the census commissions (10/2.2g) and the administrative tax commissions in accordance with the rules described at 13/4.1. Controversies other than those involving simple estimation of income or questions of fact may be appealed to the courts under the rules explained at 13/4.9.

10/2.4 Income from Movable Wealth

Income derived by a tenant (*affittuario* or *conduttore*) from the exercise of an agricultural enterprise on land which he leases from another is subject to the tax on income from movable wealth (art. 81).[91] If the taxpayer so requests on his return, however, income derived from the carrying on, under lease, of activities within the normal exercise of agriculture may be determined as the amount of agrarian income from the estate, assessed cadastrally (10/2.3b), multiplied by 12 (12/1.2), and revalued in accordance with the coefficients of variation fixed annually by the Minister of Finance, for purposes of the complementary tax, in relation to the market prices of agricultural products and their means of production (art. 114) (12/1.5a). The amount so determined takes the place of the normal assessment of income from movable wealth from that source.

Income derived from the conduct of an agricultural enterprise which is subject to the tax on income from movable wealth is normally taxed in category B. However, income derived from an agrarian leasehold may be taxed in category C/1, instead of category B, under the conditions listed below.[92]

1. The taxpayer cultivates the land exclusively with his own labor or the labor of his immediate family and does not make use of other laborers, paid either in money or in kind, except for brief seasonal work.
2. The capital invested in the agricultural enterprise is limited to what is needed for the size and requirements of the land and for its proper

---

[90] L. 2 June 1961, n. 454, art. 28.

[91] See also D.L. 4 April 1939, n. 589, art. 5. The leasing (*affitto* or *locazione*) of agricultural land is governed by article 1628 *et seq.* of the Civil Code, and in the case of a lease made directly to a person who cultivates the farm with his own labor or that of his family, by article 1647 *et seq.* of the Civil Code. The owner of the land remains subject to the tax on income from landowning (10/2.2b).

[92] C.M. 12 June 1946, n. 4090, continued in effect under C.M. 8 December 1959, n. 304250. These provisions are an application of the general rules, discussed at 7/1.2b, regarding the taxation of income derived by an individual from the exercise of an enterprise based predominantly on his personal labor and the labor of members of his family.

cultivation, and it does not include special machinery or equipment which permits industrial processing of the agricultural products.

3. Neither the leaseholder nor any member of his family operates dairy plants, milk dairies, cheese dairies, or herds taxable in category B under the law in force.

The benefit of these provisions is extended to collective leaseholds held by cooperatives which allot the farms to individual participants who manage them independently,[93] but not to cooperatives which furnish means of production, pay taxes, and oversee observance of conditions established by them.[94]

Income realized by a cooperative society or by an association, however formed, through the processing, transformation, or sale of agricultural products contributed by its members, not exceeding the production of the farms owned by the members or held by them under lease, or *mezzadria* or *colonia* (10/2.3a), is excluded from the tax on income from movable wealth to the extent that the activities of the society or association are included in the normal exercise of agriculture according to the techniques which govern it (art. 84). Such income is subject either to the tax on agrarian income or to the tax on income from movable wealth as income of the members. Cooperative societies which are entitled to the exclusion described above and cooperative societies furnishing services among direct cultivators are exempt from the corporation tax provided they fulfill the requirements described at 5/5.10.

An agricultural enterprise which is subject to the tax on income from movable wealth is entitled to the normal deductions from business income (7/2). The table of rates of amortization and depreciation (7/3.5) includes rates for the depreciation of assets used in agrarian and forestry industries (Group I), zootechnic industries (Group II), and industries manufacturing foodstuffs (Group V), whose income is subject to the tax on income from movable wealth.[95] Depreciation is not allowed for assets whose depreciation is considered to have been taken into account in the determination of income from landowning (10/2.2d).

10/3. Insurance

Insurance is a business activity (art. 8; CC art. 2195), and income derived from the exercise of an insurance business is subject to the tax on income from movable wealth, in category B, as business income (7/1.1). However, special exemptions from the tax on income from movable wealth are granted to certain entities of the public law furnishing provident or social security insurance as monopolies (5/5.6). Since net

---

[93] *Verb. conf.* October 1947, De Angelis, Potenza, and Testa, *Testo unico delle leggi sulle imposte dirette* 395; C.M. 9 March 1948, n. 300940.
[94] C.M. 24 May 1955, n. 72184.
[95] C.M. 1 March 1957, n. 350620 (Annex).

income of category B consists of the net aggregate result of all the taxpayer's activities producing income in category B (7/1.1), an insurance company which furnishes more than one type of insurance—both life insurance and casualty insurance, for example—may set off losses sustained on one type of insurance against profits earned on the other. Deduction of casualty losses resulting from events which have already occurred is permitted even if the amount has not been settled.[96] Amounts set aside as actuarial reserves by fixed premium or mutual life insurance companies (art. 83), and amounts transferred annually to reserves by agrarian mutual insurance associations,[97] are not subject to the tax on income from movable wealth.

Insurance companies formed as corporations or similar entities (5/2) and mutual insurance companies (5/2.6) are required to be taxed on the balance sheet basis under the rules discussed at 6/1.2b and, except in the case of legally formed and recognized provident entities and institutions (5/5.6), are subject to the corporation tax (6/1.1g).

The legal business period of a private insurance company, whether or not taxed on the balance sheet basis, is the calendar year; the balance sheet must be approved on or before 30 June of the following year except in the case of enterprises conducting reinsurance, for which the time limit may be extended to 30 November with the approval of the Ministry of Industry and Commerce (art. 276).[98] The return must be filed within one month of the approval of the balance sheet (art. 276).

Regarding the keeping of the special journal of payments made to individuals which is required of entities and enterprises taxed on the balance sheet basis (6/2.2), special provisions are applicable to payments made by insurance companies and their branches.[99]

Insurance enterprises are required to pay the tax on income from movable wealth, with a right of recovery against the recipient, on amounts payable as a result of contracts of capitalization, insurance, and life annuities (13/3.4).

10/4. Banking and Credit

10/4.1 In General

Credit firms and institutions (*aziende ed istituti di credito*) (art. 8), including Italian branches of foreign banks (11/3.5a), are subject to a number of special provisions. Banks, and other credit firms and institutions which carry on business activities (that is, speculative activities

---

[96] Comm. Centr. 9 March 1927, n. 71624. See Giannetta, Scandale, and Sessa, *Teoria e tecnica nell'accertamento del reddito mobiliare* 400; Traina-Portanova, *Spese e passività deducibili nell'imposta di ricchezza mobile* 31-32.

[97] R.D. 2 September 1919, n. 1759, art. 7.

[98] L. 10 August 1950, n. 792, art. 3.

[99] C.M. 18 February 1957, n. 350400.

apart from normal banking activities), are subject to the rules applicable
to business enterprises (art. 8) (7/1.2a). A credit firm or institution
formed as a corporation or similar entity (5/2) is subject to the provisions applicable to entities required to be taxed on the balance sheet
basis (art. 8) (6/1.2b).

Interest on securities issued by entities domiciled or resident in Italy
(11/1.6a), when taxable, is subject to the tax on income from movable
wealth in category A as income from capital (9/1.1). Interest received
by an Italian bank on securities issued by a foreign entity is apparently
not subject to the tax on income from movable wealth under present
law (11/1.6a). All other interest received by a credit firm or institution
is included in income of category B for purposes of the tax on income from
movable wealth (art. 85) if it is considered as produced in Italy under
the rules relating to business income (11/1.3). It appears, however,
that interest received by a foreign bank on a loan made in Italy but not
received through a permanent establishment in Italy, although it is not
considered as produced in Italy under the rules relating to business
income, would nonetheless be considered as produced in Italy under the
rules applicable to income of category A (11/1.6a) and be subject to
the tax on income from movable wealth in that category.[100] Gains and
losses on shares, bonds, and other interest-bearing securities, valued in
accordance with the rules discussed at 6/5.3, are taken into account
in category B as business income under the rules described at 9/8.1 and
9/8.4.

10/4.2 Exemptions and Reliefs

For all credit firms and institutions, the rate of the tax on income
from movable wealth is reduced by one half on that part of the income
which is set aside as reserves, under the law or bylaws, in excess of one
twentieth of the profits shown in the annual balance sheet (art. 90).
The corporation tax is reduced by 25% for credit firms and institutions
which are subject to it (art. 153). Credit firms and institutions are
exempt from the tax on income from movable wealth on interest derived
from loans made to regions, provinces, communes, religious welfare institutions (*opere pie*), and other public entities (art. 84).

Credit firms and institutions which furnish investment credit of not
less than a three-year duration are subject to a special annual fee (*abbonamento*) at the rate of 0.15% of the total of such credit outstanding
at the end of the business period.[101] This tax replaces: the tax on income
from movable wealth of category A on interest paid on bonds and other
interest-bearing securities having a term of not less than four years

---

[100] Comm. Centr., Sez. un., 3 February 1943, n. 65922.
[101] L. 27 July 1962, n. 1228, art. 1.

and not redeemed within four years from issue; the tax on income from movable wealth of category A on interest paid on funds furnished by the state or by persons domiciled abroad; the tax on income from movable wealth of category A on interest on certain foreign investments. It also replaces fees and indirect transaction taxes relative to such financing and to the documents by which it is effected. The stamp tax on certain documents connected with the financing of foreign investment is reduced to L. 100 for every L. 1 million or fraction thereof. For 10 years from the effective date of the new law, the rate of the new tax is reduced to 0.10% of the outstanding credits, for those institutions which are not already subject to a fee of *abbonamento* in higher measure under previous laws. Regarding the tax on income from movable wealth of category B, the law provides a special deduction for risks and losses (10/4.3). An annual return is filed with the Registry Office (10/4.4). Assessment, appeals, and other administrative matters are governed by the rules for the registration tax (15/7-15/10).

A number of institutions furnishing credit for economic development or for the expansion of certain sectors of the economy have been exempted, by special provisions, from the tax on income from movable wealth on income arising from specified credit operations.[102]   Among the most important of these institutions are the *Istituto Mobiliare Italiano* (IMI), the International Monetary Fund, the International Bank for Reconstruction and Development, the National Institution of Credit for Small Industries and Artisans, the Fund for Credit to Artisan Enterprises, and the industrial credit sections of the Bank of Sardinia and the Bank of Sicily. The Fund for the South (*Cassa per il Mezzogiorno*) (1/3.4a) pays an annual fee, based on its capital, replacing the tax on income from movable wealth, stamp, registration, and other taxes.[103] Substitution of an annual fee for the tax on income from movable wealth and certain other direct and indirect taxes is provided for a large number of other institutions of credit and financing, including regional institutions for the financing of medium-sized and small industries, certain institutions furnishing mining credit, and certain agrarian credit institutions.[104]

---

[102] See Mandò, *Imposta di ricchezza mobile* 83; Zappalà, Marionetti, and Lanza, *L'imposta sui redditi di ricchezza mobile* 203 *et seq.*

[103] L. 10 August 1950, n. 646, art. 26. Under article 21 of L. 29 July 1957, n. 634, communes, provinces, Chambers of Commerce, and other entities concerned are empowered to form associations (*consorzi*) for the purpose of favoring new industrial undertakings by the development of transport facilities, supplies of energy, and other public services. Such associations are now entitled to the tax reliefs granted to the Fund for the South under the 1950 law. L. 29 September 1962, n. 1462, art. 5.

[104] See Mandò, *Imposta di ricchezza mobile* 89. Exemption from "direct" taxes under these provisions does not, by itself, confer exemption from the corporation tax.

Exemptions which are granted for interest from loans made for specified purposes or to specified enterprises, whether or not the recipient is engaged in a credit business, are discussed at 9/1.7.

10/4.3 Deductions

Credit firms and institutions are in general subject to the rules discussed at 7/2 regarding deductions in determining net income from operations. Thus, usually, a bad debt can be deducted only when it becomes uncollectible (7/2.10). However, a recent law permits credit firms and institutions which furnish investment credit for a term of not less than three years to make a global deduction for risks and losses, not exceeding 0.4% of the total of their medium- and long-term credits outstanding at the end of the business period, in determining their income from movable wealth of category B.[105] That part of the deductible amount which exceeds the losses actually sustained on medium- and long-term credits during the business period must be inscribed in the balance sheet as a special reserve, which may be used to cover losses exceeding the global deduction allowable in subsequent years. The amount of the global deduction is halved if the reserve exceeds 5% of the outstanding credits, and the deduction is eliminated entirely if the reserve exceeds 10% of the outstanding credits. It has been held that a credit institution may deduct the tax on income from movable wealth which it has paid on behalf of a depositor but has failed to recover from the depositor through withholding (7/2.8, 13/3.4). With the exception of the rule relating to payments of interest to foreigners (art. 92), the deduction of interest charges by banks and other credit institutions is subject to the limitations described at 7/2.5.

Credit firms and institutions are subject to the tax on income from movable wealth, at a reduced rate, on income which is set aside as a reserve and which is in excess of one twentieth of the profits shown in the balance sheet (10/4.2).

10/4.4 Records and Returns

Credit firms and institutions are required to pay the tax on income from movable wealth, with the right to recover the tax from the recipient through withholding, on interest and premiums payable having the character of income from capital (13/3.4).[106] However, they are not required to list interest taxable through recovery on their own returns (art. 25) (13/1.4) or to keep the special chronological journal, normally required

---

[105] L. 27 July 1962, n. 1228, art. 2.
[106] Tax paid on behalf of the depositor but not recovered through withholding has been held to be deductible as an expense of producing income (7/2.8).

of persons subject to tax on the balance sheet basis (6/2.2), of payments
made to individuals (art. 43).

Credit firms and institutions which pay the annual fee of *abbonamento*
on investment credit of a duration of not less than three years (10/4.2)
must file with the Registry Office an annual return of the amount on
which the fee is measured.[107] The return must be filed in duplicate
within 30 days of the date on which the balance sheet was approved or
should have been approved; it must be signed by the legal representative,
by the general manager, and by the person in charge of the accounts;
and it must be accompanied by a copy of the balance sheet and the
profit and loss statement and a copy of the minutes of the decision
approving them. Payment is made in one installment within 20 days
of the filing of the return.

A credit firm or institution required to be taxed on the balance sheet
basis must attach to the annual return lists of shares purchased or sold
by it in the course of the business period, except for shares which it
purchased or sold as an intermediary (9/2.8, 13/1.4). Credit firms and
other persons participating as agents in transactions in securities also
must supply annually, for the card index of share certificates, information
regarding shares taken by them in *riporto* and then given in *riporto* to
others and regarding shares sold on time or with execution deferred
(9/2.8). Credit firms which act as agents for the distribution of profits
are subject to the duties otherwise incumbent on issuing companies with
regard to withholding from distributions (9/2.7a) and supplying information for the card index of share certificates (9/2.8).[108] Banks and credit
firms must make the withholdings and communications described in
9/2.7e for profits collected on foreign securities for distribution to owners
in Italy. The performance of these duties is subject to check by the
Service of Credit Control, upon request of the Minister of Finance.[109]

10/5. Investment Companies

Income derived by investment companies (*società finanziarie*) is, in
general, subject to tax under the rules applicable to business income
which are described in Chapter 7. Under the rules discussed at 9/2,
dividends are not included in income from movable wealth but are included in aggregate income for the corporation tax (6/1.1g). Gains and
losses on shares, bonds, and other interest-bearing securities, valued under
the rules described at 6/5.3, are taken into account in determining business income as explained at 9/8.1 and 9/8.4. However, certain public
entities furnishing credit for economic development or for the expansion

---

[107] L. 27 July 1962, n. 1228, art. 3.
[108] See L. 29 December 1962, n. 1745, arts. 6, 7, 8.
[109] L. 29 December 1962, n. 1745, art. 18.

of certain sectors of the economy are given special reliefs from the tax on income from movable wealth (10/4.2).

The corporation tax is reduced by 25% for companies and entities, other than those with prevailing state participation, which comply with the requirements listed below (art. 154).

1. During the business period, the company must have as objects in its bylaws, and must in fact carry on, no activities other than the participation in other companies or entities, the financing or technical coordination of the companies or entities in which it participates, and the dealing in, holding of, administration of, or placing of public and private securities.
2. During the business period, the corporate shares (*titoli azionari*) or shares of participation in limited liability companies held by the company must be carried on its balance sheet in an amount which is not less than 60% of the aggregate value of the assets inscribed in the balance sheet.
3. The securities held must be inscribed in the balance sheet, drawn up and made public by the company in accordance with the Civil Code and applicable special provisions, indicating separately securities issued by the same entity and having the same characteristics, their number, and the value attributed to them in the balance sheet.
4. The company must be inscribed in the appropriate register at the Service of Credit Control (art. 155).

The corporation tax is reduced by 40% for companies and entities, meeting the requirements listed above, which have prevailing state participation (art. 154).[110]

A company may not hold shares of other companies for a value higher than that of its own share capital.[111]

10/6.   Industrial Incentives
10/6.1   In General

The Italian government provides a number of tax reliefs and other economic incentives to further the industrialization and economic development of southern Italy and the islands. Besides tax incentives, the national laws relating to the industrialization of the south provide for capital grants to various classes of industries; the extension of industrial credit to finance the purchase of plant, equipment, and inventory; the possibility of government participation in share capital; and various other aids such as the reduction of freight rates, the possible expropriation of property needed for industrial development, special terms for the purchase or leasing of industrial sites from local governments, and the

---

[110] Companies and entities with prevailing state participation are carried on under the Ministry of State Participations for the purpose of financing or holding participations in other companies. The principal examples are *Istituto di Recostruzione Industriale* (IRI), *Ente Nazionale Idrocarburi* (ENI), and their respective holdings (1/3.2a).

[111] R.D.L. 25 October 1941, n. 1148, art. 5. Provisions for valuing and reporting of shares are made by articles 31-34 of R.D. 29 March 1942, n. 239.

reservation of a percentage of the supplying and processing ordered by the government administrative offices for bidding by industrial businesses operating in the south. The regional governments of Sardinia and Sicily (and of Trentino-Alto Adige in the north), in addition to other incentives supplementing those offered by the state, authorize new industrial and shipping companies based in their respective territories to issue bearer shares (9/2.8).[112]

The tax incentives provided by the state for industrial development in southern Italy are listed below.[113]

1. *Customs duties.* Exemption of building materials required for industrial factories.

2. *General tax on receipts.* Reduction by 50% for building materials and machinery required for industrial factories (14/4.6k).

3. *Tax on income from movable wealth.* Exemption for 10 years for industries (10/6.2); exemption for 10 years for income derived by an industrial enterprise from the total utilization of the products of its lands (10/6.2d); and a special allowance for income invested in agricultural or industrial development by entities required to be taxed on the balance sheet basis (10/6.3).[114]

4. *Registration and mortgage taxes.* Reduction to a small fixed fee for transfers of immovable property to be used for industrial projects, for mortgages on such land, and for other acts to which industrial enterprises are parties (4/3.3, 15/4.5b).

5. *Local tax on industry, commerce, arts, and professions.* Total or partial exemption, at the discretion of each commune (2/2.9).

6. *Local consumption and other taxes.* Total or partial exemption, at the discretion of each commune, from the consumption taxes (4/5.8) and other local taxes; and reduction by 50% of the consumption tax on electric power used to operate industrial plants (4/5.8).[115]

Exemptions from the tax on movable wealth are provided for limited periods for industries located in certain other industrial zones outside the south (10/6.4) and for new artisan enterprises and new small industries located outside the south (10/6.5). Tax exemptions and reliefs applicable to particular industries are listed at 10/6.6. Tax exemptions

---

[112] For a brief outline of these national and regional incentives, see SVIMEZ, *Measures To Promote Industrialization in Southern Italy.*

[113] Except as otherwise noted, these provisions are found in D.L.C.P.S. 14 December 1947, n. 1598 (provisions for the industrialization of southern and insular Italy), and L. 29 July 1957, n. 634 (measures for the south).

[114] Under article 26 of L. 5 January 1956, n. 1, entities and enterprises taxed on the balance sheet basis were permitted to deduct from business income subject to the tax on income from movable wealth a special allowance of 10% of the amount by which expenditures for new plants (*impianti*) installed during the tax period exceeded the depreciation allowed in the same period. The allowance, limited to 5% of the declared income, was granted for the three base years following the effective date of the law; thus, for a taxpayer using the calendar year as his tax period, the deduction would have been available for the tax periods 1957, 1958, and 1959. This allowance was not limited to investments made in the south.

[115] D.L. 6 October 1948, n. 1199; L. 24 September 1958, n. 918.

and reliefs for income derived from the granting of industrial credit
are discussed at 10/4.2.

A regional law of Sardinia provides for the refund of registration and
mortgage taxes on certain acts involving companies undertaking investment in its territory.[116] A regional law of Sicily provides for the reduction
of registration and mortgage taxes to a fixed fee on certain acts involving
companies undertaking investment in its territory. Sicily also grants: exemption for 10 years from the tax on income from movable wealth
attributable to new, enlarged, or converted plant installed on or before 31
March 1960;[117] exemption from the tax on income from movable wealth on
interest paid on bonds issued by industrial enterprises in Sicily on or
before 7 December 1963;[118] and, at the discretion of the President of the
region, an exemption for 10 years from the tax on income from movable
wealth analogous to the national exemption described at 10/6.2d.[119]
These provisions supplement, but do not replace, the reliefs granted by
national laws.

Subsidies received from the state or other public entities are exempt
from the tax on income from movable wealth provided they do not constitute a participation in production expenses or other deductible
charges (art. 83).

A general provision for the accelerated depreciation of new plants and
the enlargement, transformation, and reconstruction of existing plants is
discussed at 7/3.5a.

10/6.2 Exemption for Industrial Factories Built in the South

a. IN GENERAL. The industrial income of a technically organized industrial factory (10/6.2b) and its attached buildings, established in southern
Italy, Sardinia, Sicily, or certain other specified territories, is exempt
from the tax on income from movable wealth for 10 years from the date
of its activation.[120] The exemption originally was limited to factories
built on or before 27 January 1958, but it has been extended to apply
to factories built on or before 30 June 1965.[121] The exemption applies only
to industrial income, not to general business income.[122] It appears that

---

[116] L.R. Sard. 16 July 1954, n. 14.
[117] L.R. Sic. 20 March 1950, n. 29, art. 2.
[118] L.R. Sic. 7 December 1953, n. 61, art. 6.
[119] L.R. Sic. 7 December 1953, n. 61, art. 2.
[120] D.L.C.P.S. 14 December 1947, n. 1598, art. 3; ratified with modifications by L.
29 December 1948, n. 1482. In effect, the exemption applies in all of mainland Italy
south of Rome. See L. 29 December 1948, n. 1482, art. 5; L. 27 November 1951, n.
1611, art. 1; L. 19 March 1955, n. 105, art. 2. For earlier provisions favoring the
economic development of the south (*Mezzogiorno*), see L. 7 July 1904, n. 351; L.
15 July 1906, n. 383.
[121] L. 29 July 1957, n. 634, art. 29; C.M. 14 June 1958, n. 351000.
[122] Ministerial Note 27 August 1951, n. 351756.

the apportionment is based on gross receipts from the industrial activit as against total gross receipts.[123]

When the owner of the factory does not carry on the industrial enter prise himself but leases the factory to another enterprise, the factor and buildings normally are subject to the tax on income from building (9/4.2). Although the law does not provide for any exemption from th tax on income from buildings in such cases, the administration is per mitted to suspend application of the tax on income from buildings fo the duration of the exemption of the factory's income from the tax o income from movable wealth, assuming that the factory is not susceptibl of other use without radical transformation and thus would be exclude from the tax on income from buildings if the owner of the building carrie on the enterprise himself.[124]

Requests for the exemption must be made under the rules governin appeals before and after the formation of the rolls (13/4).[125] Thus when a notice of assessment is served, the request must be made withi 30 days of the service; when no notice of assessment has been served the request must be made within 30 days of the service of the paymen bill for the roll in which the tax has been finally inscribed. If thes time limits have expired for any year, the exemption, when granted, run from the date of the filing of the request until the expiration of 10 year from the date of activation of the factory.

Income exempt from the tax on income from movable wealth or the ta on income from buildings under the foregoing provisions must nonethe less be included in the income for the complementary tax and the cor poration tax.

The communal administrations are permitted to grant exemption fron the communal tax on industry, commerce, arts, and professions (2/2.9) t industrial factories which qualify for the 10-year exemption from the ta on income from movable wealth.[126]

b. TECHNICALLY ORGANIZED INDUSTRIAL FACTORIES. The exemption ap plies only to income of technically organized industrial factories. T be entitled to the exemption, an enterprise must have a fixed establish ment in which it employs machines and equipment for manufacturing, o for transforming or processing goods, or for performing some work on th goods which will increase their value. These requirements are not me

---

[123] For discussion of this problem, see Giannetta, Scandale, and Sessa, *Teoria* tecnica nell'accertamento del reddito mobiliare 676.

[124] C.M. 28 March 1949, n. 350670.

[125] C.M. 28 March 1949, n. 350670.

[126] L. 29 July 1957, n. 634, art. 33. Such exemption does not affect the provincial additional to this tax (2/2.9).

by trolley-bus lines and other transportation enterprises,[127] by theatres for projecting films,[128] or by hotels,[129] even if a building is fitted out with modern machinery and equipment which could not be removed without changing the nature of the building.[130] On the other hand, the transformation of goods is not required; an enterprise which processes them in some way, such as one which roasts coffee, may be entitled to the exemption,[131] and an establishment for washing and ironing clothes may be entitled to the exemption if it has the requisite industrial character by virtue of using modern machinery or apparatus.[132] An enterprise which employs fixed machinery in its operations may be classified as a technically organized factory even if it is small or of a kind traditionally regarded as artisan, as in the case of a mill for grinding cereals [133] or a bakery where there is an oven for baking bread.[134] Decisions made under earlier laws relating to the industrialization of the south also may be useful in construing the present law on this point.[135]

The exemption applies to income from attached structures, which are united with, or adjacent to, the factory or in some manner necessary to the purposes of the industry, as in the case of offices for the direction and management of the factory or lodgings for watchmen; but living quarters for managers and administrative employees ordinarily would not be regarded as necessary to the purposes of an industry.[136] Whether attached structures are necessary for the purposes of the industry is determined case by case.[137]

C. FACTORIES WHICH ARE EXPANDED, CONVERTED, REACTIVATED, OR TRANS-FERRED. If a technically organized factory already existing in the territories for which the exemption is available is expanded, converted, or reactivated within the prescribed period (10/6.2a), the income deriving from the expansion, conversion, or reactivation is exempt from the tax on income from movable wealth for 10 years from the effective date of

---

[127] Comm. Centr., Sez. II, 14 January 1956, n. 77795; Comm. Centr., Sez. I, 10 December 1956, n. 87343.

[128] Comm. Centr., Sez. II, 8 May 1957, n. 93217.

[129] Comm. Centr. 21 May 1957, n. 93814.

[130] Comm. Centr. 29 December 1958, n. 11245.

[131] Comm. Centr., Sez. I, 7 June 1955, n. 72790; Comm. Centr., Sez. I, 26 October 1955, n. 75334.

[132] Comm. Centr., Sez. II, 15 January 1957, n. 88246.

[133] Comm. Centr., Sez. II, 10 March 1956, n. 79929.

[134] C.M. 20 October 1955, n. 352460.

[135] C.M. 28 March 1949, n. 350670. For discussions of various decisions under earlier and present laws, see Zappalà, Marionetti, and Lanza, *L'imposta sui redditi di ricchezza mobile* 230 et seq.; SVIMEZ, *Rassegna di giurisprudenza sulle leggi per l'industrializzazione del Mezzogiorno* 55-75.

[136] C.M. 28 March 1959, n. 350670.

[137] C.M. 21 October 1949, n. 352360.

the increased capacity.[138] The income to be exempted by reason of the increased capacity is determined by comparison, from information rigorously checked by the Revenue Technical Office, of the productive potential of the factory before and after the change.[139] The proportion of the assessed income which is attributable to the increase in capacity remains constant for the 10-year period of the exemption and is applied to whatever amount is assessed as the total industrial income, even if, as a matter of fact, there is no increase in production as a result of the increased capacity.

If an enterprise which is not technically organized, such as a predominantly artisan enterprise, is given technical organization for the first time, it appears that the factory is regarded as a new plant rather than as an expanded one and that its entire industrial income is therefore entitled to the exemption.[140]

When an existing factory is reconstructed, the income attributable to the increased capacity resulting from the reconstruction is entitled to the 10-year exemption in the same manner as income attributable to expansion, conversion, or reactivation.[141] The exemption applies to income of an industrial factory transferred into the prescribed territories from other provinces, provided the transfer is authorized by the Ministry of Industry upon consultation with the Central Commission for Industry.[142] If a factory is transferred from one part of the prescribed territories to another, it is entitled only to the unexpired portion of its old exemption, and not to a new exemption. If a factory is transferred from the prescribed territories to another part of Italy, the exemption lapses.[143]

d. INCOME DERIVED FROM UTILIZATION OF AGRICULTURAL PRODUCTS. The Minister of Finance, by decree in concert with the Minister of Industry and Commerce and the Minister of Agriculture and Forests, may grant a 10-year exemption from the tax on income from movable wealth for income derived by an industrial factory from the total utilization of the products of lands purchased, taken in emphyteusis (9/4.1), or taken under a lease of more than 20 years, provided that the lands are functionally devoted to the operation of the factory in which the processing is carried on [144] and provided that they are subjected to radical transformation with

---

[138] D.L.C.P.S. 14 December 1947, n. 1598, art. 3; Comm. Centr. 12 January 1955, n. 67166.

[139] C.M. 10 April 1956, n. 350672.

[140] Comm. Centr., Sez. II, 16 June 1953, n. 49427.

[141] L. 29 December 1948, n. 1482, art. 5; C.M. 8 August 1951, n. 352150.

[142] D.L.C.P.S. 14 December 1947, n. 1598, art. 11.

[143] C.M. 28 March 1949, n. 350670.

[144] This requirement means that the entire produce of the lands must be used or processed in the factory itself; no part may be sold directly or sent to other factories for processing.

substantial investment of capital, or to reforestation.[145] The exemption
is applicable in the territories in which the Fund for the South operates.[146]
It is not restricted to income of new factories, or to the income attributable
to the increased capacity of an old factory.[147] The Tax Offices, making
use of all the elements of valuation available to them, must separate
the income derived from the use of the products of the lands in the
factory from the other income produced by the factory. The duration
of the exemption is calculated from the year in which the products
obtained from the radical transformation of the lands or from reforestation are first used.

The decree by which the exemption is granted, in which the ministers
may also grant certain reliefs from the registration and mortgage taxes
(15/4), establishes the conditions of the relief and the time limits for
their fulfillment; the right to the relief lapses if, within three months
of the end of the time limit, the fulfillment of the conditions has not been
established with attestation of the Minister of Industry and Commerce.[148]
The relief is granted provisionally by the Tax Office upon the production
of a certificate showing that a properly documented application for the
relief has been filed.

10/6.3   Allowance for Agricultural or Industrial Investment in the South

a. DIRECT INVESTMENT. For the tax periods beginning after 18 August
1957 and ending on or before 30 June 1965, an allowance for purposes of
the tax on income from movable wealth is granted to an entity required
to be taxed on the balance sheet basis or an enterprise electing to be so
taxed (6/1.2b) on income up to 50% of the annual profits declared for the
tax on income from movable wealth which are directly employed in the
execution of works of transformation or improvement of agricultural
lands, or in the construction, expansion, or reactivation of industrial
plants in the territories in which the Fund for the South operates.[149]
The total amount exempted under this provision may not exceed 50%
of the cost of the works and plants in which the investment is made.
Provided the investments are made in the prescribed territories, the

---

[145] L. 29 July 1957, n. 634, art. 37.
[146] L. 29 July 1957, n. 634, art. 37. See 10/6.3a.
[147] C.M. 14 June 1958, n. 351000.
[148] L. 29 July 1957, n. 634, art. 39.
[149] L. 29 July 1957, n. 634, art. 34. The allowance was originally granted for five
business periods commencing after 1 August 1957 but was extended to 30 June
1965 by L. 18 July 1959, n. 555. For a critical discussion of the operation of the
allowance, see Forte, "Su di alcune misure di politica fiscale per l'industrializzazione
del Sud," *Studi in onore di Achille Donato Giannini* 591.

The Fund for the South operates in Sardinia, Sicily, mainland Italy south of
Rome, and certain other territories. See L. 10 August 1950, n. 646, art. 3; L. 5
January 1955, n. 13; L. 19 March 1955, n. 105, art. 1; L. 18 July 1956, n. 760.

place where the entity or company has its fiscal domicile is immaterial.[150] The allowance applies only to income produced in the years for which the allowance is granted, not to income invested during those years but produced earlier.[151] In computing the declared income on which the allowance is calculated, income which is not taxable because it is exempt, because it is subjected to another tax or to a substitutive tax, or because it represents a distribution of profits already taxed at source, is not taken into account.

To obtain the allowance, the taxpayer must make an express request in the annual return, specifying the portion of the profits which he intends to invest in accordance with the provision. A plan of the investments, specifying the dates of beginning and completion of the works and the plan for financing them, must be attached to the return.[152] The allowance is granted on condition that the undertaking meet the criteria for the organic development of the southern economy. The allowance is applied provisionally on the basis of the return, and finally on the basis of the observance of the conditions listed below.[153]

1. The works must begin within one year, and be completed within three years, of the filing of the return.
2. The dates of the beginning and completion of the works and the total of the amounts paid in their execution must be established by certificates issued by the Revenue Technical Office.
3. The certificate must be filed with the Direct Tax Office within 60 days of the completion of the works.

If the works planned are not begun or completed within the prescribed time limits, the tax improperly exonerated is recovered within two years from the end of the prescribed three-year period, and a surcharge of 50% of the improperly exonerated tax is assessed against the taxpayer. No surcharge is imposed if the works are begun and completed within the prescribed time limits, but the allowance is denied because of failure to fulfill the formal requirements relating to the certificates.

If the taxpayer claiming the allowance is not required to be taxed on the balance sheet basis, he must make a request to be so taxed in his annual return for each year in which the allowance is claimed; if the taxpayer fails to make the request in any year, he loses the right to the allowance, and the Tax Office must proceed to recover the tax provisionally exonerated.[154] The allowance is also denied if a taxpayer who has requested taxation on the balance sheet basis fails to produce, at the request of the Tax Office, the documents required by law.[155] Since taxation on the balance sheet basis is required in order to permit a valid check

150 C.M. 14 June 1958, n. 351000.
151 C.M. 14 June 1958, n. 351000.
152 L. 29 July 1957, n. 634, art. 35.
153 L. 29 July 1957, n. 634, art. 35.
154 C.M. 14 June 1958, n. 351000.
155 C.M. 14 June 1958, n. 351000.

of the cost of the works undertaken, failure to fulfill the requirement in any year included in the period of execution of the works results in denial of the allowance for the entire investment; but after the year in which the works are completed, the taxpayer may continue to enjoy any remaining balance of the allowance even if no longer taxed on the balance sheet basis.

The income exempt under this provision is nonetheless included in income for the complementary tax or the corporation tax.

b. PARTICIPATION. The allowance described at 10/6.3a applies not only to income employed in works carried out by the investing company, but also to income invested in the form of a participation in a newly formed company or in the form of a subscription to an increase in the capital of an existing company, provided that the company in which the investment is made devotes the entire amount of the capital subscribed with the income to the realization of appropriate works, meeting the conditions prescribed for the allowance of a direct investment. The allowance is granted provisionally and is withdrawn if the participation is transferred before the works are completed.[156]   Since the total allowance for income invested in a project is limited to 50% of the cost of the project, the allowance of income invested in participation in the company which actually carries out the project is limited to that proportion of 50% of the cost of the project which the participation bears to the total capital of the company in which the investment is made, if it is a new company, or to the increase in its capital, if it is an existing company.[157]

10/6.4 Exemptions for Other Industrial Zones

Exemption from the tax on income from movable wealth has been provided for limited periods for income from factories built in certain industrial zones and for any increase in income from movable wealth resulting from the enlargement or conversion of factories in those zones. The most recent of these exemptions are listed below.

1. *Apuana industrial zone.* Exemption for 10 years for factories built, enlarged, or converted on or before 31 December 1956.[158]
2. *Province of Gorizia.* Exemption for 10 years for factories built, enlarged, or converted on or before 31 December 1957.[159]
3. *Industrial zone of Rome.* Exemption for 10 years for factories built, enlarged, or converted on or before 31 December 1956.[160]

---

[156] C.M. 14 June 1958, n. 351000.
[157] C.M. 14 June 1958, n. 351000.
[158] R.D.L. 24 July 1938, n. 1266; D.L.C.P.S. 3 April 1947, n. 372; D.L. 31 March 1948, n. 242. The territorial limits of the exemption were extended by L. 21 July 1950, n. 818.
[159] L. 1 December 1948, n. 1438.
[160] L. 6 February 1941, n. 346, art. 11; L. 4 November 1951, n. 1359.

4. *Agricultural-industrial zone of Verona.* Exemption for 10 years for factories built, enlarged, or converted on or before 3 June 1958, devoted to the preservation or processing of garden and fruit products.[161]

10/6.5 Exemption for New Artisan Enterprises and New Small Industries

a. IN GENERAL. A new artisan enterprise or new small industry which is formed in a commune with a population of less than 10,000, in an economically depressed area outside the territories in which the Fund for the South operates (10/6.5b), is exempt from direct taxes on its income for 10 years from the beginning of its activity, as evidenced by a document (*atto*) of the competent Chamber of Commerce.[162] The exemption is restricted to taxes levied specifically on the activity from which the income arises, that is, the tax on income from movable wealth and surtaxes thereon and the local tax on industry, commerce, arts, and professions (2/2.9); it does not apply to the complementary tax, the corporation tax, or the family tax (2/3, 2/4).[163]

If the enterprise owns the building in which the enterprise is carried on, the income attributable to the building is excluded from the tax on income from buildings if the building is not susceptible of other use without radical transformation (9/4.2a). If the enterprise is carried on by someone other than the owner of the building, the building is not excluded from the tax on income from buildings but is exempt from that tax by virtue of the provision under discussion, provided that the building is not susceptible of other use without radical transformation, even if it has been rented without any plant or technical equipment.[164]

Although the law itself prescribes no time limit within which an enterprise must have been formed in order to receive the exemption, the administration considers the exemption available only to enterprises formed between 18 August 1957 and 30 June 1965, by analogy with the provisions relating to new industrial factories in southern Italy (10/6.2a).[165] The procedure for filing requests for exemption is similar to that provided for the exemptions relating to the industrialization of the south (10/6.2a).[166]

The income of an artisan or of a small business is usually subject to the tax on income from movable wealth in category C/1, as income from independent work of an individual, instead of in category B, as income from business (7/1.2b).

b. TERRITORIES IN WHICH EXEMPTION MAY BE GRANTED. The exemption for income of new artisan enterprises and new small industries is limited

---

[161] D.L. 24 April 1948, n. 579.
[162] L. 29 July 1957, n. 635, art. 8.
[163] C.M. 23 January 1959, n. 350390.
[164] C.M. 5 November 1959, n. 352030.
[165] C.M. 23 January 1959, n. 350390.
[166] C.M. 23 January 1959, n. 350390. See also C.M. 28 March 1959, n. 350670.

to communes with a population of less than 10,000 in economically
depressed areas outside of the territories in which the Fund for the
South operates (10/6.2a). The designation of areas as economically
depressed is made by a Committee of Ministers instituted in connection
with the Fund for the South (10/6.3a).[167] The Committee may extend
the benefits of the exemption to enterprises formed in a commune whose
population exceeds 10,000 if the commune is located in a zone of agrarian
reform.[168] When the exemption has been granted for an enterprise formed
in a commune with less than 10,000 inhabitants, the enterprise may continue to enjoy the exemption for 10 years even if the population grows to
exceed 10,000 during the period; no further exemptions, however, may
be granted to new enterprises after that limit is reached.[169]

Territories classified as mountainous in the list compiled and kept by
the Central Census Commission,[170] and lands enclosed by such territories,
and territories included in recognized mountain reclamation zones, situated in communes with a population not exceeding 20,000 inhabitants,
are recognized by law as economically depressed, without any decision
of the Committee of Ministers.[171] An enterprise to which exemption is
granted in a commune classified as mountainous may continue to enjoy
the exemption for 10 years even if the commune is subsequently removed
from the list of mountainous territories.[172]

If an enterprise is formed after the effective date of the law in a
territory which is subsequently recognized by the Committee of Ministers
as economically depressed, it is entitled to the exemption from the date
of its formation provided that all other conditions of the law are fulfilled. If assessment has been made and the income inscribed in the rolls,
the taxpayer must file a request with the Tax Office within the time
limit prescribed for appeal against the rolls (13/4.6), starting from the
date of public notification by the commune of its recognition as an
economically depressed area.[173]

C. LIMITATIONS ON SIZE OF ENTERPRISE. For purposes of the exemption
under discussion, an industry which regularly employs not more than
100 workers is considered a small industry; in territories recognized as
mountainous by law, without decision of the Committee of Ministers
(10/6.5b), an industry which regularly employs not more than 500
workers is considered a small industry.[174] The determination of the num-

---

[167] L. 29 July 1957, n. 635, art. 8. See L. 10 August 1950, n. 646, art. 3.
[168] L. 29 July 1957, n. 635, art. 8.
[169] C.M. 23 January 1959, n. 350930.
[170] L. 30 July 1957, n. 657; C.M. 23 January 1959, n. 350390. See 10/2.2f.
[171] L. 29 July 1957, n. 635, art. 8, as modified by L. 13 June 1961, n. 526.
[172] C.M. 5 November 1959, n. 352030.
[173] C.M. 5 November 1959, n. 352030.
[174] L. 29 July 1957, n. 635, art. 8; as modified by L. 13 June 1961, n. 526.

ber of workers regularly employed is based on the capacity of the enterprise, rather than on the number actually employed at the time of the request for exemption. The legal form of the enterprise is immaterial. When exemption has been granted to an enterprise which regularly employs fewer than 100 workers, the exemption continues for 10 years unless the enterprise subsequently comes to employ regularly more than 100 workers; it is not revoked merely because the number of workers happens at some time to exceed 100.[175] Apprentices employed under the laws governing apprenticeship and employees (*impiegati*) other than workers (*operai*) are not taken into account in determining whether an industry qualifies for the exemption. Counted as workers are those who are so considered under the law or collective contract which regulates the labor relations of the industry; if no legal or contractual regulation is applicable, the Tax Office takes account of the internal regulations of the enterprise and any other elements, such as duties, holidays, pay periods, retirement, termination allowances, which may affect an employee's classification as a worker.[176]

d. INDUSTRIAL ACTIVITIES. Exemption is granted to an enterprise as a small industry only if its activity can be considered industrial activity, defined as activity regularly exercised by the employment of those plants and fixed equipment which are characteristic of industrial factories.[177] Thus, building enterprises generally are not entitled to the exemption as small industries, since, even if they operate with their own equipment and employees, which is not always the case, they move men and equipment from one job to another and therefore make no lasting contribution to the economy of the area in which a particular building site is located. In areas recognized by law as economically depressed without any decision of the Committee of Ministers (10/6.5b), however, the exemption applies also to new hotel enterprises and new enterprises conducting installations for cable transport.[178]

e. RECONSTRUCTION OR EXPANSION BY EXISTING ENTERPRISES. The exemption may be granted to an enterprise which builds a new factory to carry on the same activity as a previously existing factory which has been completely demolished by order of the public authority for reasons of safety or health, or to a newly formed enterprise which takes over the plant of a

---

[175] C.M. 23 January 1959, n. 350390.

[176] C.M. 5 November 1959, n. 352030.

[177] C.M. 10 September 1960, n. 352350. The concept of an industrial factory is similar to that which has been developed in connection with the narrower concept of "technically organized" factories under the legislation dealing with the industrialization of the south (10/6.2b).

[178] L. 29 July 1957, n. 635, art. 8, as modified by L. 13 June 1961, n. 526.

bankrupt enterprise.[179] The exemption also may be granted to the income of a new factory built by an existing enterprise which already has a factory carrying on the same activity in the same place, provided that the new factory is completely independent of the existing factory. The exemption is terminated, however, if the new factory ceases to satisfy this condition. The exemption is granted neither for income arising from the expansion, conversion, or modernization of existing factories, even if the expansion involves the execution of new works or the installation of new plants, nor for the income of enterprises or productive activities already operating elsewhere which are transferred to a territory for which the exemption is provided. The exemption is not granted to enterprises which are closed down and then reactivated for the main purpose of benefiting from the exemption.[180]

10/6.6 Incentives for Particular Industries

The industries listed below receive special exemptions.

1. *Housing.* All new buildings are exempted, for varying periods, from the tax on income from buildings, and special provisions are made for the exemption of low-cost housing (9/4.2b). Special exemptions from the tax on income from movable wealth have been made for interest on loans made to finance the construction of housing (9/1.1). Cooperative and mutual aid societies are exempt from the tax on income from movable wealth on profits paid to member-tenants to decrease rents or purchase prices.[181]

2. *Use of petroleum residues.* Income of an enterprise which makes use of the residues from the refining of petroleum is exempt from the tax on income from movable wealth, under prescribed conditions, for 10 years from the date of the activation of the enterprise.[182]

3. *Distillation of asphalt and tar.* Income of an enterprise which distills asphaltiphorous or bituminous rocks is exempt from the tax on income from movable wealth for 10 years from the date of the activation of the enterprise.[183]

4. *Export of raw tobacco.* Income of an enterprise which has as its sole purpose the exporting of raw indigenous tobacco is exempt from the tax on income from movable wealth for 5 years from the date of formation of the business.[184]

No income tax reliefs are given at present for income from ships and shipping. However, exemptions from customs duties and from the general tax on receipts are given for materials imported for the construction, rebuilding, fitting out, repair, or alteration of ships; and fuels and lubricants for merchant ships are exempt from customs duties and from

---

[179] C.M. 5 November 1959, n. 352030.
[180] C.M. 5 November 1959, n. 352030.
[181] L. 11 July 1942, n. 843, art. 3, replacing R.D. 28 April 1938, n. 1165, art. 157.
[182] R.D.L. 25 November 1926, n. 2159, art. 1.
[183] L. 27 June 1929, n. 1106, art. 1.
[184] L. 19 February 1928, n. 258.

manufacturing taxes and border surtaxes (4/5.2). Registration at fixed fee (15/6.5) and exemption from the general tax on receipts are provided for contracts for the construction, repair, and fitting out of ships, and registration at fixed fee is provided for contracts for furnishing materials for the refitting of ships by their owners.[185]

10/7.   Miscellaneous Sources

10/7.1   Lotteries, Prizes, and Awards

Winnings from *lotto* and from national lotteries are exempt from the tax on income from movable wealth [186] but are included in aggregate income for purposes of the complementary tax (6/1.1f). Prizes and winnings from other lotteries are subject to the tax on income from movable wealth in category A (art. 85) (6/1.1e); the organizers of lotteries are required to pay the tax on the winnings, with a right of recovery against the payee (13/3.4). Winnings from prize contests, games, and bets are subject to the tax on income from movable wealth in category A (art. 85), with the exception of winnings from certain contests which are subject instead to a single tax on games of skill and football pools (4/5.7).[187] Winnings on radio and television quiz shows, however, are subject to the tax on income from movable wealth in category C/1 as income from independent work.[188]

It appears that awards to scientists and artists would be excluded from the tax on income from movable wealth as capital gifts if given in recognition of work already completed but would be subject to tax in category C/1 as income from the exercise of an art or profession if the work for which they are given was undertaken for the purpose of qualifying for the awards.[189]

Regardless of their status under the tax on income from movable wealth, all winnings and prizes are subject to the complementary tax (6/1.1f).

10/7.2   Speculative Operations

Income derived from speculative operations, even if occasional, is subject to the tax on income from movable wealth in category B as business income (art. 85) (7/1.1). Taxable income from speculative operations includes capital gains (art. 81). What constitutes a speculative operation is discussed at 9/8.2.

---

[185] L. 17 July 1954, n. 522, arts. 1, 3; L. 19 July 1960, n. 764.
[186] D.L. 19 October 1938, n. 1933, art. 36; D.L.P. 27 June 1946, n. 122. The operations of the national lotteries are subject to a lottery fee (4/6.7).
[187] See L. 22 December 1951, n. 1379, modified by L. 10 March 1955, n. 110, and L. 27 May 1959, n. 358.
[188] Comm. Centr. 3 July 1959, n. 18815; Ministerial Note 24 July 1956, n. 302501.
[189] See Comm. Centr. 16 November 1960, n. 33849.

10/7.3   Scholarships and Fellowships

Scholarships (*borse di studio*) and fellowships are subject to the tax on income from movable wealth in category C/1 as income from independent work, and therefore also to the complementary tax (6/1.1f), if awarded on the basis of work undertaken for the purpose of winning them; if awarded solely in recognition of work already done independently, they are excluded as capital receipts. Scholarships paid by the state, like other state contributions and subsidies (6/1.3), are exempt from the tax on income from movable wealth unless given for work performed.[190] When taxable, scholarships paid by the government are subject to direct withholding of the tax on income from movable wealth at the rate of 8%, and to provisional withholding of the complementary tax at the rate of 1.5%, under the rules described at 13/3.3.[191]

Gratuities paid for educational purposes are deductible within the limits explained at 6/1.5f.

---

[190] See Giannetta, Scandale, and Sessa, *Teoria e tecnica nell'accertamento del reddito mobiliare* 113.

[191] Ministerial Note 31 March 1954, n. 300461, De Angelis, Potenza, and Testa, *Testo unico delle leggi sulle imposte dirette* 642.

CHAPTER 11

INTERNATIONAL ASPECTS OF INCOME TAXATION

11/1. **Introduction**

11/1.1   General Principles

11/1.2   Determination of Source of Income—In General
    a. Objective taxes
    b. Personal taxes

11/1.3   Determination of Source of Income from Business

11/1.4   Determination of Source of Income from Independent Work

11/1.5   Determination of Source of Income from Employment

11/1.6   Determination of Source of Income from Capital
    a. Interest, annuities, and pensions
    b. Dividends
    c. .Royalties
    d. Capital gains

11/2. **Taxation of Income Produced Abroad**

11/2.1   In General

11/2.2   Persons Domiciled or Resident in Italy

11/2.3   Income from Business Activities Exercised Abroad by Italian Enterprises
    a. Italian enterprises
    b. Permanent establishment abroad
    c. Apportionment of income from international transactions

11/2.4   Attribution of Payments Made to Foreign Enterprises

11/2.5   Blocked Foreign Income

11/2.6   Relief from Double Taxation

11/3. Taxation of Income of Nonresidents and Foreign Enterprises
   11/3.1 In General
   11/3.2 Individuals
      a. In general
      b. Change of residence
      c. Temporary visitors
   11/3.3 Foreign Corporations and Similar Entities
   11/3.4 Other Foreign Companies and Associations
   11/3.5 Income from Business Activities Exercised in Italy
      a. Branch or other permanent establishment in Italy
      b. Apportionment of income from international transactions
   11/3.6 Participation in Italian Enterprise
      a. Participation in a noncorporate enterprise
      b. Ownership of shares of a corporation or similar entity
   11/3.7 Shipping Income
   11/3.8 Rates of Tax
   11/3.9 Withholding at Source
   11/3.10 Restrictions on Transfer Abroad of Capital Invested in Italy and Income Therefrom

11/4. Tax Treaties
   11/4.1 Treaties in Force
   11/4.2 Taxes Covered
   11/4.3 Methods of Avoiding Double Taxation
      a. Exemption
      b. Credit for foreign taxes
   11/4.4 Definitions
      a. In general
      b. Nationality or domicile of enterprise
      c. Residence or domicile of individual
      d. Permanent establishment
   11/4.5 Industrial or Commercial Profits
      a. In general
      b. Apportionment of profits
      c. Controlled enterprises
   11/4.6 Income from Shipping and Air Transport
   11/4.7 Dividends
      a. Dividends paid by Italian corporations
      b. Dividends paid by foreign corporations

Italy

541

INTERNATIONAL ASPECTS

11/1.1

11/4.8   Interest

11/4.9   Royalties

11/4.10 Income from Immovable Property

11/4.11 Capital Gains

11/4.12 Public Salaries and Pensions

11/4.13 Private Salaries and Remuneration for Professional Services
    a. In general
    b. Services on ships and aircraft
    c. Visiting professors or teachers
    d. Students and apprentices
    e. Directors of companies

11/4.14 Private Pensions and Annuities

11/4.15 Individual Claims for Relief

11/4.16 International Administrative Cooperation

11/1. Introduction

11/1.1 General Principles

The Italian direct taxes are applicable, in general, if their bases (6/1.1a) arise in the territory of Italy (art. 6), regardless of the taxpayer's citizenship, domicile, or residence. Under this principle, known as the principle of territoriality, the taxes on income from landowning (10/2.2), agrarian income (10/2.3), and income from buildings (9/4.2) are based on the possession of immovable property in Italian territory and are payable by the owner of the land, whatever his citizenship, domicile, or residence.

Similarly, the tax on income from movable wealth is based on the production of income in Italy. However, the rules defining income which is considered produced in Italy introduce certain complications into the application of the principle of territoriality to income from movable wealth. As a result of these rules, the taxation of income derived from business activities in Italy is somewhat broader for Italian enterprises, including foreign companies based in Italy, than it is for foreign companies operating in Italy from bases abroad; Italian enterprises, including foreign companies based in Italy, are also taxed on income derived from activities abroad, under certain conditions, whereas foreign enterprises based abroad are not (11/1.3). Income of certain categories may also be taxed if payable by persons domiciled or resident in Italy (11/1.2); persons resident or domiciled in Italy are subject to tax on income produced abroad which, by virtue of an international agreement, is non-taxable in another country (11/2.2).

The complementary progressive tax, the personal tax applicable to individuals, is based on the possession of income by an individual. The tax applies to income produced in Italy, regardless of the citizenship, domicile, or residence of the taxpayer (6/1.1f, 11/3.2). If the taxpayer is resident in Italy, however, the complementary tax also applies to income produced abroad which is enjoyed by him in Italy or is non-taxable in another country by virtue of an international agreement (11/2.2).

The corporation tax is based on the possession of assets or of income by an entity formed in Italy which is required to be taxed on the balance sheet basis, or by a foreign company or association operating in Italy through a permanent establishment, even if not required to be taxed on the balance sheet basis (art. 145). In the case of a foreign company or association not required to be taxed on the balance sheet basis (6/1.2b), including a foreign corporation or a similar entity neither having its head office nor carrying on the principal activities of its enterprise in Italy (11/3.3), the application of the asset component of the tax is limited to the aggregate amount of assets devoted to operations in Italy, or in any manner employed in Italy, on 31 December of the tax period (art. 147). In the case of a foreign company or association of any type, moreover, the application of the income component of the tax is limited to income referable to the employment of assets in Italy or to a permanent establishment in Italy (art. 148) (11/3.3, 11/3.4). But the assets of a corporation or similar entity formed in Italy, or formed abroad but having its head office or carrying on the principal object of its enterprise in Italy, include assets not devoted to operations in Italy or employed in Italy; similarly, income of a corporation or similar entity which is formed in Italy includes income which is referable neither to capital employed in Italy nor to a permanent establishment in Italy.[1]

11/1.2   Determination of Source of Income—In General

a. OBJECTIVE TAXES. For purposes of the objective taxes, income is considered produced in Italy if its basis or productive source (6/1.1a) is located in Italy. The criteria for determining the location of the source of income are listed below.

1. *Location of property.* The taxes on income from landowning, agrarian income, and income from buildings are based on the possession of

---

[1] See C.M. 1 June 1955, n. 351960; Berliri, *Il testo unico delle imposte dirette* 380-381; Massimino, "Lo stabilimento permanente nel diritto fiscale nazionale ed internazionale," *RDFSF*, 1957, 201, 205. This view, which is that of the tax administration, is not accepted by all students of the subject, however. See Poli, *Imposta sulle società e imposta sulle obbligazioni* 134-136, who suggests that income produced abroad should not be subject to the corporation tax until brought into Italy.

immovable property located in Italy. These taxes do not apply to property located abroad. Income from capital guaranteed by a mortgage (*ipoteca*) on property situated in Italy is considered produced in Italy for purposes of the tax on income from movable wealth (11/1.6a).

2. *Place of exercise of activity.* Income from business (11/1.3), independent work (11/1.4), or work as an employee (11/1.5) is considered produced in Italy if the activity is exercised in Italy. Whether and to what extent a business activity is exercised in Italy depend, in part, on the status of the enterprise with respect to Italian nationality (11/1.3).

3. *Domicile or residence of payor.* The *Testo unico* contains a provision that income payable by a person domiciled or resident in Italy is considered produced in Italy (art. 82, para. 1(a)). Because of the general scheme of article 82, and because further provisions in that article otherwise would be redundant, it is understood that the provision does not apply to all categories of income but, at most, only to those which are capable of classification as income from capital, such as interest and annuities (11/1.6a) and royalties (11/1.6c).[2] But interest and royalties taxed in category B as income from business may be considered produced in Italy under this provision, even if they would not have been considered produced in Italy under the rules specifically governing business income.

Another clause of article 82 (para. 1(e)) provides that income from work rendered abroad either on behalf of the public administration or in the employment of a person domiciled or resident in Italy who does not have a distinct organization abroad with separate administration and accounting to which the compensation can be charged is considered produced in Italy (11/1.5).[3]

4. *Place of creation of obligation to pay income.* The 1877 law provided for the taxation of income inscribed at the mortgage offices in Italy or otherwise resulting from a public document (*atto publico nominativo*) made in Italy.[4] The *Testo unico* of 1958 provides that income from capital secured by a mortgage on property situated in Italy is considered produced in Italy, even if paid by persons not domiciled or resident in Italy (11/1.6a). Since no provision regarding income otherwise resulting from a public document made in Italy appears in the *Testo unico,* income resulting from such a document is subject to tax only if considered produced in Italy under some other rule.

---

[2] See Berliri, *Il testo unico delle imposte dirette* 184, n. 19. If interpreted as applying to all business income, the provision in question would also render ineffective the provision (art. 82, para. 2) which limits the taxation of income produced in Italy by enterprises formed and based abroad to income derived from activities carried on through a permanent establishment in Italy (11/1.3).

[3] Under article 3 of R.D.L. 24 August 1877, n. 4021, all salaries, pensions, and annuities paid by anyone for the account of an Italian entity were subject to tax in Italy. Salaries and other allowances paid abroad by branches having separate management were exempted by article 9 of R.D.L. 12 August 1927, n. 1463. The provision of the *Testo unico* regarding the source of income from work performed abroad preserves this restriction, but differs from prior law in making no provision for the taxation of income from independent services exercised abroad, except in the case of activity rendered on behalf of the public administration. See Berliri, *Il testo unico delle imposte dirette* 207-208.

[4] R.D.L. 24 August 1877, n. 4021, art. 3. The provision regarding income resulting from a public document was considered by some authorities to be applicable to business contracts embodied in public documents made in Italy (11/3.5a).

In general, under the rules governing the application of these criteria, income which is considered produced in Italy under one criterion would not be considered produced in another country which applied the same criterion to the same class of income. However, since the criterion for determining the source of business income of an Italian enterprise from activities exercised abroad and the criterion for determining the source of income of a foreign enterprise from activities exercised in Italy are not completely symmetrical (11/1.3), income of a foreign enterprise from activities exercised in Italy may be subject to tax in Italy, even though the base country of the enterprise, applying the criterion which Italy applies to Italian enterprises, would also tax the same income. In the case of interest received from Italy by a foreign bank without a permanent establishment in Italy (11/1.6a), royalties received by a foreign individual or enterprise from an Italian payor (11/1.6c), and income from capital secured by a mortgage on property situated in Italy (11/1.6a), the rules provide for the application of alternative criteria. As a result, income of a nonresident individual or a foreign enterprise may be subject to tax in Italy under one criterion, even though the taxpayer's base country, applying the alternative criterion which Italy applies to Italian taxpayers, would tax the same income. Thus, in Italy, as in most countries, the criteria cannot be regarded as methods of determining a single location for the source of each category or class of income, but rather as components of the definition of the country's tax jurisdiction.

There is a further provision under which income produced abroad by persons domiciled or resident in Italy is considered produced in Italy when, by virtue of an international agreement, it is not taxable in another country (art. 82) (11/2.2). The purpose of this rule is to compensate for Italy's renunciation by treaty of the taxation of the Italian income of citizens of other countries.[5] Because its application depends on the status of the taxpayer, rather than on the place where the income is actually produced, this rule is not, strictly speaking, a rule for determining the source of income, but provides an additional basis for the taxation of the income of a certain class of taxpayers.

It should be noted that although the provisions relating to the place where income from movable wealth is produced differ from the provisions in effect under the law of 1877, they reflect, for the most part, the doctrine and jurisprudence developed under the earlier provisions. Nonetheless, cases and commentary relating to the earlier provisions should now be used with caution.[6]

---

[5] See De Angelis, Potenza, and Testa, *Testo unico delle leggi sulle imposte dirette* 349; Mandò, *L'imposta di ricchezza mobile* 16.

[6] The effect of the new provisions, insofar as they differ from the prior law as interpreted in the doctrine and jurisprudence, has been discussed by Uckmar,

b. PERSONAL TAXES. Income considered produced in Italy for purposes of the objective taxes is subject automatically to the complementary tax (6/1.1f), regardless of the residence of the taxpayer (art. 133). In the case of a person resident in Italy, income produced abroad is subject to the complementary tax if "enjoyed" in Italy or exempted from tax in another country by virtue of an international agreement (11/2.2).

For purposes of the corporation tax, the source of income is irrelevant in the case of an Italian corporation or a foreign corporation having its head office or carrying on the principal activities of its enterprise in Italy (11/2.1). In the case of a foreign corporation having a permanent establishment in Italy, but neither having its head office nor carrying on the principal activities of its enterprise in Italy, income referable to capital invested in Italy or to a permanent establishment in Italy is determined as explained at 11/3.3.

11/1.3 Determination of Source of Income from Business

For purposes of the tax on income from movable wealth, the *Testo unico* provides that income derived from a business activity exercised in Italy is considered produced in Italy (art. 82). If a business enterprise operates both in Italy and abroad, the income considered to be produced in Italy is that part which is derived from activity exercised in Italy through the central office, branches, or other permanent establishments (art. 82). As a result, income derived from the exercise of a business activity in Italy by a foreign enterprise is not considered produced in Italy unless the activity is exercised through a branch or other permanent establishment in Italy (11/3.5a). In the case of an enterprise formed in Italy, however, or a company formed abroad but having its head office or the principal object of its enterprise in Italy, income derived from activities exercised abroad without a permanent establishment having separate administration and accounting is also considered produced in Italy (art. 82) (11/2.3).

Under the 1877 law, any business activity which took place in Italy was regarded as exercised in Italy;[7] in addition, if the business itself was formed in Italy, its entire activity was regarded as exercised in Italy, even if part of its activity actually took place abroad. Later, however, income produced abroad through a branch having separate management was excluded if accounts necessary for the allocation of income between the Italian enterprise and its branch were produced.[8] With the exceptions noted at 11/2.3a, this restriction is preserved in substance in the *Testo unico* of 1958. The *Testo unico* also codifies the practice under

---

"Contrasto fra alcune norme del T.U. imposte dirette e la legislazione precedente," *Dir. e prat. trib.*, 1959, I, 18.

[7] R.D.L. 24 August 1877, n. 4021, art. 3.

[8] R.D.L. 12 August 1927, n. 1463, art. 9.

ANALYSIS OF INCOME TAX

the earlier law by limiting, in effect, the concept of "business exercised in Italy" to activity exercised in Italy through the central office, branches, or other permanent establishments of an enterprise and thus excluding single or occasional transactions (11/3.5a).

Since it is the exercise of an activity which is the productive source of income from movable wealth (6/1.1a), income which is produced partly by an activity exercised in Italy and partly by an activity exercised abroad must be apportioned between the two activities whenever the income from the activity exercised abroad is not subject to tax under the foregoing rules (11/2.3c, 11/3.5b).

11/1.4 Determination of Source of Income from Independent Work

For purposes of the tax on income from movable wealth, income from independent work (8/2, 8/3), derived from an activity exercised in Italy, is considered produced in Italy (art. 82). The exercise of a professional activity in Italy includes the performance of a professional activity in Italy over a period of time, as in the case of an actor making a film; [9] whether it also includes the occasional or irregular performance of a professional activity in Italy, as in the case of a surgeon who performs a single operation, is apparently uncertain. [10] Payments made to an alien or to an Italian domiciled abroad for the exercise of an art or profession in Italy are subject to provisional withholding of the tax on income from movable wealth and the complementary tax, in accordance with the rules described at 13/3.5.

Income from independent work rendered abroad is not considered produced in Italy, except under the rules applying expressly to persons resident or domiciled in Italy (11/2.2). [11]

11/1.5 Determination of Source of Income from Employment

For purposes of the tax on income from movable wealth, income from work as an employee rendered in Italy is considered produced in Italy (art. 82). Income from work rendered abroad is considered produced in Italy if performed on behalf of the public administration (5/5.4), or in the employment (*alle dipendenze*) of a person domiciled or resident in Italy (11/2.2) who does not have a distinct organization abroad with separate administration and accounting to which the compensation can be charged (art. 82).

---

[9] Uckmar, *La tassazione degli stranieri in Italia,* Appendix, p. 14.

[10] See Uckmar, *La tassazione degli stranieri in Italia,* Appendix, p. 14; C.M. 29 December 1956, n. 303800.

[11] From the arrangement of article 82, and from article 3 of R.D.L. 24 August 1877, n. 4021, it appears that the provision governing work performed abroad on behalf of the public administration (11/1.5) does not apply to independent work.

11/1.6   Determination of Source of Income from Capital

a. INTEREST, ANNUITIES, AND PENSIONS. Interest received by a credit firm
or institution (10/4), or by any other business enterprise in the exercise
of business activities (7/1.3b), exclusive of interest on securities held,
is subject to tax in category B of income from movable wealth (9/1.1),
and is considered produced in Italy if and only if it meets the tests
provided for business income (11/1.3).[12] All other interest is considered
produced in Italy and is subject to tax in category A (9/1.1), if it is
payable by persons domiciled or resident in Italy (11/2.2) or is payable
on capital guaranteed by a mortgage (*ipoteca*) on property situated in
Italy (art. 82) (11/1.2). Annuities, pensions, and similar payments,
normally classified in category C/2 (9/3), are considered produced in
Italy if payable by persons domiciled or resident in Italy (art. 82).[13]

Interest on securities issued by a company having its office abroad is
apparently not considered produced in Italy, even if paid or received
in Italy.[14]

b. DIVIDENDS. Although dividends normally are not subject to the tax
on income from movable wealth (9/2.1), dividends received by an
Italian company on shares in a foreign company engaged in a similar
business in Italy may be regarded, in exceptional cases, as business income
produced in Italy and subjected to the tax on income from movable
wealth in category B (11/2.3b).

Dividends paid out of income considered produced in Italy for purposes of the tax on income from movable wealth, and any dividends
themselves subjected to the tax on income from movable wealth as
business income in the exceptional cases referred to above, are considered produced in Italy for purposes of the complementary tax (6/1.1f).
If a corporation formed in Italy, or having its head office or the principal
object of its enterprise in Italy, declares dividends partly out of profits
produced in Italy and partly out of profits derived from activities abroad

---

[12] It appears, however, that interest received on a loan made in Italy by a foreign
bank not having a permanent establishment in Italy may be treated as income of
category A, produced in Italy because payable by persons domiciled or resident in
Italy, rather than as business income (10/4.1).

[13] The prior law provided specifically for the taxation of interest, annuities, pensions,
and dividends paid on behalf of an entity having its office in Italy, whereas other
nonbusiness interest was covered by a general provision, similar to the present one,
regarding income payable by persons domiciled or resident in Italy. R.D.L. 24
August 1877, n. 4021, art. 3. Regarding the interpretation of these provisions, see
Uckmar, *La tassazione degli stranieri in Italia* 166-167.

[14] Cass., Sez. un., 30 August 1947, n. 1557; Comm. Centr., Sez. un., 3 February
1943, n. 65922. For decisions holding such interest subject to tax in category B
because resulting from operations connected with the banking enterprise, however,
see Comm. Centr. 22 July 1937, n. 103027; Comm. Centr. 23 June 1941, n. 46282;
and discussion in Giannetta, Scandale, and Sessa, *Teoria e tecnica nell'accertamento
del reddito mobiliare* 57.

through a branch with separate administration and accounting, it appears that the entire dividend is subject to the complementary tax. Otherwise, dividends declared out of income not considered produced in Italy are subject to the complementary tax only by virtue of the special rules applicable to persons domiciled or resident in Italy (11/2.2).

In determining the income for purposes of the corporation tax of a foreign company having a permanent establishment in Italy, dividends received on shares of a company formed in Italy, or having its head office or the principal object of its enterprise in Italy, are treated as referable to capital employed in Italy (11/3.6b).

Beginning in 1963, all distributions of profits by Italian corporations and similar entities are subject to withholding of tax under the so-called coupon tax provisions. The operation of these provisions with respect to payments to nonresident individuals and foreign companies and associations is summarized at 11/3.9; the provisions are described in detail at 9/2.7.

c. ROYALTIES. For purposes of the tax on income from movable wealth, royalties from the use of copyrights, patents, designs, trademarks, formulas, processes, and other intellectual property may be classified as income from independent work or as income from business, in accordance with the rules explained at 9/5.

When royalties are classified as income from independent work, and are not payable by a person domiciled or resident in Italy, whether or not they are considered produced in Italy depends on the application of the rules discussed at 11/1.4. When royalties are payable to a business enterprise, they are classified as income from business; and if they are not payable by a person domiciled or resident in Italy, whether or not they are considered produced in Italy depends on the application of the rules described at 11/1.3. Thus, royalties derived by an Italian enterprise from granting a foreign company the right to exploit a patented manufacturing process, or a license for the construction abroad of plants covered by patents, together with the planning of such plants, are considered produced in Italy if the studies, researches, experiments, and other work of which the processes and plants are the result are performed in Italy, or are performed abroad by the enterprise itself without having a permanent establishment with separate administration and accounting.[15]

When royalties are payable by persons domiciled or resident in Italy, they are considered produced in Italy, under the principle described at 11/1.2,[16] whether or not they would be considered produced in Italy

---

[15] See Ministerial Note 28 October 1957, n. 351830.

[16] Comm. Centr. 11 May 1959, n. 16563; see Ministerial Note 28 October 1957, n. 351830. The application of the principle to royalties has been criticized by Uckmar, *La tassazione degli stranieri in Italia*, Appendix, pp. 13, 18-21, and by Berliri, "Sulla

under the rules relating to business income or professional income. Thus, a foreign company having no permanent establishment in Italy is subject to the tax on income from movable wealth on royalties received from Italian enterprises, even though its income from other business activities exercised in Italy is not subject to tax under the rules discussed at 11/3.5.[17]

Royalties payable to aliens or to Italians domiciled abroad are subject to provisional withholding of the tax on income from movable wealth and of the complementary tax, under the rules described at 13/3.5.

d. CAPITAL GAINS. Capital gains which are subject to the tax on income from movable wealth under the rules discussed at 7/1.3d and 9/8.1 are considered produced in Italy under the rules applicable to income from business, as explained at 11/1.3. The location of the property is immaterial. Gain on the sale of shares of a foreign corporation may be considered produced in Italy under these rules.

11/2. Taxation of Income Produced Abroad

11/2.1 In General

The tax on income from landowning, the tax on agrarian income, and the tax on income from buildings are based on the possession of immovable property in Italy (11/1.1) and thus do not apply to income from the possession of immovable property abroad.[18]

Similarly, the tax on income from movable wealth applies only to income which is considered produced in Italy under the rules described at 11/1.2-11/1.6. As has been stated at 11/1.2, however, the place where income is considered to have been produced under those rules depends, in the cases listed below, on the status of the taxpayer with respect to Italian nationality (art. 82).

1. If the taxpayer is domiciled or resident in Italy, income produced abroad by him is considered produced in Italy if, by virtue of an international agreement, it is not taxable in another country (11/2.2).

---

tassazione delle redevances," *Giur. imp.*, 1959, 735, 756. See also App. Milano 11 May 1962 (*Giur. it.*, 1963, I, 2, 733), with comment by Croxatto, "Sulla tassabilità delle 'redevances' corrisposte a società straniere per la utilizzazione in Italia di beni immateriali." Treaty provisions regarding royalties are discussed at 11/4.9.

[17] See also Comm. Centr., Sez. III, 18 June 1941, n. 43071, in which a foreign enterprise which had granted an Italian enterprise the exclusive right to manufacture and sell a product in Italy was taxed on its share of the receipts from the sales made by the Italian enterprise in Italy.

[18] Under the rules stated below, however, income from the exercise of an agricultural enterprise abroad or from the renting of immovable property abroad could be subjected to the tax on income from movable wealth as business income and, even if not subject to the tax on income from movable wealth, could be included in the income of a resident for purposes of the complementary tax, under the rules explained at 11/2.2. Similarly, the value represented by immovable property situated abroad and the income therefrom could be subjected to the corporation tax.

2. If the taxpayer is an enterprise formed in Italy, or a company formed abroad with its head office or the principal object of its enterprise in Italy, its income from business activities exercised abroad is considered produced in Italy, unless those activities are carried on through a permanent establishment abroad having separate administration and accounting (11/2.3a).

Income which is subject to the tax on income from movable wealth under these provisions is also included in income for purposes of the complementary tax (11/1.1). In addition, the income of a resident for purposes of the complementary tax includes both income produced abroad which is nontaxable in another country by virtue of an international agreement and income produced abroad which is enjoyed by him in Italy (11/2.2).

For purposes of the corporation tax, capital employed abroad is taken into account in the case of a corporation or similar entity formed in Italy (5/2), or formed abroad but having its head office or carrying on the principal object of its enterprise in Italy (11/2.3a). Income which is referable neither to capital employed in Italy nor to a permanent establishment in Italy is subject to the income component of the corporation tax only in the case of a corporation or similar entity which is formed in Italy (11/1.1).

11/2.2 Persons Domiciled or Resident in Italy

Income produced abroad by a person domiciled or resident in Italy is considered to have been produced in Italy, for purposes of the tax on income from movable wealth, if, by virtue of an international agreement, it is not taxable in another country (art. 82). Under this provision would be taxed, for example, income derived by an Italian shipping company through a branch abroad, not subject to tax under the rules relating to business income (11/2.3b), if exempt from foreign tax by a treaty under the converse of one of the provisions discussed at 11/4.6.

For purposes of this provision, an individual is considered domiciled in Italy if he has established the principal seat of his affairs and interests there; he is considered resident in Italy if he has his habitual dwelling (*dimora abituale*) there (CC art. 43). It is possible to have more than one residence at a time, but not more than one domicile.[19] A wife has the same domicile as her husband unless she is legally separated from him or the husband is of unsound mind; she may, however, establish her own domicile in Italy if her husband has transferred his domicile abroad (CC art. 45). An unemancipated minor child has the same domicile as his parent or guardian; a person of unsound mind has the same domicile as his guardian (CC art. 45).

---

[19] See Trabucchi, *Istituzioni di diritto civile* 98.

The residence or domicile of a juridical person is the place where its office (*sede*) is located; if the office established by the bylaws or appearing in the register is different from the actual office, the latter may also be considered to be its office by third persons (CC art. 46). These provisions apply to personal companies (5/3) as well as to companies which are juridical persons (5/2). The nationality of a nonbusiness association is generally determined by the citizenship of its members; that of a foundation, by the location of its object or the citizenship of the beneficiaries.[20]

If an enterprise formed in Italy or a company formed abroad is domiciled or resident in Italy under these rules, income which it derives from activities exercised abroad without a permanent establishment having separate administration and accounting usually will be considered produced in Italy under the rules discussed at 11/2.3.

Domicile under these rules must be distinguished from the "fiscal domicile" described at 13/1.1d, the purpose of which is to determine for all taxpayers, wherever domiciled or resident, the proper Tax Office for the filing of returns and for other proceedings connected with assessment. Thus, one may have a fiscal domicile in Italy for that purpose without having either domicile or residence in Italy for purposes of the rules governing the taxation of income produced abroad.

For purposes of the complementary tax, the aggregate income of an individual resident in Italy includes income produced abroad which is "enjoyed" by him in Italy and income produced abroad which is nontaxable in another country by virtue of an international agreement (art. 133). Under this provision, an individual is considered resident not only if he has his habitual dwelling in Italy, but also if he has been staying in Italy for at least one year (even if not inscribed in a population register), or if he is an Italian citizen residing abroad by reason of service connected with public administration.[21] The meaning of "enjoyed" (*goduto*) includes not only expenditure for consumption but also investment in Italy. It is not certain whether income earned outside Italy, transferred to Italy, and then reinvested outside Italy would be subject to tax under this provision; but, in practice, such income generally escapes assessment for technical reasons, because banking information cannot be disclosed.

11/2.3 Income from Business Activities Exercised Abroad by Italian Enterprises

a. ITALIAN ENTERPRISES. Income derived from activities exercised abroad by a business enterprise (7/1.2a) formed in Italy, or a company formed

---

[20] See Trabucchi, *Istituzioni di diritto civile* 104.
[21] See Uckmar, *La tassazione degli stranieri in Italia* 167, 168.

abroad having its head office or the principal object of its enterprise in
Italy, is considered produced in Italy for purposes of the tax on income
from movable wealth if the activities are carried on without a permanent
establishment (*stabile organizzazione*) having separate administration
and accounting (art. 82).[22]

A business company formed abroad is subject to all provisions of
Italian law if it has its directing office (*sede della amministrazione*) or
the principal object of its enterprise in Italy (CC art. 2505) and thus
is subject to the Civil Code requirements with respect to the keeping of
books and records (6/2.1). If the company is a corporation or similar
entity, it is required to be taxed on the balance sheet basis, under the
rules described at 6/1.2b.

Regardless of its form, a company formed abroad which has its head
office or carries on the principal activities of its enterprise in Italy is
subject to the corporation tax (6/1.1g). If such a company is required
to be taxed on the balance sheet basis (6/1.2b), its taxable assets are
determined in the same manner as those of an Italian corporation; if it
is not required to be taxed on the balance sheet basis, its taxable assets
are limited to assets devoted to operations in Italy or in any way employed in Italy on 31 December of the tax period (art. 147). In either
case, its income for purposes of the corporation tax is limited to income
referable to assets employed in Italy or to a permanent establishment in
Italy (art. 148) (11/3.4).

b. PERMANENT ESTABLISHMENT ABROAD. The phrase "permanent establishment having separate administration and accounting" is apparently
intended to encompass any fixed productive organization which has
"taxable unity" (*unità imponibile*)—that is, which functions as an economic and accounting unit independently of the principal office.[23] It
should be noted that a permanent establishment abroad must have
separate administration and accounting in order to relieve the Italian
enterprise from taxation of its foreign income, whereas separate adminis-

---

[22] The provision differs from the prior law (11/1.3), as stated below.
1. It taxes income derived from activities abroad without a permanent establishment by a company having the principal object of its enterprise in Italy, even
though formed abroad and having its head office abroad.
2. It does not tax income produced abroad by an enterprise formed abroad but
having its head office in Italy if the enterprise is not conducted by a company
(*società*) but by a "private firm" (*ditta privata*).
See Uckmar, *La tassazione degli stranieri in Italia,* Appendix, p. 7.

[23] Cass., Sez. I, 14 January 1946, n. 19, held that to fulfill this requirement a
branch must have a permanent and general power of representation, enabling third
parties to enter into relations with the branch which would otherwise have to be
concluded with the principal office. See, however, Massimino, "Lo stabilimento
permanente nel diritto fiscale nazionale ed internazionale," *RDFSF,* 1957, 201, 203,
204, suggesting that the doctrine is at variance with this decision.

ration and accounting are not required in order to subject a permanent establishment of a foreign enterprise in Italy to Italian tax under the treaties for the avoidance of double taxation (11/4.4), and under Italian domestic tax law (11/3.5a).[24]

The language of the *Testo unico* seems to remove from doubt that distributions received by an Italian enterprise from a subsidiary operating abroad would not be considered produced in Italy, since a subsidiary is juridically independent of its parent.[25] On the other hand, it has been held that when an Italian company invests in shares of a foreign company which is engaged in a similar business in Italy, that part of the dividends received by the Italian company which represents income produced in Italy by the foreign company may be subjected to the tax on income from movable wealth as business income of the Italian company.[26] Presumably, however, dividends representing income already subject to the tax on income from movable wealth, because produced by a permanent establishment of the foreign company in Italy, would not again be subjected to the tax on income from movable wealth. Dividends declared by a foreign company are, in any event, included in the income of an Italian company for purposes of the corporation tax (11/1.1).

Ordinarily, a partnership formed in Italy is subject only to the objective taxes; the personal tax on the partnership income is paid by the members of the partnership (5/3.2). If one of the members of the partnership were an Italian corporation or a foreign company of any type having a permanent establishment in Italy, the profits actually distributed to it by the partnership would be subject to the corporation tax, under the rules described at 5/3.2. If one of the members of the Italian partnership were a company formed abroad having no permanent establishment in Italy, it would ordinarily not be liable for the corporation tax (11/3.6a). By administrative instructions, however, the Italian partnership itself may be subjected to the corporation tax in such a case if all the conditions listed below are established.[27]

1. The Italian partnership has been created by the foreign company or association.

---

[24] See Massimino, "Lo stabilimento permanente nel diritto fiscale nazionale ed internazionale," *RDFSF*, 1957, 201, 204.

[25] Massimino, "Lo stabilimento permanente nel diritto fiscale nazionale ed internazionale," *RDFSF*, 1957, 201, 204. The Central Commission once held, however, that dividends received by an Italian enterprise from a subsidiary operating abroad were subject to the tax on income from movable wealth under the prior law (11/1.3), whose terms provided only that income produced abroad by branches should not be taken into account. Comm. Centr., Sez. un., 12 February 1936, n. 84394.

[26] Comm. Centr., Sez. un., 15 June 1942, n. 57143; Comm. Centr., Sez. un., 27 February 1935, n. 72945; Comm. Centr. 18 October 1915, n. 73089. For discussion of this question, see Berliri, *Imposta di ricchezza mobile* 216-224.

[27] C.M. 1 June 1955, n. 351690.

2. The capital of the partnership has been predominantly supplied by th foreign company or association.

3. The Italian partnership operates as a "mere organ for the execution operations made and determined by" the foreign company or association

These instructions are based on a decision under which the former neg tiation tax (2/4.1) was applied to a foreign company which was operatin in Italy through an Italian company; [28] under the present practice, how ever, the corporation tax would be imposed on the Italian company an not on the foreign parent.

C. APPORTIONMENT OF INCOME FROM INTERNATIONAL TRANSACTION Since income from business activities exercised in Italy is considere to have been produced in Italy (11/1.3), income derived through activ ties exercised partly in Italy by the principal office and partly by branch abroad having separate administration and accounting must b apportioned between the principal office and the branch.[29] In practic this is done by estimation, employing criteria of valuation appropriat to each case.[30]

A loss sustained on activities exercised abroad by a branch or othe permanent establishment with separate administration and accountin cannot be deducted from the income from movable wealth of the princi pal office. A loss sustained on activities exercised abroad without a pe manent establishment having separate administration and accounting, o without any permanent organization abroad, would be deductible i inherent in the activity productive of income, under the principle tha in such a case, there would be no basis either for distinguishing receipt from activities abroad from receipts from activities in Italy, or for dis tinguishing expenses and charges sustained abroad from those sustaine in Italy. However, some authorities have taken the position that a los sustained on activities exercised abroad by a branch or other permanen establishment cannot be deducted from income from movable wealth whether or not the permanent establishment has separate administratio and accounting, since otherwise an Italian enterprise could determine a will, merely by failing to comply with the requirements of separat administration and accounting, whether a loss on activities exercise abroad would be deductible.[31]

---

[28] Comm. Centr., Sez. un., 5 July 1947, n. 91408.

[29] See Cass., Sez. I, 7 October 1955, n. 2887; see also Uckmar, *La tassazione deg stranieri in Italia* 191, n. 78.

[30] Massimino, "Lo stabilimento permanente nel diritto fiscale nazionale ed inter nazionale," *RDFSF*, 1957, 201, 204.

[31] See Giannetta, Scandale, and Sessa, *Teoria e tecnica nell'accertamento de reddito mobiliare* 496; Massimino, "Lo stabilimento permanente nel diritto fiscal nazionale ed internazionale," *RDFSF*, 1957, 201, 203.

1/2.4   Attribution of Payments Made to Foreign Enterprises

If a corporation or other entity required to be taxed on the balance
neet basis (6/1.2b) exercises its activities in Italy on behalf of a foreign
nterprise through the sale or disposal of raw materials or merchandise,
r through the manufacture of goods, it must include in its income any
mounts paid to the foreign enterprise in the form of a price higher than
ne current market price of the goods furnished, or in the form of broker-
ge fees, royalties, commissions, or premiums, except when such payments
re made for copyrights, patents, or similar intangibles, or for profes-
ional services and are therefore subject to provisional withholding (art.
13) (13/3.5).

1/2.5   Blocked Foreign Income

There are no provisions for postponing the taxation of income whose
ransfer to Italy or use abroad is prohibited or restricted by the laws of a
preign country.

1/2.6   Relief from Double Taxation

Apart from treaties (11/4.3) and from the normal operation of the
principle of territoriality (11/1.1), there is no provision for the relief
f double taxation. Income taxes paid abroad cannot be deducted in
letermining income from movable wealth, but are deductible in deter-
nining income subject to the complementary tax since they cannot be
ncluded in income enjoyed in Italy; foreign income subject to the
orporation tax is net of income taxes paid abroad unless Italy gives a
redit for such taxes under a treaty provision (6/1.5e).

1/3.   Taxation of Income of Nonresidents and Foreign Enterprises

1/3.1   In General

This section deals with the rules relating to the taxation of income of
persons who are neither domiciled nor resident in Italy under the rules
liscussed at 11/2.2, including foreign companies and associations which
nave neither their head offices nor the principal objects of their enterprise
n Italy.

Since the tax on income from landowning, the tax on agrarian income,
und the tax on income from buildings are completely territorial (11/1.1),
un owner of property in Italy which forms the basis of one of those
axes is subject to that tax regardless of his domicile or residence. A taxpayer who is neither domiciled nor resident in Italy is nonetheless subject
:o the tax on income from movable wealth on income which is considered
o have been produced in Italy in accordance with the rules described

at 11/1.2–11/1.6, except those which are specifically applicable only persons having Italian nationality (11/2.1). Of particular concern to ta payers of foreign nationality are the rules listed below.

1. Income of an enterprise formed abroad which has neither its hea office nor the principal object of its enterprise in Italy is considere produced in Italy only if derived from activities exercised in Ita through a branch or other permanent establishment (11/3.5).
2. Interest, annuities, and pensions (11/1.6a), royalties (11/1.6c), an certain wages and salaries (11/1.5) are considered produced in Ita if payable by persons domiciled or resident in Italy (11/1.2).

A nonresident is liable for the complementary tax on income produce in Italy (11/3.2). A foreign company or association which has neith its head office nor the principal object of its enterprise in Italy is subje to the corporation tax on capital devoted to operations in Italy or en ployed in Italy, and on income referable to such capital or to a permane establishment in Italy (11/3.3, 11/3.4). Except as provided by an inte national agreement, withholdings from profits distributable to aliens or t Italians domiciled abroad which are not subject to the complementar tax or to the corporation tax are not credited against the liability of th recipient for those taxes and thus are not refunded; the credit for witl holdings on profits payable to a foreign company or association operatin in Italy through a permanent establishment is limited to the withholding made on shares included in the taxable assets determined for purposes the corporation tax (9/2.7c, 11/3.3).

Any person who possesses income or assets subject to tax is require to file an annual return, regardless of his residence or domicile (13/1.1a The return is filed at the place where the person has his fiscal domicil under the rules described at 13/1.1d.

11/3.2 Individuals

a. IN GENERAL. An individual who is neither domiciled nor residen in Italy is subject to the objective taxes on income in the same manne as an individual domiciled or resident in Italy, with the exceptions dis cussed at 11/3.1. It should be noted, however, that an individual wh conducts in Italy a business enterprise formed abroad is not, under th *Testo unico*, subject to tax on income derived from activities exercise abroad, since the provision subjecting income derived from activitie exercised abroad to tax refers only to enterprises formed in Italy and t companies formed abroad (art. 82) (11/1.3).

An individual is subject to the complementary tax on income produce in Italy or considered produced in Italy (art. 133), regardless of hi residence or citizenship (art. 131) (11/1.2); but income produced abroa by a nonresident individual is not subject to the complementary ta even if enjoyed by him in Italy and nontaxable in another country b virtue of an international agreement (6/1.1f). An Italian citizen residing abroad by reason of service connected with public administration is considered resident in Italy for purposes of the complementary tax (11/2.2).

The exemptions available to diplomatic agents of foreign states are discussed at 5/5.1.

b. CHANGE OF RESIDENCE. If a person acquires or loses residence in Italy during the year, by adopting or abandoning a habitual dwelling there, he is subject to the complementary tax on income produced abroad but enjoyed by him in Italy, under the rules discussed at 11/2.2, although he may be able to show that the amount of income enjoyed by him in Italy is smaller than it would have been if he had resided in Italy for the entire year. It is impossible to say what apportionment, if any, could be made of income subjected to the complementary tax because nontaxable in another country by virtue of an international agreement.

c. TEMPORARY VISITORS. A temporary visitor is taxable in the same manner as a person resident or domiciled in Italy if he satisfies the tests of residence or domicile discussed at 11/2.2. A nonresident who has not established his habitual dwelling in Italy is not subject to the complementary tax on income produced abroad unless he has lived in Italy for at least one year (11/2.2).[32]

11/3.3 Foreign Corporations and Similar Entities

Any corporation or similar entity (5/2) formed abroad is subject to the objective taxes on income considered to have been produced in Italy, under the rules listed at 11/3.1. Thus, if it operates both in Italy and abroad, that part of its income which is derived from a business activity exercised in Italy through the central office, branches, or other permanent establishments is considered produced in Italy for purposes of the tax on income from movable wealth (11/3.5). However, its income derived from a business activity exercised abroad without a permanent establishment having separate administration and accounting is not subject to the tax on income from movable wealth unless the corporation has its head office or the principal object of its enterprise in Italy (art. 82) (11/2.3a).

A foreign corporation which neither has its head office nor carries on the principal activities of its enterprise in Italy is not required to be taxed on the balance sheet basis (art. 8), but may elect to be so taxed if it has one or more secondary offices with a permanent representative in Italy (art. 104) (6/1.2b).

---

[32] The *Testo unico* eliminates a provision of the prior law under which a citizen or alien who lived (*dimori*) for part of the year in Italy was subject to the complementary tax on that part of his income produced abroad which was presumed to be enjoyed by him in Italy. See R.D. 30 December 1923, n. 3062, art. 4.

ANALYSIS OF INCOME TAX

A foreign corporation which operates in Italy through a permanent establishment is subject to the corporation tax, even if it does not have its head office or carry on the principal activities of its enterprise in Italy and therefore is not required to be taxed on the balance sheet basis (art 145) (6/1.2b). The taxable assets of a foreign corporation having its head office or carrying on the principal object of its enterprise in Italy include its foreign assets (11/1.1); the taxable assets of a foreign corporation operating in Italy only through a permanent establishment are limited to the assets devoted to operations in Italy or otherwise employed in Italy in any manner on 31 December of the tax period (art. 147), since such a corporation is not required to be taxed on the balance sheet basis. However, the liability of any foreign corporation for the income component of the corporation tax is determined by reference to the receipts and expenses (6/1.1g) relating to capital devoted to operations in Italy or otherwise employed in any manner in Italy on 31 December of the tax period, or relating in any way to a permanent establishment in Italy (arts. 147, 148) (11/3.5a).

Unless otherwise provided by an international agreement, credit against the corporation tax for withholdings from distributions of profits payable to a foreign corporation operating in Italy through a permanent establishment is limited to withholdings on profits derived from shares included in the taxable assets for purposes of the corporation tax (9/2.7c). The taxation of distributions by foreign corporations is discussed at 11/1.6b.

A company formed abroad which does not have its head office or the principal object of its enterprise in Italy, but establishes one or more secondary offices there, is subject to the provisions of Italian law regarding the deposit and registration of its charter and the publication of its balance sheet and is required to publish the names and deposit the signatures of the persons who regularly represent it in Italy (CC art. 2506)

11/3.4 Other Foreign Companies and Associations

A foreign company or association which is not organized as a corporation or similar entity (5/3) is subject to the objective taxes on income considered produced in Italy, under the rules listed at 11/3.1, under the same conditions as a foreign corporation (11/3.3). However, such a company is not required to be taxed on the balance sheet basis even if it has its head office or carries on the principal activities of its enterprise in Italy, but may elect to be so taxed if it has one or more secondary offices with a permanent representative in Italy (art. 104) (6/1.2b)

If the company operates in Italy through a permanent establishment (11/3.5a), it is subject to the corporation tax on its assets employed in Italy (art. 147), and on its income referable to assets employed in Italy or to a permanent establishment in Italy (art. 148). Unless otherwise provided by an international agreement, credit for withholdings from profits payable to a foreign company or association operating in Italy through a permanent establishment is limited to withholdings on profits derived from shares included in the taxable assets for purposes of the corporation tax (9/2.7c).

A company formed abroad which has neither its head office nor the principal object of its enterprise in Italy, but establishes one or more secondary offices there, is subject to the same provisions as a foreign corporation (11/3.3) regarding registration and publication. A foreign company or association of a type different from those regulated by the Civil Code is subject to the rules applicable to corporations regarding registration and the liability of directors (CC art. 2507).

A member of the foreign company is subject to the complementary tax on his share of the company income, whether or not distributed, which is subject to the tax on income from movable wealth (5/3.2). If resident in Italy, he is also subject to the complementary tax on distributions from company income not subject to the tax on income from movable wealth which are enjoyed by him in Italy or which are nontaxable in another country by virtue of an international agreement (11/2.2).

11/3.5 Income from Business Activities Exercised in Italy

a. BRANCH OR OTHER PERMANENT ESTABLISHMENT IN ITALY. If a business enterprise operates both in Italy and abroad, the income which is considered to be produced in Italy is that part which is derived from the activity exercised in Italy through the central office, branches, or other permanent establishments (*stabili organizzazioni*) (art. 82) (11/1.3). In the absence of this provision, all income from a business activity exercised in Italy by any enterprise, wherever formed and whatever the location of its head office and the principal object of its enterprise, would be subject to the tax on income from movable wealth under the territoriality principle for business income (11/1.3). Although the language of the provision is not entirely clear, its effect is to remove from the scope of the movable wealth tax income derived from activities in Italy, not carried on through a branch or other permanent establishment there, by an enterprise formed abroad and having neither its head office nor the principal object of its enterprise in Italy.[33] It appears that an enterprise formed abroad and having its head office abroad, but having the principal object of its enterprise in Italy and therefore subject to tax on its foreign income under the

---

[33] No provision to this effect was contained in the 1877 law. With the exceptions noted below, however, the present provision represents the result reached in decisions made under the earlier law. See Uckmar, *La tassazione degli stranieri in Italia* 175; Massimino, "Lo stabilimento permanente nel diritto fiscale nazionale ed internazionale," *RDFSF*, 1957, 201, 206; Zappalà, Marionetti, and Lanza, *L'imposta sui redditi di ricchezza mobile* 65.

rules discussed at 11/2.3a, would be considered as having a permanen*
establishment in Italy. It should also be noted that certain payment
made to a foreign enterprise by an Italian corporation may be attributec
to the Italian corporation for purposes of the tax on income from movabl(
wealth (11/2.4).

A foreign company having neither its head office nor the principa
object of its enterprise in Italy and a foreign enterprise not formed as a
company are not subject to the tax on income from movable wealth or
income derived from activities abroad (11/1.3).

It appears that when applied to foreign enterprises operating in Italy
the concept of "branch or other permanent establishment" coincides with
that of "permanent establishment" used in the treaties for the avoidance
of double taxation (11/4.4d).[34] Thus, it has been held that a foreign
enterprise is subject to tax on income derived through the activities of an
agent in Italy who has the power to conclude contracts or a general power
of representation.[35] The taxation of income derived by a foreign enterprise through a permanent establishment in Italy is not conditioned or
the maintenance of separate management and accounting; if it were, the
foreign enterprise could escape taxation at will merely by neglecting to
comply with the condition.[36]

Although it had long been settled under the decisions of the courts that
a foreign enterprise could not be taxed on income from isolated sales in
Italy when the taxpayer had neither a permanent establishment nor an
agency in Italy and was not continuously exercising a productive activity
there,[37] a foreign enterprise could be taxed on income from a long series
of sales in Italy, continued for several years, and made under contracts
stipulated in Italy, even without an establishment or organization in Italy,
since under these circumstances, the sales amounted to the carrying on
of a business exercised at least in part in Italy.[38] It also appears that a
foreign enterprise could be taxed on income received under a contract
embodied in a public act stipulated in Italy (11/1.2), even if the operation were an isolated transaction.[39] Under the present law, the continued

---

[34] See Massimino, "Lo stabilimento permanente nel diritto fiscale nazionale ed
internazionale," RDFSF, 1957, 201, 206. In 1933, it was stated on behalf of the
Italian government that a foreign enterprise was subject to tax in Italy if it had
there "a permanent productive organization in the form of a branch, representative,
agency, purchase and sales office, goods depot, manufacturing establishment or some
other permanent organization showing that the foreign enterprise has transferred a
part of its activity to Italy with a view to its regular deployment in that country."
2 League of Nations, Taxation of Foreign and National Enterprises 259.
[35] Comm. Centr. 28 November 1949, n. 7559 (RDFSF, 1951, II, 305).
[36] Massimino, "Lo stabilimento permanente nel diritto fiscale nazionale ed internazionale," RDFSF, 1957, 201, 205.
[37] Cass. 23 November 1905.
[38] Comm. Centr. 3 March 1939, n. 13727.
[39] Cass. 15 January 1926; R.M. 28 October 1928; Trib. Milano 16 April 1938
(RDFSF, 1938, II, 269). See also Uckmar, La tassazione degli stranieri in Italia

efficacy of these decisions is doubtful.   Under the prevailing decisions, income realized from the sale abroad of products purchased in Italy, or from the manufacture abroad of products using goods purchased in Italy, was not subject to tax in the absence of a permanent establishment.[40]

Interest received by foreign banks (11/1.6a) and royalties (11/1.6c) received by foreign enterprises from Italian payors may be considered to have been produced in Italy, independently of the rules applicable to ordinary business income.

The maintenance of a branch or other permanent establishment in Italy gives a foreign company the option of being taxed on the balance sheet basis (6/1.2b) and also subjects it to liability for the corporation tax, under the rules discussed at 11/3.3 and 11/3.4.   For the purpose of these rules, the term "permanent establishment" includes an industrial or business establishment, an office for the purchase, sale, or advertising of products, a general agency, the possession and management of immovable property, and the like.[41]   Although a branch is not a separate taxable entity (5/2.2, 6/7), in practice, an Italian branch of a foreign company generally files the return of its income.

An Italian branch of a foreign bank is subject to the special rules applicable to credit firms and institutions (art. 8) (10/4.1).

b. APPORTIONMENT OF INCOME FROM INTERNATIONAL TRANSACTIONS. The production of business income in Italy by a foreign enterprise is the result of activities exercised in Italy, and not of the realization of income in Italy (11/1.3).[42] Since income of a foreign enterprise which is attributable to its own activities abroad is not subject to tax in Italy (11/3.5a), income which the enterprise derives through a branch or other fixed organization in Italy must be apportioned between the activities of the branch in Italy and the activities of the central office abroad.[43] When goods purchased or manufactured abroad are sold in Italy, or when goods manufactured or purchased in Italy are sold abroad, the income to be attributed to activities in Italy is a question of fact to be resolved in each

---

167-177, and Appendix, pp. 6-7. The provision under which such income was subjected to tax, whose applicability to business income was uncertain, does not appear in the *Testo unico* (11/1.2).

[40] Comm. Centr., Sez. un., 18 February 1931, n. 18416.

[41] C.M. 1 June 1955, n. 351690.

[42] Comm. Centr. 7 August 1875, n. 36901; Comm. Centr., Sez. un., 27 February 1935, n. 72945; Uckmar, *La tassazione degli stranieri in Italia* 177. See, however, Comm. Centr. 28 November 1949, n. 7559 (*RDFSF*, 1951, II, 305, with critical note by Uckmar).

[43] Cass. 21 May 1889 (*Imp. dir.*, 1889, 262); Comm. Centr. 3 March 1939, n. 13728, n. 13729, n. 13730, n. 13731. See also Uckmar, *La tassazione degli stranieri in Italia* 183, commenting on Comm. Centr. 28 November 1949, n. 7559 (*RDFSF*, 1951, II, 305).

ANALYSIS OF INCOME TAX   562

case by reference to the criteria which seem most appropriate.[44]   Where
as in the case of an Italian enterprise operating abroad, the problem o
apportionment arises only when there is a permanent establishment with
separate administration and accounting (11/2.3c), income derived by a
foreign enterprise through a permanent establishment in Italy is subjec
to tax even if the establishment does not have separate administration and
accounting (11/3.5a); hence greater reliance may have to be placed on
other criteria such as plants, offices, number of transactions, number of
employees and workers, as well as on the criteria prescribed under the
various treaties (11/4.4c).[45]   In general, the cost of goods purchased
abroad, the expenses of the branch in Italy, and a share of the general
administration expenses of the principal office abroad are deductible in
determining the income attributable to activities in Italy.   A loss incurred
by a branch is generally not recognized unless the branch has separate
management and accounting.[46]

11/3.6   Participation in Italian Enterprise

a.   PARTICIPATION IN A NONCORPORATE ENTERPRISE.   An Italian enterprise
organized as a general partnership or a limited partnership without shares
is subject to the tax on income from movable wealth on income of the
enterprise which is considered produced in Italy under the rules discussed
at 11/2.3.   If a nonresident individual is a partner in such an enterprise,
he is subject to the complementary tax on his share of the income subject
to the tax on income from movable wealth, whether or not distributed
(5/3.2, 5/3.3).   If a company or association of any type formed abroad
is a partner in the Italian enterprise and has, in addition, a permanent
establishment in Italy, the company is subject to the corporation tax on
the assets invested in the Italian enterprise or otherwise employed in Italy,
on the income received from the distribution or division of the profits of
the Italian enterprise (9/2.1), and on any income referable to the
permanent establishment (11/3.5a).   The Italian enterprise is not, by
itself, regarded as a permanent establishment of the foreign enterprise,
and a foreign company or association of any type which has no permanent establishment in Italy (independent of its participation in an Italian
enterprise) is therefore not subject to the corporation tax.   However, if
an Italian company has been created by a foreign company, its capital has
been predominantly furnished by the foreign company, and it operates as
a "mere organ for the execution of operations made and determined by"

---

[44] *Italian Government Reply to Fiscal Commission of United Nations Economic
and Social Council*, U.N. Doc. E/CN8/46/Add. 16; Massimino, "Lo stabilimento
permanente nel diritto fiscale nazionale ed internazionale," *RDFSF*, 1957, 201, 206.

[45] Massimino, "Lo stabilimento permanente nel diritto fiscale nazionale ed internazionale," *RDFSF*, 1957, 201, 206-207.

[46] Massimino, "Lo stabilimento permanente nel diritto fiscale nazionale ed internazionale," *RDFSF*, 1957, 201, 205.

the foreign company, the Italian company itself may be subject to the corporation tax (11/2.3b).

b. OWNERSHIP OF SHARES OF A CORPORATION OR SIMILAR ENTITY. An Italian corporation or similar entity is subject to the tax on income from movable wealth on income considered produced in Italy and to the corporation tax on its assets and income, under the rules discussed at 11/2.3a. Dividends paid to a foreign shareholder are not again subject to the tax on income from movable wealth (9/2.1). A nonresident individual shareholder, however, is subject to the complementary tax on distributions of the profits subject to the tax on income from movable wealth (9/2.1b). If the foreign shareholder is a company or association of any type with no permanent establishment in Italy, it incurs no liability for the corporation tax by reason of its ownership of the shares (11/3.3). However, if the foreign shareholder is a company or association of any type with a permanent establishment in Italy, amounts which it has invested in shares of an Italian company and dividends which it has received on such shares are subject to the corporation tax when the shares are inscribed to the foreign company, even if they do not appear in the accounts of the permanent establishment, and even if the activity of the Italian company is in no way connected with that of the permanent establishment of the foreign company in Italy.[47] It appears that this rule applies not only to investment in a company formed in Italy but also to investment in a company formed abroad with its head office or the principal object of its enterprise in Italy.

The rules stated above apply regardless of the proportion of the shares of the Italian corporation held by the foreign company. Even if the Italian corporation is a subsidiary of the foreign company, it is juridically independent and therefore is not itself considered a permanent establishment of the foreign company.[48]

Beginning in 1963, distributions of profits by corporations and similar entities are subject to a withholding (9/2.7a) which, in most cases, is credited against the recipient's liability for the complementary tax or the corporation tax (9/2.7c). For foreign companies and associations operating in Italy through a permanent establishment, the credit is limited, apart from provisions of international agreements, to withholdings made from profits derived from shares included in taxable assets (11/3.4) for purposes of the corporation tax.

Foreign banks are subject to the provisions discussed at 10/4.2; foreign investment companies, to the provisions discussed at 10/5.

---

[47] Ministerial Note 22 July 1958, n. 351170, De Angelis, Potenza, and Testa, *Testo unico delle leggi sulle imposte dirette* 774.

[48] Massimino, "Lo stabilimento permanente nel diritto fiscale nazionale ed internazionale," *RDFSF*, 1957, 201, 202.

11/3.7 Shipping Income

If a foreign company having neither its head office nor the principal object of its enterprise in Italy exercises shipping activities through a branch or other permanent establishment in Italy, that portion of its income which is attributable to passages and freights purchased in Italy is considered produced in Italy, under the rules discussed at 11/3.5.[49]

The Italian government formerly had express authority to grant exemption from the tax on income from movable wealth for income derived from the exercise of maritime commerce in Italian ports by foreign navigation companies having their head offices abroad and branches, agencies, or representatives in Italy, on the condition of reciprocal treatment of Italian navigation companies operating abroad.[50] This provision is abrogated by article 288A of the *Testo unico*; however, the government still has the power to grant such exemptions, subject to the constitutional provision relating to treaties (11/4.1). The treaties in effect are discussed at 11/4.6.

11/3.8 Rates of Tax

The rates of tax applied to income subject to tax are the same for all taxpayers, regardless of domicile, residence, and other elements of nationality.

11/3.9 Withholding at Source

The application of the withholding rules described at 13/3 to income produced in Italy is not affected by the residence, domicile, or nationality of the person to whom the income is payable. Thus, an employer must pay the tax on income from movable wealth of category C/2, recovering it through withholding, on payments made to its employees for work performed in Italy, and on payments made for activities carried on in Italy on his behalf by employees of a foreign enterprise not having a permanent establishment in Italy (13/3.4). The complementary tax must be provisionally withheld from all such payments, under the rules described at 13/3.5. It appears that an employer must make these withholdings even if it does not have a permanent establishment in Italy.[51] A company formed abroad which has its head office or the principal object of its enterprise in Italy is subject to these requirements in the same manner as an enterprise formed in Italy. Income from work rendered abroad is subject to withholding when considered produced in Italy under the

49 See Uckmar, *La tassazione degli stranieri in Italia* 192.
50 R.D.L. 7 May 1925, n. 587.
51 See Giannetta, Scandale, and Sessa, *Teoria e tecnica nell'accertamento del reddito mobiliare* 112; Uckmar, *La tassazione degli stranieri in Italia* 198.

rules described at 11/1.5. The tax on income from movable wealth must be withheld from the other payments listed at 13/3.4 when payable by persons domiciled or resident in Italy (11/1.6a). Thus, it appears that an entity required to be taxed on the balance sheet basis must pay the tax on income from movable wealth of category A, with a right of recovery against the recipient, on interest paid to a foreign bank which does not have a permanent establishment in Italy, unless there is a treaty provision which exempts the interest from Italian taxation.[52]

A provisional withholding of the tax on income from movable wealth and of the complementary tax, at special rates, is prescribed for payments made to aliens or to Italians domiciled abroad for copyrights, for fees or earnings for the transfer of patents, designs, processes, formulas, trademarks, and similar property, and for compensation for the exercise in Italy of an art or profession (13/3.5). Failure to make the withholding may result in denial of a deduction for the expenditures, under the provision described at 11/2.4.

Beginning in 1963, all distributions of profits by Italian corporations and similar entities are subject to a withholding (9/2.7a), to be credited in most cases against the complementary tax or the corporation tax due from the recipient (9/2.7c). In the case of dividends payable to a foreign company or association operating in Italy through a permanent establishment, the credit is limited, apart from provisions of international agreements, to withholdings made from profits derived from shares included in the taxable assets for purposes of the corporation tax (11/3.3). Apart from provisions of international agreements, no credit is given for withholdings from profits payable to aliens or Italians domiciled abroad and subject neither to the complementary tax nor to the corporation tax. Profits collected on foreign securities by Italian banks, on behalf of owners in Italy, are subject to a similar withholding, which is to be credited against the complementary tax or the corporation tax (9/2.7e).

In all cases, the person effecting the withholding must report the withholding, as explained at 13/1.4.

11/3.10 Restrictions on Transfer Abroad of Capital Invested in Italy and Income Therefrom

Under the present law governing the investment of foreign capital in Italy, the transfer abroad of capital invested and of the returns (*rendite*) thereon is dependent on the payment of all applicable direct taxes, national and local, which result from the activity to which the transfer relates.[53] The taxes which must be paid under this provision include the

---

[52] See De Angelis, Potenza, and Testa, *Testo unico delle leggi sulle imposte dirette* 652.

[53] L. 7 February 1956, n. 43, art. 8. The restriction applies only in the case of

tax on income from movable wealth, the corporation tax, and the related local surtaxes and additionals (12/1.4c), assessed or assessable against the investor in relation to the capital invested in Italy.[54] The requirement is probably not applied either to the complementary tax or to the family tax (2/3), which are not considered to be based on the activity to which the transfer relates (6/1.1a), or to the objective taxes based on the possession of immovable property in Italy, whose collection is assured by the existence of the property itself.[55] The methods of proving the payment of the taxes are prescribed by administrative instructions.[56]

The requirement relates to the liability of the investor, not that of the enterprise or entity in which the investment has been made; the mere fact that the enterprise or entity in which the investment is made has not paid its own taxes should not prevent the transfer of capital or returns to the investor.

A taxpayer who has not paid the entire tax due may nonetheless transfer the capital or the returns abroad if he deposits with the Intendant of Finance (1/4.7) suitable security for the payment of the balance of the tax due.[57] According to the administrative instructions, the amount of security required will depend on the soundness of the enterprise in which the investment is made, the amount of the tax, and any other circumstances affecting the certainty of recovering the tax.[58] The Intendant of Finance is authorized to permit the transfer of income when the capital remains invested in Italy and the enterprise in which it is invested is solvent and not likely to incur debts which would impair the ability to pay the amount due. When it is necessary to protect the tax obligation, however, the taxpayer may be required to deposit, with the Bank of Italy or a credit institution authorized to act as an agent thereof, not more than 20% of the amount to be transferred abroad.

11/4.   Tax Treaties

11/4.1   Treaties in Force

Italy has general treaties for the avoidance of double taxation of income, dating from before World War II, with Belgium,[59] France,[60] and

---

capital invested in Italy after the entry into force of the law. See D.M. 15 June 1956, art. 9.

[54] D.P.R. 6 July 1956, n. 758 (Regulations), art. 9.

[55] See Uckmar, *La tassazione degli stranieri in Italia*, Appendix, pp. 65-66; Piazza, *Tassazione degli stranieri* 172.

[56] C.M. 6 August 1956, n. 455871; C.M. 21 February 1957, n. 451467; C.M. 16 October 1957, n. 459052.

[57] L. 7 February 1956, n. 43, art. 8.

[58] C.M. 6 August 1956, n. 455871.

[59] Concluded 11 July 1931; approved by L. 31 March 1932, n. 456; ratified 8 September 1932, with effect from 1 January 1933; restored to effect by Belgian notification 10 March 1948, by virtue of Treaty of Peace 10 February 1947, art. 44.

[60] Concluded 16 June 1930; approved by L. 30 December 1931, n. 1576; ratified 27 October 1933, supplemented by additional agreement of 16 November 1931, with

Germany.[61] The German treaty is also applicable between Italy and Austria.[62] Treaties negotiated before World War II with Hungary [63] and Romania [64] are in suspension. There is also a treaty with Spain dealing with the taxation of companies.[65]

Since World War II, Italy has entered into general treaties for the avoidance of double taxation of income with the United States of America,[66] Sweden,[67] the Netherlands,[68] Great Britain,[69] France,[70] and Norway.[71]

Special treaties for the avoidance of double taxation of income from shipping (11/4.6) are in effect with Canada [72] and Greece [73] and, for the avoidance of double taxation of income from shipping and air

---

effect from 1 January 1934; restored to effect by exchange of notes 2 July 1947 and 17 February 1948.

[61] Concluded 31 October 1925; approved by D.L. 13 December 1925, n. 2161, converted in L. 15 July 1926, n. 1866; ratified 15 December 1925, with effect from 1 January 1926; restored to effect from 1 January 1951 by an exchange of notes 20 November 1951. A new treaty is under negotiation.

[62] C.M. 3 July 1952, n. 351230.

[63] R.D.L. 3 September 1926, n. 2307.

[64] L. 15 May 1939, n. 953.

[65] Concluded 28 November 1927; approved by R.D.L. 7 June 1928, n. 1493, converted in L. 28 December 1928, n. 4587; ratified 10 September 1928, with effect from 18 September 1928.

[66] Concluded 30 March 1955; approved by L. 19 July 1956, n. 943; ratified 26 October 1956, with effect from 1 January 1956. Administrative instructions governing the application of the treaty in Italy are contained in C.M. 21 January 1957, n. 350300. In the United States, Treasury Decision 6215 deals with the effect of the treaty on United States withholding provisions. The provisions of the treaty are discussed in Uckmar, *La tassazione degli stranieri in Italia*, Appendix, p. 33.

[67] Concluded 20 December 1956; approved by L. 13 March 1958, n. 280; ratified 3 June 1958, with effect from 3 June 1958. The provisions of this treaty are discussed in Uckmar, *La tassazione degli stranieri in Italia*, Appendix, p. 47; and Croxatto, "Le convenzioni fra Italia e Svezia al fine di evitare le doppie imposizioni," *Dir. e prat. trib.*, 1959, I, 26.

[68] Concluded 24 January 1957; approved by L. 18 June 1960, n. 704; ratified 18 June 1960, with effect from 1 January 1954. The provisions of this treaty are discussed by Uckmar, *La tassazione degli stranieri in Italia*, Appendix, p. 42.

[69] Concluded 4 July 1960; approved by L. 12 August 1962, n. 1378; ratified 28 November 1962, with effect from 28 November 1962.

[70] Concluded 29 October 1958; approved by L. 9 February 1963, n. 469; to become effective on ratification.

[71] Concluded 25 August 1961; approved by L. 2 March 1963, n. 534; ratified 25 July 1963, with effect from 25 July 1963.

[72] Concluded 29 March 1932; approved by R.D. 25 August 1932, n. 1265, with effect from 1 January 1928; restored to effect by notification by Canada 27 February 1948, by virtue of Treaty of Peace 10 February 1947, art. 44.

[73] Concluded 15 January 1932, approved by L. 3 June 1932, n. 853; ratified 14 January 1933, with effect from 1 April 1932; restored to effect by exchange of notes 20 May 1948, by virtue of Treaty of Peace 10 February 1947, art. 44.

transport, with Argentina,[74] Brazil,[75] Israel,[76] Switzerland,[77] and the Union of South Africa.[78] Treaties relating to exemptions accorded to international organizations and their personnel are discussed at 5/5.1. All international treaties involving burdens on the finances (*alle finanze*) or modifications of law must be ratified by Parliament (Const. art. 80), but a treaty may be placed in effect preceding ratification.

The subsections which follow deal with the general features of the Italian income tax treaties; emphasis is on those which have been concluded since World War II. The discussion is limited to the effects of the treaties on Italian tax jurisdiction and does not purport to deal with the effects of the treaties on the tax jurisdiction of the other countries, unless Italy's obligation to give a credit for foreign taxes is involved (11/4.3b).

11/4.2 Taxes Covered

All of Italy's general treaties for the avoidance of double taxation of income apply to the objective taxes (6/1.1a) and to the complementary tax (6/1.1f). The Swedish treaty is made expressly applicable to the corporation tax (6/1.1g), including the income and asset components, and the tax on bonds; [79] the new French treaty has the same scope.[80] The United States treaty contains a special provision [81] dealing with the income and asset components of the corporation tax, and, under the credit provisions of the treaty, Italy credits United States taxes against the income component of the corporation tax (11/4.3b). The treaties with the Netherlands and Germany contain provisions [82] broad enough to encompass the income and asset components of the corporation tax. The provisions of the other treaties cover only the income component of the corporation tax.

All treaties except those with the United States, Greece, and Belgium apply to all regional, provincial, communal, and Chamber of Commerce surtaxes (12/1.4d), and also to autonomous local taxes such as the tax on industry, commerce, arts, and professions (ICAP) (2/2.9). The Bel-

---

[74] Concluded 12 April 1949; approved by L. 26 November 1951, n. 1612; in force from 26 January 1952, with effect from 1 January 1946.
[75] Concluded 4 October 1957; approved by L. 12 August 1962, n. 1371; effective on ratification.
[76] Concluded 10 August 1955; approved by L. 25 April 1957, n. 359, with effect from 18 June 1957.
[77] Concluded 31 July 1958; approved by L. 2 December 1960, n. 1588; ratified 8 May 1961, with effect from 1 October 1952.
[78] Concluded 26 June 1953; approved by L. 9 August 1954, n. 873, with effect from 1 July 1948.
[79] Treaty with Sweden, art. 2(1)(a).
[80] Treaty with France, art. 2(1)(B).
[81] Treaty with the United States, art. 6.
[82] Treaty with the Netherlands, art. 1(2); Treaty with Germany, art. 1.

gian treaty applies to the surtaxes, but not to the autonomous local
taxes.[83] Except in the case of the German treaty,[84] which applies to all
direct taxes, it appears that the treaties do not apply to the family tax
(2/3); some authorities believe, however, that the family tax should be
regarded as subject to treaty provisions in the same manner as the complementary tax.[85]

11/4.3   Methods of Avoiding Double Taxation

a.   EXEMPTION. Under all of the Italian treaties, each country exempts
from tax entirely certain classes of income which otherwise would be taxable under its law, regardless of whether the other country actually taxes
the income so exempted. Thus, under all the treaties, each country exempts specified classes of income derived from sources in that country by
persons domiciled or resident in the other. The prewar treaties provided
for the application of the objective taxes (6/1.1a) on the basis of source,
with the result that each country exempted from its objective taxes certain
income otherwise subject to those taxes, which was attributable, under the
treaty provisions, to sources in the other. Article 12 of the treaty with
France and article 13 of the treaty with Belgium, in addition, exempted
persons domiciled in either of the contracting countries from personal
taxes (6/1.1a) in the other on any income, regardless of source. Article 11
of the German treaty exempted persons domiciled in one of the countries
from personal tax in the other on dividends (11/4.7), compensation for
serving as a director (11/4.13e), and interest on securities or bank
deposits (11/4.8), regardless of source; exemption of other income from
personal tax was made in accordance with the rules applicable to the
objective taxes. The allocations of source made by the postwar treaties,
however, apply to both the objective and the personal taxes.

With regard to income derived by persons domiciled or resident in one
country from sources in the other, the prewar treaties exempted from
the objective taxes in each country income attributable, under the treaty
provisions, to sources in the other. Under the French and Belgian treaties,
however, these exemptions did not apply to the personal taxes imposed
by each country on the income of persons domiciled or resident therein;
each country was permitted to impose its personal tax on all income of
such persons, regardless of source. Under the German treaty, the exemptions applied to the personal tax imposed by each country on persons
domiciled or resident therein, except in the case of dividends, compensation for serving as a director, and interest on securities or bank deposits;
in these cases, each country was empowered to impose its personal tax

---

[83] C.M. 15 March 1957, n. 350610.
[84] Treaty with Germany, art. 1.
[85] See Uckmar, *La tassazione degli stranieri in Italia* 249.

regardless of the source of income. The allocations of source made by the postwar treaties apply to both the objective and the personal taxes of each country insofar as the exemption method is applied to income of persons domiciled or resident in that country. The United States treaty, however, provides that each country may tax all or part of the income of persons resident therein, without regard to the source of such income, giving a credit for taxes paid thereon in the country of source (11/4.3b). The Swedish treaty operates by the exemption method except in the case of interest and dividends, which may be taxed in both countries; the country of domicile is required to give a credit for tax paid in the country of source (11/4.3b). The treaty with the United Kingdom also provides for crediting of the tax due in the country of source against any tax payable in the other country on the same income (11/4.3b). This treaty also contains a provision that when income from a source in one country is allocated to the other under the treaty, and the second country taxes only the amount remitted to or received in it, the exemption accorded in the first country is limited to that amount.[86]

Under article 17 of the Swedish treaty and article 19(1) of the Netherlands treaty, each country is permitted to take income allocated to the other into account in determining the rate of a progressive tax applicable to income of a taxpayer domiciled in that country, although such income is excluded from the taxable income to which the rate so determined is applied. In the case of Italy, these provisions are applicable to the complementary tax; they insure that exemptions under the treaties will not reduce the average rate of tax applicable to the domestic income of a person domiciled in Italy.

Exemption of capital from the asset component of the corporation tax, under the treaties which apply to that tax, is discussed at 11/4.5a.

Although article 18(1) of the Swedish treaty and article 22 of the Netherlands treaty expressly provide that the treaties do not increase the exercise by a country of its tax jurisdiction, Italian law now taxes persons domiciled or resident in Italy on income which, by virtue of an international agreement, is nontaxable in another country (11/2.2). Under article 18(2) of the Swedish treaty, individuals resident in one country who are taxable in the other are entitled to any exemptions, allowances, deductions, reductions, or similar benefits in relation to family obligations which that country accords to its own citizens who are domiciled abroad.[87] Article 21 of the Netherlands treaty provides that neither country may apply the taxes covered by the treaty to the citizens of the other in a manner more onerous than to its own citizens in the same situation.[88]

---

[86] Treaty with the United Kingdom, art. 2(2).
[87] See also Treaty with the United Kingdom, art. 16.
[88] Compare Treaty with the United Kingdom, art. 19.

b. CREDIT FOR FOREIGN TAXES. Under article 8 of the treaty between Italy and Sweden, each country may tax dividends paid by a domestic corporation to a person domiciled in the other country, in accordance with the rules described at 11/4.7, but the other country is required to grant a credit for the tax paid in the first. Under article 9 of this treaty, Sweden is also required to give a credit for Italian taxes paid by a taxpayer domiciled in Sweden on interest from Italian sources; there is no converse requirement for the giving of a credit for Swedish taxes by Italy because Sweden does not tax nonresidents on interest from foreign sources (11/4.8).

Under article 15 of the United States treaty, each country is permitted to tax any income of its citizens, residents, and corporations or other entities (as if the treaty had not come into effect), but must give a credit for the amount of income taxes paid to the other country on income derived from sources in the other country which is not exempt from tax in that country under the terms of the treaty. In determining the credit for United States taxes to be allowed against Italian taxes, that proportion of the United States tax which is attributable to dividends is excluded, and, instead, Italy allows a credit of 8% of the amount of the dividends.[89] However, neither country is permitted to tax income of its residents which is exempt under the provisions applicable to teachers (11/4.13c) and students or apprentices (11/4.13d) who are temporary visitors in the other country.[90]

Administrative instructions have been issued by the Italian government for the application of the United States treaty [91] in the crediting of United States taxes against the Italian taxes. If the income on which the United States tax was paid is subject to the tax on income from movable wealth, a credit is given against the tax on income from movable wealth in the amount of the United States tax, or that proportion of the tax on income from movable wealth which the income from sources in the United States bears to all income subject to the tax on income from movable wealth, whichever is lower. If part of the United States tax remains uncredited, or the income on which the United States tax was paid is not subject to the tax on income from movable wealth, a credit is given against the complementary tax or the corporation tax in the amount of any part of the United States tax which remains uncredited, or in the amount of that proportion of the complementary tax, or the income component of the corporation tax, which the income taxed in the United States bears to total income subject to the Italian personal tax, whichever is lower. The credit cannot be applied to the asset component of the corporation tax.

---

[89] Treaty with the United States, art. 15(1)(b).
[90] Treaty with the United States, art. 15(2).
[91] C.M. 21 January 1957, n. 350300.

The United States determines its credit for Italian taxes under the rules provided for its statutory foreign tax credit under the Internal Revenue Code.[92]

The treaty with the United Kingdom provides that the tax due in either country on income from sources therein is to be credited against the tax payable in the other on the same income.[93] The amount of United Kingdom tax creditable against Italian tax in this way is limited to that proportion which the income in question bears to the total income subject to Italian tax. Special provisions are made regarding the credit to be given for tax payable on dividends (11/4.7).

11/4.4 Definitions

a. IN GENERAL. The postwar treaties contain definitions of certain terms. The more important of these definitions are discussed below, with particular reference to the United States treaty.

b. NATIONALITY OR DOMICILE OF ENTERPRISE. Article 2(1)(f) of the United States treaty defines a "United States enterprise" as an enterprise carried on in the United States by a resident of the United States or by a United States company or other entity. A "United States company or other entity" is a company or other entity created or organized in the United States or under the law of the United States or of any state or territory of the United States. Article 2(1)(g) defines "Italian enterprise" in an analogous manner.

Article 3(2) of the Swedish treaty and article 2(1) of the Netherlands treaty provide that a juridical person is domiciled in the country in which the seat of its actual direction is located. Under the treaty with the United Kingdom, a company is considered a resident of the country in which its affairs are directed and controlled, and an enterprise carried on by a resident of one of the countries is considered an enterprise of that country.[94]

c. RESIDENCE OR DOMICILE OF INDIVIDUAL. Under article 3(1) of the Swedish treaty, an individual is considered domiciled in a country if he has his actual residence and his dwelling there, or sojourns there permanently. An individual who would be domiciled in both countries under this rule is considered domiciled in the country in which he has the closest personal and economic relations or, if this criterion does not resolve the problem, in the country of which he is a citizen; if he is a citizen of both or of neither, the tax authorities of the two countries are to agree case by case. Under article 2 of the treaty with the United

---

[92] Treaty with the United States, art. 15(1)(a).
[93] Treaty with the United Kingdom, art. 17.
[94] Treaty with the United Kingdom, art. 2.

Kingdom, an individual is considered resident in a country if he is resident there for purposes of its taxes, and either is not a resident of the other for purposes of the latter's taxes, or is present in the latter for not more than 91 days in the aggregate during the fiscal year.

The United States treaty contains no definition of residence, and references to resident of the United States or of Italy under that treaty therefore must be interpreted in accordance with the laws of each country.

d. PERMANENT ESTABLISHMENT. Under article 2(1)(c) of the United States treaty, a "permanent establishment" (*organizzazione permanente*) includes a branch, office, factory, warehouse, or other fixed place of business. It includes an agency if and only if the agent has and exercises a general authority to negotiate and conclude contracts on behalf of the enterprise, or has a stock of merchandise from which he regularly sells orders on its behalf. The existence of a permanent establishment does not result merely from the carrying on in one country, by an enterprise of the other country, of the activities listed below.

1. Casual or temporary using of merely storage facilities.
2. Carrying on business dealings through a bona fide commission agent, broker, or custodian, acting in the ordinary course of his business as such.
3. Maintaining a fixed place of business exclusively for the purchase of goods or merchandise.
4. Having a subsidiary corporation (*società sussidiaria*) which is a corporation of the first country or is engaged in trade or business in the first country.[95]

The definitions of "permanent establishment" (*stabile organizzazione*) in the Swedish and Netherlands treaties are substantially the same.[96] Similar also is that of article 2(1)(k) of the United Kingdom treaty, except that it makes no reference to the use of storage facilities.

11/4.5 Industrial or Commercial Profits

a. IN GENERAL

1. Foreign enterprise operating in Italy. As a general rule, income derived from activities in Italy by a foreign enterprise is subject to Italian tax, under the recent Italian treaties, only if the enterprise has a permanent establishment (11/4.4d) in Italy.

---

[95] For a subsidiary, article 2(1)(e) of the Netherlands treaty and article 2(1)(k) of the United Kingdom treaty use *"filiale";* article 3(5) of the Swedish treaty uses *"società filiale."* In ordinary Italian usage, however, a *"filiale"* is a "branch"; the terms usually adopted for a subsidiary are *"società-figlia"* and *"società sussidiaria."*

[96] Article 3(5) of the Swedish treaty expressly includes mines and other mineral deposits and construction sites whose use has exceeded or may be expected to exceed 12 months, and does not expressly exclude temporary use of merely storage facilities. Article 2(1)(e) of the Netherlands treaty expressly includes (1) the execution of works if actually directed in the country, even when there is no permanent installation there, and (2) an agent representing one enterprise exclusively.

Under article 3(1) of the United States treaty, for example, industrial or commercial profits of a United States enterprise are exempt from Italian tax unless the United States enterprise is engaged in trade or business in Italy through a permanent establishment in Italy. If the United States enterprise is engaged in trade or business in Italy through a permanent establishment in Italy, Italy may tax the entire income of the enterprise from sources within Italy; article 5(1) of the Swedish treaty and article 4(1) of the Netherlands treaty, however, restrict the imposition of tax to income derived through the permanent establishment.

Under article 3(2) of the United States treaty, industrial or commercial profits are not deemed to arise from the mere purchase of goods or merchandise in Italy by a United States enterprise; a similar limitation appears in article 4(3) of the Netherlands treaty.

The liability of a United States enterprise to the asset component of the corporation tax is limited to the tax on property used or employed in Italy in the activity of the enterprise; a United States enterprise is not subject to the income component of the corporation tax if it is exempt from tax on its income under the rules stated above or at 11/4.6.[97] Under article 15 of the Swedish treaty, Italy may impose the asset component of the corporation tax on assets attributable to a permanent establishment in Italy and on immovable property situated in Italy, but may tax assets consisting of credits guaranteed by a mortgage on immovable property only if the property is situated in Italy.

2. *Italian enterprises operating abroad.* Article 5(1) of the Swedish treaty prevents Italy from taxing income derived by an Italian enterprise through a permanent establishment in Sweden. The United States treaty, on the other hand, expressly permits Italy to tax income derived by an Italian enterprise through a permanent establishment in the United States; but Italy must give a credit against Italian tax, as explained at 11/4.3b, for the United States tax paid. The Netherlands treaty and the United Kingdom treaty contain no provisions regarding the taxation by Italy of income derived by an Italian enterprise through a permanent establishment in the other contracting country.

Under article 15 of the Swedish treaty, Italy may not impose the asset component of the corporation tax on movable property included in assets invested in a permanent establishment in Sweden. The United States treaty does not limit the application of the asset component of the corporation tax to Italian enterprises (11/4.3a).

b. APPORTIONMENT OF PROFITS. In determining income from sources within Italy, under the United States treaty, the industrial or commercial profits which a permanent establishment of the United States enterprise

---

[97] Treaty with the United States, art. 6.

might be expected to derive if it were an independent enterprise engaged in the same or similar activities, under the same or similar conditions, and dealing at arm's length with the United States enterprise, are to be attributed to the permanent establishment, and may be taxed in Italy as income from sources within Italy, in accordance with Italian law.[98] In determining the net profits of the permanent establishment, all expenses reasonably allocable to the permanent establishment, wherever incurred, are allowed as deductions, including executive and general administrative expenses.[99] Rules for the apportionment of industrial and commercial profits may be laid down by agreement between the competent authorities of the two countries.[100]

In addition to substantive allocation rules similar to those of the United States treaty, the treaty with the United Kingdom provides that profit is not to be allocated to a permanent establishment in a country merely because of the purchase of goods or products in that country by a foreign enterprise.[101] It also contains a provision for allocating income between two enterprises of different countries when one of them participates in the direction, control, or capital of the other, or the same persons participate in the direction, control, or capital of both.[102]

c. CONTROLLED ENTERPRISES. The recent Italian treaties provide that if an enterprise of one of the countries, by reason of its participation in the management or the financial structure of an enterprise of the other country, makes in its commercial or financial relations with the latter conditions different from those which would be made with an independent enterprise, any profits which would normally have accrued to one of the enterprises in the absence of those conditions may be included in the profits of that enterprise and taxed accordingly.[103]

11/4.6 Income from Shipping and Air Transport

Italy's general tax treaties contain provisions governing the taxation of income from shipping and air transport; in addition, Italy has concluded special treaties covering income from shipping or air transport with Argentina, Canada, Israel, Switzerland, and the Union of South

---

[98] Treaty with the United States, art. 3(3). Article 4(2) of the Netherlands treaty also provides that the income attributable to the permanent establishment is to be determined as if the permanent establishment were an independent enterprise, and provides further, in article 4(4), that rules for the apportionment of profits are to be fixed by the tax authorities of the two countries.

[99] Treaty with the United States, art. 3(5).

[100] Treaty with the United States, art. 3(4).

[101] Treaty with the United Kingdom, art. 3(4).

[102] Treaty with the United Kingdom, art. 4.

[103] See Treaty with the United States, art. 4; Treaty with Sweden, art. 5(2); Treaty with the Netherlands, art. 5.

Africa (11/4.1).[104] Under these provisions, income of a shipping or air transport enterprise is subject to tax in Italy only if the enterprise is domiciled or resident in Italy under the rules provided by the treaty concerned. Article 5 of the United States treaty, article 6 of the Netherlands treaty, and the Canadian treaty require, as a condition of exemption from tax in Italy of enterprises domiciled abroad, that the ships or aircraft be registered in the country in which the enterprise is domiciled. Similarly, profits derived by a British enterprise from the operation of ships or aircraft registered in the United Kingdom are exempt from tax in Italy.[105] Under an agreed interpretation of the United States treaty, income which a carrier domiciled in the United States derives from commissions on the sale of tickets on behalf of other carriers is exempt from tax in Italy, but income derived from the management of hotels, excursion buses, places of entertainment, and other activities not directly connected with the carrier's transport services is not.[106] Article 2(3) of the draft treaty with Switzerland, on the other hand, extends the benefit of exemption from Italian tax to income derived from the operation of ships flying the Swiss flag, even if the enterprise operating the ships is not domiciled in Switzerland.

In general, Italy may impose the asset component of the corporation tax on assets employed in Italy by a foreign enterprise (11/4.5a). Under article 15 of the Swedish treaty, Italy may tax business assets whose income is subject to tax, including assets of a shipping or air transport enterprise domiciled in Italy, except in the case of movable property included in assets invested in a permanent establishment in Sweden.

11/4.7 Dividends

a. DIVIDENDS PAID BY ITALIAN CORPORATIONS

1. In general. The prewar Italian treaties provide that dividends shall be subject to objective taxes only in the country in which the declaring corporation has its office, and to personal taxes only in the country in which the recipient is domiciled.[107] Since Italy imposes no objective tax on dividends as such (9/2.1), dividends paid by Italian corporations to persons domiciled abroad are not subject to any Italian tax under these provisions. The postwar treaties, making no distinction between objective and personal taxes (11/4.3a), provide for the taxation by Italy of dividends paid by Italian corporations to persons domiciled abroad.

---

[104] The special treaties with Canada and Greece deal only with income from shipping. A special arrangement with the United States, under an exchange of notes (authorized by R.D. 4 March 1926, n. 340), has been suspended by article 5 of the general treaty with the United States.

[105] Treaty with the United Kingdom, art. 6.

[106] C.M. 20 October 1962, n. 351470.

[107] See, for example, Treaty with France, art. 5.

Double taxation is avoided in accordance with the provisions described below.

2. *Dividends paid to individuals.* Under article 8(3) of the Swedish treaty and article 7(1) of the Netherlands treaty, dividends paid by a corporation domiciled in Italy to a person domiciled in the other country are subject to the complementary tax. Dividends received from sources in Italy by a resident of the United States are also subject to the complementary tax, but the rate at which the tax is imposed may not exceed 15% if the taxpayer does not have a permanent establishment in Italy.[108] The United States is required to give a credit for the Italian tax paid, in accordance with the provisions discussed at 11/4.3b; Sweden is required to give a credit for the Italian tax paid, not exceeding 10% of the gross amount of the dividends, against its coupon tax.[109]

Italy may subject dividends paid by a company resident in Italy to an individual resident in the United Kingdom to taxes in force at the date of the signing of the treaty (4 July 1960);[110] thus, such dividends are subject to the complementary tax. The United Kingdom gives a credit against its tax for the Italian tax on the dividends plus the Italian tax payable by the company on its profits.[111] Dividends paid by a company resident in Italy to a resident of the United Kingdom are exempt from any other Italian tax over and above the tax applicable to the profits of the company, provided that the recipient is subject to tax on the dividends in the United Kingdom and that he does not carry on any business or industry in Italy through a permanent establishment there.[112]

3. *Dividends paid to companies.* Dividends paid by an Italian corporation to a company domiciled abroad are subject to the income component of the Italian corporation tax only if the recipient has a permanent establishment in Italy (11/3.5a). The Swedish treaty contains no provision regarding the taxation in Italy of dividends paid by an Italian corporation to a company domiciled in Sweden, and such dividends are therefore subject to the corporation tax under the rule stated above. However, article 8(4) of the treaty extends the exemption granted by Swedish law for dividends received by a Swedish company from another Swedish company [113] to dividends received by a corporation domiciled in Sweden from a corporation domiciled in Italy of which the Swedish corporation owns 10% or more of the paid-in capital. Article 7(2) of the

---

108 Treaty with the United States, art. 7(1).

109 Treaty with Sweden, art. 8(3). See WTS: *Sweden,* 11/5.10.

110 Treaty with the United Kingdom, art. 7(1).

111 Treaty with the United Kingdom, arts. 7(1), 17(2). Under article 17(2), if a dividend payable on preferential shares involves a fixed rate of return plus a participation in the profits, the credit for the Italian tax is computed on that part of the dividend which exceeds the fixed rate of return.

112 Treaty with the United Kingdom, art. 7(1).

113 See WTS: *Sweden,* 9/2.8, 11/5.10.

ANALYSIS OF INCOME TAX   578

Netherlands treaty provides that if Italy should subject to tax dividends paid by an Italian corporation to a corporation domiciled in the Netherlands, Italy will exempt dividends paid to a company domiciled in the Netherlands which is actually and directly the owner of 75% or more of the paid-in capital of the Italian company, unless the dividends are income of a permanent establishment of the Netherlands company in Italy.

Dividends received from sources within Italy by a United States corporation or other entity not having a permanent establishment in Italy may not be subjected to the income component of the Italian corporation tax at a rate exceeding 15%.[114] However, if the shareholder is a corporation controlling, directly or indirectly, at least 95% of the entire voting power in the corporation paying the dividend, and not more than 25% of the gross income of the corporation paying the dividend is derived from interest and dividends not received from its own subsidiary corporations, the rate of Italian tax on the dividends is reduced to not more than 5%, provided that the relationship between the two corporations has not been arranged, and is not maintained, primarily with the intention of securing the reduced rate.[115] The credit provisions of article 15 of the United States treaty do not refer to the corporation tax; and although Italy, in practice, credits United States tax against the income component of the corporation tax (11/4.3b), it is not clear whether the United States grants a credit for the income component of the corporation tax.

Under article 7(1) of the treaty with the United Kingdom, dividends payable by a company resident in Italy to a company resident in the United Kingdom are exempt from Italian tax if the dividends are taxable in the United Kingdom and the recipient does not operate in Italy through a permanent establishment.

4. *Withholding of tax.* In the case of dividends payable to nonresidents who are subject neither to the complementary tax nor to the corporation tax (9/2.7c), and in the case of dividends payable on bearer shares (9/2.7d), tax withheld under the coupon tax provisions described at 9/2.7a is not credited against any complementary tax or corporation tax liability of the recipient and thus constitutes an independent tax, in the absence of a contrary provision of an international agreement. Since dividends payable by an Italian company are regarded as having an Italian source (11/1.6b), they are normally subject to the complementary tax if payable to a nonresident individual whose total income from Italian sources exceeds the taxable minimum of L. 720,000 (12/1.5c), and are subject to the corporation tax if payable to a foreign company or association which operates in Italy through a permanent establishment

---

[114] Treaty with the United States, art. 7(1).
[115] Treaty with the United States, art. 7(2).

(9/2.7c). Under most of the Italian treaties, such dividends remain subject to tax in Italy, and, in these cases, the tax withheld is credited against the liability of the nonresident recipient for the complementary tax or the corporation tax, provided that the shares on which the dividends are payable are registered.[116] Unless otherwise provided under a treaty, however, no credit or refund is given for tax withheld from dividends payable on bearer shares, from dividends payable on registered shares to a nonresident individual whose total income from Italian sources does not exceed the taxable minimum, or from dividends payable on registered shares to a foreign company or association not operating in Italy through a permanent establishment there.

Tax withheld from dividends exempted from Italian tax under a treaty provision, on the other hand, is subject to credit and refund whether or not the dividends would be subject to Italian tax in the absence of the treaty. Thus, credit is given under the treaties with the United States and the Netherlands for any tax withheld over the percentage limitations provided by those treaties (11/4.7a2, 11/4.7a3).[117] Under the United Kingdom treaty, dividends payable by a company resident in Italy to an individual resident in the United Kingdom are subject to the complementary tax because this tax was in effect when the treaty was signed; but dividends payable by a company resident in Italy to an individual or company resident in the United Kingdom are exempt from any other Italian tax provided that the recipient is subject to tax in the United Kingdom on the dividends and does not carry on a business or industry in Italy through a permanent establishment there (11/4.7a2). Since the coupon tax was levied after the date on which the treaty was signed, credit must be given for tax withheld from dividends payable to a resident of the United Kingdom who is subject to United Kingdom tax on the

---

[116] The tax liability is computed by calculating the full tax due on all income produced in Italy as if the treaty did not exist, and subtracting that proportion of it which is attributable to income taxable in the other country under the treaty. The tax withheld from dividends payable on registered shares is credited against the resulting amount, and the final difference is inscribed in the roll if positive, or refunded if negative.

In order to obtain the credit, the recipient of the dividends must file a return on the regular form on or before 31 March of the year following that in which the dividends became payable and must attach proof of residence or domicile in the other country under the treaty. To obtain a refund, he must apply, within six months of the date on which the tax withheld was paid into the Treasury, to the Intendant of Finance of the province in which the company declaring the dividends has its office.

For discussion of the requirements under the various treaties, see Poli, *Imposta complementare sui redditi derivanti da partecipazione in società e imposta cedolare* 246-260.

[117] See Poli, *Imposta complementare sui redditi derivanti da partecipazione in società e imposta cedolare* 254-258. In each case, the recipient of the dividends must file a return in order to obtain the credit and must make appropriate application if a refund is desired.

dividends and does not carry on a business or industry in Italy through a permanent establishment, as well as for tax withheld from dividends payable on registered shares to a resident of the United Kingdom who has a permanent establishment in Italy or is an individual whose income from Italian sources does not exceed the taxable minimum and who is not subject to tax in the United Kingdom on the dividends.[118]

b.   DIVIDENDS PAID BY FOREIGN CORPORATIONS

1. *In general.* Under the prewar treaties, Italy imposes its personal tax on dividends paid by corporations domiciled abroad to persons domiciled in Italy, under the rules described at 11/4.3a. The postwar treaties with the United States and Sweden, making no distinction between the objective and personal taxes (11/4.3a), permit the country in which the declaring corporation is domiciled to tax dividends paid to persons domiciled in Italy; under these treaties, Italy is also permitted to tax the dividends, but is required to give a credit for the foreign tax paid. Article 7(2) of the Netherlands treaty permits the Netherlands to tax dividends paid by a corporation domiciled in the Netherlands to a person domiciled in Italy only if they are income of a permanent establishment of the recipient in the Netherlands.

2. *Dividends paid to individuals.* Article 8(2) of the Swedish treaty allows Sweden to apply its coupon tax to dividends paid by a Swedish corporation to an individual domiciled in Italy, and requires Italy to give a credit, against its complementary tax, for the Swedish tax paid. Under article 15(1)(b) of the United States treaty, Italy may subject Italian residents to the complementary tax on dividends from sources in the United States, but must grant a credit of 8% of the amount of the dividends. Under article 14(2), dividends paid by a United States corporation to an individual who is neither a citizen nor a resident of Italy are exempt from Italian tax. Italy can apply no tax to dividends payable to a person not resident in Italy by a company resident in the United Kingdom obtaining profits or income from sources in Italy, nor apply to such a company any levy having the nature of a tax on undistributed profits, whether or not the dividends or undistributed profits represent profits or income from sources in Italy.[119] The United Kingdom may subject dividends received by an individual resident in Italy from a company resident in the United Kingdom to any United Kingdom tax in force on 4 July 1960; Italy gives a credit, not exceeding 8% of the total of the

---

[118] For discussion of the procedures for obtaining credits and refunds, and, in the case of a company resident in the United Kingdom, applying for exemption from the withholding requirements, see Poli, *Imposta complementare sui redditi derivanti da partecipazione in società e imposta cedolare* 251-254.

[119] Treaty with the United Kingdom, art. 7(2).

dividends subject to Italian tax, against the Italian tax for the United Kingdom tax payable on dividends received by individuals.[120]

3. *Dividends paid to companies.* In determining the taxes imposed on its corporations or other entities, Italy may include, under article 15(1)(b) of the United States treaty, dividends from sources within the United States, but must allow a credit against its own taxes of 8% of the amount of the dividends. Dividends paid by a United States corporation to a recipient who is neither a citizen or resident of Italy, nor an Italian corporation or other entity, are exempt from all Italian income taxes, under article 14(2) of the treaty.

Article 8(1) of the Swedish treaty allows Sweden to apply its coupon tax, limited to 5% of the gross amount of the dividends, to dividends paid by a Swedish company to a company domiciled in Italy which has a permanent establishment in Sweden. Under article 8(2), Italy is required to give a credit against its corporation tax for the Swedish tax paid.

The provision described at 11/4.7b2 regarding dividends payable by a company resident in the United Kingdom obtaining profits or income from sources in Italy also applies to dividends payable to companies not resident in Italy. However, the United Kingdom is not permitted to tax dividends payable by a company resident in the United Kingdom to a company resident in Italy,[121] and Italy gives no credit against Italian tax for United Kingdom tax payable on dividends received by companies.[122]

11/4.8   Interest

Interest paid by a United States corporation to a recipient who is neither a citizen or resident of Italy, nor an Italian corporation or other entity, is exempt from Italian tax.[123]   However, Italy may tax its residents and corporations on interest from sources in the United States, giving a credit for any United States tax paid, under the rules described at 11/4.3b. Sweden does not tax interest payable to a nonresident from a Swedish source; [124] but, when a taxpayer domiciled in Sweden is subject to Italian tax on interest from Italian sources, Sweden gives a credit for the Italian tax paid.[125]

Under article 8(1) of the Netherlands treaty, interest is taxable in Italy only if the debtor's fiscal domicile is in Italy or, under article 8(2), if the debt is contracted or the deposit received as part of the activity of a permanent establishment of the debtor in Italy. Conversely, interest

---

[120] Treaty with the United Kingdom, arts. 7(1), 17(3).
[121] Treaty with the United Kingdom, art. 7(1).
[122] Treaty with the United Kingdom, art. 17(3).
[123] Treaty with the United States, art. 14(2).
[124] See WTS: *Sweden*, 11/5.11.
[125] Treaty with Sweden, art. 9.

on a debt of a permanent establishment of an Italian enterprise in the Netherlands is not subject to tax in Italy.

Under article 8(1) of the treaty with the United Kingdom, interest derived from sources in Italy (11/1.6a) is taxable in accordance with Italian law except in the case of interest on a loan guaranteed by a mortgage on immovable property situated in the United Kingdom; but interest paid by a resident of Italy to a resident of the United Kingdom is exempt from the Italian complementary tax if the interest is subject to tax in the United Kingdom and the recipient does not carry on an industrial or business activity in Italy through a permanent establishment there.[126] If interest derived from sources in the United Kingdom is also taxable in Italy, the tax payable in the United Kingdom is credited against the tax payable in Italy.[127]

11/4.9 Royalties

In general, under the recent Italian treaties, royalties and other amounts received from sources in Italy by a recipient domiciled or resident in the other contracting country, as consideration for the right to use copyrights, patents, designs, secret processes and formulas, trademarks, and similar property, are exempt from tax in Italy if the recipient does not have a permanent establishment in Italy. The exemption generally applies also to rentals and similar payments for motion-picture films or for the use of industrial, commercial, or scientific equipment. The exemption usually does not apply when the royalties exceed the normal and intrinsic value of the rights for which they are paid.[128]

Article 6(1) of the Swedish treaty expressly precludes the taxation by Italy of royalties derived by a taxpayer domiciled in Italy through a permanent establishment in Sweden. It appears, however, that under its other postwar treaties, Italy is not precluded from taxing royalties received by persons domiciled in Italy from sources abroad, even if derived through a permanent establishment in the other contracting country. Under the United States treaty, Italy must give a credit in such cases, in accordance with the rules explained at 11/4.3b.

Provisional withholding from royalties payable to aliens or to Italians domiciled abroad, under the rules described at 13/3.5, is not required when the royalties are exempt from Italian tax under the treaty provisions, provided that the royalties are actually taxed abroad. However, withholding of local taxes on income must still be made when such taxes are not covered by the treaty.[129]

---

126 Treaty with the United Kingdom, art. 8(3).
127 Treaty with the United Kingdom, art. 8(4).
128 Treaty with the Netherlands, art. 9(2); Treaty with Sweden, art. 6(2); Treaty with the United Kingdom, art. 9.
129 For the United States treaty, see C.M. 21 January 1957, n. 350300. For earlier

Royalties from the exploitation of mines, quarries, or other natural resources are treated as income from immovable property (11/4.10).

11/4.10 Income from Immovable Property

Generally, under the postwar treaties, income from immovable property, and royalties from the exploitation of mines, quarries, or other natural resources, are taxable in Italy only if the property is situated in Italy.[130]

Article 9(2) of the United States treaty provides that a resident or company or other entity of one country deriving such income from sources in the second may elect to be subject to tax in the second country on a "net basis," as if it were engaged in trade or business in the second country through a permanent establishment situated therein. Since Italy already taxes the income in question on a net basis, this provision affects only the application of United States taxes to income derived by an Italian resident, company, or entity from sources in the United States.[131]

Income of a person resident in Italy from immovable property in the United States may be subjected to the personal taxes in Italy, but Italy is required to give a credit for United States income tax paid (11/4.3b).

11/4.11 Capital Gains

Under the treaties, the taxation of capital gains subject to tax in Italy under the rules discussed at 7/1.3 and 9/8.1 is governed by the rules explained at 11/4.5 for business income, even if, as in article 15 of the Swedish treaty, special rules are provided for increments of capital.[132] However, the rules governing royalties (11/4.9) also apply to profits derived from the transfer of rights on which royalties would be payable.[133]

11/4.12 Public Salaries and Pensions

In general, under the postwar treaties, wages, salaries, and pensions paid by the other contracting country or by a political subdivision thereof are exempt from Italian tax unless the recipient is a citizen of Italy. Article 10(1)(a) of the United States treaty also requires, as a condition of the exemption, that the recipient not have his permanent residence in

---

treaties, see C.M. 29 December 1956, n. 303800; C.M. 15 March 1957, n. 350610; and C.M. 20 May 1957, n. 350874.

[130] Under some treaties—for example, article 9 of the United States treaty—this rule does not apply to interest derived from mortgages and bonds secured by immovable property, and such interest is therefore taxed under the rules discussed at 11/4.8.

[131] See C.M. 21 January 1957, n. 350300.

[132] See Croxatto, "Le convenzioni fra Italia e Svezia al fine di evitare le doppie imposizioni," *Dir. e prat. trib.*, 1959, I, 26, 32.

[133] Treaty with Sweden, art. 6(3); Treaty with the Netherlands, art. 9(3); Treaty with the United Kingdom, art. 9(5).

Italy. The exemption usually does not apply to remuneration for services rendered in connection with a business or industrial activity carried on by the other country for purposes of profit.[134]

11/4.13 Private Salaries and Remuneration for Professional Services

a. IN GENERAL. Under article 11(1) of the Swedish treaty, compensation for labor or personal services, including the practice of the liberal professions, is taxable in Italy only if the services are rendered in Italy. The United States treaty permits Italy to tax income of Italian residents for services performed in the United States, giving a credit for tax paid in the United States (11/4.3b). Remuneration of an individual resident in the United Kingdom for personal (including professional) services rendered in Italy is exempt from tax in Italy in any tax year provided that the recipient is not present in Italy for more than 183 days during the year; that, if the recipient is a director of a company or a clerical employee, his services are rendered for or on behalf of a resident of the United Kingdom; that, in other cases, the recipient does not have an office or other fixed place of business in Italy; that the remuneration is not deductible in the determination of any income taxable in Italy; and that the remuneration is subject to tax in the United Kingdom.[135] In cases not fulfilling these conditions, Italy may tax remuneration for personal (including professional) services rendered in Italy by an individual resident in the United Kingdom; if remuneration for personal services rendered in the United Kingdom by a resident of Italy is taxed by both countries, Italy grants a credit for the tax payable in the United Kingdom under the rules described at 11/4.3b.[136] For purposes of the credit provisions, remuneration for services is considered derived from sources in the country in which the services were rendered, except in the case of services on ships or aircraft (11/4.13b).[137]

When a person domiciled in another country performs services in Italy on behalf of another person domiciled in the first country, his remuneration is generally exempt from tax in Italy if his stay in Italy does not exceed a prescribed limit, the remuneration has not been charged against income of the employer which is subject to tax in Italy, and the taxpayer is not exercising a liberal profession through a permanent establishment in Italy. Under the United States treaty, compensation received by a resident of the United States for labor or personal services performed in Italy as an employee of, or under contract with, a resident or corporation or other entity of the United States is exempt from Italian tax if his stay

---

[134] See, for example, Treaty with Sweden, art. 10(2); Treaty with the Netherlands, art. 14(1).

[135] Treaty with the United Kingdom, art. 12(2).

[136] Treaty with the United Kingdom, art. 12(1).

[137] Treaty with the United Kingdom, art. 17(5).

in Italy does not exceed a total of 90 days during the tax year; compensation received by a resident of the United States from other employers is exempt from Italian tax if his stay in Italy does not exceed a total of 90 days during the tax year and the compensation received for such services does not exceed $2,000 in the aggregate.[138]

The Netherlands treaty makes separate provision for income from the exercise of a liberal profession. Income received by a person domiciled in the Netherlands for the exercise of a liberal profession in Italy is taxable in Italy only if the profession is exercised through a permanent establishment (*organizzazione stabile*) in Italy.[139] Conversely, Italy, under the same article, may not tax income received by a person domiciled in Italy from the exercise of a liberal profession in the Netherlands through a permanent establishment in the Netherlands. Under article 11(3) of the Swedish treaty, remuneration of persons in the entertainment professions (theater, cinema, radio, television, music, and athletics) for services performed in Italy is subject to Italian tax regardless of the duration of the taxpayer's stay in Italy.

Provisional withholding applicable to remuneration paid to aliens or to Italians domiciled abroad for the exercise of an art or profession in Italy (13/3.5) does not apply if the income is exempt from Italian tax under the treaty provisions, provided that the income is actually taxed abroad.[140]

b. SERVICES ON SHIPS AND AIRCRAFT. Under article 11(4) of the Swedish treaty and article 13 of the Netherlands treaty, remuneration for personal services rendered on ships or aircraft is taxable in Italy only if the actual direction of the enterprise is situated in Italy. For purposes of the credit provisions of the United Kingdom treaty (11/4.3b), services rendered entirely or predominantly on ships or aircraft are considered performed in the country in which the enterprise managing the ships or aircraft is resident.[141]

c. VISITING PROFESSORS OR TEACHERS. If a resident of the United States who is not a citizen of Italy temporarily visits Italy with the purpose of teaching for a period not exceeding two years at an educational institution in Italy, his remuneration for such teaching during that period is

---

[138] Treaty with the United States, art. 11(2).

[139] Treaty with the Netherlands, art. 10(1). Under the German treaty, which provides that income from the exercise of a liberal profession in Italy is taxable only if the professional activity has a fixed office (*sede fissa*) in Italy, it has been established by administrative instructions that income from professional services exercised in Italy under a contract of service (*contratto di lavoro*) is taxable in Italy even in the absence of a permanent office (C.M. 30 September 1957, n. 351690).

[140] For the applicable administrative instructions, see note 129 *supra*.

[141] Treaty with the United Kingdom, art. 17(5).

exempt from Italian tax under article 13 of the treaty. Under similar provisions in article 12 of the Swedish treaty, article 16 of the Netherlands treaty, and article 14 of the United Kingdom treaty, the exemption is not restricted to persons who are not citizens of Italy; but the Netherlands treaty limits the exemption to income received from the Netherlands or from a person domiciled in the Netherlands.

d. STUDENTS AND APPRENTICES. Under article 12 of the United States treaty, a student or business apprentice who is a resident of the United States and is not a citizen of Italy, but who is temporarily present in Italy exclusively for the purpose of study or training, is exempt from Italian tax on payments made to him by persons resident in the United States for the purpose of his maintenance, education, and training. Similar provisions are found in article 13 of the Swedish treaty, article 17 of the Netherlands treaty, and article 15 of the United Kingdom treaty.

e. DIRECTORS OF COMPANIES. Under article 11(5) of the Swedish treaty and article 15(1) of the Netherlands treaty, remuneration paid by a company to a director, a member of the board of directors or overseers, or any other person who exercises analogous functions is taxable in Italy if the company is domiciled in Italy. Article 15(2) of the Netherlands treaty expressly exempts remuneration paid to a director in relation to a separate contract of work with the company. Article 12(2) of the United Kingdom treaty exempts from Italian tax remuneration received by a resident of the United Kingdom for services performed in Italy as a director on behalf of a resident of the United Kingdom, under the conditions described at 11/4.13a; if those conditions are not met, Italy may tax the income under article 12(1) of the treaty. If both Italy and the United Kingdom tax remuneration for services rendered as a director in the United Kingdom by a resident of Italy, Italy grants a credit for the tax payable in the United Kingdom (11/4.3b, 11/4.13a).

11/4.14 Private Pensions and Annuities

Private pensions and life annuities received from sources within Italy by a person domiciled in the other country are exempt from taxation in Italy under the treaties, either by express provision [142] or by virtue of a general residuary provision.[143] Article 13(1) of the treaty with the United Kingdom expressly requires, as a condition of the exemption, that the payments be subject to tax in the United Kingdom.

---

[142] See, for example, Treaty with the United States, art. 10(2).
[143] See, for example, Treaty with Sweden, art. 14.

/4.15 Individual Claims for Relief

Under most of the treaties, a taxpayer who shows proof that the action
the tax authorities of the two countries has resulted or will result in
ouble taxation, contrary to the provisions of the treaty, is entitled to
·dge a claim for relief. If the claim is upheld, the competent authorities
the two countries are required to come to an agreement for the equit-
ble avoidance of the double taxation. For Italy, the competent authority
nder all the treaties is the General Directorate of the Direct Taxes, in
ne Ministry of Finance (1/4.2). Under article 16 of the United States
·eaty, an individual should lodge such a claim with the country of which
e is a citizen, or if he is a citizen of neither country, with that of which
e is a resident; a corporation or other entity should file its claim with the
·untry in which it is created or organized.

1/4.16 International Administrative Cooperation

Italy's tax treaties generally provide for the exchange of fiscal informa-
on between the respective tax administrations of the contracting coun-
·ies.[144] The earlier treaties, in addition, provide for mutual assistance
nd support in the collection of taxes covered by the conventions.[145]
.rticle 18 of the United States treaty provides that each country may
ollect taxes governed by the conventions which are applied in the other
ountry, in such a manner as to prevent exemptions and reductions of
ites granted by the other country under the treaty from benefiting per-
ons who are not entitled to them.

---

[144] See, for example, Treaty with the United States, art. 17; Treaty with Sweden,
rt. 19.

[145] See, for example, Treaty with Belgium, art. 14; Treaty with France, art. 19;
'reaty with Germany, art. 18.

CHAPTER 12

COMPUTATION OF TAX

12/1. Individuals

12/1.1 Tax on Income from Landowning
12/1.2 Tax on Agrarian Income
12/1.3 Tax on Income from Buildings
12/1.4 Tax on Income from Movable Wealth
　　　a. Determination of income
　　　b. Allowances
　　　c. Rates
　　　d. Surtaxes and additionals
12/1.5 Complementary Tax
　　　a. Determination of income
　　　b. Allowances
　　　c. Rates and additionals
12/1.6 Withholding at Source
12/1.7 Example of Individual Tax Computation

12/2. Corporations and Similar Entities

12/2.1 Objective Taxes
12/2.2 Corporation Tax
　　　a. Determination of assets
　　　b. Determination of income
　　　c. Rates and additionals
12/2.3 Tax on Bonds
12/2.4 Withholding at Source
12/2.5 Example of Corporate Tax Computation

12/3. Other Taxpayers

12/3.1 Partnerships and Similar Companies
12/3.2 Cooperative Societies

12/4. Nonresident Taxpayers

12/5. Forms of Return

12/5.1 In General

12/5.2 Reproduction of Annual Return of Income of Individuals

12/5.3 Summary of Annual Return of Income of Partnerships and Similar Companies

12/5.4 Translation of Annual Return of Income, Assets, and Bonds of Corporations and Similar Entities

---

12/1. Individuals

12/1.1 Tax on Income from Landowning

Taxable income from landowning is the income inscribed in the rural cadaster (10/2.2c). This amount is multiplied by 12,[1] a coefficient of revaluation established to take account of the change in monetary values since the formation of the cadastral estimates.[2] No personal allowance is made in determining income from landowning except the proportional reduction of income for the objective taxes which is provided for large families (5/1.3). As of 1 January 1962, however, lands whose taxable income, after revaluation, does not exceed L. 600 are excluded from the tax (art. 49).[3]

The basic rate of the tax on income from landowning, applied to the revalued income, is 10% (art. 53). However, a provincial surtax not exceeding 30%, a communal surtax not exceeding 30%,[4] and a surtax of 0.02% for the benefit of the Chamber of Commerce[5] are also computed on the revalued income. On the total amount of the tax on income from landowning and the provincial and communal surtaxes are then computed an additional of 5% for the benefit of the communal assistance entities (ECA)[6] and an additional of 5% for Calabrian relief.[7] Collection fees are also computed on the amounts collectible through the rolls

---

[1] D.L.C.P.S. 12 May 1947, n. 356, art. 1. In practice, the Tax Offices inscribe the cadastral estimates of taxable income in the roll without revaluation; they multiply the rate, rather than the income, by 12. See De Angelis, Potenza, and Testa, *Testo unico delle leggi sulle imposte dirette* 242.

[2] The present value of the lira is about one seventieth of the 1938 value.

[3] As modified by L. 28 July 1961, n. 838, arts. 1, 2.

[4] R.D. 14 September 1931, n. 1175, art. 254; L. 16 September 1960, n. 1014, art. 19. The rates of these surtaxes are established by the communes and provinces in accordance with the powers described at 1/5.5d and 1/5.6.

[5] R.D.L. 7 December 1942, n. 1418, converted, with modifications, in L. 11 March 1943, n. 204, art. 16.

[6] R.D.L. 30 November 1937, n. 2145; D.L.L. 18 February 1946, n. 100, art. 7; L. 10 December 1961, n. 1346, art. 1.

[7] L. 26 November 1955, n. 1177, art. 18. This additional is applicable to taxes collectible through rolls (13/3.7) from 1955-1956 through 1966-1967 (2/2.9).

13/3.7). The maximum aggregate rate of tax on income from landowning may be computed as shown below.

National tax	10.00%	
Communal surtax	30.00	
Provincial surtax	30.00	
Subtotal		70.00%
Chamber of Commerce surtax	0.02	
Total tax and surtaxes		70.02%
Additional for ECA (5% × 70%)	3.50	
Additional for Calabrian relief (5% × 70%)	3.50	
Total tax, surtaxes, and additionals...................		77.02%
Collection fees (6% × 77.02%)	4.62	
Maximum aggregate rate		81.64%

12/1.2   Tax on Agrarian Income

Taxable agrarian income is the income inscribed in the rural cadaster
(10/2.3b) and, like income from landowning, must be multiplied by a
revaluation coefficient of 12. No personal allowance is made in determining agrarian income except the proportional reduction of income for
the objective taxes which is provided for large families (5/1.3). As of
1 January 1962, however, lands whose income from landowning, after
revaluation, does not exceed L. 600 are excluded from the tax on agrarian
income (art. 62).[8]

The basic rate of the tax on agrarian income, applied to the revalued
income, is 10% (art. 66). There are, at present, no surtaxes computed
on agrarian income.[9] However, additionals of 5% for ECA and 5% for
Calabrian relief and collection fees are computed on the taxes inscribed
in the rolls, as in the case of the tax on income from landowning (12/1.1).
The maximum aggregate rate of tax on agrarian income may be computed
as shown below.

National tax	10.00%	
Additional for ECA (5% × 10%)	0.50	
Additional for Calabrian relief (5% × 10%)	0.50	
Total tax and additionals............................		11.00%
Collection fees (6% × 11%)	0.66	
Maximum aggregate rate		11.66%

12/1.3   Tax on Income from Buildings

For buildings listed in the new urban building cadaster, taxable income
is the cadastral income, in 1938 lire, multiplied by coefficients of revalua-

---

[8] As modified by L. 28 July 1961, n. 838, art. 1, 2.

[9] Provincial and communal surtaxes of 5% were levied by article 6 of D.L.L. 18
February 1946, n. 100, but were abolished as of 1 January 1961 by article 15 of L. 16
September 1960, n. 1014.

tion established to take account of the change in monetary values sinc
1938 (9/4.2d). The coefficients established for various categories of build
ings for 1963 ranged from 20, for rural dwellings, to 75, for stores and
shops.[10] For buildings not listed in the cadaster and buildings whose ac
tual income exceeds the revalued cadastral income by a certain percent
age, taxable income is determined by making a standard deduction from
the rent specified in the contract, or from the current rent obtainabl
from similar buildings under similar conditions, whichever is higher
A further special deduction is granted for buildings built before 193;
(9/4.2c). No personal allowance is made in determining income from
buildings except the proportional reduction of income for the objectiv
taxes which is provided for large families (5/1.3).

The basic rate of the tax on income from buildings, applied to the
taxable income, is 5% (art. 76). A provincial surtax not exceeding 11%, ;
communal surtax not exceeding 9%,[11] and a surtax for the benefit of the
Chamber of Commerce at a rate not exceding 0.055%[12] are computed
on the net income. On the total amount of the tax and the provincia
and communal surtaxes are then computed an additional for ECA a
10%[13] and an additional for Calabrian relief at 5%, as in the case of the
tax on income from landowning (12/1.1). Collection fees are also
computed on the amounts collectible through the rolls (13/3.7). The
maximum aggregate rate of tax on income from buildings may be com
puted as shown below.

National tax	5.000%	
Provincial surtax	11.000	
Communal surtax	9.000	
Subtotal		25.000%
Chamber of Commerce surtax	0.055	
Total tax and surtaxes...........................		25.055%
Additional for ECA (10% × 25%)	2.500	
Additional for Calabrian relief (5% × 25%)	1.250	
Total tax, surtaxes, and additionals.................		28.805%
Collection fees (6% × 28.805%)	1.728	
Maximum aggregate rate...........................		30.533%

12/1.4   Tax on Income from Movable Wealth

a. DETERMINATION OF INCOME. Net income is determined separately for
each of the four categories of income from movable wealth (6/1.1e)
Net income from business activities (category B) and net income from

---

[10] D.M. 24 April 1963.

[11] R.D. 14 September 1931, n. 1175, art. 254; L. 16 September 1960, n. 1014,
art. 19.

[12] L. 4 November 1951, n. 1219, art. 3.

[13] L. 10 December 1961, n. 1346, arts. 1, 2.

professional activities (category C/1) are determined by deducting allow-able expenses from gross income (6/1.5b, 7/2, 8/2.2). At the taxpayer's election, income of a business enterprise may be assessed on the balance sheet basis (13/2.2). Income from capital (category A) and income from work as an employee (category C/2) are, in general, determined without any deductions. However, when the person paying income of category A or category C/2 has paid the tax thereon and recovered it from the recipient through withholding (12/1.6, 13/3.4), no separate assessment of the income in the hands of the recipient is made for purposes of the tax on income from movable wealth.

Income from work as an employee and income from pensions are exempt from the tax on income from movable wealth if, either alone or cumulated with other income, they do not exceed L. 300,000 when annualized (art. 89).[14] Length-of-service and social security payments made in accordance with a collective labor contract are exempt from the tax on income from movable wealth if their amount does not exceed L. 1 million.[15]

Taxable income is net income reduced by a standard allowance (12/1.4b).

b. ALLOWANCES. An annual allowance of L. 240,000 is deducted from net income of categories B, C/1, and C/2 of an individual (art. 89) (2/2.7g). For income from work as an employee classified in category C/2, the allowance is applied proportionately in each payment period. The allowance is imputed first to income of category C/2, next to income of category C/1, and finally to income of category B. The proportional reduction of the income subject to each of the objective taxes which is provided for the relief of taxpayers with large families is applied in addition to this allowance (5/1.3). The allowance is applied in full even if part of the taxpayer's income is exempt from the tax on income from movable wealth under a special law.[16]

For termination payments based on length of service and for social security and other payments made in a lump sum at the time of termination of employment, the allowance is L. 40,000 for each year of service rendered (art. 89).

Exemption from the tax on income from movable wealth is provided for income from work as an employee, pensions, and length-of-service and welfare payments not exceeding certain limits (12/1.4a).

c. RATES. The basic rates of the tax on income from movable wealth are established by article 90 of the *Testo unico*; they have recently been

---

14 Added by L. 4 December 1962, n. 1682, art. 3.
15 Added by L. 4 December 1962, n. 1682, art. 3.
16 C.M. 12 April 1957, n. 350820.

modified with effect from 1 January 1962.[17] On the first L. 720,000 of
taxable income of categories B, C/1, and C/2 of an individual, the rates
are reduced by one half, the amount subject to reduction being imputed
first to category C/2, next to category C/1, and finally to category B.
For income from work as an employee classified in category C/2, the
reduction is applied proportionately in each payment period; but for
length-of-service and social security payments, the reduction is applied
to L. 60,000 for each year of service rendered (art. 90).[18]

The basic rates of tax applicable to taxable income of the various
categories are set forth in Table 59.

Table 59:   *Rates of Tax on Income from Movable Wealth for Individuals*

Category of Income	Taxable Income (Lire)		Rate on Excess Over Lower Limit
	Lower Limit	Upper Limit	
Category A (income from capital)	0	—	26%
Category B (income from business)	0	720,000 *	9
	720,000	4,000,000	18
	4,000,000	10,000,000	20
	10,000,000	50,000,000	22
	50,000,000	100,000,000	23
	100,000,000	—	24
Category C/1 (income from independent services)	0	720,000 °°	4
	720,000	—	8
Category C/2 (income from work as an employee)	0	720,000	4
	720,000	—	8

* Portion not absorbed by category C/2 and category C/1.
** Portion not absorbed by category C/2.
Source: Article 90 of the *Testo unico,* as modified by article 1 of L. 1 April 1962,
n. 206.

d. SURTAXES AND ADDITIONALS. On the taxable income of both category
B and category C/1 are computed the communal tax on industry, commerce, arts, and professions (ICAP), and the provincial additional thereto,
which is actually a separate tax applied to the same taxable income. The
maximum rates of the communal tax are 3% on income of category B and
2.4% on income of category C/1; the maximum rates of the provincial
tax are 1.5% on income of category B and 1.2% on income of category

[17] L. 18 April 1962, n. 206.
[18] As modified by L. 4 December 1962, n. 1682, art. 4.

C/1.[19] The communal tax may also be applied to income which is exempt under a special law from the tax on income from movable wealth. In such cases, the commune assesses the income, subject to rights of appeal, and the maximum rates are 4.5% on income of category B and 3.6% on income of category C/1.[20] The province may institute the additional even if the commune has not levied the principal tax, except when the income is exempt from the tax on income from movable wealth.[21]

Chambers of Commerce, Industry, and Agriculture are also authorized to impose a tax on any form of business or industrial activity, including agricultural activity, which is subject to the tax on income from movable wealth.[22] Different maximum rates of tax have been established by law for different localities.[23] The rate of tax is the same whether the income of the activity is taxed in category B or, under the rules discussed at 7/1.2b, in category C/1. The additional for Calabrian relief is computed, at the rate of 5%, on the tax on income from movable wealth of all categories, and on the communal and provincial taxes discussed above.[24] The additional for ECA, applied to the same taxes, is imposed at the rate of 5% on the taxes relative to income from employment which is subject to the tax on income from movable wealth at 4%, and at the rate of 10% on all other taxes.[25] The additionals relative to taxes withheld are paid by the person paying the taxes (12/1.6). Collection fees are computed on the taxes inscribed in the rolls (13/3.7); if the taxes are inscribed in the rolls against the person paying the income, the collection fees are generally not recovered from the recipient through withholding, even if the taxes are.

12/1.5 Complementary Tax

a. DETERMINATION OF INCOME. Aggregate income includes (1) income assessed for the tax on income from landowning (12/1.1), multiplied by a revaluation coefficient of 2.5; (2) income assessed for the tax on agrarian income (12/1.2), multiplied by a revaluation coefficient of 3.5;[26] (3) income assessed for the tax on income from buildings (12/1.3); and

---

[19] R.D. 14 September 1931, n. 1175, arts. 162, 164. The rates of the communal tax may be increased to 2.5% and 2.8%, respectively; the rates of the provincial additional may be increased to 1.75% and 1.4%, respectively (L. 16 September 1960, n. 1014, art. 20). The rates adopted for income of category C/1 must always remain four fifths of those adopted for category B.

[20] R.D. 14 September 1931, n. 1175, art. 162.

[21] R.D. 14 September 1931, n. 1175, arts. 162, 164. See also C.M. 14 June 1958, n. 351000.

[22] R.D. 20 September 1934, n. 2011, art. 52(1)(c).

[23] R.D. 31 October 1941, n. 1418, art. 1. For Venice, see also L. 2 February 1960, n. 40.

[24] L. 26 November 1955, n. 1177, art. 18.

[25] L. 10 December 1961, n. 1346, art. 1.

[26] These coefficients are established for 1963 by D.M. 10 November 1962.

(4) income assessed for the tax on income from movable wealth (12/1.4a) or for a substitutive tax (6/1.1e). It also includes the taxpayer's share of the income of a partnership or similar company (5/3.2), income derived from participation in a corporation or similar entity (9/2.1b), income derived from serving as a director of a company (8/1.2), interest on state securities or on bonds (9/1.2, 9/1.7), and any other income received by the taxpayer (6/1.1f). Income of the taxpayer's wife and other dependents is aggregated with that of the taxpayer under the rules discussed at 5/1.2, 5/1.3, and 5/1.4. For this reason, the income of the wife and other dependents for all taxes is reported on the husband's return, although there is no aggregation of their respective incomes for purposes of objective taxes (5/1.2).

Net aggregate income is determined by deducting, from this total, interest not deductible in determining income from movable wealth (6/1.5f); and expenses, charges, and losses inherent in the production the year (6/1.5e); social security contributions not deductible in determining income from movable wealth, and life insurance premiums (6/1.5f); and expenses, charges and losses inherent in the production of income subject to the tax which by their nature (rather than because of their amount) were not deductible in the determination of that income (art. 136) (6/1.5b). In the case of income from work as an employee and from pensions, such expenses are valued at 20% of the income, with a maximum of L. 360,000 (8/1.9). If the net aggregate income is assessed by estimate, however, no deductions are permitted other than the personal allowances described at 12/1.5b (art. 13).

Taxable income is net aggregate income reduced by allowances (12/1.5b).

b. ALLOWANCES. From the net aggregate income are deducted a basic allowance of L. 240,000 (about $387) and a further allowance of L. 50,000 (about $80.60) for each member of the taxpayer's family shown to be dependent on him on 31 December of the year for which the tax is due (art. 138). The determination of the status of a wife as a dependent is discussed at 5/1.2, of children, at 5/1.3, and of other persons, at 5/1.4. If a wife has income of her own as an employee, the family is entitled to an additional basic allowance of L. 240,000 in place of her allowance as a dependent.[27]

In the case of a war widow having six or more children, and for any other taxpayer having seven or more children, the basic allowance is increased to L. 5,000,000 (about $8,060); for a taxpayer having five or more children, the basic allowance is increased to L. 2,500,000 (about $4,030) (5/1.3).

---

[27] C.M. 4 January 1960, n. 501519.

C. RATES AND ADDITIONALS. No complementary tax is imposed if the net aggregate income does not exceed L. 720,000 (about $116) before applying the allowances discussed in 12/1.5b (art. 130).[28] If the net aggregate income exceeds L. 720,000, the tax is applied to the taxable income at progressive rates, increasing from a minimum of 2% on a taxable income of L. 240,000 (about $387) or less to 6% on a taxable income of L. 5,000,000 (about $8,060), and ultimately to a maximum of 65% on a taxable income of L. 500,000,000 (about $806,000) or more (art. 139).[29] These rates are effective from 1 January 1962.[30] The law also provides a short illustrative schedule of the rates for selected values of taxable income; this schedule is set forth in Table 60.

Table 60: *Rates of Complementary Tax for Selected Values of Taxable Income*

Taxable Income (Lire)	Rate of Tax
L. 240,000	2.00%
500,000	2.50
1,000,000	3.17
2,000,000	4.12
3,000,000	4.85
5,000,000	6.00
10,000,000	11.93
20,000,000	16.27
30,000,000	19.26
40,000,000	21.69
50,000,000	23.79
100,000,000	31.85
200,000,000	43.03
300,000,000	51.55
400,000,000	58.71
500,000,000	65.00

Source: Article 139 of the *Testo unico,* as replaced by article 1 of L. 18 April 1962, n. 209.

[28] As of 1 January 1964, the taxable minimum for the complementary tax has been increased from L. 720,000 to L. 960,000. L. 1 March 1964, n. 113.

[29] The rate applicable to a taxable income which does not exceed L. 5,000,000 is determined by the formula below, where x is the taxable income in millions of lire, and y is the rate.

$$y = 0.023025 \sqrt{x} - 0.0000472\, x + 0.00874$$

The rate applicable to a taxable income which exceeds L. 5,000,000 is determined by the formula below.

$$y = 0.06 + \sqrt{x - 5}$$

[30] L. 18 April 1962, n. 209, art. 2. Under the rate table originally attached to the *Testo unico,* a maximum rate of 50% was applicable to taxable income exceeding L. 500 million. Under the present formulas, income not exceeding L. 5 million is taxed at the same rates as formerly, but a new scale of progression has been applied to the rates on income exceeding L. 5 million.

For a criticism of the erratic behavior of the curve of the rate plotted against income, see Castellino, "Note sulla progressività dell'imposta complementare," *Giorn. degli economisti,* 1963, 168.

Since income which would not otherwise have been taxed becomes fully taxable when net aggregate income exceeds L. 720,000, the imposition of tax at the scheduled rates on income just above this limit would have the effect of reducing after-tax income below the limit. To prevent this result, the law provides that the tax may not in any case exceed the difference between the net aggregate income and L. 720,000 (art. 139). Special provisions are made for determining the rates of tax applicable to social security and other payments received in connection with termination of employment (8/1.3, 8/1.8) and those applicable to income received as a result of the liquidation of a business or connected with the realization of good will on the transfer of a business (9/9.2).

The additional of 5% for Calabrian relief [31] and collection fees (13/3.7) are computed on the complementary tax collected through the rolls; the additional for ECA is computed at the rate of 10% of the tax.[32]

12/1.6 Withholding at Source

The tax on income from movable wealth is withheld directly from payments made by the state, in accordance with the provisions listed below (art. 126) (13/3.3).

1. From payments of income of category A, at the normal rate applicable to category A (12/1.4c).

2. From fixed remuneration of a state employee exceeding the personal allowance (12/1.4b), at the normal rates applicable to income of category C/2 (12/1.4c).

3. From all compensation of a state employee other than fixed remuneration, if the annualized fixed remuneration does not exceed L. 960,000, at the rate of 4%.

4. From compensation paid by the state in any other case, including compensation paid to a person not a member of a state office, at the rate of 8%.

In the cases described at 13/3.4, private persons paying income of categories A and C/2 are required to pay the tax on income from movable wealth at the normal rates (12/1.4c); they recover the tax from the recipient of the income through withholding. The tax to be withheld, in each pay period, from income of category C/2, taking account of the standard allowance (12/1.4b) and of the difference in rates on taxable income above and below L. 720,000, is determined as explained below.

1. The standard allowance of L. 240,000 is divided by the number of pay periods in the year: 12 for employees paid by the month, 24 for those paid semimonthly, 48 for those paid by the week, and 288 for those

---

[31] L. 26 November 1951, n. 1177, art. 18.
[32] R.D.L. 30 November 1937, n. 2145, art. 1; L. 10 December 1961, n. 1346, art. 1.

paid by the day. The resulting quotient is deducted from the income
on which tax is to be withheld in each pay period.[33] The entire quotient
is deducted even in the case of an employee who works for only part
of a pay period.[34]

2. The first L. 720,000 of the yearly compensation remaining after deduction of the standard allowance is divided by the number of pay periods.
The resulting quotient is subject to withholding, in each pay period, at
the rate of 4%; the balance payable in each pay period is subject to
withholding at the rate of 8%.[35]

3. If a bonus (8/1.7) caused an employee's compensation for the month
to exceed the quotient subject to withholding at 4%, the excess would
be subject to withholding at 8% even if the employee's total compensation
for the year did not exceed the standard allowance plus L. 720,000. To
avoid this result, a special method is authorized to determine the rates
of withholding on annual bonuses and Christmas gratuities, required
by law or by collective contract, which are measured by one month's
compensation or multiples thereof.[36] Under this method, the bonus is
multiplied by 13 (or by 12 plus the number of extra months); the
difference between the resulting amount and L. 960,000 is subject to
withholding at 8%, and the balance is subject to withholding at 4%.[37]
Similarly, if the resulting amount does not exceed L. 960,000, the difference between it and L. 240,000 is subject to withholding at 4%, the
balance being exempt; if the resulting amount does not exceed L.
240,000, no tax is withheld.

4. In the case of a lump-sum payment of retirement or length-of-service
benefits, the total payment is divided by the number of years of service,
and the standard allowance of L. 40,000 (8/1.8) is deducted from the
resulting quotient. Of the difference remaining, the first L. 60,000
(representing L. 720,000 divided by 12), multiplied by the number of
years of service, is subject to withholding at 4%; the balance, multiplied
by the number of years of service, is subject to withholding at 8%.[38]

Business enterprises are required to make a provisional withholding, at
the rate of 8%, on two thirds of the total compensation paid for artistic
services performed in Italy by persons domiciled there, and on two
thirds of the total compensation (excluding participations in the net
profits of the business period) paid to directors and to auditors or
overseers (art. 128) (13/3.5).

---

[33] The weekly or daily quotient is deducted for all pay periods during the year,
even though the divisor used takes holidays into account. C.M. 23 September 1952,
n. 307670.

[34] C.M. 11 November 1949, n. 307600; Ministerial Note 21 October 1958, n.
301459.

[35] C.M. 23 April 1948, n. 302130.

[36] This method is also applied when the bonus is less than one month's pay
(C.M. 20 April 1954, n. 301260), but not when an employee has received the
benefit of the full quotient for the lower rate, although working only part of the pay
period (C.M. 16 May 1949, n. 303750).

[37] C.M. 12 March 1949, n. 301970.

[38] C.M. 16 March 1960, n. 300790.

The complementary tax is withheld provisionally, at the rate of 1.5%, in each payment period, from that part of the income paid to each employee which, when annualized, exceeds L. 720,000. It is also withheld provisionally by business enterprises from payments for artistic services and from payments to directors and to auditors or overseers, at the rate of 4% on two thirds of the gross payment (art. 143). Complementary tax is withheld provisionally at the rate of 15% from distributions of profits of corporations and similar entities (9/2.7a).[39] All taxes provisionally withheld are credited toward the tax due on the net aggregate income in which the payments are included (13/3.5).

On taxes withheld directly, paid with a right of recovery through withholding, or withheld provisionally, the additional for ECA is withheld in accordance with the rules applicable to the taxes involved (art. 272).

The additional for Calabrian relief applies to all withholdings described in this section except those made by business enterprises from payments for artistic services and payments to directors and auditors or overseers; these withholdings are paid directly into the Treasury (13/3.5). Collection fees on taxes withheld and inscribed in the roll against the person paying the income may be, but usually are not, recovered from the employee through withholding. Special provisions relating to aliens and to Italians domiciled abroad are discussed at 12/4.

12/1.7 Example of Individual Tax Computation

The following example illustrates the computation of the objective taxes and the complementary tax of an individual.

Example 1

The taxpayer is a married man with three minor children. He owns a small farm which is worked by a tenant. The income from landowning inscribed in the cadaster is L. 50,000. The taxpayer owns the house in which he lives, which was built before 1938; its presumed rental value is L. 100,000, and the income assessed for 1938 was L. 2,000. The taxpayer earns a salary of L. 3,000,000, and also holds a participation of 20% in a partnership which earned profits of L. 50,000,000 during the year, and which paid a tax on income from movable wealth, on its previous year's profits, of L. 12,500,000, inclusive of surtaxes, additionals, and fees. The taxpayer also received interest of L. 60,000 on a personal loan to a relative, interest of L. 100,000 on corporate bonds, interest of L. 100,000 on government bonds exempt from the tax on income from movable wealth, and dividends of L. 1,500,000 on shares of corporations. He also owns life insurance policies on his own life, on which he paid premiums of L. 300,000 during the year.

---

[39] In certain cases, withholdings from distributions of profits are not provisional but are treated as a separate tax. See 9/2.7c, 9/2.7d.

1. Tax on income from landowning (12/1.1)

Income inscribed in cadaster, multiplied by 12 (12 × 50,000)	L. 600,000
Tax at 10%	60,000
Provincial surtax at 30% [a]	180,000
Communal surtax at 30% [a]	180,000
Surtax for Chamber of Commerce at 0.02% [a]	120
Total taxes and surtaxes	L. 420,120
Additional for ECA (5% × 420,000)	21,000
Additional for Calabrian relief (5% × 420,000)	21,000
Total tax, surtaxes, and additionals	L. 462,120
Collection fee (5% × 462,120) [b]	23,106
Total tax, surtaxes, additionals, and fee	L. 485,226

2. Tax on agrarian income. Since the agricultural enterprise on the tax-
    payer's land is conducted by a tenant, not by the taxpayer himself,
    there is no liability for the tax on agrarian income (10/2.3a).

3. Tax on income from buildings (12/1.3)

Presumed rental value of property		L. 100,000
Less: Standard deduction		
(.25 × 100,000)	25,000	
Deduction based on 1938 income		
(4.5 × 2,000)	9,000	
		34,000
Net income		L. 66,000
Tax at 5%		3,300
Provincial surtax at 11% [c]		7,260
Communal surtax at 9% [c]		5,940
Surtax for Chamber of Commerce at 0.055% [c]		36
Total tax and surtaxes		L. 16,536
Additional for ECA (10% × 16,500)		1,650
Additional for Calabrian relief (5% × 16,500)		825
Total tax, surtaxes, and additionals		L. 19,011
Collection fee (5% × 19,011)		951
Total tax, surtaxes, additionals, and fee		L. 19,962

[a] Assumed to be at the maximum rate for purposes of this example.

[b] For purposes of this example, collection fees (13/3.7) are assumed to be at the
rate of 5% throughout. Collection fees on taxes inscribed in the roll against the
person paying the income are assumed, in accordance with the usual practice, to be
borne by the payor and not recovered from the recipient. Hence they are computed
here only when the tax is inscribed in the roll against the taxpayer himself.

[c] Assumed to be at the maximum rate for purposes of this example.

4. Tax on income from movable wealth of category A not subject to withholding

Interest on personal loan............................	L. 60,000
Tax at 26%	15,600
Additional for ECA (10% × 15,600)	1,560
Additional for Calabrian relief (5% × 15,600)	780
Total tax and additionals	L. 17,940
Collection fee (5% × 17,940)	897
Total tax, additionals, and fee	L. 18,837

5. Tax on income from movable wealth of category A, inscribed in the roll against the payor of the income, with a right to recover the tax from the recipient through withholding [d]

Interest on corporate bonds...........................	L. 100,000
Tax at 26%	26,000
Additional for ECA (10% × 26,000)	2,600
Additional for Calabrian relief (5% × 26,000)	1,300
Total tax and additionals	L. 29,900

6. Tax on income from movable wealth of category C/2, inscribed in the roll against the employer, with requirement of recovery from the employee through withholding [e]

Salary (after withholding of social security)............	L. 3,000,000
Less: Standard allowance (12/1.4b)	240,000
Taxable income................................	L. 2,760,000
Tax on 720,000 at 4% (12/1.4c)	28,800
Tax on 2,040,000 at 8%	163,200
Additional for ECA	
(5% × 28,000)	1,550
(10% × 163,200)	16,320
Additional for Calabrian relief (5% × 192,000)	9,600
Total tax and additionals	L. 219,360

[d] This income is reported on the return for purposes of the complementary tax only. In this example, it is assumed, in accordance with the usual practice, that the right of recovery is not exercised. Hence the income is included in the recipient's income for the complementary tax without any deduction for the tax on income from movable wealth paid by the person paying the interest. The computation of the tax on income from movable wealth of category A is shown here solely for purposes of illustration. The payor would also bear the collection fee, amounting in this case to 5% × L. 29,900, or L. 1,495.

[e] This income is reported on the return for purposes of the complementary tax only. The employer also bears the collection fee, amounting in this case to 5% of L. 219,360, or L. 10,968, and normally does not recover it from the employee.

7. Complementary tax
   a. Aggregate income

Income assessed for tax on income from landowning, multiplied by 2.5 (2.5 × 600,000)	L.	1,500,000
Income assessed for tax on income from buildings		66,000
Interest on personal loan		60,000
Interest on corporate bonds		100,000
Salary		3,000,000
Interest on governmental bonds, exempt from tax on income from movable wealth		100,000
Participation in profits of partnership (20% × 50,000,000)		10,000,000
Dividends		1,500,000

Aggregate income .... L. 16,326,000

   b. Deductions

Taxes recovered through withholding during the year (item 6)	L.	219,360
Taxes paid during the year [f]		
item 1		485,226
item 2		19,962
item 3		18,837
Tax on income from movable wealth paid by partnership (20% × 12,500,000)		2,500,000
Other taxes [g]		2,000,000
Life insurance premiums (6/1.5f)		300,000
Standard deduction from income from work as an employee (8/1.9)		
(20% × 3,000,000)	600,000	
Limit (8/1.9)	360,000	360,000

Total deductions........................ L. 5,903,385

   c. Net aggregate income

Aggregate income	L.	16,326,000
Less: Total deductions		5,903,385

Net aggregate income..................... L. 10,422,615

   d. Taxable income

Net aggregate income	L.	10,422,615
Less: Standard allowance	240,000	
Allowance for dependents (4 × 50,000)	200,000	
		440,000

Taxable income .... L. 9,982,615

[f] Taxes on income of previous year are assumed equal to those in example.
[g] Including the family tax (2/3).

e. Rate of tax

$$y = 0.06 + 0.02652 \sqrt{x - 5}$$

$$y = 0.06 + 0.02652 \sqrt{9.9826 - 5}$$
$$y = 0.11919$$

Rate of tax 11.92%

f. Complementary tax due

Tax at 11.92% of taxable income	L.	1,189,927
Additional for ECA (10% × 1,189,927)		118,993
Additional for Calabrian relief (5% × 1,189,927)		59,497
Total tax and additionals	L.	1,368,418

g. Credit for tax provisionally withheld from salary (12/1.6)

Salary subject to withholding of complementary tax (3,000,000 − 720,000)	L.	2,280,000
Complementary tax withheld (1.5% × 2,280,000)		34,200
Additional for ECA withheld (10% × 34,200)		3,420
Additional for Calabrian relief withheld (5% × 34,200)		1,710
Total tax and additionals withheld from salary	L.	39,330

h. Credit for coupon tax provisionally withheld from dividends (12/1.6)

Dividends subject to withholding of coupon tax	L.	1,150,000
Coupon tax withheld (15% × 1,500,000)	L.	225,000

i. Total complementary tax, additionals, and fee remaining due

Total tax and additionals		L.	1,368,418
Less: Total tax and additionals			
withheld from salary	39,330		
Coupon tax withheld	225,000		264,330
Total tax and additionals remaining due		L.	1,104,088
Collection fee (5% × 1,104,088)			55,204
Total complementary tax, additionals, and fee remaining due		L.	1,159,292

8. Total taxes (including family tax) and effective rate on aggregate income

Tax on:

Income from landowning (item 1)	L.	485,226
Agrarian income		......
Income from buildings		19,962
Income from movable wealth of category A (item 4)		18,837

Income from movable wealth of category C/2
   (item 6)   219,360
Complementary tax (item 7f)   1,368,418
Collection fee for complementary tax
   (from item 7i)   55,204
Family tax (2/3)[h]   1,500,000

    Total taxes .... L. 3,666,891
    Aggregate income (item 7a) .... L. 16,326,000

$$\text{Effective rate} = \frac{3,666,891}{16,326,000} = .2246$$

Effective rate = 22.46%

[h] Assumed.

12/2.   Corporations and Similar Entities

12/2.1 Objective Taxes

The liability of a corporation or similar entity for the tax on income from landowning, the tax on agrarian income, and the tax on income from buildings is determined in the same manner as that of an individual (12/1.1-12/1.3).

For purposes of the tax on income from movable wealth, income of a corporation is generally assessed on the basis of the balance sheet (13/2.2); the determination of business income is subject to special provisions with respect to capital gains, windfalls, and hidden reserves (7/1.3). Taxable income of a corporation is determined without deduction of a standard allowance, and there is no reduction in rate for the first L. 720,000 of taxable income. A special reduction in rate is applicable to certain types of income of credit firms and institutions (10/4.2). With these exceptions, the liability of a corporation for the tax on income from movable wealth is determined in the same manner as that of an individual.

Similarly, surtaxes and additionals related to the objective taxes are applied in the same manner as in the case of an individual.

12/2.2 Corporation Tax

a. DETERMINATION OF ASSETS. The taxable assets (*patrimonio*) of a corporation are the sum of subscribed and paid-in capital (*capitale*), balance sheet reserves and positive monetary revaluation funds, and profits of previous business periods carried forward, less losses of previous business periods carried forward and the amortized value of immovable property held only for the duration of a concession (3/2.3).

b. DETERMINATION OF INCOME. Aggregate income for the corporation tax includes (1) income determined for the tax on income from land-

ANALYSIS OF INCOME TAX   606

owning (12/1.1), multiplied by a coefficient of revaluation of 2.5; [40] (2) income determined for the tax on agrarian income (12/1.2), multiplied by a coefficient of revaluation of 3.5; (3) the net income determined for the tax on income from buildings; (4) the net income from movable wealth of category B, disregarding any loss carried forward, and increased by certain payments to directors (6/1.1g); (5) amounts received as a result of the distribution or division of the profits of a company or association of any type; (6) interest not included in income from movable wealth of category B; (7) income exempt from the objective taxes; and (8) any other income not otherwise included. Deductions are allowed for certain expenses incurred in producing income subject to the tax (6/1.5b); for ordinary taxes affecting income, inscribed in the rolls, whose collection was begun during the year (6/1.5e); and for losses of the business period resulting from the application of the rules relating to the tax on income from movable wealth (7/4.1).

c. RATES AND ADDITIONALS. For purposes of the corporation tax, taxable assets are taxed at the rate of 0.75%; in addition, that part of the aggregate income which exceeds 6% of the taxable assets is taxed at the rate of 15% (art. 146). If computation of aggregate income results in a loss, the tax is reduced at the rate of 10 times the proportion between the loss and the amount of the taxable assets (art. 149).[41] In any case, the reduction cannot exceed 90% of the tax. The tax is reduced by 25% for credit firms and institutions (10/4) and for certain investment companies (10/5).

There are no surtaxes applicable to the corporation tax; and the additional for Calabrian relief does not apply to the corporation tax due on the basis of the taxpayer's return, since the tax on that amount is not collected through rolls but is paid directly into the Treasury (13/3.2). However, the additional for ECA, at the rate of 10% of the tax due, is now applicable to the corporation tax,[42] and both additionals apply to the tax assessed on amounts in excess of those originally declared.

12/2.3 Tax on Bonds

Entities required to be taxed on the balance sheet basis (6/1.2b) are subject to a tax on bonds and similar securities, measured on the aggregate value of the securities as obtained from the balance sheet; the value

---

[40] These coefficients are established for 1963 by D.M. 10 November 1962.

[41] For example, if a corporation has taxable assets of L. 100,000,000, and sustains a net loss of L. 5,000,000, the reduction would be 50%, as shown below.

$$10 \times \frac{5,000,000}{100,000,000} = .5.$$

See also C.M. 1 June 1955, n. 351690.

[42] L. 10 December 1961, n. 1346, art. 1.

of securities issued during the second half of the business period is reduced by one half (3/3.2).

12/2.4 Withholding at Source

The tax on income from movable wealth for income of category A payable to corporations is withheld directly or paid with a right of recovery through withholding; this process is governed by the rules described for payments to individuals (12/1.6). Certain payments to foreign corporations are subject to provisional withholding of the tax on income from movable wealth under the rules discussed at 12/4. Withholding is made at the rate of 15% from distributions of profits by corporations and similar entities (9/2.7a). In the case of an entity required to be taxed on the balance sheet basis which is exempt from the corporation tax, and in the case of a foreign corporation, or an Italian corporation domiciled abroad, which is not subject to the corporation tax, this is a separate, noncreditable tax; in other cases, the withholding is credited against the corporation tax (9/2.7c). Profits allocated to bearer shares are subject to an 8% withholding in addition to the corporation tax (9/2.7d).

12/2.5 Example of Corporate Tax Computation

The following example illustrates the computation of the objective taxes and the corporation tax of a manufacturing corporation.

Example 2

The corporation is a manufacturing concern; the balance sheet at the end of the business period, the profit and loss account, and the industrial or commercial account are summarized below (items 1-3). The tax on income from movable wealth, the corporation tax, and the tax on bonds are computed in items 5-9.

1. Summary of balance sheet at end of business period
   a. Assets

Fixed capital	L. 200,000,000
Inventory (raw materials and finished products)	125,000,000
Business credits	5,000,000
Government securities	50,000,000
Corporate shares	50,000,000
Corporate bonds	50,000,000
Bank accounts	100,000,000
Cash	166,500,000
Total assets	L. 746,500,000

   b. Liabilities

Capital subscribed and paid	L. 300,000,000
Reserves	100,000,000
Bonds (L. 25,000,000 issued in second half of business period)	100,000,000
Depreciation fund (7/3.1)	120,000,000
Retirement funds	50,000,000

Business debts   10,000,000
Profit of business period (from item 2)   66,500,000

Total liabilities . . . . L. 746,500,000

2. Summary of profit and loss account

Gross profit before depreciation (from item 3)   L. 102,000,000
Dividends   15,000,000
Interest on corporate bonds   2,500,000
Interest on government securities   2,500,000

                                                       L. 122,000,000

Less: General expenses   30,000,000
       Depreciation   20,000,000
       Interest on bonds   5,000,000
       Interest on business debts   500,000

                                                          55,500,000

Profit of business period before taxes . . . . L. 66,500,000

3. Summary of industrial or commercial account

Closing inventory of preceding business period   L. 100,000,000
Increase in inventory   100,000,000
Wages   25,000,000
Salaries   15,000,000
Charges relative to wages and salaries (social security) 18,000,000
Maintenance and repairs   5,000,000
Other expenses of production   10,000,000

                                                       L. 273,000,000
Less: Closing inventory   125,000,000

Cost of production . . . . L. 148,000,000

Gross receipts from business   L. 250,000,000
Less: Cost of production   148,000,000

Gross profit before depreciation . . . . L. 102,000,000

4. Tax on income from movable wealth of category A, inscribed in the roll
   against the payor of the income, with a right to recover the tax from the
   recipient through withholding [a]

Interest on corporate bonds . . . . L.   2,500,000
Tax at 26%   650,000
Additional for ECA (10% × 650,000)   65,000
Additional for Calabrian relief (5% × 650,000)   32,500

Total tax and additionals . . . . L.   747,500

[a] This income is reported on the return for purposes of the corporation tax only.
In this example, it is assumed, in accordance with the usual practice, that the right
of recovery is not exercised. Hence the income is included in the recipient's income
for the corporation tax without any deduction for the tax on income from movable
wealth paid by the person paying the interest. The computation of the tax on income
from movable wealth of category A is shown here solely for purposes of illustration.
The payor would also bear the collection fee, amounting, in this case, to 5% of
L. 747,500, or L. 37,375.

5. Tax on income from movable wealth of category B [b]

Gross profit before depreciation (from item 3)		L. 102,000,000
Less: Depreciation	20,000,000	
General expenses		
(.8 × 30,000,000) [c]	24,000,000	
Interest on bonds		
(.925 × 5,000,000) [d]	4,625,000	
Interest on business debts		
(.925 × 500,000) [d]	462,500	
		49,087,500
Net income of category B		L. 52,912,500
Less: Deductible gratuities paid to employees		
Gratuities paid	5,000,000	
Limit (7/2.11)		
(5% × 52,912,500)	2,645,625	
		2,645,625
Taxable income of category B		L. 50,266,875
Tax on 4,000,000 at 18% (12/1.4c)		720,000
Tax on 6,000,000 at 20%		1,200,000
Tax on 40,000,000 at 22%		8,800,000
Tax on 266,875 at 23%		61,381
ICAP at 3.5%		1,759,341
Provincial additional to ICAP at 1.75%		879,670
Subtotal		13,420,392
Chamber of Commerce surtax at 2%		1,005,338
Total taxes and surtaxes		14,425,730
Additional for ECA (10% × 13,420,392)		1,342,039
Additional for Calabrian relief (5% × 13,420,392)		671,019
Total tax, surtaxes, and additionals		16,438,788
Collection fee (5% × 16,438,788)		821,939
Total tax, surtaxes, additionals, and fee		L. 17,260,727

[b] In the computation of income from movable wealth of category B, the example follows the form of the return, not standard accounting practice.

[c] Proportion assumed to be allocable, under the rules discussed at 7/2.1, to income subject to tax.

[d] Deductible in the proportion of gross receipts included in income taxable in category B to aggregate amount of gross receipts (7/2.5). In this example, the proportion is gross receipts from business (L. 250,000,000, from item 3) to gross receipts from business plus dividends plus interest (L. 250,000,000 + L. 15,000,000,000 + L. 2,500,000 + L. 2,500,000, from items 2 and 3).

It is assumed that the corporation has paid the tax on income from movable wealth of category A, on the interest paid out on its own bonds, and has not exercised its right to recover the tax from the recipient, so that the tax paid is deductible by the corporation as an expense of producing income.

6. Corporation tax: Taxable assets

Capital subscribed and paid in	L. 300,000,000
Reserves	100,000,000
Taxable assets	L. 400,000,000
Tax at 0.75%	3,000,000
Additional for ECA (10% × 3,000,000)	300,000
Total tax and additionals	L. 3,300,000

7. Corporation tax: Income

Net income of category B (from item 5)	L. 52,912,500
Dividends	15,000,000
Interest on corporate bonds	2,500,000
Interest on government securities	2,500,000
Aggregate income	L. 72,912,500

Less: Deductions

Taxes related to income paid or withheld during the year (6/1.5e)

Tax on income from movable wealth on income of category B of preceding year e	10,000,000

Expenses by their nature not deductible in determining aggregate income (6/1.5b)

General expenses (30,000,000 − 24,000,000)	6,000,000
Interest on bonds (5,000,000 − 4,625,000)	375,000
Interest on business debts (500,000 − 462,500)	37,500
Total deductions	L. 16,412,500
Aggregate income	L. 72,912,500
Less: Deductions	16,412,500
Net aggregate income	L. 56,500,000
Less: 6% of taxable assets (6% × 400,000,000)	24,000,000
Taxable income	L. 32,500,000
Tax (15% × 32,500,000)	4,875,000
Additional for ECA (10% × 4,875,000)	487,500
Total tax and additional	L. 5,362,500

8. Corporation tax: Credit for coupon tax withheld (12/2.4)

Dividends subject to withholding of coupon tax		L. 15,000,000
Coupon tax withheld (15% × 15,000,000)		L. 2,250,000
Total corporation tax and additionals		
Assets (item 6)	3,300,000	
Income (item 7)	5,362,500	
		L. 8,662,500
Less: Credit for coupon tax withheld		2,250,000
Corporation tax and additionals remaining due		L. 6,412,500

e Assumed.

9. Tax on bonds

Value of bonds other than those issued in second half
  of business period   L. 75,000,000
Value of bonds issued in second half of business
  period (.5 × 25,000,000)   12,500,000

Aggregate value of securities .... L. 87,500,000
Tax (0.5% × 87,500,000) .... L.   437,500

10. Total taxes and effective rate on aggregate income

Tax:

Tax on income from movable wealth of category B
  (item 5)   L. 17,260,727
Corporation tax: Taxable assets (item 6)   3,300,000
Corporation tax: Income (item 7)   5,362,500
Tax on bonds (item 9)   437,500

Total taxes .... L. 26,360,727
Aggregate income (from item 7) .... L. 72,912,500

$$\text{Effective rate} = \frac{26,360,727}{72,912,500} = .361$$

Effective rate = 36.1%

12/3. Other Taxpayers

12/3.1 Partnerships and Similar Companies

The liability of a partnership or similar company for the tax on income from landowning, the tax on agrarian income, and the tax on income from buildings is determined in the same manner as that of an individual (5/3.2).

Apart from certain provisions regarding capital gains and hidden reserves affecting the determination of income of a business company (7/1.3), a partnership's net income from movable wealth is determined in the same manner as that of an individual. Like an individual, a partnership is entitled to a single standard allowance of L. 240,000 (art. 89) (12/1.4b) and to a reduction in rate on the first L. 720,000 of taxable income from movable wealth (art. 90) (12/1.4c). Since a partnership cannot have income from employment, the allowance and the rate reduction are applicable first to category C/1 and then to category B.

Except as noted at 12/4, a partnership, as such, is not subject to any personal tax (5/3.2).

12/3.2 Cooperative Societies

A cooperative society is entitled to a single standard allowance of L. 240,000 (art. 89) (12/1.4b) and to a reduction in rate on the first L. 720,000 of taxable income from movable wealth (art. 90) (12/1.4c).

Since a cooperative society cannot have income from employment, the allowance and the rate reduction are applicable first to category C/1 and then to category B. Certain cooperative societies are entitled to special exemptions or deductions in determining income from movable wealth (5/2.5).

Exemption from the corporation tax is provided for cooperative societies of unlimited liability which carry on operations only with their own members and for certain classes of cooperative societies which satisfy specified conditions (5/5.10). Cooperative societies which meet all these conditions, except the limitation on capital, and cooperatives established by law or in fulfillment of legislative provisions for social utility or public interest are subject to the corporation tax, but only on that part of their taxable assets which exceeds L. 5 million; income of such an entity which exceeds 6% of taxable assets is subject to the corporation tax at the reduced rate of 7.5% (art. 152).

In all other respects, the tax liability of a cooperative society is determined in the same manner as that of a corporation (5/2.5).

12/4.   Nonresident Taxpayers

The rules governing the determination of taxable income of nonresident taxpayers are discussed at 11/3. Except for the operation of those rules, the tax liability of a nonresident is computed in the same manner as that of a resident. Foreign companies and associations operating in Italy through a permanent establishment are subject to the corporation tax to the extent explained at 11/3.4 and to the tax on bonds (3/3.1), even if not required to be taxed on the balance sheet basis.

Any person paying income to aliens or to Italians domiciled abroad for the transfer or licensing of intellectual property or for the exercise in Italy of an art or profession is required to make a provisional withholding, subject to later adjustment, of the tax on income from movable wealth (13/3.5). This withholding, which is computed on two thirds of the gross amount paid, is made at the rate of 18% from payments to business enterprises taxable in category B, by virtue of copyrights or fees or earnings for the grant or licensing for use of patents, designs, processes, formulas, trademarks, and the like, and at the rate of 8% from such payments when made to persons other than business enterprises. The rate is also 8% in the case of payments for the exercise of an art or profession in Italy (arts. 128, 273). Complementary tax is provisionally withheld from all of the payments described above, when made to individuals, at the rate of 4% on two thirds of the gross amount paid (art. 143). In all cases, the additional for ECA is withheld in accordance with the rules applicable to the taxes involved (art. 272). The additional for Calabrian relief is not withheld, since the amounts withheld under these provisions are paid directly into the Treasury (13/3.2). Withholding of ICAP and the provincial additional thereto, and of the additional for ECA, are required even if, by virtue of an international agreement, the income is exempt from withholding of the tax on income from movable wealth.

A withholding of 15% is made from distributions of profits by corporations and similar entities (9/2.7a); in the case of aliens or Italians domiciled abroad who are not subject to the complementary tax or the corporation tax, this withholding is not provisional but is a separate tax (9/2.7c).

12/5. Forms of Return

12/5.1 In General

The forms of return, which are the same for residents and nonresidents, are listed below.

1. Annual return of income of individuals (12/5.2).
2. Annual return of income of collective firms not required to be taxed on the balance sheet basis (12/5.3).
3. Annual return of income, assets, and bonds of companies and entities required to be taxed on the balance sheet basis (12/5.4).

An enterprise not required to be taxed on the balance sheet basis which elects to be so taxed (6/1.2b) does not use the third form of return described above, but attaches a copy of its balance sheet to whichever of the other forms it regularly uses. A foreign company or association not taxed on the balance sheet basis which is subject to the corporation tax under the rules described at 11/3.3 must file the third form of return for purposes of determining its liability for the corporation tax; it must also file the second form of return for purposes of determining its liability for the other direct taxes.

The forms of return do not provide for computation of tax, but merely call for information from which tax may be computed by the Tax Offices (13/2.1). The notice of assessment sent to the taxpayer (13/2.1) shows the income assessed by the Tax Office for all the taxes and the computation of the complementary tax.

A booklet of instructions for the completion of the return forms is issued annually by the Ministry of Finance.[43]

12/5.2 Reproduction of Annual Return of Income of Individuals

The return form for income of individuals is translated herein. A reproduction of the first page of the return is also included.

---

[43] See Ministero delle Finanze, Direzione Generale delle Imposte Dirette, *Guida pratica per la compilazione della dichiarazione unica dei redditi nell'anno 1962.*

Scadenza: 31 marzo 1962

MODULARIO F. - Imp. - 369	1) SCHEDA UNICA (*Imp. dir.*) Modello per le persone fisiche

Comune di................................ (*prov*....................................)

Ufficio distrettuale imposte dirette di............................

Posizione schedario N.....................

Numero meccanografico....................

```
ESTREMI DELLA PRESENTAZIONE

Presentata all'Ufficio delle Imposte di...............................
il.............................. n..................    Il Procuratore

........................................................
Presentata al Comune di......................................
il.......................... n.............    Il Sindaco

........................................................
```

DICHIARAZIONE ANNUALE DEI REDDITI DELLE PERSONE FISICHE

(Testo unico delle leggi sulle imposte dirette, approvato con decreto del Presidente della Repubblica 29 gennaio 1959, n. 645)

Il sottoscritto (1).. nato a..

il (2).. con domicilio fiscale nel Comune di..

abitazione in via.. n..............., di professione..

dichiara, con questo atto, le fonti, l'importo lordo, le spese detraibili e l'importo netto dei redditi prodotti

nell'anno 1961 quali risultano dalle indicazioni dei quadri (3)..

La dichiarazione relativa al periodo d'imposta precedente è stata presentata all'Ufficio di..................

STATO DI FAMIGLIA DEL CONTRIBUENTE

In questo prospetto debbono essere elencati: il coniuge, i figli legittimi, riconosciuti, adottivi e naturali, gli affiliati, i figliastri ed in genere tutte le persone (genitori, suoceri, ecc.) che, essendo unite al contribuente da vincoli di parentela o di affinità, abbiano diritto, per legge, agli alimenti e che effettivamente siano a suo carico.

Generalità dei componenti la famiglia	Grado di parentela con il contribuente	Data e luogo di nascita	Professione, arte, mestiere

(1) Scrivere in modo leggibile, preferibilmente in stampatello, cognome e nome. — (2) Indicare giorno, mese ed anno di nascita. — (3) Indicare i quadri compilati.

1) SINGLE RETURN (*Dir. tax*)
Form for individuals

Commune of . . . . *(prov.* . . . .)

District Office of Direct Taxes of . . . .

Card file position no. . . . .

Mechanographic number . . . .

INFORMATION ON FILING
Filed at the Tax Office of · · · · · · · · · · · · · · · · ·
on · · · · · · · · · · · no. · · · · · ·   Procurator
· · · · · · · · · ·
Filed at the Commune of · · · · · · · · · · · · · · · · ·
on · · · · · · · · · · · no. · · · ·   Mayor
· · · · · · · · · ·

Due: 31 March 1962

ANNUAL RETURN OF INCOME OF INDIVIDUALS

(*Testo unico of the laws on the direct taxes, approved by decree of the President of the Republic,
29 January 1959, n. 645*)

The undersigned (1) . . . . born at . . . .

on (2) . . . . having fiscal domicile in the Commune of . . . .

living in . . . . Street, no. . . . . , of profession . . . .

declares, by this act, the sources, the gross amount, the deductible expenses, and the net amount of the income produced in the

year 1961 as appearing in the schedules (3) . . . .

The return for the preceding tax period was filed at the Office of . . . .

FAMILY STATUS OF THE TAXPAYER

In this table must be listed: the spouse, the legitimate, recognized, adopted, and natural children, the affiliates, the step-children, and in general all persons (parents, parents-in-law, etc.) who, being related to the taxpayer by blood or marriage, have a right, by law, to support and who are actually dependent on him.

Identity of members of the family	Degree of relationship with the taxpayer	Date and place of birth	Profession, craft, trade
. . . .	. . . .	. . . .	. . . .
. . . .	. . . .	. . . .	. . . .
. . . .	. . . .	. . . .	. . . .
. . . .	. . . .	. . . .	. . . .
. . . .	. . . .	. . . .	. . . .
. . . .	. . . .	. . . .	. . . .
. . . .	. . . .	. . . .	. . . .
. . . .	. . . .	. . . .	. . . .

(1) Write legibly, preferably in printing, surname and given name. — (2) Specify day, month, and year of birth. — (3) Specify the schedules filled out.

ANALYSIS OF INCOME TAX

SCHEDULE *A.*

LANDS

This schedule concerns those who possess lands. The person declaring shall specify, in addition to his own, the lands of his wife and those of other persons over which he has free disposition or administration without the duty of rendering an accounting.

No. in order	Commune in which the lands are situated	Concern inscribed in the cadaster	Number of the cadastral division	Landowning income inscribed in the cadaster multiplied by 12		Agrarian income inscribed in cadaster multi-plied by 12 (1)		Type of farming (2)	Space reserved for the Office	
				Total	Share of person declaring	Total	Share of person declaring			
1	2	3	4	5	6	7	8	9	10	11
			TOTALS							

Remarks by the person declaring: . . . .

. . . .

. . . .

(1) This information will be omitted for rented lands.
(2) For rented lands, specify in the "Remarks of the person declaring" the surname and given name of the tenant, the rent, and the area.

Signature of person declaring

Done at . . . . *on* . . . . *196* . . .

. . . .

BUILDINGS:

Schedule B forwarded _____ to the department

_____ to the office of

Concern inscribed in the cadaster (col. 3)..........

.... on .... Taxable income belonging to the person declaring (total col. 14)..........

Signature of employee

---------------- (Cut along dotted line)

Person declaring.......... *Forwarding office*..........

SCHEDULE B.

BUILDINGS

This schedule concerns those who possess buildings.

Specify first the buildings subject to tax and, afterward, those exempt, giving for the latter the date of expiration of the exemption in the space "Remarks of the person declaring." The person declaring must attach, for the income of his wife and for that of other persons, over which he has free disposition or administration without the duty of rendering an accounting, separate schedules signed by them.

In cases of community (joint ownership) between husband, wife, and dependent children, the return of the entire income must be filed by the collective concern on the form of *return of collective firms not taxable on the balance sheet basis*; in such a case, the individual return concerns the share of the taxable income which belongs to the person declaring, who shall reply only to the questions of columns 1 to 5 and column 14.

For structures devoted specifically to the exercise of business activities (including shops, workshops, garages, warehouses, etc.) must be furnished only the information required by columns 1 to 8 if the owner there carries on directly the activity to which the structures are devoted; mention must be made of this activity in the space "Remarks of person declaring."

No. in order	Commune in which the building is found	CONCERN INSCRIBED IN CADASTER	Number of cadastral division	SIZE (1)					Gross income (rent or leasehold value) (2)	FIXED DEDUCTIONS			Taxable income (col. 9–12)	Share of taxable income belonging to the person declaring in cases of joint ownership	Space reserved for the Office
				Use	Floors	Functional rooms	Accessory rooms			1/4 or 1/3 of gross income (3)	Four and one half times the taxable income of 1938 (4)	Total (col. 10+11)			
1	2	3	4	5	6	7	8		9	10	11	12	13	14	15	16
:	:	:	:	:	:	:	:		:	:	:	:	:	:	:	:
:	:	:	:	:	:	:	:		:	:	:	:	:	:	:	:

To be carried forward..........

(1) Specify the actual present size. For buildings of more than one floor all belonging to the same owner, it is sufficient to specify the total number of floors and of rooms when they are already counted in the cadaster or in the past already declared separately by floors and by rooms. When one has ownership of only parts of the building, one should say: ground floor, mezzanine, first floor, second floor, etc. Considered functional rooms are those which are principally devoted to the ordinary use of the immovables (rooms, halls, galleries, kitchens, and the like). Considered accessory rooms are those necessary to the service or to the fulfillment of the principal rooms (baths, storerooms, lockers, verandas, corridors, and the like) or which supplement their function (garrets, cellars, drying-rooms, and the like).

(2) In the rent is included the increase to which the owner is entitled in cases of sublease. The expenses of light, water, porter, elevator, heating, and the like which are included in the rent are deducted from the rent itself.

(3) The deduction is one fourth of the gross income specified in column 9 for structures suitable for habitation or a third of that income for those devoted specifically to the exercise of business activities which are subject to the buildings tax because the owner does not directly carry on in them the activity to which they are devoted.

(4) This deduction applies only for buildings built and used as intended before 29 May 1946. When a taxable income of 1938 is lacking, that income is determined by comparison with the rents, in the year 1938, of buildings in analogous conditions, in the same commune.

No. in order	Commune in which the building is found	CONCERN INSCRIBED IN CADASTER	Number of cadastral division	SIZE (1)				Gross income (rent or leasehold value) (2)	FIXED DEDUCTIONS			Taxable income (col. 9→12)	Share of taxable income belonging to the person declaring in cases of joint ownership	Space reserved for the Office	
				Use	Floors	Functional rooms	Accessory rooms		1/4 or 1/3 of gross income (3)	Four and one half times the taxable income of 1938 (4)	Total (col. 10+11)				
1	2	3	4	5	6	7	8	9	10	11	12	13	14	15	16
											Carried forward.				
											TOTALS				

REMARKS OF PERSON DECLARING

NOTE: In the space "Remarks of person declaring" specify the heading of the collector's bill for the tax for the year 1961, the changes which have occurred in the concern and the title, when they have not already been introduced in the cadaster, and also changes in the size of the building in the year 1961. In the case of buildings not yet counted in the cadaster or which are being declared for the first time, a listing is necessary, even if on a separate sheet, of the tenants with specification of the individual units of immovable property, of the essentials of the act of lease, and of the rent.

Done at . . . . *on* . . . . 196 . . .

Signature of person declaring

COMPUTATION OF TAX

SCHEDULE *C.*

INDUSTRIAL, BUSINESS, ARTISAN ACTIVITIES, AGRARIAN LEASES

This schedule concerns those who carry on any industrial, business, or artisan activities, agrarian leasing, or animal husbandry.

Tenants of rural lands may merely specify, opposite the heading *Net income* on the following page, the agrarian income belonging to the land, sessed cadastrally, multiplied by the coefficient established for purposes of the complementary tax; they must, in that case, specify, in the space served for remarks of the person declaring: the concern inscribed in the cadaster for the leased land, the number of the cadastral division, the ea of the land, and the agrarian income inscribed in the cadaster multiplied by 12.

If the person declaring carries on different activities whose incomes are not classifiable in the same category, he must fill out a schedule for ch category of income.

The person declaring must attach, for the income of his wife, separate schedules signed by her.

Surname and given name or concern . . . .

Kind of activity . . . .

Location of business: Commune of . . . . Street . . . . no. . . . . . .

Seats of branches, affiliates, factories, etc. . . . .

Does the concern request that the taxable income be assessed on the basis of the accounting records? . . . .

If so, a copy of the balance sheet and of the profit and loss account must be attached.

	Declared by the taxpayer 1	Space reserved for the Office 2	3
GROSS PROCEEDS AND PROFITS			
— Total of sales and services . . . . L.	. . . .	. . . .	. . . . . .
— Gross commissions . . . . "	. . . .	. . . .	. . . . . .
— Interest . . . . "	. . . .	. . . .	. . . . . .
— Other gross earnings . . . . "	. . . .	. . . .	. . . . . .
. . . . "	. . . .	. . . .	. . . . . .
. . . . "	. . . .	. . . .	. . . . . .
TOTAL GROSS PROCEEDS AND PROFITS. . . L.	. . . .	. . . .	. . . . . .
DEDUCTIBLE COSTS, EXPENSES, AND LOSSES			
— Inventory at the beginning of the year of merchandise, of products, of semi-processed goods, of raw materials, and of subsidiary materials . . . . . L.	. . . .	. . . .	. . . . . .
— Cost of merchandise, raw and subsidiary materials purchased during the year . . . . "	. . . .	. . . .	. . . . . .
— Total of salaries and other allowances paid during the year to clerical personnel, gross of withholdings charged to the employees. No. employees . . . . Amount L.	. . . .	. . . .	. . . . . .
— Total of wages paid during the year gross of withholdings charged to the workers. No. workers . . . . Amount L.	. . . .	. . . .	. . . . . .
— Total of contributions on salaries and on wages charged to the enterprise "	. . . .	. . . .	. . . . . .
— Expenses for electrical and heat energy, etc. . . . . "	. . . .	. . . .	. . . . . .
— Other costs:			
. . . . "	. . . .	. . . .	. . . . . .
. . . . "	. . . .	. . . .	. . . . . .
(*a*) TOTAL . . . L.	. . . .	. . . .	. . . . . .
b) less (−) inventory at the end of the year of merchandise, of products, of semiprocessed goods, of raw materials, and of subsidiary materials . . . . L.	. . . .	. . . .	. . . . . .
Cost of merchandise and of products sold during the year ($a - b$) . . . . "	. . . .	. . . .	. . . . . .
To be carried forward . . . L.	. . . .	. . . .	. . . . . .

	Declared by the taxpayer 1	Space reserved for the Office 2	3
Carried forward ... L.	....	....	....
— Depreciation: aggregate annual amount .... L. Specify — on attached sheets, if necessary — for each category of property depreciable at the same rate: 1) kind; 2) date of purchase; 3) cost; 4) amount of depreciation for the year:	....	....	....
— Interest charges: (specify the identity and the domicile of the creditor and the total interest paid). 1) ....L. 2) .... " 3) .... "	....	....	....
— Total of rents paid .... " Identity and domicile of the owner of the rented business, or of the land, or of the premises.	....	....	....
— Salaries and wages not included under previous headings .... "	....	....	....
— Other expenses and losses of the business period: 1) .... " 2) .... " 3) .... "	....	....	....
TOTAL DEDUCTIBLE COSTS, EXPENSES, AND LOSSES L.	....	....	....
Net income (total gross proceeds and profits less (—) total deductible costs, expenses, and losses) .... L.	....	....	....
Fixed deduction for allowance (insofar as applicable) .... L.	....	....	....
Taxable income L.	....	....	....

Information on payment of the governmental concession fee relative to the first inspection of the books which the return covers: Reg-

istry Office of .... c.c.p. No. ....

payment No. .... on .... for the book ....

"   "   ....   "   "   "   " ....

"   "   ....   "   "   "   " ....

— Specify whether the business enjoys total or partial exemptions from tax and the type and the duration of the exemption ....

....

— Total of the leasehold value for owned premises specified in the schedule "Buildings" in which the business activity is carried on, L.
....

— Persons of the family occupied in the business (including the taxpayer) ....

....

For income of categ. C/2 (salaries and wages to employees) taxable through recovery, specify, carrying them forward from schedule *F*:

a) taxable at 4% (total of column 13 of schedule *F*)   = L. ....;

b) taxable at 8% (total of column 14 of schedule *F*)   = L. ....;

c) taxable complementary (total of col. 16 of schedule *F*) = L. ....;

_____ *REMARKS OF PERSON DECLARING* _____

....

....

N.B.—To the questions of this schedule the person declaring may add, for each business, according to its characteristics, other headings of proceeds and of expenses.

Signature of person declaring

Done at .... on .... .196 ....

....

COMPUTATION OF TAX

SCHEDULE *D.*

PROFESSIONAL AND ARTISTIC ACTIVITIES

This schedule concerns those who carry on any profession, artistic or scientific activity, as well as ministers of worship, representatives without deposit, insurance agents, intermediaries, and the like. Representatives, insurance agents, and the like will specify the total of commissions and other earnings, giving the concern by which they were paid.

The person declaring must attach, for the income of his wife, separate schedules signed by her.

Surname and given name . . . .

Kind of profession, office, or activity . . . .

Communes and office addresses in which the activity is carried on . . . .

Street . . . . no. . . . .

Are you subject to the general tax on receipts as a professional under art. 5 of the Law of 16 December 1959, n. 1070? . . . .

	Declared by the taxpayer 1	Space reserved for the Office 2	3
GROSS EARNINGS			
— Gross total of receipts . . . . (*) L.	. . . .	. . . .	. . . .
— Amounts to be deducted because taken in as reimbursements of expenses . . "	. . . .	. . . .	. . . .
EARNINGS GROSS OF DEDUCTIBLE GENERAL EXPENSES . . L.	. . . .	. . . .	. . . .
DEDUCTIBLE EXPENSES			
— Aggregate total of salaries and wages paid to employees gross of withholdings. No. employees . . . . Amount . L.	. . . .	. . . .	. . . .
— Contributions on salaries and wages charged to the professional or artist . . "	. . . .	. . . .	. . . .
— Expenses for rental of premises of exercise . . . . "	. . . .	. . . .	. . . .
Identity and domicile of the owner of the premises of exercise:			
. . . .			
— Expenses for heating, light, etc. L.	. . . .	. . . .	. . . .
— Other expenses (books, periodicals, etc.) . . . . "	. . . .	. . . .	. . . .
. . . . "	. . . .	. . . .	. . . .
TOTAL DEDUCTIBLE EXPENSES . . L.	. . . .	. . . .	. . . .
Net income . . L.	. . . .	. . . .	. . . .
— Fixed deduction for allowance (insofar as applicable) . . . . L.	. . . .	. . . .	. . . .
Taxable income . . L.	. . . .	. . . .	. . . .

— Family members who collaborate in the professional activity, including the taxpayer:

. . . .

For income of categ. C/2 (salaries and wages to employees) taxable through recovery, specify, carrying forward from schedule *F*:

a) taxable at 4% (total of column 13 of schedule *F*)   = L. . . . . ;

b) taxable at 8% (total of column 14 of schedule *F*)   = L. . . . . ;

c) taxable complementary (total of column 16 of schedule *F*) = L. . . . .

REMARKS OF PERSON DECLARING

. . . .

. . . .

(*) For *professionals*, on the figure specified opposite "Gross total of receipts," the general tax on receipts is applied at the rate of 1.30%.

Signature of person declaring

Done at . . . . on . . . . 196 . . . .

. . . .

ANALYSIS OF INCOME TAX

SCHEDULE *E*.

OTHER INCOME (not included in the preceding schedules)

This schedule is divided into two sections: the first, for income to be declared for purposes of the movable wealth tax and the complementary tax; the second, for income already subjected to the movable wealth tax, or exempt from the same, which is to be declared only for purposes of the complementary tax.

The person declaring must attach, for the income of his wife and that of other persons over which he has free disposition or administration without the duty of rendering an accounting, separate schedules signed by them.

ASSETS	Debtor person or entity, employer	Contract establishing the income elements of the act and of its registration	Income (interest, payments in money or in kind, etc.)	Space reserved for the Office	
1	2	3	4	5	6
SECTION I					
1) Income from capital given in loan					
2) Life annuities (1).					
3) Salaries and allowances of personnel employed by private owners of rural and urban properties (stewards, porters, keepers, and the like)					
4)					
5)					
Fixed deduction for allowance from income under 2 and 3 (insofar as applicable).					
TOTAL OF INCOME (*A*) . .					

ASSETS	Employer, owner of land, issuing entity, debtor person or entity	Income (salaries and accessories, dividends, etc.)	Space reserved for the Office	
1	2	3	4	5
SECTION II				
a) Income from work as an employee subject to tax through withholding, net only of withholdings required by law or by the labor contract charged to the employee (2):				
1) salaries, wages, pensions, and cost-of-living bonus (excluding complementary payments and family allowances), and extra months (13th, 14th, etc.)				
2) remuneration for extraordinary work				
3) appointment bonus or equivalents				
4) other earnings: prizes, daily expense allowances, directors' attendance fees, fees of any kind, travel allowances (these in the measure of 40%), etc.				
b) Cadastral agrarian income of *mezzadri* and *coloni* (3)				
c) Income from public and equivalent securities, shares, bonds (4)				
d) Participations in collective concerns and nonshare companies				
e) Earnings of directors, managers, overseers, not included under letter *a*)				
f) Life annuities (5)				
g)				
h)				
TOTAL OF INCOME (*B*) . .				
TOTAL OF INCOME OF SECTIONS I AND II (*A*+*B*) . .				

———— *REMARKS OF PERSON DECLARING* ————

. . . .

. . . .

(1) Specify life annuities paid by individuals not taxed through recovery against the debtor.

(2) Employees of public administrative offices may declare income from work net of all legal withholdings, decreased by the family supplement and the special supplementary allowance and increased by withholdings of special character (*Incis* rent, transfer of salary-free insurance premiums, etc.)

(3) Specify the part of the cadastral income involved on the basis of the agrarian contract multiplied by the coefficient 12 and, then, by 3.5.

(4) On the sheet attached to this schedule, give a separate detailed list of the assets (securities of the state, shares, bonds, etc.), with specification of descriptive information for each of them (kind, issuer, quantity, denominations, nominal value, income).

(5) Specify life annuities paid by entities and subjected to tax through withholding.

Signature of person declaring

Done at . . . ., *on* . . . . 196. . .   . .

COMPUTATION OF TAX

Annex to SCHEDULE *E* section II letter *c*)

LIST OF PUBLIC AND EQUIVALENT SECURITIES, OF SHARES, AND OF BONDS

Kind of securities 1	ISSUER 2	Quantity 3	Denomi- nations 4	Aggregate nominal value 5	Aggregate income received in 1961 6	Remarks 7

To be carried forward . . . L.

ANALYSIS OF INCOME TAX

Kind of securities 1	ISSUER 2	Quantity 3	Denominations 4	Aggregate nominal value 5	Aggregate income received in 1961 6	Remarks 7
				Carried forward . . . L.	. . . .	
				TOTAL . . . L. . .	. . . .	

Done at . . . . *on* . . . . 196 . . . .

Signature of person declaring

. . . .

NOTE— 1) List in order public securities, equivalent securities, shares, and bonds, including also securities transferred during the year 1961, whenever their yields have been collected in that year. — 2) The total of column 6 must correspond to the amount given in schedule *E*, section II, column 3 of the return form, opposite "Income from public and equivalent securities, shares, and bonds."

Commune of . . . .

Card file position no. . . . .

Mechanographic number . . . .

MOVABLE WEALTH TAX CAT. C/2 AND COMPLEMENTARY TAX ON INCOME FROM WORK (RECOVERY)—RETURN FOR PURPOSES OF FINAL ADJUSTING ASSESSMENT FOR THE YEAR 1961 AND OF PROVISIONAL INSCRIPTIONS IN THE ROLL FOR THE YEAR 1963

Surname and given name or concern . . . .

Kind of business . . . .

Location of business: Commune of . . . . *Street* . . . .

This schedule must be filled out by those who have employed personnel (employees or workers), to whom have been paid individually during the year 1961 aggregate remuneration which, in relation to the pay period, has exceeded L. 20,000 monthly — L. 10,000 semimonthly — L. 5,000 weekly — L. 833.33 daily.

Done at . . . . , *on* . . . . .196 . . . .

Signature of person declaring

. . . .

NOTICES

a) Col. 5; must be declared: all recurring or occasional remuneration, ordinary or extraordinary, on whatever basis paid (double salaries, extra months, cost-of-living allowances, gratuities, percentages and participations, compensation for extraordinary work or special duties and the like), amounts paid for representation expenses, indemnities, and the value of payments in kind.

b) Col. 6; must be declared: daily travel expenses and duties away from home settled without rendering an accounting, and meal allowances paid to seamen.

c) Col. 10; the allowance for purposes of the movable wealth tax in relation to the pay period, respectively of L. 20,000 monthly; L. 10,000 semimonthly; L. 5,000 weekly; L. 833.33 daily.

d) Col. 13-14; the amount taxable at 4% (col. 13) is the amount which, in each pay period, does not exceed, net of the deductions of columns 8, 9, and 10, the total of L. 60,000 monthly, of L. 30,000 semimonthly, of L. 15,000 weekly, or L. 2,500 daily; the excesses over those limits, paid in each pay period, are the amount taxable at 8% (col. 14).

e) Col. 15; the further deductible share is of L. 40,000 monthly; L. 20,000 semimonthly; L. 10,000 weekly; L. 1,666.66 daily.

f) Col. 17; must be specified: subsidies paid by Provinces, Communes, and other Public Entities to their own employees, on a purely charitable basis; the cost-of-living allowance; remuneration exempt for a large family, and in general any other amount on which withholding of tax is not applied.

ANALYSIS OF INCOME TAX

No. in order	SURNAMES AND GIVEN NAMES OF RECIPIENTS	Domicile	Classi-fication (employee or worker)	Gross amounts paid			Deductions			
				Salaries and other allow-ances on whatever basis paid	Daily allowances for travel and meals	TOTAL (col. 5+6)	With-holdings for welfare and contri-butions	Subtract 60% of income in col. 6	Allowance	TOTAL (columns 8+9+10)
1	2	3	4	5	6	7	8	9	10	11

N.B. - Work out the sum of the figures given in the individual columns.

Include in the list, with all the information required in columns 1 to 11 and in column 17, also employed personnel for whom withholding of tax

COMPUTATION OF TAX

Net taxable AMOUNT for Movable Wealth (columns 7 – 11)	Movable Wealth Taxable amount from column 12, divided into		Complementary		Other amounts on whatever basis paid, on which tax has not been withheld	REMARKS (Period to which payments are referred when entire year is not involved)	RESERVED FOR THE OFFICE		
	taxable at 4%	taxable at 8%	Further allowance beyond that in col. 10	Excess taxable at 1.50% (col. 12 – 15)			Movable Wealth		Complementary
							taxable at 4%	taxable at 8%	Taxable
12	13	14	15	16	17	18	19	20	21

aas not been made, because the remuneration in each period has not exceeded the allowance.

ANALYSIS OF INCOME TAX

AGGREGATE TOTAL OF COMPULSORY CONTRIBUTIONS CHARGED TO THE EMPLOYER PAID DURING THE YEAR 1961

ENTITY	Information on payment		Amount	ENTITY	Information on payment		Amount
	N.	Date			N.	Date	
. . . .	. . . . .	. . .	. . . .		*Carried forward . . . L.*		. . . .
. . . .	. . . . .	. . .	. . . .				
. . . .	. . . . .	. . .	. . . .				
. . . .	. . . . .	. . .	. . . .				
. . . .	. . . . .	. . .	. . . .				
. . . .	. . . . .	. . .	. . . .				
. . . .	. . . . .	. . .	. . . .				
. . . .	. . . . .	. . .	. . . .				
. . . .	. . . . .	. . .	. . . .				
. . . .	. . . . .	. . .	. . . .				
. . . .	. . . . .	. . .	. . . .				
. . . .	. . . . .	. . .	. . . .				
. . . .	. . . . .	. . .	. . . .				
. . . .	. . . . .	. . .	. . . .				
. . . .	. . . . .	. . .	. . . .				
. . . .	. . . . .	. . .	. . . .				
. . . .	. . . . .	. . .	. . . .				
. . . .	. . . . .	. . .	. . . .				
	To be carried forward . . . L.		. . . .		*Aggregate total . . . L.*		. . . .

REMARKS: . . . .

INSCRIPTIONS IN THE ROLL AND REFUNDS (*Reserved for the Office*)

INSCRIPTIONS IN THE ROLL AND REFUNDS	Movable wealth tax - Categ. C/2		Complementary tax
	at 4%	at 8%	
1) *Aggregate taxable income shown by this return* . . . . L.	. . . .	. . . .	. . . .
2) Taxable income inscribed provisionally in the roll for the year 1961 . . . . L.	. . . .	. . . .	. . . .
3) *Provisional adjustment* (1 − 2) – SPECIAL ROLL issued in the year . . . . .due. . . . . L.	. . . .	. . . .	. . . .
4) FINAL ADJUSTMENT – SPECIAL ROLL issued in the year . . . . .due. . . . . L. (in black) – RELIEF: list no. . . . . of . . . . L. (in red)	. . . .	. . . .	. . . .
5) FINAL TAXABLE INCOME FOR THE YEAR 1961 . . . . L.	. . . .	. . . .	. . . .
6. *Provisional inscription for the year* 1963 . . . . L.	. . . .	. . . .	. . . .

SCHEDULE *G.*

INCOME AND DEDUCTIONS FOR PURPOSES OF THE COMPLEMENTARY TAX

The taxpayer must declare in this schedule his own income (even if exempt from the appropriate objective taxes), as well as that of his wife and that of other persons, over which he has free disposition or administration without the duty of rendering an accounting, included in schedules attached to this return.

Income:	Taxpayer's own income 1	Income of wife 2	Income of children and of other persons over which there is free disposition 3	Space reserved for the Office 4	5	6
1) *Lands* (Schedule *A*): — Landowning income (multiplied by 2.5)(1) . . . . . L.						
— Agrarian income (multiplied by 3.5)(1) . . . . "						
2) *Buildings* (Schedule *B*): — Taxable income . . . . "						
3) *Industries, businesses, leases* (Schedule *C*): — Net income (*) . . . . "						
4) *Professional and artistic activities* (Schedule *D*): — Net income (*) . . . . "						
5) *Other income* (Schedule *E*): — Income (*) TOTAL SECTION I AND II . . . . . "						
TOTAL . . . . L.						

(1) For purposes of the adjustment for 1961 the multipliers 3 and 4 are used.
(*) The income to be declared is income gross of the fixed deduction for allowance.

		Corrected 2	Final 3
6) *Aggregate total of income* (col. 1 + 2 + 3). . . . . L.			
Deductions:			
a) Taxes related to income from lands, from buildings, and from movable wealth inscribed in the rolls whose collection has begun in 1961, or paid through withholding in that year . . . . L.			
b) Other deductible taxes and contributions (family tax, etc.) . . . . "			
c) Annual life insurance premium (policy no. . . . . Ins. Institution . . . .) "			
d) Interest charges (excluding those deducted for the movable wealth tax) . . . . "			
e) Other deductions . . . . "			
7) Total deductions (*a* + *b* + *c* + *d* + *e*). . . . . L.			
8) *Net aggregate income* (6 — 7) . . . . L.			
f) Deductions for family burdens (L. 50,000 for the wife and for each dependent family member). . . . . "			
g) Fixed deduction for allowance . . . . "	240,000		
9) Total deductions (*f* + *g*) . . . . L.			
10) *Taxable income* (8 — 9) . . . . L.			

The undersigned states, under his own liability, that this is a complete and truthful return of his own income and of the deductible expenses.

Signature of person declaring

Done at . . . . on . . . . 196 . . . .

RESERVED FOR THE OFFICE

SETTLEMENT OF THE TAX	Declared	Corrected	Final
1) Taxable income . . . . L.			
2) Complementary tax and relative additional for ECA on emoluments of public employees declared net . . . . L.			
3) Total taxable income (1 + 2). . . . . L.			
4) Tax due on the total of net income rounded off (rate . . . .) . . . . . . L.			
Deductions:			
a) withholding of 1.50% made in 1961 by the employer or by the Public Administration . . . . L.			
b) share of adjustment of provisional withholdings under article 284 of T.U. 29 January 1958, n. 645 . . . . "			
c) tax provisionally inscribed in roll for 1961 . . . . "			
5) Total deductions for purposes of adjustment for the year 1961 . . . . L.			

12/5.3   Summary of Annual Return of Income of Partnerships and
         Similar Companies

The return form for partnerships and other companies not required to be taxed on the balance sheet basis (5/3.1) contains schedules for buildings (Schedule I); industrial, business, and artisan activities, and agrarian leases (Schedule II); movable wealth of category C/2 and the complementary tax on income from work (Schedule II-A); and other income (Schedule III). These schedules, except Schedule III, are substantially similar to the corresponding schedules of the individual return form (12/5.2), and, for this reason, the return form is not reproduced or translated here.

12/5.4   Translation of Annual Return of Income, Assets, and Bonds of
         Corporations and Similar Entities

The return form for income, assets, and bonds of corporations and other entities required to be taxed on the balance sheet basis (6/1.2b) is translated herein; Schedule C, income from buildings, has been omitted, as it is similar to Schedule B of the individual return form (12/5.2).

FORM 3 (*Dir. tax*)

INFORMATION ON FILING
Filed at the Tax Office of . . . .
on . . . . and registered at no. . . . .
Procurator
. . . .
Filed at the Commune of . . . .
on . . . . and registered at no. . . . .
Mayor
. . . .

Commune of . . . . *(Prov. of* . . . .)

District Office of Direct Taxes of . . . .

Mechanographic number . . . .

Group and subgroup . . . .

Department . . . .

ANNUAL RETURN OF INCOME, OF ASSETS, AND OF BONDS OF COMPANIES AND ENTITIES TAXABLE ON THE BALANCE SHEET BASIS (1) FOR PURPOSES OF THE DIRECT TAXES

(*Testo unico of the laws on the direct taxes, approved by decree of the President of the Republic 29 January 1958, n. 645*)

BALANCE SHEET ON . . . .

On behalf of the Company, Entity, or Association, (2) . . . .

carrying on (3) . . . . with fiscal domicile in the Commune

of . . . . Street . . . . no. . . . . (teleph. no. . . . .)

legal office in . . . . , administrative office in . . . . ,

and principal factory in . . . . , the undersigned, in the capacity of (4) . . . . .

. . . . , declares the income, the assets, and the bonds shown in the specifications

contained in the schedules and tables of this return, for purposes of the movable wealth tax, the tax on buildings, and the corpo-

ration tax and the tax on bonds. For these last two taxes, he attaches the document attesting the payment to the Provincial

Treasury Office of . . . . . . the aggregate amount of L. . . . . according to information given in

Schedule "G" of this return.

The return for the preceding tax period was filed at the Office of . . . .

Done at . . . . , *on* . . . . 196 . . .

Person declaring (legal representative)

. . . .

The president of the board of overseers or the members of other governing body

. . . .

Account chief (5)   *General manager*

. . . .

. . . .

. . . .

N.B.—To the return must be attached the annexes specified at the end of this form.

(1) For foreign Companies and Associations not subject to the movable wealth tax on the balance sheet basis, this return is filled out only for purposes of the corporation tax and the tax on bonds, in addition to the duty to file the single return for purposes of the other taxes on the appropriate form.
(2) Specify, in full, the name of the Company or Association.
(3) Specify the principal branch of economic activity carried on.
(4) Specify the capacity of the person declaring: Delegated Councilor, Single Director, and the like.
(5) The signature of the account chief is required only for the companies contemplated by the 2d paragraph of art. 2397 of the Civil Code.

SCHEDULE *A*

INCOME OF CATEGORY A

	Amount Declared	Space reserved for the Office
Interest received:		
1) Taxable in category *A* in the name of the recipient (annex 5) . . . . L.		
. . . . ,,		
. . . . ,,		
Interest charges:		
2) On deposits in c/a, savings, etc., taxable through recovery (annex 8) . . . . L.		
3) On loans, advances, etc., when not already taxed in the name of the creditor (annex 8) . . . . ,,		
4) On bonds (annex 8) . . . . ,,		
5) . . . . ,,		
6) . . . . ,,		
TOTAL . . . . L.		

SCHEDULE *B*

INCOME OF CATEGORY B

	Amount Declared	Space reserved for the Office
A) POSITIVE COMPONENTS		
1) Gross proceeds of the business period, as from table IV . . . . L.		
2) Commissions and fees received or receivable (annex 4) . . . . ,,		
3) Interest received or receivable (excluding that on state securities and on bonds - annex 5) . . . ,,		
4) Windfalls and nonexistence of charges however coming about (annex 6) . . . . ,,		
5) Capital gains realized or distributed or inscribed in the balance sheet . . . . ,,		
6) Income not taxed in previous business periods imputed to capital or distributed or in any way appearing in the balance sheet . . . . ,,		
7) Other gross proceeds (excluding income from lands, from buildings insofar as subjected to the buildings tax, and dividends on shares in portfolio) . . . . ,,		
a) . . . . ,,		
b) . . . . ,,		
TOTAL . . . . L.		
B) NEGATIVE COMPONENTS		
1) Fiscal cost of production, as from table IV . . . . L.		
2) Cancellations and discounts . . . . ,,		
3) General expenses (annex 7) . . . . ,,		
4) Salaries to administrative personnel . . . . ,,		
4/A) Charges relative to above . . . . ,,		
5) Depreciation (table I) . . . . ,,		
6) Interest and discount charges (annex 8) . . . . ,,		
7) Commissions paid or payable (annex 9) . . . . ,,		
8) Deductible taxes and fees (annex 10) . . . . ,,		
9) Various losses including capital losses on securities (annex 11) . . . . ,,		
10) Repayments and distributions to members of cooperatives (art. 111) . . . . ,,		
11) . . . . ,,		
TOTAL . . . . L.		
C) NET INCOME (*A—B*) . . . . L.		
D) DEDUCTIONS FROM NET INCOME		
1) Exemption for payments made as gratuities (art. 84, letter *g*) . . . . L.		
2) Allowance for cooperatives (art. 89, 3d paragraph) . . . . ,,		
3) Losses of previous business periods (art. 112) . . . . ,,		
TOTAL . . . . L.		
E) TAXABLE INCOME (*C—D*) . . . . L.		

Person declaring (**legal representative**)

Done at . . . . , *on* . . . . 196 . . .

. . . .

SCHEDULE *D*

Company, Association, or Entity . . . .

Fiscal domicile . . . .   *Filed at* . . . .

Mechanographic number . . . .   *Group and subgroup* . . . .   *and registered at No.* . . . . . .

CORPORATION TAX - DETERMINATION OF TAXABLE ASSETS (art. 147)

No. in order	SPECIFICATION OF ELEMENTS	Declaration of the Company	Assessment of the Office	Final Assessment
		(Lire)	(Lire)	(Lire)
I.	—Companies and Entities taxable on the balance sheet basis (arts. 8 and 145)			
	Positive elements			
1	Capital subscribed and paid in, or, for Entities, net assets			
2	a) Ordinary reserves			
	b) Extraordinary reserves (1)			
	c) Positive monetary revaluation funds (1)			
3	Financial amortization set aside for property gratuitously revertible			
4	Profits of previous business periods carried forward			
	A) TOTAL GROSS ASSETS			
	Deductions			
5	Losses of earlier business periods carried forward			
6	Share of integral value of immovable property gratuitously revertible corresponding to the time already elapsed since the concession (V. details attached)			
	B) TOTAL OF DEDUCTIONS			
	C) TAXABLE ASSETS (*A - B*)			
7	Fixed deduction of 5 million for cooperatives (article 152)			
	D) TAXABLE DIFFERENCE FOR THE ABOVE COOPERATIVES ONLY			
II.	—Foreign Companies and Associations not taxable on the balance sheet basis			
	Aggregate total of capital devoted to operations or in any way employed in the territory of the state			
	Settlement of the tax involved in this schedule			
1	Tax computed at the rate of 0.75% on the taxable assets			
2	Reduction of the tax — for companies and entities showing a loss in the computation of income (art. 149) — on the basis of the percentage of the loss reported to the assets (Reduction of . . . . %)			
3	Difference (1 - 2)			
4	Reduction of the tax for companies and entities provided for by arts. 153 and 154 (. . . .% of the total given at no. 3 above)			
5	Tax due (Difference 3-4)			

REMARKS

. . . .

. . . .

. . . .

. . . .

(1) Excluding reserves and funds set aside to cover specific charges or liabilities or for third persons.

ANALYSIS OF INCOME TAX

Determination of taxable income (art. 148)

No. in order	SPECIFICATION OF ELEMENTS	Declaration of the Company	Assessment of the Office	Final Assessment
		(Lire)	(Lire)	(Lire)
	Positive components			
1	Income from movable wealth, category *B* (letter *E* of schedule *B*)	. . . .	. . . .	. . . .
2	Losses of previous business periods (letter *D*, no. 3, of schedule *B*)	. . . .	. . . .	. . . .
3	Income from landowning resulting from the cadastral estimates (multiplied by 30).	. . . .	. . . .	. . . .
4	Agrarian income resulting from the cadastral estimates (multiplied by 42)	. . . .	. . . .	. . . .
5	Taxable income from buildings determined for purposes of the applicable tax	. . . .	. . . .	. . . .
6	Amounts received by way of distribution or division of the profits of companies and associations of any type	. . . .	. . . .	. . . .
7	Interest not included in the determination of income from movable wealth of category *B*	. . . .	. . . .	. . . .
8	Salaries, compensation, and allowances, paid to directors or to members, computable under letter *f* of art. 148	. . . .	. . . .	. . . .
9	Income exempt from the applicable taxes (here including income which in any form, even substitutive, enjoys temporary or permanent modifications or reductions of tax, determined with the criteria in effect for the taxes themselves), income exempt as gratuities, and the allowance for cooperatives under schedule *B*, letter *D* (1)			
10	Any other income not included in the preceding numbers:			
	a)	. . . .	. . . .	. . . .
	b)	. . . .	. . . .	. . . .
	A) TOTAL POSITIVE COMPONENTS			
	Deductions			
1	Expenses, charges, or losses inherent in the production of the various classes of income, insofar as by their nature they were nondeductible in the determination of the income itself	. . . .	. . . .	. . . .
2	Ordinary taxes, related to the various classes of income, inscribed in the rolls whose collection began during the tax period to which the return applies	. . . .	. . . .	. . . .
3	Loss of the business period determined by the criteria of the movable wealth tax, category *B*	. . . .	. . . .	. . . .
	B) TOTAL DEDUCTIONS	. . . .	. . . .	. . . .
	C) NET AGGREGATE INCOME (*A—B*)	. . . .	. . . .	. . . .
	D) DEDUCTION OF 6% OF THE TAXABLE ASSETS (see schedule *D* - letter *C*)	. . . .	. . . .	. . . .
	E) TAXABLE INCOME (*C—D*)	. . . .	. . . .	. . . .
	Settlement of the tax involved in this schedule			
1	Tax computed at the rate of 15% or of 7.50% on the income shown at letter *E* (2)	. . . .	. . . .	. . . .
2	Reduction of the tax for the companies and entities mentioned in articles 153 and 154 (. . % of the total shown at no. 1 above)	. . . .	. . . .	. . . .
3	Tax due (Difference 1—2)	. . . .	. . . .	. . . .

REMARKS

. . . .

. . . .

. . . .

(1) Specify in an annex the details of exempt income and the duration of the exemption.
(2) The reduced rate of 7.50% is provided by art. 152, second paragraph, for the cooperative societies specified in arts. 151, letter *a*, and 152.
N.B. — With respect to foreign companies and associations operating in Italy, the positive components and the deductions are referred to the employment, in the territory of the state, of the capital specified in schedule *D*, or in any way to a permanent establishment of the taxpayer in the territory of the state.

TAX ON BONDS

Determination of taxable values (art. 158)

SPECIFICATION OF ELEMENTS	Declaration of the Company (5+9) (Lire)	Assessment of the Office (Lire)	Final Assessment (Lire)
Companies or Entities taxable on the balance sheet basis (1)	. . . . .	. . . .	. . . . . .
Foreign Companies and Associations not taxable on the balance sheet basis (2)	. . . . .	. . . .	. . . . . .

	BONDS AND OTHER SECURITIES QUOTED ON EXCHANGE					BONDS AND OTHER SECURITIES NOT QUOTED ON EXCHANGE						
	Kind	Number	Nomin. value	Price paid (3)		Kind	Number	Nomin. value				
	1	2	3	Unit 4	Aggregate 5	6	7	Unit 8	Aggregate 9			

Left side row group label: **Bonds and other securities in circulation excluding those issued in the 2d half of the business period.**

(rows of dotted entry lines)

TOTAL *A*

Left side row group label: **Bonds and other securities issued in the 2d half of the business period.**

(rows of dotted entry lines)

TOTAL *B*

Settlement of the tax involved in this schedule			
Tax 5 o/oo corresponding to total *A* (col. 5+ col. 9)	. . . .	. . . .	. . . . . .
Tax 2.5 o/oo corresponding to total *B* (col. 5+ col. 9)	. . . .	. . . .	. . . . . .
Tax reduced to 1.25 o/oo in the cases provided by the law (art. 159, fifth paragraph)	. . . .	. . . .	. . . . . .
TAX DUE	. . . .	. . . .	. . . . . .

REMARKS

. . . .

. . . .

. . . .

(1) Declare the securities shown in the balance sheet to which the return refers.
(2) Declare the securities shown on 31 December of the year to which the return of income refers.
(3) Last exchange price paid before the closing of the business period.

SCHEDULE *G*

SETTLEMENT OF THE TAXES DUE

No. in order	BASIS OF PAYMENT	Paid on the basis of the return of the Company or Entity	Due as result of assessment of the Office	To be inscribed in the roll or paid in lump sum
		(Lire)	(Lire)	(Lire)
1	Tax computed on assets (schedule *D*)	. . . .	. . . .	. . . .
2	Tax computed on taxable income (schedule *E*)	. . . .	. . . .	. . . .
	TOTAL	. . . .	. . . .	. . . .
3	Tax on bonds and other securities (schedule *F*)	. . . .	. . . .	. . . .
	GENERAL TOTAL	. . . .	. . . .	. . . .
	Deductions by way of refund by virtue of the law of 25 February 1960, n. 163:			
	—corporation tax (1/8 of L. . . . .)	. . . .		
	—tax on bonds (1/8 of L. . . . .)	. . . .		
	TOTAL DEDUCTIONS	. . . .		
	AMOUNT TO BE PAID TO TREASURY . . .	. . . .		

Information on payment:

a) receipt no. . . . . of . . . . of the Provincial Treasury . . . .

b) payment to c/a no. . . . . of . . . . at the Post Office of . . . .

R E M A R K S

. . . .
. . . .
. . . .
. . . .

Done at . . . . , *on* . . . . 19 . . . .

Person declaring (legal representative)

. . . .

The president of the board of overseers or the members of other governing body

. . . .

Account chief   *General manager*

. . . .

Company or Entity . . . .

TABLE I

TABLE OF CHANGES IN FIXED CAPITAL (Immovables, plant, and other fixed assets, technical and otherwise)

DEVELOPMENT	TOTAL as from balance sheet (10 + 11 + 12)	Depreciable categories									Assets fiscally not depreciable	
		at . . . %	at . . . %	at . . . %	at . . . %	at . . . %	at . . . %	at . . . %	Total	By their nature (nonbusiness buildings, lands, and others)	Because completely depreciated
1	2	3	4	5	6	7	8	9	10	11	12
Balance sheet values at end of preceding business period											
Increases:											
purchases											
contributions received											
new buildings and installations . . .											
. . . .											
capital gains taken into accounts . . .											
TOTAL *A* . .											
Decreases:											
through sales, contributions, exchanges											
a) value realized											
b) profits (—), losses (+) . . .											
c) already depreciated cost (+) . .											
asset statement value of assets totally or partially destroyed or in any way eliminated . . .											
devaluations											
TOTAL *B* . .											
Balance sheet values at end of business period (*A—B*)											
Depreciation funds:											
at beginning of business period											
(+) depreciation in the business period:											
ordinary											
advanced											
(—) depreciation relative to assets in any way eliminated (sales, contributions, exchanges, etc.) . .											
(—) transfer to other accounts											
at end of business period											

Done at . . . . , on . . . . . . : 19 . . .

Person declaring   (legal representative)

TABLE II

Company or Entity. . . . .

TABLE OF CHANGES IN PARTICIPATIONS AND OTHER MOVABLE INVESTMENTS

a) Purchases and contributions received:

Securities	Quantity	Nominal Value	Cost

b) Sales and contributions made:

Securities	Quantity	Nominal Value	Proceeds

c) Remainder at end of business period:

| Securities | Quantity | Unit Value | | | Balance sheet value |
		nominal	of cost	at close of business period(1)	

(1) Art. 103 of the *testo unico*.

SUMMARY

Balance sheet value at end of preceding business period . . . . L. . . . .

Increases:

     — Purchases and contributions received . . . . L. . . . .

     — Revaluations . . . . L. . . . .

                                         L. . . . .

                 TOTAL . . . L. . . . .

Decreases:

     — Sales and contributions made. . . . . L. . . . .

     — Devaluations . . . . L. . . . .

                                         L. . . . .

Profits (—) or losses (+) over sales and contributions . . . . L. . . . .

                                         L. . . . .

Balance sheet value at end of business period . . . . L. . . . .

                          Person declaring (legal representative)

Done at . . . ., on . . . . .19 . . . .

TABLE III

Company or Entity . . . .

TABLE OF CHANGES

OF THE LEGAL, BYLAW AND EXTRAORDINARY RESERVES, EXPENSE FUNDS, RISK FUNDS, PERSONNEL SETTLEMENT FUND, TAX FUND, AMOUNTS SET ASIDE IN GENERAL, AND ANY OTHER DIVISION OF LIABILITY REFERRING TO UNLIQUIDATED CHARGES

(To be filled out separately for each heading)

DEVELOPMENT						
Amount at beginning of business period . . . . . L.						
Increases for:						
— allocation of profits of preceding business period . . . . L.						
— imputation of taxed capital gains. . . . . "						
— imputation of shares charged to business period . . . . "						
— transferred from other accounts . . . . . . "						
TOTAL . . . . L.						
Decreases for:						
— use to cover deductible expenses and liabilities . . . . L.						
— use to cover other expenses and liabilities . . . . "						
— transfer to other accounts . . . . "						
TOTAL . . . L.						
Amount at end of business period. . . . . L.						

Done at . . . . , on . . . . 19 . . . .

*Person declaring (**legal representative**)*

. . . .

Company or Entity . . . .

TABLE OF THE INDUSTRIAL OR BUSINESS ACCOUNT

Remainder at end of preceding business period of raw materials, products in processing, finished products L. . . . .

Purchases . . . . ” . . . .

Wages . . . . ” . . . .

Salaries to technical personnel . . . . ” . . . .

Charges relative to wages and salaries . . . . ” . . . .

Maintenance and repairs . . . . ” . . . .

Other expenses of production:

    a) . . . . ” . . . .

    b) . . . . ” . . . .

    c) . . . . ” . . . .

    d) . . . . ” . . . .

                                               TOTAL . . . . . . L. . . . .

Deduct: Remainder at end of business period valued according to art. 102 . . . . L. . . . .

                                 Fiscal cost of production . . . . L. . . . .

    + Devaluation of remainder . . . . ” . . . .

    — Revaluation of remainder . . . . ” . . . .

                                   Balance sheet cost . . . . L. . . . .

                                   Gross profit of business period . . . . . L. . . . .

                                   Gross total of proceeds . . . . L. . . . .

Done at . . . . , on . . . . 19 . . . . .

                                                          Person declaring (legal representative)

                                                          . . . .

                                                      The president of the board of overseers or the members of other governing body

                                                        . . . .

                                                        . . . .

        Account chief   *General manager*

. . . .

N. B.— For businesses furnishing credit, this table should be replaced by an extract of the economic account giving the gross earnings. Interest, discounts received, and other earnings should be subdivided by the various categories (discounts received on advances, *riporti,* current accounts, corresponding accounts, opening of credit, foreign services, merchandise, counters, etc.). Interest and discounts paid should also be separated by category (on advances, discounts, savings deposits, corresponding accounts, current accounts, *riporti,* personnel welfare accounts, pension fund, etc.).

    For insurance businesses, this table should likewise be replaced by an extract of the economic account with the movement of the various reserves, of premiums received and of premiums paid, and of commissions received and those paid.

Company or Entity . . . .

LIST OF DIRECTORS AND OF AUDITORS OR OVERSEERS

in office during the business period and total of compensation paid to them in relation to their office

No. in order	SURNAME AND GIVEN NAME	Functions performed (director – overseer)	Residence	Fiscal domicile	Compensation paid	Other amounts on whatever basis paid	Total	REMARKS
1	2	3	4	5	6	7	8	9

To be carried forward . . L.

No. in order	SURNAME AND GIVEN NAME	Functions performed (director - overseer)	Residence	Fiscal domicile	Compensation paid	Other amounts on whatever basis paid	Total	REMARKS
1	2	3	4	5	6	7	8	9
				Carried forward L.				
				TOTAL . . L.				

Done at . . . ., on . . . ., 19 . . . . . .

Account chief　　　　　*General manager*

The president of the board of overseers
or the members of other governing body

Person declaring (legal representative)

COMPUTATION OF TAX

ANNEXES TO BE ATTACHED TO THE RETURN

(dated and signed by the legal representative only, with exception of annex 1 which must be signed
also by the other persons required to sign the return)

1) Copy of the balance sheet and of the profit and loss statement or copy of the financial report.

2) Copy of the minutes of the shareholders' meeting which approves the balance sheet, of the report of the Board of Directors and of the Overseers, and of the schedule of division of the profits.

3) List of debtors and creditors, with their addresses, classified according to the headings of the final state of the assets, with specification of the amounts at the closing of the business period.

Businesses furnishing credit must file, instead, a copy of the quarterly position.

4) For businesses which carry on predominantly activities of representation, mediation, etc., a list by categories of the commissions and fees received, with specification of the concern which has paid them.

5) List of interest received or receivable and dividends.

6) List of windfalls.

7) List of the general administrative and overhead expenses, with separate specification of the expenses whose deduction from fiscal income is not allowed.

8) List with names of interest and discounts paid or payable. For businesses furnishing credit, what is said at no. 3 applies.

9) List by category of the commissions and fees paid, with specification of the recipients and their addresses.

10) List of the taxes and fees paid or charged during the business period, with separate specifications of those not allowed in deduction for tax purposes.

11) Details of the various losses, including negative windfalls.

12) If the Company or Entity has income exempt in whole or in part, specify the type and the duration of the exemption with a detailed description of the exempt income.

13) Comparison table between the total of salaries and wages carried forward in schedule *B* and Table IV and the total appearing in the return of income of Cat. *C-2* taxable through recovery.

Information on payment of the governmental concession fee relative to the first inspection of the books to which the return refers.

Registry Office of. . . . . .c.c.p. No. . . . .

payment no.. . . . . on. . . . . for book. . . . .

   ,,   ,, ... ,, ... ,, ,, ...

   ,,   ,, ... ,, ... ,, ,, ...

   ,,   ,, ... ,, ... ,, ,, ...

   ,,   ,, ... ,, ... ,, ,, ...

   ,,   ,, ... ,, ... ,, ,, ...

Any remarks in order on the keeping of the books and accounting records (art. 253 of the *testo unico*).

. . . .

. . . .

. . . .

Person declaring (legal representative)

. . . .

. . . ., ... 19. .

The president of the board of overseers
or the members of other governing body

. . . .

. . . .

. . . .

CHAPTER 13

ADMINISTRATION AND PROCEDURE

13/1. **Returns**
- 13/1.1 In General
  - a. Requirement of return
  - b. Signing of return
  - c. Time limits for filing
  - d. Place of filing
- 13/1.2 Content of the Return
- 13/1.3 Documents Attached to the Return
- 13/1.4 Withholding and Information Returns
- 13/1.5 Report of Termination of Activity or Other Basis of Taxation

13/2. **Assessment**
- 13/2.1 In General
- 13/2.2 Review of Returns
- 13/2.3 Estimated Assessments
- 13/2.4 Assessment by Agreement
- 13/2.5 Supplementation or Modification of the Assessment

13/3. **Payment of Tax**
- 13/3.1 In General
- 13/3.2 Direct Payment into the Treasury
- 13/3.3 Direct Withholding from Government Payments
- 13/3.4 Payment of Taxes of Others with Recovery through Withholding
- 13/3.5 Provisional Withholding

13/3.6   Inscription in the Rolls
     a. In general
     b. Effect of appeal
     c. Adjustments
13/3.7   Collection through Rolls
13/3.8   Collection of Delinquent Taxes

13/4.   Protests and Appeals
13/4.1   In General
13/4.2   Complaint to the District Commission
13/4.3   Appeal to the Provincial Commission
13/4.4   Appeal to the Central Commission
13/4.5   Appeal to the Intendant of Finance Against Withholding
13/4.6   Appeal to the Tax Office Against Inscription in the Roll
13/4.7   Appeal to the Intendant of Finance Against Acts of the Collector in Execution
13/4.8   Appeal to the Minister of Finance Against Application of Penalties
13/4.9   Appeal to the Ordinary Courts
     a. In general
     b. Competence
     c. Time limits
13/4.10 Appeal to the Supreme Court of Cassation for Violation of Law
13/4.11 Extraordinary Appeals
13/4.12 Payment of Tax Pending Review

13/5.   Refunds

13/6.   Time Limits on Assessment and Collection
13/6.1   Assessment
13/6.2   Collection

13/7.   Interest, Penalties, and Prosecutions
13/7.1   In General
13/7.2   Omitted, Late, or Incomplete Returns
13/7.3   Taxpayer's Failure To Furnish Information or To Comply with Other Requests and Orders

13/7.4   False Returns or False Statements of Taxpayer
13/7.5   Returns and Information Regarding Income of Others
13/7.6   Late Payment of Tax
13/7.7   Failure To Withhold Taxes or To Pay Taxes Withheld
13/7.8   Miscellaneous Offenses

13/1.   Returns

13/1.1   In General

a. REQUIREMENT OF RETURN. The taxpayer reports information regarding his income and expenses on return forms and in documents attached to the return. Based on the return, the required documents, and other information, an assessment of income is made by the Tax Office and is transmitted to the taxpayer in a notice of assessment if it differs from the amount of income reported on the return (13/2.1).

Whoever possesses income or capital subject to tax is required to file an annual return, even if no changes have occurred since the preceding tax period (art. 17). An individual whose aggregate income for purposes of the complementary tax, before allowances, does not exceed L. 720,000 need not file a return for income assessed under the cadastral system (9/4.2, 10/2.2, 10/2.3) or for income taxable with a right of recovery from the recipient (13/3.4). A person whose taxable income for purposes of the tax on income from buildings (9/4.2) is less than L. 2,000, and who does not possess other income subject to tax, is also not required to file a return (art. 20). Failure to file a return if required, however, results in the imposition of penalties (13/7.2) and the application of special assessment provisions (13/2.3).[1] The returns of individuals lacking legal capacity to act and of persons other than individuals must be filed by their representatives (art. 17) (1/4.11). If more than one person is required to file a return of the same income, filing by one of them relieves the others of the requirement of filing (art. 17).

A single return is filed for all of the income and capital of the taxpayer (art. 17). The forms of return are approved by decree of the Minister of Finance and are published in the *Gazzetta ufficiale*. Copies of the forms may be obtained without charge at the Tax Offices or at the town halls of communes having no Tax Offices; they may also be purchased

---

[1] It appears that the failure to file a return of income from movable wealth does not invoke the special assessment provisions if income does not exceed the standard allowance described at 12/1.4b. Comm. Centr. 8 March 1960, n. 25886; Comm. Centr. 21 April 1961, n. 42171. For contrary decisions, however, see Comm. Centr., Sez. un., 12 November 1941, n. 47391; Comm. Centr., Sez. un., 22 May 1950, n. 13610. The question is examined in Poli, "Maggiorazione del reddito, dichiarazioni tardive e ricorsi contro il ruolo," *Imp. dir. erariali*, 1962, 450.

at a standard sale price from retailers of monopoly goods (art. 18). A taxpayer who filed a return for the previous year receives a return form by mail from the tax administration.

When the return is filed at the District Office of Direct Taxes (1/4.2), or at the town hall, a receipt must be issued even if not requested by the taxpayer (art. 29). Proof of the filing of the return is given by this receipt, by the receipt for the registered letter, or by any other document of the postal administration verifying the date of mailing. No other proof may be brought to contradict or supplement the evidence of the records, registries, and office documents (art. 29).

b. SIGNING OF RETURN. The return of an individual is invalid unless signed by the taxpayer himself or by his legal or designated representative (art. 26) (1/4.11). The return of an entity taxed on the balance sheet basis (6/1.2b) is invalid unless signed by the legal representative of the taxpayer (art. 27). In addition, the return of an entity taxed on the balance sheet basis must be signed by various other officers of the entity in accordance with the provisions outlined below (art. 27).

1. The return must be signed by the person charged with the general management (*direzione generale*) of the enterprise.
2. The return of a corporation having a capital of at least L. 50 million must be signed by the person in charge of accounting (*contabilità*).
3. The return of an entity having a controlling board (*organo di controllo*) must be signed by the members of the board, or by the president if the board is collectively responsible.

Failure to comply with these requirements does not render the return invalid; however, it does permit the administration to determine the income on the basis of the economic situation of the business, deduced from elements and data available to it (arts. 27, 120) (13/2.3).

c. TIME LIMITS FOR FILING. All taxpayers other than entities required to be taxed on the balance sheet basis (6/1.2b) must file their returns on or before 31 March of each year (art. 21). An entity required to be taxed on the balance sheet basis must file its return within one month of the approval by the shareholders of the balance sheet (*bilancio*) or annual financial report (*rendiconto*). If the balance sheet or annual financial report has not been approved within the period prescribed by law or by the bylaws of the entity, the return must be filed within one month of the expiration of that period. However, entities required to be taxed on the balance sheet basis must report on or before 31 March of each year all remuneration paid by them to employees during the preceding year (13/1.4).

If a company not required to be taxed on the balance sheet basis reorganizes, without closing its business period, into a company required to be taxed on the balance sheet basis, or vice versa, the return for the tax period before the reorganization must be filed within three months of the reorganization decision (art. 22). If entities required to be taxed on the balance sheet basis are merged or consolidated, the return for the business period of any extinguished entity must be filed by the surviving or resulting entity within three months after the merger or consolidation (art. 22). The final return relating to the outcome of the liquidation of an entity required to be taxed on the balance sheet basis must be filed within three months of the deposit of the final balance sheet with the registry of enterprises.[2]

A return filed within one month of the expiration of the applicable time limit is valid, but a penalty may be imposed for the late filing (arts. 23, 243) (13/7.2). If the return of an entity taxed on the balance sheet basis is filed more than one month after the expiration of the time limit, the tax administration may determine income on the basis of the economic situation of the business, deduced from all information available to it (art. 120) (13/2.3).

d. PLACE OF FILING. The return is filed at the District Office of Direct Taxes or at the town hall of the commune in whose jurisdiction the person filing it has his fiscal domicile (*domicilio fiscale*) (art. 29). The return may also be sent to the Tax Office by registered mail; in this case, it is considered filed on the day on which it is deposited at the post office, which must stamp the date on the return. The filing of a return at an office other than one of those specified above is considered effective on the day on which the return reaches the competent Tax Office.

For tax purposes, each person is considered to have a fiscal domicile in a commune of Italy in accordance with the rules listed below (art. 9).[3]

1. An Italian citizen resident in Italy is domiciled in the commune in whose civil register he is inscribed.
2. An Italian citizen resident abroad is domiciled in the commune of last residence or, if there is no commune of last residence, in the commune in which he was born.
3. An alien is domiciled in the commune in which he resides or, if he has no residence in any commune, in a commune in which he has lived for at least one year.
4. An entity formed in Italy has its domicile in the commune in which its legal office (*sede legale*) is situated or, if it has no legal office, in the commune in which it regularly carries on its principal activity. The legal

---

[2] See CC art. 2453. Since the registry of enterprises does not yet exist, the balance sheet is deposited with the Chancellery of the Tribunal (1/4.10f); see R.D. 30 March 1942, n. 318 (provisions for the actuation of the Civil Code and transitory provisions), arts. 100, 101.

[3] Having a fiscal domicile in this sense must be distinguished from having a domicile in Italy for purposes of the rules relating to the taxation of income produced abroad (11/2.2).

office of an enterprise is considered to be located in the commune in whose registry of enterprises that enterprise is listed as having its principal office (CC arts. 2196, 2197).[4]

5. A company formed abroad which has not established secondary offices in Italy is domiciled in the commune in which its administrative office (*sede amministrativa*) is situated (that is, where its accounts are kept) or, if it has no administrative office, in the commune in which it regularly carries on its principal activity.

If the fiscal domicile of an individual or an entity cannot be determined by using these rules, it is considered to be in the commune in which the income was produced; if the income was produced in several communes, in the commune in which the greatest part of the income was produced; if the income was not produced in Italy, in the commune in which the income was enjoyed (art. 9).

If the commune of fiscal domicile determined by the application of these provisions is different from that in which the taxpayer carries on its principal activity or, if the taxpayer is a company formed abroad, is different from that in which it has its administrative office, the Office of the Intendant of Finance has the power, by an order supported by reasons, to establish the fiscal domicile in the commune in which the taxpayer regularly carries on his activities or in which the administrative office is established (art. 10). This power is exercised by the Ministry of Finance if the fiscal domicile resulting from the application of the rules is in a different province from that in which the taxpayer carries on its principal activity, or if a company formed abroad, has its administrative office. Moreover, under special circumstances, a taxpayer who submits a petition supported by reasons may be authorized by the Office of the Intendant of Finance or, when appropriate, by the Ministry of Finance, to establish his fiscal domicile in a commune different from that determined by the application of the provisions described above. Measures establishing fiscal domicile taken under these provisions must be communicated to the parties concerned, and are final (*definitivi*) (art. 10).

13/1.2   Content of the Return

The return must specify the positive and negative elements (gross income and deductions) necessary for the determination of the taxable income and capital of the tax period for purposes of the various taxes (art. 24). The return form (12/5.1) indicates the degree of specification required. If the return does not contain a detailed specification of the positive and negative elements, the notice of assessment from the Tax Office need not be supported by detailed reasons; and detailed reasons

---

[4] Since the registry of enterprises does not yet exist, the enterprise is registered with the Chancellery of the Tribunal; see note 2 *supra*.

are not required for the assessment of income which the taxpayer fails to report (art. 37) (13/2.1). If a taxpayer taxed on the balance sheet basis fails to specify the positive and negative elements of income and capital, the administration has the power to determine its income on the basis of the economic situation of the business, deduced from any available information (art. 120) (13/2.3).

The return of an entity taxed on the balance sheet basis, unless the entity is classified as a small business under the Civil Code (7/1.2b), must report the essential elements (*estremi*) of receipts of payment of the tax on governmental concessions (4/7) due at the time of the first inspection of the books and accounting records (art. 24).

If the taxpayer wishes to take advantage of the allowance of accelerated depreciation (7/3.5b), the request therefor, specifying the amounts of increased depreciation for which deduction is requested, must be made when the annual return is filed (art. 98).

13/1.3   Documents Attached to the Return

Any entity which is required to be taxed on the balance sheet basis (art. 28) and any enterprise which elects to be so taxed (art. 104) must attach to its return a copy of its balance sheet or of its annual financial report, which must also be signed by the persons required to sign the return (13/1.1b). An entity which is required to be taxed on the balance sheet basis must also attach to the return a list of the directors (*amministratori*) and auditors (*revisori*) or overseers (*sindaci*) (5/2.1) who were in office during the business period covered by the balance sheet or financial report, specifying the residence and fiscal domicile of each (art. 28); it must also attach a list of the shares purchased or sold during the business period, other than those purchased or sold by credit firms acting as intermediaries,[5] and a list of shares given or taken in *riporto* during the business period.[6] Any other association or company must attach to its return a list of the partners or associates who are personally liable for the debts of the firm, specifying the residence and the fiscal domicile of each. If these requirements are not fulfilled, the administration has the power to determine the income of the company on the basis of the economic situation of the business, deduced from any available information (art. 120) (13/2.3).

Any person who receives income subject to provisional withholding (13/3.5) must attach to his return a certificate from the payor, stating the total amount paid and the total amount withheld for each of the taxes collected by withholding (art. 28). For purposes of applying the credit for tax withheld from distributions of profits under the provisions

---

[5] L. 29 December 1962, n. 1745, art. 3.
[6] L. 29 December 1962, n. 1745, art. 8.

described at 9/2.7a, the requirement of this certificate is optional with the Tax Office.[7] When taxes are paid directly to the Treasury (13/3.2), a statement from the Provincial Treasury Office verifying payment must be attached to the return.

13/1.4 Withholding and Information Returns

Persons who pay income subject to tax recoverable through withholding (13/3.4) or income subject to provisional withholding of tax (13/3.5) must report the payment of such income on their own returns (art. 19). However, a taxpayer whose tax period differs from the calendar year (6/3.2) must report on or before 31 March of each year, on the regular form (12/5.4), the remuneration paid by it during the preceding calendar year (art. 21) (13/1.1c) and need not report it on the return.

A return reporting payments subject to tax recoverable through withholding or subject to provisional withholding of tax must specify the identities and domiciles of the recipients and the amount paid to each (art. 25). This requirement does not apply, however, to payments of interest by credit firms and institutions (10/4.4).

In the case of payments of income from work as an employee, the information listed below must be furnished on the return of the employer (art. 25).

1. The gross amount of remuneration, including employer's social security contributions, paid to each recipient, and the net amount after deducting employer's contributions, distinguishing standard allowances, amounts from which, and the rates at which, the tax on income from movable wealth was withheld, and the amounts from which the complementary tax was withheld.

2. A list of all other payments of any sort, made to individual employees, from which tax has not been withheld.

3. The total amount of compulsory social security contributions paid by the employer during the year and the essential elements (*estremi*) of their payment.

With respect to the payments which are subject to provisional withholding of the tax on income from movable wealth and of the complementary tax under the rules described at 13/3.5, the payor's return must specify, for each recipient, the amount and reasons for the payments and the amounts withheld; the return of a business enterprise must also specify amounts paid to directors and auditors or overseers in relation to their duties and not subjected to withholding (art. 25).[8]

Reports of the issue of shares by newly formed companies, of the movement of shares resulting from changes of capital, and of changes in the

---

[7] L. 29 December 1962, n. 1745, art. 18.
[8] As amended by L. 21 April 1962, n. 226, art. 1.

nominal value of shares must be made by the issuing company on or before 31 January and 31 July of each year for changes arising in the six-month period ending respectively on 31 December and 30 June.[9] The 1962 law providing for withholding from distributions of profits by corporations and similar entities (9/2.7a) introduced the additional reporting requirements listed below.

1. On or before 31 March of each year, a company must declare to the Tax Office, on a special form approved by decree of the Minister of Finance, the aggregate total of profits and of withholdings made from each distribution of profits during the preceding calendar year, attaching attestations of the Provincial Treasury Office showing the payments made.[10] If gratuitous shares have been allotted or the nominal value of the shares has been increased gratuitously (9/2.3), the declaration must contain the elements upon which the determination of the profit subjected to withholding has been based and must specify the participation attributable to each share. A limited liability company or a limited liability cooperative society in which participations are not represented by shares must specify the total amount of profit attributable to each member, giving his residence and fiscal domicile.

2. On or before 15 February of each year, a company must communicate to the general card index of share certificates information regarding the ownership of securities and withholdings from distributions of profits (9/2.8).

3. A company whose shares are held in *riporto* must make annual communications to the card index regarding the ownership of the shares (9/2.8). In addition, credit firms, exchange agents, and stock exchange commission agents must make communications to the card index regarding shares held in *riporto* which they have given in *riporto* to others (10/4.4). Similar provisions apply to sales on time and sales for cash with execution deferred.

4. A corporation or other entity required to be taxed on the balance sheet basis must file, attached to its annual return, a list of shares given and taken in *riporto* during the business period (9/2.8).

5. On or before 15 February of each year, a fiduciary company must communicate to the card index and to the competent Tax Office information regarding shares held by it on behalf of third persons (9/2.8).

These communications are required, even if tax is not withheld because the recipient is not inscribed in the rolls of the complementary tax (9/2.7b), but they are not required in the case of shares of a cooperative society which is exempt from withholding under the rules described at 9/2.7b. The communications are not required in the case of profits allocated to bearer shares issued under regional laws; such profits are subject to the special treatment described at 9/2.7d. The reports are made to the Central Section of the Tax Register (*Sezione Centrale*

---

[9] R.D. 29 March 1942, n. 239, art. 37.
[10] L. 29 December 1962, n. 1745, art. 2.

dell'Anagrafe Tributaria), at the Ministry of Finance in Rome, which enters them in a general card index of share certificates.[11]

Public administrative offices and public entities must report, without a request from the Tax Office, the essential elements of all contracts of *appalto* and *somministrazione* (8/4), specifying the identity and fiscal domicile of the contracting parties and the amount of the contract payments (art. 40). This report must be made to the Tax Office of the fiscal domicile of the contracting party within 90 days of the registration or, if registration is not necessary, within 90 days of the closing of the contract. Any Chamber of Commerce, Industry, or Agriculture and any professional organization must, on or before 31 March of each year, submit to the Tax Office in whose jurisdiction it has its office a list of the persons inscribed in or deleted from its rolls during the preceding year, specifying the identity and the fiscal domicile of each person (art. 40). Public administrative offices which pay to business enterprises subsidies or premiums subject to provisional withholding (13/3.5) must communicate information about these payments, on or before 31 March of each year, to the Tax Office at the fiscal domicile of the recipient (art. 40).

Further information on payments of income may be required during the course of assessment (13/2.2).

13/1.5   Report of Termination of Activity or Other Basis of Taxation

In case of termination of the basis of a tax (6/1.1a) during the tax period, the taxpayer may file a report of the termination in the manner prescribed for the filing of the return (art. 30) (13/1.1). The report may be filed separately from the return and before the beginning of the period during which the return must be filed (art. 30). For purposes of the complementary tax, a report of termination may be filed only in case of the taxpayer's death (art. 144). If the notice of termination is omitted, the taxpayer (or his heirs) may appeal against inscription in the roll for total or partial nonexistence of the tax liability (art. 188) (13/4.6), provided that the inscription has not been preceded by the service of a notice of assessment.[12]

13/2.   Assessment

13/2.1   In General

After examining the return (13/1), the tax administration assesses the income, rectifying taxable items erroneously declared and assessing omitted items ex officio (13/2.3), and sends the taxpayer an appropriate notice of assessment (art. 31) if the income assessed differs from that

---

[11] R.D. 29 March 1942, n. 239, arts. 35, 40. On the mechanization of the index and the availability of the information in it for use by the Tax Offices, see C.M. 30 December 1959, n. 501578.

[12] As amended by L. 21 April 1962, n. 226, art. 1.

reported in the return. The taxpayer may appeal this assessment under the rules relating to tax litigation (13/4). For the taxes on income from landowning, on agrarian income, and on income from buildings, the assessment is made by the District Office of Direct Taxes in whose jurisdiction is located the immovable property on whose income the tax is based; for the other taxes, the assessment is made by the Tax Office in whose jurisdiction the taxpayer has his fiscal domicile (art. 33) (13/1.1d). A taxpayer who owns immovable property from which he derives income subject to any of the cadastral taxes must keep the Tax Office in whose jurisdiction the property is located informed, by registered mail, of his current fiscal domicile (art. 33). Except for the fact that special deductions may be allowed (6/1.5a), the assessments of income from buildings and income from movable wealth are valid in all respects for purposes of the complementary tax (art. 141) and the corporation tax (art. 150).

The normal method of assessing the income of a taxpayer not taxed on the balance sheet basis, if not a business enterprise, is the determination of various positive and negative elements (gross income and deductions) composing the income (13/2.2). However, if such a taxpayer fails to file a return or to furnish all of the information necessary to check its completeness and accuracy, his income may be estimated by the Tax Office (13/2.3). In addition, income of an individual, for purposes of the complementary tax, may be estimated if there is evidence that his net income is greater than that resulting from a determination by the ordinary method (13/2.3).

The income of a business enterprise not taxed on the balance sheet basis is normally assessed by estimate on the basis of the economic situation of the business (13/2.3). The income of an entity or enterprise taxed on the balance sheet basis, however, is normally determined on the basis of information obtained from the balance sheet and profit and loss statement (13/2.2), subject to modification or correction of individual entries, and may be estimated only if the taxpayer has failed to comply with certain requirements regarding returns and records (13/2.3).

Provision is made also for assessment by agreement between the taxpayer and the tax administration (13/2.4). If a taxpayer has failed to file a return, the assessment of income of those classes which are subject to annual variation must be based on the assessment for the preceding tax period, increased by 10%, without prejudice to the assessment ex officio of any increment of income (13/2.3).

A notice of assessment which is not supported by detailed reasons (*analiticamente motivata*) is invalid, provided that the taxpayer takes exception to it in the proceedings before the tax commission of first degree (art. 37). Detailed reasons are not required, however, for the assessment of income which the taxpayer has failed to report, or when the return lacks a detailed specification of the positive and negative elements. The requirement of detailed reasons means, in practice, that the items of income or expense altered in the assessment must be specified, and reasons given for the changes. The requirement does not prevent the Tax Office, in the application of the provisions regulating estimated assessments (13/2.3), from estimating the amounts of the individual items changed. In addition, the amount of detail required may vary according to whether the taxpayer has filed a return on time, has kept accounts and exhibited them on demand, and, if an entity taxed on the balance sheet basis, has filed a proper balance sheet.

The service on the taxpayer of notices and other documents required by law is governed by article 38 of the *Testo unico* and by articles 137-151 of the Code of Civil Procedure.

Any person required by law to pay the tax of another person, if the tax arises exclusively out of facts or situations referable to those persons (13/3.4), has a right to intervene in the assessment proceeding, whether or not the tax is payable in advance (art. 14). The taxpayer may appeal such an assessment under the rules relating to tax litigation (art. 31) (13/4).

13/2.2   Review of Returns

The normal method of assessing the income of a taxpayer taxed on the balance sheet basis or the income of any other taxpayer except a business enterprise is by the determination of the various positive and negative elements (gross income and deductions) composing the income. Such an assessment is known as an analytical assessment (*accertamento analitico*), as distinguished from the estimated or inductive assessments discussed at 13/2.3.

If the taxpayer has filed a return within the legal time limits (13/1.1c), specifying the positive and negative elements necessary for the determination of taxable income, and has also furnished all data and produced all books, records, and documents necessary for a check of the completeness and truthfulness of the return, income from movable wealth is assessed by a determination of the various positive and negative elements which compose it (art. 117). In making the assessment of income from movable wealth, the administration is not limited to use of the return, but may consider all information furnished by the taxpayer or collected ex officio, which is pertinent to the determination of the income (art. 117).

In most cases, the income of an entity required to be taxed on the balance sheet basis or of an enterprise electing to be so taxed is determined on the basis of information obtained from the balance sheet and profit and loss statement or from the annual financial report (arts. 118, 119). The tax administration may, however, check the entries in the balance sheet with the aid of the accounting books, records, and documents, and may check the entries in the records themselves with information collected ex officio. Individual entries in the balance sheet may be corrected if found to be erroneous or irregular (13/2.3).

For purposes of assessment, the Tax Office may make use of information coming to its knowledge in any manner (art. 39). Listed below are the powers expressly granted to the Tax Office for obtaining information (arts. 39, 42).

1. To send the taxpayer interrogatories relating to the assessment, by registered letter with return receipt, with a request that they be duly returned, answered, and signed, allowing not less than 15 days for compliance.
2. To request the taxpayer to appear in person or through an agent, for reasons specified, to furnish information, explanations, or documents.
3. To summon for examination, for reasons specified, any person in a position to furnish information.
4. To empower its own officers, provided with appropriate authorization specifying the purpose of the inquiry, to visit places of business to obtain evidence and to inspect documents, and to visit other immovable property to obtain evidence regarding its size, characteristics, and use.
5. To request extracts of documents deposited with notaries, Registry Offices, and other public officials.
6. To take notice directly through its own officials of information in the possession of public entities, companies, and entities which make collections and payments on behalf of those concerned, and in the possession of insurance companies and institutes for individual taxpayers or classes of taxpayers.[13]
7. To require persons required to be taxed on the balance sheet basis, other than credit firms and institutions, to furnish data relative to sales, purchases, or supplies, taking place in a defined period, with customers and suppliers specified by name, in addition to the information regarding *riporti* and sales of securities on time which must be kept by exchange agents, credit firms and institutions, financial and fiduciary companies, and stock exchange commission agents (9/2.8).[14]
8. To inspect the writings, accounting books, records, and documents which the taxpayer is required by law to keep or to preserve.

When the taxpayer is requested to appear in person or through an agent, or officers are empowered to visit places of business or other immovable property, or books and documents are inspected, the Tax Office must prepare an official written report, of which the taxpayer must be given a copy, showing the questions of the Tax Office, the declarations of the taxpayer or his representative, and the results of the inspection of books or documents (arts. 39, 42). The report must be signed by the taxpayer or his representative, or specify the reasons for the absence of the signature. The weight given to books and records in the assessment and the consequences of failure to produce them are discussed at 6/2.5.

---

[13] Added by L. 4 December 1962, n. 1682, art. 1.
[14] Added by L. 4 December 1962, n. 1682, art. 1.

If the taxpayer alleges the existence of debts owed to credit firms or institutions, the Tax Office may request him to submit, allowing not less than 30 days for compliance, a copy of the statement of the account with the creditor and a certificate from the creditor attesting to the amount of the debts and listing all other debit or credit relations with the taxpayer at the date on which the tax period ends and at earlier or later dates specified by the Tax Office (art. 41).[15] The certificate may also be required to show transfers of securities subject to *riporti* (9/2.8) and guarantees given by third persons in conjunction with the taxpayer. The creditor must issue the certificate within 20 days of the written request of the taxpayer; this certificate must be countersigned by the service chief or by the accountant attached to the office of the credit institution and must state explicitly that it has been issued, under this provision, at the request of the taxpayer. At the request of the Minister of Finance, the Service of Credit Control (*Servizio di Vigilanza sulle Aziende di Credito*) will examine the correctness of the information contained in the certificate.

At the request of the Tax Office, public administrative offices and public entities, companies and entities which make collections and payments on behalf of persons concerned, and insurance companies and institutions are required to furnish lists of the names of persons for whom collections and payments were made, including all information in their possession about individual taxpayers or categories of taxpayers (art. 40). This requirement prevails against all contrary provisions of law, bylaw, or regulation. It does not apply, however, to the Central Statistical Institute (*Istituto Centrale di Statistica*), to the Labor Inspectorates (*Ispettorati di Lavoro*) regarding matters entrusted to them by law, to credit firms and institutions regarding matters pertaining to their relations with their clients (the so-called "*segreto bancario*"), to insurance companies and institutions regarding their relations with those whose lives they insure, or to dependent offices of the Ministry of Post and Telecommunications for matters relating to postal accounts, deposit books, and interest-bearing postal bonds. In matters pertaining to the taxes within their competence, public entities (including banks, for example) are required to furnish information concerning only those persons named specifically in a request.

13/2.3 Estimated Assessments

An estimated assessment of the taxpayer's entire income received from buildings, income from movable wealth, or income for the complementary

---

[15] Administrative instructions regarding the application of this provision are contained in C.M. 1 September 1956, n. 78, and C.M. 11 October 1956, n. 351770. The provision is not applicable in the case of a debt owed to an investment or fiduciary company; C.M. 18 December 1959, n. 84.

tax is known as an inductive or synthetic assessment (*accertamento induttivo o sintetico*), as distinguished from the analytic assessment described at 13/2.2. Provisions of the direct tax law authorize the assessment by estimate of income from movable wealth of all business enterprises not taxed on the balance sheet basis and the assessment by estimate, under certain conditions, of net aggregate income of individuals for the complementary tax. In other cases, assessment of the entire income by estimate is authorized only if the taxpayer fails to comply with requirements regarding returns, records, or information. Semi-inductive assessment, in which the various positive and negative elements composing income are specified, but individual items are estimated, is authorized for the modification or correction of individual entries in the balance sheet of an entity or enterprise taxed on the balance sheet basis.

The income of a business enterprise not taxed on the balance sheet basis is determined, inductively or by estimate, on the basis of the economic situation of the firm, derived from the information specified by the taxpayer or gathered ex officio (art. 118). In assessing the income of an enterprise, the Tax Office makes use of a ministerial decree [16] containing a detailed classification of the economic activities the income from which is subject to the tax on income from movable wealth, and applies coefficients devised by the tax administration for checking assessments. If a report of inspection (13/2.2) shows that a business enterprise, other than one classified as a small business under the Civil Code (7/1.2b), has not kept or has failed to produce the required accounting records in the manner prescribed by the Civil Code (6/2.2), the enterprise has the burden of proving the incorrectness of the assessment of the Tax Office (art. 118). In other cases, the burden is on the Tax Office to explain why the accounting records were not accepted.

The income of any other taxpayer not taxed on the balance sheet basis may be assessed without a determination of the various positive and negative elements which compose it if the taxpayer has failed to file a return, to furnish all data, or to produce all of the books, records, and documents necessary for a check of the completeness and truthfulness of the return (art. 117).

The net aggregate income for the complementary tax may be determined by estimate, with reference to the taxpayer's way of living or to other factual elements or circumstances, if these are such as to justify the presumption of a net income greater than that resulting from an analytical determination (art. 137). No deductions may be taken from income so determined except the standard allowances for the complementary tax (12/1.5b). An assessment under this provision is void unless

---

[16] D.M. 12 August 1950.

accompanied by detailed reasons (art. 37) (13/2.1).[17] It cannot be based on presumptions, but must be supported by factual evidence.[18] The provision is not applicable to persons residing abroad who are not subject to the tax on income enjoyed in Italy but produced abroad.[19] Since the assessments of income for the objective taxes are, in general, valid for the complementary tax (6/1.1f, 13/2.1), the taxpayer could presumably show that income assessed by estimate under this provision was, in fact, produced by immovable property whose income was determined cadastrally (9/4.1). When income has been assessed by estimate for the complementary tax under this provision, the Tax Office cannot proceed to modify the assessment of income for the objective taxes unless it is clear that the income is neither excluded nor exempt from objective taxation.[20]

In assessing the income of an entity or enterprise taxed on the balance sheet basis, the Tax Office may modify or correct individual entries in the balance sheet, by estimate (*induttivamente*) if necessary, when it appears (1) that nonexistent expenses and losses have been shown or that the amounts shown are in excess of the actual amounts, (2) that receipts have been omitted or shown incorrectly, or (3) that business facts have been reported incorrectly or irregularly in such a manner as to produce a result different from the correct one (art. 119). In the situations listed below, furthermore, the tax administration may disregard the balance sheet and the accounting records, and may determine income on the basis of the economic situation of the business, using any available information (art. 120).

1. When the taxpayer has not filed, within the legal time limits, a return specifying the positive and negative elements necessary for determining income (art. 24) (13/1.2), properly signed (art. 27) (13/1.1b), and accompanied by a properly signed copy of the balance sheet and the profit and loss statement (art. 28) (13/1.3).
2. When it appears from a report of inspection (6/2.3) that the taxpayer has not kept or has refused to produce the required accounting records, or that the accounting records have not been kept in the prescribed manner (6/2.2, 6/2.4).
3. When incorrect or irregular entries are so serious or so frequently repeated that they justify the conclusion that the balance sheet is unreliable.

If income is assessed under this provision, assessment cannot be made by agreement (art. 120) (13/2.4). When balance sheet entries are corrected or modified or the income is determined on the basis of the

---

[17] See *Verb. conf.* May 1957, De Angelis, Potenza, and Testa, *Testo unico delle leggi sulle imposte dirette* 728.
[18] Cass., Sez. I, 3 April 1941, n. 947; Comm. Centr., Sez. III, 12 December 1945, n. 79768; Comm. Centr., Sez. III, 4 March 1955, n. 69235; Comm. Centr., Sez. III, 9 December 1955, n. 77015. See also C.M. 15 October 1932, n. 3417.
[19] Comm. Centr., Sez. IV, 15 December 1942, n. 64043.
[20] See C.M. 15 October 1932, n. 3417.

economic situation of the business without regard to the balance sheet, the Tax Office must specify in the notice of assessment the reasons for its action; and if the reasons appear valid, the taxpayer has the burden of proving the incorrectness of the assessment (art. 121) (13/4.1). If elements relevant to these proceedings appear during an adjudication proceeding of the first degree, the commission suspends the proceedings and remands the records to the Tax Office, fixing a time limit for a new assessment (art. 122).

The provisions permitting assessment of income by estimate or on the basis of information collected ex officio do not relieve the administration of the requirement of furnishing detailed reasons for an assessment (13/2.1) in any case in which the conditions governing that requirement have been fulfilled.

In case of failure to file a return, the tax on income from buildings (art. 80) and the tax on income from movable wealth are applied to the income assessed for the preceding tax period, plus an increase of 10% for all income from movable wealth except that of category C/2 (art. 123).[21] In such cases, the complementary tax is also applied to the income assessed for the preceding tax period (art. 142), plus the increase of 10% provided for income from movable wealth (art. 141). Any further increment of income may be assessed ex officio (13/2.3). The increase of 10% for income from movable wealth is also included in the assessment for the corporation tax (art. 150).

13/2.4 Assessment by Agreement

The taxable amount of income may be determined with the agreement (*l'adesione*) of the taxpayer by means of an appropriate written document, of which the taxpayer has the right to have a copy; this document must specify the productive sources and the elements on which the determination of the taxable amount has been based, and must make express reference to the return of the taxpayer if one was filed (art. 34).[22] An assessment made in this manner may be supplemented or modified through the service of an appropriate notice, on the basis of later-acquired knowledge of new elements (art. 35) (13/2.5).

If the document fails to specify the required information or has not been signed by the representative of the Tax Office and by the taxpayer

---

[21] On the application of this provision, see Poli, "Maggiorazione del reddito, dichiarazioni tardive e ricorsi contro il ruolo," *Imp. dir. erariali*, 1962, 450.

[22] This method of assessment, known as the "pact" (*concordato*), is more accurately regarded not as a transaction, but as a unilateral administrative act drawing its effect from the concurrence of the taxpayer. See De Angelis, Potenza, and Testa, *Testo unico delle leggi sulle imposte dirette* 135. Comm. Centr., Sez. IV, 13 June 1946, n. 82988; Comm. Centr., Sez. VI, 14 March 1951, n. 21765. For further discussion of the *concordato*, see Cocivera, *Il concordato tributario*; Allorio, *Diritto processuale tributario* 138-145; Giannini, *Istituzioni di diritto tributario* 171-177; Maffezzoni, "Alcune riflessioni sul concordato tributario," *RDFSF*, 1941, I, 254.

or his representative, it may be declared invalid by the tax commission of first degree on a petition by the taxpayer within 60 days of the date of the agreement or on a petition by the Tax Office on or before 31 December of the second calendar year following that in which the agreement was made (art. 34). The declaration of invalidity does not prevent the inscription of the agreed taxable amount in the roll (13/3.6). The Tax Office must make a new assessment within 90 days of the date when the declaration of invalidity becomes final.

When the taxable amount has been determined with the concurrence of the taxpayer, the taxpayer cannot contest the assessment except by petition for a declaration of invalidity; if a protest has already been begun, the proceeding is extinguished (art. 34).

Assessment with the agreement of the taxpayer is not possible (1) when an assessment is supplemented by a decision of the tax commission of first degree which is based on knowledge of new elements acquired during the proceeding (art. 36), or (2) when an assessment of the entire income of an enterprise or entity taxed on the balance sheet basis is based on the economic situation of the firm, deduced from information however collected (art. 120) (13/2.3). Assessment by agreement for purposes of the complementary tax is not possible when the taxable amounts for the tax on income from movable wealth or for the tax on income from buildings have not been determined (art. 141).

13/2.5 Supplementation or Modification of the Assessment

The assessment, even if made with the agreement of the taxpayer, may be supplemented (*integrato*) or modified on the basis of new knowledge of new elements, by service of an appropriate notice (art. 35), within the time limit explained at 13/6.1. A taxpayer who has not previously contested the assessment is given a new time limit in which to contest the previous assessments of the same income as well as the supplementation or modification of those assessments. If the Tax Office avails itself of the power to supplement or modify an assessment of a protest proceeding, the adjudicating body before which the dispute is pending remits it ex officio to the tax commission of first degree.[23]

The supplementation of an assessment may take place by a decision of the tax commission of first degree if the commission acquires new knowledge of new elements during the course of the proceeding (art. 36). In this case, the commission suspends judgment and remands the question to the Tax Office, fixing the time limit for a new assessment. When an assessment is supplemented under this provision, the taxable amount cannot be determined with the agreement of the taxpayer (13/2.4).

---

[23] L. 5 January 1956, n. 1, art. 3.

13/3.   Payment of Tax

13/3.1   In General

The methods of collecting the taxes applicable to the various classes and categories of income are listed below.

1. The tax on income from landowning, the tax on agrarian income, the tax on income from buildings, and the tax on income from movable wealth of categories B and C/1 are inscribed in the tax rolls (13/3.6) and collected as explained at 13/3.7. The complementary tax on individuals is also inscribed in the rolls and is subject to adjustment for amounts provisionally withheld under the provisions described at 13/3.5.

2. Payments by the state of income from movable wealth of category A are subject to direct withholding of the tax on income from movable wealth (13/3.3). In the cases described at 13/3.4, the tax on income from movable wealth on other payments of income of category A is inscribed in the roll against the payor of the income, who has a right to recover the tax from the recipient through withholding.

3. Payments by government offices of salaries and other compensation are subject to direct withholding of the tax on income from movable wealth (13/3.3). The tax on income from movable wealth on other payments of income from employment is inscribed in the roll against the payor of the income, who is required to recover the tax from the recipient through withholding (13/3.4). A provisional withholding of the complementary tax on governmental and other payments of income from employment is made by the employer at less than the minimum rate (12/1.6), is inscribed against the employer in the roll, and is collected from him in the regular manner (13/3.5).

4. Payments to aliens or to Italians domiciled abroad for the transfer or licensing of intellectual property, or for the exercise of an art or profession in Italy, are subject to provisional withholding of the tax on income from movable wealth and of the complementary tax; the taxes withheld are paid directly into the Treasury or inscribed against the payor in special rolls (13/3.5).

5. Payments made by business enterprises to persons domiciled in Italy for the performance of artistic services there are subject to provisional withholding of the tax on income from movable wealth and of the complementary tax; the taxes withheld are paid directly into the Treasury or inscribed against the payor in special rolls (13/3.5).

6. Compensation paid to directors, auditors, or overseers, excluding participations in net profits, is subject to provisional withholding of the tax on income from movable wealth and of the complementary tax; the taxes withheld are paid directly into the Treasury or inscribed against the payor in special rolls (13/3.5).

7. Profits distributed by corporations, limited partnerships with shares, limited liability companies, and cooperatives with limited liability are subject to a provisional withholding (9/2.7a), which is paid over to the Provincial Treasury Office every six months (13/3.5). With the exceptions noted at 9/2.7c, the amounts withheld are credited against the complementary tax or the corporation tax due from the recipient of the distribution.

8. The corporation tax and the tax on bonds are paid directly into the Treasury, or inscribed against the taxpayer in special rolls (13/3.2).

The time limits for payment and collection are discussed at 13/6.2. Appeals connected with payment and collection proceedings are discussed at 13/4.5-13/4.7.

The heirs of a deceased taxpayer are jointly and severally liable for his tax obligations (art. 16). When a property right subject to the tax on income from landowning or to the tax on income from buildings is held jointly by more than one person, each of them is jointly and severally liable for payment of the tax (arts. 50, 70). However, when there are several distinct possessory rights in the same property, the holder of each right is liable only for the tax on the income attributable to his right. The preference accorded to the tax liability (13/3.8) extends to the entire property.

The possessor of an estate who is liable for the tax on agrarian income has a right of recovery against his associates in the conduct of the agricultural enterprise; the amount recovered from each associate is to be in proportion to the income received by him (art. 63).

New owners of immovable property and new holders of property rights in immovable property are jointly and severally liable with their predecessors for the tax charged against the property and inscribed in the roll against their predecessors for the period after the date of the document which serves as the basis of the cadastral annotation (art. 196). When the filing of a proper request for a cadastral annotation has not had effect in the rolls, the Intendant of Finance may order that the tax be collected only from the new owners, forbidding the collector to proceed against the property of the predecessors.

A purchaser of a business productive of income from movable wealth of categories B or C/1 is liable for the payment of the taxes due on the income of the enterprise and on income of category C/2 from any preceding owners of the business for the tax period during which the transaction occurred and for the preceding period (art. 197).[24] The new owner is also liable for the payment of surcharges due for violations which were already charged to a preceding owner at the time of the transfer. For purposes of these provisions, anyone who carries on the same business activity as the previous owners of the enterprise in the same premises or in a part thereof is presumed, in the absence of proof to the contrary, to be a purchaser. The purchaser or the seller of a

---

[24] For application of this provision, see C.M. 18 December 1959, n. 84. A purchaser is not liable for taxes under this provision unless he has himself been inscribed in the roll; Trib. Firenze 13 February 1952 (*Giur. tosc.*, 1952, 377). The application of the provision presupposes a bargaining relationship (*rapporto negoziale*) between the new owner and the old. Hence a person leasing a business from a commune is not a purchaser from a previous lessee from the commune under a similar arrangement; App. Firenze 17 July 1956 (*Giur. tosc.*, 1956, 694). Similarly, the purchaser of a business at a forced sale in bankruptcy cannot be held liable for taxes on previous income of the business. See Ministerial Note 16 December 1952, n. 455193.

business may obtain from the Tax Office, at his own expense, a certificate showing the tax position of the enterprise.

The liquidators of an entity required to be taxed on the balance sheet basis are personally liable for payment of taxes owed by the entity for the period of liquidation, and for the preceding tax period, if they have not fulfilled the obligation to pay them as part of the activity of liquidation (art. 265).

13/3.2 Direct Payment into the Treasury

The corporation tax and the tax on bonds must be paid by the taxpayer directly to the Provincial Treasury Office in whose jurisdiction the taxpayer has its fiscal domicile (13/1.1d); payment must be made within the time limit fixed for the filing of the return (art. 168). A statement from the Provincial Treasury Office verifying that payment has been made must be attached to the return (art. 28) (13/1.3). Any unpaid tax, any increment of tax resulting from ex officio assessment, and the corresponding surcharges (13/7.1) are inscribed in a special roll (13/3.6c) and collected in the regular manner (arts. 168, 183) (13/3.7). The taxpayer may appeal to the Intendant of Finance under the rules discussed at 13/4.5.

Payment into the Treasury is generally made through the postal current account of the Provincial Treasury Office.

13/3.3 Direct Withholding from Government Payments

In the case of payments of income arising from securities of public debt, prizes for loan lotteries on bonds issued by the state, annuities, and interest due from state offices, including those with autonomous regulation (art. 126), the state withholds the tax on income from movable wealth directly at the time of payment.

The state also withholds the tax on income from movable wealth directly from payments of salaries, remuneration, pensions, and occasional compensation owed by state offices, including those with autonomous regulation, at the rates described at 12/1.6 (art. 126). However, tax is not withheld from amounts which are paid exclusively as reimbursements of expenses or which include reimbursements of precisely determinable expenses, provided the office which makes the payment notifies the competent District Office of Direct Taxes of the amount and basis of the payment and of the identity and fiscal domicile of the recipient.

13/3.4 Payment of Taxes of Others with Recovery through Withholding

Private and public juridical persons, companies and associations of all types, entrepreneurs, and professional persons are required to pay the tax on income from movable wealth of category C/2 on all payments of compensation to employees (art. 127). The employer is required to recover the tax in each payment period by withholding at the time of payment of the income; if he fails to do so, and pays the income to the employee free of tax, the tax can be collected again from the employee by inscription in the roll (13/3.6). The withholding requirement applies also to payments of income from employment made for activities carried on in Italy, on the payor's behalf, by employees of a foreign enterprise not having a permanent establishment in Italy.

The persons making the payments specified below are required to pay the tax on income from movable wealth on such payments, with a right of recovery from the recipient through withholding (art. 127).

1. Lottery winnings.
2. Interest and premiums payable, having the character of income from capital, by persons required to be taxed on the balance sheet basis or by credit firms and institutions (9/1.1).[25]
3. Interest included in amounts payable by insurance enterprises as a result of contracts of capitalization and insurance (9/3.1).
4. Amounts payable as a result of life annuities, however established, by insurance enterprises or other entities and companies.

The return of the payor must contain the information described at 13/1.4 regarding the payments. The taxes due on these payments are inscribed in the roll against the payor and collected from him in the same manner as the taxes on his own income (13/3.6, 13/3.7).

The additional for the benefit of communal welfare entities must also be withheld from the payments discussed above (art. 272).[26]

13/3.5 Provisional Withholding

A provisional withholding (*ritenuta d'acconto*) of the tax on income from movable wealth must be made, by the person paying the income, from the payments listed below (art. 128).

1. Compensation paid in any form by business enterprises for artistic services performed in Italy by persons domiciled there.[27]

---

[25] The first two paragraphs of article 127, discussed above, relate to payments of compensation for work as an employee, all of which are taxed in category C/2. The third paragraph, however, applies to certain classes of income of category A (items 1 and 2 above), and also to certain classes of income of category C/2 (items 3 and 4 below). See 6/1.1e.

[26] It has been held that a credit firm or institution which pays the tax on behalf of a depositor but fails to recover it through withholding may deduct the tax paid as a business expense (7/2.8). It appears that the tax paid is not included in the income of the recipient of the interest. See Comm. Centr. 24 May 1928, n. 85428; but see also Berliri, *Il testo unico delle imposte dirette* 188.

[27] This provision, added by article 1 of L. 21 April 1962, n. 226, became effective as of 1 December 1962.

2. Compensation paid in any form by business enterprises to directors, auditors, or overseers, excluding participations in net profits of the business period.[28]

3. Payments to aliens or to Italians domiciled abroad by virtue of copyrights or fees or earnings for the transfer or licensing of patents, designs, processes, formulas, trademarks, and similar property. The withholding is not required if the income is exempt from tax by virtue of an international agreement (11/4.9).

4. Compensation paid to aliens or to Italians domiciled abroad for the exercise of an art or profession in Italy.[29] The withholding is not required if the income is exempt from tax by virtue of an international agreement (11/4.13).

5. Contributions or premiums paid by public administrative offices to business enterprises, when such contributions are not exempt from tax (6/1.4).[30]

In each case, the withholdings are computed on two thirds of the gross amount paid. The rates of the withholding for items 1 and 2 are given at 12/1.6; the rates for items 3 and 4, at 12/4. The complementary tax must also be withheld at special rates (12/1.6) from payments to individuals which are subject to provisional withholding of the tax on income from movable wealth under the rules described above (art. 143).

Amounts provisionally withheld under the rules described above must be paid, within 20 days, directly to the Provincial Treasury Office in whose jurisdiction the payor required to withhold has his fiscal domicile (art. 169). Amounts not paid over, increments resulting from ex officio assessment, and the corresponding surcharges (13/7.1) are inscribed in a special roll, for collection by the regular method, in the name of the person required to withhold (art. 169). The taxpayer may appeal to the Intendant of Finance as explained at 13/4.5. Payments may be made through the postal current account of the Provincial Treasury Office.

Amounts provisionally withheld by a company or its designated agent from distributions of profits, under the rules described at 9/2.7, must be paid over every six months to the Provincial Treasury Office in whose jurisdiction the company has its fiscal domicile.[31] The payment must

---

[28] This provision, added by article 1 of L. 21 April 1962, n. 226, became effective as of 1 December 1962. The withholding requirement applies to all compensation for serving as a director, including daily allowances, travel expenses, fees for attendance at meetings, and fixed reimbursements of expenses (on *"forfait"*). It does not apply to reimbursements of specific expenses, which are not taxable; to compensation for services as a director which does not satisfy the conditions for deductibility from the income of the corporation under the rules discussed at 7/2.3c; or to compensation for any other services not connected with the duties as a director. C.M. 15 June 1962, n. 60.

[29] The requirement of withholding is not affected by the fact that the recipient of the payment does not regularly exercise his art or profession in Italy. C.M. 29 December 1956, n. 303800.

[30] This provision, added by article 1 of L. 21 April 1962, n. 226, became effective as of 1 December 1962.

[31] L. 29 December 1962, n. 1745, art. 2.

be made on or before 20 January and 20 July following the distribution decision, or the publication thereof, in the legal notice sheet, and must include also the total of withholdings on profits not yet collected by the members. Amounts not paid over, increments resulting from ex officio assessment, and the corresponding surcharges are inscribed in a special roll, for collection in the regular manner (13/3.6), in the name of the person required to withhold (art. 169). The taxpayer may appeal to the Intendant of Finance (art. 171) (13/4.5), who must provide for a refund where proper (art. 172) (13/5).

Private and public juridical persons, companies and associations of all types, entrepreneurs, and professional persons are required to make a provisional withholding of the complementary tax from all payments of compensation to employees. The withholding must be made in each payment period, at the rate given at 12/1.6 on that part of the income paid to an employee which, when annualized, exceeds L. 720,000 (art. 143). Provisional withholding of the complementary tax is made by the state, at the rate given at 12/1.6, (1) on that part of the fixed compensation of a government employee (13/3.3) which, when annualized, exceeds L. 720,000; (2) on the entire amount of other compensation of a government employee if the annualized total of fixed remuneration exceeds L. 720,000; and (3) on the entire amount of compensation paid to persons not members of the state administration (art. 143). The taxes due on these payments are inscribed in the roll against the payor (13/3.6) and collected from him in the regular manner (13/3.7).

The additional tax for the benefit of communal welfare entities (2/2.9) must be withheld from all payments subject to provisional withholding of the tax on income from movable wealth or of the complementary tax (art. 272). Local taxes must also be withheld at prescribed rates (12/4) from payments to aliens or to Italians domiciled abroad for the transfer or the licensing of intellectual property or for the exercise of an art or profession in Italy (art. 273).

The recipient of income subject to provisional withholding must attach to his return a certificate from the person who effected the withholding, attesting separately for each of the taxes involved the total of the amounts paid and the total of the amounts withheld from them (art. 28) (13/1.3). The return of the person effecting the withholding must contain the information described at 13/1.4.

Except in the case of certain distributions of profits by corporations (9/2.7c, 9/2.7d), all amounts provisionally withheld are credited against the taxes due on the income in which the amounts subjected to withholding are included (arts. 128, 143) (13/3.6). If the amount of tax provisionally withheld exceeds the amount to be inscribed in the roll, the taxpayer is entitled to a refund (13/5).[32] International conventions affecting the applicability of the provisional withholding rules are discussed at 11/4.7a4, 11/4.9, and 11/4.13. The provisional withholdings of the complementary tax are computed in payment of the tax due, from the persons against whom the withholdings are made, on the net aggregate income in which the compensation and fixed allowances are included (art. 143).[33]

13/3.6   Inscription in the Rolls

a. IN GENERAL. Taxes which are not collected through direct withholding (13/3.3) or through direct payment into the Treasury (13/3.2) are collected by the collectors (*esattori*) of the communes or associations of communes (13/3.7) on the basis of rolls (*ruoli*) made up by the Tax Offices (art. 173).

The Tax Office makes up a roll for each commune of the district and for each tax. The roll contains the names of the taxpayers in alphabetical order, giving the tax period, the taxable amount, and the amount of the tax, including commissions (art. 181). It also lists the fiscal domicile of the taxpayer unless, in the case of the tax on income from landowning, the tax on agrarian income, or the tax on income from buildings, the taxpayer has failed to keep the competent Tax Office informed of changes in his fiscal domicile (13/1.1d). Each roll is signed by the representative of the Tax Office.

Ordinary rolls are prepared and sent to the Intendant of Finance on or before 15 June (first series) and on or before 15 December (second series) of each year (art. 182). There is no difference between these two series; inscription in one or the other depends merely on when the right of the administration to inscribe the taxes in the roll arises. Special rolls may be prepared for the collection of certain taxes (13/3.6c). Extraordinary rolls may be authorized by the Intendant of Finance if there is a well-founded danger of loss of the tax due (art. 182), such as in the case of imminent bankruptcy.

The tax on income from landowning and the tax on agrarian income are inscribed in the rolls, for each tax period, on the basis of the information in the cadastral registers on 31 August of the preceding year (art. 179), but taking account of reductions and supplemental inscriptions arising from changes in taxable income and from the exemptions provided by the rules relating to those taxes (10/2.2f, 10/2.3c).

The tax on income from buildings, the tax on income from movable wealth, and the complementary tax are provisionally inscribed in the rolls, computed on the taxable amounts relative to the second preceding

---

[32] Regarding refunds to persons domiciled abroad, see C.M. 29 December 1956.
[33] Added by L. 4 December 1962, n. 1682, art. 6.

tax period, unless a report of termination (13/1.5) has been received by the Tax Office before the making of the roll (art. 176). The taxable amounts of the preceding tax period, however, are used for the tax on income from movable wealth of categories A and B of entities taxed on the balance sheet basis, and are also used for taxes for which no taxable amount was inscribed for the second preceding tax period. In the case of a company which reorganized during the base period, the taxable amounts of the tax periods before the reorganization are provisionally inscribed in accordance with the foregoing rules, and the fractions of the year or business period before and after the reorganization are both taken into account; the taxable amount for an entity or company surviving or resulting from a merger is the sum of the taxable amounts of all the entities participating in the merger. Provisional inscription of taxes on income whose assessment for the tax period taken as the base has not become final is determined on the basis of the income for which taxes have been provisionally inscribed for the base period under the rules discussed at 13/3.6b.[34] The amount to be provisionally inscribed may be reduced, on the authorization of the chief of the District Tax Office, if the income on which the tax previously inscribed was calculated includes receipts of an exceptional character, or if intervening circumstances give firm grounds for concluding that the taxable income has been substantially reduced.[35] Taxes withheld provisionally (13/3.5) during the tax period for which the provisional inscription is made are deducted from the amount provisionally inscribed against the recipient for the tax on income from movable wealth of categories B and C/1 and the complementary tax (art. 177).

Final inscriptions for the tax on income from buildings, the tax on income from movable wealth, the complementary tax, and the related surcharges (13/7.1) are based on the return or on the amount assessed in the absence of a return if no return was filed (13/1.1a), and on the taxable amounts finally assessed (art. 174). Taxes provisionally withheld (13/3.5) are deducted from the taxes to be finally inscribed in the roll (art. 177). If the amount of tax withheld exceeds the amount to be inscribed in the roll, the taxpayer is entitled to a refund (13/5).

Inscription in the roll is suspended for the tax on income from movable wealth with respect to unreceived income which, for specified reasons, is uncollected or uncollectible.[36]

b. EFFECT OF APPEAL. When an assessment for the tax on income from buildings, the tax on income from movable wealth, or the complementary tax has not become final, the tax attributable to the difference between

---

[34] C.M. 18 May 1960, n. 301520.

[35] C.M. 18 May 1960, n. 301520.

[36] See R.D.L. 24 August 1877, n. 4021, art. 64; L. 8 June 1936, n. 1231, art. 32.

the taxable amount assessed by the tax administration and the taxable
amount already inscribed is provisionally inscribed in the roll as explained below (art. 175).

1. After 60 days from the transmission of the taxpayer's appeal to the tax
   commission of first degree (13/4.2), one half of the tax attributable to
   the greater taxable amount assessed by the Tax Office is inscribed.
2. After the decision of the tax commission of first degree, two thirds of the
   tax attributable to the greater taxable amount assessed by that commission is inscribed.
3. After the decision of the tax commission of second degree (13/4.3), the
   tax attributable to the entire greater taxable amount assessed by that
   commission is inscribed.

If no tax was previously inscribed, the tax corresponding to the entire
amount assessed is inscribed in each case.

c. ADJUSTMENTS. The amount of tax inscribed in the roll is increased
or reduced if the tax due is greater or less than the tax previously inscribed (art. 178). If the tax on the taxable amount finally assessed
or the tax to be finally inscribed is less than the total of provisional
inscriptions and provisional withholdings, the taxpayer has a right
to a reduction of the inscription (arts. 178, 198) and, consequently, to
a refund, or application to installments due but uncollected, of any
overpayment (13/5).

Special rolls, which may be prepared and sent to the Intendant of
Finance at any time (art. 182) within the applicable time limit (13/6.2),
for collection of the tax inscribed in one payment at the next bimonthly
payment date (13/3.7), are prepared for the taxes listed below (art. 183).

1. The tax on income from movable wealth and the complementary tax due
   on income of category C/2 in excess of the taxes provisionally inscribed
   in the roll, and the corresponding surcharges (13/7.1).
2. The corporation tax and the tax on bonds not paid into the Treasury
   (13/3.2), any increases resulting from the assessment of the Tax Office,
   and the corresponding surcharges.
3. Amounts withheld provisionally for the tax on movable wealth and for
   the complementary tax but not paid into the Treasury (13/3.5), any
   increases resulting from the assessment of the Tax Office, and the
   corresponding surcharges.

Increases in taxes imposed on a taxpayer who has failed to file a
return, has compiled an incomplete or false return (13/7.2), or has deferred payment of tax (13/3.7) are inscribed with the collection fees
in the roll of the taxes to which they apply (arts. 184 *bis*, 184 *quater*).

13/3.7   Collection through Rolls

After ascertaining that the roll conforms to the provisions of the law,
the Intendant of Finance affixes his approval for enforcement (art. 185).
The roll is then sent to the commune for publication, which is made by

deposit in the town hall and the affixing of an appropriate notice on the court bulletin board for five consecutive days; in the case of an extraordinary roll, the Intendant of Finance may order that, instead of publication, the Tax Office serve on each taxpayer inscribed in the roll a notice containing the information on the entry which concerns him. Publication or service of the roll renders the taxes payable on their respective due dates. The roll, with the attestation of completed publication, is then delivered by the Mayor to the collector (*esattore*) (art. 187).

The collector performs the functions of collecting the direct taxes and paying them over to the Treasury under a contract of *appalto* (8/4) with a commune or association of communes which are under the jurisdiction of a single District Office of Direct Taxes.[37] Thus, a collector is neither a public official nor an employee of the commune, but a grantee of a concession to exercise a public function;[38] generally, collectors are banks or credit institutions. A collectorship is normally awarded at public auction to the bidder willing to accept the lowest collection fee (*aggio di riscossione*).[39] A collectorship is conferred for 10 years[40] and can normally be renewed for a second decade, subject to the approval of the Prefect (1/5.1), the Intendant of Finance, and the Communal Council (1/5.2).[41] The present maximum collection fee is 6.72% of the collection made; the collection fees, together with indemnities for lateness (13/7.6) and expenses of execution (13/3.8), constitute the collector's compensation.[42]

If the amount of a tax inscribed in the roll (13/3.6) does not exceed L. 1,000, it is collected in one payment. If the amount inscribed in an ordinary or extraordinary roll exceeds L. 1,000, it is divided into six installments, which fall due consecutively on the tenth day of each even-numbered month (art. 184). The first installment is due on 10 August for ordinary rolls of the first series, on 10 February for ordinary rolls of the second series, and on the first bimonthly due date for extraordinary rolls. However, the Intendant of Finance may order division into

---

[37] The basic law governing the collection of the direct taxes, and of all other state and local tax receipts which are collectible through rolls, is contained in a new *Testo unico* of the laws on the services of collection of the direct taxes, approved by D.P.R. 15 May 1963, n. 858, and issued under authority of L. 6 November 1962, n. 1608. For a discussion of the operation of this system under the legislative provisions replaced by this new *Testo unico*, see Scandale, *Riscossione delle imposte dirette*.

[38] See Scandale, *Riscossione delle imposte dirette* 11 *et seq.* Service as a collector is limited to persons inscribed in a collectors' list kept by a special commission in the Ministry of Finance; D.P.R. 15 May 1963, n. 858, arts. 5, 7.

[39] D.P.R. 15 May 1963, n. 858, arts. 21, 26.

[40] D.P.R. 15 May 1963, n. 858, art. 17.

[41] D.P.R. 15 May 1963, n. 858, art. 36.

[42] D.P.R. 15 May 1963, n. 858, art. 56. See also Scandale, *Riscossione delle imposte dirette* 125 *et seq.* For a discussion of the costs of the system of collection, see Gazzero, "I costi d'imposizione e di riscossione delle imposte dirette e ripercussioni di essi nel MEC," *Boll. trib. informazioni*, 1959, 835.

fewer installments or collection in one payment. In case of late payment of four consecutive installments of a tax inscribed in the roll, the entire amount becomes collectible in one payment. Taxes inscribed in the special rolls (13/3.6c) are collected in one payment on the first bimonthly due date (art. 184).

Except in the case of taxes inscribed in a special roll (13/3.6c), the tax administration has the power to permit the collection of a tax debt inscribed or to be inscribed in the rolls, relative to past tax periods, in not more than 18 bimonthly installments, if the payments of the ordinary installments would be excessively burdensome (art. 184 *ter*).[43] If an installment due under this provision is not paid on the due date, the collector proceeds to recover immediately the entire remaining debt (art. 184 *ter*). For each six-month period or fraction thereof following the due date of the last normal installment, there is applied an increase of 2.5% on the amount of the tax whose payment has been deferred beyond the due date of the last normal installment (art. 184 *quater*). This increase is collected, with the fees, with the installments of tax; at each due date, the amount consists of the installment plus 2.5% of the amount of the installment for each six-month period or fraction thereof since the due date of the last normal installment.[44] If the collector proceeds to recover the entire remaining debt, because of omitted or late payment of an installment, the increase is owed only for the installments already due (art. 184 *quater*).

The collector must serve a bill for payment on the taxpayer not later than the fifth day of the month in which the first installment following the delivery of the roll is due (arts. 189, 190). Service of a bill is not necessary for taxes inscribed in an extraordinary roll, notice of which has been served on the taxpayer (art. 189). Payment must be made to the collector within eight days of the due date (art. 191). Provision is made for payment in cash, in matured coupons of public securities, or in unmatured coupons in cases provided by law, and for payment in cash through postal current accounts (art. 192). The collector must issue a receipt for each payment and make an appropriate annotation in the roll or on the taxpayer's file card (art. 193). Penalties for late payment are discussed at 13/7.6.

The tax rolls for all national and local taxes are now in the process of being mechanized on punched cards. The formation of the mechanized rolls is being carried out, under the supervision of the tax administration, by an association (*consorzio obbligatorio*) to which all collectors are required to belong.[45]

---

[43] This provision was added by article 1 of L. 25 October 1960, n. 1316. Its operation is explained in C.M. 10 December 1960, n. 333.

[44] The computation of the increase is described in C.M. 10 December 1960, n. 333.

[45] See L. 13 June 1952, n. 693; D.P.R. 2 August 1952, n. 1141; D.M. 3 June 1958.

13/3.8   Collection of Delinquent Taxes

After serving a notice of lateness on the taxpayer (art. 201), the collector may proceed to enforced expropriation of movable property (arts. 219-230) or, if that is insufficient, to the expropriation of immovable property (arts. 231-241) or of ships and aircraft (art. 242).

The collector's credit for any direct tax of the state inscribed in the roll of the year of the collection proceeding is entitled to a general preference against the movable property of the debtor (art. 211; CC art. 2752). The collector's credit for the tax on income from landowning inscribed in the rolls of the year of execution and of the preceding year, and credits for the communal and provincial surtaxes for the same period, are entitled to preference against all immovable property of the taxpayer situated in the commune in which the tax is collected and against the fruits and rents of the property (CC art. 2771). Under both of these provisions, the preference is limited to the amount of the tax due for the last two years if supplemental rolls (special or extraordinary rolls) are involved. Credits for the tax on income from movable wealth based on the exercise of business or professional activities, for the tax period during which execution was commenced and for the preceding period, are entitled to preference against movable property serving the exercise of the activity and against merchandise on the premises or in the taxpayer's dwelling (art. 211; CC art. 2759). This preference applies to any property satisfying the stated conditions even if it does not belong to the taxpayer, except lost or stolen property, merchandise entrusted to the taxpayer for processing, and merchandise provided with a regular customs entry bill but not yet legally brought into the country (art. 211). These preferences are extended to the increases of taxes which are imposed in case of failure to file a return, filing a false or incomplete return (13/7.2), or failure to pay an extended installment of taxes (art. 184 *quater*) (13/3.7).

13/4.   Protests and Appeals

13/4.1   In General

The taxpayer may appeal (*ricorrere*) the assessment of the Tax Office under the rules relating to tax litigation (art. 31). The rules in force regarding administrative litigation of direct tax matters and the litigation of direct tax matters in the courts are to be found principally in the law governing administrative litigation,[46] the decree law and law on the reform of tax provisions (*ordinamenti tributari*),[47] and the decree concerning the rules for the constitution and functioning of the tax com-

---

[46] L. 20 March 1865, n. 2248, Annex E, art. 6. The second paragraph of this article, however, has recently been declared unconstitutional (13/4.12).

[47] R.D.L. 7 August 1936, n. 1639, converted in L. 7 June 1937, n. 1016.

missions.[48] Except as regulated by special laws, litigation of direct tax matters in the courts (13/4.9) is also governed by the Code of Civil Procedure.[49] Certain provisions of the law concerning the tax on income from movable wealth,[50] certain provisions of the tax reform law of 1956 (Tremelloni law),[51] and certain provisions of the regulations for the tax on income from movable wealth [52] remain in effect (art. 288B); these provisions are also applicable to the complementary tax and the corporation tax.[53] With regard to the tax on income from landowning (10/2.2), the tax on agrarian income (10/2.3), and, insofar as assessed cadastrally, the tax on income from buildings (9/4.2), the administrative tax commissions are competent only for controversies concerning the tax liability, errors, reductions of tax, and exemptions and reliefs established exclusively in relation to the person of the taxpayer.[54] Controversies regarding the cadastral entries, the determination of the kind and grade of lands, and the drawing up and application of the schedules of estimated values are within the exclusive competence of the census commissions (10/2.2g).[55]

The first appeal (*ricorso*) must always go to the administrative commission of first degree (the District Commission) (13/4.2); the decision of that commission may, however, be taken on appeal (*appello*) to the Provincial Commission (13/4.3) or, if the tax has been inscribed in the roll, to the ordinary courts (13/4.9). A decision of the Provincial Commission may be appealed only on questions of law; the appeal may be made to the Central Commission (13/4.4) or, if the tax has been inscribed in the roll, to the ordinary courts. A decision of the Central Commission may also be appealed to the ordinary courts on questions of law. Questions of mere estimation of income may be appealed to the Central Commission only if they involve the determination of income from capital giving an unspecified yield (13/4.4); with this exception, questions of the estimation of income are excluded from the competence of the Central Commission and from the competence of the ordinary courts, unless they involve questions of law or other juridical questions (13/4.4, 13/4.9). An appeal from a decision of the Central Commission

---

[48] R.D. 8 July 1937, n. 1516. The commissions are further described at 1/4.10.

[49] The composition and functioning of the courts are discussed at 1/4.10. For a discussion of the sources of the law of tax procedure and of the relations between the law of tax procedure and the civil procedural law, see Allorio, *Diritto processuale tributario* 34-56.

[50] R.D.L. 24 August 1877, n. 4021.

[51] L. 5 January 1956, n. 1, arts. 6, 50.

[52] R.D. 11 July 1907, n. 560.

[53] See R.D. 30 December 1923, n. 3062, art. 26, abrogated by art. 288A of the *Testo unico*; and L. 6 August 1954, n. 603, art. 11, abrogated by art. 288C of the *Testo unico*.

[54] L. 8 March 1943, n. 153, art. 23, as modified by D.L. 8 April 1948, n. 514, art. 5.

[55] See also C.M. 10 November 1952, n. 201600, quoted in Vizzini, *Fabbricati e terreni nell'imposizione diretta erariale* 347.

or of an ordinary court of appeal is allowed to the Supreme Court of Cassation in the case of violation of law (13/4.10).

An assessment made with the agreement of the taxpayer cannot be contested except on the basis of certain defects in the document of assessment (13/2.4), for which a special petition to the District Commission is provided; any other proceeding in progress at the time of the assessment is extinguished (art. 34). If the taxpayer contends that a notice of assessment is void because not supported by detailed reasons, he must make this objection before the District Commission in order to avoid the lapse of the objection (art. 37) (13/2.1). With this exception, objections not raised before the administrative commission of the first degree may nonetheless be raised in appeals to other administrative commissions or to the courts, provided that no new claims (*domande*) are made (CPC art. 345). An appeal to the Tax Office against inscription in the roll is provided for, but an objection to the assessment cannot be made in such a proceeding if a notice of assessment has been served (13/4.6).

If the taxpayer has failed to file a return or if the income declared in the return is less than one half of the income assessed by the Tax Office, the commission or court hearing the appeal has the power to put the taxpayer to his oath on specific facts, not involving judgments or opinion, which are directly relevant to the application of the direct taxes, are such as must be known by the person required to swear, and do not involve estimates.[56] The taxpayer cannot be put to his oath if the assessment in controversy does not exceed L. 720,000.[57] If the taxpayer is not a physical person or lacks legal capacity, the oath may be required of the legal representative and of others required to sign the return (13/1.1b). The oath cannot be administered to prove an illegal act, or to deny an act which is shown by a public document (*atto pubblico*) to have occurred in the presence of the public official who drew the document. If the taxpayer fails to give the oath without a legitimate reason, his conclusions on the points of fact on which the oath has been requested are considered unfounded. The giving of a false oath is punishable by imprisonment (13/7.4). On a conviction for giving a false oath, the Tax Office may proceed to a new assessment, to be served on the taxpayer not later than 31 December of the second calendar year following that in which the sentence of conviction has become final (13/6.1).

If the income of an entity or enterprise taxed on the balance sheet basis has been determined by modification or correction of omitted or incorrect entries in the balance sheet, or has been assessed on the basis of the economic situation of the business, under the rules explained at 13/2.3, the income assessed by estimate under those provisions cannot

---

[56] L. 5 January 1956, n. 1, art. 6.
[57] L. 5 January 1956, n. 1, art. 6; L. 28 May 1959, n. 361, art. 2.

be reduced or declared nonexistent, in case of contest, unless the taxpayer
has furnished proof of the incorrectness of the modifications or corrections or proof of the total or partial nonexistence of the income (art.
121). The adjudicating body may require the taxpayer to furnish proof
under oath, under the provision discussed above (art. 121).

Administrative appeals against assessments and against the rolls,
against corrections, and against decisions of the commissions of first
and second degree, with respect to income subject to the direct taxes,
are filed with the assessing Tax Office in accordance with the rules
prescribed for the filing of returns (13/1.1).[58] However, an administrative appeal to a commission may also be filed with the commission itself.[59]

13/4.2 Complaint to the District Commission

With respect to the acts (*operato*) of the Tax Office in relation to
the direct taxes, the taxpayer may complain (*reclamare*) to the District
Commission for Direct Taxes within 30 days of the service (*notificazione*)
of the measure (*provvedimento*) to which he objects.[60] If the notice
of assessment has been served in accordance with the rules discussed at
13/2.1, the taxpayer's failure to complain to the District Commission
within 30 days renders final the amount of income determined by the
Tax Office.[61]

The taxpayer must be notified of the date of the hearing at least
20 days in advance,[62] and the Commission must hear him or his representative at his request.[63] If the taxpayer has been given regular communication of the hearing, his failure to be present does not prevent the
Commission from deciding the controversy; the decision on a request
for postponement for the alleged impossibility of the taxpayer's being
present is left to the discretion of the Commission.[64] Up to the day
before the hearing, the taxpayer has the right to consult the report of
the Tax Office and the documents annexed to it. Up to five days before
the hearing, he has the right to file supplementary notes and documents
with the Commission; documents which have not been so filed, in

---

[58] R.D. 8 July 1937, n. 1516, art. 23; R.D.L. 7 August 1936, n. 1639, art. 43.
Article 12 of R.D. 17 September 1931, n. 1608, cited in the 1936 law, was abrogated
by article 25 of D.P.R. 5 July 1951, n. 573, and is now replaced by article 29 of the
Testo unico.
[59] Regarding the Provincial Commission, see R.D. 8 July 1937, n. 1516, art. 37.
Regarding the District Commission, see Comm. Centr., Sez. III, 25 June 1958, n.
6845; Comm. Centr. 15 June 1959, n. 17998.
[60] R.D. 8 July 1937, n. 1516, art. 23. See also R.D.L. 7 August 1936, n. 1639,
art. 22.
[61] R.D. 11 July 1907, n. 560, art. 91. See also R.D.L. 7 August 1936, n. 1639,
art. 41.
[62] L. 5 January 1956, n. 1, art. 50.
[63] R.D. 11 July 1907, n. 560, art. 94.
[64] L. 5 January 1956, n. 1, art. 51.

duplicate, cannot be taken into consideration without the explicit assent of the representative of the tax administration.[65] The Procurator of Taxes (1/4.2) may intervene at the hearings of the Commission, personally or through his representative; [66] but both the taxpayer and the representative of the Tax Office must withdraw before the decision, which is made immediately after the hearing.[67]

If the District Commission has not made a decision within three months of the filing of the complaint, either the Tax Office or the taxpayer may request the President of the Commission to set a day for the discussion, which cannot be deferred beyond the 45th day from the filing of the request. The petitioner must receive 15 days' notice of the hearing.[68]

The District Commissions have all the powers conferred on the direct tax officials with respect to investigation, access, inspection, checking, and the requiring of data, information, and clarifications (13/2.2).[69] The taxpayer's failure to permit inspection of books, writings, or documents has the same effect as it has in the case of the assessment process itself (13/2.3).[70] If the Commission acquires knowledge of new elements during a proceeding before it (that is, elements not taken into account in the assessment), it may withhold decision and remand the question to the Tax Office, fixing a time limit for a new assessment (art. 36). In such a case, the taxable amount cannot be determined with the agreement of the taxpayer under the procedure described at 13/2.4. The decision of the Commission may not extend beyond the limits of the contest.[71]

The decision of the Commission is considered published only when a copy is sent to the Tax Office.[72] It must be served on the taxpayer, at the responsibility of the Tax Office, within 60 days of its receipt.[73]

13/4.3   Appeal to the Provincial Commission

The taxpayer may contest the decision of the District Commission before the Provincial Commission within 30 days from the date of service of that decision.[74] The Tax Office may also appeal within the same time limit, informing the taxpayer of the decision to appeal and

---

[65] R.D. 8 July 1937, n. 1516, art. 24.

[66] R.D. 11 July 1907, n. 560, art. 94; R.D. 8 July 1937, n. 1516, art. 29.

[67] L. 5 January 1956, n. 1, art. 50. Before the enactment of this provision, the representative of the Tax Office could be present at the voting. See R.D. 8 July 1937, n. 1516, art. 29; C.M. 12 August 1955, n. 10526.

[68] R.D. 8 July 1937, n. 1516, art. 33.

[69] R.D. 8 July 1937, n. 1516, art. 25.

[70] R.D. 8 July 1937, n. 1516, art. 26.

[71] R.D. 11 July 1907, n. 560, art. 94.

[72] L. 5 January 1956, n. 1, art. 50.

[73] R.D. 8 July 1937, n. 1516, art. 35.

[74] R.D. 8 July 1937, n. 1516, art. 37. See also R.D.L. 7 August 1936, n. 1639, art. 22.

of the reasons on which it is based.[75] However, if the Tax Office fails to serve a decision of the District Commission on the taxpayer within 60 days of its receipt by the Tax Office (13/4.2), the right of the Office to appeal lapses unless the notice serving the decision was sent at least 10 days before the expiration of the time limit.[76]

In cases before the Provincial Commission, either of the parties may make an incidental appeal against the appeal of the other.[77] It appears that an incidental appeal by the Tax Office, unlike a principal appeal, is not barred by the failure of the Office to fulfill the requirement of serving the taxpayer, within 60 days, with the dispositive part of the decision of the District Commission.[78] An incidental appeal must be made in the same form as a principal appeal (CPC art. 333), and must be made within 30 days of the service on the taxpayer or the deposit at the Tax Office of the principal appeal.[79] An incidental appeal may be made even if the time limit for making a principal appeal or counterappeal has expired or if the party making it has acquiesced in the previous decision; the incidental appeal loses its efficacy if the principal appeal is declared inadmissible (CPC art. 334).

Appeals for revocation for certain grave irregularities in the process may be made to the Commission before which the irregularities occurred.[80]

In general, the rules governing the conduct of the hearing and the publication and notification of the decision of the District Commission also apply to appeals before the Provincial Commission.[81] The additional provisions listed below also apply.[82]

1. The Compartmental Inspector (1/4.2) or his representative has the right to take part in the hearing, but not to be present at the decision.[83]

---

[75] R.D. 8 July 1937, n. 1516, art. 38.

[76] R.D. 8 July 1937, n. 1516, art. 35.

[77] R.D. 8 July 1937, n. 1516, art. 40. An incidental appeal, like the principal appeal, is an appeal against the original decision; a counterappeal, on the other hand, is made in opposition to the grounds of the principal appeal and thus ordinarily seeks to sustain the original decision.

[78] See Comm. Centr., Sez. un., 12 November 1941, n. 47398, and discussion in Biscotto and Ozzola, *Il processo tributario di accertamento* 313.

[79] Comm. Centr., Sez. un., 16 July 1952, n. 38979. For a discussion of this point, see Biscotto and Ozzola, *Il processo tributario di accertamento* 307-312.

[80] R.D. 8 July 1937, n. 1516, art. 44; CPC arts. 395, 396. An appeal for revocation seeks annulment of the proceedings and the re-examination of the controversy. For discussion of the cases in which this procedure is available, see Allorio, *Diritto processuale tributario* 400; Biscotto and Ozzola, *Il processo tributario di accertamento* 232 *et seq.* (District Commission), 342 *et seq.* (Provincial Commission), 401 (Central Commission); Rotondi, "L'istituto della revocazione nel processo tributario," *Dir. e prat. trib.*, 1950, I, 45.

[81] R.D. 8 July 1937, n. 1516, art. 41.

[82] R.D. 8 July 1937, n. 1516, arts. 41, 42.

[83] L. 5 January 1956, n. 1, art. 50.

2. The decision cannot be pronounced before 30 days have passed from the date of the service of the appeal.

3. Whenever the Provincial Commission pronounces on questions of law, it must specify the reasons for its decision.

The Provincial Commission also decides questions relating to duplication of assessment between communes located in different districts.[84]

13/4.4 Appeal to the Central Commission

A decision of the Provincial Commission may be appealed to the Central Commission within the same time limits as apply to appeals to the Provincial Commission (13/4.3).[85] An appeal to the Central Commission must contain a description of the contested decision and a specification of the articles of law or regulations which are alleged to have been violated or erroneously applied.[86]

The Central Commission is competent to decide appeals from decisions of the Provincial Commission on questions concerning the application of the law, including errors of procedure in the administrative process, but not questions concerning the mere estimation of taxable income (*estimazione semplice*) [87] unless they arise with respect to the existence or determination, for purposes of the tax on income from movable wealth, of income from capital for which no interest has been stipulated.[88] The Central Commission may consider errors of procedure in the administrative process as well as errors of substantive law and is competent to decide questions of fact or of estimation of income which also involve juridical questions (*estimazione complessa*), whether substantive or procedural.[89]

The provisions governing the setting of dates for hearings and the publication of decisions of the District and Provincial Commissions apply also to the Central Commission.[90] Ordinarily, judgments before the

---

[84] R.D. 11 July 1907, n. 560, arts. 100, 101.

[85] R.D. 8 July 1937, n. 1516, arts. 35, 38, 45. See also R.D.L. 7 August 1936, n. 1639, art. 22.

[86] R.D. 8 July 1937, n. 1516, art. 46.

[87] R.D.L. 24 August 1877, n. 4021, art. 48.

[88] R.D.L. 24 August 1877, n. 4021, art. 50.

[89] On the distinctions between questions of fact and questions of law and between *estimazione semplice* and *estimazione complessa*, see Allorio, *Diritto processuale tributario* 341; Allorio, *La vita e la scienza del diritto in Italia e in Europa* 343-359; Berliri, *Il processo tributario* 74; Biscotto and Ozzola, *Il processo tributario di accertamento* 365-367; Cocivera, *Guida alle imposte dirette* 141-144; Giannini, *Istituzioni di diritto tributario* 198-200; Capaccioli, "L'estimazione semplice," *RDFSF*, 1956, I, 375-392; *RDFSF*, 1957, I, 76-89. Compare the principles governing the jurisdiction of the ordinary courts (13/4.9b). Even if a decision on the merits involves mere estimation, the Central Commission is competent to inquire into the method by which the judgment of estimation was reached. Comm. Centr., Sez. I, 2 May 1946, n. 82032.

[90] R.D. 8 July 1937, n. 1516, art. 47.

Central Commission proceed without intervention of either the taxpayer
or the representative of the tax administration; each presents his arguments in the appeal, the counterappeal, or attached memorials.[91] However, the Central Commission must hear a complainant who has made
an express request to be heard when it recognizes the existence of and
estimates the value of income from capital, taxable in category A of
income from movable wealth, for which no interest is stipulated.[92] In
such a case, the invitation to appear must be sent to the party at least
15 days before the day fixed for the hearing.

The taxpayer may file a counterappeal within 60 days of the service
of a notice of an appeal of the Tax Office, and the Tax Office may file
a counterappeal within 60 days of its receipt of an appeal of the taxpayer.
Other communications regarding the appeal must be filed by the Tax
Office with the Secretariat of the Commission, and by the taxpayer
with the Tax Office, at least seven days before the hearing.[93] Incidental
appeals may be made under the same conditions as incidental appeals
to the Provincial Commission (13/4.3).[94]

The Central Commission must specify the reasons for its decision
when it pronounces on a question of law,[95] and the Tax Office must
notify the taxpayer of the decision within 60 days.[96] The Tax Office
need serve only the dispositive part of the decision on the taxpayer;
the persons concerned, however, may ask to see the text of the decision
and may obtain copies of the decision upon payment of a fee.[97]

An appeal to the Central Commission is allowed in the case of con-
flicting jurisdiction between communes in different provinces over the
income of the taxpayer.[98]

13/4.5 Appeal to the Intendant of Finance Against Withholding

Against direct withholding of the direct taxes (13/3.3) and provisional
withholdings paid directly to the Provincial Treasury Office (13/3.5),
the taxpayer may appeal to the Intendant of Finance of the province
in which he has his fiscal domicile, on the grounds of material error,
duplication, or total or partial nonexistence of the tax obligation (art.
171). The appeal must be made within six months of the date of withholding or payment and must be accompanied by a request for

---

91 R.D. 8 July 1937, n. 1516, art. 48.
92 R.D. 8 July 1937, n. 1516, art. 48; R.D.L. 24 August 1877, n. 4021, art. 50.
93 R.D. 8 July 1937, n. 1516, art. 48.
94 R.D. 8 July 1937, n. 1516, art. 48. Regarding appeals for revocation, see note
80 supra.
95 R.D. 11 July 1907, n. 560, art. 104.
96 R. D. 11 July 1907, n. 560, arts. 97, 105.
97 R.D. 8 July 1937, n. 1516, art. 49.
98 R.D.L. 24 August 1877, n. 4021, art. 48; see also R.D. 11 July 1907, n. 560,
arts. 100, 101.

reimbursement. If the Intendant does not allow the appeal, he sends it to the competent tax commission within 60 days of its receipt, giving notice to the appellant.

13/4.6 Appeal to the Tax Office Against Inscription in the Roll

The taxpayer may appeal to the Tax Office, on the grounds listed below, against inscription in the roll (art. 188).

1. Omitted or improper service of the notice of assessment.
2. Material error or duplication of the inscription.
3. Total or partial nonexistence of the tax obligation, provided that the inscription was not preceded by the service of a notice of assessment.[99]
4. Violation of the rules governing inscription in the roll, provided that the taxpayer has an interest in raising the question.

The appeal must be made within 30 days of the service of a bill for payment or, in the absence thereof, of the service of a notice of lateness, or of the service of a notice of inscription in an extraordinary roll (13/3.6c). If the Tax Office decides not to accept the appeal, it sends the appeal to the competent tax commission within 60 days of its receipt, giving notice to the appellant.

An appeal against inscription in the roll does not suspend collection, but the Intendant of Finance has the power to suspend collection temporarily, on the proposal of the Tax Office, by an order supported by reasons (art. 188).

13/4.7 Appeal to the Intendant of Finance Against Acts of the Collector in Execution

Against acts of the collector in execution, appeal may be made to the Intendant of Finance by the taxpayer and his co-obligors (heirs, transferees of a business, members of a *de facto* company) and by directors and liquidators of an entity required to be taxed on the balance sheet basis, if the proceeding is brought against them as personally liable for payment of the tax (art. 208) (see 13/3.1). The spouse and relations by blood or by marriage within the third degree of the taxpayer or of a co-obligor may also appeal, unless entitled to an appeal to the judge

---

[99] This provision permits a taxpayer who has not received a notice of assessment to contest his liability to pay a tax if the basis of the tax has terminated but he has not filed a report of termination (13/1.5), or if the income subjected to the tax is exempt or does not exceed the applicable allowances (12/1.4b). See De Angelis, Potenza, and Testa, *Testo unico delle leggi sulle imposte dirette* 906; C.M. 18 December 1959, n. 84. For a discussion of the possibility of appeal against inscription in the roll, on the ground that income does not exceed the applicable allowance, in cases where income has been inscribed in the roll on the basis of income of the preceding tax period because of failure to file a return (13/2.3), see Poli, "Maggiorazione del reddito, dichiarazioni tardive, ricorsi contro il ruolo," *Imp. dir. erariali*, 1962, 450.

in execution by virtue of a claim of ownership or of other property right in the property subject to execution (arts. 207, 208; CPC art. 619).

The Intendant of Finance must hear the Tax Office and give the collector 15 days in which to present his arguments; his decision must be made within 30 days of the filing of the appeal (art. 208). His order is final, and the time limit for extraordinary appeal to the Head of State (13/4.11) is reduced to 60 days. The Intendant may suspend the acts of execution by an order supported by reasons during the time that the appeal is before him.

13/4.8 Appeal to the Minister of Finance Against Application of Penalties

A decree of suspension of the exercise of a professional activity for nonpayment of the tax, under the provisions described at 13/7.6, may be appealed within 15 days to the Minister of Finance (art. 262). An appeal against the imposition of a pecuniary penalty by the Intendant of Finance may be made to the Minister of Finance within 30 days of notification, provided that the maximum penalty prescribed by law for the offense is not less than L. 10,000.[100]

13/4.9 Appeal to the Ordinary Courts

a. IN GENERAL. A final decision of the Central Commission [101] or of the Provincial or District Commission [102] may be appealed to the courts on questions other than those concerning the mere estimation of income, provided that the tax has been inscribed in the roll (13/4.12). An appeal to the courts is allowed only if there has been a final (*definitiva*) decision of an administrative commission,[103] that is, a conclusive disposition of the tax controversy. Thus, an order for the production of documents or other evidence or an order of the Central Commission remanding the case to the Provincial Commission for further proceedings cannot be appealed to the courts.[104]

In controversies concerning the direct taxes, jurisdiction of the ordinary courts is exercised in the first instance by the District Tribunals (*Tribunali di Circondario*) and, in the second, by the Courts of Appeal (*Corti d'Appello*) (1/4.10f).[105] Further appeal to the Supreme Court of Cassation is allowed for violation of law, in accordance with the rules discussed at 13/4.10.

---

[100] L. 7 January 1929, n. 4, art. 56.
[101] R.D.L. 24 August 1877, n. 4021, art. 53 (movable wealth); L. 8 March 1943, n. 153, art. 23 (cadastral taxes).
[102] R.D.L. 7 August 1936, n. 1639, art. 22.
[103] R.D.L. 7 August 1936, n. 1639, art. 22; Cass., Sez. I, 13 April 1960, n. 861.
[104] See Allorio, *Diritto processuale tributario* 300.
[105] L. 20 March 1865, n. 2248, Annex E, art. 6. See also CPC art. 9.

b. COMPETENCE. The courts are not competent to consider questions of simple estimation (*estimazione semplice*) (13/4.9a). However, simple estimation has been defined in the decisions to include not only the determination of value or quantity, as suggested by a literal interpretation of the law, but also the resolution of any question of fact which is possible by an empirical investigation without juridical inquiry (*indagine giuridica*).[106] Thus, under the prevailing jurisprudence, the competence of the ordinary courts in direct tax matters is limited to questions of law (*diritto*) and to questions of complex estimation (*estimazione complessa*), that is, questions requiring a juridical inquiry in addition to an empirical investigation. When determination of whether a tax is due involves juridical questions, or juridical questions and questions of fact together (*collegate*), the competence of the courts extends to the entire controversy, without distinction between juridical questions and questions of fact.[107]

Except in appeals to the Supreme Court of Cassation for violation of law (13/4.10), the courts are not competent to consider errors of procedure [108] or questions of illegitimacy (*illegittimità*) in matters of form [109] in the proceedings before the tax commissions.

Since the proceedings before the ordinary courts are regarded as independent proceedings of first instance,[110] questions and exceptions not raised before the administrative commissions may be raised before the court of first instance, although the objective of the proceeding may not be changed.[111] However, the decision of the court cannot modify or annul the decision of a tax commission regarding the direct taxes, but can only declare its legitimacy or illegitimacy. If the decision of the commission was illegitimate, the judgment of the court requires the administration to restore tax installments already paid (13/5) and renders illegitimate the claim for those not yet due.[112]

c. TIME LIMITS. Appeal by the taxpayer to the courts against administrative decisions relating to the direct taxes can be made only within the six months following publication of the roll or direct withholding of the tax.[113] However, on questions which have not been finally resolved administratively before the formation of the roll, on questions for which appeal to the Tax Office against inscription in the roll is allowed

---

[106] For criticisms of this interpretation of the law, see Allorio, *Diritto processuale tributario* 288; and Giannini, *Istituzioni di diritto tributario* 216. Compare the principles governing the competence of the Central Commission (13/4.4).

[107] Cass., Sez. un., 14 May 1945, n. 339; Cass., Sez. I, 24 March 1952, n. 806.

[108] Cass., Sez. I, 17 April 1952, n. 1023.

[109] Cass., Sez. un., 19 January 1957, n. 128.

[110] This view, however, is criticized by Allorio, *Diritto processuale tributario* 382.

[111] Cass., Sez. I, 13 March 1947, n. 367.

[112] Giannini, *Istituzioni di diritto tributario* 231.

[113] R.D.L. 24 August 1877, n. 4021, art. 53.

13/4.6),[114] and on questions regarding relief from the tax on income rom buildings for the total or partial destruction of buildings,[115] appeal o the courts may be made at any time within six months from the date f service on the taxpayer of the last final administrative decision.

The tax administration may appeal a decision of the Central Commission to the courts at any time within 12 months of the date of service f the decision on the taxpayer, provided the decision has been served n the taxpayer within three months of its arrival at the Tax Office. f the decision of the Central Commission has not been served on the axpayer within three months of its arrival at the Tax Office, the decision ecomes final with respect to the administration unless the taxpayer ppeals to the courts within six months of the service.[116]

3/4.10   Appeal to the Supreme Court of Cassation for Violation of Law

Against decisions of the courts and decisions of the Central Commission,[117] an appeal may be made to the Supreme Court of Cassation or violation of law (Const. art. 111). Under this provision, both subtantive and procedural questions may be raised, whereas the procedural questions cannot be considered in appeals from the commissions to the ordinary courts (13/4.9). Any further appeal to the ordinary courts on he question of the legitimacy of the tax assessment is precluded by an ppeal to the Supreme Court for violation of substantive law,[118] but not oy an appeal to the Supreme Court on a defect of jurisdiction of the commission or on a violation of procedural law. Appeal to the Supreme Court from decisions of the District and Provincial Commissions is not llowed.[119]

Even before the recent decision of the Constitution Court regarding payment as a condition of appeal (13/4.12),[120] payment of installments of the tax due was not a prerequisite of appeal to the Supreme Court from a decision of the Central Commission.[121]

Appeal to the Supreme Court must be made within 60 days of the service of the decision being appealed (CPC art. 325).[122]

---

[114] R.D. 11 July 1907, n. 560, art. 120.
[115] R.D. 24 August 1877, n. 4024, art. 57 (Regulations).
[116] L. 8 June 1936, n. 1231, art. 34.
[117] Cass., Sez. I, 17 April 1952, n. 1023.
[118] Cass., Sez. I, 10 March 1952 (RDFSF, 1953, II, 57); Cass., Sez. I, 17 April 1952, n. 1023.
[119] Cass. 20 November 1957, n. 4450.
[120] Corte Cost. 31 March 1961, n. 21.
[121] Cass., Sez. un., 6 April 1951, n. 800 (RDFSF, 1951, II, 211).
[122] Cass., Sez. I, 21 June 1957, n. 2369; Cass., Sez. un., 13 March 1954, n. 703 (Dir. e prat. trib., 1956, II, 36).

13/4.11 Extraordinary Appeals

Provision is made for an extraordinary appeal to the Head of State [12] in which the Council of State (1/4.10g) must be heard; [124] provision i: made also for an appeal to the Council of State, in its judicial capacity against administrative acts (Const. arts. 103, 113), provided that th(appeal does not fall within the competence of the courts or of ar administrative adjudicating body.[125] With regard to the direct taxes the jurisdiction of the Council of State is therefore limited to questions concerning collection.

13/4.12 Payment of Tax Pending Review

There is no requirement that taxes be paid prior to the start of proceedings before the administrative commissions. However, after the decision of an administrative commission, the taxes are inscribed in the rolls in accordance with the rules discussed at 13/3.6b, and the amounts sc inscribed must then be paid in the regular manner. The Intendant of Finance has the power to suspend collection of the tax pending an appeal against inscription in the roll (13/4.6) or an appeal against acts of the collector in execution (13/4.7).

As explained at 13/4.9, the ordinary courts have no competence in appeals relating to direct taxes unless publication of the roll has taken place. Until recently, no protest in direct tax matters was allowed in the courts unless accompanied by a certificate attesting payment of the tax.[126] However, the Constitutional Court has recently declared this requirement to be contrary to the Constitution of Italy, and payment of the tax is therefore no longer a condition of appealing to the courts in tax matters.[127]

13/5. Refunds

When amounts greater than those due have been directly withheld (13/3.3) or provisionally withheld and paid into the Treasury (13/3.2)

---

[123] R.D. 21 April 1942, n. 444, art. 60.

[124] R.D. 26 June 1924, n. 1054, art. 16.

[125] R.D. 26 June 1924, n. 1054, art. 26.

[126] L. 20 March 1865, n. 2248, Annex E, art. 6; R.D. 11 July 1907, n. 560, art. 120 (movable wealth); R.D. 24 August 1877, n. 4024, art. 57 (buildings). For discussions of this rule, sometimes referred to as the rule of "solve et repete," see Allorio, Diritto processuale tributario LIV-LIX, 120; Giannini, Istituzioni di diritto tributario 219; Biscotto and Ozzola, Il processo tributario di accertamento 440.

[127] Corte Cost. 31 March 1961, n. 21. The constitutional provisions under which the requirement was held invalid were: article 3, dealing with the equality of all citizens before the law; article 24, dealing with the right of anyone to proceed in court for the protection of his own rights and legitimate interests; and article 113, allowing jurisdictional protection, against acts of the public administration, of rights and legitimate interests before ordinary and administrative organs of jurisdiction. See also 1/4.10a. For comments on the decision, see Maffezzoni, "Motivi e limiti di efficacia della abolizione del 'solve et repete,'" Riv. dir. proc., 1961, 641; Micheli, "Considerazioni sulla incostituzionalità del 'solve et repete,'" Giur. cost., 1961, 1183.

art. 172), or the amount of tax provisionally withheld exceeds the amount of tax to be inscribed in the roll (art. 177), the Intendant of Finance is required to provide for a refund (*rimborso*) by means of an order of payment.

Similarly, when the tax due on the basis of the final assessment or inscribed in the roll after a decision of the tax commission of the first or second degree (13/3.6b) is less than the aggregate amount of the provisional inscriptions in the rolls and provisional withholdings (if any), and, in general, when amounts not due have been inscribed in the roll, the taxpayer is entitled to a reduction (13/3.6c). The reduction is made by a written order of the Tax Office and notice is given to the taxpayer (art. 198). When the tax provisionally inscribed in the roll exceeds the tax finally inscribed on the basis of the return (13/3.6a), the taxpayer's right to a reduction does not arise immediately, but only on the expiration of the time limit for making the assessment; however, the Tax Office may provide for the reduction immediately if it decides to accept the return.[128] When the tax provisionally inscribed for the tax period exceeds the amount finally inscribed, in the absence of a return, after assessment under the rules discussed at 13/2.3, the Tax Office provides for the reduction as soon as the tax finally due for the period has been determined. Collection fees are included in the reduction except in cases of relief from the tax on income from landowning and from the tax on agrarian income by reason of adverse weather conditions (art. 198) (10/2.2). The reductions are inscribed in a list, specifying the reasons and the justifying documents (art. 198); the list is delivered to the collector (13/3.7), who refunds the amounts already collected or applies them to installments due but uncollected (art. 199). The taxpayer is also entitled to an indemnity, which amounts to 2.5% of the difference between the tax actually paid on the basis of the provisional inscription and the tax finally assessed for the same period, for each full six-month period, after the first, between the due date of the last installment of the roll in which the higher tax was inscribed and the date of the reduction list (art. 199 *bis*).[129]

Whenever an appeal to the courts is resolved in the taxpayer's favor, any overpayment of tax is refunded after the passing of the decree of the court, and the appropriate annotations are made in the register and on the roll.[130] In the case of an appeal to the Intendant of Finance against withholding (13/4.5), the appeal must be accompanied by a request for reimbursement (art. 171).

The Tax Office compiles special refund lists of taxpayers whose returns show that the withholdings on distributions of profits made under the rules described at 9/2.7a exceed the tax finally to be inscribed in the roll,

---

[128] C.M. 18 May 1960, n. 301520.
[129] This provision was added by L. 25 October 1960, n. 1316, art. 1.
[130] R.D. 11 July 1907, n. 560, art. 120.

and these lists must be delivered to the collector at the same time as the rolls in which the taxes are inscribed.[131] The indemnity for the difference between the tax paid on the basis of the provisional inscription and the tax finally assessed is due starting from the second six-month period following the filing of the return.

13/6. Time Limits on Assessment and Collection

13/6.1 Assessment

If a return has been filed within the prescribed time limit (13/1.1c) or if income has been assessed without a return, proceedings to correct the amount of income (art. 32), or to modify or supplement the assessment (art. 35), must be commenced, to avoid lapse, on or before 31 December of the third year following that in which the return was, or should have been, filed. The same time limit applies to assessments of increases in income from landowning (art. 57) and in agrarian income (art. 68).

In the case of the assessment ex officio of unreported income which has not been the object of a return or of an assessment for the preceding tax period, proceedings for assessment (art. 32), or for modification or supplementation of the assessment (art. 35), must be commenced, to avoid lapse, on or before 31 December of the fourth year following that in which the return should have been filed.

In the cases specified below, assessment may be made even if the time limits described above have expired.

1. When an assessment made with the agreement of the taxpayer has been declared void (13/2.4), the Tax Office has 90 days in which to make a new assessment (art. 34).
2. When the tax commission of first degree supplements an assessment (art. 36) (13/2.5), or remands to the Tax Office the assessment of an entity or enterprise taxed on the balance sheet basis for an estimated assessment (art. 122) (13/2.3), the commission is authorized to fix a time limit for the new assessment.
3. If the taxpayer has been sentenced for giving a false oath (13/4.1), the Tax Office may proceed to a new assessment, which is to be served on the taxpayer on or before 31 December of the second calendar year following that in which the sentence of conviction has become final.[132]

All time limits pending on the date of a taxpayer's death are extended for six months (art. 16).

13/6.2 Collection

Proceedings for the final inscription in the roll of taxes on income declared by the taxpayer, and of taxes applied to income assessed under articles 80, 123, or 142, because of the taxpayer's failure to file a return, must be commenced, to avoid lapse, on or before 31 December of the

---

[131] L. 29 December 1962, n. 1745, art. 3.
[132] L. 5 January 1956, n. 1, art. 6.

second year following that in which the return was, or should have been, filed (art. 180). In all other cases, taxes or increased taxes on income assessed by the Tax Office must be inscribed in the rolls on or before 31 December of the second year following that in which the assessment became final (art. 180).

In the case of the taxpayer's death, all time limits are extended for six months (art. 16).

13/7. Interest, Penalties, and Prosecutions

13/7.1 In General

Penalties are provided for violation of various rules governing the assessment and payment of the direct taxes. The types of penalties which may be imposed under various conditions are listed below.

1. *Surcharge.* A surcharge (*sopratassa*) is a fixed amount measured as a fraction or multiple of the tax due. Liability for the payment of a surcharge is a civil obligation.[133]

2. *Pecuniary penalty.* A pecuniary penalty (*pene pecuniaria*) may be imposed for a violation which does not constitute a crime (*reato*); liability for the payment of a pecuniary penalty is a civil obligation.[134] In setting a pecuniary penalty between the maximum and the minimum established by the law, the gravity of the violation and the character of the offender, inferred from his previous penal and judicial record and from his conduct, are considered.[135]

3. *Fine.* A fine (*ammenda*) is a payment to the state, within the maximum and minimum established by the tax law, imposed for a contravention (*contravvenzione*), which is the less serious type of crime (CP arts. 17, 26).[136] If the fine established by law can be presumed to be inefficacious by reason of the offender's economic condition, it may be tripled (CP art. 26).[137]

4. *Mulct.* A mulct (*multa*) is a payment to the state, within the maximum and minimum established by the tax law, imposed for a delict (*delitto*), which is the more serious type of crime (CP arts. 17, 24).[138] The mulct established by a tax law may also be tripled if it can be presumed to be inefficacious by reason of the offender's economic condition (CP art. 24).[139]

5. *Detention.* Detention (*arresto*) in places established for that purpose or in special sections of prisons is provided, in addition to or as an alternative to a fine, for certain contraventions (CP arts. 17, 25).

---

[133] L. 7 January 1929, n. 4 (general rules for the repression of violations of the tax laws), art. 5.

[134] L. 7 January 1929, n. 4, art. 3.

[135] L. 7 January 1929, n. 4, art. 4.

[136] A violation for which the tax law provides a fine is classified as a contravention. L. 7 January 1929, n. 4, art. 2.

[137] As modified by D.L.C.P.S. 21 October 1947, n. 1250, art. 2.

[138] A violation for which the tax specifies a mulct is classified as a delict. L. 7 January 1929, n. 4, art. 2.

[139] As modified by D.L. 21 October 1947, n. 1250, art. 1.

6. *Imprisonment.* Imprisonment (*reclusione*) is provided, in addition to or as an alternative to a mulct, for certain delicts (CP arts. 17, 23).

7. *Indemnity for late payment.* After the expiration of the time limit for payment of an installment of taxes, a taxpayer is required to pay a percentage of the unpaid amount as an indemnity for lateness (*indennità di mora*) (13/7.6).

8. *Increase in tax.* An increase in tax of 2.5% for each six-month period, after the first, between the date of publication of the roll based on the return and the date of publication of the roll based on the assessment of the Tax Office is imposed when the taxpayer has failed to file a return or has filed an incomplete or false return (13/7.2). A similar increase is imposed on taxes whose collection has been extended beyond the normal period (13/3.7).[140]

9. *Tax bankruptcy.* When taxes of a person engaged in the exercise of a business, profession, or other profitable activity are in arrears, the Intendant of Finance may order the collector to file a petition for a declaration of tax bankruptcy (*fallimento fiscale*) (13/7.6).

10. *Suspension of exercise of activity.* When taxes of a person engaged in the exercise of a business, profession, or other profitable activity are in arrears, the Intendant of Finance may decree the suspension of the activity for as long as the taxes remain unpaid (13/7.6). A similar penalty may also be imposed on credit firms for improper certification of debts and on agents engaged in the transfer of shares who fail to report transactions (13/7.5).

11. *Prohibition from serving as member of controlling board.* Persons who have been convicted of tax fraud (13/7.4) or of failure to state the absence of books or accounting records of an entity taxed on the balance sheet basis (13/7.2) are prohibited for five years from serving as members of controlling boards of entities taxed on the balance sheet basis (art. 259).

The surcharges are applied by the Tax Office, either through the notice of assessment or through a separate notice (art. 268). Violations for which other penalties are imposed are reported in writing by the Tax Office to the Intendant of Finance (art. 270), who has cognizance of violations of rules of tax laws for which a pecuniary penalty is provided,[141] and of crimes for which the only penalty, other than a surcharge, is a fine.[142] The authorization of a bankruptcy proceeding and the suspension of the exercise of the taxpayer's activity for nonpayment of taxes are also within the cognizance of the Intendant of Finance (13/7.6). The application of a sanction against a credit firm or institution for false or late attestation of debts owed to it is referred by the Intendant of Finance to the Minister of Finance for decision in concert

---

[140] These provisions were introduced by article 1 of L. 25 October 1960, n. 1316. Administrative instructions are contained in C.M. 10 December 1960, n. 333.

[141] The procedure for the application of a pecuniary penalty is set forth in articles 55-59 of L. 7 January 1929, n. 4.

[142] L. 7 January 1929, n. 4, art. 21. The decree of the Intendant of Finance imposing penalties within his competence is governed by articles 36-45 of this law.

with the Minister of the Treasury (13/7.5). The application of other penalties is referred by the Intendant of Finance to the courts (art. 270).[143]

Surcharges are inscribed in the roll for collection with the taxes due (13/3.6). Unpaid fines may be collected by mortgage or sequestration of the taxpayer's property.[144] The right of the state to the collection of a pecuniary penalty lapses with the passage of five years from the day on which the violation was committed; the right to the collection of a surcharge lapses with the passage of the time established for the prescription of the tax itself.[145] The time limits for seeking bankruptcy or suspension are the same as for the collection of the tax.[146]

The transferee of a business productive of income from movable wealth of categories B or C/1 is liable for the payment of surcharges due for violations which were already charged to the transgressor at the time of the transfer of the business (art. 197) (13/3.1).

13/7.2 Omitted, Late, or Incomplete Returns

If a taxpayer fails to file a return or files an incomplete or false return, the tax on the unreported income is increased by 2.5% for each six-month period, after the first, between the date of publication of the roll in which the taxes based on the return were inscribed and the date of publication of the roll in which the unreported income is inscribed (art. 184 *bis*).[147] However, the taxpayer may request, in his appeal to the commission of first degree, that the taxes and higher taxes resulting from the assessment of the Tax Office be inscribed provisionally in the roll in their entire amount, rather than in installments, with the matured six-month increases of 2.5%; in that case, the increases relating to subsequent six-month periods are excused (art. 184 *bis*).

A taxpayer who fails to file a return of his own income is subject to a single fine of between L. 30,000 and L. 300,000 and also to a surcharge of one third of the amount of each tax due (art. 243). If the aggregate of taxes due exceeds L. 600,000, the taxpayer is subject to a fine of not less than the amount of each tax due. On the first repetition of the offense, the fine is doubled; for further repetitions, it is tripled. If the amount of income finally assessed exceeds L. 6,000,000, the taxpayer is subject to detention for up to six months, and the conviction includes publication of the sentence.

---

[143] The Tribunal (1/4.10f) has cognizance of all crimes established by the tax laws which involve penalties other than surcharges and fines. L. 7 January 1929, n. 4, art. 21.

[144] See L. 7 January 1929, n. 4, arts. 26, 27.

[145] L. 7 January 1929, n. 4, art. 21.

[146] C.M. 3 September 1935, n. 4100.

[147] This provision was added by article 1 of L. 25 October 1960, n. 1316.

If a return has been filed within one month of the expiration of the time limit (13/1.1c), the taxpayer is subject only to a surcharge at the rate of one sixth of the amount of each tax due (arts. 23, 243).

If the taxpayer's return does not include all of his income and capital, the taxpayer is subject to a fine of between L. 500 and L. 20,000 and also to a surcharge of one third of the amount of each tax due (art. 244). A person who has signed the return of a person lacking legal capacity, or a legal representative or general manager who has signed the return of an entity or enterprise taxed on the balance sheet basis, is jointly and severally liable with the taxpayer for payment of the surcharge. A taxpayer who fails to declare increases in income from landowning and from agrarian income within the prescribed time limit (10/2.2; 10/2.3) is subject to a surcharge of one third of the difference between (1) the objective tax and local surtax due on that income and (2) the tax payable on the previous income (art. 247). A pecuniary penalty of between L. 10,000 and L. 500,000 is imposed for failure of an entity or enterprise taxed on the balance sheet basis to attach a list of the directors and auditors or overseers to the return and for the failure of a company or association to attach to the return a list of the partners or associates who are personally liable for the debts of the firm (art. 251) (13/1.3). Directors and members of controlling boards of entities taxed on the balance sheet basis are subject to a mulct of between L. 15,000 and L. 1,000,000 if the annual report or the return fails to state the absence of any of the prescribed books or accounting records (6/2.2), and to a fine of between L. 10,000 and L. 1,000,000 if the annual report or the return fails to disclose other violations of the rules governing the keeping of accounting records (art. 253). A person convicted of either of these offenses is prohibited for a period of five years from serving as a member of a board of overseers of an entity taxed on the balance sheet basis (art. 259).

The penalties provided for the omission, lateness, or incompleteness of the return are not applicable if the requirement of the return can be contested on reasonable grounds for objective uncertainty of the existence of the basis of the tax obligation (art. 248). The surcharge, under these provisions, is reduced to one half, and the fine to one quarter, if the assessment of the Tax Office is made final without the taxpayer's opposition, or with the taxpayer's agreement, before a decision of the tax commission of first degree has intervened (art. 249).

The failure to file a return reporting income derived from a credit which is productive of income from movable wealth of category A deprives the creditor of legal actions otherwise available to him for the collection of the credit (art. 250).

In connection with the introduction of the withholding from distributions of profits (9/2.7a), penalties which would have been applicable as a result of the failure to declare distributions received in 1961 and earlier years were made inapplicable if the taxpayer filed a special supplementary return of such distributions.[148] If a taxpayer fails to declare distributions of profits subject to the withholding provisions described at 9/2.7a, and the aggregate taxable income assessable against him for purposes of the complementary tax does not exceed L. 16 million, the penalties otherwise applicable are reduced to one tenth, and the taxpayer loses the right to a refund of any excess of the withholding over the amount of the tax actually due.[149]

The penalties described above are applied in addition to the special assessment provisions applicable in cases of failure to file a return (13/2.3). Decisions of the courts in proceedings for the penalties provided for failure to file a return within the proper time limits do not affect the validity of measures of the tax authorities or decisions of the administrative commissions with respect to the existence of income and its estimation.[150]

13/7.3 Taxpayer's Failure To Furnish Information or To Comply with Other Requests and Orders

A taxpayer who does not return answers to interrogatories relating to the assessment within the time limit assigned (13/2.2), or who returns them with incomplete or false replies, is subject to a fine of between L. 2,000 and L. 50,000 (art. 254). A taxpayer who fails, without justification, to appear at the Tax Office within the time limit assigned to him, when requested to do so, is subject to a pecuniary penalty of between L. 125 and L. 750 (art. 254). If a taxpayer fails to comply with other requests or orders of the Tax Office in the exercise of its powers (13/2.2), he is subject to a fine of between L. 500 and L. 20,000 if such failure results in any impediment to the assessment (art. 254). Refusal or failure to comply with requests for information made by a District or Provincial Commission is punishable by a fine of between L. 500 and L. 20,000.[151]

13/7.4 False Returns or False Statements of Taxpayer

If the taxable amount specified in a return is less by at least one fourth than the amount finally assessed, the taxpayer is subject to a surcharge of one third of the difference between the tax due and the tax payable on the basis of the return—unless the difference results from adding back

---

[148] L. 29 December 1962, n. 1745, art. 21.
[149] L. 29 December 1962, n. 1745, art. 21.
[150] R.D. 17 September 1931, n. 1608, art. 34.
[151] R.D. 8 July 1937, n. 1516, arts. 25, 41.

nondeductible expenses, liabilities, and charges (art. 245). In computing the surcharge for a false return with reference to the complementary tax and the corporation tax, changes resulting from the rectification of income subject to the tax on income from movable wealth or to the tax on income from buildings are not taken into account. Penalties for incomplete returns are discussed at 13/7.2. Persons signing the return who are liable for payment of the surcharge in the case of an incomplete return are also liable for payment of the surcharge in the case of a false return.

In addition to any other penalties which may be applicable, the punishment of imprisonment for six months and a mulct of between L. 50,000 and L. 600,000 may be imposed on anyone required to sign a return of an entity taxed on the balance sheet basis who does so without correcting information based on entries or omissions, known by him to be false, in the statement of assets or the balance sheet, or on records or documents known by him to have been altered (art. 252). The same penalties may be imposed on anyone who claims deduction of nonexistent charges or liabilities (*passività*) in the return and on anyone who commits other fraudulent acts for the purpose of withdrawing income from the direct taxes. If the tax evaded exceeds L. 600,000, the mulct is equal to the amount of tax for which the evasion was attempted. Imprisonment is not imposed if the amount of tax evaded is extremely small (art. 252). A person convicted of an offense under article 252 is prohibited for five years from serving as a member of the controlling board of an entity taxed on the balance sheet basis (art. 259).

The filing of a false return also results in imposition of the increase of tax described at 13/7.2.

A taxpayer who returns false answers to interrogatories is subject to a fine (13/7.3). The giving of a false oath by a taxpayer in an appeal proceeding (13/4.1) is punishable by imprisonment for from six months to three years, unless the false matter is retracted before the pronouncement of the final judgment on the question at issue.[152]

13/7.5 Returns and Information Regarding Income of Others

The penalties provided for omitted, late, or false returns (13/7.2, 13/7.4) apply also to returns of income of others which is taxable with a right of recovery through withholding (13/3.4) or subject to provisional withholding (13/3.5) (art. 246). The surtax is reduced to one half, and the fine to one quarter, if the taxable amount is made final without opposition to the assessment of the Tax Office by the person required to withhold, or with his agreement, before a decision of the tax commission of first degree has intervened (art. 249). The penalties provided by article 252 for fraudulent returns (13/7.4) are also applicable if the omission

---

[152] L. 5 January 1956, n. 1, art. 6; CP art. 371.

or falsity of the return concerns income from work as an employee from which the tax on income from movable wealth has been recovered through withholding under article 127 and from which the complementary tax has been provisionally withheld under article 143 (art. 246). A pecuniary penalty of between L. 10,000 and L. 500,000 is applicable if the return reporting payments to employees which are taxable through recovery or which are subject to provisional withholding does not contain the required list (13/1.4) of all other payments made to employees from which tax has not been withheld (art. 251). For omission or incompleteness of the declaration by a company of its profits and withholdings therefrom, under the rules discussed at 9/2.7a, there is a pecuniary penalty of between L. 50,000 and L. 500,000.[153]

A person, other than a taxpayer, who fails to furnish information or to comply with other requests and orders of the Tax Office is also subject to the penalties described at 13/7.3 (art. 254). Public administrative offices and public entities are subject to pecuniary penalties for failure to report the terms of contracts of *appalto* and *somministrazione* (8/4) and for failure to report provisional withholdings as required by article 40 (art. 255) (13/1.4). The Secretary of a Chamber of Commerce or professional order which fails to submit to the Tax Office a list of the persons inscribed or deleted from the roles of the organization during the preceding year (13/1.3) is subject to a fine of L. 5,000 for each name omitted (art. 256). A credit firm or institution which submits a false certificate of debts owed to it by a taxpayer or issues a certificate more than 20 days after the taxpayer's written request (13/1.3) is subject to a pecuniary penalty of between L. 5,000 and L. 5,000,000; any person signing the certificate is subject to a pecuniary penalty of up to L. 1,500,000 (art. 257). These pecuniary penalties are applied by decree of the Minister of Finance after consultation with the Minister of the Treasury (art. 269). If such offenses are repeated, the dissolution of the directing organs of the firm may be ordered, and, in cases of exceptional gravity, the authorization to grant credit may be revoked (art. 257). These measures are adopted on proposal by the Minister of Finance in concert with the Minister of the Treasury (art. 269). A public official who certifies books or accounting records without transcribing thereon the elements of the receipt of payment of the tax on governmental concessions, or who fails to affix his signature or the stamp on the receipt, is subject to a fine (art. 258).

In addition to the pecuniary penalty for omission or incompleteness of a company's declaration of profits and withholdings of tax therefrom under the rules discussed at 9/2.7a, the penalties listed below are prescribed for various acts and omissions in connection with the measures

---

[153] L. 29 December 1962, n. 1745, art. 12.

enacted in 1962 for obtaining information regarding the ownership of shares (9/2.8).

1. A pecuniary penalty of between L. 20,000 and L. 100,000 is imposed for every security returned to its owner without stamping after the last endorsement and for each entry omitted or not made in conformity to law in the register of shareholders.[154]

2. Companies, their designated agents, and fiduciary companies, which fail to make the communications required regarding the ownership of shares (13/1.4), are subject to a pecuniary penalty of one fifth of the total profits with regard to which the communications have been omitted.[155] In the case of a company which has not distributed profits, the pecuniary penalty is between L. 20,000 and L. 100,000 for each name omitted. The pecuniary penalties are doubled if false or fictitious names are used. The same penalties are provided for omitted or false communications from *riportatori*, sellers on time, credit firms, and stock exchange commission agents. If the offense is a fraudulent act, done for the purpose of removing income from tax, a mulct and imprisonment may be imposed under the provision described at 13/7.4.

3. Intermediaries who have themselves fictitiously listed as owners of securities belonging to others are subject to a pecuniary penalty equal to 10% of the nominal value of the securities.[156] If the act is done for the purpose of removing the income of the securities from the direct taxes, both the actual owners and the persons fictitiously listed are subject to a mulct and to imprisonment, in accordance with the provision described at 13/7.4.

4. Exchange agents, credit firms, financial and fiduciary companies, and stock exchange commission agents are subject to a fine of between L. 50,000 and L. 500,000 for failure to keep regularly the required daily records of time transactions and *riporti*, for refusal to produce them, and for impeding their inspection.[157]

5. In cases of repeated or particularly serious violations of the duties prescribed by the coupon tax law, a credit enterprise or investment company can be subject to the dissolution of its governing body and to liquidation, the authorization of a fiduciary company to carry on its fiduciary activity can be suspended, and an exchange agent or stock exchange commission agent can be excluded from the stock exchange.[158]

13/7.6 Late Payment of Tax

In the case of the expiration of the time limit for payment of an installment of taxes, a taxpayer who has failed to pay all or a part of the installment is required to pay an indemnity for lateness; the rate of the

---

[154] L. 29 December 1962, n. 1745, art. 13. For omitted or improper entries in the register of shareholders, directors, general managers, and liquidators are subject to a fine of between L. 100,000 and L. 500,000.

[155] L. 29 December 1962, n. 1745, art. 14. The persons required to sign the communications are subject to a fine of between L. 50,000 and L. 500,000.

[156] L. 29 December 1962, n. 1745, art. 15.

[157] L. 29 December 1962, n. 1745, art. 16.

[158] L. 12 December 1962, n. 1745, art. 17; R.D.L. 12 March 1936, n. 375, arts. 55, 66; R.D.L. 12 April 1940, n. 531, art. 4; L. 20 March 1913, n. 272, art. 59.

indemnity is 2% of the unpaid amount if payment is made within three days of the due date and 6% of the unpaid amount if payment is made thereafter (art. 194). If the bill for payment was not served until after the expiration of the time limit established for its service (13/3.7), the indemnity for lateness becomes due after the expiration of 12 days from the day of the service. If the collector has not served the bill for payment or, in the case of collections outside his jurisdiction, has not complied with the requirements for giving public notice (13/3.7), the indemnity for lateness is not due until after the expiration of five days from the service of the notice of lateness (art. 194). No indemnity for lateness is due if the taxpayer pays the tax through postal current accounts and the certificate of booking or of credit reaches the collector within the time limit applicable to the payment of the installment, even if the taxpayer has paid the tax after the 12th day of the month in which the installment was due (art. 194).

When collection extending beyond the normal period is permitted, taxes remaining due after the expiration of the normal period are subject to the increase described at 13/3.7.

When 50% or more of the taxpayers inscribed in a roll have not paid the amount due at the due date of an installment of the direct taxes, each taxpayer who has not made payment on or before the last day of the month during which the payment fell due is required to pay to the Treasury a surcharge equal to the indemnity for lateness owed to the collector.[159]

Failure to pay six consecutive installments, of an aggregate amount of not less than L. 12,000, of taxes inscribed in the rolls is punishable by a fine of between L. 1,000 and L. 20,000 (art. 261). If the unpaid taxes include taxes on income from the exercise of a business enterprise or of an activity requiring inscription in professional rolls or a special authorization, no fine is imposed, but the tax administration proceeds, instead, to have the taxpayer declared bankrupt or to suspend the exercise of the activity. However, neither the fine nor the suspension is applied if the taxpayer proves that his failure to pay the tax results from economic impossibility (art. 261).

In addition to the penalties described above, a taxpayer is subject to imprisonment for not more than three months if, for the purpose of avoiding payment of taxes due, he has rendered the collector's execution ineffective, wholly or in part, by fraudulent transactions with his own property or with the property of others (art. 261).

In the cases to which these penalties are applicable, the collector informs the Tax Office, within 60 days of the due date of the sixth installment, of the failure of payment (art. 262). The Tax Office serves on the

---

[159] D.L.C.P.S. 7 November 1947, n. 1559, art. 4.

taxpayer a report of lateness, containing a summons to appear before the Intendant of Finance within 30 days, with a notice that the penalties will be applied if the taxpayer fails to appear and fails to pay the taxes due within the time limit established. If the taxpayer appears, the Intendant of Finance may assign a new time limit for the payment of the taxes due. If the taxpayer does not appear and does not make timely payment, the Intendant of Finance imposes the appropriate penalty. If he issues a decree suspending the exercise of the professional activity, the decree is served on the party concerned, who may appeal within 15 days to the Minister of Finance (13/4.8); if no appeal is filed or an appeal is rejected, the decree is sent for implementation to the Office charged with maintaining the professional roll or to the authority which granted the authorization for the exercise of the activity (art. 262).[160] Apparently, the suspension of a professional activity continues until the tax has been paid.[161]

The payment of taxes due and of expenses extinguishes the offense of late payment and, if a sentence of conviction has been passed, extinguishes the penalty. If suspension from the professional roll has been ordered, it is revoked (art. 263).

If the corporation tax or the tax on bonds has not been paid into the Treasury in full, the taxpayer is subject to a surcharge of 5% of the unpaid tax if payment is made with a delay of not more than one month, or to a surcharge of 10% of the unpaid tax if the delay exceeds one month (art. 260).

13/7.7   Failure To Withhold Taxes or To Pay Taxes Withheld

The penalty for failure to pay into the Treasury taxes on income of others which is taxable with a right of recovery through withholding (13/3.4) or income which is subject to provisional withholding (13/3.5) is a surcharge equal to the total tax remaining due, plus detention for not more than six months if the tax has been withheld (art. 260).

The failure to pay in one settlement the taxes on income for labor paid to employees inscribed in a special roll (13/3.6c) results in the penalties described at 13/7.6 for late payment of taxes collected through rolls (art. 261). The collector informs the Tax Office of the delay within 60 days of the due date of the single payment (art. 262). Payment of the taxes due does not extinguish the offense or the penalty (art. 263).

In addition to any penalty for failure to pay to the Treasury the taxes due on income of others taxable through recovery or subject to pro-

---

[160] The procedures for the declaration of tax bankruptcy and suspension of the taxpayer's activity are set forth in C.M. 3 September 1935, n. 4100. See also Merlino, *Dizionario delle infrazioni e delle relative conseguenze nel campo delle imposte dirette* 279 *et seq.*, 331 *et seq.*

[161] See R.D. 17 September 1931, n. 1608, art. 26.

visional withholding, failure to make the withholdings or provisional withholdings prescribed results in a surcharge equal to one half of the amount of tax not withheld (art. 264).[162]

13/7.8 Miscellaneous Offenses

In addition to any other penalties which may be applicable, imprisonment for from six months to five years is provided for promoting or organizing agreements or understandings among taxpayers for the purpose of delaying, suspending, or refraining from the payment of taxes (including the direct taxes), or for instigating taxpayers in public or at meetings to delay, suspend, or refrain from the payment of taxes.[163] When such an agreement or instigation has the effect intended, the minimum sentence is one year. The penalty for causing any other interruption or disturbance of the regular functioning of the services of assessment or collection of taxes is imprisonment for from three months to two years, and the chief promoters or organizers are subject to imprisonment for from one to six years.[164]

Imprisonment for from six months to one year is provided for any public official or appointee to a public office who omits or delays acts of his own office or service with the purpose of interrupting or disturbing the regular functioning of the services of assessment and collection of taxes.[165]

Former tax officials who exercise functions of assistance or representation in tax matters in violation of the provisions of article 13 (1/4.11) are subject to a mulct of between L. 50,000 and L. 500,000 (art. 266). The conviction involves exclusion for one year from the exercise of those functions.

---

[162] If an employer fails to withhold the tax on income from movable wealth from payments of income from employment made by him, the tax can be recovered again from the employee even if the employer has already paid it (13/3.4).

[163] D.L.C.P.S. 7 November 1947, n. 1559, art. 1.

[164] D.L.C.P.S. 7 November 1947, n. 1559, art. 2.

[165] D.L.C.P.S. 7 November 1947, n. 1559, art. 3.

PART III

ANALYSIS OF TAXES OTHER THAN INCOME TAX

This part analyzes those taxes other than the income tax which deserve discussion in addition to the summary in Part I. In this volume, the general tax on receipts and the registration tax are analyzed in Part III.

CHAPTER 14

THE GENERAL TAX
ON RECEIPTS

14/1. **History of the Tax**

14/2. **Persons Subject to Tax**
14/2.1 In General
14/2.2 Integrated Companies
a. In general
b. Sales departments of producing enterprises
c. Other internal transfers
14/2.3 Commercial Intermediaries and Auxiliaries
a. In general
b. Agents
c. Commercial travelers
d. Commission agents
e. Brokers
f. Other intermediaries
14/2.4 Government Stockpiling Agencies
14/2.5 Tax Substitutes
14/2.6 Persons Liable
14/2.7 Shifting of the Tax Burden

14/3. **Taxable Receipts**
14/3.1 In General
14/3.2 Receipts of Persons Other than Industrialists or Merchants
14/3.3 Business Receipts
a. Sales
b. Barters
c. Internal transfers

703

        d. Public entertainments
        e. Public services
        f. Hotels and restaurants
        g. Advertising
14/3.4   Receipts from the Exercise of Professions and Arts
14/3.5   Receipts of Commercial Intermediaries
14/3.6   Receipts from Leases
14/3.7   Receipts from Contracts of *Appalto*
14/3.8   Receipts of Credit Institutions
14/3.9   Receipts of Insurance Firms
14/3.10 Other Receipts
14/3.11 Transfers on Approval
14/3.12 Transfers on Consignment
14/3.13 Transfers for Purposes of Processing

14/4.   **Nontaxable Receipts**

14/4.1   In General
14/4.2   Capital Receipts and Interest on Capital
14/4.3   Salaries, Wages, and Other Remuneration
14/4.4   Taxes and Similar Receipts
14/4.5   Receipts Without Consideration
14/4.6   Exemptions and Reliefs Favoring Certain Sectors of
         the Economy
        a. Reconstruction
        b. Shipbuilding
        c. Gold
        d. Aviation
        e. Bread and milk
        f. Distillation wine
        g. Cereals
        h. Fish imports
        i. Newspapers
        j. Printing
        k. Regional development
14/4.7   Sales Between Private Individuals
14/4.8   Retail Stage
        a. Retail sales
        b. Retail services
14/4.9   Foreign Diplomatic and Consular Offices
14/4.10 Other Exemptions

14/5. Determination of the Tax Base

    14/5.1 In General

    14/5.2 Charges Included

    14/5.3 Charges Excluded

14/6. The Tax Rates

    14/6.1 In General

    14/6.2 The Standard Tax Rate

    14/6.3 The Special Rates

        a. Increased rates

        b. Reduced rates

        c. Annual fees in *abbonamento*

    14/6.4 The *Una Tantum* Rates

14/7. Assessment and Collection

    14/7.1 In General

    14/7.2 Collection for Each Transaction

        a. In general

        b. Self-assessment

        c. Payment

        d. Appeals and refunds

    14/7.3 Annual Fee (*Abbonamento*)

        a. In general

        b. Classes of taxpayers

        c. Assessment

        d. Payment

        e. Administrative appeals

        f. Judicial appeals

        g. Single annual payment of aggregate tax due

    14/7.4 Other Methods of Collection

        a. Subscription contracts subject to reconciliation

        b. Annual payment of fixed amount

    14/7.5 Rules Regarding Books and Records

14/8. International Aspects

    14/8.1 Territoriality

    14/8.2 Exemption of Export Sales

        a. Direct exports

        b. Indirect exports

    14/8.3 Refund of IGE on Exported Products

14/8.4   Taxation of Imports
     a.   Imported merchandise
     b.   Temporary imports
     c.   Exempt merchandise
14/8.5   Equalization Tax on Imported Products

14/9.   Penalties
14/9.1   In General
14/9.2   Civil Penalties
     a.   Penalties of general character
     b.   Special penalties for violations of the rules on
        postal current accounts
     c.   Special penalties for violations of the rules on pay-
        ment by annual fee
14/9.3   Criminal Penalties
     a.   Penalties of general character
     b.   Special penalties for violations of the rules gov-
        erning the import taxes
     c.   Special penalties for violations of the rules on
        postal current accounts
14/9.4   Special Penalties for Serious or Habitual Violations

14/10.   Time Limits
14/10.1   Collection of Tax and Penalties
14/10.2   Refunds

14/1.   History of the Tax

The first sales taxes in Italy, like those adopted by many other countries, were designed to relieve the financial burdens of World War I
and of the succeeding years. These taxes, called luxury taxes (*tasse di
lusso*), were levied on sales to private consumers of luxury articles,[1]
among which were included perfumes and patent medicines,[2] bottled
mineral waters and sparkling wines,[3] gloves and selected textiles,[4] and
jewelry and other precious objects.[5] The rate of tax varied with the
category of goods taxed.[6] Most of these taxes were paid directly by buy-

---

[1] Stammati, *L'imposta generale sull'entrata* 75-76.   See also Due, *Sales Taxation*
100.
[2] D.L. 9 November 1916, n. 1525; R.D.L. 28 December 1922, n. 1671.
[3] D.L.L. 24 November 1918, n. 2086.
[4] D.L. 24 November 1919, n. 2165.
[5] R.D.L. 28 December 1922, n. 1670.
[6] See Stammati, *L'imposta generale sull'entrata* 75-76.

ing stamps to be affixed to the goods sold or by an annual fee (*abbona-mento*) assessed on the basis of the taxpayer's gross receipts (14/7.3).

In 1919, a law was enacted imposing a stamp tax that was confined to retail sales and imposed not only on luxuries but on other goods. The rate of the tax was 10% for luxuries and 2% for other goods. The law excluded sales of certain goods from the scope of the tax, namely, necessary foods, commonly used merchandise costing less than L. 5, and goods sold by the state monopoly enterprise (4/6.1).[7] This tax was collected only on an annual-fee system.

A new period in the history of Italian sales taxation began in 1923 with the introduction of a stamp tax on commercial exchanges (*tassa generale di bollo sugli scambi commerciali*),[8] a multistage levy on the full value of the goods sold. In contrast to the earlier taxes which it replaced or modified, the 1923 tax was imposed on exchanges of merchandise classifiable as commercial transactions, rather than on sales to private consumers. It did not, however, apply to the furnishing of services. For purposes of the law, an exchange meant any exchange of merchandise taking place in Italy between industrialists, merchants, or tradesmen (*industriali, commercianti ed esercenti*), in the course of their industrial or commercial activities, even if the merchandise was intended to be used, employed, or consumed in the commercial or industrial enterprise (*azienda*) of the purchaser.[9] Also subject to the tax were transactions involving the importation of goods from abroad, whether or not the importer was a merchant and irrespective of the destination of the goods imported.[10]

The tax on exchanges did not, however, apply to merchandise exported directly by Italian producers and merchants. Neither was it applied if the exportation was carried out by export intermediaries, provided, however, that the merchandise passed directly from the place of production or sale to the foreign market.[11] Exemptions from the tax were provided for necessary foods, fuel, laundry soap, irrigation and drinking water and water for motive power, goods sold by the state monopoly enterprise, books, periodicals, and newspapers, other than publications

---

[7] R.D.L. 24 November 1919, n. 2163, Annex B.

[8] R.D. 30 December 1923, n. 3273, replacing R.D. 18 March 1923, n. 550; this decree, as modified by R.D.L. 28 July 1930, n. 1011, and the corresponding instructions in D.M. 27 September 1930, n. 43202, was the basis of the tax until 1940. On the tax on exchanges, see also Rogari, "La tassa generale di bollo sugli scambi commerciali," De Stefani, *Lezioni sugli ordinamenti finanziari italiani*; see also Jammarino, *Legge sulla tassa di scambi*; Stammati, *L'imposta generale sull'entrata* 75-86; Due, *Sales Taxation* 100-101.

[9] R.D.L. 28 July 1930, n. 1011, art. 1.

[10] R.D.L. 28 July 1930, n. 1011, art. 1.

[11] R.D.L. 28 July 1930, n. 1011, art. 35, as amended by R.D.L. 26 September 1935, n. 1749, arts. 3, 4.

for publicity or fashion purposes.[12] A transaction was not subject to the tax if it had already been subject to a proportional registration tax (15/6.3) not less than the tax on exchanges.[13]

The methods of payment employed were stamps, postal money orders, direct payment (*in modo virtuale*) to the Registry Office, and the annual-fee system.[14] Single-stage or *una tantum* collection was provided for certain commodities in industries where the discrimination in favor of integrated companies had caused complaints.[15]

The second major reform of Italian sales taxation occurred in 1940 with the repeal of the tax on exchanges and the introduction of the general tax on receipts (*imposta generale sull'entrata*) (IGE),[16] a modified form of the German turnover tax (*Umsatzsteuer*).[17] The primary goal of the reform was to give the Italian economy a simple and powerful revenue-producing tool during World War II. The basic innovation of the law of 1940 was the substantial broadening of the concept of taxable exchange over that of the repealed 1930 law. Almost every economic activity, including the furnishing of services, comes within the scope of the general tax on receipts (14/3).[18] Another objective of the reform legislation was the simplification of the rate structure. Since 1940, however, the rates have been increased and differentiated, and, at the present time, the rate structure of IGE is perhaps even more elaborate and complex than that of the old tax on exchanges (14/6).

14/2. Persons Subject to Tax

14/2.1 In General

The general tax on receipts is a multistage levy applied cumulatively on sales of goods by manufacturers and wholesalers, on payments for services furnished by professionals and others, and on all other receipts for consideration, except those specifically excluded or exempted. It is imposed on taxable receipts obtained by "individuals, juridical persons, and entities of all kinds, both national and foreign" (IGE art. 1). From

---

[12] R.D.L. 28 July 1930, n. 1011, art. 58.

[13] R.D.L. 28 July 1930, n. 1011, art. 1, paras. 3, 4.

[14] R.D.L. 28 July 1930, n. 1011, arts. 44, 57.

[15] Due, *Sales Taxation* 100. For a list of merchandise on which *una tantum* collection was applied, see Stammati, *L'imposta generale sull'entrata* 84; on *una tantum* rates under the regime of the general tax on receipts (IGE), see 14/6.4.

[16] R.D.L. 9 January 1940, n. 2, converted in L. 19 June 1940, n. 762; an article of the decree-law will hereinafter be cited: "IGE art." The regulations for the execution of the decree-law are contained in R.D. 26 January 1940, n. 10, an article of which will hereinafter be cited: "IGE Reg. art." In addition, many rules relative to IGE, both of substantive and procedural nature, are contained in other laws and decrees, the most important of which may be found in Mandò, *Imposta generale sull'entrata* 1077-1144.

[17] Due, *Sales Taxation* 101. See WTS: *Germany, 16/.*

[18] Cass., Sez. un., 12 October 1955, n. 3041.

the use of the phrase "entities of all kinds," it may be inferred that organizations of persons or property devoid of legal capacity under civil law may be subject to the tax if they obtain receipts from taxable transactions.[19] Thus, the criterion for determining liability for IGE is economic—whether or not a person or association carries on activities subject to the tax—and not the legal structure of the person or association.

The concept of "taxpayer" for purposes of IGE is both wider and narrower than that of "entrepreneur" (*imprenditore*), defined by the Civil Code as one "who professionally exercises economic activity organized for purposes of production or exchange of goods and services" (CC art. 2082).[20] However, production as such, as well as certain classes of exchanges, is excluded from the scope of IGE. On the other hand, receipts obtained from the furnishing of services by professionals (14/3.4) and any receipts resulting from the leasing of property (14/3.6) are subject to IGE. In effect, anyone obtaining receipts must pay the tax unless the receipts are specifically excluded (as retail sales are now) or unless the transaction is an occasional one between private individuals with no connotation of trade.[21] In general, liability for IGE is not dependent on the intent to realize profit.[22]

14/2.2   Integrated Companies

a. IN GENERAL.. Special provisions govern transfers of merchandise performed in Italy through an intermediary entity such as a branch office, sales department, or retail outlet, of an integrated company. The IGE law contains only a general reference to this class of taxpayers (IGE art. 13), leaving the formulation of the detailed rules to the regulations (IGE Reg. arts. 20-30). With respect to dependent branches of integrated companies, two situations must be distinguished: first, transfers of merchandise between the producing firm and its sales outlets; and second, transfers between the head office of an industrial or commercial firm and its dependent entities other than sales outlets.

b. SALES DEPARTMENTS OF PRODUCING ENTERPRISES. Transfers of merchandise between a producing firm and its own stores, retail outlets, and

---

[19] On the question of the relation between taxable capacity and legal capacity in general under civil or public law, see Giannini, *Concetti fondamentali del diritto tributario* 206-211, and the literature cited therein.

[20] The Civil Code defines "small entrepreneurs" to include "direct cultivators of land, artisans, small merchants, and those who exercise professional activity organized merely with labor of their own and of members of their family" (CC art. 2083). Regarding entrepreneurs, see also Bigiavi, *La professionalità dell'imprenditore*.

[21] See Romani, *L'entrata imponibile nel sistema dell'IGE* 208 *et seq.*, and literature quoted therein. See, in particular, the discussion of the transfer of soccer players at 229 *et seq.*

[22] See Romani, *L'entrata imponibile nel sistema dell'IGE* 249.

departments of direct sales to the public are transactions subject to IGE (IGE art. 3).[23] Such transfers are taxable also if the store or sale department is managed by the producer through an intermediary, whether or not it belongs to the intermediary.[24] This provision is directed against those integrated firms which not only produce but also distribute and sell their merchandise. The transfers described below, however, are excluded from the scope of IGE.

1. Transfers of merchandise by the producing firm to its premises open to the public for the exhibition of the merchandise, provided that no direct sales are made (IGE art. 3).

2. Transfers of merchandise from the workshop to a public store belonging to the same owner, if the workshop produces merchandise exclusively on the specific order of the customer made through the store (IGE art. 3).

3. Transfers of merchandise to the store from the workshop directly adjacent, provided that the firm runs only one workshop and one store, and that the workshop supplies the store.[25]

c. OTHER INTERNAL TRANSFERS. Transfers between a parent commercial or industrial firm and its branches, depots, stores, warehouses, and the like, other than sales outlets, are considered nontaxable. Also nontaxable are transfers of merchandise between these branches, stores, warehouses, and depots. The exclusion is granted only if all of the conditions listed below are met (IGE Reg. art. 20).[26]

1. The dependent entities must, before the transfer of merchandise, be listed as dependent entities of the parent firm with the competent Chamber of Commerce, Industry, and Agriculture.

2. A certificate issued to each of the dependent entities by such Chamber of Commerce, Industry, and Agriculture must certify that the entity actually carries on commercial or industrial activity in the name and in the exclusive interest of the parent firm.

3. The entities in question must, on every invoice, bill, receipt, and any other document relative to their commercial or industrial activities, indicate their dependent status with relation to the parent firm and specify the Chamber of Commerce, Industry, and Agriculture with which they are listed.

14/2.3 Commercial Intermediaries and Auxiliaries

a. IN GENERAL. Transfers of merchandise performed through the services of certain commercial intermediaries and auxiliaries (*ausiliari ed intermediari di commercio*) give rise to only one taxable receipt, namely that between the seller and the buyer, the intermediate stage being

---

[23] As modified by R.D.L. 3 June 1943, n. 452, art. 13.

[24] D.L. 3 May 1948, n. 799, art. 9; L. 5 April 1952, n. 341.

[25] D.L. 3 May 1948, n. 799, art. 9.

[26] See also Cass., Sez. I, 23 October 1959, n. 3051, confirming the condition of inscription with the Chamber of Commerce. App. Torino 23 December 1955 (Cordaro, *Dizionario del contribuente* 578).

excluded from the application of IGE (IGE Reg. arts. 21-26). This exclusion, however, is subject to strict requisites specified in the regulations, without whose observance the transfers effected through these intermediaries are treated as two separate transactions, each subject to the tax (IGE Reg. art. 29).[27] The IGE regulations contain separate provisions concerning agents (*rappresentanti*), commercial travelers (*commessi viaggiatori*), commission agents (*commissionari*), middlemen or brokers (*mediatori*), and other commercial intermediaries and auxiliaries.

b. AGENTS. Agents (*rappresentanti*) include those who are authorized to conclude transactions on behalf of and for the account of the principal firm (CC arts. 1387, 1703, 1752). Transfers of merchandise between a commercial or industrial firm and its agents who are depositaries of the merchandise for the account of the principal firm do not give rise to taxable receipts, provided that all of the conditions listed below are met.

1. The agency must be granted by express mandate (*mandato*) in the form of a public act or private contract attested by a notary public and duly registered.
2. The agent must issue invoices in the name of the principal firm.
3. The transactions performed by the agent must be recorded chronologically by him in his journal, separately for each firm represented.
4. The agent must not receive or make payments for the transactions performed unless expressly authorized in his contract or by a special authorization granted also by means of commercial correspondence kept according to law and registered at the Registry Office.
5. The agent must not make advance payments to the represented firm unless authorized to do so in the manner described in item 4.

In the case of agents who are not depositaries of merchandise, the agency may also be based on an appropriate letter bearing a date prior to the day on which the intermediary activity began and filed with the Registry Office within whose jurisdiction the firm has its seat (IGE Reg. art. 21).

c. COMMERCIAL TRAVELERS. Sales made by a commercial traveler (CC arts. 2210-2213) with direct delivery of merchandise result in only one taxable receipt, provided that the firm employing him has authorized the sale and delivery in a public act or proper document (*scrittura*) attested by a notary public and registered, and provided that he issues invoices in the name of and on behalf of that firm (IGE Reg. art. 22).

---

[27] Cass., Sez. I, 15 March 1958, n. 854 (Cordaro, *Dizionario del contribuente* 759). The nonobservance of the requisites results in an absolute presumption of a double transfer; see Trib. Genova 29 November 1957 (Cordaro, *Dizionario del contribuente* 716).

d. COMMISSION AGENTS. Transfers of merchandise made by merchants and industrialists through commission agents [28] result in only one taxable receipt provided that all of the conditions listed below are met (IGE Reg. art. 23).[29]

1. The relationship of commission agent must be based on a public act or private registered contract, or simple letter, a copy of which is kept by the principal and registered and filed with the Registry Office, before the performance of the transaction.
2. The agent must be listed as such with the Chamber of Commerce, Industry, and Agriculture within whose jurisdiction he carries on his transactions.
3. The agent must record his transactions chronologically in his journal, separately for each principal.
4. If the agent is also depositary of the merchandise, the ownership of such merchandise by his principal must appear from duly kept commercial correspondence, filed with the Registry Office, and the merchandise for each principal must be kept separately.

e. BROKERS. In order to take advantage of the exclusion described at 14/2.3a, a broker (CC art. 1754) must be listed with the Chamber of Commerce, must enter in detail in his general book (CC art. 1760) all transfers of merchandise made through him, and must not make or receive payments related to such transfers.

f. OTHER INTERMEDIARIES. Transfers of merchandise made through an intermediary other than those described above result in only one taxable receipt, provided that such an intermediary is authorized to buy or sell merchandise by a public act or private registered contract, or by a commission letter drawn up in two copies and filed with the Registry Office before the commencement of the intermediary activities. This condition does not apply to commercial travelers who limit their activities to an offer or to a conclusion of a transaction without actual delivery of merchandise. The deposit of merchandise with an intermediary must be based on a public act or private contract, registered and attested by a notary public. Transfers of merchandise must be recorded in the intermediary's journal of goods received and shipped (IGE Reg. art. 25).

14/2.4 Government Stockpiling Agencies

Taxation of obligatory transfers of raw materials, merchandise, and products, including food and agricultural products, to government

---

[28] Included are commission agents selling and buying in their own names for the accounts of their principals, forwarding agents, commercial agencies, commission syndicates, and so forth (CC arts. 1731, 1737, 1742, 2602 et seq.). The IGE provisions are also applicable to agents who buy merchandise. See R.M. 30 August 1957, n. 215887.

[29] R.D.L. 3 June 1943, n. 452.

stockpiling agencies (*ammassi*) and similar entities, as well as the distribution of such products through similar agencies, is governed by special provisions. IGE is due not on delivery, but on sale of the products by such entities. Similarly, various government-authorized syndicates, companies, and the like, which make collective purchases, pay IGE not at the moment of the purchase of the commodities in Italy, but at the moment of resale or distribution. In the case of products coming from abroad, IGE is due at the time of the act of importation, but subsequent resale or distribution of those products is exempt from IGE.[30]

14/2.5 Tax Substitutes

The general rule of tax liability is that, except as otherwise provided, the person subject to IGE is the person in whose favor the receipt is given—that is, the seller of the goods or services (IGE art. 6). Thus, for example, if a manufacturer sells goods and receives money therefor, he is bound to pay the tax on the transaction. In the cases listed below, however, the tax is due not from the person who obtains the receipts, but from the person who pays them—that is, the purchaser.

1. Purchase by merchants and industrialists of agricultural products from owners, possessors, and leaseholders of farm land (IGE Reg. art. 35).
2. Purchase by merchants and industrialists of raw materials and products (excluding those mentioned in item 1) from individuals and entities which are not merchants or industrialists (IGE Reg. art. 37).
3. Management by others of individual or collective activities (*prestazioni*) of artists (IGE Reg. art. 42).
4. Direct payment by managers or other persons of fees to the authors holding the rights (IGE Reg. art. 63).

In Italian doctrine and practice, the persons required to pay the tax under these provisions are called "tax substitutes" (*sostituti d'imposta*).[31]

14/2.6 Persons Liable

The IGE law also provides that, in some cases, another person, in addition to the person subject to the tax, is jointly and severally responsible for the satisfaction of the tax liability. These persons, who are called "persons liable" (*responsabili d'imposta*),[32] are listed below.

---

[30] R.D.L. 3 June 1943, n. 452, as modified by L. 7 January 1949, n. 1.

[31] See, for example, Giannini, *Concetti fondamentali del diritto tributario* 255; Stammati, *L'imposta generale sull'entrata* 102. *Cf.* also 13/3.

[32] See Giannini, *Concetti fondamentali del diritto tributario* 251, n. 1, and the literature cited therein. Giannini defines *responsabile d'imposta* as "a person upon whom the law imposes the duty to pay the tax affecting another person," and distinguishes him from the person subject to the tax. But see, for example, Pugliese, "I soggetti passivi dell'obbligazione tributaria nel diritto italiano," *Riv. it. sc. econ.*, 1935, 337, representing the view that the *responsabile d'imposta* is also subject to the tax.

1. Persons who provide for the slaughtering of cattle and those charged with the collection of the consumption tax (4/5.8f) on meat or on wines and grapes (IGE art. 14).
2. Persons who clear merchandise of foreign origin through customs (IGE art. 17).
3. Guaranty banks and clearing houses (*casse di garanzia e di compensazione*) operating in the commodity market, are liable for the tax due on the endorsements of the delivery notes (*buoni di consegna*) issued on the closing of term contracts (*contratti a termine*).[33]

14/2.7 Shifting of the Tax Burden

The person in whose favor a receipt is given is the *de jure* taxpayer (*contribuente di diritto*). Thus, for example, in the case of the sale of merchandise, the tax is payable by the seller. However, article 6 of the law grants the person in whose favor the receipt is made the right to shift the burden of the tax to the other contracting party, for example, the buyer, by increasing the price in an amount corresponding to the tax due. Therefore, the person who makes the payment of the sum constituting the receipt becomes, as a rule, the *de facto* taxpayer of IGE (*contribuente di fatto*). The right of the *de jure* taxpayer to recover the sum is only a right and not a duty.[34] This right of recovery (*rivalsa*) is protected by the same preferences as the right of the state to recover the tax due under the laws in force (IGE art. 6).

The right of recovery is not granted, and the tax burden may not be shifted, for the receipts listed below (IGE art. 6).

1. Payments by the state administration and by entities which, for tax purposes, are treated in the same manner as units of the state administration.
2. Payments by the National Entity for Assistance to Workers (*Ente Nazionale Assistenza Lavoratori* (ENAL)), and to employees of Workers' Assistance Recreation Clubs (*Circoli Ricreativi Assistenza Lavoratori* (CRAL)).[35]
3. Amounts received by the collectors of national, provincial, and communal taxes as collection fees (13/3.7), and amounts received as subsidies and grants by firms operating subsidized public services.

These prohibitions do not operate in the case of "retail services" (*prestazioni al dettaglio*) (14/3.4), where the right of recovery may always be exercised (IGE art. 6).[36]

---

[33] L. 13 July 1954, n. 502, art. 2.

[34] Cass., Sez. I, 29 May 1947; Cass., Sez. III, 5 January 1953, n. 1.

[35] These are the entities which succeeded the former fascist organizations specified in article 6, paragraph 3, of the IGE law. See R.M. 23 July 1946, n. 63631, and R.M. 15 June 1949, n. 60214. See also Mandò, *Imposta generale sull'entrata* 356.

[36] L. 31 October 1961, n. 1196, art. 3. For the definitions of retail sale, see R.D.L. 3 June 1943, n. 452, art. 16; regarding retail services, see IGE art. 8(c), and L. 31 October 1961, n. 1196, art. 3. Most such transactions are exempt, however; see 14/4.8b.

In cases where IGE is collected by annual fee (*abbonamento*) on the basis of total receipts for a determined period of time (14/7.3), recovery from the purchaser is permitted for the actual amount of the tax to be paid to the state. In cases where the aggregate tax due for the year is paid in a lump sum (14/7.3g), the actual amount of the tax payable may be recovered from the purchaser (IGE art. 6).[37]

In the case of subsidies, contributions, bonuses, and similar grants by provinces, communes, and other public entities, IGE is always payable by the recipient.[38] In the case of sales, supplies, and all kinds of services (*prestazioni*) rendered to foreign military units and offices functioning in Italy, IGE is payable by the person effecting the supply or rendering the service, without the right of recovery from the purchaser.[39]

14/3. Taxable Receipts

14/3.1 In General

A taxable receipt (*entrata imponibile*) is any receipt in money or means of payment substitutive of money, obtained by persons subject to the tax (14/2.1), as a counterpart of (*in corrispondenza di*) the transfer of goods or rendition of services, effected in Italy (IGE art. 1). The payment of the receipt may be made by the purely formal movement of money as, for example, in credit operations. Means of payment substitutive of money include checks and other negotiable instruments. There is no agreement on whether bills of exchange are considered means of payment for purposes of IGE.[40] When goods are exchanged for services, the goods are the taxable receipt (IGE art. 1). Taxable also are receipts obtained from the leasing of immovable property, or from the lease, sublease, or other transfer for consideration of the right of enjoyment of immovable property for a definite period, except receipts arising from "passive" leases to state offices and agencies (IGE art. 3(a)) and from leases for a definite period of urban immovable

---

[37] See also C.M. 22 January 1947, n. 60144; C.M. 3 January 1948, n. 72014; R. M. 14 January 1955, n. 81968. See Mandò, *Imposta generale sull'entrata* 350, 360.

[38] L. 4 July 1941, n. 770, art. 1, para. 2.

[39] D.L.L. 7 June 1945, n. 386, art. 10. However, there are no exemptions from IGE with regard to foreign diplomatic and consular agents, except receipts from the renting of immovable property to them (14/4.9). Hence, the right of recovery provided by the general rule of article 6 is allowed. See R.M. 16 May 1947, n. 62307; R.M. 21 June 1947, n. 64128. See also Mandò, *Imposta generale sull'entrata* 350.

[40] Bills of exchange have been stated to be means of payment by C.M. 5 August 1947, n. 65403. *Contra*, Cass. pen. 25 March 1953. On the nature of bills of exchange, see De Semo, *Diritto cambiario;* Stammati, *L'imposta generale sull'entrata* 95-97. See also Romani, *L'entrata imponibile nel sistema dell'IGE* 20, n. 16, where the literature on the subject is cited.

property.[41] The expression "transfer of goods" also includes supplies (pur
veyances) and contracts for transfers of movables manufactured or
order.[42]

In general terms, the types of receipts listed below are subject to IGE

1. Receipts obtained as a result of the transfer of merchandise and product
between merchants and industrialists.
2. Receipts obtained by private individuals or agriculturalists as a resul
of the sale of goods to merchants or industrialists.
3. Receipts obtained as a result of sales made by merchants to direct con
sumers (except in the case of sales by retailers, since 1959).
4. Receipts obtained from the rendition of services.

The general notion of taxable receipt as given by article 1 of the
IGE law is elaborated by articles 2, 3, and 8. Article 2 classifies the
receipts by reference to the persons subject to the tax. Article 3 subjects
to IGE receipts which do not come within the scope of transfer of
goods or rendition of services, and article 8 analyzes in detail various
categories of receipts from the point of view of the payment of the tax.
The provisions of these articles are further developed by the regulations.
Excluded and exempted receipts are discussed at 14/4.1.

If a receipt is subject to IGE, liability for the tax is not affected by
the fact that the transaction giving rise to the receipt is also subject to
the registration tax (Chapter 15). IGE must be paid on the basis of the
document evidencing the transaction within the time limits and by the
methods prescribed by the IGE law (IGE art. 23; IGE Reg. art. 110).
On receipts from the leasing of urban immovable property, however, the
registration tax now replaces both IGE and the stamp tax (4/2.4, 15/6.3).

14/3.2 Receipts of Persons Other than Industrialists or Merchants

Receipts obtained by persons who are not industrialists or merchants
for economic acts carried out with merchants and industrialists include
payments resulting from the sale of agricultural products (excluding
cattle and wine products) by owners, possessors, and leaseholders of
land, and other persons who are not merchants or industrialists, to merchants or industrialists, but not to private consumers (IGE arts. 2(a),
8(e); IGE Reg. art. 35). In these cases, the merchant or industrialist
is the person subject to the payment of the tax.

14/3.3 Business Receipts

a. SALES. Receipts obtained by commercial or industrial firms and
companies of any type, and by individuals or entities carrying out eco-

---

[41] L. 29 December 1962, n. 1744, art. 1. The IGE due on receipts from the
leasing of urban immovable property is included in the registration tax payable
on them (15/6.3). See 14/3.6.
[42] See L. 31 October 1961, n. 1196, art. 1.

nomic acts which result in receipts inherent (*inerente*) in the activities carried on, are subject to tax even if the acts in question are only occasional (IGE art. 2(b)). Sales of movable property between individuals and entities not engaged in business do not give rise to taxable receipts unless the sales constitute "occasional acts of commerce" as contemplated by article 2(b) of the IGE law (IGE Reg. art. 1) (14/2.1, 14/4.7).[43] Among the receipts contemplated by article 2(b), the receipts derived from the transfer of merchandise between merchants and industrialists constitute the bulk of those to which IGE is applicable.

In case of the rescission of the original sale followed by the return of the merchandise to the seller and the repayment of the sale price to the buyer, no tax is imposed provided that certain formalities have been observed in returning the merchandise.[44] Gratuitous transfers of merchandise, other than mere samples of goods, have been held subject to the tax.[45] As of 1 January 1960, receipts obtained from retail sales to private consumers are not subject to IGE (14/4.8a).[46]

b. BARTERS. Ordinary barter (*permuta*) (CC art. 1552) of movables between private individuals does not give rise to a taxable receipt (IGE Reg. art. 1); but all other barters are taxable,[47] and IGE is applied in relation to the exchanged thing having the higher value. If the bartered things are subject to different tax rates, the tax is applied in relation to the thing for whose transfer the higher tax is due. If merchandise subject to the tax is exchanged for exempt merchandise, or for merchandise for which the tax has already been paid, the tax is applied on the value of the exchanged merchandise subject to the tax (IGE Reg. art. 1).[48] In the exchange of movables for immovables, the tax is due on the value of the movables, since immovables are not subject to IGE.

c. INTERNAL TRANSFERS. The treatment of internal transfers is discussed at 14/2.2.

d. PUBLIC ENTERTAINMENTS. Taxable business receipts include receipts derived from public entertainments, whether or not subject to revenue fees (4/5.4) (IGE arts. 8(m), 8(o); IGE Reg. arts. 47, 54), and from betting and games (IGE art. 8(u); IGE Reg. arts. 48, 53).

---

[43] On the notion of "economic act" and "act of commerce," see Romani, *L'entrata imponibile nel sistema dell'IGE* 209-223, and the literature quoted therein.

[44] C.M. 16 February 1941, n. 98967. See also Mandò, *Imposta generale sull'entrata* 125-216, 676-681.

[45] Mandò, *Imposta generale sull'entrata* 629-631.

[46] L. 16 December 1959, n. 1070, art. 1, paras. 1, 2.

[47] For the view that a barter represents two distinct transactions, see Stammati, *L'imposta generale sull'entrata* 169; *contra*, Romani, *L'entrata imponibile nel sistema dell'IGE* 24.

[48] As modified by R.D.L. 3 June 1943, n. 452, art. 10.

e. PUBLIC SERVICES. An important group of business receipts consist of receipts resulting from the supplying of public services, such as water gas, and electricity (IGE art. 15; IGE Reg. arts. 83-87, 95), and from the transport of persons or things, excluding state transportation service (IGE art. 8(i); IGE Reg. art. 46). A taxable receipt arises from the furnishing of public services without regard to whether the service are rendered directly to the users or indirectly by concessionary firms

f. HOTELS AND RESTAURANTS. Also considered business receipts are re ceipts derived from the management of hotels, boarding houses, inns dormitories, restaurants, cafés, bars, cafeterias, and similar establish ments (IGE arts. 8(r), 8(s); IGE Reg. arts. 57, 58, 60).

g. ADVERTISING. Within the scope of business receipts are also receipt obtained by publishers for advertisements (IGE art. 8(u); IGE Reg art. 64).[49]

14/3.4   Receipts from the Exercise of Professions and Arts

Receipts obtained by persons habitually or occasionally practicing professions, arts, and crafts are subject to IGE (IGE arts. 2(c), 8(f) IGE Reg. arts. 38-43). However, receipts resulting from "retail services" (*prestazioni al dettaglio*) obtained by persons exercising arts and trades including itinerant persons, whose incomes for purposes of income from movable wealth are classifiable in category C/1 as professional income (8/2.1) are not subject to IGE. On the other hand, the receipts of such persons are subject to IGE if they are classifiable in category B as business income (7/1.2).[50] "Retail services" include

> all renditions of private services of a personal nature, processing, mainte nance, repairs of movable and immovable things, and installations of im movables, made by anyone for private consumers, provided that the con siderations agreed upon by oral or written agreement do not, in thei total amount, exceed L. 400,000, including all expenses incurred and the value of any material used.[51]

As of 1 January 1962, receipts of a professional whose income i classifiable in category C/1 for purposes of the tax on income from movable wealth (8/2.1) are subject to IGE at the rate of 1.3% of the amount of gross earnings which the taxpayer is required to report in his annual return of income (13/1.2).[52] A professional having income classifiable in category C/1 must file a return of his income even if, as a

---

[49] There is also a special tax on advertising, regulated by D.P.R. 24 June 1954, n 342 (4/5.3).

[50] L. 16 December 1959, n. 1070, arts. 5(a), 5(f), 6.

[51] L. 31 October 1961, n. 1196, art. 3.

[52] L. 31 October 1961, n. 1196. art. 4.

result of exemptions or the personal allowance, he is not liable for the tax on income from movable wealth. The rules governing the direct taxes are applicable to the assessment (13/2) and collection (13/3) of IGE on these receipts; the time limits governing assessment and collection of the direct taxes (13/6) also apply.[53]

14/3.5   Receipts of Commercial Intermediaries

Receipts obtained by commercial intermediaries and, in general, by all individuals or entities carrying out the activities of intermediaries, whose incomes are classifiable in categories B or C/1 as business or professional income for purposes of the tax on movable wealth, are subject to IGE. Such intermediaries include agents, commission agents, brokers, commercial travelers, and other persons in any way engaged in intermediary activities in the exchange of goods and services, and receiving remuneration in the form of commissions, brokerage fees, and the like (14/2.3).

14/3.6   Receipts from Leases

Also subject to IGE are receipts in money or in kind resulting from the leasing (*locazione*) of movables and the leasing and subleasing, or any other form of transfer for consideration, for a definite period, of the right of enjoyment of immovable property, except consideration from leases to the state administration or to entities which are treated for fiscal purposes like units of the state administration (IGE art. 3(a)).[54]

Receipts from the leasing of urban immovable property have been excluded from IGE since 7 January 1963 and subjected to an increased registration tax (15/6.3) at 6% of the cadastral rent if the property is listed in the new urban building cadaster. The registration tax is 4% of the agreed rent if the property is not yet listed in the cadaster.[55]

14/3.7   Receipts from Contracts of Appalto

IGE is applied to receipts obtained from contracts for the execution of a work or service, that is, from contracts of *appalto* in general,[56] and from contracts of purveyance (*somministrazione*) of materials, foodstuffs,

---

[53] L. 31 October 1961, n. 1196, art. 5.

[54] FAO (Food and Agricultural Organization) enjoys the same privileges as the state offices; R.M. 23 July 1952, n. 76402. Receipts from the leasing of immovable property to diplomatic agents do not constitute taxable receipts; R.M. 7 April 1940, n. 91932; R.M. 27 February 1953, n. 79419.

[55] L. 29 December 1962, n. 1744, art. 1.

[56] *Appalto* is "a contract by which a person assumes with organization of the necessary means and with management at his own risk the fulfillment of a work or service for consideration in money" (CC art. 1655).

and commodities, which are equivalent to contracts of *appalto* for purposes of the application of the registration tax (IGE art. 3(b)).[57]

14/3.8 Receipts of Credit Institutions

Interest payments obtained on any basis by credit institutions and companies and not classifiable in category A for purposes of the tax on income from movable wealth (10/4.1), and commissions and compensation received for operations and services rendered for clients, constitute another class of taxable receipts (IGE art. 3(c)).[58] The broad formulation of the law permits the application of IGE to receipts for any services rendered by credit institutions to their clients, with the exclusion of interest classifiable for purposes of tax on movable wealth in category A (9/1.1) and certain other classes of interest (14/4.2). Receipts for similar services rendered by entities which are not credit institutions are subject to IGE under the general provision of article 1 of the IGE law.[59]

14/3.9 Receipts of Insurance Firms

Insurance premiums and accessory payments paid by insured persons to insurance firms, institutions, and companies, including amounts paid for life annuities, are included in taxable receipts up to 40% of their amount (art. 3(d)).[60] This percentage includes the tax on the transfer of premiums to another insurer for reinsurance or reassignment (*retrocessione*), as well as the tax on commissions, profit sharing, refunds, and similar payments. Whether the risk concerns economic persons or entities in Italy or abroad and whether the premium is paid in Italy or abroad do not affect the taxability of the receipts. On the other hand, if the contract assuming the risk was made abroad and the obligation to pay the insurance arises abroad, the premiums are not taxable receipts, whether paid in Italy or abroad. But if the assumption of risk results from a policy executed in Italy, even if executed with a branch office or agency of an insurance company having its head office abroad, the assumption of risk which constitutes the service is considered

---

[57] See L. 19 July 1941, n. 771, art. 1, specifying services made equivalent for tax purposes to the contract of *appalto*. Among the purveyance contracts are also those for the transfer of movables manufactured on order; L. 31 October 1961, n. 1196, art. 1. On the difference between *appalto* and sale, see Cass., Sez. I, 24 July 1958, n. 2679.

[58] See also the elaboration of this article given by R.M. 27 December 1951, n. 60481. The assessment and payment are regulated by article 8(p) of the IGE law and article 55 of the regulations.

[59] See Stammati, *L'imposta generale sull'entrata* 183.

[60] Assessment and payment are governed by article 8(q) of the IGE law and article 56 of the regulations.

to take place in Italy, and the premiums are subject to IGE regardless of where they were paid.[61]

14/3.10 Other Receipts

Examples of other taxable receipts are receipts from auctions (IGE art. 8(d); IGE Reg. art. 34); compensation obtained by collectors of taxes for collection of fees of a nontax character, such as those for certain services to the public (IGE art. 8(t); IGE Reg. art. 61),[62] and receipts obtained from radio and television broadcast subscription fees (IGE art. 8(z); IGE Reg. art. 62).

14/3.11 Transfers on Approval

Transfer of merchandise on approval (*in sospeso*) occurs when one enterprise delivers merchandise to another for examination and selection. In such cases, IGE is due not upon the delivery of the merchandise, but upon the fulfillment of a contract of sale, and only on the amount of the merchandise actually sold (IGE art. 13). The postponement of taxation to the moment of sale is subject to the conditions that both enterprises keep books specifying all operations concerning delivery of the merchandise, and that each delivery and return of merchandise be evidenced by documents specifying the kind, quantity, and price of the merchandise. The time limit for the completion of the operation is three months from the delivery or forwarding of the merchandise. Within 10 days of this date, the enterprise which delivered or shipped the merchandise must pay the tax by stamps or postal current account (14/7.2b) on the value of all merchandise not returned (IGE Reg. art. 13).

14/3.12 Transfers on Consignment

Transfer of merchandise on consignment (*in conto deposito*) occurs when one enterprise delivers merchandise to another and the latter undertakes to sell it to its customers. The tax is due upon the sale of the merchandise or upon failure to return it within a determined period of time. The rules listed below govern the transaction (IGE art. 13; IGE Reg. arts. 14, 15).

1. The relationship of consignment must be evidenced by a public act or a private contract registered or attested by a notary public, or by properly kept commercial correspondence.
2. Both firms must keep special books of merchandise on consignment.
3. Each consignment or return must be specified in a note listing the kind, quantity, and price of the merchandise with reference to the book of merchandise on consignment.

---

[61] See R.M. 9 January 1954, n. 76374.
[62] On the interpretation of these provisions, see R.M. 21 May 1942, n. 62355; Giorgis, *Imposta generale sull'entrata* 35, 271.

4. At least once every three months, the consignee must forward to the consignor an extract of the book showing merchandise sold within the period.
5. Within five days of the receipt of such an extract, the consignor must issue an invoice subjected to IGE.

The time limit for the contract of consignment is one year from the forwarding of the merchandise. It can be extended subject to the first condition listed above. Within 10 days of the expiration of the time limit, the consignor must pay the tax by affixing stamps in the book of merchandise on consignment or by postal current account (14/7.2b).

14/3.13   Transfers for Purposes of Processing

Excluded from the application of IGE are transfers of merchandise effected in Italy for purposes of processing, either between two industrialists, or between a merchant (ordering the processing) and an industrialist (executing it). However, the total cost of the processing, including labor and any material used, constitutes a taxable receipt (IGE art. 13).

The provisions listed below govern transfers of merchandise for purposes of processing (IGE Reg. arts. 16, 17).

1. Any debiting of merchandise delivered for processing must be done exclusively against the guarantee of the consignee's liability for the return of the merchandise.
2. The processing must be done for the supplier of the merchandise to be processed.
3. The products obtained after processing must be in an appropriate quantitative relation to the merchandise received for processing; it is not necessary that the resulting product be obtained from the identical merchandise received.
4. The processed products must be returned to the supplier of merchandise or shipped on his account to a third party.
5. Both contracting parties must keep books of merchandise in processing.[63]
6. Each delivery of merchandise for processing must be accompanied by a note in two copies, describing the merchandise and specifying the nature of the transaction.
7. The processed product must be accompanied by an invoice which, among other items, must indicate the price of the processing (labor or labor and materials). The invoice must discount IGE on the total amount even if the cost of labor is specified separately from that of the material used. In the case of processing on a continuing basis, the invoice may be cumulative and include processings done over biweekly or monthly periods.

---

[63] Artisans whose income is classified or classifiable in category C/1 for purposes of tax on movable wealth are not required to keep books of merchandise in processing; C.M. 15 January 1953, n. 90101, para. 1, n. 2. On merchandise in processing, see Montagni, *IGE. "Merci in lavorazione."*

14/4. Nontaxable Receipts

14/4.1 In General

The general tax on receipts (IGE) was conceived as a tax covering all transfers of goods and renditions of services taking place in Italy. However, receipts from certain transactions involving transfer of goods or performance of services are expressly excluded or exempted from IGE. Receipts not subject to IGE are specified in article 1 of the IGE law and by subsequent legal provisions adding other exclusions and exemptions based on fiscal, economic, political, or social considerations. Nontaxable receipts are discussed in the following subsections.

14/4.2 Capital Receipts and Interest on Capital

Exclusion from the scope of IGE is provided for all receipts resulting from the pure and simple movement of capital, including amounts constituting consideration for the transfer of immovable property, businesses, public and private securities, or resulting from the creation or extinction of debts (IGE art. 1(a)). The reason for this exclusion is that these movements of capital are subject to other transfer taxes (registration, mortgage, stamp, and the like). The list in the law of receipts from the movement of capital that are excluded from the application of IGE is not exhaustive.[64] In the interpretation of the administration, the transactions listed below, among others, do not give rise to taxable receipts.

1. The distribution among creditors of property sold in bankruptcy proceedings.[65]
2. The sale of immovables, even if payment is deferred and even if the installments include interest on the deferred payments.[66]
3. The transfer of an entire business enterprise, even if the price is agreed upon separately for various units of the business. The essential condition is that the transfer be effected in one contract.[67]
4. The transfer to credit institutions by business enterprises of annual fees payable to the enterprises by the state. However, the tax is levied on the difference between the discounted annuities and the payments made by the credit institutions.[68]
5. Receipts in the form of subsidies, bonuses, and other forms of financial contribution granted by the state, regions, provinces, and other public

---

[64] Cass., Sez. un., 10 July 1954, n. 13.
[65] I.M. 1 August 1940, n. 91915, para. 1, n. 1.
[66] Mandò, *Imposta generale sull'entrata* 12.
[67] R.M. 21 June 1947, n. 60633. The transfer of ships presents some problems of interpretation. As movables, they should be considered subject to IGE, being only one element of the enterprise; R.M. 23 July 1940, n. 93091; Cass. pen., Sez. I, 14 January 1952. However, a more recent judicial decision excluded the sale of a ship from application of IGE, regarding the ship as a whole business, and not only one element thereof; Cass., Sez. un., 10 July 1954, n. 13.
[68] Stammati, *L'imposta generale sull'entrata* 140-141.

entities to various persons or entities to cover expenses of construction or conversion (but not the current expenses of running the enterprise) insofar as they present only simple movement of capital.[69]

Also excluded is interest derived from the pure investment of capital, classifiable for purposes of the tax on movable wealth in category A; dividends and interest derived from the investment of capital in securities of the state, other public entities, and corporations; and interest derived from bank deposits or current accounts, from rediscounts between credit institutions, and from rediscounts or advances with the issuing bank (IGE art. 1(f)).[70]

Similarly, the so-called "consumption loan" (*prestito di consumo* or *prestito di uso*) is not subject to IGE since the lender does not realize a receipt and the borrower only stipulates to return the equivalent of the thing borrowed.[71] In order not to constitute a taxable receipt, a consumption loan must result from a public act or a private writing signed by the competent official of the Registry Office before the time of the transfer.[72] On the question of the taxability of interest on the loan, the administrative interpretation has not been consistent.[73]

Amounts paid as compensation for damage are not taxable for purposes of IGE insofar as they do not constitute consideration for transfer of goods or rendition of services and result from a written agreement of the parties or a judicial decision.[74]

Time installment contracts made orally on the commodity market, if not executed by issuance of a delivery note, are not taxable.[75] These contracts, being only promises to sell, do not fall within the definition of taxable transactions.

14/4.3 Salaries, Wages, and Other Remuneration

Exclusion is provided for receipts for services as an employee in the form of salaries, wages, premiums, subsidies, and all kinds of remuneration classifiable in category C/2 for purposes of the tax on income from

---

[69] I.M. 1 August 1940, n. 91915, para. II, n. 4(b). See Mandò, *Imposta generale sull'entrata* 375-382. See also Stammati, *L'imposta generale sull'entrata* 141.

[70] See R.M. 23 January 1956, n. 217273 (interest owed by banks on money borrowed by them is exempt from IGE); R.M. 18 September 1941, n. 64876; R.M. 16 March 1957, n. 216754 (distributions of profits among partners of a joint venture are exempt from IGE); I.M. 1 August 1940, n. 91915, para. II, n. 2 (distributions of profits resulting from investment of capital in partnerships are exempt from IGE).

[71] Trib. Genova 9 August 1955; see also I.M. 1 August 1940, n. 91915, para. II, n. 1.

[72] R.M. 25 November 1947, n. 70182.

[73] I.M. 1 August 1940, n. 91915, para. II, n. 2(a), recognizes the exemption from IGE of the interest on a consumption loan. *Contra*, R.M. 13 May 1948, n. 71382; R.M. 23 February 1948, n. 70705. See Mandò, *Imposta generale sull'entrata* 12, n. 3, 384-385.

[74] R.M. 2 April 1942, n. 61404; R.M. 12 February 1947, n. 69598. See also Stammati, *L'imposta generale sull'entrata* 139.

[75] L. 13 July 1954, n. 502, art. 1.

movable wealth (8/1.1); for commissions paid on the sale of state monopoly goods and revenue stamps; and for pensions, life annuities, and the like (IGE art. 1(g)).[76]

Contributions and the corresponding accessory amounts paid as social security and other forms of providence and assistance established by law, collective bargaining, or equivalent provisions, or by regulations of the enterprise, are also excluded from the application of IGE, as an implementation of wages (IGE art. 1(c)).[77]

14/4.4 Taxes and Similar Receipts

Among the exclusions from IGE are amounts received by the state, provinces, communes, and other public entities as taxes,[78] obligatory contributions, and participations in tax receipts; amounts received by collectors of direct taxes, by provincial collectors, by persons charged with the collection of local consumption taxes, and by other persons and entities charged with the collection of taxes for the account of the state, as compensation for the collection of taxes; amounts received by public entities and administrative organs as administrative and authentication fees; and, in general, emoluments and fees which may be received under the law by the state administration or its functionaries (IGE art. 1(d)).[79] Receipts from the sale of state monopoly goods (4/6.1) and stamped paper are also excluded (IGE art. 1(b)).

All these are taxes which are not received in payment for services and therefore are excluded from the scope of IGE. However, the tax is due on amounts received by provinces, communes, and other entities which constitute specific consideration for services, immediate or deferred, direct or indirect, or for the enjoyment of goods or rights pertaining to these entities.[80] Thus, for example, fees for municipal services such as sewerage, water supply, and the like constitute direct consideration for the rendition of service and are subject to IGE.[81] But amounts received by the state from the direct management of public services and from the operation of the game of lotto and the lotteries are exempt from IGE (IGE art. 1(e)). The condition for this exemption is that the public service be managed directly by the state administration under the state budget, not by another organization managing it as a private law enter-

---

[76] See Mandò, *Imposta generale sull'entrata* 197-210; Giorgis, *Imposta generale sull'entrata* 42-49, giving the official interpretation of various kinds of doubtful cases.

[77] See Mandò, *Imposta generale sull'entrata* 484-491.

[78] Supervised by the Minister of Finance under article 1 of R.D.L. 7 August 1936, n. 1639.

[79] For cases and administrative interpretation, see Mandò, *Imposta generale sull'entrata* 397-414.

[80] R.D.L. 3 June 1943, n. 452, art. 12. See also Cass., Sez. I, 12 April 1956, n. 1065; R.M. 22 September 1951, n. 60469.

[81] R. M. 4 June 1958, n. 276039.

prise. Thus, for example, if the state administration carries on transportation of goods directly by its own personnel, the receipts resulting from such management are exempt from IGE.[82] But if a commune entrusts a municipal service such as slaughtering or street-cleaning to an enterprise (*appaltatore*), the tax is due on the fees paid by the users for the service and on the compensation of the *appaltatore*, the latter representing the difference between the fees collected from the users and those paid to the administration of the commune.[83]

14/4.5 Receipts Without Consideration

Receipts in money, goods, or services obtained for no consideration, lacking the reciprocity contemplated by the definition of a taxable receipt, are not taxable. Thus, specific exclusion is provided for donations made to entities and institutions having religious, charitable, cultural, educational, health, and public utility purposes; for donations made by such entities and institutions; and for hospitalization and similar charges paid by public entities or charitable institutions, without reciprocal service, direct or indirect, or any form of insurance between the entities and the beneficiaries (IGE art. 1(c)).[84] Contributions and membership fees paid to trade unions, political parties, and several similar organizations are not subject to IGE (IGE art. 1(c)),[85] provided that they are paid strictly as contributions or membership fees. If they are paid as consideration for services, the tax is due.[86]

14/4.6 Exemptions and Reliefs Favoring Certain Sectors of the Economy

a. RECONSTRUCTION. Payments under contracts of *appalto* for the reconstruction or repair of buildings, highways, railroads, and other facilities destroyed or damaged by war are exempt from IGE provided that the contracts are registered.[87] The exemption does not apply to payments

---

[82] R.M. 29 March 1947, n. 62072.
[83] R.M. 21 May 1942, n. 62355.
[84] R.D.L. 3 June 1943, n. 452, art. 12; I.M. 1 August 1940, n. 91915, para. II, n. 4. The following have been held not subject to IGE: voluntary contributions to Chambers of Commerce (R.M. 31 August 1940, n. 94261), subsidies to hospitals to cover ordinary expenses (Cass., Sez. I, 24 September 1954, n. 3123). The following donations made by institutions and entities have, among others, been held excluded from IGE: subsidies and premiums paid to farmers (I.M. 1 August 1940, n. 91915, para. II, n. 4), subsidies for land improvement (R.M. 1 September 1944, n. 72409).
[85] R.M. 28 November 1946, n. 63964; R.M. 7 April 1954, n. 75451.
[86] R.M. 5 April 1956, n. 215528.
[87] D.L.L. 7 June 1945, n. 322; D.L.L. 26 March 1946, n. 221, arts. 2, 3. For administrative and judicial interpretation, see Giorgis, *Imposta generale sull'entrata* 101-104.

under subcontracts or contracts for purchases of materials.[88] The exemption has been extended until 31 December 1967.[89]

b. SHIPBUILDING. Amounts received from sales to shipyards of imported materials used in the shipbuilding industry or under contracts connected with shipbuilding are exempt from the import tax provided by article 17 of the IGE law (14/8.4a).[90]

c. GOLD. Amounts received from trade in unrefined gold and its alloys, including gold in bulk, gold in bullion, grains, and scrap, are exempt.[91] Importation of gold in these forms (which is reserved to the Italian Exchange Office) and of gold and silver coins is exempt from the payment of IGE.[92]

d. AVIATION. Italian airline companies are exempt, for a 10-year period following the commencement of operations, from IGE (and several other levies) due on transactions involving fuel and lubricants. Imported flight equipment (aircraft, engines, instruments, and the like) enjoy exemption as well, provided that the equipment is not used for foreign flights. The exemptions do not apply to airlines whose activity is exclusively the transport of merchandise.[93]

Civil aviation schools training pilots are exempt from IGE (and from several other levies) on fuel and lubricants up to 1,000 tons of fuel and 1,000 tons of lubricants per year.[94]

All economic acts, contributions, and donations connected with the construction and operation of the airport of Genoa-Sestri are exempt from all taxes and levies, including IGE.[95]

e. BREAD AND MILK. Also exempt are receipts from sale of bread and milk in their natural states, intended for direct consumption as food (IGE art. 1(1)).[96]

f. DISTILLATION WINE. Receipts obtained from the sale of wine intended for distillation are exempt.[97]

---

[88] R.M. 31 August 1945, n. 63468.
[89] See L. 2 February 1960, n. 35, art. 3.
[90] L. 17 July 1954, n. 522.
[91] L. 12 June 1955, n. 481, art. 1.
[92] L. 12 June 1955, n. 481, arts. 1, 2.
[93] D.L. 3 May 1948, n. 937, arts. 1-3, as modified by L. 6 March 1950, n. 181.
[94] L. 6 March 1950, n. 181, art. 4.
[95] L. 16 April 1954, n. 156; R.M. 10 March 1955, n. 215002.
[96] See also Mandò, *Imposta generale sull'entrata* 438-443; Giorgis, *Imposta generale sull'entrata* 58-61.
[97] D.L. 18 April 1950, n. 142, art. 18.

g. CEREALS. Receipts from sale of wheat, corn, rye flour, and cereal products made exclusively from flour are exempt from IGE and also from the import equalization tax (14/8.5).[98]

h. FISH IMPORTS. Importation of fresh or frozen fish intended for direct consumption as food in its natural state is exempt.[99]

i. NEWSPAPERS. Amounts received from the sale of daily newspapers of all kinds and periodicals with "prevailingly political character" are also exempt from IGE (IGE art. 1(m)).[100] In order to qualify for the exemption, a periodical must publish exclusively or predominantly news, information, and articles of substantially political nature. Periodicals designed for other purposes (illustrated magazines, economic and financial periodicals, art, fashion, or sport magazines, and the like) are not exempt even if, in addition, they publish political news or articles. Satirical periodicals are regarded as having a predominantly political character and, consequently, are exempt from IGE. Amounts received by news agencies for daily bulletins are always exempt; on the other hand, amounts received for periodic bulletins or special bulletins at the request of customers are exempt only insofar as they are of a predominantly political character.[101]

j. PRINTING. Amounts received by printing offices for the composition and printing of daily newspapers and other periodicals of political, labor, or cultural character are exempt from IGE.[102] Of "political character" are daily newspapers and periodicals "from which the citizen draws the basic elements and orientation for his political education," such as common political periodicals and those informing of national and international events, as well as periodic publications of critical, polemic, and informative character. Humoristic and satirical periodicals are also included.. Of "labor character" are "periodicals published by trade unions, which deal with problems reflecting the protection of the interests of the classes represented." Of "cultural character" are "not only periodicals

---

98 L. 24 December 1949, n. 941, art. 1. See also Mandò, *Imposta generale sull'entrata* 49-50, 543-550.

99 L. 13 November 1940, n. 1700, as amended by D.L.P. 27 December 1946, n. 469, art. 9. Sales of fish intended for industry (for example, the canning industry) are subject to IGE (Cass., Sez. I, 11 October 1952). By "imported" fish are meant fish caught on the high seas or within the territorial waters and brought within the customs line as defined under L. 25 September 1940, n. 1424.

100 As amended by D.L.L. 7 June 1945, n. 386, art. 3.

101 C.M. 24 July 1945, n. 62632. See also Trib. Milano 12 January 1951, discussed in Giorgis, *Imposta generale sull'entrata* 62; Forte, "Sulla esenzione dalla imposta generale sull'entrata per i giornali periodici aventi carattere prevalentemente politico," *Dir. e prat. trib.*, 1956, I, 113.

102 L. 1 August 1949, n. 482, art. 1.

of higher standard (science, learning, literature, art, technique, and the like), but also those designed to provide cultural information for an average reader."

Amounts received for the printing of catalogues, yearbooks, lists, and periodicals publishing exclusively novels and stories are subject to IGE.[103]

k. REGIONAL DEVELOPMENT. The reductions listed below were designed as a relief for and activation of depressed or underdeveloped regions.

1. The IGE for the purchase of materials and machinery for new industrial plant, or for the activation or transfer of a technically organized factory, in certain areas of southern Italy and in insular Italy, and for interest on loans for these activities, is reduced by one half.[104] In 1950, a law was enacted setting up for a period of 10 years the Fund for the South (*Cassa per il Mezzogiorno*) (10/6.2). The Fund was granted the privilege of paying an annual fee (*abbonamento*), based on its capital, in substitution of all other taxes.[105] The annual fee paid by the Fund also replaces other taxes on contracts of *appalto* and other transactions made by entities which are concessionaires of the Fund.[106] The activities of the Fund for the South have been extended until 30 June 1965.[107]

2. The first transfers of certain goods introduced into the territory of Valle d'Aosta for local consumption are exempt from IGE.[108] For this territory, a free zone is provided,[109] and the same goods are also exempt to a limited extent from customs duties and consumption taxes.[110]

3. The law for the industrialization of Trieste provides complete exemption from IGE for purchases of materials and machinery intended for new industrial plant, or for the activation or transfer of technically organized industrial factories, in the region of Trieste.[111]

14/4.7 Sales Between Private Individuals

Sales of movable property between private individuals and, in general, between nonbusiness entities are not subject to IGE unless they constitute the so-called "occasional acts of commerce" provided for by article 2(b) (IGE Reg. art. 1) (14/2.1). Sales of used automobiles in

---

[103] R.M. 7 June 1951, n. 61371. See also Giorgis, *Imposta generale sull'entrata* 62-65; Mandò, *Imposta generale sull'entrata* 443-445.

[104] D.L. 14 December 1947, n. 1598, confirmed by L. 29 December 1948, n. 1482; L. 12 February 1955, n. 38; L. 29 July 1957, n. 634, art. 29. See also Mandò, *Imposta generale sull'entrata* 37-43, 524-543; Stammati, *L'imposta generale sull'entrata* 152-153. If the materials are imported, they are exempt from the import equalization tax (14/8.5).

[105] L. 10 August 1950, n. 646, art. 26. The tax reliefs granted to the Fund under this law have been extended to associations of local governments formed for the purpose of favoring industrial development.

[106] L. 29 July 1957, n. 634, art. 31.

[107] L. 29 July 1957, n. 634, art. 1.

[108] L. 3 August 1949, n. 623, art. 2.

[109] L. Cost. 26 February 1948, n. 4, art. 14.

[110] L. 3 August 1949, n. 623, art. 1.

[111] Under L. 18 December 1960, n. 1608, the exemption obtains until 31 May 1969. See Giorgis, *Imposta generale sull'entrata* 104.

some cases have been held nontaxable, except for trucks or similar vehicles which, by their nature, are destined to be used for business purposes by the buyer,[112] but are now taxed at the rate of 3.3%, except in the case of excluded transactions between private persons having no commercial intent.

14/4.8 Retail Stage

a. RETAIL SALES. Receipts obtained from sales of raw materials, merchandise, and products made in places of public sale provided with an appropriate license, or by itinerant vendors, including sales and purveyances in public accommodations, are exempt from IGE. Similarly exempt are sales made to private consumers by handicraft workshops, by market stands, by cooperatives and military stores, or by stores run by enterprises and factories even if they do not have public sales licenses, as well as purveyances in the shops and restaurants of enterprises, factories, and recreation clubs which pay IGE on the basis of the number of members.[113]

b. RETAIL SERVICES. Receipts from "retail services" (14/3.4) obtained by persons exercising arts and trades, including itinerant persons, whose incomes are classifiable in category C/1 for purposes of the tax on income from movable wealth (8/2.1) are exempt from IGE.[114]

14/4.9 Foreign Diplomatic and Consular Offices

Although there is no general exemption from IGE for receipts from sales to foreign diplomatic and consular offices, the receipts obtained from rental of immovables to them do not constitute taxable receipts; the exemption also applies to cardinals of the Church and to officials of FAO (Food and Agricultural Organization), which has its seat in Rome.[115] In addition, sales and services rendered to FAO, CARE, the Administration of Allied War Cemeteries, and a few similar organizations are exempt from IGE.[116]

---

[112] R.M. 17 January 1948, n. 68112; R.M. 25 June 1954, n. 82334; Cass., Sez. I, 30 March 1953.

[113] L. 16 December 1959, n. 1070, art. 1. Purveyances in luxury or first category establishments, taxed under the 1959 law, were exempted by L. 5 March 1963, n. 270. Those in luxury hotels and spa accommodations are still subject to tax. See C.M. 9 May 1963, n. 35.

[114] L. 16 December 1959, n. 1070, arts. 5(a), 5(f), 6.

[115] R.M. 7 April 1940, n. 91932; R.M. 27 February 1953, n. 79419; R.M. 5 July 1941, n. 68863; R.M. 11 December 1953, n. 82015.

[116] R.M. 23 July 1957, n. 248310; R.M. 9 September 1957, n. 217046; R.M. 29 August 1958, n. 190950.

14/4.10 Other Exemptions

In addition, the receipts listed below are exempt from IGE.

1. Receipts obtained from the sale of state monopoly goods and stamped paper, and from the game of lotto and the lotteries (IGE arts. 1(b), 1(e)). The latter exemption also includes amounts paid by the state to the winners.
2. Receipts from the operation of railway, streetcar, and inland navigation facilities carried out under concession by private enterprises that are subject to the national stamp tax on the transport of passengers and merchandise (IGE art. 1(i)) (4/4.5).
3. Receipts from games of skill and football pools are exempt because direct and indirect taxes on promoters of these activities are levied in one tax on the gross receipts from these games (4/5.7).[117]
4. Receipts from the delivery (but not sale) of agricultural produce to cooperatives, syndicates, and similar entities, by their members who are direct producers, as well as from the delivery to members of the processed product and the consideration paid in money or in kind by the members as processing expenses, or charged to their respective entities.[118]

14/5. Determination of the Tax Base

14/5.1 In General

The base of IGE is measured as a rule by the total amount of the consideration resulting from the taxable transaction. The general rule is that, in determining the amount of the receipt, no deduction is admissible for production costs, taxes, fees, profit sharing (*compartecipazioni*), or any other expense, even if such burdens bear directly on the receipt itself (IGE art. 4). Thus, in the case of the transfer of goods, the tax base is the gross amount which is the consideration for the sale of the merchandise; in case of services, the amount obtained from the rendition of these services; and, for commercial intermediaries, the amount of the commissions received by them (IGE art. 2).

For insurance companies, the tax base is reduced to 40% of the amount of premiums and accessory payments (IGE art. 3(d)) (14/3.9).

In the case of an exchange of movables between merchants or between merchants and nonmerchants, IGE is applied in relation to the exchanged thing which has the higher value (IGE Reg. art. 1). The IGE due on receipts in kind for services is computed on the basis of the market price of the goods obtaining at the place and on the day nearest to that on which the economic act took place. The tax base in the transfer of merchandise subject to an official price is computed on the basis of that price (IGE Reg. art. 3). The base of the import equalization tax is discussed in 14/8.5.

---

[117] L. 22 December 1951, n. 1379, arts. 1, 5.
[118] L. 7 January 1949, n. 1, art. 8; L. 25 July 1959, n. 609; R.M. 14 April 1949, n. 60344. See also Mandò, *Imposta generale sull'entrata* 604-618.

14/5.2 Charges Included

For receipts from the transfer of merchandise, the general rule of article 4 of the IGE law is further elaborated by article 12 and by articles 4, 5, 6, and 7 of the regulations.[119] Under these provisions, the tax base includes not only the price of the merchandise specified in the invoice, but also the additional charges listed below, even if they result from a document separate from that embodying the transfer of the merchandise (IGE art. 12).

1. Transportation expenses charged in the invoice or billed separately in the case of merchandise bought f.o.b. destination (*franco destino*). Merchandise carried by the seller in his own means of transport directly to the domicile of the buyer is presumed to be sold f.o.b. destination unless proved to the contrary.[120] If, in derogation of the contract of sale, the buyer requests the goods to be forwarded by a more expensive means of transport than that prepaid by the seller, the resulting difference in expense, charged separately in the invoice, is not included in the tax base.[121] In case of sale f.o.b. destination with the price of the goods to be paid on delivery (*porto assegnato*), freight expenses specified in the invoice separately from the price of the merchandise are excluded from the tax base (IGE Reg. art. 5). If goods are sold f.o.b. point of departure (*franco stazione di partenza*), shipping costs paid in advance by the seller and charged to the buyer are not included in the tax base (IGE Reg. art. 4).[122]

2. Charges of packing, crating, containers, and the like that accompany the merchandise are included in the tax base, except when the return of the containers has been agreed upon and the charges are specified separately in the invoice (IGE Reg. art. 7).[123] If the containers have not been returned in spite of the agreement, the resulting charge is subject to IGE.

3. Taxes and other fees directly charged against the merchandise upon its entering the commercial cycle or direct consumption are included—for example, manufacturing taxes, local consumption taxes, the stamp tax on playing cards, radiophonic tax, and monopoly fees.

4. Postage charges, handling expenses, and overhead expenses are included in the base of IGE, but not insurance premiums paid by the seller on behalf of the buyer.

14/5.3 Charges Excluded

The charges listed below are not included in the tax base of IGE (IGE art. 12).

1. Unconditional rebates or discounts granted in the invoice. By an "unconditional" rebate or discount is meant one not dependent upon any condition, such as, for example, payment by the buyer within

---

[119] See also Mandò, *Imposta generale sull'entrata* 635-658.
[120] R.M. 3 August 1940, n. 92039.
[121] R.M. 4 August 1942, n. 61464.
[122] I.M. 1 August 1940, n. 91915, para. VI, n. 2; R.M. 15 May 1941, n. 98878.
[123] I.M. 1 August 1940, n. 91915, para. VI, n. 2.

certain time limits (IGE Reg. art. 6). The question whether discounts granted in kind may be deductible is controversial.[124]
2. The amount of IGE specified in the invoice.
3. Interest payable on delay in payment, if separately specified in the invoice, insofar as it does not exceed the official discount rate by 3% or more.

14/6. The Tax Rates

14/6.1 In General

Although one of the main objectives of the IGE law of 1940 was the simplification of the rate structure of the tax,[125] this structure soon became as complex as it had been before the reform. Although a standard general rate was established (14/6.2), a large number of taxable events, in particular, sales of various articles, are subject either to increased or reduced rates. And although, as a rule, the rate is applied to each particular transaction, a large number of commodities are subject to single-stage collection (*una tantum*) under which a consolidated rate is applied only to one transaction covering all prior and subsequent ones except the sale by the retailer. These rates are fixed annually by the decree of the Minister of Finance. For these reasons, it is possible to give only a general outline of the complex rate structure of IGE, emphasizing its essential characteristics. For details, reference must be made to the numerous provisions regulating the rates of particular taxable transactions.[126]

14/6.2 The Standard Tax Rate

The standard general rate was originally established at 2% of the taxable receipt (IGE art. 7), and subsequently raised to 4%.[127] Effective 1 January 1947, the standard rate was fixed at 3%, with lower or higher rates for certain commodities.[128] However, as of 1 January 1960, all of the rates of tax on receipts resulting from sales of commodities were increased by 0.3% if they were not lower than 1%, and by 0.1% if lower than 1%. Hence the basic rate is now 3.3%.[129]

---

[124] See R.M. 12 May 1950, n. 64533; C.M. 31 October 1959, n. 176666. See also Mandò, *Imposta generale sull'entrata* 122-123; Stammati, *L'imposta generale sull'-entrata* 165.

[125] See Stammati, *L'imposta generale sull'entrata* 186-188; Due, *Sales Taxation* 102.

[126] For a review of the variations in the tax rate, see the "Tables of Variation of the Rate" in Mandò, *Imposta generale sull'entrata* 1146-1147, brought up to date as of 1 January 1960; see also the alphabetical list of the commodities subject to special rates, at 1168-1171. For an alphabetical list of commodities with corresponding rates and method of taxation, see Cordaro, *Codice fiscale* 1731-1741.

[127] D.L.L. 19 October 1944, n. 348, art. 1.

[128] D.L. 27 December 1946, n. 469, art. 1.

[129] L. 16 December 1959, n. 1070, art. 2, as modified by L. 31 October 1961, n. 1196, art. 2.

ANALYSIS OF OTHER TAXES   734

14/6.3 The Special Rates

a. INCREASED RATES. The purpose of the higher rates, in most cases, is to discriminate against luxury articles or to tax expanding sectors of the economy considered capable of bearing a heavier burden, or not bearing manufacturing taxes. The receipts from the transactions listed below are taxed at rates higher than the standard rate.

1. Sale of various kinds of cement and cement products by producers: 9.3%.[130]
2. Internal transfers of cement from cement plants to factories making cement products: 6%.[131] This is the only case in which internal transfers are taxed (14/2.2c).
3. Sale of luxury furs, precious stones, pearls, and gold, platinum, and silver objects,[132] and natural and sparkling wines: 8.3%.[133]
4. Sale of a wide range of articles regarded as luxuries, including liquors, antiques, photographic equipment, phonographs, records, sporting goods, playing cards, and cosmetics,[134] and watches with gold or platinum cases: 5.3%.[135]

b. REDUCED RATES. Reduced rates are applied to transactions involving certain goods of popular consumption, listed below.

1. Sales of certain foodstuffs, such as butter, cheese, vegetables, fish, sugar,[136] tomato preserves; [137] processing and sales of certain textile products, such as jute and many common articles of clothing,[138] and of most fertilizers: 2.3%.[139]
2. Sales of marble, granite, alabaster, and similar minerals: 0.6%.[140]

c. ANNUAL FEES IN *ABBONAMENTO*. When the tax is paid in the form of an annual fee (*abbonamento*) (14/7.3), instead of on each separate transaction, the regular rate is 1% of the estimated gross receipts. For the establishments and products listed below, however, receipts are subject to special rates.[141]

---

[130] D.L. 21 November 1956, n. 1284 (converted in L. 27 December 1956, n. 1412), art. 1.

[131] D.L. 21 November 1956, n. 1284 (converted in L. 27 December 1956, n. 1412), art. 2.

[132] L. 7 January 1949, n. 1, art. 1. Sales of luxury furs are now taxed under the *una tantum* system of collection (14/6.4). See Mandò, *Imposta generale sull'entrata* 89, n. 6.

[133] L. 18 December 1959, n. 1079, art. 12; L. 16 December 1959, n. 1070, art. 2.

[134] D.L. 3 May 1948, n. 799, art. 1; L. 4 March 1952, n. 110, art. 2. The 3.3% rate is, however, applied to certain photographic and phonographic equipment; see L. 26 November 1957, n. 1153, art. 3.

[135] L. 4 March 1952, n. 110, art. 2(d).

[136] D.L. 27 December 1946, n. 469, art. 5.

[137] L. 4 March 1952, n. 110, art. 2(a). Most processed foods are, however, subject to higher rates.

[138] L. 12 August 1957, n. 755, arts. 11, 13.

[139] L. 7 January 1949, n. 1, art. 5; L. 26 November 1957, n. 1153, arts. 1, 7.

[140] L. 29 December 1949, n. 955, art. 3; L. 27 May 1959, n. 359.

[141] L. 26 November 1957, n. 1153, art. 2, as substituted by L. 27 May 1959, n. 359.

1. Luxury tearooms, ballrooms, clubs, and similar establishments, including those in hotels: 8% (standard 5% plus 3% additional).
2. Establishments listed in item 1, if they are not luxury but first class: 7% (5% plus 2% additional).
3. Luxury restaurants, cafés, and bars: 7% (4% plus 3% additional).
4. Luxury hairdressers, and the establishments listed in item 3, if they are first class, and not located in the south: 5% (3% plus 2% additional).
5. Sales of products subject under the normal method of taxation (14/6.3a) to an 8% rate on each transfer: 4%.
6. Sales of products subject under the normal method of taxation (14/6.3a) to a 5% rate on each transfer: 3%.
7. Luxury hotels: 3% (1% plus 2% additional).

A rate of 0.5% applies to sales of products subject under the normal methods of taxation to a 0.5% rate on each transfer.

14/6.4   The *Una Tantum* Rates

For receipts on sales of certain commodities, tax is collected in a single stage, *una tantum:* a consolidated rate is applied once to take account of all of the stages through which a given commodity passes in its production and distribution cycle. The consolidated rate to be applied to a given commodity is determined on the basis of the number of stages through which the commodity passes in its production and distribution cycle, the average value of the commodity at each stage of the cycle, and the rate which would be due at each stage if taxed in the normal manner. The law providing for the *una tantum* collection usually indicates at which stage the tax is to be imposed. This may be the initial stage of the cycle, for example, the introduction of the merchandise into national territory, or the final one, the last wholesale transaction. It may also be some intermediate point, such as subjection to the local consumption tax. Typically, however, the tax at the *una tantum* rate is collected from the manufacturer or importer; this system has been designed to reduce the advantages of integrated firms.[142] The general legal basis of the *una tantum* rates was established by a legislative decree of 1944 which allowed the government to apply *una tantum* rates to particular commodities.[143] Subsequent legislative measures extended this authorization to other commodities. Detailed specification of the commodities subject to *una tantum* rates, the rates themselves, the phase at which the tax must be paid, and other provisions are, for some commodities, fixed by special laws or by an annual ministerial decree.[144] The 0.3% or 0.1% addition introduced in 1959 (see 14/6.2) does not apply to *una tantum* rates comprising the tax due on retail sales.[145]

[142] See Due, *Sales Taxation* 104, 106.
[143] D.L.L. 19 October 1944, n. 348. The decree also authorized the government to establish the annual-fee (*abbonamento*) system for such commodities (14/7.3).
[144] For 1963, see D.M. 22 December 1962.
[145] L. 31 October 1961, n. 1196, art. 2.

Some examples of merchandise and products for which *una tantum* rates are imposed by legislative provisions are listed below.

1. Wines and grapes exempt from the local consumption tax and used in the production of other goods not subject to the special regime established for wine by article 14 of the IGE law (14/7.2a),[146] and certain textile products: 3%.[147]
2. Books, maps, music, and periodicals, excluding daily newspapers and periodicals of a predominantly political character (14/4.6i): 2%.[148]
3. Secondhand books, excluding antique books,[149] and rice: 2%.[150]
4. Imported hides, excluding sheepskins for the fur industry;[151] cattle, sheep, pigs, and horses sold for immediate slaughtering, and meats therefrom which are exempt from the local consumption tax;[152] canned beef, pork and lamb, and meat products;[153] fresh horse meat, and canned horse meat and horse meat products: 5%.[154]
5. Fine wines (excluding sparkling wines): 6%.[155]
6. Fresh beef, pork, and lamb,[156] and certain textile raw materials: 6%.[157]

The more important *una tantum* rates established by the annual decree for 1963 are listed below.[158]

1. Vegetables, fruit, fish products, eggs: 2.3%.
2. Fresh flowers, poultry, rabbits, game: 3.3%.
3. Domestic or foreign beer: 5.8%.
4. Imported coffee: 12%; coffee substitutes: 5.3%.
5. Tea and maté: 12%.
6. Fertilizers: 5%.
7. Petroleum products, fuels, and lubricants: gasoline, 5.8%; lubricants, 7% (if used for internal consumption by refineries, the rate is 1%); oil for heating purposes, 6%; mineral oil fuels, 4%; paraffin, 4%.
8. Domestic or imported solid fuels: 4%.
9. Domestic or imported patent medicines: 4.3%.
10. Herring: 6.3%; codfish and stockfish: 7.3%.
11. Domestic or imported sugar: 5.3%; sugar for industrial purposes: 2.3%.
12. Spices: 14%.
13. Methane gas: 5%.
14. Propane and butane gas and their blends, for fuels: 10%; for other purposes: 14%.
15. Domestic or imported yeast for baking bread: 5.3%.
16. Carbonated beverages, ice: 4.3%.

---

[146] D.L. 27 December 1946, n. 469, art. 2.
[147] L. 12 August 1957, n. 757.
[148] D.L.L. 7 June 1945, n. 386, art. 4; D.L. 27 November 1946, n. 469.
[149] L. 31 October 1961, n. 1196, art. 2.
[150] L. 24 December 1949, n. 941, art. 2.
[151] D.L. 3 May 1948, n. 799, arts. 2, 3; L. 4 February 1956, n. 33, art. 6.
[152] L. 4 February 1956, n. 33, art. 3.
[153] L. 4 February 1956, n. 33, arts. 2(b), 4(a).
[154] L. 4 February 1956, n. 33, arts. 2, 4(b).
[155] D.L. 27 December 1946, n. 469, art. 2.
[156] L. 4 February 1956, n. 33, arts. 2, 4(a).
[157] L. 12 August 1957, n. 757, art. 2.
[158] D.M. 22 December 1962.

17. Resinous timbers: domestic, 8%; imported, 6, 7, or 8%, depending on the class.
18. Italian fur skins: common, 3.3%; luxury, 8.3%; imported: luxury, 23.3%.

14/7.   Assessment and Collection

14/7.1   In General

The central administration of IGE lies within the competence of the General Directorate of the Fees and Indirect Taxes on Transactions (1/4.3). The Registry Offices are the local organs of the Directorate charged with the collection of the tax. Insofar as IGE is self-assessed and paid through postal current accounts, its collection is supervised by five large mechanized Registry Offices, called "first offices of IGE" (*primi uffici IGE*).[159] Other smaller offices, numbering about one thousand, deal with the collection of IGE paid by other methods.

Two methods of collection of IGE should be distinguished: (1) collection separately on each transaction; and (2) collection of the tax for a period of time, by annual fee (*abbonamento*) or another method of payment. Under the original text of the IGE law of 1940, direct payment for each transaction was almost universally required. This technique of collection, particularly difficult to administer with regard to retailers (who are often small stores not keeping regular records for each sale and not issuing receipts) was motivated by the fear of the government that, if it were not used, firms would accumulate large tax liabilities which they would be unable to meet.[160] Soon, however, it became apparent that collection by this method was not feasible for many categories of small taxpayers; thus, the annual-fee system was developed and prescribed for a number of taxable transactions, the tax to be paid generally at the final stage. The scope of the annual-fee method has been rather narrow, however, since the exclusion of most retail sales from IGE (14/4.8a).

The general rule still is that IGE is applied separately and distinctly to each transaction rather than on the basis of periodic returns, a practice common in other countries; any other systems of collection are established by the annual decree of the Minister of Finance, on the basis of legislative authorization.

14/7.2   Collection for Each Transaction

a. IN GENERAL. The general rule is that IGE is due only after the date on which one of the contracting parties, the person selling commodities or rendering service, receives payment from the other party, the buyer

---

[159] The five "first offices of IGE" are in Milan, Rome, Florence, Genoa, and Palermo; D.M. 5 June 1952; D.M. 5 November 1952. For the jurisdictions of these five offices, see Stammati, *L'imposta generale sull'entrata* 115-117.

[160] Due, *Sales Taxation* 105.

or the person for whom the service has been rendered. In a few particular cases dictated by necessity to provide for a more efficient method of collection of the tax, the law sets the tax duty on a different basis. Some of these cases are listed below.

1. The tax on the sale of wines (excluding sparkling wines), grapes (IGE art. 14), cattle, and meat products [161] is due when the goods are subjected to the communal consumption tax (4/5.8).
2. The tax on the transfer of merchandise between a producing firm and its own retail sales departments is due at the time of transfer (14/2.2b).
3. The tax on the importation of merchandise from abroad is due at the time of importation (IGE art. 17).[162]

b. SELF-ASSESSMENT. The burden of assessment, in the majority of cases, falls upon the taxpayer, who himself determines whether the tax is due and applies the appropriate tax rate to the given transaction. This self-assessment is typical for a large number of exchanges of merchandise between manufacturers and wholesalers, and also for the rendition of services. In the case of payment for each transaction, the self-assessment is made on the basis of the appropriate document, whose issuance is obligatory under the law and which must specify the amount of elements constituting the receipt and any other elements which can identify the particular economic act subject to the tax (IGE art. 8). The document usually takes the form of an invoice, note, account, or receipt and is issued in duplicate; in the case of the transfer of merchandise between businessmen, the document must be issued within five weekdays of the day of the dispatching or delivery of the merchandise, and, in any case, within five weekdays of the day of payment, total or partial, whenever the payment occurs before the forwarding or delivery of the merchandise (IGE Reg. art. 9).

c. PAYMENT

1. Time limits. The provisions regulating the payment of IGE for each transaction are contained in articles 8 through 11 of the IGE law and elaborated by various provisions of the regulations. The time limit for the payment of IGE, as applied to each transaction, varies with the nature of the transaction. Payment may be immediate or in installments. Immediate payment is simultaneous with the receiving of the consideration constituting the taxable receipt or the fulfillment of the economic act incurring the tax, and is provided for receipts resulting from the furnishing of services in general, including consideration for contracts of *appalto,* rentals, sales at public auctions, importation of merchandise, registration of insurance contracts, and so forth. The payment may be made a short

---

[161] L. 4 February 1956, n. 33, art. 1.
[162] See Cass. 27 May 1952; Cass. 25 October 1951. See also 14/8.4.

time following the moment at which the transaction took place, such as, for example, in the case of transactions between businessmen or purchases made by businessmen from farmers, when the tax is due within five days of the issuance of the invoice.

2. *Payment in installments.* The Intendant of Finance has the power to grant the taxpayer the right to pay the tax (as well as surcharges, pecuniary penalties, and fines) in installments spread over a maximum of four years, with 5% interest on the unpaid balance. In the case of late payment of an installment by more than 20 days, the entire amount becomes collectible in one payment, together with interest and a surcharge of 10% of the tax due. The extension of the time limit for payment must be based on a written document (IGE art. 46; IGE Reg. art. 117).

The credit of the state for the tax not paid has a preference against the movable property of the debtor, according to the rules of the civil law (IGE art. 44; CC art. 2758).

3. *Methods.* Payment is made either by applying revenue stamps to the appropriate document, through postal current accounts, or by direct payment (*in modo virtuale*) to the competent Registry Office. The tax on receipts whose amount is less than L. 100 must be paid by means of stamps. For receipts exceeding L. 100, but not exceeding L. 2,000, the seller may use either the stamp method or the postal current account. In cases where the taxes are collected by means of stamps, the taxpayer may use the postal current account for that part of each receipt which exceeds L. 100 (IGE art. 9).[163] Payment by means of stamps is made through the application and cancellation of the prescribed double stamps; one section of the stamp is applied to the invoice or other document, the other to the seller's copy (IGE Reg. art. 65). If the receipt exceeds L. 2,000, the tax must be paid through a postal current account.[164] The holders of postal current accounts pay the tax by means of a draft (*postagiro*) drawn on the current account of the taxpayer in favor of the current account of the competent Registry Office. A taxpayer who has no current account makes direct payment through any post office to the postal current account of the competent Registry Office (IGE art. 11).

Each person inscribed in the rolls of the tax on income from movable wealth for income of category B in an amount not less than L. 150,000 has the duty to open his own postal current account within three months of the last day of the publication of the roll in which the income was inscribed. Such persons, on opening an account, must pay the sum of L. 20,000 as a guarantee deposit to be used by the tax authorities in cases of deficient payment and for penalties and fines arising from violations of the law

---

[163] As modified by D.L. 3 May 1948, n. 799, art. 7.

[164] Payment by means of postal current account is regulated by articles 10 and 11 of the IGE law and articles 66-82 of the regulations.

(IGE art. 10).[165] Leaseholders and owners of farm land are not required to open a postal account, unless they are inscribed in the rolls of the tax on income from movable wealth for income of category B derived from agriculture or cattle-raising (IGE Reg. art. 67).

As a result of the setting up of mechanized centers, payment of the tax is now made to the postal account of the competent "first office of IGE." In each of these offices, elaborate mechanical tabulating equipment records all transactions and payments.

The tax must be paid separately for each taxable transaction on the basis of the documents issued in connection with the transaction, not on the amount of total sales over a period of time. However, certain large firms, in particular, those which are inscribed in the rolls for income from movable wealth in an amount not less than L. 200,000, are permitted to make weekly payments (*postagiro settimanale*) rather than having to pay the tax on each transaction (IGE art. 9; IGE Reg. arts. 75, 76). This method involves certain formalities, in particular the keeping of a register of invoices in an officially prescribed manner. An extract of the register specifying each individual transaction with the name and address of the purchaser must be sent to the competent "first office of IGE" on the same day on which the tax for the invoices of the week is paid through the postal current account. The cumulative payment on the weekly basis should be made not later than Friday of each week for the invoices issued in the week which ended on the preceding Sunday.

4. Joint and several liability for payment. The taxpayer of IGE is the person who receives payment—that is, the seller of goods or the person furnishing services. However, both the seller and the buyer, being connected by a single contractual bond subject to the tax, are jointly and severally liable (*obbligati in solido*) for the payment of any unpaid tax and for the payment of the resulting surcharges and pecuniary penalties (IGE art. 43). As an exception to this rule, the law provides that the person making the payment is exempt from joint and several liability if the economic act in question is not connected with his industrial or commercial activity (IGE art. 43). This means that if the purchaser performs the economic act for a purpose not connected with his industrial or commercial business, he is not liable for the tax. If the economic act in question is performed as a result of direct or indirect connection with his industrial or commercial activity, the purchaser is jointly and severally liable with the seller for any penalty imposed for violation of the tax law. But if the violation is proved imputable to only one of the parties, only that party is liable (IGE art. 43).[166]

---

[165] As modified by D.L. 3 May 1948, n. 799, art. 5.

[166] Article 14 of D.L. 3 May 1948, n. 799, incorporated into article 43 of the IGE law, introduced a radical change in the matter of liability, the former rule being

In cases of transfers of merchandise between merchants and industrialists made without the issuance of the prescribed documents (14/7.2b), the purchaser is free from liability for the payment of pecuniary penalties and surcharges if, within 15 days from the receipt of the merchandise, he issues the document in question and pays the tax due.[167]

d. APPEALS AND REFUNDS.   In cases where IGE is assessed by the taxpayer himself and paid currently on each transaction, litigation may arise, first, if the Intendant of Finance ascertains violation of the law (IGE arts. 48-52) and, proceeding according to the general rules on the repression of fiscal evasion,[168] imposes a pecuniary penalty upon the taxpayer.   The taxpayer may appeal to the Minister of Finance, and against the decision of the latter may file a complaint before the courts in civil proceedings (IGE art. 53).   The rule that an appeal in tax matters cannot be taken before a court unless the tax has been paid (the rule of *solve et repete*) is included in the IGE law, but has been declared unconstitutional by the Constitutional Court.[169]   The unconstitutionality of the rule of *solve et repete* has been extended to all provisions containing that rule.

Tax erroneously paid by means of stamps cannot be refunded.   Refund is allowable on petition in case of erroneous payment made by postal current account or by direct payment.   A request for refund must be filed within one year of the date of payment.   The competence to grant a refund lies with the Intendant of Finance if the amount does not exceed L. 1 million and, in other cases, with the Ministry of Finance (IGE art. 47).   The taxpayer may also demand refund by judicial proceedings. This action is independent of the administrative proceedings, that is, it may be brought without previous exhaustion of the administrative remedies.[170]

---

that only the *de jure* taxpayer was liable for the payment of the tax due, surcharges, and pecuniary penalties.   See Mandò, *Imposta generale sull'entrata* 329, 1014.

[167] R.D.L. 3 June 1943, n. 452, art. 24.

[168] L. 7 January 1929, n. 4.

[169] See Corte Cost. 29-30 December 1961, n. 79 (*Riv. leg. fisc.*, 1962, 1015-1019) declaring article 58, second paragraph, second sentence, of the IGE law unconstitutional under articles 3, 24, and 113 of the Constitution; this decision also declares the unconstitutionality of article 149 of R.D. 30 December 1923, n. 3269 (registration law) and article 24, paragraph 3, of L. 25 September 1940, n. 1424 (customs law).   See also Corte Cost. 31 March 1961, nn. 21, 24-31, in which the Court for the first time held unconstitutional article 6, paragraph 2, of L. 30 March 1865, n. 2248, Annex E, which sanctioned the rule of *solve et repete* (see 13/4.11).

[170] App. Roma 4 July 1955; Cass., Sez. un., 7 November 1957, n. 4259, reported in Giorgis, *Imposta generale sull'entrata* 571; Mandò, *Imposta generale sull'entrata* 1019-1020.

14/7.3   Annual Fee (*Abbonamento*)

a. IN GENERAL. The method of payment by annual fee (*abbonamento* or *forfait*), which had legislative precedents even before 1940,[171] was included in the original 1940 IGE law in the special regime applied to receipts resulting from sales of cattle, sheep, pigs, grapes, and wines: the law provides for payment by annual fee in cases in which the local consumption tax is collected by this method (IGE art. 14).[172] The annual-fee method has been widely used since 1944, when the same legislative decree that authorized the application of the *una tantum* rates (14/6.4) granted the Minister of Finance the power to establish it for certain categories of taxpayers.[173] The provisions of the 1944 decree were eventually extended to other classes of taxpayers.[174] Since 1 January 1954, the annual-fee system of collection has been, in general, regulated by a decree passed in 1953,[175] but important changes were introduced (as of 1 January 1960) by a law in 1959, amended in 1961. In 1959, the retail stage, which had used the annual-fee system since 1953, was excused from IGE altogether (14/4.8);[176] for the other sectors in which the annual-fee system was previously applied, it has been made optional, and the respective classes of taxpayers now have the choice of paying IGE either by an annual fee or by a single annual payment of the actual aggregate amount of the tax due on individual transactions (14/7.3g).[177]

b. CLASSES OF TAXPAYERS. The classes of taxpayers listed below have the choice of payment by annual fee or by an annual payment of the aggregate tax.[178]

1. Professionals whose income is not classified in category C/1 for purposes of the tax on income from movable wealth.[179]
2. Stockbrokers and commission agents in the money and stock exchanges.
3. Forwarding and shipping agents, city agencies of state railroads, travel and tourist agencies and offices, river, lake, and lagoon navigation agencies, loading and unloading carriers, carters, cabmen, and boatmen,

---

[171] See Stammati, *L'imposta generale sull'entrata* 120-121.

[172] L. 4 February 1956, n. 33.

[173] D.L.L. 19 October 1944, n. 348, art. 10.

[174] D.L.C.P.S. 27 December 1946, n. 469, arts. 14, 17; D.L. 3 May 1948, n. 799, arts. 16-22, 26-28.

[175] D.M. 10 December 1953.

[176] L. 16 December 1959, n. 1070, art. 1.

[177] L. 16 December 1959, n. 1070, as modified by L. 31 October 1961, n. 1196. See also I.M. 15 December 1961, n. 62/170503.

[178] L. 16 December 1959, n. 1070, art. 5, as modified by L. 31 October 1961, n. 1196, arts. 3-6. Regarding institutions furnishing medium- and long-term credit, see L. 27 July 1962, n. 1228.

[179] Receipts of professionals whose income is classified in category C/1 are subject to IGE at the rate of 1.3%, applied to the gross earnings reported on the return of income from movable wealth, and assessed and collected in accordance with the provisions applicable to the direct taxes (14/3.4).

even if associated in cooperatives, whose incomes, for purposes of the tax on movable wealth, are classified or classifiable in category C/1.

4. Hotels, boarding houses, and tourist camps.
5. Billiard rooms and bathing establishments.
6. Persons furnishing retail services (*prestazioni al dettaglio*), including itinerant persons (14/3.4, 14/4.8b), whose incomes are classified or classifiable in category B for purposes of the tax on income from movable wealth (7/1.2).
7. Persons engaged in the transportation of persons by automobiles, boats, or gondolas.
8. Cattle-breeding stations.[180]

c. ASSESSMENT. The general principle of the annual-fee system is that the tax is paid on the basis of the gross receipts obtained by the taxpayer in the preceding year. The assessment is made on the basis of a return (*dichiarazione*) which is due at the Registry Office by the end of February of each year. The return indicates the gross receipts or turn-over (*volume degli affari*) realized in the preceding year. Persons commencing business operations must submit the statement within two months of the initiation of the activity and indicate the estimated gross receipts for the year. Persons engaged in seasonal activities—for example, bathing establishments—must submit two statements: the first within one month of the start of their activities, indicating anticipated receipts, and the other within one month of the cessation of the business activities, indicating the actual receipts of the season.[181] On the basis of the taxpayer's return, the Registry Office determines the annual tax amount to be paid by the taxpayer. The return is examined by the Registry Office and, whenever the receipts assessed by the Office exceed those declared by the taxpayer, a notice of assessment is forwarded to him. If the taxpayer fails to file the required statement, the Registry Office may determine the tax due on the basis of its own records.[182]

d. PAYMENT. The payment of the tax is made through a postal current account to the postal current account of the competent Registry Office, in four quarterly installments due respectively on the last day of March, June, September, and December. If the yearly tax (*canone*) does not exceed L. 2,000, it must be paid in full by the end of March. The payment of any supplementary amount due as a result of a rectification by the taxpayer which is accepted by the Registry Office must be made within two years of rectification in bimonthly installments beginning with the month following that in which the rectification was accepted by the

---

[180] L. 16 December 1959, n. 1070, art. 5, as modified by L. 31 October 1961, n. 1196, arts. 3-6.
[181] D.L.C.P.S. 27 December 1946, n. 469, art. 14; D.M. 10 December 1953, art. 15.
[182] D.M. 10 December 1953, art. 16.

Office. Within the same period of time must be paid the difference due as a result of an assessment which has become final because of failure to file an appeal or because of filing a late appeal.[183]

e. ADMINISTRATIVE APPEALS. The protest procedures in cases relating to the payment of IGE by annual fee are similar to those for the direct taxes (13/4). The Registry Office forwards a notice of assessment (*avviso di accertamento*), against which the taxpayer may appeal within 30 days to the District Commission, in which a special section is organized to decide in the first instance cases resulting from the application of IGE, and which may add to the taxable amount as determined by the Registry Office. The taxpayer's appeal must be accompanied by supporting reasons. Upon receipt of an adverse decision by the District Commission, the taxpayer may appeal within 30 days to the Provincial Commission, also with accompanying reasons. The rule of *solve et repete* (14/7.2d) has never been applied to administrative appeals, and therefore failure to pay has never excluded appeal to the Provincial Commission.[184] The decision of the Provincial Commission is final.[185] This finality, however, must be interpreted as referring only to the determination of the amount of the tax base; it does not exclude the possibility of an appeal to the Central Commission on the question of legitimacy or legality, on which that Commission may decide under the general rules of administrative litigation,[186] or the possibility of an appeal to the courts on such a question (14/7.3f).

The decision of the District Commission is final if the taxpayer fails to appeal against it within the time limit of 30 days. Generally, the taxpayer's failure to file a timely appeal to the District Commission, or his having entered into an agreement (*concordato*) with the Registry Office within 30 days of the original notice, terminates his right to contest the assessment of the tax base. However, on the request of the taxpayer, filed within 30 days of the date of the notice of the Office or the payment of the tax, the tax administration may reduce the amount assessed if the assessment has proved to be insufficient or erroneous. This power is exercised by the Intendant of Finance if the assessed receipts for the year do not exceed L. 10 million and by the Minister of Finance in other cases.[187]

The dispute may also be settled by mutual agreement between the taxpayer and the Registry Office within 30 days of the notice of assessment.

---

[183] D.M. 10 December 1953, art. 17.

[184] Comm. Centr., Sez. VI, 10 November 1950, n. 17248.

[185] D.L. 3 May 1948, n. 799, arts. 18-21.

[186] Comm. Centr., Sez. un., 6 July 1949, n. 5156; Cass., Sez. un., 13 March-6 June 1952. The Central Commission has this power under R.D.L. 7 August 1936, n. 1639, and R.D. 8 July 1937, n. 1516. See 13/4.4.

[187] D.L. 3 May 1948, n. 799, art. 17. See also I.M. 8 June 1954, n. 92353.

If the taxpayer has already filed an appeal with the District Commission, he can make an agreement within 120 days from the notice of assessment, provided that the District Commission has not rendered a decision within this period.[188] The taxpayer may modify his return also after receipt of the notice of assessment, and file an appeal, provided that he does so before the day set for the appellate argument. The acceptance of the modified return serves as a mutual agreement and cancels the appellate proceedings.[189] It must be formally signed by the Registry Office.[190]

Payment during the appellate proceedings is only provisional if a timely appeal is filed with the Provincial Commission. It is final if no appeal has been made, in which situation the taxpayer must also pay a surcharge determined by the Registry Office. If the amount of the tax exceeds L. 20,000, the Intendant of Finance may permit payment by installments over a period of not more than six months.[191] The taxpayer must submit his request for payment in installments on the appropriate stamped paper to the Intendant of Finance, who decides on the number of installments and the amount of each payment; there is an interest charge of 4%. The taxpayer must submit formally to the decision and give a valid personal guarantee or security. If the tax paid in the provisional payment is larger than that due under the final decision, the difference is used in satisfaction of any surtaxes due, or applied to taxes for the succeeding years (IGE art. 46; IGE Reg. art. 117).[192]

f. JUDICIAL APPEALS. Appeal to judicial authority may be made only on questions of law (*legittimità*), or law and fact combined, but not on the mere determination of value.[193] Appeal has also been allowed for gross and evident error in appraisal or for defective or insufficient calculation.[194] Appeal to the court does not depend on any previous administrative action such as compulsory collection or on the exhaustion of the administrative remedies.[195]

g. SINGLE ANNUAL PAYMENT OF AGGREGATE TAX DUE. A taxpayer who is subject to payment of tax by annual fee has the option in the alternative of making a single annual payment directly to the Registry Office (*in modo virtuale*) of the aggregate tax actually due on the individual taxable

---

[188] D.L. 3 May 1948, n. 799, art. 16.

[189] L. 29 December 1949, n. 955, art. 5.

[190] C.M. 31 December 1949, n. 66631.

[191] D.L.C.P.S. 27 December 1946, n. 469, art. 17.

[192] As amended by D.P.R. 4 February 1955, n. 72, art. 16.

[193] Cass., Sez. un., 14 June 1952; Cass., Sez. un., 3 May 1954, n. 1361; Cass. 9 September 1953, n. 2995; Cass. 30 January 1957, n. 326. See also 13/4.9.

[194] See Trib. Firenze 23 January 1950.

[195] Cass., Sez. un., 12 October 1955, n. 3041; Cass., Sez. un., 7 November 1957, n. 4259.

transactions.[196] For payment by this method, the taxpayer must file with the Registry Office, within 10 days of the end of each year, an appropriate report (*denuncia*) of the receipts obtained, specifying the essential elements of the payment of the tax, and pay the tax through the postal current account of the Registry Office. A taxpayer who wishes to change from one system to the other must file an appropriate declaration with the Registry Office on or before 30 November of the year before that in which the change is to become effective.[197]

14/7.4   Other Methods of Collection

a. SUBSCRIPTION CONTRACTS SUBJECT TO RECONCILIATION. The tax on receipts derived from the supply of water, gas, and electricity is collected by means of subscription contracts (*convenzioni di abbonamento*) (IGE art. 15).

The assessment of the tax is based on an annual return submitted by the taxpayer, specifying the transactions carried out during the preceding year. On the basis of this declaration, the Registry Office determines, finally, the amount of the tax due for the year to which the declaration refers and, provisionally, the tax due for the following year. The tax provisionally assessed is paid in one sum if it does not exceed L. 2,000. Otherwise, payment in six bimonthly installments is allowed. If the Office has assessed a higher amount than that declared by the taxpayer, the difference must be paid within 20 days of the service of the assessment notice. If a larger amount than that due has been paid provisionally, the difference is credited against future assessments (IGE Reg. arts. 83, 85-87).

b. ANNUAL PAYMENT OF FIXED AMOUNT. Until the end of 1959, the IGE for certain transactions was paid in fixed annual amounts regardless of actual or estimated receipts. This system applied to military or factory messes and stores and eating places of welfare institutions. Since the IGE law exempted sales made by such establishments from IGE, the payment of IGE by fixed annual amount remains in force only for the receipts obtained as premiums by mutual associations providing cattle insurance. The tax on premiums for cattle insured in 1960 amounted to L. 15 for each head of cattle insured.[198]

---

[196] L. 16 December 1959, n. 1070, art. 5.

[197] L. 16 December 1959, n. 1070, art. 5. Under the fourth paragraph of this article, taxpayers who wished to avail themselves of the method of a single annual payment of the aggregate tax due on actual receipts were required to file, within the month of January 1960, a declaration that they would follow this method for 1960 and subsequent years. However, this requirement apparently does not preclude later choices of this method or of the method of payment by annual fee. See R.M. 27 December 1960, n. 58/65240.

[198] D.M. 14 December 1959, art. 5.

14/7.5 Rules Regarding Books and Records

To ensure the assessment and collection of the tax, the law provides a number of rules regarding the keeping of books and records by taxpayers. These rules are listed below (IGE arts. 26, 27; IGE Reg. arts. 112-114).

1. Preservation for five years of books, registers, counterfoil books, and other documents prescribed for purposes of payment of IGE (14/7.2b). In some cases, the Minister of Finance may, at the request of the person concerned, consent to the destruction of counterfoil books before the expiration of the five-year term.
2. Progressive numeration for each calendar year of the obligatory documents and their copies, in all cases by those who issue them, and by merchants or manufacturers who receive them.
3. Presentation of the prescribed books and records at the Registry Office for numbering before use.
4. Production of the required documents for purposes of proving the payment of the tax. In particular, anyone who keeps in his store or warehouse merchandise not produced by him must, at the request of the competent Office, be able to prove the payment of the tax. Wholesalers must prove by the production of the corresponding invoice the payment of the tax on sales of merchandise which, in relation to merchandise purchased, does not appear on the premises of the firm. The absence of such proof creates the legal presumption that the merchandise not to be found on the premises has been sold without the payment of the tax. The documents must be produced directly at the request of the competent authority; documents produced at a later time have no effect as evidence of payment.

Judges, functionaries, and other public officials are prohibited from issuing measures, carrying out legalizations, authentications, and other acts relative to documents which violate the IGE law or relative to transactions occasioning receipts for which IGE has not been paid (IGE art. 29). Recorders, secretaries, attorneys, notaries, archivists, tax consultants, agents of the tax administration, arbiters, experts, judicial employees, ushers, bailiffs, and messengers are forbidden to perform any functions involving invoices, bills, receipts, or other documents which contravene the IGE law (IGE art. 29).

Notaries may not issue copies and abstracts of documents unless a copy of the document or of the original book, register, or counterfoil book on which the tax has been lawfully paid has been produced before them (IGE Reg. art. 115).

14/8. International Aspects

14/8.1 Territoriality

IGE applies only to payments for the transfer of goods, or the rendition of services, carried out in Italy (IGE art. 1). If a receipt constitutes payment for the transfer of goods or the rendition of services outside

Italy, it is not subject to IGE even if payment is made in Italy. Where the agreement on which the receipt is based was concluded and where the payment is received are irrelevant.

National territory for purposes of IGE is coextensive with the area of Italy for customs purposes. Hence the receipts obtained for transfer of goods and services effected in the buildings of foreign embassies and other diplomatic representations are subject to IGE.[199]

Amounts due to foreign firms for the utilization of patents in Italy are subject to IGE because the service rendered by the foreign firm is performed where the utilization of the patent takes place.[200] On the other hand, commissions paid to foreign agents for transactions concluded by them abroad on behalf of Italian export firms do not come within the scope of the application of IGE, because the services of such agents are performed outside Italy.[201] However, commissions received by agents of foreign firms for services rendered in Italy are subject to IGE, even if the agents have no possibility of recovering the tax from the firms.[202]

14/8.2 Exemption of Export Sales

a. DIRECT EXPORTS. Receipts obtained from the exportation of raw materials, merchandise, and products, and for freights and other payments relative to international services, are excluded from IGE (IGE art. 1(h)). The export invoices are subject to the regular stamp tax (4/4.2). The exporter must give evidence of the exportation by means of a customs bill or a copy of the exporter's invoice issued to the foreign buyer, duly signed by the Customs Office (IGE Reg. art. 106). By international services are meant those which take place between the Italian and foreign territories.[203] Commissions received by agents and intermediaries carrying on their activities in Italy on behalf of foreign enterprises are not considered receipts from international services and are therefore subject to tax.[204] Also among the articles excluded from the tax are sales of ship's stores necessary for a voyage abroad.[205]

b. INDIRECT EXPORTS. If one Italian businessman buys merchandise from another in order to sell it abroad, the transaction is excluded from IGE provided that the merchandise is shipped by the seller directly abroad or the seller stores it in a deposit or free zone (*punto franco*) in

---

[199] Romani, *L'entrata imponibile nel sistema dell'IGE* 329-331.

[200] R.M. 9 May 1951, n. 65214, and R.M. 19 May 1953, n. 78985.

[201] R.M. 13 February 1952, n. 62222.

[202] R.M. 7 October 1953, n. 81660. For other examples see Mandò, *Imposta generale sull'entrata* 339-344.

[203] C.M. 12 May 1959, n. 19/248699.

[204] C. M. 12 May 1959, n. 19/248699. See, however, Cass., Sez. I, 21 December 1962, n. 3401.

[205] See Mandò, *Imposta generale sull'entrata* 445-447. For the list of ship's stores, see I.M. 1 August 1940, n. 91915; see also Mandò 20-22, n. 2.

Italy or in premises or storehouses of a Customs Office. Evidence of the exportation must be shown by an attestation placed by the competent Customs Office on the copy of the invoice issued to the purchaser by the seller. The copies of the invoice are subject to the stamp tax (IGE art. 21) (4/4.2). In cases of exportation by parcel post, the attestation is issued by the post office from which the parcel is sent abroad (IGE art. 21).

14/8.3   Refund of IGE on Exported Products

The refund of IGE on exported products is a measure designed to promote export of Italian products by returning IGE paid at earlier stages and thus placing exported products on an equal footing with foreign goods in foreign markets. It was introduced in 1954 with the equalization tax on imported products (14/8.5).[206] The right to the refund is enjoyed by all businessmen, domestic or foreign, exporting articles specified in the classification table.[207] The refund is not limited to Italian exporters, but is available also to representatives and branches of foreign firms carrying on in Italy the export of Italian products.[208] The refund is granted on the basis of the actual sale price of the merchandise as shown in the copy of the invoice to be submitted at the Customs Office.[209] The decrees specifying the classes of goods for which IGE is to be refunded also specify the rates at which the refunded tax is computed. In general, these rates correspond to the rates of the import equalization tax (14/8.5) which is applied to products of the same kind on importation. The tax refunded is computed at the rate applicable to the merchandise. Therefore, the tax on the value of the crating or containers is reimbursed at the same rate as the merchandise itself, even if ordinarily subject to IGE at a different rate. No refund is allowed for the packing if the merchandise is excluded from the benefit of refund. Accessory expenses such as insurance or freight are not included in the sale price. The refund is made on the value of the merchandise as specified in the invoice net of any discount.[210] If the price is stated in foreign currency, it is converted

206 L. 31 July 1954, n. 470, amended by L. 9 November 1961, n. 1233, has since been followed by D.P. 14 August 1954, n. 676 (containing tables of industrial products concerned); D.P. 27 February 1955, n. 192 (implementing the previous decree); L. 26 June 1959, n. 487 (regulating the taxation of vegetables and fruits); L. 7 July 1960, n. 633 (delegating to the government the power to issue decree-laws in the matter in question); D.P. 22 July 1960, n. 794; D.P. 23 August 1960, n. 905; D.P. 31 August 1960, n. 909 (the decrees specifying rates). More recently, new rates have been established by D.P.R. 10 February 1962, n. 15, issued under the delegation of authority granted by L. 25 January 1962, n. 3.

207 See D.P. 14 August 1954, n. 676, Table A, Annex, and D.M. 18 August 1954, n. 93782, Table.

208 R.M. 9 April 1955, n. 94525.

209 D.P. 27 February 1955, n. 192, art. 3.

210 R.M. 9 April 1955, n. 94525.

into Italian lire at the rate of exchange on the day on which the exports are cleared through customs. If the exported products have been made from raw materials imported temporarily, the amount of IGE refunded at exportation of these products is reduced by the amount of IGE applicable to the foreign materials admitted on their bills of temporary importation.[211]

14/8.4 Taxation of Imports

a. IMPORTED MERCHANDISE. Imported merchandise which would be subject to IGE if produced in Italy is subject to a corresponding tax at the moment of importation (IGE art. 17). The purpose of this corresponding tax is to impose on imported goods the same tax as is imposed on a single sale of similar domestic goods. The tax is not a customs duty; it is imposed because of the objective fact of importation and is not conditioned on any transfer of goods within the national territory.[212] Receipts resulting subsequently from transactions carried out in Italy with respect to the imported merchandise are subject to IGE (IGE art. 17).

The tax on imported merchandise is applied and collected directly by the Customs Office when the merchandise is declared (IGE art. 17). The tax is paid by the person clearing the merchandise at customs, whether or not he is the owner of the merchandise. The rate is the same as the rate of IGE regularly provided for domestic merchandise of the same kind (14/6.2).[213] The basis for the application and collection is the customs declaration (4/8.4), which must contain the value or price of the merchandise. In cases of merchandise imported by parcel post, the value must appear on the customs declaration accompanying the parcel.

The tax base for IGE is the value of the imported merchandise, plus costs of freight, packing, and insurance, plus customs duties and all other fees, taxes, and surcharges due on the clearing of the merchandise. If the customs tariff provides an official value of the merchandise for customs purposes, that value is also used as the base for IGE. The Minister of Finance has the power to fix periodically the values of specified kinds of merchandise imported from abroad, and, in such cases, the tax is applied by customs officials exclusively on the basis of this value, increased by customs duties and all other duties, taxes, or surcharges due at the clearing of the merchandise (IGE art. 18; IGE Reg. art. 96).

Sales in Italy of foreign merchandise located abroad, in customs, or in transit through Italy, and not intended for import, are not subject to tax, provided that the invoice has been subjected to the stamp tax (4/4.2)

---

[211] L. 31 July 1954, n. 570, art. 3.

[212] Cass. 27 May 1952; Cass. 25 October 1951; Cass. 5 March 1951.

[213] L. 16 December 1959, n. 1070, art. 2, as modified by L. 31 October 1961, n. 1196, art. 2.

and bears a cancellation by a Registry or Customs Office showing that the sale preceded importation (IGE art. 17).[214] However, this exemption no longer applies to sales carried out in Italy by a firm operating in Italy,[215] including sales made by a foreign firm normally or occasionally carrying on its activity in Italy, or to sales made by a foreign firm through an intermediary to other firms operating in Italy, unless the intermediary is limited to promoting transactions later concluded directly by the foreign firm itself.[216]

b. TEMPORARY IMPORTS. In order to facilitate the import of raw materials and products which, after appropriate processing, are to be exported, the IGE law declares that merchandise admitted for temporary importation under the customs law (4/8.3)[217] enjoys similar treatment for purposes of IGE (IGE art. 19). The tax, assessed at the time of temporary importation, becomes due in whole or in part if the merchandise is not exported within the time limit fixed in the import license (*bolletta doganale*) for purposes of the customs duties. The Minister of Finance has the power to allow temporary importation of merchandise for purposes of IGE, independently of the customs procedure (IGE art. 19).

c. EXEMPT MERCHANDISE. The classes of imported merchandise listed below are exempt (IGE art. 20; IGE Reg. art. 105).

1. Merchandise imported directly by units of the state administration, including autonomous state enterprises (*aziende statali autonome*). Among the latter services are the state monopolies (4/6), the state railroads, post and telecommunications, forests, state highways (*Azienda Nazionale Autonoma delle Strade Statali*) (ANAS).[218]
2. Certain merchandise admitted free of customs duties under the provisions of the customs tariff (4/8.2).
3. Italian merchandise admitted for reimportation free of customs duties under the provisions of the customs law.
4. Italian merchandise admitted for reimportation under bills of temporary exportation.
5. The processing waste of foreign merchandise imported temporarily to be processed, insofar as it is calculable for purposes of the discharge of the temporary import license.
6. Cows, sheep, and pigs.
7. Wines (exclusive of sparkling wines) and grapes.

Among other merchandise exempt from IGE on importation are grain and grain products,[219] fresh and canned meat, and horses intended for

---

[214] As modified by L. 24 March 1959, n. 112.

[215] L. 16 August 1962, n. 1347.

[216] C.M. 9 November 1962, n. 72.

[217] L. 18 December 1913, n. 1453.

[218] This exemption is subject to a condition that the sale be made between the foreign seller and the unit of the administration and that the merchandise be forwarded to the address of the administration and cleared by the latter directly or through a forwarding agent (IGE Reg. art. 104).

[219] L. 24 December 1949, n. 941, art. 1.

ANALYSIS OF OTHER TAXES

immediate slaughtering,[220] and fabrics for the textile industry.[221] Special tax reliefs are also provided for import of materials for the shipbuilding industry.[222]

14/8.5 Equalization Tax on Imported Products

The general rule is that imported merchandise is subject to an import tax corresponding to IGE (14/8.4a). In addition, industrial products imported into Italy are subject to an equalization tax (*imposta di conguaglio*); [223] this tax applies to the same classes of goods that receive a refund of IGE if exported. The regular tax levied on importation (14/8.4a) represents only one stage. The equalization tax takes the place of the taxes which would have been imposed on the goods at earlier stages if these earlier stages had taken place in Italy, and thus is the counterpart of the export refund described at 14/8.3. Another purpose of the equalization tax is to provide the Treasury with the funds necessary for the refund of IGE on exported goods. With this tax and the export refund, Italy follows the principle of taxation at destination, now generally adopted for indirect taxes by the Common Market.[224]

The equalization tax is due from anyone importing products, not only Italian import firms, but also representatives and branch offices of foreign firms importing foreign products in Italy. The taxable transaction is the importation of merchandise subject to the tax. The tax base is the price of the merchandise, not including the amount of IGE paid at the importation stage (14/8.4a), but including charges for packaging (taxed at the same rate as the merchandise itself), customs duties, and any other duty or fee that may be payable at the clearing of the merchandise. The tax is applied and collected directly at the time of clearing the merchandise, according to the method and criteria prescribed for the tax on imports (IGE Reg. arts. 102, 103). The rules on assessment, payment, and penalties for the IGE on imports are also applicable to the equalization tax. The exemptions provided by article 20 of the IGE law also hold for the equalization tax. However, exemptions envisaged by special laws normally do not apply.[225] The rates of the equalization tax originally varied from 1% to 4%, being equal to the rates of IGE which would have been paid on the goods in question if they had been produced in Italy. They are also the same as the refund rates for the same products

---

[220] L. 4 February 1956, n. 33, art. 6.

[221] L. 12 August 1957, n. 757, art. 9.

[222] L. 17 July 1954, n. 522. See 14/4.6b.

[223] L. 31 July 1954, n. 570. This Italian tax is similar to the German *Ausgleichsteuer* (WTS: *Germany*, 16/9.3a).

[224] Treaty of Rome (The Common Market Treaty), concluded 27 March 1957, arts. 95-99; 3 *United Nations Treaty Series* 298 (1958).

[225] L. 31 July 1954, n. 570; R.M. 9 April 1955, n. 94525.

on export (14/8.3).[226] The rates were subsequently raised, in some cases to 8%. The highest rates have been recently reduced from 8% and 7.5% to 6.5%, from 7% to 6.25%, from 6.5% to 6%, from 6% to 5.5%, and from 5.5% to 5.25%.[227]

Building materials, machines, and other things needed for the first installation, enlargement, or modernization of industrial factories in the south, if imported from abroad, are exempt from the equalization tax during the period in which the Fund for the South (10/6.2, 14/4.6k) operates.[228]

14/9. Penalties

14/9.1 In General

The general principles relating to penalties for violation of fiscal laws are governed by a special law of 1929.[229] The particular tax laws in turn establish penalties for the nonobservance of the duties relating to each tax. The basic IGE law regulates the system of penalties according to the general principles of the law of 1929, with certain exceptions (IGE arts. 30-42). These original articles have undergone certain modifications since 1940.[230]

Penalties for the violation of the laws governing IGE can be classed as civil, criminal, and special.

14/9.2 Civil Penalties

a. PENALTIES OF GENERAL CHARACTER. Civil penalties (*sanzioni di carattere civile*) are imposed in the form of pecuniary penalties or surcharges (IGE arts. 30, 31). The most important of these are listed below.

1. A pecuniary penalty of from two to eight times the tax due if the transaction subject to IGE lacks the prescribed document.
2. A pecuniary penalty of from two to six times the tax due if a document prescribed for the application of IGE has wholly or partially escaped tax.
3. A pecuniary penalty of from two to six times the tax due for failure to comply with the provisions of the regulations in cases of transfers on approval, on consignment, for purposes of processing, and in cases of transfer through commercial auxiliaries. In cases of violations of minor

---

[226] See D.P. 14 August 1954, n. 676, Table, Annex B.

[227] D.P.R. 10 February 1962, n. 15, issued under the delegation of authority granted by L. 25 January 1962, n. 3.

[228] L. 29 July 1957, n. 634, art. 29, as modified by L. 29 September 1962, n. 1462, art. 14.

[229] L. 7 January 1929, n. 4. See 13/7.1. See also Stammati, *L'imposta generale sull'entrata* 275-278; Lampis, *Le norme per la repressione delle violazioni delle leggi finanziarie;* Spinelli, *Le preleggi penali finanziarie;* Spinelli, *La repressione delle violazioni delle leggi finanziarie.*

[230] See R.D.L. 3 June 1943, n. 452, arts. 19-22; D.L.L. 19 October 1944, n. 348; D.L.C.P.S. 5 October 1947, n. 1208 (fixing new amounts of pecuniary penalties and fines in connection with monetary devaluation).

importance, the pecuniary penalty is not less than one tenth and not more than one half of the tax due.

4. A pecuniary penalty from L. 300 to L. 1,200 is imposed on judges, public functionaries, officials, attorneys, and consultants who, in carrying out their functions, make use of documents not properly taxed (14/7.5).
5. A pecuniary penalty of from L. 25 to L. 100 is imposed for each document not preserved in accordance with article 26 of the IGE law (14/7.5).

If the tax is paid after the due date, but before the ascertainment of one of the violations specified in items 1-3, the pecuniary penalties for these violations are replaced by a surcharge of one tenth of the tax (IGE art. 30). If the rules regarding registration of transfers or merchandise on approval, on consignment, or for processing have been observed, the failure to observe other rules applicable to such transfers is subject to a pecuniary penalty of from one tenth to one half of the tax instead of the penalties described in items 1-3 above (IGE art. 31).

If there has been improper application or cancellation of stamps, a pecuniary penalty of from one twentieth to one tenth of the tax amount improperly paid is imposed (IGE art. 30).

A pecuniary penalty of from L. 1,000 to L. 40,000 is imposed for failure to file or late filing of the statement prescribed by the decrees introducing payment by annual fee (14/7.3). In addition, a surcharge equal to the amount of tax due is imposed. However, this may be reduced to one tenth of the tax due if the statement is filed within 90 days of its due date. A pecuniary penalty of from L. 200 to L. 40,000 is imposed if any of the statements required proves to be false. To this is added a surcharge of one half of the tax amount not paid to the Treasury.[231] These sanctions are not applied when the controversy on the assessment is settled by "agreement" (*concordato*) (14/7.3e).

A pecuniary penalty of from L. 25 to L. 500 is imposed for any violation of the law or regulations for which a penalty is not explicitly provided.

b. SPECIAL PENALTIES FOR VIOLATIONS OF THE RULES ON POSTAL CURRENT ACCOUNTS. The penalties listed below are provided for violations of the rules regarding postal current accounts (IGE art. 35).

1. A pecuniary penalty of from one tenth to one half of the tax improperly paid, for payment of the tax by stamps instead of by postal current account or postal draft (*postagiro*).
2. The same penalty is provided for splitting a taxable receipt in order to make payment of tax by stamps.
3. A pecuniary penalty of from one twentieth to one fourth of the tax improperly paid, for payment of the tax by means of direct payment (*in modo virtuale*) to the post office instead by draft on the taxpayer's postal current account.

---

[231] D.L.L. 19 October 1944, n. 348, art. 13.

4. A pecuniary penalty of from one half to the whole of the tax due, for failure to open a postal current account or for the late opening thereof and the consequent failure to make or lateness of the required deposit.

5. A pecuniary penalty of from one half to the whole of the tax due, for omitted or late restoration of a deposit reduced below the limit fixed by the law.

C. SPECIAL PENALTIES FOR VIOLATIONS OF THE RULES ON PAYMENT BY ANNUAL FEE. The penalties listed below are provided for violations of the rules regarding payment by annual fee (*abbonamento*) or other methods of direct payment (*in modo virtuale*) (14/7.3).

1. A pecuniary penalty of from one tenth to one half of the tax improperly paid, for payment by stamps or postal current account instead of by direct payment (IGE art. 37).

2. A pecuniary penalty of from L. 500 to L. 5,000, for failure to file declarations and statements, or for the late filing thereof (IGE art. 37).

3. A surcharge equal to one tenth of the tax due, for failure to pay or late payment of the tax. In case of late payment of the tax by installments, the surcharge is measured on the amount of the installment due and not paid, and the taxpayer loses the privilege of paying in installments,

4. A pecuniary penalty of from L. 1,000 to L. 10,000, for failure to file, within the prescribed term, the annual statement by a taxpayer who has chosen to pay IGE to the Registry Office in a single annual payment rather than by annual fee. In addition, a pecuniary penalty of from two to six times the amount of the tax evaded, is imposed for total or partial failure to pay the tax.[232]

14/9.3 Criminal Penalties

a. PENALTIES OF GENERAL CHARACTER. The criminal penalties (13/7.1) provided for violations of the IGE law are listed below (IGE art. 32).

1. A fine (*ammenda*) of from three to nine times the tax due, if the document drawn up for the application of the tax specifies an amount lower than that of the actual receipt. (In addition, a surcharge equal to the tax due must be paid.) The same penalties are applied if, in the case of direct payment (*in modo virtuale*) or on the basis of a document, a receipt lower than that actually obtained has been declared.

2. A fine of from L. 1,000 to L. 10,000 is imposed on a taxpayer who refuses to submit his books and records to competent tax authorities.

In all cases, the tax not paid remains due. Article 41 of the IGE law also incorporates Title 9 of the stamp tax law,[233] which provides penalties for forgery, sale, and reuse of stamps. Irrespective of the penalty for forgery contained in the Penal Code, the person who renews stamps previously used or keeps or uses such stamps is punishable by imprisonment for up to one year.

---

[232] L. 16 December 1959, n. 1070, art. 7.
[233] D.P. 25 June 1953, n. 492 (4/4.1).

b. SPECIAL PENALTIES FOR VIOLATIONS OF THE RULES GOVERNING THE IM-
PORT TAXES. If a value lower than that assessed by the customs is declared for imported merchandise (14/8.4, 14/8.5), a fine is imposed of
from one half to double the amount of tax due on the difference between
the value assessed and the value declared. The same penalty is applied
for the incorrect declaration of the kind or quantity of the merchandise
subjected to the tax on the basis of an official value. In the case of insufficient payment of the tax due on imported merchandise, a fine is
imposed of from two to six times the amount of the deficiency. A violation of the law on IGE connected with a corresponding violation of the
customs law which is of a criminal nature is considered a crime and is
punishable by a mulct (*multa*) of from two to ten times the amount of
the tax evaded (IGE art. 33).

C. SPECIAL PENALTIES FOR VIOLATIONS OF THE RULES ON POSTAL CURRENT
ACCOUNTS. Whoever, in order to avoid payment of IGE, falsely declares
on the prescribed document that he has paid the tax is punishable by
payment of a mulct of up to L. 30,000, irrespective of other penalties
provided by the Penal Code and by the IGE law (IGE art. 36).

14/9.4   Special Penalties for Serious or Habitual Violations

In cases of violations of exceptional gravity or habitual violations, the
Intendant of Finance may, without prejudice to other sanctions, order
the closing of a business for a period of from three days to one month,
or, in the case of an itinerant commercial activity, may order the withdrawal of the license (IGE art. 40).[234] The decision, supported by
reasons, is forwarded immediately to the offender, who may appeal to the
Minister of Finance within five days of the notice of the decision. The
appeal suspends the execution of the decision. The decision of the
Minister of Finance is not subject to appeal or complaint. The order of
closing may be revoked by the Intendant of Finance upon the request
of the taxpayer if the latter deposits a sum fixed by the Intendant as a
guarantee of the payment of the tax due, the related penalties, and the
cost of the dispute. The order of closing may also be revoked by the
Intendant ex officio.

14/10.   Time Limits

14/10.1   Collection of Tax and Penalties

The right of the state to collect IGE and corresponding surcharges expires after 10 years (IGE art. 45). The time limit for collecting taxes

---

[234] The application of this penalty is governed by L. 7 January 1929, n. 4 (see
13/7.1).

arising from imported goods and the equalization tax is five years (IGE art. 47).[235]

The IGE law leaves in effect the two provisions on time limits contained in the general law on tax violations (13/7.1), namely, the time limit of five years for the collection of pecuniary penalties, running from the date of the commission of the fiscal violation, and the time limit of three years for the prosecution of the lesser offenses known as "contraventions" (*contravvenzioni*); the latter period also applies to the right of collection of the corresponding fine.[236] Under the provisions of the Penal Code, an offense for which the law provides a mulct is subject to a five-year limitation (CP art. 27).

From the general provisions governing the duty of the taxpayer to pay the tax and the right of the state to collect the tax (IGE art. 1; IGE Reg. art. 8), it follows that the time limits for collection begin to run in accordance with the rules described below.

1. For receipts obtained by the rendition of services, from the day on which the payment was received, since the duty to pay the tax arises at that time.
2. For receipts obtained for the sale of merchandise, from the day of consignment or shipment of the merchandise; or from the day of total or partial payment if this precedes delivery or shipment of merchandise; or, finally, from the day of the issuance of the document of sale if the issuance took place before the delivery or shipment of merchandise.

In cases where IGE is paid annually or in installments (14/7.3), the time limit begins to run from the due date of the payment or installment, since the right of the state to collect the tax accrues at that time. If the taxpayer is required to file a return and fails to do so, the period of limitation runs from the day on which the return should have been filed.[237]

The interruption and suspension of the limitation period are regulated by the general rules of the Civil Code (CC arts. 2941-2944). The corresponding rules of the Penal Code (CP arts. 157-161) govern the question of interruption and suspension in the case of amounts due because of violations constituting crimes and other criminal offenses.

In general, the interruption of the limitation period occurs on the serving of a payment injunction on the party or the commencement of administrative or judicial action to obtain payment of the tax due on the initiation of criminal proceedings, or on the serving of the notice of a pecuniary penalty by the Intendant of Finance.

---

[235] By virtue of reference to the customs law, L. 25 September 1940, n. 1424, art. 27.
[236] L. 7 January 1929, n. 4, arts. 7, 17.
[237] See Stammati, *L'imposta generale sull'entrata* 272-273.

14/10.2   Refunds

If the taxpayer has paid tax in excess of the amount due, he has a time limit of one year from payment within which to seek a refund (14/7.2c). However, in cases of payment by stamps no refund is allowed. If the taxpayer paying by annual fee terminates his business activity before the end of the year, he is entitled to a credit or refund for the excess tax paid. The action must be commenced within one year of the date of the taxpayer's receipt from the Registry Office of the notice of the credit for the excess tax paid (IGE art. 47). This time limit applies only to the administrative assertion of the claim and does not prejudice judicial action by the taxpayer to contest the existence of the tax obligation as such (14/7.3f).[238]

---

[238] Cass. 7 November 1957, n. 4259; compare App. Genova 11 June 1952.

CHAPTER 15

THE REGISTRATION TAX

15/1. **Introduction**
    15/1.1   In General
    15/1.2   Historical Background

15/2. **Persons Subject to the Tax**
    15/2.1   Nonjudicial Acts
    15/2.2   Judicial Acts
    15/2.3   Liability of Notaries and Public Officials

15/3. **Taxable Transactions**
    15/3.1   Written Acts
    15/3.2   The Principle of Economic Reality
    15/3.3   Determination of Taxable Transactions
        a. In general
        b. Acts with several provisions
        c. Partly gratuitous contracts
        d. Transfers of enterprises
        e. Appurtenances
        f. Acts with suspensive conditions
        g. Partition of common property
        h. Exchange or barter
        i. *Appalto* and sale
        j. Agreement to forbear or discontinue litigation
        k. Cancellation of contract
        l. Void acts

    15/3.4   *De Facto* Transfers
        a. General presumptions
        b. Transfers of business enterprises
        c. Transfers resulting from *appalti* and concessions to carry on public services
    15/3.5   Oral Agreements

15/4. Exemptions and Reductions

    15/4.1   In General

    15/4.2   Acts Completely Exempt from Registration

    15/4.3   Acts Subject to Gratuitous Registration

    15/4.4   Acts Subject to Registration and Tax in Case of Use

    15/4.5   Reductions of Tax

        a. In general

        b. Fixed fees

        c. Reduced tax rates

15/5. Valuation

    15/5.1   In General

    15/5.2   Immovables

    15/5.3   Movables

15/6. Tax Rates

    15/6.1   In General

    15/6.2   Progressive Rates

    15/6.3   Proportional Rates

        a. In general

        b. Transfers of immovables

        c. Transfers of movables

        d. Leases of movables or immovables

        e. Rights to income, annuities, and pensions

        f. Obligations

        g. Miscellaneous contracts

        h. Organization, reorganization, and dissolution of business

    15/6.4   Graduated Rates

    15/6.5   Fixed Fees

15/7. Assessment and Collection

    15/7.1   Assessment

    15/7.2   Payment

        a. General conditions

        b. Refunds

        c. Registration on account

15/8. Penalties

    15/8.1 In General
    15/8.2 Surcharges
    15/8.3 Pecuniary Penalties
    15/8.4 Fines

15/9. Time Limits

    15/9.1 Refunds
    15/9.2 Collection
    15/9.3 Interruption of the Limitation Periods

15/10. Protests and Appeals

15/11. International Aspects

    15/11.1 Transactions Executed Abroad
    15/11.2 Transactions Involving Property Located Abroad or
            Activities Carried on Abroad

15/1. Introduction

15/1.1 In General

Registration taxes (*tasse di registro* or *imposte di registro*) are, in general, levies imposed and collected by the state at the time of the registration of a large variety of acts and transactions (*atti*). These acts and transactions include transfers of property and property rights and, in general, any document intended to produce legal effects, such as a private, civil, or commercial agreement, a judicial or extrajudicial document, or an oral agreement concerning the lease, sublease, or rental of immovable property. The institution of registration, that is, entry in a public register, serves to certify the legal existence of acts and transactions in general, and to certify the date of private writings with respect to third parties.[1]

The institution of registration and the levy connected with it have been known since ancient times.[2] At first, registration was a public service under which the state offered its citizens protection against forgeries of private deeds, particularly conveyances, and public documents; the documents were registered and deposited in special offices and special fees were collected. Eventually, with the consolidation of the state's authority and the increase in its financial needs, registration became a fiscal instrument and a source of revenue for the state. This development

---

[1] R.D. 30 December 1923, n. 3269, art. 1; this 1923 decree is the basic registration tax law and will hereinafter be cited "LR."

[2] On the historical evolution of the registration taxes, see 1 Uckmar, *La legge del registro* 7-44; Rastello, *Il tributo di registro* 12-19.

ANALYSIS OF OTHER TAXES   762

is still reflected in discussions concerning the nature of the registration tax, namely, whether it is a fee (tassa) or a tax pure and simple (imposta). Although the basic law of 1923 uses tassa, imposta is found in most of the subsequent legislation, and the majority of writers on the subject have agreed in using it.[3]

As a fiscal tool, however, the registration tax has not proved especially significant; its yield was L. 93,000 million, or 3.2% of total state revenues, in the fiscal year 1959-1960.[4] Nevertheless, because of its juridical aspects, it has received much attention in the doctrine and in decisions.[5]

15/I.2 Historical Background

The first registration law of the unified Italian state was enacted in 1862 [6] and, although modeled on a law of the French Revolution, took into account previously existing legislation of the various Italian states.[7] The law of 1862 introduced the principle of taxation according to the nature of a transaction rather than according to its apparent form; it also distinguished between a fixed and a proportional levy. After several modifications by special laws, a Testo unico, which included the inheritance tax within its scope, was approved in 1897.[8] Regulations [9] were enacted in the same year and, despite subsequent legislative modifications, continue in force today.

The Testo unico of 1897 underwent a large number of modifications until 1923. At this time, there was an over-all reform of taxation in Italy, and the registration law was brought up to date by a royal decree [10] which is still the basic law on the subject. The 1923 law excluded from its discipline the inheritance tax, for which a separate law was enacted (3/4).[11]

Since 1923, however, there have been more than 300 legislative modifications of the law.[12] The duty of registration was extended to oral

---

[3] See 1 Uckmar, La legge del registro 60; Berliri, Principi di diritto tributario 206 et seq. Some authors hold that the registration tax has the character of both fee and tax; see Graziani, Istituzioni di scienza delle finanze 260-261; Griziotti, Primi elementi di scienza delle finanze 122. Rastello calls the tax tributo (Il tributo di registro).

[4] Berliri, Le imposte di bollo e di registro 61. See also 1/6.8d.

[5] See 1 Jammarino, Commento alla legge sulle imposte di registro 3-4.

[6] L. 21 April 1862, n. 585.

[7] Law of 22 Frimaire VII (12 December 1798). See 1 Uckmar, La legge del registro 23 et seq.; Rastello, Il tributo di registro 15 et seq.

[8] R.D. 20 May 1897, n. 217.

[9] R.D. 23 December 1897, n. 549; this decree will hereinafter be cited "Reg. R."

[10] R.D. 30 December 1923, n. 3269; see note 1 supra.

[11] R.D. 30 December 1923, n. 3270.

[12] For a list of the laws passed between 1923 and 1957, see 1 Uckmar, La legge del registro 33-44. See also Stammati, Armani, and Ceccarelli, Codice della imposta di registro, which contains a chronological list of all laws and decrees relating to the registration tax.

contracts for the performance of work or services (*appalto*),[13] and criteria were established to distinguish between *appalto* and sale (15/3.3i).[14] The taxation of the transfer of immovables was changed from proportional to progressive in 1943,[15] and subsequently reverted to proportional following World War II.[16] The penalties for violations of the tax duty were increased in 1947.[17] A general revision of the levy, beginning in 1952, has brought about reductions in the rates of the tax, especially for transfers of immovables, *appalti*, loans, sales of ships, and industrial establishments.[18] These modifications are some of the most important ones occurring in the last 40 years.

15/2. Persons Subject to the Tax

15/2.1 Nonjudicial Acts

All contracting parties (*le parti contraenti*), and those in whose interest registration is requested, are jointly and severally liable for the payment of the registration tax due on transactions subject to registration within a fixed time limit (civil acts and contracts) (15/3.1), on those oral agreements which are subject to registration, and on taxable transactions concluded abroad (LR art. 93). Although the law contains no express provision, the same rule applies to gratuitous transfers inter vivos.[19]

Judicial decisions have interpreted the term "contracting parties" to include as persons jointly and severally liable for payment of the tax agents and representatives participating at the conclusion of the transaction.[20] It has also been held by the Supreme Court of Cassation, on the principle of the indivisibility of registration,[21] that even if one act contains several transactions which are distinct from each other in nature and which have different parties, all of the persons concerned are jointly and

---

[13] R.D.L. 15 November 1937, n. 1924.

[14] L. 19 July 1941, n. 771.

[15] L. 19 August 1943, n. 737.

[16] D.L.L. 5 April 1945, n. 141.

[17] D.L.C.P.S. 5 October 1947, n. 1208.

[18] L. 4 April 1953, n. 216; L. 6 August 1954, n. 603; L. 27 May 1959, n. 355.

[19] See 3 Uckmar, *La legge del registro* 99; Berliri, *Le leggi di registro* 443; Rastello, *Il tributo di registro* 166; Guglielmi and Azzariti, *Le imposte di registro* 46-47.

[20] See Cass. 13 January 1928 (Stammati, Armani, and Ceccarelli, *Codice della imposta di registro* 474); Cass., Sez. III, 14 January 1933 (Stammati, Armani, and Ceccarelli, *Codice della imposta di registro* 475). For criticism of the latter decision, see Vanoni, "Sulla presunta responsabilità del mandatario per la tassa di registro," *Foro it.*, 1933, I, 1798. See also Cass., Sez. un., 23 January 1956, n. 202 (*Foro it.*, 1956, I, 515); Comm. Centr. 15 July 1944, n. 63775 (*Riv. leg. fisc.*, 1955, 66). Contra, see Giannini, *Istituzioni di diritto tributario* 398-399; Berliri, *Le leggi di registro* 446; 3 Uckmar, *La legge del registro* 100. But see Rastello, *Il tributo di registro* 171-172, for the opinion that, in the case of an agency without representation, the agent is a contracting party.

[21] See Rastello, *Il tributo di registro* 121.

ANALYSIS OF OTHER TAXES   764

severally liable for submitting the act for registration and for paying the tax on all of the transactions.[22]

The notion of persons interested in registration is not limited to the contracting parties, but includes anyone who has requested registration and whose name must therefore be indicated in the registration record (LR art. 73). Any such person is liable for payment of the tax (LR art. 93).[23]

With respect to acts subject to registration only in case of use (15/4.4), the law does not state explicitly the person from whom the tax is due. The generally accepted interpretation, however, is that the tax is due only from the persons who request registration.[24]

In addition, the rules listed below apply to particular nonjudicial acts (LR art. 93).

1. Payment of taxes on acts which are subject to suspensive conditions, and thus become operative only on the fulfillment of the condition or the execution of the contract, is due not only from the contracting parties but also from all persons who benefit by the fulfillment of the condition or execution of the contract.
2. Payment of taxes on the merger of usufruct (9/4.1) with bare ownership of the estate (see 3/4.3b) is due from those who effect the merger, and from their heirs and other successors in title (*aventi causa*).
3. The payment of succession taxes (3/4) and mortgage taxes (4/3.3) on testaments and acts of last will is due from heirs, legatees, their guardians, custodians, administrators of the estate, and testamentary executors, since testaments are registrable only after the testator's death.

15/2.2   Judicial Acts

The persons listed below are liable for payment of taxes on judicial acts resulting from litigation (LR art. 93).

1. The parties to the suit (*parti istanti*) and those who make use of acts subject to registration.
2. Attorneys (*procuratori*) of such parties.
3. The parties charged with the costs of the proceedings.

The parties to the suit and those who make use of acts subject to registration are liable for payment not only of the taxes due on judicial acts as such (judicial fees, *tasse giudiziali*), but also of taxes applying to acts and contracts recorded in the judicial acts (title fees, *imposte*

---

[22] Cass., Sez. I, 5 December 1934 (Stammati, Armani, and Ceccarelli, *Codice della imposta di registro* 476). Comm. Centr., Sez. V, 23 March 1953, n. 46183 (*Giur. imp. dir.*, 1953, 521). See also Berliri, *Le leggi di registro* 449-450; Rastello, *Il tributo di registro* 170; but see Giannini, *Istituzioni di diritto tributario* 399-400.

[23] Cass., Sez. I, 17 April 1944, n. 260 (Stammati, Armani, and Ceccarelli, *Codice della imposta di registro* 478).

[24] 3 Uckmar, *La legge del registro* 105-106; Berliri, *Le leggi di registro* 445, 448; Giannini, *Istituzioni di diritto tributario* 400. *Contra*, Guglielmi and Azzariti, *Le imposte di registro* 59-60.

(*tasse*) *di titolo*). Attorneys are liable only for payment of judicial fees.[25] The taxes applied to decrees and orders enforcing arbitral awards and foreign judgments are due from the parties who requested the decrees or orders, and from their attorneys (LR art. 93). Payment of taxes on judicial acts having business contents is due from the respective court official (recorder, *cancelliere*) (LR arts. 80, 93; Reg. R. art. 14).

15/2.3 Liability of Notaries and Public Officials

In certain cases, the law, in order to facilitate collection, makes another person, along with the principal tax debtor, jointly and severally responsible for the satisfaction of the tax liability. Such a person, known in the doctrine as a *responsabile d'imposta*, after having paid the tax due from another, has the right of recovery against the latter.[26] Thus, the duty to request registration of acts and to provide for payment of the tax is incumbent upon notaries public for acts drawn up in the fulfillment of their office and for private documents authenticated by them; upon recorders for acts issued by judicial authority; upon judicial officials and bailiffs for acts issued by them; and upon public officials and representatives of the public administration for acts drawn up with their official participation (LR art. 80). All public officials and, in general, those who paid the tax for the person primarily liable enter into all rights, actions, and preferences of the public administration and, in order to recover the sum paid, may obtain from the competent Magistrate (*Pretore*) an order of payment to be executed within 24 hours. In the execution of this order, it is no defense that the taxes paid were not due or were overpaid; the debtor may not appeal against the tax administration unless he proves that he has reimbursed those who paid the tax for him as *responsabili d'imposta*. The rules on subrogation, applied under the succession taxes (3/4.10f), are also applicable to the registration tax (LR art. 98).

15/3. Taxable Transactions

15/3.1 Written Acts

Unless expressly excluded or exempted by the law, the transactions subject to registration and the corresponding tax include all written acts

---

[25] Judicial fees (*tasse giudiziali*) are those applied to judicial decisions and acts specified in Schedule, Annex A, Part II, attached to the registration law. The title fees are those which, although collected on judgments, do not apply to the latter, but to the agreement resulting therefrom (LR art. 72).

[26] On the concept of the *responsabile d'imposta*, see Giannini, *Istituzioni di diritto tributario* 105-107; see also Pugliese, "I soggetti passivi dell'obbligazione tributaria nel diritto italiano," *Riv. it. sc. econ.*, 1935, 337 *et seq.* See also Rastello, *Il tributo di registro* 178-184; Guglielmi and Azzariti, *Le imposte di registro* 42-45.

entered into in Italy, in public [27] or private form, of civil or business content, of judicial or extrajudicial nature (LR art. 1). Transactions entered into abroad are subject to registration and tax if they contain transfers of property, of usufruct, use, or enjoyment of immovable property located in Italy, or if they establish servitudes, mortgages or other charges, or leases, subleases, renovations, or releases, assignments, reassignments, or resolutions of leases of immovable property located in Italy (LR art. 1).

Various more common written acts, subject to registration and tax within a fixed term, are specified in the Schedule, Annex A, attached to the law. The Schedule is divided into three parts; Part I deals with civil acts and contracts such as (1) "onerous" civil contracts—that is, contracts for good and valid consideration; (2) gratuitous civil contracts; (3) civil acts; (4) business acts and documents; (5) copies of private acts; and (6) certifications of signatures. Part II relates to judgments and other judicial acts and acts of court officials; Part III deals with gratuitous acts inter vivos.

The specification of acts in the Schedule is not exhaustive, and the law expressly provides for application by analogy. A transaction which is not specified by name in the Schedule is subject to the progressive, proportional, or graduated tax imposed on the act with which it has the greatest similarity in nature and effects (LR art. 8). Since fixed fees are not mentioned in this provision, they may not be applied by analogy, but refer only to acts expressly specified in the Schedule.[28]

15/3.2   The Principle of Economic Reality

The determination of the taxable event is governed by the civil law principle that, in interpreting a contract, the real intention of the parties should be ascertained without limiting the inquiry to the literal meaning of the words (CC art. 1362). Similarly, article 8 of the registration law provides that the tax is to be applied according to the intrinsic nature and effects of an act or transfer even if the apparent title or form of the act or transfer does not correspond to the nature and effects. This rule is directed against avoidance of the registration tax by taxpayers who attempt to disguise an economic transaction under the form of a legal act subject to a lower tax. Thus, in order to determine the category of acts to which a given act belongs, the tax authorities must refer to

---

[27] A public act (*atto pubblico*) is a document drawn up according to the prescribed rules, by a notary public or other official, the certification by a notary serving only to prove the authenticity of the signatures (CC arts. 2702-2707).

[28] See Cass. Roma 11 January 1899; see also 1 Uckmar, *La legge del registro* 199, n. 3.

the economic contents of the act rather than to its legal form.[29] However, proof that the apparent form of an act does not correspond to the substance and effects of the act may be derived only from the act itself and not from acts and elements extraneous to it.[30]

15/3.3 Determination of Taxable Transactions

a. IN GENERAL. Since in many cases it is difficult for the tax administration to prove that the transaction actually sought by the parties to a document differs from the one apparently embodied in the document ("relative simulation"), the law establishes certain legal presumptions by virtue of which an act concluded in a certain way and with certain provisions is considered to embody a transaction different from that suggested by the name of the act.[31] Such a presumption is found, for instance, in article 45 of the law which provides that an irrevocable agency (*mandato*) with a release from the duty to render an accounting is considered a transfer and is taxed on the effect which it produces with respect to the object of the agency (15/6.3g). Thus, for example, if A grants B an irrevocable agency to sell for his account immovable property, and exempts B from the duty to render an accounting, the law conclusively presumes that A has conveyed that property to B and hence subjects the apparent agency to the tax provided for a sale of immovable property.[32]

b. ACTS WITH SEVERAL PROVISIONS. If an act contains several provisions which are independent and not necessarily derived from each other, each provision is subject to tax as if it were a separate act. If, however, the provisions are, because of their intrinsic nature, necessarily connected and derived from one another, the act is taxed as if it contained only one provision, the one which occasions the higher tax (LR art.

---

[29] Cass. 19 July 1940; Cass. 16 June 1943; Trib. Milano 23 December 1954. See also Comm. Centr. 8 June 1953, n. 49073; Comm. Centr. 20 October 1954, n. 64558; 1 Jammarino, *Commento alla legge sulle imposte di registro* 30-32. *Contra,* Berliri, *Le leggi di registro* 150.

[30] Cass. 9 January 1947; Cass., Sez. I, 9 July 1949; Cass., Sez. I, 30 March 1951. See also Comm. Centr., Sez. un., 16 July 1952, n. 38978; Griziotti, "Il principio della realtà economica negli art. 8 e 68 della legge di registro," *RDFSF,* 1941, II, 202; Giannini, *Istituzioni di diritto tributario* 124-125, 382-383. On the controversy between the economic and legal interpretations of the "effects" contemplated by article 8 of the registration law, see Rastello, *Il tributo di registro* 258 *et seq.*; 1 Uckmar, *La legge del registro* 193-196.

[31] See Rastello, *Il tributo di registro* 282. On simulation, see CC art. 1414. "Absolute simulation" is the declaration of a nonexistent transaction. See Cordaro, *Dizionario del contribuente* 865-866.

[32] See Cass. 27 July 1933; Cass., Sez. un., 9 August 1934; 1 Jammarino, *Commento alla legge sulle imposte di registro* 389-391. The agencies contemplated by article 45 are those granted exclusively for the benefit of the agent. On the concept of agency (*mandato*), see CC arts. 1703-1730.

9).[33] Thus, for example, an obligation to pay a certain price or a receipt of price contained in the same act in which a transfer was stipulated is not subject to a separate tax (LR art. 43). In the case of judgments and decisions subject to a fixed fee, there is only one levy no matter how many provisions the given decision contains (LR art. 68).

c. PARTLY GRATUITOUS CONTRACTS. If a contract, either because of the agreement which it contains or because of the effects it produces, is partly gratuitous and partly for consideration, it is taxed as two separate contracts, one gratuitous, the other for consideration (LR art. 42).[34]

d. TRANSFERS OF ENTERPRISES. An act of transfer, for consideration, of ownership, usufruct, or other property right, covering both movables and immovables, is subject to the proportional tax established for transfers of immovables (15/6.3b) unless a particular price has been stipulated for the movables and these have not been made equivalent to immovables under the civil law (LR art. 46). This provision finds its application in cases of transfers of commercial enterprises, which encompass immovables, movables, credits, merchandise, and other property. For a long time, the tax administration and also the courts held that such transfers should be subject to the tax as transfers of immovables, even though separate prices were contemplated for each category of goods.[35] This position, which regarded a commercial enterprise as a unit (*universitas facti*), was overcome for the first time in 1926 in a decision of the Supreme Court of Cassation, which held that if separate prices were fixed for various items, the rate fixed for transfers of immovables should be applied only to the value of the immovables, whereas the other categories of goods should be taxed according to their nature (LR art. 46).[36] This modification is also applied in cases of

---

[33] On the question whether the word "provisions" (*disposizioni*) refers to the whole transaction or only to the elements thereof, see Rastello, *Il tributo di registro* 413-426; 1 Jammarino, *Commento alla legge sulle imposte di registro* 190-199, and cases and literature cited therein. The judicial decisions agree that it is not enough that the various parts of an act be connected economically or by the mere will of the parties; it is necessary that they be objectively and juridically inseparable. See, for example, Cass., Sez. I, 3 August 1936 (Stammati, Armani, and Ceccarelli, *Codice della imposta di registro* 42-43). See also Comm. Centr. 15 May 1939, n. 15751; Comm. Centr., Sez. IV, 17 February 1948, n. 95619 (Stammati, Armani, and Ceccarelli, *Codice della imposta di registro* 45).

[34] See 1 Jammarino, *Commento alla legge sulle imposte di registro* 291.

[35] See, for example, Cass. Roma 24 April 1922 (Stammati, Armani, and Ceccarelli, *Codice della imposta di registro* 195).

[36] Cass. 26 May 1926 (Stammati, Armani, and Ceccarelli, *Codice della imposta di registro* 196). See also Cass., Sez. I, 4 August 1936 (Stammati, Armani, and Ceccarelli, *Codice della imposta di registro* 198); Cass., Sez. I, 6 May 1958, n. 1480 (Cordaro, *Dizionario del contribuente* 779). See also 2 Uckmar, *La legge del registro*

mergers of companies.[37] If an act refers also to credits (*crediti*), their amount, if proved, is taxed according to rates fixed for transfers of credit (LR art. 46). The provisions of article 46 are designed to protect the Treasury against the intentional exaggeration of the price of movables or of the amount of credit in order to take advantage of the lower rates applicable to them.

e. APPURTENANCES. The law also makes a presumption on the much-debated question of whether appurtenances are transferred along with immovables. In the case of transfers of immovables for consideration, the appurtenances which are in the service of or for cultivation of the land are considered, for purposes of the registration tax, to be transferred to the purchaser of the immovable, even if the document of transfer expressly excludes them. To overcome this presumption, the purchaser must prove that he has obtained the appurtenances from others, or that they belong to others by virtue of a previously registered act (LR art. 47). A similar presumption applies to transfers or grants of land from which trees, hanging fruits, and buildings or plantings (*accessioni*) (CC art. 983) have been excluded (LR art. 47).

If movable goods considered under civil law to be "immovables by destination" are sold by a separate act to the purchaser of the immovable to which those movables were annexed, the tax is determined at the rate applicable to the transfer of immovables (LR art. 47) (15/6.3b). Since the Civil Code of 1942 does not contain the notion of "immovables by destination," differences of opinion have arisen as to whether this rule should still be applied.[38] In the absence of clear legislative regulation, the prevailing doctrine and judicial decisions follow the opinion that, as a result of the change in the terminology of the Civil Code from "immovables by destination" to "appurtenances," movable appurtenances of immovables should be taxed separately as movables.[39]

191-212; Rastello, *Il tributo di registro* 334; 1 Jammarino, *Commento alla legge sulle imposte di registro* 407-412.

[37] Cass. Roma 7 February 1928. See 2 Uckmar, *La legge del registro* 116.

[38] The term "immovables by destination," used in the registration tax law, was also used in article 407 of the Civil Code of 1865. In articles 817-819 of the Civil Code of 1942, it was replaced by "appurtenances" (*pertinenze*), defined as "things intended in a durable way to serve or embellish another thing."

[39] See Comm. Centr., Sez. VI, 23 June 1949, n. 4743; Comm. Centr. 6 November 1947, n. 6762; Comm. Centr. 9 May 1952, n. 36105; Comm. Centr., Sez. V, 1 July 1955, n. 73720; Cass., Sez. I, 27 July 1956, n. 2908. *Contra*, Cass., Sez. un., 3 July 1957, n. 2599. See also C.M. 31 March 1952, n. 170999. See also, for example, Berliri, *Le leggi di registro* 235-238; 2 Uckmar, *La legge del registro* 232-235; 1 Jammarino, *Commento alla legge sulle imposte di registro* 419; Griziotti, "Il regime delle pertinenze nel Codice Civile vigente e gli immobili per destinazione secondo l'art. 47 della legge del registro e la legge di successione," *RDFSF*, 1953, II, 112; Sciello, "Le pertinenze e le imposte sui trasferimenti," *Riv. not.*, 1952, 478. *Contra*, Rastello, *Il tributo di registro* 334 *et seq.*; Rastello, "Le pertinenze: Aspetti civilistici ed aspetti tributari, *RDFSF*, 1954, I, 354.

If the machinery serving a plant is not dismantled and removed but remains in the service of the plant, it is presumed sold to the purchaser of the plant, even if excluded in the document of sale of the plant and purchased by a person other than the purchaser of the plant (LR art. 47). Separate contracts under which immovable property, raw materials, and other natural produce are sold to the same purchaser, to be extracted or separated from the immovable property, or already extracted or separated but not yet carried away, are subject to the tax due for the transfer of immovables (LR art. 47).

f. ACTS WITH SUSPENSIVE CONDITIONS. Special treatment is given in the law to transactions which are subject to "suspensive conditions"—that is, to conditions which make the effectiveness of the transactions depend on the occurrence of uncertain future events (see CC art. 1353). Examples of acts with suspensive conditions are donations not yet accepted, agreements relative to dowry benefits, gifts of all kinds subject to the possibility of survival, and acts subject to approval, such as contracts of public bodies and acts modifying the charter of a corporation.

In all of these cases, only a fixed fee is paid on the registration of the act, and the progressive, proportional, or graduated tax relative to the transfer is due when the condition is fulfilled or when the act or transfer becomes effective before the fulfillment of the condition (LR art. 17).

There is universal agreement that acts forming corporations are not considered subject to the condition of fulfillment of the formalities prescribed by the Civil Code for legal formation, and are subject to registration from the very beginning, with the corresponding duty to pay the tax.[40] Moreover, sales of movables or immovables with the stipulation of reserved ownership (CC arts. 1523-1526) are not considered conditional for tax purposes.[41]

g. PARTITION OF COMMON PROPERTY. In Italian civil law, partition of common property (CC art. 713) is of declaratory nature; the share falling pro rata to each of the persons dividing the property is presumed to belong to him even before the actual partition (CC art. 757). Consequently, since there is no transfer of value, partition is subject to tax at graduated, not proportional, rates (15/6.3), provided that, in the case of the partition of an estate of inheritance, the exact amount of the movables and all income are declared for purposes of succession taxes, and that, in other cases, the common property appears in previously registered

---

[40] Cass., Sez. un., 25 July 1930; Cass., Sez. III, 13 July 1938. Comm. Centr., Sez. V, 7 March 1949, n. 1171. However, acts modifying the charter come within the scope of article 17 of the law. See Comm. Centr. 18 October 1939, n. 18213.

[41] R.D.L. 26 September 1935, n. 1749, art. 4, Annex A. See also Cass. 4 August 1949.

acts or in the balance sheet of a corporation (*bilancio sociale*). The income from inherited or common property is considered, for purposes of the registration tax, to belong to the heirs or co-owners in proportion to their respective shares. However, if one of the co-owners is alloted more than his share and thus has the duty to compensate the others, a proportional tax is due for the excess value (LR art. 48). Similar rules apply if only one share is separated from the common property (*stralcio di quota*), the rest remaining undivided.[42]

h. EXCHANGE OR BARTER. In the case of an exchange (*permuta*) (CC art. 1552), the tax is applied to the exchanged property which has the higher value (LR art. 51). Exchanges of immovables for other property are taxed at the rate applicable to transfers of immovables for consideration, up to the value of the immovables; the excess value of the exchanged property is taxed at the rate applicable to transfers of that kind of property for consideration (LR art. 51).

i. APPALTO AND SALE. The civil law distinction between *appalto* and *vendita* (sale) may cause interpretative difficulties in the law of taxation.[43] For purposes of the registration tax, the distinction is clarified by special legislative provisions, listed below, which define the characteristics of *appalto* and sale.[44]

1. A contract for the supply of raw materials, merchandise or products, and rendition of work is considered *appalto* whenever the price or value of the materials, merchandise, or products does not constitute the greater proportion of the total price or value.

2. Periodic supplies (*somministrazioni*)[45] and continuous provisions (*approvvigionamenti*) are treated in the same manner as *appalti* if the contractor must produce or obtain the promised goods after the conclusion of the contract.

3. Considered as *appalti*, whatever the consideration, are contracts whose object is the rendition of work by persons other than those who have contracted the obligation.

4. Considered as sales, whatever the relative value of the materials, merchandise, or products, are contracts under which a firm agrees to deliver goods which are the object of its ordinary production, by which

---

[42] Comm. Centr., Sez. V, 12 May 1949, n. 3304; Comm. Centr., Sez. VI, 2 March 1951, n. 21281; Comm. Centr., Sez. VI, 17 December 1951, n. 30835; Comm. Centr., Sez. IV, 23 March 1954, n. 59156.

[43] *Appalto* is "a contract by which a party assumes, with the organization of necessary means and management at his own risk, the execution of a work or service for consideration in money" (CC art. 1655). Sale is "a contract which has as its object transfer of ownership of a thing or transfer of another right in consideration of a price" (CC art. 1470).

[44] L. 19 July 1941, n. 771, art. 1.

[45] *Somministrazione* (supply, purveyance) is "a contract under which one party binds itself, in consideration of a price, to carry out, to the benefit of the other party, periodic or continuous furnishing of things (*prestazioni di cose*)" (CC art. 1559).

ANALYSIS OF OTHER TAXES

is meant the production of the ordinary industrial organization or technical equipment of the firm inferable from its trade classification, from declarations submitted to Chambers of Commerce, or from contracts and accounting records of the firms, even if the products delivered undergo modifications at the request of the purchaser.

j. AGREEMENT TO FORBEAR OR DISCONTINUE LITIGATION. An agreement of the parties to a suit to forbear or discontinue litigation (*transazione*) (CC art. 1965) is subject to a fixed fee if it is declaratory, that is, if it involves a mutual waiver of claims. If the agreement contains a novation of rights belonging to the parties under previous titles, a transfer of ownership or other property rights, a transfer of goods, creation of annuities, monetary obligations, or other contracts, it is subject to tax according to the nature of the contract (LR art. 60).[46]

k. CANCELLATION OF CONTRACT. The cancellation of a contract by mutual consent of the parties (*risoluzione*) (CC arts. 1453-1459) is subject to proportional, graduated, or progressive tax according to the nature of the contract. Only a fixed fee is due, however, if cancellation takes place, independently of the will of the parties, as a result of a "resolutory" (dissolving) condition stipulated in the contract, or by virtue of an authenticated document executed on the day following that on which the contract was concluded (LR art. 64).[47] Any additional provision of the contract beyond cancellation pure and simple which is not a necessary consequence thereof is taxed separately according to its nature (LR art. 64).

l. VOID ACTS. The registration tax cannot be applied unless the act has at least the external appearance of a legal act (see CC arts. 1325, 1346). For example, a private act not signed by the party or parties concerned would not be an act at all.[48] However, the tax is due in the case of acts which are null and void (*atti nulli*); there is no distinction between acts of absolutely no legal effect and acts which are voidable (LR art. 11).[49] The taxpayer cannot obtain a refund of tax collected, even if the nullity of the transaction has been declared and recognized, unless refund of the tax is expressly allowed by the law (LR arts. 11, 12).[50]

---

[46] See also Comm. Centr. 27 July 1939, n. 17738; Comm. Centr. 12 December 1949, n. 8129; Cass. 10 May 1946.

[47] On the term "*atto autentico*," see 2 Uckmar, *La legge del registro* 487-488.

[48] Comm. Centr. 6 July 1949, n. 5151; Comm. Centr., Sez. V, 19 January 1955, n. 67464; Comm. Centr., Sez. V, 23 March 1956, n. 80438. Cass., Sez. I, 10 July 1954, n. 2446.

[49] See 1 Jammarino, *Commento alla legge sulle imposte di registro* 38-39. See also 1 Uckmar, *La legge del registro* 210 *et seq.*; Berliri, *Le leggi di registro* 139-140; Griziotti, "Il regime della legge di registro per gli ati nulli, annullabili e revocabili nel controllo dell'interpretazione funzionale," *RDFSF*, 1941, II, 260.

[50] For the cases in which refund of the tax is allowed, see 15/7.3b.

15/3.4   De Facto Transfers

a.   GENERAL PRESUMPTIONS. Transfers of ownership, usufruct, use, enjoyment, or other property rights in immovables situated in Italy are subject to the registration tax even if they do not result from written acts (LR art. 1). This rule seems to conflict with the civil law rule which, under the sanction of nullity, prescribes the written form for transfers of rights in immovables (CC art. 1350). However, the rule is not concerned with transfers of immovables by oral contract, which, lacking an essential requisite, are null and void (15/3.5). Rather, a transfer is presumed in the absence of proof to the contrary, if a new owner has been inscribed in the rolls of the tax on income from landowning or the tax on income from buildings and has paid on his account at least one installment of that tax; or if there is an agreement (*convenzione*) justifying the inference that a new owner has the right of ownership or usufruct (LR art. 18). These presumptions are only mentioned by way of example; transfer may be presumed also from other relevant circumstances.[51] In absence of direct proof to the contrary, even the enjoyment of an immovable, under a lease or antichresis, can be subject to the registration tax.[52] The lessee has the duty to report to the Registry Office any oral contract of lease of immovables the annual rent from which exceeds L. 5,000 (LR art. 18).[53] In absence of such a report, the existence of a lease is presumed if there are facts or written transactions from which it can be inferred, or the Office has obtained knowledge of the payment of rent or other consideration (LR art. 18).[54]

All these presumptions can be rebutted by contrary proof, other than proof by witnesses (LR art. 18).

b.   TRANSFERS OF BUSINESS ENTERPRISES. Before the enactment of the Royal Decree of 30 December 1923, n. 2882, *de facto* transfers of the ownership or the right to the profits of an industrial or commercial enterprise for which no written act is required by civil law usually

---

[51] See Cass., Sez. I, 7 June 1954, n. 1862; App. Casale 29 January 1919; App. Bari 11 January 1937. *Contra*, Comm. Centr. 18 June 1941, n. 43099. Berliri, *Le leggi di registro* 77. However, in order to presume that a *de jure* transfer corresponds to the *de facto* transfer, there must be an actual transfer of possession. See Cass., Sez. I, 13 August 1948 (*Foro it.*, 1949, I, 943).

[52] Antichresis (*anticresi*) is "a contract by which the debtor or a third person binds himself to transfer an immovable to the creditor as security of the credit for the creditor to enjoy the fruits thereof on account of interest, if due, and hence of capital" (CC art. 1960).

[53] R.D.L. 7 August 1936, n. 1657; L. 15 February 1949, n. 33, art. 6.

[54] This presumption is also applicable in the case of antichresis. See also Cass., Sez. I, 3 June 1933, in which the Supreme Court of Cassation for the first time examined the question whether the tax authority may ex officio tax contracts of leases of immovables. For a comment on the decision, see Zappulli, "La registrazione d'ufficio dei contratti di locazione d'immobile," *Foro it.*, 1957, I, 780.

escaped the registration tax.[55] But such transfers must now be reported to the Registry Office (LR art. 79); in the absence of such a report, the law establishes a presumption of transfer of the enterprise as a whole. This presumption may be based on the transfer or succession of the firm with the continuation of the business in the same premises; on the alteration of the business license obtained by the new owner in his own name; on notification of the Chamber of Commerce or inscription in the tax rolls; or on proof of an agreement which justifies the legal presumption of the right of ownership or enjoyment of the enterprise in the new owner (LR art. 18).[56] The presumption can be rebutted by contrary proof, other than proof by witnesses.

C. TRANSFERS RESULTING FROM APPALTI AND CONCESSIONS TO CARRY ON PUBLIC SERVICES. The Registry Office must be notified and the tax must be paid in the case of oral contracts of *appalto* and concession for the exercise of public services, oral agreements thereof, oral contracts of *subappalto* and subconcession, and oral extensions of written or oral contracts of *appalto* and concession.[57] Exempt from the requirement, except when used (15/4.4), are contracts of *appalto* concluded orally or by way of business correspondence, if the total price does not exceed L. 250,000, and contracts between businessmen concluded for repair or processing of materials and merchandise, if that is the ordinary object of the firm's activity.[58] If the contracts in question have not been reported, the tax authorities may impose the tax whenever the contracts appear from facts, acts, or documents, or other adequate evidence of the transaction, without prejudice to contrary proof other than proof by witnesses.[59]

15/3.5 Oral Agreements

With the exceptions discussed above, oral agreements are not subject to registration or tax. However, if an oral agreement is mentioned in a written act, it, as well as that act, is subject to tax whenever it has a direct connection with the contents of the act, unless the agreement has already expired or expires with the act which mentions it (LR art. 62). This provision finds its justification in the concept expressly formulated in articles 13-18 of the Civil Code of 1865, that a written act furnishes the proof of an oral agreement mentioned in it whenever this agreement

---

55 Article 3 of R.D. 30 December 1923, n. 2882, is now integrated with article 18 of the basic registration law of 1923.

56 See also 1 Uckmar, *La legge del registro* 262-263; 1 Jammarino, *Commento alla legge sulle imposte di registro* 86-88; Celoria, "Cessione di azienda e legge di registro," *Foro padano*, 1956, I, 209.

57 R.D.L. 15 November 1937, n. 1924, Annex B, arts. 2 and 3.

58 L. 19 July 1941, n. 771, art. 3; L. 15 February 1949, n. 33, art. 4.

59 R.D.L. 15 November 1937, n. 1924, Annex B, art. 6.

has a direct relationship with the act itself. Thus, it is logical that it should be subject to the tax as if it were reduced into writing at the same moment. The tax is not due if the written act fails to establish the oral agreement, as, for example, if the parties to the oral agreement do not participate in the act.[60]

Whenever a judgment decided on a claim based on an oral agreement, there is due, besides the fee on the judgment, the tax to which an agreement of that kind would be subject if it had been registered (LR art. 72). By virtue of this provision, the tax relative to the oral agreement is payable if the agreement has been set forth in the judgment and constitutes the basis of the claim or of the exception on which the judgment itself has been pronounced.

15/4. Exemptions and Reductions

15/4.1 In General

Numerous exemptions and reductions are granted in the basic law of 1923 and in subsequent legislation to acts which would otherwise be subject to tax under the rules described at 15/3.[61] These exemptions and reductions vary in range and nature and can be classified into four major groups according to the four Tables annexed to the 1923 law (LR art. 5).[62]

1. Acts completely exempt both from registration and the corresponding tax (LR Table, Annex E).
2. Acts subject to registration but exempt from the corresponding tax (LR Table, Annex C).
3. Acts which are subject to both registration and the tax, not within a fixed term, but only in case of use (LR Table, Annex D).
4. Acts registrable within a fixed term but subject to a small fixed fee or to a reduced tax (LR Table, Annex B).

15/4.2 Acts Completely Exempt from Registration

Among the acts completely exempt both from registration and the tax are those listed below (LR Table, Annex E).

1. Acts connected with insurance operations such as insurance contracts and policies for which the special tax on insurance is applied (4/3.4).
2. Acts issued by mortgage offices, which are subject to the mortgage tax (4/3.3).
3. Shares, bonds, and other securities of Italian and foreign corporations, and acts connected with operations of negotiation of the securities. If,

---

[60] Comm. Centr. 21 December 1938; see also Giannini, *Istituzioni di diritto tributario* 393.

[61] About 2,300 legislative acts were passed in the period 1924-1958; see Stammati, Armani, and Ceccarelli, *Codice delle imposte di registro* 1612 *et seq.*

[62] The list of acts and contracts in the Tables B, C, D, and E is not exhaustive (see the note introducing the Tables).

for purposes of the negotiation, a public act or private document separate from the securities was executed, the act or document is subject to a fixed fee under article 108 of the Schedule, Annex A. The exemption of shares and bonds is not applied if they are the object of judgments or gratuitous transfers inter vivos, in which cases the taxes provided in Parts II and III of the Schedule, Annex A, are applicable.[63]

4. Acts of civil proceedings and powers of attorney.
5. Acts effected in savings banks and pawnshops, relative to the deposit or pledging of merchandise and securities.
6. Decisions and minutes of Conciliator courts and decisions of the Council of State, Provincial Administrative Boards, and the Court of Accounts (1/4.10).

15/4.3   Acts Subject to Gratuitous Registration

Among acts subject to gratuitous registration are those listed below (LR Table, Annex C).

1. Acts and contracts effected in the interest of the state and the administrative entities treated for tax purposes in the same manner as the state. Gratuitous registration is granted only for that part of the tax which would be charged to the state or administrative entities under article 94 of the law.
2. Acts involving social security and accident insurance, certain charitable institutions, and agrarian credit.
3. Acts establishing cooperative societies, mutual aid societies, and agricultural associations.
4. Acts of recognition of natural children and acts relating to guardianship and custody.
5. Acts relating to small bankruptcies.

Among other acts exempt from the tax are gifts for the benefit of provinces, communes, and other legally recognized Italian entities or institutions founded or to be founded, made for the specific purpose of

---

[63] The exemption of shares and other securities was introduced as a result of the abolition of the tax on negotiating instruments and the introduction of the corporation tax; L. 6 August 1954, n. 603. The shares in a limited liability company do not clearly fall within the meaning of "other securities of Italian and foreign corporations" mentioned in article 108 of the Schedule, Annex A (15/6.5), and in article 10 of Table, Annex E, and, consequently, transfers of such shares were held to be subject to the proportional tax under article 27 of the law. See Comm. Centr., Sez. V, 10 December 1956, n. 87361; Comm. Centr., Sez. V, 7 January 1957, n. 87977; Comm. Centr., Sez. un., 24 March 1958, n. 3338. However, a limited liability company is subject to the corporation tax in the same manner as a corporation (5/2.3). It has therefore been held, more recently, that transfers of participations in limited liability companies are entitled to the same treatment, for registration tax purposes, as transfers of shares of corporations. Cass. Sez. I, 16 January 1961, n. 56; Comm. Centr., Sez. VII, 14 March 1962, n. 86553. For discussion of this question, see Piccatti, "Regime fiscale della circolazione di quote delle società a responsabilità limitata," *Temi trib.*, 1960, 147; Piccatti, "Ancora sul regime fiscale della circolazione di quote delle società a responsabilità limitata," *Temi trib.*, 1961, 226; Braccini, "Requisiti per la registrazione a tassa fissa della cessione di quote di società a responsabilità limitata," *Dir. e prat. trib.*, 1962, II, 116.

charity, instruction, or education,[64] and gifts to entities having the purpose of religion or worship.[65] In addition, gratuitous transfers of artistic collections, made by acts inter vivos to libraries, museums, galleries, universities, or other institutions legally existing in Italy, are not subjected to registration taxes unless they are business stock-in-trade. The exemption ceases to have effect if a collection is sold within a decade of the date of the gift and, in that case, tax is due both on the sale and on the preceding gift (LR art. 16).

15/4.4   Acts Subject to Registration and Tax in Case of Use

Certain acts, specified in Table, Annex D, are subject to registration and payment of tax, not within a fixed period of time, but only in case of use in one of the ways listed below (LR art. 2).

1. The acts are produced in judicial proceedings or in administrative proceedings before the Council of State, Court of Accounts, Provincial Administrative Boards, and Councils of Prefectures and any other special jurisdiction, or are produced before arbitral tribunals.
2. The acts are reported, even partially, in public or private documents subject to registration, and are made a part of the documents in the recorder's office or in offices of the public administration.

Use does not occur if a document is produced in court as a simple historical fact, and not in order to derive some juridical effect.[66]

Table, Annex D, specifies at what time each act subject to registration in case of use should be registered. Among those acts are certain types of invoices and receipts; documents pertaining to savings-bank activities, such as charter agreements, bank books, and account statements; written offers to public auctions; admission documents for hospitals and public schools; stock exchange contracts and related documents; contracts involving the rendering of transportation services; business correspondence; nonauthenticated agreements relating to the purchase or resale of machines and other industrial products; and agreements for the supply of water, heat, and electricity.

15/4.5   Reductions of Tax

a. IN GENERAL. A number of acts enjoy a reduction in the rate of tax normally due. In most cases, only a fixed fee is paid; in others, only a part of the regular tax is required. In a few cases, the registration tax is included in an annual fee (*abbonamento*) paid in substitution of taxes. However, all acts and contracts for which a reduction of registration tax

---

[64] R.D.L. 9 April 1925, n. 380, art. 1.

[65] Concordat with the Holy See (L. 27 May 1929, n. 810), art. 29(h); R.D. 28 February 1930, n. 289, art. 12. Apart from these provisions, gifts to such entities are subject to a 5% tax (see LR art. 44; LR Schedule, Annex A, art. 141). See Berliri, *Le leggi di registro* 265.

[66] Cass., Sez. I, 5 July 1949, n. 1681. See also Giannini, *Istituzioni di diritto tributario* 395, n. 28.

has been granted lose this privilege and are subject to ordinary taxes and relative surcharges if not presented for registration within the fixed period of time (LR art. 110).[67]

b. FIXED FEES. Fixed fees have been provided for a number of acts which would otherwise be subject to proportional, progressive, or graduated rates. These fees are now fixed at the standard rate of L. 2,000 (about $3.22).[68] Fixed fees are due, for example, for acts granting private concessions for the construction of public railroads; for the establishment of companies for concessions of auxiliary railroads and grants and subsidies for tramway and automobile services; for civil acts pertaining to certain associations formed for the exploitation of natural resources; for acts relative to the formation of new cadasters; for acts establishing companies dealing in citrus fruits; for certain contracts of emphyteusis (9/4.1) relative to land in southern and insular Italy; for contracts of loan for reconstruction of houses in new towns in Basilicata and Calabria; for acts establishing associations of production and work cooperatives for *appalti* for public works; for acts relative to land reclamation, acquisition of land for and building of elementary schools, and construction of artificial lakes; for contracts relative to the acquisition or exchange of land by communes for the purpose of division among farmers; for acts of endowment of artistic, literary, or scientific collections; and for acts for the transfer of objects of art and antiquities to provinces, communes, or other legally recognized lay Italian entities or institutions founded or to be founded (LR Table, Annex B).

The 1923 law and special legislation also provide fixed fees for other acts. For example, all acts relative to the operations of popular banks and cooperative societies are subject to fixed minimum fees, provided that they are governed by principles of mutual benefit (LR art. 66) and that the acts are effected within 10 years of the date of the establishment of the institution and before the capital actually paid exceeds L. 3 million (LR art. 65).[69] In order to enjoy the tax reliefs, a cooperative must fulfill the civil law formalities concerning inscription in the register of enterprises of the charter and its modifications, the balance sheet, and acts of merger, and must deposit the acts of formation with the Ministry of Industry.[70]

The exemption of the acts of agrarian and building cooperatives is limited to the first assignment of rural land or house to each member;

---

[67] As modified by R.D. 13 January 1936, n. 2313.

[68] L. 21 July 1961, n. 707, art. 1.

[69] L. 15 February 1949, n. 33, art. 3; D.L.C.P.S. 14 December 1947, n. 1577. See also Comm. Centr., Sez. VI, 23 May 1952, n. 36668; Comm. Centr., Sez. VI, 26 May 1952, n. 36755.

[70] R.D.L. 11 December 1930, n. 1882, art. 2; for the prescribed formalities, see CC arts. 2435, 2502, 2516, 2519, 2537, 2538.

the value of the assigned immovable cannot exceed L. 5 million, and the immovable cannot be sold by the member for five years. If the member has previously had other assignments of the same kind, with the same tax benefits, their value is included in the determination of the limit.[71]

The first transfer of ownership of land and buildings for the construction and activation of new industrial factories in southern and insular Italy is subject to a fixed rate of registration tax and mortgage fees (4/3.3).[72] The same rate has been extended to mortgages entered into at the same time in order to guarantee the unpaid price and to secure debts contracted for purposes of payment.[73] This reduction has recently been extended to the first transfer made for the benefit of an association of local government entities formed to further industrial development, and to transfers made by such associations for the benefit of industrial enterprises.[74]

c. REDUCED TAX RATES. Under Table, Annex B, taxes are reduced by one half for judicial acts submitted by tax collectors for the enforcement of tax collection; judicial acts regarding Chambers of Commerce, communes, or certain associations for the use of natural resources; acts regarding agrarian credit; sales of immovables situated in the reclamation areas of the plain surrounding Rome (*agro romano*); and acts relative to the redemption of ground rents (*canoni*), perpetual rent charges (*censi*), and other perpetual payments. A substantial reduction is granted for transfers of property for the construction of nonluxury housing (15/6.3). Reductions to one quarter or even to one tenth of the tax ordinarily due are granted in a few other cases, for example, acts of corporations established for the acquisition of agrarian land.

Acts pertaining to the production and distribution of sulphur, contracts of loan concluded with institutions of land credit, acts involving credit associations for public works, and acts involving the National Credit Institute for Italian Labor Abroad (*Istituto Nazionale di Credito per il Lavoro Italiano all'Estero*) are subject to special treatment, since registration taxes are included in the annual fee (*abbonamento*) paid by the respective taxpayers in substitution of all taxes (LR Table, Annex B).

---

[71] R.D.L. 19 August 1943, n. 737, art. 3; L. 15 February 1949, n. 33, art. 3. See also Comm. Centr., Sez. V, 21 March 1956, n. 80331. See also Gualandi, "Le imposte di registro ed ipotecarie relative agli atti di assegnazione di immobile a socio de cooperativa edilizia priva di contributo statale," *Riv. leg. fisc.*, 1954, 481.

[72] D.L.C.P.S. 14 December 1947, n. 1598, art. 5, converted in L. 29 December 1948, n. 1482.

[73] L. 29 July 1957, n. 634, art. 37.

[74] L. 29 September 1962, n. 1462, art. 6.

15/5. Valuation

15/5.1 In General

Except in the case of fixed fees, where there is no need to evaluate the taxable amount, the taxable basis is determined under the principles listed below.

1. Gratuitous transfers inter vivos are subject to the same rules as transfers at death (3/4.5).
2. In transfers for consideration, two elements are taken into account: the salable or market value (*valore venale*) of the transferred property and the consideration (*corrispettivo*) agreed upon by the parties.

In general, the rules of valuation are the same as those discussed at 3/4.5. The tax should be applied to the market value of the property even if no price or consideration has been fixed or no value declared, the market value being the value which the property has in common commerce on the day of transfer.[75] In the case of public acts (15/3.1) containing transfers of immovables, commercial enterprises, and the like, the taxable amount must be determined by reference to the date on which the acts occasioning the transfer were made. Private acts regarding transfers of property susceptible of valuation are valued with reference to the date of the registration of the act.

In the valuation of the taxable basis both of immovables and of movables, the law provides certain criteria which should be taken into account in the first place (*principalmente*), which means that the specification of the criteria is not exhaustive and that consequently any other element or fact relevant to the determination or value can be considered.[76]

15/5.2 Immovables

The law provides that the elements listed below should be taken into account in the valuation of immovable property.

1. Transfers, partitions, and judicial appraisals made within the past three years, relative to the property itself or to other property situated in the same locality and in analogous conditions.
2. Net income from the property, taking into account the average capitalization rate adopted in the locality for similar immovable investments at the time of the transfer.[77]
3. The current market value of the immovable at the time of the transfer.[78]

Rural land, other than forests and building lots, is valued for the registration taxes in the same manner as for the succession taxes,[79] that

---

[75] R.D.L. 7 August 1936, n. 1639, art. 15, replacing LR art. 30, para. 1. For the interpretation of the phrase "market value," see 3/4.5a.

[76] Cass., Sez. I, 21 May 1930 (*Dir. e prat. trib.*, 1930, 395); Cass., Sez. I, 17 May 1937 (*Riv. leg. fisc.*, 1937, 438); Comm. Centr., Sez. VI, 31 October 1952, n. 40455.

[77] R.D.L. 7 August 1936, n. 1639, art. 16.

[78] R.D.L. 5 March 1942, n. 186, art. 1, modified by L. 21 June 1942, n. 840.

[79] L. 27 May 1959, n. 355, art. 3.

is, on the basis of tables of valuation compiled by the Central Census Commission (10/2.2g) for the former extraordinary progressive tax on wealth, adjusted to take account of changes in the price level (3/4.5c).[80]

The value of usufruct in land (9/4.1) and of bare ownership is determined by a proportional computation taking into account the extent and duration of the right of the respective holders; the rules for gratuitous transfers inter vivos are the same as those for the inheritance tax (3/4.3b). If bare ownership has previously been transferred for consideration and the bare ownership and the usufruct are later merged, a merger tax is applied to the difference between the value of full ownership at the moment of the merger and the price or consideration taxed at the time of the transfer of the bare ownership (LR art. 21).[81]

15/5.3 Movables

In the case of the transfer of movables, account is taken of the value declared by the parties, the value resulting from the inventory estimate, or the value resulting from a contract concerning the movables made within six months before or after the transfer.[82] These tests give the tax authority the power either to determine the taxable amount from the act of transfer or to use the higher value resulting from the inventory estimate, contract, or other documentary evidence.[83] Shares, bonds, and public securities, Italian or foreign, are valued at the legal exchange rate for cash prices as specified in the stock exchange lists on the date of transfer, or calculated at their market value on the date of transfer if they are not listed.[84]

In the case of taxable transfers of commodities and other commercial goods the tax is applied either to the value resulting from market reports, listings, or books of Chambers of Commerce, or else to the value resulting from the records and books of commercial intermediaries, taking into account the market reports or contracts nearest in time to the date of the transaction in question. The prices or consideration in foreign currency or gold are converted to lire at the exchange rate on the date of the transaction unless the parties themselves have fixed a different date.[85] Annuities and pensions are valued in the same manner as for purposes of the succession taxes (3/4.3e).

---

[80] L. 20 October 1954, n. 1044, art. 1.

[81] This provision is the subject of rich literature and many judicial decisions. See Stammati, Armani, and Ceccarelli, *Codice della imposta di registro* 85-98. The rules of articles 19-21 are also applicable in the case of the transfer of the rights of use or habitation (9/4.1). See article 22, corresponding to article 24 of the inheritance tax law (3/4.3b). For transfers of emphyteusis (9/4.1), see 3/4.3f.

[82] R.D.L. 7 August 1936, n. 1639, art. 16.

[83] See Cass. Roma 31 December 1902.

[84] R.D.L. 7 August 1936, n. 1639, art. 16.

[85] R.D.L. 7 August 1936, n. 1639, art. 16.

In transfers for consideration of credits (*crediti*), pensions, and annuities, the tax is applied to the amount of the credit assigned. If the price of the assignment is lower than the amount of the credit and a reason for the lower price is explained in the act, the tax is applied to the price agreed upon by the parties.

In cases of transfer of credits, pensions, and annuities made at public auction, the tax is always applied to the sale price (LR art. 52). In the case of the assignment of credits as a guarantee for financing, the tax is applied to the amount of the credits assigned.[86]

For purposes of the registration law, obligations and shares which have sums of money as their exclusive object are considered credit rights. Rights and obligations which have movables as their object, and shares (*azioni*) of business corporations (*società de commercio*), are treated as movables. Participations in general partnerships (*società in nome collettivo*) and simple limited partnerships (*società in accomandita semplice*) are considered movables or immovables according to the nature of the partnership capital. If the capital includes both movables and immovables, the participation is considered as immovable up to the amount of the value of immovables (LR art. 27).[87]

Industrial and commercial enterprises and participations in commercial partnerships are valued on the basis of the amount and value of merchandise existing at the date of transfer of the enterprise and on the basis of the kind and value of other property, including good will and monopoly rights.[88] In the case of the creation or merger of corporations, the tax is applied to the gross value of the assets conferred. With respect to acts creating foreign corporations, the tax is applied only to the amount of capital intended for operations in Italy or actually invested there.

15/6. Tax Rates

15/6.1 In General

The rates of the registration taxes are progressive, proportional, graduated, or fixed (LR art. 4). In no case may the amount of the registration tax (whether graduated, proportional, or progressive) be lower than the minimum fixed fee of L. 1,000 (about $1.61).[89] In each case, the total amount of the tax is increased by the additional for the benefit of the communal assistance entities (ECA) at the rate of 10% of the tax (2/2.9).

15/6.2 Progressive Rates

Progressive rates are applied to gratuitous transfers (LR art. 4). The rates, fixed in brackets, increase with the amount of the tax base, up to

---

[86] See Comm. Centr., Sez. IV, 19 December 1946, n. 86366.
[87] Compare the inheritance tax law, arts. 28, 29 (3/4.3h).
[88] R.D.L. 7 August 1936, n. 1639, art. 19.
[89] L. 21 July 1961, n. 707, art. 1.

a maximum limit of 80% for the top bracket, beyond which the rate is invariable. The original Part III of the Schedule, Annex A, entitled "Taxes on gratuitous transfers inter vivos," was replaced, in 1949, by the rate table of taxes on inheritances and gifts; the same system of rates now applies to virtually all gratuitous transfers (3/4.7).[90]

15/6.3 Proportional Rates

a. IN GENERAL. The proportional rate is one in which the measure remains invariable, whatever the taxable basis. The fractions of one hundred are computed in their precise amount (LR art. 10). The rates differ according to the nature of the acts or transfers subject to tax. Proportional rates are applied to transfers for consideration of ownership, usufruct, use, and enjoyment of immovables or movables or of any other property right; to acts which contain an obligation for or a release from payments or services (*prestazioni*) (LR art. 4); and to gratuitous transfers for the benefit of certain legal entities (LR art. 44) (see 3/4.7c). There are certain exceptions to the rule, for example, acts containing obligations of compensation for instruction in arts and crafts (LR Schedule, Annex A, art. 33(b)), and releases and receipts for loans in maritime exchange (LR Schedule, Annex A, art. 61), which are subject to a fixed fee. With respect to obligations, only those which arise from contracts are subject to a proportional rate; natural obligations or those resulting from the law (CC art. 2034) are subject to a fixed fee.[91]

The more important of the rates in the group of proportional taxes are specified below.

b. TRANSFERS OF IMMOVABLES. Transfers of immovable property and property rights in immovable property situated in Italy are taxed at the rate of 7.5% of the value of the property or right transferred (LR Schedule, Annex A, art. 1).[92] If the same property has been transferred for consideration within the previous three years in a transaction on which tax was paid at the normal rate, the rate on the new transfer is reduced by one fourth on that part of the value which does not exceed the value taxed in the previous transfer. The same rate applies to exchanges of immovable property situated in Italy for other immovable property, whether situated in Italy or abroad (LR Schedule, Annex A,

---

[90] Annex A of L. 12 May 1949, n. 206.

[91] C.M. 2 September 1869, n. 567. 1 Uckmar, *La legge del registro* 174, n. 4; see also Cass. Roma 3 May 1916 (*Giur. it.*, 1916, I, 820).

[92] Immovable property includes the soil, springs and watercourses, trees, buildings and other structures, even if attached to the soil for transitory purposes, and, in general, anything that is naturally or artificially attached to the soil. Floating structures which are firmly secured to the bank or riverbed and intended to remain so permanently for their use are also considered immovables. All other property is movable. CC art. 812.

art. 7(a)). Transfers of immovables situated abroad are taxed at the rate of 1% (LR Schedule, Annex A, art. 1).[93]

Transfers of nonluxury dwellings which are exempt from the tax on income from buildings (9/4.2c) [94] are entitled to a special rate of 2.5% if they take place within four years of the declaration of inhabitability or actual habitation.[95] This relief is not applicable to sales or exchanges of business premises unless they are transferred en bloc with the whole building.[96]

When a debtor transfers the enjoyment of immovable property to a creditor until the extinction of a debt, a rate of 2% is applied either to the capital amount of the debt or to the total of interest charges met by the yield of the property, depending on whether or not the yield of the property can be applied to reduce the debt (LR Schedule, Annex A, art. 19).

c. TRANSFERS OF MOVABLES. Transfers and exchanges of movable property and of property rights in movable property are taxed at the rate of 2% of the value transferred (LR Schedule, Annex A, arts. 2, 7(b)). This rate applies to acts of conveyance (*compravendita*) of goods between merchants (LR Schedule, Annex A, art. 3). Sales of ships are taxed at the rate of 0.5%.[97] A rate of 1% is provided for transfers of cattle and agricultural products (LR Schedule, Annex A, art. 2).

A special schedule of fixed fees is provided for acts embodying transfers of motor vehicles (4/3.6).

d. LEASES OF MOVABLES OR IMMOVABLES. A lease of movable property or immovable property for a definite period is taxed at the rate of 0.5% (LR Schedule, Annex A, art. 44),[98] applied to the aggregate rents and other payments agreed upon for the duration of the lease (LR art. 54).

Since 1 January 1963, however, leases of urban immovable property are subject to registration taxes at the special rate of 6% of the cadastral income, for property listed in the cadaster (9/4.2d), and at the rate of 4% of the annual rent, for property not yet listed in the cadaster.[99] These new rates include the general tax on receipts and the stamp taxes formerly imposed on such leases.

e. RIGHTS TO INCOME, ANNUITIES, AND PENSIONS. The establishment of an annuity in the income of land, or the dissolution or redemption of such

---

[93] As modified by L. 27 May 1959, n. 355, art. 1, and by L. 27 September 1963, n. 1317.

[94] See L. 2 February 1960, n. 35, art. 1.

[95] L. 2 July 1949, n. 408, art. 17; L. 27 May 1959, n. 355, art. 2.

[96] L. 2 July 1949, n. 408, art. 17; Comm. Centr., Sez. IV, 13 March 1956, n. 80170.

[97] L. 6 August 1954, n. 603, art. 34.

[98] As modified by D.L.L. 5 April 1945, n. 141, art. 8.

[99] L. 29 December 1962, n. 1744, art. 1.

an annuity by retransfer of the land, is subject to the rates described at 15/6.3b for transfers of immovables (LR Schedule, Annex A, art. 17). In other cases, the creation or transfer of a right to income, or of an annuity or pension, is taxed at the rate of 2% (LR Schedule, Annex A, art. 21), applied to the capital value expressed in the instrument, or to the capitalized value of the annual payments if no capital value is expressed in the instrument (LR art. 24).

f. OBLIGATIONS. Acts and contracts containing nongratuitous money obligations, promises to pay, loans, promises of loans, opening of credit and the like are subject to tax at the rate of 1.5%, provided that they do not represent consideration for the transfer of movables or immovables and have not previously been taxed (LR Schedule, Annex A, art 28). Opening of credit, advances, and other financing extended by credit firms to business or industrial concerns are taxed at the rate of 0.5%; credit extended to public entities or to units of the public administration is taxed at 0.25% (LR Schedule, Annex A, art. 28). The novation of a debt is taxed at the rate of 2%, applied to the capital amount of the debt plus accrued interest (LR Schedule, Annex A, art. 29). Obligations of compensation or indemnification for work in liberal arts or professions are taxed at 0.5%; for teaching, personal services, or other work, to a fixed fee of L. 1,000 (LR Schedule, Annex A, art. 33).

g. MISCELLANEOUS CONTRACTS. The rate generally applicable to contracts of *appalto* (15/3.3i) is 1% of the contract price (LR Schedule, Annex A, art. 52).[100] However, special rates are provided for contracts for supplies to the state administration (0.5%),[101] *appalti* for the construction of ships in Italy for foreign companies (0.1%), and other *appalti* for the construction of ships (0.5%) (LR Schedule, Annex A, art. 53). The rate for the charter of a ship is 0.5% of the price (LR Schedule, Annex A, art. 49). Concessions for the exercise of public services are taxed at 0.75% of the consideration agreed and the gross proceeds (LR art. 56), except in the case of concessions to supply water, gas, or electricity, for which the rate is 0.3% (LR Schedule, Annex A, art. 51 *bis*).

An irrevocable mandate (*mandato*) with release from the duty to render an accounting is taxed at rates ranging from 0.5% to 3%, depending on the subject matter of the mandate (LR Schedule, Annex A, art. 15). A mandate or power of attorney (*procura*) with compensation to the agent is taxed at 3% of the capitalized value of the annual payments if the term of the agency is indefinite or exceeds 10 years; in other cases, the rate is 0.5% of the total compensation, but not less than L. 1,000

---

[100] As modified by D.L.L. 5 April 1945, n. 141, art. 5.
[101] L. 4 April 1953, n. 261, art. 4; L. 6 August 1954, n. 603, art. 33.

(LR Schedule, Annex A, art. 92). A mandate or power of attorney without compensation is subject to a fixed fee of L. 1,000 (LR Schedule, Annex A, art. 91).

h. ORGANIZATION, REORGANIZATION, AND DISSOLUTION OF BUSINESS. On the formation of a company of any kind or of an association in participation (5/3.5), contributions of money or of movable property are taxed at the rate of 1%; contributions of industrial factories or workshops, at 2.5%, applied to the gross value of the property contributed; [102] and contributions of other immovables, at the rates applicable to transfers of immovables (15/6.3b) (LR Schedule, Annex A, art. 81). The same rates are applied to the gross assets of a cooperative society when it is transformed into a business company (LR Schedule, Annex A, art. 82), and to increases of the capital of a company already formed (LR Schedule, Annex A, art. 85). The transformation of a business company from one type to another (CC arts. 2498-2500) is taxed at 0.5% of the gross assets (LR Schedule, Annex A, art. 83). Transfers of enterprises are taxed at the rate applicable to the classification of the assets transferred, determined under the rules discussed at 15/3.3d.

The admission to a partnership of a new member who contributes only work is subject to a fixed fee of L. 1,000 (LR Schedule, Annex A, art. 84). A similar fixed fee is payable on the total or partial dissolution of a company (LR Schedule, Annex A, art. 87). On the dissolution of a corporation or similar entity, distributions of immovables to shareholders are subject to the rates described at 15/6.3b. On the dissolution of a partnership or similar company, distributions of immovables made to a member other than the original contributor are subject to the same rates unless the immovables were purchased or built by the company; distributions of immovables to the original contributor, of immovables purchased or built by the company, or of movables are subject to graduated rates (15/6.4) (LR Schedule, Annex A, art. 88).

15/6.4 Graduated Rates

A graduated rate is imposed in the form of a certain fee for the first L. 1,000 and a lower fee for each successive L. 1,000. A fraction of the taxable amount lower than L. 1,000 is considered a whole thousand; if the taxable amount exceeds L. 1,000, a fraction of 1,000 lower than 100 is not computed (LR art. 10). The graduated rates provided by Part II of the Schedule for judicial acts are L. 10 on the first L. 1,000 and L. 5 on each successive L. 1,000.[103] The graduated rates provided for other acts in the Schedule are L. 20 on the first L. 1,000 and L. 10 on each successive L. 1,000.

---

[102] L. 6 August 1954, n. 603, art. 35.
[103] D.L.L. 5 April 1945, n. 141, art. 8.

Graduated rates are applied to transactions not involving obligation or release but merely a declaration or attribution of rights or values without a transfer thereof (LR art. 4). Among such acts are partition of property among heirs or other co-owners (LR Schedule, Annex A, art. 98) and cancellation of a lease for consideration (LR Schedule, Annex A, art. 44). Also subject to graduated rates are transfers of securities of the public debt or equivalent securities for a price paid in cash under a notarized transaction or private writing (LR Schedule, Annex A, art. 24) and distributions to members of partnerships, following dissolution or liquidation, of movables, of immovables returned to the original contributor, or of immovables purchased or built by the partnership (LR Schedule, Annex A, art. 88).

15/6.5   Fixed Fees

Fixed fees are applied to all other acts which can serve as legal documents (LR art. 4). The fees must be expressly specified in the Schedule and cannot be applied by analogy.[104] For example, a fixed fee is applied to a separate public act or private writing negotiating securities of Italian or foreign companies when the price is paid with the buyer's act, in cash, or in securities (LR Schedule, Annex A, art. 108).[105]

The fixed fee for acts contemplated by Part I of the Schedule, Annex A, is L. 1,000. However, for acts on which a fixed fee is imposed under special provisions (15/4.5b), instead of a proportional, progressive, or graduated tax, the minimum fixed fee amounts to L. 2,000. The judicial fees are L. 2,000, L. 4,000, or L. 8,000.[106]

15/7.   Assessment and Collection

15/7.1   Assessment

In the case of a written act, the process of assessment begins with the filing of the document with the Registry Office. A public document or certified private document must be filed by the notary or official who is required to request registration and is liable for the tax (*responsabile d'imposta*) under the rules described at 15/2.3 (LR art. 80). An uncertified private document must be filed by the persons subject to the tax under the rules discussed at 15/2.1. Oral contracts and other unwritten transactions subject to tax must be reported to the Registry Office by the persons subject to the tax.

Filing must take place within 20 days of the date of the act, the oral agreement, or the event occasioning the tax liability (LR art. 80). For certified acts, the time limit runs from the date of certification (LR art.

---

[104] I.M. 10 September 1961, art. 2.
[105] As replaced by L. 6 August 1954, n. 603, art. 36.
[106] L. 21 July 1961, n. 707, arts. 1, 2.

80); for acts subject to approval or court confirmation (*omologazione*), the time limit runs from the date on which the notice of approval or confirmation was received by the official responsible for registration (LR art. 81). For acts drawn up abroad, the time limit is six months from their date for acts made in Europe, and 18 months for acts made outside Europe (LR art. 82).

If the elements necessary for the determination of the tax base are not evident from the act or declaration, the person subject to tax must supply a declaration of estimate signed by him (LR art. 30).

On the basis of the act or declaration, or ex officio in the case of undeclared transfers, the Registry Office proceeds to the assessment of the tax. If the value or consideration for a transfer or elements necessary for the determination thereof appear in the act or declaration, the tax is collected on the value or consideration declared or determined. If the act or declaration does not express the taxable value and does not contain elements necessary for the determination thereof, the Registry Office calls upon the taxpayer to furnish a declaration giving the estimate of the value; upon failure to furnish such a declaration, the Office determines the value ex officio. The debtor has the right to appeal the determination to the District Commission within 30 days of the payment of the tax.[107]

In the case of the transfer of immovables whose price is to be determined in the future, in the case of *appalti* with a presumed price, and, in general, in the case of any contract with an undetermined or variable consideration, the tax is collected provisionally on the basis of the taxpayer's declaration. Subsequently, either a complementary tax is collected or the excess payment is refunded within the four-year time limitation provided by article 137 of the law (15/7.2c). If, as a result of absolute impossibility, an *appalto* has not been fulfilled, the amount of tax attributable to the value of the service actually performed is collected (LR art. 132).[108] If the Registry Office obtains knowledge of a *de facto* transfer subject to tax, it calls upon the parties fo file a declaration of value within 10 days. Failure to do so results in ex officio valuation.[109]

If, in any of the foregoing cases, the Registry Office claims that the value appearing in the document or the declaration of the parties is lower than the market price of the thing transferred, it serves notice

---

[107] R.D.L. 7 August 1936, n. 1639, art. 17.

[108] See also Cass., Sez. I, 30 June 1933 (*Riv. leg. fisc.*, 1933, 674); Comm. Centr. 24 January 1939, n. 12456; and other cases in Stammati, Armani, and Ceccarelli, *Codice della imposta di registro* 123-131.

[109] R.D.L. 7 August 1936, n. 1639, art. 18. Late filing of the declaration does not result in any penalty or surcharge, but only gives the tax authority the right to determine the taxable amount and collect the tax, without prejudice to the taxpayer's right of appeal. Comm. Centr., Sez. V, 1 February 1954, n. 56800.

of the Office's valuation within one year of the payment of tax or of the grant of an extension. The taxpayer may appeal to the District Commission within 30 days.[110] In view of the provision that the tax on sales and *appalti* at public auction is due on the price of the last bid (LR art. 50), it has been held that the tax authorities may not notify assessment of a higher value in these cases.[111] Other rules of assessment are similar to those applicable to the succession taxes (3/4.9).

15/7.2 Payment

a. GENERAL CONDITIONS. As a rule, payment of tax must be made simultaneously with the registration of the act. However, in certain cases, where the principal or complementary tax is due on the occurrence of a determined event following the act (for example, merger of usufruct with ownership, fulfillment of a suspensive condition, or final determination of the price or value), the payment must be made within two months following the expiration of the time limits fixed for reporting the event in question (LR art. 91).

Besides the principal tax collected at the time of registration, the taxes described below are imposed (LR art. 7).[112]

1. Complementary tax, which is applied after registration, and which could not be collected with the principal tax because of a lack of the elements necessary for its valuation, or whose collection was suspended by law.

2. Supplementary tax, which is collected after registration if, at the time of registration, the Registry Office made a mistake or omission either regarding the amount of the tax or surcharge due or regarding the tax base appearing in the act or declaration. However, the tax demanded on an act erroneously registered gratuitously has the character of a principal tax.

The taxpayer has the duty to observe the time limit without previous notice from the tax administration. In case of failure to pay the tax, the filing of the document or the declaration of oral agreement for registration is considered as not having occurred; and, on the expiration of the time limit, the taxpayer incurs the penalties established by the law.[113]

At the taxpayer's request, payment of taxes on merger of usufruct with ownership in immovables and the corresponding surcharges may be made in installments over not more than four years, with the payment of 5% interest. Payment by installments may be allowed by the tax administration, in writing, for the similar taxes on movable values. If the permission is granted before the expiration of the time limit fixed

---

[110] R.D.L. 7 August 1936, n. 1639, arts. 20, 21; D.L.C.P.S. 21 January 1947, n. 25, art. 1.

[111] Cass., Sez. I, 17 May 1933 (*Foro it.*, 1933, I, 1171); Comm. Centr. 24 January 1940 (*Foro it.*, 1941, III, 38).

[112] Substituted by R.D. 13 January 1936, n. 2313, art. 1.

[113] Comm. Centr. 27 December 1952, n. 33523 (*Rass. tasse*, 1952, 359).

for the payment of the tax, the taxpayer incurs no surcharge for late payment. If payment of an installment is delayed more than 20 days beyond its due date, the taxpayer loses the benefit of extension and must pay the full tax with matured interest plus a surcharge for the amount still due (LR art. 92).

Payment in installments is also allowed for taxes due on continuing contracts of *appalto* whose duration exceeds three years, or to which the state, a province, or a commune is a party, provided that its annual value is not less than L. 300,000.[114]

b. REFUNDS. As in the case of succession taxes (3/4.10g), the general rule is that registration taxes collected according to the law cannot be refunded. Exceptions are made for taxes on gifts of which the taxpayer was deprived by eviction or other deprivation (*spoglio*), under the same conditions as for the succession taxes. Other exceptions are the annulment of a compulsory sale; annulment by final judgment of an act void from the beginning because of an essential defect (*vizio radicale*); and cancellation or annulment of a nuptial agreement. The time limit for filing a request for refund is six months from the date of the judgment declaring the annulment (LR art. 14).

c. REGISTRATION ON ACCOUNT. Special rules of payment apply in the case of registration on account (*registrazione a debito*), under which the document is registered in a special register (*campione*), and the tax is collected at a later date or, in certain cases, not at all. It must be distinguished from gratuitous registration, which never involves payment of tax. In registration on account, payment of tax is left in abeyance, subject to the condition that the pending action with regard to which the document has been registered will bring benefit to the party granted the right to register on account.

The right to register on account is granted by law to the state and entities treated, for tax purposes, in the same manner as the state; and on request, to persons declared bankrupt, in cases where the assets of the bankrupt are insufficient to defray the expenses of the bankruptcy proceedings, and to persons and entities granted the right to free legal assistance (*gratuito patrocinio*).

For nonjudicial acts subject to registration within a fixed time limit, registration on account is granted only if the acts come into being after the commencement of the proceedings for which the right of *gratuito patrocinio* was granted. For nonjudicial acts subject to registration only in case of use, the date of the act in question is irrelevant, but the request for registration on account must follow the granting of the right of *gratuito patrocinio*. Judicial acts may be registered on account only if

---

[114] L. 23 March 1940, n. 283, arts. 1, 2.

they are issued on behalf of or at the request of the party who enjoys the right of *gratuito patrocinio*. If the other party is subsequently required to pay the litigation costs, the state has the right to collect from it within three months the tax registered on account, in proportion to its share of the costs. Also, if the person granted *gratuito patrocinio* subsequently receives as a result of the judicial proceedings an amount of at least six times his share of the tax, he becomes personally liable to pay his share of the tax within three months (LR art. 115). Thus, for example, if the rich party has been adjudged liable for two thirds of the costs, and the poor one (granted the right of *gratuito patrocinio*), one third, the state will demand two thirds of the tax from the rich party, and the rest from the poor party if the latter has obtained at least six times the amount of that one third in the proceedings. Consequently, if the total costs are charged to the rich party, the other litigant will never be liable for the fees.[115]

15/8. Penalties

15/8.1 In General

The penalties for the violation of the legal provisions concerning registration taxes are of two kinds. First, although failure to register does not invalidate an act, the use of the nonregistered act is limited.[116] In particular, notaries, judicial officials, and officials of the public administration may not issue an act subject to registration unless it has been previously registered (LR art. 117).[117] In addition, public officials are prohibited from inserting in their acts, or receiving in deposit, acts subject to registration but not registered, and from issuing orders on the basis of such acts. Civil judges and arbiters are prohibited from rendering judgments, awards, or orders on the basis of such acts, and attorneys may not use or cite them in their pleadings and court proceedings. Violators of the above rules are required to pay the tax and surcharges due, but have the right of recovery against the parties to the act (LR art. 118).[118] Furthermore, all acts and contracts for which a reduction of tax has been granted by law lose the reduction if they have not been registered within the prescribed time limits (LR art. 110) (15/4.5a).[119] This rule is applied also in cases of acts subject to a fixed fee.[120]

---

[115] *Gratuito patrocinio* is regulated by R.D. 30 December 1923, n. 3282. On registration on account, see Berliri, *Le leggi di registro* 479-492; 2 Jammarino, *Commento alla legge sulle imposte di registro* 137-165; 3 Uckmar, *La legge del registro* 231-263.

[116] Cass., Sez. un, 30 July 1947; Cass., Sez. un., 10 October 1956, n. 3487.

[117] R.D. 13 January 1936, n. 2313, art. 1.

[118] The violation by a judge of the prohibition provided by article 118 does not make the judgment null and void. See Cass. 27 May 1955, n. 1619.

[119] R.D. 13 January 1936, n. 2313, art. 1.

[120] Comm. Centr., Sez. VI, 10 April 1954, n. 60205; Comm. Centr., Sez. IV, 12 January 1956, n. 77727.

In addition to these consequences, a surcharge, a pecuniary penalty, and, in a very few cases, a fine are provided for specified violations (15/8.2-15/8.4).

15/8.2 Surcharges

A surcharge (*sopratassa*) constitutes a certain compensation for the damage done to the state by the violation of the law. It is imposed for failure to register acts or late filing of the declaration required by the law for the assessment of the principal and complementary taxes, and for late payment of the tax finally assessed.

The most important instance in which a surcharge is imposed is that of public officials and notaries who fail, within the prescribed time limit, to make a registration or to carry out other duties imposed by the registration laws; the surcharge is equal to six tenths of the tax due. If the act was registered on account (15/7.2c), the surcharge is applied in the amount of one twentieth of the tax due. The surcharge is not applied if the delay was caused by absolute necessity justified and recognized by the Intendant of Finance and, in case of dispute, by competent judicial authority, provided that the registration is made within 10 days of the cessation of the reason for delay. The public officials and notaries have the right of recovery against the parties if the funds to pay the registration tax have not been supplied by them (LR art. 99).[121]

For noncertified private writings, acts stipulated abroad, and wills not registered within the prescribed time limits, the surcharge is equal to the amount of the tax due plus one fifth, that is, 120% of the tax due (LR art. 100). The surcharge for omitted or late registration of leases of immovables, made in noncertified writings or oral agreements, is six times the tax due (LR art. 101).[122]

A surcharge of six tenths of the tax due is imposed in cases of failure to declare or late declaration of any of the acts listed below (LR art. 102).[123]

1. Merger of usufruct and bare ownership.
2. Devolution of total benefits and the fulfillment of a condition of survival to which a gift is subject.
3. Fulfillment of suspensive conditions (15/3.3f) in contracts.
4. The final price or value of transfers of immovables, and of contracts of *appalto* based on a presumed price.
5. Amount of actual gross proceeds in contracts of concession for carrying on public services (15/6.3g) and related acts of transfer.[124]

---

[121] R.D. 13 January 1936, n. 2313, art. 1.
[122] R.D. 13 January 1936, n. 2313, art. 1. The surcharge is due only from the person declaring the act. See Comm. Centr. 17 October 1939, n. 18144.
[123] R.D. 13 January 1936, n. 2313, art. 1.
[124] R.D.L. 9 May 1935, n. 606, art. 3.

There is a surcharge of one tenth of the tax due if the payment of the tax and the surcharge has not been made within the time limits for payment. A similar surcharge is due for insufficient valuation or higher value determined by agreement between the taxpayer and the Registry Office (15/7.1) if payment has not been made within 20 days from that on which the taxpayer was notified by the bailiff of the settlement (*liquidazione*) (LR art. 103).[125]

The surcharges for late declaration or registration and for late payment are reduced to one half of their amount if the payment of the amount due is made before the initiation of an injunction procedure. The surcharges are, besides, reduced to one tenth if the declaration, registration, and payment are made within 60 days of the expiration of the applicable time limit (LR art. 104).

15/8.3 Pecuniary Penalties

A pecuniary penalty (*pena pecuniaria*) fulfills the function of a sanction and is imposed for a violation which is not a crime. It is measured not only according to the seriousness of the violation but also according to the character and behavior of the offender. The penalty may vary between a fixed minimum and maximum.

Anyone who conceals a part of the agreed value in the execution of a public act, a private writing, or the declaration of an oral contract of lease of immovables is subject to a pecuniary penalty of not less than the tax due and not more than twice the tax due on the undisclosed value. If the value has been assessed by agreement or by judicial decision, the tax is applied to the difference between the value agreed upon or assessed in court and the larger value proved to have been concealed. The pecuniary penalty is calculated on the difference between the value originally declared by the taxpayer and that resulting from the proof of concealment, but the amount of any pecuniary penalty to which the taxpayer may be subject on final valuation, under article 40, discussed below, is deducted from the amount of the pecuniary penalty so applied. The public official who drew up the act and anyone who has used it are jointly and severally liable for the tax due and the pecuniary penalty if they had knowledge of the concealment (LR art. 105).

A pecuniary penalty may also be imposed in connection with the collection of the complementary tax (15/7.2a) as a result of a final decision of an administrative commission. If the value assessed by the commission, reduced by one fourth, exceeds the value declared by the taxpayer, he must pay, besides the tax on the difference between the two values, a pecuniary penalty of not less than one tenth of the tax and not more than the amount of the tax plus one fifth (LR art. 40).

---

[125] R.D. 13 January 1936, n. 2313, art. 1.

Various pecuniary penalties are also imposed on public officials for violations of their duties with regard to registration (see LR arts. 68, 81, 117, 131, 135).

15/8.4   Fines

The penalty of a fine (*ammenda*) imposed in cases of lesser criminal offenses (*contravvenzioni*) has limited application in the registration tax laws. A fine of from L. 500 to L. 20,000 is imposed, for example, in the case of refusal to produce accounting books for purposes of valuation of enterprises and participation shares in companies.[126] Refusal to permit inspection and check by the District Commission is subject to the same fine.[127]

15/9.   Time Limits

15/9.1   Refunds

The right of the taxpayer to request the refund of a tax not due must be exercised within a three-year limitation period running from the date of payment (LR art. 136). In cases where the tax is due on the fulfillment of an event following the act (for example, merger of usufruct and bare ownership) which the taxpayer must declare, the limitation period runs from the date of the declaration (LR art. 137).[128] The right to the refund of the higher tax paid at the registration of contracts with a variable consideration is also governed by a three-year limitation period running from the date on which the final value was assessed (LR art. 137).

15/9.2   Collection

The right of the state to demand supplementary payment of taxes must be exercised within a three-year limitation period running from the date of the registration of the act or contract (LR art. 136). This is true even if gratuitous registration has been erroneously granted.[129]

The right of the state to obtain taxes and surcharges due for unregistered acts, oral agreements, and undeclared transfers is subject to a 20-year limitation period. Such acts, however, may not be used in court or in administrative acts or before government offices unless they have been registered and the basic tax (but not the surcharge) has been paid.

---

[126] R.D.L. 7 August 1936, n. 1639, art. 19; R.D. 17 September 1931, n. 1608, art. 20.

[127] R.D. 8 July 1937, n. 1516, art. 25.

[128] In the case of a legal transaction assessed by a judgment, the limitation period runs from the date of the judgment. See Cass. 6 February 1957.

[129] App. Roma 26 March 1946 (*Foro it.*, 1947, I, 306); Comm. Centr. 7 June 1946 (*Foro it.*, 1947, III, 99). This period of limitation is applied also for complementary taxes. See Giannini, *Istituzioni di diritto tributario* 410, n. 43; 3 Uckmar, *La legge del registro* 374.

However, if the act is inserted or declared in other acts in public or private form, the tax due on the act inserted or declared is applied even if 20 years have elapsed, but no interest is due (LR art. 138).

The power of the state to revise prices and values resulting from the declaration of the taxpayer or determined ex officio is subject to a one-year limitation period running from the date of the payment of principal tax or from the date of the act granting an extension, if any.[130]

15/9.3   Interruption of the Limitation Periods

The rules regarding the interruption of the limitation periods are the same as those with respect to the succession taxes (LR arts. 140, 141) (3/4.12).[131]

15/10. Protests and Appeals

The rules governing protests and appeals are the same as those described at 3/4.11 for the inheritance tax.

15/11. International Aspects

15/11.1   Transactions Executed Abroad

Transactions executed abroad are subject to registration and tax in Italy if they contain transfers of ownership of other property rights in, or of the enjoyment of, immovable property situated in Italy, or if they establish servitudes, mortgages, or other charges, or leases or contracts relating to leases, of immovable property situated in Italy (15/3.1).

All contracting parties and all those in whose interest registration is requested are jointly and severally liable for payment of registration taxes on taxable transactions concluded abroad (15/2.1).

15/11.2   Transactions Involving Property Located Abroad or Activities Carried on Abroad

Transfers of immovable property situated abroad are subject to Italian registration taxes if made by inter vivos transactions in Italy (LR art. 15); the rate of tax on such transfers is 1% of the value (15/6.3b). Movable property and credits existing abroad and services to be performed abroad are subject to the ordinary Italian registration taxes when they form the object of an instrument executed (*stipulazione*) in Italy (LR art. 15).

Shares, bonds, and other securities of foreign companies and transactions connected with their negotiation are exempt from the registration tax, or subject to a fixed fee, in the same manner as securities of Italian

---

[130] R.D.L. 7 August 1936, n. 1639, arts. 20, 21; D.L.C.P.S. 21 January 1947, n. 25, art. 1.

[131] Compare articles 89 and 90 of R.D. 30 December 1923, n. 3270.

companies (15/4.2). Gifts for the benefit of legally recognized foreign institutions for charity, education, or welfare are subject to registration tax at the rate of 5% in the same manner as gifts to Italian institutions which are not entitled to a special exemption (LR art. 44) (15/4.3).[132]

---

[132] This provision also applies to gifts to an entity whose principal office is situated abroad. R.D.L. 6 November 1930, n. 1509, art. 1.

REFERENCES

Table of Cases

Decisions of the Constitutional Court, the Supreme Court of Cassation, the Courts of Appeal, the Tribunals, and the Central and Provincial Tax Commissions are listed below chronologically.

Comm. Centr. 24 September 1870, n. 12949   7/2.8

Comm. Centr. 6 March 1873, n. 13772   7/2.8

Comm. Centr. 7 August 1875, n. 36901   11/3.5b

Comm. Centr. 1 July 1877, n. 46687   7/5.1

Cass. Roma 29 December 1877   3/4.10a

Cass. 21 May 1889   11/3.5b

Cass. Roma 15 May 1894   3/4.10a

Cass. Roma 11 January 1899   15/3.1

Comm. Centr. 16 April 1901, n. 80390   10/2.2a

Cass. Roma 31 December 1902   15/5.3

Cass. 23 November 1905   11/3.5a

Cass. 21 October 1910   9/1.3

Comm. Centr. 18 October 1915, n. 73089   11/2.3b

Cass. 15 April 1916   9/8.2

Cass. Roma 3 May 1916   15/6.3a

App. Casale 29 January 1919   15/3.4a

Comm. Centr. 10 March 1921, n. 6228   9/8.2

Cass. 31 March 1921   3/4.3a

Cass. Roma 24 April 1922   15/3.3d

Cass. 15 January 1926   11/3.5a

Cass. 26 May 1926   15/3.3d

Cass., Sez. un., 14 January 1927   9/8.2

Comm. Centr. 9 March 1927, n. 71624   10/3

Cass. 13 January 1928   15/2.1

Cass. Roma 7 February 1928   15/3.3d

Comm. Centr. 9 February 1928, n. 82469   10/1.1

Comm. Centr. 4 April 1928, n. 83883   9/8.3

Comm. Centr. 24 May 1928, n. 85428   13/3.4

Comm. Centr. 6 June 1928, n. 86122   9/3.1

Cass. 12 November 1928   3/4.10f

Cass. 6 April 1929   3/4.3a

Comm. Centr. 8 May 1929, n. 95507   8/1.7

Trib. Bari 12 March 1930   3/4.10f

Comm. Centr. 22 March 1930, n. 3685   8/1.9

Cass., Sez. I, 21 May 1930   15/5.1

Comm. Centr. 8 July 1930, n. 9421   9/3.1

Cass., Sez. un., 25 July 1930   15/3.3f

Comm. Centr. 6 December 1930, n. 15070   10/2.3a

Comm. Centr. 15 December 1930, n. 15569   7/2.8

Comm. Centr. 16 December 1930, n. 15606   6/1.3

Comm. Centr., Sez. un., 18 February 1931, n. 18416   11/3.5a

Comm. Centr., Sez. un., 25 March 1931, n. 20441   9/9.4

Comm. Centr. 3 October 1931, n. 27299   8/3.1

Cass. 16 November 1931   3/4.6a

Cass. 11 December 1931   3/4.6a

Comm. Centr., Sez. un., 16 December 1931, n. 31938   10/1.3

Comm. Centr., Sez. un., 16 December 1931, n. 31939   10/1.3

Comm. Centr. 1 March 1932, n. 34551   7/2.10

Cass. 29 March 1932   3/4.3b

Comm. Centr., Sez. un., 6 April 1932, n. 35619   7/4.5

Cass. 28 April 1932   3/4.6c

Comm. Centr. 1 October 1932, n. 40667   7/2.3

Cass., Sez. III, 14 January 1933   15/2.1

REFERENCES

Cass., Sez. I, 17 May 1933   15/7.1
Cass., Sez. I, 3 June 1933   15/3.4a
Cass., Sez. I, 30 June 1933   15/7.1
Comm. Centr., Sez. un., 26 July 1933, n. 53445   10/1.3
Cass. 27 July 1933   15/3.3a
Comm. Centr., Sez. un., 15 November 1933, n. 55447   9/9.7
App. Bologna 12 January 1934   3/4.6a
Cass. 7 May 1934   9/9.4
Cass., Sez. un., 9 August 1934   15/3.3a
Cass., Sez. I, 5 December 1934   15/2.1
App. Torino 18 January 1935   3/4.6a
Cass., Sez. I, 22 January 1935   3/4.6a
Comm. Centr. 25 February 1935, n. 72870   9/9.2
Comm. Centr., Sez. un., 27 February 1935, n. 72945   11/2.3b; 11/3.5b
Comm. Centr., Sez. un., 12 February 1936, n. 84394   11/2.3b
Comm. Centr. 30 April 1936, n. 87472   9/9.2
Comm. Centr. 7 July 1936, n. 90523   10/1.1
Cass., Sez. I, 3 August 1936   15/3.3b
Cass., Sez. I, 4 August 1936   15/3.3d
Cass., Sez. un., 5 November 1936   9/9.2
Cass., Sez. I, 1 December 1936   7/2.7
App. Bari 11 January 1937   15/3.4a
Comm. Centr., Sez. un., 13 January 1937, n. 96279   9/2.1b
Comm. Centr., Sez. un., 13 January 1937, n. 96282   9/2.1b
Cass., Sez. un., 4 March 1937   9/9.7
Comm. Centr. 8 March 1937, n. 98532   9/2.1b
Comm. Centr. 16 March 1937, n. 98848   9/9.2
Cass. 23 March 1937   3/4.6a
Cass., Sez. I, 17 May 1937   15/5.1
Comm. Centr. 21 June 1937, n. 101792   9/9.7
Comm. Centr. 22 July 1937, n. 103027   11/1.6a
Comm. Centr. 23 July 1937, n. 103098   9/2.1b
Cass., Sez. I, 4 January-23 February 1938   3/4.10f
Trib. Milano 16 April 1938   11/3.5a
Comm. Centr., Sez. un., 1 June 1938, n. 6599   9/2.1b
Cass., Sez. III, 13 July 1938   15/3.3f
Comm. Centr. 21 December 1938   15/3.5
Comm. Centr. 24 January 1939, n. 12456   15/7.1
Comm. Centr. 3 March 1939, n. 13727   11/3.5a

Comm. Centr. 3 March 1939, n. 13728   11/3.5b
Comm. Centr. 3 March 1939, n. 13729   11/3.5b
Comm. Centr. 3 March 1939, n. 13730   11/3.5b
Comm. Centr. 3 March 1939, n. 13731   11/3.5b
Comm. Centr., Sez. un., 22 March 1939, n. 14411   9/3.1
Comm. Centr. 15 May 1939, n. 15751   15/3.3b
Comm. Centr., Sez. un., 25 May 1939, n. 15993   9/9.4
Comm. Centr. 12 June 1939, n. 16494   3/4.3b
Comm. Centr., Sez. un., 30 June 1939, n. 16967   7/2.4
Comm. Centr. 20 July 1939, n. 17681   10/2.2d
Comm. Centr. 27 July 1939, n. 17738   15/3.3j
Comm. Centr. 17 October 1939, n. 18115   9/9.4; 9/9.7
Comm. Centr. 17 October 1939, n. 18144   15/8.2
Comm. Centr. 18 October 1939, n. 18213   15/3.3f
Comm. Centr. 24 January 1940   15/7.1
Comm. Centr. 30 January 1940, n. 21811   3/4.6a
Comm. Centr., Sez. un., 21 February 1940, n. 22715   7/2.3; 8/1.6; 9/2.1a
Cass. 19 July 1940   15/3.2
Comm. Centr., Sez. VII, 25 July 1940, n. 30237   3/4.3a
Cass., Sez. I, 29 July 1940, n. 2575   7/1.3
Comm. Centr., Sez. III, 25 October 1940, n. 31481   9/9.4
Comm. Centr. 10 January 1941, n. 35143   8/3.1
Comm. Centr., Sez. III, 4 March 1941, n. 38141   7/2.8
Cass., Sez. I, 10 March 1941, n. 698   9/2.1b
Cass., Sez. I, 3 April 1941, n. 947   13/2.3
Comm. Centr., Sez. II, 29 May 1941, n. 42054   10/2.3a
Comm. Centr., Sez. III, 18 June 1941, n. 43071   11/1.6c
Comm. Centr. 18 June 1941, n. 43099   15/3.4a
Comm. Centr. 23 June 1941, n. 46282   11/1.6a
Comm. Centr., Sez. III, 21 July 1941, n. 44759   10/1.1

Comm. Centr., Sez. II, 7 October
1941, n. 45437   10/2.3a
Comm. Centr., Sez. un., 12 November 1941, n. 47391   13/1.1a
Comm. Centr., Sez. un., 12 November 1941, n. 47398   13/4.3
Comm. Centr., Sez. un., 12 November 1941, n. 53296   6/9.2
Cass. 2 January 1942   3/4.8b
Comm. Centr., Sez. un., 31 January
1942, n. 50514   9/9.9a
Comm. Centr., Sez. II, 2 March
1942, n. 52059   8/1.4
Comm. Centr., Sez. III, 26 March
1942, n. 53346   7/3.9
Comm. Centr., Sez. III, 11 May
1942, n. 55406   10/2.3a
Comm. Centr., Sez. un., 15 June
1942, n. 57143   11/2.3b
Comm. Centr., Sez. IV, 15 December 1942, n. 64043   13/2.3
Comm. Centr., Sez. VI, 21 January
1943, n. 65284   3/4.8b
Cass., Sez. un., 27 January 1943, n.
184   9/9.4
Comm. Centr., Sez. un., 3 February
1943, n. 65922   10/4.1; 11/1.6a
Comm. Centr., Sez. VII, 18 February 1943, n. 66798   3/4.10e
Cass. 16 June 1943   15/3.2
Cass., Sez. un., 25 February 1944, n.
115   7/1.3
Cass., Sez. I, 17 April 1944, n.
260   15/2.1
Comm. Centr. 15 June 1944, n.
63775   15/2.1
Cass., Sez. un., 14 May 1945, n.
339   13/4.9b
Comm. Centr., Sez. III, 15 June
1945, n. 76996   8/1.5
Comm. Centr., Sez. un., 9 July 1945,
n. 77517   3/4.6a
Comm. Centr., Sez. III, 20 July
1945, n. 77842   8/2.1
Comm. Centr., Sez. I, 15 October
1945, n, 78315   9/3.1
Comm. Centr., Sez. un., 24 November 1945, n. 79346   9/8.4; 9/9.2
Comm. Centr., Sez. I, 3 December
1945, n. 79522   9/9.4
Comm. Centr., Sez. III, 12 December 1945, n. 79768   13/2.3
Cass., Sez. I, 14 January 1946, n.
19   11/2.3a
Cass., Sez. I, 11 February 1946, n.
115   8/2.1
Comm. Centr., Sez. I, 22 March
1946, n. 81623   8/2.1

Comm. Centr., Sez. II, 25 March
1946, n. 81693   10/2.3a
App. Roma 26 March 1946   15/9.2
Comm. Centr., Sez. I, 2 May 1946,
n. 82032   13/4.4
Comm. Centr., Sez. I, 6 May 1946,
n. 82273   10/1.1
Cass., Sez. I, 10 May 1946   15/3.3j
Comm. Centr. 7 June 1946   15/9.2
Comm. Centr., Sez. IV, 13 June
1946, n. 82988   13/2.4
Comm. Centr., Sez. I, 10 July 1946,
n. 83514   8/1.5
Comm. Centr., Sez. un., 8 November 1946, n. 84911   3/4.2
Comm. Centr., Sez. un., 9 November
1946, n. 85001   9/9.3
Comm. Centr., Sez. IV, 19 December 1946, n. 86366   15/5.3
Cass. 9 January 1947   15/3.2
Cass., Sez. I, 22 February 1947, n.
253   7/1.3
Cass., Sez. I, 22 February 1947,
n. 254   9/3.1
Cass., Sez. I, 13 March 1947, n.
367   13/4.9b
Comm. Centr., Sez. III, 16 April
1947, n. 89084   8/1.2
Comm. Centr., Sez. VII, 26 May
1947, n. 90214   3/4.10e
Cass., Sez. I, 29 May 1947   14/2.7
Comm. Centr., Sez. un., 5 July 1947,
n. 91408   11/2.3b
Comm. Centr., Sez. un., 7 July 1947,
n. 91418   8/2.1
Comm. Centr., Sez. VII, 14 July
1947, n. 91672   3/4.8c
Cass., Sez. un., 30 July 1947   15/8.1
Cass., Sez. un., 30 August 1947, n.
1557   11/1.6a
Cass., Sez. I, 3 September 1947, n.
1559   5/5.6
Comm. Centr., Sez. VII, 13 October
1947, n. 92132   3/6
Comm. Centr. 6 November 1947, n.
6762   15/3.3e
Comm. Centr., Sez. VII, 7 November
1947, n. 92817   3/4.6a
Comm. Centr., Sez. II, 19 January
1948, n. 94657   9/8.4
Comm. Centr., Sez. un., 7 February
1948, n. 95317   9/3.1
Comm. Centr., Sez. IV, 17 February
1948, n. 95619   15/3.3b
Comm. Centr., Sez. VII, 14 April
1948, n. 97052   3/4.3f
Comm. Centr., Sez. II, 9 June 1948,
n. 98766   10/1.3

Comm. Centr., Sez. II, 14 June 1948,
n. 98897   7/1.3; 10/1.3
Comm. Centr., Sez. II, 23 June 1948,
n. 99181   7/2.1
Cass., Sez. I, 13 August 1948   15/3.4a
Comm. Centr., Sez. I, 20 October
1948, n. 100768   9/8.2
Comm. Centr., Sez. V, 7 March
1949, n. 1171   15/3.3f
Comm. Centr., Sez. V, 12 May 1949,
n. 3304   15/3.3g
Comm. Centr., Sez. VI, 23 June
1949, n. 4743   15/3.3e
Cass. 5 July 1949   15/4.4
Comm. Centr. 6 July 1949, n. 5151
15/3.3j
Comm. Centr., Sez. un., 6 July 1949,
n. 5156   14/7.3e
Cass., Sez. I, 9 July 1949   15/3.2
Comm. Centr. 19 July 1949, n.
100077   3/5.5
Cass. 4 August 1949   15/3.3f
Comm. Centr., Sez. VI, 9 November
1949, n. 6875   3/4.8c
Comm. Centr. 28 November 1949,
n. 7559   11/3.5a
Comm. Centr. 12 December 1949,
n. 8129   15/3.3j
Comm. Centr., Sez. II, 17 January
1950, n. 8923   9/9.4
Trib. Firenze 23 January 1950   14/7.3f
Comm. Centr., Sez. I, 22 March
1950, n. 11531   10/2.3a
Comm. Centr., Sez. un., 22 May
1950, n. 13610   13/1.1a
Comm. Centr., Sez. VI, 10 Novem-
ber 1950, n. 17248   14/7.3e
Comm. Centr., Sez. II, 11 Novem-
ber 1950, n. 17275   9/8.8
Comm. Centr., Sez. VI, 13 Novem-
ber 1950, n. 17364   3/4.7a
Trib. Milano 12 January 1951   14/4.6i
Comm. Centr. 8 February 1951, n.
20288   2/3.3b
Comm. Centr., Sez. II, 24 February
1951, n. 20995   9/9.2
Comm. Centr., Sez. VI, 2 March
1951, n. 21281   15/3.3g
Cass. 5 March 1951   14/8.4a
Comm. Centr., Sez. VI, 14 March
1951, n. 21765   13/2.4
Cass., Sez. I, 30 March 1951   15/3.2
Cass., Sez. un., 6 April 1951, n.
800   13/4.10
Comm. Centr., Sez. VI, 7 May 1951,
n. 23509   3/5.4
Comm. Centr., Sez. II, 9 October
1951, n. 27911   10/2.3a

Cass. 25 October 1951   14/7.2a;
14/8.4a
Cass., Sez. un., 30 October 1951,
n. 2651   10/2.3a
Comm. Centr., Sez. un., 10 Novem-
ber 1951, n. 29243   10/2.3a
Comm. Centr., Sez. VI, 17 December 1951, n. 30835   15/3.3g
Comm. Centr., Sez. VI, 17 Decem-
ber 1951, n. 30839   3/4.3g
Cass. Pen., Sez. I, 14 January 1952
14/4.2
Comm. Centr., Sez. VI, 18 February
1952, n. 33116   3/4.3a
Cass., Sez. I, 10 March 1952   13/4.10
Cass., Sez. un., 13 March-6 June
1952   14/7.3e
Cass., Sez. I, 24 March 1952, n.
806   13/4.9b
Comm. Centr., Sez. VI, 4 April 1952,
n. 35020   3/4.3a
Cass., Sez. I, 17 April 1952, n. 1023
13/4.9b; 13/4.10
Comm. Centr. 9 May 1952, n. 36105
15/3.3e
Comm. Centr., Sez. VI, 23 May
1952, n. 36668   15/4.5b
Comm. Centr., Sez. VI, 26 May
1952, n. 36755   15/4.5b
Cass. 27 May 1952   14/7.2a; 14/8.4a
App. Genova 11 June 1952   14/10.2
Cass., Sez. un., 14 June 1952   14/7.3f
Comm. Centr., Sez. VI, 16 June
1952, n. 37532   3/4.3g
Comm. Centr., Sez. un., 16 July
1952, n. 38978   15/3.2
Comm. Centr., Sez. un., 16 July
1952, n. 38979   13/4.3
Cass., Sez. I, 11 October 1952   14/4.6h
Comm. Centr., Sez. VI, 31 October
1952, n. 40455   15/5.1
Comm. Centr. 27 December 1952,
n. 33523   15/7.2a
Cass., Sez. III, 5 January 1953, n. 1
14/2.7
Trib. Firenze 13 February 1953   13/3.1
Comm. Centr., Sez. V, 23 March
1953, n. 46183   15/2.1
Cass. Pen. 25 March 1953   14/3.1
Cass., Sez. I, 30 March 1953   14/4.7
Comm. Centr., Sez. VI, 13 April
1953, n. 46704   3/4.7a
Cass., Sez. I, 14 April 1953, n. 962
10/2.3a
Comm. Centr., Sez. II, 19 May 1953,
n. 48280   9/9.2; 9/9.4
Comm. Centr., Sez. un., 26 May
1953, n. 48558   10/2.3a

Comm. Centr. 8 June 1953, n. 49073
                 15/3.2
Comm. Centr., Sez. II, 16 June 1953,
  n. 49427   10/6.2c
Cass. 9 September 1953, n. 2995 14/7.3f
Comm. Centr., Sez. II, 24 October
  1953, n. 52485   8/1.2
Comm. Centr., Sez. II, 3 November
  1953, n. 52908   10/2.3a
Comm. Centr., Sez. VI, 9 January
  1954, n. 55700   3/4.6c
Comm. Centr., Sez. V, 1 February
  1954, n. 56800   15/7.1
Cass., Sez. un., 13 March 1954, n.
  703   13/4.10
Comm. Centr., Sez. IV, 23 March
  1954, n. 59156   15/3.3g
Comm. Centr., Sez. VI, 10 April
  1954, n. 60205   15/8.1
Cass., Sez. un., 3 May 1954, n. 1361
                14/7.3f
Cass., Sez. I, 7 June 1954, n. 1862
                15/3.4a
Cass., Sez. un., 10 July 1954, n. 13
                14/4.2
Cass., Sez. I, 10 July 1954, n. 2446
                15/3.31
Cass., Sez. I, 24 September 1954,
  n. 3123   14/4.5
Comm. Centr. 20 October 1954, n.
  64558   15/3.2
Trib. Milano 23 December 1954 15/3.2
Comm. Centr. 12 January 1955, n.
  67166   10/6.2c
Comm. Centr., Sez. V, 19 January
  1955, n. 67464   15/3.31
Comm. Centr., Sez. un., 21 February
  1955, n. 68742   9/8.4; 9/9.2
Comm. Centr., Sez. III, 4 March
  1955, n. 69235   13/2.3
Cass. 27 May 1955, n. 1619   15/8.1
Comm. Centr., Sez. I, 7 June 1955,
  n. 72790   10/6.2b
Comm. Prov. Cremona 10 June 1955
                3/5.5
Comm. Centr., Sez. II, 11 June 1955,
  n. 72945   7/1.3
Comm. Centr., Sez. VI, 27 June
  1955, n. 73598   3/6
Comm. Centr., Sez. V, 1 July 1955,
  n. 73720   15/3.3e
App. Roma 4 July 1955   14/7.2d
Trib. Genova 9 August 1955   14/4.2
Cass., Sez. I, 7 October 1955, n.
  2887   11/2.3c
Cass., Sez. un., 12 October 1955, n.
  3041   14/1; 14/7.3f

Comm. Centr., Sez. I, 26 October
  1955, n. 75334   10/6.2b
Comm. Centr., Sez. III, 28 November 1955, n. 76536   9/5
Comm. Centr., Sez. III, 9 December
  1955, n. 77015   13/2.3
App. Torino 23 December 1955 14/2.2c
Comm. Centr., Sez. IV, 12 January
  1956, n. 77727   15/8.1
Comm. Centr., Sez. II, 14 January
  1956, n. 77795   10/6.2b
Cass., Sez. un., 23 January 1956,
  n. 202   15/2.1
Comm. Centr. 6 February 1956,
  n. 78608   3/6
Comm. Centr., Sez. un., 6 February
  1956, n. 78639   10/1.1
Comm. Centr., Sez. II, 10 March
  1956, n. 79929   10/6.2b
Comm. Centr., Sez. IV, 13 March
  1956, n. 80070   15/6.3b
Comm. Centr., Sez. V, 21 March
  1956, n. 80331   15/4.5b
Comm. Centr., Sez. V, 23 March
  1956, n. 80438   15/3.31
Comm. Centr., Sez. I, 24 March
  1956, n. 80477   7/2.1
Cass., Sez. I, 12 April 1956, n. 1065
                14/4.4
Comm. Centr., Sez. II, 28 April
  1956, n. 81431   9/9.9a
Comm. Prov. Napoli 8 May 1956 8/1.9
App. Firenze 17 July 1956   13/3.1
Cass., Sez. I, 27 July 1956, n. 2908
                15/3.3e
Cass., Sez. un., 10 October 1956, n.
  3487   15/8.1
Cass. 2 November 1956   3/6
Comm. Centr., Sez. II, 16 November
  1956, n. 86364   7/2.3
Comm. Centr., Sez. VI, 3 December
  1956, n. 87103   3/4.6a
Comm. Centr., Sez. I, 10 December
  1956, n. 87343   10/6.2b
Comm. Centr., Sez. V, 10 December
  1956, n. 87361   15/4.2
Comm. Centr., Sez. V, 7 January
  1957, n. 87977   15/4.2
Comm. Centr., Sez. II, 15 January
  1957, n. 88246   10/6.2b
Cass., Sez. un., 19 January 1957, n.
  127   10/2.3a
Cass., Sez. un., 19 January 1957, n.
  128   10/2.3a; 13/4.9b
Corte Cost. 26 January 1957, n. 12
                1/4.10b
Cass. 30 January 1957, n. 326 14/7.3f
Cass. 6 February 1957   15/9.1

Corte Cost. 11 March 1957, n. 41
                        1/4.10a; 1/4.10b
Corte Cost. 11 March 1957, n. 42
                                1/4.10b
Cass., Sez. I, 16 March 1957, n. 921
                                    3/6
Comm. Centr., Sez. II, 8 May 1957,
  n. 93217   10/6.2b
Comm. Centr. 21 May 1957, n.
  93814   10/6.2b
Cass., Sez. I, 21 June 1957, n. 2369
                                13/4.10
Cass., Sez. un., 3 July 1957, n. 2599
                                15/3.3e
Cass. 19 October 1957, n. 3985   3/4.3b
Cass., Sez. un., 7 November 1957, n.
  4259   14/7.2d; 14/7.3f; 14/10.2
Cass., Sez. I, 15 March 1958, n. 854
                                14/2.3a
Comm. Centr., Sez. un., 24 March
  1958, n. 3338   15/4.2
Comm. Centr., Sez. II, 25 March
  1958, n. 3377   10/2.3a
Comm. Centr., Sez. I, 3 May 1958,
  n. 4605   10/2.3a
Cass., Sez. I, 6 May 1958, n. 1480
                                15/3.3d
Comm. Centr., Sez. I, 28 May 1958,
  n. 5633   7/2.3
Comm. Centr., Sez. III, 6 June 1958,
  n. 6015   9/2.1b
Cass. 14 June 1958, n. 8024   5/3.2
Comm. Centr., Sez. III, 25 June
  1958, n. 6845   13/4.1
Comm. Centr., Sez. I, 16 July 1958,
  n. 7744   10/2.3a
Cass., Sez. I, 24 July 1958, n. 2679
                                 14/3.7
Cass. 23 September 1958, n. 3035
                                  5/3.2
Comm. Centr., Sez. II, 15 December
  1958, n. 11014   7/1.2
Comm. Centr. 29 December 1958,
  n. 11245   10/6.2b
Comm. Centr., Sez. III, 11 March
  1959, n. 14440   7/2.7
Cass. 3 April 1959, n. 993   5/3.2
Comm. Centr. 11 May 1959, n.
  16563   11/1.6c
Comm. Centr., Sez. II, 13 May 1959,
  n. 16625   8/2.1
Comm. Centr., Sez. V, 25 May 1959,
  n. 17176   3/4.10g
Comm. Prov. Milano 5 June 1959 7/2.8
Comm. Centr., Sez. I, 15 June 1959,
  n. 17998   13/4.1
Comm. Centr., Sez. III, 3 July 1959,
  n. 18815   10/7.1

Comm. Centr., Sez. I, 20 July 1959,
  n. 19617   9/9.4
Cass., Sez. un., 14 August 1959, n.
  2542   2/3.3b
Cass., Sez. I, 23 October 1959, n.
  3051   14/2.2c
Comm. Centr., Sez. III, 28 October
  1959, n. 20600   7/1.2
Comm. Centr., Sez. I, 19 January
  1960, n. 23620   9/9.4
Comm. Centr., Sez. III, 19 February
  1960, n. 25110   9/9.4
Comm. Centr. 8 March 1960, n.
  25886   13/1.1a
Cass., Sez. I, 13 April 1960, n. 861
                                13/4.9a
Comm. Centr., Sez. III, 25 May
  1960, n. 29038   6/1.5
Corte Cost. 15 June 1960, n. 41
                                1/4.10a
Cass. 3 August 1960, n. 2283   6/4.1
Comm. Centr., Sez. I, 12 October
  1960, n. 32148   7/2.1; 7/2.8
Comm. Centr., Sez. III, 16 Novem-
  ber 1960, n. 33849   10/7.1
Comm. Centr., Sez. I, 23 November
  1960, n. 34217   9/9.4
Cass., Sez. I, 16 December 1960,
  n. 3261   6/1.5
Cass., Sez. I, 16 January 1961, n. 56
                                 15/4.2
Cass., Sez. I, 13 March 1961   3/4.6a
Corte Cost. 31 March 1961, n. 21
                        13/4.10; 13/4.12
Comm. Centr., Sez. I, 21 April 1961,
  n. 42171   13/1.1a
Comm. Centr. 8 May 1961, n. 43503
                                 9/9.9b
Corte Cost. 9 June 1961, n. 30   1/3.1d
Comm. Centr. 1 December 1961, n.
  50892   9/9.9b
Comm. Centr., Sez. II, 6 December
  1961, n. 51283   7/2.8
Corte Cost. 30 December 1961, n. 79
                                 14/7.2d
Cass., Sez. I, 11 January 1962, n. 21
                                  5/3.2
Comm. Centr., Sez. VII, 14 March
  1962, n. 86553   15/4.2
Corte Cost. ord. 16 March 1962,
  n. 110   1/2.7
Cass., Sez. I, 21 December 1962,
  n. 3401   14/8.2a
Corte Cost. 13 July 1963, n. 132
                                1/4.10b

Table of Statutes

Albertine Statute

Statuto degli Stati Sardi, 4 March 1848
(Statute of the Sardinian States *or*
Statute of Carlo Alberto)   1/2.2;
                 1/4.10g; 1/5.1
art. 25   1/2.3
art. 30   1/2.2

Constitution

Costituzione della Repubblica Italiana,
approved 22 December 1947, promulgated and published 27 December
1947, entered into force 1 January
1948   1/2.1; 1/4.10g; 1/5.1
Const.

art. 3	1/2.5; 13/4.12
art. 4	1/2.5
art. 5	1/2.7; 1/3.4a; 1/5.1
art. 7	1/2.7
art. 14	1/4.12
art. 15	1/4.12
art. 16	1/2.7
art. 18	1/2.7
art. 20	1/2.7
art. 21	1/2.7
art. 23	1/2.2; 1/3.1b; 1/3.1c; 1/5.5b; 1.5/5c
art. 24	13/4.12
art. 25	1/2.2
art. 31	1/2.5
art. 39	1/2.7
art. 41	1/2.6; 3/7.3b
art. 42	1/2.6
art. 43	1/2.6; 3/7.3b
art. 44	1/2.6
art. 45	1/2.6
art. 47	1/2.6
art. 53	1/2.3; 1/2.4; 1/2.5; 1/2.6; 1/2.8; 3/7.3b
art. 55	1/3.1a
art. 56	1/3.1a
art. 57	1/3.1a
art. 58	1/3.1a
art. 60	1/3.1a
art. 70	1/3.1b
art. 71	1/3.1b
art. 72	1/3.1b
art. 73	1/3.1b
art. 74	1/3.1b
art. 75	1/3.1b
art. 76	1/3.1d
art. 77	1/3.1c
art. 80	1/3.1e; 11/4.1
art. 81	1/3.4a; 1/3.4b; 1/3.4c
art. 83	1/3.2a

Constitution (*continued*)
Const.

art. 85	1/3.2a
art. 87	1/3.2a; 1/3.2c
art. 88	1/3.2a
art. 89	1/3.1c; 1/3.1d
art. 92	1/3.2a
art. 95	1/3.2b
art. 99	1/3.1b; 1/3.3
art. 102	1/4.10a; 1/4.10b; 1/4.13
art. 103	1/4.10a; 13/4.11
art. 104	1/4.10a
art. 105	1/4.10a
art. 106	1/4.10a
art. 107	1/4.10a
art. 111	13/4.10
art. 113	1/4.10a; 1/4.10b; 1/4.13; 13/4.11; 13/4.12
art. 114	1/5.1
art. 115	1/5.1; 1/5.5c
art. 116	1/5.1
art. 117	1/5.3
art. 118	1/5.2; 1/5.3
art. 119	1/3.4a; 1/5.5c
art. 120	1/2.7; 1/5.5c
art. 121	1/5.2
art. 122	1/5.2
art. 128	1/3.4a; 1/5.1; 1/5.3; 1/5.5c
art. 129	1/5.1
art. 134	1/4.10g
art. 135	1/4.10g
art. 136	1/4.10g
Transitory and Final Provisions art. VI	1/4.10a; 1/4.10b

Constitutional Laws

L. Cost. 9 February 1948, n. 1 1/4.10g

L. Cost. 26 February 1948, n. 3 (Stat. Sard).
    art. 8   1/5.5e

L. Cost. 26 February 1948, n. 4 (Stat. Valle d'Aosta)
    art. 12   1/5.5e
    art. 14   14/4.6k

L. Cost. 26 February 1948, n. 5 (Stat. Trentino-Alto Adige)
    arts. 60-70   1/5.5e

L. Cost. 11 March 1953, n. 87
    art. 1   1/4.10g
    art. 2   1/4.10g
    art. 3   1/4.10g
    art. 4   1/4.10g
    art. 23   1/4.10g

Civil Code

Codice civile, approved by R.D. 25 June
June 1865

arts. 13-18	15/3.5
arts. 20-22	3/4.1a
art. 407	15/3.3e
art. 423	3/4.3a

Codice civile, approved by R.D. 16
March 1942, n. 262
CC
—

art. 2	5/1.3
art. 11	5/2.7
art. 12	5/3.8
art. 17	3/4.10c
art. 36	5/3.8
art. 43	11/2.2
art. 45	11/2.2
art. 46	11/2.2
art. 49	3/4.1a
arts. 58-68	3/4.1a
arts. 74-78	3/4.7b
arts. 74-77	2/3.2
art. 77	2/3.2
art. 390	5/1.3
art. 391	5/1.3
art. 392	5/1.3
art. 394	5/1.3
arts. 404-413	3/4.7b
art. 456	5/3.9
art. 457	3/4.1a
art. 459	5/3.9
art. 460	5/3.9
art. 473	3/4.10c
art. 490	3/4.8c; 5/3.9
arts. 528-532	5/3.9
arts. 536-564	3/4.1a
art. 565	3/4.1a
art. 580	3/4.3e
art. 588	3/4.1a
arts. 641-644	5/3.9
art. 649	5/3.9
art. 669	5/3.9
art. 678	3/4.3b
arts. 688-691	3/4.3d
arts. 692-699	3/4.3d
art. 692	3/4.3d
art. 697	3/4.3d
art. 698	3/4.3b
art. 700	5/3.9
art. 703	5/3.9
art. 713	15/3.3g
art. 757	15/3.3g
arts. 769-809	3/6
art. 812	3/4.3a
arts. 817-819	15/3.3e
art. 822	9/4.2a
art. 824	9/4.2a

Civil Code (*continued*)
CC
—

art. 826	10/1.1
art. 832	9/4.1
art. 952	9/4.1
arts. 957-977	3/4.3f
art. 959	9/4.1
art. 960	9/4.1
art. 964	9/4.1
arts. 978-1020	3/4.3b
art. 979	3/4.3b; 9/4.1
art. 981	9/4.1
art. 982	9/4.1
art. 983	15/3.3e
art. 984	9/4.1
art. 985	9/4.1
art. 986	9/4.1
art. 987	9/4.1
arts. 989-1007	9/4.1
art. 1008	9/4.1
art. 1014	3/4.3b
art. 1021	3/4.3c; 9/4.1
art. 1022	3/4.3c; 9/4.1
art. 1025	9/4.1
art. 1026	9/4.1
art. 1140	9/4.1
arts. 1201-1205	3/4.10f
art. 1203	3/4.10b
art. 1203, n. 3	3/4.10f
art. 1277	2/2.6b
art. 1325	15/3.3j
art. 1346	15/3.3j
art. 1350	15/3.4a
art. 1353	15/3.3f
art. 1362	15/3.2
art. 1387	14/2.3b
art. 1414	15/3.3a
arts. 1453-1459	15/3.3j
art. 1470	15/3.3i
arts. 1523-1526	15/3.3f
art. 1531	9/2.8
art. 1548	9/2.8
art. 1550	9/2.8
art. 1552	14/3.3b; 15/3.3h
arts. 1559-1677	8/4
art. 1559	15/3.3i
art. 1575	9/4.2c
art. 1576	9/4.2c
art. 1609	4/5.8c
arts. 1647 *et seq.*	10/2.4
art. 1655	8/4; 14/3.7; 15/3.3i
arts. 1703-1730	15/3.3a
art. 1703	14/2.3b
art. 1731	14/2.3d
art. 1737	14/2.3d
art. 1742	14/2.3d
art. 1752	14/2.3b
art. 1754	14/2.3e

Civil Code (*continued*)
CC

art. 1760	14/2.3e
art. 1861	3/4.3e; 9/3.1
art. 1863	3/4.3e
art. 1864	3/4.3e
art. 1872	3/4.3e
art. 1920	3/4.3i
art. 1960	15/3.4a
art. 1965	15/3.3j
art. 2034	15/6.3a
art. 2082	7/1.2; 14/2.1
art. 2083	7/1.2; 14/2.1
art. 2094	8/1.2
art. 2099	7/2.3
art. 2117	7/2.4
art. 2120	7/2.3
art. 2121	7/2.3
art. 2135	10/2.3a
arts. 2141 *et seq.*	10/2.3a
arts. 2164 *et seq.*	10/2.3a
arts. 2170 *et seq.*	10/2.3a
art. 2195	7/1.2; 10/3
art. 2196	13/1.1d
art. 2197	13/1.1d
art. 2200	7/1.3; 9/8.1; 9/8.3; 9/8.4
art. 2202	7/1.2
arts. 2210-2213	14/2.3c
art. 2214	6/2.2; 7/1.2
art. 2215	4/7.2; 6/2.3
art. 2216	6/2.3
art. 2217	6/2.2; 6/2.3
art. 2218	6/2.3
art. 2219	6/2.3
art. 2220	6/2.3
art. 2247	5/2.1
art. 2249	5/3.4
art. 2251	5/3.4
art. 2257	5/3.2
art. 2258	5/3.2
art. 2259	5/3.2
art. 2291	5/3.2
art. 2293	5/3.2
art. 2304	6/2.2
art. 2313	5/3.3
art. 2315	5/3.3
art. 2318	5/3.3
art. 2325	5/2.2
art. 2331	5/2.1; 5/2.3; 5/2.5
art. 2349	3/2.3
art. 2353	3/2.3
art. 2364	5/2.2; 6/3.2
art. 2380	5/2.2
art. 2381	5/2.2
art. 2383	5/2.2
art. 2397	5/2.2

Civil Code (*continued*)
CC

art. 2421	6/2.2; 6/2.3
art. 2423	6/2.4
art. 2424	6/2.4
art. 2425	6/5.2; 6/5.3; 7/3.1; 7/3.9
art. 2427	7/3.9
art. 2428	6/6.2
art. 2429	6/6.2
art. 2433	9/2.1a
art. 2435	15/4.5b
art. 2440	3/2.3
art. 2442	9/2.3
art. 2446	6/5.3
art. 2462	5/2.4
art. 2464	5/2.4; 6/2.2
art. 2465	5/2.4
art. 2468	5/2.4
art. 2472	5/2.3
art. 2475	5/2.3
art. 2486	5/2.3
art. 2487	5/2.3
art. 2488	5/2.3
art. 2490	6/2.2
arts. 2498-2500	15/6.3h
art. 2502	15/4.5b
art. 2505	11/2.3a
art. 2506	11/3.3
art. 2507	11/3.4
art. 2511	5/2.5
art. 2513	5/2.5
art. 2514	5/2.5
art. 2516	5/2.5; 6/2.2; 15/4.5b
art. 2519	5/2.5; 15/4.5b
art. 2536	6/6.2
art. 2537	15/4.5b
art. 2538	15/4.5b
art. 2541	5/2.5
art. 2546	5/2.6
art. 2547	5/2.6; 6/2.2
art. 2549	5/3.5
art. 2551	5/3.5
art. 2552	5/3.5
art. 2555	3/4.6a; 5/3.7
arts. 2602 *et seq.*	14/2.3d
art. 2644	4/3.2a
art. 2699	3/4.6a
arts. 2702-2707	15/3.1
art. 2702	3/4.6a
art. 2703	3/4.6a
art. 2704	3/4.6a
arts. 2745-2783	3/4.10e
art. 2752	13/3.8
art. 2754	13/3.8
art. 2758	3/4.10e; 14/7.2c
art. 2771	13/3.8

Civil Code (*continued*)
CC

art. 2772	3/4.10e
arts. 2934-2963	3/4.12a
arts. 2941-2944	14/10.1

Code of Civil Procedure

Codice di procedura civile, approved by
R.D. 28 October 1940, n. 1443
CPC

art. 9	13/4.9a
arts. 137-151	13/2.1
art. 324	3/4.6a
art. 325	13/4.10
art. 333	13/4.3
art. 334	13/4.3
art. 345	13/4.1
art. 395	3/4.11; 4/4.2g; 13/4.3
art. 396	13/4.3
art. 598	9/1.1
art. 619	13/4.7
art. 796	3/4.14c
art. 797	3/4.14c

Penal Code

Codice penale, approved by R.D. 19 October 1930, n. 1948
CP

art. 17	13/7.1
art. 23	13/7.1
art. 24	13/7.1
art. 25	13/7.1
art. 26	13/7.1
art. 27	14/10.1
arts. 157-161	14/10.1
art. 371	13/7.4

**Laws and Decrees
(Chronological)**

L. 21 April 1862, n. 585	3/4.1b; 15/1.2
L. 26 January 1865, n. 2136	9/1.4
art. 18	9/4.2b
L. 20 March 1865, n. 2248	
Annex E	10/2.2g
Annex E, art. 6	13/4.1; 13/4.9a; 13/4.12
Annex E, art. 6, para. 2	14/7.2d
L. 30 August 1868, n. 4613	
art. 5	1/5.5c
art. 6	1/5.5c
art. 7	1/5.5c
R.D. 5 June 1871, n. 267	9/4.2d

R.D.L. 24 August 1877, n. 4021   13/4.1

art. 3	11/1.2a; 11/1.3; 11/1.4; 11/1.6a
art. 29	5/3.5; 5/3.6
art. 31	7/2.5
art. 32	7/2.1
art. 48	13/4.4
art. 50	13/4.4
art. 53	13/4.9a; 13/4.9c
art. 54	8/2.1
art. 64	13/3.6a
R.D. 24 August 1877, n. 4024	9/4.2d
art. 57	13/4.9c; 13/4.12
L. 1 March 1886, n. 3682	9/4.1; 10/1.1
L. 15 April 1886, n. 3818	3/4.7c
L. 11 July 1889, n. 6214	9/4.2d
art. 8	9/4.2b
L. 4 July 1895, n. 390	1/5.5c
L. 8 August 1895, n. 486	9/1.2
Annex E, art. 3	4/6.5
R.D. 20 May 1897, n. 217	3/4.1b; 15/1.2

R.D. 23 December 1897, n. 549 (*Regolamento per l'esecuzione del T.U. delle tasse di registro 20 maggio 1897, n. 217*)   3/4.8d; 15/1.2
Reg. R.

art. 14	15/2.2
L. 23 January 1902, n. 25	3/4.1b
R.D. 23 March 1902, n. 114	3/4.1b; 3/4.8d
arts. 14-18	3/4.10d
L. 7 July 1904, n. 351	10/6.2a
L. 15 July 1906, n. 383	10/6.2a
R.D. 11 July 1907, n. 560	13/4.1
art. 55	7/2.1
art. 91	13/4.2
art. 94	13/4.2
art. 97	13/4.3
art. 100	13/4.3
art. 101	13/4.3
art. 104	13/4.3
art. 105	13/4.3
art. 120	13/4.9c; 13/4.12; 13/5
R.D. 22 May 1910, n. 316	
art. 8	3/4.6c
R.D. 9 April 1911, n. 330	4/8.4
art. 2	1/4.10i
art. 3	1/4.10i
L. 23 April 1911, n. 509	3/4.1b
L. 18 December 1913, n. 1453	4/8.3; 14/8.4b
R.D. 27 September 1914, n. 1042	3/4.1b
D.L. 9 November 1916, n. 1525	14/1
D.L.L. 21 April 1918, n. 629	3/4.1b

D.L.L. 24 November 1918, n. 2086
14/1'
R.D. 2 September 1919, n. 1759
art. 7   10/3
D.L. 24 November 1919, n. 2165   14/1
R.D.L. 24 November 1919, n. 2163
3/4.1b
Annex B   14/1
L. 24 September 1920, n. 1300   3/4.1b
R.D. 17 October 1922, n. 1401   13/3.7
R.D.L. 28 December 1922, n. 1670
14/1
R.D. 4 January 1923, n. 16   10/2.3b
R.D. 11 March 1923, n. 560
art. 1   4/6.5
art. 5   4/6.5
art. 7   4/6.5
R.D. 18 March 1923, n. 550   14/1
R.D.L. 14 June 1923, n. 1281
art.1   1/4.8
R.D. 20 August 1923, n. 1802   3/4.1b
R.D. 15 September 1923, n. 2090
13/3.7
R.D. 6 December 1923, n. 2722   9/4.1
art. 1   10/1.1
R.D. 30 December 1923, n. 2882
art. 3   15/3.4b
R.D. 30 December 1923, n. 3062
art. 3   9/2.1b
art. 4   11/3.2c
art. 26   13/4.1
R.D. 30 December 1923, n. 3069
9/4.2d
R.D. 30 December 1923, n. 3268   4/5.3a
R.D. 30 December 1923, n. 3269 (*Testo unico di legge del registro*)   4/3.2a;
15/1.2
LR
art. 1   15/1.1; 15/3.1; 15/3.4a
art. 2   15/4.4
art. 4   3/6; 15/6.1; 15/6.2;
15/6.3a; 15/6.4; 15/6.5
art. 5   15/4.1
art. 7   15/7.2a
art. 8   15/3.1; 15/3.2
art. 9   15/3.3b
art. 10   15/6.3a; 15/6.4
art. 11   15/3.3j
art. 12   15/3.3j
art. 15   15/11.2
art. 16   15/4.3
art. 17   15/3.3f
art. 18   15/3.4a; 15/3.4b
art. 21   15/5.2
art. 22   15/5.2
art. 24   15/6.3e
art. 27   15/4.2; 15/5.3

R.D. 30 December 1923, n. 3269 (*continued*)
LR
art. 30   15/7.1
art. 30, para. 1   15/5.1
art. 40   15/8.3
art. 42   15/3.3c
art. 43   15/3.3b
art. 44   3/6; 15/4.3; 15/6.3a;
15/11.2
art. 45   15/3.3a
art. 46   15/3.3d
art. 47   15/3.3e
art. 48   15/3.3g
art. 50   15/7.1
art. 51   15/3.3h
art. 52   15/5.3
art. 54   15/6.3d
art. 56   15/6.3g
art. 60   15/3.3j
art. 61   3/6
art. 62   15/3.5
art. 64   15/3.3j
art. 65   15/4.5b
art. 66   15/4.5b
art. 68   15/3.3b; 15/8.3
art. 72   15/2.2; 15/3.5
art. 73   15/2.1
art. 79   15/3.4b
art. 80   15/2.2; 15/2.3; 15/7.1
art. 81   15/7.1; 15/8.3
art. 82   15/7.1
art. 91   15/7.2a
art. 92   15/7.2a
art. 93   15/2.1; 15/2.2
art. 94   15/4.3
art. 98   3/4.10b; 3/4.10f; 15/2.3
art. 99   15/8.2
art. 100   15/8.2
art. 101   15/8.2
art. 102   15/8.2
art. 103   15/8.2
art. 104   15/8.2
art. 105   15/8.3
art. 110   15/4.5a; 15/8.1
art. 115   15/7.2b
art. 117   15/8.1; 15/8.3
art. 118   15/8.1
art. 131   15/8.3
art. 132   15/7.1
art. 135   15/8.3
art. 136   15/9.1; 15/9.2
art. 137   15/9.1
art. 138   15/9.2
art. 140   15/9.3
art. 141   15/9.3
art. 149   14/7.2d

R.D. 30 December 1923, n. 3269 (*continued*)

Schedule, Annex A	4/3.2b; 15/3.1
Part I	15/6.5
art. 1	15/6.3b
art. 2	15/6.3c
art. 3	15/6.3c
art. 3 *bis*	4/3.6
art. 7(a)	15/6.3b
art. 7(b)	15/6.3c
art. 15	15/6.3g
art. 17	15/6.3e
art. 19	15/6.3b
art. 21	15/6.3e
art. 24	15/6.4
art. 28	15/6.3f
art. 29	15/6.3f
art. 33	15/6.3f
art. 33(b)	15/6.3a
art. 44	15/6.3d; 15/6.4
art. 49	15/6.3g
art. 51 *bis*	15/6.3g
art. 52	15/6.3g
art. 53	15/6.3g
art. 61	15/6.3a
art. 78	3/6
art. 81	15/6.3h
art. 82	15/6.3h
art. 83	15/6.3h
art. 84	15/6.3h
art. 87	15/6.3h
art. 88	15/6.3h; 15/6.4
art. 91	15/6.3g
art. 92	15/6.3g
art. 98	15/6.4
art. 105	3/6
art. 108	15/4.2; 15/6.5
Part II	15/2.2
Part III	15/6.2
art. 139	3/6
art. 141	15/4.3
Table, Annex B	4/3.2b; 15/4.1; 15/4.5b; 15/4.5c
Table, Annex C	4/3.2b; 15/4.1; 15/4.3
Table, Annex D	4/3.2b; 15/4.1; 15/4.4
Table, Annex E	4/3.2b; 15/4.1
art. 10	15/4.2

R.D. 30 December 1923, n. 3270 (*Legge tributaria sulle successioni*) 3/4.1b; 3/4.7c; 3/5.2; 15/1.2

LS

art. 1	3/4.1a; 3/4.3b
art. 2	3/4.1a; 3/4.7a; 3/4.7b; 3/4.7c
art. 3	3/4.3a; 3/4.7e

R.D. 30 December 1923, n. 3270 (*continued*)

LS

art. 5	3/4.10a
art. 6	3/4.2
art. 7	3/4.10g
art. 8	3/4.10d
art. 9	3/4.10g
art. 10	3/4.7b
art. 11	3/4.7c
art. 12	3/4.7c
art. 15	3/4.7a; 3/4.10b
art. 17	3/4.13a
art. 19	3/4.7d
art. 20	3/4.1a; 3/4.14a; 3/4.14b
art. 21	3/4.4b
art. 22	3/4.3a; 3/4.3c
art. 23	3/4.3b; 3/4.3c
art. 24	3/4.3b
art. 26	3/4.3e
art. 27	3/4.3e; 3/4.5d
art. 28	3/4.3h; 15/5.3
art. 29	3/4.3g; 3/4.3h; 15/5.3
art. 30	3/4.3f
art. 31	3/4.3a
art. 32	3/4.10g
art. 34	3/4.5b; 3/4.5f; 3/4.9
art. 36	3/4.9
art. 37	3/4.9
art. 38	3/4.9
art. 43	3/4.13a
art. 44	3/4.9
arts. 45-50	3/4.3a
art. 45	3/4.6a
art. 46	3/4.6b
art. 47	3/4.14c
art. 48	3/4.6a
art. 49	3/4.13a
art. 50	3/4.6a; 3/4.6c; 3/4.10g
art. 50, para. 2	3/4.6c
art. 51	3/4.8a; 3/4.8d
art. 52	3/4.8d
art. 53	3/4.8a
art. 54	3/4.3j; 3/4.8d
art. 55	3/4.8b; 3/4.8c; 3/4.8d; 3/4.10b; 3/4.10c; 3/4.10g
art. 56	3/4.8c
art. 57	3/4.8c
art. 58	3/4.8c
art. 60	3/4.8d
art. 61	3/4.8a
art. 63	3/4.8a
art. 64	3/4.10c
art. 65	3/4.10d; 3/4.10e; 3/4.10f
art. 66	3/4.10b
art. 67	3/4.10a
art. 68	3/4.10e

R.D. 30 December 1923, n. 3270 (*continued*)
LS

art. 69	3/4.10b; 3/4.10f
art. 70	3/4.10b
art. 71	3/4.10c
art. 72	3/4.10b; 3/4.13a
art. 73	3/4.13c
art. 74	3/4.13a
art. 75	3/4.13a
art. 76	3/4.13c
art. 77	3/4.13b
art. 79	3/4.13b
art. 80	3/4.13b
art. 81	3/4.13b
art. 82	3/4.13b
art. 83	3/4.13b
art. 84	3/4.13b
art. 86	3/4.10g; 3/4.12a
art. 87	3/4.12a
art. 88	3/4.12a
art. 89	3/4.12b; 15/9.3
art. 90	3/4.12b; 15/9.3
art. 92	3/4.10h
art. 93	3/4.10h
art. 94	3/4.10h; 3/4.11
art. 95	3/4.10h
art. 96	3/4.10h
art. 102	3/4.7b

R.D. 30 December 1923, n. 3273   14/1
R.D. 30 December 1923, n. 3276

| art. 1 | 4/5.4 |

R.D. 30 December 1923, n. 3277
                                                  4/5.2a
R.D. 30 December 1923, n. 3278 (*Legge delle tasse sui contratti di borsa*)
LTCB

art. 1	4/4.3a
art. 3	4/4.3c
art. 4	4/4.3c
art. 7	4/4.3a
art. 8	4/4.3a; 4/4.3c
arts. 9-15	4/4.3c
art. 15	4/4.3a
arts. 16-21	4/4.3c

R.D. 30 December 1923, n. 3280 (*Legge sulle tasse in surrogazione del bollo e del registro*)   4/3.1
LTSBR

art. 20	4/3.5
art. 21	4/3.5
art. 23	4/3.5
art. 24	4/3.5
Annex A, art. 5	4/3.5
Annex A, art. 6	4/3.5

R.D. 30 December 1923, n. 3281 (*Legge tributaria sulle assicurazioni*)
LTA

art. 1	4/3.4
art. 5	4/3.4
art. 6	4/3.4
art. 8	4/3.4
art. 16	4/3.4
art. 18	4/3.4
art. 28	4/3.4
art. 29	4/3.4
art. 33	4/3.4
art. 39	4/3.4
Annex A, Schedule	4/3.4
Annex B	4/3.4
Annex C	4/3.4

R.D. 30 December 1923, n. 3282
                                                  15/7.2c

R.D.L. 15 May 1924, n. 749   5/5.7
R.D. 23 May 1924, n. 827

| art. 145 | 5/5.11 |
| art. 146 | 5/5.11 |

R.D. 26 June 1924, n. 1054

| art. 16 | 13/4.11 |
| art. 26 | 13/4.11 |

R.D.L. 16 October 1924, n. 1613

| art. 1 | 8/1.1 |

R.D.L. 5 April 1925, n. 396

| art. 1 | 4/6.5 |
| art. 3 | 4/6.5 |

R.D.L. 9 April 1925, n. 380   3/4.2

| art. 1 | 15/4.3 |

R.D.L. 7 May 1925, n. 587   11/3.7
D.L. 13 December 1925, n. 2161
                                                  11/4.1
R.D.L. 3 January 1926, n. 63   1/4.8
R.D. 4 March 1926, n. 340   11/4.6
L. 15 July 1926, n. 1866   11/4.1
R.D.L. 3 September 1926, n. 2307
                                                  11/4.1
R.D.L. 7 September 1926, n. 1511   6/6.2
R.D.L. 16 September 1926, n. 1606
                                                  10/2.2f
R.D.L. 20 September 1926, n. 1643

| art. 10 | 9/1.2; 9/1.7 |

R.D.L. 25 November 1926, n. 2159

| art. 1 | 10/6.6 |

R.D.L. 26 December 1926, n. 2334
                                                  5/5.11
R.D.L. 14 March 1927, n. 372

| art. 1 | 5/5.11 |

L. 16 June 1927, n. 1100   10/2.2f
R.D.L. 29 June 1927, n. 1509

| art. 21 | 9/1.7 |

R.D. 29 July 1927, n. 1443   10/1.1
R.D.L. 12 August 1927, n. 1463

| art. 9 | 11/1.2a; 11/1.3 |

L. 19 February 1928, n. 258 — 10/6.6
R.D.L. 7 June 1928, n. 1493 — 11/4.1
L. 14 June 1928, n. 1312 — 2/3.4a
R.D.L. 13 November 1928, n. 2579
— 5/5.11
L. 28 December 1928, n. 4587 — 11/4.1
L. 7 January 1929, n. 4 — 3/4.13a;
14/7.2d; 14/9.1; 14/9.4
    art. 2 — 13/7.1
    art. 3 — 13/7.1
    art. 4 — 13/7.1
    art. 5 — 13/7.1
    art. 7 — 14/10.1
    art. 17 — 3/4.12a; 14/10.1
    art. 21 — 13/7.1
    art. 26 — 13/7.1
    art. 27 — 13/7.1
    arts. 36-45 — 13/7.1
    arts. 55-59 — 13/7.1
    art. 56 — 13/4.8
L. 27 May 1929, n. 810 — 5/5.5
    art. 29 — 3/4.2
    art. 29(h) — 15/4.3
L. 24 June 1929, n. 1154 — 3/4.2
L. 27 June 1929, n. 1106
    art. 1 — 10/6.6
L. 11 July 1929, n. 1260 — 9/4.1
R.D.L. 26 February 1930, n. 105
    art. 1 — 4/6.6
R.D. 28 February 1930, n. 289
    art. 12 — 3/4.2; 15/4.3
R.D.L. 30 April 1930, n. 431 — 3/4.1b
L. 12 June 1930, n. 742
    art. 8 — 3/4.9
    art. 12 — 3/4.13a
    art. 38 — 3/4.9
R.D.L. 28 July 1930, n. 1011 — 14/1
    art. 1, para. 3 — 14/1
    art. 1, para. 4 — 14/1
    art. 35 — 14/1
    art. 44 — 14/1
    art. 57 — 14/1
    art. 58 — 14/1
R.D.L. 6 November 1930, n. 1509
    art. 1 — 15/11.2
R.D.L. 11 December 1930, n. 1882
    art. 2 — 15/4.5b
R.D. 14 September 1931, n. 1175
(*Testo unico per la finanza locale*)
    TUFL
    art. 3 — 4/5.8c
    art. 10 — 1/5.5c; 1/5.5d
    art. 10(7) — 1/5.5c
    art. 11 — 1/5.6
    art. 20 — 4/5.8b; 4/5.8c
    art. 21 — 4/5.8d
    art. 22 — 4/5.8d

R.D. 14 September 1931, n. 1175 (*continued*)
    TUFL
    art. 29 — 4/5.8c
    art. 30 — 4/5.8c
    art. 32 — 4/5.8e
    art. 33 — 4/5.8e
    art. 34 — 4/5.8e
    art. 35 — 4/5.8e
    art. 37 — 4/5.8e
    art. 38 — 4/5.8e
    art. 39 — 4/5.8e
    art. 40 — 4/5.8e
    art. 42 — 4/5.8e
    art. 46 — 4/5.8e
    art. 50 — 4/5.8e
    art. 51 — 4/5.8c; 4/5.8e
    art. 52 — 4/5.8c; 4/5.8e
    art. 53 — 4/5.8e
    art. 54 — 4/5.8g
    art. 55 — 4/5.8g
    art. 56 — 4/5.8g
    art. 59 — 4/5.8g
    art. 62 — 4/5.8g
    art. 70 — 4/5.8g
    arts. 71-75 — 4/5.8f
    art. 71 — 4/5.8f
    arts. 76-89 — 4/5.8f
    art. 78 — 4/5.8f
    art. 80 — 4/5.8f
    art. 86 — 4/5.8f
    art. 88 — 4/5.8f
    art. 89 — 4/5.8f
    art. 91 — 4/5.8h
    art. 93 — 4/5.8f
    art. 95 — 4/5.8d
    art. 101 — 2/3.7
    art. 102 — 2/3.7
    art. 104 — 2/3.7
    arts. 111-121 — 2/3.1
    art. 111 — 2/3.7
    art. 112 — 2/3.2
    art. 113 — 2/3.2
    art. 114 — 2/3.2; 2/3.5
    art. 115 — 2/3.6
    art. 117 — 2/3.3b
    art. 118 — 2/3.4a; 2/3.4b
    art. 119 — 2/3.3b
    arts. 122-126 — 1/5.5c
    arts. 130-136 — 1/5.5c
    arts. 137-147 — 1/5.5c
    arts. 149-152 — 2/3.1
    arts. 155-160 — 1/5.5c; 2/3.1
    art. 162 — 12/1.4d
    art. 164 — 12/1.4d
    arts. 165-167 — 2/2.9
    art. 183 — 4/5.10
    art. 184 — 4/5.10

R.D. 14 September 1931, n. 1175 (continued)
TUFL

art. 185	4/5.10
art. 187	4/5.10
art. 189	4/5.10
art. 190	4/5.10
art. 192	4/5.11
art. 194	4/5.11
art. 195	4/5.11
art. 197	4/5.11
art. 198	4/5.11
art. 200	4/5.11
art. 201	4/5.12
art. 202	4/5.12
art. 203	4/5.12
art. 204	4/5.12
art. 209	4/5.13
art. 212	4/5.13
art. 214	4/5.14
art. 215	4/5.14
art. 216	4/5.14
art. 217	4/5.14
art. 220	4/5.14
art. 236	3/7.3b
art. 241	3/7.3a
art. 254	1/5.6; 12/1.1; 12/1.3
art. 255	1/5.6
arts. 268-272	1/5.5c
arts. 274 et seq.	2/3.8
arts. 277-294	3/7.2e
art. 277	2/3.8
art. 278	1/4.10j
art. 279	1/4.10j
art. 280	1/4.10j; 1/4.11
art. 281	1/4.10j
art. 282	1/4.10j; 2/3.8
art. 283	1/4.10j
art. 284 bis	1/4.10j; 2/3.8
art. 285	1/4.10j
arts. 286-290	2/3.9
art. 289	2/3.8
art. 297	2/3.9

R.D. 17 September 1931, n. 1608

art. 12	13/4.1
art. 20	15/8.4
art. 26	13/7.6
art. 34	13/7.2

R.D. 8 October 1931, n. 1572

art. 2	10/2.2c
art. 12	10/2.2c
art. 13	10/2.2c
art. 15	10/2.2c
art. 16	10/2.2a
art. 18	9/4.1; 10/1.1; 10/2.2c
art. 19	10/2.2g
art. 20	10/2.2g

R.D. 8 October 1931, n. 1572 (continued)

art. 23	10/2.2g
art. 45	10/2.2e
art. 55	10/2.2b

L. 30 December 1931, n. 1576	11/4.1
L. 31 March 1932, n. 456	11/4.1
L. 3 June 1932, n. 853	11/4.1
R.D. 25 August 1932, n. 1265	11/4.1
R.D.L. 22 September 1932, n. 1346	
	10/1.1
R.D.L. 20 December 1932, n. 1607	
	4/4.3c

R.D. 13 February 1933, n. 215

| art. 44 | 10/2.2f |
| R.D. 31 August 1933, n. 1592 | 5/5.7 |

R.D. 12 October 1933, n. 1539

arts. 127 et seq.	10/2.2g
art. 131	10/2.2g
art. 140	1/4.11
art. 157	10/2.2g
art. 158	10/2.2g
art. 161	10/2.2g
art. 162	10/2.2g
art. 164	10/2.2g
art. 166	10/2.2g
art. 172	10/2.2g

R.D. 30 October 1933, n. 1611

art. 7	3/4.10h
art. 11	3/4.10h
R.D.L. 3 February 1934, n. 60	3/4.4c

R.D. 3 March 1934, n. 383 (Legge
communale e provinciale)
LCP

art. 19	1/5.1
art. 91	1/5.4
art. 92	1/5.4
art. 102	1/5.3
art. 144	1/5.4
art. 290	1/5.5g
art. 299	1/5.5h
art. 300	1/5.5h
art. 306	1/5.6; 4/5.8d
art. 312	1/5.4
art. 314	1/5.4
art. 316	1/5.4
art. 328	1/5.3
art. 332	1/5.6
art. 336	1/5.6

R.D.L. 5 July 1934, n. 1128

art. 1	10/1.1
art. 4	10/1.1
R.D.L. 18 September 1934, n. 1465	
	9/1.7

R.D. 20 September 1934, n. 2011

art. 52(1)(c)	12/1.4d
R.D. 28 September 1934, n. 1591	10/1.1
R.D.L. 17 January 1935, n. 67	5/5.7

R.D.L. 9 May 1935, n. 606
  art. 3   15/8.2
R.D. 17 August 1935, n. 1765
  art. 71   5/5.6; 8/1.3b
R.D.L. 20 September 1935, n. 1684
                                            3/4.4c
R.D.L. 26 September 1935, n. 1749
                                            3/4.2
  art. 3   14/1
  art. 4   14/1; 15/3.3f
  Annex A   15/3.3f
  Annex B   3/4.1b
  Annex B, art. 11   3/4.6a; 3/4.8d
  Annex B, art. 13   3/4.10c
R.D.L. 4 October 1935, n. 1827
  art. 122   5/5.6
  art. 124   8/1.3b
R.D. 13 January 1936, n. 2313   15/4.5a
  art. 1   3/4.10h; 3/4.13a;
                   15/7.2a; 15/8.1; 15/8.2
R.D.L. 13 January 1936, n. 70
  art. 1   4/6.4
  art. 3   4/6.4
  art. 11   4/6.4
R.D.L. 3 February 1936, n. 287   9/1.7
L. 6 April 1936, n. 1155   5/5.6; 8/1.3b
R.D.L. 27 April 1936, n. 635
  art. 10   4/5.2b
R.D. 30 April 1936, n. 1138
  art. 102   4/5.8c
L. 28 May 1936, n. 1027   3/4.1b
L. 4 June 1936, n. 1342   4/6.4
L. 8 June 1936, n. 1231
  art. 4   5/3.5; 5/3.6
  art. 7   8/4
  art. 8   7/1.1; 8/4; 9/4.2b
  art. 13   7/1.1
  art. 16   9/9.7
  art. 19   6/6.3
  art. 28   9/4.2a
  art. 32   13/3.6a
  art. 34   13/4.9c
R.D.L. 7 August 1936, n. 1639   3/4.5a;
              3/4.10e; 13/4.1; 14/7.3e
  art. 1   1/3.1c; 14/4.4
  art. 14   3/4.9; 3/4.10d
  art. 15   3/4.5b; 15/5.1
  art. 16   3/4.5c; 15/5.2; 15/5.3
  art. 17   3/4.9; 15/7.1
  art. 18   15/7.1
  art. 19   3/4.9; 15/5.3; 15/8.4
  art. 20   3/4.9; 15/7.1; 15/9.2
  art. 21   3/4.9; 15/7.1; 15/9.2
  art. 22   13/4.3; 13/4.4; 13/4.9a
  art. 28   3/4.11
  art. 29   3/4.11
  art. 31   1/4.10c; 3/4.11
  art. 40   3/4.10h

R.D.L. 7 August 1936, n. 1639 (con-
  tinued)
  art. 41   3/4.11; 13/4.2
  art. 43   13/4.1
R.D.L. 7 August 1936, n. 1657   15/3.4a
R.D.L. 21 August 1936, n. 1632
  art. 10   8/1.3b
R.D.L. 5 October 1936, n. 1743   3/4.4c
R.D.L. 26 December 1936, n. 2394
  art. 3   1/4.10j
L. 7 June 1937, n. 1016   1/3.1c; 13/4.1
R.D.L. 17 June 1937, n. 1048
  art. 23   8/1.3b
R.D. 8 July 1937, n. 1516   1/4.10c;
              1/4.10d; 1/4.10e; 3/4.5a;
              3/4.11; 13/4.1; 14/7.3e
  art. 23   13/4.1; 13/4.2
  art. 24   13/4.2
  art. 25   13/4.2; 13/7.3; 15/8.4
  art. 26   13/4.2
  art. 29   13/4.2
  art. 33   13/4.2
  art. 35   13/4.2; 13/4.3; 13/4.4
  art. 37   13/4.1; 13/4.3; 13/4.11
  art. 38   13/4.3; 13/4.4
  art. 40   13/4.3
  art. 41   13/4.3; 13/7.3
  art. 42   13/4.3
  art. 44   13/4.3; 13/4.11
  art. 45   13/4.4; 13/4.11
  art. 46   13/4.4
  art. 47   13/4.4
  art. 48   13/4.4
  art. 49   13/4.4
R.D.L. 9 September 1937, n. 1769
  art. 1   2/3.7
R.D.L. 15 November 1937, n. 1924
                                            15/1.2
  Annex B, art. 2   15/3.4c
  Annex B, art. 3   15/3.4c
  Annex B, art. 6   15/3.4c
R.D.L. 30 November 1937, n. 2145
                   1/5.5d; 12/1.1
  art. 1   1/5.5d; 2/2.9; 12/1.5c
R.D.L. 16 December 1937, n. 1669
  art. 17   9/4.2b
R.D.L. 21 February 1938, n. 246   4/5.6
R.D.L. 3 March 1938, n. 261
  art. 1   4/3.4
L. 11 April 1938, n. 709   4/8.3
R.D. 28 April 1938, n. 1165
  art. 71   9/1.7
  art. 157   10/6.6
  art. 159   9/4.2b
  art. 160   9/4.2b
  art. 161   9/4.2b
  art. 168   9/4.2b
  art. 252   9/4.2b

R.D. 28 April 1938, n. 1165 (continued)
  art. 274   9/4.2b
  art. 323   9/4.2b
  art. 340   9/4.2b
  art. 392   9/4.2b
R.D.L. 16 June 1938, n. 954
  art. 1   4/5.2a
R.D.L. 21 June 1938, n. 1094
  art. 2   9/4.2b
  art. 3   9/4.2b
  art. 7   9/4.2b
R.D.L. 24 July 1938, n. 1266   10/6.4
R.D. 5 September 1938, n. 1530 1/4.10j
R.D.L. 19 October 1938, n. 1933
(Riforma delle leggi sul lotto
pubblico)
  LLP
  ―――
  art. 1   4/6.7
  art. 3   4/6.7
  art. 4   4/6.7
  art. 8   4/6.7
  art. 36   10/7.1
  art. 39   4/6.7
  art. 40   4/6.7
  art. 41   4/6.7
  art. 42   4/6.7
  art. 43   4/6.7
  art. 44   4/6.7
  arts. 45-49   4/6.7
  art. 50   4/6.7
R.D.L. 24 November 1938, n. 1926
(Imposta di soggiorno)
  IS
  ―
  art. 1   4/5.9
  art. 4   4/5.9
  art. 7   4/5.9
R.D.L. 28 November 1938, n. 2,000
(Applicazione dei contributi di
miglioria per le opere eseguite
dallo Stato o col suo concorso) 3/7.1
  ACM
  ―――
  art. 1   3/7.4
  art. 2   3/7.4
  art. 5   3/7.4
  art. 6   3/7.4
  art. 7   3/7.4
  art. 8   3/7.4
  art. 12   3/7.4
  art. 14   3/7.4
  art. 15   3/7.4
  art. 16   3/7.4
  art. 19   3/7.4
R.D. 8 December 1938, n. 2153
  art. 131   10/2.2e
R.D.L. 15 December 1938, n. 1975 4/3.1
D.L. 28 February 1939, n. 334   4/5.2a

R.D.L. 4 April 1939, n. 589
  art. 2   10/2.2c; 10/2.2d
  art. 4   10/2.3b
  art. 5   10/2.4
R.D.L. 13 April 1939, n. 652   9/4.2d
  art. 9   9/4.2d
L. 15 May 1939, n. 953   11/4.1
L. 5 June 1939, n. 973   4/6.7
L. 11 August 1939, n. 1249   9/4.2d
R.D.L. 9 January 1940, n. 2 (Istituzione di una imposta generale sull'
entrata)   1/3.1d; 14/1
  IGE
  ―――
  art. 1   14/2.1; 14/3.1; 14/3.8;
            14/4.1; 14/8.1; 14/10.1
  art. 1(a)   14/4.2
  art. 1(b)   14/4.4; 14/4.10
  art. 1(c)   14/4.3; 14/4.5
  art. 1(d)   14/4.4
  art. 1(e)   14/4.4; 14/4.10
  art. 1(f)   14/4.2
  art. 1(g)   14/4.3
  art. 1(h)   14/8.2a
  art. 1(i)   14/4.10
  art. 1(l)   14/4.6e
  art. 1(m)   14/4.6i
  art. 2   14/3.1; 14/5.1
  art. 2(a)   14/3.2
  art. 2(b)   14/3.3a; 14/4.7
  art. 2(c)   14/3.4
  art. 3   14/2.2b; 14/3.1
  art. 3(a)   14/3.6
  art. 3(b)   14/3.7
  art. 3(c)   14/3.8
  art. 3(d)   14/3.9; 14/5.1
  art. 4   14/5.1
  art. 6   14/2.5; 14/2.7
  art. 7   14/6.1
  arts. 8-11   14/7.2c
  art. 8   14/3.1; 14/7.2b
  art. 8(d)   14/3.10
  art. 8(e)   14/2.7; 14/3.2
  art. 8(f)   14/3.4
  art. 8(i)   14.3/3e
  art. 8(m)   14/3.3d
  art. 8(o)   14/3.3d
  art. 8(p)   14/3.8
  art. 8(q)   14/3.9
  art. 8(r)   14/3.3f
  art. 8(s)   14/3.3f
  art. 8(t)   14/3.10
  art. 8(u)   14/3.3d; 14/3.3g
  art. 8(z)   14/3.10
  art. 9   14/7.2c
  art. 10   14/7.2c
  art. 11   14/7.2c
  art. 12   14/5.2; 14/5.3

R.D.L. 9 January 1940, n. 2 (*continued*)
IGE

art. 13	14/2.2; 14/3.11; 14/3.12; 14/3.13
art. 14	14/2.6; 14/6.4; 14/7.2a; 14/7.3a
art. 15	14/3.3e; 14/7.4a
art. 17	14/2.6; 14/4.6b; 14/7.2a; 14/8.4a
art. 18	14/8.4a
art. 19	14/8.4b
art. 20	14/8.4c; 14/8.5
art. 21	14/8.2b
art. 23	14/2.1
art. 24	4/4.2b; 14/2.1
art. 25	4/4.2b; 14/2.1
art. 26	14/7.5; 14/9.2a
art. 27	14/7.5
art. 29	14/7.5
arts. 30-42	14/9.1
art. 30	14/9.2a
art. 31	14/9.2a
art. 32	14/9.3a
art. 33	14/9.3b
art. 35	14/9.2b
art. 36	14/9.3c
art. 37	14/9.2c
art. 40	14/9.4
art. 41	14/9.3a
art. 43	14/7.2c
art. 44	14/7.2c
art. 45	14/10.1
art. 46	14/7.2c; 14/7.3e
art. 47	14/7.2d; 14/10.1; 14/10.2
arts. 48-52	14/7.2d
art. 53	14/7.2d
art. 58	14/7.2d

R.D. 26 January 1940, n. 10 (*Regolamento per l'esecuzioni del R.D.L. 9 gennaio 1940, n. 2, istitutivo di una imposta generale sull'entrata*)   14/1
IGE Reg.

art. 1	14/3.3a; 14/3.3b; 14/4.7; 14/5.1
art. 3	14/5.1
art. 4	14/5.2
art. 5	14/5.2
art. 6	14/5.2; 14/5.3
art. 7	14/5.2
art. 8	14/10.1
art. 9	14/7.2b
art. 13	14/3.11
art. 14	14/3.12
art. 15	14/3.12
art. 16	14/3.13
art. 17	14/3.13

R.D. 26 January 1940, n. 10 (*continued*)
IGE Reg.

arts. 20-30	14/2.2a
art. 20	14/2.2c
arts. 21-26	14/2.3a
art. 21	14/2.3b
art. 22	14/2.3c
art. 23	14/2.3d
art. 25	14/2.3f
art. 29	14/2.3a
art. 34	14/3.10
art. 35	14/2.5; 14/3.2
art. 37	14/2.5
arts. 38-43	14/3.4
art. 42	14/2.5
art. 46	14/3.3e
art. 47	14/3.3d
art. 48	14/3.3d
art. 53	14/3.3d
art. 54	14/3.3d
art. 55	14/3.8
art. 56	14/3.9
art. 57	14/3.3f
art. 58	14/3.3f
art. 60	14/3.3f
art. 61	14/3.10
art. 62	14/3.10
art. 63	14/2.5
art. 64	14/3.3g
art. 65	14/7.2c
arts. 66-82	14/7.2c
art. 67	14/7.2c
art. 75	14/7.2c
art. 76	14/7.2c
arts. 83-87	14/3.3e
art. 83	14/7.4a
arts. 85-87	14/7.4a
art. 95	14/3.3e
art. 96	14/8.4a
art. 102	14/8.5
art. 103	14/8.5
art. 104	14/8.4c
art. 105	14/8.4c
art. 106	14/8.2a
art. 110	14/2.1
art. 111	4/4.2b; 14/2.1
arts. 112-114	14/7.5
art. 115	14/7.5
art. 117	14/7.2c; 14/7.3e

L. 23 March 1940, n. 283

| art. 1 | 15/7.2a |
| art. 2 | 15/7.2a |

L. 19 June 1940, n. 762   1/3.1d; 14/1

L. 29 June 1940, n. 877   3/4.1b

L. 25 September 1940, n. 1424
(*Legge doganale*) 4/5.2e; 4/8.1;
14/4.6h
LD
art. 4 4/8.1
art. 5 4/8.4
art. 7 4/8.1
arts. 16-19 4/8.4
art. 24, para. 3 14/7.2d
art. 27 14/10.1
art. 54 4/8.4
art. 57 4/8.3
arts. 97-116 4/8.5
arts. 117-130 4/8.5
art. 144 4/8.5
L. 13 November 1940, n. 1700 14/4.6h
R.D. 30 January 1941, n. 12 1/4.10f
L. 6 February 1941, n. 346
art. 11 10/6.4
L. 4 July 1941, n. 770
art. 1, para. 2 14/2.7
L. 19 July 1941, n. 771 15/1.2
art. 1 14/3.7; 15/3.3i
art. 3 15/3.4c
R.D.L. 25 October 1941, n. 1148
art. 1 9/2.8
art. 2 9/2.8
art. 5 10/5
R.D. 31 October 1941, n. 1418
art. 1 12/1.4d
L. 24 November 1941, n. 1506
art. 7 9/4.2b
L. 19 January 1942, n. 23 3/4.1b
art. 1 3/4.13e
R.D.L. 5 March 1942, n. 186
art. 1 3/4.5c; 15/5.2
L. 16 March 1942, n. 267
art. 118(4) 9/1.1
R.D. 29 March 1942, n. 239
art. 1 9/2.8
art. 4 9/2.8
arts. 31-34 10/5
arts. 35-37 9/2.8
art. 35 13/1.4
art. 37 13/1.4
art. 40 9/2.8; 13/1.4
art. 42 9/2.8
R.D. 21 April 1942, n. 444
art. 60 13/4.11
R.D.L. 4 May 1942, n. 434 3/4.1b;
3/5.1
L. 21 June 1942, n. 840 3/4.5c;
15/5.2
L. 11 July 1942, n. 843
art. 3 10/6.6
art. 5 9/4.2b
art. 7 9/4.2b

L. 11 July 1942, n. 843 (*continued*)
art. 8 9/4.2b
art. 10 9/4.2a
L. 17 July 1942, n. 907 (*Legge sul
monopolio dei sali e dei tabacchi*)
LMST
art. 1 4/6.2
art. 19 4/6.2
art. 45 4/6.3
art. 49 4/6.3
art. 54 4/6.3
L. 18 October 1942, n. 1220 3/4.1b;
3/5.1
R.D.L. 7 December 1942, n. 1418
12/1.1
L. 11 January 1943, n. 138
art. 35 5/5.6; 8/1.3b
L. 8 March 1943, n. 153 1/4.10h;
9/4.2e
arts. 20-23 9/4.2d
art. 20 10/2.2g
art. 22 10/2.2g
art. 23 10/2.2g; 13/4.1; 13/4.9a
art. 360 9/4.2e
L. 11 March 1943, n. 204
art. 16 12/1.1
R.D.L. 12 April 1943, n. 205 7/1.1
R.D.L. 12 April 1943, n. 243
art. 6 9/4.2b
R.D.L. 26 May 1943, n. 398
art. 2 3/4.4c
R.D.L. 3 June 1943, n. 452 14/2.3d;
14/2.4
art. 10 14/3.3b
art. 12 14/4.4; 14/4.5
art. 13 14/2.2b
art. 16 14/2.7
arts. 19-22 14/9.1
art. 24 14/7.2c
L. 25 June 1943, n. 540 4/3.3
R.D.L. 19 August 1943, n. 734
art. 2 3/4.2
R.D.L. 19 August 1943, n. 737
art. 3 15/4.5b
R.D.L. 19 August 1943, n. 738
art. 13 4/3.5
R.D.L. 13 March 1944, n. 88 1/4.10c;
1/4.10d
D.L.L. 28 September 1944, n. 359 5/5.7
D.L.L. 12 October 1944, n. 334 1/4.10e
art. 3 1/4.10j
D.L.L. 19 October 1944, n. 348 14/6.4;
14/9.1
art. 1 14/6.1
art. 10 14/7.3a
art. 13 14/9.2a

D.L.L. 19 October 1944, n. 384
   art. 4   8/1.1
D.L.L 23 November 1944, n. 403 1/4.10h
R.D.L. 21 December 1944, n. 458   4/5.6
D.L.L. 8 March 1945, n. 62   2/3.3b;
                         4/5.8c
   art. 5   4/5.8c
   art. 9   4/5.8c
   art. 15   2/3.7
D.L.L. 8 March 1945, n. 90 (*Modificazioni delle imposte sulle successioni e sulle donazioni*)   3/4.1b;
                         3/5.1
MSD
   art. 1   3/4.7b
   art. 3   3/6
   art. 4   3/6
   art. 5   3/6
   art. 6   3/5.3; 3/5.5
   art. 7   3/5.5
   art. 8   3/5.3
   art. 9   3/6
   art. 10   3/5.3; 3/6
   art. 11   3/4.5g; 3/4.8a;
                         3/5.2; 3/5.7
   art. 12   3/5.4
   art. 13   3/4.6d; 3/5.2
   art. 14   3/4.13a
   art. 16   3/4.2
D.L.L. 5 April 1945, n. 141   15/1.2
   art. 5   15/6.3g
   art. 8   15/6.3d; 15/6.4
D.L.L. 26 April 1945, n. 223
   Annex B   4/5.2a
   Annex E   4/5.2a
D.L.L. 7 June 1945, n. 322   14/4.6a
D.L.L. 7 June 1945, n. 386
   art. 3   14/4.6i
   art. 4   14/6.4
   art. 10   14/2.7
D.L.L. 18 June 1945, n. 399   4/3.6
   art. 2   4/3.6
   art. 9   3/4.4d
   art. 11   3/4.11
   Table, Annex A   3/4.4d
D.L.L. 8 August 1945, n. 498   4/8.1
D.L.L. 1 December 1945, n. 834
   art. 3   4/5.6
D.L.L. 18 February 1946, n. 100
   art. 6   12/1.2
   art. 7   12/1.1
D.L.L. 22 February 1946, n. 43   3/4.4c
D.L.L. 26 March 1946, n. 221
   art. 2   14/4.6a
   art. 3   14/4.6a
D.L.L. 24 April 1946, n. 350   9/4.2c

R.D.L. 15 May 1946, n. 455 (Stat.
   Reg. Sic.)
   art. 36   1/5.5e
   art. 37   1/5.5e
   art. 38   1/5.5e; 1/5.5f
   art. 39   1/5.5e
R.D.L. 29 May 1946, n. 452
   art. 12   9/4.2b
D.L.P. 27 June 1946, n. 87
   art. 6   2/3.4a
D.L.P. 27 June 1946, n. 122   10/7.1
   art. 1   4/6.7
D.L.C.P.S. 21 October 1946, n. 236
                         4/5.2a
D.L.C.P.S. 26 October 1946, n. 262
                         3/4.4c
D.L.C.P.S. 27 December 1946, n.
   469   14/6.4
   art. 1   14/6.1
   art. 1, para. 1   14/6.2
   art. 2   14/6.4
   art. 5   14/6.3b
   art. 9   14/4.6h
   art. 14   14/7.3a; 14/7.3c
   art. 17   14/7.3a; 14/7.3e
D.L.P. 3 January 1947, n. 1   4/5.2a
D.L.C.P.S. 21 January 1947, n. 25
   art. 1   3/4.9; 15/7.1; 15/9.2
L. 23 March 1947, n. 132   5/5.1
D.L.P. 29 March 1947, n. 177
   art. 16   4/5.10
D.L.C.P.S. 3 April 1947, n. 372   10/6.4
D.L.C.P.S. 10 April 1947, n. 261   9/4.2b
   art. 90   9/1.7
D.L.C.P.S. 12 May 1947, n. 356
   art. 1   12/1.1
L. 9 June 1947, n. 530   1/5.3
D.L.P. 1 September 1947, n. 892   2/3.4a
D.L.C.P.S. 5 September 1947, n.
   1173   4/3.1
D.L.C.P.S. 5 October 1947, n. 1208
               3/4.13a; 14/9.1; 15/1.2
   art. 1, para. 2   3/4.13a
   art. 2   3/4.13c
D.L.C.P.S. 14 October 1947, n.
   1472   1/4.10h
D.L.C.P.S. 21 October 1947, n. 1250
   art. 1   13/7.1
   art. 2   13/7.1
D.L.C.P.S. 7 November 1947, n. 1559
   art. 1   13/7.8
   art. 2   13/7.8
   art. 3   13/7.8
   art. 4   13/7.6
D.L.C.P.S. 14 December 1947, n.
   1577   15/4.5b
   art. 26   5/5.10

D.L.C.P.S. 14 December 1947, n.
  1598   10/6.1; 14/4.6k
    art. 3   10/6.2a; 10/6.2c
    art. 5   15/4.5b
    art. 11   10/6.2c
L. 31 December 1947, n. 1629   10/2.2f
L. 6 February 1948, n. 29   1/3.1a
D.L. 24 February 1948, n. 114   10/2.2f
D.L. 26 March 1948, n. 261
    art. 2   1/5.5e; 4/5.4
D.L. 31 March 1948, n. 242   10/6.4
D.L. 8 April 1948, n. 514   1/4.10b;
                                   1/4.10d
    art. 2   9/4.2d
    art. 5   9/4.2e; 10/2.2g; 13/4.1
D.L. 12 April 1948, n. 507   1/5.5e
D.L. 13 April 1948, n. 917   5/5.1
D.L. 14 April 1948, n. 496
    art. 1   4/5.7
D.L. 17 April 1948, n. 740   9/4.2b
D.L. 24 April 1948, n. 579   10/6.4
D.L. 3 May 1948, n. 799
    art. 1   14/6.3a
    art. 2   14/6.4
    art. 3   14/6.4
    art. 5   14/7.2c
    art. 7   14/7.2c
    art. 9   14/2.2b
    art. 14   14/7.2c
    arts. 16-22   14/7.3a
    art. 16   14/7.3e
    art. 17   14/7.3e
    arts. 18-21   14/7.3e
    arts. 26-28   14/7.3a
D.L. 3 May 1948, n. 937
    arts. 1-3   14/4.6d
D.L. 7 May 1948, n. 1173
    art. 1   4/4.4
    Annex A, Schedule   4/4.4
L. 4 August 1948, n. 1107   5/5.1
L. 9 August 1948, n. 1102
    art. 3   5/5.4
D.L. 6 October 1948, n. 1199   10/6.1
L. 1 December 1948, n. 1438   10/6.4
D.P. 14 December 1948, n. 1421   4/6.2
L. 29 December 1948, n. 1482   10/6.2a;
                                  14/4.6k
    art. 5   10/6.2a; 10/6.2c
L. 7 January 1949, n. 1   14/2.4
    art. 1   14/6.3a
    art. 5   14/6.3b
    art. 8   14/4.10
L. 15 February 1949, n. 33
    art. 3   15/4.5b
    art. 4   15/3.4c
    art. 6   15/3.4a
L. 28 February 1949, n. 43   7/2.4;
                                   9/4.2b

L. 8 March 1949, n. 277   1/5.1
D.P.R. 9 May 1949, n. 250
    arts. 32-35   1/5.5e
L. 12 May 1949, n. 206   3/4.1b; 3/5.1
    art. 3   3/4.3d; 3/4.7d
    art. 4   3/4.6a
    art. 5   3/4.10d
    art. 6   3/4.3d; 3/5.4
    art. 7   3/4.6b
    art. 8   3/5.3; 3/5.5
    art. 9   3/5.5
    Annex A   15/6.2
    Annex A, Table 1   3/4.7b
    Annex A, Table 3   3/4.7b
L. 25 June 1949, n. 409
    art. 33   9/4.2b
L. 2 July 1949, n. 408
    art. 1   9/4.2b
    art. 13   9/4.2b
    art. 15   9/1.7
    art. 17   15/6.3b
    art. 18   9/1.7
    art. 19   9/1.7
    art. 24   9/4.2b
L. 1 August 1949, n. 482
    art. 1   **14/4.6j**
L. 3 August 1949, n. 623
    art. 1   14/4.6k
    art. 2   14/4.6k
L. 12 November 1949, n. 996   4/5.6
D.P.R. 1 December 1949, n. 1142 9/4.2d
    art. 1   9/4.2d
    art. 2   9/4.2d
L. 24 December 1949, n. 941
    art. 1   14/4.6g; 14/8.4c
    art. 2   14/6.4
L. 29 December 1949, n. 955
    art. 3   14/6.3b
    art. 5   14/7.3e
L. 6 March 1950, n. 181
    art. 4   14/4.6d
D.P. 10 March 1950, n. 52   4/6.6
D.L. 11 March 1950, n. 50
    art. 5   4/5.2a
L. 5 April 1950, n. 295   4/8.2
D.L. 18 April 1950, n. 142
    art. 18   14/4.6f
L. 12 May 1950, n. 230   10/2.2f
    art. 8   3/4.4c
L. 15 July 1950, n. 585
    art. 2   4/6.7
L. 21 July 1950, n. 818   10/6.4
L. 10 August 1950, n. 646
    art. 3   10/6.5b
    art. 26   10/4.2; 14/4.6k
L. 10 August 1950, n. 792
    art. 3   10/3

L. 21 October 1950, n. 841 — 10/2.2f
L. 9 January 1951, n. 11 — 5/5.1
L. 11 January 1951, n. 25 — 2/1
  art. 9 — 6/5.1
  art. 10 — 6/5.1
  art. 11 — 6/5.1
  art. 18 — 6/3.1
D.P. 7 February 1951, n. 69
  art. 1 — 10/2.2f
L. 2 April 1951, n. 302 — 5/5.10
D.P.R. 30 June 1951, n. 574
  arts. 57-63 — 1/5.5e
D.P.R. 5 July 1951, n. 573
  art. 2 — 5/3.5; 5/3.6
  art. 25 — 13/4.1
L. 24 July 1951, n. 1740 — 5/5.1
D.L. 8 September 1951, n. 750 — 4/5.2a
L. 27 October 1951, n. 1578 — 5/5.1
L. 4 November 1951, n. 1219
  art. 1, letter b — 9/4.2c
  art. 3 — 12/1.3
L. 4 November 1951, n. 1359 — 10/6.4
L. 26 November 1951, n. 1612 — 11/4.1
L. 27 November 1951, n. 1611
  art. 1 — 10/6.2a
L. 22 December 1951, n. 1379 — 4/5.7; 10/7.1
  art. 1 — 14/4.10
  art. 5 — 14/4.10
L. 11 February 1952, n. 74 — 6/5.6; 9/8.1
L. 4 March 1952, n. 110
  art. 2 — 14/6.3a
  art. 2(a) — 14/6.3b
  art. 2(d) — 14/6.3a
L. 5 April 1952, n. 341 — 14/2.2b
L. 8 April 1952, n. 212
  art. 29 — 5/5.4
L. 13 June 1952, n. 693 — 13/3.7
L. 25 June 1952, n. 766 — 4/8.2; 5/5.1
L. 28 June 1952, n. 677
  art. 3 — 9/4.2b
L. 2 July 1952, n. 703 — 1/5.5e
  art. 2 — 1/5.5e
  art. 24 — 4/5.8
  art. 28 — 2/3.2
  art. 29 — 2/3.2
  art. 30 — 2/3.4b
  art. 31 — 4/5.10; 4/5.12
  art. 33 — 4/5.10
  art. 34 — 4/5.10
  art. 36 — 4/5.10
  art. 38 — 4/5.10
  art. 39 — 4/5.11
  art. 47 — 1/4.10j
  art. 52 — 2/3.8

L. 25 July 1952, n. 991 — 10/2.2f
D.P.R. 2 August 1952, n. 1141 — 13/3.7
L. 31 October 1952, n. 1976 — 4/8.2
L. 27 December 1952, n. 3596
  art. 1 — 4/4.2a
D.P.R. 5 February 1953, n. 39 (*Testo unico delle leggi sulle tasse automobilistiche*)
  TUTA
  art. 1 — 4/5.5
  art. 2 — 4/5.5
  art. 8 — 4/5.5
  art. 10 — 1/5.5e
  art. 17 — 4/5.5
  art. 18 — 4/5.5
  art. 39 — 4/5.5
L. 10 February 1953, n. 59 — 3/4.1b; 3/4.2
L. 10 February 1953, n. 136
  art. 26 — 10/1.1
L. 4 April 1953, n. 261 — 15/1.2
  art. 4 — 15/6.3g
D.P.R. 25 June 1953, n. 492 (*Nuove norme sulla imposta di bollo*) — 4/4.2a
  IB
  art. 1 — 4/4.2a
  art. 2 — 4/4.2b; 4/4.2c
  art. 4 — 4/4.2f
  art. 5 — 4/4.2f
  art. 6 — 4/4.2c
  art. 7 — 4/4.2b
  arts. 10-21 — 4/4.2f
  art. 23 — 4/4.2f
  art. 25 — 4/4.2f
  art. 26 — 4/4.2f
  art. 27 — 4/4.2h
  art. 28 — 4/4.2h
  art. 30 — 4/4.2g
  art. 33 — 4/4.2h
  art. 35 — 4/4.2h
  art. 36 — 4/4.2h
  art. 37 — 4/4.2h
  art. 38 — 4/4.2h
  art. 39 — 4/4.2h
  art. 40 — 4/4.2h
  art. 42 — 4/4.2h
  art. 46 — 4/4.2f
  Schedule, Annex A
    art. 1 — 4/4.2b
    art. 5 — 4/4.2d
    art. 64 — 4/4.2c
    Part II — 4/4.2c
  Table, Annex B, art. 9 — 3/4.8d
D.L. 20 November 1953, n. 843 — 4/5.2a
D.L. 3 December 1953, n. 878 — 4/5.2a
L. 17 December 1953, n. 935
  art. 1 — 9/4.2b

L. 27 December 1953, n. 968
   art. 69   9/4.2b
   art. 70   9/4.2b
L. 31 January 1954, n. 2
   art. 1   4/5.2a
L. 16 April 1954, n. 156   14/4.6d
D.P.R. 24 June 1954, n. 342 (*Nuove
norme sulla imposta di pubblicità*)   4/5.3a; 14/3.3g
   IP
   art. 6   4/5.3b
   art. 7   4/5.3b
   art. 8   4/5.3b
   art. 9   4/5.3b
   art. 10   4/5.3b
   art. 11   4/5.3c
   art. 13   4/5.3c
   art. 14   4/5.3c
   art. 15   4/5.3d
   art. 16   4/5.3d
   art. 17   4/5.3d
   art. 18   4/5.3f
   Schedule, Annex   4/5.3f
   Annex B   4/5.3e
L. 13 July 1954, n. 502
   art. 1   14/4.2
   art. 2   14/2.6
L. 17 July 1954, n. 522   14/4.6b
L. 31 July 1954, n. 570   14/8.3;
                14/8.4c; 14/8.5
   art. 3   14/8.3
L. 6 August 1954, n. 603   7/2.8;
                15/1.2; 15/4.2
   art. 5   6/1.5
   art. 11   13/4.1
   art. 26   4/3.1
   art. 33   15/6.3g
   art. 34   15/6.3c
   art. 35   15/6.3h
   art. 36   15/6.5
L. 9 August 1954, n. 645
   art. 1   1/5.5f
   art. 2   1/5.5f
L. 9 August 1954, n. 873   11/4.1
D.P. 14 August 1954, n. 676   14/8.3
   Table A, Annex   14/8.3
   Table B, Annex   14/8.5
D.P.R. 19 August 1954, n. 968
   art. 3   4/5.8d
   art. 5   1/5.6
   art. 17   1/5.5d
L. 20 October 1954, n. 1044   3/4.1b
   art. 1   3/4.5c; 3/4.9; 15/5.2
   art. 2   3/4.9
L. 22 October 1954, n. 974
   art. 3   3/4.4c
   art. 8   3/4.4c

L. 29 October 1954, n. 1050
   art. 5   3/4.4c
D.L. 7 November 1954, n. 1025
   art. 2   1/5.5d
   art. 3   1/5.5d
L. 10 November 1954, n. 1079
   art. 1   4/4.3a
   Table A   4/4.3b
   Table B   4/4.3b
L. 10 November 1954, n. 1226   5/5.1
D.L. 24 November 1954, n. 1068   4/5.2a
D.L. 24 November 1954, n. 1071   4/5.2a
D.L. 26 November 1954, n. 1080   4/5.2a
L. 10 December 1954, n. 1166   4/5.2a
D.P. 22 December 1954, n. 1217   4/5.2a
D.P.R. 4 February 1955, n. 72   4/4.2f
   art. 16   14/7.3e
L. 12 February 1955, n. 38   14/4.6k
D.P. 27 February 1955, n. 192   14/8.3
   art. 3   14/8.3
L. 10 March 1955, n. 110   10/7.1
L. 19 March 1955, n. 105
   art. 2   10/6.2a
L. 31 March 1955, n. 240   10/2.2f
L. 21 May 1955, n. 463
   Schedule C   4/5.5
L. 12 June 1955, n. 481
   art. 1   14/4.6c
   art. 2   14/4.6c
D.P.R. 28 June 1955, n. 620   10/1.1
D.L. 6 October 1955, n. 873   4/5.2a
L. 20 November 1955, n. 1123   3/4.1b;
                3/4.7b
L. 26 November 1955, n. 1109
   art. 1   4/5.4
   Table A   4/5.4
   Table B   4/5.4
   Table C   4/5.4
L. 26 November 1955, n. 1177
   art. 18   1/5.5d; 2/2.9;
            12/1.1; 12/1.4d; 12/1.5c
L. 29 November 1955, n. 1179
   art. 2   1/5.5e
L. 30 November 1955, n. 1335   5/5.1
L. 30 November 1955, n. 1338   5/5.1
L. 3 December 1955, n. 1110   4/5.2a
L. 5 January 1956, n. 1   2/1
   art. 3   13/2.5
   art. 6   13/4.1; 13/6.1; 13/7.4
   art. 17   9/2.8
   art. 20   9/8.1; 9/8.2; 9/8.3
   art. 22   6/6.3
   art. 23   7/2.1; 7/2.5
   art. 24   5/3.7; 7/1.1; 8/4
   art. 25   7/2.13
   art. 26   10/6.1
   art. 28   6/1.5
   art. 50   13/4.1; 13/4.2

L. 5 January 1956, n. 1 (*continued*)
   art. 51   13/4.2
   art. 63   1/3.1d
L. 11 January 1956, n. 2
   art. 1   4/6.6
   art. 2   4/6.6
   art. 3   4/6.6
L. 4 February 1956, n. 33   14/7.3a
   art. 1   14/7.2a
   art. 2   14/6.4
   art. 2(b)   14/6.4
   art. 3   14/6.4
   art. 4(a)   14/6.4
   art. 4(b)   14/6.4
   art. 6   14/6.4; 14/8.4c
L. 7 February 1956, n. 43
   art. 8   11/3.10
D.P.R. 6 July 1956, n. 758
   art. 9   11/3.10
L. 19 July 1956, n. 943   3/4.14d;
                          11/4.1
D.L. 31 October 1956, n. 1194   4/5.2a
D.L. 21 November 1956, n. 1284
   art. 1   14/6.3a
   art. 2   14/6.3a
L. 27 December 1956, n. 1412 14/6.3a
L. 27 December 1956, n. 1416 9/4.2b
L. 5 January 1957, n. 33
   art. 8   1/3.3
   art. 10   1/3.3
   art. 12   1/3.3
D.P.R. 30 March 1957, n. 361   1/3.1a
L. 25 April 1957, n. 359   11/4.1
L. 29 July 1957, n. 634   10/6.1
   art. 1   14/4.6k
   art. 21   10/4.2
   art. 29   10/6.2a; 14/4.6k; 14/8.5
   art. 31   14/4.6k
   art. 33   4/5.8c; 10/6.2a
   art. 35   10/6.3a
   art. 37   10/6.2d; 15/4.5b
   art. 39   10/6.2d
L. 29 July 1957, n. 635
   art. 8   10/6.5a; 10/6.5b;
                  10/6.5c; 10/6.5d
L. 30 July 1957, n. 654   1/3.1d
L. 30 July 1957, n. 657   10/2.2f;
                        10/6.5b
D.P.R. 1 August 1957, n. 649   10/1.1
D.P.R. 2 August 1957, n. 278
   art. 8   3/4.6a
L. 12 August 1957, n. 755
   art. 11   14/6.3b
   art. 13   14/6.3b
L. 12 August 1957, n. 757   14/6.4
   art. 2   14/6.4
   art. 9   14/8.4c

L. 14 October 1957, n. 1203   4/8.2
   art. 14   4/8.2
L. 26 November 1957, n. 1153
   art. 1   14/6.3b
   art. 2   14/6.3c
   art. 3   14/6.3a
   art. 7   14/6.3b
L. 10 December 1957, n. 1218   9/1.7
D.P.R. 29 January 1958, n. 645
(*Testo unico delle leggi sulle imposte dirette*)   1/1.5; 1/3.1d;
                  2/1; 2/2.4d; 3/2.1
   art. 3   6/1.2; 6/3.1; 6/3.2;
                  6/3.3; 7/4.2; 8/1.1;
                  8/2.1; 9/4.2a; 9/9.4
   art. 4   6/3.1; 7/4.2
   art. 5   6/3.4; 6/3.5
   art. 6   1/2.3; 11/1.1
   art. 7   2/2.6a; 6/1.1
   art. 8   5/1.1;
            5/2.2; 5/2.3; 5/2.4;
            5/2.5; 5/2.6; 5/2.7;
            5/2.8; 5/3.1; 5/3.5;
            6/1.2; 7/1.2; 10/3;
        10/4.1; 11/3.3; 11/3.5a
   art. 9   13/1.1d
   art. 10   13/1.1d
   art. 12   1/4.11
   art. 13   1/4.11; 12/1.5a; 13/7.8
   art. 14   13/2.1
   art. 16   5/3.9; 13/3.1;
                  13/6.1; 13/6.2
   art. 17   13/1.1a; 13/7.5
   art. 18   13/1.1a
   art. 19   13/1.4
   art. 20   13/1.1a
   art. 21   6/1.2; 13/1.1c; 13/1.4
   art. 22   6/1.2; 9/9.4;
         9/9.7; 9/9.9c; 13/1.1c
   art. 23   13/1.1c; 13/7.2
   art. 24   6/2.3; 13/1.2; 13/2.3
   art. 25   13/1.4
   art. 26   13/1.1b
   art. 27   13/1.1b; 13/2.3
   art. 28   6/1.2; 13/1.3;
        13/2.3; 13/3.2; 13/3.5
   art. 29   13/1.1a; 13/1.1d; 13/4.1
   art. 30   6/3.5; 13/1.5
   art. 31   13/2.1; 13/4.1
   art. 32   13/6.1
   art. 33   13/2.1
   art. 34   13/2.4; 13/4.1; 13/6.1
   art. 35   13/2.4; 13/2.5; 13/6.1
   art. 36   13/2.4; 13/2.5;
                  13/4.2; 13/6.1
   art. 37   13/1.2; 13/2.1; 13/4.1
   art. 38   13/2.1
   art. 39   13/2.2

D.P.R. 29 January 1958, n. 645 (*continued*)

art. 40	13/1.4; 13/2.2; 13/7.5
art. 41	13/2.2
art. 42	3/4.5e; 6/2.1; 6/2.3; 6/2.5; 13/2.2
art. 43	6/1.2; 6/2.2; 6/5.6; 7/2.5; 10/4.4
art. 44	6/1.2; 6/2.3; 6/2.4; 6/5.2
art. 45	6/1.2; 6/2.2; 6/2.4
art. 49	5/5.11; 10/2.2a; 10/2.2b; 12/1.1
art. 50	10/2.2b; 13/3.1
art. 51	10/2.2b
art. 52	10/2.2c
art. 53	12/1.1
art. 54	10/2.2e
art. 55	10/2.2e
art. 56	10/2.2e
art. 57	10/2.2e; 13/6.1
art. 58	10/2.2f
art. 59	10/2.2f
art. 60	10/2.2f
art. 61	10/2.2f
art. 62	10/2.3a; 12/1.2
art. 63	13/3.1
art. 64	10/2.3a
art. 65	10/2.3a; 10/2.3b
art. 66	12/1.2
art. 67	10/2.3a
art. 68	10/2.3a; 10/2.3b; 10/2.3c; 13/6.1
art. 69	9/4.2a
art. 70	9/4.2a; 13/3.1
art. 71	10/2.2a
art. 72	9/4.2a; 9/4.2b
art. 74	9/4.2c
art. 75	9/4.2c
art. 76	12/1.3
art. 77	5/5.5; 5/5.11; 9/4.2a
art. 78	5/5.5; 5/5.11; 9/4.2b
art. 79	9/4.2a
art. 80	13/2.3; 13/6.2
art. 81	6/1.1; 6/1.4; 8/1.4; 9/4.3; 10/2.4; 10/7.2
art. 82	8/1.1; 8/2.1; 11/1.3; 11/1.4; 11/1.5; 11/1.6a; 11/2.1; 11/2.2; 11/2.3a; 11/3.2a; 11/3.3; 11/3.5a
art. 82, para. 1, a	11/1.2a
art. 82, para. 1, e	11/1.2a
art. 82, para. 2	11/1.2a
art. 83	5/3.2; 6/1.3; 6/1.4; 7/1.3; 9/2.1a; 9/9.3; 10/3; 10/6.1

D.P.R. 29 January 1958, n. 645 (*continued*)

art. 84	5/2.5; 5/5.1; 5/5.2; 5/5.4; 5/5.10; 6/1.4; 6/1.5; 7/2.4; 7/2.11; 9/1.2; 10/2.4; 10/4.2
art. 85	6/1.1; 7/1.1; 7/1.2; 7/1.3; 8/1.1; 8/1.3b; 8/2.1; 8/3.1; 9/1.1; 9/3.1; 9/3.2; 9/3.3; 10/4.1; 10/7.1; 10/7.2
art. 86	6/1.1; 6/1.5; 6/4.1; 9/1.1; 9/3.1
art. 87	6/1.4; 6/1.5; 6/4.1; 7/2.4; 8/1.1; 8/1.3a; 8/1.3b; 8/1.5; 8/1.7; 8/1.8; 8/1.9
art. 88	7/1.1
art. 89	5/1.1; 5/2.5; 5/3.2; 5/3.5; 5/3.7; 12/1.4a; 12/1.4b; 12/3.1; 12/3.2
art. 90	5/1.1; 5/2.5; 5/3.2; 5/3.5; 5/3.7; 10/4.2; 12/1.4c; 12/3.1; 12/3.2
art. 91	7/1.1; 7/2.1; 8/2.2; 8/3.2
art. 92	7/2.5; 8/2.2; 10/4.3
art. 93	7/2.5
art. 94	7/2.3; 8/2.2
art. 95	2/2.7h; 5/3.7; 6/9.2; 7/1.1; 8/2.1
art. 96	7/2.1
art. 97	7/2.1; 7/2.3; 7/2.13; 8/2.2; 9/9.3
art. 98	7/2.6; 7/3.1; 7/3.5; 7/3.9; 8/2.2; 13/1.2
art. 99	7/2.7; 7/2.10; 7/3.6; 9/8.8
art. 100	7/1.3; 7/2.7; 7/2.10; 7/3.6; 9/8.1; 9/8.3; 9/8.8; 9/9.2
art. 101	7/2.7; 9/8.4
art. 102	6/5.1
art. 103	6/5.3
art. 104	5/3.2; 6/1.2; 11/3.3; 11/3.4; 13/1.3
art. 105	6/1.2
art. 106	6/1.2; 7/1.3; 9/8.1
art. 107	6/6.3
art. 108	6/1.5; 7/2.3
art. 109	6/1.2; 6/1.5; 7/2.3; 7/2.5; 7/2.7; 7/2.12; 7/3.1; 7/3.9; 7/5.4
art. 110	6/1.2; 6/1.5; 7/2.5
art. 111	5/2.5; 6/1.5; 7/2.3; 7/2.14; 9/2.7b
art. 112	6/1.2; 6/1.5; 7/4.2
art. 113	6/1.2; 6/8.2; 11/2.4
art. 114	10/2.4

D.P.R. 29 January 1958, n. 645 (*continued*)

art. 115	6/4.1; 8/2.1; 8/2.2
art. 116	6/4.3; 8/4
art. 117	6/9.1; 13/2.2; 13/2.3
art. 118	6/2.5; 13/2.2; 13/2.3
art. 119	6/1.2; 6/2.5; 13/2.2; 13/2.3
art. 120	13/1.1b; 13/1.1c; 13/1.2; 13/1.3; 13/2.3; 13/2.4
art. 121	13/2.3; 13/4.1
art. 122	13/2.3; 13/6.1
art. 123	13/2.3; 13/6.2
art. 124	6/1.2; 9/9.4; 9/9.7
art. 125	6/1.2; 9/9.9c
art. 126	12/1.6; 13/3.3
art. 127	13/3.4; 13/7.5
art. 128	12/1.6; 12/4; 13/3.5
art. 129	9/1.1
arts. 130-144	2/3.1
art. 130	6/1.1; 12/1.5c
art. 131	5/1.2; 5/1.3; 5/1.4; 6/1.1; 11/3.2a
art. 132	5/5.1
art. 133	6/1.1; 6/1.4; 7/1.3; 11/1.2b; 11/2.2; 11/3.2a
art. 134	5/5.2; 5/5.4; 6/1.4
art. 135	5/3.2; 6/1.1; 6/4.1; 8/1.2; 8/2.1; 9/1.1; 9/1.2; 9/2.1b; 10/2.1
art. 136	6/1.1; 6/1.5; 7/2.1; 7/2.5; 7/2.8; 8/1.3a; 8/1.9; 9/3.2; 12/1.5a
art. 137	13/2.3
art. 138	5/1.1; 5/1.2; 5/1.3; 5/1.4; 6/1.1; 9/3.1; 12/1.5b
art. 139	12/1.5c
art. 140	8/1.3b; 8/1.8; 9/9.2; 9/9.9c
art. 141	13/2.1; 13/2.3; 13/2.4
art. 142	13/2.3; 13/6.2
art. 143	12/1.6; 12/4; 13/3.5; 13/7.5
art. 144	5/3.9; 13/1.5
art. 145	5/2.8; 6/1.1; 6/1.4; 11/1.1; 11/3.3
art. 146	3/2.4; 6/1.1; 12/2.2c
art. 147	3/2.3; 6/5.6; 6/6.1; 7/3.9; 7/4.2; 11/1.1; 11/2.3a; 11/3.3; 11/3.4
art. 148	5/3.2; 6/1.1; 6/1.5; 6/4.1; 7/1.3; 7/2.1; 7/2.3; 7/2.5; 7/2.7; 7/2.8; 7/4.1; 7/4.2; 9/1.1; 9/1.2; 9/2.1c; 9/9.7; 9/9.9c; 10/2.1; 11/1.1; 11/2.3a; 11/3.3; 11/3.4
art. 149	12/2.2c

D.P.R. 29 January 1958, n. 645 (*continued*)

art. 150	3/2.3; 9/9.9c; 13/2.1; 13/2.3
art. 151	5/5.5; 5/5.6; 5/5.7; 5/5.8; 5/5.9; 5/5.10; 5/5.11
art. 152	3/2.2; 5/5.10; 12/3.2
art. 153	10/4.2
art. 154	10/5
art. 155	10/5
art. 156	3/3.1
art. 157	3/3.3
art. 158	3/3.2
art. 159	3/3.1
art. 161	5/1.3
art. 163	5/1.3
art. 164	5/1.3
art. 165	5/1.3
art. 168	13/3.2
art. 169	13/3.5
art. 171	13/3.5; 13/4.5; 13/5
art. 172	13/3.5; 13/5
art. 173	13/3.6a
art. 174	13/3.6a
art. 175	13/3.6b
art. 176	9/9.4; 9/9.7; 13/3.6a
art. 177	13/3.6a; 13/5
art. 178	13/3.6c
art. 179	13/3.6a
art. 180	13/6.2
art. 181	13/3.6a
art. 182	13/3.6a; 13/3.6c
art. 183	13/3.2; 13/3.6c
art. 184 *bis*	13/3.6c; 13/7.2
art. 184 *ter*	13/3.7
art. 184 *quater*	13/3.6c; 13/3.8
art. 185	13/3.7
art. 187	13/3.7
art. 188	5/3.9; 13/1.5; 13/4.6
art. 189	13/3.7
art. 190	13/3.7
art. 191	13/3.7
art. 192	13/3.7
art. 193	13/3.7
art. 194	13/7.6
art. 196	13/3.1
art. 197	13/3.1; 13/7.1
art. 198	13/3.6c; 13/5
art. 199	13/5
art. 199 *bis*	13/5
art. 201	13/3.8
art. 207	13/4.7
art. 208	13/4.7
art. 211	13/3.8
arts. 219-230	13/3.8
arts. 231-241	13/3.8
art. 242	13/3.8
art. 243	13/1.1c; 13/7.2

D.P.R. 29 January 1958, n. 645 (*continued*)

art. 244	13/7.2
art. 245	13/7.4
art. 246	13/7.5
art. 247	10/2.2e; 13/7.2
art. 248	13/7.2
art. 249	13/7.2; 13/7.5
art. 250	13/7.2
art. 251	13/7.2; 13/7.5
art. 252	13/7.4; 13/7.5
art. 253	13/7.2
art. 254	3/4.5e; 13/7.3; 13/7.5
art. 255	13/7.5
art. 256	13/7.5
art. 257	13/7.5
art. 258	13/7.5
art. 259	13/7.1; 13/7.2; 13/7.4
art. 260	13/7.6; 13/7.7
art. 261	13/7.6; 13/7.7
art. 262	13/4.8; 13/7.6; 13/7.7
art. 263	13/7.6; 13/7.7
art. 264	13/7.7
art. 265	13/3.1
art. 266	13/7.8
art. 268	13/7.1
art. 269	13/7.5
art. 270	13/7.1
art. 272	12/1.6; 12/4; 13/3.4; 13/3.5
art. 273	12/4; 13/3.5
art. 274	6/1.4; 9/4.2a; 9/4.2b
art. 276	10/3
art. 288(A)	11/3.7; 13/4.1
art. 288(B)	13/4.1
art. 288(C)	9/4.2a; 13/4.1
art. 289	6/5.1

L. 12 February 1958, n. 126

art. 18	1/5.5f

L. 4 March 1958, n. 174

	4/5.9
art. 8	2/2.9

L. 13 March 1958, n. 280 — 11/4.1

L. 18 March 1958, n. 228 — 3/4.6a

D.L. 24 September 1958, n. 918 — 10/6.1

L. 19 December 1958, n. 1085

art. 1	4/6.1
art. 2	4/6.2; 4/6.3

D.P.R. 26 December 1958, n. 1105

(*Tariffa doganale*)	4/8.1

TD

art. 2	4/8.2

Preliminary Provisions

art. 3	4/8.4
art. 8	4/8.2
art. 9	4/8.2
art. 10	4/8.2
art. 11	4/8.2

D.P.R. 26 December 1958, n. 1105 (*continued*)

TD

art. 16	4/8.3
art. 28	4/8.4

D.P.R. 29 December 1958, n. 1103

	4/8.2

D.P.R. 29 December 1958, n. 1104

art. 1	4/8.2
art. 2	4/8.2

L. 24 March 1959, n. 112 — 14/8.4a

L. 11 April 1959, n. 137 — 4/6.2

D.P.R. 18 April 1959, n. 167 — 4/6.3

L. 9 May 1959, n. 266 — 4/5.2a

L. 27 May 1959, n. 324

art. 1	5/5.4
art. 16	5/5.4

L. 27 May 1959, n. 355 — 15/1.2

art. 1	15/6.3b
art. 2	15/6.3b
art. 3	15/5.2

L. 27 May 1959, n. 356

art. 1	4/5.5

L. 27 May 1959, n. 358 — 10/7.1

art. 1	4/5.7

L. 27 May 1959, n. 359 — 14/6.3b; 14/6.3c

L. 27 May 1959, n. 360 — 4/5.2b

L. 28 May 1959, n. 361

art. 2	13/4.1

L. 11 June 1959, n. 405 — 4/5.2a

L. 26 June 1959, n. 487 — 14/8.3

L. 25 July 1959, n. 609 — 14/4.10

L. 25 November 1959, n. 1001 — 9/1.7

L. 16 December 1959, n. 1070

art. 1	14/4.8a; 14/7.3a
art. 1, para. 1	14/3.3a
art. 1, para. 2	14/3.3a
art. 2	14/6.1; 14/6.2; 14/6.3a; 14/8.4a
art. 5	14/7.3b; 14/7.3g
art. 5(a)	14/3.4; 14/4.8b
art. 5(f)	14/3.4; 14/4.8b
art. 6	14/3.4; 14/4.8b
art. 7	14/9.2c

L. 18 December 1959, n. 1079

art. 1	4/5.8d
art. 5	1/5.5e
art. 8	4/5.8b
art. 12	4/5.8b; 14/6.3a
art. 13	4/5.8b

L. 20 December 1959, n. 1102

art. 4	1/5.5e; 4/5.4

L. 2 February 1960, n. 35

art. 1	9/1.7; 9/4.2b; 15/6.3b
art. 2	9/1.7
art. 3	14/4.6a

L. 2 February 1960, n. 40 — 12/1.4d
L. 23 February 1960, n. 131
    art. 1 — 9/4.2d
    art. 2 — 9/4.2d
    art. 4 — 9/4.2e
L. 16 June 1960, n. 623
    art. 1 — 4/5.2a
L. 18 June 1960, n. 704 — 11/4.1
D.L. 30 June 1960, n. 589 — 4/4.3b
    art. 2 *bis* — 4/4.3c
L. 7 July 1960, n. 633 — 14/8.3
L. 13 July 1960, n. 661 — 4/5.2a; 4/5.2b
L. 21 July 1960, n. 739
    art. 9 — 10/2.2f
    art. 11 — 10/2.2f
D.P. 22 July 1960, n. 794 — 14/8.3
L. 14 August 1960, n. 822 — 4/5.2a
L. 14 August 1960, n. 826 — 4/4.3c
D.P. 23 August 1960, n. 905 — 14/8.3
D.P. 31 August 1960, n. 909 — 14/8.3
L. 16 September 1960, n. 1014
    art. 3 — 1/5.6
    art. 7 — 1/5.5f
    art. 8 — 1/5.5f
    art. 10 — 1/5.5f
    art. 15 — 1/5.5c; 12/1.2
    art. 16 — 1/5.5e
    art. 18 — 2/3.3b; 2/3.4b
    art. 19 — 12/1.1; 12/1.3
    art. 20 — 1/5.6; 2/3.4b; 2/3.7; 12/1.4d
    art. 23 — 1/5.6
L. 21 October 1960, n. 1371
    art. 2 — 1/5.5c
L. 25 October 1960, n. 1316
    art. 1 — 13/3.7; 13/5; 13/7.1; 13/7.2
L. 2 December 1960, n. 1588 — 11/4.1
L. 15 December 1960, n. 1560 — 4/5.2a; 4/5.6
L. 18 December 1960, n. 1608 — 14/4.6k
L. 21 December 1960, n. 1521
    art. 6 — 9/4.2c
D.P.R. 1 March 1961, n. 121 (*Testo unico delle leggi vigenti in materia di tasse sulle concessioni governative*) — 4/7.1
    TUCG — 4/7.1
    art. 1 — 4/7.1
    art. 2 — 4/7.3
    art. 3 — 4/7.3
    art. 4 — 4/7.3
    art. 5 — 4/7.3
    art. 14 — 4/7.4
    art. 15 — 4/7.4
    Table Annex A, Schedule — 4/7.1

D.P.R. 1 March 1961, n. 121 (*continued*)
    TUCG
    art. 15 — 4/7.2
    art. 16 — 4/7.2
    art. 22 — 4/7.2
    art. 29 — 4/7.2
    art. 30 — 4/7.2
    art. 75 — 4/7.2
    art. 83 — 4/7.2
    art. 84 — 4/7.2
    art. 108 — 4/7.2
    art. 110 — 4/7.2
    art. 111 — 4/7.2
    art. 136 — 4/7.2
    art. 146 — 4/7.2
    art. 163 — 4/7.2
    art. 166 — 4/7.2
    Table, Annex B — 4/7.1
D.P.R. 9 March 1961, n. 390 — 4/6.2; 4/6.4
L. 2 June 1961, n. 454
    art. 28 — 10/2.2f; 10/2.3c
    art. 37 — 10/2.2f
L. 13 June 1961, n. 526 — 10/6.5b; 10/6.5c; 10/6.5d
L. 27 June 1961, n. 551
    art. 10 — 5/1.3
L. 1 July 1961, n. 569 — 4/5.2b
L. 19 July 1961, n. 659
    art. 1 — 9/4.2b
    art. 2 — 9/4.2b
    art. 4 — 5/5.10
L. 21 July 1961, n. 707
    art. 1 — 15/4.5b; 15/6.1; 15/6.5
    art. 2 — 15/6.5
L. 24 July 1961, n. 729 — 1/5.5f
L. 28 July 1961, n. 838
    art. 1 — 10/2.2a; 10/2.3a; 12/1.1; 12/1.2
    art. 2 — 10/2.2a; 10/2.3a; 12/1.1; 12/1.2
L. 31 October 1961, n. 1196 — 14/7.3a
    art. 1 — 14/3.1; 14/3.7
    art. 2 — 14/6.1; 14/6.2; 14/6.4; 14/8.4a
    arts. 3-6 — 14/7.3b
    art. 3 — 14/2.7; 14/3.4
    art. 4 — 14/3.4
    art. 5 — 14/3.4
L. 9 November 1961, n. 1233 — 14/8.3
L. 10 December 1961, n. 1346 — 1/5.5d; 6/3.1
    art. 1 — 2/2.9; 12/1.1; 12/1.3; 12/1.4d; 12/1.5c; 12/2.2c
    art. 2 — 12/1.3

L. 16 December 1961, n. 1425   4/5.2a
L. 25 January 1962, n. 3   14/8.3; 14/8.5
D.P.R. 10 February 1962, n. 15   14/8.3;
                                    14/8.5
L. 18 April 1962, n. 206
    art. 1   12/1.4c
L. 18 April 1962, n. 209   12/1.5c
    art. 2   12/1.5c
L. 21 April 1962, n. 226   12/1.6
    art. 1   7/2.3; 8/1.2; 13/1.4;
                            13/1.5; 13/3.5
L. 27 July 1962, n. 1228   14/7.3b
    art. 1   10/4.2
    art. 2   10/4.3
    art. 3   10/4.4
L. 16 August 1962, n. 1347   14/8.4a
L. 29 September 1962, n. 1462
    art. 5   10/4.2
    art. 6   15/4.5b
    art. 14   14/8.5
L. 4 December 1962, n. 1682
    art. 1   13/2.2
    art. 2   8/1.3b; 8/1.8
    art. 3   12/1.4a
    art. 4   12/1.4c
    art. 5   8/1.9
    art. 6   13/3.5
L. 29 December 1962, n. 1744
    art. 1   14/3.1; 14/3.6; 15/6.3d
L. 29 December 1962, n. 1745
    art. 1   9/2.2; 9/2.3; 9/2.7a; 9/2.7b
    art. 2   13/1.4; 13/3.5
    art. 3   9/2.7c; 13/1.3; 13/5
    art. 4   9/2.8
    art. 5   9/2.8
    art. 6   10/4.4
    art. 7   9/2.8, 10/4.4
    art. 8   9/2.7c; 9/2.8; 10/4.4;
                                13/1.3
    art. 9   9/2.8
    art. 10   9/2.7d
    art. 11   9/2.7e
    art. 12   13/7.5
    art. 13   13/7.5
    art. 14   13/7.5
    art. 15   13/7.5
    art. 16   13/7.5
    art. 18   9/2.8; 10/4.4; 13/1.3
    art. 21   13/7.2
    art. 22   9/2.7a
L. 31 December 1962, n. 1852   4/5.2a
L. 11 January 1963, n. 39   4/8.2
D.P.R. 12 February 1963, n. 169   4/8.1
L. 21 February 1963, n. 263   4/5.2a

L. 5 March 1963, n. 246 (*Imposta sugli
    incrementi di valore delle aree fab-
    bricabili*)   3/7.1
    IAF
    art. 1   3/7.3a
    art. 2   3/7.3b
    art. 3   3/7.3a
    art. 4   3/7.3b
    art. 5   3/7.3b
    art. 6   3/7.3d
    art. 7   3/7.3d
    arts. 8-11   3/7.3b
    art. 12   3/7.3d
    art. 13   3/7.3d
    art. 14   3/7.3b
    art. 15   3/7.3b
    art. 18   3/7.3d
    art. 21   3/7.3c
    art. 24   3/7.3a; 3/7.3c
    art. 25   3/7.3b
    art. 27   3/7.3d
    art. 31   3/7.2b
    art. 32   3/7.2b
    art. 33   3/7.2b; 3/7.2d
    art. 35   3/7.4
    art. 36   3/7.2a; 3/7.2e
    art. 37   3/7.2b; 3/7.2c
    art. 38   3/7.2e
    art. 43   3/7.3d
    art. 44   3/7.2e; 3/7.3d
    art. 46   3/7.2a; 3/7.3a
    art. 47   3/7.3a
L. 5 March 1963, n. 270   14.4/8a
L. 27 September 1963, n. 1317   15/6.3b
D.L. 23 February 1964, n. 25   4/5.2b
D.L. 23 February 1964, n. 26   4/3.6
D.L. 23 February 1964, n. 27   9/2.7a
    art. 1   9/2.7d
L. 1 March 1964, n. 62
    art. 1   1/3.4b
L. 1 March 1964, n. 113   12/1.5c

**Regional Laws
(Chronological)**

L.R. Sic. 8 July 1948, n. 32   9/2.8
L.R. Sic. 20 March 1950, n. 29
    art. 2   10/6.1
L.R. Sic. 27 December 1950, n. 104
                                  10/2.2f
L.R. Sic. 7 December 1953, n. 61
    art. 2   10/6.1
    art. 6   10/6.1
L.R. Sard. 16 July 1954, n. 14   10/6.1
L.R. Sard. 12 April 1957, n. 10   9/2.8
L.R. Trent. 8 August 1959, n. 10 9/2.8

Table of Ministerial Decrees

D.M. 8 July 1924 (*Testo unico* for the tax on beer)   4/5.2a

D.M. 8 July 1924 (*Testo unico* for the tax on coffee substitutes) art. 1   4/5.2a

D.M. 8 July 1924 (*Testo unico* for the tax on spirits) art. 14   4/5.2a

D.M. 8 July 1924 (*Testo unico* for the tax on sugar)   4/5.2a

D.M. 8 July 1924 (*Testo unico* for the tax on the consumption of gas and electric energy)   4/5.2a

D.M. 5 May 1930 art. 3   9/1.2

D.M. 27 September 1930, n. 43202   14/1

D.M. 26 February 1933   4/5.11

D. Intermin. 25 June 1940   4/5.9

D.M. 20 July 1946   1/5.5d

D.M. 20 August 1947   4/5.3a

D.M. 1 March 1949   10/2.2g

D.M. 10 March 1949 Table A   4/5.2a

D.M. 12 August 1950   13/2.3

D.M. 5 June 1952   14/7.2c

D.M. 10 August 1952   4/5.9

D.M. 5 November 1952   14/7.2c

D.M. 15 June 1953   4/3.6

D.M. 1 October 1953   4/8.4

D.M. 10 December 1953   14/7.3a

    art. 15   14/7.3c

    art. 16   14/7.3c

    art. 17   14/7.3d

D.M. 18 August 1954, n. 93782 Table   14/8.3

D.M. 15 June 1956 art. 9   11/3.10

D.M. 3 June 1958   13/3.7

D.M. 1 March 1959   10/2.2e

D.M. 14 December 1959 art. 5   14/7.4b

D.M. 4 December 1961   9/4.2d

D.M. 19 February 1962   12/1.3

D.M. 28 September 1962   4/8.4

D.M. 31 October 1962 Table A   4/8.4

D.M. 10 November 1962   12/1.5a; 12/2.2b

D.M. 22 December 1962   14/6.4

D.M. 24 April 1963   9/4.2d

Table of Administrative Instructions

I.M. 10 September 1866
    art. 23   3/4.10c
C.M. 2 September 1869, n. 567   15/6.3a
C.M. 1 July 1902, n. 11959   7/2.1;
                            7/2.9; 7/5.1
R.M. 6 August 1903, n. 52723   3/4.10g
R.M. 18 June 1906, n. 53059   3/4.14a
C.M. 29 March 1924, n. 4314   7/2.16
C.M. 12 March 1925   6/1.5; 8/1.3a;
                               9/2.1b
R.M. 28 October 1928   11/3.5a
I.M. 10 April 1930, n. 92127   3/4.2
C.M. 8 June 1932, n. 5169   7/2.9; 7/2.10
C.M. 15 October 1932, n. 3417   13/2.3
C.M. 19 January 1934, n. 600   7/2.4;
                               8/1.3a
C.M. 14 July 1934, n. 7120   8/1.3a
C.M. 21 September 1934, n. 9460
                               9/1.7
I.M. 10 October 1934, n. 361   3/4.5b
C.M. 3 September 1935, n. 4100
                         13/7.1; 13/7.6
C.M. 17 October 1936, n. 10560   8/1.5
C.M. 28 June 1937, n. 6200   9/4.2a;
                       9/9.7; 10/2.3a
I.M. 21 April 1938, n. 8478   3/4.9
R.M. 7 April 1940, n. 91932   14/3.6;
                               14/4.9
R.M. 23 July 1940, n. 93091   14/4.2
I.M. 1 August 1940, n. 91915   14/8.2a
    para. I, n. 1   14/4.2
    para. II, n. 1   14/4.2
    para. II, n. 2   14/4.2
    para. II, n. 2(a)   14/4.2
    para. II, n. 4   14/4.5
    para. II, n. 4(b)   14/4.2
    para. VI, n. 2   14/5.2
R.M. 3 August 1940, n. 92039   14/5.2
R.M. 31 August 1940, n. 94261   14/4.5
C.M. 22 January 1941, n. 690   5/5.2
C.M. 16 February 1941, n. 98967
                               14/3.3a
R.M. 15 May 1941, n. 98878   14/5.2
Ministerial Note 28 May 1941, n.
    3087   8/1.2
R.M. 5 July 1941, n. 68863   14/4.9
R.M. 18 September 1941, n. 64876
                               14/4.2
R.M. 2 April 1942, n. 61404   14/4.2
R.M. 21 May 1942, n. 62355   14/3.10;
                               14/4.4
R.M. 4 August 1942, n. 61464   14/5.2
C.M. 23 May 1944, n. 3660   10/2.3b
R.M. 1 September 1944, n. 72409
                               14/4.5
C.M. 27 March 1945, n. 770   8/1.4

I.M. 6 April 1945, n. 120156   3/5.3
C.M. 24 July 1945, n. 62632   14/4.6i
I.M. 10 August 1945, n. 90960   3/4.4d
R.M. 31 August 1945, n. 63468   14/4.6a
C.M. 5 April 1946, n. 2160   7/1.2
C.M. 12 June 1946, n. 4080   7/1.2
C.M. 12 June 1946, n. 4090   10/2.4
R.M. 23 July 1946, n. 63631   14/2.7
R.M. 28 November 1946, n. 63964
                               14/4.5
C.M. 22 January 1947, n. 60144   14/2.7
R.M. 12 February 1947, n. 69598
                               14/4.2
R.M. 29 March 1947, n. 62072   14/4.4
R.M. 16 May 1947, n. 62307   14/2.7
R.M. 21 June 1947, n. 60633   14/4.2
R.M. 21 June 1947, n. 64128   14/2.7
C.M. 5 August 1947, n. 65403   14/3.1
Verb. conf. October 1947   9/9.2;
                               10/2.4
R.M. 25 November 1947, n. 70182
                               14/4.2
C.M. 3 January 1948, n. 72014   14/2.7
R.M. 17 January 1948, n. 68112   14/4.7
R.M. 23 February 1948, n. 70705
                               14/4.2
C.M. 9 March 1948, n. 300940   10/2.4
C.M. 23 April 1948, n. 302130   12/1.6
R.M. 13 May 1948, n. 71382   14/4.2
R.M. 23 July 1948, n. 122011   3/4.6a
C.M. 7 February 1949, n. 501   2/3.4a
C.M. 12 March 1949, n. 301970   12/1.6
C.M. 17 March 1949, n. 500280   2/3.4a
C.M. 28 March 1949, n. 350670
           10/6.2a; 10/6.2b; 10/6.2c
R.M. 14 April 1949, n. 60344   14/4.10
C.M. 16 May 1949, n. 303750   12/1.6
R.M. 15 June 1949, n. 60214   14/2.7
I.M. 16 June 1949, n. 121579   3/4.7b;
                               3/5.5
C.M. 21 October 1949, n. 352360
                              10/6.2b
C.M. 11 November 1949, n. 307600
                               12/1.6
C.M. 31 December 1949, n. 66631
                              14/7.3e
C.M. 25 April 1950, n. 131556   3/4.9
R.M. 12 May 1950, n. 64533   14/5.3
R.M. 9 May 1951, n. 65214   14/8.1
R.M. 7 June 1951, n. 61371   14/4.6j
C.M. 8 August 1951, n. 352150   10/6.2c
Ministerial Note 27 August 1951, n.
    351756   10/6.2a
R.M. 22 September 1951, n. 60469
                               14/4.4

R.M. 27 December 1951, n. 60481
14/3.8
C.M. 10 January 1952, n. 200100   9/4.2c
R.M. 13 February 1952, n. 62222
14/8.1
C.M. 20 March 1952, n. 301340   7/2.3
C.M. 31 March 1952, n. 170999   15/3.3e
R.M. 31 March 1952, n. 190631   3/5.4
C.M. 13 May 1952, n. 301430   7/2.8
C.M. 3 July 1952, n. 351230   11/4.1
R.M. 23 July 1952, n. 76402   14/3.6
C.M. 23 September 1952, n. 307670
12/1.6
C.M. 26 September 1952, n. 371700
7/2.4
C.M. 10 November 1952, n. 201600
13/4.1
R.M. 29 November 1952, n. 163772   3/6
Ministerial Note 16 December 1952,
n. 455193   13/3.1
C.M. 15 January 1953, n. 90101
para. 1, n. 2   14/3.13
R.M. 27 February 1953, n. 79419
14/3.6; 14/4.9
C.M. 2 April 1953, n. 2/4025/5   2/3.4b
Annex   2/3.4a
C.M. 14 April 1953, n. 177124   3/4.2
R.M. 19 May 1953, n. 78985   14/8.1
R.M. 29 August 1953, n. 166955   3/6
R.M. 7 October 1953, n. 81660   14/8.1
C.M. 1 December 1953, n. 501370
6/1.5
R.M. 11 December 1953, n. 82015
14/4.9
R.M. 9 January 1954, n. 76374   14/3.9
R.M. 18 January 1954, n. 170758
3/4.6c
Ministerial Note 31 March 1954, n.
300461   10/7.3
C.M. 2 April 1954, n. 350650   7/3.5
R.M. 7 April 1954, n. 75451   14/4.5
C.M. 20 April 1954, n. 301260   12/1.6
R.M. 30 April 1954, n. 178646   3/5.4
I.M. 8 June 1954, n. 92353   14/7.3e
R.M. 25 June 1954, n. 82334   14/4.7
C.M. 7 December 1954, n. 303932
7/2.3
R.M. 14 January 1955, n. 81968   14/2.7
R.M. 10 March 1955, n. 215002
14/4.6d
R.M. 9 April 1955, n. 94525   14/8.3;
14/8.5
C.M. 2 May 1955, n. 301660   5/2.7
C.M. 14 May 1955, n. 351440   7/3.5
C.M. 24 May 1955, n. 72184   10/2.4

C.M. 1 June 1955, n. 351690   2/4.4;
3/2.3; 5/5.10; 6/1.5; 6/3.4;
6/3.5; 6/3.6; 11/1.1; 11/2.3b;
11/3.5a; 12/2.2c
C.M. 4 June 1955, n. 302220   7/1.2
C.M. 12 August 1955, n. 10526   13/4.2
C.M. 20 October 1955, n. 352460
10/6.2b
R.M. 23 January 1956, n. 217273
14/4.2
C.M. 1 March 1956, n. 350660   6/2.3
C.M. 7 March 1956, n. 300770   9/5
R.M. 5 April 1956, n. 215528   14/4.5
C.M. 10 April 1956, n. 350672   10/6.2c
C.M. 15 June 1956, n. 351038   7/2.8
Ministerial Note 24 July 1956, n.
302501   10/7.1
C.M. 6 August 1956, n. 455871   11/3.10
C.M. 1 September 1956, n. 78   13/2.2
C.M. 7 September 1956, n. 351253
9/9.4
C.M. 11 October 1956, n. 351770
13/2.2
C.M. 29 December 1956, n. 303800
11/4.9; 13/3.5
C.M. 21 January 1957, n. 350300
11/4.1; 11/4.3b; 11/4.9;
11/4.10; 11/4.13a
C.M. 18 February 1957, n. 350400
10/3
C.M. 21 February 1957, n. 451467
11/3.10
C.M. 25 February 1957, n. 500116
8/1.9
Ministerial Note 25 February 1957,
n. 352173   7/2.10
C.M. 1 March 1957, n. 350620   7/2.15;
7/3.1; 7/3.3; 7/3.5; 7/3.6;
7/3.7; 7/3.9
Annex   7/3.2; 7/3.5; 10/2.4
Annex, Group IV   10/1.5
C.M. 15 March 1957, n. 350610
11/4.2; 11/4.9
R.M. 16 March 1957, n. 216754   14/4.2
C.M. 12 April 1957, n. 350820   12/1.4b
C.M. 15 April 1957, n. 350860   6/5.3;
6/6.3; 7/1.1;
7/2.1; 7/2.5; 7/3.3;
8/4; 9/8.3; 9/8.6
C.M. 23 April 1957, n. 300635   7/2.10
Verb. conf. May 1957   13/2.3
C.M. 20 May 1957, n. 350874   11/4.9
C.M. 25 May 1957, n. 351190   7/2.8;
7/2.13
C.M. 21 June 1957, n. 302020   10/2.3a
R.M. 23 July 1957, n. 248310   14/4.9
C.M. 29 July 1957, n. 351420   5/5.6

R.M. 30 August 1957, n. 215887 14/2.3d
R.M. 9 September 1957, n. 217046 14/4.9
C.M. 30 September 1957, n. 351690
    11/4.13a
C.M. 16 October 1957, n. 459052 11/3.10
Ministerial Note 28 October 1957,
  n. 351830   11/1.6c
Verb. conf. November 1957   7/2.3
C.M. 7 December 1957, n. 352040 7/2.5
C.M. 23 December 1957, n. 352114 7/2.5
C.M. 15 February 1958, n. 500051 8/1.3b
C.M. 5 March 1958, n. 10   7/3.6;
    9/8.1; 9/8.3
Verb. conf. May 1958   10/1.4
R.M. 4 June 1958, n. 276039   14/4.4
C.M. 14 June 1958, n. 351000 10/6.2a;
    10/6.2d; 10/6.3a;
    10/6.3b; 12/1.4d
C.M. 30 June 1958, n. 351060   6/2.3
Ministerial Note 22 July 1958, n.
  351170   11/3.6b
R.M. 23 July 1958, n. 122011   3/4.6a;
    3/4.6c
C.M. 27 July 1958, n. 500701   6/1.5
R.M. 29 August 1958, n. 190950 14/4.9
Ministerial Note 21 October 1958,
  n. 301459   12/1.6
C.M. 23 January 1959, n. 350390
    10/6.5a; 10/6.5b; 10/6.5c
C.M. 25 March 1959, n. 200400 9/4.2c;
    10/2.2f
C.M. 28 March 1959, n. 350670 10/6.5a
C.M. 14 April 1959, n. 350710   7/3.1
C.M. 12 May 1959, n. 19/248699
    14/8.2a
C.M. 31 October 1959, n. 176666 14/5.3
C.M. 5 November 1959, n. 352030
    10/6.5a; 10/6.5b;
    10/6.5c; 10/6.5e
C.M. 18 December 1959, n. 84   6/1.5;
    6/6.3; 7/2.3;
    8/1.2; 10/2.2f;
    13/2.2; 13/3.1; 13/4.6
C.M. 18 December 1959, n. 304250
    7/1.2; 10/2.4

C.M. 30 December 1959, n. 501578
    13/1.4
C.M. 4 January 1960, n. 501519 8/1.9;
    12/1.5b
Ministerial Note 8 March 1960, n.
  352412   9/1.7
C.M. 16 March 1960, n. 300790 12/1.6
C.M. 13 April 1960, n. 350890 7/2.15
C.M. 13 April 1960, n. 350900 7/2.3
C.M. 9 May 1960, n. 351110   9/9.2;
    9/9.4
C.M. 18 May 1960, n. 301520 13/3.6a;
    13/5
C.M. 9 September 1960, n. 204650
    10/2.2f
C.M. 10 September 1960, n. 352350
    10/6.5d
C.M. 10 December 1960, n. 333 13/3.7;
    13/7.1
R.M. 27 December 1960, n.
  58/65240   14/7.3g
Ministerial Note 10 April 1961, n.
  201259   9/4.2b
Verb. conf. 16-19 May 1961   9/9.4
Ministerial Note 24 May 1961, n.
  500240   9/4.2c
C.M. 20 July 1961, n. 204210   10/2.2f
C.M. 3 August 1961, n. 500816   5/1.3
I.M. 10 September 1961
  art. 2   15/6.5
C.M. 23 October 1961, n. 302187 9/9.9b
C.M. 30 November 1961, n. 500719
    9/2.8
I.M. 15 December 1961, n.
  62/170503   14/7.3a
C.M. 15 June 1962, n. 60   7/2.3;
    8/1.2; 13/3.5
C.M. 20 October 1962, n. 351470 11/4.6
C.M. 9 November 1962, n. 72 14/8.4a
C.M. 2 April 1963, n. 110   9/2.3;
    9/2.7c; 9/2.7d
C.M. 9 May 1963, n. 35   14/4.8a
C.M. 12 June 1963, n. 360120   9/2.7c
C.M. 31 October 1963, n. 320590 7/3.5a

Table of International Agreements

Income Tax Treaties

Argentina (1949)	11/4.1; 11/4.6
Belgium (1931)	11/4.1; 11/4.2
art. 13	11/4.3a
art. 14	11/4.16
Brazil (1957)	11/4.1
Canada (1932)	11/4.1; 11/4.6
France (1930)	11/4.1
art. 5	11/4.7a
art. 19	11/4.16
France (1958)	11/4.1
art. 2(1)(B)	11/4.2
art. 12	11/4.3a
Germany (1925)	11/4.1
art. 1	11/4.2
art. 11	11/4.3a
art. 18	11/4.16
Greece (1932)	11/4.1; 11/4.2; 11/4.6
Hungary (1926)	11/4.1
The Netherlands (1957)	11/4.1
art. 1(2)	11/4.2
art. 2(1)	11/4.4b
art. 2(1)(e)	11/4.4d
art. 4(1)	11/4.5a
art. 4(2)	11/4.5b
art. 4(3)	11/4.5a
art. 4(4)	11/4.5b
art. 5	11/4.5c
art. 6	11/4.6
art. 7(1)	11/4.7a
art. 7(2)	11/4.7a; 11/4.7b
art. 8(1)	11/4.8
art. 8(2)	11/4.8
art. 9(2)	11/4.9
art. 9(3)	11/4.11
art. 10(1)	11/4.13a
art. 13	11/4.13b
art. 14(1)	11/4.12
art. 15(1)	11/4.13e
art. 15(2)	11/4.13e
art. 16	11/4.13c
art. 17	11/4.13d
art. 19(1)	11/4.3a
art. 21	11/4.3a
art. 22	11/4.3a
Norway (1961)	11/4.1
Israel (1955)	11/4.1; 11/4.6
Romania (1939)	11/4.1
Spain (1927)	11/4.1
Sweden (1956)	11/4.1
art. 2(1)(a)	11/4.2
art. 3(1)	11/4.4c
art. 3(2)	11/4.4b
art. 3(5)	11/4.4d

Sweden (1956) (*continued*)	
art. 5(1)	11/4.5a
art. 5(2)	11/4.5c
art. 6(1)	11/4.9
art. 6(2)	11/4.9
art. 6(3)	11/4.11
art. 8	11/4.3b
art. 8(1)	11/4.7b
art. 8(2)	11/4.7b
art. 8(3)	11/4.7a
art. 8(4)	11/4.7a
art. 9	11/4.3b; 11/4.8
art. 10(2)	11/4.12
art. 11(1)	11/4.13a
art. 11(3)	11/4.13a
art. 11(4)	11/4.13b
art. 11(5)	11/4.13e
art. 12	11/4.13c
art. 13	11/4.13d
art. 14	11/4.14
art. 15	11/4.5a; 11/4.6; 11/4.11
art. 17	11/4.3a
art. 18(1)	11/4.3a
art. 18(2)	11/4.3a
art. 19	11/4.16
Switzerland (1958)	11/4.1; 11/4.6
Union of South Africa (1953)	11/4.1; 11/4.6
United Kingdom (1960)	11/4.1
art. 2	11/4.4b; 11/4.4c
art. 2(1)(k)	11/4.4d
art. 2(2)	11/4.3a
art. 3(4)	11/4.5b
art. 4	11/4.5b
art. 6	11/4.6
art. 7(1)	11/4.7a; 11/4.7b
art. 7(2)	11/4.7b
art. 8(1)	11/4.8
art. 8(3)	11/4.8
art. 8(4)	11/4.8
art. 9	11/4.9
art. 9(5)	11/4.11
art. 12(1)	11/4.13a; 11/4.13e
art. 12(2)	11/4.13a; 11/4.13e
art. 13(1)	11/4.14
art. 14	11/4.13c
art. 15	11/4.13d
art. 16	11/4.3a
art. 17	11/4.3b
art. 17(2)	11/4.7a
art. 17(3)	11/4.7b
art. 17(5)	11/4.13a; 11/4.13b
art. 19	11/4.3a
United States (1955)	11/4.1; 11/4.2
art. 2(1)(c)	11/4.4d
art. 2(1)(f)	11/4.4b

United States (1955) (*continued*)
art. 2(1)(g)	11/4.4b
art. 3(1)	11/4.5a
art. 3(2)	11/4.5a
art. 3(3)	11/4.5b
art. 3(4)	11/4.5b
art. 3(5)	11/4.5b
art. 4	11/4.5c
art. 5	11/4.6
art. 6	11/4.2; 11/4.5a
art. 7(1)	11/4.7a
art. 7(2)	11/4.7a
art. 9	11/4.10
art. 9(2)	11/4.10
art. 10(1)(a)	11/4.12
art. 10(2)	11/4.14
art. 11(2)	11/4.13a
art. 12	11/4.13d
art. 13	11/4.13c
art. 14(2)	11/4.7b; 11/4.8
art. 15	11/4.3b; 11/4.7a
art. 15(1)(a)	11/4.3b
art. 15(1)(b)	11/4.3b; 11/4.7b
art. 15(2)	11/4.3b
art. 16	11/4.15
art. 17	11/4.16
art. 18	11/4.16

Succession Tax Treaties

Sweden (1956)
art. 3	3/4.14d
art. 4	3/4.14d
art. 5	3/4.14d
art. 6	3/4.14d
art. 9	3/4.14d

United States (1955)
art. III(1)	3/4.14d
art. IV	3/4.14d
art. V	3/4.14d
art. VIII	3/4.14d

**Other International Agreements
(Chronological)**

Lateran Treaty, 11 February 1929	1/2.7
arts. 13-16	9/4.2b
art. 29	5/5.5
Treaty of Peace, 10 February 1947	
art. 44	11/4.1
General Agreement on Tariffs and Trade, 30 October 1947	4/8.2
Resolution of the United Nations General Assembly for the Unification of Privileges and Immunities, 21 November 1947	5/5.1
General Agreement on Privileges and Immunities, 2 September 1949	5/5.1
Protocol of Annecy, 10 October 1949	4/8.2
Treaty of Brussels, 11 January 1951	4/8.2
European Coal and Steel Community Treaty, 18 April 1951	4/8.2
Treaty of Rome (establishing the European Economic Community), 27 March 1957	1/2.7; 1/3.1e; 4/8.2
arts. 95-99	14/8.5

INDEX

The References—to legal provisions, decisions, and administrative instructions—which appear immediately in front of this Index, as well as the detailed table of contents at the beginning of each chapter, are also helpful as a means of finding material.

All references to Chapters 5/ through 13/ are to the income taxes

A

Abbonamento. See Annual fee *(abbonamento)*

Ability to pay, contribution in accordance with, 1/2.3

Accelerated depreciation, 7/3.5b

Accident insurance, 4/3.4; 9/3.3

Accounting, branches, 6/7

Accounting methods, 6/4
. cash and accrual, 6/4.1
. revaluations and devaluations, 6/5.6

Accounting periods, 6/3
. base year, 6/3.1
. calendar year, 6/3.2
. change, 6/3.3
. commencement of operations, 6/3.4
. fiscal year, 6/3.2
. mergers, 6/3.6
. reorganizations, 6/3.6
. tax year, 6/3.1
. termination of operations, 6/3.5

Additionals
. generally, 1/5.5d
. objective taxes, 2/2.9
. personal taxes, 2/3.4b
. rates, 12/1.4d; 12/1.5c. See also Tax rates

Administration of Allied War Cemeteries, exempt, 14/4.9

Administration of Cadaster and of Revenue Technical Services, 10/2.2g

Administration of tax, 1/4; 13/
. advertising tax, 4/5.3g
. appeals. See Taxpayers' remedies
. assessment. See Assessment of tax
. complementary tax, 2/3.8; 13/
. customs duties, 1/4.4; 4/8.4
. family tax, 2/3.8
. income from landowning, 10/2.2g
. international cooperation, 11/4.16

Administration of tax *(Continued)*
. local consumption taxes, 4/5.8f
. manufacturing taxes, 4/5.2c
. penalties. See Penalties
. public shows, 4/5.4
. returns. See Returns
. stock exchange contracts, 4/4.3c
. taxpayers' remedies, 1/4.10. See also Taxpayers' remedies

Administration of the Cadaster, 9/4.2d

Administrative commissions. See Tax commissions

Administrators. See Executors and administrators

Adopted children, 5/1.3

Advertising, general tax on receipts, 14/3.3g

Advertising tax, 4/5.3

Affiliated children, 3/4, *n.* 84; 5/1.3

Affinità, 2/3, *n.* 20

Agents, general tax on receipts, 4/2.2; 14/2.3

Agriculture, 10/2
. agrarian associations, 3/2.2
. agrarian income, 2/2.2a; 2/2.3; 6/1.1c; 10/2.3b
. . corporations, 12/2.1
. . individuals, 12/1.2
. . sale of produce of nonagricultural land, 10/2.3a
. . tax period, 6/3.4
. agricultural entrepreneur, 10/2, *n.* 75
. agricultural products
. . general tax on receipts, 14/4.10
. . registration tax, 15/6.3c
. buildings
. . exclusion from tax, 9/4.2a
. . presumed income, 9/4.1
. cadastral register and schedule of estimated values, 10/2.2c
. changes in production or costs, 10/2.2e

All references to Chapters 5/ through 13/ are to the income taxes

Agriculture *(Continued)*
. consumption, investment, and production of industry, agriculture, and the tertiary sector, 1/6.10e, Table 42
. expenditures, 1/5.4
. farm or agrarian credit, loans for, exemption of interest, 9/1.7
. generally, 10/2.1
. housing for farmers and agricultural workers, 9/4.2b
. landowning, income from, 10/2. *See also* Landowning, income from
. movable wealth, income from, 10/2.4
. presumed income, 6/1.1b; 9/4.1; 10/2
. subsidies and premiums paid to farmers, general tax on receipts, 14/4, *n.* 84
. termination and sale of property, 6/3.5
. value added and net product of the principal agricultural activities, 1951 and 1961, 1/6.10g, Table 47

Aircraft and air transportation
. general tax on receipts, 14/4.6d
. income tax treaties, 11/4.6
. insurance, tax on, 4/3.4
. personal services, income tax treaties, 11/4.13b
. stamp tax, 4/4.4

Alcoholic beverages
. general tax on receipts, 14/4.6e; 14/4.6f
. local consumption tax, 4/5.8b
. manufacturing tax, border surtax, and license fee, 4/5.2b

Aliens
. dividends payable to, 9/2.7c
. family tax, 2/3.5
. income taxes, 11/1.1; 11/3.1
. withholding of tax, 9/2.7c; 13/3.5

Allowances. *See* Expense allowances and reimbursements *and* Personal allowances

Amortization, 7/3
. assets reverting to grantor of concessions, 7/3.10
. good will, 7/2.13
. intangibles, 7/3.9
. leasehold improvements, 7/3.8
. mineral rights, 10/1.2
. obsolete machinery, 7/3.11
. royalties, 9/5
. study, research, and experimentation, expenses for, 7/3.9

Animal-drawn vehicles, local fee, 4/5.14

Annual fee *(abbonamento),* 4/5.8e; 14/6.3c; 14/7.3

Annuities, 9/3
. general tax on receipts, 14/4.3
. in kind, valuation for inheritance tax, 3/4.5d
. inheritance tax, 3/4.3e
. international aspects, inheritance tax, 3/4.14b
. Italian source, 11/1.6a
. life insurance annuity contract, 4/3.4
. payments by employer, 8/1.3b
. perpetual or life, good will, 9/9.2
. registration tax rates, 15/6.3e
. treaty effect, 11/4.14
. withholding of tax, 13/3.4

Appalto
. collection of taxes
. . income taxes, 13/3.7
. . local consumption taxes, 4/5.8f
. taxation of contracts of
. . general tax on receipts, 14/3.7
. . income taxes, 8/4
. . registration tax, 15/3.3i; 15/6.3f; 15/7.2a

Appeals. *See* Taxpayers' remedies

Apprentices, treaties, income tax, 11/4.13d

Approval, transfer on, general tax on receipts, 14/3.11

Archives, local expenditures, 1/5.4

Argentina, treaty, 11/4.1

Armed forces
. barracks, tax on income from buildings, 9/4.2b
. expenditures, 1/5.4
. pensions and allowances, 5/5.4; 8/1.3b

Art collections, inheritance tax, 3/4.4b

Artisans
. housing for, 9/4.2b
. income of, classification, 7/2.1b
. industrial activities of new enterprises, 10/6.5
. receipts from retail services performed by, 4/2.5; 14/4.8b

Arts and professions. *See* Professional services

Ascendants
. income tax, 5/1.4
. inheritance tax, 3/4.2

Asphalt, 10/6.6

All references to Chapters 5/ through 13/ are to the income taxes

Assessment of tax, 13/2
. agrarian income, 6/3.4; 10/2.3b
. agreement, 13/2.1; 13/2.4
. agriculture, 10/2.2g
. analytical, 13/2.2
. annual fee, 14/7.3c
. appeal. *See* Taxpayers' remedies
. burden of proof of incorrectness, 13/2.3
. change of period, 6/3.1
. dividends, 9/2.8
. estimated, 13/2.3
. finality, 13/2.1
. general tax on receipts, 14/7
. governmental concessions, fees for, 4/7.3
. income taxes, generally, 13/2.1
. increases in value of building lots, new local tax, 3/7.3d
. inductive or synthetic, 13/2.3
. inheritance tax, 3/4.9
. inspection of books and records, 6/2.3; 13/2.2
. landowning income, 6/3.4; 10/2.2
. local consumption taxes, 4/5.8e
. local entities, specific betterment contribution, 3/7.2e
. notice, 13/2.1
. receipt, appeal, 2/3.8
. review of return, 13/2.2
. supplementation or modification, 13/2.5
. time limits
. . income taxes, 13/6.1
. . inheritance tax, 3/4.12

Assets
. corporation tax, 3/2.3; 12/2.2a
. depreciation, 7/3
. purchase, 9/9.3
. sale, 9/8; 9/9.2
. valuation, 3/2.3; 6/5

Assistance entities, corporation tax, 3/2.2; 5/5.5

Associations, 5/3.8
. foreign, 11/3.4

Associations in participation, 5/3.5

Attribution rules, 6/8

Auctions, general tax on receipts, 14/3.10

Austria, treaty, 11/4.1

Authorizations, 4/7, *n.* 110

Authors, 5/5.3; 8/4; 9/5

Automobiles and trucks. *See* Motor vehicles

Awards and winnings, 10/7.1

B

Bad debts, 7/2.10

Balance sheet
. assessment on basis of, 5/2.1; 6/1.2b; 13/2
. example, 12/2.5
. national economic balance sheet, 1951 and 1961, 1/6.10e, Table 41

Bank of Italy, 1/3.4a

Bankruptcy
. general tax on receipts, distribution among creditors, 14/4.2
. inheritance tax, 3/4.6a
. registration on account, 15/7.2c

Banks and banking, 10/4. *See also* Credit institutions
. credit institutions, exemption of interest, 9/1.7
. deposit and loan banks, fees for governmental concessions, 4/7.1
. foreign banks, 11/3.5a
. general tax on receipts, 14/3.8
. risk allowances, 8/1.5
. Service of Credit Control, 13/2.2
. tax paid on behalf of depositor, 10/4, *n.* 106

Bare ownership. *See* Ownership of immovable property

Barters, general tax on receipts, 14/3.3b

Basis. *See* Tax base

Beach and seacoast, fees for governmental concessions, 4/7.1

Bearer shares, 9/2.7d; 9/2.8

Beer, manufacturing tax, 4/5.2b

Belgium, treaty, 11/4.1

Benefits in kind, 6/1.1e; 8/1.4; 14/5.1

Bequests
. income tax, 6/1.3
. inheritance tax. *See* Inheritance tax

Betterment contributions and increases in value of building lots, taxation, 1/5.5c; 3/7

Betting and games, general tax on receipts, 14/3.3d

Boardinghouses, general tax on receipts, 14/7.3b

Bonds
. amortization of amount owed and received, 7/3.9
. income from, 9/1
. tax on, 3/3
. . computation of tax, 12/2.3; 12/2.5
. . receipts of corporation tax and tax on bonds, 1/6.7d, Table 16

All references to Chapters 5/ through 13/ are to the income taxes

Bonuses
. deduction by employer, 7/2.3b
. income of employees, 8/1.7; 12/1.7
Books and records
. banks and banking, 10/4.4
. failure to keep, denial of deduction, 7/5.4
. general tax on receipts, 14/7.5
. income tax, 6/2
. manufacturing taxes, 4/5.2c
. stamping of, 4/4.2b
Branches
. accounting, 6/7
. foreign corporation, 11/3.5a
. loss carry-over, 7/4.3
. return, 5/2.2
Brazil, treaty, 11/4.1
Bread, general tax on receipts, 4/2.5; 14/4.6e
Brokers, general tax on receipts, 14/2.3e
Brothers and sisters, inheritance tax, 3/4.2
Budget policy, 1/3.4
Budget surplus or deficit, 1/6.1b, Table 4
Building Increment Fund, 1/3.4a
Building lots, tax on increases in value of, 3/7.3
Building materials
. general tax on receipts, 14/4.6
. local consumption tax, 4/5.8b
Buildings
. agricultural buildings, 10/2.2a
. business, buildings used in, 9/4.2a
. nonluxury dwellings, interest on loans for, 9/1.7
. profession, buildings used in, 8/1.1; 8/2.2
. subletting, income from, 9/4.3
. tax on income from, 2/2.2a; 9/4.2
. . corporations, 12/2.1
. . individuals, 12/1.3
. . "personalization" of tax, 2/2.7c
. . receipts of tax, 1/6.7c, Table 13
. urban cadaster, 9/4.2d
Business enterprise
. books and records, 6/2
. buildings used in, 9/4.2b
. capital gains, 7/1.3d; 9/8
. commencement of operations. *See* Commencement of business
. controlled enterprise, 11/4.5c
. defined, 4/2.1; 7/1.2
. enterprise, defined, 3/4.6a

Business enterprise *(Continued)*
. enterprise income, 2/2.2c
. entrepreneur *(imprenditore)*, 7/1.2a; 14/2.1
. good will, 9/9.2
. income, 7/. *See also* Business income
. integrated companies, 14/2.2
. internal transfers, 14/2.2c
. organization, reorganization, and dissolution
. . income taxes, 9/9
. . registration taxes, 15/6.3h
. owners, payments to, 7/2.3c; 7/5.2
. permanent establishment. *See* Permanent establishment
. receipts, 14/3.3
. separate businesses and activities, 5/3.7
. small businesses, 7/1.2b
. termination. *See* Termination of business
. transfer
. . general tax on receipts, 14/4.2
. . income taxes, 9/9
. . registration taxes, 15/3.3d

Business income, 7/
. buildings, presumed income, 9/4.1
. exchange of shares for shares, 9/9.5
. foreign enterprise, 11/3.5
. good will, 9/9.2
. gross income, 7/1
. "hidden reserves," 7/1.3f; 9/9.2
. interest, 7/1.3b
. Italian source, 11/1.3; 11/3.5
. mines, quarries, peat bogs, and salt deposits, 10/1.1
. participation in Italian enterprise, 11/3.6
. price paid for own share, 9/8.4
. productive activities, 7/1.2a
. rental
. . agricultural land, 10/2.1
. . movable property, 9/4.4
. . subleasing of immovables, 9/4.3
. royalties, 7/1.3c; 9/5; 11/1.6c
. sale of enterprise, 9/8.1
. separate businesses and activities, 5/3.7
. source in international transactions, 11/1.3
. speculative dealing in property used in exercise of a profession, 8/2.1
. speculative operations, 9/8; 10/7.2
. sublease, 9/4.1; 9/4.3
. treaties, 11/4.5

All references to Chapters 5/ through 13/ are to the income taxes

C

Cadaster and Revenue Technical Services, 1/4.6
. rural cadaster, 10/2.2c
. urban cadaster, 9/4.2d

Calabrian relief, additional for, 1/5.5d; 2/2.9; 3/5.5; 12/1.4d; 12/1.5c

Canada, treaty, 11/4.1

Candy, local consumption tax, 4/5.8b

Capital
. agricultural enterprise, 10/2.3b
. contribution, 9/9.3
. corporation tax. *See* Assets
. distributions in reduction of, 9/2.4
. foreign
. . participation in Italian enterprise, 11/3.6
. . registration tax, 15/11.1
. . restrictions on transfer abroad, 11/3.10
. increase, expense deductible, 7/2.13; 9/9.3
. movements of capital, local finance, 1/5.5g
. receipts of, general tax on receipts, 4/2.4; 14/4.2
. restrictions on transfer abroad, 11/3.10
. subscribed and paid-in, 3/2.3
. taxes on, 3/

Capital and capital transactions, income from, 2/2.2b; 9/
. annuities, 9/3
. capital gains and losses, 9/8. *See also* Capital gains and losses
. dividends and other distributions, 9/2. *See also* Dividends and other distributions
. insurance, 9/3
. interest, 9/1. *See also* Interest
. pensions, 9/3
. presumed income, 9/6
. rent, 9/4. *See also* Rent
. royalties, 9/5
. source of income from, 11/1.6

Capital gains and losses, 2/2.6; 6/1.1e; 9/8
. building lots, local tax on increases in value of, 3/7.3
. business income, 7/1.3d
. determination, 9/8.7
. patents and copyrights, sale of, 9/8.5
. production in Italy, 9/8.1; 11/1.6d

Capital gains and losses *(Continued)*
. reorganization of business, 9/9
. set-off of losses, 6/1.5b; 9/8.8
. source of income, 11/1.6b
. speculative operations, 8/2.1; 9/8.1; 9/8.2; 9/8.4; 10/7.2
. treaty effect, 11/4.11

Capital receipts, general tax on receipts, 14/4.2

Capitalization, contract of, 9/3.1

CARE, sales and services to, 14/4.9

Carry-back of losses, 7/4.4

Carry-over
. depreciation, 7/3.7
. losses, 7/4.2

Casualty insurance premiums, 6/1.3

Casualty losses, deductibility, 7/2.7; 10/3

Catholic Church
. clergy, remuneration by Holy See, 5/5.2
. constitutional provisions regarding, 1/2.7
. income of, 5/5.5
. receipts from sales to cardinals, 14/4.9

Cattle
. general tax on receipts, 14/8.4c
. income from breeding of, 10/2.3a
. insurance, tax on, 4/3.4
. train service, registration tax, 15/6.3c

Cemeteries
. exemption, 9/4.2a
. expenditures by local governments, 1/5.4

Central Census Commission, 1/4.10h; 9/4.2d; 10/2.2g

Central Commission for Direct Taxes, 1/4.10j; 2/3.8; 13/4.4

Central Commission for Local Finance, 1/5.3

Central Section of Tax Register, 9/2.8

Central Tax School, 1/4.1; 1/4.9

Cereals, general tax on receipts, 14/4.6g

Chamber of Commerce, Industry, and Agriculture, 1/5.7
. exemption, 3/2.2; 5/5.11
. voluntary contribution, general tax on receipts, 14/4, *n.* 84

Chancellery of the Tribunal, 13/1.1d

Charges. *See* Deductions

All references to Chapters 5/ through 13/ are to the income taxes

Charitable organizations
. contributions, deduction of, 6/1.5f; 7/2.11
. exemption of income, 5/5.5

Church. *See* Catholic Church

Cigarettes, fiscal monopoly
: lighters and flints, 4/6.6
. packages and papers, 4/6.4
. tobacco, 4/6.3

Cinema
. advertising, 4/5.3d
. governmental concessions, 4/7.2
. insurance, 4/3.4

Citizenship and civil status, fees for governmental concessions, 4/7.1

Classes of communes, 1/5.6, Table 1

Classes of taxpayers. *See* Taxpayers, classes of

Clergy, income of, 5/5.2

Clothing, furs, local consumption tax, 4/5.8b

Coffee
. *espresso* machines, local license tax, 4/5.10
. substitutes, manufacturing tax and license fee, 4/5.2b

Collection and payment of tax
. advertising tax, 4/5.3g
. appeal, effect of, 13/3.6b
. cigarette lighters and flints, state monopoly, 4/6.6
. complementary tax, 2/3.9
. computation, 12/1.4d
. executors and administrators, 5/3.9
. family tax, 2/3.9
. fees
. . complementary tax, 12/1.5c
. . inscribed in roll, 12/1.7
. . refund, 13/5
. . withholding at source, 12/1.6
. general tax on receipts, 14/7
. government payments, direct withholding from, 13/3.1; 13/3.3
. governmental concessions, fees for, 4/7.3
. heirs, 5/3.9
. income taxes, 13/3
. increases in value of building lots, local tax on, 3/7.3d
. inheritance tax, 3/4.10
. insurance tax, 4/3.4
. international administrative cooperation, 11/4.16

Collection and payment of tax *(Continued)*
. local consumption taxes, 4/5.8e; 4/5.8f
. local entities, specific betterment contribution, 3/7.2e
. local fee for the circulation of animal-drawn vehicles, 4/5.14
. motor vehicle fees, 4/5.5
. national betterment contributions, 3/7.4
. public shows, tax on, 4/5.4
. radio and television reception fees, 4/5.6
. registration tax, 15/7
. rolls, 13/3.7
. single payment of aggregate tax due, 14/7.3g
. stamp tax, 4/4.2f
. stock exchange contracts, 4/4.3c
. subscription contracts for, 14/7.4a
. time limits, 13/6.2; 14/10.1. *See also* Time limits

Commencement of business
. expenses deductible, 7/2.8; 7/2.13; 9/9.3
. registration tax, proportional rate, 15/6.3h

Common expenditures by general categories, 1951 and 1961, 1/6.10h, Table 48

Communal assistance entities, additional for, 1/5.5d; 2/2.9; 3/5.5; 12/1.4d; 12/1.5c

Communal Census Commission, 1/4.10h; 9/4.2d; 10/2.2g

Communal Commission for Local Taxes, 1/4.10j; 4/5.8e
. family tax, appeal, 2/3.8

Communal Council, 1/5.2

Communes, 1/5.1
. administration, 1/5.4
. building lots, power to purchase, 3/7.3d
. classes of, 1/5.6, Table 1
. Communal Council, 1/5.2
. "dormitory," defined, 2/3.6
. expenditures, 1/5.4. *See also* Expenditures
. "factory," defined, 2/3.6
. family tax, 5/1.2
. . aggregation of income of minor child, 5/1.3
. . jurisdiction to impose, 2/3.6
. local surtaxes on state taxes, 1/5.5d

All references to Chapters 5/ through 13/ are to the income taxes

Communes *(Continued)*
. Municipal Board, 1/5.2
. participation in yields of state taxes, 1/5.5e
. receipts, current, 1/6.9a, Table 28
. receipts of communal and provincial direct taxes, 1/6.9b, Table 32
. receipts of communal consumption taxes, 1/6.9c, Table 34
. receipts of communal consumption taxes by region, 1959, 1/6.9c, Table 35
. receipts of communal consumption taxes in provincial capitals, 1959, 1/6.9c, Table 36
. reforms in local finances, 1/5.6
. subsidies, 1/5.5f
. supercontributions, 1/5.6
. tax on leasehold values, 2/3.7
. "tertiary," defined, 2/3.6
. tourism, 1/5.4

Company *(società)*, 5/2.1. *See also* Corporations *and* Partnerships

Compartmental Inspectorates, 1/4.2; 1/4.3

Complementary progressive tax on income, 2/3; 5/1.1; 6/1.1f
. allowances, 12/1.5b
. computation of tax, 12/1.5
. historical background, 2/3.1
. rates and additionals, 2/3.4b; 12/1.5c
. rates of complementary tax for selected values of taxable income, 12/1.5c, Table 48

Computation of tax
. bonds, tax on, 3/3.3
. complementary tax, 2/3.4; 12/1.5
. estate tax, 3/5.5
. family tax, 2/3.3
. income taxes, 12/
. inheritance tax, 3/4.7
. movable wealth, income, 12/1.4

Computation table for the estate tax, 3/5.5, Table 57

Computation table for the inheritance tax, 3/4.7b, Table 55

Concessions. *See also* Governmental concessions, fees for
. amortization of rights to, 7/3.9

Conciliator, 1/4.10f
. registration tax on decisions of, 15/4.2

Consignment note, 4/5.2a; 4/5.8e

Constitution of the Italian Republic
. jurisdiction in tax matters, provisions regarding, 1/4.10
. principles affecting tax policy, 1/2

Constitutional Court, 1/2.8; 1/4.10g
. payment as condition of appeal, decisions concerning, 13/4.10
. principles affecting taxation decisions on, 1/2.8

Consulting College of Customs Experts, 4/8.4

Consumption, investment, and production of industry, agriculture, and the tertiary sector, 1/6.10e, Table 42

Consumption taxes, 4/5.2a; 4/5.8
. appeals, 1/4.10i. *See also* Taxpayers' remedies
. receipts, 1/6.8e, Table 23

Contracts
. *appalto*. *See Appalto*
. long-term, accounting method, 6/4.3
. registration tax
. . cancellation of contracts, 15/3.3k
. . proportional rates, 15/6.3g

Contraventions, 13/7.1; 14/10.1

Cooperative societies, 5/2.5
. accounting methods, 6/4.1
. agricultural products, 10/2.4
. books required, 6/2.2
. computation of tax, 12/3.2
. corporate assets, tax on, 3/2.2
. dividends and other distributions
. . complementary tax, 9/2.1b
. . coupon tax, 9/2.7a
. . deductibility, 7/2.14
. domicile or residence, 11/2.2
. exemption, 2/4.6; 5/5.10
. limited liability, 5/2.5
. sale of business enterprise, 9/8.1
. taxable assets, 3/2.3
. unlimited liability, 5/2.5

Corporate assets, tax on. *See* Corporation tax

Corporation tax
. asset component, 3/2
. computation, 3/2.4; 12/2.2
. deductions, 6/1.5e; 7/2.1. *See also* Deductions
. distributions
. . basis of tax, 9/2.1c
. . intercorporate, 2/4.5
. . exemptions, 3/2.2; 5/5. *See also* Exemptions

All references to Chapters 5/ through 13/ are to the income taxes

Corporation tax *(Continued)*
. foreign companies or associations, 3/2.2; 11/3
. historical background, 2/4.1
. income component, 2/4; 5/2.2; 6/1.1g; 12/2.2
. liquidation of business, 6/3.5; 9/9.9c
. public entities, 2/4.6; 3/2.2; 5/2.7; 5/5.11
. rates and additionals, 3/2.4; 12/2.2c. *See also* Tax rates
. receipts of corporation tax and tax on bonds, 1/6.7d, Table 16
. taxable assets, 2/4.1; 3/2.3
. . defined, 2/4.3; 12/2.2a
. . determination, 12/2.2a

Corporations, 5/2.2
. assessment on balance sheet basis, 6/1.2b; 13/2.2
. auditors or overseers, withholding at source, 12/1.6
. bonds. *See* Bonds
. bonus securities, 9/2.3
. books required, 6/2.2
. computation of income taxes, 12/2
. contributions to capital, deductibility, 7/2.8
. corporation tax. *See* Corporation tax
. coupon tax, 9/2.7a
. directors, auditors, and overseers
. . payments to, 7/2.3c; 7/5.2; 8/1.2; 8/3.1; 9/2.5
. . profit sharing, 8/1.6
. . withholding at source, 8/1.10; 12/1.6; 13/3.5
. dividends, 9/2. *See also* Dividends and other distributions
. fiscal domicile, 13/1.1d
. foreign, income of, 11/3.3
. formation
. . income taxation, 9/9
. . registration tax, 15/3.3f
. integrated companies, general tax on receipts, 14/2.2
. Liechtenstein, 2/4.4
. merger. *See* Merger of business *and* Reorganization of business
. negotiation tax, 2/4.1; 3/1
. public enterprises, 2/4.6; 5/2.7; 5/5.11
. residence or domicile, 11/2.2
. returns
. . forms, 12/5.4
. . signing of, 13/1.1b
. shareholders, payments to. *See* Dividends and other distributions

Corporations *(Continued)*
. surcharge and adjustment paid for shares, 9/9.3
. surtaxes and additionals, 12/2.1
. Swiss, 2/4.4
. treaty effect, 11/4.13e
. withholding at source, 9/2.7; 12/2.4

Council of Europe, 5/5.1
Council of Ministers, 1/3.2b
Council of State, 1/4.10a; 1/4.10g
. decisions, registration tax on, 15/4.2
. Head of State, appeal to, 13/4.11

Coupon tax, 9/2.1; 9/2.7
Court of Accounts, 1/3.4a
. decisions, registration tax on, 15/4.2
. public expenditures and accounts, 1/4.10a

Court of Appeal, 1/4.10f; 13/4.9
Court of Cassation, 1/2.8; 1/4.10f; 13/4.10
Courts, 1/2.8; 1/4.10; 13/4.9; 13/4.10
Credit institutions
. corporation tax, 3/2.2; 10/4
. general tax on receipts, 14/3.8; 14/4.2
. income taxation, 10/4
. interest. *See* Interest
. Italian branch of foreign bank, 11/3.5a

Cultural institutions, 3/2.2
Curators, 3/4.10b; 5/1.3
Current expenditures of the state, 1/6.10e, Table 45
Current receipts of the communes, 1/6.9a, Table 28
Current receipts of the provinces, 1/6.9a, Table 29
Current receipts of the regions, 1/6.9a, Table 30
Customs duties, 1/4.4; 4/8
. deductibility, 7/2.8
. merchandise admitted free of, 14/8.4c
. receipts, 1/6.8g, Table 25
. tobacco, 4/6.3

D

Dairy products
. general tax on receipts, 4/2.5; 14/4.6e
. local consumption tax, 4/5.8b
. processing, income from, 10/2.3a
De facto **companies,** 5/3.6

All references to Chapters 5/ through 13/ are to the income taxes

De Viti De Marco, 2/2.1

Death, time limits on assessment and collection, 13/6.1

Debts
. bad, deductible, 7/2.10
. cancellation, 6/1.1e; 7/1.3e
. cessation of business, 9/9.9b
. foreign
. . income of foreign enterprise, 11/3.5b
. . income of Italian enterprise, 11/2.3c; 11/2.4
. . inheritance tax, 3/4.14c
. inheritance tax, deduction, 3/4.6a

Decedents' estates, 3/4; 3/5; 5/3.9. *See also* Heirs

Decree-laws, 1/3.1c

Deductions
. agrarian income, 10/2.3b
. banking and credit, 10/4.3
. bonuses, 7/2.3b
. buildings, income from, 9/4.2c
. business income, 7/2
. business losses, 7/4
. capital losses, 9/8.8
. corporations, 12/2.2b
. depreciation 7/3. *See also* Depreciation
. employee, income from services as, 8/1.9
. foreign enterprise, 11/3.5b
. foreign income, 11/2.3c; 11/2.4
. health insurance, amount withheld or paid for, 9/3.3
. income taxes, 6/1.5
. inheritance tax, 3/4.6
. landowning, income from, 10/2.2d
. merger of corporations, 9/9.7
. mining expenses, 10/1.3
. miscellaneous services, 8/3.2
. professional services, income from, 8/2.2
. standard allowance, 6/1.5b
. support payments, 9/3.1

Deficit of the budget of the state, 1/6.1b, Table 4

Delegated regulations, 1/3.2c

Delict (*delitto*), 13/7.1

Dependents, 5/1.4. *See also* Incompetent persons *and* Minors

Depletion, natural resources, 10/1.4

Deposit and Loan Fund, 1/3.4a

Deposits of merchandise and securities, 15/4.2

Depreciation, 6/1.5c
. business assets, 7/3
. loans, 9/1.3
. natural resource extraction, 10/1.5
. professional assets, 8/2.2

Descendants
. income tax, 5/1.4
. inheritance tax, 3/4.2

Detention (*arresto*), defined, 13/7.1

Diplomatic officers and employees
. buildings, tax on income from, 9/4.2b
. general tax on receipts, 14/4.9; 14/8.1
. income taxation, 5/5.1; 11/3.2a
. inheritance tax, 3/4.14a

Direct taxes. *See also* Income taxes
. administration, 1/4.2
. receipts, 1/6.7
. receipts of national direct taxes, 1/6.7a, Table 11

Director General, 1/4.1

Directors of companies
. accounting methods, 6/4.1
. deduction of payments to, 7/2.3c; 7/5.2
. income from serving as, 8/1.2
. services outside scope of duties, 8/1.2
. withholding, 8/1.2; 13/3.5

Dissolution of business, 9/9.9. *See also* Termination of business

District Offices of Direct Taxes, 1/4.2; 13/2

District Procurator, 1/4.2

Dividends and other distributions
. accounting methods, 6/4.1
. cooperative societies, deduction, 7/2.14
. coupon tax (*imposta cedolare*), 9/2.1a; 9/2.1b; 9/2.7
. foreign enterprise, Italian participation in, 11/4.7b
. foreign participation in Italian enterprise, 11/3.6b; 11/4.7a
. general tax on receipts, 14/4.2
. intercorporate, 2/4.5; 9/2.1c; 10/5
. . in kind, 9/2.2
. Italian source, 11/1.6b; 11/3.6b
. liquidation, 9/2.4; 9/9.9c
. reduction of capital, 9/2.4
. stock dividends, 9/2.3
. transfers of, 9/2.6
. treaty effect, 11/4.7
. withholding, 9/2.7; 13/3.5

All references to Chapters 5/ through 13/ are to the income taxes

Domicile
. defined, 11/2.2
. enterprise, 11/3.4b
. fiscal, 13/1.1d
. treaty provisions, 11/4.4c

Double taxation of income, 2/2.5;
11/2.6; 11/4

Draw-back, 4/5.2d

E

Earthquake damage
. additional for relief of, 1/5.5d
. buildings, repair of, 9/4.2b

Economy
. government intervention in, 1/2.6
. tax policy as related to, 1/6.10

Education
. bequests for, 3/4.2
. deduction of contributions for, 6/1.5f
. expenditures by local governments,
  1/5.4

Educational institutions, exemption,
3/2.2; 5/5.7

Electricity and electrical equipment
. local consumption tax, 4/5.8b
. manufacturing tax, border surtax,
  and license fee, 4/5.2b
. stamp tax, 4/4.2b

Emphyteusis *(enfiteusi),* 3/4.3f; 9/4.1;
10/2.2b

Employment accident insurance
. benefits, 8/1.3b
. contributions, 7/2.4; 8/1.3a; 8/1.9
. insurance tax, 4/3.4

Employment, income from
. accounting methods, 6/4.1
. bonuses, 8/1.7
. deductions, 7/2.3; 8/1.9; 8/2.2; 8/3.2
. expense allowances and reimbursements, 7/2.3f; 8/1.5
. general tax on receipts, 14/5.1
. gifts of property, 6/1, *n.* 9
. gratuities, 7/2.4; 7/2.11; 8/1.7
. housing, 7/2.4; 9/4.2b
. income from employment and its
  relation to national income, 1954
  and 1961, 1/6.10d, Table 39
. independent work distinguished, 8/1.2;
  8/2
. irregular or seasonal employment,
  8/1.2

Employment, income from *(Continued)*
. labor force and value added per employee in the major sectors, 1951
  and 1961, 1/6.10d, Table 40
. length-of-service payments, 8/1.3b
. pensions, 8/1.3b
. profit sharing, 7/2.3d; 8/1.6
. social security and welfare benefits,
  8/1.3
. source, 11/1.5
. termination of employment, 7/2.3e;
  8/1.3b; 8/1.8
. treaties, effect of, 11/4.12; 11/4.13
. withholding at source, 8/1.10; 12/1.6;
  13/3.4; 13/3.5

Entertainment
. general tax on receipts, 14/3.3d
. governmental concessions, 4/7.2
. tax on public shows, 4/5.4

Entities taxed as corporations, 5/2. *See
also* Corporations

Entrepreneur, defined, 7/1.2a; 14/2.1.
See also Business enterprise

Equality of taxation, 1/2.5

Equalization tax on imported products,
14/8.5

Espresso **coffee machines, local license
tax,** 4/5.10

Estate tax, 3/5
. computation table, 3/5.5, Table 57
. gift tax, credit for, 3/5.5
. gifts before death, 3/5.3
. inheritance tax, relation to, 3/4.7a;
  3/5.2
. net value of entire estate, 3/5.1
. persons subject, 3/5.4
. rates, 3/5.5, Table 56
. receipts of taxes on gratuitous transfers, 1/6.7e, Table 17
. returns, 3/5.6
. second succession within two years,
  3/5.5

Estimated income, 6/9.1; 13/2.3

**European Coal and Steel Community
(CECA),** 5/5.1

**European Economic Community (Com-
mon Market),** 1/2.7; 4/8.2

Evidence
. books and records, weight given,
  6/2.5
. burden of proof
. . assessment, 7/2.1; 13/2.3
. . correctness of account, 13/2.3
. . deductions, 7/5.4

All references to Chapters 5/ through 13/ are to the income taxes

Evidence, burden of proof *(Continued)*
. . distribution of corporate profits,
    9/2.1b
. . termination of income from mov-
    able wealth of category A, 9/1.1
. . worthlessness of debt, 7/2.10
. presumptions under inheritance tax,
    3/4.3a
. presumptions under registration tax,
    15/3.3; 15/3.4

Exchange
. foreign exchange, losses on, 7/4.5
. securities, gains or losses on, 9/8.6

Exchanges
. movables, 14/5.1
. receipts of taxes on, 1/6.8b, Table 20
. taxes on, 1/6.8b. *See also* General
    tax on receipts

Exclusions
. buildings, 9/4.2a
. general tax on receipts, 4/2.4; 14/4
. . agents, 14/2.3b
. . brokers, 14/2.3e
. . integrated companies, 14/2.2
. . international services, 4/2.4; 14/8.3
. . leasing of urban immovable prop-
    erty, 4/2.4; 14/3.6
. . processing in Italy, 4/2.4; 14/8.4b
. income taxes, 6/1.3
. local consumption taxes, 4/5.8c
. social security and welfare, 9/3.1

Executive branch, 1/3.2

Executors and administrators
. bequests to, 8/3.1
. *curatore,* 5/3.9
. income tax return, 5/3.9
. inheritance tax
. . payment, 3/4.10b
. . return, 3/4.8b

Executory regulations, 1/3.2c

Exemptions
. advertising tax, 4/5.3e
. agrarian income, 10/2.3c
. agricultural products, income de-
    rived from utilization of, 10/6.2d
. agriculture, 10/2.2f
. banking and credit, 10/4.2
. buildings, 9/4.2b
. coupon tax, 9/2.7b
. double taxation, avoidance, 11/4.3a
. equalization tax, 14/8.5
. factories which are expanded, con-
    verted, reactivated, or transferred,
    10/6.2c

Exemptions *(Continued)*
. gas and electrical energy, 4/5.2b
. general tax on receipts, 4/2.5; 14/4
. . exported goods, 14/8.2
. . imported goods, 14/8.4c
. government interest, 9/1.2; 9/1.7
. gratuitous registration, 15/4.3
. income taxes, 5/5; 6/1.4
. increases in value of building lots,
    new local tax, 3/7.3a
. industrial factories built in the south,
    10/6.2
. industrial zones, 10/6.4
. inheritance tax, 3/4.4
. insurance tax, 4/3.4
. interest, 9/1.1; 9/1.7
. length of service, remuneration,
    12/1.4a
. local consumption taxes, 4/5.8c
. local fee for occupation of public
    spaces and areas, 4/5.11
. local fee for the circulation of ani-
    mal-drawn vehicles, 4/5.14
. local visitors tax, 4/5.9
. lotto and lotteries, 4/6.7
. movable wealth, remuneration for
    services, 12/1.4a
. national betterment contributions,
    3/7.4
. new artisan enterprises and small
    industries, 10/6.5
. pensions, income, 12/1.4a
. radio and television reception fees,
    4/5.6
. reforestation, 10/2.2f
. registration tax, 15/4
. stamp tax, 4/4.2b; 4/4.2d
. technically organized industrial fac-
    tories, 10/6.2b
. transfers, intermediate stages, 4/2.5;
    14/2.2; 14/2.3; 14/2.4
. welfare payments, 12/1.4b

Expenditures
. common expenditures by general
    categories, 1951 and 1961, 1/6.10h,
    Table 48
. local governments, 1/5.4
. state, current, 1/6.10e, Table 45

**Expense allowances and reimburse-
ments**
. deduction by employer, 7/2.3f
. income of employee, 8/1.5

Expenses, deduction of
. agrarian income, 10/2.3b
. banking and credit, 10/4.3

All references to Chapters 5/ through 13/ are to the income taxes

Expenses, deduction of *(Continued)*
. business income, 7/2; 7/5
. foreign enterprise, 11/3.5b
. foreign source income, 11/2.3c; 11/2.4
. formation of company, 9/9.3
. immovable property, 9/4.1; 9/4.2c
. income taxes, 6/1.5b
. increase in capital, 7/2.13; 9/9.3
. landowning, income from, 10/2.2d
. mineral extraction, 10/1.3
. miscellaneous sources, income from, 8/3.2
. professional income, 8/2.2
. recovery of expenses previously deducted, 6/1.1e

Exports
. customs duties, 4/8.1
. general tax on receipts, 4/2.4; 14/8.2; 14/8.3

F

Fairs, local expenditures, 1/5.4

Family, attribution of income, 2/3.2; 6/8.1

Family tax, 1/5.5c; 2/3
. deduction of, 6/1.5e

Fascist period, 1/1.3

Fees
. circulation of animal-drawn vehicles, 4/5.14
. fixed, proportional tax rate, 15/6.5
. governmental concessions, 4/7
. "objective" taxes, 2/2.9
. occupation of public spaces and areas, 4/5.11
. public weights and measures and the renting of public counters, 4/5.13

Fees and indirect taxes on transactions, administration of, 1/4.3; 14/7.1

Fideicommissary (trust) substitution, 3/5.4

Fiduciary warehouses, 4/5.2a

Filiale, 5/2, *n. 7*

Finance Guard, 1/4.8

Fines. *See also* Penalties
. defined, 13/7.1
. registration tax, 15/8.4

Firearms, fees for governmental concessions, 4/7.1

First Offices of General Tax on Receipts, 1/4.3

Fiscal burden, 1/6.1

Fiscal consultant, 1/4.11

Fiscal monopolies of the state, 1/4.5; 4/6
. general tax on receipts on sales of monopoly goods, 14/4.10

Fish and fishing
. canning, general tax on receipts, 14/4, *n.* 99
. expenditures by local governments, 1/5.4
. fees for governmental concessions, 4/7.1
. imports, general tax on receipts, 14/4.6h
. local consumption taxes, 4/5.8b

Fixed assets
. depreciation, 7/3; 10/1.3
. valuation, 3/2.3; 6/5.4

Flowers, local consumption tax, 4/5.8b

Food
. agricultural products, processing of, 10/2.3a
. bread, general tax on receipts, 14/4.6e
. butter and substitutes, local consumption tax, 4/5.8b
. candy, local consumption tax, 4/5.8b
. cereals, general tax on receipts, 14/4.6g
. cheese and dairy products, local consumption tax, 4/5.8b
. meats, local consumption tax, 4/5.8b
. milk, exempt from general tax on receipts, 14/4.6e
. poultry, rabbits, game, and fish, local consumption tax, 4/5.8b
. sugar, glucose, maltose, and sugar products, manufacturing tax, border surtax, and license fee, 4/5.2b
. various, local consumption tax, 4/5.8b
. wheat, flour, and spaghetti, general tax on receipts, 4/2.5; 14/4.6g

Food and Agriculture Organization of the United Nations (FAO), 5/5.1; 14/4.9

Foreign companies and entities
. apportionment of income from international transactions, 11/3.5b; 11/4.5a
. attribution of payments made to, 6/8.2; 11/2.4
. bonds, tax on, 3/3.1
. corporation tax, 3/2.2; 11/3.3
. dividends
. . source of income, 11/1.6b
. . treaty provisions, 11/4.7b
. . withholding, 9/2.7e

All references to Chapters 5/ through 13/ are to the income taxes

Foreign companies and entities *(Continued)*
. inheritance tax, 3/4.2
. partnerships, 5/3.2; 11/3.4
. registration tax, 15/5.3
. secondary office in Italy, 11/3.3
. taxable assets, 3/2.3
. taxation of income, 11/3
. taxes, deductible, 7/2.8

Foreign debts
. income tax. *See* International transactions
. inheritance tax, 3/4.14c

Foreign diplomats. *See* Diplomatic officers and employees

Foreign exchange, losses, 7/4.5

Foreign income, 11/2

Foreign securities
. registration tax, 15/4.2
. source of income from, 11/1.6b
. stamp taxes, 4/4.2c; 4/4.3
. withholding of income taxes, 9/2.7c; 11/4.7b

Foreign taxes
. credit, 11/4.3b
. deduction, 6/1.5e; 7/2.8

Forestry, 10/2
. exemptions, reforestation, 10/2.2f

Foundations, 5/3.8

France, treaty, 11/4.1

Freight charges, 4/2.4; 14/5.2

Fund for Small Farming Property, 1/3.4a

Fund for Solidarity, 1/5.5f

Fund for the South, 1/3.4a; 10/4.2

Fund for Training of Workers, 1/3.4a

Fund for Winter Relief, 1/3.4a

Funeral expenses, 3/4.6b

Furniture, household
. defined, 3/4.3a
. local consumption tax, 4/5.8b

G

Gambling
. fiscal monopoly, 4/6.7
. general tax on receipts, 14/3.3d; 14/4.4; 14/4.10
. income from, 10/7.1; 13/3.4
. prize operations, 4/6.7

Games of skill and football pools, tax on, 4/5.7

Gas
. local consumption tax, 4/5.8d
. manufacturing tax and license fee, 4/5.2b
. stamp tax, 4/4.2b

General Agreement on Tariffs and Trade, 4/8.2

General balance of current payments, 1/6.10a, Table 37

General Directorate of Cadaster and Revenue Technical Services, 1/4.1

General Directorate of Customs Duties and Indirect Taxes, 1/4.4

General Directorate of General Matters and Personnel, 1/4.1; 1/4.7

General Directorate of the Fees and Indirect Taxes on Transactions, 1/4.3; 3/4.8a; 4/4.2h; 4/5.4

General Directorate of the Public Domain, 1/4.1

General Inspectorate for Lotto and Lotteries, 1/4.1

General partnerships, 5/3.2. *See also* Partnerships

General tax on receipts (IGE), 4/2; 14/
. *appalto,* contracts of, 14/3.7
. approval, transfer on, 14/3.11
. assessment and collection, 14/7
. auctions, 14/3.10
. books and records, rules regarding, 14/7.5
. business receipts, 14/3.3
. capital, 14/4.2
. collection for each transaction, 14/7.2
. commercial intermediaries, 14/3.5
. commercial travelers, 14/2.3c
. compensation for damages, 14/4.2
. consignment, transfers on, 14/3.12
. consumption loan, 14/4.2
. contributions and membership fees, 14/4.5
. credit institutions, 14/3.8
. equalization, 4/2.2; 14/2.2
. equalization tax on imported products, 14/8.5
. exclusions, 4/2.4; 14/4
. exemptions, 4/2.5; 14/4; 14/8.4c
. exports
. . refund on products, 14/8.3
. . sales, exempt, 14/8.2
. fees of nontax character, 14/3.10
. foreign diplomatic and consular offices, 14/4.9; 14/8.1
. government stockpiling agencies, 14/2.4

All references to Chapters 5/ through 13/ are to the income taxes

General tax on receipts (IGE) *(Continued)*
. historical background, 4/2.1; 14/1
. imports, 14/8.4
. . collection on merchandise, 14/8.4a
. . equalization tax, 14/8.5
. . shipbuilding materials, sale, 14/4.6b; 14/4.8c
. . silver coins, exempt, 14/4.6c
. . temporary, 14/8.4b
. in kind for services, 14/5.1
. independent public services, 4/2.4
. insurance companies, 14/3.9; 14/5.1
. integrated companies, 14/2.2
. interest on capital, 14/4.2
. international aspects, 14/8
. leases, 14/3.6
. payment, annual fee *(abbonamento)*, 14/7.3
. penalties, 14/9. *See also* Penalties
. persons other than industrialists or merchants, 14/3.2
. persons subject, 4/2.2; 14/2
. postal current account, 14/7.2c
. printing, 14/4.6j
. processing, transfer for purposes of, 4/3.13
. professions and arts, exercise of, 14/3.4
. radio and television broadcast subscription, 14/3.10
. refunds, 14/10.2
. retail outlet, transfer by parent to, 4/2.5; 14/2.2b
. retail sales, 14/4.8
. retail services
. . defined, 14/3.4
. . performed by artisans, 4/2.5; 14/4.8b
. salaries, wages, and other remuneration, 14/4.3
. sale between private individuals, 14/4.7
. sale of monopoly goods, 14/4.4
. shifting of tax burden, 14/2.7
. stamp tax as included, 4/4.2b
. subsidies for land improvements, 14/4, *n.* 84
. tax base, 4/2.3; 14/5
. tax rates, 4/2.1; 14/6
. tax substitutes, 14/2.5
. taxes and similar receipts, 14/4.4
. time installment contracts, 14/4.2
. time limits, 14/10

Germany, treaty, 11/4.1

Gift tax, 3/6
. estate tax, credit, 3/5.5
. receipts of taxes on gratuitous transfers, 1/6.7e, Table 17

Gifts. *See also* Estate tax *and* Gift tax
. excluded from income, 6/1.3

Giolitti, 1/5.1

Glass and crystal products, local consumption tax, 4/5.8b

Gold, general tax on receipts, 14/4.6c

Good will
. agreement not to compete, 9/9.2
. amortization, 7/2.13
. merger of corporation, 9/9.7
. sale of business, 9/9.2
. transfer of corporation, 9/9.4
. valuation, 9/9.2
. withdrawing partner, 9/9.9b

Government officials and employees
. exemptions, 5/5.4
. treaties, 11/4.12
. withholding, 13/3.3

Government participations
. corporation tax, 3/2.2; 10/5
. Ministry of State Participations, 1/3.4a

Governmental bodies, 5/2.7; 5/5.11. *See also* Public enterprises and entities
. amounts received by state from management of public services, 4/2.4; 14/4.4
. receipts of public services, 14/3.3e

Governmental concessions, fees for, 4/7
. deduction from business income, 7/2.8

Grain and grain products, general tax on receipts, 14/8.4c

Gratuities paid to employees
. deduction, 7/2.4; 7/2.11; 8/1.7
. income, 8/1.3b

Great Britain, treaty, 11/4.1

Greece, treaty, 11/4.1

Gross income, 6/1.1; 7/1; 8/2.1. *See also* Income

Gross investments by major categories, 1951 and 1961, 1/6.10e, Table 44

Guardians and curators
. income taxes, 5/1.3
. inheritance tax, 3/4.8c; 3/4.10b

All references to Chapters 5/ through 13/ are to the income taxes

H

Habitation *(abitazione)*, 3/4.3c; 9/4.1

Health
. contributions, local visitors tax, 4/5.9
. expenditures by local governments, 1/5.4
. fees for governmental concessions, 4/7.1
. insurance, 4/3.4; 9/3.3

Heirs. *See also* Decedents' estates
. acceptance of succession with benefit of inventory, 3/4, *n.* 91; 5/3.9
. joint and several liability
. . estate tax, 3/5.4
. . income taxes, 5/3.9; 13/3.1
. . inheritance tax, 3/4.8b; 3/4.10b

"Hidden reserves," 6/6.3; 7/1.3f; 9/9

High Council of the Magistracy, 1/3.2a; 1/4.10a

Historical background of the fiscal system, 1/1

Holding companies, 3/2.2; 10/5

Hospitals, exemptions, housing built by entity, 9/4.2b

Hotels
. buildings, tax on income from, 9/4.2b
. general tax on receipts, 14/3.3f; 14/4, *n.* 114; 14/7.3b

Household furniture *(mobilia)*, 3/4.3a

Housing
. employees', deduction of contributions from business income, 7/2.4
. exemptions from tax on income from buildings, 9/4.2b
. incentives, 10/6.6. *See also* Building materials *and* Buildings

Hunting
. expenditures by local governments, 1/5.4
. fees for governmental concessions, 4/7.1

I

IGE. *See* General tax on receipts

Immovable property
. defined, 15/6, *n.* 92
. general tax on receipts, 14/4.2
. income
. . imputed, 2/2.4b; 9/4.1; 10/2.2
. . treaty effect, 11/4.10
. inheritance tax, 3/4.8a
. ownership, 9/4.1
. registration, 3/4.8a; 15/6.3b

Immovable property *(Continued)*
. rights in, 9/4.1
. sublease, 9/4.1
. treaty effect, 11/4.10
. valuation, 3/4.5c; 15/5.2

Imports
. customs duties, 4/8
. equalization tax, 14/8.5
. fish, 14/4, *n.* 99
. general tax on receipts, 14/8.4
. gold, exempt, 14/4.6c
. lighters and flints, 4/6.6
. manufacturing tax, border surtax corresponding to, 4/5.2
. salt, 4/6.2
. temporary
. . customs duties, 4/8.3
. . manufacturing taxes, 4/5.2d

Improvement associations, 3/2.2

Improvements. *See* Betterment contributions and increases in value of building lots, taxation

"Imputed" income, 2/2.4. *See also* Presumed income

Incentives. *See* Industrial incentives

Income
. agricultural activities, 10/2.3
. agricultural land, 10/2.2
. allowance received by taxpayer from family, 9/3.1
. annuities, 6/1.1e; 9/3.1
. buildings, 6/1.1d; 9/4.2a. *See also* Buildings
. business activities exercised abroad, 11/2.3
. business activities exercised in Italy, 11/3.5
. business income, 7/1
. cancellation of indebtedness, 6/1.1e
. capital employed so as to derive, 9/3.1
. capital gains, 6/1.1e; 9/8
. commissions, 7/2.3b
. complementary progressive tax, 6/1.1f
. corporation tax, 6/1.1g
. determination, 6/; 12/
. determination of gain, 9/8.7
. determined by agreement, tax base, 6/9.3
. dissolution of business, 9/9.9
. "enjoyed" in Italy, 11/2.2
. estimated, 6/9.1
. exemptions. *See* Exemptions
. fixed, category A and category C/2, 2/2.2d

All references to Chapters 5/ through 13/ are to the income taxes

Income *(Continued)*
. foreign enterprises, 11/3
. gift of property as income, 6/1, *n.* 9
. gross. *See* Gross income
. health insurance proceeds, 9/3.3
. heirs, 9/9.9a
. imputed income, 2/2.4; 9/4.1
. . movable property, 2/2.4d
. . pure work, 2/2.4c
. in kind, 6/1.1e
. methods of determining, 6/1.2
. movable wealth, 6/1.1e
. movables, subject to rent, 9/4.4
. net aggregate income, 6/1.1f
. net income method, 6/1.2a
. net national income, 1/6.1a, Table 2
. net worth comparison method, 6/1.2b
. nonresidents, 11/3
. occasional, 6/1.1e
. perpetual annuities, 9/3.1
. presumed, 6/9.2
. prizes in lotteries, 4/6.7
. produced abroad, 11/2
. production of, 2/2.2; 6/1.1a
. recovery of previously deducted expenses, 6/1.1e
. rent, 9/4.3
. rights, proportional tax rates, 15/6.3e
. shipping, 11/3.7
. spreading, 8/2.1; 8/4
. support allowance received by wife, 9/3.1
. taxable, 6/1.1

Income determination, principles of, 6/. *See also* Computation of tax *and* Income

Income from business. *See* Business income

Income from capital and capital transactions. *See* Capital and capital transactions, income from

Income from employment and its relation to national income, 1954 and 1961, 1/6.10b, Table 39

Income from personal services. *See* Employment, income from, *and* Professional services, income from

Income from special activities and miscellaneous sources. *See* Special activities and miscellaneous sources, income from

Income taxes, 2/; 5/-13/
. administration, 1/4.2; 13/
. local and surtaxes, additionals and fees, 2/2.9

Income taxes *(Continued)*
. receipts, 1/6.7
. structure, 6/1.1
. summary, 2/

Incompetent persons, 5/1.3

Increases in value of building lots, local tax on, 3/7.3

Independent regulations, 1/3.2c

Independent work, income from. *See* Miscellaneous services, income from, *and* Professional services, income from

Indirect taxes
. administration, 1/4.1; 1/4.3; 1/4.4
. defined, 1/6.6
. receipts of, 1/6.8

Individuals
. computation of tax, 12/1
. example of tax computation, 12/1.7
. fiscal domicile, 13/1.1d
. general tax on receipts, 4/2.2
. income taxation, 5/1
. nonresidents, 11/3.2
. receipts of national personal taxes, 1/6.7d, Table 15
. residence and domicile, 11/2.2
. return form, 12/5.2
. signing of return, 13/1.1b
. withholding at source, 12/1.6

Industrial incentives, 10/6
. allowance for agricultural or industrial investment in the south, 10/6.3
. general tax on receipts, 14/4.6k

Industry
. consumption, investment, and production of industry, agriculture, and the tertiary sector, 1/6.10e, Table 42
. value added and net product of industrial activities, 1951 and 1961, 1/6.10g, Table 46

Inheritance tax, 3/4
. assessment, 3/4.9
. compulsory collection, 3/4.10h
. computation, 3/4.7
. computation table, 3/4.7b, Table 55
. credit, 3/4.3h
. deductions, 3/4.6
. estate tax
. . distinguished, 3/4.7a
. . relation, 3/5.2
. exemptions, 3/4.4
. history, 3/4.1b
. international aspects, 3/4.14
. payment, 3/4.10

All references to Chapters 5/ through 13/ are to the income taxes

Inheritance tax *(Continued)*
. penalties, 3/4.13
. protests and appeals, 3/4.11
. rates, 3/4.7; 3/4.7b, Table 54
. receipts of taxes on gratuitous transfers, 1/6.7e, Table 17
. returns, 3/4.8
. tax base, 3/4.3
. taxes on previous gifts, credit for, 3/4.7e
. territorial compensation, 3/4.1a
. time limits, 3/4.10c; 3/4.12
. transfers to surviving spouses, 3/4.2
. trusts, 3/4.3d
. universal and particular dispositions defined, 3/4.1a
. valuation, 3/4.5

Initiative petition, 1/3, *n.* 16

Insolvency, insurance against, 7/2.10

Inspection, 1/4.12; 13/2.2

Installment sales, 6/4.2

Insurance companies
. corporation tax, 10/3
. general tax on receipts, 14/3.9; 14/5.1
. movable wealth, tax on income, 10/3
. mutual
. . books required, 6/2.2
. . profits of, 6/1.1e

Insurance policies
. registration tax, 15/4.2
. tax on insurance, 4/3.4

Insurance premiums
. accident and health insurance, 9/3.3
. casualty insurance, 6/1.3
. deductible, 6/1.5f; 7/2.9; 9/3.2
. general tax on receipts, 14/3.9
. insolvency, 7/2.10

Insurance proceeds
. accident, income tax, 9/3.3
. employment accident insurance, tax on insurance, 4/3.4
. health, income tax, 9/3.3
. life
. . income tax, 9/3.2
. . inheritance tax, 3/4.3i
. payments as income from employment, 8/1.3a

Insurance tax, 4/3.4

Intangibles
. amortization, 7/3.9
. valuation, 6/5.5

Intellectual property
. amortization, 7/3.9
. artistic services performed in Italy, provisional withholding, 13/3.5
. copyrights, fees for governmental concessions, 4/7.1
. general tax on receipts, 14/3.4
. income from, 8/3
. income-spreading from sale of, 8/4
. patents and copyrights, sale of, 9/8.5
. patents and trademarks, fees for governmental concessions, 4/7.1
. royalties. *See* Royalties
. withholding at source, 8/2.3; 11/3.9; 12/1.6

Intendant of Finance, 1/4.7; 4/5.5; 9/4.2e; 13/4.7

Interest
. accounting methods, 6/4.1
. banks, 10/4
. business income, 7/1.3b
. capitalized, 9/1.4
. deduction, 6/1.5d; 7/2.5; 8/2.2
. exemptions, 9/1.1; 9/1.7
. foreign banks, 11/3.5a
. foreign sources, 11/1.6a; 11/1, *n.* 12
. general tax on receipts, 14/4.2
. government or public entities, payment by, 9/1.2
. income, 9/1
. loan premiums and prizes, 9/1.3
. professional income, 8/2.2
. sale of obligation with accrued interest, 9/1.5
. sales of, 9/1.6
. treaty effect, 11/4.8
. withholding of tax, 13/3.4

International Monetary Fund (IMF), employees, 5/5.1

International transactions
. apportionment of income, 11/2.3c; 11/3.5b; 11/4.5b
. complementary tax, 2/3.5; 11/2.2; 11/3.2
. constitutional doctrine, 1/2.3
. domicile, 11/2.2
. family tax, 2/3.5
. foreign enterprises, 11/3
. general tax on receipts, 14/8
. income enjoyed in Italy, 2/3.5; 11/2.2
. income produced abroad, 11/2; 11/2.1
. income produced in Italy, 2/3.5; 11/1.2a

All references to Chapters 5/ through 13/ are to the income taxes

International transactions *(Continued)*
. income taxes, 2/2.5; 11/
. inheritance tax, 3/4.14
. Italian enterprises, 11/2.3a; 11/4.4b; 11/4.5a
. manufacturing taxes, 4/5.2d
. nonresidents, 11/3.2
. registration tax, 15/11
. residence, 11/2.2
. shipping, 11/3.7
. treaties, 3/4.14d; 11/4

Inventors, 5/5.3; 8/3; 8/4; 9/5

Inventory valuation, 6/5.1

Investigative Tax Police, 1/4.8

Investment
. foreign capital, restrictions on transfer of, 11/3.10
. foreign enterprise participating in Italian enterprise, 11/3.6
. gross investments by major categories, 1951 and 1961, 1/6.10e, Table 44
. income from, 5/2; 5/3; 9/2; 10/5

Investment companies, 10/5

Irrigation, 3/2.2; 10/2.2d

Israel, treaty, 11/4.1

Italian Society of Authors and Publishers, 4/5.4

Italian Sulphur Agency, 10/1.1

Italian Tobacco Enterprise, 1/4.5

Itinerant vendors, 4/2.5; 14/4.8

J

Joint and several liability
. general tax on receipts, 14/2.6; 14/7.2c
. income taxes, 13/3.1

Judicial proceedings
. courts, 1/4.10f; 13/4.9; 13/4.10
. fees, 15/2.2

Juridical persons, 5/2.1. *See also* Corporations
. general tax on receipts, 4/2.2; 14/2.1
. governmental concessions, fees for, 4/7.1

Jurisdiction. *See* Taxpayers' remedies

Justice, local expenditures for, 1/5.4

L

Labor force and value added per employee in the major sectors, 1951 and 1961, 1/6.10d, Table 40

Labor, housing for employees, 9/4.2b

Labor organizations, contributions to
. general tax on receipts, 14/4.5
. income tax
. . deduction, 7/2.16
. . exemption, 5/5, *n.* 45
. trade association dues, 7/2.16

Labor periodicals, 14/4.6j

Land, presumed income, 2/2.4b; 9/4.1

Landowning, income from, 2/2.2a; 6/1.1a; 6/1.1b; 10/2.2
. computation of tax
. . corporations, 12/2.1
. . individuals, 12/1.1
. example of tax computation, 12/1.7
. gross income of land capital, 10/2.2d
. imputed income, 2/2.4b
. "personalization" of tax, 2/2.7b; 12/1.1
. "productive source," 2/2.2
. receipts of tax, 1/6.7c, Table 12
. relief from taxation, 10/2.2f
. tax period, 6/3.4

Large families, reliefs for, 5/1.3; 6/1.5b

Laws, 1/2.2; 1/3.1b

Leases and leaseholds
. amortization of leasehold improvements, 7/3.8
. communal tax on leasehold values, 2/3.7
. general tax on receipts, 14/3.6
. mines and quarries, 10/1.1
. registration tax, 4/4.2b; 15/6.3d
. rent, 9/4. *See also* Rent

Legality, 1/2.2

Legatees. *See also* Decedents' estates
. estate tax, 3/5.4
. income taxes, 5/3.9
. inheritance tax, 3/4.10b

Legislature, 1/3.1

Legitimate interest, 1/4, *n.* 38

Liberties, constitutional provisions, 1/2.7

Licenses
. deductibility, 7/2.8
. local taxes, 4/5.10
. manufacturing taxes, 4/5.2

All references to Chapters 5/ through 13/ are to the income taxes

Life annuities
. income taxes, 9/3.1; 9/3.2
. inheritance tax, 3/4.3e
. insurance tax, 4/3.4

Life insurance. *See also* Insurance *and* Insurance companies
. deduction of premiums, 6/1.5f
. proceeds, 3/4.3i; 9/3.2

Limited liability companies, 5/2.3
. accounting methods, 6/4.1
. books required, 6/2.2
. corporation tax, 3/2.2
. coupon tax, 9/2.7a
. dividends and other distributions, complementary tax, 9/2.1b
. sale of business enterprise, 9/8.1; 9/8, *n.* 141
. taxable assets, 3/2.3
. transfers of participations, registration tax, 15/4, *n.* 63

Limited partnerships, sale of business enterprise, 9/8.1; 9/8, *n.* 141

Limited partnerships with shares, 5/2.4
. accounting methods, 6/4.1
. books reqiured, 6/2.2
. corporation tax, 3/2.2; 5/2.4
. coupon tax, 9/2.7a
. dividends and other distributions, complementary tax, 9/2.1b
. sale of business enterprise, 9/8.1; 9/8, *n.* 141
. taxable assets, 3/2.3

Limited partnerships without shares, 5/3.3

Liquidation of corporation, 9/9.9c
. distributions, 9/2.4
. liquidators, liability for tax, 13/3.1
. tax period, 6/3.5

Loan premiums and prizes, 9/1.3

Loans
. interest. *See* Interest
. registration tax, 15/6.3f
. tax on secured loans, 4/3.5

Local consumption taxes, 1/5.5c; 4/5.8
. receipts, 1/6.9c, Table 34
. . by region, 1959, 1/6.9c, Table 35
. . in provincial capitals, 1959, 1/6.9c, Table 36
. register of loading and unloading, 4/5.8e
. taxable goods, 4/5.8b
. valuation, 4/5.8d

Local entities, 1/5
. administrative functions, 1/5.3; 1/5.4
. classes of communes, 1/5.6, Table 1
. corporation tax, 3/2.2; 5/2.7; 5/5.11
. current receipts of the communes, 1/6.9a, Table 28
. current receipts of the provinces, 1/6.9a, Table 29
. current receipts of the regions, 1/6.9a, Table 30
. expenditures, 1/5.4
. family tax, jurisdiction to impose, 2/3.6
. inheritance tax, 3/4.2
. legislative functions, 1/5.3
. limitations on tax powers, 1/5.6
. local finance, diminished importance, 1/6.3
. participations in yields of state taxes, 1/5.5e
. receipts, 1/5.5
. receipts of communal and provincial direct taxes, 1/6.9b, Table 32
. receipts of communal consumption taxes, 1/6.9c, Table 34
. receipts of communal consumption taxes by region, 1959, 1/6.9c, Table 35
. receipts of communal consumption taxes in provincial capitals, 1959, 1/6.9c, Table 36
. receipts of local direct taxes, 1/6.9b, Table 31
. receipts of local indirect taxes, 1/6.9c, Table 33
. structures, 1/5.2
. supercontributions, 1/5.6
. tax receipts of the local governments, 1/6.3, Table 7

Long-term contracts, 6/4.3

Losses
. business income, 2/2.7h; 5/3.7; 7/2.1; 7/4
. capital losses, 9/8.8
. insurance, 10/3
. reorganization, 9/9

Lotto and lotteries. *See also* Gambling
. fiscal monopoly, 4/6.7
. General Inspectorate for Lotto and Lotteries, 1/4.1
. general tax on receipts, 14/4.10
. income tax, 10/7.1
. receipts, 1/6.8i, Table 27

All references to Chapters 5/ through 13/ are to the income taxes

M

Magistrate, 1/4.10f

Maintenance. *See* Repairs and maintenance, deduction of

Mandate
. registration tax, 15/6.3g

Manufacturing taxes, 4/5.2
. fiduciary warehouses, defined, 4/5.2a
. final stage, defined, 4/5.2a
. international aspects, 4/5.2d
. matches, 4/6.5
. products taxed, 4/5.2b
. receipts, 1/6.8e, Table 23
. Technical Offices of Manufacturing Taxes, 1/4.4; 4/5.2c

Margarine
. local consumption tax, 4/5.8b
. manufacturing tax, 4/5.2b

Markets, local expenditures, 1/5.4

Married persons
. aggregation of income, 5/1.2
. domicile of wife, 11/2.2
. effect of separation, 5/1.2
. family tax, 2/3.2
. personal allowance granted to wife, 8/1.9
. support allowance received by wife, 9/3.1

Matches, fiscal monopoly, 4/6.5

Mayor, 1/5.2

Meat
. general tax on receipts, 14/8.4c
. local consumption tax, 4/5.8b

Merger of business, 6/3.6; 9/9.7

Methane gas, manufacturing tax, 4/5.2b

Military expenditures
. local entities, 1/5.4
. national budget, 1/6.10e

Military hospitals and establishments, radio and television reception fees, 4/5.6

Milk, general tax on receipts, 4/2.5; 14/4.6e

Mines and minerals
. fees for governmental concessions, 4/7.1
. income from, 10/1

Minister of Finance, 1/3.2b; 1/3.4c; 4/5.5
. family tax, appeal, 2/3.8
. income tax, appeal to, 13/4.8

Minister of Finance *(Continued)*
. specific betterment contributions, approval, 3/7.2e
. transfer of motor vehicle at death of owner, 3/4, *n.* 124

Minister of the Budget, 1/3.2b

Minister of the Treasury, 1/3.2b

Ministerial circulars, 1/3.2e

Ministerial decrees, 1/3.2d

Ministry of Finance, 1/3.2b; 1/4.1; 4/6.7; 13/1.1

Ministry of Internal Affairs, 1/5.3
. Central Commission for Local Finance, 1/5.3

Ministry of State Participations, 1/3.4a

Minors
. domicile, 11/2.2
. income of, 5/1.3

Miscellaneous services, income from, 8/3

Monopolies. *See* Fiscal monopolies of the state

Mortgages
. registration of immovable property, 3/4.8a; 15/4.2
. tax on, 4/3.3
. . receipts, 1/6.8c, Table 21
. treaty effect, 11/4, *n.* 130

Motion pictures. *See* Cinema

Motor vehicles
. fees for operation of, 4/5.5
. receipts of fees and manufacturing taxes on petroleum and gasoline, 1/6.8f, Table 24
. registration tax, 15/6.3c
. special tax on transfers, 3/4.4d; 4/3.6
. stamp tax, 4/4.4
. used trucks, general tax on receipts, 14/4.7

Mountainous lands, reliefs for, 10/2.2f

Movable property
. furniture and other movables, 6/1.1e
. rental income, 9/4.4
. transfers, registration tax, 15/6.3c
. valuation, inheritance tax, 3/4.5f

Movable wealth, tax on income from, 2/2; 6/1.1e
. agricultural industry, income from, 10/2.4
. allowances, 12/1.4b
. computation, 12/1.4; 12/2.1

All references to Chapters 5/ through 13/ are to the income taxes

Movable wealth, tax on income from *(Continued)*
. example of tax computation, 12/1.7
. productive source, 2/2.2a
. rates, 12/1.4c, Table 59
. receipts, 1/6.7c, Table 14
. rental income subject to, 9/4.3
. surtaxes and additionals, 12/1.4d
. taxable income, defined, 12/1.4a
. withholding at source, 12/1.6

Mulct, 13/7.1

Municipal Board, 1/5.2

Mutual aid societies, exemption, 5/5.8

Mutual insurance companies, 3/2.2; 3/2.3; 5/2.6

N

National Autonomous Road Enterprise, 1/5.5f

National betterment contributions, 3/7.4

National Economic and Labor Council, 1/3.3; 1/3, *n.* 15

National economic balance sheet, 1951 and 1961, 1/6.10e, Table 41

National income and total fiscal burden, 1/6.1

National Institute of Health Insurance
. exemption, 5/5.6
. pensions, allowances, and subsidies, 8/1.3b

National Institute of Social Security
. exemption, 5/5.6
. pensions, allowances, and subsidies, 8/1.3b

National Institute of Work Accident Insurance
. exemption, 5/5.6
. payments, 8/1.3b

National Petroleum Agency, 10/1.1

Nationality. *See* Domicile *and* Residence

Natural resource extraction, 10/1
. mining credit, loans for, exemption of interest, 9/1.7
. treaty effect, 11/4.10

Navigation. *See* Ships and shipping

Negotiation tax, 2/4.1; 3/1

Net national income, 1/6.1a, Table 2

Netherlands, treaty, 11/4.1

Newspapers. *See* Printing

Nonprofit educational, scientific, and cultural institutions, 3/2.2; 5/5.5; 5/5.7

Nonresidents
. computation of tax, 12/4
. individuals, 11/3.2
. payments to, nondeductible, 7/5.3
. provisional withholding, 13/3.5
. taxation of income, 11/3

North Atlantic Treaty Organization (NATO), 5/5.1

Norway, treaty, 11/4.1

Notaries and public officials, liability for registration tax, 15/2.3

Notice of assessment, 13/2.1

Notices to the public, advertising tax, 4/5.3b

O

Oath in contest of assessment, 13/4.1

"Objective" taxes, 2/2; 5/1.1; 6/1.1a
. source of income, 11/1.2a

Obsolete machinery, 7/3.11

Official Collection of Laws and Decrees, 1/3.1b

Official Gazette, 1/3.1b

Oil and gas. *See* Petroleum and petroleum products

Organisation for European Economic Co-operation (OEEC), 5/5.1

Organization of business, 7/2.13; 9/9. *See also* Commencement of business

Overhead expenses
. general tax on receipts, 14/5.2
. income tax deduction, 7/2.1

Owners of business, payments to, 7/2.3c; 7/5.2; 9/2.5

Ownership of immovable property, 2/2.4b; 9/4.1
. agricultural land, 10/2.2a; 10/2.2b
. buildings, income from, 9/4.2a
. estate tax, 3/5.4
. inheritance tax, 3/4.3a; 3/4.3b

P

Packaging
. general tax on receipts, 14/5.2
. local consumption tax, 4/5.8b

Paper, local consumption tax, 4/5.8b

Parentela, 2/3, *n.* 20

All references to Chapters 5/ through 13/ are to the income taxes

Parliament
. allowance and per diem of members, exempt, 5/5.4
. composition and election, 1/2.2; 1/3.1a
. initiative and referendum, 1/3, *n.* 16

Participations. *See* Dividends and other distributions, Investment, *and* Partnerships

Partnerships, 5/3.2
. books required, 6/2.2
. cessation of business, 9/9.9b
. computation of tax, 12/3.1
. corporation tax, 2/4.4; 5/3.2; 11/2.3b
. domicile or residence, 11/2.2
. foreign, 11/3.4
. foreign enterprise as member, 11/3.6a
. income taxes, 5/3.2
. inheritance tax, 3/4.3g
. merger, 9/9.4
. noncommercial, 5/3.4
. partners
. . distributions as income, 5/3.2; 9/2.1a
. . distributions, general tax on receipts, 14/4, *n.* 70
. . foreign partner in Italian enterprise, 11/3.6a
. . liability, 6/2.2
. . payments to, 7/2.3c; 7/5.2
. . remuneration, 8/1.2
. . shares of, inheritance tax, 3/4.3g
. returns, form of, 12/5.3
. sale of business enterprise, 9/8.1; 9/8, *n.* 141
. simple limited, 5/3.3
. taxes deductible, 7/2.8
. transfer of profits or reserves to capital, 9/2.1a

Passports, fees for governmental concessions, 4/7.1

Peat bogs, income from, 10/1

Pecuniary penalty, 13/7.1

Penalties, 13/7
. advertising tax, 4/5.3g
. appeals. *See* Taxpayers' remedies
. civil, 14/9.2
. contravention, 13/7.1
. coupon tax, 13/7.5
. customs duties, 4/8.5
. degree of relationship, failure to state, 3/6
. delict, 13/7.1
. detention, 13/7.1

Penalties *(Continued)*
. failure to furnish information or to comply with other requests and orders, 13/7.3
. failure to withhold taxes or to pay taxes withheld, 13/7.7
. false oath, 13/4.1
. false returns or false statements, 13/7.4
. fines, 13/7.1
. general tax on receipts, 14/9
. import taxes, 14/9.3b
. imprisonment *(reclusione),* 13/7.1
. income taxes, 13/7
. increase of tax, 13/7.1
. indemnity for late payment, 13/7.1
. inheritance tax, 3/4.5e; 3/4.13
. instigating taxpayers to delay or refrain from payment, 13/7.8
. insurance tax, 4/3.4
. late filing of return, 13/1.1c
. late payment, 13/7.6
. liability
. . employee, 13/7.7
. . transferee of business, 13/7.1
. local consumption taxes, 4/5.8e; 4/5.8h
. manufacturing taxes, 4/5.2c
. miscellaneous offenses, 13/7.8
. mulct, 13/7.1
. omitted, late, or incomplete returns, 13/7.2
. payment by annual fee, violations, 14/9.2c
. pecuniary, defined, 13/7.1
. postal current accounts, violations, 14/9.2b; 14/9.3c
. prohibition from serving as member of controlling board, 13/7.1
. public officials, 13/7.5
. registration tax, 15/8
. . fines, 15/8.4
. . pecuniary, 15/8.3
. . surcharges, 15/8.2
. returns and information regarding income of others, 13/7.5
. stamp tax, 4/4.2h
. stock exchange contracts, 4/4.3c
. suspension of exercise of activity, 13/7.1
. tax bankruptcy, 13/7.1
. taxpayer assistance or representation contrary to law, 13/7.8

Pensions, 9/3
. deductions, 7/2.4
. exemption, 12/1.4a

All references to Chapters 5/ through 13/ are to the income taxes

Pensions *(Continued)*
. foreign source income, 11/1.6a
. general tax on receipts, 14/4.3
. grants annexed, exempt, 5/5.4
. income from movable wealth, 8/1.3b
. registration tax, 15/6.3e
. treaties, 11/4.12; 11/4.14
.. war pensions, family supplements to, exempt, 5/5.4

Percentage distribution of certain indirect taxes in the regions of ordinary statute, 1958, 1/6.10i, Table 51

Percentage distribution of national permanent direct taxes in the regions of ordinary statute, 1958, 1/6.10i, Table 50

Percentage distribution of principal national tax receipts in the regions of ordinary statute, 1958, 1/6.10i, Table 49

Periodicals. *See* Printing

Permanent establishment, 2/2.5
. abroad, 11/2.3b
. in Italy, 11/3.5b
. treaty, 11/4.4d

Perpetual annuities, 3/4.3e; 9/3.1

Personal allowances
. complementary tax, 2/3.4a; 12/1.5b
. cooperative society, 5/2.5; 12/3.2
. dependents, 5/1.2; 5/1.3; 5/1.4; 6/1.5b
. family tax, 2/3.4a
. large families, 5/1.3
. movable wealth income tax, 12/1.4b
. partnership, 5/3.2; 12/3.1
. "personalization" of income, 2/2.7g
. war widows with six children, 5/1.3

Personal services, income from, 8/

"Personal taxes," 2/3; 5/1.1; 6/1.1a

"Personalization" of income taxes, 2/2.7a

Petroleum and petroleum products
. incentive for use of residues, 10/6.6
. income from extraction and processing, 10/1
. manufacturing tax, border surtax, and license fee, 4/5.2b
. National Petroleum Agency, annual fee, 10/1.1

Phonograph records and other devices for reproduction of sound, manufacturing tax, 4/5.2b

Pledges of merchandise and securities
. general tax on receipts, 15/4.2
. tax on secured loans, 4/3.5

Police, expenditures for, 1/5.4

Political periodicals, general tax on receipts, 14/4.6j

Population registers, 1/5.4

Postage expenses, general tax on receipts, 14/5.2

President of the Council of Ministers, 1/3.2a; 1/3.2c

President of the Republic, 1/3.2a
. annual grant, exempt, 5/5.4
. decrees, 1/3.1d
. extraordinary appeal to, 13/4.11

Presidential decrees, 1/3.1d

Presumed income, 6/9.2; 9/6

Printing
. advertising, 4/3.5c
. general tax on receipts, 4/2.5; 14/4.6i

Prizes
. games of skill, 4/5.7
. income taxes, 10/7.1
. lotto and lotteries, 4/6.7; 10/7.1

Procedure and practice
. advertising tax, 4/5.3g
. appeals, 1/4.10; 13/4. *See also* Taxpayers' remedies
. bonds, tax on, 3/3.4
. complementary tax, 2/3.8; 13/
. customs duties, 4/8.4
. family tax, 2/3.8
. income taxes, 13/
. returns. *See* Returns

Processing
. agricultural products, 10/2.3a; 10/2.4
. transfer for purposes of, 14/3.13
. waste from foreign merchandise, 14/8.4c

Production and consumption, taxes on, 4/5

Professional associations, 5/5.9

Professional services
. deduction of payments for, 7/2.13
. general tax on receipts, 14/3.4
. income taxes, 2/2.2d; 6/1.1e; 8/2
.. accounting methods, 6/4.1
.. directors, 8/1.2. *See also* Directors of companies

All references to Chapters 5/ through 13/ are to the income taxes

Professional services, income taxes
(*Continued*)
. . source of income, 2/2.5; 11/1.4
. . spreading of income, 8/4
. . treaties, 11/4.13
. . withholding from payments to
persons domiciled abroad, 8/2.3;
11/3.9; 13/3.5

Professions and arts, fees for governmental concessions, 4/7.1

Professors, visiting, 11/4.13

Profit sharing, 7/2.3d; 8/1.6

Progressivity, 1/2.4

Protests, 1/4.10; 13/4. *See also* Taxpayers' remedies

Provident associations and institutions,
exempt, 3/2.2; 5/5.6

Provinces, 1/5.1
. Chamber of Commerce, Industry,
and Agriculture, 1/5.7
. current receipts, 1/6.9a, Table 29
. president, 1/5.1
. Provincial Council, 1/5.1; 1/5.2
. receipts of communal and provincial
direct taxes, 1/6.9b, Table 32
. receipts of communal consumption
taxes, 1959, 1/6.9c, Table 36
. revenues 1/5.5

Provincial Administrative Board,
1/4.10a; 1/5.2; 1/5.3
. audit of merit over expenditures,
1/5.4
. family tax, appeal, 2/3.8
. local taxes, 1/4.10j
. registration tax on decisions, 15/4.2
. supercontributions (*eccedenze*), 1/5.6

Provincial Census Commission,
1/4.10h; 10/2.2g

Provincial Council, 1/5.2

Provincial Tax Commission, 1/4.10d;
13/4.3

Public accommodations, retail sales in,
4/2.5; 14/4.8

Public act (*atto pubblico*), 15/3, *n.* 27

Public counters, local fee, 4/5.13

Public debt, 1/6.5, Table 10
. local governments, 1/5.5h
. securities of, 3/4.4c; 9/1.2

Public domain, 1/4.1; 10/1.1

Public enterprises and entities, 5/2.7;
5/5.11
. amounts received by, general tax on
receipts, 4/2.4; 14/3.3e; 14/4.4
. autonomous, defined, 1/3.4a
. bequests for provinces, communes,
and other Italian legal entities,
3/4.2
. budgets, 1/3.4
. corporation tax, 2/4.6; 3/2.2; 3/2.3;
5/2.7; 5/5.11
. merchandise imported directly by
units of state, 14/8.4c

Public order, local expenditures, 1/5.4

Public services
. general tax on receipts, 4/2.5;
14/3.3e; 14/4.4
. local expenditures, 1/5.4

Public shows, tax on, 4/5.4

Public spaces and areas, fee for occupation, 4/5.11; 7/2.8

Public weights and measures, local fee,
4/5.13

Public works
. expenditures, 1/5.4
. fees for governmental concessions,
4/7.1

Q

Quarries, income from, 10/1

R

Radio and television
. advertising tax, 4/5.3d
. broadcasting
. . general tax on receipts, 14/3.10
. . radio broadcast fees, 4/5.2b; 4/5.6
. consumption tax, 4/5.8b
. governmental concessions, fees for,
4/7.1
. reception fee, 4/5.6

Railroads
. general tax on receipts, 4/2.4; 14/4.10
. insurance, provident institutions for
personnel, 4/3.4
. stamp tax, 4/4.4

Rates. *See* Tax rates

"Real" or "objective" taxes, 2/2; 5/1.1;
6/1.1a

Real property. *See* Immovable property

Rebate, general tax on receipts, 14/5.3

All references to Chapters 5/ through 13/ are to the income taxes

Receipts, stamp tax, 4/4.2b

Receivables, valuation, 6/5.2

Reclamation association, 3/2.2

Reconstruction of war damage, 14/4.6a

Recreation clubs, sales by, 4/2.5; 14/4.8

Referendum, 1/3, *n.* 116

Reforestation, income from landowning, 10/2.2f

Refunds
. exported products, tax on, 14/8.3
. general tax on receipts, 14/7.2d
. income taxes, 13/3.6c; 13/5
. inheritance tax, 3/4.10g
. local consumption taxes, 4/5.8e
. registration tax, 15/3.3 l; 15/7.2b

Regional development incentives
. general tax on receipts, 14/4.6k
. income taxes, 10/6

Regions, 1/5.1
. current receipts, 1/6.9a, Table 30
. legislative rules, 1/5.3
. limitations on powers, 1/5.5c
. participations in yields of state taxes, 1/5.5e
. receipts of communal consumption taxes, 1959, 1/6.9c, Table 35
. Regional Board, 1/5.2
. Regional Council, 1/5.2
. tax autonomy, 1/5.5c

Registration
. books and records, 6/2.3
. motor vehicles, fees, 4/3.6
. shares, 9/2.8

Registration tax, 4/3; 15/
. acts forming corporations, 15/3.3f
. acts with several provisions, 15/3.3b
. acts with suspensive conditions, 15/3.3f
. agreement to forbear or discontinue litigation, 15/3.3j
. *appalto* and sale, 15/3.3i
. appeals, 15/10
. appurtenances, 15/3.3e
. assessment, 15/7.1
. collection, 15/7.2
. contracting parties, defined, 15/2.1
. contracts
. . cancellation of, 15/3.3k
. . partly gratuitous, 15/3.3c
. . rates, 15/6.3
. *de facto* transfers, 15/3.4

Registration tax *(Continued)*
. deduction from business income, 7/2.13
. economic reality, principle of, 15/3.2
. exchange or barter, 15/3.3h
. exemptions, 15/4.1
. historical background, 15/1.2
. international aspects, 15/11
. judicial acts, 15/2.2
. judicial fees, 15/2, *n.* 25
. mandates, 15/6.3g
. nonjudicial acts, 15/2.1
. notaries and public officials, liability, 15/2.3
. oral agreements, 15/3.5
. partition of common property, 15/3.3g
. payment, 15/7.2
. penalties. *See* Penalties
. persons subject, 15/2
. protests, 15/10
. public act, 15/3, *n.* 27
. rates, 4/3.2c; 15/4.1; 15/4.5a
. . fixed fees, 15/4.5b
. . proportional, 15/6.3h
. . reduced, 15/4.5c
. receipts, 1/6.8c, Table 21
. registration on account, 15/7.2c
. subrogation, 15/2.3
. surcharges, 15/8.2
. time limits, 15/9
. transfers of enterprises, 15/3.3d; 15/3.4b
. valuation, 4/3.2d; 15/5
. void acts, 15/3.3 l
. written acts, 15/3.1

Registry Offices, 1/4.3; 14/7.1; 15/7.1

Registry Procurator, 1/4.3

Reimbursements of expenses, 7/2.3f; 8/1.5

Reimportation of merchandise, 14/8.4c

Relatives
. bequests to, 3/4.7c
. dependent, 5/1.4

Reliefs. *See* Exemptions, Personal allowances, *and* Tax rates

Religious organizations, exemptions, 3/4.2; 5/5.5; 9/4.2a

Remuneration for services, 8/

Rendita perpetua, 9/3, *n.* 65

Renewal projects, 3/7; 9/4.2b

All references to Chapters 5/ through 13/ are to the income taxes

Rent, 9/4
. agricultural land, 10/2.1
. buildings, net income from, 9/4.2c
. deduction from business income, 7/2.2
. general tax on receipts, 14/3.6
. movable wealth, income from, 6/1.1e;
   9/4.3; 9/4.4
. urban building cadaster, 9/4.2d

Reorganization of business, 6/3.6; 9/9
. assets
. . division, 9/9.8
. . purchase, 9/9.3
. . sale, 9/9.2
. balance sheet, 9/9.4
. exchange of shares for shares, 9/9.5
. expenses deductible, 9/9.3
. merger, 9/9.4; 9/9.7
. registration tax, 15/6.3h
. subsidiaries, creation of, 9/9.6
. surcharge, 9/9.3
. time limit for filing return, 13/1.1c

Repairs and maintenance, deduction of
. business income, 7/2.6
. professional income, 8/2.2

Representation of taxpayers, 1/4.11

Research expenses, deduction of, 7/2.15

Reservation on account (*prenotazione
   à debito*), 4/4.2f; 15/7.2c

Reserves, 6/6
. "hidden reserves," 6/6.3; 7/1.3f
. required by law, 6/6.2
. transfer of business, 9/9.2

Residence. *See also* Domicile
. defined, 11/2.2
. family tax, 2/3.6
. treaty provisions, 11/4.4c

Restaurants, general tax on receipts,
   14/3.3f

Retail sales, general tax on receipts,
   4/2.5; 14/4.8a

Retail services, general tax on receipts,
   14/3.4; 14/4.8b; 14/7.3b

Returns, 13/1
. banks and banking, 10/4.4
. content and form, 12/5; 13/1.2
. corporations, 5/2.2
. . form, 12/5.4
. . merger, 9/9.7
. . reorganization, 9/9.4
. credit institutions, 10/4.4
. documents attached, 13/1.3

Returns *(Continued)*
. estate tax, 3/5.6
. executors and administrators, 5/3.9
. failure to file, 13/1.1a; 13/1, *n.* 1.
   See also Penalties
. family tax, 2/3.8
. forms of, 12/5
. heirs, 5/3.9
. incompetent persons, 5/1.3
. individuals, 5/1.1; 12/5.2
. information, 13/1.4
. inheritance tax, 3/4.8
. liquidation, 9/9.9c
. minors, 5/1.3
. partnerships, 5/3.2; 12/5.3
. penalties, 13/7.2
. place of filing, 13/1.1d
. review, 13/2.2
. signing, 13/1.1b
. termination of business, report of,
   9/9.2; 13/1.5
. time limits for filing, 13/1.1c
. withholding, 13/1.4

Revenue Technical Offices, 1/4.6;
   9/4.2d; 10/2.2g

Rolls, collection through, 13/3.5; 13/3.6;
   13/3.7

Royalties, 9/5
. amortization, 9/5
. business income, 7/1.3c
. deduction of, 7/2.12
. received by foreign enterprises from
   Italian payor, 11/3.5a
. source of income, 11/1.6c
. treaties, effect of, 11/4.9

S

Salaries and wages. *See* Employment,
   income from

Sales
. general tax on receipts, 14/3.3a
. installment, accounting for, 6/4.2
. interest, 9/1.6
. obligations with accrued interest,
   9/1.5
. registration tax, 15/3.3i
. retail sales nontaxable, 14/4.8a
. transfer of goods, 14/5.1

Salt deposits, income from, 10/1

Salt, fiscal monopoly, 4/6.2

Sanctions. *See* Penalties

All references to Chapters 5/ through 13/ are to the income taxes

Savings, 1954-1959, 1/6.10e, Table 43

Scholarships and fellowships, 10/7.3; 11/4.13d

Schools. *See also* Education
. buildings, tax on income from, 9/4.2b
. local expenditures, 1/5.4
. subsidies for construction of, 1/5.5f

Scientific institutions, 3/2.2

Seacoast, fee for governmental concessions, 4/7.1

Search and seizure, 1/4.12; 13/2.2

Securities
. bearer shares, 9/2.7d
. dividends, 9/2
. exchange of shares for shares, 9/9.5
. exemptions, 15/4.2
. foreign ownership, 11/3.6b
. foreign securities, 9/2.7e
. gratuitous shares, 9/2.3; 9/2.7a
. inheritance tax, 3/4.4c; 3/4.5g; 3/4.14b
. registration of shares, 9/2.8
. stamp tax, 4/4.2
. transactions in
. . capital gains, 9/8.4
. . registration tax, 15/4.2; 15/5.3; 15/6.3; 15/6.4; 15/6.5
. valuation, 6/5.3; 15/5.3

Seed oils, manufacturing tax, border surtax, and license fee, 4/5.2b

Self-assessment, 2/2.8; 14/7.2b

Services. *See also* Employment, income from, Miscellaneous services, income from, *and* Professional services
. general tax on receipts, 4/2.4; 14/3
. income taxes, 8/

Set-off
. losses, 7/4; 9/8.8
. separate businesses and activities, 5/3.7
. unused depreciation, 7/3.7

Shareholders
. dividends, 9/2
. liquidation of business, 9/9.9c
. payments to, 7/2.3c; 9/2.5
. unabsorbed losses, 9/9.9c

Ships and shipping
. accelerated depreciation, 7/3, *n.* 74
. foreign exercise, 11/3.7

Ships and shipping *(Continued)*
. governmental concessions, fees for, 4/7.1
. imported materials for shipbuilding, 14/4.6b; 14/8.4c
. incentives, 10/6.6
. inheritance tax, international aspects, 3/4.14a
. marine insurance, 4/3.4
. motor boats, fees, 4/5.5
. personal services, effect of treaty, 11/4.13b
. registration tax, 15/6.3c; 15/6.3g
. stamp tax, 4/4.4
. treaty provisions, 11/4.6

Shoes, local consumption tax, 4/5.8b

Signs, local tax on, 4/5.12

Silver coins, imported, 14/4.6c

Simple limited partnership, 5/3.3

Slaughterhouses
. expenditures of local governments, 1/5.4
. general tax on receipts, 14/4.4

Small businesses
. income of, 7/1.2b
. industrial activities of new enterprises, 10/6.5

Social insurance and social security
. compulsory, burden of, 1/6.4
. contributions, 1/6.4, Table 8
. . deduction of, 6/1.5f; 7/2.4
. . general tax on receipts, 4/2.4; 14/4.3
. . income, 8/1.3a
. income of entities furnishing, 5/5.6
. institutions, fees for concessions, 4/7.1
. insurance tax, 4/3.4
. nature, 1/6.6
. payments
. . general tax on receipts, 4/2.4; 14/4.3
. . income, 8/1.3b
. receipts by source, 1/6.4, Table 9
. receipts of national and local taxes, and social insurances, 1/6.1c, Table 5

Somministrazione, 8/4, *n.* 33; 15/3, *n.* 45

Sources of income
. international transactions, 11/1
. "productive sources," 2/2.2; 6/1.1a

All references to Chapters 5/ through 13/ are to the income taxes

Spain, treaty, 11/4.1

Special activities and miscellaneous sources, income from, 10/
. agriculture, 10/2. *See also* Agriculture
. banking and credit, 10/4. *See also* Banks and banking
. forestry, 10/2
. industrial incentives, 10/6. *See also* Industrial incentives
. insurance, 10/3. *See also* Insurance companies *and* Insurance policies
. investment companies, 10/5. *See also* Investment companies
. lotteries, prizes, and awards, 10/7.1
. natural resource extraction, 10/1. *See also* Natural resource extraction
. scholarships and fellowships, 10/7.3
. speculative operations, 10/7.2

Specific betterment contribution, 3/7.2

Spirits. *See* Alcoholic beverages

Sporting goods, local consumption tax, 4/5.8b

Spouse
. estate tax, 3/5.5
. income tax, 5/1.2
. inheritance tax, 3/4.2; 3/4.7b

Spreading of income, 6/4.1; 8/4

Stamp tax, 4/4
. authentication of document, 4/3.1; 4/4
. claim for refund, 3/4.12b
. copy of invoice, 14/8.2b
. deduction from income, 7/2.13
. foreign investment, 10/4.2
. general tax on receipts as including, 4/4.2b
. general tax on receipts on sales of stamped paper, 14/4.10
. general tax on receipts paid by stamps, 14/7.2c
. "paper," defined, 4/4.2a
. registration tax as replacing IGE and stamp tax, 4/4.2b
. securities issued abroad, 4/4.2c
. stock exchange contracts, 4/4.3
. transportation documents, 4/4.4

Stepchildren, 5/1.3

Stock brokers, general tax on receipts, 14/7.3b

Stock exchange contracts, stamp tax, 4/4.3

Subjective right, 1/4, *n.* 38

Subsidiaries, creation of, 9/9.6

Subsidies
. general tax on receipts, 14/4.2
. income from movable wealth, 8/1.3b
. local entities, 1/5.5f

Succession taxes. *See* Estate tax *and* Inheritance tax

Succursale, 5/2, *n.* 7

Sugar, glucose, maltose, and sugar products, manufacturing tax, border surtax, and license fee, 4/5.2b

Sulphur, special tax, 10/1.1

Supercontributions, 1/5.6

Supervening assets, 3/4.3j

Supreme Court of Cassation, 1/4.10f; 13/4.10

Surcharge (penalty)
. income tax, 13/7.1
. registration tax, 15/8.2

Surcharges on issue of shares, 9/9.3

Surplus or deficit of the budget of the state, 1/6.1b, Table 4

Surtaxes of local entities, 1/5.5d
. corporations and similar entities, 12/2.1; 12/2.2c
. movable wealth, 12/1.4d
. "objective" taxes, 2/2.9; 12/1
. receipts of local direct taxes, 1/6.9b, Table 31

Surviving spouse. *See* Spouse

Suspensive conditions, 15/3.3f

Sweden, treaty, 3/4.14d; 11/4.1

Switzerland, treaty, 11/4.1

T

Tables
. 1: Classes of Communes, 1/5.6
. 2: Net National Income, 1/6.1a
. 3: Tax Receipts of the National and Local Governments, 1/6.1a
. 4: Surplus or Deficit of the Budget of the State, 1/6.1b
. 5: Receipts of National and Local Taxes and Social Insurances, 1/6.1c

All references to Chapters 5/ through 13/ are to the income taxes

Tables *(Continued)*

. 6: Tax Receipts of the National Government, 1/6.2
. 7: Tax Receipts of the Local Governments, 1/6.3
. 8: Social Insurance Contributions, 1/6.4
. 9: Social Insurance Receipts by Source, 1955 and 1959, 1/6.4
. 10: Public Debt, 1/6.5
. 11: Receipts of National Direct Taxes, 1/6.7a
. 12: Receipts of Tax on Income from Landowning, 1/6.7c
. 13: Receipts of Tax on Income from Buildings, 1/6.7c
. 14: Receipts of Tax on Income from Movable Wealth, 1/6.7c
. 15: Receipts of National Personal Taxes on Income of Individuals, 1/6.7d
. 16: Receipts of Corporation Tax and Tax on Bonds, 1/6.7d
. 17: Receipts of Taxes on Gratuitous Transfers, 1/6.7e
. 18: Receipts of Transitory and Extraordinary Direct Taxes on Wealth, 1/6.7f
. 19: Receipts of National Indirect Taxes, 1/6.8a
. 20: Receipts of Taxes on Exchanges, 1/6.8b
. 21: Receipts of Registration and Mortgage Taxes, 1/6.8c
. 22: Receipts of Miscellaneous Transaction Taxes, 1/6.8d
. 23: Receipts of National Manufacturing and Consumption Taxes, 1/6.8e
. 24: Receipts of Motor Vehicle Fees and Manufacturing Taxes on Petroleum and Gasoline, 1/6.8f
. 25: Receipts of Customs Duties, 1/6.8g
. 26: Receipts of Fiscal Monopolies, 1/6.8h
. 27: Receipts of Lotto and Lotteries, 1/6.8i
. 28: Current Receipts of the Communes, 1/6.9a
. 29: Current Receipts of the Provinces, 1/6.9a
. 30: Current Receipts of the Regions, 1/6.9a

Tables *(Continued)*

. 31: Receipts of Local Direct Taxes, 1/6.9b
. 32: Receipts of Communal and Provincial Direct Taxes, 1/6.9b
. 33: Receipts of Local Indirect Taxes, 1/6.9c
. 34: Receipts of Communal Consumption Taxes, 1/6.9c
. 35: Receipts of Communal Consumption Taxes by Region, 1959, 1/6.9c
. 36: Receipts of Communal Consumption Taxes in Provincial Capitals, 1959, 1/6.9c
. 37: General Balance of Current Payments, 1/6.10a
. 38: Value Added and Net Product of the Private Sector, 1/6.10b
. 39: Income from Employment and Its Relation to National Income, 1954 and 1961, 1/6.10d
. 40: Labor Force and Value Added Per Employee in the Major Sectors, 1951 and 1961, 1/6.10d
. 41: National Economic Balance Sheet, 1951 and 1961, 1/6.10e
. 42: Consumption, Investment, and Production of Industry, Agriculture, and the Tertiary Sector, 1/6.10e
. 43: Savings, 1954-1959, 1/6.10e
. 44: Gross Investments by Major Categories, 1951 and 1961, 1/6.10e
. 45: Current Expenditures of the State, 1/6.10e
. 46: Value Added and Net Product of Industrial Activities, 1951 and 1961, 1/6.10g
. 47: Value Added and Net Product of the Principal Agricultural Activities, 1951 and 1961, 1/6.10g
. 48: Common Expenditures by General Categories, 1951 and 1961, 1/6.10h
. 49: Percentage Distribution of Principal National Tax Receipts in the Regions of Ordinary Statute, 1958, 1/6.10i
. 50: Percentage Distribution of National Permanent Direct Taxes in the Regions of Ordinary Statute, 1958, 1/6.10i
. 51: Percentage Distribution of Certain Indirect Taxes in the Regions of Ordinary Statute, 1958, 1/6.10i

All references to Chapters 5/ through 13/ are to the income taxes

Tables *(Continued)*
. 52: Range of Allowance for Income Subject to the Family Tax, by Class of Commune, 2/3.4a
. 53: Rates of the Family Tax, 2/3.4b
. 54: Rates of the Inheritance Tax, 3/4.7b
. 55: Computation Table for the Inheritance Tax, 3/4.7b
. 56: Rates of the Estate Tax, 3/5.5
. 57: Computation Table for the Estate Tax, 3/5.5
. 58: Rates of Tax on Increases in the Value of Building Lots, 3/7.3c
. 59: Rates of Tax on Income from Movable Wealth for Individuals, 12/1.4c
. 60: Rates of Complementary Tax for Selected Values of Taxable Income, 12/1.5c

Tar, 10/6.6

Tax administration, 1/4. *See also* Administration of tax

Tax base
. agrarian income, 6/1.1c; 10/2.3a; 10/2.3b; 12/1.2
. building lots, tax on increases in value, 3/7.3b
. buildings, tax on income from, 6/1.1d; 9/4.2c; 12/1.3
. complementary tax, 2/3.3a; 2/4.2; 6/1.1f; 12/1.5a
. corporation tax, 2/4.2; 2/4.3; 6/1.1g; 12/2.2
. estate tax, 3/5.3
. estimated income, 6/9.1
. family tax, 2/3.3b
. general tax on receipts, 4/2.3; 14/3.1; 14/5
. income determined by agreement, 6/9.3
. inheritance tax, 3/4.3
. landowning, tax on income from, 6/1.1b; 10/2.2d; 12/1.1
. movable wealth, income from, 6/1.1e; 12/1.4a
. "objective" taxes on income, 2/2; 6/1.1; 12/1
. presumed income, 6/9.2
. specific betterment contribution, 3/7.2b

Tax burden, 1/6

Tax commissions, 1/4.10; 3/4.11; 13/2; 13/4

Tax credit
. building lots, tax on increases in value of, 3/7.3c
. coupon tax, 9/2.7c
. estate tax, 3/5.5
. foreign income taxes, 11/4.3b
. inheritance tax, 3/4.7e
. provisional withholdings, 13/3.5

Tax incentives. *See* Industrial incentives

Tax legislation, 1/3

Tax rates
. additionals, 2/2.9; 3/4.7f; 12/1
. advertising tax, 4/5.3f
. animal-drawn vehicles, fee for circulation of, 4/5.14
. annual fee *(abbonamento)*. *See* Annual fee *(abbonamento)*
. betterment contributions
. . national, 3/7.4
. . specific, 3/7.2d
. bonds, tax on, 3/3.3
. building lots, tax on increases in value of, 3/7.3c, Table 58
. class of commune, 1/5.6, Table 1
. complementary tax, 2/3.4b; 12/1.5c, Table 60
. consumption taxes, 4/5.8d
. corporation tax, 2/4.3; 3/2.4; 12/2.2c
. customs duties, 4/8.2
. estate tax, 3/5.5, Table 56
. European Economic Community, 4/8.2
. family tax, 2/3.4b, Table 53
. games of skill and football pools, 4/5.7
. General Agreement on Tariffs and Trade, 4/8.2
. general tax on receipts, 14/6
. governmental concessions, fees for, 4/7.2
. income taxes
. . corporations, 12/2.1; 12/2.2c
. . individuals, 12/1.4c, Table 59; 12/1.5c
. inheritance tax, 3/4.7; 3/4.7b, Table 54
. insurance tax, 4/3.4
. license taxes, 4/5.10
. manufacturing taxes, 4/5.2b
. matches, 4/6.5
. mortgage tax, 4/3.3
. motor vehicle fees, 4/5.5
. movable wealth, 12/1.4c, Table 59
. occupation of public spaces and areas, 4/5.11

All references to Chapters 5/ through 13/ are to the income taxes

Tax rates *(Continued)*
. public shows, tax on, 4/5.4
. public weights and measures and the renting of public counters, fee for, 4/5.13
. radio and television fees, 4/5.6
. registration tax, 4/3.2c; 15/6
. signs, tax on, 4/5.12
. stamp tax, 4/4.2e
. stock exchange contracts, tax on, 4/4.3b
. termination pay, 8/1.8
. *una tantum,* 14/6.4
. visitors tax, 4/5.9

Tax receipts of the local governments, 1/6.3, Table 7

Tax receipts of the national and local governments, 1/6.1a, Table 3

Tax receipts of the national government, 1/6.2, Table 6

Tax regulations, 1/3.2c

Tax substitutes, 13/3.1; 14/2.5

Tax system in relation to economic structure, 1/6

Taxes paid or payable
. deduction of, 6/1.5e; 7/2.8; 9/4.1; 9/9.9c; 10/4, *n.* 106
. receipts for general tax on receipts, 4/2.4; 14/4.4; 14/5.2

Taxpayers, classes of
. agrarian income, tax on, 10/2.3a
. bonds, tax on, 3/3.1
. estate tax, 3/5.4
. general tax on receipts, 14/2
. income taxes, 5/
. registration tax, 15/2
. separate businesses and activities, 5/3.7
. visitors tax, 4/5.9

Taxpayers' remedies, 1/4.10
. advertising tax, 4/5.3g
. agrarian income, 10/2.3d
. buildings, tax on income from, 9/4.2e
. Census Commissions, 1/4.10h; 10/2.2g
. Central Tax Commission, 1/4.10e; 13/4.4
. constitutional provisions, 1/4.10a; 1/4.10b
. Council of State, 1/4.10a; 13/4.11
. counterappeals, 13/4.4; 13/4, *n.* 74
. courts, 2/3.8; 13/4.9b
. Courts of Appeal, 1/4.10f; 13/4.9a

Taxpayers' remedies *(Continued)*
. customs duties, 1/4.10i; 4/8.4
. District Tax Commission, 1/4.10c; 3/4.9; 13/4.2
. District Tribunals, 1/4.10f; 13/4.9
. family tax, 2/3.8
. general tax on receipts, 14/7.2d; 14/7.3e; 14/7.3f
. governmental concessions, fees for, 4/7.4
. incidental appeals, 13/4.3
. income taxes, 13/4
. increases in value of building lots, tax on, 3/7.3d
. inheritance tax, 3/4.10h; 3/4.11
. inscription in roll, 13/4.6
. Intendant of Finance, 1/4.7; 13/4.5; 13/4.7
. landowning, tax on income from, 10/2.2g
. legitimate interest, defined, 1/4, *n.* 38
. local consumption taxes, 4/5.8e; 4/5.8g
. local taxes, 1/4.10j
. manufacturing taxes, 1/4.10i
. Minister of Finance, 13/4.8; 14/7.2d
. motor vehicle fees, 4/5.5
. national betterment contributions, 3/7.4
. ordinary courts, 1/4.10f; 13/4.9
. payment of tax pending review, 13/4.12; 14/7.2d
. Provincial Tax Commission, 1/4.10d; 13/4.3
. reform of tax litigation, proposals for, 1/4.10a; 1/4.13
. registration tax, 15/10
. representation of taxpayers, 1/4.11
. revocation appeal, 3/4.11
. special courts, 1/4.10g
. specific betterment contribution, 3/7.2e
. stamp tax, 4/4.2g
. subjective right, defined, 1/4, *n.* 38
. Supreme Court of Cassation, 13/4.9a; 13/4.10
. tax commissions, 1/4.10b; 1/4, *n.* 40
. time limits, 13/4.9c
. treaties, 11/4.15

Teachers
. income of, 5/5.3
. treaties, 11/4.13c

Technical Offices of Manufacturing Taxes, 4/5.2c

Telephone, stamp tax, 4/4.2b

Temporary importation, 4/5.2d; 4/8.3

All references to Chapters 5/ through 13/ are to the income taxes

Temporary visitors, 11/3.2c

Termination of business
. corporation or similar entity, 9/9.9c
. liquidation, 9/9.4
. partnerships or similar companies, 9/9.9b
. registration tax, 15/6.3h
. report of, 9/9.2; 13/1.5
. sole proprietorship, 9/9.9a
. surcharge, return of, 9/9.3
. tax period, 6/3.5
. time limit for filing return, 13/1.1c

Termination of employment, 7/2.3e; 8/1.8

Territoriality, 1/2.3; 2/2.5; 11/. *See also* International transactions

Testo unico of the laws on direct taxes, 1/3.1d; 2/1; 5/-13/

Textiles
. imported, general tax on receipts, 14/8.4c
. local consumption tax, 4/5.8b
. manufacturing tax, 4/5.2b

Time limits
. bankruptcy or suspension, 13/7.1
. existence of debts, proving, 3/4.6c
. general tax on receipts, 14/10
. income taxes, 13/6
. interruption of, 3/4.12b; 14/10.1
. payment, inheritance tax, 3/4.10c
. penalties and surcharges, 13/7.1; 14/10.1
. refunds, 14/10.2; 15/7.2b; 15/9.1. *See also* Refunds
. registration tax, 15/9.1; 15/9.2
. returns
. . income tax, 13/1.1c
. . inheritance tax, 3/4.8c

Tobacco
. exportation, incentives for, 10/6.6
. fiscal monopoly, 4/6.3

Tourism. *See also* Hotels
. general tax on receipts, 14/7.3b
. local expenditures for, 1/5.4
. visitors tax, 4/5.9

Toys, local consumption tax, 4/5.8b

Trade unions. *See* Labor organizations, contributions to

Tramways
. general tax on receipts, 4/2.4; 14/4.10
. stamp tax, 4/4.4

Transactions, taxes on, 4/
. consumption, 4/5
. customs duties, 4/8
. general tax on receipts, 4/2; 14/
. governmental concessions, fees for, 4/7
. insurance tax, 4/3.4
. mortgage tax, 4/3.3
. receipts, 1/6.8d, Table 22
. registration taxes, 4/3; 15/3
. registry of motor vehicles, tax on, 4/3.6
. secured loans, 4/3.5
. stamp taxes, 4/4
. state fiscal monopolies, 4/6

Transportation. *See also* Ships and shipping
. general tax on receipts, 14/5.2
. governmental concessions, fees for, 4/7.1
. stamp tax, 4/4.4; 14/4.10

Treaties, 1/3.1e
. income taxes, 11/4
. inheritance tax, 3/4.14d
. withholding from income exempt under, 13/3.5

Tremelloni law, 2/1

Tribunal, 1/4.10f; 13/4.9

Trusts, 3/4.3d; 3/5.4

U

Una tantum, 8/4; 14/6.1

Union of South Africa, treaty, 11/4.1

United Kingdom, treaty, 11/4.3a

United Nations agencies, 5/5.1

United States
. company or enterprise, 11/4.4b
. income tax treaty, 11/4.1
. inheritance tax treaty, 3/4.14d

Universal disposition, 3/4.1a

Unrecognized natural children, 5/1.3

Urban affairs, 1/5.4; 3/7

Use *(uso)*, 3/4.3c; 9/4.1

Usufruct *(usufrutto)*
. estate tax, 3/5.4
. income taxes, 9/4.1; 10/2.2a
. inheritance tax, 3/4.3b
. merger with bare ownership, 3/4.3b
. registration tax, 15/5.2

All references to Chapters 5/ through 13/ are to the income taxes

V

Valuation, 6/5
. accounts receivable, 6/5.2
. annuities in kind, 3/4.5d
. average value, local consumption tax, 4/5.8d
. building lots, tax on increases in value of, 3/7.3b
. business assets, 9/9.2
. business enterprises, 3/4.5e
. devaluation, 6/5.6
. fixed assets, 6/5.4
. good will, 9/9.2
. "hidden reserve" taxable, 6/5.2
. immovable property, 3/4.5c; 15/5.2
. inheritance tax, 3/4.3a; 3/4.5
. intangibles, 6/5.5
. inventory, 6/5.1
. last-in-first-out, 6/5.1
. local consumption taxes, 4/5.8d
. local entities, specific betterment contribution, 3/7.2c
. movable property, 3/4.5f; 15/5.3
. partnership interest, 3/4.5e
. registration tax, 4/3.2d; 15/5
. revaluation, 6/5.6
. "saleable" (market) value, 3/4.5b
. securities, 3/4.5g; 6/5.3; 15/5.3

Value added, 2/2.1

Value added and net product of industrial activities, 1951 and 1961, 1/6.10g, Table 46

Value added and net product of the principal agricultural activities, 1951 and 1961, 1/6.10g, Table 47

Value added and net product of the private sector, 1/6.10b, Table 38

Vanoni law, 2/1

Visitors
. local tax, 4/5.9
. temporary, income of, 11/3.2c

W

Wages. *See* Employment, income from

War
. materials for reconstruction, 14/4.6a
. reliefs for large families, 5/1.3
. repair of damage to buildings, 9/4.2b

Water
. associations for water works, 3/2.2

Water *(Continued)*
. buildings for supply of, 9/4.2b
. stamp tax, 4/4.2b

Wealth, receipts of transitory and extraordinary direct taxes, 1/6.7f, Table 18

Welfare entities
. communal, additional, 13/3.4
. exempt, 3/2.2
. housing built by, exempt, 9/4.2b

Welfare, local expenditures for, 1/5.4

Welfare payments
. deduction of, 7/2.4
. income from, 8/1.3b; 12/1.4b

Well-being, assessment of family tax, 2/3.3b

Wills. *See also* Decedents' estates *and* Heirs
. bequests, 6/1.3
. legatees, duty to file return, 3/4.8b

Windfalls
. business income, 7/1.3e
. recovery by insurance, 7/2.7
. recovery of bad debts, 7/2.10

Wine
. general tax on receipts, 14/4.6e; 14/4.6f; 14/8.4c
. local consumption tax, 4/5.8b

Withholding at source
. aliens, 11/3.9
. capital, income from, 9/7
. certificate of payor, 13/1.3
. computation, 12/1.6
. dividends and other distributions, 9/2.7; 11/3.3; 11/3.4; 11/4.7
. foreign company, 11/3.3; 11/3.4; 11/3.9; 11/4.7
. foreign recipient, 11/3.6b; 11/3.9
. foreign securities, 9/2.7e
. generally, 13/3.1
. government interest payments, 9/1.2
. government payments, 13/3.3
. independent work, 8/2.3
. intellectual property, 8/3.1; 12/1.6
. nonresidents, 11/3.3; 11/3.4; 11/3.9; 11/4.7
. professional income, 8/2.3
. provisional, 13/3.5
. rates
. . corporations, 12/2.4
. . individuals, 12/1.6
. . nonresidents, 12/4

All references to Chapters 5/ through 13/ are to the income taxes

Withholding at source *(Continued)*
. recovery of taxes paid for others, 13/3.4
. registration of shares, 9/2.8
. returns, 13/1.4
. treaty provision, 11/4.7a
. wages and salaries, 8/1.10

Work, income from, 8/. *See also* Employment, income from, Miscellaneous services, income from, *and* Professional services, income from

Work, income from *(Continued)*
. agriculture, manual labor of owner, 10/2, *n.* 34
. mixed capital and work, 2/2.2b
. pure work, 2/2.2a; 2/2.2d

World Health Organization (WHO), employees, 5/5.1

Worthless assets, 7/2.7

The Harvard Law School International Program in Taxation acknowledges the generous financial support received on behalf of the following contributors:

Abbott Laboratories
The Alcoa Foundation
Allis-Chalmers Manufacturing
    Company
American Can Company Foundation
American Chicle Company
American Cyanamid Company
American Express Foundation
American Home Products Corporation
American Metal Climax, Inc.
American Metal Products Company
American Optical Company
American Radiator & Standard
    Sanitary Corporation
American Viscose Corporation
American Zinc, Lead and Smelting
    Company
The Anaconda Company
Anderson, Clayton & Co.
Armour and Company
Asarco Foundation
Automatic Electric Company
Bechtel Foundation
Beneficial Finance Co.
Bethlehem Steel Company
Bingham, Dana & Gould
E. W. Bliss Company
The Borden Company
Borg-Warner Corporation
Bucyrus-Erie Company
The Budd Company
Burroughs Corporation
Cabot Corporation
Campbell Soup Company
Canada Dry Corporation
Cargill, Incorporated
Caterpillar Tractor Co.
Celanese Corporation of America
The Chase Manhattan Bank
Chrysler Corporation
Clark Equipment Company
The Coca-Cola Export Corporation
Colgate-Palmolive Company
Columbia Broadcasting System, Inc.
Corn Products Company
Crown Zellerbach Corporation
John Deere Foundation
Delhi-Taylor Oil Corporation

Diamond Alkali Company
The Dow Chemical Company
Dresser Industries, Inc.
E. I. duPont de Nemours &
    Company
Eastman Kodak Company
The Firestone Tire & Rubber Company
The First National Bank of Boston
Ford Motor Company
The Foxboro Company
General Foods Corporation
General Motors Overseas Operations
General Telephone Services
    Corporation
The General Tire & Rubber
    Company
The Gillette Company
The B. F. Goodrich Fund, Inc.
The Goodyear Tire & Rubber
    Company
W. R. Grace & Co.
Gulf Oil Foundation
The Hanna Mining Company Fund
Hercules Powder Company
Instron Engineering Corporation
International Bank for Reconstruction
    & Development
International Business Machines
    Corporation
International Finance Corporation
International General Electric
    Company
International Harvester Foundation
International Minerals & Chemical
    Corporation
The International Nickel Company,
    Inc.
International Telephone and
    Telegraph Corporation
Johnson & Johnson
S. C. Johnson & Son, Inc.
The Koppers Foundation
Lambert & Co.
Libbey-Owens-Ford Glass Company
Liberty Mutual Fire Insurance
    Company
Eli Lilly International Corporation
Lily Cups Overseas Limited